SCRABBLE®

DICTIONARY

SCRABBLE®

DICTIONARY

Collins

This edition first published 2008

© HarperCollins Publishers 2008

HarperCollins Publishers
Westerhill Road, Bishopbriggs
Glasgow G64 2QT
Great Britain

www.collins.co.uk

Collins® is a registered trademark of
HarperCollins Publishers Limited

Scrabble® is a registered trademark of
J. W. Spear & Sons Ltd., a subsidiary of Mattel, Inc
© 2008 Mattel, Inc.

ISBN 978-0-00-780998-1

A catalogue record for this book is available from the British Library

This book is set in CollinsFedra, a typeface specifically
created for Collins dictionaries by Peter Bil'ak.

Printed and bound in Germany by Bercker

Contributors

Editors
Sandra Anderson
Kay Cullen
Penny Hands
Andrew Holmes
Mike Munro

Project Manager
Justin Crozier

For the Publisher
Morven Dooner
Elaine Higgleton

Computing Support
Thomas Callan

Collins Corpus Programmer
Nigel Rochford

Typesetting
Wordcraft

Contents

Introduction

Collins Scrabble Dictionary – Every Word Counts

The *Collins Scrabble Dictionary* is the ideal reference book for people who play Scrabble for enjoyment, in a social or family setting. This dictionary doesn't include every word eligible for Scrabble, but does contain the most commonly used of the 260,000 words in *Collins Scrabble Words 2005*, the definitive Scrabble wordlist. The concise definitions in the *Scrabble Dictionary* allow players to check the meaning of words, as well as using the book for settling arguments during games.

The *Collins Scrabble Dictionary* contains only words of up to 15 letters in length, as longer words cannot be used in Scrabble. Because the dictionary is designed for family play, it does not include offensive terms. Such words are included in *Collins Scrabble Words 2005*, the complete wordlist for tournaments and club competitions.

Word order

In the *Collins Scrabble Dictionary*, words are listed in alphabetical order, rather than being grouped at the base form as in a conventional dictionary. Where words are inflections of a base form, only the base form has a definition, but the inflections are listed alphabetically as individual entries for easy reference during a game. Base forms and inflections are shown in black; inflections are indented, with a cross-reference to the base form in blue.

Special Scrabble Words

To help family players learn and use some of the rarer and higher-scoring words in the game, the Collins Scrabble Dictionary includes a number of special panel entries. These are unusual words which are particularly useful in Scrabble, either because they use the high-scoring 'power tiles' (J, Q, X, and Z), or because they have only two or three letters. There are also panel entries at the start of every letter section, which offer advice on useful words beginning with that letter.

The *Collins Scrabble Dictionary* is designed to be useful to new players and Scrabble veterans alike – we hope you enjoy using it!

Forming Words

The key to successful Scrabble is constant awareness of the opportunities for forming words on the board. The obvious way to play a new word is to place it so that it intersects a word already on the board through a common letter:

			D_2		
			O_1		
	L_1	U_1	C_3	K_5	
			T_1		
			O_1		
			R_1		

Other methods of forming words, however, create more than one new word in the process, giving a higher score. The two main ways of doing this are 'hooking' and 'tagging'.

Hooking

Hooking involves 'hanging' one word on another – the word already on the board acts as a 'hook' on which the other word can be hung – changing the first word in the process. When you form a word by hooking, you add a letter to the beginning or end of a word on the board, transforming it into a longer word as you do so:

C_3	O_1	M_3	E_1	T_1	

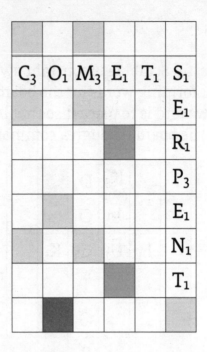

In this example, you get the points for COMETS as well as for SERPENTS. Plurals ending in S provide some of the most obvious – and useful – end-hooks. But there are plenty of other end-hooks as well. There are also lots of useful front-hooks. Consider the following example:

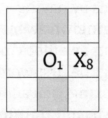

If you happened to have CEFIKL among the letters on your rack, you could play the following, taking full advantage of the valuable X played by your opponent:

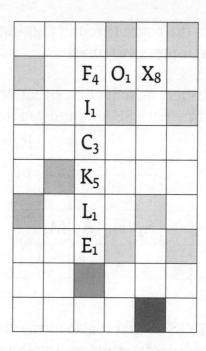

Here you get the 13 points for FOX as well as those for FICKLE. So you can see that hooking is generally a much more profitable method of word-formation than simply playing a word through one that is already on the board.

Obviously, only certain words can act as hooks. Some words cannot form other words by having a letter added to their front or back; these are known as 'blockers', as they prevent other players from adding words by hooking.

Tagging

Playing a word parallel to one already on the board, so that one or more tiles are in contact, is known as tagging. Tagging is more difficult than hooking because you need to form one additional word for each tile in contact with the word on the board. In most circumstances, these will be two-letter words, which is why short words are so vital to the game. The more two-letter words you know, the greater your opportunities for

fitting words onto the board through tagging – and of
running up some impressive scores!

For example, consider the following situation (your opponent
has started the game with SHAM, and you have EEHISTX on
your rack):

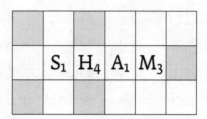

You could play HEXES so that it also forms SH, HE, AX and ME
(all valid two-letter words), thus adding the scores for these
three words to the points you make from HEXES:

	S_1	H_4	A_1	M_3	
H_4	E_1	X_8	E_1	S_1	

A particular advantage of tagging is that it allows you to
benefit from valuable tiles twice in one go, as in the example
above where X is used in both HEXES and AX.

Two-letter words are very important for tagging. The panel
sections of this dictionary contain a number of unusual two-
letter words: learning these is a good method of improving
your game immediately!

ABBREVIATIONS USED IN THIS DICTIONARY

AD	anno Domini	Meteorol	Meteorology
adj	adjective	Mil	Military
adv	adverb	n	noun
Anat	Anatomy	N	North
Archit	Architecture	Naut	Nautical
Astrol	Astrology	NZ	New Zealand
Aust	Australia(n)	Obs	Obsolete
BC	before Christ	Offens	Offensive
Biol	Biology	orig.	originally
Brit	British	Photog	Photography
Chem	Chemistry	pl	plural
C of E	Church of England	prep	preposition
conj	conjunction	pron	pronoun
E	East	Psychol	Psychology
e.g.	for example	®	Trademark
esp.	especially	RC	Roman Catholic
etc.	et cetera	S	South
fem	feminine	S Afr	South Africa(n)
foll.	followed	Scot	Scottish
Geom	Geometry	sing	singular
Hist	History	US	United States
interj	interjection	usu.	usually
Lit	Literary	v	verb
masc	masculine	W	West
Med	Medicine	Zool	Zoology

Aa

A forms a two-letter word when followed by any one of A, B, D, E, G, H, I, M, N, R, S, T, W, X and Y – 15 letters out of 26 – so it's a really useful tile. There are also a number of short high-scoring words beginning with A. **Axe** (10 points) and **adze** (14 points) are good examples, but don't forget their US variants, **ax** (9 points) and **adz** (13 points). Also remember their plurals and the verb form **axed** (12 points). **Aye** (6) and **ay** (5) are handy for tight corners.

a *adj* indefinite article, used before a noun being mentioned for the first time

> **aa** aa *n* (**aas**). Aa is a type of volcanic rock. Aa scores 2 points, and is a good way of getting rid of annoying multiples of A.
>
> **aah** *interj*. Aah is a sound people make when they're pleased or amazed. Aah scores 6 points.
>
> **aal** *adj* Aal is a Scots word for **all**. Aal scores 3 points.

aardvark *n* (*pl* **-s**) S African anteater with long ears and snout

aardvarks *n* ▷ **aardvark**

ab *n* (*pl* **-s**) (*Informal*) (usually plural) abdominal muscle

> **aba** *noun* (**abas**). Cloth made from goat or camel hair. This is a useful word to remember for when you have more than one A on your rack. Aba scores 5 points.

aback *adv* startled or disconcerted

abacus (*pl* **-es**) *n* beads on a wire frame, used for doing calculations

abacuses *n* ▷ **abacus**

abalone (*pl* **-s**) [ab-a-**lone**-ee] *n* edible sea creature with a shell lined with mother of pearl

abalones *n* ▷ **abalone**

abandon *v* (**-s**, **-ing**, **-ed**) desert or leave (one's wife, children, etc.) ▶ *n* lack of inhibition > **abandonment** *n* (*pl* **-s**)

abandoned *adj* deserted ▶ *v* ▷ **abandon**

abandoning *v* ▷ **abandon**

abandonment *n* ▷ **abandon**

abandonments *n* ▷ **abandon**

abandons *v* ▷ **abandon**

abase *v* (**-ses**, **-sing**, **-sed**) humiliate or degrade (oneself) > **abasement** *n* (*pl* **-s**)

abased *v* ▷ **abase**

abasement *n* ▷ **abase**

abasements *n* ▷ **abase**

abases *v* ▷ **abase**

abashed *adj* embarrassed and ashamed

abasing *v* ▷ **abase**

abate *v* (**-tes**, **-ting**, **-ted**) make or become less strong > **abatement** *n* (*pl* **-s**)

abated *v* ▷ **abate**

abatement *n* ▷ **abate**

abatements *n* ▷ **abate**

abates *v* ▷ **abate**

abating *v* ▷ **abate**

abattoir [ab-a-twahr] *n* place where animals are killed for food (*pl* **-s**)

abattoirs *n* ▷ **abattoir**

> **abb** *noun* (**abbs**). Abb is yarn used in weaving. Remember this word for when you have two Bs on your rack, as there will probably already be an A on the board that you can use. Abb scores 7 points.

abbess *n* (*pl* **-es**) nun in charge of a convent

abbesses *n* ▷ **abbess**

abbey *n* (*pl* **-s**) dwelling place of, or a church belonging to, a community of monks or nuns

abbeys *n* ▷ **abbey**

abbot *n* (*pl* **-s**) head of an abbey of monks

abbots *n* ▷ **abbot**

abbreviate *v* (**-tes**, **-ting**, **-ted**) shorten (a word) by leaving out some letters

abbreviated *v* ▷ **abbreviate**

abbreviates *v* ▷ **abbreviate**

abbreviating *v* ▷ **abbreviate**

abbreviation *n* (*pl* **-s**) shortened form of a word or words

abbreviations *n* ▷ **abbreviation**

abdicate v (-tes, -ting, -ted) give up (the throne or a responsibility) > **abdication** n (pl -s)
  abdicated v ▷ abdicate
  abdicates v ▷ abdicate
  abdicating v ▷ abdicate
  abdication n ▷ abdicate
  abdications n ▷ abdicate
abdomen n (pl -s) part of the body containing the stomach and intestines > **abdominal** adj
  abdomens n ▷ abdomen
  abdominal adj ▷ abdomen
abduct v (-s, -ing, -ed) carry off, kidnap > **abduction** n (pl -s) > **abductor** n (pl -s)
  abducted v ▷ abduct
  abducting v ▷ abduct
  abduction n ▷ abduct
  abductions n ▷ abduct
  abductor n ▷ abduct
  abductors n ▷ abduct
  abducts v ▷ abduct
aberrant adj showing aberration
aberration n (pl -s) sudden change from what is normal, accurate, or correct
  aberrations n ▷ aberration
abet v (-s, -ting, -ted) help or encourage in wrongdoing > **abettor** n (pl -s)
  abets v ▷ abet
  abetted v ▷ abet
  abetting v ▷ abet
  abettor n ▷ abet
  abettors n ▷ abet
abeyance n (pl -s) not in use
  abeyances n ▷ abeyance
abhor v (-s, -horring, -horred) detest utterly > **abhorrence** n (pl -s)
  abhorred v ▷ abhor
  abhorrence n ▷ abhor
  abhorrences n ▷ abhor
abhorrent adj hateful, loathsome
  abhorring v ▷ abhor
  abhors v ▷ abhor
abide v (-des, -ding, -ded) endure, put up with
  abided v ▷ abide
  abides v ▷ abide
abiding adj lasting ▶ v ▷ abide
  abilities n ▷ ability
ability n (pl -ties) competence, power
abject adj utterly miserable > **abjectly** adv
  abjectly adv ▷ abject
abjure v (-res, -ring, -red) deny or renounce on oath
  abjured v ▷ abjure
  abjures v ▷ abjure
  abjuring v ▷ abjure

ablative n (pl -s) case of nouns in Latin and other languages, indicating source, agent, or instrument of action
  ablatives n ▷ ablative
ablaze adj burning fiercely
able adj (-r, -st) capable, competent > **ably** adv
  abler adj ▷ able
  ablest adj ▷ able
ablution n (pl -s) (usually plural) act of washing
  ablutions n ▷ ablution
  ably adv ▷ able
abnormal adj not normal or usual > **abnormally** adv > **abnormality** n (pl -ties)
  abnormalities n ▷ abnormal
  abnormality n ▷ abnormal
  abnormally adv ▷ abnormal
aboard adv, prep on, in, onto, or into (a ship, train, or plane)
abode n (pl -s) home, dwelling
  abodes n ▷ abode
abolish v (-shes, -shing, -shed) do away with > **abolition** n (pl -s)
  abolished v ▷ abolish
  abolishes v ▷ abolish
  abolishing v ▷ abolish
  abolition n ▷ abolish
abolitionist n (pl -s) person who wishes to do away with something, esp. slavery
  abolitionists n ▷ abolitionist
  abolitions n ▷ abolish
abominable adj detestable, very bad > **abominably** adv
  abominably adv ▷ abominable
abomination n (pl -s) someone or something that is detestable
  abominations n ▷ abomination
  aboriginal n, adj ▷ aborigine
  aboriginals n ▷ aborigine
aborigine, aboriginal [ab-or-**rij**-in-ee] n (pl -s) original inhabitant of a country or region, esp. (A-) Australia > **aboriginal** adj
  aborigines n ▷ aborigine
abort v (-s, -ing, -ed) have an abortion or perform an abortion on
  aborted v ▷ abort
  aborting v ▷ abort
abortion n (pl -s) operation to end a pregnancy
abortionist n (pl -s) person who performs abortions, esp. illegally
  abortionists n ▷ abortionist
  abortions n ▷ abortion
abortive adj unsuccessful
  aborts v ▷ abort
abound v (-s, -ing, -ed) be plentiful

> **abounding** *adj*
abounded *v* ▷ **abound**
abounding *v*, *adj* ▷ **abound**
abounds *v* ▷ **abound**
about *prep* concerning, on the subject of ▶ *adv* nearly, approximately
above *adv*, *prep* over or higher (than)
abracadabra *n* (*pl* -**s**) supposedly magic word
abracadabras *n* ▷ **abracadabra**
abrasion *n* (*pl* -**s**) scraped area on the skin
abrasions *n* ▷ **abrasion**
abrasive *adj* harsh and unpleasant in manner ▶ *n* (*pl* -**s**) substance for cleaning or polishing by rubbing
abrasives *n* ▷ **abrasive**
abreast *adv*, *adj* side by side
abridge *v* (-**ges**, -**ging**, -**ged**) shorten by using fewer words > **abridgment, abridgement** *n* (*pl* -**s**)
abridged *v* ▷ **abridge**
abridgement *n* ▷ **abridge**
abridgements *n* ▷ **abridge**
abridges *v* ▷ **abridge**
abridging *v* ▷ **abridge**
abridgment *n* ▷ **abridge**
abridgments *n* ▷ **abridge**
abroad *adv* to or in a foreign country
abrogate *v* (-**tes**, -**ting**, -**ted**) cancel (a law or agreement) formally > **abrogation** *n* (*pl* -**s**)
abrogated *v* ▷ **abrogate**
abrogates *v* ▷ **abrogate**
abrogating *v* ▷ **abrogate**
abrogation *n* ▷ **abrogate**
abrogations *n* ▷ **abrogate**
abrupt *adj* (-**er**, -**est**) sudden, unexpected > **abruptly** *adv* > **abruptness** *n* (*pl* -**es**)
abrupter *adj* ▷ **abrupt**
abruptest *adj* ▷ **abrupt**
abruptly *adv* ▷ **abrupt**
abruptness *n* ▷ **abrupt**
abruptnesses *n* ▷ **abrupt**
abs *n* ▷ **ab**
abscess *n* (*pl* **abscesses**) inflamed swelling containing pus
abscesses *n* ▷ **abscess**
abscond *v* (-**s**, -**ing**, -**ed**) leave secretly
absconded *v* ▷ **abscond**
absconding *v* ▷ **abscond**
absconds *v* ▷ **abscond**
abseil [ab-sale] *v* (-**s**, -**ing**, -**ed**) go down a steep drop by a rope fastened at the top and tied around one's body
abseiled *v* ▷ **abseil**
abseiling *v* ▷ **abseil**
abseils *v* ▷ **abseil**

absence *n* (*pl* -**s**) being away
absences *n* ▷ **absence**
absent *adj* not present ▶ *v* (-**s**, -**ing**, -**ed**) stay away > **absently** *adv*
absented *v* ▷ **absent**
absentee *n* (*pl* -**s**) person who should be present but is not
absenteeism *n* (*pl* -**s**) persistent absence from work or school
absenteeisms *n* ▷ **absenteeism**
absentees *n* ▷ **absentee**
absenting *v* ▷ **absent**
absently *adv* ▷ **absent**
absents *v* ▷ **absent**
absinthe *n* (*pl* -**s**) strong green aniseed-flavoured liqueur
absinthes *n* ▷ **absinthe**
absolute *adj* complete, perfect
absolutely *adv* completely ▶ *interj* certainly, yes
absolution *n* ▷ **absolve**
absolutions *n* ▷ **absolve**
absolutism *n* (*pl* -**s**) government by a ruler with unrestricted power
absolutisms *n* ▷ **absolutism**
absolve *v* (-**ves**, -**ving**, -**ved**) declare to be free from blame or sin > **absolution** *n* (*pl* -**s**)
absolved *v* ▷ **absolve**
absolves *v* ▷ **absolve**
absolving *v* ▷ **absolve**
absorb *v* (-**s**, -**ing**, -**ed**) soak up (a liquid) > **absorption** *n* (*pl* -**s**) > **absorbency** *n* (*pl* -**s**)
absorbed *v* ▷ **absorb**
absorbencies *n* ▷ **absorb**
absorbency *n* ▷ **absorb**
absorbent *adj* able to absorb liquid
absorbing *v* ▷ **absorb**
absorbs *v* ▷ **absorb**
absorption *n* ▷ **absorb**
absorptions *n* ▷ **absorb**
abstain *v* (-**s**, -**ing**, -**ed**) choose not to do something > **abstainer** *n* (*pl* -**s**)
abstained *v* ▷ **abstain**
abstainer *n* ▷ **abstain**
abstainers *n* ▷ **abstain**
abstaining *v* ▷ **abstain**
abstains *v* ▷ **abstain**
abstemious *adj* taking very little alcohol or food > **abstemiousness** *n* (*pl* -**es**)
abstemiousness *n* ▷ **abstemious**
abstemiousnesses *n* ▷ **abstemious**
abstention *n* (*pl* -**s**) abstaining, esp. from voting
abstentions *n* ▷ **abstention**
abstinence *n* (*pl* -**s**) abstaining, esp. from

drinking alcohol > **abstinent** adj
abstinences n ▷ **abstinence**
abstinent adj ▷ **abstinence**
abstract adj (**-er, -est**) existing as a quality or idea rather than a material object ▶ n (pl -s) summary ▶ v (**-s, -ing, -ed**) summarize > **abstraction** n (pl -s)
abstracted adj lost in thought v ▷ **abstract**
abstracter adj ▷ **abstract**
abstractest adj ▷ **abstract**
abstracting adj ▷ **abstract**
abstraction n ▷ **abstract**
abstractions n ▷ **abstract**
abstracts n, v ▷ **abstract**
abstruse adj (**-er, -est**) not easy to understand
abstruser adj ▷ **abstruse**
abstrusest adj ▷ **abstruse**
absurd adj (**-er, -est**) incongruous or ridiculous > **absurdly** adv > **absurdity** n (pl **-ties**)
absurder adj ▷ **absurd**
absurdest adj ▷ **absurd**
absurdities n ▷ **absurd**
absurdity n ▷ **absurd**
absurdly adv ▷ **absurd**
abundance n ▷ **abundant**
abundances n ▷ **abundant**
abundant adj plentiful > **abundantly** adv > **abundance** n (pl -s)
abundantly adv ▷ **abundant**
abuse v (**-ses, -sing, -sed**) use wrongly ▶ n (pl -s) prolonged ill-treatment > **abuser** n (pl -s) > **abusive** adj > **abusively** adv > **abusiveness** n (pl **-es**)
abused v ▷ **abuse**
abuser n ▷ **abuse**
abusers n ▷ **abuse**
abuses v, n ▷ **abuse**
abusing v ▷ **abuse**
abusive adj ▷ **abuse**
abusively adv ▷ **abuse**
abusiveness n ▷ **abuse**
abusivenesses n ▷ **abuse**
abut v (**-s, abutting, abutted**) be next to or touching
abuts v ▷ **abut**
abutted v ▷ **abut**
abutting v ▷ **abut**

> **aby** verb (**abys abying abought**). Aby is an old word meaning to pay a penalty. If someone plays this word, remember that it can be expanded to **baby**, **abysmal** or **abyss**. Aby scores 8 points.

abysmal adj (Informal) extremely bad, awful > **abysmally** adv
abysmally adv ▷ **abysmal**

abyss n (pl **-es**) very deep hole or chasm
abysses n ▷ **abyss**
acacia [a-kay-sha] n (pl **-s**) tree or shrub with yellow or white flowers
acacias n ▷ **acacia**
academic adj of an academy or university ▶ n (pl **-s**) lecturer or researcher at a university > **academically** adv
academically adv ▷ **academic**
academician n (pl **-s**) member of an academy
academicians n ▷ **academician**
academics n ▷ **academician**
academies n ▷ **academy**
academy n (pl **-mies**) society to advance arts or sciences
acanthus n (pl **-es**) prickly plant
acanthuses n ▷ **acanthus**
accede v (**-des, -ding, -ded**) consent or agree (to)
acceded v ▷ **accede**
accedes v ▷ **accede**
acceding v ▷ **accede**
accelerate v (**-tes, -ting, -ted**) (cause to) move faster > **acceleration** n (pl -s)
accelerated v ▷ **accelerate**
accelerates v ▷ **accelerate**
accelerating v ▷ **accelerate**
acceleration n ▷ **accelerate**
accelerations n ▷ **accelerate**
accelerator n (pl **-s**) pedal in a motor vehicle to increase speed
accelerators n ▷ **accelerator**
accent n (pl **-s**) distinctive style of pronunciation of a local, national, or social group ▶ v (**-s, -ing, -ed**) place emphasis on
accented v ▷ **accent**
accenting v ▷ **accent**
accents n, v ▷ **accent**
accentuate v (**-tes, -ting, -ted**) stress, emphasize > **accentuation** n (pl -s)
accentuated v ▷ **accentuate**
accentuates v ▷ **accentuate**
accentuating v ▷ **accentuate**
accentuation n ▷ **accentuate**
accentuations n ▷ **accentuate**
accept v (**-s, -ing, -ed**) receive willingly > **acceptance** n (pl -s)
acceptabilities n ▷ **acceptable**
acceptability n ▷ **acceptable**
acceptable adj tolerable > **acceptably** adv > **acceptability** n (pl **-ties**)
acceptably adv ▷ **acceptable**
acceptance n ▷ **accept**
acceptances n ▷ **accept**
accepted v ▷ **accept**

accepting v ▷ accept
accepts v ▷ accept
access n (pl **-es**) means of or right to approach or enter ▶ v (**-es, -ing, -ed**) obtain (data) from a computer
accessed v ▷ access
accesses n, v ▷ access
accessibilities n ▷ accessible
accessibility n ▷ accessible
accessible adj easy to reach > **accessibility** n (pl **-ties**)
accessing v ▷ access
accession n (pl **-s**) taking up of an office or position
accessions n ▷ accession
accessories n ▷ accessory
accessory n (pl **-ries**) supplementary part or object
accident n (pl **-s**) mishap, often causing injury
accidental adj happening by chance or unintentionally ▶ n (pl **-s**) (MUSIC) symbol indicating that a sharp, flat, or natural note is not a part of the key signature > **accidentally** adv
accidentally adv ▷ accidental
accidentals n ▷ accidental
accidents n ▷ accident
acclaim v (**-s, -ing, -ed**) applaud, praise ▶ n (pl **-s**) enthusiastic approval > **acclamation** n (pl **-s**)
acclaimed v ▷ acclaim
acclaiming v ▷ acclaim
acclaims v, n ▷ acclaim
acclamation n ▷ acclaim
acclamations n ▷ acclaim
acclimatization n ▷ acclimatize
acclimatizations n ▷ acclimatize
acclimatize v (**-zes, -zing, -zed**) adapt to a new climate or environment > **acclimatization** n (pl **-s**)
acclimatized v ▷ acclimatize
acclimatizes v ▷ acclimatize
acclimatizing v ▷ acclimatize
accolade n (pl **-s**) award, honour, or praise
accolades n ▷ accolade
accommodate v (**-tes, -ting, -ted**) provide with lodgings
accommodated v ▷ accommodate
accommodates v ▷ accommodate
accommodating adj obliging ▶ v ▷ accommodate
accommodation n (pl **-s**) house or room for living in
accommodations n ▷ accommodation
accompanied v ▷ accompany

accompanies v ▷ accompany
accompaniment n (pl **-s**) something that accompanies
accompaniments n ▷ accompaniment
accompanist n ▷ accompany
accompanists n ▷ accompany
accompany v (**-nies, -nying, -nied**) go along with > **accompanist** n (pl **-s**)
accompanying v ▷ accompany
accomplice n (pl **-s**) person who helps another to commit a crime
accomplices n ▷ accomplice
accomplish v (**-es, -ing, -ed**) manage to do
accomplished adj expert, proficient ▶ v ▷ accomplish
accomplishes v ▷ accomplish
accomplishing v ▷ accomplish
accomplishment n (pl **-s**) completion
accomplishments n ▷ accomplishment
accord n (pl **-s**) agreement, harmony ▶ v (**-s, -ing, -ed**) fit in with
accordance n (pl **-s**) conforming to or according to
accordances n ▷ accordance
accorded v ▷ accord
according adv as stated by ▶ v ▷ accord
accordingly adv in an appropriate manner
accordion n (pl **-s**) portable musical instrument played by moving the two sides apart and together, and pressing a keyboard or buttons to produce the notes > **accordionist** n
accordionist n (pl **-s**) ▷ accordion
accordionists n ▷ accordion
accordions n ▷ accordion
accords v ▷ accord
accost v (**-s, -ing, -ed**) approach and speak to, often aggressively
accosted v ▷ accost
accosting v ▷ accost
accosts v ▷ accost
account n (pl **-s**) report, description ▶ v (**-s, -ing, -ed**) judge to be
accountabilities n ▷ accountable
accountability n ▷ accountable
accountable adj responsible to someone or for something > **accountability** n (pl **-ties**)
accountancies n ▷ accountant
accountancy n ▷ accountant
accountant n (pl **-s**) person who maintains and audits business accounts > **accountancy** n (pl **-cies**)
accountants n ▷ accountant
accounted v ▷ account
accounting n (pl **-s**) skill or practice of

maintaining and auditing business accounts
▶ v ▷ **account**

accountings n ▷ accounting

accounts n, v ▷ account

accoutrement n (pl -s) an item of clothing and equipment for a particular activity

accoutrements n ▷ accoutrement

accredited adj authorized, officially recognized

accretion [ak-**kree**-shun] n (pl -s) gradual growth

accretions n ▷ accretion

accrual n ▷ accrue

accruals n ▷ accrue

accrue v (-crues, -cruing, -crued) increase gradually ▶ **accrual** n (pl -s)

accrued v ▷ accrue

accrues v ▷ accrue

accruing v ▷ accrue

accumulate v (-tes, -ting, -ted) gather together in increasing quantity ▶ **accumulation** n (pl -s) ▶ **accumulative** adj

accumulated v ▷ accumulate

accumulates v ▷ accumulate

accumulating v ▷ accumulate

accumulation n ▷ accumulate

accumulations v ▷ accumulate

accumulative adj ▷ accumulate

accumulator n (pl -s) (BRIT & AUST) rechargeable electric battery

accumulators n ▷ accumulator

accuracies n ▷ accurate

accuracy n ▷ accurate

accurate adj exact, correct ▶ **accurately** adv ▶ **accuracy** n (pl -cies)

accurately adv ▷ accurate

accursed adj under a curse

accusation n ▷ accuse

accusations n ▷ accuse

accusative n (pl -s) grammatical case indicating the direct object

accusatives n ▷ accusative

accusatory adj ▷ accuse

accuse v (-ses, -sing, -sed) charge with wrongdoing ▶ **accused** n ▶ **accuser** n (pl -s) ▶ **accusing** adj ▶ **accusation** n (pl -s) ▶ **accusatory** adj

accused v ▷ accuse

accused n ▷ accuse

accuser n ▷ accuse

accusers n ▷ accuser

accuses v ▷ accuse

accusing v, adj ▷ accuse

accusing adj ▷ accuse

accustom v (-s, -ing, -ed) make used to

accustomed adj usual v ▷ **accustom**

accustoming v ▷ accustom

accustoms v ▷ accustom

ace n (pl -s) playing card with one symbol on it ▶ adj (Informal) excellent

acerbic [ass-**sir**-bik] adj harsh or bitter ▶ **acerbity** n (pl -ties)

acerbities n ▷ acerbic

acerbity n ▷ acerbic

aces n ▷ ace

acetate [**ass**-it-tate] n (pl -s) (CHEM) salt or ester of acetic acid

acetates n ▷ acetate

acetic [ass-**see**-tik] adj of or involving vinegar

acetone [**ass**-it-tone] n (pl -s) colourless liquid used as a solvent

acetones n ▷ acetone

acetylene [ass-**set**-ill-een] n (pl -s) colourless flammable gas used in welding metals

acetylenes n ▷ acetylene

ache n (pl -s) dull continuous pain ▶ v (-ches, -ching, -ched) be in or cause continuous dull pain

ached n ▷ ache

aches v, n ▷ ache

achieve v (-ves, -ving, -ved) gain by hard work or ability

achieved v ▷ achieve

achievement n (pl -s) something accomplished

achievements n ▷ achievement

achieves v ▷ achieve

achieving v ▷ achieve

aching v ▷ ache

achromatic adj colourless

acid n (pl -s) (CHEM) one of a class of compounds, corrosive and sour when dissolved in water, that combine with a base to form a salt ▶ adj containing acid ▶ **acidic** adj ▶ **acidify** v ▶ **acidity** n (pl -ties)

acidic adj ▷ acid

acidify v ▷ acid

acidities n ▷ acid

acidity n ▷ acid

acids n ▷ acid

acknowledge v (-ges, -ging, -ged) admit, recognize ▶ **acknowledgment, acknowledgement** n (pl -s)

acknowledged v ▷ acknowledge

acknowledgement n ▷ acknowledge

acknowledgements n ▷ acknowledge

acknowledges v ▷ acknowledge

acknowledging v ▷ acknowledge

acknowledgment n ▷ acknowledge

acknowledgments n ▷ acknowledge

acme [ak-mee] n (pl -s) highest point of achievement or excellence
  acmes n ▷ **acme**
acne [ak-nee] n (pl -s) pimply skin disease
  acnes n ▷ **acne**
acolyte n (pl -s) follower or attendant
  acolytes n ▷ **acolyte**
aconite n (pl -s) poisonous plant with hoodlike flowers
  aconites n ▷ **aconite**
acorn n (pl -s) nut of the oak tree
  acorns n ▷ **acorn**
acoustic adj of sound and hearing
  > **acoustically** adv
  acoustically adv ▷ **acoustic**
acoustics n science of sounds
acquaint v (-s, -ing, -ed) make familiar, inform
  > **acquainted** adj
acquaintance n (pl -s) person known
  acquaintances n ▷ **acquaintance**
  acquainted v, adj ▷ **acquaint**
  acquainting v ▷ **acquaint**
  acquaints v ▷ **acquaint**
acquiesce [ak-wee-ess] v (-sces, -scing, -sced) agree to what someone wants
  > **acquiescence** n (pl -s) > **acquiescent** adj
  acquiesced v ▷ **acquiesce**
  acquiescence n ▷ **acquiesce**
  acquiescences n ▷ **acquiesce**
  acquiescent adj ▷ **acquiesce**
  acquiesces v ▷ **acquiesce**
  acquiescing v ▷ **acquiesce**
acquire v (-res, -ring, -red) gain, get
  acquired v ▷ **acquire**
  acquires v ▷ **acquire**
  acquiring v ▷ **acquire**
acquisition n (pl -s) thing acquired
  acquisitions n ▷ **acquisition**
acquisitive adj eager to gain material possessions > **acquisitiveness** n (pl -es)
  acquisitiveness n ▷ **acquisitive**
  acquisitivenesses n ▷ **acquisitive**
acquit v (-s, -quitting, -quitted) pronounce (someone) innocent > **acquittal** n (pl -s)
  acquits v ▷ **acquit**
  acquittal n ▷ **acquit**
  acquittals n ▷ **acquit**
  acquitted v ▷ **acquit**
  acquitting v ▷ **acquit**
acre n (pl -s) measure of land, 4840 square yards (4046.86 square metres)
acreage [ake-er-rij] n (pl -s) land area in acres
  acreages n ▷ **acreage**
  acres n ▷ **acre**
acrid [ak-rid] adj (-er, -est) pungent, bitter

acrider adj ▷ **acrid**
acridest adj ▷ **acrid**
acrimonies n ▷ **acrimonious**
acrimonious adj bitter in speech or manner
  > **acrimony** n (pl -ies)
acrimony n ▷ **acrimonious**
acrobat n (pl -s) person skilled in gymnastic feats requiring agility and balance
  > **acrobatic** adj
  acrobatic adj ▷ **acrobatic**
acrobatics pl n acrobatic feats
  acrobats n ▷ **acrobat**
acronym n (pl -s) word formed from the initial letters of other words, such as NASA
  acronyms n ▷ **acronym**
across adv, prep from side to side (of)
acrostic n (pl -s) lines of writing in which the first or last letters of each line spell a word or saying
  acrostics n ▷ **acrostic**
acrylic n (pl -s) ▶ adj (synthetic fibre, paint, etc.) made from acrylic acid
  acrylics n ▷ **acrylic**
act n (pl -s) thing done ▶ v (-s, -ing, -ed) do something
  acted v ▷ **act**
acting n (pl -s) art of an actor ▶ adj temporarily performing the duties of ▶ v ▷ **act**
  actings n ▷ **acting**
actinium n (pl -s) (CHEM) radioactive chemical element
  actiniums n ▷ **actinium**
action n (pl -s) process of doing something
actionable adj giving grounds for a lawsuit
  actions n ▷ **action**
activate v (-tes, -ting, -ted) make active
  > **activation** n (pl -s) > **activator** n (pl -s)
  activated v ▷ **activate**
  activates v ▷ **activate**
  activating v ▷ **activate**
  activation n ▷ **activate**
  activations n ▷ **activate**
  activator n ▷ **activate**
  activators n ▷ **activate**
active adj moving, working > **actively** adv
  actively adv ▷ **active**
  activism n ▷ **activist**
  activisms n ▷ **activist**
activist n (pl -s) person who works energetically to achieve political or social goals > **activism** n (pl -s)
  activists n ▷ **activist**
  activities n ▷ **activity**
activity n (pl -ties) state of being active
actor n (pl -s) person who acts in a play, film,

etc.

actors *n* ▷ **actor**

actress *n* (*pl* **-es**) woman who acts in a play, film, etc.

actresses *n* ▷ **actress**

acts *n, v* ▷ **act**

actual *adj* existing in reality > **actuality** *n* (*pl* **-ties**)

actualities *n* ▷ **actual**

actuality *n* ▷ **actual**

actually *adv* really, indeed

actuarial *adj* ▷ **actuary**

actuaries *n* ▷ **actuary**

actuary *n* (*pl* **-ries**) statistician who calculates insurance risks > **actuarial** *adj*

actuate *v* (**-tes, -ting, -ted**) start up (a device)

actuated *v* ▷ **actuate**

actuates *v* ▷ **actuate**

actuating *v* ▷ **actuate**

acuities *n* ▷ **acuity**

acuity [ak-**kew**-it-ee] *n* (*pl* **-ties**) keenness of vision or thought

acumen [ak-yew-men] *n* (*pl* **-s**) ability to make good judgments

acumens *n* ▷ **acumen**

acupuncture *n* (*pl* **-s**) medical treatment involving the insertion of needles at various points on the body > **acupuncturist** *n* (*pl* **-s**)

acupunctures *n* ▷ **acupuncture**

acupuncturist *n* ▷ **acupuncture**

acupuncturists *n* ▷ **acupuncture**

acute *adj* (**-r, -st**) severe ▶ *n* (*pl* **-s**) accent (´) over a letter to indicate the quality or length of its sound, as in café > **acutely** *adv* > **acuteness** *n*

acutely *adv* ▷ **acute**

acuteness *n* ▷ **acute**

acuter *adj* ▷ **acute**

acutes *n* ▷ **acute**

acutest *adj* ▷ **acute**

ad *n* (*pl* **-s**) (*Informal*) advertisement

adage *n* (*pl* **-s**) wise saying, proverb

adages *n* ▷ **adage**

adagio *n* (*pl* **-gios**) ▶ *adv* (MUSIC) (piece to be played) slowly and gracefully

adagios *n* ▷ **adagio**

adamant *adj* unshakable in determination or purpose > **adamantly** *adv*

adamantly *adv* ▷ **adamant**

adapt *v* (**-s, -ing, -ed**) alter for new use or new conditions > **adaptable** *adj* > **adaptability** *n* (*pl* **-ties**)

adaptabilities *n* ▷ **adapt**

adaptability *n* ▷ **adapt**

adaptable *adj* ▷ **adapt**

adaptation *n* (*pl* **-s**) thing produced by adapting something

adaptations *n* ▷ **adaptation**

adapted *v* ▷ **adapt**

adapter *n* ▷ **adaptor**

adapters *n* ▷ **adaptor**

adapting *v* ▷ **adapt**

adaptor, adapter *n* (*pl* **-s**) device for connecting several electrical appliances to a single socket

adaptors *n* ▷ **adaptor**

adapts *v* ▷ **adapt**

add *v* (**-s, -ing, -ed**) combine (numbers or quantities)

added *v* ▷ **add**

addenda *n* ▷ **addendum**

addendum *n* (*pl* **-da**) addition

adder *n* (*pl* **-s**) small poisonous snake

adders *n* ▷ **adder**

addict *n* (*pl* **-s**) person who is unable to stop taking drugs > **addicted** *adj* > **addiction** *n* (*pl* **-s**)

addicted *adj* ▷ **addict**

addiction *n* ▷ **addict**

addictions *n* ▷ **addict**

addictive *adj* causing addiction

addicts *n* ▷ **addict**

adding *v* ▷ **add**

addition *n* (*pl* **-s**) adding > **additional** *adj* > **additionally** *adv*

additional *adj* ▷ **addition**

additionally *adv* ▷ **addition**

additions *n* ▷ **addition**

additive *n* (*pl* **-s**) something added, esp. to a foodstuff, to improve it or prevent deterioration

additives *n* ▷ **additive**

addled *adj* confused or unable to think clearly

address *n* (*pl* **-es**) place where a person lives ▶ *v* (**-es, -ing, -ed**) mark the destination, as on an envelope

addressed *v* ▷ **address**

addressee *n* (*pl* **-s**) person addressed

addressees *n* ▷ **addressee**

addresses *n, v* ▷ **address**

addressing *v* ▷ **address**

adds *v* ▷ **add**

adduce *v* (**-ces, -cing, -uced**) mention something as evidence or proof

adduced *v* ▷ **adduce**

adduces *v* ▷ **adduce**

adducing *v* ▷ **adduce**

adenoid [ad-in-oid] *n* (*pl* **-s**) (usually plural) mass of tissue at the back of the throat

adenoidal *adj* having a nasal voice caused by

swollen adenoids
adenoids *n* ▷ **adenoid**
adept *adj* (**-er, -est**) ▶ *n* (*pl* **-s**) very skilful (person)
adepter *adj* ▷ **adept**
adeptest *adj* ▷ **adept**
adepts *n* ▷ **adept**
adequacies *n* ▷ **adequate**
adequacy *n* ▷ **adequate**
adequate *adj* sufficient, enough > **adequately** *adv* > **adequacy** *n* (*pl* **-ies**)
adequately *adv* ▷ **adequate**
adhere *v* (**-res, -ring, -red**) stick (to)
> **adherence** *n* (*pl* **-ces**)
adhered *v* ▷ **adhere**
adherence *n* ▷ **adhere**
adherences *n* ▷ **adhere**
adherent *n* (*pl* **-s**) devotee, follower
adherents *n* ▷ **adherent**
adheres *v* ▷ **adhere**
adhering *v* ▷ **adhere**
adhesion *n* (*pl* **-s**) sticking (to)
adhesions *n* ▷ **adhesion**
adhesive *n* (*pl* **-s**) substance used to stick things together ▶ *adj* able to stick to things
adhesives *n* ▷ **adhesive**
adieu [a-**dew**] *interj* (*Lit*) farewell, goodbye
adipose *adj* of or containing fat
adjacent *adj* near or next (to)
adjectival *adj* ▷ **adjective**
adjective *n* (*pl* **-es**) word that adds information about a noun or pronoun > **adjectival** *adj*
adjectives *n* ▷ **adjective**
adjoin *v* (**-s, -ing, -ed**) be next to > **adjoining** *adj*
adjoined *v* ▷ **adjoin**
adjoining *v, adj* ▷ **adjoin**
adjoins *v* ▷ **adjoin**
adjourn *v* (**-s, -ing, -ed**) close (a court) at the end of a session > **adjournment** *n* (*pl* **-s**)
adjourned *v* ▷ **adjourn**
adjourning *v* ▷ **adjourn**
adjournment *n* ▷ **adjourn**
adjournments *n* ▷ **adjourn**
adjourns *v* ▷ **adjourn**
adjudge *v* (**-ges, -ging, -ged**) declare (to be)
adjudged *v* ▷ **adjudge**
adjudges *v* ▷ **adjudge**
adjudging *v* ▷ **adjudge**
adjudicate *v* (**-tes, -ting, -ted**) give a formal decision on (a dispute) > **adjudication** *n* (*pl* **-s**)
> **adjudicator** *n* (*pl* **-s**)
adjudicated *v* ▷ **adjudicate**
adjudicates *v* ▷ **adjudicate**
adjudicating *v* ▷ **adjudicate**
adjudication *n* ▷ **adjudicate**

adjudications *n* ▷ **adjudicate**
adjudicator *n* ▷ **adjudicate**
adjudicators *n* ▷ **adjudicate**
adjunct *n* (*pl* **-s**) subordinate or additional person or thing
adjuncts *n* ▷ **adjunct**
adjure *v* (**-res, -ring, -red**) command (to do)
adjured *v* ▷ **adjure**
adjures *v* ▷ **adjure**
adjuring *v* ▷ **adjure**
adjust *v* (**-s, -ing, -ted**) adapt to new conditions > **adjustable** *adj* > **adjuster** *n* (*pl* **-s**)
> **adjustment** *n* (*pl* **-s**)
adjustable *adj* ▷ **adjust**
adjusted *v* ▷ **adjust**
adjuster *n* ▷ **adjust**
adjusters *n* ▷ **adjust**
adjustment *n* ▷ **adjust**
adjustments *n* ▷ **adjust**
adjusts *v* ▷ **adjust**
adjutant [**aj**-oo-tant] *n* (*pl* **-s**) army officer in charge of routine administration
adjutants *n* ▷ **adjutant**
admin *n* (*pl* **-s**) (*Informal*) administration
administer *v* (**-s, -ing, -ed**) manage (business affairs)
administered *v* ▷ **administer**
administering *v* ▷ **administer**
administers *v* ▷ **administer**
administrate *v* (**-tes, -ting, -ated**) manage (an organization) > **administrator** *n* (*pl* **-s**)
administrated *v* ▷ **administrate**
administrates *v* ▷ **administrate**
administrating *v* ▷ **administrate**
administration *n* (*pl* **-s**) management of an organization
administrations *n* ▷ **administration**
administrative *adj* of the management of an organization
administrator *n* ▷ **administrate**
administrators *n* ▷ **administrate**
admins *n* ▷ **admin**
admirable *adj* ▷ **admire**
admirably *adv* ▷ **admire**
admiral *n* (*pl* **-s**) highest naval rank
admirals *n* ▷ **admiral**
admiralties *n* ▷ **admiralty**
admiralty *n* (*pl* **-ties**) the office or jurisdiction of an admiral
admiration *n* ▷ **admire**
admirations *n* ▷ **admire**
admire *v* (**-res, -ring, -red**) regard with esteem and approval > **admirable** *adj* > **admirably** *adv* > **admiration** *n* (*pl* **-s**) > **admirer** *n* (*pl* **-s**)
> **admiring** *adj* > **admiringly** *adv*

admired v ▷ admire
admirer n ▷ admire
admirers n ▷ admire
admires v ▷ admire
admiring v, adj ▷ admire
admiringly adv ▷ admire
admissibilities n ▷ admissible
admissibility n ▷ admissible
admissible adj allowed to be brought in as evidence in court > **admissibility** n (pl -ties)
admission n (pl -s) permission to enter
admissions n ▷ admission
admit v (-mits, -mitting, -mitted) confess, acknowledge
admits v ▷ admit
admittance n (pl -s) permission to enter
admittances n ▷ admittance
admitted v ▷ admit
admittedly adv it must be agreed
admitting v ▷ admit
admixture n (pl -s) mixture
admixtures n ▷ admixture
admonish v (-es, -ing, -ed) reprove sternly > **admonition** n (pl -s)
admonished v ▷ admonish
admonishes v ▷ admonish
admonishing v ▷ admonish
admonition n ▷ admonish
admonitions n ▷ admonish
ado n (pl -s) (Lit) fuss, trouble
adobe [ad-oh-bee] n (pl -s) sun-dried brick
adobes n ▷ adobe
adolescence n (pl -s) period between puberty and adulthood
adolescences n ▷ adolescence
adolescent n (pl -s), adj (person) between puberty and adulthood
adolescents n ▷ adolescent
adopt v (-s, -ing, -ed) take (someone else's child) as one's own > **adoption** n (pl -s)
adopted v ▷ adopt
adopting v ▷ adopt
adoption n ▷ adopt
adoptions n ▷ adopt
adoptive adj related by adoption
adopts v ▷ adopt
adorable adj ▷ adore
adoration n ▷ adore
adorations n ▷ adore
adore v (-res, -ring, -red) love intensely > **adorable** adj > **adoration** n (pl -s) > **adoring** adj > **adoringly** adv
adored v ▷ adore
adores v ▷ adore
adoring v, adj ▷ adore

adoringly adv ▷ adore
adorn v (-s, -ing, -ed) decorate, embellish > **adornment** n (pl -s)
adorned v ▷ adorn
adorning v ▷ adorn
adornment n ▷ adorn
adornments n ▷ adorn
adorns v ▷ adorn
ados n ▷ ado
adrenal [ad-reen-al] adj near the kidneys
adrenalin, adrenaline n (pl -s) hormone secreted by the adrenal glands in response to stress
adrenaline n ▷ adrenalin
adrenalines n ▷ adrenalin
adrenalins n ▷ adrenalin
adrift adj, adv drifting
adroit adj quick and skilful > **adroitly** adv > **adroitness** n
adroitly adv ▷ adroit
adroitness n ▷ adroit
ads n ▷ ad
adsorb v (-s, -ing, -ed) (of a gas or vapour) condense and form a thin film on a surface > **adsorption** n (pl -s)
adsorbed v ▷ adsorb
adsorbing v ▷ adsorb
adsorbs v ▷ adsorb
adsorption n ▷ adsorb
adsorptions n ▷ adsorb
adulation n (pl -s) uncritical admiration
adulations n ▷ adulation
adult adj fully grown, mature ▶ n (pl -s) adult person or animal > **adulthood** n (pl -s)
adulterate v (-tes, -ting, -ted) spoil something by adding inferior material > **adulteration** n (pl -s)
adulterated v ▷ adulterate
adulterates v ▷ adulterate
adulterating v ▷ adulterate
adulteration n ▷ adulterate
adulterations n ▷ adulterate
adulterer n ▷ adultery
adulterers n ▷ adultery
adulteress n ▷ adultery
adulteresses n ▷ adultery
adulteries n ▷ adultery
adulterous adj ▷ adultery
adultery n (pl -teries) sexual unfaithfulness of a husband or wife > **adulterer** n (pl -s) > **adulteress** n (pl -es) > **adulterous** adj
adulthood n ▷ adult
adulthoods n ▷ adult
adults n ▷ adult
advance v (-ces, -cing, -ced) go or bring

forward ▶ n (pl **-s**) forward movement ▶ adj done or happening before an event

advanced adj at a late stage in development ▶ v ▷ advance

advancement n (pl **advancements**) promotion

advancements n ▷ advancement

advances v, n ▷ advance

advancing v ▷ advance

advantage n (pl **-s**) more favourable position or state > **advantageous** adj > **advantageously** adv

advantageous adj ▷ advantage

advantageously adv ▷ advantage

advantages n ▷ advantage

advent n (pl **-s**) arrival

adventitious adj added or appearing accidentally

advents n ▷ advent

adventure n (pl **-s**) exciting and risky undertaking or exploit > **adventurous** adj

adventurer n (pl **-s**) person who unscrupulously seeks money or power

adventurers n ▷ adventurer

adventures n ▷ adventure

adventuress n (pl **-es**) woman who unscrupulously seeks money or power

adventuresses n ▷ adventuress

adventurous adj ▷ adventure

adverb n (pl **-s**) word that adds information about a verb, adjective, or other adverb > **adverbial** adj

adverbial adj ▷ adverb

adverbs n ▷ adverb

adversaries n ▷ adversary

adversary [ad-verse-er-ree] n (pl **-ries**) opponent or enemy

adverse adj unfavourable > **adversely** adv

adversely adv ▷ adverse

adversities n ▷ adversity

adversity n (pl **-ties**) very difficult or hard circumstances

advert n (pl **-s**) (Informal) advertisement

advertise v (**-ses, -sing, -sed**) present or praise (goods or services) to the public in order to encourage sales > **advertiser** n (pl **-s**) > **advertising** adj, n (pl **-s**)

advertised v ▷ advertise

advertisement n (pl **-s**) public announcement to sell goods or publicize an event

advertisements n ▷ advertisement

advertiser n ▷ advertise

advertises v ▷ advertise

advertising v, adj n ▷ advertise

advertisings n ▷ advertise

adverts n ▷ advert

advice n (pl **-s**) recommendation as to what to do

advices n ▷ advice

advisabilities n ▷ advisable

advisability n ▷ advisable

advisable adj prudent, sensible > **advisability** n (pl **-ties**)

advise v (**-ses, -sing, -sed**) offer advice to

advised adj considered, thought-out ▶ v ▷ advise

advisedly adv deliberately

adviser, advisor n (pl **-s**) person who offers advice, e.g. on careers to students or school pupils

advisers n ▷ adviser

advises v ▷ advise

advising v ▷ advise

advisor n ▷ adviser

advisors n ▷ adviser

advisory adj giving advice

advocaat n (pl **-s**) liqueur with a raw egg base

advocaats n ▷ advocaat

advocacies n ▷ advocate

advocacy n ▷ advocate

advocate v (**-tes, -ting, -ted**) propose or recommend ▶ n (pl **-s**) person who publicly supports a cause > **advocacy** n (pl **-cies**)

advocated v ▷ advocate

advocates v, n ▷ advocate

advocating v ▷ advocate

adz n ▷ adze

adze, adz n (pl **adzes**) tool with an arched blade at right angles to the handle

adzes n ▷ adze

ae adj. Ae is a Scots word that means **one**. This is a useful word to remember when you want to form words in two directions at once. Ae scores 2 points.

aegis [ee-jiss] n (pl **-es**) sponsorship, protection

aegises n ▷ aegis

aeon [ee-on] n (pl **-s**) immeasurably long period of time

aeons n ▷ aeon

aerate v (**-tes, -ting, -ted**) put gas into (a liquid), as when making a fizzy drink > **aeration** n (pl **-s**)

aerated v ▷ aerate

aerates v ▷ aerate

aerating v ▷ aerate

aeration n ▷ aerate

aerations n ▷ aerate

aerial adj in, from, or operating in the air ▶ n (pl **-ls**) metal pole, wire, etc., for receiving or transmitting radio or TV signals

aerials *n* ▷ aerial
aerobatic *adj* ▷ aerobatics
aerobatics *pl n* stunt flying > **aerobatic** *adj*
aerobic *adj* ▷ aerobics
aerobics *n* exercises designed to increase the
   amount of oxygen in the blood > **aerobic** *adj*
aerodrome *n* (*pl* -s) small airport
aerodromes *n* ▷ aerodrome
aerodynamic *adj* ▷ aerodynamics
aerodynamics *n* study of how air flows
   around moving solid objects > **aerodynamic**
   adj
aerofoil *n* (*pl* -s) part of an aircraft, such as the
   wing, designed to give lift
aerofoils *n* ▷ aerofoil
aerogram *n* (*pl* -s) airmail letter on a single
   sheet of paper that seals to form an envelope
aerograms *n* ▷ aerogram
aeronautical *adj* ▷ aeronautics
aeronautics *n* study or practice of aircraft
   flight > **aeronautical** *adj*
aeroplane *n* (*pl* -s) powered flying vehicle with
   fixed wings
aeroplanes *n* ▷ aeroplane
aerosol *n* (*pl* -s) pressurized can from which a
   substance can be dispensed as a fine spray
aerosols *n* ▷ aerosol
aerospace *n* (*pl* -s) earth's atmosphere and
   space beyond
aerospaces *n* ▷ aerospace
aesthete [eess-theet] *n* (*pl* -s) person who
   has or affects an extravagant love of art
   > **aestheticism** *n* (*pl* -s)
aesthetes *n* ▷ aesthete
aesthetic [iss-thet-ik] *adj* relating to
   the appreciation of art and beauty
   > **aesthetically** *adv*
aesthetically *adv* ▷ aesthetic
aestheticism *n* ▷ aesthete
aestheticisms *n* ▷ aesthete
aesthetics *n* study of art, beauty, and good
   taste
aether *n* (*pl* -s) ▷ ether
aethers *n* ▷ aether
aetiologies *n* ▷ aetiology
aetiology [ee-tee-ol-a-jee] *n* (*pl* -gies) ▷ etiology
afar *adv* from or at a great distance
affabilities *n* ▷ affable
affability *n* ▷ affable
affable *adj* friendly and easy to talk to > **affably**
   adv > **affability** *n* (*pl* -ties)
affably *adv* ▷ affable
affair *n* (*pl* -s) event or happening
affairs *n* ▷ affair
affect[1] *v* (-s, -ing, -ed) act on, influence

affect[2] *v* (-s, -ing, -ed) put on a show of
affectation *n* (*pl* -s) attitude or manner put on
   to impress
affectations *n* ▷ affectation
affected *adj* displaying affectation ▶ *v*
   ▷ affect[1, 2]
affecting *v* ▷ affect[1, 2]
affection *n* (*pl* -s) fondness or love
affectionate *adj* loving > **affectionately** *adv*
affectionately *adv* ▷ affectionate
affections *n* ▷ affection
affects *v* ▷ affect[1, 2]
affianced [af-fie-anst] *adj* (*Old-fashioned*)
   engaged to be married
affidavit [af-fid-dave-it] *n* (*pl* -s) written
   statement made on oath
affidavits *n* ▷ affidavit
affiliate *v* (-tes, -ting, -ted) (of a group) link up
   with a larger group > **affiliation** *n* (*pl* -s)
affiliated *v* ▷ affiliate
affiliates *v* ▷ affiliate
affiliating *v* ▷ affiliate
affiliation *n* ▷ affiliate
affiliations *n* ▷ affiliate
affinities *n* ▷ affinity
affinity *n* (*pl* -ties) close connection or liking
affirm *v* (-s, -ing, -ed) declare to be true
   > **affirmation** *n* (*pl* -s)
affirmation *n* ▷ affirm
affirmations *n* ▷ affirm
affirmative *n* (*pl* -s), *adj* (word or phrase)
   indicating agreement
affirmatives *n* ▷ affirmative
affirmed *v* ▷ affirm
affirming *v* ▷ affirm
affirms *v* ▷ affirm
affix *v* (-fixes, -fixing, -fixed) attach or fasten
   ▶ *n* (*pl* -fixes) word or syllable added to a word
   to change its meaning
affixed *v* ▷ affix
affixes *v*, *n* ▷ affix
affixing *v* ▷ affix
afflict *v* (-s, -ing, -ed) give pain or grief to
   > **affliction** *n* (*pl* -s)
afflicted *v* ▷ afflict
afflicting *v* ▷ afflict
affliction *n* ▷ afflict
afflictions *n* ▷ afflict
afflicts *v* ▷ afflict
affluence *n* (*pl* -s) wealth
affluences *n* ▷ affluence
affluent *adj* having plenty of money
afford *v* (-s, -ing, -ed) have enough money to
   buy > **affordable** *adj*
affordable *adj* ▷ afford

afforded v ▷ afford
affording v ▷ afford
affords v ▷ afford
afforest v (-s, -ing, -ed) plant trees on
> **afforestation** n (pl -s)
afforestation n ▷ afforest
afforestations n ▷ afforest
afforested v ▷ afforest
afforesting v ▷ afforest
afforests v ▷ afforest
affray n (pl -s) (BRIT, AUST & NZ) (LAW) noisy fight,
brawl
affrays n ▷ affray
affront v (-s, -ing, -ed), n (pl -s) insult
affronted v ▷ affront
affronting v ▷ affront
affronts v, n ▷ affront
afghan adj of Afghanistan or its language
aficionado [af-fish-yo-**nah**-do] n (pl -dos)
enthusiastic fan of something or someone
aficionados n ▷ aficionado
afield adv far away
aflame adj burning
afloat adv, adj floating
afoot adv, adj happening, in operation
aforementioned adj referred to previously
aforesaid adj referred to previously
aforethought adj premeditated
afraid adj frightened
afresh adv again, anew
aft adv at or towards the rear of a ship or
aircraft
after prep following in time or place ▶ conj at a
later time than ▶ adv at a later time
afterbirth n (pl -s) material expelled from the
womb after childbirth
afterbirths n ▷ afterbirth
aftercare n (pl -s) support given to a person
discharged from a hospital or prison
aftercares n ▷ aftercare
aftereffect n (pl -s) result occurring some time
after its cause
aftereffects n ▷ aftereffect
afterglow n (pl -s) glow left after a source of
light has gone
afterglows n ▷ afterglow
afterlife n (pl -lives) life after death
afterlives n ▷ afterlife
aftermath n (pl -s) results of an event
considered together
aftermaths n ▷ aftermath
afternoon n (pl -s) time between noon and
evening
afternoons n ▷ afternoon
afters pl n (BRIT) (Informal) dessert

aftershave n (pl -s) lotion applied to the face
after shaving
aftershaves n ▷ aftershave
afterthought n (pl -s) idea occurring later
afterthoughts n ▷ afterthought
afterward adv ▷ afterwards
afterwards, afterward adv later

> **ag** adj. Ag means to do with
agriculture. This is a good short word
to remember, as it can come in handy
when you need to form words in more
than one direction. Ag scores 3 points.

again adv once more
against prep in opposition or contrast to
agape adj (of the mouth) wide open
agaric n (pl -s) fungus with gills on the
underside of the cap, such as a mushroom
agarics n ▷ agaric
agate [ag-git] n (pl -s) semiprecious form of
quartz with striped colouring
agates n ▷ agate
age n (pl -s) length of time a person or thing
has existed ▶ v (-s, ageing or aging, -d) make
or grow old > **ageing, aging** n, adj
aged adj [ay-jid] old ▷ age
ageing v, n, adj ▷ age
ageless adj apparently never growing old
agencies n ▷ agency
agency n (pl -cies) organization providing a
service
agenda n (pl -s) list of things to be dealt with,
esp. at a meeting
agendas n ▷ agenda
agent n (pl -s) person acting on behalf of
another
agents n ▷ agent
ages n, v ▷ age
agglomeration n (pl -s) confused mass or
cluster
agglomerations n ▷ agglomeration
aggrandize v (-zes, -zing, -zed) make greater
in size, power, or rank > **aggrandizement**
n (pl -s)
aggrandized v ▷ aggrandize
aggrandizement n ▷ aggrandize
aggrandizements n ▷ aggrandize
aggrandizes v ▷ aggrandize
aggrandizing v ▷ aggrandize
aggravate v (-tes, -ting, -ted) make worse
> **aggravating** adj > **aggravation** n (pl -s)
aggravated v ▷ aggravate
aggravates v ▷ aggravate
aggravating v, adj ▷ aggravate
aggravation n ▷ aggravate
aggravations n ▷ aggravate

aggregate n (pl -s) total ▶ adj gathered into
a mass ▶ v (-tes, -ting, -ted) combine into a
whole > **aggregation** n (pl -s)
  aggregated v ▷ **aggregate**
  aggregates n, v ▷ **aggregate**
  aggregating v ▷ **aggregate**
  aggregation n ▷ **aggregate**
  aggregations n ▷ **aggregate**
aggression n (pl -s) hostile behaviour
  > **aggressor** n (pl -s)
  aggressions n ▷ **aggression**
aggressive adj showing aggression
  > **aggressively** adv > **aggressiveness** n
  aggressively adv ▷ **aggressive**
  aggressiveness n ▷ **aggressive**
  aggressor n ▷ **aggression**
  aggressors n ▷ **aggression**
aggrieved adj upset and angry
aggro n (pl -s) (BRIT, AUST & NZ) (Slang) aggressive
behaviour
  aggros n ▷ **aggro**
aghast adj overcome with amazement or
horror
agile adj (-r, -st) nimble, quick-moving > **agility**
n (pl -ties)
  agiler adj ▷ **agile**
  agilest adj ▷ **agile**
  agilities n ▷ **agile**
  agility n ▷ **agile**
  aging v, n, adj ▷ **age**
agitate v (-tes, -ting, -ted) disturb or excite
  > **agitation** n (pl -s) > **agitator** n (pl -s)
  agitated v ▷ **agitate**
  agitates v ▷ **agitate**
  agitating v ▷ **agitate**
  agitation n ▷ **agitate**
  agitations n ▷ **agitate**
  agitator n ▷ **agitate**
  agitators n ▷ **agitate**
aglow adj glowing
agnostic n (pl -s) person who believes that it is
impossible to know whether God exists ▶ adj
of agnostics > **agnosticism** n (pl -s)
  agnosticism n ▷ **agnostic**
  agnosticisms n ▷ **agnostic**
  agnostics n ▷ **agnostic**
ago adv in the past
agog adj eager or curious
  agonies n ▷ **agony**
agonize v (-zes, -zing, -zed) worry greatly
  > **agonizing** adj
  agonized v ▷ **agonize**
  agonizes v ▷ **agonize**
  agonizing v, adj ▷ **agonize**
agony n (pl -nies) extreme physical or mental
pain

agoraphobia n (pl -s) fear of open spaces
  > **agoraphobic** n (pl -s), adj
  agoraphobias n ▷ **agoraphobia**
  agoraphobic n, adj ▷ **agoraphobia**
  agoraphobics n ▷ **agoraphobic**
agrarian adj of land or agriculture
agree v (-s, -ing, -d) be of the same opinion
agreeable adj pleasant and enjoyable
  > **agreeably** adv
  agreeably adv ▷ **agreeable**
  agreed v ▷ **agree**
  agreeing v ▷ **agree**
agreement n (pl agreements) agreeing
  agreements n ▷ **agreement**
  agrees v ▷ **agree**
  agricultural adj ▷ **agriculture**
  agriculturalist n ▷ **agriculture**
  agriculturalists n ▷ **agriculture**
agriculture n (pl -s) raising of crops and
livestock > **agricultural** adj > **agriculturalist**
n (pl -s)
  agricultures n ▷ **agriculture**
  agronomies n ▷ **agronomy**
  agronomist n ▷ **agronomy**
  agronomists n ▷ **agronomy**
agronomy [ag-ron-om-mee] n (pl -mies) science
of soil management and crop production
  > **agronomist** n (pl -s)
aground adv onto the bottom of shallow
water
ague [aig-yew] n (pl -s) (Old-fashioned) periodic
fever with shivering
  agues n ▷ **ague**

> **ah** interj. Ah is a sound people make
> to show pleasure or pain. Ah scores 5
> points, and is a good word to form as a
> result of playing a longer word.

ahead adv in front
ahoy interj shout used at sea to attract
attention

> **ai** n (ais). An ai is a three-toed sloth.
> Although ai only scores 2 points, it's a
> useful word to remember when you're
> trying to form several words at once.

aid v (-s, -ing, -ed) ▶ n (pl -s) (give) assistance
or support
aide n (pl -s) assistant
  aided v ▷ **aid**
  aides n ▷ **aide**
  aiding v ▷ **aid**
  aids v, n ▷ **aid**
ail v (-s, -ing, -ed) trouble, afflict
  ailed v ▷ **ail**
aileron n (pl -s) movable flap on an aircraft

wing which controls rolling

ailerons n ▷ aileron

ailing adj sickly ▶ v ▷ ail

ailment n (pl -s) illness

ailments n ▷ ailment

ails v ▷ ail

aim v (-s, -ing, -ed) point (a weapon or missile) or direct (a blow or remark) at a target ▶ n (pl -s) aiming

aimed v ▷ aim

aiming v ▷ aim

aimless adj having no purpose > **aimlessly** adv

aimlessly adv ▷ aimless

aims v, n ▷ aim

air n (pl -s) mixture of gases forming the earth's atmosphere ▶ v (-s, -ing, -ed) make known publicly

airborne adj carried by air

airbrush n (pl -es) atomizer spraying paint by compressed air

airbrushes n ▷ airbrush

aircraft n any machine that flies, such as an aeroplane

aired v ▷ air

airfield n (pl -s) place where aircraft can land and take off

airfields n ▷ airfield

airier adj ▷ airy

airiest adj ▷ airy

airily adv ▷ airy

airing n (pl -s) exposure to air for drying or ventilation ▶ v ▷ air

airings n ▷ airing

airless adj stuffy

airlift n (pl -s) transport of troops or cargo by aircraft when other routes are blocked ▶ v (-s, -ing, -ed) transport by airlift

airlifted v ▷ airlift

airlifting v ▷ airlift

airlifts n, v ▷ airlift

airline n (pl -s) company providing scheduled flights for passengers and cargo

airliner n (pl -s) large passenger aircraft

airliners n ▷ airliner

airlines n ▷ airline

airlock n (pl -s) air bubble blocking the flow of liquid in a pipe

airlocks n ▷ airlock

airmail n system of sending mail by aircraft

airman n (pl -men) member of the air force

airmen n ▷ airman

airplay n (pl -s) broadcast performances of a record on radio

airplays n ▷ airplay

airport n (pl -s) airfield for civilian aircraft,

with facilities for aircraft maintenance and passengers

airports n ▷ airport

airs n, v ▷ air

airship n (pl -s) lighter-than-air self-propelled aircraft

airships n ▷ airship

airspace n (pl -s) atmosphere above a country, regarded as its territory

airspaces n ▷ airspace

airstrip n (pl -s) cleared area where aircraft can take off and land

airstrips n ▷ airstrip

airtight adj sealed so that air cannot enter

airworthiness n ▷ airworthy

airworthinesses n ▷ airworthy

airworthy adj (of aircraft) fit to fly > **airworthiness** n (pl -es)

airy adj (-rier, -riest) well-ventilated > **airily** adv

aisle [rhymes with **mile**] n (pl -s) passageway separating seating areas in a church, theatre, etc., or row of shelves in a supermarket

aisles n ▷ aisle

ajar adj, adv (of a door) partly open

akimbo adv with hands on hips and elbows outwards

akin adj similar, related

al conj. Al is an old word for **if** or **although**. Al scores 2 points.

alabaster n (pl -s) soft white translucent stone

alabasters n ▷ alabaster

alacrities n ▷ alacrity

alacrity n (pl -ies) speed, eagerness

alarm n (pl -s) sudden fear caused by awareness of danger ▶ v (-s, -ing, -med) fill with fear > **alarming** adj

alarmed v ▷ alarm

alarming v, adj ▷ alarm

alarmist n (pl -s) person who alarms others needlessly

alarmists n ▷ alarmist

alarms n, v ▷ alarm

alas adv unfortunately, regrettably

albatross n (pl -es) large sea bird with very long wings

albatrosses n ▷ albatross

albeit conj even though

albino n (pl -nos) person or animal with white skin and hair and pink eyes

albinos n ▷ albino

album n (pl -s) book with blank pages for keeping photographs or stamps in

albumen n (pl -s) egg white

albumens n ▷ albumen

albumin n (pl -s) protein found in blood

plasma, egg white, milk, and muscle
albumins *n* ▷ **albumin**
albums *n* ▷ **album**
alchemies *n* ▷ **alchemy**
alchemist *n* ▷ **alchemy**
alchemists *n* ▷ **alchemy**
alchemy *n* (*pl* **-ies**) medieval form of chemistry concerned with trying to turn base metals into gold and to find the elixir of life
> **alchemist** *n* (*pl* **-s**)
alcohol *n* (*pl* **-s**) colourless flammable liquid present in intoxicating drinks
alcoholic *adj* of alcohol ▶ *n* (*pl* **-s**) person addicted to alcohol
alcoholics *n* ▷ **alcoholic**
alcoholism *n* (*pl* **-s**) addiction to alcohol
alcoholisms *n* ▷ **alcoholism**
alcohols *n* ▷ **alcohol**
alcopop *n* (*pl* **-s**) (BRIT, AUST & S AFR) (*Informal*) alcoholic drink that tastes like a soft drink
alcopops *n* ▷ **alcopop**
alcove *n* (*pl* **-s**) recess in the wall of a room
alcoves *n* ▷ **alcove**
aldehyde *n* (*pl* **-s**) one of a group of chemical compounds derived from alcohol by oxidation
aldehydes *n* ▷ **aldehyde**
alder *n* (*pl* **-s**) tree related to the birch
alderman *n* (*pl* **-men**) formerly, senior member of a local council
aldermen *n* ▷ **alderman**
alders *n* ▷ **alder**
ale *n* (*pl* **-s**) kind of beer
alert *adj* (**-er, -est**) watchful, attentive ▶ *n* (*pl* **-s**) warning of danger ▶ *v* (**-s, -ing, -ed**) warn of danger > **alertness** *n* (*pl* **-es**)
alerted *v* ▷ **alert**
alerter *adj* ▷ **alert**
alertest *adj* ▷ **alert**
alerting *v* ▷ **alert**
alertness *n* ▷ **alert**
alertnesses *n* ▷ **alert**
alerts *n, v* ▷ **alert**
ales *n* ▷ **ale**
alfalfa *n* (*pl* **-s**) kind of plant used to feed livestock
alfalfas *n* ▷ **alfalfa**
alfresco *adv, adj* in the open air
alga *n* (*pl* **-e**) (usually plural) plant which lives in or near water and has no true stems, leaves, or roots
algae [al-jee] *n* ▷ **alga**
algebra *n* (*pl* **-s**) branch of mathematics using symbols to represent numbers > **algebraic** *adj*
algebraic *adj* ▷ **algebra**

algebras *n* ▷ **algebra**
algorithm *n* (*pl* **-s**) logical arithmetical or computational procedure for solving a problem
algorithms *n* ▷ **algorithm**
alias *adv* also known as ▶ *n* (*pl* **-ses**) false name
aliases *n* ▷ **alias**
alibi *n* (*pl* **-s**) plea of being somewhere else when a crime was committed
alibis *n* ▷ **alibi**
alien *adj* foreign ▶ *n* (*pl* **-s**) foreigner
alienate *v* (**-tes, -ting, -ted**) cause to become hostile > **alienation** *n* (*pl* **-s**)
alienated *v* ▷ **alienate**
alienates *v* ▷ **alienate**
alienating *v* ▷ **alienate**
alienation *n* ▷ **alienate**
alienations *n* ▷ **alienate**
aliens *n* ▷ **alien**
alight[1] *v* (**-s, -ing, -ed**) step out of (a vehicle)
alight[2] *adj* on fire
alighted *v* ▷ **alight**[1]
alighting *v* ▷ **alight**[1]
alights *v* ▷ **alight**[1]
align [a-line] *v* (**-s, -ing, -ed**) bring (a person or group) into agreement with the policy of another > **alignment** *n* (*pl* **-s**)
aligned *v* ▷ **align**
aligning *v* ▷ **align**
alignment *n* ▷ **align**
alignments *n* ▷ **align**
aligns *v* ▷ **align**
alike *adj* like, similar ▶ *adv* in the same way
alimentary *adj* of nutrition
alimonies *n* ▷ **alimony**
alimony *n* (*pl* **-nies**) allowance paid under a court order to a separated or divorced spouse
aliquot (MATHS) *adj* of or denoting an exact divisor of a number ▶ *n* (*pl* **-s**) exact divisor
aliquots *n* ▷ **aliquot**
alive *adj* living, in existence
alkali [alk-a-lie] *n* (*pl* **-s**) substance which combines with acid and neutralizes it to form a salt > **alkaline** *adj* > **alkalinity** *n* (*pl* **-ties**)
alkaline *adj* ▷ **alkali**
alkalinities *n* ▷ **alkali**
alkalinity *n* ▷ **alkali**
alkalis *n* ▷ **alkali**
alkaloid *n* (*pl* **-s**) any of a group of organic compounds containing nitrogen
alkaloids *n* ▷ **alkaloid**
all *adj* whole quantity or number (of) ▶ *adv* wholly, entirely
allay *v* (**-s, -ing, -ed**) reduce (fear or anger)
allayed *v* ▷ **allay**

allaying v ▷ allay
allays v ▷ allay
allegation n (pl -s) unproved accusation
  allegations n ▷ allegation
allege v (-ges, -ging, -ged) state without proof
  > **alleged** adj > **allegedly** adv
  alleged v, adj ▷ allege
  allegedly adv ▷ allege
  alleges v ▷ allege
allegiance n (pl -s) loyalty to a person, country,
or cause
  allegiances n ▷ allegiance
  alleging v ▷ allege
  allegorical adj ▷ allegory
  allegories n ▷ allegory
allegory n (pl -ries) story with an underlying
meaning as well as the literal one
  > **allegorical** adj
allegretto n (pl -s) ▶ adv (MUSIC) (piece to be
played) fairly quickly or briskly
  allegrettos n ▷ allegretto
allegro n (pl -s) ▶ adv (MUSIC) (piece to be
played) in a brisk lively manner
  allegros n ▷ allegro
  alleluia interj ▷ hallelujah
allergen n (pl -s) substance capable of causing
an allergic reaction
  allergens n ▷ allergen
allergic adj having or caused by an allergy
  allergies n ▷ allergy
allergy n (pl -gies) extreme sensitivity to a
substance, which causes the body to react
to it
alleviate v (-tes, -ting, -ted) lessen (pain or
suffering) > **alleviation** n (pl -s)
  alleviated v ▷ alleviate
  alleviates v ▷ alleviate
  alleviating v ▷ alleviate
  alleviation n ▷ alleviate
  alleviations n ▷ alleviate
alley n (pl -s) narrow street or path
  alleys n ▷ alley
alliance n (pl -s) state of being allied
  alliances n ▷ alliance
  allied v, adj ▷ ally
  allies n, v ▷ ally
alligator n (pl -s) reptile of the crocodile family,
found in the southern US and China
  alligators n ▷ alligator
alliteration n (pl -s) use of the same sound at
the start of words occurring together, e.g.
moody music > **alliterative** adj
  alliterations n ▷ alliteration
  alliterative adj ▷ alliteration
allocate v (-tes, -ting, -ted) assign to someone

or for a particular purpose > **allocation** n
(pl -s)
  allocated v ▷ allocate
  allocates v ▷ allocate
  allocating v ▷ allocate
  allocation n ▷ allocate
  allocations n ▷ allocate
allot v (-lots, -lotting, -lotted) assign as a share
or for a particular purpose
allotment n (pl -s) distribution
  allotments n ▷ allotment
allotrope n (pl -s) any of two or more physical
forms in which an element can exist
  allotropes n ▷ allotrope
  allots v ▷ allot
  allotted v ▷ allot
  allotting v ▷ allot
allow v (-s, -ing, -ed) permit > **allowable** adj
  allowable adj ▷ allow
allowance n (pl -s) amount of money given at
regular intervals
  allowances n ▷ allowance
  allowed v ▷ allow
  allowing v ▷ allow
  allows v ▷ allow
alloy n (pl -s) mixture of two or more metals ▶ v
(-s, -ing, -ed) mix (metals)
  alloyed v ▷ alloy
  alloying v ▷ alloy
  alloys n, v ▷ alloy
allspice n (pl -s) spice made from the berries of
a tropical American tree
  allspices n ▷ allspice
allude v (-des, -ding, -ded) (foll. by to) refer
indirectly
  alluded v ▷ allude
  alludes v ▷ allude
  alluding v ▷ allude
allure n (pl -s) attractiveness ▶ v (-s, -ing, -ed)
entice or attract > **alluring** adj
  allured v ▷ allure
  allures n, v ▷ allure
  alluring v, adj ▷ allure
allusion n (pl -s) indirect reference > **allusive**
adj
  allusions n ▷ allusion
  allusive adj ▷ allusion
  alluvial adj ▷ alluvium
alluvium n (pl -s) fertile soil deposited by
flowing water > **alluvial** adj
  alluviums n ▷ alluvium
ally n (pl -lies) country, person, or group with
an agreement to support another ▶ v (-lies,
-lying, -lied) > **allied** adj
  allying v ▷ ally

almanac n (pl -s) yearly calendar with detailed information on anniversaries, phases of the moon, etc.
  almanacs n ▷ **almanac**
almighty adj having absolute power
almond n (pl -s) edible oval-shaped nut which grows on a small tree
  almonds n ▷ **almond**
almoner n (pl -s) (BRIT) formerly, a hospital social worker
  almoners n ▷ **almoner**
almost adv very nearly
alms [ahmz] pl n (Old-fashioned) gifts to the poor
aloe n (pl -s) plant with fleshy spiny leaves
  aloes n ▷ **aloe**
aloft adv in the air
alone adj, adv without anyone or anything else
along prep over part or all the length of ▶ adv forward
alongside prep, adv beside (something)
aloof adj distant or haughty in manner
  > **aloofness** n (pl -es)
  aloofness n ▷ **aloof**
  aloofnesses n ▷ **aloof**
alopecia [al-loh-**pee**-sha] n (pl -s) loss of hair
  alopecias n ▷ **alopecia**
aloud adv in an audible voice
alpaca n (pl -s) Peruvian llama
  alpacas n ▷ **alpaca**
alpenstock n (pl -s) iron-tipped stick used by climbers
  alpenstocks n ▷ **alpenstock**
alpha n (pl -s) first letter in the Greek alphabet
alphabet n (pl -s) set of letters used in writing a language
alphabetical adj in the conventional order of the letters of an alphabet > **alphabetically** adv
  alphabetically adv ▷ **alphabetical**
alphabetize v (-zes, -zing, -zed) put in alphabetical order
  alphabetized v ▷ **alphabetize**
  alphabetizes v ▷ **alphabetize**
  alphabetizing v ▷ **alphabetize**
  alphabets n ▷ **alphabet**
  alphas n ▷ **alpha**
alpine adj of high mountains ▶ n (pl -s) mountain plant
  alpines n ▷ **alpine**
already adv before the present time
alright adj, interj all right
also adv in addition, too
altar n (pl -s) table used for Communion in Christian churches
altarpiece n (pl -s) work of art above and

behind the altar in some Christian churches
  altarpieces n ▷ **altarpiece**
  altars n ▷ **altar**
alter v (-s, -ing, -ed) make or become different
  > **alteration** n (pl -s)
  alteration n ▷ **alter**
  alterations n ▷ **alter**
altercation n (pl -s) heated argument
  altercations n ▷ **altercation**
  altered v ▷ **alter**
  altering v ▷ **alter**
alternate v (-tes, -ting, -ted) (cause to) occur by turns ▶ adj occurring by turns
  > **alternately** adv > **alternation** n (pl -s)
  alternated v ▷ **alternate**
  alternately adv ▷ **alternate**
  alternates v ▷ **alternate**
  alternating v ▷ **alternate**
  alternation n ▷ **alternate**
  alternations n ▷ **alternate**
alternative n (pl -s) one of two choices ▶ adj able to be done or used instead of something else > **alternatively** adv
  alternatively adv ▷ **alternative**
  alternatives n ▷ **alternative**
alternator n (pl -s) electric generator for producing alternating current
  alternators n ▷ **alternator**
  alters v ▷ **alter**
although conj despite the fact that
altimeter [al-**tim**-it-er] n (pl -s) instrument that measures altitude
  altimeters n ▷ **altimeter**
altitude n (pl -s) height above sea level
  altitudes n ▷ **altitude**
alto n (pl -s) (MUSIC) (singer with) the highest adult male voice
altogether adv entirely
  altos n ▷ **alto**
altruism n (pl -s) unselfish concern for the welfare of others > **altruist** n (pl -s) > **altruistic** adj > **altruistically** adv
  altruisms n ▷ **altruism**
  altruist n ▷ **altruism**
  altruists n ▷ **altruism**
  altruistic adj ▷ **altruism**
  altruistically adv ▷ **altruism**
aluminium n (pl -s) (CHEM) light silvery-white metal that does not rust
  aluminiums n ▷ **aluminium**
  alumna n ▷ **alumnus**
  alumnae n ▷ **alumnus**
  alumni n ▷ **alumnus**
alumnus [al-**lumm**-nuss] n (pl -ni) [-nie] graduate of a college > **alumna** [al-**lumm**-na]

▶ *n fem* (*pl* **-nae**) [-nee]
always *adv* at all times
alyssum *n* (*pl* **-s**) garden plant with small yellow or white flowers
  alyssums *n* ▷ **alyssum**
am *v* ▷ **be**
amalgam *n* (*pl* **-s**) blend or combination
amalgamate *v* (**-tes, -ting, -ted**) combine or unite > **amalgamation** *n* (*pl* **-s**)
  amalgamated *v* ▷ **amalgamate**
  amalgamates *v* ▷ **amalgamate**
  amalgamating *v* ▷ **amalgamate**
  amalgamation *n* ▷ **amalgamate**
  amalgamations *n* ▷ **amalgamate**
  amalgams *n* ▷ **amalgam**
amandla [ah-**mand**-lah] *n* (S AFR) political slogan calling for power to the Black population
  amanuenses *n* ▷ **amanuensis**
amanuensis [am-man-yew-**en**-siss] *n* (*pl* **-ses**) [-seez] person who writes from dictation
amaranth *n* (*pl* **-s**) imaginary flower that never fades
  amaranths *n* ▷ **amaranth**
amaryllis *n* (*pl* **-ses**) lily-like plant with large red, pink, or white flowers
  amaryllises *n* ▷ **amaryllis**
amass *v* (**-ses, -sing, -sed**) collect or accumulate
  amassed *v* ▷ **amass**
  amasses *v* ▷ **amass**
  amassing *v* ▷ **amass**
amateur *n* (*pl* **-s**) person who engages in a sport or activity as a pastime rather than as a profession
amateurish *adj* lacking skill > **amateurishly** *adv*
  amateurishly *adv* ▷ **amateurish**
  amateurs *n* ▷ **amateur**
amatory *adj* relating to romantic or sexual love
amaze *v* (**-zes, -zing, -zed**) surprise greatly, astound > **amazing** *adj* > **amazingly** *adv* > **amazement** *n* (*pl* **-s**)
  amazed *v* ▷ **amaze**
  amazement *n* ▷ **amaze**
  amazements *n* ▷ **amaze**
  amazes *v* ▷ **amaze**
  amazing *v, adj* ▷ **amaze**
  amazingly *adv* ▷ **amaze**
amazon *n* (*pl* **-s**) strong and powerful woman > **amazonian** *adj*
  amazonian *adj* ▷ **amazon**
  amazons *n* ▷ **amazon**
ambassador *n* (*pl* **-s**) senior diplomat who represents his or her country in another country > **ambassadorial** *adj*
  ambassadorial *adj* ▷ **ambassador**
  ambassadors *n* ▷ **ambassador**
amber *n* (*pl* **-s**) clear yellowish fossil resin ▶ *adj* brownish-yellow
ambergris [**am**-ber-greece] *n* (*pl* **-es**) waxy substance secreted by the sperm whale, used in making perfumes
  ambergrises *n* ▷ **ambergris**
  ambers *n* ▷ **amber**
ambidextrous *adj* able to use both hands with equal ease
ambience *n* (*pl* **-s**) atmosphere of a place
  ambiences *n* ▷ **ambience**
ambient *adj* surrounding
  ambiguities *n* ▷ **ambiguous**
  ambiguity *n* ▷ **ambiguous**
ambiguous *adj* having more than one possible meaning > **ambiguously** *adv* > **ambiguity** *n* (*pl* **-ties**)
  ambiguously *adv* ▷ **ambiguous**
ambit *n* (*pl* **-s**) limits or boundary
ambition *n* (*pl* **-s**) desire for success > **ambitious** *adj* > **ambitiously** *adv*
  ambitions *n* ▷ **ambition**
  ambitious *adj* ▷ **ambition**
  ambitiously *adv* ▷ **ambition**
  ambits *n* ▷ **ambit**
ambivalence *n* (*pl* **-s**) state of feeling two conflicting emotions at the same time > **ambivalent** *adj* > **ambivalently** *adv*
  ambivalences *n* ▷ **ambivalence**
  ambivalent *adj* ▷ **ambivalence**
  ambivalently *adv* ▷ **ambivalence**
amble *v* (**-les, -ling, -led**) walk at a leisurely pace ▶ *n* (*pl* **-s**) leisurely walk or pace
  ambled *v* ▷ **amble**
  ambles *v, n* ▷ **amble**
  ambling *v* ▷ **amble**
ambrosia *n* (*pl* **-s**) (MYTH) food of the gods > **ambrosial** *adj*
  ambrosial *adj* ▷ **ambrosia**
  ambrosias *n* ▷ **ambrosia**
ambulance *n* (*pl* **-s**) motor vehicle designed to carry sick or injured people
  ambulances *n* ▷ **ambulance**
ambush *n* (*pl* **-es**) act of waiting in a concealed position to make a surprise attack ▶ *v* (**-shes, -shing, -shed**) attack from a concealed position
  ambushed *v* ▷ **ambush**
  ambushes *n, v* ▷ **ambush**
  ambushing *v* ▷ **ambush**
ameliorate [am-**meal**-yor-rate] *v* (**-tes,**

-ting, -ted) make (something) better
> **amelioration** n (pl -s)
ameliorated v ▷ **ameliorate**
ameliorates v ▷ **ameliorate**
ameliorating v ▷ **ameliorate**
amelioration n ▷ **ameliorate**
ameliorations n ▷ **ameliorate**
amen interj so be it: used at the end of a prayer
amenable adj likely or willing to cooperate
amend v (-s, -ing, -ed) make small changes to correct or improve (something)
> **amendment** n (pl -s)
amended v ▷ **amend**
amending v ▷ **amend**
amendment n ▷ **amend**
amends pl n compensation for ▶ v ▷ **amend**
amenities n ▷ **amenity**
amenity n (pl -ties) useful or enjoyable feature
amethyst [am-myth-ist] n (pl -s) bluish-violet variety of quartz used as a gemstone
amethysts n ▷ **amethyst**
amiabilities n ▷ **amiable**
amiability n ▷ **amiable**
amiable adj friendly, pleasant-natured
> **amiably** adv > **amiability** n (pl -ties)
amiably adv ▷ **amiable**
amicable adj friendly > **amicably** adv
amicably adv ▷ **amicable**
amid, amidst prep in the middle of, among
amidships adv at or towards the middle of a ship
amidst prep ▷ **amid**
amiss adv wrongly, badly ▶ adj wrong, faulty
amities n ▷ **amity**
amity n (pl -ties) friendship
ammeter n (pl -s) instrument for measuring electric current
ammeters n ▷ **ammeter**
ammonia n (pl -s) strong-smelling alkaline gas containing hydrogen and nitrogen
ammonias n ▷ **ammonia**
ammonite n (pl -s) fossilized spiral shell of an extinct sea creature
ammonites n ▷ **ammonite**
ammunition n (pl -s) bullets, bombs, and shells that can be fired from or as a weapon
ammunitions n ▷ **ammunition**
amnesia n (pl -s) loss of memory > **amnesiac** adj, n (pl -s)
amnesiac adj, n ▷ **amnesia**
amnesiacs n ▷ **amnesia**
amnesias n ▷ **amnesia**
amnesties n ▷ **amnesty**
amnesty n (pl -ties) general pardon for offences against a government

amniocenteses n ▷ **amniocentesis**
amniocentesis n (pl -ses) removal of some amniotic fluid to test for possible abnormalities in a fetus
amoeba [am-mee-ba] n (pl -bae, -bas) microscopic single-celled animal able to change its shape
amoebae n ▷ **amoeba**
amoebas n ▷ **amoeba**
amok [a-muck, a-mock] adv in a violent frenzy
among, amongst prep in the midst of
amongst prep ▷ **among**
amoral [aim-mor-ral] adj without moral standards > **amorality** n (pl -ties)
amoralities n ▷ **amoral**
amorality n ▷ **amoral**
amorous adj feeling, showing, or relating to sexual love > **amorously** adv
amorously adv ▷ **amorous**
amorphous adj without distinct shape
amortize v (-zes, -zing, -zed) pay off (a debt) gradually by periodic transfers to a sinking fund
amortized v ▷ **amortize**
amortizes v ▷ **amortize**
amortizing v ▷ **amortize**
amount n (pl -s) extent or quantity ▶ v (-s, -ing, -ed) (foll. by to) be equal or add up to
amounted v ▷ **amount**
amounting v ▷ **amount**
amounts n, v ▷ **amount**
amour n (pl -s) (secret) love affair
amours n ▷ **amour**
amp n (pl -s) ampere
ampere [am-pair] n (pl -s) basic unit of electric current
amperes n ▷ **ampere**
ampersand n (pl -s) the character (&) meaning and
ampersands n ▷ **ampersand**
amphetamine [am-fet-am-mean] n (pl -s) drug used as a stimulant
amphetamines n ▷ **amphetamine**
amphibian n (pl -s) animal that lives on land but breeds in water
amphibians n ▷ **amphibian**
amphibious adj living or operating both on land and in water
amphitheatre n (pl -s) open oval or circular building with tiers of seats rising round an arena
amphitheatres n ▷ **amphitheatre**
amphora [am-for-ra] n (pl -phorae) two-handled ancient Greek or Roman jar
amphorae n ▷ **amphora**

ample *adj* (**-r, -st**) more than sufficient > **amply**
adv
  ampler *adj* ▷ **ample**
  amplest *adj* ▷ **ample**
  amplification *n* ▷ **amplify**
  amplifications *n* ▷ **amplify**
  amplified *v* ▷ **amplify**
amplifier *n* (*pl* **-s**) device used to amplify a
current or sound signal
  amplifiers *n* ▷ **amplifier**
  amplifies *v* ▷ **amplifly**
amplify *v* (**-fies, -fying, -fied**) increase the
strength of (a current or sound signal) of
  > **amplification** *n* (*pl* **-s**)
  amplifying *v* ▷ **amplify**
amplitude *n* (*pl* **-s**) greatness of extent
  amplitudes *n* ▷ **amplitude**
  amply *adv* ▷ **ample**
ampoule *n* (*pl* **-s**) small sealed glass vessel
containing liquid for injection
  ampoules *n* ▷ **ampoule**
  amps *n* ▷ **amp**
amputate *v* (**-tes, -ting, -ted**) cut off (a
limb or part of a limb) for medical reasons
  > **amputation** *n* (*pl* **-s**)
  amputated *v* ▷ **amputate**
  amputates *v* ▷ **amputate**
  amputating *v* ▷ **amputate**
  amputation *n* ▷ **amputate**
  amputations *n* ▷ **amputate**
  amuck *adv* ▷ **amok**
amulet *n* (*pl* **-s**) something carried or worn as a
protection against evil
  amulets *n* ▷ **amulet**
amuse *v* (**-ses, -sing, -sed**) cause to laugh or
smile > **amusing** *adj*
  amused *v* ▷ **amuse**
amusement *n* (*pl* **-s**) state of being amused
  amusements *n* ▷ **amusement**
  amuses *v* ▷ **amuse**
  amusing *v, adj* ▷ **amuse**
an *adj* form of **a** used before vowels, and
sometimes before *h*
anachronism [an-**nak**-kron-iz-zum] *n* (*pl*
-s) person or thing placed in the wrong
historical period or seeming to belong to
another time > **anachronistic** *adj*
  anachronisms *n* ▷ **anachronism**
  anachronistic *adj* ▷ **anachronism**
anaconda *n* (*pl* **-s**) large S American snake
which kills by constriction
  anacondas *n* ▷ **anaconda**
anaemia [an-**neem**-ee-a] *n* (*pl* **-s**) deficiency in
the number of red blood cells
  anaemias *n* ▷ **anaemia**

anaemic *adj* having anaemia
anaesthesia [an-niss-**theez**-ee-a] *n* (*pl* **-s**) loss of
bodily feeling
  anaesthesias *n* ▷ **anaesthesia**
anaesthetic [an-niss-**thet**-ik] *n* (*pl* **-s**), *adj*
(substance) causing loss of bodily feeling
  anaesthetics *n* ▷ **anaesthetic**
anaesthetist [an-**neess**-thet-ist] *n* (*pl* **-s**)
doctor trained to administer anaesthetics
  > **anaesthetize** *v* (**-zes, -zing, -zed**)
  anaesthetists *n* ▷ **anaesthetist**
  anaesthetize *v* ▷ **anaesthetist**
  anaesthetized *v* ▷ **anaesthetist**
  anaesthetizes *v* ▷ **anaesthetist**
  anaesthetizing *v* ▷ **anaesthetist**
anagram *n* (*pl* **-s**) word or phrase made by
rearranging the letters of another word or
phrase
  anagrams *n* ▷ **anagram**
anal [**ain**-al] *adj* of the anus
analgesia *n* (*pl* **-s**) absence of pain
  analgesias *n* ▷ **analgesia**
analgesic [an-nal-**jeez**-ik] *n* (*pl* **-s**) ▶ *adj* (drug)
relieving pain
  analgesics *n* ▷ **analgesic**
  analogical *adj* ▷ **analogy**
  analogies *n* ▷ **analogy**
analogous *adj* similar in some respects
analogue *n* (*pl* **-s**) something that is similar
in some respects to something else ▶ *adj*
displaying information by means of a dial
  analogues *n* ▷ **analogue**
analogy *n* (*pl* **-gies**) similarity in some respects
  > **analogical** *adj*
analyse *v* (**-ses, -sing, -sed**) make an analysis
of (something)
  analysed *v* ▷ **analyse**
  analyses *v* ▷ **analyse** ▶ *n* ▷ **analysis**
  analysing *v* ▷ **analyse**
analysis *n* (*pl* **-ses**) separation of a whole
into its parts for study and interpretation
  > **analytical, analytic** *adj* > **analytically** *adv*
analyst *n* (*pl* **-s**) person skilled in analysis
  analysts *n* ▷ **analyst**
  analytic *adj* ▷ **analysis**
  analytical *adj* ▷ **analysis**
  analytically *adv* ▷ **analysis**
  anarchic *adj* ▷ **anarchy**
  anarchies *n* ▷ **anarchy**
anarchism *n* (*pl* **-s**) doctrine advocating the
abolition of government
  anarchisms *n* ▷ **anarchism**
anarchist *n* (*pl* **-s**) person who advocates the
abolition of government > **anarchistic** *adj*
  anarchistic *adj* ▷ **anarchist**

anarchists *n* ▷ **anarchist**
anarchy [an-ark-ee] *n* (*pl* **-ies**) lawlessness and disorder > **anarchic** *adj*
anathema [an-**nath**-im-a] *n* (*pl* **-s**) detested person or thing
  anathemas *n* ▷ **anathema**
  anatomical *adj* ▷ **anatomy**
  anatomically *adv* ▷ **anatomy**
  anatomies *n* ▷ **anatomy**
anatomist *n* (*pl* **-s**) expert in anatomy
  anatomists *n* ▷ **anatomist**
anatomy *n* (*pl* **-mies**) science of the structure of the body > **anatomical** *adj* > **anatomically** *adv*
ancestor *n* (*pl* **-s**) person from whom one is descended > **ancestral** *adj*
  ancestors *n* ▷ **ancestor**
  ancestral *adj* ▷ **ancestor**
  ancestries *n* ▷ **ancestry**
ancestry *n* (*pl* **-ries**) lineage or descent
anchor *n* (*pl* **-s**) heavy hooked device attached to a boat by a cable and dropped overboard to fasten the ship to the sea bottom ▶ *v* (**-s, -ing, -ed**) fasten with or as if with an anchor
anchorage *n* (*pl* **-s**) place where boats can be anchored
  anchorages *n* ▷ **anchorage**
  anchored *v* ▷ **anchor**
  anchoring *v* ▷ **anchor**
anchorite *n* (*pl* **-s**) religious recluse
  anchorites *n* ▷ **anchorite**
anchorman *n* (*pl* **-men**) broadcaster in a central studio who links up and presents items from outside camera units and other studios
  anchormen *n* ▷ **anchorman**
  anchors *n, v* ▷ **anchor**
anchorwoman *n* (*pl* **-women**) female broadcaster in a central studio who links up and presents items from outside camera units and other studios
  anchorwomen *n* ▷ **anchorwoman**
  anchovies *n* ▷ **anchovy**
anchovy [an-chov-ee] *n* (*pl* **-vies**) small strong-tasting fish
ancient *adj* dating from very long ago
ancients *pl n* people who lived very long ago
ancillary *adj* supporting the main work of an organization
and *conj* in addition to
andante [an-dan-tay] *n* (*pl* **-s**) ▶ *adv* (MUSIC) (piece to be played) moderately slowly
  andantes *n* ▷ **andante**
andiron *n* (*pl* **-s**) iron stand for supporting logs in a fireplace

andirons *n* ▷ **andiron**
androgynous *adj* having both male and female characteristics
android *n* (*pl* **-s**) robot resembling a human
  androids *n* ▷ **android**
  anecdotal *adj* ▷ **anecdote**
anecdote *n* (*pl* **-s**) short amusing account of an incident > **anecdotal** *adj*
  anecdotes *n* ▷ **anecdote**
anemometer *n* (*pl* **-s**) instrument for recording wind speed
  anemometers *n* ▷ **anemometer**
anemone [an-**nem**-on-ee] *n* (*pl* **-s**) plant with white, purple, or red flowers
  anemones *n* ▷ **anemone**
  aneurism *n* ▷ **aneurysm**
  aneurisms *n* ▷ **aneurysm**
aneurysm, aneurism [an-new-riz-zum] *n* (*pl* **-s**) permanent swelling of a blood vessel
  aneurysms *n* ▷ **aneurysm**
anew *adv* once more
angel *n* (*pl* **-s**) spiritual being believed to be an attendant or messenger of God > **angelic** *adj* > **angelically** *adv*
  angelic *adj* ▷ **angel**
angelica *n* (*pl* **-s**) aromatic plant
  angelically *adv* ▷ **angel**
  angelicas *n* ▷ **angelica**
  angels *n* ▷ **angel**
angelus [an-jell-uss] *n* (*pl* **-es**) (in the Roman Catholic Church) prayers recited in the morning, at midday, and in the evening
  angeluses *n* ▷ **angelus**
anger *n* (*pl* **-s**) fierce displeasure or extreme annoyance ▶ *v* (**-s, -ing, -ed**) make (someone) angry
  angered *v* ▷ **anger**
  angering *v* ▷ **anger**
  angers *n, v* ▷ **anger**
angina [an-jine-a] *n* (*pl* **-s**) heart disorder causing sudden severe chest pains
  anginas *n* ▷ **angina**
angle[1] *n* (*pl* **-s**) space between or shape formed by two lines or surfaces that meet ▶ *v* (**-s, -ing, -ed**) bend or place (something) at an angle
angle[2] *v* (**-s, -ing, -ed**) fish with a hook and line > **angling** *n* (*pl* **-s**)
  angled *v* ▷ **angle**[1, 2]
angler *n* (*pl* **-s**) person who fishes with a hook and line
  anglers *n* ▷ **angler**
  angles *n* ▷ **angle**[1] ▶ *v* ▷ **angle**[1, 2]
anglicize *v* (**-zes, -zing, -zed**) make or become English in outlook, form, etc.
  anglicized *v* ▷ **anglicize**

anglicizes v ▷ anglicize
anglicizing v ▷ anglicize
angling n ▷ angle² ▶ v ▷¹,²
anglings n ▷ angle²
angophora n (pl -s) Australian tree related to the eucalyptus
angophoras n ▷ angophora
angora n (pl -s) variety of goat, cat, or rabbit with long silky hair
angoras n ▷ angora
angrier adj ▷ angry
angriest adj ▷ angry
angrily adv ▷ angry
angry adj (-grier, -griest) full of anger > **angrily** adv
angst n feeling of anxiety
angstrom n (pl **angstroms**) unit of length used to measure wavelengths
angstroms n ▷ angstrom
anguish n (pl -es) great mental pain
> **anguished** adj
anguished adj ▷ anguish
anguishes n ▷ anguish
angular adj (of a person) lean and bony
> **angularity** n (pl -ties)
angularities n ▷ angular
angularity n ▷ angular
anhydrous adj (CHEM) containing no water
aniline n (pl -s) colourless oily liquid obtained from coal tar and used for making dyes, plastics, and explosives
anilines n ▷ aniline
animal n (pl -s) living creature with specialized sense organs and capable of voluntary motion, esp. one other than a human being
▶ adj of animals
animals n ▷ animal
animate v (-tes, -ting, -ted) give life to ▶ adj having life > **animated** adj > **animator** n (pl -s)
animated v, adj ▷ animate
animates v ▷ animate
animating v ▷ animate
animation n (pl -s) technique of making cartoon films
animations n ▷ animation
animator n ▷ animate
animators n ▷ animate
animism n (pl -s) belief that natural objects possess souls > **animist** n (pl -s) adj
> **animistic** adj
animisms n ▷ animism
animist n, adj ▷ animism
animistic adj ▷ animism
animists n ▷ animism
animosities n ▷ animosity

animosity n (pl -ties) hostility, hatred
animus n (pl -es) hatred, animosity
animuses n ▷ animus
anion [an-eye-on] n (pl -s) ion with negative charge
anions n ▷ anion
anise [an-niss] n (pl -s) plant with liquorice-flavoured seeds
aniseed n (pl -s) liquorice-flavoured seeds of the anise plant
aniseeds n ▷ aniseed
anises n ▷ anise
ankle n (pl -s) joint between the foot and leg
ankles n ▷ ankle
anklet n (pl -s) ornamental chain worn round the ankle
anklets n ▷ anklet
annal n (usually plural) yearly record of events
annals n ▷ annal
anneal v (-s, -ing, -ed) toughen (metal or glass) by heating and slow cooling
annealed v ▷ anneal
annealing v ▷ anneal
anneals v ▷ anneal
annelid n (pl -s) worm with a segmented body, such as an earthworm
annelids n ▷ annelid
annex v (-es, -ing, -ed) seize (territory)
> **annexation** n (pl -s)
annexation n ▷ annex
annexations n ▷ annex
annexe n (pl -s) extension to a building
annexed v ▷ annex
annexes v ▷ annex ▶ n ▷ annexe
annexing v ▷ annex
annihilate v (-tes, -ting, -ted) destroy utterly
> **annihilation** n (pl -s)
annihilated v ▷ annihilate
annihilates v ▷ annihilate
annihilating v ▷ annihilate
annihilation n ▷ annihilate
annihilations n ▷ annihilate
anniversaries n ▷ anniversary
anniversary n (pl -ries) date on which something occurred in a previous year
annotate v (-tes, -ting, -ted) add notes to (a written work) > **annotation** n (pl -s)
annotated v ▷ annotate
annotates v ▷ annotate
annotating v ▷ annotate
annotation n ▷ annotate
annotations n ▷ annotate
announce v (-ces, -cing, -ced) make known publicly > **announcement** n (pl -s)
announced v ▷ announce

announcement *n* ▷ announce

announcements *n* ▷ announce

announcer *n* (*pl* -s) person who introduces radio or television programmes

announcers *n* ▷ announcer

announces *v* ▷ announce

announcing *v* ▷ announce

annoy *v* (-s, -ing, -ed) irritate or displease > **annoyance** *n* (*pl* -s)

annoyance *n* ▷ annoy

annoyances *n* ▷ annoy

annoyed *v* ▷ annoy

annoying *v* ▷ annoy

annoys *v* ▷ annoy

annual *adj* happening once a year ▶ *n* (*pl* -s) plant that completes its life cycle in a year > **annually** *adv*

annually *adv* ▷ annual

annuals *n* ▷ annual

annuities *n* ▷ annuity

annuity *n* (*pl* -ties) fixed sum paid every year

annul *v* (-ls, -lling, -lled) declare (something, esp. a marriage) invalid > **annulment** *n* (*pl* -s)

annular [an-new-lar] *adj* ring-shaped

annulled *v* ▷ annul

annulling *v* ▷ annul

annulment *n* ▷ annul

annulments *n* ▷ annul

annuls *v* ▷ annul

anode *n* (*pl* -s) (ELECTRICITY) positive electrode in a battery, valve, etc.

anodes *n* ▷ anode

anodize *v* (-zes, -zing, -zed) coat (metal) with a protective oxide film by electrolysis

anodized *v* ▷ anodize

anodizes *v* ▷ anodize

anodizing *v* ▷ anodize

anodyne *n* (*pl* -s) something that relieves pain or distress ▶ *adj* relieving pain or distress

anodynes *n* ▷ anodyne

anoint *v* (-s, -ing, -ed) smear with oil as a sign of consecration

anointed *v* ▷ anoint

anointing *v* ▷ anoint

anoints *v* ▷ anoint

anomalies *n* ▷ anomaly

anomalous *adj* ▷ anomaly

anomaly [an-nom-a-lee] *n* (*pl* -lies) something that deviates from the normal, irregularity > **anomalous** *adj*

anon *adv* (*Obs*) in a short time, soon

anonymity *n* ▷ anonymous

anonymous *adj* by someone whose name is unknown or withheld > **anonymously** *adv* > **anonymity** *n*

anonymously *adv* ▷ anonymous

anorak *n* (*pl* -s) light waterproof hooded jacket

anoraks *n* ▷ anorak

anorexia *n* (*pl* -s) psychological disorder characterized by fear of becoming fat and refusal to eat > **anorexic** *adj*, *n*

anorexias *n* ▷ anorexia

anorexic *adj*, *n* ▷ anorexia

another *adj*, *pron* one more

answer *n* (*pl* -s) reply to a question, request, letter, etc. ▶ *v* (-s, -ing, -ed) give an answer (to)

answerable *adj* (*foll. by* **for** *or* **to**) responsible for or accountable to

answered *v* ▷ answer

answering *v* ▷ answer

answers *n*, *v* ▷ answer

ant *n* (*pl* -s) small insect living in highly organized colonies

antacid *n* (*pl* -s) substance that counteracts acidity, esp. in the stomach

antacids *n* ▷ antacid

antagonism *n* (*pl* -s) open opposition or hostility

antagonisms *n* ▷ antagonism

antagonist *n* (*pl* -s) opponent or adversary > **antagonistic** *adj*

antagonistic *adj* ▷ antagonist

antagonists *n* ▷ antagonist

antagonize *v* (-zes, -zing, -zed) arouse hostility in, annoy

antagonized *v* ▷ antagonize

antagonizes *v* ▷ antagonize

antagonizing *v* ▷ antagonize

antarctic *n* area around the South Pole ▶ *adj* of this region

ante *n* (*pl* -s) player's stake in poker ▶ *v* (-tes, -teing, -ted *or* -teed) place (one's stake) in poker

anteater *n* (*pl* -s) mammal which feeds on ants by means of a long snout

anteaters *n* ▷ anteater

antecedent *n* (*pl* -s) event or circumstance happening or existing before another ▶ *adj* preceding, prior

antecedents *n* ▷ antecedent

anted *v* ▷ ante

antedate *v* (-tes, -ting, -ted) precede in time

antedated *v* ▷ antedate

antedates *v* ▷ antedate

antedating *v* ▷ antedate

antediluvian *adj* of the time before the biblical Flood

anteed *v* ▷ ante

anteing *v* ▷ ante

antelope *n* (*pl* -s) deerlike mammal with long

legs and horns
antelopes *n* ▷ **antelope**
antenatal *adj* during pregnancy, before birth
antenna *n* (*pl* **-e**) insect's feeler; (*pl* **-s**) aerial
antennae *n* ▷ **antenna**
antennas *n* ▷ **antenna**
anterior *adj* to the front
anteroom *n* (*pl* **-s**) small room leading into a
larger one, often used as a waiting room
anterooms *n* ▷ **anteroom**
antes *n*, *v* ▷ **ante**
anthem *n* (*pl* **-s**) song of loyalty, esp. to a
country
anthems *n* ▷ **anthem**
anther *n* (*pl* **-s**) part of a flower's stamen
containing pollen
anthers *n* ▷ **anther**
anthologies *n* ▷ **anthology**
anthologist *n* ▷ **anthology**
anthologists *n* ▷ **anthology**
anthology *n* (*pl* **-gies**) collection of poems
or other literary pieces by various authors
> **anthologist** *n* (*pl* **-s**)
anthraces *n* ▷ **anthrax**
anthracite *n* (*pl* **-s**) hard coal burning slowly
with little smoke or flame but intense heat
anthracites *n* ▷ **anthracite**
anthrax *n* (*pl* **-thraces**) dangerous disease of
cattle and sheep, communicable to humans
anthropoid *adj* like a human ▶ *n* (*pl* **-s**) ape,
such as a chimpanzee, that resembles a
human
anthropoids *n* ▷ **anthropoid**
anthropological *adj* ▷ **anthropology**
anthropologies *n* ▷ **anthropology**
anthropologist *n* ▷ **anthropology**
anthropologists *n* ▷ **anthropology**
anthropology *n* (*pl* **-ies**) study of human
origins, institutions, and beliefs
> **anthropological** *adj* > **anthropologist** *n*
(*pl* **-s**)
anthropomorphic *adj* attributing human
form or personality to a god, animal, or
object > **anthropomorphism** *n* (*pl* **-s**)
anthropomorphism *n* ▷ **anthropomorphic**
anthropomorphisms *n* ▷ **anthropomorphic**
antibiotic *n* (*pl* **-s**) chemical substance capable
of destroying bacteria ▶ *adj* of antibiotics
antibiotics *n* ▷ **antibiotic**
antibodies *n* ▷ **antibody**
antibody *n* (*pl* **-dies**) protein produced in the
blood, which destroys bacteria
anticipate *v* (**-tes, -ting, -ted**) foresee and
act in advance of > **anticipation** *n* (*pl* **-s**)
> **anticipatory** *adj*

anticipated *v* ▷ **anticipate**
anticipates *v* ▷ **anticipate**
anticipating *v* ▷ **anticipate**
anticipation *n* ▷ **anticipate**
anticipations *n* ▷ **anticipate**
anticipatory *adj* ▷ **anticipate**
anticlimax *n* (*pl* **-es**) disappointing conclusion
to a series of events
anticlimaxes *n* ▷ **anticlimax**
anticlockwise *adv*, *adj* in the opposite
direction to the rotation of the hands of a
clock
antics *pl n* absurd acts or postures
anticyclone *n* (*pl* **-s**) area of moving air of high
pressure in which the winds rotate outwards
anticyclones *n* ▷ **anticyclone**
antidote *n* (*pl* **-s**) substance that counteracts
a poison
antidotes *n* ▷ **antidote**
antifreeze *n* (*pl* **-s**) liquid added to water to
lower its freezing point, used esp. in car
radiators
antifreezes *n* ▷ **antifreeze**
antigen [an-tee-jen] *n* (*pl* **-s**) substance,
usu. a toxin, causing the blood to produce
antibodies
antigens *n* ▷ **antigen**
antihero *n* (*pl* **-roes**) central character in a
book, film, etc., who lacks the traditional
heroic virtues
antiheroes *n* ▷ **antihero**
antihistamine *n* (*pl* **-s**) drug used to treat
allergies
antihistamines *n* ▷ **antihistamine**
antimacassar *n* (*pl* **-s**) cloth put over a chair-
back to prevent soiling
antimacassars *n* ▷ **antimacassar**
antimonies *n* ▷ **antimony**
antimony *n* (*pl* **-ies**) (CHEM) brittle silvery-
white metallic element
antipathetic *adj* ▷ **antipathy**
antipathies *n* ▷ **antipathy**
antipathy [an-tip-a-thee] *n* (*pl* **-thies**) dislike,
hostility > **antipathetic** *adj*
antiperspirant *n* (*pl* **-s**) substance used to
reduce or prevent sweating
antiperspirants *n* ▷ **antiperspirant**
antiphon *n* (*pl* **-s**) hymn sung in alternate parts
by two groups of singers > **antiphonal** *adj*
antiphonal *adj* ▷ **antiphon**
antiphons *n* ▷ **antiphon**
antipodean *adj* ▷ **antipodes**
antipodes [an-**tip**-pod-deez] *pl n* any two places
diametrically opposite one another on the
earth's surface > **antipodean** *adj*

antipyretic *adj* reducing fever ▶ *n* (*pl* -**s**) drug that reduces fever

antipyretics *n* ▷ **antipyretic**

antiquarian *adj* of or relating to antiquities or rare books ▶ *n* (*pl* -**s**) antiquary

antiquarians *n* ▷ **antiquarian**

antiquaries *n* ▷ **antiquary**

antiquary *n* (*pl* -**ries**) student or collector of antiques or ancient works of art

antiquated *adj* out-of-date

antique *n* (*pl* -**s**) object of an earlier period, valued for its beauty, workmanship, or age ▶ *adj* made in an earlier period

antiques *n* ▷ **antique**

antiquities *pl n* objects dating from ancient times ▶ *n* ▷ **antiquity**

antiquity *n* (*pl* -**ties**) great age

antiracism *n* (*pl* -**s**) policy of challenging racism and promoting racial tolerance

antiracisms *n* ▷ **antiracism**

antirrhinum *n* (*pl* -**s**) two-lipped flower of various colours

antirrhinums *n* ▷ **antirrhinum**

antiseptic *adj* preventing infection by killing germs ▶ *n* (*pl* -**s**) antiseptic substance

antiseptics *n* ▷ **antiseptic**

antisocial *adj* avoiding the company of other people

antistatic *adj* reducing the effects of static electricity

antitheses *n* ▷ **antithesis**

antithesis [an-tith-iss-iss] *n* (*pl* -**ses**) [-seez] exact opposite > **antithetical** *adj*

antithetical *adj* ▷ **antithesis**

antitoxin *n* (*pl* -**s**) (serum containing) an antibody that acts against a toxin

antitoxins *n* ▷ **antitoxin**

antitrust *adj* (AUST & S AFR) (of laws) opposing business monopolies

antler *n* (*pl* -**s**) branched horn of male deer

antlers *n* ▷ **antler**

antonym *n* (*pl* -**s**) word that means the opposite of another

antonyms *n* ▷ **antonym**

ants *n* ▷ **ant**

anus [ain-uss] *n* (*pl* -**es**) opening at the end of the alimentary canal, through which faeces are discharged

anuses *n* ▷ **anus**

anvil *n* (*pl* -**s**) heavy iron block on which metals are hammered into particular shapes

anvils *n* ▷ **anvil**

anxieties *n* ▷ **anxiety**

anxiety *n* (*pl* -**ties**) state of being anxious

anxious *adj* worried and tense > **anxiously** *adv*

anxiously *adv* ▷ **anxious**

any *adj, pron* one or some, no matter which ▶ *adv* at all > **anything** *pron*

anybody *pron* anyone

anyhow *adv* anyway

anyone *pron* any person

anything *pron* ▷ **any**

anyway *adv* at any rate, nevertheless

anywhere *adv* in, at, or to any place

aorta [eh-or-ta] *n* (*pl* -**s**) main artery of the body, carrying oxygen-rich blood from the heart

aortas *n* ▷ **aorta**

apace *adv* (*Lit*) swiftly

apalled *v* ▷ **appal**

apart *adv* to or in pieces

apartheid *n* (*pl* -**s**) former official government policy of racial segregation in S Africa

apartheids *n* ▷ **apartheid**

apartment *n* (*pl* -**s**) room in a building

apartments *n* ▷ **apartment**

apathetic *adj* ▷ **apathy**

apathy *n* (*pl* -**thies**) lack of interest or enthusiasm > **apathetic** *adj*

apethies *n* ▷ **apathy**

ape *n* (*pl* -**s**) tailless monkey such as the chimpanzee or gorilla ▶ *v* (**apes, aping, aped**) imitate

aped *v* ▷ **ape**

aperient [ap-**peer**-ee-ent] *adj* having a mild laxative effect ▶ *n* (*pl* -**s**) mild laxative

aperients *n* ▷ **aperient**

aperitif [ap-per-rit-**teef**] *n* (*pl* -**s**) alcoholic drink taken before a meal

aperitifs *n* ▷ **aperitif**

aperture *n* (*pl* -**s**) opening or hole

apertures *n* ▷ **aperture**

apes *n, v* ▷ **ape**

apex *n* (*pl* -**es**) highest point

apexes *n* ▷ **apex**

aphasia *n* disorder of the central nervous system that affects the ability to speak and understand words

aphid [**eh**-fid], **aphis** [**eh**-fiss] *n* (*pl* **aphids**) small insect which sucks the sap from plants

aphids *n* ▷ **aphid**

aphis *n* ▷ **aphid**

aphorism *n* (*pl* -**s**) short clever saying expressing a general truth

aphorisms *n* ▷ **aphorism**

aphrodisiac [af-roh-**diz**-zee-ak] *n* (*pl* -**s**) substance that arouses sexual desire ▶ *adj* arousing sexual desire

aphrodisiacs *n* ▷ **aphrodisiac**

apiaries *n* ▷ **apiary**

apiary *n* (*pl* -**ries**) place where bees are kept

apiculture n (pl -s) breeding and care of bees
  apicultures n ▷ apiculture
apiece adv each
  aping v ▷ ape
aplomb n (pl -s) calm self-possession
  aplombs n ▷ aplomb
apocalypse n (pl -s) end of the world
  > **apocalyptic** adj
  apocalypses n ▷ apocalypse
  apocalyptic adj ▷ apocalypse
apocryphal [ap-**pok**-rif-al] adj (of a story) of
  questionable authenticity
apogee [**ap**-oh-jee] n (pl -s) point of the moon's
  or a satellite's orbit that is farthest from
  the earth
  apogees n ▷ apogee
apologetic adj showing or expressing regret
  > **apologetically** adv
  apologetically adv ▷ apologetic
apologetics n branch of theology concerned
  with the reasoned defence of Christianity
  apologies n ▷ apology
apologist n (pl -s) person who formally
  defends a cause
  apologists n ▷ apologist
apologize v (-zes, -zing, -zed) make an apology
  apologized v ▷ apologize
  apologizes v ▷ apologize
  apologizing v ▷ apologize
apology n (pl -gies) expression of regret for
  wrongdoing
apoplectic adj of apoplexy
  apoplexies n ▷ apoplexy
apoplexy n (pl -xies) (MED) stroke
  apostasies n ▷ apostasy
apostasy [ap-**poss**-stass-ee] n (pl -sies)
  abandonment of one's religious faith or other
  belief > **apostate** n (pl -s) adj
  apostate n, adj ▷ apostasy
  apostates n ▷ apostasy
apostle n (pl -s) ardent supporter of a cause or
  movement > **apostolic** adj
  apostles n ▷ apostle
  apostolic adj ▷ apostle
apostrophe [ap-**poss**-trof-fee] n (pl -s)
  punctuation mark (') showing the omission
  of a letter or letters in a word, e.g. don't, or
  forming the possessive, e.g. Jill's car
  apostrophes n ▷ apostrophe
  apothecaries n ▷ apothecary
apothecary n (pl -ries) (Obs) chemist
  apotheoses n ▷ apotheosis
apotheosis [ap-poth-ee-oh-siss] n (pl -ses)
  [-seez] perfect example
appal v (-s, -lling, -lled) dismay, terrify

appalled v ▷ appal
appalling adj dreadful, terrible ▶ v ▷ appal
  appals v ▷ appal
apparatus n (pl -es) equipment for a particular
  purpose
  apparatuses n ▷ apparatus
apparel n (pl -s) (Old-fashioned) clothing
  apparels n ▷ apparel
apparent adj readily seen, obvious
  > **apparently** adv
  apparently adv ▷ apparent
apparition n (pl -s) ghost or ghostlike figure
  apparitions n ▷ apparition
appeal v (-s, -ing, -ed) make an earnest request
  ▶ n (pl -s) earnest request > **appealing** adj
  appealed v ▷ appeal
  appealing v, adj ▷ appeal
  appeals v, n ▷ appeal
appear v (-s, -ing, -ed) become visible or
  present
appearance n (pl -s) appearing
  appearances n ▷ appearance
  appeared v ▷ appear
  appearing v ▷ appear
  appears v ▷ appear
appease v (-s, -ing, -ed) pacify (a person)
  by yielding to his or her demands
  > **appeasement** n (pl -s)
  appeased v ▷ appease
  appeasement n ▷ appeal
  appeasements n ▷ appeal
  appeases v ▷ appease
  appeasing v ▷ appease
appellant n (pl -s) person who makes an
  appeal to a higher court
  appellants n ▷ appellant
appellation n (pl -s) (Formal) name, title
  appellations n ▷ appellation
append v (-s, -ing, -ed) join on, add
appendage n (pl -s) thing joined on or added
  appendages n ▷ appendage
  appended v ▷ append
  appendices n ▷ appendix
appendicitis n (pl -es) inflammation of the
  appendix
  appendicitises n ▷ appendicitis
  appending v ▷ append
appendix n (pl -dices, -dixes) separate
  additional material at the end of a book
  appendixes n ▷ appendix
  appends v ▷ append
appertain v (-s, -ing, -ed) (foll. by to) belong to
  appertained v ▷ appertain
  appertaining v ▷ appertain
  appertains v ▷ appertain

appetite n (pl -s) desire for food or drink
  appetites n ▷ appetite
appetizer n (pl -s) thing eaten or drunk to stimulate the appetite > **appetizing** adj stimulating the appetite
  appetizers n ▷ appetizer
  appetizing adj ▷ appetizer
applaud v (-s, -ing, -ed) show approval of by clapping one's hands
  applauded v ▷ applaud
  applauding v ▷ applaud
  applauds v ▷ applaud
applause n (pl -s) approval shown by clapping one's hands
  applauses n ▷ applause
apple n (pl -s) round firm fleshy fruit that grows on trees
  apples n ▷ apple
appliance n (pl -s) device with a specific function
  appliances n ▷ appliance
  applicabilities n ▷ applicable
  applicability n ▷ applicable
applicable adj relevant, appropriate
  > **applicability** n (pl -ties)
applicant n (pl -s) person who applies for something
  applicants n ▷ applicant
application n (pl -s) formal request
  applications n ▷ application
applied adj (of a skill, science, etc.) put to practical use ▶ v ▷ apply
  applies v ▷ apply
appliqué [ap-**plee**-kay] n (pl -s) kind of decoration in which one material is cut out and attached to another
  appliqués n ▷ appliqué
apply v (-plies, -plying, -plied) make a formal request
  applying v ▷ apply
appoint v (-s, -ing, -ed) assign to a job or position
  appointed v ▷ appoint
  appointing v ▷ appoint
appointment n (pl -s) arrangement to meet a person
  appointments n ▷ appointment
  appoints v ▷ appoint
apportion v (-s, -ing, -ed) divide out in shares
  apportioned v ▷ apportion
  apportioning v ▷ apportion
  apportions v ▷ apportion
apposite adj suitable, apt
apposition n (pl -s) grammatical construction in which two nouns or phrases referring to

the same thing are placed one after another without a conjunction
  appositions n ▷ apposition
  appraisal n ▷ appraise
  appraisals n ▷ appraise
appraise v (-ses, -sing, -sed) estimate the value or quality of > **appraisal** n (pl -s)
  appraised v ▷ appraise
  appraises v ▷ appraise
  appraising v ▷ appraise
appreciable adj enough to be noticed
  > **appreciably** adv
  appreciably adv ▷ appreciable
appreciate v (-tes, -ting, -ted) value highly
  > **appreciation** n (pl -s)
  appreciated v ▷ appreciate
  appreciates v ▷ appreciate
  appreciating v ▷ appreciate
  appreciation n ▷ appreciate
  appreciations n ▷ appreciate
appreciative adj feeling or showing appreciation
apprehend v (-s, -ing, -ed) arrest and take into custody
  apprehended v ▷ apprehend
  apprehending v ▷ apprehend
  apprehends v ▷ apprehend
apprehension n (pl -s) dread, anxiety
  apprehensions n ▷ apprehension
apprehensive adj fearful or anxious
apprentice n (pl -s) someone working for a skilled person for a fixed period in order to learn his or her trade ▶ v (-ces, -cing, -ced) take or place (someone) as an apprentice
  > **apprenticeship** n (pl -s)
  apprenticed v ▷ apprentice
  apprentices n, v ▷ apprentice
  apprenticing v ▷ apprentice
apprise v (-ses, -sing, -sed) make aware (of)
  apprised v ▷ apprise
  apprises v ▷ apprise
  apprising v ▷ apprise
appro n (pl -s) (BRIT, AUST, NZ & S AFR) (Informal) on approval
approach v (-ches, -ching, -ched) come near or nearer (to) ▶ n (pl -es) approaching or means of approaching > **approachable** adj
  approachable adj ▷ approach
  approached v ▷ approach
  approaches v, n ▷ approach
  approaching v ▷ approach
approbation n (pl -s) approval
  approbations n ▷ approbation
appropriate adj suitable, fitting ▶ v (-tes, -ting, -ted) take for oneself > **appropriately**

adv > **appropriateness** *n* > **appropriation**
n (*pl* **-s**)
appropriated *v* ▷ **appropriate**
appropriately *adv* ▷ **appropriate**
appropriateness *n* ▷ **appropriate**
appropriates *v* ▷ **appropriate**
appropriating *v* ▷ **appropriate**
appropriation *n* ▷ **appropriate**
appropriations *n* ▷ **appropriate**
appros *n* ▷ **appro**
approval *n* (*pl* **-s**) consent
approvals *n* ▷ **approval**
approve *v* (**-ves, -ving, -ved**) consider good
or right
approved *v* ▷ **approve**
approves *v* ▷ **approve**
approving *v* ▷ **approve**
approximate *adj* almost but not quite exact
▶ *v* (**-tes, -ting, -ted**) (*foll. by* **to**) come close to
> **approximately** *adv* > **approximation** *n* (*pl* **-s**)
approximated *v* ▷ **approximate**
approximately *adv* ▷ **approximate**
approximates *v* ▷ **approximate**
approximating *v* ▷ **approximate**
approximation *n* ▷ **approximate**
approximations *n* ▷ **approximate**
appurtenance *n* (*pl* **-s**) a minor or additional
feature
appurtenances *n* ▷ **appurtenance**
apricot *n* (*pl* **-s**) yellowish-orange juicy fruit
like a small peach ▶ *adj* yellowish-orange
apricots *n* ▷ **apricot**
apron *n* (*pl* **-s**) garment worn over the front of
the body to protect the clothes
aprons *n* ▷ **apron**
apropos [ap-prop-**poh**] *adj, adv* appropriate(ly)
apse *n* (*pl* **-s**) arched or domed recess, esp. in
a church
apses *n* ▷ **apse**
apt *adj* having a specified tendency > **aptly** *adv*
> **aptness** *n* (*pl* **-es**)
aptitude *n* (*pl* **-s**) natural ability
aptitudes *n* ▷ **aptitude**
aptly *adv* ▷ **apt**
aptness *n* ▷ **apt**
aptnesses *n* ▷ **apt**
aqualung *n* (*pl* **-s**) mouthpiece attached to air
cylinders, worn for underwater swimming
aqualungs *n* ▷ **aqualung**
aquamarine *n* (*pl* **-s**) greenish-blue gemstone
▶ *adj* greenish-blue
aquamarines *n* ▷ **aquamarine**
aquaplane *n* (*pl* **-s**) board on which a person
stands to be towed by a motorboat ▶ *v* (**-nes,
-ning, -ned**) ride on an aquaplane

aquaplaned *v* ▷ **aquaplane**
aquaplanes *n, v* ▷ **aquaplane**
aquaplaning *v* ▷ **aquaplane**
aquaria *n* ▷ **aquarium**
aquarium *n* (*pl* **-s, -ria**) tank in which fish and
other underwater creatures are kept
aquariums *n* ▷ **aquarium**
aquatic *adj* living in or near water
aquatics *pl n* water sports
aquatint *n* (*pl* **-s**) print like a watercolour,
produced by etching copper
aquatints *n* ▷ **aquatint**
aqueduct *n* (*pl* **-s**) structure carrying water
across a valley or river
aqueducts *n* ▷ **aqueduct**
aqueous *adj* of, like, or containing water
aquiline *adj* (of a nose) curved like an eagle's
beak

> **ar** *n* (**ars**). Ar is the letter R. This is a
> good two-letter word to remember
> because it uses two very common tiles,
> and so is easy to fit on the board. Ar
> scores 2 points.

arabesque [ar-ab-**besk**] *n* (*pl* **-s**) ballet position
in which one leg is raised behind and the
arms are extended
arabesques *n* ▷ **arabesque**
arable *adj* suitable for growing crops on
arachnid [ar-**rak**-nid] *n* (*pl* **-s**) eight-legged
invertebrate, such as a spider, scorpion, tick,
or mite
arachnids *n* ▷ **arachnid**
arbiter *n* (*pl* **-s**) person empowered to judge
in a dispute
arbiters *n* ▷ **arbiter**
arbitrarily *adv* ▷ **arbitrary**
arbitrary *adj* based on personal choice or
chance, rather than reason > **arbitrarily** *adv*
arbitrate *v* ▷ **arbitration**
arbitrated *v* ▷ **arbitration**
arbitrates *v* ▷ **arbitration**
arbitrating *v* ▷ **arbitration**
arbitration *n* (*pl* **-s**) hearing and settling of
a dispute by an impartial referee chosen
by both sides > **arbitrate** *v* (**-tes, -ting, -ted**)
> **arbitrator** *n* (*pl* **-s**)
arbitrations *n* ▷ **arbitration**
arbitrator *n* ▷ **arbitration**
arbitrators *n* ▷ **arbitration**
arboreal *adj* of or living in trees
arboreta *n* ▷ **arboretum**
arboretum [ahr-bore-**ee**-tum] *n* (*pl* **-ta**) place
where rare trees or shrubs are cultivated
arboriculture *n* (*pl* **-s**) cultivation of trees or
shrubs

arboricultures *n* ▷ **arboriculture**
arbour *n* (*pl* -**s**) glade sheltered by trees
   arbours *n* ▷ **arbour**
arc *n* (*pl* -**s**) part of a circle or other curve ▶ *v* (-**s**, -**ing**, -**ed**) form an arc
arcade *n* (*pl* -**s**) covered passageway lined with shops
   arcades *n* ▷ **arcade**
arcane *adj* mysterious and secret
   arced *v* ▷ **arc**
arch¹ *n* (*pl* -**es**) curved structure supporting a bridge or roof ▶ *v* (-**es**, -**ing**, -**ed**) (cause to) form an arch
arch² *adj* (-**er**, -**est**) superior, knowing > **archly** *adv* > **archness** *n* (*pl* -**es**)
archaeological *adj* ▷ **archaeology**
archaeologies *n* ▷ **archaeology**
archaeologist *n* ▷ **archaeology**
archaeologists *n* ▷ **archaeology**
archaeology *n* (*pl* -**ies**) study of ancient cultures from their physical remains > **archaeological** *adj* > **archaeologist** *n* (*pl* -**s**)
archaic [ark-kay-ik] *adj* ancient > **archaism** [ark-kay-iz-zum] ▶ *n* (*pl* -**s**) archaic word or phrase
   archaism *n* ▷ **archaic**
   archaisms *n* ▷ **archaic**
archangel [ark-ain-jell] *n* (*pl* -**s**) chief angel
   archangels *n* ▷ **archangel**
archbishop *n* (*pl* -**s**) chief bishop
   archbishops *n* ▷ **archbishop**
archdeacon *n* (*pl* -**s**) priest ranking just below a bishop
   archdeacons *n* ▷ **archdeacon**
archdiocese *n* (*pl* -**es**) diocese of an archbishop
   archdioceses *n* ▷ **archdiocese**
   arched *v* ▷ **arch¹**
archer *n* (*pl* -**s**) person who shoots with a bow and arrow ▶ *adj* ▷ **arch²** > **archery** *n* (*pl* -**ries**)
   archeries *n* ▷ **archer**
   archers *n* ▷ **archer**
   archery *n* ▷ **archer**
   arches *n*, *v* ▷ **arch¹**
   archest *adj* ▷ **arch²**
   archetypal *adj* ▷ **archetype**
archetype [ark-ee-type] *n* (*pl* -**s**) perfect specimen > **archetypal** *adj*
   archetypes *n* ▷ **archetype**
   arching *v* ▷ **arch¹**
archipelago [ark-ee-pel-a-go] *n* (*pl* -**gos**) group of islands
   archipelagos *n* ▷ **archipelago**
architect *n* (*pl* -**s**) person qualified to design and supervise the construction of buildings
   architects *n* ▷ **architect**

architectural *adj* ▷ **architecture**
architecture *n* (*pl* -**s**) style in which a building is designed and built > **architectural** *adj*
   architectures *n* ▷ **architecture**
architrave *n* (*pl* -**s**) (ARCHIT) beam that rests on columns
   architraves *n* ▷ **architrave**
   archival *adj* ▷ **archive**
archive [ark-ive] *n* (*pl* -**s**) (*often pl* collection of records or documents > **archival** *adj*
   archives *n* ▷ **archive**
archivist [ark-iv-ist] *n* (*pl* -**s**) person in charge of archives
   archivists *n* ▷ **archivist**
   archly *adv* ▷ **arch²**
   archness *n* ▷ **arch²**
   archnesses *n* ▷ **arch²**
archway *n* (*pl* -**s**) passageway under an arch
   archways *n* ▷ **archway**
   arcing *v* ▷ **arc**
   arcs *n*, *v* ▷ **arc**
arctic *n* (*pl* -**s**) area around the North Pole ▶ *adj* of this region
   arctics *n* ▷ **arctic**
ardent *adj* passionate > **ardently** *adv*
   ardently *adv* ▷ **ardent**
ardour *n* (*pl* -**s**) passion
   ardours *n* ▷ **ardour**
arduous *adj* hard to accomplish, strenuous > **arduously** *adv*
   arduously *adv* ▷ **arduous**
are¹ *v* ▷ **be**
are² *n* (*pl* -**s**) unit of measure, 100 square metres
area *n* (*pl* -**s**) part or region
   areas *n* ▷ **area**
arena *n* (*pl* -**s**) seated enclosure for sports events
   arenas *n* ▷ **arena**
areola *n* (*pl* -**lae**, -**las**) small circular area, such as the coloured ring around the human nipple
   areolae *n* ▷ **areola**
   areolas *n* ▷ **areola**
   ares *n* ▷ **are²**
argon *n* (*pl* -**s**) (CHEM) inert gas found in the air
   argons *n* ▷ **argon**
argot [ahr-go] *n* (*pl* -**s**) slang or jargon
   argots *n* ▷ **argot**
   arguable *adj* ▷ **argue**
   arguably *adv* ▷ **argue**
argue *v* (-**gues**, -**guing**, -**gued**) try to prove by giving reasons > **arguable** *adj* > **arguably** *adv*
   argued *v* ▷ **argue**
   argues *v* ▷ **argue**

arguing *v* ▷ **argue**
argument *n* (*pl* -**s**) quarrel
argumentation *n* (*pl* -**s**) process of reasoning methodically
  argumentations *n* ▷ **argumentation**
argumentative *adj* given to arguing
  arguments *n* ▷ **argument**
aria [ah-ree-a] *n* (*pl* -**s**) elaborate song for solo voice, esp. one from an opera
  arias *n* ▷ **aria**
arid *adj* parched, dry > **aridity** *n* (*pl* -**ties**)
  aridities *n* ▷ **arid**
  aridity *n* ▷ **arid**
aright *adv* rightly
arise *v* (**arises, arising, arose, arisen**) come about
  arisen *v* ▷ **arise**
  arises *v* ▷ **arise**
  arising *v* ▷ **arise**
  aristocracies *n* ▷ **aristocracy**
aristocracy *n* (*pl* -**cies**) highest social class
aristocrat *n* (*pl* -**s**) member of the aristocracy > **aristocratic** *adj*
  aristocratic *adj* ▷ **aristocrat**
  aristocrats *n* ▷ **aristocrat**
arithmetic *n* (*pl* -**s**) calculation by or of numbers ▶ *adj* of arithmetic > **arithmetical** *adj* > **arithmetically** *adv*
  arithmetical *adj* ▷ **arithmetic**
  arithmetically *adv* ▷ **arithmetic**
  arithmetics *n* ▷ **arithmetic**
ark *n* (*pl* -**s**) (OLD TESTAMENT) boat built by Noah, which survived the Flood
  arks *n* ▷ **ark**
arm¹ *n* (*pl* -**s**) either of the upper limbs from the shoulder to the wrist
arm² *v* (-**s, -ing, -ed**) supply with weapons
armada *n* (*pl* -**s**) large number of warships
  armadas *n* ▷ **armada**
armadillo *n* (*pl* -**s**) small S American mammal covered in strong bony plates
  armadillos *n* ▷ **armadillo**
armament *n* (*pl* -**s**) military weapons
  armaments *n* ▷ **armament**
armature *n* (*pl* -**s**) revolving structure in an electric motor or generator, wound with coils carrying the current
  armatures *n* ▷ **armature**
armchair *n* (*pl* -**s**) upholstered chair with side supports for the arms
  armchairs *n* ▷ **armchair**
  armed *v* ▷ **arm²**
armful *n* (*pl* -**s**) as much as can be held in the arms
  armfuls *n* ▷ **armful**
armhole *n* (*pl* -**s**) opening in a garment

through which the arm passes
  armholes *n* ▷ **armhole**
  armies *n* ▷ **army**
  arming *v* ▷ **arm²**
armistice [arm-miss-stiss] *n* (*pl* -**s**) agreed suspension of fighting
  armistices *n* ▷ **armistice**
armour *n* (*pl* -**s**) metal clothing formerly worn to protect the body in battle
armourer *n* (*pl* -**s**) maker, repairer, or keeper of arms or armour
  armourers *n* ▷ **armourer**
  armouries *n* ▷ **armoury**
  armours *n* ▷ **armour**
armoury *n* (*pl* -**ries**) place where weapons are stored
armpit *n* (*pl* -**s**) hollow under the arm at the shoulder
  armpits *n* ▷ **armpit**
arms *pl n* weapons ▶ *n* ▷ **arm¹** ▶ *v* ▷ **arm²**
army *n* (*pl* -**mies**) military land forces of a nation
aroma *n* (*pl* -**s**) pleasant smell > **aromatic** *adj*
  aromas *n* ▷ **aroma**
  aromatherapies *n* ▷ **aromatherapy**
aromatherapy *n* (*pl* -**pies**) massage with fragrant oils to relieve tension
  aromatic *adj* ▷ **aroma**
  arose *v* ▷ **arise**
around *prep, adv* on all sides (of)
arouse *v* (-**ses, -sing, -sed**) stimulate, make active
  aroused *v* ▷ **arouse**
  arouses *v* ▷ **arouse**
  arousing *v* ▷ **arouse**
arpeggio [arp-**pej**-ee-oh] *n* (*pl* -**s**) (MUSIC) notes of a chord played or sung in quick succession
  arpeggios *n* ▷ **arpeggio**
arraign [ar-**rain**] *v* (-**s, -ing, -ed**) bring (a prisoner) before a court to answer a charge > **arraignment** *n* (*pl* -**s**)
  arraigned *v* ▷ **arraign**
  arraigning *v* ▷ **arraign**
  arraignment *n* ▷ **arraign**
  arraignments *n* ▷ **arraign**
  arraigns *v* ▷ **arraign**
arrange *v* (-**ges, -ging, -ged**) plan > **arrangement** *n* (*pl* -**s**)
  arranged *v* ▷ **arrange**
  arrangement *n* ▷ **arrange**
  arrangements *n* ▷ **arrange**
  arranges *v* ▷ **arrange**
  arranging *v* ▷ **arrange**
arrant *adj* utter, downright
arras *n* (*pl* -**es**) tapestry wall-hanging
  arrases *n* ▷ **arras**
array *n* (*pl* -**s**) impressive display or collection

(*Poetic*) ▶ *v* (**-s, -ing, -ed**) arrange in order
arrayed *v* ▷ **array**
arraying *v* ▷ **array**
arrays *n, v* ▷ **array**
arrear *n* (*p* **-s**) (usually plural) money owed
arrears *n* ▷ **arrear**
arrest *v* (**-s, -ing, -ed**) take (a person) into
custody ▶ *n* (*pl* **-s**) act of taking a person into
custody
arrested *v* ▷ **arrest**
arresting *adj* attracting attention, striking
▶ *v* ▷ **arrest**
arrests *v, n* ▷ **arrest**
arrival *n* (*pl* **-s**) arriving
arrivals *n* ▷ **arrival**
arrive *v* (**-ves, -ving, -ved**) reach a place or
destination
arrived *v* ▷ **arrive**
arrives *v* ▷ **arrive**
arriving *v* ▷ **arrive**
arrogance *n* ▷ **arrogant**
arrogances *n* ▷ **arrogant**
arrogant *adj* proud and overbearing
> **arrogantly** *adv* > **arrogance** *n* (*pl* **-s**)
arrogantly *adv* ▷ **arrogant**
arrogate *v* (**-tes, -ting, -ted**) claim or seize
without justification
arrogated *v* ▷ **arrogate**
arrogates *v* ▷ **arrogate**
arrogating *v* ▷ **arrogate**
arrow *n* (*pl* **-s**) pointed shaft shot from a bow
arrowhead *n* (*pl* **-s**) pointed tip of an arrow
arrowheads *n* ▷ **arrowhead**
arrowroot *n* (*pl* **-s**) nutritious starch obtained
from the root of a W Indian plant
arrowroots *n* ▷ **arrowroot**
arrows *n* ▷ **arrow**
arsenal *n* (*pl* **-s**) place where arms and
ammunition are made or stored
arsenals *n* ▷ **arsenal**
arsenic *n* (*pl* **-s**) toxic grey element > **arsenical**
adj
arsenical *adj* ▷ **arsenic**
arsenics *n* ▷ **arsenic**
arson *n* (*pl* **-s**) crime of intentionally setting
property on fire > **arsonist** *n* (*pl* **-s**)
arsonist *n* ▷ **arson**
arsonists *n* ▷ **arson**
arsons *n* ▷ **arson**
art *n* (*pl* **-s**) creation of works of beauty, esp.
paintings or sculpture
artefact *n* (*pl* **-s**) something made by human
beings
artefacts *n* ▷ **artefact**
arterial *adj* of an artery

arteries *n* ▷ **artery**
artery *n* (*pl* **-ries**) one of the tubes carrying
blood from the heart
artful *adj* cunning, wily > **artfully** *adv*
> **artfulness** *n* (*pl* **-es**)
artfully *adv* ▷ **artful**
artfulness *n* ▷ **artful**
artfulnesses *n* ▷ **artful**
arthritic *adj, n* ▷ **arthritis**
arthritics *n* ▷ **arthritis**
arthritis *n* (*pl* **-es**) painful inflammation of a
joint or joints > **arthritic** *adj, n* (*pl* **-s**)
arthritises *n* ▷ **arthritis**
arthropod *n* (*pl* **-s**) animal, such as a spider or
insect, with jointed limbs and a segmented
body
arthropods *n* ▷ **arthropod**
artichoke *n* (*pl* **-s**) flower head of a thistle-like
plant, cooked as a vegetable
artichokes *n* ▷ **artichoke**
article *n* (*pl* **-s**) written piece in a magazine or
newspaper
articled *adj* bound (as an apprentice) by a
written contract
articles *n* ▷ **article**
articulate *adj* able to express oneself clearly
and coherently ▶ *v* (**-tes, -ting, -ted**) speak or
say clearly and coherently > **articulately** *adv*
> **articulation** *n* (*pl* **-s**)
articulated *adj* jointed ▶ *v* ▷ **articulate**
articulates *v* ▷ **articulate**
articulating *v* ▷ **articulate**
articulation *n* ▷ **articulate**
articulations *n* ▷ **articulate**
artier *adj* ▷ **arty**
artiest *adj* ▷ **arty**
artifice *n* (*pl* **-s**) clever trick
artificer [art-**tiff**-iss-er] *n* (*pl* **-s**) craftsman
artificers *n* ▷ **artificer**
artifices *n* ▷ **artifice**
artificial *adj* man-made, not occurring
naturally > **artificially** *adv* > **artificiality** *n*
(*pl* **-ties**)
artificialities *n* ▷ **artificial**
artificiality *n* ▷ **artificial**
artificially *adv* ▷ **artificial**
artilleries *n* ▷ **artillery**
artillery *n* (*pl* **-ies**) large-calibre guns
artisan *n* (*pl* **-s**) skilled worker, craftsman
artisans *n* ▷ **artisan**
artist *n* (*pl* **-s**) person who produces works of
art, esp. paintings or sculpture > **artistic** *adj*
> **artistically** *adv*
artiste *n* (*pl* **-s**) professional entertainer such
as a singer or dancer

artistes *n* ▷ artiste
artistic *adj* ▷ artist
artistically *adv* ▷ artist
artistries *n* ▷ artistry
artistry *n* (*pl* -ries) artistic skill
artists *n* ▷ artist
artless *adj* free from deceit or cunning
> **artlessly** *adv*
artlessly *adv* ▷ artless
arts *n* ▷ art
arty *adj* (-tier, -tiest) (*Informal*) having an
affected interest in art
arvie *n* (*pl* -s) (S AFR) (*Informal*) afternoon
arvies *n* ▷ arvie
as *conj* while, when ▸ *adv, conj* used to indicate
amount or extent in comparisons ▸ *prep* in
the role of, being
asafoetida *n* (*pl* -s) strong-smelling plant resin
used as a spice in Eastern cookery
asafoetidas *n* ▷ asafoetida
asbestos *n* (*pl* -es) fibrous mineral which does
not burn
asbestoses *n* ▷ asbestos, asbestosis
asbestosis *n* (*pl* -ses) lung disease caused by
inhalation of asbestos fibre
ascend *v* (-s, -ing, -ed) go or move up
ascendancies *n* ▷ ascendancy
ascendancy *n* (*pl* -cies) condition of being
dominant
ascendant *adj* dominant or influential
ascended *v* ▷ ascend
ascending *v* ▷ ascend
ascends *v* ▷ ascend
ascent *n* (*pl* -s) ascending
ascents *n* ▷ ascent
ascertain *v* (-s, -ing, -ed) find out definitely
> **ascertainable** *adj* > **ascertainment** *n* (*pl* -s)
ascertainable *adj* ▷ ascertain
ascertained *v* ▷ ascertain
ascertaining *v* ▷ ascertain
ascertainment *n* ▷ ascertain
ascertainments *n* ▷ ascertain
ascertains *v* ▷ ascertain
ascetic [ass-**set**-tik] *n* (*pl* -s) ▸ *adj* (person)
abstaining from worldly pleasures and
comforts > **asceticism** *n* (*pl* -s)
asceticism *n* ▷ ascetic
asceticisms *n* ▷ ascetic
ascetics *n* ▷ ascetic
ascribe *v* (-bes, -bing, -bed) attribute, as to a
particular origin > **ascription** *n* (*pl* -s)
ascribed *v* ▷ ascribe
ascribes *v* ▷ ascribe
ascribing *v* ▷ ascribe
ascription *n* ▷ ascribe

ascriptions *n* ▷ ascribe
aseptic [eh-**sep**-tik] *adj* free from harmful
bacteria
asexual [eh-**sex**-yew-al] *adj* without sex
> **asexually** *adv*
asexually *adv* ▷ asexual
ash[1] *n* (*pl* -es) powdery substance left when
something is burnt
ash[2] *n* (*pl* -es) tree with grey bark
ashamed *adj* feeling shame
ashen *adj* pale with shock
ashes *n* ▷ ash[1, 2]
ashlar *n* (*pl* -s) square block of hewn stone used
in building
ashlars *n* ▷ ashlar
ashore *adv* towards or on land
ashram *n* (*pl* -s) religious retreat where a
Hindu holy man lives
ashrams *n* ▷ ashram
ashtray *n* (*pl* -s) receptacle for tobacco ash and
cigarette butts
ashtrays *n* ▷ ashtray
aside *adv* to one side ▸ *n* (*pl* -s) remark not
meant to be heard by everyone present
asides *n* ▷ aside
asinine *adj* stupid, idiotic
ask *v* (-s, -ing, -ed) say or write (something) in
a form that requires an answer
askance [ass-**kanss**] *adv* with an oblique glance
asked *v* ▷ ask
askew *adv, adj* to one side, crooked
asking *v* ▷ ask
asks *v* ▷ ask
aslant *adv, prep* at a slant (to), slanting (across)
asleep *adj* sleeping
asp *n* (*pl* -s) small poisonous snake
asparagus *n* (*pl* -es) plant whose shoots are
cooked as a vegetable
asparaguses *n* ▷ asparagus
aspect *n* (*pl* -s) feature or element
aspects *n* ▷ aspect
aspen *n* (*pl* -s) kind of poplar tree
aspens *n* ▷ aspen
asperities *n* ▷ asperity
asperity *n* (*pl* -ties) roughness of temper
aspersion *n* (*pl* -s) derogatory remark
aspersions *n* ▷ aspersion
asphalt *n* (*pl* -s) black hard tarlike substance
used for road surfaces etc.
asphalts *n* ▷ asphalt
asphodel *n* (*pl* -s) plant with clusters of yellow
or white flowers
asphodels *n* ▷ asphodel
asphyxia [ass-**fix**-ee-a] *n* (*pl* -s) suffocation
asphyxiate *v* (-tes, -ting, -ted) suffocate

> **asphyxiation** *n* (*pl* **-s**)
asphyxiated *v* ▷ **asphyxiate**
asphyxiates *v* ▷ **asphyxiate**
asphyxiating *v* ▷ **asphyxiate**
asphyxiation *n* ▷ **asphyxiate**
asphyxiations *n* ▷ **asphyxiate**
aspic *n* (*pl* **-s**) savoury jelly used to coat meat, eggs, fish, etc.
aspics *n* ▷ **aspic**
aspidistra *n* (*pl* **-s**) plant with long tapered leaves
aspidistras *n* ▷ **aspidistra**
aspirant *n* (*pl* **-s**) person who aspires
aspirants *n* ▷ **aspirant**
aspirate (PHONETICS) *v* (**-tes, -ting, -ted**) pronounce with an *h* sound ▶ *n* (*pl* **-s**) *h* sound
aspirated *v* ▷ **aspirate**
aspirates *v*, *n* ▷ **aspirate**
aspirating *v* ▷ **aspirate**
aspiration *n* (*pl* **-s**) strong desire or aim
aspirations *n* ▷ **aspiration**
aspire *v* (**-res, -ring, -red**) (*foll. by* **to**) yearn (for), hope (to do or be)
aspired *v* ▷ **aspire**
aspires *v* ▷ **aspire**
aspirin *n* (*pl* **-s**) drug used to relieve pain and fever
aspiring *v* ▷ **aspire**
aspirins *n* ▷ **aspirin**
asps *n* ▷ **asp**
ass *n* (*pl* **-es**) donkey
assail *v* (**-s, -ing, -ed**) attack violently
> **assailant** *n* (*pl* **-s**)
assailant *n* ▷ **assail**
assailants *n* ▷ **assail**
assailed *v* ▷ **assail**
assailing *v* ▷ **assail**
assails *v* ▷ **assail**
assassin *n* (*pl* **-s**) person who murders a prominent person
assassinate *v* (**-tes, -ting, -ted**) murder (a prominent person) > **assassination** *n* (*pl* **-s**)
assassinated *v* ▷ **assassinate**
assassinates *v* ▷ **assassinate**
assassinating *v* ▷ **assassinate**
assassination *n* ▷ **assassinate**
assassinations *n* ▷ **assassinate**
assassins *n* ▷ **assassin**
assault *n* (*pl* **-ts**) violent attack ▶ *v* (**-s, -ing, -ed**) attack violently
assaulted *v* ▷ **assault**
assaulting *v* ▷ **assault**
assaults *n*, *v* ▷ **assault**
assay *n* (*pl* **-s**) analysis of a substance, esp. a metal, to ascertain its purity ▶ *v* (**-s, -ing, -ed**)

assayed *v* ▷ **assay**
assaying *v* ▷ **assay**
assays *n*, *v* ▷ **assay**
assegai [**ass**-a-guy] *n* (*pl* **-s**) slender spear used in S Africa
assegais *n* ▷ **assegai**
assemblage *n* (*pl* **-s**) collection or group
assemblages *n* ▷ **assemblage**
assemble *v* (**-bles, -bling, -bled**) collect or congregate
assembled *v* ▷ **assemble**
assembles *v* ▷ **assemble**
assemblies *n* ▷ **assembly**
assembling *v* ▷ **assemble**
assembly *n* (*pl* **-blies**) assembled group
assent *n* (*pl* **-s**) agreement or consent ▶ *v* (**-s, -ing, -ed**) agree or consent
assented *v* ▷ **assent**
assenting *v* ▷ **assent**
assents *n*, *v* ▷ **assent**
assert *v* (**-s, -ing, -ed**) declare forcefully
> **assertion** *n* (*pl* **-s**) > **assertive** *adj*
> **assertively** *adv*
asserted *v* ▷ **assert**
asserting *v* ▷ **assert**
assertion *n* ▷ **assert**
assertions *n* ▷ **assert**
assertive *adj* ▷ **assert**
assertively *adv* ▷ **assert**
asserts *v* ▷ **assert**
asses *n* ▷ **ass**
assess *v* (**-es, -ing, -ed**) judge the worth or importance of > **assessment** *n* (*pl* **-s**)
> **assessor** *n* (*pl* **-s**)
assessed *v* ▷ **assess**
assesses *v* ▷ **assess**
assessing *v* ▷ **assess**
assessment *n* ▷ **assess**
assessments *n* ▷ **assess**
assessor *n* ▷ **assess**
assessors *n* ▷ **assess**
asset *n* (*pl* **-s**) valuable or useful person or thing
assets *n* ▷ **asset**
asseverate *v* (**-tes, -ting, -ted**) declare solemnly
asseverated *v* ▷ **asseverate**
asseverates *v* ▷ **asseverate**
asseverating *v* ▷ **asseverate**
assiduities *n* ▷ **assiduous**
assiduity *n* ▷ **assiduous**
assiduous *adj* hard-working > **assiduously** *adv*
> **assiduity** *n* (*pl* **-ties**)
assiduously *adv* ▷ **assiduous**
assign *v* (**-s, -ing, -ed**) appoint (someone) to a job or task

assignation n (pl -s) assigning
  assignations n ▷ **assignation**
  assigned v ▷ **assign**
  assigning v ▷ **assign**
assignment n (pl -s) task assigned
  assignments n ▷ **assignment**
  assigns v ▷ **assign**
  assimilable adj ▷ **assimilate**
assimilate v (-tes, -ting, -ted) learn and
  understand (information) > **assimilable** adj
  > **assimilation** n (pl -s)
  assimilated v ▷ **assimilate**
  assimilates v ▷ **assimilate**
  assimilating v ▷ **assimilate**
  assimilation n ▷ **assimilate**
  assimilations n ▷ **assimilate**
assist v (-s, -ing, -ed) give help or support
  > **assistance** n (pl -s)
  assistance n ▷ **assist**
  assistances n ▷ **assist**
assistant n (pl -s) helper ▶ adj junior or deputy
  assistants n ▷ **assistant**
  assisted v ▷ **assist**
  assisting v ▷ **assist**
  assists v ▷ **assist**
assizes pl n (BRIT) court sessions formerly held
  in each county of England and Wales
associate v (-tes, -ting, -ted) connect in the
  mind ▶ n (pl -s) partner in business ▶ adj
  having partial rights or subordinate status
  associated v ▷ **associate**
  associates v, n ▷ **associate**
  associating v ▷ **associate**
association n (pl -s) society or club
  associations n ▷ **association**
assonance n (pl -s) rhyming of vowel sounds
  but not consonants, as in time and light
  assonances n ▷ **assonance**
assorted adj consisting of various types mixed
  together
assortment n (pl -s) assorted mixture
  assortments n ▷ **assortment**
assuage [ass-wage] v (-ges, -ging, -ged) relieve
  (pain, grief, thirst, etc.)
  assuaged v ▷ **assuage**
  assuages v ▷ **assuage**
  assuaging v ▷ **assuage**
assume v (-mes, -ming, -med) take to be true
  without proof
  assumed v ▷ **assume**
  assumes v ▷ **assume**
  assuming v ▷ **assume**
assumption n (pl -s) thing assumed
  assumptions n ▷ **assumption**
assurance n (pl -s) assuring or being assured

assurances n ▷ **assurance**
assure v (-res, -ring, -red) promise or
  guarantee
assured adj confident ▶ v ▷ **assure**
assuredly adv definitely
  assures v ▷ **assure**
  assuring v ▷ **assure**
astatine n (pl -s) (CHEM) radioactive
  nonmetallic element
  astatines n ▷ **astatine**
aster n (pl -s) plant with daisy-like flowers
asterisk n (pl -s) star-shaped symbol (*) used
  in printing or writing to indicate a footnote
  etc. ▶ v (-s, -ing, -ed) mark with an asterisk
  asterisked v ▷ **asterisk**
  asterisking v ▷ **asterisk**
  asterisks n, v ▷ **asterisk**
astern adv at or towards the stern of a ship
asteroid n (pl -s) any of the small planets that
  orbit the sun between Mars and Jupiter
  asteroids n ▷ **asteroid**
  asters n ▷ **aster**
asthma [ass-ma] n (pl -s) illness causing
  difficulty in breathing > **asthmatic** adj, n
  (pl -s)
  asthmas n ▷ **asthma**
  asthmatic adj, n ▷ **asthma**
  asthmatics n ▷ **asthma**
astigmatism [eh-stig-mat-tiz-zum] n (pl -s)
  inability of a lens, esp. of the eye, to focus
  properly
  astigmatisms n ▷ **astigmatism**
astir adj (Old-fashioned) out of bed
astonish v (-es, -ing, -ed) surprise greatly
  > **astonishment** n (pl -s)
  astonished v ▷ **astonish**
  astonishes v ▷ **astonish**
  astonishing v ▷ **astonish**
  astonishment n ▷ **astonish**
  astonishments n ▷ **astonish**
astound v (-s, -ing, -ed) overwhelm with
  amazement > **astounding** adj
  astounded v ▷ **astound**
  astounding v, adj ▷ **astound**
  astounds v ▷ **astound**
astrakhan n (pl -s) dark curly fleece of lambs
  from Astrakhan in Russia
  astrakhans n ▷ **astrakhan**
astral adj of stars
astray adv off the right path
astride adv, prep with a leg on either side (of)
  astringencies n ▷ **astringent**
  astringency n ▷ **astringent**
astringent adj causing contraction of body
  tissue ▶ n (pl -s) astringent substance

> **astringency** *n* (*pl* -**cies**)
astringents *n* ▷ **astringent**
astrolabe *n* (*pl* -**s**) instrument formerly used to measure the altitude of stars and planets
astrolabes *n* ▷ **astrolabe**
astrologer *n* ▷ **astrology**
astrologers *n* ▷ **astrology**
astrological *adj* ▷ **astrology**
astrologies *n* ▷ **astrology**
astrology *n* (*pl* -**gies**) study of the alleged influence of the stars, planets, and moon on human affairs > **astrologer** *n* (*pl* -**s**)
> **astrological** *adj*
astronaut *n* (*pl* -**s**) person trained for travelling in space
astronautical *adj* ▷ **astronautics**
astronautics *n* science and technology of space flight > **astronautical** *adj*
astronauts *n* ▷ **astronaut**
astronomer *n* ▷ **astronomy**
astronomers *n* ▷ **astronomy**
astronomical *adj* very large > **astronomically** *adv*
astronomically *adv* ▷ **astronomical**
astronomies *n* ▷ **astronomy**
astronomy *n* (*pl* -**mies**) scientific study of heavenly bodies > **astronomer** *n* (*pl* -**s**)
astrophysical *adj* ▷ **astrophysics**
astrophysicist *n* ▷ **astrophysics**
astrophysicists *n* ▷ **astrophysics**
astrophysics *n* science of the physical and chemical properties of stars, planets, etc.
> **astrophysical** *adj* > **astrophysicist** *n* (*pl* -**s**)
astute *adj* perceptive or shrewd > **astutely** *adv*
> **astuteness** *n* (*pl* -**es**)
astutely *adv* ▷ **astute**
astuteness *n* ▷ **astute**
astutenesses *n* ▷ **astute**
asunder *adv* (*Obs or poetic*) into parts or pieces
asylum *n* (*pl* -**s**) refuge or sanctuary
asylums *n* ▷ **asylum**
asymmetric *adj* ▷ **asymmetry**
asymmetrical *adj* ▷ **asymmetry**
asymmetries *n* ▷ **asymmetry**
asymmetry *n* (*pl* -**tries**) lack of symmetry
> **asymmetrical, asymmetric** *adj*
asymptote [ass-im-tote] *n* (*pl* -**s**) straight line closely approached but never met by a curve
asymptotes *n* ▷ **asymptote**
at *prep* indicating position in space or time, movement towards an object, etc.
atavism [at-a-viz-zum] *n* (*pl* -**s**) recurrence of a trait present in distant ancestors > **atavistic** *adj*
atavisms *n* ▷ **atavism**
atavistic *adj* ▷ **atavism**

ate *v* ▷ **eat**
atheism [aith-ee-iz-zum] *n* (*pl* -**s**) belief that there is no God > **atheist** *n* (*pl* -**s**) > **atheistic** *adj*
atheisms *n* ▷ **atheism**
atheist *n* ▷ **atheism**
atheistic *adj* ▷ **atheism**
atheists *n* ▷ **atheism**
atherosclerosis *n* disease in which deposits of fat cause the walls of the arteries to thicken
athlete *n* (*pl* -**s**) person trained in or good at athletics
athletes *n* ▷ **athlete**
athletic *adj* physically fit or strong
> **athletically** *adv* > **athleticism** *n* (*pl* -**s**)
athletically *adv* ▷ **athletic**
athleticism *n* ▷ **athletic**
athleticisms *n* ▷ **athletic**
athletics *pl n* track-and-field sports such as running, jumping, throwing, etc.
athwart *prep* across ▶ *adv* transversely
atlas *n* (*pl* -**es**) book of maps
atlases *n* ▷ **atlas**
atmosphere *n* (*pl* -**s**) mass of gases surrounding a heavenly body, esp. the earth
> **atmospheric** *adj*
atmospheres *n* ▷ **atmosphere**
atmospheric *adj* ▷ **atmosphere**
atmospherics *pl n* radio interference due to electrical disturbance in the atmosphere
atoll *n* (*pl* -**s**) ring-shaped coral reef enclosing a lagoon
atolls *n* ▷ **atoll**
atom *n* (*pl* -**s**) smallest unit of matter which can take part in a chemical reaction
atomic *adj* of or using atomic bombs or atomic energy
atomize *v* (-**zes, -zing, -zed**) reduce to atoms or small particles
atomized *v* ▷ **atomize**
atomizer *n* (*pl* -**s**) device for discharging a liquid in a fine spray
atomizers *n* ▷ **atomizer**
atomizes *v* ▷ **atomize**
atomizing *v* ▷ **atomize**
atoms *n* ▷ **atom**
atonal [eh-tone-al] *adj* (of music) not written in an established key
atone *v* (-**nes, -ning, -ned**) make amends (for sin or wrongdoing) > **atonement** *n* (*pl* -**s**)
atoned *v* ▷ **atone**
atonement *n* ▷ **atone**
atonements *n* ▷ **atone**
atones *v* ▷ **atone**
atoning *v* ▷ **atone**

atop *prep* (*Lit*) on top of
   atria *n* ▷ **atrium**
atrium *n* (*pl* **atria**) upper chamber of either half
   of the heart
atrocious *adj* extremely cruel or wicked
   > **atrociously** *adv*
   atrociously *adv* ▷ **atrocious**
   atrocities *n* ▷ **atrocity**
atrocity *n* (*pl* **-ties**) wickedness
   atrophied *v* ▷ **atrophy**
   atrophies *n, v* ▷ **atrophy**
atrophy [at-trof-fee] *n* (*pl* **-phies**) wasting
   away of an organ or part ▶ *v* (**-phies, -phying,
   -phied**) (cause to) waste away
   atrophying *v* ▷ **atrophy**
attach *v* (**-es, -ing, -ed**) join, fasten, or
   connect > **attached** *adj* (*foll. by* **to**) fond of
   > **attachment** *n* (*pl* **-s**)
attaché [at-**tash**-shay] *n* (*pl* **-s**) specialist
   attached to a diplomatic mission
attached *v, adj* ▷ **attach**
   attaches *v* ▷ **attach**
   attachés *n* ▷ **attaché**
   attaching *v* ▷ **attach**
attack *v* (**-s, -ing, -ed**) launch a physical assault
   (against) ▶ *n* (*pl* **-s**) act of attacking > **attacker**
   n (*pl* **-s**)
   attacked *v* ▷ **attack**
   attacker *n* ▷ **attack**
   attackers *n* ▷ **attack**
   attacking *v* ▷ **attack**
attacks *v, n* ▷ **attack**
attain *v* (**-s, -ing, -ed**) achieve or accomplish (a
   task or aim) > **attainable** *adj*
   attainable *adj* ▷ **attain**
   attained *v* ▷ **attain**
   attaining *v* ▷ **attain**
attainment *n* (*pl* **-s**) accomplishment
   attainments *n* ▷ **attainment**
   attains *v* ▷ **attain**
attar *n* (*pl* **-s**) fragrant oil made from roses
   attars *n* ▷ **attar**
attempt *v* (**-s, -ing, -ed**) try, make an effort ▶ *n*
   (*pl* **-s**) effort or endeavour
   attempted *v* ▷ **attempt**
   attempting *v* ▷ **attempt**
   attempts *v, n* ▷ **attempt**
attend *v* (**-s, -ing, -ed**) be present at
attendance *n* (*pl* **-s**) attending
   attendances *n* ▷ **attendance**
attendant *n* (*pl* **-s**) person who assists, guides,
   or provides a service ▶ *adj* accompanying
   attendants *n* ▷ **attendant**
   attended *v* ▷ **attend**
   attending *v* ▷ **attend**

attends *v* ▷ **attend**
attention *n* (*pl* **-s**) concentrated direction of
   the mind
   attentions *n* ▷ **attention**
attentive *adj* giving attention > **attentively**
   adv > **attentiveness** *n* (*pl* **-es**)
   attentively *adv* ▷ **attentive**
   attentiveness *n* ▷ **attentive**
   attentivenesses *n* ▷ **attentive**
attenuated *adj* weakened > **attenuation** *n* (*pl* **-s**)
   attenuation *n* ▷ **attenuated**
   attenuations *n* ▷ **attenuated**
attest *v* (**-s, -ing, -ed**) affirm the truth of, be
   proof of > **attestation** *n* (*pl* **-s**)
   attestation *n* ▷ **attest**
   attestations *n* ▷ **attest**
   attested *v* ▷ **attest**
   attesting *v* ▷ **attest**
   attests *v* ▷ **attest**
attic *n* (*pl* **-s**) space or room within the roof
   of a house
   attics *n* ▷ **attic**
attire *n* (*pl* **-s**) (*Formal*) fine or formal clothes
attired *adj* dressed in a specified way
   attires *n* ▷ **attire**
attitude *n* (*pl* **-s**) way of thinking and behaving
   attitudes *n* ▷ **attitude**
attorney *n* (*pl* **-s**) person legally appointed to
   act for another (US & S AFR)
   attorneys *n* ▷ **attorney**
attract *v* (**-s, -ing, -ed**) arouse the interest or
   admiration of
   attracted *v* ▷ **attract**
   attracting *v* ▷ **attract**
attraction *n* (*pl* **-s**) power to attract
   > **attractive** *adj* > **attractively** *adv*
   > **attractiveness** *n*
   attractions *n* ▷ **attraction**
   attractive *adj* ▷ **attraction**
   attractively *adv* ▷ **attraction**
   attractiveness *n* ▷ **attraction**
   attracts *v* ▷ **attract**
attributable *adj* ▷ **attribute**
attribute *v* (**-tes, -ting, -ted**) (*usu. foll. by* **to**)
   regard as belonging to or produced by ▶ *n*
   (*pl* **-s**) quality or feature representative
   of a person or thing > **attributable** *adj*
   > **attribution** *n* (*pl* **-s**)
   attributed *v* ▷ **attribute**
   attributes *v, n* ▷ **attribute**
   attributing *v* ▷ **attribute**
attributive *adj* (GRAMMAR) (of an adjective)
   preceding the noun modified
attrition *n* (*pl* **-s**) constant wearing down to
   weaken or destroy

attritions *n* ▷ **attrition**
attune *v* (**-nes, -ning, -ned**) adjust or accustom (a person or thing)
  attuned *v* ▷ **attune**
  attunes *v* ▷ **attune**
  attuning *v* ▷ **attune**
atypical [eh-**tip**-ik-al] *adj* not typical
aubergine [oh-bur-zheen] *n* (*pl* **-s**) (BRIT) dark purple tropical fruit, cooked and eaten as a vegetable
  aubergines *n* ▷ **aubergine**
aubrietia [aw-bree-sha] *n* (*pl* **-s**) trailing plant with purple flowers
  aubrietias *n* ▷ **aubrietia**
auburn *adj* (of hair) reddish-brown
auction *n* (*pl* **-s**) public sale in which articles are sold to the highest bidder ▶ *v* (**-s, -ing, -ed**) sell by auction
  auctioned *v* ▷ **auction**
auctioneer *n* (*pl* **-s**) person who conducts an auction
  auctioneers *n* ▷ **auctioneer**
  auctioning *v* ▷ **auction**
  auctions *n, v* ▷ **auction**
audacious *adj* recklessly bold or daring
  > **audaciously** *adv* > **audacity** *n* (*pl* **-ties**)
  audaciously *adv* ▷ **audacious**
  audacities *n* ▷ **audacious**
  audacity *n* ▷ **audacious**
  audibilities *n* ▷ **audible**
  audibility *n* ▷ **audible**
audible *adj* loud enough to be heard > **audibly** *adv* > **audibility** *n* (*pl* **-ties**)
  audibly *adv* ▷ **audible**
audience *n* (*pl* **-s**) group of spectators or listeners
  audiences *n* ▷ **audience**
audio *adj* of sound or hearing > **audiovisual** *adj* (esp. of teaching aids) involving both sight and hearing
  audiovisual *adj* ▷ **audio**
audit *n* (*pl* **-s**) official examination of business accounts ▶ *v* (**-s, -ing, -ted**) examine (business accounts) officially > **auditor** *n* (*pl* **-s**)
  audited *v* ▷ **audit**
  auditing *v* ▷ **audit**
audition *n* (*pl* **-s**) test of a performer's ability for a particular role or job ▶ *v* (**-s, -ing, -ed**) test or be tested in an audition
  auditioned *v* ▷ **audition**
  auditioning *v* ▷ **audition**
  auditions *n, v* ▷ **audition**
  auditor *n* ▷ **audit**
  auditoria *n* ▷ **auditorium**
auditorium *n* (*pl* **-riums, -ria**) area of a concert hall or theatre where the audience sits

auditoriums *n* ▷ **auditorium**
  auditors *n* ▷ **audit**
auditory *adj* of or relating to hearing
  audits *n, v* ▷ **audit**

  auf *n* (**aufs**). An auf is an elf-child left in place of a human baby. Auf scores 6 points.

auger *n* (*pl* **-s**) tool for boring holes
  augers *n* ▷ **auger**
aught *pron* (Obs) anything whatever
augment *v* (**-s, -ing, -ed**) increase or enlarge
  > **augmentation** *n* (*pl* **-s**)
  augmentation *n* ▷ **augment**
  augmentations *n* ▷ **augment**
  augmented *v* ▷ **augment**
  augmenting *v* ▷ **augment**
  augments *v* ▷ **augment**
augur *v* (**-s, -ing, -ed**) be a sign of (future events)
  augured *v* ▷ **augur**
  auguries *n* ▷ **augury**
  auguring *v* ▷ **augur**
  augurs *v* ▷ **augur**
augury *n* (*pl* **-ries**) foretelling of the future
august [aw-**gust**] *adj* dignified and imposing
auk *n* (*pl* **-s**) northern sea bird with short wings and black-and-white plumage
  auks *n* ▷ **auk**
aunt *n* (*pl* **-s**) father's or mother's sister
auntie, aunty *n* (*pl* **-ties**) (Informal) aunt
  aunties *n* ▷ **auntie**
  aunts *n* ▷ **aunt**
  aunty *n* ▷ **auntie**
aura *n* (*pl* **-s**) distinctive air or quality of a person or thing
aural *adj* of or using the ears or hearing
  auras *n* ▷ **aura**
  aureola *n* ▷ **aureole**
  aureolas *n* ▷ **aureole**
aureole, aureola *n* (*pl* **-s**) halo
  aureoles *n* ▷ **aureole**
auricle *n* (*pl* **-s**) upper chamber of the heart
  > **auricular** *adj*
  auricles *n* ▷ **auricle**
  auricular *adj* ▷ **auricle**
aurochs *n* (*pl* **aurochs**) recently extinct European wild ox
aurora *n* (*pl* **-ras, -rae**) bands of light sometimes seen in the sky in polar regions
  aurorae *n* ▷ **aurora**
  auroras *n* ▷ **aurora**
auscultation *n* (*pl* **-s**) listening to the internal sounds of the body, usu. with a stethoscope, to help with diagnosis
  auscultations *n* ▷ **auscultation**

auspice [aw-spiss] n (pl -s) (usually plural) patronage or guidance
    auspices n ▷ **auspice**
auspicious adj showing signs of future success, favourable > **auspiciously** adv
    auspiciously adv ▷ **auspicious**
austere adj (-r, -st) stern or severe > **austerely** adv > **austerity** n (pl -ties)
    austerely adv ▷ **austere**
    austerer adj ▷ **austere**
    austerest adj ▷ **austere**
    austerities n ▷ **austere**
    austerity n ▷ **austere**
    autarchies n ▷ **autarchy**
autarchy [aw-tar-kee] n (pl -chies) absolute power or autocracy
    autarkies n ▷ **autarky**
autarky [aw-tar-kee] n (pl -kies) policy of economic self-sufficiency
authentic adj known to be real, genuine > **authentically** adv > **authenticity** n (pl -ties)
    authentically adv ▷ **authentic**
authenticate v (-tes, -ting, -ted) establish as genuine > **authentication** n (pl -s)
    authenticated v ▷ **authenticate**
    authenticates v ▷ **authenticate**
    authenticating n ▷ **authenticate**
    authentication n ▷ **authenticate**
    authentications n ▷ **authenticate**
    authenticities n ▷ **authentic**
    authenticity n ▷ **authentic**
author n (pl -s) writer of a book etc. > **authorship** n (pl -s)
authoritarian n (pl -s) ▶ adj (person) insisting on strict obedience to authority
    authoritarians n ▷ **authoritarian**
authoritative adj recognized as being reliable > **authoritatively** adv
    authoritatively adv ▷ **authoritative**
    authorities n ▷ **authority**
authority n (pl -ties) power to command or control others
    authorization n ▷ **authorize**
    authorizations n ▷ **authorize**
authorize v (-zes, -zing, -zed) give authority to > **authorization** n (pl -s)
    authorized v ▷ **authorize**
    authorizes v ▷ **authorize**
    authorizing v ▷ **authorize**
    authors n ▷ **author**
    authorship n ▷ **author**
    authorships n ▷ **author**
autism n (pl -s) (PSYCHIATRY) disorder, usu. of children, characterized by lack of response to people and limited ability to communicate

> **autistic** adj
    autisms n ▷ **autism**
    autistic adj ▷ **autism**
    autobiographical adj ▷ **autobiography**
    autobiographically adv ▷ **autobiography**
    autobiographies n ▷ **autobiography**
autobiography n (pl -phies) account of a person's life written by that person
> **autobiographical** adj > **autobiographically** adv
    autocracies n ▷ **autocracy**
autocracy n (pl -cies) government by an autocrat
autocrat n (pl -s) ruler with absolute authority > **autocratic** adj > **autocratically** adv
    autocratic adj ▷ **autocrat**
    autocratically adv ▷ **autocrat**
    autocrats n ▷ **autocrat**
autocross n (pl -es) motor-racing over a rough course
    autocrosses n ▷ **autocross**
autocue n (pl **autocues**)® electronic television prompting device displaying a speaker's script, unseen by the audience
    autocues n ▷ **autocue**
autogiro, autogyro n (pl -ros) self-propelled aircraft resembling a helicopter but with an unpowered rotor
    autogiros n ▷ **autogiro**
autograph n (pl -s) handwritten signature of a (famous) person ▶ v (-s, -ing, -ed) write one's signature on or in
    autographed v ▷ **autograph**
    autographing v ▷ **autograph**
    autographs n, v ▷ **autograph**
    autogyro n ▷ **autogiro**
    autogyros n ▷ **autogiro**
automat n (pl -s) (US) vending machine
automate v (-tes, -ting, -ted) make (a manufacturing process) automatic > **automation** n (pl -s)
    automated v ▷ **automate**
    automates v ▷ **automate**
automatic adj (of a device) operating mechanically by itself ▶ n (pl -s) self-loading firearm > **automatically** adv
    automatically adv ▷ **automatic**
    automatics n ▷ **automatic**
    automating v ▷ **automate**
    automation n ▷ **automate**
    automations n ▷ **automate**
automaton n (pl -s) robot
    automatons n ▷ **automaton**
    automats n ▷ **automat**
automobile n (pl -s) (US) motor car

automobiles *n* ▷ **automobile**
autonomies *n* ▷ **autonomy**
autonomous *adj* ▷ **autonomy**
autonomy *n* (*pl* **-mies**) self-government
> **autonomous** *adj*
autopsies *n* ▷ **autopsy**
autopsy *n* (*pl* **-sies**) examination of a corpse to determine the cause of death
autosuggestion *n* (*pl* **-s**) process in which a person unconsciously influences his or her own behaviour or beliefs
autosuggestions *n* ▷ **autosuggestion**
autumn *n* (*pl* **-s**) season between summer and winter > **autumnal** *adj*
autumnal *adj* ▷ **autumn**
autumns *n* ▷ **autumn**
auxiliaries *n* ▷ **auxiliary**
auxiliary *adj* secondary or supplementary ▶ *n* (*pl* **-ries**) person or thing that supplements or supports
avail *v* (**-s**, **-ing**, **-ed**) be of use or advantage (to) ▶ *n* (*pl* **-s**) use or advantage
availabilities *n* ▷ **available**
availability *n* ▷ **available**
available *adj* obtainable or accessible
> **availability** *n* (*pl* **-ties**)
availed *v* ▷ **avail**
availing *v* ▷ **avail**
avails *v*, *n* ▷ **avail**
avalanche *n* (*pl* **-s**) mass of snow or ice falling down a mountain
avalanches *n* ▷ **avalanche**
avarice [av-a-riss] *n* (*pl* **-s**) greed for wealth
> **avaricious** *adj*
avarices *n* ▷ **avarice**
avaricious *adj* ▷ **avarice**
avast *interj* (NAUT) stop
avatar *n* (*pl* **-s**) (HINDUISM) appearance of a god in animal or human form
avatars *n* ▷ **avatar**
avenge *v* (**-ges**, **-ging**, **-ged**) take revenge in retaliation for (harm done) or on behalf of (a person harmed) > **avenger** *n* (*pl* **-s**)
avenged *v* ▷ **avenge**
avenger *n* ▷ **avenge**
avengers *n* ▷ **avenge**
avenges *v* ▷ **avenge**
avenging *v* ▷ **avenge**
avenue *n* (*pl* **-s**) wide street
avenues *n* ▷ **avenue**
aver [av-vur] *v* (**avers**, **averring**, **averred**) state to be true
average *n* (*pl* **-s**) typical or normal amount or quality ▶ *adj* usual or typical ▶ *v* (**-ges**, **-ging**, **-ged**) calculate the average of

averaged *v* ▷ **average**
averages *n*, *v* ▷ **average**
averred *v* ▷ **aver**
averring *v* ▷ **aver**
avers *v* ▷ **aver**
averages *n*, *v* ▷ **average**
averse *adj* (*usu. foll. by* **to**) disinclined or unwilling
aversion *n* (*pl* **-s**) strong dislike
aversions *n* ▷ **aversion**
avert *v* (**-s**, **-ing**, **-ed**) turn away
averted *v* ▷ **avert**
averting *v* ▷ **avert**
averts *v* ▷ **avert**
aviaries *n* ▷ **aviary**
aviary *n* (*pl* **-ries**) large cage or enclosure for birds
aviation *n* (*pl* **-s**) art of flying aircraft > **aviator** *n* (*pl* **-s**)
aviations *n* ▷ **aviation**
aviator *n* ▷ **aviation**
aviators *n* ▷ **aviation**
avid *adj* (**-er**, **-est**) keen or enthusiastic > **avidly** *adv* > **avidity** *n* (*pl* **-ties**)
avider *adj* ▷ **avid**
avidest *adj* ▷ **avid**
avidities *n* ▷ **avid**
avidity *n* ▷ **avid**
avidly *adv* ▷ **avid**
avocado *n* (*pl* **-dos**) pear-shaped tropical fruit with a leathery green skin and yellowish-green flesh
avocados *n* ▷ **avocado**
avocation *n* (*pl* **-s**) (Old-fashioned) occupation
avocations *n* ▷ **avocation**
avocet *n* (*pl* **-s**) long-legged wading bird with a long slender upward-curving bill
avocets *n* ▷ **avocet**
avoid *v* (**-s**, **-ing**, **-ed**) prevent from happening
> **avoidable** *adj* > **avoidance** *n* (*pl* **-s**)
avoidable *adj* ▷ **avoid**
avoidance *n* ▷ **avoid**
avoidances *n* ▷ **avoid**
avoided *v* ▷ **avoid**
avoiding *v* ▷ **avoid**
avoids *v* ▷ **avoid**
avoirdupois [av-er-de-**poise**] *n* (*pl* **-es**) system of weights based on pounds and ounces
avoirdupoises *n* ▷ **avoirdupois**
avow *v* (**-s**, **-ing**, **-ed**) state or affirm > **avowal** *n* (*pl* **-s**) > **avowed** *adj* > **avowedly** *adv*
avowal *n* ▷ **avow**
avowals *n* ▷ **avow**
avowed *v*, *adj* ▷ **avow**
avowedly *adv* ▷ **avow**

avowing v ▷ avow
avows v ▷ avow
avuncular adj (of a man) friendly, helpful, and caring towards someone younger

aw interj. A sound people make when they're feeling sorry for someone. Aw scores 5 points.

await v (-s, -ing, -ed) wait for
awaited v ▷ await
awaiting v ▷ await
awaits v ▷ await
awake v (awakes, awaking, awoke, awoken) emerge or rouse from sleep ▶ adj not sleeping
awaken v (-s, -ing, -ed) awake
awakened v ▷ awaken
awakening v ▷ awaken
awakens v ▷ awaken
awakes v ▷ awake
awaking v ▷ awake
award v (-s, -ing, -ed) give (something, such as a prize) formally ▶ n (pl -s) something awarded, such as a prize
awarded v ▷ award
awarding v ▷ award
awards v, n ▷ award
aware adj having knowledge, informed > **awareness** n (pl -es)
awareness n ▷ aware
awarenesses n ▷ aware
awash adv washed over by water
away adv from a place ▶ adj not present
awe n (pl -s) wonder and respect mixed with dread ▶ v (awes, awing, awed) fill with awe
awed v ▷ awe
awes n, v ▷ awe
awesome adj inspiring awe
awestruck adj filled with awe
awful adj (-ller, -llest) very bad or unpleasant
awfuller adj ▷ awful
awfullest adj ▷ awful
awfully adv in an unpleasant way
awhile adv for a brief time
awing v ▷ awe
awkward adj (-er, -est) clumsy or ungainly > **awkwardly** adv > **awkwardness** n (pl -es)
awkwarder adj ▷ awkward
awkwardest adj ▷ awkward
awkwardly adv ▷ awkward
awkwardness n ▷ awkward
awkwardnesses n ▷ awkward
awl n (pl -s) pointed tool for piercing wood, leather, etc.
awls n ▷ awl
awning n (pl -s) canvas roof supported by a frame to give protection against the weather
awnings n ▷ awning
awoke v ▷ awake
awoken v ▷ awake
awry [a-rye] adv, adj with a twist to one side, askew
ax n ▷ axe
axe, ax n (pl axes) tool with a sharp blade for felling trees or chopping wood (Informal) ▶ v (axes, axing, axed) (Informal) dismiss (employees), restrict (expenditure), or terminate (a project)
axed v ▷ axe
axes n, v ▷ axe, axis
axial adj ▷ axis
axil n (pl -s) angle where the stalk of a leaf joins a stem
axils n ▷ axil
axing v ▷ axe
axiom n (pl -s) generally accepted principle
axiomatic adj self-evident
axioms n ▷ axiom
axis n (pl axes) (imaginary) line round which a body can rotate or about which an object or geometrical figure is symmetrical > **axial** adj
axle n (pl -s) shaft on which a wheel or pair of wheels turns
axles n ▷ axle
axolotl n (pl -s) aquatic salamander of central America
axolotls n ▷ axolotl
ay interj ▷ aye
ayatollah n (pl -s) Islamic religious leader in Iran
ayatollahs n ▷ ayatollah
aye, ay interj yes ▶ n (pl -s) affirmative vote or voter
ayes n ▷ aye
azalea [az-**zale**-ya] n (pl -s) garden shrub grown for its showy flowers
azaleas n ▷ azalea
azimuth n (pl -s) arc of the sky between the zenith and the horizon
azimuths n ▷ azimuth

azo adj. Azo describes a kind of chemical. Azo scores 12 points, and so is a very high-scoring word for only three letters.
azulejo n (azulejos). An azulejo is a painted and glazed tile. Azulejo scores 23 points, and if you are lucky enough to have all seven letters needed for it, you'll get the 50-point bonus for using all of your tiles.

azure adj, n (pl -s) (of) the colour of a clear blue sky
azures n ▷ azure

Bb

B forms a two-letter word with every vowel except U – and with Y as well. With a B in your rack, you can play lots of short everyday words that will give you relatively high scores. The best of these is **box** (12 points), but don't forget **bay** (8), **by** (7), **bow** (8), **boy** (8), **buy** (8) and **bye** (8).

ba *n* (**bas**). A ba is the human soul in Egyptian mythology, shown in paintings as a bird with a human head. Ba scores 4 points.

baa *v* (**-s, -ing, -ed**) make the characteristic bleating sound of a sheep ▶ *n* (*pl* **-s**) cry made by a sheep
  baaed *v* ▷ **baa**
  baaing *v* ▷ **baa**
  baas *v*, *n* ▷ **baa**
babble *v* (**-les, -ling, -led**) talk excitedly or foolishly ▶ *n* (*pl* **-s**) muddled or foolish speech
  babbled *v* ▷ **babble**
  babbles *v*, *n* ▷ **babble**
  babbling *v* ▷ **babble**
babe *n* (*pl* **-s**) baby
babel *n* (*pl* **-s**) confused mixture of noises or voices
  babels *n* ▷ **babel**
  babes *n* ▷ **babe**
  babies *n* ▷ **baby**
baboon *n* (*pl* **-s**) large monkey with a pointed face and a long tail
  baboons *n* ▷ **baboon**
baby *n* (*pl* **-bies**) very young child or animal ▶ *adj* comparatively small of its type
  > **babyish** *adj*
  babyish *adj* ▷ **baby**
babysitter *n* (*pl* **-s**) someone who looks after children when the parents are out
  babysitters *n* ▷ **babysitter**
baccarat [back-a-rah] *n* (*pl* **-s**) card game involving gambling
  baccarats *n* ▷ **baccarat**
bacchanalia [back-a-**nail**-ee-a] *n* (*pl* **-s**) wild drunken party or orgy
  bacchanalias *n* ▷ **bacchanalia**
bach [batch] (NZ) *n* (*pl* **-es**) small holiday cottage ▶ *v* (**-es, -ing, -ed**) look after oneself when one's spouse is away

bached *v* ▷ **bach**
bachelor *n* (*pl* **-s**) unmarried man
  bachelors *n* ▷ **bachelor**
  baches *n*, *v* ▷ **bach**
  baching *v* ▷ **bach**
  bacilli *n* ▷ **bacillus**
bacillus [bass-**ill**-luss] *n* (*pl* **-li**) [-lie] rod-shaped bacterium
back *n* (*pl* **-s**) rear part of the human body, from the neck to the pelvis ▶ *v* (**-s, -ing, -ed**) (cause to) move backwards ▶ *adv* at, to, or towards the rear
backbencher *n* (*pl* **-s**) Member of Parliament who does not hold office in the government or opposition
  backbenchers *n* ▷ **backbencher**
backbiting *n* (*pl* **-s**) spiteful talk about an absent person
  backbitings *n* ▷ **backbiting**
backbone *n* (*pl* **-s**) spinal column
  backbones *n* ▷ **backbone**
backchat *n* (*pl* **-s**) (*Informal*) impudent replies
  backchats *n* ▷ **backchat**
backcloth *n* (*pl* **-s**) painted curtain at the back of a stage set
  backcloths *n* ▷ **backcloth**
backdate *v* (**-tes, -ting, -ted**) make (a document) effective from a date earlier than its completion
  backdated *v* ▷ **backdate**
  backdates *v* ▷ **backdate**
  backdating *v* ▷ **backdate**
backdrop *n* (*pl* **-s**) painted curtain at the back of a stage set
  backdrops *n* ▷ **backdrop**
  backed *v* ▷ **back**
backer *n* (*pl* **-s**) person who gives financial support
  backers *n* ▷ **backer**
backfire *v* (**-res, -ring, -red**) (of a plan) fail to

have the desired effect

backfired v ▷ **backfire**

backfires v ▷ **backfire**

backfiring v ▷ **backfire**

backgammon n (pl -s) game played with counters and dice

backgammons n ▷ **backgammon**

background n (pl -s) events or circumstances that help to explain something

backgrounds n ▷ **background**

backhand n (pl -s) (TENNIS ETC.) stroke played with the back of the hand facing the direction of the stroke

backhanded adj ambiguous or implying criticism

backhander n (pl -s) (Slang) bribe

backhanders n ▷ **backhander**

backhands n ▷ **backhand**

backing n (pl -s) support ▶ v ▷ **back**

backings n ▷ **backing**

backlash n (pl -es) sudden and adverse reaction

backlashes n ▷ **backlash**

backlog n (pl -s) accumulation of things to be dealt with

backlogs n ▷ **backlog**

backpack n (pl -s) large pack carried on the back

backpacks n ▷ **backpack**

backs n, v ▷ **back**

backside n (pl -s) (Informal) buttocks

backsides n ▷ **backside**

backslid v ▷ **backslide**

backslide v (-slides, -sliding, -slid) relapse into former bad habits > **backslider** n (pl -s)

backslider n ▷ **backslide**

backsliders n ▷ **backslide**

backslides v ▷ **backslide**

backsliding v ▷ **backslide**

backstage adv, adj behind the stage in a theatre

backstroke n (pl -s) swimming stroke performed on the back

backstrokes n ▷ **backstroke**

backtrack v (-s, -ing, -ed) return by the same route by which one has come

backtracked v ▷ **backtrack**

backtracking v ▷ **backtrack**

backtracks v ▷ **backtrack**

backup n (pl -s) support or reinforcement

backups n ▷ **backup**

backward adj directed towards the rear > **backwardness** n (pl -es)

backwardness n ▷ **backward**

backwardnesses n ▷ **backwardness**

backwards adv towards the rear

backwash n (pl -es) water washed backwards by the motion of a boat

backwashes n ▷ **backwash**

backwater n (pl -s) isolated or backward place or condition

backwaters n ▷ **backwater**

backwood n (pl -s) (usually plural) remote sparsely populated area

backwoods n ▷ **backwood**

bacon n (pl -s) salted or smoked pig meat

bacons n ▷ **bacon**

bacteria pl n (sing -rium) large group of microorganisms, many of which cause disease > **bacterial** adj

bacterial adj ▷ **bacteria**

bacteriologist n ▷ **bacteriology**

bacteriologists n ▷ **bacteriology**

bacteriology n study of bacteria > **bacteriologist** n (pl -s)

bacterium n ▷ **bacteria**

bad adj (**worse, worst**) of poor quality > **badly** adv > **badness** n (pl -es)

bade v ▷ **bid**

badge n (pl -s) emblem worn to show membership, rank, etc.

badger n (pl -s) nocturnal burrowing mammal of Europe, Asia, and N America with a black and white head ▶ v (-s, -ing, -ed) pester or harass

badgered v ▷ **badger**

badgering v ▷ **badger**

badgers n, v ▷ **badger**

badges n ▷ **badge**

badinage [bad-in-nahzh] n (pl -s) playful and witty conversation

badinages n ▷ **badinage**

badly adv ▷ **bad**

badminton n (pl -s) game played with rackets and a shuttlecock, which is hit back and forth over a high net

badmintons n ▷ **badminton**

badness n ▷ **bad**

badnesses n ▷ **bad**

baffle v (-les, -ling, -led) perplex or puzzle ▶ n (pl -s) device to limit or regulate the flow of fluid, light, or sound > **bafflement** n

baffled v ▷ **baffle**

bafflement n ▷ **baffle**

baffles v, n ▷ **baffle**

baffling v ▷ **baffle**

bag n (pl -s) flexible container with an opening at one end ▶ v (**bags, bagging, bagged**) put into a bag

bagatelle n (pl -s) something of little value

bagatelles n ▷ bagatelle

bagel n (pl -s) hard ring-shaped bread roll

bagels n ▷ bagel

baggage n (pl -s) suitcases packed for a journey

baggages n ▷ baggage

bagged n ▷ bag

baggier adj ▷ baggy

baggiest adj ▷ baggy

bagging n ▷ bag

baggy adj (-ggier, -ggiest) (of clothes) hanging loosely

bagpipes pl n musical wind instrument with reed pipes and an inflatable bag

bags n, v ▷ bag

> **bah** interj. Bah is something people say when they are annoyed or disgusted. Bah scores 8 points.

bail¹ n (pl -s) (LAW) money deposited with a court as security for a person's reappearance in court ▶ v (-s, -ing, -ed) pay bail for (a person)

bail², **bale** v (-s, -ing, -ed) (foll. by **out**) remove (water) from (a boat) (Informal)

bail³ n (pl -s) (CRICKET) either of two wooden bars across the tops of the stumps

bailed v ▷ bail¹, ²

bailey n (pl -s) outermost wall or court of a castle

baileys n ▷ bailey

bailiff n (pl -s) sheriff's officer who serves writs and summonses

bailiffs n ▷ bailiff

bailing v ▷ bail¹, ²

bails n ▷ bail¹, ³ ▶ v ▷ bail¹, ²

bairn n (pl -s) (SCOT) child

bairns n ▷ bairn

bait n (pl -s) piece of food on a hook or in a trap to attract fish or animals ▶ v (-s, -ing, -ed) put a piece of food on or in (a hook or trap)

baited v ▷ bait

baiting v ▷ bait

baits n, v ▷ bait

baize n (pl -s) woollen fabric used to cover billiard and card tables

baizes n ▷ bait

bake v (-kes, -king, -ked) cook by dry heat as in an oven

baked v ▷ bake

baker n (pl -s) person whose business is to make or sell bread, cakes, etc.

bakeries n ▷ bakery

bakers n ▷ baker

bakery n (pl -eries) place where bread, cakes, etc. are baked or sold

bakes v ▷ bake

baking v ▷ bake

bakkie n (pl -s) (S AFR) small truck

bakkies n ▷ bakkie

balaclava n (pl -s) close-fitting woollen hood that covers the ears and neck

balaclavas n ▷ balaclava

balalaika n (pl -s) guitar-like musical instrument with a triangular body

balalaikas n ▷ balalaika

balance n (pl -s) state in which a weight or amount is evenly distributed ▶ v (-ces, -cing, -ced) weigh in a balance

balanced v ▷ balance

balances n, v ▷ balance

balancing v ▷ balance

balconies n ▷ balcony

balcony n (pl -nies) platform on the outside of a building with a rail along the outer edge

bald adj (-er, -est) having little or no hair on the scalp > **baldness** n (pl -es)

balder adj ▷ bald

balderdash n (pl -es) stupid talk

balderdashes n ▷ balderdash

baldest adj ▷ bald

balding adj becoming bald

baldness n ▷ bald

baldnesses n ▷ bald

bale¹ n (pl -s) large bundle of hay or goods tightly bound together ▶ v (-les, -ling, -led) make or put into bales

bale² v ▷ bail²

baled v ▷ bale¹, ²

baleful adj vindictive or menacing > **balefully** adv

balefully adv ▷ baleful

bales n, v ▷ bale¹, ²

baling v ▷ bale¹, ²

balk, **baulk** v (-s, -ing, -ed) be reluctant to (do something)

balked v ▷ balk

balking v ▷ balk

balks v ▷ balk

ball¹ n (pl -s) round or nearly round object, esp. one used in games ▶ v (-lls, -lling, -lled) form into a ball

ball² n (pl -s) formal social function for dancing > **ballroom** n (pl -s)

ballad n (pl -s) narrative poem or song

ballads n ▷ ballad

ballast n (pl -s) substance, such as sand, used to stabilize a ship when it is not carrying cargo

ballasts n ▷ ballast

balled v ▷ ball¹

ballerina *n* (*pl* -**s**) female ballet dancer
  ballerinas *n* ▷ **ballerina**
ballet *n* (*pl* -**s**) classical style of expressive
  dancing based on conventional steps
  ballets *n* ▷ **ballet**
  balling *v* ▷ **ball¹**
  ballistic *adj* ▷ **ballistics**
ballistics *n* study of the flight of projectiles,
  such as bullets > **ballistic** *adj*
balloon *n* (*pl* -**s**) inflatable rubber bag used as a
  plaything or decoration ▸ *v* (-**s**, -**ing**, -**ed**) fly in
  a balloon > **balloonist** *n* (*pl* -**s**)
  ballooned *v* ▷ **balloon**
  ballooning *v* ▷ **balloon**
  balloonist *n* ▷ **balloon**
  balloonists *n* ▷ **balloonist**
  balloons *n*, *v* ▷ **balloon**
ballot *n* (*pl* -**s**) method of voting ▸ *v* (-**lots**,
  -**loting**, -**loted**) vote or ask for a vote from
  balloted *v* ▷ **ballot**
  balloting *v* ▷ **ballot**
  ballots *n*, *v* ▷ **ballot**
ballpoint *n* (*pl* -**s**) pen with a tiny ball bearing
  as a writing point
  ballpoints *n* ▷ **ballpoint**
  ballroom *n* ▷ **ball²**
  ballrooms *n* ▷ **ball²**
  balls *n* ▷ **ball¹, ²** ▸ *v* ▷ **ball¹**
ballyhoo *n* (*pl* -**s**) exaggerated fuss
  ballyhoos *n* ▷ **ballyhoo**
balm *n* (*pl* -**s**) aromatic substance used for
  healing and soothing
  balmier *adj* ▷ **balmy**
  balmiest *adj* ▷ **balmy**
  balms *n* ▷ **balm**
balmy *adj* (-**mier**, -**miest**) (of weather) mild
  and pleasant
baloney, boloney *n* (*pl* -**s**) (*Informal*) nonsense
  baloneys *n* ▷ **baloney**
balsa [bawl-sa] *n* (*pl* -**s**) very light wood from a
  tropical American tree
balsam *n* (*pl* -**s**) soothing ointment
  balsams *n* ▷ **balsam**
  balsas *n* ▷ **balsa**
baluster *n* (*pl* -**s**) set of posts supporting a rail
  balusters *n* ▷ **baluster**
balustrade *n* (*pl* -**s**) ornamental rail supported
  by balusters
  balustrades *n* ▷ **balustrade**
bamboo *n* (*pl* -**s**) tall treelike tropical grass
  with hollow stems
  bamboos *n* ▷ **bamboo**
bamboozle *v* (-**zles**, -**zling**, -**zled**) (*Informal*)
  cheat or mislead
  bamboozled *v* ▷ **bamboozle**

bamboozles *v* ▷ **bamboozle**
  bamboozling *v* ▷ **bamboozle**
ban *v* (-**s**, -**nning**, -**nned**) prohibit or forbid
  officially ▸ *n* (*pl* -**s**) official prohibition
banal [ban-nahl] *adj* (-**er**, -**est**) ordinary and
  unoriginal > **banality** *n* (*pl* -**ties**)
  banaler *adj* ▷ **banal**
  banalest *adj* ▷ **banal**
  banalities *n* ▷ **banal**
  banality *n* ▷ **banal**
banana *n* (*pl* -**s**) yellow crescent-shaped fruit
  bananas *n* ▷ **banana**
band¹ *n* (*pl* -**s**) group of musicians playing
  together > **bandsman** *n* (*pl* -**men**)
band² *n* (*pl* -**s**) strip of some material, used to
  hold objects
bandage *n* (*pl* -**s**) piece of material used to
  cover a wound or wrap an injured limb ▸ *v*
  (-**ges**, -**ging**, -**ged**) cover with a bandage
  bandaged *v* ▷ **bandage**
  bandages *n*, *v* ▷ **bandage**
  bandaging *v* ▷ **bandage**
  bandana *n* ▷ **bandanna**
  bandanas *n* ▷ **bandanna**
bandanna, bandana *n* (*pl* -**s**) large brightly
  coloured handkerchief or neckerchief
  bandannas *n* ▷ **bandanna**
bandicoot *n* (*pl* -**s**) ratlike Australian
  marsupial
  bandicoots *n* ▷ **bandicoot**
  bandied *v* ▷ **bandy**
  bandier *adj* ▷ **bandy**
  bandies *v* ▷ **bandy**
  bandiest *n* ▷ **bandy**
bandit *n* (*pl* -**s**) robber, esp. a member of an
  armed gang > **banditry** *n*
  banditry *n* ▷ **bandit**
  bandits *n* ▷ **bandit**
bandolier *n* (*pl* -**s**) shoulder belt for holding
  cartridges
  bandoliers *n* ▷ **bandolier**
  bands *n* ▷ **band¹, ²**
  bandsman *n* ▷ **band¹**
  bandsmen *n* ▷ **band¹**
bandstand *n* (*pl* -**s**) roofed outdoor platform
  for a band
  bandstands *n* ▷ **bandstand**
bandwagon *n* (*pl* -**s**) a party or movement that
  seems assured of success
  bandwagons *n* ▷ **bandwagon**
bandy *adj* (-**dier**, -**diest**) ▸ *v* (-**dies**, -**dying**, -**died**)
  exchange (words) in a heated manner
  bandying *v* ▷ **bandy**
bane *n* (*pl* -**s**) person or thing that causes
  misery or distress > **baneful** *adj*

baneful *adj* ▷ bane
banes *n* ▷ bane
bang *n* (*pl* -s) short loud explosive noise ▶ *v* (-s, -ging, -ged) hit or knock, esp. with a loud noise ▶ *adv* precisely
banged *v* ▷ bang
banger *n* (*pl* -s) (*Informal*) (BRIT & AUST) old decrepit car
bangers *n* ▷ banger
banging *v* ▷ bang
bangle *n* (*pl* -s) bracelet worn round the arm or the ankle
bangles *n* ▷ bangle
bangs *n*, *v* ▷ bang
banish *v* (-es, -ing, -ed) send (someone) into exile > **banishment** *n* (*pl* -s)
banished *v* ▷ banish
banishes *v* ▷ banish
banishing *v* ▷ banish
banishment *n* ▷ banish
banishments *n* ▷ banish
banisters, bannisters *pl n* railing supported by posts on a staircase
banjax *v* (**banjaxes, banjaxing, banjaxed**). If you banjax something, you wreck or ruin it. This is a great word to remember, with its high-scoring combination of J and X. Look out for chances to form it from either **ban** or **ax**. Banjax scores 22 points.
banjo *n* (*pl* -jos, -joes) guitar-like musical instrument with a circular body
banjoes *n* ▷ banjo
banjos *n* ▷ banjo
bank¹ *n* (*pl* -s) institution offering services such as the safekeeping and lending of money ▶ *v* (-s, -ing, -ed) deposit (cash or cheques) in a bank > **banking** *n*
bank² *n* (*pl* -s) raised mass, esp. of earth ▶ *v* (-s, -ing, -ed) form into a bank
bank³ *n* (*pl* -s) arrangement of switches, keys, oars, etc. in a row or in tiers
banked *v* ▷ bank¹, ²
banker *n* (*pl* -s) manager or owner of a bank
bankers *n* ▷ banker
banking *v* ▷ bank¹, ² ▶ *n* ▷ bank¹
banknote *n* (*pl* -s) piece of paper money
banknotes *n* ▷ banknote
bankrupt *n* (*pl* -s) person declared by a court to be unable to pay his or her debts ▶ *adj* financially ruined ▶ *v* (-s, -ing, -ed) make bankrupt > **bankruptcy** *n* (*pl* -cies)
bankruptcies *n* ▷ bankrupt
bankruptcy *n* ▷ bankrupt
bankrupted *v* ▷ bankrupt

bankrupting *v* ▷ bankrupt
bankrupts *n*, *v* ▷ bankrupt
banks *n* ▷ bank¹, ², ³ ▶ *v* ▷ bank¹, ²
banksia *n* (*pl* -s) Australian evergreen tree or shrub
banksias *n* ▷ banksia
banned *v* ▷ ban
banner *n* (*pl* -s) long strip of cloth displaying a slogan, advertisement, etc.
banners *n* ▷ banner
banning *v* ▷ ban
bannisters *pl n* ▷ banisters
banns *pl n* public declaration, esp. in a church, of an intended marriage
banquet *n* (*pl* -s) elaborate formal dinner
banquets *n* ▷ banquet
bans *v*, *n* ▷ ban
banshee *n* (*pl* -s) (in Irish folklore) female spirit whose wailing warns of a coming death
banshees *n* ▷ banshee
bantam *n* (*pl* -s) small breed of chicken
bantams *n* ▷ bantam
bantamweight *n* (*pl* -s) boxer weighing up to 118lb (professional) or 54kg (amateur)
bantamweights *n* ▷ bantamweight
banter *v* (-s, -ing, -ed) tease jokingly ▶ *n* (*pl* -s) teasing or joking conversation
bantered *v* ▷ banter
bantering *v* ▷ banter
banters *v*, *n* ▷ banter
baobab [bay-oh-bab] *n* (*pl* -s) African tree with a thick trunk and angular branches
baobabs *n* ▷ baobab
baptism *n* (*pl* -s) Christian religious ceremony in which a person is immersed in or sprinkled with water as a sign of being cleansed from sin and accepted into the Church > **baptismal** *adj*
baptismal *adj* ▷ baptism
baptisms *n* ▷ baptism
baptist *n* (*pl* -s) member of a Protestant denomination that believes in adult baptism by immersion
baptists *n* ▷ baptist
baptize *v* (-zes, -zing, -zed) perform baptism on
baptized *v* ▷ baptize
baptizes *v* ▷ baptize
baptizing *v* ▷ baptize
bar¹ *n* (*pl* -s) rigid length of metal, wood, etc. ▶ *v* (**bars, barring, barred**) secure with a bar > **barman** (*pl* -men), **barmaid** (*pl* -s) ▶ *n*
bar² *n* (*pl* -s) unit of atmospheric pressure
barb *n* (*pl* -s) cutting remark > **barbed** *adj*
barbarian *n* (*pl* -s) member of a primitive or

uncivilized people
barbarians n ▷ **barbarian**
barbaric adj cruel or brutal
barbarism n (pl **-s**) condition of being backward or ignorant
barbarisms n ▷ **barbarism**
barbarities n ▷ **barbarity**
barbarity n (pl **-ties**) state of being barbaric or barbarous
barbarous adj uncivilized
barbecue n (pl **-s**) grill on which food is cooked over hot charcoal, usu. outdoors ▶ v (**-cues, -cuing, -cued**) cook (food) on a barbecue
barbecued v ▷ **barbecue**
barbecues n, v ▷ **barbecue**
barbecuing v ▷ **barbecue**
barbed adj ▷ **barb**
barber n (pl **-s**) person who cuts men's hair and shaves beards
barbers n ▷ **barber**
barbiturate n (pl **-s**) drug used as a sedative
barbiturates n ▷ **barbiturate**
barbs n ▷ **barb**
bard n (pl **-s**) (Lit) poet
bards n ▷ **bard**
bare adj (**-r, -st**) unclothed, naked ▶ v (**-res, -ring, -red**) uncover > **bareness** n (pl **-es**)
bareback adj, adv (of horse-riding) without a saddle
bared v ▷ **bare**
barefaced adj shameless or obvious
barely adv only just
bareness n ▷ **bare**
barenesses n ▷ **bare**
barer adj ▷ **bare**
bares v ▷ **bare**
barest adj ▷ **bare**
bargain n (pl **-s**) agreement establishing what each party will give, receive, or perform in a transaction ▶ v (**-s, -ing, -ed**) negotiate the terms of an agreement
bargained v ▷ **bargain**
bargaining v ▷ **bargain**
bargains n, v ▷ **bargain**
barge n (pl **-s**) flat-bottomed boat used to transport freight ▶ v (**-ges, -ging, -ged**) (Informal) push violently
barged v ▷ **barge**
barges n, v ▷ **barge**
barging v ▷ **barge**
baring v ▷ **bare**
barista [bar-ee-sta] n (pl **-s**) person who makes and sells coffee in a coffee bar
baristas n ▷ **barista**
baritone n (pl **-s**) (singer with) the second

lowest adult male voice
baritones n ▷ **baritone**
barium n (pl **-s**) (CHEM) soft white metallic element
bariums n ▷ **barium**
bark¹ n (pl **-s**) loud harsh cry of a dog ▶ v (**-s, -ing, -ed**) (of a dog) make its typical cry
bark² n (pl **-s**) tough outer layer of a tree
barked v ▷ **bark¹**
barking v ▷ **bark¹**
barks n, v ▷ **bark¹** ▶ n ▷ **bark²**
barley n (pl **-s**) tall grasslike plant cultivated for grain
barleys n ▷ **barley**
barmaid n ▷ **bar¹**
barmaids n ▷ **bar¹**
barman n ▷ **bar¹**
barmen n ▷ **bar¹**
barmier adj ▷ **barmy**
barmiest adj ▷ **barmy**
barmy adj (**-mier, -miest**) (Slang) insane
barn n (pl **-s**) large building on a farm used for storing grain
barnacle n (pl **-s**) shellfish that lives attached to rocks, ship bottoms, etc.
barnacles n ▷ **barnacle**
barney n (pl **-s**) (Informal) noisy fight or argument
barneys n ▷ **barney**
barns n ▷ **barn**
barometer n (pl **-s**) instrument for measuring atmospheric pressure > **barometric** adj
barometers n ▷ **barometer**
barometric adj ▷ **barometer**
baron n (pl **-s**) member of the lowest rank of nobility > **baroness** n (pl **-es**) > **baronial** adj
baroness n ▷ **baron**
baronesses n ▷ **baron**
baronet n (pl **baronets**) commoner who holds the lowest hereditary British title
baronets n ▷ **baronet**
baronial adj ▷ **baron**
barons n ▷ **baron**
baroque [bar-rock] n (pl **-s**) highly ornate style of art, architecture, or music from the late 16th to the early 18th century ▶ adj ornate in style
baroques n ▷ **baroque**
barque [bark] n (pl **-s**) sailing ship, esp. one with three masts
barques n ▷ **barque**
barra n (pl **-s**) (AUST) (Informal) ▷ **barramundi**
barrack v (**-s, -ing, -ed**) criticize loudly or shout against (a team or speaker)
barracked v ▷ **barrack**

barracking v ▷ **barrack**

barracks v ▷ **barrack** ▶ pl n building used to accommodate military personnel

barracouta n (pl -s) large Pacific fish with a protruding lower jaw and strong teeth

barracoutas n ▷ **barracouta**

barracuda n (pl **barracuda**) tropical sea fish

barrage [bar-rahzh] n (pl -s) continuous delivery of questions, complaints, etc.

barrages n ▷ **barrage**

barramundi n (pl -s) edible Australian fish

barramundis n ▷ **barramundi**

barras n ▷ **barra**

barred v ▷ **bar¹**

barrel n (pl -s) cylindrical container with rounded sides and flat ends

barrels n ▷ **barrel**

barren adj (-er, -est) (of a woman or female animal) incapable of producing offspring
> **barrenness** n (pl -es)

barrener adj ▷ **barren**

barrenest adj ▷ **barren**

barrenness n ▷ **barren**

barrennesses n ▷ **barren**

barricade n (pl -s) barrier, esp. one erected hastily for defence ▶ v (-des, -ding, -ded) erect a barricade across (an entrance)

barricaded v ▷ **barricade**

barricades n, v ▷ **barricade**

barricading v ▷ **barricade**

barrier n (pl -s) anything that prevents access, progress, or union

barriers n ▷ **barrier**

barring v ▷ **bar¹** ▶ prep except for

barrister n (pl -s) (BRIT, AUST & NZ) lawyer qualified to plead in a higher court

barristers n ▷ **barrister**

barrow¹ n (pl -s) wheelbarrow

barrow² n (pl -s) mound of earth over a prehistoric tomb

barrows n ▷ **barrow¹, ²**

bars n ▷ **bar¹, ²** ▶ v ▷ **bar¹**

barter v (-s, -ing, -ed) trade (goods) in exchange for other goods ▶ n (pl -s) trade by the exchange of goods

bartered v ▷ **barter**

bartering v ▷ **barter**

barters v, n ▷ **barter**

basalt [bass-awlt] n (pl -s) dark volcanic rock
> **basaltic** adj

basaltic adj ▷ **basalt**

basalts n ▷ **basalt**

base¹ n (pl -s) bottom or supporting part of anything ▶ v (**bases, basing, based**) (foll. by **on** or **upon**) use as a basis (for) > **baseless** adj

base² adj (-r, -st) dishonourable or immoral
> **baseness** n

baseball n (pl -s) team game in which runs are scored by hitting a ball with a bat then running round four bases

baseballs n ▷ **baseball**

based v ▷ **base¹**

baseless adj ▷ **base¹**

basement n (pl -s) partly or wholly underground storey of a building

basements n ▷ **basement**

baseness n ▷ **base²**

baser adj ▷ **base²**

bases n ▷ **base¹**, **basis** ▶ v ▷ **base¹**

basest adj ▷ **base²**

bash (Informal) v (-es, -ing, -ed) hit violently or forcefully ▶ n (pl **bashes**) heavy blow

bashed v ▷ **bash**

bashes v, n ▷ **bash**

bashful adj shy or modest > **bashfully** adv
> **bashfulness** n

bashfully adv ▷ **bash**

bashfulness n ▷ **bash**

bashing v ▷ **bash**

basic adj of or forming a base or basis
> **basically** adv

basically adv ▷ **basic**

basics pl n fundamental principles, facts, etc.

basil n (pl -s) aromatic herb used in cooking

basilica n (pl -s) rectangular church with a rounded end and two aisles

basilicas n ▷ **basilica**

basilisk n (pl -s) legendary serpent said to kill by its breath or glance

basilisks n ▷ **basilisk**

basils n ▷ **basil**

basin n (pl -s) round open container

basing v ▷ **base¹**

basins n ▷ **basin**

basis n (pl -ses) fundamental principles etc. from which something is started or developed

bask v (-s, -ing, -ed) lie in or be exposed to something, esp. pleasant warmth

basked v ▷ **bask**

basket n (pl -s) container made of interwoven strips of wood or cane > **basketwork** n (pl -s)

basketball n (pl -s) team game in which points are scored by throwing the ball through a high horizontal hoop

basketballs n ▷ **basketball**

baskets n ▷ **basket**

basketwork n ▷ **basket**

basketworks n ▷ **basket**

basking v ▷ **bask**

basks v ▷ **bask**

bass¹ [base] n (pl **-es**) (singer with) the lowest adult male voice ▶ adj of the lowest range of musical notes

bass² n (pl **bass**) edible sea fish

basses n ▷ **bass¹**

bassoon n (pl **-s**) low-pitched woodwind instrument

bassoons n ▷ **bassoon**

bastard n (pl **-s**) (Offens) obnoxious or despicable person

bastards n ▷ **bastard**

baste¹ v (**bastes, basting, basted**) moisten (meat) during cooking with hot fat

baste² v (**bastes, basting, basted**) sew with loose temporary stitches

basted v ▷ **baste¹, ²**

bastes v ▷ **baste¹, ²**

basting v ▷ **baste¹, ²**

bastion n (pl **-s**) projecting part of a fortification

bastions n ▷ **bastion**

bat¹ n (pl **-s**) any of various types of club used to hit the ball in certain sports ▶ v (**bats, batting, batted**) strike with or as if with a bat

bat² n (pl **-s**) nocturnal mouselike flying animal

batch n (pl **-es**) group of people or things dealt with at the same time

batches n ▷ **batch**

bath n (pl **-s**) large container in which to wash the body ▶ pl public swimming pool ▶ v (**-s, -ing, -ed**) wash in a bath

bathe v (**-thes, -thing, -thed**) swim in open water for pleasure > **bather** n (pl **-s**)

bathed v ▷ **bath** ▷ **bathe**

bather n ▷ **bathe**

bathers n ▷ **bathe**

bathes v ▷ **bath** ▷ **bathe**

bathing v ▷ **bath** ▷ **bathe**

bathos [bay-thoss] n (pl **-es**) sudden ludicrous change in speech or writing from a serious subject to a trivial one

bathoses n ▷ **bathos**

bathroom n (pl **-s**) room with a bath, sink, and usu. a toilet

bathrooms n ▷ **bathe**

baths n, v ▷ **bath**

batik [bat-teek] n (pl **-s**) process of printing fabric using wax to cover areas not to be dyed

batiks n ▷ **batik**

batman n (pl **-men**) officer's servant in the armed forces

batmen n ▷ **batman**

baton n (pl **-s**) thin stick used by the conductor of an orchestra

batons n ▷ **baton**

bats n ▷ **bat¹, ²** ▶ v ▷ **bat¹**

batsman n (pl **-men**) (CRICKET) person who bats or specializes in batting

batsmen n ▷ **batsman**

battalion n (pl **-s**) army unit consisting of three or more companies

battalions n ▷ **battalion**

batted v ▷ **bat¹**

batten n (pl **-s**) strip of wood fixed to something, esp. to hold it in place

battens n ▷ **batten**

batter¹ v (**-s, -ing, -ed**) hit repeatedly

batter² n (pl **-s**) mixture of flour, eggs, and milk, used in cooking

battered v ▷ **batter¹**

batteries n ▷ **battery**

battering v ▷ **batter¹**

batters v, n ▷ **batter¹, ²**

battery n (pl **-teries**) device that produces electricity in a torch, radio, etc. ▶ adj kept in series of cages for intensive rearing

battier adj ▷ **batty**

battiest adj ▷ **batty**

batting adj ▷ **bat¹**

battle n (pl **-s**) fight between large armed forces ▶ v (**battles, battling, battled**) struggle

battled v ▷ **battle**

battlement n (pl **-s**) wall with gaps along the top for firing through

battlements n ▷ **battlement**

battles n, v ▷ **battle**

battleship n (pl **-s**) large heavily armoured warship

battleships n ▷ **battleship**

battling v ▷ **battle**

batty adj (**-tier, -tiest**) (Slang) eccentric or crazy

bauble n (pl **-s**) trinket of little value

baubles n ▷ **bauble**

bauera n (pl **-s**) small evergreen Australian shrub

baueras n ▷ **bauera**

baulk v (**-s, -ing, -ed**) ▷ **balk**

baulked v ▷ **baulk**

baulking v ▷ **baulk**

baulks v ▷ **baulk**

bauxite n (pl **-s**) claylike substance that is the chief source of aluminium

bauxites n ▷ **bauxite**

bawdier adj ▷ **bawdy**

bawdiest adj ▷ **bawdy**

bawdy adj (**-ier, -iest**) (of writing etc.) containing humorous references to sex

bawl v (**-s, -ing, -ed**) shout or weep noisily

bawled v ▷ **bawl**

bawling v ▷ **bawl**
bawls v ▷ **bawl**
bay¹ n (pl **-s**) stretch of coastline that curves inwards
bay² n (pl **-s**) recess in a wall
bay³ v (**-s, -ing, -ed**) howl in deep prolonged tones
bay⁴ n (pl **-s**) Mediterranean laurel tree
bay⁵ adj, n (pl **-s**) reddish-brown (horse)
bayed v ▷ **bay³**
baying v ▷ **bay³**
bayonet n (pl **-s**) sharp blade that can be fixed to the end of a rifle ▶ v (**-nets, -neting, -neted**) stab with a bayonet
bayoneted v ▷ **bayonet**
bayoneting v ▷ **bayonet**
bayonets n, v ▷ **bayonet**
bays n ▷ **bay¹, ², ⁴, ⁵** ▶ v³
bazaar n (pl **-s**) sale in aid of charity
bazaars n ▷ **bazaar**
bazooka n (pl **-s**) portable rocket launcher that fires an armour-piercing projectile
bazookas n ▷ **bazooka**
be v (present sing (1st person **am**) (2nd person **are**) (3rd person **is**) (present pl **are**) (past sing (1st person **was**) (2nd person **were**) (3rd person **was**) (past pl **were**) (present participle **being**) (past participle **been**) exist or live
beach n (pl **-es**) area of sand or pebbles on a shore ▶ v (**-es, -ing, -ed**) run or haul (a boat) onto a beach
beached v ▷ **beach**
beaches n, v ▷ **beach**
beachhead n (pl **-s**) beach captured by an attacking army on which troops can be landed
beachheads v ▷ **beachhead**
beaching v ▷ **beach**
beacon n (pl **-s**) fire or light on a hill or tower, used as a warning
beacons n ▷ **beacon**
bead n (pl **-s**) small piece of plastic, wood, etc., pierced for threading on a string to form a necklace etc. > **beaded** adj
beaded n ▷ **bead**
beadier adj ▷ **beady**
beadiest adj ▷ **beady**
beading n strip of moulding used for edging furniture
beads n ▷ **bead**
beady adj (**-ier, -iest**) small, round, and glittering
beagle n (pl **-s**) small hound with short legs and drooping ears
beagles n ▷ **beagle**

beak¹ n (pl **-s**) projecting horny jaws of a bird
> **beaky** adj (**-ier, -iest**)
beak² n (pl **-s**) (BRIT, AUST & NZ) (Slang) judge, magistrate, or headmaster
beaker n (pl **-s**) large drinking cup
beakers n ▷ **beaker**
beakier adj ▷ **beak¹**
beakiest adj ▷ **beak¹**
beaks n ▷ **beak¹, ²**
beaky adj ▷ **beak¹**
beam n (pl **-s**) broad smile ▶ v (**-s, -ing, -ed**) smile broadly
beamed v ▷ **beam**
beaming v ▷ **beam**
beams n, v ▷ **beam**
bean n (pl **-s**) seed or pod of various plants, eaten as a vegetable or used to make coffee etc.
beanie n (pl **-s**) close-fitting woollen hat
beanies n ▷ **beanie**
beans n ▷ **bean**
bear¹ v (**bears, bearing, bore, borne**) support or hold up (passive **born**) > **bearable** adj
bear² n (pl **-s**) large heavy mammal with a shaggy coat
bearable adj ▷ **bear¹**
beard n (pl **-s**) hair growing on the lower parts of a man's face > **bearded** adj
bearded adj ▷ **beard**
beards n ▷ **beard**
bearer n (pl **-s**) person who carries, presents, or upholds something
bearers n ▷ **bearer**
bearing n (pl **-s**) relevance (to) ▶ pl sense of one's own relative position ▶ v ▷ **bear¹**
bearings n ▷ **bearing**
bears v ▷ **bear¹** ▶ n ▷ **bear²**
bearskin n (pl **-s**) tall fur helmet worn by some British soldiers
bearskins n ▷ **bearskin**
beast n (pl **-s**) large wild animal
beastliness n ▷ **beastly**
beastly adj unpleasant or disagreeable
> **beastliness** n
beasts n ▷ **beast**
beat v (**beats, beating, beat, beaten** or **beat**) hit hard and repeatedly ▶ n (pl **beats**) regular throb
beaten v ▷ **beat**
beatific adj displaying great happiness
beatification n ▷ **beatify**
beatifications n ▷ **beatify**
beatified v ▷ **beatify**
beatifies v ▷ **beatify**
beatify [bee-at-if-fie] v (**-fies, -fying, -fied**) (RC

CHURCH) declare (a dead person) to be among the blessed in heaven: the first step towards canonization > **beatification** n (pl -**s**)
beatifying v ▷ **beatify**
beating v ▷ **beat**
beatitude n (pl -**s**) (CHRISTIANITY) any of the blessings on the poor, meek, etc., in the Sermon on the Mount
beatitudes n ▷ **beatitude**
beats v, n ▷ **beat**
beau [boh] n (pl **beaux, beaus**) boyfriend or admirer
beaus n ▷ **beau**
beautician n (pl -**s**) person who gives beauty treatments professionally
beauticians n ▷ **beautician**
beauties n ▷ **beauty**
beautification n ▷ **beautify**
beautified v ▷ **beautify**
beautifies v ▷ **beautify**
beautiful adj very attractive to look at > **beautifully** adv
beautifully adv ▷ **beautiful**
beautify v (-**fies, -fying, -fied**) make beautiful > **beautification** n
beautifying v ▷ **beautify**
beauty n (pl -**ties**) combination of all the qualities of a person or thing that delight the senses and mind
beaux n ▷ **beau**
beaver n (pl -**s**) amphibious rodent with a big flat tail
beavers n ▷ **beaver**
becalmed adj (of a sailing ship) motionless through lack of wind
became v ▷ **become**
because conj on account of the fact that
beck n (pl -**s**) (N ENGLISH) stream
beckon v (-**s, -ing, -ed**) summon with a gesture
beckoned v ▷ **beckon**
beckoning v ▷ **beckon**
beckons v ▷ **beckon**
becks n ▷ **beck**
become v (-**coming, -came, -come**) come to be
becoming adj attractive or pleasing
bed n (pl -**s**) piece of furniture on which to sleep > **bedroom** n (pl -**s**)
bedding n (pl -**s**) sheets and covers that are used on a bed
beddings n ▷ **bedding**
bedevil v (-**s, -illing, -illed**) harass, confuse, or torment
bedevilled v ▷ **bedevil**
bedevilling v ▷ **bedevil**
bedevils v ▷ **bedevil**

bedlam n (pl -**s**) noisy confused situation
bedlams n ▷ **bedlam**
bedpan n (pl -**s**) shallow bowl used as a toilet by bedridden people
bedpans n ▷ **bedpan**
bedraggled adj untidy, wet, or dirty
bedridden adj confined to bed because of illness or old age
bedrock n (pl -**s**) solid rock beneath the surface soil
bedrocks n ▷ **bedrock**
bedroom n ▷ **bed**
bedrooms n ▷ **bed**
beds n ▷ **bed**
bedsit, bedsitter n (pl -**s**) furnished sitting room with a bed
bedsits n ▷ **bedsit**
bedsitters n ▷ **bedsit**
bee n (pl -**s**) insect that makes wax and honey
beech n (pl -**es**) tree with a smooth greyish bark
beeches n ▷ **beech**
beef n (pl **beeves**) flesh of a cow, bull, or ox
beefburger n (pl -**s**) flat grilled or fried cake of minced beef
beefburgers n ▷ **beefburger**
beefeater n (pl -**s**) yeoman warder at the Tower of London
beefeaters n ▷ **beefeater**
beefier adj ▷ **beefy**
beefiest adj ▷ **beefy**
beefy adj (-**fier, -fiest**) like beef
beehive n (pl -**s**) structure in which bees live
beehives n ▷ **beehive**
been v ▷ **be**
beep n (pl -**s**) high-pitched sound, like that of a car horn ▶ v (-**s, -ing, -ed**) (cause to) make this noise
beeped v ▷ **beep**
beeping v ▷ **beep**
beeps n, v ▷ **beep**
beer n (pl -**s**) alcoholic drink brewed from malt and hops > **beery** (-**ier, -iest**) ▶ adj
beerier adj ▷ **beer**
beeriest adj ▷ **beer**
beers n ▷ **beer**
beery adj ▷ **beer**
bees n ▷ **bee**
beeswax n (pl -**es**) wax secreted by bees, used in polishes etc.
beeswaxes n ▷ **beeswax**
beet n (pl -**s**) plant with an edible root and leaves
beetle n (pl -**s**) insect with a hard wing cover on its back

beetles *n* ▷ **beetle**
beetroot *n* (*pl* **-s**) type of beet plant with a dark red root
beetroots *n* ▷ **beetroot**
beets *n* ▷ **beet**
beeves *n* ▷ **beef**
befall *v* (**-falls, -falling, -fell, -fallen**) (*Old-fashioned*) happen to (someone)
befallen *v* ▷ **befall**
befalling *v* ▷ **befall**
befalls *v* ▷ **befall**
befell *v* ▷ **befall**
befit *v* (**-fits, -fitting, -fitted**) be appropriate or suitable for > **befitting** *adj*
befits *v* ▷ **befit**
befitted *v* ▷ **befit**
befitting *v*, *adj* ▷ **befit**
before *conj*, *prep adv* indicating something earlier in time, in front of, or preferred to
beforehand *adv* in advance
befriend *v* (**-s, -ing, -ed**) become friends with
befriended *v* ▷ **befriend**
befriending *v* ▷ **befriend**
befriends *v* ▷ **befriend**
beg *v* (**begs, begging, begged**) solicit (for money or food), esp. in the street
began *v* ▷ **begin**
begat *v* ▷ **beget**
beget *v* (**-gets, -getting, -got** *or* **-gat; -gotten** *or* **-got**) (*Old-fashioned*) cause or create
begets *v* ▷ **beget**
begetting *v* ▷ **beget**
beggar *n* (*pl* **s**) person who lives by begging > **beggarly** *adj* > **beggarliness** *n*
beggarliness *n* ▷ **beggar**
beggarly *adj* ▷ **beggar**
beggars *n* ▷ **beggar**
begged *v* ▷ **beg**
begging *v* ▷ **beg**
begin *v* (**-gins, -ginning, -gan, -gun**) start > **beginning** *n* (*pl* **-s**)
beginner *n* (*pl* **-s**) person who has just started learning to do something
beginners *n* ▷ **begin**
beginning *v*, *n* ▷ **begin**
begins *v* ▷ **begin**
begonia *n* (*pl* **-s**) tropical plant with waxy flowers
begonias *n* ▷ **begonia**
begot *v* ▷ **beget**
begotten *v* ▷ **beget**
begrudge *v* (**-grudges, -grudging, -grudged**) envy (someone) the possession of something
begrudged *v* ▷ **begrudge**
begrudges *v* ▷ **begrudge**

begrudging *v* ▷ **begrudge**
begs *v* ▷ **beg**
beguile [big-gile] *v* (**-guiles, -guiling, -guiled**) cheat or mislead > **beguiling** *adj*
beguiled *v* ▷ **beguile**
beguiles *v* ▷ **beguile**
beguiling *v*, *adj* ▷ **beguile**
begun *v* ▷ **begin**
behalf *n* in the interest of or for the benefit of
behave *v* (**-haves, -having, -haved**) act or function in a particular way
behaved *v* ▷ **behave**
behaves *v* ▷ **behave**
behaving *v* ▷ **behave**
behaviour *n* (*pl* **-s**) manner of behaving
behaviours *n* ▷ **behaviour**
behead *v* (**-s, -ing, -ed**) remove the head from
beheaded *v* ▷ **behead**
beheading *v* ▷ **behead**
beheads *v* ▷ **behead**
beheld *v* ▷ **behold**
behest *n* (*pl* **-s**) order or earnest request
behests *n* ▷ **behest**
behind *prep*, *adv* indicating position to the rear, lateness, responsibility, etc. ▶ *n* (*pl* **-s**) (*Informal*) buttocks
behinds *n* ▷ **behind**
behold *v* (**-holds, -holding, -held**) (*Old-fashioned*) look (at) > **beholder** *n* (*pl* **-s**)
beholden *adj* indebted or obliged
beholder *n* ▷ **behold**
beholders *n* ▷ **behold**
beholding *v* ▷ **behold**
beholds *v* ▷ **behold**
behove *v* (**-hoves, -hoving, -hoved**) (*Old-fashioned*) be necessary or fitting for
behoved *v* ▷ **behove**
behoves *v* ▷ **behove**
behoving *v* ▷ **behove**
beige *adj* pale brown
being *n* (*pl* **-s**) state or fact of existing ▶ *v* ▷ **be**
beings *n* ▷ **being**
belabour *v* (**-s, -ing, -ed**) attack verbally or physically
belaboured *v* ▷ **belabour**
belabouring *v* ▷ **belabour**
belabours *v* ▷ **belabour**
belated *adj* late or too late > **belatedly** *adv*
belatedly *adv* ▷ **belated**
belch *v* (**-es, -ing, -ed**) expel wind from the stomach noisily through the mouth ▶ *n* (*pl* **belches**) act of belching
belched *v* ▷ **belch**
belches *v*, *n* ▷ **belch**
belching *v* ▷ **belch**

beleaguered *adj* struggling against difficulties or criticism
  belfries *n* ▷ **belfry**
belfry *n* (*pl* **-fries**) part of a tower where bells are hung
belie *v* (**belies, belying, belied**) show to be untrue
  belied *v* ▷ **belie**
belief *n* (*pl* **-s**) faith or confidence
  beliefs *n* ▷ **belief**
  belies *v* ▷ **belie**
  believable *adj* ▷ **believe**
believe *v* (**-lieves, -lieving, -lieved**) accept as true or real > **believable** *adj* > **believer** *n* (*pl* **-s**)
  believed *v* ▷ **believe**
  believer *n* ▷ **believe**
  believers *n* ▷ **believe**
  believes *v* ▷ **believe**
  believing *v* ▷ **believe**
belittle *v* (**-ttles, -ttling, -ttled**) treat as having little value or importance
  belittled *v* ▷ **belittle**
  belittles *v* ▷ **belittle**
  belittling *v* ▷ **belittle**
bell *n* (*pl* **-s**) hollow, usu. metal, cup-shaped instrument that emits a ringing sound when struck
belladonna *n* (*pl* **-s**) (drug obtained from) deadly nightshade
  belladonnas *n* ▷ **belladonna**
bellbird *n* (*pl* **-s**) Australasian bird with bell-like call
  bellbirds *n* ▷ **bellbird**
belle *n* (*pl* **-s**) beautiful woman, esp. the most attractive woman at a function
  belles *n* ▷ **belle**
bellicose *adj* warlike and aggressive
  bellied *v* ▷ **belly**
  bellies *n, v* ▷ **belly**
  belligerence *n* ▷ **belligerent**
belligerent *adj* hostile and aggressive ▶ *n* (*pl* **-s**) person or country engaged in war > **belligerence** *n*
  belligerents *n* ▷ **belligerent**
bellow *v* (**-s, -ing, -ed**) make a low deep cry like that of a bull ▶ *n* (*pl* **-s**) loud deep roar
  bellowed *v* ▷ **bellow**
  bellowing *v* ▷ **bellow**
bellows *v, n* ▷ **bellow** ▶ *pl n* instrument for pumping a stream of air into something
  bells *n* ▷ **bell**
belly *n* (*pl* **-lies**) part of the body of a vertebrate which contains the intestines ▶ *v* (**-lies, -lying, -lied**) (cause to) swell out
bellyful *n* (*pl* **-s**) (*Slang*) more than one can tolerate
  bellyfuls *n* ▷ **bellyful**
  bellying *v* ▷ **belly**
belong *v* (**-s, -ing, -ed**) (*foll. by* **to**) be the property of
  belonged *v* ▷ **belong**
  belonging *v* ▷ **belong**
belongings *pl n* personal possessions
  belongs *v* ▷ **belong**
beloved *adj* dearly loved ▶ *n* (*pl* **-s**) person dearly loved
  beloveds *n* ▷ **beloved**
below *prep, adv* at or to a position lower than, under
belt *n* (*pl* **-s**) band of cloth, leather, etc., worn usu. around the waist ▶ *v* (**-s, -ing, -ed**) fasten with a belt
  belted *v* ▷ **belt**
  belting *v* ▷ **belt**
  belts *n, v* ▷ **belt**
  belying *v* ▷ **belie**
bemoan *v* (**-s, -ing, -ed**) express sorrow or dissatisfaction about
  bemoaned *v* ▷ **bemoan**
  bemoaning *v* ▷ **bemoan**
  bemoans *v* ▷ **bemoan**
bemused *adj* puzzled or confused
bench *n* (*pl* **-es**) long seat
  benches *n* ▷ **bench**
benchmark *n* (*pl* **-s**) criterion by which to measure something
  benchmarks *n* ▷ **benchmark**
bend *v* (**-s, -ing, bent**) (cause to) form a curve ▶ *n* curved part > **bendy** *adj* (**-dier, -diest**) > **bendiness** *n* (*pl* **-es**)
  bendier *adj* ▷ **bend**
  bendiest *adj* ▷ **bend**
  bendiness *n* ▷ **bend**
  bendinesses *n* ▷ **bend**
  bending *v* ▷ **bend**
bends *v* ▷ **bend** ▶ *pl n* (*Informal*) decompression sickness
  bendy *adj* ▷ **bend**
beneath *adv, prep* below
benediction *n* (*pl* **-s**) prayer for divine blessing
  benedictions *n* ▷ **benediction**
  benefaction *n* ▷ **benefactor**
  benefactions *n* ▷ **benefactor**
benefactor, benefactress *n* (*pl* **-s, -esses**) someone who supports a person or institution by giving money > **benefaction** *n* (*pl* **-s**)
  benefactors *n* ▷ **benefactor**
  benefactress *n* ▷ **benefactor**
  benefactresses *n* ▷ **benefactor**

beneficence n ▷ **beneficent**
beneficent [bin-eff-iss-ent] adj charitable or generous > **beneficence** n
beneficial adj helpful or advantageous
beneficiaries n ▷ **beneficiary**
beneficiary n (pl -ciaries) person who gains or benefits
benefit n (pl -s) something that improves or promotes ▶ v (-s, -fiting, -fited) do or receive good
benefited v ▷ **benefit**
benefiting v ▷ **benefit**
benefits n, v ▷ **benefit**
benevolence n (pl -s) inclination to do good > **benevolent** adj > **benevolently** adv
benevolences n ▷ **benevolence**
benevolent adj ▷ **benevolence**
benevolently adv ▷ **benevolence**
benighted adj ignorant or uncultured
benign [bin-nine] adj showing kindliness > **benignly** adv
benignly adv ▷ **benign**
bent v ▷ **bend** ▶ adj curved ▶ n (pl -s) personal inclination or aptitude
bento n (pl -s) thin lightweight box divided into compartments, which contain small separate dishes comprising a Japanese meal
bentos n ▷ **bento**
bents n ▷ **bent**
benzene n (pl -s) flammable poisonous liquid used as a solvent, insecticide, etc.
benzenes n ▷ **benzene**
bequeath v (-s, -ing, -ed) dispose of (property) as in a will
bequeathed v ▷ **bequeath**
bequeathing v ▷ **bequeath**
bequeaths v ▷ **bequeath**
bequest n (pl -s) legal gift of money or property by someone who has died
bequests v ▷ **bequest**
berate v (-ates, -ating, -ated) scold harshly
berated v ▷ **berate**
berates v ▷ **berate**
berating v ▷ **berate**
bereaved adj having recently lost a close friend or relative through death > **bereavement** n (pl -s)
bereavements n ▷ **bereavement**
bereft adj (foll. by of) deprived
beret [ber-ray] n (pl -s) round flat close-fitting brimless cap
berets n ▷ **beret**
berg[1] n (pl -s) iceberg
berg[2] n (pl -s) (S AFR) mountain
bergamot n (pl -s) small Asian tree, the fruit of

which yields an oil used in perfumery
bergamots n ▷ **bergamot**
bergs n ▷ **berg**[1, 2]
beriberi n (pl -s) disease caused by vitamin B deficiency
beriberis n ▷ **beriberi**
berk n (pl -s) (BRIT, AUST & NZ) (Slang) stupid person
berks n ▷ **berk**
berm n (pl -s) (NZ) narrow grass strip between the road and the footpath in a residential area
berms n ▷ **berm**
berries n ▷ **berry**
berry n (pl -ries) small soft stoneless fruit
berserk adj violent or destructive
berth n (pl -s) bunk in a ship or train ▶ v (-s, -ing, -ed) dock (a ship)
berthed v ▷ **berth**
berthing v ▷ **berth**
berths n, v ▷ **berth**
beryl n (pl -s) hard transparent mineral
beryllium n (pl -s) (CHEM) toxic silvery-white metallic element
berylliums n ▷ **beryllium**
beryls n ▷ **beryl**
beseech v (-seeches, -seeching, -sought or -seeched) ask earnestly; beg
beseeched v ▷ **beseech**
beseeches v ▷ **beseech**
beseeching v ▷ **beseech**
beset v (-sets, -setting, -set) trouble or harass constantly
besets v ▷ **beset**
besetting v ▷ **beset**
beside prep at, by, or to the side of
besides adv, prep in addition
besiege v (-sieges, -sieging, -sieged) surround with military forces
besieged v ▷ **besiege**
besieges v ▷ **besiege**
besieging v ▷ **besiege**
besotted adj infatuated
besought v ▷ **beseech**
bespeak v (-speaks, -speaking, -spoke, -spoken) indicate or suggest
bespeaking v ▷ **bespeak**
bespeaks v ▷ **bespeak**
bespoke v ▷ **bespeak** ▶ adj (esp. of a suit) made to the customer's specifications
bespoken v ▷ **bespeak**
best adj most excellent of a particular group etc. ▶ adv in a manner surpassing all others ▶ n (pl -s) most outstanding or excellent person, thing, or group in a category

bestial *adj* brutal or savage > **bestiality** *n* (*pl* -ities)
bestialities *n* ▷ **bestial**
bestiality *n* ▷ **bestial**
bestir *v* (-stirs, -stirring, -stirred) cause (oneself) to become active
bestirred *v* ▷ **bestir**
bestirring *v* ▷ **bestir**
bestirs *v* ▷ **bestir**
bestow *v* (-s, -ing, -ed) present (a gift) or confer (an honour) > **bestowal** *n* (*pl* -s)
bestowal *n* ▷ **bestow**
bestowals *n* ▷ **bestow**
bestowed *v* ▷ **bestow**
bestowing *v* ▷ **bestow**
bestows *v* ▷ **bestow**
bestridden *v* ▷ **bestride**
bestride *v* (-strides, -striding, -strode, -stridden) have or put a leg on either side of
bestrides *v* ▷ **bestride**
bestriding *v* ▷ **bestride**
bestrode *v* ▷ **bestride**
bests *n* ▷ **best**
bestseller *n* (*pl* -s) book or other product that has sold in great numbers
bestsellers *n* ▷ **bestseller**
bet *n* (*pl* -s) the act of staking a sum of money or other stake on the outcome of an event ▶ *v* (bets, betting, bet *or* betted) make or place (a bet)
betel [bee-tl] *n* (*pl* -s) Asian climbing plant, the leaves and nuts of which can be chewed
betels *n* ▷ **betels**
betide *v* (-tides, -tiding, -tided) happen (to)
betided *v* ▷ **betide**
betides *v* ▷ **betide**
betiding *v* ▷ **betide**
betoken *v* (-s, -ing, -ed) indicate or signify
betokened *v* ▷ **betoken**
betokening *v* ▷ **betoken**
betokens *v* ▷ **betoken**
betray *v* (-s, -ing, -ed) hand over or expose (one's nation, friend, etc.) treacherously to an enemy > **betrayal** *n* (*pl* -s) > **betrayer** *n* (*pl* -s)
betrayal *n* ▷ **betray**
betrayals *n* ▷ **betray**
betrayed *v* ▷ **betray**
betrayer *n* ▷ **betray**
betrayers *n* ▷ **betray**
betraying *v* ▷ **betray**
betrays *v* ▷ **betray**
betrothal *n* ▷ **betrothed**
betrothals *n* ▷ **betrothed**
betrothed *adj* engaged to be married > **betrothal** *n* (*pl* -s)

bets *n*, *v* ▷ **bet**
betted *v* ▷ **bet**
better *adj* more excellent than others ▶ *adv* in a more excellent manner ▶ *pl n* one's superiors ▶ *v* (-s, -ing, -ed) improve upon
bettered *v* ▷ **better**
bettering *v* ▷ **better**
betters *n*, *v* ▷ **better**
betting *v* ▷ **bet**
bettong *n* (*pl* -s) short-nosed rat kangaroo
bettongs *n* ▷ **bettong**
between *prep*, *adv* indicating position in the middle, alternatives, etc.
betwixt *prep*, *adv* (Old-fashioned) between
bevel *n* (*pl* -s) slanting edge ▶ *v* (-els, -elling, -elled) cut a bevel on (a piece of timber etc.)
bevelled *v* ▷ **bevel**
bevelling *v* ▷ **bevel**
bevels *n*, *v* ▷ **bevel**
beverage *n* (*pl* -s) drink
beverages *n* ▷ **beverage**
bevies *n* ▷ **bevy**
bevy *n* (*pl* bevies) flock or group
bewail *v* (-s, -ing, -ed) express great sorrow over
bewailed *v* ▷ **bewail**
bewailing *v* ▷ **bewail**
bewails *v* ▷ **bewail**
beware *v* (-wares, -waring, -wared) be on one's guard (against)
bewared *v* ▷ **beware**
bewares *v* ▷ **beware**
bewaring *v* ▷ **beware**
bewilder *v* (-s, -ing, -ed) confuse utterly > **bewildering** *adj* > **bewilderment** *n* (*pl* -s)
bewildered *v* ▷ **bewilder**
bewildering *v*, *adj* ▷ **bewilder**
bewilderment *n* ▷ **bewilder**
bewilderments *n* ▷ **bewilder**
bewilders *v* ▷ **bewilder**
bewitch *v* (-es, -ing, -ed) attract and fascinate > **bewitching** *adj*
bewitched *v* ▷ **bewitch**
bewitches *v* ▷ **bewitch**
bewitching *v*, *adj* ▷ **bewitch**

bey *n* (beys). A bey was an official in the Ottoman empire, and scores 8 points
beyond *prep* at or to a point on the other side of ▶ *adv* at or to the far side of something
bez *n* (bezes). A bez is the second spike of a deer's antler. This is a really handy word when you have Z on your rack. Bez scores 14 points.
bezique *n* (beziques). Bezique is a card game; if you're lucky enough to be able

▨▨▨ to play it, you'll score 27 points.
bi *adj, n* (*pl* **-s**) short for bisexual
biannual *adj* occurring twice a year
 > **biannually** *adv*
 biannually *adv* ▷ **biannual**
bias *n* (*pl* **-es**) mental tendency, esp. prejudice
 ▶ *v* (**-ases, -asing, -ased** *or* **-asses** *or* **-assing**
 or **-assed**) cause to have a bias > **biased,**
 biassed *adj*
 biased *v* ▷ **bias**
 biases *n, v* ▷ **bias**
 biasing *v* ▷ **bias**
 biassed *v* ▷ **bias**
 biasses *n, v* ▷ **bias**
 biassing *v* ▷ **bias**
bib *n* (*pl* **-s**) piece of cloth or plastic worn to
 protect a young child's clothes when eating
bible *n* (*pl* **-s**) book regarded as authoritative
 > **biblical** *adj*
 bibles *n* ▷ **bible**
 biblical *n* ▷ **bible**
 bibliographer *n* ▷ **bibliography**
 bibliographers *n* ▷ **bibliography**
 bibliographies *n* ▷ **bibliography**
bibliography *n* (*pl* **-phies**) list of books on a
 subject > **bibliographer** *n* (*pl* **-s**)
bibliophile *n* (*pl* **-s**) person who collects or is
 fond of books
 bibliophiles *n* ▷ **bibliophile**
 bibs *n* ▷ **bib**
bibulous *adj* addicted to alcohol
bicarbonate *n* (*pl* **-s**) salt of carbonic acid
 bicarbonates *n* ▷ **bicarbonate**
 bicentenaries *n* ▷ **bicentenary**
bicentenary *n* (*pl* **-naries**) 200th anniversary
biceps *n* (*pl* **-es**) muscle with two origins, esp.
 the muscle that flexes the forearm
bicker *v* (**-s, -ing, -ed**) argue over petty matters
 bickered *v* ▷ **bicker**
 bickering *v* ▷ **bicker**
 bickers *v* ▷ **bicker**
bicycle *n* (*pl* **-s**) vehicle with two wheels, one
 behind the other, pedalled by the rider
 bicycles *n* ▷ **bicycle**
bid *v* (**bids, bidding, bade, bidden**) say (a
 greeting) (*past* **bid**) ▶ *n* (*pl* **-s**) offer of a
 specified amount > **bidder** *n* (*pl* **-s**)
biddable *adj* obedient
 bidden *v* ▷ **bid**
 bidder *n* ▷ **bid**
 bidders *n* ▷ **bid**
bidding *n* (*pl* **-s**) command ▶ *v* ▷ **bid**
bide *v* (**bides, biding, bided**) wait patiently for
 an opportunity
 bided *v* ▷ **bide**

 bides *v* ▷ **bide**
bidet [bee-day] *n* (*pl* **-s**) low basin for washing
 the genital area
 bidets *n* ▷ **bidet**
 biding *v* ▷ **bide**
 bids *v, n* ▷ **bid**
biennial *adj* occurring every two years ▶ *n*
 (*pl* **-s**) plant that completes its life cycle in
 two years
 biennials *n* ▷ **biennial**
bier *n* (*pl* **-s**) stand on which a corpse or coffin
 rests before burial
 biers *n* ▷ **bier**
bifocals *pl n* spectacles with lenses permitting
 near and distant vision
big *adj* (**bigger, biggest**) of considerable size,
 height, number, or capacity ▶ *adv* on a grand
 scale
 bigamies *n* ▷ **bigamy**
 bigamist *n* ▷ **bigamy**
 bigamists *n* ▷ **bigamy**
 bigamous *adj* ▷ **bigamy**
 bigamously *adv* ▷ **bigamy**
bigamy *n* (*pl* **-mies**) crime of marrying a
 person while still legally married to someone
 else > **bigamist** *n* (*pl* **-s**) > **bigamous** *adj*
 > **bigamously** *adv*
 bigger *adj* ▷ **big**
 biggest *adj* ▷ **big**
bighead *n* (*pl* **-s**) (*Informal*) conceited person
 > **bigheaded** *adj*
 bigheaded *n* ▷ **bighead**
 bigheads *n* ▷ **bighead**
bigot *n* (*pl* **-s**) person who is intolerant, esp.
 regarding religion or race > **bigoted** *adj*
 > **bigotry** *n* (*pl* **-tries**)
 bigoted *adj* ▷ **bigot**
 bigotries *n* ▷ **bigot**
 bigotry *n* ▷ **bigot**
 bigots *n* ▷ **bigot**
bigwig *n* (*pl* **-s**) (*Informal*) important person
 bigwigs *n* ▷ **bigwig**

▨▨ **bijou** *n* (**bijoux**). A bijou is an intricate
 trinket. The plural form, bijoux, uses an
 X and allows you to score 22 points.

bike *n* (*pl* **-s**) (*Informal*) bicycle or motorcycle
 bikes *n* ▷ **bike**
bikini *n* (*pl* **-s**) woman's brief two-piece
 swimming costume
 bikinis *n* ▷ **bikini**
bilateral *adj* affecting or undertaken by two
 parties > **bilaterally** *adv*
 bilaterally *adv* ▷ **bilateral**
 bilberries *n* ▷ **bilberry**
bilberry *n* (*pl* **-berries**) bluish-black edible berry

bilbies *n* ▷ **bilby**

bilby *n* (*pl* -**bies**) Australian marsupial with long pointed ears and grey fur

bile *n* (*pl* -**s**) bitter yellow fluid secreted by the liver

biles *n* ▷ **bile**

bilge *n* (*pl* -**s**) (*Informal*) nonsense

bilges *n* ▷ **bilge**

bilingual *adj* involving or using two languages

bilious *adj* sick, nauseous > **biliousness** *n*

biliousness *n* ▷ **bilious**

bill[1] *n* (*pl* -**s**) statement of money owed for goods or services supplied ▶ *v* (-**s**, -**ing**, -**ed**) send or present a bill to

bill[2] *n* (*pl* -**s**) bird's beak

billabong *n* (*pl* -**s**) (AUST) stagnant pool in an intermittent stream

billabongs *n* ▷ **billabong**

billed *v* ▷ **bill**[1]

billet *v* (-**lets**, -**leting**, -**leted**) assign a lodging to (a soldier) ▶ *n* (*pl* -**s**) accommodation for a soldier in civil lodgings

billeted *v* ▷ **billet**

billeting *v* ▷ **billet**

billets *v*, *n* ▷ **billet**

billhook *n* (*pl* -**s**) tool with a hooked blade, used for chopping etc.

billhooks *n* ▷ **billhook**

billiards *n* game played on a table with balls and a cue

billies *n* ▷ **billy**

billing *v* ▷ **bill**[1]

billion *n* (*pl* -**s**) one thousand million > **billionth** *adj*

billions *n* ▷ **billion**

billionth *adj* ▷ **billion**

billow *n* (*pl* -**s**) large sea wave ▶ *v* (-**s**, -**ing**, -**ed**) rise up or swell out > **billowy, billowing** *adj*

billowed *v* ▷ **billow**

billowing *v*, *adj* ▷ **billow**

billows *n*, *v* ▷ **billow**

billowy *adj* ▷ **billow**

bills *n* ▷ **bill**[1, 2] ▶ *v* ▷ **bill**[1]

billy, billycan *n* (*pl* -**lies**, -**s**) metal can or pot for cooking on a camp fire

billycan *n* ▷ **billy**

billycans *n* ▷ **billy**

biltong *n* (*pl* -**s**) (S AFR) strips of dried meat

biltongs *n* ▷ **biltong**

bimbo *n* (*pl* -**s**) (*Slang*) attractive but empty-headed young person, esp. a woman

bimbos *n* ▷ **bimbo**

bin *n* (*pl* -**s**) container for rubbish or for storing grain, coal, etc.

binary *adj* composed of two parts (MATHS)

(COMPUTERS)

bind *v* (**binds, binding, bound**) make secure with or as if with a rope ▶ *n* (*pl* -**s**) (*Informal*) annoying situation

binder *n* (*pl* -**s**) firm cover for holding loose sheets of paper together

binders *n* ▷ **binder**

binding *n* (*pl* -**s**) anything that binds or fastens ▶ *n* ▷ **bind**

bindings *n* ▷ **binding**

bindweed *n* (*pl* -**s**) plant that twines around a support

bindweeds *n* ▷ **bindweed**

binge *n* (*pl* -**s**) (*Informal*) bout of excessive indulgence, esp. in drink

binges *n* ▷ **binge**

bingo *n* (*pl* -**s**) gambling game in which numbers are called out and covered by the players on their individual cards

bingos *n* ▷ **bingo**

binoculars *pl n* optical instrument consisting of two small telescopes joined together

binomial *n* (*pl* -**s**), *adj* (mathematical expression) consisting of two terms

binomials *n* ▷ **binomial**

bins *n* ▷ **bin**

biochemistries *n* ▷ **biochemistry**

biochemistry *n* (*pl* -**ries**) study of the chemistry of living things > **biochemist** *n* (*pl* -**s**)

biochemists *n* ▷ **biochemistry**

biodegradable *adj* capable of being decomposed by natural means

biodiversities *n* ▷ **biodiversity**

biodiversity *n* (*pl* -**ities**) existence of a wide variety of species in their natural environment

biographer *n* (*pl* -**s**) person who writes an account of another person's life

biographers *n* ▷ **biographer**

biographical *n* ▷ **biography**

biographies *n* ▷ **biography**

biography *n* (*pl* -**phies**) account of a person's life by another person > **biographical** *adj*

biological *adj* of or relating to biology > **biologically** *adv*

biologically *adv* ▷ **biological**

biologies *n* ▷ **biology**

biologist *n* ▷ **biology**

biologists *n* ▷ **biology**

biology *n* (*pl* -**ogies**) study of living organisms > **biologist** *n* (*pl* -**s**)

biometric *adj* of any automated system using physiological or behavioural traits as a means of identification.

bionic *adj* having a part of the body that is operated electronically
biopsies *n* ▷ **biopsy**
biopsy *n* (*pl* -**sies**) examination of tissue from a living body
biotechnologies *n* ▷ **biotechnology**
biotechnology *n* (*pl* -**ologies**) use of microorganisms, such as cells or bacteria, in industry and technology
bioterrorism *n* (*pl* -**s**) use of viruses, bacteria, etc., by terrorists > **bioterrorist** *n* (*pl* -**s**)
bioterrorisms *n* ▷ **bioterrorism**
bioterrorists *n* ▷ **bioterrorism**
biped [**bye**-ped] *n* (*pl* -**s**) animal with two feet
bipeds *n* ▷ **biped**
biplane *n* (*pl* -**s**) aeroplane with two sets of wings, one above the other
biplanes *n* ▷ **biplane**
birch *n* (*pl* -**es**) tree with thin peeling bark
birches *n* ▷ **birch**
bird *n* (*pl* -**s**) creature with feathers and wings, most types of which can fly
birdie *n* (*pl* -**s**) (GOLF) score of one stroke under par for a hole
birdies *n* ▷ **birdie**
birds *n* ▷ **bird**
biretta *n* (*pl* -**s**) stiff square cap worn by the Catholic clergy
birettas *n* ▷ **biretta**
birth *n* (*pl* -**s**) process of bearing young; childbirth
birthday *n* (*pl* -**s**) anniversary of the day of one's birth
birthdays *n* ▷ **birthday**
birthmark *n* (*pl* -**s**) blemish on the skin formed before birth
birthmarks *n* ▷ **birthmark**
birthright *n* (*pl* -**s**) privileges or possessions that someone is entitled to as soon as he or she is born
birthrights *n* ▷ **birthright**
births *n* ▷ **birth**
bis *n* ▷ **bi**
biscuit *n* (*pl* -**s**) small flat dry sweet or plain cake
biscuits *n* ▷ **biscuit**
bisect *v* (-**s**, -**ing**, -**ed**) divide into two equal parts
bisected *v* ▷ **bisect**
bisecting *v* ▷ **bisect**
bisects *v* ▷ **bisect**
bisexual *adj* sexually attracted to both men and women > **bisexuality** *n* (*pl* -**ties**)
bisexualities *n* ▷ **bisexual**
bisexuality *n* ▷ **bisexual**

bishop *n* (*pl* -**s**) clergyman who governs a diocese
bishopric *n* (*pl* -**s**) diocese or office of a bishop
bishoprics *n* ▷ **bishopric**
bishops *n* ▷ **bishop**
bismuth *n* (*pl* -**s**) (CHEM) pinkish-white metallic element
bismuths *n* ▷ **bismuth**
bison *n* (*pl* -**bison**) large hairy animal of the cattle family, native to N America and Europe
bistro *n* (*pl* -**s**) small restaurant
bistros *n* ▷ **bistro**
bit[1] *n* (*pl* -**s**) small piece, portion, or quantity
bit[2] *n* (*pl* -**s**) metal mouthpiece on a bridle
bit[3] *v* ▷ **bite**
bit[3] *n* (*pl* -**s**) (MATHS) (COMPUTERS) single digit of binary notation, either 0 or 1
bitch *n* (*pl* -**es**) female dog, fox, or wolf ▶ *v* (-**es**, -**ing**, -**ed**) (*Informal*) complain or grumble > **bitchy** *adj* (-**ier**, -**iest**) > **bitchiness** *n*
bitched *v* ▷ **bitch**
bitches *n*, *v* ▷ **bitch**
bitchier *adj* ▷ **bitch**
bitchiest *adj* ▷ **bitch**
bitching *v* ▷ **bitch**
bitchy *adj* ▷ **bitch**
bite *v* (**bites**, **biting**, **bit**, **bitten**) grip, tear, or puncture the skin, as with the teeth or jaws ▶ *n* (*pl* -**s**) act of biting > **biter** *n* (*pl* -**s**)
biter *n* ▷ **bite**
biters *n* ▷ **bite**
bites *v*, *n* ▷ **bite**
biting *adj* piercing or keen ▶ *v* ▷ **bite**
bits *n* ▷ **bit**[1, 2, 4]
bitten *v* ▷ **bite**
bitter *adj* (-**er**, -**est**) having a sharp unpleasant taste ▶ *n* (*pl* -**s**) beer with a slightly bitter taste ▶ *pl* bitter-tasting alcoholic drink > **bitterly** *adv* > **bitterness** *n* (*pl* -**es**)
bitterer *adj* ▷ **bitter**
bitterest *adj* ▷ **bitter**
bitterly *adv* ▷ **bitter**
bittern *n* (*pl* -**s**) wading marsh bird with a booming call
bitterness *n* ▷ **bitter**
bitternesses *n* ▷ **bitter**
bitterns *n* ▷ **bittern**
bitters *n* ▷ **bitter**
bitumen *n* (*pl* -**s**) black sticky substance obtained from tar or petrol
bitumens *n* ▷ **bitumen**
bivalve *n* (*pl* -**s**) ▶ *adj* (marine mollusc) with two hinged segments to its shell
bivalves *n* ▷ **bivalve**
bivouac *n* (*pl* -**s**) temporary camp in the

open air ▶ *v* (**-acs, -acking, -acked**) camp in a bivouac

bivouacked *v* ▷ bivouac

bivouacking *v* ▷ bivouac

bivouacs *n*, *v* ▷ bivouac

bizarre *adj* odd or unusual > **bizarrely** *adv* > **bizarreness** *n*

bizarrely *adv* ▷ bizarre

bizarreness *n* ▷ bizarre

blab *v* (**blabs, blabbing, blabbed**) reveal (secrets) indiscreetly

blabbed *v* ▷ blab

blabbing *v* ▷ blab

blabs *v* ▷ blab

black *adj* (**-er, -est**) of the darkest colour, like coal ▶ *n* (*pl* **-s**) darkest colour ▶ *v* (**-s, -ing, -ed**) make black > **blackness** *n*

blackball *v* (**-balls, -balling, -balled**) exclude from a group ▶ *n* (*pl* **-balls**) (NZ) hard boiled sweet with black-and-white stripes

blackballed *v* ▷ blackball

blackballing *v* ▷ blackball

blackballs *v*, *n* ▷ blackball

blackberries *n* ▷ blackberry

blackberry *n* (*pl* **-rries**) small blackish edible fruit

blackbird *n* (*pl* **-s**) common European thrush

blackbirds *n* ▷ blackbird

blackboard *n* (*pl* **-s**) hard black surface used for writing on with chalk

blackboards *n* ▷ blackboard

blackboy *n* (*pl* **-s**) Australian plant with grasslike leaves and a spike of small white flowers

blackboys *n* ▷ blackboy

blackbutt *n* (*pl* **-s**) Australian eucalyptus tree with hard wood used as timber

blackbutts *n* ▷ blackbutt

blackcurrant *n* (*pl* **-s**) very small blackish edible fruit that grows in bunches

blackcurrants *n* ▷ blackcurrant

blacked *v* ▷ black

blacken *v* (**-s, -ing, -ed**) make or become black

blackened *v* ▷ blacken

blackening *v* ▷ blacken

blackens *v* ▷ blacken

blacker *adj* ▷ black

blackest *adj* ▷ black

blackfish *n* (*pl* **blackfish**) small dark Australian estuary fish

blackguard [**blag**-gard] *n* (*pl* **-s**) unprincipled person

blackguards *n* ▷ blackguard

blackhead *n* (*pl* **-s**) black-tipped plug of fatty matter clogging a skin pore

blackheads *n* ▷ blackhead

blacking *v* ▷ black

blackleg *n* (*pl* **-s**) person who continues to work during a strike

blacklegs *n* ▷ blackleg

blacklist *n* (*pl* **-s**) list of people or organizations considered untrustworthy etc.

blacklists *n* ▷ blacklist

blackmail *n* (*pl* **-s**) act of attempting to extort money by threats ▶ *v* (**-s, -ing, -ed**) (attempt to) obtain money by blackmail

blackmailed *v* ▷ blackmail

blackmailing *v* ▷ blackmail

blackmails *n*, *v* ▷ blackmail

blackness *n* ▷ black

blackout *n* (*pl* **-s**) extinguishing of all light as a precaution against an air attack

blackouts *n* ▷ blackout

blacks *n*, *v* ▷ black

blacksmith *n* (*pl* **-s**) person who works iron with a furnace, anvil, etc.

blacksmiths *n* ▷ blacksmith

bladder *n* (*pl* **-s**) sac in the body where urine is held

bladders *n* ▷ bladder

blade *n* (*pl* **-s**) cutting edge of a weapon or tool

blades *n* ▷ blade

blame *v* (**-mes, -ming, -med**) consider (someone) responsible for ▶ *n* (*pl* **-s**) responsibility for something that is wrong > **blameless** *adj*

blamed *v* ▷ blame

blameless *adj* ▷ blame

blames *v*, *n* ▷ blame

blameworthy *adj* deserving blame

blaming *v* ▷ blame

blanch *v* (**-es, -ing, -ed**) become white or pale

blanched *v* ▷ blanch

blanches *v* ▷ blanch

blanching *v* ▷ blanch

blancmange [blam-**monzh**] *n* (*pl* **-s**) jelly-like dessert made with milk

blancmanges *n* ▷ blancmange

bland *adj* (**-er, -est**) dull and uninteresting > **blandly** *adv*

blander *adj* ▷ bland

blandest *adj* ▷ bland

blandishments *pl* *n* flattery intended to coax or persuade

blandly *adj* ▷ bland

blank *adj* not written on ▶ *n* (*pl* **-s**) empty space > **blankly** *adv*

blanket *n* (*pl* **-s**) large thick cloth used as covering for a bed ▶ *v* (**-s, -ing, -ed**) cover as with a blanket

blanketed v ▷ blanket
blanketing v ▷ blanket
blankets n, v ▷ blanket
blankly adv ▷ blank
blanks n ▷ blank
blare v (**blares, blaring, blared**) sound loudly and harshly ▶ n (pl **-s**) loud harsh noise
blared v ▷ blare
blares v, n ▷ blare
blaring v ▷ blare
blarney n (pl **-s**) flattering talk
blarneys n ▷ blarney
blasé [blah-zay] adj indifferent or bored through familiarity
blaspheme v (**-phemes, -pheming, -phemed**) speak disrespectfully of (God or sacred things) > **blasphemy** n (pl **-phemies**) > **blasphemous** adj > **blasphemously** adv > **blasphemer** n (pl **-s**)
blasphemed v ▷ blaspheme
blasphemer n ▷ blaspheme
blasphemers n ▷ blaspheme
blasphemes v ▷ blaspheme
blasphemies n ▷ blaspheme
blaspheming v ▷ blaspheme
blasphemous v ▷ blaspheme
blasphemously v ▷ blaspheme
blast n (pl **-s**) explosion ▶ v (**-s, -ing, -ed**) blow up (a rock etc.) with explosives
blasted v ▷ blast
blasting v ▷ blast
blastoff n (pl **-s**) launching of a rocket
blastoffs n ▷ blastoff
blasts n, v ▷ blast
blatant adj glaringly obvious > **blatantly** adv
blatantly adv ▷ blatant
blaze¹ n (pl **-s**) strong fire or flame ▶ v (**-s, -ing, -d**) burn or shine brightly
blaze² n (pl **-s**) mark made on a tree to indicate a route
blazed v ▷ blaze¹
blazer n (pl **-s**) lightweight jacket, often in the colours of a school etc.
blazers n ▷ blazer
blazes n ▷ blaze¹, ² ▶ v ▷ blaze¹
blazing v ▷ blaze¹
blazon v (**-s, -ing, -ed**) proclaim publicly
blazoned v ▷ blazon
blazoning v ▷ blazon
blazons v ▷ blazon
bleach v (**-es, -ing, -ed**) make or become white or colourless ▶ n (pl **-es**) bleaching agent
bleached v ▷ bleach
bleaches v, n ▷ bleach
bleaching v ▷ bleach

bleak adj (**-er, -est**) exposed and barren > **bleakly** adv > **bleakness** n (pl **-es**)
bleaker adj ▷ bleak
bleakest adj ▷ bleak
bleakly adv ▷ bleak
bleakness n ▷ bleak
bleaknesses n ▷ bleak
blearier adj ▷ bleary
bleariest adj ▷ bleary
blearily adv ▷ bleary
bleariness n ▷ bleary
blearinesses n ▷ bleary
bleary adj (**-rier, -riest**) with eyes dimmed, as by tears or tiredness > **blearily** adv > **bleariness** n (pl **-es**)
bleat v (**-s, -ing, -ed**) (of a sheep, goat, or calf) utter its plaintive cry ▶ n (pl **-s**) cry of sheep, goats, and calves
bleated v ▷ bleat
bleating v ▷ bleat
bleats v, n ▷ bleat
bled v ▷ bleed
bleed v (**-s, -ing, bled**) lose or emit blood
bleeding v ▷ bleed
bleeds v ▷ bleed
bleep n (pl **-s**) short high-pitched sound made by an electrical device ▶ v (**-s, -ing, -ed**) make a bleeping sound
bleeped v ▷ bleep
bleeper n (pl **-s**) small portable radio receiver that makes a bleeping signal
bleepers n ▷ bleeper
bleeping v ▷ bleep
bleeps n, v ▷ bleep
blemish n (pl **-es**) defect or stain ▶ v (**-es, -ing, -ed**) spoil or tarnish
blemished v ▷ blemish
blemishes n, v ▷ blemish
blemishing v ▷ blemish
blench v (**-es, -ing, -ed**) shy away, as in fear
blenched v ▷ blench
blenches v ▷ blench
blenching v ▷ blench
blend v (**-s, -ing, -ed**) mix or mingle (components or ingredients) ▶ n (pl **-s**) mixture
blended v ▷ blend
blender n (pl **-s**) electrical appliance for puréeing vegetables etc.
blenders n ▷ blender
blending v ▷ blend
blends v, n ▷ blend
bless v (**-es, -ing, -ed**) make holy by means of a religious rite
blessed adj holy ▶ v ▷ blessed > **blessedness** n

blessedness *n* ▷ **blessed**
blesses *v* ▷ **bless**
blessing *n* (*pl* -**s**) invoking of divine aid ▶ *v*
▷ **bless**
blessings *n* ▷ **blessing**
blether (Scot) *v* (-**s**, -**ing**, -**ed**) talk, esp. foolishly
or at length ▶ *n* (*pl* -**s**) conversation
blethered *v* ▷ **blether**
blethering *v* ▷ **blether**
blethers *v*, *n* ▷ **blether**
blew *v* ▷ **blow**¹
blight *n* (*pl* -**s**) person or thing that spoils or
prevents growth ▶ *v* (-**s**, -**ing**, -**ed**) frustrate or
disappoint
blighted *v* ▷ **blight**
blighter *n* (*pl* -**s**) (*Informal*) irritating person
blighters *n* ▷ **blighter**
blighting *v* ▷ **blight**
blights *n*, *v* ▷ **blight**
blimp *n* (*pl* -**s**) small airship
blimps *n* ▷ **blimp**
blind *adj* (-**er**, -**est**) unable to see ▶ *v* (-**s**, -**ing**,
-**ed**) deprive of sight ▶ *n* (*pl* -**s**) covering for a
window > **blindly** *adv* > **blindness** *n* (*pl* -**es**)
blinded *v* ▷ **blind**
blinder *adj* ▷ **blind**
blindest *adj* ▷ **blind**
blindfold *v* (-**s**, -**ing**, -**ed**) prevent (a person)
from seeing by covering the eyes ▶ *n* (*pl* -**s**)
piece of cloth used to cover the eyes
blindfolded *v* ▷ **blindfold**
blindfolding *v* ▷ **blindfold**
blindfolds *v*, *n* ▷ **blindfold**
blinding *adj*, *v* ▷ **blind**
blindly *adv* ▷ **blind**
blindness *n* ▷ **blind**
blindnesses *n* ▷ **blind**
blinds *v*, *n* ▷ **blind**
blink *v* (-**s**, -**ing**, -**ed**) close and immediately
reopen (the eyes) ▶ *n* (*pl* -**s**) act of blinking
blinked *v* ▷ **blink**
blinkers *pl n* leather flaps on a horse's bridle to
prevent sideways vision
blinking *v* ▷ **blink**
blinks *v*, *n* ▷ **blink**
blip *n* (*pl* -**s**) spot of light on a radar screen
indicating the position of an object
blips *n* ▷ **blip**
bliss *n* (*pl* -**es**) perfect happiness > **blissful** *adj*
> **blissfully** *adv*
blisses *n* ▷ **bliss**
blissful *adj* ▷ **bliss**
blissfully *adv* ▷ **bliss**
blister *n* (*pl* -**s**) small bubble on the skin ▶ *v* (-**s**,
-**ing**, -**ed**) (cause to) have blisters

blistered *v* ▷ **blister**
blistering *adj* (of weather) very hot ▶ *v* ▷ **blister**
> **blisteringly** *adv*
blisteringly *adv* ▷ **blistering**
blisters *n*, *v* ▷ **blister**
blithe *adj* (-**r**, -**st**) casual and indifferent
> **blithely** *adv* > **blitheness** *n* (*pl* -**es**)
blithely *adv* ▷ **blithe**
blitheness *n* ▷ **blithe**
blithenesses *n* ▷ **blithe**
blither *adj* ▷ **blithe**
blithest *adj* ▷ **blithe**
blitz *n* (*pl* -**es**) violent and sustained attack by
aircraft ▶ *v* (-**es**, -**ing**, -**ed**) attack suddenly and
intensively
blitzed *v* ▷ **blitz**
blitzes *n*, *v* ▷ **blitz**
blitzing *v* ▷ **blitz**
blizzard *n* (*pl* -**s**) blinding storm of wind and
snow
blizzards *n* ▷ **blizzard**
bloat *v* (-**s**, -**ing**, -**ed**) cause to swell, as with
liquid or air
bloated *v* ▷ **bloat**
bloater *n* (*pl* -**s**) (BRIT) salted smoked herring
bloaters *n* ▷ **bloater**
bloating *v* ▷ **bloat**
bloats *v* ▷ **bloat**
blob *n* (*pl* -**s**) soft mass or drop
blobs *n* ▷ **blob**
bloc *n* (*pl* -**s**) people or countries combined by a
common interest
block *n* (*pl* -**s**) large solid piece of wood, stone,
etc. ▶ *v* (-**s**, -**ing**, -**ed**) obstruct or impede by
introducing an obstacle > **blockage** *n* (*pl* -**s**)
blockade *n* (*pl* -**s**) sealing off of a place to
prevent the passage of goods ▶ *v* (-**ades**,
-**ading**, -**aded**) impose a blockade on
blockaded *n* ▷ **blockade**
blockades *n*, *v* ▷ **blockade**
blockading *v* ▷ **blockade**
blockage *n* ▷ **block**
blockages *n* ▷ **block**
blocked *v* ▷ **block**
blockhead *n* (*pl* -**s**) stupid person
blockheads *n* ▷ **blockhead**
blockie *n* (*pl* -**s**) (AUST) owner of a small
property, esp. a farm
blockies *n* ▷ **blockie**
blocking *v* ▷ **block**
blocks *n*, *v* ▷ **block**
blocs *n* ▷ **bloc**
blog *n* (*pl* -**s**) ▷ **weblog**
blogs *n* ▷ **blog**
bloke *n* (*pl* -**s**) (*Informal*) man

blokes *n* ▷ bloke
blonde, *masc* **blond** *adj*, *n* (*pl* **-es, -s**) fair-haired (person)
  blondes *n* ▷ blonde
  blonds *n* ▷ blonde
blood *n* (*pl* **-s**) red fluid that flows around the body > **bloodless** *adj* > **bloodlessness** *n*
bloodhound *n* (*pl* **-s**) large dog formerly used for tracking
  bloodhounds *n* ▷ bloodhound
  bloodied *v* ▷ bloody
  bloodies *v* ▷ bloody
  bloodily *adv* ▷ bloody
  bloodiness *n* ▷ bloody
  bloodless *adj* ▷ blood
  bloodlessness *n* ▷ blood
  bloods *n* ▷ blood
bloodshed *n* (*pl* **-s**) slaughter or killing
  bloodsheds *n* ▷ bloodshed
bloodshot *adj* (of an eye) inflamed
bloodstream *n* (*pl* **-s**) flow of blood round the body
  bloodstreams *n* ▷ bloodstream
bloodsucker *n* (*pl* **-s**) animal that sucks blood
  bloodsuckers *n* ▷ bloodsucker
  bloodthirstily *adv* ▷ bloodthirsty
  bloodthirstiness *n* ▷ bloodthirsty
bloodthirsty *adj* taking pleasure in violence > **bloodthirstily** *adv* > **bloodthirstiness** *n*
bloody *adj* covered with blood ▶ *adj*, *adv* (*Slang*) extreme or extremely ▶ *v* (**-dies, -dying, -died**) stain with blood > **bloodily** *adv* > **bloodiness** *n*
  bloodying *v* ▷ bloody
bloom *n* (*pl* **-s**) blossom on a flowering plant ▶ *v* (**-s, -ing, -ed**) bear flowers
  bloomed *v* ▷ bloom
bloomer *n* (*pl* **-s**) (BRIT) (*Informal*) stupid mistake
bloomers *n* ▷ bloomer ▶ *pl n* woman's baggy knickers
  blooming *v* ▷ bloom
  blooms *n*, *v* ▷ bloom
blooper *n* (*pl* **-s**) (CHIEFLY US) (*Informal*) stupid mistake
  bloopers *n* ▷ blooper
blossom *n* (*pl* **-s**) flowers of a plant ▶ *v* (**-s, -ing, -ed**) (of plants) flower
  blossomed *v* ▷ blossom
  blossoming *v* ▷ blossom
  blossoms *n*, *v* ▷ blossom
blot *n* (*pl* **-s**) spot or stain ▶ *v* (**-s, -tting, -tted**) cause a blemish in or on > **blotter** *n* (*pl* **-s**)
blotch *n* (*pl* **-es**) discoloured area or stain > **blotchy** *adj*
  blotches *n* ▷ blotch
  blotchy *adj* ▷ blotch

blots *n*, *v* ▷ blot
blotted *v* ▷ blot
blotter *n* ▷ blot
blotters *n* ▷ blot
blotting *v* ▷ blot
blotto *adj* (BRIT, AUST & NZ) (*Slang*) extremely drunk
blouse *n* (*pl* **-s**) woman's shirtlike garment
  blouses *n* ▷ blouse
blow[1] *v* (**-s, -ing, blew, blown**) (of air, the wind, etc.) move > **blower** *n* (*pl* **-s**)
blow[2] *n* (*pl* **-s**) hard hit
  blower *n* ▷ blow[1]
  blowers *n* ▷ blow[1]
blowie *n* (*pl* **blowies**) (AUST) (*Informal*) bluebottle
  blowier *n* ▷ blowy
  blowies *n* ▷ blowie
  blowiest *n* ▷ blowy
  blowing *v* ▷ blow[1]
  blown *v* ▷ blow[1]
blowout *n* (*pl* **-s**) sudden loss of air in a tyre
  blowouts *n* ▷ blowout
  blows *v* ▷ blow[1] ▶ *n* ▷ blow[2]
  blowsier *n* ▷ blowsy
  blowsiest *n* ▷ blowsy
blowsy *adj* (**-sier, -siest**) fat, untidy, and red-faced
blowy *adj* (**-wier, -wiest**) windy
blubber *n* (*pl* **-s**) fat of whales, seals, etc. ▶ *v* (**-s, -ing, -ed**) sob without restraint
  blubbered *v* ▷ blubber
  blubbering *v* ▷ blubber
  blubbers *n*, *v* ▷ blubber
bludge (*Informal*) *v* (**-s, -ging, -d**) (AUST & NZ) evade work (AUST & NZ) ▶ *n* (*pl* **-s**) (AUST) easy task
  bludged *v* ▷ bludge
bludgeon *n* (*pl* **-s**) short thick club ▶ *v* (**-s, -ing, -ed**) hit with a bludgeon
  bludgeoned *v* ▷ bludgeon
  bludgeoning *v* ▷ bludgeon
  bludgeons *n*, *v* ▷ bludgeon
bludger *n* (*pl* **-s**) person who scrounges
  bludgers *n* ▷ bludger
  bludges *v*, *n* ▷ bludge
  bludging *v* ▷ bludge
blue *n* (*pl* **-s**) colour of a clear unclouded sky ▶ *pl* feeling of depression ▶ *adj* (**bluer, bluest**) of the colour blue > **bluish** *adj*
bluebell *n* (*pl* **-s**) flower with blue bell-shaped flowers
  bluebells *n* ▷ bluebell
bluebottle *n* (*pl* **-s**) large fly with a dark-blue body
  bluebottles *n* ▷ bluebottle

blueprint n (pl -s) photographic print of a plan
blueprints n ▷ **blueprint**
bluer adj ▷ **blue**
blues n ▷ **blue**
bluest adj ▷ **blue**
bluetongue n (pl -s) Australian lizard with a blue tongue
bluetongues n ▷ **bluetongue**
bluff¹ v (-s, -ing, -ed) pretend to be confident in order to influence (someone) ▶ n (pl -s) act of bluffing
bluff² n (pl -s) steep cliff or bank ▶ adj good-naturedly frank and hearty
bluffed v ▷ **bluff¹**
bluffing v ▷ **bluff¹**
bluffs v, n ▷ **bluff¹, ²**
bluish adj ▷ **blue**
blunder n (pl -s) clumsy mistake ▶ v (-s, -ing, -ed) make a blunder
blunderbuss n (pl -es) obsolete gun with a wide flared muzzle
blunderbusses n ▷ **blunderbuss**
blundered v ▷ **blunder**
blundering v ▷ **blunder**
blunders n, v ▷ **blunder**
blunt adj (blunter, bluntest) not having a sharp edge or point ▶ v (-s, -ing, -ed) make less sharp > **bluntly** adv > **bluntness** n
blunted v ▷ **blunt**
blunter adj ▷ **blunt**
bluntest adj ▷ **blunt**
blunting v ▷ **blunt**
bluntly adv ▷ **blunt**
bluntness n ▷ **blunt**
blunts v ▷ **blunt**
blur v (-s, -rring, -rred) make or become vague or less distinct ▶ n (pl -s) something vague, hazy, or indistinct > **blurry** adj (-rier, -rriest)
blurb n (pl -s) promotional description, as on the jacket of a book
blurbs n ▷ **blurb**
blurred v ▷ **blur**
blurrier adj ▷ **blur**
blurriest adj ▷ **blur**
blurring v ▷ **blur**
blurry adj ▷ **blur**
blurs v, n ▷ **blur**
blurt v (-s, -ing, -ed) (foll. by out) utter suddenly and involuntarily
blurted v ▷ **blurt**
blurting v ▷ **blurt**
blurts v ▷ **blurt**
blush v (-es, -ing, -ed) become red in the face, esp. from embarrassment or shame ▶ n (pl -es) reddening of the face

blushed v ▷ **blush**
blushes v, n ▷ **blush**
blushing v ▷ **blush**
bluster v (-s, -ing, -ed) speak loudly or in a bullying way ▶ n (pl -s) empty threats or protests
blustered v ▷ **bluster**
blusteriness n ▷ **blustery**
blustering v ▷ **bluster**
blusters v, n ▷ **bluster**
blustery adj (of weather) rough and windy > **blusteriness** n

bo or **boh** interjection. Bo is an exclamation used to startle someone. Bo scores 4 points, while boh scores 8.

boa n (pl -s) large nonvenomous snake
boab [boh-ab] n (pl -s) (AUST) (Informal) ▷ **baobab**
boabs n ▷ **boab**
boar n (pl -s) uncastrated male pig
board n (pl -s) long flat piece of sawn timber ▶ v (-s, -ing, -ed) go aboard (a train, aeroplane, etc.)
boarded v ▷ **board**
boarder n (pl -s) person who pays rent in return for accommodation in someone else's home
boarders n ▷ **boarder**
boarding v ▷ **board**
boardroom n (pl -s) room where the board of a company meets
boardrooms n ▷ **boardroom**
boards n, v ▷ **board**
boars n ▷ **boar**
boas n ▷ **boa**
boast v (-s, -ing, -ed) speak too proudly about one's talents etc. ▶ n (pl -s) bragging statement > **boastful** adj > **boastfully** adv > **boastfulness** n
boasted v ▷ **boast**
boastful adj ▷ **boast**
boastfully adv ▷ **boast**
boastfulness n ▷ **boast**
boasting v ▷ **boast**
boasts v, n ▷ **boast**
boat n (pl -s) small vehicle for travelling across water > **boating** n
boater n (pl -s) flat straw hat
boaters n ▷ **boater**
boating n ▷ **boat**
boats n ▷ **boat**
boatswain n (pl -s) ▷ **bosun**
boatswains n ▷ **boatswain**
bob¹ v (bobs, bobbing, bobbed) move up and down repeatedly ▶ n (pl -s) short abrupt movement
bob² n (pl -s) hairstyle in which the hair is cut

short evenly all round the head ▶ v (**bobs, bobbing, bobbed**) cut (the hair) in a bob
bobbed v ▷ **bob**[1, 2]
bobbies n ▷ **bobby**
bobbin n (pl -s) reel on which thread is wound
bobbing v ▷ **bob**[1, 2]
bobbins n ▷ **bobbin**
bobble n (pl -s) small ball of material, usu. for decoration
bobbles n ▷ **bobble**
bobby n (pl -**bies**) (BRIT) (Informal) policeman
bobotie [ba-**boot**-ee] n (pl -s) (S AFR) dish of curried mince
boboties n ▷ **bobotie**
bobs v ▷ **bob**[1, 2] ▶ n[1, 2]
bobsleigh n (pl -s) sledge for racing down an icy track ▶ v (-**s, -ing, -ed**) ride on a bobsleigh
bobsleighed v ▷ **bobsleigh**
bobsleighing v ▷ **bobsleigh**
bobsleighs n, v ▷ **bobsleigh**
bode v (-**s, -ding, -ed**) be an omen of (good or ill)
boded v ▷ **bode**
bodes v ▷ **bode**
bodice n (pl -s) upper part of a dress
bodices n ▷ **bodice**
bodies n ▷ **body**
bodily adj relating to the body ▶ adv by taking hold of the body
boding v ▷ **bode**
bodkin n (pl -s) blunt large-eyed needle
bodkins n ▷ **bodkin**
body n (pl -**dies**) entire physical structure of an animal or human
bodyboard n (pl -s) small polystyrene surfboard
bodyboards n ▷ **bodyboard**
bodyguard n (pl -s) person or group of people employed to protect someone
bodyguards n ▷ **bodyguard**
bodywork n (pl -s) outer shell of a motor vehicle
bodyworks n ▷ **bodywork**
boerewors n (S AFR) spiced sausage
boffin n (pl -s) (BRIT, AUST, NZ & S AFR) (Informal) scientist or expert
boffins n ▷ **boffin**
bog n (pl -s) wet spongy ground > **boggy** adj (**boggier, boggiest**)
bogan n (pl -s) (AUST DATED & NZ) (Slang) youth who dresses and behaves rebelliously
bogans n ▷ **bogan**
bogey, bogy n (pl **bogeys, bogies**) something that worries or annoys
bogeys n ▷ **bogey**

boggier adj ▷ **bog**
boggiest adj ▷ **bog**
boggle v (**boggles, boggling, boggled**) be surprised, confused, or alarmed
boggled v ▷ **boggle**
boggles v ▷ **boggle**
boggling v ▷ **boggle**
boggy adj ▷ **bog**
bogies n ▷ **bogey**
bogong, bugong n (pl -s, -s) large nocturnal Australian moth
bogongs n ▷ **bogong**
bogs n ▷ **bog**
bogus adj not genuine
bogy n (pl -**gies**) ▷ **bogey**
bohemian n (pl -s) ▶ adj (person) leading an unconventional life
bohemians n ▷ **bohemian**
boil[1] v (-**s, -ing, -ed**) (cause to) change from a liquid to a vapour so quickly that bubbles are formed ▶ n (pl -s) state or action of boiling
boil[2] n (pl -s) red pus-filled swelling on the skin
boiled v ▷ **boil**[1]
boiler n (pl -s) piece of equipment which provides hot water
boilers n ▷ **boiler**
boiling v ▷ **boil**[1]
boils v, n ▷ **boil**[1, 2]
boisterous adj noisy and lively > **boisterously** adv > **boisterousness** n
boisterously adv ▷ **boisterous**
boisterousness n ▷ **boisterous**

bok n (**boks**). A bok is a goat or antelope. Bok scores 9 points.

bold adj (-**er, -est**) confident and fearless > **boldly** adv > **boldness** n (pl -**es**)
bolder adj ▷ **bold**
boldest adj ▷ **bold**
boldly adv ▷ **bold**
boldness n ▷ **bold**
boldnesses n ▷ **bold**
bole n (pl -s) tree trunk
bolero n (pl -s) (music for) traditional Spanish dance
boleros n ▷ **bolero**
boles n ▷ **bole**
bollard n (pl -s) short thick post used to prevent the passage of motor vehicles
bollards n ▷ **bollard**
boloney n (pl -s) ▷ **baloney**
boloneys n ▷ **boloney**
bolshie, bolshy adj (Informal) difficult or rebellious
bolshy n ▷ **bolshie**
bolster v (-**s, -ing, -ed**) support or strengthen

▶ *n* (*pl* -s) long narrow pillow
bolstered *v* ▷ **bolster**
bolstering *v* ▷ **bolster**
bolsters *v*, *n* ▷ **bolster**
bolt *n* (*pl* -s) sliding metal bar for fastening a door etc. ▶ *v* (-s, -ing, -ed) run away suddenly
bolted *v* ▷ **bolt**
bolting *v* ▷ **bolt**
bolts *n*, *v* ▷ **bolt**
bomb *n* (*pl* -s) container fitted with explosive material ▶ *v* (-s, -ing, -ed) attack with bombs
bombard *v* (-s, -ing, -ed) attack with heavy gunfire or bombs > **bombardment** *n* (*pl* -s)
bombarded *v* ▷ **bombard**
bombarding *v* ▷ **bombard**
bombardment *n* ▷ **bombard**
bombardments *n* ▷ **bombard**
bombards *n* ▷ **bombard**
bombast *n* (*pl* -s) pompous language > **bombastic** *adj*
bombastic *adj* ▷ **bombast**
bombasts *n* ▷ **bombast**
bombed *v* ▷ **bomb**
bomber *n* (*pl* -s) aircraft that drops bombs
bombers *n* ▷ **bomber**
bombing *v* ▷ **bomb**
bombs *n*, *v* ▷ **bomb**
bombshell *n* (*pl* -s) shocking or unwelcome surprise
bombshells *n* ▷ **bombshell**
bonanza *n* (*pl* -s) sudden good luck or wealth
bonanzas *n* ▷ **bonanza**
bond *n* (*pl* -s) something that binds, fastens or holds together ▶ *pl* something that restrains or imprisons ▶ *v* (-s, -ing, -ed) bind > **bonded** *adj*
bondage *n* (*pl* -s) slavery
bondages *n* ▷ **bondage**
bonded *v*, *adj* ▷ **bond**
bonding *v* ▷ **bond**
bonds *n*, *v* ▷ **bond**
bone *n* (*pl* -s) any of the hard parts in the body that form the skeleton ▶ *v* (-s, -ing, -d) remove the bones from (meat for cooking etc.) > **boneless** *adj*
boned *v* ▷ **bone**
boneless *adj* ▷ **bone**
bones *n*, *v* ▷ **bone**
bonfire *n* (*pl* -s) large outdoor fire
bonfires *n* ▷ **bonfire**
bongo *n* (*pl* -gos, -goes) small drum played with the fingers
bongoes *n* ▷ **bongo**
bongos *n* ▷ **bongo**
bonhomie [bon-om-ee] *n* (*pl* -s) cheerful

friendliness
bonhomies *n* ▷ **bonhomie**
boning *v* ▷ **bone**
bonito [ba-nee-toh] *n* (*pl* -s) small tunny-like marine food fish
bonitos *n* ▷ **bonito**
bonnet *n* (*pl* -s) metal cover over a vehicle's engine
bonnets *n* ▷ **bonnet**
bonnier *adj* ▷ **bonny**
bonniest *adj* ▷ **bonny**
bonnily *adv* ▷ **bonny**
bonny *adj* (-nier, -niest) (Scot) beautiful > **bonnily** *adv*
bonsai *n* (*pl* **bonsai**) ornamental miniature tree or shrub
bonus *n* (*pl* -es) something given, paid, or received above what is due or expected
bonuses *n* ▷ **bonus**
bony *adj* having many bones
boo *interj* shout of disapproval ▶ *v* (-s, -ing, -ed) shout 'boo' to show disapproval
boob (Slang) *n* (*pl* -s) foolish mistake
boobies *n* ▷ **booby**
boobook [boo-book] *n* (*pl* -s) small spotted Australian brown owl
boobooks *n* ▷ **boobook**
boobs *n* ▷ **boob**
booby *n* (*pl* -bies) foolish person
booed *v* ▷ **boo**
boogie *v* (-s, -ing, -ied) (Informal) dance to fast pop music
boogied *v* ▷ **boogie**
boogieing *v* ▷ **boogie**
boogies *v* ▷ **boogie**
booing *v* ▷ **boo**
book *n* (*pl* -s) number of pages bound together between covers ▶ *pl* record of transactions of a business or society ▶ *v* (-s, -ing, -ed) reserve (a place, passage, etc.) in advance
booked *n* ▷ **book**
booking *v* ▷ **book**
booklet *n* (*pl* -s) thin book with paper covers
booklets *v* ▷ **booklet**
bookmaker *n* (*pl* -s) person whose occupation is taking bets
bookmakers *n* ▷ **bookmaker**
bookmark *n* (*pl* -s) strip of material used to mark a place in a book ▶ *v* (-s, -ing, -ed) (COMPUTERS) identify and store (a website) so that one can return to it quickly and easily
bookmarked *v* ▷ **bookmark**
bookmarking *v* ▷ **bookmark**
bookmarks *n*, *v* ▷ **bookmark**
books *n*, *v* ▷ **book**

bookworm *n* (*pl* **-s**) person devoted to reading
  bookworms *n* ▷ **bookworm**
boom[1] *v* (**-s**, **-ing**, **-ed**) make a loud deep
  echoing sound ▶ *n* (*pl* **-s**) loud deep echoing
  sound
boom[2] *n* (*pl* **-s**) pole to which the foot of a sail
  is attached
  boomed *v* ▷ **boom**[1]
boomer *n* (*pl* **-s**) (AUST) large male kangaroo
boomerang *n* (*pl* **-s**) curved wooden missile
  which can be made to return to the
  thrower ▶ *v* (**-s**, **-ing**, **-ed**) (of a plan) recoil
  unexpectedly
  boomeranged *n* ▷ **boomerang**
  boomeranging *v* ▷ **boomerang**
  boomerangs *n*, *v* ▷ **boomerang**
  boomers *n* ▷ **boomer**
  booming *v* ▷ **boom**[1]
  booms *v*, *n* ▷ **boom**[1, 2]
boon *n* (*pl* **-s**) something helpful or beneficial
  boongaries *n* ▷ **boongary**
boongary [boong-gar-ree] *n* (*pl* **-garies**) tree
  kangaroo of NE Queensland, Australia
  boons *n* ▷ **boon**
boor *n* (*pl* **-s**) rude or insensitive person
  > **boorish** *adj* > **boorishly** *adv* > **boorishness** *n*
  boorishly *adv* ▷ **boor**
  boorishness *n* ▷ **boor**
  boors *n* ▷ **boor**
  boos *v* ▷ **boo**
boost *n* (*pl* **-s**) encouragement or help ▶ *v* (**-s**,
  -ing, **-ed**) improve
  boosted *v* ▷ **boost**
booster *n* (*pl* **-s**) small additional injection of
  a vaccine
  boosters *n* ▷ **booster**
  boosting *v* ▷ **boost**
  boosts *n*, *v* ▷ **boost**
boot *n* (*pl* **-s**) outer covering for the foot that
  extends above the ankle ▶ *v* (**-s**, **-ing**, **-ed**)
  (*Informal*) kick
  booted *v* ▷ **boot**[1]
bootee *n* (*pl* **-s**) baby's soft shoe
  bootees *n* ▷ **bootee**
booth *n* (*pl* **-s**) small partly enclosed cubicle
  booths *n* ▷ **booth**
  booties *n* ▷ **booty**
  booting *v* ▷ **boot**[1]
bootleg *adj* produced, distributed, or sold
  illicitly ▶ *v* (**-legs**, **-legging**, **-legged**) make,
  carry, or sell (illicit goods) > **bootlegger** *n*
  (*pl* **-s**)
  bootlegged *v* ▷ **bootleg**
  bootlegger *n* ▷ **bootleg**
  bootleggers *n* ▷ **bootleg**

bootlegging *v* ▷ **bootleg**
  bootlegs *v* ▷ **bootleg**
  boots *n* ▶ *v* ▷ **boot**
booty *n* (*pl* **-ties**) valuable articles obtained
  as plunder
booze *v* (**-zes**, **-zing**, **-zed**) ▶ *n* (*pl* **-s**) (*Informal*)
  (consume) alcoholic drink > **boozy** *adj* (**-zier**,
  -ziest) > **boozily** *adv*
  boozed *v* ▷ **booze**
boozer *n* (*pl* **-s**) (*Informal*) person who is fond
  of drinking
  boozers *n* ▷ **booze**
  boozes *v*, *n* ▷ **booze**
  boozier *adj* ▷ **booze**
  booziest *adj* ▷ **booze**
  boozily *adv* ▷ **booze**
  boozing *v* ▷ **booze**
  boozy *adj* ▷ **booze**
bop *v* (**-s**, **-pping**, **-pped**) (*Informal*) dance to
  pop music
  bopped *v* ▷ **bop**
  bopping *v* ▷ **bop**
  bops *v* ▷ **bop**
bora *n* (*pl* **-s**) (AUST) Aboriginal ceremony
  boras *n* ▷ **bora**
borax *n* (*pl* **-es**) white mineral used in making
  glass
  boraxes *n* ▷ **borax**
border *n* (*pl* **-s**) dividing line between political
  or geographical regions ▶ *v* (**-s**, **-ing**, **-ed**)
  provide with a border
  bordered *v* ▷ **border**
  bordering *v* ▷ **border**
  borders *n*, *v* ▷ **border**
bore[1] *v* (**-s**, **-ring**, **-d**) make (a hole) with a drill
  etc. ▶ *n* (*pl* **-s**) (diameter of) the hollow of a
  gun barrel or other tube
bore[2] *v* (**-s**, **-ring**, **-d**) make weary by being dull
  or repetitious ▶ *n* dull or repetitious person or
  thing > **bored** *adj* > **boredom** *n*
bore[3] *n* (*pl* **-s**) high wave in a narrow estuary,
  caused by the tide
bore[4] *v* ▷ **bear**[1]
  bored *v*, *n* ▷ **bore**[1, 2]
boree [baw-ree] *n* (*pl* **-s**) (AUST) ▷ **myall**
  borees *n* ▷ **boree**
  bores *n* ▷ **bore**[1, 2, 3] ▶ *v* ▷ **bore**[1, 2]
  boring *v* ▷ **bore**[1, 2]
born *v* ▷ **bear**[1] ▶ *adj* possessing certain
  qualities from birth
  borne *v* ▷ **bear**[1]
boron *n* (*pl* **-s**) (CHEM) element used in
  hardening steel
boronia *n* (*pl* **-s**) Australian aromatic flowering
  shrub

boronias *n* ▷ boronia
borons *n* ▷ boron
borough *n* (*pl* -s) (CHIEFLY BRIT) town or district with its own council
boroughs *n* ▷ borough
borrow *v* (-s, -ing, -ed) obtain (something) temporarily > **borrower** *n* (*pl* -s)
borrowed *v* ▷ borrow
borrower *n* ▷ borrow
borrowers *n* ▷ borrow
borrowing *v* ▷ borrow
borrows *v* ▷ borrow
borstal *n* (*pl* -s) (formerly in Britain) prison for young criminals
borstals *n* ▷ borstal
borzoi *n* (*pl* -s) tall dog with a long silky coat
borzois *n* ▷ borzoi
bosh *n* (*pl* -es) (BRIT, AUST & NZ) (*Informal*) empty talk, nonsense
boshes *n* ▷ bosh
bosom *n* (*pl* -s) chest of a person, esp. the female breasts ▶ *adj* very dear
bosoms *n* ▷ bosom
boss¹ *n* (*pl* -es) person in charge of or employing others ▶ *v* (-es, -ing, -ed) be domineering towards > **bossy** *adj* > **bossiness** *n*
boss² *n* (*pl* -es) raised knob or stud
bossed *v* ▷ boss¹
bosses *n* ▷ boss¹, ² ▶ *v* ▷ boss¹
bossiness *n* ▷ boss¹
bossing *v* ▷ boss¹
bossy *adj* ▷ boss¹
bosun *n* (*pl* -s) officer responsible for the maintenance of a ship
bosuns *n* ▷ bosun
botanic *adj* ▷ botany
botanical *adj* ▷ botany
botanies *n* ▷ botany
botanist *n* ▷ botany
botanists *n* ▷ botany
botany *n* (*pl* -ies) study of plants > **botanical, botanic** *adj* > **botanist** *n* (*pl* -s)
botch *v* (-es, -ing, -ed) spoil through clumsiness ▶ *n* (*pl* -es) (*also* **botch-up**) (*pl* -s) badly done piece of work or repair
botched *v* ▷ botch
botches *v*, *n* ▷ botch
botching *v* ▷ botch
both *adj*, *pron* two considered together
bother *v* (-s, -ing, -ed) take the time or trouble ▶ *n* (*pl* -s) trouble, fuss, or difficulty > **bothersome** *adj*
bothered *v* ▷ bother
bothering *v* ▷ bother

bothers *v*, *n* ▷ bother
bothersome *adj* ▷ bother
bottle *n* (*pl* -s) container for holding liquids ▶ *v* (-s, -ttling, -d) put in a bottle
bottled *v* ▷ bottle
bottleneck *n* (*pl* -s) narrow stretch of road where traffic is held up
bottlenecks *n* ▷ bottleneck
bottles *n*, *v* ▷ bottle
bottling *v* ▷ bottle
bottom *n* (*pl* -s) lowest, deepest, or farthest removed part of a thing ▶ *adj* lowest or last > **bottomless** *adj*
bottomless *adj* ▷ bottom
bottoms *n* ▷ bottom
botulism *n* (*pl* -s) severe food poisoning
botulisms *n* ▷ botulism
boudoir [boo-dwahr] *n* (*pl* -s) woman's bedroom or private sitting room
boudoirs *n* ▷ boudoir
bougainvillea *n* (*pl* -s) climbing plant with red or purple flowers
bougainvilleas *n* ▷ bougainvillea
bough *n* (*pl* -s) large branch of a tree
boughs *n* ▷ bough
bought *v* ▷ buy
boulder *n* (*pl* -s) large rounded rock
boulders *n* ▷ boulder
boulevard *n* (*pl* -s) wide, usu. tree-lined, street
boulevards *n* ▷ boulevard
bounce *v* (-s, -cing, -d) (of a ball etc.) rebound from an impact (*Slang*) ▶ *n* (*pl* -s) act of rebounding
bounced *v* ▷ bounce
bouncer *n* (*pl* -s) person employed at a disco etc. to remove unwanted people
bouncers *n* ▷ bouncer
bounces *v*, *n* ▷ bounce
bouncing *v* ▷ bounce ▶ *adj* vigorous and robust
bound¹ *v* (-s, -ing, -ed) ▷ bind ▶ *adj* destined or certain
bound² *v* (-s, -ing, -ed) move forwards by jumps ▶ *n* (*pl* -s) jump upwards or forwards
bound³ *v* (-s, -ing, -ed) form a boundary of ▶ *pl n* limit
bound⁴ *adj* going or intending to go towards
boundaries *n* ▷ boundary
boundary *n* (*pl* -aries) dividing line that indicates the farthest limit
bounded *v* ▷ bound², ³
bounding *v* ▷ bound², ³
bounds *v*, *n* ▷ bound², ³
bounteous *adj* ▷ bounty
bounties *n* ▷ bounty

bountiful *adj* ▷ **bounty**

bounty *n* (*pl* **-ties**) generosity > **bountiful, bounteous** *adj*

bouquet *n* (*pl* **-s**) bunch of flowers

bouquets *n* ▷ **bouquet**

bourbon [bur-bn] *n* (*pl* **-s**) whiskey made from maize

bourbons *n* ▷ **bourbon**

bourgeois [boor-zhwah] *adj, n* (*pl* **bourgeois**) middle-class (person)

bout *n* (*pl* **-s**) period of activity or illness

boutique *n* (*pl* **-s**) small clothes shop

boutiques *n* ▷ **boutique**

bouts *n* ▷ **bout**

bovine *adj* relating to cattle

bow¹ [rhymes with **now**] *v* (**-s, -ing, -ed**) lower (one's head) or bend (one's knee or body) as a sign of respect or shame ▶ *n* (*pl* **-s**) movement made when bowing

bow² [rhymes with **go**] *n* (*pl* **-s**) knot with two loops and loose ends

bow³ [rhymes with **now**] *n* (*pl* **-s**) front end of a ship

bowdlerize *v* (**-zes, -zing, -zed**) remove words regarded as indecent from (a play, novel, etc.)

bowdlerized *v* ▷ **bowdlerize**

bowdlerizes *v* ▷ **bowdlerize**

bowdlerizing *v* ▷ **bowdlerize**

bowed *v* ▷ **bow¹**

bowel *n* (*pl* **-s**) intestine, esp. the large intestine ▶ *pl* innermost part

bowels *n* ▷ **bowel**

bower *n* (*pl* **-s**) shady leafy shelter

bowerbird *n* (*pl* **-s**) songbird of Australia and New Guinea, the males of which build bower-like display grounds to attract females

bowerbirds *n* ▷ **bowerbird**

bowers *n* ▷ **bower**

bowing *v* ▷ **bow¹**

bowl¹ *n* (*pl* **-s**) round container with an open top

bowl² *n* (*pl* **-s**) large heavy ball ▶ *pl* game played on smooth grass with wooden bowls ▶ *v* (**-s, -ing, -ed**) (CRICKET) send (a ball) towards the batsman

bowled *v* ▷ **bowl²**

bowlegged *adj* having legs that curve outwards at the knees

bowler¹ *n* (*pl* **-s**) (CRICKET) player who sends (a ball) towards the batsman

bowler² *n* (*pl* **-s**) stiff felt hat with a rounded crown

bowlers *n* ▷ **bowler¹, ²**

bowling *n* game in which bowls are rolled at a group of pins ▶ *v* ▷ **bowl²**

bowls *n* ▷ **bowl¹, ²** ▶ *v* ▷ **bowl²**

bows *v* ▷ **bow¹** ▶ *n* ▷ **bow¹, ², ³**

box¹ *n* (*pl* **-es**) container with a firm flat base and sides ▶ *v* (**-es, -ing, -ed**) put into a box

box² *v* (**-es, -ing, -ed**) fight (an opponent) in a boxing match

box³ *n* (*pl* **-es**) evergreen tree with shiny leaves bark

boxed *v* ▷ **box¹, ²**

boxer *n* (*pl* **-s**) person who participates in the sport of boxing

boxers *n* ▷ **boxer**

boxes *v* ▷ **box¹, ²** ▶ *n* ▷ **box¹, ², ³**

boxing *n* sport of fighting with the fists ▶ *v* ▷ **box¹, ²**

boy *n* (*pl* **-s**) male child > **boyish** *adj* > **boyhood** *n* (*pl* **-s**)

boycott *v* (**-cotts, -cotting, -cotted**) refuse to deal with (an organization or country) ▶ *n* (*pl* **-s**) instance of boycotting

boycotted *v* ▷ **boycott**

boycotting *v* ▷ **boycott**

boycotts *v, n* ▷ **boycott**

boyfriend *n* (*pl* **-s**) male friend with whom a person is romantically or sexually involved

boyfriends *n* ▷ **boyfriend**

boyhood *n* ▷ **boy**

boyhoods *n* ▷ **boy**

boyish *n* ▷ **boy**

boys *n* ▷ **boy**

bra *n* (*pl* **-s**) woman's undergarment for supporting the breasts

braai *n* ▷ **braaivlies**

braaied *v* ▷ **braaivlies**

braaiing *v* ▷ **braaivlies**

braais *n, v* ▷ **braaivlies**

braaivlies [brye-flayss], **braai** (S AFR) *n* (*pl* **braais**) grill on which food is cooked over hot charcoal, usu. outdoors ▶ *v* (**braais, braaiing, braaied**) cook (food) on in this way

brace *n* (*pl* **-s**) object fastened to something to straighten or support it ▶ *pl* straps worn over the shoulders to hold up trousers ▶ *v* (**-ces, -cing, -ced**) steady or prepare (oneself) for something unpleasant

braced *n, v* ▷ **brace**

bracelet *n* (*pl* **-s**) ornamental chain or band for the wrist

bracelets *n* ▷ **bracelet**

braces *n, v* ▷ **brace**

bracing *adj* refreshing and invigorating ▶ *v* ▷ **brace**

bracken *n* (*pl* **-s**) large fern

brackens *n* ▷ **bracken**

bracket *n* (*pl* **-s**) either of a pair of characters

used to enclose a section of writing ▶ v (**-ets, -eting, -eted**) put in brackets
bracketed v ▷ **bracket**
bracketing v ▷ **bracket**
brackets n, v ▷ **bracket**
brackish adj (of water) slightly salty
> **brackishness** n
brackishness n ▷ **bracket**
bract n (pl **-s**) leaf at the base of a flower
bracts n ▷ **bract**
brag v (**-s, -gging, -gged**) speak arrogantly and boastfully > **braggart** n (pl **-s**)
braggart n ▷ **brag**
braggarts n ▷ **brag**
bragged v ▷ **brag**
bragging v ▷ **brag**
brags v ▷ **brag**
braid v (**-s, -ing, -ed**) interweave (hair, thread, etc.) ▶ n (pl **-s**) length of hair etc. that has been braided
braided v ▷ **braid**
braiding v ▷ **braid**
braids v, n ▷ **braid**
braille n (pl **-s**) system of writing for the blind, consisting of raised dots interpreted by touch
brailles n ▷ **braille**
brain n (pl **-s**) soft mass of nervous tissue in the head ▶ v (**-s, -ing, -ed**) hit (someone) hard on the head
brainchild n (pl **-children**) idea produced by creative thought
brainchildren n ▷ **brainchild**
brained v ▷ **brain**
brainier adj ▷ **brainy**
brainiest adj ▷ **brainy**
braininess n ▷ **brainy**
braininesses n ▷ **brainy**
braining v ▷ **brain**
brainless adj stupid
brains n, v ▷ **brain**
brainwash v (**-es, -ing, -ed**) cause (a person) to alter his or her beliefs, esp. by methods based on isolation, sleeplessness, etc.
brainwashed v ▷ **brainwash**
brainwashes v ▷ **brainwash**
brainwashing v ▷ **brainwash**
brainwave n (pl **-s**) sudden idea
brainwaves v ▷ **brainwave**
brainy adj (**-nier, -niest**) (Informal) clever
> **braininess** n (pl **-es**)
braise v (**-ses, -sing, -sed**) cook slowly in a covered pan with a little liquid
braised v ▷ **braise**
braises v ▷ **braise**

braising v ▷ **braise**
brake n (pl **-s**) device for slowing or stopping a vehicle ▶ v (**-kes, -king, -ked**) slow down or stop by using a brake
braked v ▷ **brake**
brakes n, v ▷ **brake**
braking v ▷ **brake**
bramble n (pl **-s**) prickly shrub that produces blackberries
brambles n ▷ **bramble**
bran n (pl **-s**) husks of cereal grain
branch n (pl **-es**) secondary stem of a tree ▶ v (**-es, -ing, -ed**) (of stems, roots, etc.) divide, then develop in different directions
branched n ▷ **branch**
branches n, v ▷ **branch**
branching v ▷ **branch**
brand n (pl **-s**) particular product ▶ v (**-s, -ing, -ed**) mark with a brand
branded v ▷ **brand**
brandies n ▷ **brandy**
branding v ▷ **brand**
brandish v (**-es, -ing, -ed**) wave (a weapon etc.) in a threatening way
brandished v ▷ **brandish**
brandishes v ▷ **brandish**
brandishing v ▷ **brandish**
brands n, v ▷ **brand**
brandy n (pl **-dies**) alcoholic spirit distilled from wine
brans n ▷ **bran**
bras n ▷ **bra**
brash adj offensively loud, showy, or self-confident > **brashness** n
brashness n ▷ **brash**
brass n (pl **-es**) alloy of copper and zinc
brasses n ▷ **brass**
brassier adj ▷ **brassy**
brassiere n (pl **-s**) bra
brassieres n ▷ **brassiere**
brassiest adj ▷ **brassy**
brassiness adj ▷ **brassy**
brassinesses adj ▷ **brassy**
brassy adj (**-ssier, -ssiest**) brazen or flashy
> **brassiness** n (pl **-es**)
brat n (pl **-s**) unruly child
brats n ▷ **brat**
bravado n (pl **-oes**) showy display of self-confidence
bravadoes n ▷ **bravado**
brave adj (**-r, -st**) having or showing courage, resolution, and daring ▶ n (pl **-s**) Native American warrior ▶ v (**-ves, -ving, -ved**) confront with resolution or courage
> **bravery** n (pl **-ies**)

braved v ▷ **brave**
braver adj ▷ **brave**
braveries n ▷ **brave**
bravery n ▷ **brave**
braves n, v ▷ **brave**
bravest adj ▷ **brave**
braving v ▷ **brave**
bravo interj well done!
brawl n (pl -s) noisy fight ▶ v (-s, -ing, -ed) fight
noisily
brawled v ▷ **brawl**
brawling v ▷ **brawl**
brawls n, v ▷ **brawl**
brawn n (pl -s) physical strength > **brawny**
(-nier, -niest) adj
brawnier adj ▷ **brawn**
brawniest adj ▷ **brawn**
brawns n ▷ **brawn**
brawny adj ▷ **brawn**
bray v (-s, -ing, -ed) (of a donkey) utter its loud
harsh sound ▶ n (pl -s) donkey's loud harsh
sound
brayed v ▷ **bray**
braying v ▷ **bray**
brays v, n ▷ **bray**
brazen adj shameless and bold ▶ v (-s, -ing, -ed)
> **brazenly** adv > **brazenness** n
brazened v ▷ **brazen**
brazening v ▷ **brazen**
brazenly adv ▷ **brazen**
brazenness n ▷ **brazen**
brazens v ▷ **brazen**
brazier [bray-zee-er] n (pl -s) portable container
for burning charcoal or coal
braziers n ▷ **brazier**
breach n (pl -es) breaking of a promise,
obligation, etc. ▶ v (-es, -ing, -ed) break (a
promise, law, etc.)
breached v ▷ **breach**
breaches n, v ▷ **breach**
breaching v ▷ **breach**
bread n (pl -s) food made by baking a mixture
of flour and water or milk
breads n ▷ **bread**
breadth n (pl -s) extent of something from
side to side
breadths n ▷ **breadth**
breadwinner n (pl -s) person whose earnings
support a family
breadwinners n ▷ **breadwinner**
break v (breaks, breaking, broke, broken)
separate or become separated into two or
more pieces ▶ n (pl -s) act or result of breaking
> **breakable** adj > **breakage** n (pl -s)
breakable adj ▷ **break**

breakage n ▷ **break**
breakages n ▷ **break**
breakdown n (pl -s) act or instance of breaking
down
breakdowns n ▷ **breakdown**
breaker n (pl -s) large wave
breakers n ▷ **breaker**
breakfast v (-s, -ing, -ed) ▶ n (pl -s) (eat) the
first meal of the day
breakfasted v ▷ **breakfast**
breakfasting v ▷ **breakfast**
breakfasts v, n ▷ **breakfast**
breaking v ▷ **break**
breakneck adj fast and dangerous
breaks v, n ▷ **break**
breakthrough n (pl -s) important
development or discovery
breakthroughs n ▷ **breakthrough**
breakwater n (pl -s) wall that extends into the
sea to protect a harbour or beach from the
force of waves
breakwaters n ▷ **breakwater**
bream n (pl bream) freshwater fish with silvery
scales
breast n (pl -s) either of the two soft fleshy
milk-secreting glands on a woman's chest
breastbone n (pl -s) long flat bone in the front
of the body, to which most of the ribs are
attached
breastbones n ▷ **breastbone**
breasts n ▷ **breast**
breaststroke n (pl -s) swimming stroke in
which the arms are extended in front of the
head and swept back on either side
breaststrokes n ▷ **breaststroke**
breath n (pl -s) taking in and letting out
of air during breathing > **breathless** adj
> **breathlessly** adv > **breathlessness** n
breathalysed v ▷ **breathalyser**
breathalyser n (pl -s) ® device for estimating
the amount of alcohol in the breath
> **breathalyse** v (-ses, -sing, -sed)
breathalysers n ▷ **breathalyser**
breathalyses v ▷ **breathalyser**
breathalysing v ▷ **breathalyser**
breathe v (-thes, -thing, -thed) take in oxygen
and give out carbon dioxide > **breathing** n
breathed v ▷ **breathe**
breather n (pl -s) (Informal) short rest
breathers n ▷ **breather**
breathes v ▷ **breathe**
breathing v, n ▷ **breathe**
breathless adj ▷ **breath**
breathlessly adv ▷ **breath**
breathlessness n ▷ **breath**

breaths *n* ▷ **breath**
breathtaking *adj* causing awe or excitement
bred *v* ▷ **breed**
breech *n* (*pl* **-es**) buttocks
breeches *pl n* trousers extending to just below
the knee ▶ *n* ▷ **breech**
breed *v* (**-s, -ding, bred**) produce new or
improved strains of (domestic animals or
plants) ▶ *n* (*pl* **-s**) group of animals etc. within
a species that have certain clearly defined
characteristics > **breeder** *n* (*pl* **-s**)
breeder *n* ▷ **breed**
breeders *n* ▷ **breed**
breeding *n* (*pl* **-s**) result of good upbringing or
training ▶ *v* ▷ **breed**
breedings *n* ▷ **breeding**
breeds *v, n* ▷ **breed**
breeze *n* (*pl* **-s**) gentle wind ▶ *v* (**-zes, -zing,
-zed**) move quickly or casually
breezed *v* ▷ **breeze**
breezes *n, v* ▷ **breeze**
breezier *adj* ▷ **breezy**
breeziest *adj* ▷ **breezy**
breezily *adj* ▷ **breezy**
breezing *v* ▷ **breeze**
breezy *adj* (**-zier, -ziest**) windy > **breezily** *adv*
brethren *pl n* (*Old-fashioned*) (used in religious
contexts) brothers
brevities *n* ▷ **brevity**
brevity *n* (*pl* **-ities**) shortness
brew *v* (**-s, -ing, -ed**) make (beer etc.) by
steeping, boiling, and fermentation ▶ *n* (*pl* **-s**)
beverage produced by brewing
brewed *v* ▷ **brew**
brewer *n* (*pl* **-s**) person or company that brews
beer
breweries *n* ▷ **brewery**
brewers *n* ▷ **brewer**
brewery *n* (*pl* **-eries**) place where beer etc. is
brewed
brewing *v* ▷ **brew**
brews *v, n* ▷ **brew**
briar¹, brier *n* (*pl* **-s**) European shrub with a
hard woody root
briar2 *n* (*pl* **-s**) ▷ **brier¹**
briars *n* ▷ **briar¹, ²**
bribe *v* (**bribes, bribing, bribed**) offer or give
something to someone to gain favour,
influence, etc. ▶ *n* (*pl* **-s**) something given or
offered as a bribe > **bribery** *n*
bribed *v* ▷ **bribe**
bribes *v, n* ▷ **bribe**
bribing *v* ▷ **bribe**
brick *n* (*pl* **-s**) (rectangular block of) baked clay
used in building ▶ *v* (**-s, -ing, -ed**) (*foll.* by **up** or

over) build, enclose, or fill with bricks
bricked *v* ▷ **brick**
bricking *v* ▷ **brick**
bricklayer *n* (*pl* **-s**) person who builds with
bricks
bricklayers *n* ▷ **bricklayer**
bricks *n, v* ▷ **brick**
bridal *adj* ▷ **bride**
bride *n* (*pl* **-s**) woman who has just been or is
about to be married > **bridal** *adj*
bridegroom *n* (*pl* **-s**) man who has just been or
is about to be married
bridegrooms *n* ▷ **bridegroom**
brides *n* ▷ **bride**
bridesmaid *n* (*pl* **-s**) girl or woman who
attends a bride at her wedding
bridesmaids *n* ▷ **bridesmaid**
bridge¹ *n* (*pl* **-s**) structure for crossing a river
etc. ▶ *v* (**-dges, -dging, -dged**) build a bridge
over (something)
bridge² *n* (*pl* **-s**) card game based on whist,
played between two pairs
bridged *v* ▷ **bridge¹**
bridgehead *n* (*pl* **-s**) fortified position at the
end of a bridge nearest the enemy
bridgeheads *n* ▷ **bridgehead**
bridges *n* ▷ **bridge¹, ²** ▶ *v* ▷ **bridge¹**
bridging *v* ▷ **bridge¹**
bridle *n* (*pl* **-s**) headgear for controlling a
horse ▶ *v* (**-dles, -dling, -dled**) show anger or
indignation
bridled *v* ▷ **bridle**
bridles *n, v* ▷ **bridle**
bridling *v* ▷ **bridle**
brief *adj* (**-er, -est**) short in duration ▶ *n* (*pl* **-s**)
condensed statement or written synopsis
(*also* **briefing**) (*pl* **-s**) ▶ *pl* men's or women's
underpants ▶ *v* (**-s, -ing, -ed**) give information
and instructions to (a person) > **briefly** *adv*
briefcase *n* (*pl* **-s**) small flat case for carrying
papers, books, etc.
briefcases *n* ▷ **briefcase**
briefed *v* ▷ **brief**
briefer *adj* ▷ **brief**
briefest *adj* ▷ **brief**
briefing *v, n* ▷ **brief**
briefings *n* ▷ **brief**
briefly *adv* ▷ **brief**
briefs *n, v* ▷ **brief**
brier¹, briar *n* (*pl* **-s**) wild rose with long thorny
stems
brier² *n* (*pl* **-s**) ▷ **briar¹**
briers *n* ▷ **brier¹, ²**
brig *n* (*pl* **-s**) two-masted square-rigged ship
brigade *n* (*pl* **-s**) army unit smaller than a

division
brigades *n* ▷ **brigade**
brigadier *n* (*pl* **-s**) high-ranking army officer
brigadiers *n* ▷ **brigadier**
brigalow *n* (*pl* **-s**) (AUST) type of acacia tree
brigalows *n* ▷ **brigalow**
brigand *n* (*pl* **-s**) (*Lit*) bandit
brigands *n* ▷ **brigand**
brigantine *n* (*pl* **-s**) two-masted sailing ship
brigantines *n* ▷ **brigantine**
bright *adj* (**-er, -est**) emitting or reflecting
much light > **brightly** *adv* > **brightness** *n*
> **brighten** *v* (**-s, -ing, -ed**)
brighten *v* ▷ **bright**
brightened *v* ▷ **bright**
brightening *v* ▷ **bright**
brightens *v* ▷ **bright**
brighter *adj* ▷ **bright**
brightest *adj* ▷ **bright**
brightly *adj* ▷ **bright**
brigs *n* ▷ **brig**
brilliance *n* ▷ **brilliant**
brilliancy *n* ▷ **brilliant**
brilliant *adj* shining with light > **brilliance,**
brilliancy *n* > **brilliantly** *adv*
brilliantly *adv* ▷ **brilliant**
brim *n* (*pl* **-s**) upper rim of a cup etc. ▶ *v* (**brims,**
brimming, brimmed) be full to the brim
brimmed *v* ▷ **brim**
brimming *v* ▷ **brim**
brims *n*, *v* ▷ **brim**
brimstone *n* (*pl* **-s**) (*Obs*) sulphur
brimstones *n* ▷ **brimstone**
brine *n* (*pl* **-s**) salt water
brines *n* ▷ **brine**
bring *v* (**-s, -ing, brought**) carry, convey, or take
to a designated place or person
bringing *v* ▷ **bring**
brings *v* ▷ **bring**
brinier *adj* ▷ **briny**
briniest *adj* ▷ **briny**
brinjal *n* (*pl* **-s**) (S AFR) aubergine
brinjals *n* ▷ **brinjal**
brink *n* (*pl* **-s**) edge of a steep place
brinks *n* ▷ **brink**
briny (**brinier, briniest**) *adj* very salty
brisk *adj* (**-er, -est**) lively and quick > **briskly** *adv*
brisker *adj* ▷ **brisk**
briskest *adj* ▷ **brisk**
brisket *n* (*pl* **-s**) beef from the breast of a cow
briskets *n* ▷ **brisket**
briskly *adv* ▷ **brisk**
bristle *n* (*pl* **-s**) short stiff hair ▶ *v* (**-les, -ling,**
-led) (cause to) stand up like bristles > **bristly**
adj (**-lier, -liest**)

bristled *v* ▷ **bristle**
bristles *n*, *v* ▷ **bristle**
bristlier *adj* ▷ **bristle**
bristliest *adj* ▷ **bristle**
bristling *v* ▷ **bristle**
bristly *adj* ▷ **bristle**
brit *n* (*pl* **-s**) (*Informal*) British person
brits *n* ▷ **brit**
brittle *adj* (**-r, -st**) hard but easily broken
> **brittleness** *n* (*pl* **-es**)
brittleness *n* ▷ **brittle**
brittlenesses *n* ▷ **brittle**
brittler *adj* ▷ **brittle**
brittlest *adj* ▷ **brittle**
broach *v* (**-es, -ing, -ed**) introduce (a topic) for
discussion
broached *v* ▷ **broach**
broaches *v* ▷ **broach**
broaching *v* ▷ **broach**
broad *adj* (**-er, -est**) having great breadth or
width > **broadly** *adv* > **broaden** *v* (**-s, -ing, -ed**)
broadband *n* (*pl* **-s**) telecommunication
transmission technique using a wide range
of frequencies
broadbands *n* ▷ **broadband**
broadcast *n* (*pl* **-s**) programme or
announcement on radio or television ▶ *v*
(**-s, -ing, broadcast**) transmit (a programme
or announcement) on radio or television
> **broadcaster** *n* (*pl* **-s**) > **broadcasting** *n*
broadcaster *n* ▷ **broadcast**
broadcasters *n* ▷ **broadcast**
broadcasting *v*, *n* ▷ **broadcast**
broadcasts *n*, *v* ▷ **broadcast**
broaden *v* ▷ **broad**
broadened *v* ▷ **broad**
broadening *v* ▷ **broad**
broadens *v* ▷ **broad**
broader *adj* ▷ **broad**
broadest *adj* ▷ **broad**
broadly *adv* ▷ **broad**
broadminded *adj* tolerant
broadside *n* (*pl* **-s**) strong verbal or written
attack
broadsides *n* ▷ **broadside**
brocade *n* (*pl* **-s**) rich fabric woven with a
raised design
brocades *n* ▷ **brocade**
broccoli *n* (*pl* **-s**) type of cabbage with greenish
flower heads
broccolis *n* ▷ **broccoli**
brochure *n* (*pl* **-s**) booklet that contains
information about a product or service
brochures *n* ▷ **brochure**
broekies [brook-eez] *pl n* (S AFR) (*Informal*)

underpants

brogue[1] *n* (*pl* **-s**) sturdy walking shoe

brogue[2] *n* (*pl* **-s**) strong accent, esp. Irish

brogues *n* ▷ **brogue**[1, 2]

broil *v* (**-s, -ing, -ed**) (AUST, NZ, US & CANADIAN) cook by direct heat under a grill

broiled *v* ▷ **broil**

broiling *v* ▷ **broil**

broils *v* ▷ **broil**

broke *v* ▷ **break** ▶ *adj* (*Informal*) having no money

broken *v* ▷ **break** ▶ *adj* fractured or smashed

brokenhearted *adj* overwhelmed by grief

broker *n* (*pl* **-s**) agent who buys or sells goods, securities, etc.

brokers *n* ▷ **broker**

brolga *n* (*pl* **-s**) large grey Australian crane with a trumpeting call

brolgas *n* ▷ **brolga**

brollies *n* ▷ **brolly**

brolly *n* (*pl* **-lies**) (*Informal*) umbrella

bromide *n* (*pl* **-s**) chemical compound used in medicine and photography

bromides *n* ▷ **bromide**

bromine *n* (*pl* **-s**) (CHEM) dark red liquid element that gives off a pungent vapour

bromines *n* ▷ **bromine**

bronchi *n* ▷ **bronchus**

bronchial [bronk-ee-al] *adj* of the bronchi

bronchitis [bronk-**eye**-tiss] *n* inflammation of the bronchi

bronchus [bronk-uss] *n* (*pl* **bronchi**) [bronk-**eye**] either of the two branches of the windpipe

bronco *n* (*pl* **-s**) (in the US) wild or partially tamed pony

broncos *n* ▷ **bronco**

brontosaurus *n* (*pl* **-es**) very large plant-eating four-footed dinosaur

brontosauruses *n* ▷ **brontosaurus**

bronze *n* (*pl* **-s**) alloy of copper and tin ▶ *adj* made of, or coloured like, bronze ▶ *v* (**-zes, -zing, -zed**) (esp. of the skin) make or become brown

bronzed *v* ▷ **bronze**

bronzes *n, v* ▷ **bronze**

bronzing *v* ▷ **bronze**

brooch *n* (*pl* **-es**) ornament with a pin, worn fastened to clothes

brooches *n* ▷ **brooch**

brood *n* (*pl* **-s**) number of birds produced at one hatching ▶ *v* (**-s, -ing, -ed**) think long and unhappily > **broody** *adj* moody and sullen (*Informal*)

brooded *v* ▷ **brood**

brooding *v* ▷ **brood**

broods *n, v* ▷ **brood**

broody *adj* ▷ **brood**

brook[1] *n* (*pl* **-s**) small stream

brook[2] *v* (**-s, -ing, -ed**) bear or tolerate

brooked *v* ▷ **brook**[2]

brooking *v* ▷ **brook**[2]

brooks *n* ▷ **brook**[1] ▶ *v* ▷ **brook**[2]

broom *n* (*pl* **-s**) long-handled sweeping brush

brooms *n* ▷ **broom**

broomstick *n* (*pl* **-s**) handle of a broom

broomsticks *n* ▷ **broomstick**

broth *n* (*pl* **-s**) soup, usu. containing vegetables

brothel *n* (*pl* **-s**) house where men pay to have sex with prostitutes

brothels *n* ▷ **brothel**

brother *n* (*pl* **-s**) boy or man with the same parents as another person > **brotherly** *adj*

brotherhood *n* (*pl* **-s**) fellowship

brotherhoods *n* ▷ **brotherhood**

brotherly *adj* ▷ **brother**

brothers *n* ▷ **brother**

broths *n* ▷ **broth**

brought *v* ▷ **bring**

brow *n* (*pl* **-s**) part of the face from the eyes to the hairline

browbeat *v* (**-s, -ing, browbeat, -en**) frighten (someone) with threats

browbeaten *v* ▷ **browbeat**

browbeating *v* ▷ **browbeat**

browbeats *v* ▷ **browbeat**

brown *n* (*pl* **-s**) colour of earth or wood ▶ *adj* (**-er, -est**) of the colour brown ▶ *v* (**-s, -ing, -ed**) make or become brown > **brownish** *adj*

browned *v* ▷ **brown**

browner *adj* ▷ **brown**

brownest *adj* ▷ **brown**

browning *v* ▷ **brown**

brownish *adj* ▷ **brown**

browns *n, v* ▷ **brown**

brows *n* ▷ **brow**

browse *v* (**-ses, -sing, -sed**) look through (a book or articles for sale) in a casual manner ▶ *n* (*pl* **-s**) instance of browsing

browsed *v* ▷ **browse**

browser *n* (*pl* **-s**) (COMPUTERS) software package that enables a user to read hypertext, esp. on the Internet

browsers *n* ▷ **browser**

browses *v, n* ▷ **browse**

browsing *v* ▷ **browse**

bruise *n* (*pl* **-s**) discoloured area on the skin caused by an injury ▶ *v* (**-ses, -sing, -sed**) cause a bruise on

bruised *v* ▷ **bruise**

bruiser *n* (*pl* **-s**) strong tough person

bruisers n ▷ bruiser
bruises n, v ▷ bruise
bruising v ▷ bruise
brumbies n ▷ brumby
brumby n (pl -bies) (AUST) wild horse
brunch n (pl -es) (Informal) breakfast and lunch
combined
brunches n ▷ brunch
brunette n (pl -s) girl or woman with dark
brown hair
brunettes n ▷ brunette
brunt n (pl -s) main force or shock of a blow,
attack, etc.
brunts n ▷ brunt
brush¹ n (pl -es) device made of bristles, wires,
etc. used for cleaning, painting, etc. ▶ v (-es,
-ing, -ed) clean, scrub, or paint with a brush
brush² n (pl -es) thick growth of shrubs
brushed v ▷ brush¹
brushes v ▷ brush¹ ▶ n ▷ brush¹, ²
brushing v ▷ brush¹
brusque adj (-r, -st) blunt or curt in manner
or speech > **brusquely** adv > **brusqueness**
n (pl -es)
brusquely adv ▷ brusque
brusqueness n ▷ brusque
brusquenesses n ▷ brusque
brusquer adj ▷ brusque
brusquest adj ▷ brusque
brutal adj cruel and vicious > **brutally** adv
> **brutality** n (pl -alities) > **brutalize** v (-lizes,
-lizing, -lized)
brutalities n ▷ brutal
brutality n ▷ brutal
brutalized v ▷ brutal
brutalizes v ▷ brutal
brutalizing v ▷ brutal
brutally adv ▷ brutal
brute n (pl -s) brutal person ▶ adj wholly
instinctive or physical, like an animal
brutes n ▷ brute
brutish adj of or like an animal > **brutishly** adv
> **brutishness** n
brutishly adv ▷ brutish
brutishness n ▷ brutish
bubble n (pl -s) ball of air in a liquid or solid ▶ v
(-les, -ling, -led) form bubbles
bubbled v ▷ bubble
bubbles n, v ▷ bubble
bubblier adj ▷ bubbly
bubbliest adj ▷ bubbly
bubbling v ▷ bubble
bubbly adj (-lier, -liest) excited and lively
buccaneer n (pl -s) (HIST) pirate
buccaneers n ▷ buccaneer

buck¹ n (pl -s) male of the goat, hare, kangaroo,
rabbit, and reindeer ▶ v (-s, -ing, -ed) (of a
horse etc.) jump with legs stiff and back
arched
buck² n (pl -s) (US, CANADIAN, AUST & NZ) (Slang)
dollar
bucked v ▷ buck¹
bucket n (pl -s) open-topped round container
with a handle ▶ v (-ets, -eting, -eted) rain
heavily > **bucketful** n (pl -s)
bucketed v ▷ bucket
bucketful n ▷ bucket
bucketfuls n ▷ bucket
bucketing v ▷ bucket
buckets n, v ▷ bucket
bucking v ▷ buck¹
buckle n (pl -s) clasp for fastening a belt
or strap ▶ v (-les, -ling, -led) fasten or be
fastened with a buckle
buckled v ▷ buckle
buckles n, v ▷ buckle
buckling v ▷ buckle
bucks v ▷ buck¹ ▶ n ▷ buck¹, ²
buckshee adj (Slang) free
buckteeth pl n projecting upper front teeth
> **buck-toothed** adj
buck-toothed adj ▷ buckteeth
buckwheat n (pl -s) small black grain used for
making flour
buckwheats n ▷ buckwheat
bucolic [bew-koll-ik] adj of the countryside or
country life
bud n (pl -s) swelling on a tree or plant that
develops into a leaf or flower ▶ v (buds,
budding, budded) produce buds
budded v ▷ bud
buddies n ▷ buddy
budding adj beginning to develop or grow
▶ v ▷ bud
buddleia n (pl -s) shrub with long spikes of
purple flowers
buddleias n ▷ buddleia
buddy n (pl -dies) (Informal) friend
budge v (budges, budging, budged) move
slightly
budged v ▷ budge
budgerigar n (pl -s) small cage bird bred in
many different-coloured varieties
budgerigars n ▷ budgerigar
budges v ▷ budge
budget n (pl -s) financial plan for a period
of time ▶ v (-ets, -eting, -eted) plan the
expenditure of (money or time) ▶ adj cheap
> **budgetary** adj
budgeted v ▷ budget

budgeting *v* ▷ budget
budgets *n*, *v* ▷ budget
budgie *n* (*pl* **-s**) (*Informal*) ▷ **budgerigar**
budgies *n* ▷ budgie
budging *v* ▷ budge
buds *n*, *v* ▷ bud
buff¹ *adj* dull yellowish-brown ▶ *v* (**-s, -ing, -ed**) clean or polish with soft material
buff² *n* (*pl* **-s**) (*Informal*) expert on or devotee of a given subject
buffalo *n* (*pl* **-oes**) type of cattle (us)
buffaloes *n* ▷ buffalo
buffed *v* ▷ buff¹
buffer *n* (*pl* **-s**) something that lessens shock or protects from damaging impact, circumstances, etc.
buffers *n* ▷ buffer
buffet¹ [boof-ay, buff-ay] *n* (*pl* **-s**) counter where drinks and snacks are served
buffet² [buff-it] *v* (**-s, -feting, -feted**) knock against or about
buffeted *v* ▷ buffet²
buffeting *v* ▷ buffet²
buffets *n* ▷ buffet¹ ▶ *v* ▷ buffet²
buffing *v* ▷ buff¹
buffoon *n* (*pl* **-s**) clown or fool > **buffoonery** *n* (*pl* **-ries**)
buffooneries *n* ▷ buffoon
buffoonery *n* ▷ buffoon
buffoons *n* ▷ buffoon
buffs *v* ▷ buff¹ ▶ *n* ▷ buff²
bug *n* (*pl* **-s**) small insect ▶ *v* (**bugs, bugging, bugged**) (*Informal*) irritate (someone)
bugbear *n* (*pl* **-s**) thing that causes obsessive anxiety
bugbears *n* ▷ bugbear
bugged *v* ▷ bug
bugging *v* ▷ bug
bugle *n* (*pl* **-s**) instrument like a small trumpet > **bugler** *n* (*pl* **-s**)
bugler *n* ▷ bugle
buglers *n* ▷ bugle
bugles *n* ▷ bugle
bugong *n* ▷ bogong
bugongs *n* ▷ bogong
bugs *n*, *v* ▷ bug
build *v* (**builds, building, built**) make, construct, or form by joining parts or materials ▶ *n* (*pl* **-s**) shape of the body > **builder** *n* (*pl* **-s**)
builder *n* ▷ build
builders *n* ▷ build
building *v* ▷ build ▶ *n* (*pl* **-s**) structure with walls and a roof
buildings *n* ▷ building

builds *v*, *n* ▷ build
built *v* ▷ build
bulb *n* (*pl* **-s**) onion-shaped root which grows into a flower or plant
bulbous *adj* round and fat
bulbs *n* ▷ bulb
bulge *n* (*pl* **-s**) swelling on a normally flat surface ▶ *v* (**bulges, bulging, bulged**) swell outwards > **bulging** *adj*
bulged *v* ▷ bulge
bulges *n*, *v* ▷ bulge
bulging *v*, *adj* ▷ bulge
bulimia *n* (*pl* **-s**) disorder characterized by compulsive overeating followed by vomiting > **bulimic** *adj*, *n* (*pl* **-s**)
bulimias *n* ▷ bulimia
bulimic *adj*, *n* ▷ bulimia
bulimics *n* ▷ bulimia
bulk *n* (*pl* **-s**) size or volume, esp. when great > **bulky** *adj* (**-ier, -iest**)
bulkhead *n* (*pl* **-s**) partition in a ship or aeroplane
bulkheads *n* ▷ bulkhead
bulkier *adj* ▷ bulk
bulkiest *adj* ▷ bulk
bulks *n* ▷ bulk
bulky *adj* ▷ bulk
bull¹ *n* (*pl* **-s**) male of some animals, such as cattle, elephants, and whales
bull² *n* (*pl* **-s**) (*Informal*) complete nonsense
bull³ *n* (*pl* **-s**) papal decree
bulldog *n* (*pl* **-s**) thickset dog with a broad head and a muscular body
bulldogs *n* ▷ bulldog
bulldoze *v* ▷ bulldozer
bulldozed *v* ▷ bulldozer
bulldozer *n* (*pl* **-s**) powerful tractor for moving earth > **bulldoze** *v* (**-zes, -zing, -zed**)
bulldozers *n* ▷ bulldozer
bulldozes *v* ▷ bulldozer
bulldozing *v* ▷ bulldozer
bullet *n* (*pl* **-s**) small piece of metal fired from a gun
bulletin *n* (*pl* **-s**) short official report or announcement
bulletins *n* ▷ bulletin
bullets *n* ▷ bullet
bullfight *n* (*pl* **-s**) public show in which a matador kills a bull > **bullfighter** *n* (*pl* **-s**)
bullfighter *n* ▷ bullfight
bullfighters *n* ▷ bullfight
bullfights *n* ▷ bullfight
bullied *v* ▷ bully
bullies *n*, *v* ▷ bully

bullion n (pl -s) gold or silver in the form of bars
  bullions n ▷ **bullion**
bullock n (pl -s) castrated bull
  bullocks n ▷ **bullock**
  bulls n ▷ **bull**[1, 2, 3]
bullswool n (AUST DATED & NZ) (Slang) nonsense
bully n (pl -lies) person who hurts, persecutes,
  or intimidates a weaker person ▶ v (-lies,
  -lying, -lied) hurt, intimidate, or persecute (a
  weaker person)
  bullying v ▷ **bully**
bulrush n (pl -es) tall stiff reed
  bulrushes n ▷ **bulrush**
bulwark n (pl -s) wall used as a fortification
  bulwarks n ▷ **bulwark**
bum[1] n (pl -s) (Slang) buttocks or anus
bum[2] (Informal) n (pl -s) disreputable idler ▶ adj
  of poor quality
bumble v (-bles, -bling, -bled) speak, do, or
  move in a clumsy way > **bumbling** adj, n
bumblebee n (pl -s) large hairy bee
  bumblebees n ▷ **bumblebee**
  bumbled v ▷ **bumble**
  bumbles v ▷ **bumble**
  bumbling v, adj n ▷ **bumble**
bumf, bumph n (pl -s) (Informal) official
  documents or forms
  bumfs n ▷ **bumf**
bump v (-s, -ing, -ed) knock or strike with a jolt
  ▶ n (pl -s) dull thud from an impact or collision
  > **bumpy** adj (-ier, -iest)
  bumped v ▷ **bump**
bumper[1] n (pl -s) bar on the front and back of a
  vehicle to protect against damage
bumper[2] adj unusually large or abundant
  bumpers n ▷ **bumper**[1]
  bumph n ▷ **bumf**
  bumphs n ▷ **bumf**
  bumpier adj ▷ **bump**
  bumpiest adj ▷ **bump**
  bumping v ▷ **bump**
bumpkin n (pl -s) awkward simple country
  person
  bumpkins n ▷ **bumpkin**
  bumps v, n ▷ **bump**
bumptious adj offensively self-assertive
  > **bumptiously** adv > **bumptiousness** n
  bumptiously adj ▷ **bumptious**
  bumptiousness adj ▷ **bumptious**
  bumpy adj ▷ **bump**
  bums n ▷ **bum**[1, 2]
bun n (pl -s) small sweet bread roll or cake
bunch n (pl -es) number of things growing,
  fastened, or grouped together ▶ v (-es, -ing,
  -ed) group or be grouped together in a bunch

  bunched v ▷ **bunch**
  bunches n, v ▷ **bunch**
  bunching v ▷ **bunch**
bundle n (pl -s) number of things gathered
  loosely together ▶ v (-dles, -dling, -dled) cause
  to go roughly or unceremoniously
  bundled v ▷ **bundle**
  bundles n, v ▷ **bundle**
  bundling v ▷ **bundle**
bung n (pl -s) stopper for a cask etc. ▶ v (-s, -ing,
  -ed) (foll. by up) (Informal) close with a bung
bungalow n (pl -s) one-storey house
  bungalows n ▷ **bungalow**
  bunged v ▷ **bung**
  bunging v ▷ **bung**
bungle v (-gles, -gling, -gled) spoil through
  incompetence > **bungler** n (pl -s) > **bungling**
  adj, n
  bungled v ▷ **bungle**
  bungler n ▷ **bungle**
  bunglers n ▷ **bungle**
  bungles v ▷ **bungle**
  bungling v, adj n ▷ **bungle**
  bungs n, v ▷ **bung**
bunion n (pl -s) inflamed swelling on the big
  toe
  bunions n ▷ **bunion**
bunk[1] n (pl -s) narrow shelflike bed
bunk[2] n (pl -s) ▷ **bunkum**
bunk[3] (Slang) n (pl -s) (BRIT) make a hurried and
  secret departure ▶ v (-s, -ing, -ed) (BRIT, NZ & S
  AFR) be absent without permission
  bunked v ▷ **bunk**[3]
bunker n (pl -s) sand-filled hollow forming an
  obstacle on a golf course
  bunkers n ▷ **bunker**
  bunking v ▷ **bunk**[3]
  bunks n ▷ **bunk**[1, 2, 3] ▶ v ▷ **bunk**[3]
bunkum n (pl -s) nonsense
  bunkums n ▷ **bunkum**
  bunnies n ▷ **bunny**
bunny n (pl -nies) child's word for a rabbit
  buns n ▷ **bun**
bunting n (pl -s) decorative flags
  buntings n ▷ **bunting**
bunya n (pl -s) tall dome-shaped Australian
  coniferous tree
  bunyas n ▷ **bunya**
bunyip n (pl -s) (AUST) legendary monster said
  to live in swamps and lakes
  bunyips n ▷ **bunyip**
buoy n (pl -s) floating marker anchored in the
  sea ▶ v (-s, -ing, -ed) prevent from sinking
  buoyancy n ▷ **buoyant**
buoyant adj able to float > **buoyancy** n

buoyed v ▷ buoy
buoying v ▷ buoy
buoys n, v ▷ buoy
bur n (pl -s) ▷ burr¹
burble v (-bles, -bling, -bled) make a bubbling
sound
burbled v ▷ burble
burbles v ▷ burble
burbling v ▷ burble
burden¹ n (pl -s) heavy load ▶ v (-s, -ing, -ed) put
a burden on > **burdensome** adj
burden² n (pl -s) theme of a speech etc.
burdened v ▷ burden¹
burdening v ▷ burden¹
burdens v ▷ burden¹ ▶ n ▷ burden¹, ²
burdensome adj ▷ burden¹
bureau n (pl -reaus, -reaux) office that
provides a service
bureaucracies n ▷ bureaucracy
bureaucracy n (pl -cies) administrative system
based on complex rules and procedures
> **bureaucrat** n (pl -s) > **bureaucratic** adj
bureaucrat n ▷ bureaucracy
bureaucratic adj ▷ bureaucracy
bureaucrats n ▷ bureaucracy
bureaus n ▷ bureau
bureaux n ▷ bureau
burgeon v (-s, -ing, -ed) develop or grow
rapidly
burgeoned v ▷ burgeon
burgeoning v ▷ burgeon
burgeons v ▷ burgeon
burgh n (pl -s) Scottish borough
burghs n ▷ burgh
burglar n (pl -s) person who enters a building
to commit a crime, esp. theft > **burglary** n
(pl -glaries) > **burgle** v (burgles, burgling,
burgled)
burglaries n ▷ burglar
burglars n ▷ burglar
burglary n ▷ burglar
burgled v ▷ burglar
burgles v ▷ burglar
burgling v ▷ burglar
burgundy adj dark-purplish red
burial n (pl -s) burying of a dead body
burials n ▷ burial
buried v ▷ bury
buries v ▷ bury
burlesque n (pl -s) artistic work which
satirizes a subject by caricature
burlesques n ▷ burlesque
burlier adj ▷ burly
burliest adj ▷ burly
burly adj (-lier, -liest) (of a person) broad and

strong
burn¹ v (-s, -ing, -t or -ed) be or set on fire ▶ n
(pl burns) injury or mark caused by fire or
exposure to heat
burn² n (pl -s) (Scot) small stream
burned v ▷ burn¹
burning adj intense ▶ v ▷ burn¹
burnish v (-es, -ing, -ed) make smooth and
shiny by rubbing
burnished v ▷ burnish
burnishes v ▷ burnish
burnishing v ▷ burnish
burns n ▷ burn¹, ² ▶ v ▷ burn¹
burnt v ▷ burn¹
burp v (-s, -ing, -ed) ▶ n (pl -s) (Informal) belch
burped v ▷ burp
burping v ▷ burp
burps v, n ▷ burp
burr¹, **bur** n (pl -s) head of a plant with prickles
or hooks
burr² n (pl -s) soft trilling sound given to the
letter r in some dialects
burrawang n (pl -s) Australian plant with
fernlike leaves and an edible nut
burrawangs n ▷ burrawang
burrow n (pl -s) hole dug in the ground by a
rabbit etc. ▶ v (-s, -ing, -ed) dig holes in the
ground
burrowed v ▷ burrow
burrowing v ▷ burrow
burrows n, v ▷ burrow
burrs n ▷ burr¹, ²
burs n ▷ bur
bursar n (pl -s) treasurer of a school, college,
or university
bursaries n ▷ bursary
bursars n ▷ bursar
bursary n (pl -ries) scholarship
burst v (-s, -ing, burst) (cause to) break open or
apart noisily and suddenly ▶ n (pl -s) instance
of breaking open suddenly
bursting v ▷ burst
bursts v, n ▷ burst
bury v (buries, burying, buried) place in a grave
burying v ▷ bury
bus n (pl buses) large motor vehicle for carrying
passengers ▶ v (busses, bussing, bussed)
travel or transport by bus
busbies n ▷ busby
busby n (pl -bies) tall fur hat worn by some
soldiers
buses n ▷ bus
bush n (pl -es) dense woody plant, smaller
than a tree
bushbabies n ▷ bushbaby

bushbaby n (pl **-babies**) small African tree-living mammal with large eyes

bushel n (pl **-s**) obsolete unit of measure equal to 8 gallons (36.4 litres)

bushels n ▷ **bushel**

bushes n ▷ **bush**

bushier adj ▷ **bushy**

bushiest adj ▷ **bushy**

bushy adj (**-shier, -shiest**) (of hair) thick and shaggy

busied v ▷ **busy**

busier adj ▷ **busy**

busies v ▷ **busy**

busiest adj ▷ **busy**

business n (pl **-es**) purchase and sale of goods and services > **businessman** n (pl **-men**), **businesswoman** (pl **-women**)

businesses n ▷ **business**

businesslike adj efficient and methodical

businessman n ▷ **business**

businessmen n ▷ **business**

businesswoman n ▷ **business**

businesswomen n ▷ **business**

busk v (**-s, -ing, -ed**) act as a busker

busked v ▷ **busk**

busker n (pl **-s**) street entertainer

buskers n ▷ **busker**

busking v ▷ **busk**

busks v ▷ **busk**

bussed v ▷ **bus**

busses v ▷ **bus**

bussing v ▷ **bus**

bust[1] n (pl **-s**) woman's bosom

bust[2] (Informal) v (**busts, busting, bust** or **busted**) burst or break ▶ adj broken

bustard n (pl **-s**) bird with long strong legs, a heavy body, a long neck, and speckled plumage

bustards n ▷ **bustard**

busted v ▷ **bust**[2]

busting v ▷ **bust**[2]

bustle[1] v (**-les, -ling, -led**) hurry with a show of activity or energy ▶ n (pl **-s**) energetic and noisy activity > **bustling** adj

bustle[2] n (pl **-s**) cushion or framework formerly worn under the back of a woman's skirt to hold it out

bustled v ▷ **bustle**[1]

bustles v ▷ **bustle**[1] ▶ n ▷ **bustle**[1, 2]

bustling v, adj ▷ **bustle**[1]

busts n ▷ **bust**[1] ▶ v ▷ **bust**[2]

busy adj (**busier, busiest**) actively employed ▶ v (**busies, busying, busied**) keep (someone, esp. oneself) busy > **busily** adv

busybodies n ▷ **busybody**

busybody n (pl **-bodies**) meddlesome or nosy person

busying v ▷ **busy**

but conj contrary to expectation ▶ prep except ▶ adv only

butane n (pl **-s**) gas used for fuel

butanes n ▷ **butane**

butch adj (**-er, -est**) (Slang) markedly or aggressively masculine

butcher n (pl **-s**) person who slaughters animals or sells their meat ▶ v (**-s, -ing, -ed**) kill and prepare (animals) for meat > **butchery** n (pl **-ries**) adj ▷ **butch**

butcherbird n (pl **-s**) Australian magpie that impales its prey on thorns

butcherbirds n ▷ **butcherbird**

butchered v ▷ **butcher**

butcheries n ▷ **butcher**

butchering v ▷ **butcher**

butchers n, v ▷ **butcher**

butchery n ▷ **butcher**

butchest adj ▷ **butch**

butler n (pl **-s**) chief male servant

butlers n ▷ **butler**

butt[1] n (pl **-s**) thicker end of something

butt[2] n (pl **-s**) person or thing that is the target of ridicule

butt[3] v (**-s, -ing, -ed**) strike with the head or horns

butt[4] n (pl **-s**) large cask

butted v ▷ **butt**[3]

butter n (pl **-s**) edible fatty solid made by churning cream ▶ v (**-s, -ing, -ed**) put butter on > **buttery** adj

buttercup n (pl **-s**) small yellow flower

buttercups n ▷ **buttercup**

buttered v ▷ **butter**

butterfingers n (pl **-s**) (Informal) person who drops things by mistake

butterflies n ▷ **butterfly**

butterfly n (pl **-flies**) insect with brightly coloured wings

buttering v ▷ **butter**

buttermilk n (pl **-s**) sourish milk that remains after the butter has been separated from milk

buttermilks n ▷ **buttermilks**

butters n, v ▷ **butter**

butterscotch n (pl **-es**) kind of hard brittle toffee

butterscotches n ▷ **butterscotch**

buttery adj ▷ **butter**

butting v ▷ **butt**[3]

buttock n (pl **-s**) either of the two fleshy masses that form the human rump

buttocks n ▷ **buttock**

button *n* (*pl* -**s**) small disc or knob sewn to clothing, which can be passed through a slit in another piece of fabric to fasten them ▶ *v* (**-s, -ing, -ed**) fasten with buttons
buttoned *v* ▷ **button**
buttonhole *n* (*pl* -**s**) slit in a garment through which a button is passed ▶ *v* (**-holes, -holing, -holed**) detain (someone) in conversation
buttonholed *v* ▷ **buttonhole**
buttonholes *n*, *v* ▷ **buttonhole**
buttonholing *v* ▷ **buttonhole**
buttoning *v* ▷ **button**
buttons *n*, *v* ▷ **button**
buttress *n* (*pl* -**es**) structure to support a wall ▶ *v* (**-es, -ing, -ed**) support with, or as if with, a buttress
buttressed *v* ▷ **buttress**
buttresses *n*, *v* ▷ **buttress**
buttressing *v* ▷ **buttress**
butts *n* ▷ **butt**[1, 2, 4] ▶ *v* ▷ **butt**[3]
buxom *adj* (**-er, -est**) (of a woman) healthily plump and full-bosomed
buxomer *adj* ▷ **buxom**
buxomest *adj* ▷ **buxom**
buy *v* (**-s, -ing, bought**) acquire by paying money for ▶ *n* (*pl* -**s**) thing acquired through payment
buyer *n* (*pl* -**s**) customer
buyers *n* ▷ **buyer**
buying *v* ▷ **buy**
buys *v*, *n* ▷ **buy**
buzz *n* (*pl* -**es**) rapidly vibrating humming sound (*Informal*) ▶ *v* (**-es, -ing, -ed**) make a humming sound > **buzzer** *n* (*pl* -**s**)
buzzard *n* (*pl* -**s**) bird of prey of the hawk family

buzzards *n* ▷ **buzzard**
buzzed *v* ▷ **buzz**
buzzer *n* ▷ **buzz**
buzzers *n* ▷ **buzz**
buzzes *n*, *v* ▷ **buzz**
buzzing *v* ▷ **buzz**
by *prep* indicating the doer of an action, nearness, movement past, time before or during which, etc. ▶ *adv* near
bye *interj* (*Informal*) goodbye
byelaw *n* ▷ **bylaw**
byelaws *n* ▷ **bylaw**
bygone *adj* past or former
bylaw, byelaw *n* (*pl* -**s**) rule made by a local authority
bylaws *n* ▷ **bylaw**
bypass *n* (*pl* -**es**) main road built to avoid a city ▶ *v* (**-es, -ing, -ed**) go round or avoid
bypassed *v* ▷ **bypass**
bypasses *n*, *v* ▷ **bypass**
bypassing *v* ▷ **bypass**
byre *n* (*pl* -**s**) (BRIT) shelter for cows
byres *n* ▷ **byre**
bystander *n* (*pl* -**s**) person present but not involved
bystanders *n* ▷ **bystander**
byte *n* (*pl* -**s**) (COMPUTERS) group of bits processed as one unit of data
bytes *n* ▷ **byte**
byway *n* (*pl* -**s**) minor road
byways *n* ▷ **byway**
byword *n* (*pl* -**s**) person or thing regarded as a perfect example of something
bywords *n* ▷ **byword**

Cc

C can be a tricky letter to use, especially as it only forms a single two-letter word **ch**. But if you remember this, you won't waste time racking your brains for two-letter words. There are, however, plenty of good three-letter words beginning with C. **Cox** scores 12 points, while **caw**, **cow** and **coy** are each worth 8. It's also a good idea to remember the short words starting with C that don't contain any vowels: **cly** and **cwm** as well as **ch**.

cab n (pl -**s**) taxi

cabal [kab-**bal**] n (pl -**s**) small group of political plotters
cabals n ▷ **cabal**

cabaret [kab-a-ray] n (pl -**s**) dancing and singing show in a nightclub
cabarets n ▷ **cabaret**

cabbage n (pl -**s**) vegetable with a large head of green leaves
cabbages n ▷ **cabbage**

cabbie, cabby n (pl -**bies**) (*Informal*) taxi driver
cabbies n ▷ **cabbie**
cabby n ▷ **cabbie**

caber n (pl -**s**) tree trunk tossed in competition at Highland games
cabers n ▷ **caber**

cabin n (pl -**s**) compartment in a ship or aircraft

cabinet n (pl -**s**) piece of furniture with drawers or shelves

cabinetmaker n (pl -**s**) person who makes fine furniture
cabinetmakers n ▷ **cabinetmaker**
cabinets n ▷ **cabinet**
cabins n ▷ **cabin**

cable n (pl -**s**) strong thick rope ▶ v (-**les**, -**ling**, -**led**) send (someone) a message by cable
cabled v ▷ **cable**
cables n, v ▷ **cable**
cabling v ▷ **cable**

caboodle n (*Informal*) the whole lot

cabriolet [kab-ree-oh-**lay**] n (pl -**s**) small horse-drawn carriage with a folding hood
cabriolets n ▷ **cabriolet**
cabs n ▷ **cab**

cacao [kak-**kah**-oh] n (pl -**s**) tropical tree with seed pods from which chocolate and cocoa are made
cacaos n ▷ **cacao**

cache [kash] n (pl -**s**) hidden store of weapons or treasure
caches n ▷ **cache**

cachet [**kash**-shay] n (pl -**s**) prestige, distinction
cachets n ▷ **cachet**

cackle v (-**les**, -**ling**, -**led**) laugh shrilly ▶ n (pl -**s**) cackling noise
cackled v ▷ **cackle**
cackles v, n ▷ **cackle**
cackling v ▷ **cackle**
cacophonies n ▷ **cacophony**
cacophonous adj ▷ **cacophony**

cacophony [kak-**koff**-on-ee] n (pl -**phonies**) harsh discordant sound > **cacophonous** adj
cacti n ▷ **cactus**

cactus n (pl -**tuses**, -**ti**) fleshy desert plant with spines but no leaves
cactuses n ▷ **cactus**

cad n (pl -**s**) (*Old-fashioned*) dishonourable man > **caddish** adj

cadaver [kad-**dav**-ver] n (pl -**s**) corpse

cadaverous adj pale, thin, and haggard
cadavers n ▷ **cadaver**

caddie, caddy n (pl -**dies**) person who carries a golfer's clubs ▶ v (-**dies**, -**dying**, -**died**) act as a caddie
caddies n ▷ **caddie, caddy** ▶ v ▷ **caddie**
caddish adj ▷ **cad**

caddy n (pl -**dies**) small container for tea ▷ **caddie**

cadence [**kade**-enss] n (pl -**s**) rise and fall in the pitch of the voice
cadences n ▷ **cadence**

cadenza n (pl -**s**) complex solo passage in a piece of music
cadenzas n ▷ **cadenza**

cadet n (pl -**s**) young person training for the armed forces or police

cadets n ▷ cadet
cadge v (**cadges, cadging, cadged**) (*Informal*) get (something) by taking advantage of someone's generosity > **cadger** n (pl -s)
cadged v ▷ cadge
cadger n ▷ cadge
cadgers n ▷ cadge
cadges v ▷ cadge
cadging v ▷ cadge
cadmium n (pl -s) (CHEM) bluish-white metallic element used in alloys
cadmiums n ▷ cadmium
cadre [kah-der] n (pl -s) small group of people selected and trained to form the core of a political organization or military unit
cadres n ▷ cadre
cads n ▷ cad
caeca n ▷ caecum
caecum [seek-um] n (pl -ca) [-ka] pouch at the beginning of the large intestine
caesium n (pl -s) (CHEM) silvery-white metallic element used in photocells
caesiums n ▷ caesium
café n (pl -s) small or inexpensive restaurant serving light refreshments
cafés n ▷ café
cafeteria n (pl -s) self-service restaurant
cafeterias n ▷ cafeteria
caffeine n (pl -s) stimulant found in tea and coffee
caffeines n ▷ caffeine
caftan n (pl -s) ▷ kaftan
caftans n ▷ caftan
cage n (pl -s) enclosure of bars or wires, for keeping animals or birds
caged adj kept in a cage
cages n ▷ cage
cagey adj (**cagier, cagiest**) (*Informal*) reluctant to go into details
cagier adj ▷ cagey
cagiest adj ▷ cagey
cagoule n (pl -s) (BRIT) lightweight hooded waterproof jacket
cagoules n ▷ cagoule
cahoots pl n (*Informal*) conspiring together
cairn n (pl -s) mound of stones erected as a memorial or marker
cairns n ▷ cairn
cajole v (-les, -ling, -led) persuade by flattery > **cajolery** n
cajoled v ▷ cajole
cajolery n ▷ cajole
cajoles v ▷ cajole
cajoling v ▷ cajole
cake n (pl -s) sweet food baked from a mixture of flour, eggs, etc. ▶ v (**cakes, caking, caked**) form into a hardened mass or crust
caked v ▷ cake
cakes n, v ▷ cake
caking v ▷ cake
calamine n (pl -s) pink powder consisting chiefly of zinc oxide, used in skin lotions and ointments
calamines n ▷ calamine
calamities n ▷ calamity
calamitous adj ▷ calamity
calamity n (pl -ties) disaster > **calamitous** adj
calcification v ▷ calcify
calcified v ▷ calcify
calcifies v ▷ calcify
calcify v (-fies, -fying, -fied) harden by the depositing of calcium salts > **calcification** n
calcifying v ▷ calcify
calcium n (pl -s) (CHEM) silvery-white metallic element found in bones, teeth, limestone, and chalk
calciums n ▷ calcium
calculable adj ▷ calculate
calculate v (-lates, -lating, -lated) solve or find out by a mathematical procedure or by reasoning > **calculable** adj > **calculation** n (pl -s)
calculated v ▷ calculate
calculates v ▷ calculate
calculating adj selfishly scheming ▶ v ▷ calculate
calculation n ▷ calculate
calculations n ▷ calculate
calculator n (pl -s) small electronic device for making calculations
calculators n ▷ calculator
calculus n (pl -es) branch of mathematics dealing with infinitesimal changes to a variable number or quantity
calculuses n ▷ calculus
calendar n (pl -s) chart showing a year divided up into months, weeks, and days
calendars n ▷ calendar
calendula n (pl -s) marigold
calendulas n ▷ calendula
calf¹ n (pl calves) young cow, bull, elephant, whale, or seal
calf² n (pl calves) back of the leg between the ankle and knee
calibrate v (-brates, -brating, -brated) mark the scale or check the accuracy of (a measuring instrument) > **calibration** n (pl -s)
calibrated v ▷ calibrate
calibrates v ▷ calibrate
calibrating v ▷ calibrate

calibration n ▷ **calibrate**
calibrations n ▷ **calibrate**
calibre n (pl -**s**) person's ability or worth
calibres n ▷ **calibre**
calico n (pl -**coes**) white cotton fabric
calicoes n ▷ **calico**
caliph n (pl -**s**) (HIST) Muslim ruler
caliphs n ▷ **caliph**
call v (-**s, -ing, -ed**) name ▶ n (pl -**s**) cry, shout
> **caller** n (pl -**s**)
called v ▷ **call**
caller n ▷ **call**
callers n ▷ **call**
calligrapher n ▷ **calligraphy**
calligraphers n ▷ **calligraphy**
calligraphies n ▷ **calligraphy**
calligraphy n (pl -**phies**) (art of) beautiful
handwriting > **calligrapher** n (pl -**s**)
calling n (pl -**s**) vocation, profession ▶ v ▷ **call**
callings n ▷ **calling**
calliper n (pl -**s**) metal splint for supporting
the leg
callipers n ▷ **calliper**
callisthenics pl n light keep-fit exercises
callous adj showing no concern for other
people's feelings > **callously** adv > **callousness**
n
calloused adj (of skin) thickened and hardened
callously adv ▷ **callous**
callousness adv ▷ **callous**
callow adj (-**er, -est**) young and inexperienced
> **callowness** n (pl -**es**)
callower adj ▷ **callow**
callowest adj ▷ **callow**
callowness adv ▷ **callow**
callownesses adv ▷ **callow**
calls v, n ▷ **call**
callus n (pl -**es**) area of thick hardened skin
calluses n ▷ **callus**
calm adj (-**er, -est**) not agitated or excited ▶ n
(pl -**s**) peaceful state ▶ v (-**s, -ing, -ed**) (often
foll. by **down**) make or become calm > **calmly**
adv > **calmness** n (pl -**es**)
calmed v ▷ **calm**
calmer adj ▷ **calm**
calmest adj ▷ **calm**
calming v ▷ **calm**
calmly adv ▷ **calm**
calmness adv ▷ **calm**
calmnesses adv ▷ **calm**
calms n, v ▷ **calm**
calorie n (pl -**s**) unit of measurement for the
energy value of food
calories n ▷ **calorie**
calorific adj of calories or heat

calumnies n ▷ **calumny**
calumny n (pl -**nies**) false or malicious
statement
calve v (**calves, calving, calved**) give birth
to a calf
calved v ▷ **calve**
calves v ▷ **calve** ▶ n ▷ **calf**[1, 2]
calving v ▷ **calve**
calyces n ▷ **calyx**
calypso n (pl -**s**) West Indian song with
improvised topical lyrics
calypsos n ▷ **calypso**
calyx n (pl **calyxes, calyces**) outer leaves that
protect a flower bud
calyxes n ▷ **calyx**
cam n (pl -**s**) device that converts a circular
motion to a to-and-fro motion
camaraderie n (pl -**s**) comradeship
camaraderies n ▷ **camaraderie**
camber n (pl -**s**) slight upward curve to the
centre of a surface
cambers n ▷ **camber**
cambric n (pl -**s**) fine white linen fabric
cambrics n ▷ **cambric**
camcorder n (pl -**s**) combined portable video
camera and recorder
camcorders n ▷ **camcorder**
came v ▷ **come**
camel n (pl -**s**) humped mammal that can
survive long periods without food or water in
desert regions
camellia [kam-**meal**-ya] n (pl -**s**) evergreen
ornamental shrub with white, pink, or red
flowers
camellias n ▷ **camellia**
camels n ▷ **camel**
cameo n (pl -**s**) brooch or ring with a profile
head carved in relief
cameos n ▷ **cameo**
camera n (pl -**s**) apparatus used for taking
photographs or pictures for television or
cinema
cameraman n (pl -**men**) man who operates a
camera for television or cinema
cameramen n ▷ **cameraman**
cameras n ▷ **camera**
camiknickers pl n (BRIT) woman's
undergarment consisting of knickers
attached to a camisole
camisole n (pl -**s**) woman's bodice-like
garment
camisoles n ▷ **camisole**
camomile n (pl -**s**) aromatic plant, used to
make herbal tea
camomiles n ▷ **camomile**

camouflage [**kam**-moo-flahzh] *n* (*pl* -**s**) use of natural surroundings or artificial aids to conceal or disguise something ▶ *v* (-**lages, -flaging, -flaged**) conceal by camouflage
  camouflaged *v* ▷ **camouflage**
  camouflages *n, v* ▷ **camouflage**
  camouflaging *v* ▷ **camouflage**
camp¹ *n* (*pl* -**s**) (place for) temporary lodgings consisting of tents, huts, or cabins ▶ *v* (-**s, -ing, -ed**) stay in a camp > **camper** *n* (*pl* -**s**)
camp² *adj* (-**er, -est**) (*Informal*) effeminate or homosexual
campaign *n* (*pl* -**s**) series of coordinated activities designed to achieve a goal ▶ *v* (-**s, -ing, -ed**) take part in a campaign
  campaigned *v* ▷ **campaign**
  campaigning *v* ▷ **campaign**
  campaigns *n, v* ▷ **campaign**
  campanologies *n* ▷ **campanology**
campanology *n* (*pl* -**gies**) art of ringing bells
campanula *n* (*pl* -**s**) plant with blue or white bell-shaped flowers
  campanulas *n* ▷ **campanula**
  camped *v* ▷ **camp¹**
  camper *n* ▷ **camp¹** ▶ *adj* ▷ **camp²**
  campers *n* ▷ **camp¹**
  campest *adj* ▷ **camp²**
camphor *n* (*pl* -**s**) aromatic crystalline substance used medicinally and in mothballs
  camphors *n* ▷ **camphor**
  camping *v* ▷ **camp¹**
campion *n* (*pl* -**s**) red, pink, or white wild flower
  campions *n* ▷ **campion**
  camps *n, v* ▷ **camp¹**
campus *n* (*pl* -**es**) grounds of a university or college
  campuses *n* ▷ **campus**
  cams *n* ▷ **cam**
camshaft *n* (*pl* -**s**) part of an engine consisting of a rod to which cams are fixed
  camshafts *n* ▷ **camshaft**
can¹ *v* (*past* **could**) be able to
can² *n* (*pl* -**s**) metal container for food or liquids ▶ *v* (**cans, canning, canned**) put (something) into a can
canal *n* (*pl* -**s**) artificial waterway
  canals *n* ▷ **canal**
canapé [**kan**-nap-pay] *n* (*pl* -**s**) small piece of bread or toast with a savoury topping
  canapés *n* ▷ **canapé**
  canaries *n* ▷ **canary**
canary *n* (*pl* -**ries**) small yellow songbird often kept as a pet
canasta *n* (*pl* -**s**) card game like rummy, played with two packs
  canastas *n* ▷ **canasta**
cancan *n* (*pl* -**s**) lively high-kicking dance performed by a female group
  cancans *n* ▷ **cancan**
cancel *v* (-**cels, -celling, -celled**) stop (something that has been arranged) from taking place > **cancellation** *n* (*pl* -**s**)
  cancellation *n* ▷ **cancel**
  cancellations *n* ▷ **cancel**
  cancelled *v* ▷ **cancel**
  cancelling *v* ▷ **cancel**
  cancels *v* ▷ **cancel**
cancer *n* (*pl* -**s**) serious disease resulting from a malignant growth or tumour > **cancerous** *adj*
  cancerous *adj* ▷ **cancer**
  cancers *n* ▷ **cancer**
candela [kan-**dee**-la] *n* (*pl* -**s**) unit of luminous intensity
  candelabra *n* ▷ **candelabrum**
candelabrum *n* (*pl* -**bra**) large branched candle holder
  candelas *n* ▷ **candela**
candid *adj* (-**er, -est**) honest and straightforward > **candidly** *adv* > **candidness** *n* (*pl* -**es**)
  candidacies *n* ▷ **candidate**
  candidacy *n* ▷ **candidate**
candidate *n* (*pl* -**s**) person seeking a job or position > **candidacy** (*pl* -**acies**), **candidature** *n* (*pl* -**s**)
  candidates *n* ▷ **candidate**
  candidature *n* ▷ **candidate**
  candidatures *n* ▷ **candidate**
  candider *adj* ▷ **candid**
  candidest *adj* ▷ **candid**
  candidly *adv* ▷ **candid**
  candidness *n* ▷ **candid**
  candidnesses *n* ▷ **candid**
candied *adj* coated with sugar
  candies *n* ▷ **candy**
candle *n* (*pl* -**s**) stick of wax enclosing a wick, which is burned to produce light
  candles *n* ▷ **candle**
candlestick *n* (*pl* -**s**) holder for a candle
  candlesticks *n* ▷ **candlestick**
candlewick *n* (*pl* -**s**) cotton fabric with a tufted surface
  candlewicks *n* ▷ **candlewick**
candour *n* (*pl* -**s**) honesty and straightforwardness
  candours *n* ▷ **candour**
candy *n* (*pl* -**dies**) (*us*) sweet or sweets
candyfloss *n* (*pl* -**es**) light fluffy mass of spun sugar on a stick

candyflosses *n* ▷ **candyfloss**

cane *n* (*pl* -**s**) stem of the bamboo or similar plant ▶ *v* (**canes, caning, caned**) beat with a cane

caned *v* ▷ **cane**

canes *n*, *v* ▷ **cane**

canine *adj* of or like a dog ▶ *n* (*pl* -**s**) sharp pointed tooth between the incisors and the molars

canines *n* ▷ **canine**

caning *v* ▷ **cane**

canister *n* (*pl* -**s**) metal container

canisters *n* ▷ **canister**

canker *n* (*pl* -**s**) ulceration, ulcerous disease

cankers *n* ▷ **canker**

cannabis *n* (*pl* -**es**) Asian plant with tough fibres

cannabises *n* ▷ **cannabis**

canned *adj* preserved in a can ▶ *v* ▷ **can²**

cannelloni *pl n* tubular pieces of pasta filled with meat etc.

canneries *n* ▷ **cannery**

cannery *n* (*pl* -**ries**) factory where food is canned

cannibal *n* (*pl* -**s**) person who eats human flesh > **cannibalism** *n*

cannibalize *v* (-**lizes, -lizing, -lized**) use parts from (one machine) to repair another

cannibalized *v* ▷ **cannibalize**

cannibalizes *v* ▷ **cannibalize**

cannibalizing *v* ▷ **cannibalize**

cannibals *n* ▷ **cannibal**

cannier *adj* ▷ **canny**

canniest *adj* ▷ **canny**

cannily *adv* ▷ **canny**

canning *v* ▷ **can²**

cannon *n* (*pl* -**s**) large gun on wheels

cannonade *n* (*pl* -**s**) continuous heavy gunfire

cannonades *n* ▷ **cannonade**

cannonball *n* (*pl* -**s**) heavy metal ball fired from a cannon

cannonballs *n* ▷ **cannonball**

cannons *n* ▷ **cannon**

cannot *v* can not

canny *adj* (-**nier, -niest**) shrewd, cautious > **cannily** *adv*

canoe *n* (*pl* -**s**) light narrow open boat propelled by a paddle or paddles > **canoeist** *n* (*pl* -**s**)

canoeing *n* sport of rowing in a canoe

canoeist *n* ▷ **canoe**

canoeists *n* ▷ **canoe**

canoes *n* ▷ **canoe**

canon¹ *n* (*pl* -**s**) priest serving in a cathedral

canon² *n* (*pl* -**s**) Church decree regulating morals or religious practices > **canonical** *adj*

canonical *adj* ▷ **canon²**

canonization *n* ▷ **canonize**

canonizations *n* ▷ **canonize**

canonize *v* (-**izes, -izing, -ized**) declare (a person) officially to be a saint > **canonization** *n* (*pl* -**s**)

canonized *v* ▷ **canonize**

canonizes *v* ▷ **canonize**

canonizing *v* ▷ **canonize**

canons *n* ▷ **canon¹, ²**

canoodle *v* (-**les, -ling, -led**) (*Slang*) kiss and cuddle

canoodled *v* ▷ **canoodle**

canoodles *v* ▷ **canoodle**

canoodling *v* ▷ **canoodle**

canopied *adj* covered with a canopy

canopies *n* ▷ **canopy**

canopy *n* (*pl* -**pies**) covering above a bed, door, etc

cans *n*, *v* ▷ **can²**

cant¹ *n* (*pl* -**s**) insincere talk

cant² *n* (*pl* -**s**) tilted position ▶ *v* (-**s, -ing, -ed**) tilt, overturn

cantaloupe, cantaloup *n* (*pl* -**s**) kind of melon with sweet orange flesh

cantaloupes *n* ▷ **cantaloupe**

cantaloups *n* ▷ **cantaloupe**

cantankerous *adj* quarrelsome, bad-tempered

cantata *n* (*pl* -**s**) musical work consisting of arias, duets, and choruses

cantatas *n* ▷ **cantata**

canted *v* ▷ **cant²**

canteen *n* (*pl* -**s**) restaurant attached to a workplace or school

canteens *n* ▷ **canteen**

canter *n* (*pl* -**s**) horse's gait between a trot and a gallop ▶ *v* (-**s, -ing, -ed**) move at a canter

cantered *v* ▷ **canter**

cantering *v* ▷ **canter**

canters *n*, *v* ▷ **canter**

canticle *n* (*pl* -**s**) short hymn with words from the Bible

canticles *n* ▷ **canticle**

cantilever *n* (*pl* -**s**) beam or girder fixed at one end only

cantilevers *n* ▷ **cantilever**

canting *v* ▷ **cant²**

canto *n* (*pl* -**s**) main division of a long poem

canton *n* (*pl* -**s**) political division of a country, esp. Switzerland

cantons *n* ▷ **canton**

cantor *n* (*pl* -**s**) man employed to lead services in a synagogue

cantors n ▷ **cantor**
cantos n ▷ **canto**
cants n ▷ **cant¹, ²** ▶ v ▷ **cant²**
canvas n (pl **-es**) heavy coarse cloth used for sails and tents, and for oil painting
canvases n ▷ **canvas**
canvass v (**-es, -ing, -ed**) try to get votes or support (from) ▶ n (pl **-es**) canvassing
canvassed v ▷ **canvass**
canvasses v, n ▷ **canvass**
canvassing v ▷ **canvass**
canyon n (pl **-s**) deep narrow valley
canyons n ▷ **canyon**
cap n (pl **-s**) soft close-fitting covering for the head ▶ v (**caps, capping, capped**) cover or top with something
capabilities n ▷ **capable**
capability n ▷ **capable**
capable adj (foll. by **of**) having the ability (for) > **capably** adv > **capability** n (pl **-ties**)
capably adv ▷ **capable**
capacious adj roomy
capacitance n (pl **-s**) (measure of) the ability of a system to store electrical charge
capacitances n ▷ **capacit**
capacities n ▷ **capacity**
capacitor n (pl **-s**) device for storing electrical charge
capacitors n ▷ **capacitor**
capacity n (pl **-ties**) ability to contain, absorb, or hold
caparisoned adj magnificently decorated
cape¹ n (pl **-s**) short cloak
cape² n (pl **-s**) large piece of land that juts out into the sea
caper n (pl **-s**) high-spirited prank ▶ v (**-s, -ing, -ed**) skip about
capercaillie, capercailzie [kap-per-**kale**-yee] n (pl **-s**) large black European grouse
capercaillies n ▷ **capercaillie**
capercailzie n ▷ **capercaillie**
capercailzies n ▷ **capercaillie**
capered v ▷ **caper**
capering v ▷ **caper**
capers pl n pickled flower buds of a Mediterranean shrub used in sauces ▶ n ▷ **caper** ▶ v ▷ **caper**
capes n ▷ **cape¹, ²**
capillaries n ▷ **capillary**
capillary n (pl **-laries**) very fine blood vessel
capital¹ n (pl **-s**) chief city of a country ▶ adj involving or punishable by death
capital² n (pl **-s**) top part of a pillar
capitalism n (pl **-s**) economic system based on the private ownership of industry

capitalisms n ▷ **capitalism**
capitalist adj of capitalists or capitalism ▶ n (pl **-s**) supporter of capitalism > **capitalistic** adj
capitalistic adj ▷ **capitalist**
capitalists n ▷ **capitalist**
capitalize v (**-lizes, -lizing, -lized**) write or print (words) in capitals
capitalized v ▷ **capitalize**
capitalizes v ▷ **capitalize**
capitalizing v ▷ **capitalize**
capitals n ▷ **capital¹, ²**
capitation n (pl **-s**) tax of a fixed amount per person
capitations n ▷ **capitation**
capitulate v (**-lates, -lating, -lated**) surrender on agreed terms > **capitulation** n (pl **-s**)
capitulated v ▷ **capitulate**
capitulates v ▷ **capitulate**
capitulating v ▷ **capitulate**
capitulation n ▷ **capitulate**
capitulations n ▷ **capitulate**
capon n (pl **-s**) castrated cock fowl fattened for eating
capons n ▷ **capon**
capped v ▷ **cap**
capping v ▷ **cap**
cappuccino [kap-poo-**cheen**-oh] n (pl **-s**) coffee with steamed milk, sprinkled with powdered chocolate
cappuccinos n ▷ **cappuccino**
caprice [kap-**reess**] n (pl **-s**) sudden change of attitude
caprices n ▷ **caprice**
capricious adj tending to have sudden changes of attitude > **capriciously** adv
capriciously adv ▷ **capricious**
caps n, v ▷ **cap**
capsicum n (pl **-s**) kind of pepper used as a vegetable or as a spice
capsicums n ▷ **capsicum**
capsize v (**-sizes, -sizing, -sized**) (of a boat) overturn accidentally
capsized v ▷ **capsize**
capsizes v ▷ **capsize**
capsizing v ▷ **capsize**
capstan n (pl **-s**) rotating cylinder round which a ship's rope is wound
capstans n ▷ **capstan**
capsule n (pl **-s**) soluble gelatine case containing a dose of medicine
capsules n ▷ **capsule**
captain n (pl **-s**) commander of a ship or civil aircraft ▶ v (**-s, -ing, -ed**) be captain of > **captaincy** n (pl **-cies**)
captaincies n ▷ **captain**

captaincy n ▷ captain
captained v ▷ captain
captaining v ▷ captain
captains n, v ▷ captain
caption n (pl -s) title or explanation accompanying an illustration ▶ v (-s, -ing, -ed) provide with a caption
captioned v ▷ caption
captioning v ▷ caption
captions n, v ▷ caption
captious adj tending to make trivial criticisms > **captiously** adv > **captiousness** n
captiously adv ▷ captious
captiousness n ▷ captious
captivate v (-ates, -ating, -ated) attract and hold the attention of > **captivating** adj
captivated v ▷ captivate
captivates v ▷ captivate
captivating adj, v ▷ captivate
captive n (pl -s) person kept in confinement ▶ adj kept in confinement > **captivity** n
captives n ▷ captive
captivity n ▷ captive
captor n (pl -s) person who captures a person or animal
captors n ▷ captor
capture v (-tures, -turing, -tured) take by force ▶ n (pl -s) capturing
captured v ▷ capture
captures v, n ▷ capture
capturing v ▷ capture
car n (pl -s) motor vehicle designed to carry a small number of people
carafe [kar-raff] n (pl -s) glass bottle for serving water or wine
carafes n ▷ carafe
caramel n (pl -s) chewy sweet made from sugar and milk
caramelize v (-izes, -izing, -ized) turn into caramel
caramelized v ▷ caramelize
caramelizes v ▷ caramelize
caramelizing v ▷ caramelize
caramels n ▷ caramel
carapace n (pl -s) hard upper shell of tortoises and crustaceans
carapaces n ▷ carapace
carat n (pl -s) unit of weight of precious stones
carats n ▷ carat
caravan n (pl -s) large enclosed vehicle for living in, designed to be towed by a car or horse
caravans n ▷ caravan
caraway n (pl -s) plant whose seeds are used as a spice

caraways n ▷ caraway
carbide n (pl -s) compound of carbon with a metal
carbides n ▷ carbide
carbine n (pl -s) light automatic rifle
carbines n ▷ carbine
carbohydrate n (pl -s) any of a large group of energy-producing compounds in food, such as sugars and starches
carbohydrates n ▷ carbohydrate
carbon n (pl -s) nonmetallic element occurring as charcoal, graphite, and diamond, found in all organic matter
carbonate n (pl -s) salt or ester of carbonic acid
carbonated adj (of a drink) containing carbon dioxide
carbonates n ▷ carbonate
carbonize v (-izes, -izing, -ized) turn into carbon as a result of heating
carbonized v ▷ carbonize
carbonizes v ▷ carbonize
carbonizing v ▷ carbonize
carbons n ▷ carbon
carbuncle n (pl -s) inflamed boil
carbuncles n ▷ carbuncle
carburettor n (pl -s) device which mixes petrol and air in an internal-combustion engine
carburettors n ▷ carburettor
carcase n ▷ carcass
carcases n ▷ carcass
carcass, carcase n (pl -es, -es) dead body of an animal
carcasses n ▷ carcass
carcinogen n (pl -s) substance that produces cancer > **carcinogenic** adj
carcinogenic adj ▷ carcinogen
carcinogens n ▷ carcinogen
carcinoma n (pl -s) malignant tumour
carcinomas n ▷ carcinoma
card n (pl -s) piece of thick stiff paper or cardboard used for identification, reference, or sending greetings or messages ▶ pl any card game, or card games in general
cardboard n (pl -s) thin stiff board made from paper pulp
cardboards n ▷ cardboard
cardiac adj of the heart
cardigan n (pl -s) knitted jacket
cardigans n ▷ cardigan
cardinal n (pl -s) any of the high-ranking clergymen of the RC Church who elect the Pope and act as his counsellors ▶ adj fundamentally important
cardinals n ▷ cardinal
cardiogram n (pl -s) electrocardiogram

cardiograms *n* ▷ **cardiogram**
cardiograph *n* (*pl* **-s**) electrocardiograph
cardiographs *n* ▷ **cardiograph**
cardiologist *n* ▷ **cardiology**
cardiologists *n* ▷ **cardiology**
cardiology *n* study of the heart and its
diseases > **cardiologist** *n* (*pl* **-s**)
cardiovascular *adj* of the heart and the blood
vessels
cards *n* ▷ **card**
cardsharp *n* (*pl* **-s**) professional card player
who cheats
cardsharps *n* ▷ **cardsharp**
care *v* (**cares, caring, cared**) be concerned ▶ *n*
(*pl* **-s**) careful attention, caution > **careful**
adj (**-ller, -llest**) > **carefully** *adv* > **carefulness**
n (*pl* **-es**) > **careless** *adj* > **carelessly** *adv*
> **carelessness** *n*
cared *v* ▷ **care**
careen *v* (**-s, -ing, -ed**) tilt over to one side
careened *v* ▷ **careen**
careening *v* ▷ **careen**
careens *v* ▷ **careen**
career *n* (*pl* **-s**) series of jobs in a profession or
occupation that a person has through their
life ▶ *v* (**-s, -ing, -ed**) rush in an uncontrolled
way
careered *v* ▷ **career**
careering *v* ▷ **career**
careerist *n* (*pl* **-s**) person who seeks
advancement by any possible means
careerists *n* ▷ **careerist**
careers *n, v* ▷ **career**
carefree *adj* without worry or responsibility
careful *adj* ▷ **care**
carefuller *adj* ▷ **care**
carefullest *adj* ▷ **care**
carefully *adv* ▷ **care**
carefulness *n* ▷ **care**
carefulnesses *n* ▷ **care**
careless *adj* ▷ **care**
carelessly *adv* ▷ **care**
carelessness *adv* ▷ **care**
cares *v, n* ▷ **care**
caress *n* (*pl* **-es**) gentle affectionate touch or
embrace ▶ *v* (**-es, -ing, -ed**) touch gently and
affectionately
caressed *v* ▷ **caress**
caresses *n, v* ▷ **caress**
caressing *v* ▷ **caress**
caret [kar-rett] *n* (*pl* **-s**) symbol (ʌ) indicating
a place in written or printed matter where
something is to be inserted
caretaker *n* (*pl* **-s**) person employed to look
after a place

caretakers *n* ▷ **caretaker**
carets *n* ▷ **caret**
careworn *adj* showing signs of worry
cargo *n* (*pl* **-es**) goods carried by a ship, aircraft,
etc.
cargoes *n* ▷ **cargo**
caribou *n* (*pl* **-bou** *or* **-bous**) large N American
reindeer
caribous *n* ▷ **caribou**
caricature *n* (*pl* **-s**) drawing or description of
a person that exaggerates features for comic
effect ▶ *v* (**-tures, -turing, -tured**) make a
caricature of
caricatured *v* ▷ **caricature**
caricatures *n, v* ▷ **caricature**
caricaturing *v* ▷ **caricature**
caries [care-reez] *n* (*pl* **caries**) tooth decay
carillon [kar-**rill**-yon] *n* (*pl* **-s**) set of bells played
by keyboard or mechanically
carillons *n* ▷ **carillon**
caring *v* ▷ **care**
cark *v* (**-s, -ing, -ed**) (AUST & NZ) (*Slang*) die
carked *v* ▷ **cark**
carking *v* ▷ **cark**
carks *v* ▷ **cark**
carmine *adj* vivid red
carnage *n* (*pl* **-s**) extensive slaughter of people
carnages *n* ▷ **carnage**
carnal *adj* of a sexual or sensual nature
> **carnally** *adv*
carnally *adv* ▷ **carnal**
carnation *n* (*pl* **-s**) cultivated plant with
fragrant white, pink, or red flowers
carnations *n* ▷ **carnation**
carnival *n* (*pl* **-s**) festive period with
processions, music, and dancing in the street
carnivals *n* ▷ **carnival**
carnivore *n* (*pl* **-s**) meat-eating animal
> **carnivorous** *adj*
carnivores *n* ▷ **carnivore**
carnivorous *adj* ▷ **carnivore**
carob *n* (*pl* **-s**) pod of a Mediterranean tree,
used as a chocolate substitute
carobs *n* ▷ **carob**
carol *n* (*pl* **-s**) joyful Christmas hymn ▶ *v* (**-ls,
-lling, -lled**) sing carols
carolled *v* ▷ **carol**
carolling *v* ▷ **carol**
carols *n, v* ▷ **carol**
carotid *adj, n* (*pl* **-s**) (of) either of the two
arteries supplying blood to the head
carotids *n* ▷ **carotid**
carouse *v* (**-ouses, -ousing, -oused**) have a
merry drinking party
caroused *v* ▷ **carouse**

carousel [kar-roo-**sell**] *n* (*pl* **-s**) revolving conveyor belt for luggage or photographic slides
carousels *n* ▷ **carousel**
carouses *v* ▷ **carouse**
carousing *v* ▷ **carouse**
carp¹ *n* (*pl* **carp**) large freshwater fish
carp² *v* (**-s, -ing, -ed**) complain, find fault
carped *v* ▷ **carp²**
carpel *n* (*pl* **-s**) female reproductive organ of a flowering plant
carpels *n* ▷ **carpel**
carpenter *n* (*pl* **-s**) person who makes or repairs wooden structures > **carpentry** *n*
carpenters *n* ▷ **carpenter**
carpentry *n* ▷ **carpenter**
carpet *n* (*pl* **-s**) heavy fabric for covering floors ▶ *v* (**-s, -ing, -ed**) cover with a carpet
carpeted *v* ▷ **carpet**
carpeting *v* ▷ **carpet**
carpets *n, v* ▷ **carpet**
carpi *n* ▷ **carpus**
carping *v* ▷ **carp²**
carps *v* ▷ **carp²**
carpus *n* (*pl* **-pi**) set of eight bones of the wrist
carriage *n* (*pl* **-s**) one of the sections of a train for passengers
carriages *n* ▷ **carriage**
carriageway *n* (*pl* **-s**) (BRIT) part of a road along which traffic passes in one direction
carriageways *n* ▷ **carriageway**
carried *v* ▷ **carry**
carrier *n* (*pl* **-s**) person or thing that carries something
carriers *n* ▷ **carrier**
carries *v* ▷ **carry**
carrion *n* (*pl* **-s**) dead and rotting flesh
carrions *n* ▷ **carrion**
carrot *n* (*pl* **-s**) long tapering orange root vegetable
carrots *n* ▷ **carrot**
carroty *adj* (of hair) reddish-orange
carry *v* (**-ries, -rying, -ried**) take from one place to another
carrying *v* ▷ **carry**
cars *n* ▷ **car**
cart *n* (*pl* **-s**) open two-wheeled horse-drawn vehicle for carrying goods or passengers ▶ *v* (**-s, -ing, -ed**) carry, usu. with some effort
carted *v* ▷ **cart**
cartel *n* (*pl* **-s**) association of competing firms formed to fix prices
cartels *n* ▷ **cartel**
carthorse *n* (*pl* **-s**) large heavily built horse
carthorses *n* ▷ **carthorse**

cartilage *n* (*pl* **-s**) strong flexible tissue forming part of the skeleton > **cartilaginous** *adj*
cartilages *n* ▷ **cartilage**
cartilaginous *n* ▷ **cartilage**
carting *v* ▷ **cart**
cartographer *n* ▷ **cartography**
cartographers *n* ▷ **cartography**
cartographic *adj* ▷ **cartography**
cartographically *adj* ▷ **cartography**
cartographies *n* ▷ **cartography**
cartography *n* (*pl* **-ies**) map making > **cartographer** *n* (*pl* **-s**) > **cartographic** *adj* > **cartographically** *adv*
carton *n* (*pl* **-s**) container made of cardboard or waxed paper
cartons *n* ▷ **carton**
cartoon *n* (*pl* **-s**) humorous or satirical drawing > **cartoonist** *n* (*pl* **-s**)
cartoonist *n* ▷ **cartoon**
cartoonists *n* ▷ **cartoon**
cartoons *n* ▷ **cartoon**
cartridge *n* (*pl* **-s**) casing containing an explosive charge and bullet for a gun
cartridges *n* ▷ **cartridge**
carts *n, v* ▷ **cart**
cartwheel *n* (*pl* **-s**) sideways somersault supported by the hands with legs outstretched
cartwheels *n* ▷ **cartwheel**
carve *v* (**carves, carving, carved**) cut to form an object > **carving** *n* (*pl* **-s**)
carved *v* ▷ **carve**
carves *v* ▷ **carve**
carving *v, n* ▷ **carve**
carvings *n* ▷ **carve**
caryatid [kar-ree-**at**-id] *n* (*pl* **-s**) supporting column in the shape of a female figure
caryatids *n* ▷ **caryatid**
casbah *n* (*pl* **-s**) citadel of a N African city
casbahs *n* ▷ **casbah**
cascade *n* (*pl* **-s**) waterfall ▶ *v* (**-cades, -cading, -caded**) flow or fall in a cascade
cascaded *v* ▷ **cascade**
cascades *n, v* ▷ **cascade**
cascading *v* ▷ **cascade**
case¹ *n* (*pl* **-s**) instance, example
case² *n* (*pl* **-s**) container, protective covering ▶ *v* (**cases, casing, cased**) (Slang) inspect (a building) with the intention of burgling it
cased *v* ▷ **case²**
casement *n* (*pl* **-s**) window that is hinged on one side
casements *n* ▷ **casement**
cases *n* ▷ **case¹, ²** ▶ *v* ▷ **case²**

cash n banknotes and coins ▸ v (**-es, -ing, -ed**) obtain cash for
  cashed v ▷ **cash**
  cashes v ▷ **cash**
cashew n (pl **-s**) edible kidney-shaped nut
  cashews n ▷ **cashew**
cashier[1] n (pl **-s**) person responsible for handling cash in a bank, shop, etc.
cashier[2] v (**-s, -ing, -ed**) dismiss with dishonour from the armed forces
  cashiered v ▷ **cashier**[2]
  cashiering v ▷ **cashier**[2]
  cashiers n ▷ **cashier**[1] ▸ v ▷ **cashier**[2]
  cashing v ▷ **cash**
cashmere n (pl **-s**) fine soft wool obtained from goats
  cashmeres n ▷ **cashmere**
casing n (pl **-s**) protective case, covering ▸ v ▷ **case**[2]
  casings n ▷ **casing**
casino n (pl **-s**) public building or room where gambling games are played
  casinos n ▷ **casino**
cask n (pl **-s**) barrel used to hold alcoholic drink
casket n (pl **-s**) small box for valuables
  caskets n ▷ **casket**
  casks n ▷ **cask**
cassava n (pl **-s**) starch obtained from the roots of a tropical American plant, used to make tapioca
  cassavas n ▷ **cassava**
casserole n (pl **-s**) covered dish in which food is cooked slowly, usu. in an oven ▸ v (**-oles, -oling, -oled**) cook in a casserole
  casseroled v ▷ **casserole**
  casseroles n, v ▷ **casserole**
  casseroling v ▷ **casserole**
cassette n (pl **-s**) plastic case containing a reel of film or magnetic tape
  cassettes n ▷ **cassette**
cassock n (pl **-s**) long tunic, usu. black, worn by priests
  cassocks n ▷ **cassock**
  cassowaries n ▷ **cassowary**
cassowary n (pl **-waries**) large flightless bird of Australia and New Guinea
cast n (pl **-s**) actors in a play or film collectively ▸ v (**casts, casting, cast**) select (an actor) to play a part in a play or film
castanets pl n musical instrument, used by Spanish dancers, consisting of curved pieces of hollow wood clicked together in the hand
castaway n (pl **-s**) shipwrecked person
  castaways n ▷ **castaway**
caste n (pl **-s**) any of the hereditary classes into

which Hindu society is divided
castellated adj having battlements
  castes n ▷ **caste**
castigate v (**-gates, -gating, -gated**) reprimand severely > **castigation** n
  castigated v ▷ **castigate**
  castigates v ▷ **castigate**
  castigating v ▷ **castigate**
  castigation v ▷ **castigate**
  casting v ▷ **cast**
castle n (pl **-s**) large fortified building, often built as a ruler's residence
  castles n ▷ **castle**
castoff adj, n (pl **-s**) discarded (person or thing)
  castoffs n ▷ **castoff**
castor n (pl **-s**) small swivelling wheel fixed to the bottom of a piece of furniture for easy moving
  castors n ▷ **castor**
castrate v (**-tes, -ting, -ted**) remove the testicles of > **castration** n (pl **-s**)
  castrated v ▷ **castrate**
  castrates v ▷ **castrate**
  castrating v ▷ **castrate**
  castration n ▷ **castrate**
  castrations n ▷ **castrate**
  casts n, v ▷ **cast**
casual adj careless, nonchalant > **casually** adv
  casually adv ▷ **casual**
  casualties n ▷ **casualty**
casualty n (pl **-ties**) person killed or injured in an accident or war
casuarina [kass-yew-a-**reen**-a] n (pl **-s**) Australian tree with jointed green branches
  casuarinas n ▷ **casuarina**
  casuistries n ▷ **casuistry**
casuistry n (pl **-ries**) reasoning that is misleading or oversubtle
cat n (pl **-s**) small domesticated furry mammal
cataclysm [**kat**-a-kliz-zum] n (pl **-s**) violent upheaval > **cataclysmic** adj
  cataclysmic adj ▷ **cataclysm**
  cataclysms n ▷ **cataclysm**
catacombs [**kat**-a-koomz] pl n underground burial place consisting of tunnels with recesses for tombs
catafalque [**kat**-a-falk] n (pl **-s**) raised platform on which a body lies in state before or during a funeral
  catafalques n ▷ **catafalque**
  catalepsies n ▷ **catalepsy**
catalepsy n (pl **-sies**) trancelike state in which the body is rigid > **cataleptic** adj
  cataleptic adj ▷ **catalepsy**
catalogue n (pl **-s**) book containing details of

items for sale ▶ v (**-logues, -loguing, -logued**) make a systematic list of

catalogued v ▷ **catalogue**

catalogues n, v ▷ **catalogue**

cataloguing v ▷ **catalogue**

catalyse v (**-lyses, -lysing, -lysed**) speed up (a chemical reaction) by a catalyst

catalysed v ▷ **catalyse**

catalyses v ▷ **catalyse**

catalysing v ▷ **catalyse**

catalysis n ▷ **catalyst**

catalyst n (pl **-s**) substance that speeds up a chemical reaction without itself changing > **catalysis** n > **catalytic** adj > **catalytically** adv

catalysts n ▷ **catalyst**

catalytic adj ▷ **catalyst**

catalytically adv ▷ **catalyst**

catamaran n (pl **-s**) boat with twin parallel hulls

catamarans n ▷ **catamaran**

catapult n (pl **-s**) Y-shaped device with a loop of elastic, used by children for firing stones ▶ v (**-s, -ing, -ed**) shoot forwards or upwards violently

catapulted v ▷ **catapult**

catapulting v ▷ **catapult**

catapults n, v ▷ **catapult**

cataract n (pl **-s**) eye disease in which the lens becomes opaque

cataracts n ▷ **cataract**

catarrh [kat-**tar**] n (pl **-s**) excessive mucus in the nose and throat, during or following a cold > **catarrhal** adj

catarrhal adj ▷ **catarrh**

catarrhs n ▷ **catarrh**

catastrophe [kat-**ass**-trof-fee] n (pl **-s**) great and sudden disaster > **catastrophic** adj > **catastrophically** adv

catastrophes n ▷ **catastrophe**

catastrophic adj ▷ **catastrophe**

catastrophically adv ▷ **catastrophe**

catcall n (pl **-s**) derisive whistle or cry

catcalls n ▷ **catcall**

catch v (**catches, catching, caught**) seize, capture ▶ n (pl **-es**) device for fastening a door, window, etc.

catches v, n ▷ **catch**

catchier adj ▷ **catchy**

catchiest adj ▷ **catchy**

catchily adv ▷ **catchy**

catchiness n ▷ **catchy**

catchinesses n ▷ **catchy**

catching adj infectious ▶ v ▷ **catch**

catchword n (pl **-s**) well-known and frequently used phrase

catchwords n ▷ **catchword**

catchy adj (**-chier, -chiest**) (of a tune) pleasant and easily remembered > **catchily** adv > **catchiness** n (pl **-es**)

catechism [kat-ti-kiz-zum] n (pl **-s**) instruction on the doctrine of a Christian Church in a series of questions and answers

catechisms n ▷ **catechism**

categorical adj absolutely clear and certain > **categorically** adv

categorically adv ▷ **categorical**

categories n ▷ **category**

categorization n ▷ **categorize**

categorizations n ▷ **categorize**

categorize v (**-izes, -izing, -ized**) put in a category > **categorization** n (pl **-s**)

categorized v ▷ **categorize**

categorizes v ▷ **categorize**

categorizing v ▷ **categorize**

category n (pl **-ries**) class, group

cater v (**-s, -ing, -ed**) provide what is needed or wanted, esp. food or services > **caterer** n (pl **-s**)

catered v ▷ **cater**

caterer n ▷ **cater**

caterers n ▷ **cater**

catering v ▷ **cater**

caterpillar n (pl **-s**) wormlike larva of a moth or butterfly

caterpillars n ▷ **caterpillar**

caters v ▷ **cater**

caterwaul v (**-s, -ing, -ed**) wail, yowl

caterwauled v ▷ **caterwaul**

caterwauling v ▷ **caterwaul**

caterwauls v ▷ **caterwaul**

catfish n (pl **catfish, catfishes**) fish with whisker-like barbels round the mouth

catfishes n ▷ **catfish**

catgut n (pl **-s**) strong cord used to string musical instruments and sports rackets

catguts n ▷ **catgut**

catharses n ▷ **catharsis**

catharsis [kath-**thar**-siss] n (pl **-ses**) relief of strong suppressed emotions > **cathartic** adj

cathartic adj ▷ **catharsis**

cathedral n (pl **-s**) principal church of a diocese

cathedrals n ▷ **cathedral**

catheter [kath-it-er] n (pl **-s**) tube inserted into a body cavity to drain fluid

catheters n ▷ **catheter**

cathode n (pl **-s**) negative electrode, by which electrons leave a circuit

cathodes n ▷ **cathode**

catholic adj (of tastes or interests) covering a wide range > **catholicism** n (pl **-s**)

catholicism n ▷ **catholic**

catholicisms n ▷ **catholic**
cation [kat-eye-on] n (pl -**s**) positively charged ion
cations n ▷ **cation**
catkin n (pl -**s**) drooping flower spike of certain trees
catkins n ▷ **catkin**
catnap n (pl -**s**) ▶ v (-**naps, -napping, -napped**) doze
catnapped v ▷ **catnap**
catnapping v ▷ **catnap**
catnaps n, v ▷ **catnap**
cats n ▷ **cat**
cattier adj ▷ **catty**
cattiest adj ▷ **catty**
cattily adv ▷ **catty**
cattiness n ▷ **catty**
cattle pl n domesticated cows and bulls
catty adj (**cattier, cattiest**) (Informal) spiteful > **cattily** adv > **cattiness** n
catwalk n (pl -**s**) narrow pathway or platform
catwalks n ▷ **catwalk**
caucus n (pl -**es**) local committee or faction of a political party
caught v ▷ **catch**
cauldron n (pl -**s**) large pot used for boiling
cauldrons n ▷ **cauldron**
cauliflower n (pl -**s**) vegetable with a large head of white flower buds surrounded by green leaves
cauliflowers n ▷ **cauliflower**
caulk v (-**s, -ing, -ed**) fill in (cracks) with paste etc.
caulked v ▷ **caulk**
caulking v ▷ **caulk**
caulks v ▷ **caulk**
causal adj of or being a cause > **causally** adv
causality n ▷ **causation**
causally adv ▷ **causal**
causation, causality n relationship of cause and effect
cause n (pl -**s**) something that produces a particular effect ▶ v (**causes, causing, caused**) be the cause of
caused v ▷ **cause**
causes n, v ▷ **cause**
causeway n (pl -**s**) raised path or road across water or marshland
causeways n ▷ **causeway**
causing v ▷ **cause**
caustic adj capable of burning by chemical action > **caustically** adv
caustically adv ▷ **caustic**
cauterize v (-**izes, -izing, -ized**) burn (a wound) with heat or a caustic agent to prevent infection
cauterized v ▷ **cauterize**
cauterizes v ▷ **cauterize**
cauterizing v ▷ **cauterize**
caution n (pl -**s**) care, esp. in the face of danger ▶ v (-**s, -ing, -ed**) warn, advise
cautionary adj warning
cautioned v ▷ **caution**
cautioning v ▷ **caution**
cautions n, v ▷ **caution**
cautious adj showing caution > **cautiously** adv
cautiously adv ▷ **cautious**
cavalcade n (pl -**s**) procession of people on horseback or in cars
cavalcades n ▷ **cavalcade**
cavalier adj showing haughty disregard ▶ n (pl -**s**) (**C-**) supporter of Charles I in the English Civil War > **cavalierly** adv
cavalierly adv ▷ **cavalier**
cavaliers n ▷ **cavalier**
cavalries n ▷ **cavalry**
cavalry n (pl -**ries**) part of the army orig. on horseback, but now often using fast armoured vehicles
cave n (pl -**s**) hollow in the side of a hill or cliff
caveat [kav-vee-at] n (pl -**s**) warning
caveats n ▷ **caveat**
caveman n (pl -**men**) prehistoric cave dweller
cavemen n ▷ **caveman**
cavern n (pl -**s**) large cave > **cavernous** adj
cavernous adj ▷ **cavern**
caverns n ▷ **cavern**
caves n ▷ **cave**
caviar, caviare n (pl -**s**) salted sturgeon roe, regarded as a delicacy
caviare n ▷ **caviar**
caviares n ▷ **caviar**
caviars n ▷ **caviar**
cavil v (-**ils, -illing, -illed**) make petty objections ▶ n (pl -**s**) petty objection
cavilled v ▷ **cavil**
cavilling v ▷ **cavil**
cavils v, n ▷ **cavil**
caving n sport of exploring caves
cavities v ▷ **cavity**
cavity n (pl -**ties**) hollow space
cavort v (-**s, -ing, -ed**) skip about
cavorted v ▷ **cavort**
cavorting v ▷ **cavort**
cavorts v ▷ **cavort**
caw n (pl -**s**) cry of a crow, rook, or raven ▶ v (-**s, -ing, -ed**) make this cry
cawed v ▷ **caw**
cawing v ▷ **caw**

caws n, v ▷ **caw**

cay n (**cays**). A cay is a small low island. Cay scores 8 points.

cayman n (pl -**s**) S American reptile similar to an alligator

caymans n ▷ **cayman**

caz adj. Caz is a slang word for **casual**. It's a great word to have up your sleeve as it scores 14 points.

cazique n (**caziques**). A cazique is a chief among certain American Indian tribes. Cazique scores 27 points, and will earn you a 50-point bonus if you manage to use all of your tiles to form it.

cease v (**ceases, ceasing, ceased**) bring or come to an end > **ceaseless** adj > **ceaselessly** adv

ceased v ▷ **cease**

ceasefire n (pl -**s**) temporary truce

ceasefires n ▷ **ceasefire**

ceaseless adj ▷ **cease**

ceaselessly adv ▷ **cease**

ceases v ▷ **cease**

ceasing v ▷ **cease**

cedar n (pl -**s**) evergreen coniferous tree

cedars n ▷ **cedar**

cede v (**cedes, ceding, ceded**) surrender (territory or legal rights)

ceded v ▷ **cede**

cedes v ▷ **cede**

cedilla n (pl -**s**) character (ˌ) placed under a c in some languages, to show that it is pronounced s, not k

cedillas n ▷ **cedilla**

ceding v ▷ **cede**

ceilidh [kay-lee] n (pl -**s**) informal social gathering for singing and dancing, esp. in Scotland

ceilidhs n ▷ **ceilidh**

ceiling n (pl -**s**) inner upper surface of a room

ceilings n ▷ **ceiling**

celandine n (pl -**s**) wild plant with yellow flowers

celandines n ▷ **celandine**

celebrant n (pl -**s**) person who performs a religious ceremony

celebrants n ▷ **celebrant**

celebrate v (-**rates, -rating, -rated**) hold festivities to mark (a happy event, anniversary, etc.) > **celebration** n (pl -**s**)

celebrated adj well known ▶ v ▷ **celebrate**

celebrates v ▷ **celebrate**

celebrating v ▷ **celebrate**

celebration n ▷ **celebrate**

celebrations n ▷ **celebrate**

celebrities n ▷ **celebrity**

celebrity n (pl -**rities**) famous person

celeriac [sill-**ler**-ee-ak] n (pl -**s**) variety of celery with a large turnip-like root

celeriacs n ▷ **celeriac**

celeries n ▷ **celery**

celerities n ▷ **celerity**

celerity [sill-**ler**-rit-tee] n (pl -**ties**) swiftness

celery n (pl -**ries**) vegetable with long green crisp edible stalks

celestial adj heavenly, divine > **celestially** adv

celestially adv ▷ **celestial**

celibacy n ▷ **celibate**

celibate adj unmarried or abstaining from sex, esp. because of a religious vow of chastity ▶ n (pl -**s**) celibate person > **celibacy** n

celibates n ▷ **celibate**

cell n (pl -**s**) smallest unit of an organism that is able to function independently

cellar n (pl -**s**) underground room for storage

cellars n ▷ **cellar**

cellist n ▷ **cello**

cellists n ▷ **cello**

cello [**chell**-oh] n (pl -**s**) large low-pitched instrument of the violin family > **cellist** n (pl -**s**)

cellophane n (pl -**s**) ® thin transparent cellulose sheeting used as wrapping

cellophanes n ▷ **cellophane**

cellos n ▷ **cello**

cells n ▷ **cell**

cellular adj of or consisting of cells

celluloid n (pl -**s**) kind of plastic used to make toys and, formerly, photographic film

celluloids n ▷ **celluloid**

cellulose n (pl -**s**) main constituent of plant cell walls, used in making paper, plastics, etc.

celluloses n ▷ **cellulose**

cement n (pl -**s**) fine grey powder mixed with water and sand to make mortar or concrete ▶ v (-**s, -ing, -ed**) join, bind, or cover with cement

cemented v ▷ **cement**

cementing v ▷ **cement**

cements n, v ▷ **cement**

cemeteries n ▷ **cemetery**

cemetery n (pl -**ries**) place where dead people are buried

cenotaph n (pl -**s**) monument honouring soldiers who died in a war

cenotaphs n ▷ **cenotaph**

censer n (pl -**s**) container for burning incense

censers n ▷ **censer**

censor n (pl -**s**) person authorized to examine

films, books, etc., to ban or cut anything considered obscene or objectionable ▶ v (**-s, -ing, -ed**) ban or cut parts of (a film, book, etc.) > **censorship** n
censored v ▷ **censor**
censoring v ▷ **censor**
censorious adj harshly critical > **censoriously** adv
censoriously adv ▷ **censorious**
censors n, v ▷ **censor**
censorship n ▷ **censor**
censure n (pl -s) severe disapproval ▶ v (**-sures, -suring, -sured**) criticize severely
censured v ▷ **censure**
censures n, v ▷ **censure**
censuring v ▷ **censure**
census n (pl -**es**) official count of a population
censuses n ▷ **census**
cent n (pl -**s**) hundredth part of a monetary unit such as the dollar or euro
centaur n (pl -**s**) mythical creature with the head, arms, and torso of a man, and the lower body and legs of a horse
centaurs n ▷ **centaur**
centenarian n (pl -**s**) person at least 100 years old
centenarians n ▷ **centenarian**
centenaries n ▷ **centenary**
centenary [sen-**teen**-a-ree] n (CHIEFLY BRIT) (pl -**naries**) 100th anniversary or its celebration
centennial n (pl -**s**) 100th anniversary or its celebration
centennials n ▷ **centennial**
centigrade adj of the temperature in which water freezes at 0° and boils at 100°
centigram, centigramme n (pl -**s**) one hundredth of a gram
centigramme n ▷ **centigram**
centigrammes n ▷ **centigram**
centigrams n ▷ **centigram**
centilitre n (pl -**s**) one hundredth of a litre
centilitres n ▷ **centilitre**
centimetre n (pl -**s**) one hundredth of a metre
centimetres n ▷ **centimetre**
centipede n (pl -**s**) small wormlike creature with many legs
centipedes n ▷ **centipede**
central adj of, at, or forming the centre > **centrally** adv > **centrality** n
centralism n principle of central control of a country or organization > **centralist** n (pl -**s**)
centralist n ▷ **centralism**
centralists n ▷ **centralism**
centrality n ▷ **central**
centralization n ▷ **centralize**

centralizations n ▷ **centralize**
centralize v (**-izes, -izing, -ized**) bring under central control > **centralization** n (pl -**s**)
centralized v ▷ **centralize**
centralizes v ▷ **centralize**
centralizing v ▷ **centralize**
centrally adv ▷ **central**
centre n (pl -**s**) middle point or part (SPORT) ▶ v (**centres, centring, centred**) put in the centre of something
centred v ▷ **centre**
centres n, v ▷ **centre**
centrifugal adj moving away from a centre > **centrifugally** adv
centrifugally adv ▷ **centrifugal**
centrifuge n (pl -**s**) machine that separates substances by centrifugal force
centrifuges n ▷ **centrifuge**
centring v ▷ **centre**
centripetal adj moving towards a centre > **centripetally** adv
centripetally adv ▷ **centripetal**
centrist n (pl -**s**) person favouring political moderation
centrists n ▷ **centrist**
cents n ▷ **cent**
centuries n ▷ **century**
centurion n (pl -**s**) (in ancient Rome) officer commanding 100 men
centurions n ▷ **centurion**
century n (pl -**ries**) period of 100 years
cep n (**ceps**). A cep is an edible fungus. Cep scores 7 points.
cephalopod [**seff**-a-loh-pod] n (pl -**s**) sea mollusc with a head and tentacles, such as the octopus
cephalopods n ▷ **cephalopod**
ceramic n (pl -**s**) hard brittle material made by heating clay to a very high temperature ▶ pl art of producing ceramic objects ▶ adj made of ceramic
ceramics n ▷ **ceramic**
cereal n (pl -**s**) grass plant with edible grain, such as oat or wheat
cereals n ▷ **cereal**
cerebra n ▷ **cerebrum**
cerebral [ser-rib-ral, ser-**reeb**-ral] adj of the brain
cerebrum [**serr**-rib-rum] n (pl -**brums, -bra**) [-bra] main part of the brain
cerebrums n ▷ **cerebrum**
ceremonial adj ▷ **ceremony**
ceremonially adv ▷ **ceremony**
ceremonials n ▷ **ceremony**
ceremonies n ▷ **ceremony**
ceremonious adj excessively polite or formal

> **ceremoniously** adv
ceremoniously adv ▷ **ceremonious**
ceremony n (pl **-nies**) formal act or ritual
> **ceremonial** adj, n (pl **-s**) > **ceremonially** adv
cerise [ser-**reess**] adj cherry-red
certain adj (**-er, -est**) positive and confident
> **certainly** adv
certainer adj ▷ **certain**
certainest adj ▷ **certain**
certainly adv ▷ **certain**
certainties n ▷ **certainty**
certainty n (pl **-ties**) state of being sure
certifiable adj considered legally insane
> **certifiably** adv
certifiably n ▷ **certifiable**
certificate n (pl **-s**) official document stating
the details of a birth, academic course, etc.
certificates n ▷ **certificate**
certification n ▷ **certify**
certifications n ▷ **certify**
certified v ▷ **certify**
certifies v ▷ **certify**
certify v (**-fies, -fying, -fied**) confirm, attest to
> **certification** n (pl **-s**)
certifying v ▷ **certify**
certitude n (pl **-s**) confidence, certainty
certitudes n ▷ **certitude**
cervical adj ▷ **cervix**
cervices n ▷ **cervix**
cervix n (pl **cervixes, cervices**) narrow
entrance of the womb > **cervical** adj
cervixes n ▷ **cervix**
cessation n (pl **-s**) ceasing
cessations n ▷ **cessation**
cesspit, cesspool n (pl **-s**) covered tank or pit
for sewage
cesspits n ▷ **cesspit**
cesspool n ▷ **cesspit**
cesspools n ▷ **cesspit**
cetacean [sit-**tay**-shun] n (pl **-s**) fish-shaped sea
mammal such as a whale or dolphin
cetaceans n ▷ **cetacean**

> **ch** pron. This is an old dialect form of **I**.
It's the only two-letter word that can
be formed with the letter C, and it's
a good word to remember because
it doesn't use any vowels. Ch scores
7 points.
cha n (**chas**). Cha is a slang word for
tea. Cha scores 8 points.

chafe v (**chafes, chafing, chafed**) make sore or
worn by rubbing
chafed v ▷ **chafe**
chafes v ▷ **chafe**
chaff¹ n (pl **-s**) grain husks

chaff² v (**-s, -ing, -ed**) (Old-fashioned) tease
good-naturedly
chaffed v ▷ **chaff²**
chaffinch n (pl **-es**) small European songbird
chaffinches n ▷ **chaffinch**
chaffing v ▷ **chaff²**
chaffs n ▷ **chaff¹** ▶ v ▷ **chaff²**
chafing v ▷ **chafe**
chagrin [**shag**-grin] n (pl **-s**) annoyance and
disappointment
chagrined adj annoyed and disappointed
chagrins n ▷ **chagrin**
chain n (pl **-s**) flexible length of connected
metal links ▶ v (**-s, -ing, -ed**) restrict or fasten
with or as if with a chain
chained v ▷ **chain**
chaining v ▷ **chain**
chains n, v ▷ **chain**
chair n (pl **-s**) seat with a back, for one person
▶ v (**-s, -ing, -ed**) preside over (a meeting)
chaired v ▷ **chair**
chairing v ▷ **chair**
chairlift (pl **-s**) series of chairs suspended from
a moving cable for carrying people up a slope
chairlifts n ▷ **chairlift**
chairman, chairwoman n (pl **-men, -women**)
person in charge of a company's board of
directors or a meeting (also **chairperson**)
(pl **-s**)
chairmen n ▷ **chairman**
chairperson n ▷ **chairman**
chairpersons n ▷ **chairman**
chairs n, v ▷ **chair**
chairwoman n ▷ **chairman**
chairwomen n ▷ **chairman**
chaise [**shaze**] n (pl **-s**) (HIST) light horse-drawn
carriage
chaises n ▷ **chaise**
chalcedonies n ▷ **chalcedony**
chalcedony [kal-**sed**-don-ee] n (pl **-nies**) variety
of quartz
chalet n (pl **-s**) kind of Swiss wooden house
with a steeply sloping roof
chalets n ▷ **chalet**
chalice n (pl **-s**) large goblet
chalices n ▷ **chalice**
chalk n (pl **-s**) soft white rock consisting of
calcium carbonate ▶ v (**-s, -ing, -ed**) draw or
mark with chalk > **chalky** adj (**-kier, -kiest**)
chalked v ▷ **chalk**
chalkier adj ▷ **chalk**
chalkiest adj ▷ **chalk**
chalking v ▷ **chalk**
chalks n, v ▷ **chalk**
chalky adj ▷ **chalk**

challenge n (pl -s) demanding or stimulating situation ▸ v (-ges, -ging, -ged) issue a challenge to > **challenger** n (pl -s)

challenged adj disabled as specified ▸ v ▷ **challenge**

challenger n ▷ **challenge**

challengers n ▷ **challenge**

challenges n, v ▷ **challenge**

challenging v ▷ **challenge**

chamber n (pl -s) hall used for formal meetings (Old-fashioned) ▸ pl set of rooms used as offices by a barrister

chamberlain n (pl -s) (HIST) officer who managed the household of a king or nobleman

chamberlains n ▷ **chamberlain**

chambermaid n (pl -s) woman employed to clean bedrooms in a hotel

chambermaids n ▷ **chambermaid**

chambers n ▷ **chamber**

chameleon [kam-**meal**-yon] n (pl -s) small lizard that changes colour to blend in with its surroundings

chameleons n ▷ **chameleon**

chamfer [**cham**-fer] v (-s, -ing, -ed) bevel the edge of

chamfered v ▷ **chamfer**

chamfering v ▷ **chamfer**

chamfers v ▷ **chamfer**

chamois [**sham**-wah] n (pl -ois) small mountain antelope

chamomile [**kam**-mo-mile] n (pl -s) ▷ **camomile**

chamomiles n ▷ **chamomile**

champ¹ v (-s, -ing, -ed) chew noisily

champ² n (pl -s) ▷ **champion**

champagne n (pl -s) sparkling white French wine

champagnes n ▷ **champagne**

champed v ▷ **champ¹**

champing v ▷ **champ¹**

champion n (pl -s) overall winner of a competition (foll. by of) ▸ v (-s, -ing, -ed) support ▸ adj (Dialect) excellent > **championship** n (pl -s)

championed v ▷ **champion**

championing v ▷ **champion**

champions n, v ▷ **champion**

championship n ▷ **champion**

championships n ▷ **champion**

champs v ▷ **champ¹** ▸ n ▷ **champ²**

chance n (pl -s) likelihood, probability ▸ v (chances, chancing, chanced) risk, hazard

chanced v ▷ **chance**

chancel n (pl -s) part of a church containing the altar and choir

chancellor n (pl -s) head of government in some European countries > **chancellorship** n (pl -s)

chancellors n ▷ **chancellor**

chancellorship n ▷ **chancellor**

chancellorships n ▷ **chancellor**

chancels n ▷ **chancel**

chances n, v ▷ **chance**

chancier adj ▷ **chancy**

chanciest adj ▷ **chancy**

chancing v ▷ **chance**

chancy adj (-cier, -ciest) uncertain, risky

chandelier [shan-dill-**eer**] n (pl -s) ornamental light with branches and holders for several candles or bulbs

chandeliers n ▷ **chandelier**

chandler n (pl -s) dealer, esp. in ships' supplies

chandlers n ▷ **chandler**

change n (pl -s) becoming different ▸ v (changes, changing, changed) make or become different

changeable adj changing often

changed v ▷ **change**

changeling n (pl -s) child believed to have been exchanged by fairies for another

changelings n ▷ **changeling**

changes n, v ▷ **change**

changing v ▷ **change**

channel n (pl -s) band of broadcasting frequencies ▸ v (-nels, -nelling, -nelled) direct or convey through a channel

channelled v ▷ **channel**

channelling v ▷ **channel**

channels n, v ▷ **channel**

chant v (-s, -ing, -ed) utter or sing (a slogan or psalm) ▸ n (pl -s) rhythmic or repetitious slogan

chanted v ▷ **chant**

chanter n (pl -s) (on bagpipes) pipe on which the melody is played

chanters n ▷ **chanter**

chanting v ▷ **chant**

chants v, n ▷ **chant**

chaos n complete disorder or confusion > **chaotic** adj > **chaotically** adv

chaotic adj ▷ **chaos**

chaotically adv ▷ **chaos**

chap n (pl -s) (Informal) man or boy

chapati, chapatti n (pl -s) (in Indian cookery) flat thin unleavened bread

chapatis n ▷ **chapati**

chapatti n ▷ **chapati**

chapattis n ▷ **chapati**

chapel n (pl -s) place of worship with its own altar, within a church

chapels n ▷ **chapel**

chaperone [shap-per-rone] n (pl -s) older person who accompanies and supervises a young person or young people on a social occasion ▶ v (-ones, -oning, -oned) act as a chaperone to

chaperoned v ▷ **chaperone**

chaperones n, v ▷ **chaperone**

chaperoning v ▷ **chaperone**

chaplain n (pl -s) clergyman attached to a chapel, military body, or institution > **chaplaincy** n (pl -cies)

chaplaincies n ▷ **chaplain**

chaplaincy n ▷ **chaplain**

chaplains n ▷ **chaplain**

chaplet n (pl -s) garland for the head

chaplets n ▷ **chaplet**

chapped adj (of the skin) raw and cracked, through exposure to cold

chaps n ▷ **chap**

chapter n (pl -s) division of a book

chapters n ▷ **chapter**

char¹ v (chars, charring, charred) blacken by partial burning

char² (BRIT) (Informal) n (pl -s) charwoman ▶ v (chars, charring, charred) clean other people's houses as a job

char³ n (BRIT) (Old-fashioned slang) tea

charabanc [shar-rab-bang] n (pl -s) (Old-fashioned) coach for sightseeing

charabancs n ▷ **charabanc**

character n (pl -s) combination of qualities distinguishing a person, group, or place

characteristic n (pl -s) distinguishing feature or quality ▶ adj typical > **characteristically** adv

characteristically n ▷ **characteristic**

characteristics n ▷ **characteristic**

characterization n ▷ **characterize**

characterizations n ▷ **characterize**

characterize v (-rizes, -rizing, -rized) be a characteristic of (foll. by as) > **characterization** n (pl -s)

characterized v ▷ **characterize**

characterizes v ▷ **characterize**

characterizing v ▷ **characterize**

characters n ▷ **character**

charade [shar-rahd] n (pl -s) absurd pretence ▶ pl game in which one team acts out a word or phrase, which the other team has to guess

charades n ▷ **charade**

charcoal n (pl -s) black substance formed by partially burning wood

charcoals n ▷ **charcoal**

charge v (charges, charging, charged) ask as a price ▶ n (pl -s) price charged > **chargeable** adj

chargeable adj ▷ **charge**

charged v ▷ **charge**

charger n (pl -s) device for charging an accumulator

chargers n ▷ **charger**

charges v, n ▷ **charge**

charging v ▷ **charge**

charier adj ▷ **chary**

chariest adj ▷ **chary**

chariot n (pl -s) two-wheeled horse-drawn vehicle used in ancient times in wars and races

charioteer n (pl -s) chariot driver

charioteers n ▷ **charioteer**

chariots n ▷ **chariot**

charisma [kar-rizz-ma] n (pl -s) person's power to attract or influence people > **charismatic** [kar-rizz-mat-ik] ▶ adj

charismas n ▷ **charisma**

charismatic adj ▷ **charisma**

charitable adj ▷ **charity**

charitably adv ▷ **charity**

charities n ▷ **charity**

charity n (pl -ties) organization that gives help, such as money or food, to those in need > **charitable** adj > **charitably** adv

charladies n ▷ **charlady**

charlady n (pl -ladies) (BRIT) (Informal) ▷ **charwoman**

charlatan [shar-lat-tan] n (pl -s) person who claims expertise that he or she does not have

charlatans n ▷ **charlatan**

charleston n (pl -s) lively dance of the 1920s

charlestons n ▷ **charleston**

charm n (pl -s) attractive quality ▶ v (-s, -ing, -ed) attract, delight > **charmer** n (pl -s)

charmed v ▷ **charm**

charmer n ▷ **charm**

charmers n ▷ **charm**

charming adj attractive ▶ v ▷ **charm**

charms n, v ▷ **charm**

charred v ▷ **char¹, ²**

charring v ▷ **char¹, ²**

chars v ▷ **char¹, ²** ▶ n ▷ **char²**

chart n (pl -s) graph, table, or diagram showing information ▶ v (-s, -ing, -ed) plot the course of

charted v ▷ **chart**

charter n (pl -s) document granting or demanding certain rights ▶ v (-s, -ing, -ed) hire by charter

chartered adj officially qualified to practise a profession ▶ v ▷ **charter**

chartering v ▷ **charter**

charters *n*, *v* ▷ **charter**
charting *v* ▷ **chart**
chartreuse [shar-**trerz**] *n* (*pl* **-s**) sweet-smelling green or yellow liqueur
  chartreuses *n* ▷ **chartreuse**
  charts *n*, *v* ▷ **chart**
charwoman *n* (*pl* **charwomen**) woman whose job is to clean other people's homes
  charwomen *n* ▷ **charwoman**
chary [**chair**-ee] *adj* (**-rier**, **-riest**) wary, careful
chase[1] *v* (**chases, chasing, chased**) run after quickly in order to catch or drive away ▶ *n* (*pl* **-s**) chasing, pursuit
chase[2] *v* (**chases, chasing, chased**) engrave or emboss (metal)
  chased *v* ▷ **chase**[1, 2]
chaser *n* (*pl* **-s**) milder drink drunk after another stronger one
  chasers *n* ▷ **chaser**
  chases *v* ▷ **chase**[1, 2] ▶ *n* ▷ **chase**[1]
  chasing *v* ▷ **chase**[1, 2]
chasm [**kaz**-zum] *n* (*pl* **-s**) deep crack in the earth
  chasms *n* ▷ **chasm**
chassis [**shass**-ee] *n* (*pl* **-sis**) frame, wheels, and mechanical parts of a vehicle
chaste *adj* (**-r**, **-st**) abstaining from sex outside marriage or altogether > **chastely** *adv* > **chasteness** *n* (*pl* **-es**) > **chastity** *n* (*pl* **-ties**)
  chastely *adv* ▷ **chaste**
chasten [**chase**-en] *v* (**-s**, **-ing**, **-ed**) subdue by criticism
  chastened *v* ▷ **chasten**
  chasteness *n* ▷ **chaste**
  chastenesses *n* ▷ **chaste**
  chastening *v* ▷ **chasten**
  chastens *v* ▷ **chasten**
  chaster *adj* ▷ **chaste**
  chastest *adj* ▷ **chaste**
chastise *v* (**-ises**, **-ising**, **-ised**) scold severely > **chastisement** *n* (*pl* **-s**)
  chastised *v* ▷ **chastise**
  chastisement *n* ▷ **chastise**
  chastisements *n* ▷ **chastise**
  chastises *v* ▷ **chastise**
  chastising *v* ▷ **chastise**
  chastities *n* ▷ **chaste**
  chastity *n* ▷ **chaste**
chat *n* (*pl* **-s**) informal conversation ▶ *v* (**chats, chatting, chatted**) have an informal conversation > **chatty** *adj* (**-ttier**, **-ttiest**) > **chattily** *adv* > **chattiness** *n* (*pl* **-es**)
chateau [**shat**-toe] *n* (*pl* **-teaux**, **-teaus**) French castle
  chateaus *n* ▷ **chateau**

chateaux *n* ▷ **chateau**
chatelaine [**shat**-tell-lane] *n* (*pl* **-s**) (formerly) mistress of a large house or castle
  chatelaines *n* ▷ **chatelaine**
chatroom *n* (*pl* **-s**) site on the Internet where users have group discussions by e-mail
  chatrooms *n* ▷ **chatroom**
  chats *n*, *v* ▷ **chat**
  chatted *v* ▷ **chat**
chattel *n* (*pl* **-s**) (usually plural) possessions
  chattels *n* ▷ **chattel**
chatter *v* (**-s**, **-ing**, **-ed**) speak quickly and continuously about unimportant things ▶ *n* (*pl* **-s**) idle talk
chatterbox *n* (*pl* **-es**) person who chatters a lot
  chatterboxes *n* ▷ **chatterbox**
  chattered *v* ▷ **chatter**
  chattering *v* ▷ **chatter**
  chatters *v*, *n* ▷ **chatter**
  chattier *adj* ▷ **chat**
  chattiest *adj* ▷ **chat**
  chattily *adv* ▷ **chat**
  chattiness *n* ▷ **chat**
  chattinesses *n* ▷ **chat**
  chatting *v* ▷ **chat**
  chatty *adj* ▷ **chat**
chauffeur *n* (*pl* **-s**) person employed to drive a car for someone
  chauffeurs *n* ▷ **chauffeur**
chauvinism [**show**-vin-iz-zum] *n* (*pl* **-s**) irrational belief that one's own country, race, group, or sex is superior > **chauvinist** *n* (*pl* **-s**) *adj* > **chauvinistic** *adj* > **chauvinistically** *adv*
  chauvinisms *n* ▷ **chauvinism**
  chauvinist *n* ▷ **chauvinism**
  chauvinistic *adj* ▷ **chauvinism**
  chauvinistically *adv* ▷ **chauvinism**
  chauvinists *n* ▷ **chauvinism**
  che *pron*. Like **ch**, che is an old dialect form of **I**. Che scores 8 points.
cheap *adj* (**-er**, **-est**) costing relatively little > **cheaply** *adv*
cheapen *v* (**-s**, **-ing**, **-ed**) lower the reputation of
  cheapened *v* ▷ **cheapen**
  cheapening *v* ▷ **cheapen**
  cheapens *v* ▷ **cheapen**
  cheaper *adj* ▷ **cheap**
  cheapest *adj* ▷ **cheap**
  cheaply *adv* ▷ **cheap**
cheapskate *n* (*pl* **-s**) (*Informal*) miserly person
  cheapskates *n* ▷ **cheapskate**
cheat *v* (**-s**, **-ing**, **-ed**) act dishonestly to gain profit or advantage ▶ *n* (*pl* **-s**) person who cheats

cheated v ▷ cheat
cheating v ▷ cheat
cheats v, n ▷ cheat
check v (-s, -ing, -ed) examine, investigate ▶ n
(pl -s) test to ensure accuracy or progress
checked v ▷ check
checking v ▷ check
checkmate n (pl -s) (CHESS) winning position
in which an opponent's king is under attack
and unable to escape ▶ v (-mates, -mating,
-mated) (CHESS) place the king of (one's
opponent) in checkmate
checkmated v ▷ checkmate
checkmates n, v ▷ checkmate
checkmating v ▷ checkmate
checkout n (pl -s) counter in a supermarket,
where customers pay
checkouts n ▷ checkout
checks v, n ▷ check
checkup n (pl -s) thorough medical
examination
checkups n ▷ checkup
cheddar n (pl -s) firm orange or yellowy-white
cheese
cheddars n ▷ cheddar
cheek n (pl -s) either side of the face below the
eye (Informal) ▶ v (-s, -ing, -ed) (BRIT, AUST & NZ)
(Informal) speak impudently to
cheeked v ▷ cheek
cheekier adj ▷ cheeky
cheekiest adj ▷ cheeky
cheekily adv ▷ cheeky
cheekiness n ▷ cheeky
cheekinesses n ▷ cheeky
cheeking v ▷ cheek
cheeks n, v ▷ cheek
cheeky adj (-kier, -kiest) impudent,
disrespectful > cheekily adv > cheekiness
n (pl -es)
cheep n (pl -s) young bird's high-pitched cry ▶ v
(-s, -ing, -ed) utter a cheep
cheeped v ▷ cheep
cheeping v ▷ cheep
cheeps n, v ▷ cheep
cheer v (-s, -ing, -ed) applaud or encourage
with shouts ▶ n (pl -s) shout of applause or
encouragement > cheerful adj (-ller, -llest)
> cheerfully adv > cheerfulness n > cheery adj
(-rier, -riest) > cheerily adv
cheered v ▷ cheer
cheerful adj ▷ cheer
cheerfuller adj ▷ cheer
cheerfullest adj ▷ cheer
cheerfully adv ▷ cheer
cheerfulness n ▷ cheer

cheerier adj ▷ cheer
cheeriest adj ▷ cheer
cheerily adv ▷ cheer
cheering v ▷ cheer
cheerio interj (Informal) goodbye ▶ n (pl -s) (AUST
& NZ) small red cocktail sausage
cheerios n ▷ cheerio
cheerless adj dreary, gloomy > cheerlessly adv
> cheerlessness n
cheerlessly adv ▷ cheerless
cheerlessness n ▷ cheerless
cheers v, n ▷ cheer
cheery adj ▷ cheer
cheese n (pl -s) food made from coagulated
milk curd > cheesy adj (pl -sier, -siest)
> cheesily adv > cheesiness n
cheeseburger n (pl -s) hamburger topped with
melted cheese
cheeseburgers n ▷ cheeseburger
cheesecake n (pl -s) dessert with a biscuit-
crumb base covered with a sweet cream-
cheese mixture
cheesecakes n ▷ cheesecake
cheesecloth n (pl -s) light cotton cloth
cheesecloths n ▷ cheesecloth
cheeses n ▷ cheese
cheesier adj ▷ cheese
cheesiest adj ▷ cheese
cheesily adv ▷ cheese
cheesiness n ▷ cheese
cheesy adj ▷ cheese
cheetah n (pl -s) large fast-running spotted
African wild cat
cheetahs n ▷ cheetah
chef n (pl -s) cook in a restaurant
chefs n ▷ chef
chemical n (pl -s) substance used in or
resulting from a reaction involving changes
to atoms or molecules ▶ adj of chemistry or
chemicals > chemically adv
chemically adv ▷ chemical
chemicals n ▷ chemical
chemise [shem-meez] n (pl -s) (Old-fashioned)
woman's loose-fitting slip
chemises n ▷ chemise
chemist n (pl -s) shop selling medicines and
cosmetics
chemistries n ▷ chemistry
chemistry n (pl -ries) science of the
composition, properties, and reactions of
substances
chemists n ▷ chemist
chemotherapies n ▷ chemotherapy
chemotherapy n (pl -apies) treatment of
disease, often cancer, using chemicals

chenille [shen-**neel**] *n* (*pl* -**s**) (fabric of) thick tufty yarn
chenilles *n* ▷ **chenille**

cheque *n* (*pl* -**s**) written order to one's bank to pay money from one's account

chequer *n* (*pl* **chequers**) piece used in Chinese chequers ▶ *pl* game of draughts

chequered *adj* marked by varied fortunes
chequers *n* ▷ **chequer**
cheques *n* ▷ **cheque**

cherish *v* (-**es**, -**ing**, -**ed**) cling to (an idea or feeling)
cherished *v* ▷ **cherish**
cherishes *v* ▷ **cherish**
cherishing *v* ▷ **cherish**

cheroot [sher-**root**] *n* (*pl* -**s**) cigar with both ends cut flat
cheroots *n* ▷ **cheroot**
cherries *n* ▷ **cherry**

cherry *n* (*pl* -**ries**) small red or black fruit with a stone ▶ *adj* deep red

cherub *n* (*pl* -**s**, -**ubim**) angel, often represented as a winged child > **cherubic** [cher-**rew**-bik] ▶ *adj*
cherubic *adj* ▷ **cherub**
cherubim *n* ▷ **cherub**
cherubs *n* ▷ **cherub**

chervil *n* (*pl* -**s**) aniseed-flavoured herb
chervils *n* ▷ **chervil**

chess *n* (*pl* -**es**) game for two players with 16 pieces each, played on a chequered board of 64 squares
chesses *n* ▷ **chess**

chessman *n* (*pl* -**men**) piece used in chess
chessmen *n* ▷ **chessman**

chest *n* (*pl* -**s**) front of the body, from neck to waist

chesterfield *n* (*pl* -**s**) couch with high padded sides and back
chesterfields *n* ▷ **chesterfield**

chestnut *n* (*pl* -**s**) reddish-brown edible nut (*Informal*) ▶ *adj* (of hair or a horse) reddish-brown
chestnuts *n* ▷ **chestnut**
chests *n* ▷ **chest**

chevron [**shev**-ron] *n* (*pl* -**s**) V-shaped pattern, esp. on the sleeve of a military uniform to indicate rank
chevrons *n* ▷ **chevron**

chew *v* (-**s**, -**ing**, -**ed**) grind (food) between the teeth
chewed *v* ▷ **chew**
chewier *adj* ▷ **chewy**
chewiest *adj* ▷ **chewy**
chewiness *n* ▷ **chewy**

chewinesses *n* ▷ **chewy**
chewing *v* ▷ **chew**
chews *v* ▷ **chew**

chewy *adj* (-**ier**, -**iest**) requiring a lot of chewing > **chewiness** *n* (*pl* -**es**)

chi *n* (chis). Chi is a letter of the Greek alphabet, and is worth 8 points.

chianti [kee-**ant**-ee] *n* (*pl* -**s**) dry red Italian wine
chiantis *n* ▷ **chianti**

chiaroscuro [kee-ah-roh-**skew**-roh] *n* (*pl* -**s**) distribution of light and shade in a picture
chiaroscuros *n* ▷ **chiaroscuro**

chic [**sheek**] *adj* (-**er**, -**est**) stylish, elegant ▶ *n* (*pl* -**s**) stylishness, elegance

chicane [shik-**kane**] *n* (*pl* -**s**) obstacle in a motor-racing circuit
chicaneries *n* ▷ **chicanery**

chicanery *n* (*pl* -**eries**) trickery, deception
chicanes *n* ▷ **chicane**
chicer *adj* ▷ **chic**
chicest *adj* ▷ **chic**

chick *n* (*pl* -**s**) baby bird

chicken *n* (*pl* -**s**) domestic fowl ▶ *adj* (*Slang*) cowardly

chickenpox *n* (*pl* -**es**) infectious disease with an itchy rash
chickenpoxes *n* ▷ **chickenpox**
chickens *n* ▷ **chicken**

chickpea *n* (*pl* -**s**) edible yellow pealike seed
chickpeas *n* ▷ **chickpea**
chicks *n* ▷ **chick**

chickweed *n* (*pl* -**s**) weed with small white flowers
chickweeds *n* ▷ **chickweed**
chicories *n* ▷ **chicory**

chicory *n* (*pl* -**ries**) plant whose leaves are used in salads
chics *n* ▷ **chic**
chid *v* ▷ **chide**
chidden *v* ▷ **chide**

chide *v* (**chiding**, **chided** *or* **chid**) (**chid** *or* **chidden**) rebuke, scold
chided *v* ▷ **chide**
chiding *v* ▷ **chide**

chief *n* (*pl* -**s**) head of a group of people ▶ *adj* most important

chiefly *adv* especially
chiefs *n* ▷ **chief**

chieftain *n* (*pl* -**s**) leader of a tribe
chieftains *n* ▷ **chieftain**

chiffon [**shif**-fon] *n* (*pl* -**s**) fine see-through fabric
chiffons *n* ▷ **chiffon**

chignon [**sheen**-yon] *n* (*pl* -**s**) knot of hair pinned up at the back of the head

chignons *n* ▷ **chignon**
chihuahua [chee-**wah**-wah] *n* (*pl* -**s**) tiny short-haired dog
chihuahuas *n* ▷ **chihuahua**
chilblain *n* (*pl* -**s**) inflammation of the fingers or toes, caused by exposure to cold
chilblains *n* ▷ **chilblain**
child *n* (*pl* **children**) young human being, boy or girl > **childhood** *n* (*pl* -**s**) > **childless** *adj* > **childlessness** *n*
childbirth *n* (*pl* -**s**) giving birth to a child
childbirths *n* ▷ **childbirth**
childhood *n* ▷ **child**
childhoods *n* ▷ **child**
childish *adj* immature, silly > **childishly** *adv* > **childishness** *n*
childishly *adv* ▷ **childish**
childishness *n* ▷ **childish**
childless *adj* ▷ **child**
childlessness *n* ▷ **child**
childlike *adj* innocent, trustful
children *n* ▷ **child**
chili *n* ▷ **chilli**
chilies *n* ▷ **chilli**
chill *n* (*pl* -**s**) feverish cold ▶ *v* (-**s**, -**ing**, -**ed**) make (something) cool or cold ▶ *adj* unpleasantly cold
chilled *v* ▷ **chill**
chilli, chili *n* (*pl* -**es**) small red or green hot-tasting capsicum pod, used in cooking
chillier *adj* ▷ **chilly**
chillies *n* ▷ **chilli**
chilliest *adj* ▷ **chilly**
chilliness *n* ▷ **chilly**
chillinesses *n* ▷ **chilly**
chilling *v* ▷ **chill**
chills *n*, *v* ▷ **chill**
chilly *adj* (-**lier**, -**liest**) moderately cold > **chilliness** *n* (*pl* -**es**)
chime *n* (*pl* -**s**) musical ringing sound of a bell or clock ▶ *v* (-**mes**, -**ming**, -**med**) make a musical ringing sound
chimed *v* ▷ **chime**
chimera [kime-**meer**-a] *n* (*pl* -**s**) unrealistic hope or idea
chimeras *n* ▷ **chimera**
chimes *n*, *v* ▷ **chime**
chiming *v* ▷ **chime**
chimney *n* (*pl* -**s**) hollow vertical structure for carrying away smoke from a fire
chimneys *n* ▷ **chimney**
chimp *n* (*pl* -**s**) (*Informal*) ▷ **chimpanzee**
chimpanzee *n* (*pl* -**s**) intelligent black African ape
chimpanzees *n* ▷ **chimpanzee**

chimps *n* ▷ **chimp**
chin *n* (*pl* -**s**) part of the face below the mouth
china *n* (*pl* -**s**) fine earthenware or porcelain
chinas *n* ▷ **china**
chinchilla *n* (*pl* -**s**) S American rodent bred for its soft grey fur
chinchillas *n* ▷ **chinchilla**
chine *n* (*pl* -**s**) cut of meat including part of the backbone
chines *n* ▷ **chine**
chink[1] *n* (*pl* -**s**) small narrow opening
chink[2] *v* (-**s**, -**ing**, -**ed**) ▶ *n* (*pl* -**s**) (make) a light ringing sound
chinked *v* ▷ **chink**[2]
chinking *v* ▷ **chink**[2]
chinks *n* ▷ **chink**[1, 2] ▶ *v* ▷ **chink**[2]
chins *n* ▷ **chin**
chintz *n* (*pl* -**es**) printed cotton fabric with a glazed finish
chintzes *n* ▷ **chintz**
chinwag *n* (*pl* -**s**) (BRIT, AUST & NZ) (*Informal*) chat
chinwags *n* ▷ **chinwag**
chip *n* (*pl* -**s**) strip of potato, fried in deep fat ▶ *v* (**chips, chipping, chipped**) break small pieces from
chipboard *n* (*pl* -**s**) thin board made of compressed wood particles
chipboards *n* ▷ **chipboard**
chipmunk *n* (*pl* -**s**) small squirrel-like N American rodent with a striped back
chipmunks *n* ▷ **chipmunk**
chipped *v* ▷ **chip**
chippie *n* (*pl* -**s**) (BRIT, AUST & NZ) (*Informal*) carpenter
chippies *n* ▷ **chippie**
chipping *v* ▷ **chip**
chips *n*, *v* ▷ **chip**
chiropodist [kir-**rop**-pod-ist] *n* (*pl* -**s**) person who treats minor foot complaints > **chiropody** *n*
chiropodists *n* ▷ **chiropodist**
chiropody *n* ▷ **chiropodist**
chiropractic [kire-oh-**prak**-tik] *n* (*pl* -**s**) system of treating bodily disorders by manipulation of the spine > **chiropractor** *n* (*pl* -**s**)
chiropractics *n* ▷ **chiropractic**
chiropractor *n* ▷ **chiropractic**
chiropractors *n* ▷ **chiropractic**
chirp *v* (-**s**, -**ing**, -**ed**) (of a bird or insect) make a short high-pitched sound ▶ *n* (*pl* -**s**) chirping sound
chirped *v* ▷ **chirp**
chirpier *adj* ▷ **chirpy**
chirpiest *adj* ▷ **chirpy**
chirpily *adv* ▷ **chirpy**

chirpiness n ▷ **chirpy**
chirping v ▷ **chirp**
chirps v, n ▷ **chirp**
chirpy adj (**-pier, -piest**) (Informal) lively and cheerful > **chirpily** adv > **chirpiness** n
chisel n (pl **-s**) metal tool with a sharp end for shaping wood or stone ▶ v (**-els, -elling, -elled**) carve or form with a chisel
chiselled v ▷ **chisel**
chiselling v ▷ **chisel**
chisels n, v ▷ **chisel**
chit[1] n (pl **-s**) short official note, such as a receipt
chit[2] n (pl **-s**) (BRIT, AUST & NZ) (old-fashioned) pert or impudent girl
chitchat n (pl **-s**) chat, gossip
chitchats n ▷ **chitchat**
chits n ▷ **chit**[1, 2]
chitterlings pl n pig's intestines cooked as food
chivalries n ▷ **chivalry**
chivalrous adj ▷ **chivalry**
chivalrously adv ▷ **chivalry**
chivalry n (pl **-ries**) courteous behaviour, esp. by men towards women > **chivalrous** adj > **chivalrously** adv
chives pl n herb with a mild onion flavour
chivvied v ▷ **chivvy**
chivvies v ▷ **chivvy**
chivvy v (**-vies, -vying, -vied**) (Informal) harass, nag
chivvying v ▷ **chivvy**
chloride n (pl **-s**) compound of chlorine and another substance
chlorides n ▷ **chloride**
chlorinate v (**-ates, -ating, -ated**) disinfect (water) with chlorine > **chlorination** n
chlorinated v ▷ **chlorinate**
chlorinates v ▷ **chlorinate**
chlorinating v ▷ **chlorinate**
chlorination n ▷ **chlorinate**
chlorine n (pl **-s**) strong-smelling greenish-yellow gaseous element, used to disinfect water
chlorines n ▷ **chlorine**
chlorofluorocarbon n (pl **-s**) any of various gaseous compounds of carbon, hydrogen, chlorine, and fluorine, used in refrigerators and aerosol propellants, some of which break down the ozone in the atmosphere
chlorofluorocarbons n ▷ **chlorofluorocarbon**
chloroform n (pl **-s**) strong-smelling liquid formerly used as an anaesthetic
chloroforms n ▷ **chloroform**
chlorophyll n (pl **-s**) green colouring matter of plants, which enables them to convert sunlight into energy
chlorophylls n ▷ **chlorophyll**
chock n (pl **-s**) block or wedge used to prevent a heavy object from moving
chockablock adj completely full
chocks n ▷ **chock**
chocolate n (pl **-s**) sweet food made from cacao seeds ▶ adj dark brown
chocolates n ▷ **chocolate**
choice n (pl **-s**) choosing ▶ adj (**choicer, choicest**) of high quality
choicer adj ▷ **choice**
choices n ▷ **choice**
choicest adj ▷ **choice**
choir n (pl **-s**) organized group of singers, esp. in church
choirs n ▷ **choir**
choke v (**chokes, choking, choked**) hinder or stop the breathing of (a person) by strangling or smothering ▶ n (pl **-s**) device controlling the amount of air that is mixed with the fuel in a petrol engine
choked v ▷ **choke**
choker n (pl **-s**) tight-fitting necklace
chokers n ▷ **choker**
chokes v, n ▷ **choke**
choking v ▷ **choke**
cholera [kol-ler-a] n (pl **-s**) serious infectious disease causing severe vomiting and diarrhoea
choleras n ▷ **cholera**
choleric [kol-ler-ik] adj bad-tempered
cholesterol [kol-**lest**-er-oll] n (pl **-s**) fatty substance found in animal tissue, an excess of which can cause heart disease
cholesterols n ▷ **cholesterol**
chomp v (**-s, -ing, -ed**) chew noisily
chomped v ▷ **chomp**
chomping v ▷ **chomp**
chomps v ▷ **chomp**
chook n (pl **-s**) (AUST & NZ) hen or chicken
chooks n ▷ **chook**
choose v (**chooses, choosing, chose, chosen**) select from a number of alternatives
chooses v ▷ **choose**
choosier adj ▷ **choosy**
choosiest adj ▷ **choosy**
choosing v ▷ **choose**
choosy adj (**-sier, -siest**) (Informal) fussy, hard to please
chop[1] v (**chops, chopping, chopped**) cut with a blow from an axe or knife (BOXING) (KARATE) ▶ n (pl **-s**) cutting or sharp blow
chop[2] v (**chops, chopping, chopped**) change

one's mind repeatedly

chopped v ▷ **chop**[1, 2]

chopper n (pl -**s**) (Informal) helicopter

choppers n ▷ **chopper**

choppier adj ▷ **choppy**

choppiest adj ▷ **choppy**

choppiness n ▷ **choppy**

choppinesses n ▷ **choppy**

chopping v ▷ **chop**[1, 2]

choppy adj (-**pier**, -**ppiest**) (of the sea) fairly rough > **choppiness** n (pl -**es**)

chops pl n (BRIT, AUST & NZ) (Informal) jaws, cheeks ▶ v ▷ **chop**[1, 2] ▶ n ▷ **chop**[1]

chopsticks pl n pair of thin sticks used to eat Chinese food

choral adj of a choir

chorale [kor-**rahl**] n (pl -**s**) slow stately hymn tune

chorales n ▷ **chorale**

chord[1] n (pl -**s**) (MATHS) straight line joining two points on a curve

chord[2] n (pl -**s**) simultaneous sounding of three or more musical notes

chords n ▷ **chord**[1, 2]

chore n (pl -**s**) routine task

choreographer n ▷ **choreography**

choreographers n ▷ **choreography**

choreographic adj ▷ **choreography**

choreographies n ▷ **choreography**

choreography n (pl -**phies**) composition of steps and movements for dancing > **choreographer** n (pl -**s**) > **choreographic** adj

chores n ▷ **chore**

chorister n (pl -**s**) singer in a choir

choristers n ▷ **chorister**

chortle v (-**tles**, -**tling**, -**tled**) chuckle in amusement ▶ n (pl -**s**) amused chuckle

chortled v ▷ **chortle**

chortles v, n ▷ **chortle**

chortling v ▷ **chortle**

chorus n (pl -**es**) large choir ▶ v (-**es**, -**ing**, -**ed**) sing or say together

chorused v ▷ **chorus**

choruses n, v ▷ **chorus**

chorusing v ▷ **chorus**

chose v ▷ **choose**

chosen v ▷ **choose**

chow n (pl -**s**) thick-coated dog with a curled tail, orig. from China

chowder n (pl -**s**) thick soup containing clams or fish

chowders n ▷ **chowder**

chows n ▷ **chow**

christen v (-**s**, -**ing**, -**ed**) baptize > **christening** n (pl -**s**)

christened v ▷ **christen**

christening v, n ▷ **christen**

christenings n ▷ **christen**

christens v ▷ **christen**

chromatic adj of colour or colours > **chromatically** adv

chromatically adv ▷ **chromatic**

chromatographies n ▷ **chromatic**

chromatography n (pl -**phies**) separation and analysis of the components of a substance by slowly passing it through an adsorbing material

chrome n ▷ **chromium**

chromes n ▷ **chromium**

chromium, chrome n (pl -**s**) (CHEM) grey metallic element used in steel alloys and for electroplating

chromiums n ▷ **chromium**

chromosome n (pl -**s**) microscopic gene-carrying body in the nucleus of a cell

chromosomes n ▷ **chromosome**

chronic adj (of an illness) lasting a long time > **chronically** adv

chronically adv ▷ **chronic**

chronicle n (pl -**s**) record of events in order of occurrence ▶ v (-**les**, -**ing**, -**led**) record in or as if in a chronicle > **chronicler** n (pl -**s**)

chronicled v ▷ **chronicle**

chronicler n ▷ **chronicle**

chroniclers n ▷ **chronicle**

chronicles v ▷ **chronicle**

chronicling v ▷ **chronicle**

chronological adj ▷ **chronology**

chronologically adv ▷ **chronology**

chronologies n ▷ **chronology**

chronology n (pl -**gies**) arrangement or list of events in order of occurrence > **chronological** adj > **chronologically** adv

chronometer n (pl -**s**) timepiece designed to be accurate in all conditions

chronometers n ▷ **chronometer**

chrysalis [**kriss**-a-liss] n (pl -**es**) insect in the stage between larva and adult, when it is in a cocoon

chrysalises n ▷ **chrysalis**

chrysanthemum n (pl -**s**) garden flower with a large head made up of thin petals

chrysanthemums n ▷ **chrysanthemum**

chub n (pl **chub**) European freshwater fish of the carp family

chubbier adj ▷ **chubby**

chubbiest adj ▷ **chubby**

chubbiness n ▷ **chubby**

chubby adj (-**bier**, -**biest**) plump and round > **chubbiness** n

chuck¹ v (**-s, -ing, -ed**) (*Informal*) throw
chuck² n (*pl* **-s**) cut of beef from the neck to the
shoulder
  chucked v ▷ **chuck¹**
  chucking v ▷ **chuck¹**
chuckle v (**-les, -ling, -led**) laugh softly ▶ n (*pl*
-s) soft laugh
  chuckled v ▷ **chuckle**
  chuckles v, n ▷ **chuckle**
  chuckling v ▷ **chuckle**
  chucks v ▷ **chuck¹** ▶ n ▷ **chuck²**
chuffed adj (*Informal*) very pleased
chug n (*pl* **-s**) short dull sound like the noise
of an engine ▶ v (**chugs, chugging, chugged**)
operate or move with this sound
  chugged v ▷ **chug**
  chugging v ▷ **chug**
  chugs n, v ▷ **chug**
chukka n (*pl* **-s**) period of play in polo
  chukkas n ▷ **chukka**
chum (*Informal*) n (*pl* **-s**) close friend ▶ v
(**chums, chumming, chummed**) form a close
friendship with > **chummy** adj (**-mmier,
-mmiest**) > **chumminess** n (*pl* **-es**)
  chummed v ▷ **chum**
  chummier adj ▷ **chum**
  chummiest adj ▷ **chum**
  chumminess n ▷ **chum**
  chumminesses n ▷ **chum**
  chumming v ▷ **chum**
  chummy adj ▷ **chum**
chump n (*pl* **-s**) (*Informal*) stupid person
  chumps n ▷ **chump**
  chums n, v ▷ **chum**
chunk n (*pl* **-s**) thick solid piece
  chunkier adj ▷ **chunky**
  chunkiest adj ▷ **chunky**
  chunkiness n ▷ **chunky**
  chunkinesses n ▷ **chunky**
  chunks n ▷ **chunk**
chunky adj (**-kier, -kiest**) (of a person) broad
and heavy > **chunkiness** n (*pl* **-es**)
church n (*pl* **-s**) building for public Christian
worship
  churches n ▷ **church**
churchgoer n (*pl* **-s**) person who attends
church regularly
  churchgoers n ▷ **churchgoer**
churchwarden n (*pl* **-s**) member of a
congregation who assists the vicar
  churchwardens n ▷ **churchwarden**
churchyard n (*pl* **-s**) grounds round a church,
used as a graveyard
  churchyards n ▷ **churchyard**
churlish adj surly and rude > **churlishly** adv

  > **churlishness** n
  churlishly adv ▷ **churlish**
  churlishness n ▷ **churlish**
churn n (*pl* **-s**) machine in which cream is
shaken to make butter ▶ v (**-s, -ing, -ed**) stir
(cream) vigorously to make butter
  churned v ▷ **churn**
  churning v ▷ **churn**
  churns n, v ▷ **churn**
chute¹ [shoot] n (*pl* **-s**) steep slope down which
things may be slid
chute² n (*pl* **-s**) (*Informal*) ▷ **parachute**
  chutes n ▷ **chute¹, ²**
chutney n (*pl* **-s**) pickle made from fruit,
vinegar, spices, and sugar
  chutneys n ▷ **chutney**
cicada [sik-kah-da] n (*pl* **-s**) large insect that
makes a high-pitched drone
  cicadas n ▷ **cicada**
  cicatrices n ▷ **cicatrix**
cicatrix [sik-a-trix] n (*pl* **-trices**) scar
  cid n (**cids**). A cid is a hero or
  commander. Cid scores 6 points.
cider n (*pl* **-s**) alcoholic drink made from
fermented apple juice
  ciders n ▷ **cider**
cigar n (*pl* **-s**) roll of cured tobacco leaves for
smoking
cigarette n (*pl* **-s**) thin roll of shredded tobacco
in thin paper, for smoking
  cigarettes n ▷ **cigarette**
  cigars n ▷ **cigar**
cinch [sinch] n (*pl* **-es**) (*Informal*) easy task
  cinches n ▷ **cinch**
cinder n (*pl* **-s**) piece of material that will not
burn, left after burning coal
  cinders n ▷ **cinder**
cinema n (*pl* **-s**) place for showing films
  > **cinematic** adj
  cinemas n ▷ **cinema**
  cinematic adj ▷ **cinema**
  cinematographer n ▷ **cinematography**
  cinematographers n ▷ **cinematography**
cinematography n technique of making films
  > **cinematographer** n (*pl* **-s**)
cineraria n (*pl* **-s**) garden plant with daisy-like
flowers
  cinerarias n ▷ **cineraria**
cinnamon n (*pl* **-s**) spice obtained from the
bark of an Asian tree
  cinnamons n ▷ **cinnamon**
cipher, cypher [sife-er] n (*pl* **-s**) system of secret
writing
  ciphers n ▷ **cipher**
circa [sir-ka] *prep* (LATIN) approximately, about

circle n (pl -s) perfectly round geometric figure,
line, or shape ▶ v (**circles, circling, circled**)
move in a circle (round)
  circled v ▷ **circle**
  circles n, v ▷ **circle**
circlet n (pl -s) circular ornament worn on
the head
  circlets n ▷ **circlet**
  circling v ▷ **circle**
circuit n (pl -s) complete route or course, esp.
a circular one
circuitous [sir-**kew**-it-uss] adj indirect and
lengthy > **circuitously** adv
  circuitously adv ▷ **circuitous**
circuitry [sir-kit-tree] n electrical circuit(s)
  circuits n ▷ **circuit**
circular adj in the shape of a circle ▶ n (pl -s)
letter for general distribution > **circularity** n
  circularity n ▷ **circular**
  circulars n ▷ **circular**
circulate v (-lates, -lating, -lated) send, go, or
pass from place to place or person to person
> **circulatory** adj
  circulated v ▷ **circulate**
  circulates v ▷ **circulate**
  circulating v ▷ **circulate**
circulation n flow of blood around the body
  circulatory adj ▷ **circulate**
circumcise v (-cises, -cising, -cised) remove
the foreskin of > **circumcision** n (pl -s)
  circumcised v ▷ **circumcise**
  circumcises v ▷ **circumcise**
  circumcising v ▷ **circumcise**
  circumcision n ▷ **circumcise**
  circumcisions n ▷ **circumcise**
circumference n (pl -s) boundary of a specified
area or shape, esp. of a circle
  circumferences n ▷ **circumference**
circumflex n (pl -es) mark (^) over a vowel to
show that it is pronounced in a particular
way
  circumflexes n ▷ **circumflex**
circumlocution n (pl -s) indirect way of saying
something
  circumlocutions n ▷ **circumlocution**
circumnavigate v (-gates, -gating, -gated)
sail right round > **circumnavigation** n (pl -s)
  circumnavigated v ▷ **circumnavigate**
  circumnavigates v ▷ **circumnavigate**
  circumnavigating v ▷ **circumnavigate**
  circumnavigation n ▷ **circumnavigate**
  circumnavigations n ▷ **circumnavigate**
circumscribe v (-scribes, -scribing, -scribed)
limit, restrict > **circumscription** n (pl -s)
  circumscribed v ▷ **circumscribe**

  circumscribes v ▷ **circumscribe**
  circumscribing v ▷ **circumscribe**
  circumscription n ▷ **circumscribe**
  circumscriptions n ▷ **circumscribe**
circumspect adj cautious and careful
not to take risks > **circumspectly** adv
> **circumspection** n
  circumspection n ▷ **circumspect**
  circumspectly adv ▷ **circumspect**
circumstance n (pl -s) (usu. pl occurrence or
condition that accompanies or influences a
person or event
  circumstances n ▷ **circumstance**
circumstantial adj (of evidence) strongly
suggesting something but not proving it
circumvent v (-s, -ing, -ed) avoid or get round
(a rule etc.) > **circumvention** n (pl -s)
  circumvented v ▷ **circumvent**
  circumventing v ▷ **circumvent**
  circumvention n ▷ **circumvent**
  circumventions n ▷ **circumvent**
  circumvents v ▷ **circumvent**
circus n (pl -es) (performance given by) a
travelling company of acrobats, clowns,
performing animals, etc.
  circuses n ▷ **circus**
cirrhosis [sir-**roh**-siss] n serious liver disease,
often caused by drinking too much alcohol
> **cirrhotic** adj
  cirrhotic adj ▷ **cirrhosis**
  cirri n ▷ **cirrus**
cirrus n (pl -ri) high wispy cloud
cistern n (pl -s) water tank, esp. one that holds
water for flushing a toilet
  cisterns n ▷ **cistern**
citadel n (pl -s) fortress in a city
  citadels n ▷ **citadel**
  citation n ▷ **cite**
  citations n ▷ **cite**
cite v (cites, citing, cited) quote, refer to
> **citation** n (pl -s)
  cited v ▷ **cite**
  cites v ▷ **cite**
  cities n ▷ **city**
  citing v ▷ **cite**
citizen n (pl -s) native or naturalized member
of a state or nation > **citizenship** n (pl -s)
  citizens n ▷ **citizen**
  citizenship n ▷ **citizen**
  citizenships n ▷ **citizen**
city n (pl -ties) large or important town
civet [**siv**-vit] n (pl -s) spotted catlike African
mammal
  civets n ▷ **civet**
civic adj of a city or citizens

civics *n* study of the rights and responsibilities of citizenship
civil *adj* relating to the citizens of a state as opposed to the armed forces or the Church > **civilly** *adv*
civilian *n* (*pl* -**s**) ▶ *adj* (person) not belonging to the armed forces
  civilians *n* ▷ **civilian**
  civilities *n* ▷ **civility**
civility *n* (*pl* -**ities**) polite or courteous behaviour
civilization *n* (*pl* -**s**) high level of human cultural and social development
  civilizations *n* ▷ **civilization**
civilize *v* (-**izes**, -**izing**, -**ized**) refine or educate (a person)
  civilized *v* ▷ **civilize**
  civilizes *v* ▷ **civilize**
  civilizing *v* ▷ **civilize**
  civilly *adv* ▷ **civil**
civvies *pl n* (BRIT, AUST & NZ) (*Slang*) ordinary clothes that are not part of a uniform
clack *n* (*pl* -**s**) sound made by two hard objects striking each other ▶ *v* (-**s**, -**ing**, -**ed**) make this sound
  clacked *v* ▷ **clack**
  clacking *v* ▷ **clack**
  clacks *n, v* ▷ **clack**
clad *v* (**clads, cladding, clad**) ▷ **clothe**
cladding *n* (*pl* -**s**) material used to cover the outside of a building ▶ *v* ▷ **clad**
  claddings *n* ▷ **cladding**
  clads *v* ▷ **clad**
claim *v* (-**s**, -**ing**, -**ed**) assert as a fact ▶ *n* (*pl* -**s**) assertion that something is true > **claimant** *n* (*pl* -**s**)
  claimant *n* ▷ **claim**
  claimants *n* ▷ **claim**
  claimed *v* ▷ **claim**
  claiming *v* ▷ **claim**
  claims *v, n* ▷ **claim**
clairvoyance *n* (*pl* -**s**) power of perceiving things beyond the natural range of the senses > **clairvoyant** *n* (*pl* -**s**) *adj*
  clairvoyances *n* ▷ **clairvoyance**
  clairvoyant *n, adj* ▷ **clairvoyance**
  clairvoyants *n* ▷ **clairvoyance**
clam *n* (*pl* -**s**) edible shellfish with a hinged shell ▶ *v* (**clams, clamming, clammed**) (*Informal*) stop talking, esp. through nervousness
clamber *v* (-**s**, -**ing**, -**ed**) climb awkwardly
  clambered *v* ▷ **clamber**
  clambering *v* ▷ **clamber**
  clambers *v* ▷ **clamber**

clammed *v* ▷ **clam**
clammier *adj* ▷ **clammy**
clammiest *adj* ▷ **clammy**
clamming *v* ▷ **clam**
clammy *adj* (-**mier**, -**miest**) unpleasantly moist and sticky
clamour *n* (*pl* -**s**) loud protest ▶ *v* (-**s**, -**ing**, -**ed**) make a loud noise or outcry > **clamorous** *adj* > **clamorously** *adv* > **clamorousness** *n*
  clamoured *v* ▷ **clamour**
  clamouring *v* ▷ **clamour**
  clamourous *adj* ▷ **clamour**
  clamourously *adj* ▷ **clamour**
  clamourousness *n* ▷ **clamour**
  clamours *n, v* ▷ **clamour**
clamp *n* (*pl* -**s**) tool with movable jaws for holding things together tightly ▶ *v* (-**s**, -**ing**, -**ed**) fasten with a clamp
  clamped *v* ▷ **clamp**
  clamping *v* ▷ **clamp**
  clamps *n, v* ▷ **clamp**
  clams *v, n* ▷ **clam**
clan *n* (*pl* -**s**) group of families with a common ancestor, esp. among Scottish Highlanders
clandestine *adj* secret and concealed > **clandestinely** *adv*
  clandestinely *adv* ▷ **clandestine**
clang *v* (-**s**, -**ing**, -**ed**) make a loud ringing metallic sound ▶ *n* (*pl* -**s**) ringing metallic sound
  clanged *v* ▷ **clang**
clanger *n* (*pl* -**s**) (*Informal*) obvious mistake
  clangers *n* ▷ **clanger**
  clanging *v* ▷ **clang**
clangour *n* (*pl* -**s**) loud continuous clanging sound
  clangours *n* ▷ **clangour**
  clangs *v, n* ▷ **clang**
clank *n* (*pl* -**s**) harsh metallic sound ▶ *v* (-**s**, -**ing**, -**ed**) make such a sound
  clanked *v* ▷ **clank**
  clanking *v* ▷ **clank**
  clanks *n, v* ▷ **clank**
clannish *adj* (of a group) tending to exclude outsiders > **clannishness** *n*
  clannishness *n* ▷ **clannish**
  clans *n* ▷ **clan**
clap *v* (**claps, clapping, clapped**) applaud by hitting the palms of one's hands sharply together ▶ *n* (*pl* -**s**) act or sound of clapping
  clapped *v* ▷ **clap**
clapper *n* (*pl* -**s**) piece of metal inside a bell, which causes it to sound when struck against the side
clapperboard *n* (*pl* -**s**) pair of hinged boards

clapped together during filming to help in synchronizing sound and picture

clapperboards *n* ▷ **clapperboard**

clappers *n* ▷ **clapper**

clapping *v* ▷ **clap**

claps *v, n* ▷ **clap**

claptrap *n* (*pl* **-s**) (*Informal*) foolish or pretentious talk

claptraps *n* ▷ **claptrap**

claret [klar-rit] *n* (*pl* **-s**) dry red wine from Bordeaux

clarets *n* ▷ **claret**

clarification *n* ▷ **clarify**

clarifications *n* ▷ **clarify**

clarified *v* ▷ **clarify**

clarifies *v* ▷ **clarify**

clarify *v* (**-fies, -fying, -fied**) make (a matter) clear and unambiguous > **clarification** *n* (*pl* **-s**)

clarifying *v* ▷ **clarify**

clarinet *n* (*pl* **-s**) keyed woodwind instrument with a single reed > **clarinettist** *n* (*pl* **-s**)

clarinets *n* ▷ **clarinet**

clarinettist *n* ▷ **clarinet**

clarinettists *n* ▷ **clarinet**

clarion *n* (*pl* **-s**) obsolete high-pitched trumpet

clarions *n* ▷ **clarion**

clarities *n* ▷ **clarity**

clarity *n* (*pl* **-ities**) clearness

clash *v* (**-es, -ing, -ed**) come into conflict ▶ *n* (*pl* **-es**) fight, argument

clashed *v* ▷ **clash**

clashes *v, n* ▷ **clash**

clashing *v* ▷ **clash**

clasp *n* (*pl* **-s**) device for fastening things ▶ *v* (**-s, -ing, -ed**) grasp or embrace firmly

clasped *v* ▷ **clasp**

clasping *v* ▷ **clasp**

clasps *n, v* ▷ **clasp**

class *n* (*pl* **-es**) group of people sharing a similar social position ▶ *v* (**-es, -ing, -ed**) place in a class

classed *v* ▷ **class**

classes *n, v* ▷ **class**

classic *adj* being a typical example of something ▶ *n* (*pl* **-s**) author, artist, or work of art of recognized excellence ▶ *pl* study of ancient Greek and Roman literature and culture

classical *adj* of or in a restrained conservative style > **classically** *adv*

classically *adv* ▷ **classical**

classicism *n* artistic style showing emotional restraint and regularity of form > **classicist** *n* (*pl* **-s**)

classicist *n* ▷ **classicism**

classicists *n* ▷ **classicism**

classics *n* ▷ **classic**

classier *adj* ▷ **classy**

classiest *adj* ▷ **classy**

classifiable *adj* ▷ **classify**

classification *n* ▷ **classify**

classifications *n* ▷ **classify**

classified *v* ▷ **classify**

classifies *v* ▷ **classify**

classify *v* (**-fies, -fying, -fied**) divide into groups with similar characteristics > **classifiable** *adj* > **classification** *n* (*pl* **-s**)

classifying *v* ▷ **classify**

classing *v* ▷ **class**

classy *adj* (**classier, classiest**) (*Informal*) stylish and elegant

clatter *v* (**-s, -ing, -ed**) ▶ *n* (*pl* **-s**) (make) a rattling noise

clattered *v* ▷ **clatter**

clattering *v* ▷ **clatter**

clatters *v, n* ▷ **clatter**

clause *n* (*pl* **-s**) section of a legal document

clauses *n* ▷ **clause**

claustrophobia *n* (*pl* **-s**) abnormal fear of confined spaces > **claustrophobic** *adj*

claustrophobia *n* ▷ **claustrophobia**

claustrophobias *n* ▷ **claustrophobia**

claustrophobic *adj* ▷ **claustrophobia**

clavichord *n* (*pl* **-s**) early keyboard instrument

clavichords *n* ▷ **clavichord**

clavicle *n* (*pl* **-s**) ▷ **collarbone**

clavicles *n* ▷ **clavicle**

claw *n* (*pl* **-s**) sharp hooked nail of a bird or beast ▶ *v* (**-s, -ing, -ed**) tear with claws or nails

clawed *v* ▷ **claw**

clawing *v* ▷ **claw**

claws *n, v* ▷ **claw**

clay *n* (*pl* **-s**) fine-grained earth, soft when moist and hardening when baked, used to make bricks and pottery > **clayey** *adj*

clayey *adj* ▷ **clay**

claymore *n* (*pl* **-s**) large two-edged sword formerly used by Scottish Highlanders

claymores *n* ▷ **claymore**

clays *n* ▷ **clay**

clean *adj* (**-er, -est**) free from dirt or impurities ▶ *v* (**-s, -ing, -ed**) make (something) free from dirt ▶ *adv* (*Not standard*) completely > **cleaner** *n* (*pl* **-s**) > **cleanly** *adv* > **cleanliness** *n* (*pl* **-es**)

cleaned *v* ▷ **clean**

cleaner *n, adj* ▷ **clean**

cleaners *n* ▷ **clean**

cleanest *adj* ▷ **clean**

cleaning *v* ▷ **clean**

cleanliness n ▷ **clean**
cleanlinesses n ▷ **clean**
cleanly adv ▷ **clean**
cleans v ▷ **clean**
cleanse v (-ses, -sing, -sed) make clean
> **cleanser** n (pl -s)
cleansed v ▷ **cleanse**
cleanser n ▷ **cleanse**
cleansers n ▷ **cleanse**
cleanses v ▷ **cleanse**
cleansing v ▷ **cleanse**
clear adj (-er, -est) free from doubt or confusion
▶ adv out of the way ▶ v (-s, -ing, -ed) make or
become clear > **clearly** adv
clearance n (pl -s) clearing
clearances n ▷ **clear**
cleared v ▷ **clear**
clearer adj ▷ **clear**
clearest adj ▷ **clear**
clearing n (pl -s) treeless area in a wood ▶ v
▷ **clear**
clearings n ▷ **clearing**
clearly adv ▷ **clear**
clears v ▷ **clear**
clearway n (pl -s) stretch of road on which
motorists may stop in an emergency
clearways n ▷ **clearway**
cleat n (pl -s) wedge
cleats n ▷ **cleat**
cleavage n (pl -s) space between a woman's
breasts, as revealed by a low-cut dress
cleavages n ▷ **cleavage**
cleave[1] v (-ves, -ving, cleft, -ved or clove) (cleft,
cleaved or cloven) split apart
cleave[2] v (-ves, -ving, cleft, cleft) cling or stick
cleaved v ▷ **cleave**[1]
cleaver n (pl -s) butcher's heavy knife with a
square blade
cleavers n ▷ **cleaver**
cleaves v ▷ **cleave**[1, 2]
cleaving v ▷ **cleave**[1, 2]
clef n (pl -s) (MUSIC) symbol at the beginning of
a stave to show the pitch
clefs n ▷ **clef**
cleft n (pl -s) narrow opening or crack ▶ v
▷ **cleave**[1, 2]
clefted v ▷ **cleft**
clefting v ▷ **cleft**
clefts n, v ▷ **cleft**
clematis n climbing plant with large colourful
flowers
clemencies n ▷ **clemency**
clemency n (pl -cies) kind or lenient treatment
clement adj (of weather) mild
clementine n (pl -s) small orange citrus fruit

clementines n ▷ **clementine**
clench v (-es, -ing, -ed) close or squeeze (one's
teeth or fist) tightly
clenched v ▷ **clench**
clenches v ▷ **clench**
clenching v ▷ **clench**
clerestories n ▷ **clerestory**
clerestory [clear-store-ee] n (pl -ries) row
of windows at the top of a wall above an
adjoining roof
clergies n ▷ **clergy**
clergy n (pl clergies) priests and ministers as a
group > **clergyman** n (pl -men)
clergyman n ▷ **clergy**
clergymen n ▷ **clergy**
cleric n (pl -s) member of the clergy
clerical adj of clerks or office work
clerics n ▷ **cleric**
clerk n (pl -s) employee in an office, bank, or
court who keeps records, files, and accounts
clerks n ▷ **clerk**
clever adj (-er, -est) intelligent, quick at
learning > **cleverly** adv > **cleverness** n (pl -es)
cleverer adj ▷ **clever**
cleverest adj ▷ **clever**
cleverly adv ▷ **clever**
cleverness n ▷ **clever**
cleverness n ▷ **clever**
clianthus [klee-anth-us] n (pl -es) Australian or
NZ plant with slender scarlet flowers
clianthuses n ▷ **clianthus**
cliché [klee-shay] n (pl -s) expression or idea
that is no longer effective because of overuse
> **clichéd** adj
clichéd n ▷ **cliché**
clichés n ▷ **cliché**
click n (pl -s) short sharp sound ▶ v (-s, -ing, -ed)
make this sound
clicked v ▷ **click**
clicking v ▷ **click**
clicks n, v ▷ **click**
client n (pl -s) person who uses the services of a
professional person or company
clientele [klee-on-tell] n (pl -s) clients
collectively
clienteles n ▷ **clientele**
clients n ▷ **client**
cliff n (pl -s) steep rock face, esp. along the
sea shore
cliffhanger n (pl -s) film, game, etc., that is
tense and exciting because its outcome is
uncertain
cliffhangers n ▷ **cliffhanger**
cliffs n ▷ **cliff**
climactic adj ▷ **climax**

climate n (pl **-s**) typical weather conditions of an area > **climatic** adj
climates n ▷ **climate**
climatic adj ▷ **climate**
climax n (pl **-es**) most intense point of an experience, series of events, or story > **climactic** adj
climaxes n ▷ **climax**
climb v (**-s, -ing, -ed**) go up, ascend ▶ n (pl **-s**) climbing > **climber** n (pl **-s**)
climbed v ▷ **climb**
climber n ▷ **climb**
climbers n ▷ **climb**
climbing v ▷ **climb**
climbs v, n ▷ **climb**
clime n (pl **-s**) (Poetic) place or its climate
climes n ▷ **clime**
clinch v (**-es, -ing, -ed**) settle (an argument or agreement) decisively
clinched v ▷ **clinch**
clincher n (pl **-s**) (Informal) something decisive
clinchers n ▷ **clincher**
clinches v ▷ **clinch**
clinching v ▷ **clinch**
cling v (**clings, clinging, clung**) hold tightly or stick closely
clingfilm n (pl **-s**) thin polythene material for wrapping food
clingfilms n ▷ **clingfilm**
clinging v ▷ **cling**
clings v ▷ **cling**
clinic n (pl **-s**) building where outpatients receive medical treatment or advice
clinical adj of a clinic > **clinically** adv
clinically adv ▷ **clinic**
clinics n ▷ **clinic**
clink¹ v (**-s, -ing, -ed**) ▶ n (pl **-s**) (make) a light sharp metallic sound
clink² n (pl **-s**) (BRIT, AUST & NZ) (Slang) prison
clinked v ▷ **clink¹**
clinker n (pl **-s**) fused coal left over in a fire or furnace
clinkers n ▷ **clinker**
clinking v ▷ **clink¹**
clinks n ▷ **clink¹, ²** ▶ v ▷ **clink¹**
clip¹ v (**clips, clipping, clipped**) cut with shears or scissors ▶ n (**-s**) short extract of a film
clip² n device for attaching or holding things together ▶ v (**clips, clipping, clipped**) attach or hold together with a clip
clipped v ▷ **clip¹, ²**
clipper n (pl **-s**) fast commercial sailing ship
clippers pl n tool for clipping ▶ n ▷ **clipper**
clipping n (**-s**) something cut out, esp. an article from a newspaper ▶ v ▷ **clip¹, ²**

clippings n ▷ **clipping**
clips n, v ▷ **clip¹, ²**
clique [kleek] n (pl **-s**) small exclusive group
cliques n ▷ **clique**
clitoral adj ▷ **clitoris**
clitoris [klit-or-iss] n (pl **-es**) small sexually sensitive organ at the front of the vulva > **clitoral** adj
clitorises n ▷ **clitoris**
cloak n (pl **-s**) loose sleeveless outer garment ▶ v (**-s, -ing, -ed**) cover or conceal
cloaked v ▷ **cloak**
cloaking v ▷ **cloak**
cloakroom n (pl **-s**) room where coats may be left temporarily
cloakrooms n ▷ **cloakroom**
cloaks n, v ▷ **cloak**
clobber¹ v (**-s, -ing, -ed**) (Informal) hit
clobber² n (pl **-s**) (BRIT, AUST & NZ) (Informal) belongings, esp. clothes
clobbered v ▷ **clobber¹**
clobbering v ▷ **clobber¹**
clobbers v ▷ **clobber¹** ▶ n ▷ **clobber²**
cloche [klosh] n (pl **-s**) cover to protect young plants
cloches n ▷ **cloche**
clock n (pl **-s**) instrument for showing the time
clocks n ▷ **clock**
clockwise adv, adj in the direction in which the hands of a clock rotate
clockwork n mechanism similar to the kind in a clock, used in wind-up toys
clod n (pl **-s**) lump of earth
clods n ▷ **clod**
clog v (**clogs, clogging, clogged**) obstruct ▶ n (pl **-s**) wooden or wooden-soled shoe
clogged v ▷ **clog**
clogging v ▷ **clog**
clogs v, n ▷ **clog**
cloister n (pl **-s**) covered pillared arcade, usu. in a monastery
cloistered adj sheltered
cloisters n ▷ **cloister**
clone n (pl **-s**) animal or plant produced artificially from the cells of another animal or plant, and identical to the original (Informal) ▶ v (**clones, cloning, cloned**) produce as a clone
cloned v ▷ **clone**
clones n, v ▷ **clone**
cloning v ▷ **clone**
close¹ v (**-ses, -sing, -sed**) [rhymes with **nose**] shut ▶ n (pl **-s**) end, conclusion
close² adj (**-r, -st**) [rhymes with **dose**] near ▶ adv closely, tightly > **closely** adv > **closeness** n

(*pl* -**es**)
closed *v* ▷ **close¹**
closely *adv* ▷ **close²**
closeness *n* ▷ **close²**
closenesses *n* ▷ **close²**
closer *adj* ▷ **close²**
closes *v, n* ▷ **close¹**
closest *adj* ▷ **close²**
closet *n* (*pl* -**s**) (us) cupboard ▶ *adj* private,
secret ▶ *v* (**-s, -ing, -ed**) shut (oneself) away
in private
closeted *v* ▷ **closet**
closeting *v* ▷ **closet**
closets *n, v* ▷ **closet**
closing *v* ▷ **close¹**
closure *n* (*pl* -**s**) closing
closures *n* ▷ **closure**
clot *n* (*pl* -**s**) soft thick lump formed from liquid
▶ *v* (**-s, -tting, -tted**) form soft thick lumps
cloth *n* (*pl* -**s**) (piece of) woven fabric
clothe *v* (**clothes, clothing, clothed** *or* **clad**) put
clothes on
clothed *v* ▷ **clothe**
clothes *pl n* articles of dress ▶ *v* ▷ **clothe**
clothing *n* clothes collectively ▶ *v* ▷ **clothe**
cloths *n* ▷ **cloth**
clots *n, v* ▷ **clot**
clotted *v* ▷ **clot**
clotting *v* ▷ **clot**
cloud *n* (*pl* -**s**) mass of condensed water vapour
floating in the sky ▶ *v* (**-s, -ing, -ed**) (*foll. by*
over) become cloudy > **cloudless** *adj*
cloudburst *n* (*pl* -**s**) heavy fall of rain
cloudbursts *n* ▷ **cloudburst**
clouded *v* ▷ **cloud**
cloudier *adj* ▷ **cloud**
cloudiest *adj* ▷ **cloud**
cloudiness *n* ▷ **cloudy**
clouding *v* ▷ **cloud**
cloudless *adj* ▷ **cloud**
clouds *n, v* ▷ **cloud**
cloudy *adj* (**-dier, -diest**) having a lot of clouds
> **cloudiness** *n*
clout (*Informal*) *n* (*pl* -**s**) hard blow ▶ *v* (**-s, -ed,
-ing**) hit hard
clouted *v* ▷ **clout**
clouting *v* ▷ **clout**
clouts *n, v* ▷ **clout**
clove¹ *n* (*pl* -**s**) dried flower bud of a tropical
tree, used as a spice
clove² *n* (*pl* -**s**) segment of a bulb of garlic
clove³ *v* ▷ **cleave¹**
cloven *v* ▷ **cleave¹**
clover *n* (*pl* -**s**) plant with three-lobed leaves
clovers *n* ▷ **clover**

cloves *n* ▷ **clove¹, ²**
clown *n* (*pl* -**s**) comic entertainer in a circus ▶ *v*
(**-s, -ing, -ed**) behave foolishly > **clownish** *adj*
> **clownishly** *adv* > **clownishness** *n*
clowned *v* ▷ **clown**
clowning *v* ▷ **clown**
clownish *adj* ▷ **clown**
clownishly *adv* ▷ **clown**
clownishness *n* ▷ **clown**
clowns *n, v* ▷ **clown**
club *n* (*pl* -**s**) association of people with
common interests ▶ *v* (**clubs, clubbing,
clubbed**) hit with a club
clubbed *v* ▷ **club**
clubbing *v* ▷ **club**
clubs *n, v* ▷ **club**
cluck *n* (*pl* -**s**) low clicking noise made by a hen
▶ *v* (**-s, -ing, -ed**) make this noise
clucked *v* ▷ **cluck**
clucking *v* ▷ **cluck**
clucks *n, v* ▷ **cluck**
clue *n* (*pl* -**s**) something that helps to solve a
mystery or puzzle
clueless *adj* stupid > **cluelessly** *adv*
> **cluelessness** *n*
cluelessly *adv* ▷ **clueless**
cluelessness *n* ▷ **clueless**
clues *n* ▷ **clue**
clump *n* (*pl* -**s**) small group of things or people
▶ *v* (**-s, -ing, -ed**) walk heavily
clumped *v* ▷ **clump**
clumping *v* ▷ **clump**
clumps *n, v* ▷ **clump**
clumsier *adj* ▷ **clumsy**
clumsiest *adj* ▷ **clumsy**
clumsily *adv* ▷ **clumsy**
clumsiness *n* ▷ **clumsy**
clumsy *adj* (**-sier, -siest**) lacking skill or
physical coordination > **clumsily** *adv*
> **clumsiness** *n*
clung *v* ▷ **cling**
clunk *n* (*pl* -**s**) dull metallic sound ▶ *v* (**-s, -ing,
-ed**) make such a sound
clunked *v* ▷ **clunk**
clunking *v* ▷ **clunk**
clunks *n, v* ▷ **clunk**
cluster *n* (*pl* -**s**) small close group ▶ *v* (**-s, -ing,
-ed**) gather in clusters
clustered *v* ▷ **cluster**
clustering *v* ▷ **cluster**
clusters *n, v* ▷ **cluster**
clutch¹ *v* (**-es, -ing, -ed**) grasp tightly (*foll. by*
at) ▶ *n* (*pl* -**es**) device enabling two revolving
shafts to be connected and disconnected,
esp. in a motor vehicle

clutch² n (pl -es) set of eggs laid at the same time
  clutched v ▷ **clutch¹**
  clutches v ▷ **clutch¹** ▶ n ▷ **clutch¹, ²**
  clutching v ▷ **clutch¹**
clutter v (-s, -ing, -ed) scatter objects about (a place) untidily ▶ n (pl -s) untidy mess
  cluttered v ▷ **clutter**
  cluttering v ▷ **clutter**
  clutters v, n ▷ **clutter**

> **cly** verb (**clys, clying, clyed**). Cly is an old word meaning steal. The various forms of this word can be useful when you are short of vowels. Cly scores 8 points.

coach n (pl -es) long-distance bus ▶ v (-es, -ing, -ed) train, teach
  coached v ▷ **coach**
  coaches n, v ▷ **coach**
  coaching v ▷ **coach**
coagulant n (pl -s) substance causing coagulation
  coagulants n ▷ **coagulant**
coagulate [koh-**ag**-yew-late] v (-lates, -lating, -lated) change from a liquid to a semisolid mass > **coagulation** n (pl -s)
  coagulated v ▷ **coagulate**
  coagulates v ▷ **coagulate**
  coagulating v ▷ **coagulate**
  coagulation n ▷ **coagulate**
  coagulations n ▷ **coagulate**
coal n (pl -s) black rock consisting mainly of carbon, used as fuel
coalesce [koh-a-**less**] v (-lesces, -lescing, -lesced) come together, merge > **coalescence** n (pl -s)
  coalesced v ▷ **coalesce**
  coalescence n ▷ **coalesce**
  coalescences n ▷ **coalesce**
  coalesces v ▷ **coalesce**
  coalescing v ▷ **coalesce**
coalfield n (pl -s) area with coal under the ground
  coalfields n ▷ **coalfield**
coalition [koh-a-**lish**-un] n (pl -s) temporary alliance, esp. between political parties
  coalitions n ▷ **coalition**
  coals n ▷ **coal**
coarse adj (-r, -st) rough in texture > **coarsely** adv > **coarseness** n (pl -es) > **coarsen** v (-s, -ing, -ed)
  coarsely adv ▷ **coarse**
  coarsen v ▷ **coarse**
  coarsened v ▷ **coarse**
  coarseness n ▷ **coarse**
  coarsenesses n ▷ **coarse**

  coarsening v ▷ **coarse**
  coarsens v ▷ **coarse**
  coarser adj ▷ **coarse**
  coarsest adj ▷ **coarse**
coast n (pl -s) place where the land meets the sea ▶ v (-s, -ing, -ed) move by momentum, without the use of power > **coastal** adj
  coastal adj ▷ **coast**
  coasted v ▷ **coast**
coaster n (pl -s) small mat placed under a glass
  coasters n ▷ **coaster**
coastguard n (pl -s) organization that aids ships and swimmers in trouble and prevents smuggling
  coastguards n ▷ **coastguard**
  coasting v ▷ **coast**
coastline n (pl -s) outline of a coast
  coastlines n ▷ **coastline**
  coasts n, v ▷ **coast**
coat n (pl -s) outer garment with long sleeves ▶ v (-s, -ing, -ed) cover with a layer
  coated v ▷ **coat**
coating n (pl -s) covering layer ▶ v ▷ **coat**
  coatings n ▷ **coating**
  coats n, v ▷ **coat**
coax v (-es, -ing, -ed) persuade gently
  coaxed v ▷ **coax**
  coaxes v ▷ **coax**
coaxial [koh-**ax**-ee-al] adj (of a cable) transmitting by means of two concentric conductors separated by an insulator
  coaxing v ▷ **coax**
cob n (pl -s) stalk of an ear of maize
cobalt n (pl -s) (CHEM) brittle silvery-white metallic element
  cobalts n ▷ **cobalt**
cobber n (pl -s) (AUST & OLD-FASHIONED NZ) (Informal) friend
  cobbers n ▷ **cobber**
cobble n (pl -s) cobblestone
cobbler n (pl -s) shoe mender
  cobblers n ▷ **cobbler**
  cobbles n ▷ **cobble**
cobblestone n (pl -s) rounded stone used for paving
  cobblestones n ▷ **cobblestone**
cobia [koh-bee-a] n (pl -s) large dark-striped game fish of tropical and subtropical seas
  cobias n ▷ **cobia**
cobra n (pl -s) venomous hooded snake of Asia and Africa
  cobras n ▷ **cobra**
  cobs n ▷ **cob**
cobweb n (pl -s) spider's web
  cobwebs n ▷ **cobweb**

cocaine n (pl -s) addictive drug used as a narcotic and as an anaesthetic
cocaines n ▷ cocaine
coccyges n ▷ coccyx
coccyx [kok-six] n (pl coccyges) [kok-**sije**-eez] bone at the base of the spinal column
cochineal n (pl -s) red dye obtained from a Mexican insect, used for food colouring
cochineals n ▷ cochineal
cock n (pl -s) male bird, esp. of domestic fowl ▶ v (-s, -ing, -ed) draw back (the hammer of a gun) to firing position
cockade n (pl -s) feather or rosette worn on a hat as a badge
cockades n ▷ cockade
cockateel n ▷ cockatiel
cockateels n ▷ cockatiel
cockatiel, cockateel n (pl -s) crested Australian parrot with a greyish-brown and yellow plumage
cockatiels n ▷ cockatiel
cockatoo n (pl -s) crested parrot of Australia or the East Indies
cockatoos n ▷ cockatoo
cocked v ▷ cock
cockerel n (pl -s) young domestic cock
cockerels n ▷ cockerel
cockeyed adj (Informal) crooked, askew
cockie, cocky n (pl -kies) (AUST & NZ) (Informal) farmer
cockier adj ▷ cocky
cockies n ▷ cockie
cockiest adj ▷ cocky
cockily adv ▷ cocky
cockiness n ▷ cocky
cocking v ▷ cock
cockle n (pl -s) edible shellfish
cockles n ▷ cockle
cockney n (pl -s) native of the East End of London
cockneys n ▷ cockney
cockpit n (pl -s) pilot's compartment in an aircraft
cockpits n ▷ cockpit
cockroach n (pl -es) beetle-like insect which is a household pest
cockroaches n ▷ cockroach
cocks n, v ▷ cock
cocksure adj overconfident, arrogant
cocktail n (pl -s) mixed alcoholic drink
cocktails n ▷ cocktail
cocky adj (cockier, cockiest) conceited and overconfident ▶ n ▷ cockie > **cockily** adv > **cockiness** n
cocoa n (pl -s) powder made from the seed of

the cacao tree
cocoas n ▷ cocoa
coconut n (pl -s) large hard fruit of a type of palm tree
coconuts n ▷ coconut
cocoon n (pl -s) silky protective covering of a silkworm ▶ v (-s, -ing, -ed) wrap up tightly for protection
cocooned v ▷ cocoon
cocooning v ▷ cocoon
cocoons n, v ▷ cocoon
cod n (pl cod) large food fish of the North Atlantic
coda n (pl -s) final part of a musical composition
codas n ▷ coda
coddle v (coddles, coddling, coddled) pamper, overprotect
coddled v ▷ coddle
coddles v ▷ coddle
coddling v ▷ coddle
code n (pl -s) system of letters, symbols, or prearranged signals by which messages can be communicated secretly or briefly ▶ v (codes, coding, coded) put into code
coded v ▷ code
codeine [kode-een] n (pl -s) drug used as a painkiller
codeines v ▷ codeine
codes n, v ▷ code
codex n (pl codices) volume of manuscripts of an ancient text
codger n (pl -s) (BRIT, AUST & NZ) (Informal) old man
codgers n ▷ codger
codices n ▷ codex
codicil [kode-iss-ill] n (pl -s) addition to a will
codicils n ▷ codicil
codification n ▷ codify
codifications n ▷ codify
codified v ▷ codify
codifies v ▷ codify
codify v (-fies, -fying, -fied) organize (rules or procedures) systematically > **codification** n (pl -s)
codifying v ▷ codify
coding v ▷ code
coeducation n education of boys and girls together > **coeducational** adj
coeducational adj ▷ coeducation
coefficient n (pl -s) (MATHS) number or constant placed before and multiplying a quantity
coefficients n ▷ coefficient
coelacanth [seel-a-kanth] n (pl -s) primitive marine fish

coelacanths n ▷ coelacanth

coerce [koh-urss] v (-ces, -cing, -ced) compel, force > coercion n > coercive adj
coerced v ▷ coerce
coerces v ▷ coerce
coercing v ▷ coerce
coercion n ▷ coerce
coercive adj ▷ coerce

coeval [koh-eev-al] adj, n (pl -s) contemporary
coevals n ▷ coeval

coexist v (-s, -ing, -ed) exist together, esp. peacefully despite differences > coexistence n
coexisted v ▷ coexist
coexistence n ▷ coexist
coexisting v ▷ coexist
coexists v ▷ coexist

coffee n (pl -s) drink made from the roasted and ground seeds of a tropical shrub ▶ adj medium-brown
coffees n ▷ coffee

coffer n (pl -s) chest for valuables ▶ pl store of money
coffers n ▷ coffer

coffin n (pl -s) box in which a corpse is buried or cremated
coffins n ▷ coffin

cog n (pl -s) one of the teeth on the rim of a gearwheel
cogency n ▷ cogent

cogent [koh-jent] adj forcefully convincing > cogency n > cogently adv
cogently n ▷ cogent

cogitate [koj-it-tate] v (-tates, -tating, -tated) think deeply about > cogitation n (pl -s)
cogitated v ▷ cogitate
cogitates v ▷ cogitate
cogitating v ▷ cogitate
cogitation n ▷ cogitate
cogitations n ▷ cogitate

cognac [kon-yak] n (pl -s) French brandy
cognacs n ▷ cognac

cognate adj derived from a common original form

cognition n (pl -s) act or experience of knowing or acquiring knowledge > cognitive adj
cognitions n ▷ cognition
cognitive adj ▷ cognition

cognizance n (pl -s) knowledge, understanding > cognizant adj
cognizances n ▷ cognizance
cognizant adj ▷ cognizance

cognoscenti [kon-yo-shen-tee] pl n connoisseurs

cogs n ▷ cog

cohabit v (-s, -ing, -ed) live together as husband and wife without being married > cohabitation n (pl -s)
cohabitation n ▷ cohabit
cohabitations n ▷ cohabit
cohabited v ▷ cohabit
cohabiting v ▷ cohabit
cohabits v ▷ cohabit

cohere v (-heres, -hering, -hered) hold or stick together
cohered v ▷ cohere
coherence n ▷ coherent

coherent adj logical and consistent > coherence n > coherently adv
coherently n ▷ coherent
coheres v ▷ cohere
cohering v ▷ cohere

cohesion n sticking together

cohesive adj sticking together to form a whole

cohort n (pl -s) band of associates
cohorts n ▷ cohort
coiffeur n ▷ coiffure
coiffeurs n ▷ coiffure
coiffeuse n ▷ coiffure
coiffeuses n ▷ coiffure

coiffure n (pl -s) hairstyle > coiffeur, coiffeuse n (pl -s) hairdresser
coiffures n ▷ coiffure

coil v (-s, -ing, -ed) wind in loops ▶ n (pl -s) something coiled
coiled v ▷ coil
coiling v ▷ coil
coils v, n ▷ coil

coin n (pl -s) piece of metal money ▶ v (-s, -ing, -ed) invent (a word or phrase)

coinage n (pl -s) coins collectively
coinages n ▷ coinage

coincide v (-cides, -ciding, -cided) happen at the same time
coincided v ▷ coincide

coincidence n (pl -s) occurrence of simultaneous or apparently connected events
coincidences n ▷ coincidence

coincident adj in agreement

coincidental adj resulting from coincidence > coincidentally adv
coincidentally adv ▷ coincidental
coincides v ▷ coincide
coinciding v ▷ coincide
coined v ▷ coin
coining v ▷ coin
coins n, v ▷ coin

coir n (pl -s) coconut fibre, used for matting

coirs *n* ▷ **coir**
coital *adj* ▷ **coitus**
coition *n* ▷ **coitus**
coitions *n* ▷ **coitus**
coitus [koh-it-uss], **coition** [koh-ish-un] *n* (*pl* **-s**) sexual intercourse > **coital** *adj*
coke[1] *n* (*pl* **-s**) solid fuel left after gas has been distilled from coal
coke[2] *n* (*pl* **-s**) (*Slang*) cocaine
cokes *n* ▷ **coke**[1,2]
col *n* (*pl* **-s**) high mountain pass
cola *n* (*pl* **-s**) dark brown fizzy soft drink
colander *n* (*pl* **-s**) perforated bowl for straining or rinsing foods
colanders *n* ▷ **colander**
colas *n* ▷ **cola**
cold *adj* (**-er**, **-est**) lacking heat ▶ *n* (*pl* **-s**) lack of heat > **coldly** *adv* > **coldness** *n* (*pl* **-es**)
colder *adj* ▷ **cold**
coldest *adj* ▷ **cold**
coldly *adv* ▷ **cold**
coldness *n* ▷ **cold**
coldnesses *n* ▷ **cold**
colds *n* ▷ **cold**
coleslaw *n* (*pl* **-s**) salad dish of shredded raw cabbage in a dressing
coleslaws *n* ▷ **coleslaw**
coley *n* (*pl* **-s**) codlike food fish of the N Atlantic
coleys *n* ▷ **coley**
colic *n* (*pl* **-s**) severe pains in the stomach and bowels > **colicky** *adj* (**-ckier**, **-ckiest**)
colickier *adj* ▷ **colic**
colickiest *adj* ▷ **colic**
colicky *adj* ▷ **colic**
colics *n* ▷ **colic**
colitis [koh-**lie**-tiss] *n* inflammation of the colon
collaborate *v* (**-ates**, **-ating**, **-ated**) work with another on a project > **collaboration** *n* (*pl* **-s**) > **collaborative** *adj* > **collaboratively** *adv* > **collaborator** *n* (*pl* **-s**)
collaborated *v* ▷ **collaborate**
collaborates *v* ▷ **collaborate**
collaborating *v* ▷ **collaborate**
collaboration *n* ▷ **collaborate**
collaborations *n* ▷ **collaborate**
collaborative *adj* ▷ **collaborate**
collaboratively *adv* ▷ **collaborate**
collaborator *n* ▷ **collaborate**
collaborators *n* ▷ **collaborate**
collage [kol-**lahzh**] *n* (*pl* **-s**) art form in which various materials or objects are glued onto a surface
collages *n* ▷ **collage**
collapse *v* (**-lapses**, **-lapsing**, **-lapsed**) fall down

suddenly ▶ *n* (*pl* **-s**) collapsing > **collapsible** *adj*
collapsed *v* ▷ **collapse**
collapses *v*, *n* ▷ **collapse**
collapsible *adj* ▷ **collapse**
collapsing *v* ▷ **collapse**
collar *n* (*pl* **-s**) part of a garment round the neck ▶ *v* (**-s**, **-ing**, **-ed**) (BRIT, AUST & NZ) (*Informal*) seize, arrest
collarbone *n* (*pl* **-s**) bone joining the shoulder blade to the breastbone
collarbones *n* ▷ **collarbone**
collared *v* ▷ **collar**
collaring *v* ▷ **collar**
collars *n*, *v* ▷ **collar**
collate *v* (**-lates**, **-lating**, **-lated**) gather together, examine, and put in order
collated *v* ▷ **collate**
collateral *n* (*pl* **-s**) security pledged for the repayment of a loan
collaterals *n* ▷ **collateral**
collates *v* ▷ **collate**
collating *v* ▷ **collate**
collation *n* (*pl* **-s**) collating
collations *n* ▷ **collation**
colleague *n* (*pl* **-s**) fellow worker, esp. in a profession
colleagues *n* ▷ **colleague**
collect[1] *v* (**-s**, **-ing**, **-ed**) gather together > **collector** *n* (*pl* **-s**)
collect[2] *n* (*pl* **-s**) short prayer
collected *adj* calm and controlled ▶ *v* ▷ **collect**[1] > **collectedly** *adv* > **collectedness** *n*
collectedly *adv* ▷ **collected**
collectedness *n* ▷ **collected**
collecting *v* ▷ **collect**[1]
collection *n* (*pl* **-s**) things collected
collections *n* ▷ **collection**
collective *adj* of or done by a group ▶ *n* (*pl* **-s**) group of people working together on an enterprise and sharing the benefits from it > **collectively** *adv*
collectively *adv* ▷ **collective**
collectives *n* ▷ **collective**
collects *v* ▷ **collect**[1] ▶ *n* ▷ **collect**[2]
colleen *n* (*pl* **-s**) (IRISH) girl
colleens *n* ▷ **colleen**
college *n* (*pl* **-s**) place of higher education > **collegiate** *adj*
colleges *n* ▷ **college**
collegiate *adj* ▷ **college**
collide *v* (**-lides**, **-liding**, **-lided**) crash together violently > **collision** *n* (*pl* **-s**)
collided *v* ▷ **collide**
collides *v* ▷ **collide**
colliding *v* ▷ **collide**

collie *n* (*pl* -**s**) silky-haired sheepdog
collier *n* (*pl* -**s**) coal miner
  collieries *n* ▷ colliery
  colliers *n* ▷ collier
colliery *n* (*pl* -**lieries**) coal mine
  collies *n* ▷ collie
  collision *n* ▷ collide
  collisions *n* ▷ collide
collocate *v* (-**cates**, -**cating**, -**cated**) (of words)
  occur together regularly > **collocation** *n* (*pl* -**s**)
  collocated *v* ▷ collocate
  collocates *v* ▷ collocate
  collocating *v* ▷ collocate
  collocation *n* ▷ collocate
  collocations *n* ▷ collocate
colloid *n* (*pl* -**s**) suspension of particles in a
  solution
  colloids *n* ▷ colloid
colloquial *adj* suitable for informal speech or
  writing > **colloquially** *adv*
colloquialism *n* (*pl* -**s**) colloquial word or
  phrase
  colloquialisms *n* ▷ colloquialism
  colloquially *adv* ▷ colloquial
collude *v* (-**ludes**, -**luding**, -**luded**) act in
  collusion
  colluded *v* ▷ collude
  colludes *v* ▷ collude
  colluding *v* ▷ collude
collusion *n* (*pl* -**s**) secret or illegal cooperation
  collusions *n* ▷ collusion
collywobbles *pl n* (*Slang*) nervousness
cologne *n* (*pl* -**s**) mild perfume
  colognes *n* ▷ cologne
colon[1] *n* (*pl* -**s**) punctuation mark (:)
colon[2] *n* (*pl* -**s**) part of the large intestine
  connected to the rectum
colonel *n* (*pl* -**s**) senior commissioned army or
  air-force officer
  colonels *n* ▷ colonel
colonial *adj*, *n* (*pl* -**s**) (inhabitant) of a colony
colonialism *n* policy of acquiring and
  maintaining colonies
  colonials *n* ▷ colonial
  colonies *n* ▷ colony
colonist *n* (*pl* -**s**) settler in a colony
  colonists *n* ▷ colonist
  colonization *n* ▷ colonize
  colonizations *n* ▷ colonize
colonize *v* (-**izes**, -**izing**, -**ized**) make into a
  colony > **colonization** *n* (*pl* -**s**)
  colonized *v* ▷ colonize
  colonizes *v* ▷ colonize
  colonizing *v* ▷ colonize
colonnade *n* (*pl* -**s**) row of columns

  colonnades *n* ▷ colonnade
  colons *n* ▷ colon[1, 2]
colony *n* (*pl* -**nies**) group of people who settle
  in a new country but remain under the rule of
  their homeland
coloration *n* (*pl* -**s**) arrangement of colours
  colorations *n* ▷ coloration
  colosally *adv* ▷ colossal
colossal *adj* very large > **colossally** *adv*
  colossi *n* ▷ colossus
colossus *n* (*pl* -**si**, -**suses**) huge statue
  colossuses *n* ▷ colossus
  colostomies *n* ▷ colostomy
colostomy *n* (*pl* -**mies**) operation to form an
  opening from the colon onto the surface of
  the body, for emptying the bowel
colour *n* (*pl* -**s**) appearance of things as a result
  of reflecting light ▶ *pl* flag of a country or
  regiment (SPORT) ▶ *v* (-**s**, -**ing**, -**ed**) apply colour
  to > **colourless** *adj* > **colourlessly** *adv*
coloured *adj* having colour ▶ *v* ▷ **colour**
colourful *adj* with bright or varied colours
  > **colourfully** *adv*
  colourfully *adv* ▷ colourful
  colouring *v* ▷ colour
  colourless *adj* ▷ colour
  colourlessly *adv* ▷ colour
colours *n*, *v* ▷ colour
  cols *n* ▷ col
colt *n* (*pl* -**s**) young male horse
  colts *n* ▷ colt
columbine *n* (*pl* -**s**) garden flower with five
  petals
  columbines *n* ▷ columbine
column *n* (*pl* -**s**) pillar
columnist *n* (*pl* -**s**) journalist who writes a
  regular feature in a newspaper
  columnists *n* ▷ columnist
  columns *n* ▷ column
coma *n* (*pl* -**s**) state of deep unconsciousness
  comas *n* ▷ coma
comatose *adj* in a coma
comb *n* (*pl* -**s**) toothed implement for
  arranging the hair ▶ *v* (-**s**, -**ing**, -**ed**) use a
  comb on
combat *n* (*pl* -**s**) ▶ *v* (-**s**, -**ing**, -**ed**) fight, struggle
  > **combatant** *n* (*pl* -**s**) > **combative** *adj*
  > **combativeness** *n*
  combatant *n* ▷ combat
  combatants *n* ▷ combat
  combated *v* ▷ combat
  combating *v* ▷ combat
  combats *n*, *v* ▷ combat
  combed *v* ▷ comb
combination *n* (*pl* -**s**) combining ▶ *pl* (BRIT) old-

fashioned undergarment with long sleeves and long legs

combinations *n* ▷ **combination**
combine *v* (**-bines, -bining, -bined**) join together ▶ *n* (*pl* **-s**) association of people or firms for a common purpose
combined *v* ▷ **combine**
combines *v, n* ▷ **combine**
combing *v* ▷ **comb**
combining *v* ▷ **combine**
combs *n, v* ▷ **comb**
combustible *adj* burning easily
combustion *n* (*pl* **-s**) process of burning
combustions *n* ▷ **combustion**
come *v* (**comes, coming, came, come**) move towards a place, arrive
comeback *n* (*pl* **-s**) (*Informal*) return to a former position
comebacks *n* ▷ **comeback**
comedian, comedienne *n* (*pl* **-s**) entertainer who tells jokes
comedians *n* ▷ **comedian**
comedienne *n* ▷ **comedian**
comediennes *n* ▷ **comedian**
comedies *n* ▷ **comedy**
comedown *n* (*pl* **-s**) decline in status
comedowns *n* ▷ **comedown**
comedy *n* (*pl* **-dies**) humorous play, film, or programme
comelier *adj* ▷ **comely**
comeliest *adj* ▷ **comely**
comeliness *n* ▷ **comely**
comely *adj* (**-lier, -liest**) (*Old-fashioned*) nice-looking > **comeliness** *n*
comes *v* ▷ **come**
comestibles *pl n* (*Formal*) food
comet *n* (*pl* **-s**) heavenly body with a long luminous tail
comets *n* ▷ **comet**
comeuppance *n* (*Informal*) deserved punishment
comfier *adj* ▷ **comfy**
comfiest *adj* ▷ **comfy**
comfit *n* (*pl* **-s**) (*Old-fashioned*) sugar-coated sweet
comfits *n* ▷ **comfit**
comfort *n* (*pl* **-s**) physical ease or wellbeing ▶ *v* (**-s, -ing, -ed**) soothe, console > **comforter** *n* (*pl* **-s**)
comfortable *adj* giving comfort > **comfortably** *adv*
comfortably *adv* ▷ **comfortable**
comforted *v* ▷ **comfort**
comforter *n* ▷ **comfort**
comforters *n* ▷ **comfort**

comforting *v* ▷ **comfort**
comforts *n, v* ▷ **comfort**
comfrey *n* (*pl* **-s**) tall plant with bell-shaped flowers
comfreys *n* ▷ **comfrey**
comfy *adj* (**-fier, -fiest**) (*Informal*) comfortable
comic *adj* humorous, funny ▶ *n* (*pl* **-s**) comedian
comical *adj* amusing > **comically** *adv*
comically *adv* ▷ **comical**
comics *n* ▷ **comic**
coming *v* ▷ **come**
comma *n* (*pl* **-s**) punctuation mark (,)
command *v* (**-s, -ing, -ed**) order ▶ *n* (*pl* **-s**) authoritative instruction that something must be done
commandant *n* (*pl* **-s**) officer commanding a military group
commandants *n* ▷ **commandant**
commanded *v* ▷ **command**
commandeer *v* (**-s, -ing, -ed**) seize for military use
commandeered *v* ▷ **commandeer**
commandeering *v* ▷ **commandeer**
commandeers *v* ▷ **commandeer**
commander *n* (*pl* **-s**) military officer in command of a group or operation
commanders *n* ▷ **commander**
commanding *v* ▷ **command**
commandment *n* (*pl* **-s**) command from God
commandments *n* ▷ **commandment**
commando *n* (*pl* **-dos, -does**) (member of) a military unit trained for swift raids in enemy territory
commandoes *n* ▷ **commando**
commandos *n* ▷ **commando**
commands *v, n* ▷ **command**
commas *n* ▷ **comma**
commemorate *v* (**-rates, -rating, -rated**) honour the memory of > **commemoration** *n* (*pl* **-s**) > **commemorative** *adj*
commemorated *v* ▷ **commemorate**
commemorates *v* ▷ **commemorate**
commemorating *v* ▷ **commemorate**
commemoration *n* ▷ **commemorate**
commemorations *n* ▷ **commemorate**
commemorative *adj* ▷ **commemorate**
commence *v* (**-mences, -mencing, -menced**) begin > **commencement** *n* (*pl* **-s**)
commenced *v* ▷ **commence**
commencement *n* ▷ **commence**
commencements *n* ▷ **commence**
commences *v* ▷ **commence**
commencing *v* ▷ **commence**
commend *v* (**-s, -ing, -ed**) praise

> **commendable** *adj* > **commendably** *adv*
> **commendation** *n* (*pl* -s)
commendable *adj* ▷ **commend**
commendably *adv* ▷ **commend**
commendation *n* ▷ **commend**
commendations *n* ▷ **commend**
commended *v* ▷ **commend**
commending *v* ▷ **commend**
commends *v* ▷ **commend**
commensurable *adj* measurable by the same standards
commensurate *adj* corresponding in degree, size, or value
comment *n* (*pl* -s) remark ▶ *v* (-s, -ing, -ed) make a comment
commentaries *n* ▷ **commentary**
commentary *n* (*pl* -taries) spoken accompaniment to a broadcast or film
commentate *v* (-tates, -tating, -tated) provide a commentary > **commentator** *n* (*pl* -s)
commentated *v* ▷ **commentate**
commentates *v* ▷ **commentate**
commentating *v* ▷ **commentate**
commentator *n* ▷ **commentate**
commentators *n* ▷ **commentate**
commented *v* ▷ **comment**
commenting *v* ▷ **comment**
comments *n*, *v* ▷ **comment**
commerce *n* (*pl* -s) buying and selling, trade
commerces *n* ▷ **commerce**
commercial *adj* of commerce ▶ *n* (*pl* -s) television or radio advertisement
commercialization *n* ▷ **commercialize**
commercialize *v* (-izes, -izing, -ized) make commercial > **commercialization** *n*
commercialized *v* ▷ **commercialize**
commercializes *v* ▷ **commercialize**
commercializing *v* ▷ **commercialize**
commercials *n* ▷ **commercial**
commiserate *v* (-rates, -rating, -rated) (*foll. by* **with**) express sympathy (for) > **commiseration** *n* (*pl* -s)
commiserated *v* ▷ **commiserate**
commiserates *v* ▷ **commiserate**
commiserating *v* ▷ **commiserate**
commiseration *n* ▷ **commiserate**
commiserations *n* ▷ **commiserate**
commissar *n* (*pl* -s) (formerly) official responsible for political education in Communist countries
commissariat *n* (*pl* -s) (BRIT, AUST & NZ) military department in charge of food supplies
commissariats *n* ▷ **commissariat**
commissars *n* ▷ **commissar**

commission *n* (*pl* -s) piece of work that an artist is asked to do (MIL) ▶ *v* (-s, -ing, -ed) place an order for
commissionaire *n* (*pl* -s) uniformed doorman at a hotel, theatre, etc.
commissionaires *n* ▷ **commissionaire**
commissioned *v* ▷ **commission**
commissioner *n* (*pl* -s) appointed official in a government department
commissioners *n* ▷ **commissioner**
commissioning *v* ▷ **commission**
commissions *n*, *v* ▷ **commission**
commit *v* (-mits, -mitting, -mitted) perform (a crime or error)
commitment *n* (*pl* -s) dedication to a cause
commitments *n* ▷ **commitment**
commits *v* ▷ **commit**
committal *n* (*pl* -s) sending someone to prison or hospital
committals *n* ▷ **committal**
committed *v* ▷ **commit**
committee *n* (*pl* -s) group of people appointed to perform a specified service or function
committees *n* ▷ **committee**
committing *v* ▷ **commit**
commode *n* (*pl* -s) seat with a hinged flap concealing a chamber pot
commodes *n* ▷ **commode**
commodious *adj* roomy
commodities *n* ▷ **commodity**
commodity *n* (*pl* -ities) something that can be bought or sold
commodore *n* (*pl* -s) senior commissioned officer in the navy
commodores *n* ▷ **commodore**
common *adj* (-er, -est) occurring often ▶ *n* (*pl* -s) area of grassy land belonging to a community > **commonly** *adv*
commoner *n* (*pl* -s) person who does not belong to the nobility ▶ *adj* ▷ **common**
commoners *n* ▷ **commoner**
commonest *adj* ▷ **common**
commonly *adv* ▷ **common**
commonplace *adj* ordinary, everyday ▶ *n* (*pl* -s) trite remark
commonplaces *n* ▷ **commonplace**
commons *n* ▷ **common**
commonwealth *n* (*pl* -s) state or nation viewed politically
commonwealths *n* ▷ **commonwealth**
commotion *n* (*pl* -s) noisy disturbance
commotions *n* ▷ **commotion**
communal *adj* shared > **communally** *adv*
communally *n* ▷ **communal**
commune[1] *n* (*pl* -s) group of people who live

together and share everything

commune² v (-**munes, -muning, -muned**) (foll. by **with**) feel very close (to)
  communed v ▷ commune²
  communes n ▷ commune¹ ▶ v ▷ commune²
communicable adj (of a disease) able to be passed on
communicant n (pl -**s**) person who receives Communion
  communicants n ▷ communicant
communicate v (-**cates, -cating, -cated**) make known or share (information, thoughts, or feelings)
  communicated v ▷ communicate
  communicates v ▷ communicate
communicating adj (of a door) joining two rooms ▶ v ▷ communicate
communication n communicating ▶ pl (-**s**) means of travelling or sending messages
  communications n ▷ communication
communicative adj talking freely
  communing v ▷ commune²
communion n (pl -**s**) sharing of thoughts or feelings
  communions n ▷ communion
communiqué [kom-**mune**-ik-kay] n (pl -**s**) official announcement
  communiqués n ▷ communiqué
communism n belief that all property and means of production should be shared by the community > **communist** n (pl -**s**) adj
  communists n ▷ communism
  communities n ▷ community
community n (pl -**ties**) all the people living in one district
commutator n (pl -**s**) device used to change alternating electric current into direct current
  commutators n ▷ commutator
commute v (-**mutes, -muting, -muted**) travel daily to and from work
  commuted v ▷ commute
commuter n (pl -**s**) person who commutes to and from work
  commuters n ▷ commuter
  commutes v ▷ commute
  commuting v ▷ commute
compact¹ adj (-**er, -est**) closely packed ▶ n (pl -**s**) small flat case containing a mirror and face powder ▶ v (-**s, -ing, -ed**) pack closely together > **compactly** adv > **compactness** n
compact² n (pl -**s**) contract, agreement
  compacted v ▷ compact¹
  compacter adj ▷ compact¹
  compactest adj ▷ compact¹

  compacting v ▷ compact¹
  compactly adv ▷ compact¹
  compactness n ▷ compact¹
  compacts n ▷ compact¹, ² ▶ v ▷ compact¹
  companies n ▷ company
companion n (pl -**s**) person who associates with or accompanies someone > **companionship** n (pl -**s**)
companionable adj friendly > **companionably** adv
  companionably adv ▷ companionable
  companions n ▷ companion
  companionship n ▷ companion
  companionships n ▷ companion
companionway n (pl -**s**) ladder linking the decks of a ship
  companionways n ▷ companionway
company n (pl -**nies**) business organization
  comparability n ▷ compare
  comparable adj ▷ compare
comparative adj relative ▶ n (pl -**s**) (GRAMMAR) comparative form of a word > **comparatively** adv
  comparatively adv ▷ comparative
  comparatives n ▷ comparative
compare v (-**pares, -paring, -pared**) examine (things) and point out the resemblances or differences (foll. by **to**) (foll. by **with**) > **comparable** adj > **comparability** n
  compared v ▷ compare
  compares v ▷ compare
  comparing v ▷ compare
comparison n (pl -**s**) comparing
  comparisons n ▷ comparison
compartment n (pl -**s**) section of a railway carriage
  compartments n ▷ compartment
compass n (pl -**es**) instrument for showing direction, with a needle that points north ▶ pl hinged instrument for drawing circles
  compasses n ▷ compass
compassion n pity, sympathy > **compassionate** adj > **compassionately** adv
  compassionate adj ▷ compassion
  compassionately adj ▷ compassion
  compatibility n ▷ compatible
compatible adj able to exist, work, or be used together > **compatibility** n
compatriot n (pl -**s**) fellow countryman or countrywoman
  compatriots n ▷ compatriot
compel v (-**pels, -pelling, -pelled**) force (to be or do)
  compelled v ▷ compel
  compelling v ▷ compel

compels v ▷ compel
compendia n ▷ compendium
compendious adj brief but comprehensive
compendium n (pl -diums, -dia) selection of board games in one box
compendiums n ▷ compendium
compensate v (-sates, -sating, -sated) make amends to (someone), esp. for injury or loss (foll. by for) > **compensatory** adj
compensated v ▷ compensate
compensates v ▷ compensate
compensating v ▷ compensate
compensation n (pl -s) payment to make up for loss or injury
compensations n ▷ compensation
compensatory adj ▷ compensate
compere n (pl -s) person who presents a stage, radio, or television show ▶ v (-peres, -pering, -pered) be the compere of
compered v ▷ compere
comperes n, v ▷ compere
compering v ▷ compere
compete v (-petes, -peting, -peted) try to win or achieve (a prize, profit, etc.) > **competitive** adj > **competitively** adv > **competitiveness** n > **competitor** n (pl -s)
competed v ▷ compete
competence n ▷ competent
competent adj having the skill or knowledge to do something well > **competently** adv > **competence** n
competently adv ▷ competent
competes v ▷ compete
competing v ▷ compete
competition n (pl -s) competing
competitions n ▷ competition
competitive adj ▷ compete
competitively adv ▷ compete
competitiveness n ▷ compete
competitor n ▷ compete
competitors n ▷ compete
compilation n ▷ compile
compilations n ▷ compile
compile v (-piles, -piling, -piled) collect and arrange (information), esp. to make a book > **compilation** n (pl -s) > **compiler** n (pl -s)
compiled v ▷ compile
compiler n ▷ compile
compilers n ▷ compile
compiles v ▷ compile
compiling v ▷ compile
complacencies n ▷ complacent
complacency n ▷ complacent
complacent adj self-satisfied > **complacently** (pl -cies) adv > **complacency** n

complacently adv ▷ complacent
complain v (-s, -ing, -ed) express resentment or displeasure
complainant n (pl -s) (LAW) plaintiff
complainants n ▷ complainant
complained v ▷ complain
complaining v ▷ complain
complains v ▷ complain
complaint n (pl -s) complaining
complaints n ▷ complaint
complaisance n ▷ complaisant
complaisant [kom-**play**-zant] adj willing to please > **complaisance** n
complement n (pl -s) thing that completes something (GRAMMAR) ▶ v (-s, -ing, -ed) make complete > **complementary** adj
complementary adj ▷ complement
complemented v ▷ complement
complementing v ▷ complement
complements n, v ▷ complement
complete adj thorough, absolute ▶ v (-pletes, -pleting, -pleted) finish > **completely** adv > **completeness** n
completed v ▷ complete
completely adv ▷ complete
completeness n ▷ complete
completes v ▷ complete
completing v ▷ complete
completion n finishing
complex adj (-er, -est) made up of parts ▶ n (pl -es) whole made up of parts > **complexity** n (pl -ities)
complexer adj ▷ complex
complexes n ▷ complex
complexest adj ▷ complex
complexion n (pl -s) skin of the face
complexions n ▷ complexion
complexities n ▷ complex
complexity n ▷ complex
compliance n (pl -s) complying > **compliant** adj
compliances n ▷ compliance
compliant adj ▷ compliance
complicate v (-cates, -cating, -cated) make or become complex or difficult to deal with > **complication** n (pl -s)
complicated v ▷ complicate
complicates v ▷ complicate
complicating v ▷ complicate
complication n ▷ complicate
complications n ▷ complicate
complicities n ▷ complicity
complicity n (pl -ities) fact of being an accomplice in a crime
complied v ▷ comply

complies *v* ▷ comply

compliment *n* (*pl* -**s**) expression of praise ▶ *pl* formal greetings ▶ *v* (-**s**, -**ing**, -**ed**) praise

complimentary *adj* expressing praise

complimented *v* ▷ compliment

complimenting *v* ▷ compliment

compliments *n*, *v* ▷ compliment

compline *n* (*pl* -**s**) last service of the day in the Roman Catholic Church

complines *n* ▷ compline

comply *v* (-**plies**, -**plying**, -**plied**) (*foll. by* **with**) act in accordance (with)

complying *v* ▷ comply

component *n* (*pl* -**s**) ▶ *adj* (being) part of a whole

components *n* ▷ component

comport *v* (-**s**, -**ing**, -**ed**) (*Formal*) behave (oneself) in a specified way

comported *v* ▷ comport

comporting *v* ▷ comport

comports *v* ▷ comport

compose *v* (-**poses**, -**posing**, -**posed**) put together

composed *v* ▷ compose

composer *n* (*pl* -**s**) person who writes music

composers *n* ▷ composer

composes *v* ▷ compose

composing *v* ▷ compose

composite *n* (*pl* -**s**) ▶ *adj* (something) made up of separate parts

composites *n* ▷ composite

composition *n* (*pl* -**s**) way that something is put together or arranged

compositions *n* ▷ composition

compositor *n* (*pl* -**s**) person who arranges type for printing

compositors *n* ▷ compositor

compost *n* (*pl* -**s**) decayed plants used as a fertilizer

composts *n* ▷ compost

composure *n* calmness

compote *n* (*pl* -**s**) fruit stewed with sugar

compotes *n* ▷ compote

compound[1] *n* (*pl* -**s**) ▶ *adj* (thing, esp. chemical) made up of two or more combined parts or elements ▶ *v* (-**s**, -**ing**, -**ed**) combine or make by combining

compound[2] *n* (*pl* -**s**) fenced enclosure containing buildings

compounded *v* ▷ compound[1]

compounding *v* ▷ compound[1]

compounds *v* ▷ compound[1] ▶ *n* ▷ compound[1, 2]

comprehend *v* (-**s**, -**ing**, -**ed**) understand
> **comprehensible** *adj* > **comprehensibly** *adv*
> **comprehension** *n* (*pl* -**s**)

comprehended *v* ▷ comprehend

comprehending *v* ▷ comprehend

comprehends *v* ▷ comprehend

comprehensible *adj* ▷ comprehend

comprehensibly *adv* ▷ comprehend

comprehension *n* ▷ comprehend

comprehensions *n* ▷ comprehend

comprehensive *adj* of broad scope, fully inclusive ▶ *n* (*pl* -**s**) (BRIT) comprehensive school > **comprehensively** *adv*
> **comprehensiveness** *n*

comprehensively *adv* ▷ comprehensive

comprehensiveness *n* ▷ comprehensive

comprehensives *n* ▷ comprehensive

compress *v* (-**es**, -**ing**, -**ed**) [kum-**press**] squeeze together ▶ *n* (*pl* -**es**) [kom-press] pad applied to stop bleeding or cool inflammation
> **compression** *n* (*pl* -**s**)

compressed *v* ▷ compress

compresses *v*, *n* ▷ compress

compressing *v* ▷ compress

compression *n* ▷ compress

compressions *n* ▷ compress

compressor *n* (*pl* -**s**) machine that compresses gas or air

compressors *n* ▷ compressor

comprise *v* (-**ises**, -**ising**, -**ised**) be made up of or make up

comprised *v* ▷ comprise

comprises *v* ▷ comprise

comprising *v* ▷ comprise

compromise [kom-prom-mize] *n* (*pl* -**s**) settlement reached by concessions on each side ▶ *v* (-**ises**, -**ising**, -**ised**) settle a dispute by making concessions

compromised *v* ▷ compromise

compromises *n*, *v* ▷ compromise

compromising *v* ▷ compromise

comptroller *n* (*pl* -**s**) (in titles) financial controller

comptrollers *n* ▷ comptroller

compulsion *n* (*pl* -**s**) irresistible urge
> **compulsive** *adj* > **compulsively** *adv*

compulsions *n* ▷ compulsion

compulsive *adj* ▷ compulsion

compulsively *adv* ▷ compulsion

compulsorily *adv* ▷ compulsory

compulsoriness *n* ▷ compulsory

compulsory *adj* required by rules or laws
> **compulsorily** *adv* > **compulsoriness** *n*

compunction *n* (*pl* -**s**) feeling of guilt or shame

compunctions *n* ▷ compunction

computation *n* ▷ compute

computations *n* ▷ compute

compute *v* (-**putes**, -**puting**, -**puted**) calculate,

esp. using a computer > **computation** *n* (*pl* -**s**)
 computed *v* ▷ **compute**
computer *n* (*pl* -**s**) electronic machine that
 stores and processes data > **computerize** *v*
 (-**izes, -izing, -ized**) adapt (a system) to be
 handled by computer > **computerization**
 n (*pl* -**s**)
 computerization *n* ▷ **computerize**
 computerizations *v* ▷ **computerize**
 computerized *v* ▷ **computerize**
 computerizes *v* ▷ **computerize**
 computerizing *v* ▷ **computerize**
 computers *n* ▷ **computer**
 computes *v* ▷ **compute**
 computing *v* ▷ **compute**
comrade *n* (*pl* -**s**) fellow member of a union or
 socialist political party > **comradeship** *n*
 comrades *n* ▷ **comrade**
 comradeship *n* ▷ **comrade**
con¹ (*Informal*) *n* (*pl* -**s**) ▷ **confidence trick** ▶ *v*
 (**cons, conning, conned**) deceive, swindle
con² *n* (*pl* -**s**) ▷ **pro¹**
concatenation *n* (*pl* -**s**) series of linked events
 concatenations *n* ▷ **concatenation**
concave *adj* curving inwards
conceal *v* (-**s, -ing, -ed**) cover and hide
 > **concealment** *n*
 concealed *v* ▷ **conceal**
 concealing *v* ▷ **conceal**
 concealment *n* ▷ **conceal**
 conceals *v* ▷ **conceal**
concede *v* (-**cedes, -ceding, -ceded**) admit to
 be true
 conceded *v* ▷ **concede**
 concedes *v* ▷ **concede**
 conceding *v* ▷ **concede**
conceit *n* (*pl* -**s**) too high an opinion of
 oneself > **conceited** *adj* > **conceitedly** *adv*
 > **conceitedness** *n*
 conceited *adj* ▷ **conceit**
 conceitedly *adv* ▷ **conceit**
 conceitedness *adv* ▷ **conceit**
 conceits *n* ▷ **conceit**
conceivable *adj* imaginable, possible
 > **conceivably** *adv*
 conceivably *adv* ▷ **conceivable**
conceive *v* (-**ceives, -ceiving, -ceived**) imagine,
 think
 conceived *v* ▷ **conceive**
 conceives *v* ▷ **conceive**
 conceiving *v* ▷ **conceive**
concentrate *v* (-**rates, -rating, -rated**) fix one's
 attention or efforts on something ▶ *n* (*pl* -**s**)
 concentrated liquid
 concentrated *v* ▷ **concentrate**

 concentrates *v, n* ▷ **concentrate**
 concentrating *v* ▷ **concentrate**
concentration *n* (*pl* -**s**) concentrating
 concentrations *n* ▷ **concentration**
concentric *adj* having the same centre
concept *n* (*pl* -**s**) abstract or general idea
conception *n* (*pl* -**s**) general idea
 conceptions *n* ▷ **conception**
 concepts *n* ▷ **concept**
conceptual *adj* of or based on concepts
 > **conceptually** *adv*
conceptualize *v* (-**izes, -izing, -ized**) form a
 concept of
 conceptualized *v* ▷ **conceptualize**
 conceptualizes *v* ▷ **conceptualize**
 conceptualizing *v* ▷ **conceptualize**
 conceptually *adv* ▷ **conceptual**
concern *n* (*pl* -**s**) anxiety, worry ▶ *v* (-**s, -ing, -ed**)
 worry (someone)
concerned *adj* interested, involved ▶ *v*
 ▷ **concern**
concerning *prep* about, regarding ▶ *v*
 ▷ **concern**
 concerns *n, v* ▷ **concern**
concert *n* (*pl* -**s**) musical entertainment
concerted *adj* done together
 concerti *n* ▷ **concerto**
concertina *n* (*pl* -**s**) small musical instrument
 similar to an accordion ▶ *v* (-**nas, -naing,
 -naed**) collapse or fold up like a concertina
 concertinaed *v* ▷ **concertina**
 concertinaing *v* ▷ **concertina**
 concertinas *n, v* ▷ **concertina**
concerto [kon-**chair**-toe] *n* (*pl* -**tos, -ti**) large-
 scale composition for a solo instrument and
 orchestra
 concertos *n* ▷ **concerto**
 concerts *n* ▷ **concert**
concession *n* (*pl* -**s**) grant of rights, land, or
 property > **concessionary** *adj*
 concessionary *adj* ▷ **concession**
 concessions *n* ▷ **concession**
conch *n* (*pl* -**s**) shellfish with a large spiral shell
 conchs *n* ▷ **conch**
concierge [kon-see-**airzh**] *n* (*pl* -**s**) (in France)
 caretaker in a block of flats
 concierges *n* ▷ **concierge**
conciliate *v* (-**ates, -ating, -ated**) try to end
 a disagreement (with) > **conciliation** *n*
 > **conciliator** *n* (*pl* -**s**)
 conciliated *v* ▷ **conciliate**
 conciliates *v* ▷ **conciliate**
 conciliating *v* ▷ **conciliate**
 conciliation *n* ▷ **conciliate**
 conciliator *n* ▷ **conciliate**

conciliators n ▷ conciliate
conciliatory adj intended to end a disagreement
concise adj (-r, -st) brief and to the point > **concisely** adv > **concision, conciseness** n (pl -s, -es)
concisely adv ▷ concise
conciseness n ▷ concise
concisenesses n ▷ concise
conciser adj ▷ concise
concisest adj ▷ concise
concision n ▷ concise
concisions n ▷ concise
conclave n (pl -s) secret meeting
conclaves n ▷ conclave
conclude v (-cludes, -cluding, -cluded) decide by reasoning
concluded v ▷ conclude
concludes v ▷ conclude
concluding v ▷ conclude
conclusion n (pl -s) decision based on reasoning
conclusions n ▷ conclusion
conclusive adj ending doubt, convincing > **conclusively** adv
conclusively adv ▷ conclusive
concoct v (-s, -ing, -ed) make up (a story or plan) > **concoction** n (pl -s)
concocted v ▷ concoct
concocting v ▷ concoct
concoction n ▷ concoct
concoctions n ▷ concoct
concocts v ▷ concoct
concomitant adj existing along with something else
concord n (pl -s) state of peaceful agreement, harmony
concordance n (pl -s) similarity or consistency
concordances n ▷ concordance
concordant adj agreeing > **concordantly** adv
concordantly adv ▷ concordant
concords n ▷ concord
concourse n (pl -s) large open public place where people can gather
concourses n ▷ concourse
concrete n (pl -s) mixture of cement, sand, stone, and water, used in building ▶ adj made of concrete
concretes n ▷ concrete
concubine [kon-kew-bine] n (pl -s) (HIST) woman living in a man's house but not married to him and kept for his sexual pleasure
concubines n ▷ concubine
concupiscence [kon-**kew**-piss-enss] n (Formal)

lust
concur v (-curs, -curring, -curred) agree > **concurrence** n (pl -s)
concurred v ▷ concur
concurrence n ▷ concur
concurrent adj happening at the same time or place
concurrently adv at the same time
concurring v ▷ concur
concurs v ▷ concur
concussed adj having concussion
concussion n (pl -s) period of unconsciousness caused by a blow to the head
concussions n ▷ concussion
condemn v (-s, -ing, -ed) express disapproval of > **condemnation** n (pl -s) > **condemnatory** adj
condemnation n ▷ condemn
condemnations n ▷ condemn
condemnatory adj ▷ condemn
condemned v ▷ condemn
condemning v ▷ condemn
condemns v ▷ condemn
condensation n ▷ condense
condense v (-denses, -densing, -densed) make shorter > **condensation** n
condensed v ▷ condense
condenser n (pl -s) (ELECTRICITY) capacitor
condensers n ▷ condenser
condenses v ▷ condense
condensing v ▷ condense
condescend v (-s, -ing, -ed) behave patronizingly towards someone > **condescension** n
condescended v ▷ condescend
condescending v ▷ condescend
condescends v ▷ condescend
condescension n ▷ condescend
condiment n (pl -s) seasoning for food, such as salt or pepper
condiments n ▷ condiment
condition n (pl -s) particular state of being ▶ pl circumstances ▶ v (-s, -ed, -ing) train or influence to behave in a particular way
conditional adj depending on circumstances > **conditionally** adv
conditionally adv ▷ conditional
conditioned v ▷ condition
conditioner n (pl -s) thick liquid used when washing to make hair or clothes feel softer
conditioning v ▷ condition
conditioners n ▷ condition
conditions n, v ▷ condition
condolence n (pl -s) sympathy ▶ pl expression of sympathy

condolences n ▷ condolence
condom n (pl -s) rubber sheath worn on the penis or in the vagina during sexual intercourse to prevent conception or infection
condominium n (pl -s) (AUST, US & CANADIAN) block of flats in which each flat is owned by the occupant
  condominiums n ▷ condominium
  condoms n ▷ condom
condone v (-dones, -doning, -doned) overlook or forgive (wrongdoing)
  condoned v ▷ condone
  condones v ▷ condone
  condoning v ▷ condone
condor n (pl -s) large vulture of S America
  condors n ▷ condor
conducive adj (foll. by to) likely to lead (to)
conduct n (pl -s) management of an activity ▶ v (-s, -ing, -ed) carry out (a task)
  conducted v ▷ conduct
  conducting v ▷ conduct
conduction n transmission of heat or electricity
  conductive adj ▷ conductivity
  conductivities n ▷ conductivity
conductivity n (pl -vities) ability to transmit heat or electricity > **conductive** adj
conductor n (pl -s) person who conducts musicians, fem **conductress** ▶ n (pl -es)
  conductors n ▷ conductor
  conductress n ▷ conductor
  conductresses n ▷ conductor
  conducts n, v ▷ conduct
conduit [kon-dew-it] n (pl -s) channel or tube for fluid or cables
  conduits n ▷ conduit
cone n (pl -s) object with a circular base, tapering to a point
  cones n ▷ cone
coney n (pl -s) ▷ cony
  coneys n ▷ coney
confab n (pl -s) (Informal) conversation (also **confabulation**)
  confabs n ▷ confab
  confabulation n ▷ confab
  confabulations n ▷ confab
confection n (pl -s) any sweet food (Old-fashioned)
confectioner n (pl -s) maker or seller of confectionery
  confectioneries n ▷ confectionery
  confectioners n ▷ confectioner
confectionery n (pl -eries) sweets
  confections n ▷ confection

confederacies n ▷ confederacy
confederacy n (pl -cies) union of states or people for a common purpose
confederate n (pl -s) member of a confederacy ▶ adj united, allied ▶ v (-rates, -rating, -rated) unite in a confederacy
  confederated v ▷ confederate
  confederates n, v ▷ confederate
  confederating v ▷ confederate
confederation n (pl -s) alliance of political units
  confederations n ▷ confederation
confer v (-fers, -ferring, -ferred) discuss together
conference n (pl -s) meeting for discussion
  conferences n ▷ conference
conferment n (pl -s) granting, giving
  conferments n ▷ conferment
  conferred v ▷ confer
  conferring v ▷ confer
  confers v ▷ confer
confess v (-es, -ing, -ed) admit (a fault or crime)
  confessed v ▷ confess
  confesses v ▷ confess
  confessing v ▷ confess
confession n (pl -s) something confessed
confessional n (pl -s) small stall in which a priest hears confessions
  confessionals n ▷ confessional
  confessions n ▷ confession
confessor n (pl -s) priest who hears confessions
  confessors n ▷ confessor
confetti n (pl -s) small pieces of coloured paper thrown at weddings
  confettis n ▷ confetti
confidant n (pl -s) person confided in > **confidante** n fem (pl -s)
  confidante n ▷ confidant
  confidantes n ▷ confidant
  confidants n ▷ confidant
confide v (-fides, -fiding, -fided) tell someone (a secret)
  confided v ▷ confide
confidence n (pl -s) trust
  confidences n ▷ confidence
confident adj sure, esp. of oneself > **confidently** adv
confidential adj private, secret > **confidentially** adv > **confidentiality** n
  confidentiality n ▷ confidential
  confidentially adv ▷ confidential
  confidently adv ▷ confident
  confides v ▷ confide

confiding v ▷ confide
configuration n (pl -s) arrangement of parts
  configurations n ▷ configuration
confine v (-fines, -fining, -fined) keep within
  bounds
  confined v ▷ confine
confinement n (pl -s) being confined
confines pl n boundaries, limits ▶ v ▷ **confine**
  confining v ▷ confine
confirm v (-s, -ing, -ed) prove to be true
confirmation n (pl -s) confirming
  confirmations n ▷ confirmation
confirmed adj firmly established in a habit or
  condition ▶ v ▷ confirm
  confirming v ▷ confirm
  confirms v ▷ confirm
confiscate v (-cates, -cating, -cated) seize
  (property) by authority > **confiscation** n (pl -s)
  confiscated v ▷ confiscate
  confiscates v ▷ confiscate
  confiscating v ▷ confiscate
  confiscation n ▷ confiscate
  confiscations n ▷ confiscate
conflagration n (pl -s) large destructive fire
  conflagrations n ▷ conflagration
conflate v (-ates, -ating, -ated) combine or
  blend into a whole > **conflation** n (pl -s)
  conflated v ▷ conflate
  conflates v ▷ conflate
  conflating v ▷ conflate
  conflation n ▷ conflate
  conflations n ▷ conflate
conflict n (pl -s) disagreement ▶ v (-s, -ing, -ed)
  be incompatible
  conflicted v ▷ conflict
  conflicting v ▷ conflict
  conflicts n, v ▷ conflict
confluence n (pl -s) place where two rivers join
  confluences n ▷ confluence
conform v (-s, -ing, -ed) comply with accepted
  standards or customs (foll. by **to** or **with**)
  conformed v ▷ conform
  conforming v ▷ conform
conformist n (pl -s) ▶ adj (person) complying
  with accepted standards or customs
  conformists n ▷ conformist
  conformities n ▷ conformity
conformity n (pl -ities) compliance with
  accepted standards or customs
  conforms v ▷ conform
confound v (-s, -ing, -ed) astound, bewilder
confounded adj (Old-fashioned) damned ▶ v
  ▷ confound > **confoundedly** adv
  confoundedly adv ▷ confounded
  confounding v ▷ confound

confounds v ▷ confound
confront v (-s, -ing, -ed) come face to face with
confrontation n (pl -s) serious argument
  > **confrontational** adj
  confrontational adj ▷ confrontation
  confrontations n ▷ confrontation
  confronted v ▷ confront
  confronting v ▷ confront
  confronts v ▷ confront
confuse v (-fuses, -fusing, -fused) mix up
  > **confusion** n (pl -s)
  confused v ▷ confuse
  confuses v ▷ confuse
  confusing v ▷ confuse
  confusion n ▷ confuse
  confusions n ▷ confuse
confute v (-futes, -futing, -futed) prove wrong
  confuted v ▷ confute
  confutes v ▷ confute
  confuting v ▷ confute
conga n (pl -s) dance performed by a number of
  people in single file
  congas n ▷ conga
congeal v (-s, -ing, -ed) (of a liquid) become
  thick and sticky
  congealed v ▷ congeal
  congealing v ▷ congeal
  congeals v ▷ congeal
congenial adj pleasant, agreeable
  > **congeniality** n > **congenially** adv
  congeniality n ▷ congenial
  congenially adv ▷ congenial
congenital adj (of a condition) existing from
  birth > **congenitally** adv
  congenitally adv ▷ congenital
conger n (pl -s) large sea eel
  congers n ▷ conger
congested adj crowded to excess
  > **congestion** n
  congestion n ▷ congested
conglomerate n (pl -s) large corporation made
  up of many companies ▶ v (-rates, -rating,
  -rated) form into a mass ▶ adj made up of
  several different elements > **conglomeration**
  n (pl -s)
  conglomerated v ▷ conglomerate
  conglomerates n, v ▷ conglomerate
  conglomerating v ▷ conglomerate
  conglomeration n ▷ conglomerate
  conglomerations n ▷ conglomerate
congratulate v (-lates, -lating, -lated) express
  one's pleasure to (someone) at his or her
  good fortune or success > **congratulations** pl
  n, interj > **congratulatory** adj
  congratulated v ▷ congratulate

congratulates v ▷ congratulate
congratulating v ▷ congratulate
congratulations n ▷ congratulate
congratulatory adj ▷ congratulate
congregate v (-gates, -gating, -gated) gather together in a crowd
congregated v ▷ congregate
congregates v ▷ congregate
congregating v ▷ congregate
congregation n (pl -s) people who attend a church > **congregational** adj
congregational adj ▷ congregation
congregations n ▷ congregation
congress n (pl **congresses**) formal meeting for discussion > **congressional** adj
congresses n ▷ congress
congressional n ▷ congress
congressman, congresswoman n (pl -men, -women) member of Congress
congressmen n ▷ congressman
congresswoman n ▷ congressman
congresswomen n ▷ congressman
congruence n ▷ congruent
congruent adj similar, corresponding
   > **congruence** n
conical adj cone-shaped
conies n ▷ cony
conifer n (pl -s) cone-bearing tree, such as the fir or pine > **coniferous** adj
coniferous adj ▷ conifer
conifers n ▷ conifer
conjectural adj ▷ conjecture
conjecture n (pl -s) ▶ v (-tures, -turing, -tured) guess > **conjectural** adj
conjectured v ▷ conjecture
conjectures n, v ▷ conjecture
conjecturing v ▷ conjecture
conjugal adj of marriage > **conjugally** adv
conjugally adv ▷ conjugal
conjugate v (-gates, -gating, -gated) give the inflections of (a verb)
conjugated v ▷ conjugate
conjugates v ▷ conjugate
conjugating v ▷ conjugate
conjugation n (pl -s) complete set of inflections of a verb
conjugations n ▷ conjugation
conjunction n (pl -s) combination
conjunctions n ▷ conjunction
conjunctiva n (pl -s) the membrane covering the eyeball and inner eyelid
conjunctivas n ▷ conjunctiva
conjunctivitis n inflammation of the conjunctiva
conjure v (-jures, -juring, -jured) perform

tricks that appear to be magic > **conjuror** n (pl -s)
conjured v ▷ conjure
conjures v ▷ conjure
conjuring v ▷ conjure
conjuror n ▷ conjure
conjurors n ▷ conjure
conk n (pl -s) (BRIT, AUST & NZ) (Slang) nose
conker n (pl -s) (Informal) nut of the horse chestnut
conkers n ▷ conker
conks n ▷ conk
connect v (-s, -ing, -ed) join together
   > **connection, connexion** n (pl -s) relationship, association > **connective** adj
connected v ▷ connect
connecting v ▷ connect
connection n ▷ connect
connections n ▷ connect
connective n ▷ connect
connects v ▷ connect
conned v ▷ con¹
connexion n ▷ connect
connexions n ▷ connect
conning v ▷ con¹
connivance n ▷ connive
connivances n ▷ connive
connive v (-nives, -niving, -nived) (foll. by at) allow (wrongdoing) by ignoring it
   > **connivance** n (pl -s)
connived v ▷ connive
connives v ▷ connive
conniving v ▷ connive
connoisseur [kon-noss-sir] n (pl -s) person with special knowledge of the arts, food, or drink
connoisseurs n ▷ connoisseur
connotation n (pl -s) associated idea conveyed by a word > **connote** v (-notes, -noting, -noted)
connotations n ▷ connotation
connoted v ▷ connotation
connotes v ▷ connotation
connoting v ▷ connotation
connubial adj (Formal) of marriage
conquer v (-s, -ing, -ed) defeat > **conqueror** n (pl -s)
conquered v ▷ conquer
conquering v ▷ conquer
conqueror n ▷ conquer
conquerors n ▷ conquer
conquers v ▷ conquer
conquest n (pl -s) conquering
conquests n ▷ conquest
cons n ▷ con¹,²
conscience n (pl -s) sense of right or wrong as

regards thoughts and actions
consciences *n* ▷ conscience
conscientious *adj* painstaking
> **conscientiously** *adv*
conscientiously *adv* ▷ conscientious
conscious *adj* alert and awake > **consciously**
adv > **consciousness** *n*
consciously *adv* ▷ conscious
consciousness *n* ▷ conscious
conscript *n* (*pl* -**s**) person enrolled for
compulsory military service ▶ *v* (-**s**, -**ing**, -**ed**)
enrol (someone) for compulsory military
service > **conscription** *n* (*pl* -**s**)
conscripted *v* ▷ conscript
conscripting *v* ▷ conscript
conscription *n* ▷ conscript
conscriptions *n* ▷ conscript
conscripts *n*, *v* ▷ conscript
consecrate *v* (-**rates**, -**rating**, -**rated**) make
sacred > **consecration** *n* (*pl* -**s**)
consecrated *v* ▷ consecrate
consecrates *v* ▷ consecrate
consecrating *v* ▷ consecrate
consecration *n* ▷ consecrate
consecrations *n* ▷ consecrate
consecutive *adj* in unbroken succession
> **consecutively** *adv*
consecutively *adv* ▷ consecutive
consensus *n* general agreement
consent *n* (*pl* -**s**) agreement, permission ▶ *v* (-**s**,
-**ing**, -**ed**) (*foll. by* **to**) permit, agree to
consented *v* ▷ consent
consenting *v* ▷ consent
consents *v*, *n* ▷ consent
consequence *n* (*pl* -**s**) result, effect
consequences *n* ▷ consequence
consequent *adj* resulting
consequential *adj* important
consequently *adv* as a result, therefore
conservancies *n* ▷ conservancy
conservancy *n* (*pl* -**cies**) environmental
conservation
conservation *n* (*pl* -**s**) protection of
natural resources and the environment
> **conservationist** *n* (*pl* -**s**)
conservationist *n* ▷ conservation
conservationists *n* ▷ conservation
conservations *n* ▷ conservation
conservatism *adv* ▷ conservative
conservative *adj* opposing change ▶ *n* (*pl* -**s**)
conservative person > **conservatively** *adv*
> **conservatism** *n*
conservatively *adv* ▷ conservative
conservatives *n* ▷ conservative
conservatoire [kon-**serv**-a-twahr] *n* (*pl* -**s**)
school of music
conservatoires *n* ▷ conservatoire
conservatories *n* ▷ conservatory
conservatory *n* (*pl* -**ries**) room with glass walls
and a glass roof, attached to a house
conserve *v* (-**serves**, -**serving**, -**served**) protect
from harm, decay, or loss ▶ *n* (*pl* -**s**) jam
containing large pieces of fruit
conserved *v* ▷ conserve
conserves *v*, *n* ▷ conserve
conserving *v* ▷ conserve
consider *v* (-**s**, -**ing**, -**ed**) regard as
considerable *adj* large in amount or degree
> **considerably** *adv*
considerably *adv* ▷ considerable
considerate *adj* thoughtful towards others
> **considerately** *adv*
considerately *adv* ▷ considerate
consideration *n* (*pl* -**s**) careful thought
considerations *n* ▷ consideration
considered *v* ▷ consider
considering *prep* taking (a specified fact) into
account ▶ *v* ▷ consider
considers *v* ▷ consider
consign *v* (-**s**, -**ing**, -**ed**) put somewhere
consigned *v* ▷ consign
consigning *v* ▷ consign
consignment *n* (*pl* -**s**) shipment of goods
consignments *n* ▷ consignment
consigns *v* ▷ consign
consist *v* (-**s**, -**ing**, -**ed**) be made up of
consisted *v* ▷ consist
consistencies *n* ▷ consistency
consistency *n* (*pl* -**cies**) being consistent
consistent *adj* unchanging, constant (*foll. by*
with) > **consistently** *adv*
consistently *adv* ▷ consistent
consisting *v* ▷ consist
consists *v* ▷ consist
consolation *n* (*pl* -**s**) consoling
consolations *n* ▷ consolation
console[1] *v* (-**soles**, -**soling**, -**soled**) comfort in
distress
console[2] *n* (*pl* -**s**) panel of controls for
electronic equipment
consoled *v* ▷ console[1]
consoles *v* ▷ console[1] ▶ *n* ▷ console[2]
consolidate *v* (-**dates**, -**dating**, -**dated**)
make or become stronger or more stable
> **consolidation** *n* (*pl* -**s**)
consolidated *v* ▷ consolidate
consolidates *v* ▷ consolidate
consolidating *v* ▷ consolidate
consolidation *n* ▷ consolidate
consolidations *n* ▷ consolidate

consoling v ▷ **console¹**
consommé [kon-**som**-may] n (pl -**s**) thin clear meat soup
consommés n ▷ **consommé**
consonance n agreement, harmony
consonant n (pl -**s**) speech sound made by partially or completely blocking the breath stream, such as b or f ▶ adj (foll. by **with**) agreeing (with) > **consonantly** adv
consonantly adv ▷ **consonant**
consonants n ▷ **consonant**
consort v (-**s**, -**ing**, -**ed**) (foll. by **with**) keep company (with) ▶ n (pl -**s**) husband or wife of a monarch
consorted v ▷ **consort**
consortia n ▷ **consortium**
consorting v ▷ **consort**
consortium n (pl -**tia**) association of business firms
consorts v, n ▷ **consort**
conspectus n (pl -**es**) (Formal) survey or summary
conspectuses n ▷ **conspectus**
conspicuous adj clearly visible > **conspicuously** adv > **conspicuousness** n
conspicuously adv ▷ **conspectus**
conspicuousness n ▷ **conspectus**
conspiracies n ▷ **conspiracy**
conspiracy n (pl -**cies**) conspiring > **conspirator** n (pl -**s**) > **conspiratorial** adj
conspirator n ▷ **conspiracy**
conspiratorial adj ▷ **conspiracy**
conspirators n ▷ **conspiracy**
conspire v (-**spires**, -**spiring**, -**spired**) plan a crime together in secret
conspired v ▷ **conspire**
conspires v ▷ **conspire**
conspiring v ▷ **conspire**
constable n (pl -**s**) police officer of the lowest rank
constables n ▷ **constable**
constabularies n ▷ **constabulary**
constabulary n (pl -**laries**) police force of an area
constancy n ▷ **constant**
constant adj continuous ▶ n (pl -**s**) unvarying quantity > **constantly** adv > **constancy** n
constantly adv ▷ **constant**
constants n ▷ **constant**
constellation n (pl -**s**) group of stars
constellations n ▷ **constellation**
consternation n anxiety or dismay
constipated adj having constipation
constipation n difficulty in defecating
constituencies n ▷ **constituency**

constituency n (pl -**cies**) area represented by a Member of Parliament
constituent n (pl -**s**) member of a constituency ▶ adj forming part of a whole
constituents n ▷ **constituent**
constitute v (-**tutes**, -**tuting**, -**tuted**) form, make up
constituted v ▷ **constitute**
constitutes v ▷ **constitute**
constituting v ▷ **constitute**
constitution n (pl -**s**) principles on which a state is governed
constitutional adj of a constitution ▶ n (pl -**s**) walk taken for exercise > **constitutionally** adv
constitutionally adv ▷ **constitutional**
constitutionals n ▷ **constitutional**
constitutions n ▷ **constitution**
constrain v (-**s**, -**ing**, -**ed**) compel, force > **constraint** n (pl -**s**)
constrained v ▷ **constrain**
constraining v ▷ **constrain**
constrains v ▷ **constrain**
constraint n ▷ **constrain**
constraints n ▷ **constrain**
constrict v (-**s**, -**ing**, -**ed**) make narrower by squeezing > **constriction** n (pl -**s**) > **constrictive** adj
constricted v ▷ **constrict**
constricting v ▷ **constrict**
constriction n ▷ **constrict**
constrictions n ▷ **constrict**
constrictive adj ▷ **constrict**
constrictor n (pl -**s**) large snake that squeezes its prey to death
constrictors n ▷ **constrictor**
constricts v ▷ **constrict**
construct v (-**s**, -**ing**, -**ed**) build or put together
constructed v ▷ **construct**
constructing v ▷ **construct**
construction n (pl -**s**) constructing
constructions n ▷ **construction**
constructive adj (of advice, criticism, etc.) useful and helpful > **constructively** adv
constructively adv ▷ **constructive**
constructs v ▷ **construct**
construe v (-**strues**, -**struing**, -**strued**) interpret
construed v ▷ **construe**
construes v ▷ **construe**
construing v ▷ **construe**
consul n (pl -**s**) official representing a state in a foreign country > **consular** adj > **consulship** n (pl -**s**)
consular adj ▷ **consul**
consulate n (pl -**s**) workplace or position of

a consul
consulates n ▷ consulate
consuls n ▷ consul
consulship n ▷ consul
consulships n ▷ consul
consult v (**-s, -ing, -ed**) go to for advice or information
consultancies n ▷ consultancy
consultancy n (pl -**cies**) work or position of a consultant
consultant n (pl -**s**) specialist doctor with a senior position in a hospital
consultants n ▷ consultant
consultation n (pl -**s**) (meeting for) consulting
consultations n ▷ consultation
consultative adj giving advice
consulted v ▷ consult
consulting v ▷ consult
consults v ▷ consult
consume v (**-sumes, -suming, -sumed**) eat or drink
consumed v ▷ consume
consumer n (pl -**s**) person who buys goods or uses services
consumers n ▷ consumer
consumes v ▷ consume
consuming v ▷ consume
consummate [kon-sum-mate] v (**-mates, -mating, -mated**) make (a marriage) legal by sexual intercourse ▶ adj [kon-**sum**-mit] supremely skilled > **consummately** adv > **consummation** n (pl -**s**)
consummated v ▷ consummate
consummately adv ▷ consummate
consummates v ▷ consummate
consummating v ▷ consummate
consummation n ▷ consummate
consummations n ▷ consummate
consumption n (pl -**s**) amount consumed
consumptions n ▷ consumption
consumptive n (pl -**s**) ▶ adj (Old-fashioned) (person) having tuberculosis
consumptives n ▷ consumptive
contact n (pl -**s**) communicating ▶ v (**-s, -ing, -ed**) get in touch with
contacted v ▷ contact
contacting v ▷ contact
contacts n, v ▷ contact
contagion n (pl -**s**) passing on of disease by contact
contagions n ▷ contagion
contagious adj spreading by contact, catching
contain v (**-s, -ing, -ed**) hold or be capable of holding

contained v ▷ contain
container n (pl -**s**) object used to hold or store things in
containers n ▷ container
containing v ▷ contain
containment n prevention of the spread of something harmful
contains v ▷ contain
contaminant n (pl -**s**) contaminating substance
contaminants n ▷ contaminant
contaminate v (**-nates, -nating, -nated**) make impure, pollute > **contamination** n (pl -**s**)
contaminated v ▷ contaminate
contaminates v ▷ contaminate
contaminating v ▷ contaminate
contamination n ▷ contaminate
contaminations n ▷ contaminate
contemplate v (**-lates, -lating, -lated**) think deeply > **contemplation** n (pl -**s**) > **contemplative** adj
contemplated v ▷ contemplate
contemplates v ▷ contemplate
contemplating v ▷ contemplate
contemplation n ▷ contemplate
contemplations n ▷ contemplate
contemplative adj ▷ contemplate
contemporaneous adj happening at the same time
contemporaries n ▷ contemporary
contemporary adj present-day, modern ▶ n (pl -**raries**) person or thing living or occurring at the same time as another
contempt n (pl -**s**) dislike and disregard
contemptible adj deserving contempt > **contemptibly** adv
contemptibly adv ▷ contemptible
contempts n ▷ contempt
contemptuous adj showing contempt > **contemptuously** adv
contemptuously adv ▷ contemptuous
contend v (**-s, -ing, -ed**) (foll. by **with**) deal with
contended v ▷ contend
contender n (pl -**s**) competitor, esp. a strong one
contenders n ▷ contender
contending v ▷ contend
contends v ▷ contend
content[1] n (pl -**s**) meaning or substance of a piece of writing ▶ pl what something contains
content[2] adj satisfied with things as they are ▶ v (**-s, -ing, -ed**) make (someone) content ▶ n happiness and satisfaction > **contented** adj > **contentedly** adv > **contentment** n

contented v, adj ▷ content²
contentedly adv ▷ content²
contenting v ▷ content²
contention n (pl -s) disagreement or dispute
contentions n ▷ contention
contentious adj causing disagreement
> **contentiously** adv > **contentiousness** n
contentiously adv ▷ contentious
contentiousness n ▷ contentious
contentment n ▷ content²
contents n ▷ content¹ ▶ v ▷ content²
contest n (pl -s) competition or struggle ▶ v
(-s, -ing, -ed) dispute, object to > **contestant**
n (pl -s)
contestant n ▷ contest
contestants n ▷ contest
contested v ▷ contest
contesting v ▷ contest
contests n, v ▷ contest
context n (pl -s) circumstances of an event or
fact > **contextual** adj
contexts n ▷ context
contextual adj ▷ context
contiguous adj very near or touching
> **contiguously** adv
contiguously adv ▷ contiguous
continence n ▷ continent²
continent¹ n (pl -s) one of the earth's
large masses of land > **continental** adj
> **continentally** adv
continent² adj able to control one's bladder
and bowels > **continence** n
continental adj ▷ continent¹
continentally adv ▷ continent¹
continents n ▷ continent¹
contingencies n ▷ contingency
contingency n (pl -cies) something that may
happen
contingent n (pl -s) group of people that
represents or is part of a larger group ▶ adj
(foll. by **on**) dependent on (something
uncertain)
contingents n ▷ contingent
continua n ▷ continuum
continual adj constant > **continually** adv
continually adv ▷ continual
continuance n continuing
continuation n (pl -s) continuing
continuations n ▷ continuation
continue v (-tinues, -tinuing, -tinued) (cause
to) remain in a condition or place
continued v ▷ continue
continues v ▷ continue
continuing v ▷ continue
continuities n ▷ continuity

continuity n (pl -ities) smooth development
or sequence
continuo n (pl -s) (MUSIC) continuous bass part,
usu. played on a keyboard instrument
continuos n ▷ continuo
continuous adj continuing uninterrupted
> **continuously** adv
continuously adv ▷ continuous
continuum n (pl -tinua, -tinuums) continuous
series
continuums n ▷ continuum
contort v (-s, -ing, -ed) twist out of shape
> **contortion** n (pl -s)
contorted v ▷ contort
contorting v ▷ contort
contortion n ▷ contort
contortionist n (pl -s) performer who contorts
his or her body to entertain
contortionists n ▷ contortionist
contortions n ▷ contort
contorts v ▷ contort
contour n (pl -s) outline
contours n ▷ contour
contraband n, adj smuggled (goods)
contraception n (pl -s) prevention of
pregnancy by artificial means
contraceptions n ▷ contraception
contraceptive n (pl -s) device used or pill
taken to prevent pregnancy ▶ adj preventing
pregnancy
contraceptives n ▷ contraceptive
contract n (pl -s) (document setting out) a
formal agreement ▶ v (-s, -ing, -ed) make
a formal agreement (to do something)
> **contraction** n (pl -s) > **contractual** adj
> **contractually** adv
contracted v ▷ contract
contracting v ▷ contract
contraction n ▷ contract
contractions n ▷ contract
contractor n (pl -s) firm that supplies
materials or labour
contractors n ▷ contractor
contracts n, v ▷ contract
contractual adj ▷ contract
contractually adv ▷ contract
contradict v (-s, -ing, -ed) declare the opposite
of (a statement) to be true > **contradiction** n
(pl -s) > **contradictory** adj
contradicted v ▷ contradict
contradicting v ▷ contradict
contradiction n ▷ contradict
contradictions n ▷ contradict
contradictory adj ▷ contradict
contradicts v ▷ contradict

contraflow n (pl -s) flow of traffic going alongside but in an opposite direction to the usual flow
  contraflows n ▷ contraflow
contralto n (pl -s) (singer with) the lowest female voice
  contraltos n ▷ contralto
contraption n (pl -s) strange-looking device
  contraptions n ▷ contraption
contrapuntal adj (MUSIC) of or in counterpoint
  > **contrapuntally** adv
  contrapuntally adv ▷ contrapuntal
  contraries n ▷ contrary
  contrarily adv ▷ contrary
  contrariness n ▷ contrary
  contrariwise adv ▷ contrary
contrary n (pl -aries) complete opposite
  ▶ adj opposed, completely different ▶ adv in opposition > **contrarily** adv > **contrariness** n
  > **contrariwise** adv
contrast n (pl -s) obvious difference ▶ v
  (-s, -ing, -ed) compare in order to show differences (foll. by **with**)
  contrasted v ▷ contrast
  contrasting v ▷ contrast
  contrasts n, v ▷ contrast
contravene v (-venes, -vening, -vened) break (a rule or law) > **contravention** n (pl -s)
  contravened v ▷ contravene
  contravenes v ▷ contravene
  contravening v ▷ contravene
  contravention n ▷ contravene
  contraventions n ▷ contravene
contretemps [kon-tra-tahn] n (pl -temps) embarrassing minor disagreement
contribute v (-butes, -buting, -buted) give for a common purpose or fund (foll. by **to**)
  > **contribution** n (pl -s) > **contributor** n (pl -s)
  > **contributory** adj
  contributed v ▷ contribute
  contributes v ▷ contribute
  contributing v ▷ contribute
  contribution n ▷ contribute
  contributions n ▷ contribute
  contributor n ▷ contribute
  contributors n ▷ contribute
  contributory adj ▷ contribute
contrite adj sorry and apologetic > **contritely** adv > **contrition** n
  contritely adv ▷ contrite
  contrition n ▷ contrite
contrivance n (pl -s) device
  contrivances n ▷ contrivance
contrive v (-trives, -triving, -trived) make happen

contrived adj planned or artificial ▶ v
  ▷ contrive
  contrives v ▷ contrive
  contriving v ▷ contrive
control n (pl -s) power to direct something ▶ pl instruments used to operate a machine ▶ v
  (-trols, -trolling, -trolled) have power over
  > **controllable** adj > **controller** n (pl -s)
  controllable adj ▷ control
  controlled v ▷ control
  controller n ▷ control
  controllers n ▷ control
  controlling v ▷ control
  controls n, v ▷ control
controversial adj causing controversy
  > **controversially** adv
  controversially adv ▷ controversial
  controversies adv ▷ controversy
controversy n (pl -sies) fierce argument or debate
  contumelies n ▷ contumely
contumely [kon-tume-mill-ee] n (pl -melies) (Lit) scornful or insulting treatment
contusion n (pl -s) (Formal) bruise
  contusions n ▷ contusion
conundrum n (pl -s) riddle
  conundrums n ▷ conundrum
conurbation n (pl -s) large urban area formed by the growth and merging of towns
  conurbations n ▷ conurbation
convalesce v (-lesces, -lescing, -lesced) recover after an illness or operation
  > **convalescence** n (pl -s) > **convalescent** n
  (pl -s) adj
  convalesced v ▷ convalesce
  convalescence n ▷ convalesce
  convalescences n ▷ convalesce
  convalescent n ▷ convalesce
  convalescents n ▷ convalesce
  convalesces v ▷ convalesce
  convalescing v ▷ convalesce
convection n (pl -s) transmission of heat in liquids or gases by the circulation of currents
  convections n ▷ convection
convector n (pl -s) heater that gives out hot air
  convectors n ▷ convector
convene v (-venes, -vening, -vened) gather or summon for a formal meeting
  convened v ▷ convene
convener, convenor n (pl -s) person who calls a meeting
  conveners n ▷ convener
  convenes v ▷ convene
convenience n (pl -s) quality of being convenient

conveniences *n* ▷ convenience
convenient *adj* suitable or opportune
> **conveniently** *adv*
conveniently *adv* ▷ convenient
convening *v* ▷ convene
convenor *n* ▷ convener
convenors *n* ▷ convener
convent *n* (*pl* -**s**) building where nuns live
convention *n* (*pl* -**s**) widely accepted view of
proper behaviour
conventional *adj* (unthinkingly) following
the accepted customs > **conventionally** *adv*
> **conventionality** *n*
conventionality *n* ▷ conventional
conventionally *adv* ▷ conventional
conventions *n* ▷ convention
convents *n* ▷ convent
converge *v* (-**verges**, -**verging**, -**verged**) meet
or join > **convergence** *n*
converged *v* ▷ converge
converges *v* ▷ converge
converging *v* ▷ converge
conversant *adj* having knowledge or
experience of
conversation *n* (*pl* -**s**) informal talk
> **conversational** *adj*
conversational *adj* ▷ conversation
conversationalist *n* (*pl* -**s**) person with a
specified ability at conversation
conversationalists *n* ▷ conversationalist
conversations *n* ▷ conversation
converse¹ *v* (-**verses**, -**versing**, **versed**) have a
conversation
converse² *adj*, *n* (*pl* -**s**) opposite or contrary
> **conversely** *adv*
conversed *v* ▷ converse¹
conversely *adv* ▷ converse²
converses *v* ▷ converse¹ ▶ *n* ▷ converse²
conversing *v* ▷ converse¹
conversion *n* (*pl* -**s**) (thing resulting from)
converting
conversions *n* ▷ conversion
convert *v* (-**s**, -**ing**, **ed**) change in form,
character, or function ▶ *n* (*pl* -**s**) person who
has converted to a different belief or religion
converted *v* ▷ convert
convertible *adj* capable of being converted ▶ *n*
(*pl* -**s**) car with a folding or removable roof
convertibles *n* ▷ convertible
converting *v* ▷ convert
converts *v*, *n* ▷ convert
convex *adj* curving outwards
convey *v* (-**s**, -**ing**, -**ed**) communicate
(information)
conveyance *n* (*pl* -**s**) (*Old-fashioned*) vehicle

conveyances *n* ▷ conveyance
conveyancing *n* branch of law dealing with
the transfer of ownership of property
conveyed *v* ▷ convey
conveying *v* ▷ convey
conveys *v* ▷ convey
convict *v* (-**s**, -**ing**, -**ed**) declare guilty ▶ *n* (*pl* -**s**)
person serving a prison sentence
convicted *v* ▷ convict
convicting *v* ▷ convict
conviction *n* (*pl* -**s**) firm belief
convictions *n* ▷ conviction
convicts *v*, *n* ▷ convict
convince *v* (-**vinces**, -**vincing**, -**vinced**)
persuade by argument or evidence
> **convincing** *adj* > **convincingly** *adv*
convinced *v* ▷ convince
convinces *v* ▷ convince
convincing *v*, *adj* ▷ convince
convincingly *adv* ▷ convince
convivial *adj* sociable, lively > **conviviality** *n*
> **convivially** *adv*
conviviality *n* ▷ convivial
convivially *adv* ▷ convivial
convocation *n* (*pl* -**s**) calling together
convocations *n* ▷ convocation
convoke *v* (-**vokes**, -**voking**, -**voked**) call
together
convoked *v* ▷ convoke
convokes *v* ▷ convoke
convoking *v* ▷ convoke
convoluted *adj* coiled, twisted > **convolution**
n (*pl* -**s**)
convolution *n* ▷ convoluted
convolutions *n* ▷ convoluted
convolvulus *n* (*pl* -**es**) twining plant with
funnel-shaped flowers
convolvuluses *n* ▷ convolvulus
convoy *n* (*pl* -**s**) group of vehicles or ships
travelling together
convoys *n* ▷ convoy
convulse *v* (-**vulses**, -**vulsing**, -**vulsed**) (of
part of the body) undergo violent spasms
(*Informal*) > **convulsive** *adj* > **convulsively** *adv*
convulsed *v* ▷ convulse
convulses *v* ▷ convulse
convulsing *v* ▷ convulse
convulsion *n* (*pl* -**s**) violent muscular spasm
▶ *pl* uncontrollable laughter
convulsions *n* ▷ convulsion
convulsive *adj* ▷ convulse
convulsively *adv* ▷ convulse
cony, coney *n* (*pl* **conies, -s**) (BRIT) rabbit
coo *v* (**coos, cooing, cooed**) (of a dove or
pigeon) make a soft murmuring sound

cooed v ▷ **coo**
cooee *interj* (BRIT, AUST & NZ) call to attract attention
cooing v ▷ **coo**
cook v (**-s, -ing, -ed**) prepare (food) by heating ▶ n (*pl* **-s**) person who cooks food
cooked v ▷ **cook**
cooker n (*pl* **-s**) (CHIEFLY BRIT) apparatus for cooking heated by gas or electricity
cookers n ▷ **cooker**
cookery n art of cooking
cookie n (*pl* **-s**) (US) biscuit
cookies n ▷ **cookie**
cooking v ▷ **cook**
cooks v, n ▷ **cook**
cool *adj* (**-er, -est**) moderately cold (*Informal*) ▶ v (**-s, -ing, -ed**) make or become cool ▶ n (*pl* **-s**) coolness > **coolly** *adv* > **coolness** n (*pl* **-es**)
coolant n (*pl* **-s**) fluid used to cool machinery while it is working
coolants n ▷ **coolant**
cooled v ▷ **cool**
cooler n (*pl* **-s**) container for making or keeping things cool ▶ *adj* ▷ **cool**
coolers n ▷ **cooler**
coolest *adj* ▷ **cool**
coolibah n (*pl* **-s**) Australian eucalypt that grows beside rivers
coolibahs n ▷ **coolibah**
cooling v ▷ **cool**
coolly *adv* ▷ **cool**
coolness n ▷ **cool**
coolnesses n ▷ **cool**
cools v, n ▷ **cool**
coomb, coombe n (*pl* **-s**) (S ENGLISH) short valley or deep hollow
coombe n ▷ **coomb**
coombes n ▷ **coomb**
coombs n ▷ **coomb**
coop¹ n (*pl* **-s**) cage or pen for poultry
coop² [koh-op] n (*pl* **-s**) (BRIT, US & AUST) (shop run by) a cooperative society
cooper n (*pl* **-s**) person who makes or repairs barrels
cooperate v (**-rates, -rating, -rated**) work or act together > **cooperation** n
cooperated v ▷ **cooperate**
cooperates v ▷ **cooperate**
cooperating v ▷ **cooperate**
cooperation n ▷ **cooperate**
cooperative *adj* willing to cooperate ▶ n (*pl* **-s**) cooperative organization
cooperatives n ▷ **cooperative**
coopers n ▷ **cooper**
coops n ▷ **coop¹, ²**

coopt [koh-opt] v (**-s, -ing, -ed**) add (someone) to a group by the agreement of the existing members
coopted v ▷ **coopt**
coopting v ▷ **coopt**
coopts v ▷ **coopt**
coordinate v (**-nates, -nating, -nated**) bring together and cause to work together efficiently ▶ n (*pl* **-s**) (MATHS) any of a set of numbers defining the location of a point ▶ *pl* clothes designed to be worn together > **coordination** n > **coordinator** n (*pl* **-s**)
coordinated v ▷ **coordinate**
coordinates v, n ▷ **coordinate**
coordinating v ▷ **coordinate**
coordination n ▷ **coordinate**
coordinator n ▷ **coordinate**
coordinators n ▷ **coordinate**
coos v ▷ **coo**
coot n (*pl* **-s**) small black water bird
coots n ▷ **coot**
cop (*Slang*) n (*pl* **-s**) policeman ▶ v (**cops, copping, copped**) take or seize
cope¹ v (**copes, coping, coped**) (*often foll. by* **with**) deal successfully (with)
cope² n (*pl* **-s**) large ceremonial cloak worn by some Christian priests
coped v ▷ **cope¹**
copes v ▷ **cope¹** ▶ n ▷ **cope²**
copied v ▷ **copy**
copies n, v ▷ **copy**
coping v ▷ **cope¹** ▶ n (*pl* **-s**) sloping top row of a wall
copings n ▷ **coping**
copious [kope-ee-uss] *adj* abundant, plentiful > **copiously** *adv*
copiously *adv* ▷ **copious**
copped v ▷ **cop**
copper¹ n (*pl* **-s**) soft reddish-brown metal
copper² n (*pl* **-s**) (BRIT) (*Slang*) policeman
copperplate n (*pl* **-s**) fine handwriting style
copperplates n ▷ **copperplate**
coppers n ▷ **copper¹, ²**
coppice, copse n (*pl* **-s**) small group of trees growing close together
coppices n ▷ **coppice**
copping v ▷ **cop**
copra n (*pl* **-s**) dried oil-yielding kernel of the coconut
copras n ▷ **copra**
cops n, v ▷ **cop**
copse n ▷ **coppice**
copses n ▷ **coppice**
copulate v (**-lates, -lating, -lated**) have sexual intercourse > **copulation** n (*pl* **-s**)

copulated v ▷ copulate
copulates v ▷ copulate
copulating v ▷ copulate
copulation n ▷ copulate
copulations n ▷ copulate
copy n (pl **copies**) thing made to look exactly like another ▶ v (**copies, copying, copied**) make a copy of
copying v ▷ copy
copyright n (pl -**s**) exclusive legal right to reproduce and control a book, work of art, etc. ▶ v (-**s, -ing, -ed**) take out a copyright on ▶ adj protected by copyright
copyrighted v ▷ copyright
copyrighting v ▷ copyright
copyrights n, v ▷ copyright
copywriter n (pl -**s**) person who writes advertising copy
copywriters n ▷ copywriter
coquette n (pl -**s**) woman who flirts
> **coquettish** adj
coquettes n ▷ coquette
coquettish adj ▷ coquette
coracle n (pl -**s**) small round boat of wicker covered with skins
coracles n ▷ coracle
coral n (pl -**s**) hard substance formed from the skeletons of very small sea animals ▶ adj orange-pink
corals n ▷ coral
cord n (pl -**s**) thin rope or thick string ▶ pl corduroy trousers
cordial adj warm and friendly ▶ n (pl -**s**) drink with a fruit base > **cordially** adv > **cordiality** n
cordiality n ▷ cordial
cordially adv ▷ cordial
cordials n ▷ cordial
cordite n (pl -**s**) explosive used in guns and bombs
cordites n ▷ cordite
cordon n (pl -**s**) chain of police, soldiers, etc., guarding an area
cordons n ▷ cordon
cords n ▷ cord
corduroy n (pl -**s**) cotton fabric with a velvety ribbed surface
corduroys n ▷ corduroy
core n (pl -**s**) central part of certain fruits, containing the seeds ▶ v (**cores, coring, cored**) remove the core from
cored v ▷ core
corella n (pl -**s**) white Australian cockatoo
corellas n ▷ corella
cores n, v ▷ core
corgi n (pl -**s**) short-legged sturdy dog

corgis n ▷ corgi
coriander n (pl -**s**) plant grown for its aromatic seeds and leaves
corianders n ▷ coriander
coring v ▷ core
cork n (pl -**s**) thick light bark of a Mediterranean oak ▶ v (-**s, -ing, -ed**) seal with a cork
corkage n (pl -**s**) restaurant's charge for serving wine bought elsewhere
corkages n ▷ corkage
corked v ▷ cork
corking v ▷ cork
corks n, v ▷ cork
corkscrew n (pl -**s**) spiral metal tool for pulling corks from bottles
corkscrews n ▷ corkscrew
corm n (pl -**s**) bulblike underground stem of certain plants
cormorant n (pl -**s**) large dark-coloured long-necked sea bird
cormorants n ▷ cormorant
corms n ▷ corm
corn[1] n (pl -**s**) cereal plant such as wheat or oats
corn[2] n (pl -**s**) painful hard skin on the toe
cornea [korn-ee-a] n (pl -**neas, -neae**) transparent membrane covering the eyeball
> **corneal** adj
corneae n ▷ cornea
corneal adj ▷ cornea
corneas n ▷ cornea
corner n (pl -**s**) area or angle where two converging lines or surfaces meet (SPORT) ▶ v (-**s, -ing, -ed**) force into a difficult or inescapable position
cornered v ▷ corner
cornering v ▷ corner
corners n, v ▷ corner
cornerstone n (pl -**s**) indispensable part or basis
cornerstones n ▷ cornerstone
cornet n (pl -**s**) brass instrument similar to the trumpet
cornets n ▷ cornet
cornflakes pl n breakfast cereal made from toasted maize
cornflour n (pl -**s**) (CHIEFLY BRIT) fine maize flour
cornflours n ▷ cornflour
cornflower n (pl -**s**) plant with blue flowers
cornflowers n ▷ cornflower
cornice n (pl -**s**) decorative moulding round the top of a wall
cornices n ▷ cornice
cornier adj ▷ corny
corniest adj ▷ corny

corns n ▷ **corn**[1, 2]
cornucopia [korn-yew-**kope**-ee-a] n (pl -**s**) great abundance
  cornucopias n ▷ **cornucopia**
corny (-**nier**, -**niest**) adj (Slang) unoriginal or oversentimental
corolla n (pl -**s**) petals of a flower collectively
  corollaries n ▷ **corollary**
corollary n (pl -**laries**) idea, fact, or proposition which is the natural result of something else
  corollas n ▷ **corolla**
corona n (pl -**nas**, -**nae**) ring of light round the moon or sun
  coronae n ▷ **corona**
  coronaries n ▷ **coronary**
coronary [**kor**-ron-a-ree] adj of the arteries surrounding the heart ▶ n (pl -**naries**)
  coronas n ▷ **corona**
coronation n (pl -**s**) ceremony of crowning a monarch
  coronations n ▷ **coronation**
coroner n (pl -**s**) (BRIT, AUST & NZ) official responsible for the investigation of violent, sudden, or suspicious deaths
  coroners n ▷ **coroner**
coronet n (pl -**s**) small crown
  coronets n ▷ **coronet**
  corpora n ▷ **corpus**
corporal[1] n (pl -**s**) noncommissioned officer in an army
corporal[2] adj of the body > **corporally** adv
  corporally adv ▷ **corporal**[2]
  corporals n ▷ **corporal**[1]
corporate adj of business corporations
corporation n (pl -**s**) large business or company
  corporations n ▷ **corporation**
corporeal [kore-**pore**-ee-al] adj physical or tangible
corps [kore] n (pl **corps**) military unit with a specific function
corpse n (pl -**s**) dead body
  corpses n ▷ **corpse**
  corpulence n ▷ **corpulent**
corpulent adj fat or plump > **corpulence** n
corpus n (pl **corpora**) collection of writings, esp. by a single author
corpuscle n (pl -**s**) red or white blood cell
  corpuscles n ▷ **corpuscle**
corral (US) n (pl -**s**) enclosure for cattle or horses ▶ v (-**rals**, -**ralling**, -**ralled**) put in a corral
  corralled v ▷ **corral**
  corralling v ▷ **corral**
  corrals n, v ▷ **corral**
correct adj free from error, true ▶ v (-**s**, -**ing**, -**ed**)

put right > **correctly** adv > **correctness** n
  corrected v ▷ **correct**
  correcting v ▷ **correct**
correction n (pl -**s**) correcting
  corrections n ▷ **correction**
corrective adj intended to put right something wrong
  correctly adv ▷ **correct**
  correctness n ▷ **correct**
  corrects v ▷ **correct**
correlate v (-**lates**, -**lating**, -**lated**) place or be placed in a mutual relationship > **correlation** n (pl -**s**)
  correlated v ▷ **correlate**
  correlates v ▷ **correlate**
  correlating v ▷ **correlate**
  correlation n ▷ **correlate**
  correlations n ▷ **correlate**
correspond v (-**s**, -**ing**, -**ed**) be consistent or compatible (with) > **corresponding** adj > **correspondingly** adv
  corresponded v ▷ **correspond**
correspondence n communication by letters
correspondent n (pl -**s**) person employed by a newspaper etc. to report on a special subject or from a foreign country
  correspondents n ▷ **correspondent**
  corresponding v, adj ▷ **correspond**
  correspondingly adv ▷ **correspond**
  corresponds v ▷ **correspond**
corridor n (pl -**s**) passage in a building or train
  corridors n ▷ **corridor**
  corrigenda n ▷ **corrigendum**
corrigendum [kor-rij-**end**-um] n (pl -**da**) error to be corrected
corroborate v (-**rates**, -**rating**, -**rated**) support (a fact or opinion) by giving proof > **corroboration** n (pl -**s**) > **corroborative** adj
  corroborated v ▷ **corroborate**
  corroborates v ▷ **corroborate**
  corroborating v ▷ **corroborate**
  corroboration n ▷ **corroborate**
  corroborations n ▷ **corroborate**
  corroborative adj ▷ **corroborate**
corroboree n (pl -**s**) (AUST) Aboriginal gathering or dance
  corroborees n ▷ **corroboree**
corrode v (-**rodes**, -**roding**, -**roded**) eat or be eaten away by chemical action or rust > **corrosion** n > **corrosive** adj > **corrosively** adv > **corrosiveness** n
  corroded v ▷ **corrode**
  corrodes v ▷ **corrode**
  corroding v ▷ **corrode**
  corrosion n ▷ **corrode**

corrosive v ▷ corrode

corrosively adv ▷ corrode

corrosiveness n ▷ corrode

corrugated adj folded into alternate grooves and ridges

corrupt adj (-er, -est) open to or involving bribery ▶ v (-s, -ing, -ed) make corrupt > **corruptly** adv > **corruption** n > **corruptible** adj

corrupted v ▷ corrupt

corrupter adj ▷ corrupt

corruptest adj ▷ corrupt

corruptible adj ▷ corrupt

corrupting v ▷ corrupt

corruption n ▷ corrupt

corruptly adv ▷ corrupt

corrupts v ▷ corrupt

corsage [kor-**sahzh**] n (pl -s) small bouquet worn on the bodice of a dress

corsages n ▷ corsage

corsair n (pl -s) pirate

corsairs n ▷ corsair

corset n (pl -s) women's close-fitting undergarment worn to shape the torso

corsets n ▷ corset

cortege [kor-**tayzh**] n (pl -s) funeral procession

corteges n ▷ cortege

cortex n (pl -tices) (ANAT) outer layer of the brain or other internal organ > **cortical** adj

cortical adj ▷ cortex

cortices n ▷ cortex

cortisone n (pl -s) steroid hormone used to treat various diseases

cortisones n ▷ cortisone

corundum n (pl -s) hard mineral used as an abrasive

corundums n ▷ corundum

coruscate v (-cates, -cating, -cated) (Formal) sparkle

coruscated v ▷ coruscate

coruscates v ▷ coruscate

coruscating v ▷ coruscate

corvette n (pl -s) lightly armed escort warship

corvettes n ▷ corvette

cosh n (pl -es) (BRIT) heavy blunt weapon ▶ v (-es, -ing, -ed) hit with a cosh

coshed v, n ▷ cosh

coshes v ▷ cosh

coshing v ▷ cosh

cosier adj ▷ cosy

cosies adj ▷ cosy

cosiest adj ▷ cosy

cosily adv ▷ cosy

cosine [**koh**-sine] n (pl -s) (in trigonometry) ratio of the length of the adjacent side to that of the hypotenuse in a right-angled triangle

cosines n ▷ cosine

cosiness n ▷ cosy

cosmetic n (pl -s) preparation used to improve the appearance of a person's skin ▶ adj improving the appearance only

cosmetics n ▷ cosmetic

cosmic adj of the whole universe > **cosmically** adv

cosmically adv ▷ cosmic

cosmological adj ▷ cosmology

cosmologist n ▷ cosmology

cosmologists n ▷ cosmology

cosmology n study of the origin and nature of the universe > **cosmological** adj > **cosmologist** n (pl -s)

cosmonaut n (pl -s) Russian name for an astronaut

cosmonauts n ▷ cosmonaut

cosmopolitan adj composed of people or elements from many countries ▶ n (pl -s) cosmopolitan person > **cosmopolitanism** n

cosmopolitanism n ▷ cosmopolitan

cosmopolitans n ▷ cosmopolitan

cosmos n (pl cosmos) the universe

cossack n (pl -s) member of a S Russian people famous as horsemen and dancers

cossacks n ▷ cossack

cosset v (-s, -ing, -ed) pamper

cosseted v ▷ cosset

cosseting v ▷ cosset

cossets v ▷ cosset

cost n (pl -s) amount of money, time, labour, etc., required for something ▶ pl expenses of a lawsuit ▶ v (costs, costing, cost) have as its cost

costermonger n (pl -s) (BRIT) person who sells fruit and vegetables from a street barrow

costermongers n ▷ costermonger

costing v ▷ cost

costlier adj ▷ costly

costliest adj ▷ costly

costliness n ▷ costly

costlinesses n ▷ costly

costly adj (-lier, -liest) expensive > **costliness** n (pl -es)

costs n, v ▷ cost

costume n (pl -s) style of dress of a particular place or time, or for a particular activity

costumes n ▷ costume

costumier n (pl -s) maker or seller of costumes

costumiers n ▷ costumier

cosy adj (-sier, -siest) warm and snug ▶ n (pl -sies) cover for keeping things warm > **cosily** adv > **cosiness** n

cot n (pl **-s**) baby's bed with high sides
cote n (pl **-s**) shelter for birds or animals
coterie [kote-er-ee] n (pl **-s**) exclusive group, clique
  coteries n ▷ coterie
  cotes n ▷ cote
cotoneaster [kot-tone-ee-**ass**-ter] n (pl **-s**) garden shrub with red berries
  cotoneasters n ▷ cotoneaster
  cots n ▷ cot
cottage n (pl **-s**) small house in the country
  cottages n ▷ cottage
cotter n (pl **-s**) pin or wedge used to secure machine parts
  cotters n ▷ cotter
cotton n (pl **-s**) white downy fibre covering the seeds of a tropical plant > **cottony** adj
  cottons n ▷ cotton
  cottony adj ▷ cotton
cotyledon [kot-ill-ee-don] n (pl **-s**) first leaf of a plant embryo
  cotyledons n ▷ cotyledon
couch n (pl **couches**) piece of upholstered furniture for seating more than one person ▶ v (**-es, -ing, -ed**) express in a particular way
  couched v ▷ couch
  couches n, v ▷ couch
couchette [koo-**shett**] n (pl **-s**) bed converted from seats on a train or ship
  couchettes n ▷ couchette
  couching v ▷ couch
cougan n (pl **-s**) (AUST) (Slang) drunk and rowdy person
  cougans n ▷ cougan
cougar n (pl **-s**) puma
  cougars n ▷ cougar
cough v (**-s, -ing, -ed**) expel air from the lungs abruptly and noisily ▶ n (pl **-s**) act or sound of coughing
  coughed v ▷ cough
  coughing v ▷ cough
  coughs v, n ▷ cough
  could v ▷ can¹
coulomb [koo-lom] n (pl **-s**) SI unit of electric charge
  coulombs n ▷ coulomb
coulter n (pl **-s**) blade at the front of a ploughshare
  coulters n ▷ coulter
council n (pl **-s**) group meeting for discussion or consultation ▶ adj of or by a council
councillor n (pl **-s**) member of a council
  councillors n ▷ councillor
  councils n ▷ council
counsel n (pl **-s**) advice or guidance ▶ v

(**-sels, -selling, -selled**) give guidance to > **counsellor** n (pl **-s**)
  counselled v ▷ counsel
  counselling v ▷ counsel
  counsellor n ▷ counsel
  counsellors n ▷ counsel
  counsels n, v ▷ counsel
count¹ v (**-s, -ing, -ed**) say numbers in order ▶ n (pl **-s**) counting
count² n (pl **-s**) European nobleman
countdown n (pl **-s**) counting backwards to zero of the seconds before an event
  countdowns n ▷ countdown
  counted v ▷ count¹
countenance n (pl **-s**) (expression of) the face ▶ v (**-nances, -nancing, -nanced**) allow or tolerate
  countenanced v ▷ countenance
  countenances n, v ▷ countenance
  countenancing v ▷ countenance
counter¹ n (pl **-s**) long flat surface in a bank or shop, on which business is transacted
counter² v (**-s, -ing, -ed**) oppose, retaliate against ▶ adv in the opposite direction ▶ n (pl **-s**) opposing or retaliatory action
counteract v (**-s, -ing, -ed**) act against or neutralize > **counteraction** n
  counteracted v ▷ counteract
  counteracting v ▷ counteract
  counteraction n ▷ counteract
  counteracts v ▷ counteract
counterattack n (pl **-s**) ▶ v (**-s, -ing, -ed**) attack in response to an attack
  counterattacked v ▷ counterattack
  counterattacking v ▷ counterattack
  counterattacks n, v ▷ counterattack
counterbalance n (pl **-s**) weight or force balancing or neutralizing another ▶ v (**-ces, -cing, -ced**) act as a counterbalance to
  counterbalanced v ▷ counterbalance
  counterbalances n, v ▷ counterbalance
  counterbalancing v ▷ counterbalance
counterblast n (pl **-s**) aggressive response to a verbal attack
  counterblasts n ▷ counterblast
  countered v ▷ counter
counterfeit adj fake, forged ▶ n (pl **-s**) fake, forgery ▶ v (**-s, -ing, -ed**) fake, forge
  counterfeited v ▷ counterfeit
  counterfeiting v ▷ counterfeit
  counterfeits n, v ▷ counterfeit
counterfoil n (pl **-s**) part of a cheque or receipt kept as a record
  counterfoils n ▷ counterfoil
  countering v ▷ counter

countermand v (-s, -ing, -ed) cancel (a previous order)

countermanded v ▷ countermand

countermanding v ▷ countermand

countermands v ▷ countermand

counterpane n (pl -s) bed covering

counterpanes n ▷ counterpane

counterpart n (pl -s) person or thing complementary to or corresponding to another

counterparts n ▷ counterpart

counterpoint n (pl -s) (MUSIC) technique of combining melodies

counterpoints n ▷ counterpoint

counterpoise n (pl -s) ▶ v (-ses, -sing, -sed) counterbalance

counterpoised v ▷ counterpoise

counterpoises n, v ▷ counterpoise

counterpoising v ▷ counterpoise

counterproductive adj having an effect opposite to the one intended

counters n ▷ counter[1,2] ▶ v ▷ counter[2]

countersank v ▷ countersink

countersign v (-s, -ing, -ed) sign (a document already signed by someone) as confirmation

countersigned v ▷ countersign

countersigning v ▷ countersign

countersigns v ▷ countersign

countersink v (-sinks, -sinking, -sank, -sunk) drive (a screw) into a shaped hole so that its head is below the surface

countersinking v ▷ countersink

countersinks v ▷ countersink

countersunk v ▷ countersink

countertenor n (pl -s) male alto

countertenors n ▷ countertenor

counterterrorism n measures to prevent terrorist attacks or eradicate terrorist groups

countess n (pl -es) woman holding the rank of count or earl

countesses n ▷ countess

counties n ▷ county

counting v ▷ count[1]

countless adj too many to count

countries n ▷ country

countrified adj rustic in manner or appearance

country n (pl -tries) nation

countryman, countrywoman n (pl -men, -women) person from one's native land

countrymen n ▷ countryman

countryside n land away from cities

countrywoman n ▷ countryman

countrywomen n ▷ countryman

counts v ▷ count[1] ▶ n ▷ count[1,2]

county n (pl -ties) (in some countries) division of a country

coup [koo] n (pl -s) successful action

coupé [koo-pay] n (pl -s) sports car with two doors and a sloping fixed roof

coupés n ▷ coupé

couple n (pl -s) two people who are married or romantically involved ▶ v (-ples, -pling, -pled) connect, associate

coupled v ▷ couple

couples n, v ▷ couple

couplet n (pl -s) two consecutive lines of verse, usu. rhyming and of the same metre

couplets n ▷ couplet

coupling n (pl -s) device for connecting things, such as railway carriages ▶ v ▷ couple

couplings n ▷ coupling

coupon n (pl -s) piece of paper entitling the holder to a discount or gift

coupons n ▷ coupon

coups n ▷ coup

courage n ability to face danger or pain without fear > **courageous** adj > **courageously** adv

courageous adj ▷ courage

courageously adv ▷ courage

courgette n (pl -s) type of small vegetable marrow

courgettes n ▷ courgette

courier n (pl -s) person employed to look after holiday-makers

couriers n ▷ courier

course n (pl -s) series of lessons or medical treatment ▶ v (-ses, -sing, -sed) (of liquid) run swiftly

coursed v ▷ course

courses n, v ▷ course

coursing v ▷ course

court n (pl -s) body which decides legal cases ▶ v (-s, -ing, -ed) (Old-fashioned) try to gain the love of

courted v ▷ court

courteous adj polite > **courteously** adv

courteously adv ▷ courteous

courtesan [kor-tiz-zan] n (pl -s) (HIST) mistress or high-class prostitute

courtesans n ▷ courtesan

courtesies n ▷ courtesy

courtesy n (pl -sies) politeness, good manners

courtier n (pl -s) attendant at a royal court

courtiers n ▷ courtier

courting v ▷ court

courtlier adj ▷ courtly

courtliest adj ▷ courtly

courtliness n ▷ courtly

courtlinesses *n* ▷ **courtly**
courtly *adj* (**-lier, -liest**) ceremoniously polite
> **courtliness** *n* (*pl* **-es**)
  courts *n, v* ▷ **court**
courtship *n* (*pl* **-s**) courting of an intended
  spouse or mate
  courtships *n* ▷ **courtship**
courtyard *n* (*pl* **-s**) paved space enclosed by
  buildings or walls
  courtyards *n* ▷ **courtyard**
cousin *n* (*pl* **-s**) child of one's uncle or aunt
  cousins *n* ▷ **cousin**
couture [koo-**toor**] *n* (*pl* **-s**) high-fashion
  designing and dressmaking
  coutures *n* ▷ **couture**
couturier *n* (*pl* **-s**) person who designs
  women's fashion clothes
  couturiers *n* ▷ **couturier**
cove *n* (*pl* **-s**) small bay or inlet
coven [**kuv**-ven] *n* (*pl* **-s**) meeting of witches
covenant [**kuv**-ven-ant] *n* (*pl* **-s**) contract ▶ *v* (**-s,
  -ing, -ed**) agree by a covenant
  covenanted *v* ▷ **covenant**
  covenanting *v* ▷ **covenant**
  covenants *n, v* ▷ **covenant**
  covens *n* ▷ **coven**
cover *v* (**-s, -ing, -ed**) place something over, to
  protect or conceal ▶ *n* (*pl* **-s**) anything that
  covers
coverage *n* amount or extent covered
  covered *v* ▷ **cover**
  covering *v* ▷ **cover**
coverlet *n* (*pl* **-s**) bed cover
  coverlets *v* ▷ **coverlet**
  covers *v, n* ▷ **cover**
covert *adj* concealed, secret ▶ *n* (*pl* **-s**) thicket
  giving shelter to game birds or animals
  > **covertly** *adv*
  covertly *adv* ▷ **covert**
  coverts *n* ▷ **covert**
  coves *n* ▷ **cove**
covet *v* (**-s, -ing, -ed**) long to possess (what
  belongs to someone else) > **covetous** *adj*
  > **covetousness** *n*
  coveted *v* ▷ **covet**
  coveting *v* ▷ **covet**
  covetous *adj* ▷ **covet**
  covetousness *n* ▷ **covet**
  covets *v* ▷ **covet**
covey [**kuv**-vee] *n* (*pl* **-s**) small flock of grouse
  or partridge
  coveys *n* ▷ **covey**
cow[1] *n* (*pl* **-s**) mature female of cattle and of
  certain other mammals, such as the elephant
  or seal

cow[2] *v* (**-s, -ing, -ed**) intimidate, subdue
coward *n* (*pl* **-s**) person who lacks courage
  > **cowardly** *adj* > **cowardliness** *n*
cowardice *n* lack of courage
  cowardliness *n* ▷ **coward**
  cowardly *adj* ▷ **coward**
  cowards *n* ▷ **coward**
cowboy *n* (*pl* **-s**) (in the US) ranch worker who
  herds and tends cattle, usu. on horseback
  cowboys *n* ▷ **cowboy**
  cowed *v* ▷ **cow**[2]
cower *v* (**-s, -ing, -ed**) cringe in fear
  cowered *v* ▷ **cower**
  cowering *v* ▷ **cower**
  cowers *v* ▷ **cower**
  cowing *v* ▷ **cow**[2]
cowl *n* (*pl* **-s**) loose hood
cowling *n* (*pl* **-s**) cover on an engine
  cowlings *n* ▷ **cowling**
  cowls *n* ▷ **cowl**
cowrie *n* (*pl* **-s**) brightly-marked sea shell
  cowries *n* ▷ **cowrie**
  cows *n* ▷ **cow**[1] ▶ *v* ▷ **cow**[2]
cowslip *n* (*pl* **-s**) small yellow wild European
  flower
  cowslips *n* ▷ **cowslip**
cox *n* (*pl* **-es**) coxswain ▶ *v* (**-es, -ing, -ed**) act as
  cox of (a boat)
  coxed *v* ▷ **cox**
  coxes *n, v* ▷ **cox**
  coxing *v* ▷ **cox**
coxswain [**kok**-sn] *n* (*pl* **-s**) person who steers
  a rowing boat
  coxswains *n* ▷ **coxswain**
coy *adj* (**-er, -est**) affectedly shy or modest
  > **coyly** *adv* > **coyness** *n* (*pl* **-es**)
  coyer *adj* ▷ **coy**
  coyest *adj* ▷ **coy**
  coyly *adv* ▷ **coy**
  coyness *n* ▷ **coy**
  coynesses *n* ▷ **coy**
coyote [koy-**ote**-ee] *n* (*pl* **-s**) prairie wolf of N
  America
  coyotes *n* ▷ **coyote**
coypu *n* (*pl* **-s**) beaver-like aquatic rodent
  native to S America, bred for its fur
  coypus *n* ▷ **coypu**

> **coz** *n* (**cozes**). Coz is an old word for
> **cousin**, and a good one to know as it
> scores 14 points.

cozen *v* (**-s, -ing, -ed**) (*Lit*) cheat, trick
  cozened *v* ▷ **cozen**
  cozening *v* ▷ **cozen**
  cozens *v* ▷ **cozen**
crab *n* (*pl* **-s**) edible shellfish with ten legs, the

first pair modified into pincers

crabbed *adj* (of handwriting) hard to read (*also*
crabby) (**crabbier, crabbiest**)

crabbier *adj* ▷ **crabbed**

crabbiest *adj* ▷ **crabbed**

crabby *adj* ▷ **crabbed**

crabs *n* ▷ **crab**

crack *v* (**-s, -ing, -ed**) break or split partially
▶ *n* (*pl* **-s**) sudden sharp noise ▶ *adj* (*Informal*)
first-rate, excellent

crackdown *n* (*pl* **-s**) severe disciplinary
measures

crackdowns *n* ▷ **crackdown**

cracked *v* ▷ **crack**

cracker *n* (*pl* **-s**) thin dry biscuit

crackers *n* ▷ **cracker** ▶ *adj* (*Slang*) insane

cracking *adj* very good ▶ *v* ▷ **crack**

crackle *v* (**-ckles, -ckling, -ckled**) make small
sharp popping noises ▶ *n* (*pl* **-ckles**) crackling
sound

crackled *v* ▷ **crackle**

crackles *v, n* ▷ **crackle**

crackling *n* crackle ▶ *v* ▷ **crackle**

crackpot *n* (*pl* **-s**) ▶ *adj* (*Informal*) eccentric
(person)

crackpots *n* ▷ **crackpot**

cracks *v, n* ▷ **crack**

cradle *n* (*pl* **-s**) baby's bed on rockers ▶ *v* (**-dles,
-dling, -dled**) hold gently as if in a cradle

cradled *v* ▷ **cradle**

cradles *n, v* ▷ **cradle**

cradling *v* ▷ **cradle**

craft *n* (*pl* **-s**) occupation requiring skill with
the hands

craftier *adj* ▷ **crafty**

craftiest *adj* ▷ **crafty**

craftily *adv* ▷ **crafty**

craftiness *n* ▷ **crafty**

craftinesses *n* ▷ **crafty**

crafts *n* ▷ **craft**

craftsman, craftswoman *n* (*pl* **-men,
-women**) skilled worker > **craftsmanship**
n (*pl* **-s**)

craftsmanship *n* ▷ **craftsman**

craftsmanships *n* ▷ **craftsman**

craftsmen *n* ▷ **craftsman**

craftswoman *n* ▷ **craftsman**

craftswomen *n* ▷ **craftsman**

crafty *adj* (**-tier, -tiest**) skilled in deception
> **craftily** *adv* > **craftiness** *n* (*pl* **-es**)

crag *n* (*pl* **-s**) steep rugged rock > **craggy** *adj*
(**-ggier, -ggiest**)

craggier *adj* ▷ **crag**

craggiest *adj* ▷ **crag**

craggy *adj* ▷ **crag**

crags *n* ▷ **crag**

cram *v* (**-s, -mming, -mmed**) force into too
small a space

crammed *v* ▷ **cram**

cramming *v* ▷ **cram**

cramp[1] *n* (*pl* **-s**) painful muscular contraction

cramp[2] *v* (**-s, -ing, -ed**) confine, restrict

cramped *v* ▷ **cramp**[2]

cramping *v* ▷ **cramp**[2]

crampon *n* (*pl* **-s**) spiked plate strapped to a
boot for climbing on ice

crampons *n* ▷ **crampon**

cramps *n* ▷ **cramp**[1] ▶ *v* ▷ **cramp**[2]

crams *v* ▷ **cram**

cranberries *n* ▷ **cranberry**

cranberry *n* (*pl* **-berries**) sour edible red berry

crane *n* (*pl* **-s**) machine for lifting and moving
heavy weights ▶ *v* (**cranes, craning, craned**)
stretch (one's neck) to see something

craned *v* ▷ **crane**

cranes *n, v* ▷ **crane**

crania *n* ▷ **cranium**

cranial *adj* ▷ **cranium**

craning *v* ▷ **crane**

cranium *n* (*pl* **-niums, -nia**) (ANAT) skull
> **cranial** *adj*

craniums *n* ▷ **cranium**

crank *n* (*pl* **-s**) arm projecting at right angles
from a shaft, for transmitting or converting
motion (*Informal*) ▶ *v* (**-s, -ing, -ed**) start (an
engine) with a crank

cranked *v* ▷ **crank**

crankier *adj* ▷ **cranky**

crankiest *adj* ▷ **cranky**

cranking *v* ▷ **crank**

cranks *n, v* ▷ **crank**

crankshaft *n* (*pl* **-s**) shaft driven by a crank

crankshafts *n* ▷ **crankshaft**

cranky *adj* (**-kier, -kiest**) (*Informal*) eccentric

crannies *n* ▷ **cranny**

cranny *n* (*pl* **-nies**) narrow opening

crape *n* (*pl* **-s**) ▷ **crepe**

crapes *n* ▷ **crape**

craps *n* gambling game played with two dice

crash *n* (*pl* **-es**) collision involving a vehicle or
vehicles ▶ *v* (**-es, -ing, -ed**) (cause to) collide
violently with a vehicle, a stationary object,
or the ground

crashed *v* ▷ **crash**

crashes *n, v* ▷ **crash**

crashing *v* ▷ **crash**

crass *adj* (**-er, -est**) stupid and insensitive
> **crassly** *adv* > **crassness** *n* (*pl* **-es**)

crasser *adj* ▷ **crass**

crassest *adj* ▷ **crass**

crassly *adv* ▷ **crass**
crassness *n* ▷ **crass**
crassnesses *n* ▷ **crass**
crate *n* (*pl* -s) large wooden container for packing goods
crater *n* (*pl* -s) very large hole in the ground or in the surface of the moon
craters *n* ▷ **crater**
crates *n* ▷ **crate**
cravat *n* (*pl* -s) man's scarf worn like a tie
cravats *n* ▷ **cravat**
crave *v* (**craves, craving, craved**) desire intensely > **craving** *n* (*pl* -s)
craved *v* ▷ **crave**
craven *adj* cowardly
craves *v* ▷ **crave**
craving *n, v* ▷ **crave**
cravings *n* ▷ **crave**
crawfish *n* (*pl* **crawfish**) ▷ **crayfish**
crawl *v* (-s, -ing, -ed) move on one's hands and knees ▶ *n* (*pl* -s) crawling motion or pace > **crawler** *n* (*pl* -s)
crawled *v* ▷ **crawl**
crawler *n* ▷ **crawl**
crawlers *n* ▷ **crawl**
crawling *v* ▷ **crawl**
crawls *v, n* ▷ **crawl**
crayfish *n* (*pl* **crayfish**) edible shellfish like a lobster
crayon *v* (-s, -ing, -ed), *n* (*pl* -s) (draw or colour with) a stick or pencil of coloured wax or clay
crayoned *v* ▷ **crayon**
crayoning *v* ▷ **crayon**
crayons *v, n* ▷ **crayon**
craze *n* (*pl* -s) short-lived fashion or enthusiasm
crazed *adj* wild and uncontrolled
crazes *n* ▷ **craze**
crazier *adj* ▷ **crazy**
craziest *adj* ▷ **crazy**
crazily *adv* ▷ **crazy**
craziness *n* ▷ **crazy**
crazinesses *n* ▷ **crazy**
crazy *adj* (-zier, -ziest) ridiculous > **crazily** *adv* > **craziness** *n* (*pl* -es)
creak *v, n* (*pl* -s) (make) a harsh squeaking sound > **creaky** *adj* (-kier, -kiest)
creakier *adj* ▷ **creak**
creakiest *adj* ▷ **creak**
creaks *n* ▷ **creak**
creaky *adj* ▷ **creak**
cream *n* (*pl* -s) fatty part of milk ▶ *adj* yellowish-white ▶ *v* (-s, -ing, -ed) beat to a creamy consistency > **creamy** *adj* > **creaminess** *n*

creamed *v* ▷ **cream**
creaminess *n* ▷ **cream**
creaming *v* ▷ **cream**
creams *n, v* ▷ **cream**
creamy *adj* ▷ **cream**
crease *n* (*pl* -s) line made by folding or pressing ▶ *v* (**creases, creasing, creased**) crush or line
creased *v* ▷ **crease**
creases *n, v* ▷ **crease**
creasing *v* ▷ **crease**
create *v* (**creates, creating, created**) make, cause to exist > **creation** *n* (*pl* -s) > **creator** *n* (*pl* -s)
created *v* ▷ **create**
creates *v* ▷ **create**
creating *v* ▷ **create**
creation *n* ▷ **create**
creations *n* ▷ **create**
creative *adj* imaginative or inventive > **creatively** *adv* > **creativity** *n*
creatively *adv* ▷ **creative**
creativity *n* ▷ **creative**
creator *n* ▷ **create**
creators *n* ▷ **create**
creature *n* (*pl* -s) animal, person, or other being
creatures *n* ▷ **creature**
crèche *n* (*pl* -s) place where small children are looked after while their parents are working, shopping, etc.
crèches *n* ▷ **crèche**
credence *n* (*pl* -s) belief in the truth or accuracy of a statement
credences *n* ▷ **credence**
credentials *pl n* document giving evidence of a person's identity or qualifications
credibility *n* ▷ **credible**
credible *adj* believable > **credibly** *adv* > **credibility** *n*
credibly *adv* ▷ **credible**
credit *n* (*pl* -s) system of allowing customers to receive goods and pay later ▶ *v* (-s, -ing, -ed) enter as a credit in an account
creditable *adj* praiseworthy > **creditably** *adv*
creditably *adv* ▷ **creditable**
credited *v* ▷ **credit**
crediting *v* ▷ **credit**
creditor *n* (*pl* -s) person to whom money is owed
creditors *n* ▷ **creditor**
credits *n, v* ▷ **credit**
credulity *n* ▷ **credulous**
credulous *adj* too willing to believe > **credulity** *n* > **credulously** *adv*
credulously *adv* ▷ **credulous**

creed *n* (*pl* -s) statement or system of (Christian) beliefs or principles
  creeds *n* ▷ **creed**
creek *n* (*pl* -s) narrow inlet or bay (AUST, NZ, US & CANADIAN)
  creeks *n* ▷ **creek**
creel *n* (*pl* -s) wicker basket used by anglers
  creels *n* ▷ **creel**
creep *v* (**creeps, creeping, crept**) move quietly and cautiously ▶ *n* (*pl* -s) (*Slang*) obnoxious or servile person
creeper *n* (*pl* -s) creeping plant
  creepers *n* ▷ **creeper**
  creepier *adj* ▷ **creepy**
  creepiest *adj* ▷ **creepy**
  creepily *adv* ▷ **creepy**
  creepiness *n* ▷ **creepy**
  creepinesses *n* ▷ **creepy**
  creeping *v* ▷ **creep**
  creeps *v*, *n* ▷ **creep**
creepy *adj* (**-pier, -piest**) (*Informal*) causing a feeling of fear or disgust > **creepily** *adv* > **creepiness** *n* (*pl* -es)
cremate *v* (**-mates, -mating, -mated**) burn (a corpse) to ash > **cremation** *n* (*pl* -s)
  cremated *v* ▷ **cremate**
  cremates *v* ▷ **cremate**
  cremating *v* ▷ **cremate**
  cremation *n* ▷ **cremate**
  cremations *n* ▷ **cremate**
  crematoria *n* ▷ **crematorium**
crematorium *n* (*pl* -iums, -ia) building where corpses are cremated
  crematoriums *n* ▷ **crematorium**
crenellated *adj* having battlements
creole *n* (*pl* -s) language developed from a mixture of languages
  creoles *n* ▷ **creole**
creosote *n* (*pl* -s) dark oily liquid made from coal tar and used for preserving wood ▶ *v* (**-sotes, -soting, -soted**) treat with creosote
  creosoted *v* ▷ **creosote**
  creosotes *n*, *v* ▷ **creosote**
  creosoting *v* ▷ **creosote**
crepe, crape [krayp] *n* (*pl* -s) fabric or rubber with a crinkled texture
  crepes *n* ▷ **crepe**
  crept *v* ▷ **creep**
crepuscular *adj* (*Lit*) of or like twilight
crescendo [krish-end-oh] *n* (*pl* -s) gradual increase in loudness, esp. in music
  crescendos *n* ▷ **creep**
crescent *n* (*pl* -s) (curved shape of) the moon as seen in its first or last quarter
  crescents *n* ▷ **crescent**

cress *n* (*pl* -es) plant with strong-tasting leaves, used in salads
  cresses *n* ▷ **cress**
crest *n* (*pl* -s) top of a mountain, hill, or wave > **crested** *adj*
  crested *adj* ▷ **crest**
crestfallen *adj* disheartened
  crests *n* ▷ **crest**
cretin *n* (*pl* -s) (*Informal*) stupid person > **cretinous** *adj*
  cretinous *adj* ▷ **cretin**
  cretins *n* ▷ **cretin**
crevasse *n* (*pl* -s) deep open crack in a glacier
  crevasses *n* ▷ **crevasse**
crevice *n* (*pl* -s) narrow crack or gap in rock
  crevices *n* ▷ **crevice**
crew *n* (*pl* -s) people who work on a ship or aircraft (*Informal*) ▶ *v* (**-s, -ing, -ed**) serve as a crew member (on)
  crewed *v* ▷ **crew**
crewel *n* (*pl* -s) fine worsted yarn used in embroidery
  crewels *n* ▷ **crewel**
  crewing *v* ▷ **crew**
  crews *n*, *v* ▷ **crew**
crib *n* (*pl* -s) piece of writing stolen from elsewhere ▶ *v* (**cribs, cribbing, cribbed**) copy (someone's work) dishonestly
cribbage *n* card game for two to four players
  cribbed *v* ▷ **crib**
  cribbing *v* ▷ **crib**
  cribs *n*, *v* ▷ **crib**
crick *n* (*pl* -s) muscle spasm or cramp in the back or neck ▶ *v* (**-s, -ing, -ed**) cause a crick in
  cricked *v* ▷ **crick**
cricket[1] *n* (*pl* -s) outdoor game played with bats, a ball, and wickets by two teams of eleven > **cricketer** *n* (*pl* -s)
cricket[2] *n* (*pl* -s) chirping insect like a grasshopper
  cricketer *n* ▷ **cricket**[1]
  cricketers *n* ▷ **cricket**[1]
  crickets *n* ▷ **cricket**[1, 2]
  cricking *v* ▷ **crick**
  cricks *n*, *v* ▷ **crick**
  cried *v* ▷ **cry**
  cries *v* ▷ **cry**
crime *n* (*pl* -s) unlawful act
  crimes *n* ▷ **crime**
criminal *n* (*pl* -s) person guilty of a crime ▶ *adj* of crime > **criminally** *adv* > **criminality** *n*
  criminality *n* ▷ **criminal**
  criminally *adv* ▷ **criminal**
  criminals *n* ▷ **criminal**
  criminologist *n* ▷ **criminology**

criminologists *n* ▷ criminology
criminology *n* study of crime > **criminologist**
  n (pl **-s)**
crimp *v* (**-s, -ing, -ed**) fold or press into ridges
  crimped *v* ▷ crimp
  crimping *v* ▷ crimp
  crimps *v* ▷ crimp
crimson *adj* deep purplish-red
cringe *v* (**cringes, cringing, cringed**) flinch
  in fear
  cringed *v* ▷ cringe
  cringes *v* ▷ cringe
  cringing *v* ▷ cringe
crinkle *v* (**-kles, -kling, -kled**) ▶ *n (pl* **-s**) wrinkle,
  crease, or fold
  crinkled *v* ▷ crinkle
  crinkles *v, n* ▷ crinkle
  crinkling *v* ▷ crinkle
crinoline *n (pl* **-s**) hooped petticoat
  crinolines *n* ▷ crinoline
cripple *n (pl* **-s**) person who is lame or disabled
  ▶ *v* (**-pples, -ppling, -ppled**) make lame or
  disabled
  crippled *v* ▷ cripple
  cripples *n, v* ▷ cripple
  crippling *v* ▷ cripple
  crises *n* ▷ crisis
crisis *n (pl* **-ses**) crucial stage, turning point
crisp *adj* (**-er, -est**) fresh and firm ▶ *n (pl* **-s**) (BRIT)
  very thin slice of potato fried till crunchy
  > **crisply** *adv* > **crispness** *n (pl* **-es**)
crispbread *n (pl* **-s**) thin dry biscuit
  crispbreads *n* ▷ crispbread
  crisper *adj* ▷ crisp
  crispest *adj* ▷ crisp
  crispier *adj* ▷ crisp
  crispiest *adj* ▷ crisp
  crisply *adv* ▷ crisp
  crispness *adv* ▷ crisp
  crispnesses *adv* ▷ crisp
  crisps *n* ▷ crisp
crispy *adj* (**-pier, -piest**) hard and crunchy
crisscross *v* (**-es, -ing, -ed**) move in or mark
  with a crosswise pattern ▶ *adj* (of lines)
  crossing in different directions
  crisscrossed *v* ▷ crisscross
  crisscrosses *v* ▷ crisscross
  crisscrossing *v* ▷ crisscross
  criteria *n* ▷ criterion
criterion *n (pl* **-ria**) standard of judgment
critic *n (pl* **-s**) professional judge of any of
  the arts
critical *adj* very important or dangerous
  > **critically** *adv*
  critically *adv* ▷ critical

criticism *n (pl* **-s**) fault-finding
  criticisms *n* ▷ criticism
criticize *v* (**-cizes, -cizing, -cized**) find fault
  with
  criticized *v* ▷ criticize
  criticizes *v* ▷ criticize
  criticizing *v* ▷ criticize
  critics *n* ▷ critic
critique *n (pl* **-s**) critical essay
  critiques *n* ▷ critique
croak *v* (**-s, -ing, -ed**) (of a frog or crow) give a
  low hoarse cry ▶ *n (pl* **-s**) low hoarse sound
  croaked *v* ▷ croak
  croakiness *n* ▷ croaky
  croaking *v* ▷ croak
  croaks *v, n* ▷ croak
croaky *adj* hoarse > **croakiness** *n*
crochet [kroh-shay] *v* (**-chets, -cheting,**
  -cheted) make by looping and intertwining
  yarn with a hooked needle ▶ *n (pl* **-s**) work
  made in this way
  crocheted *v* ▷ crochet
  crocheting *v* ▷ crochet
  crochets *v, n* ▷ crochet
crock[1] *n (pl* **-s**) earthenware pot or jar
crock[2] *n (pl* **-s**) (BRIT, AUST & NZ) (*Informal*) old or
  decrepit person or thing
crockery *n* dishes
  crocks *n* ▷ crock[1, 2]
crocodile *n (pl* **-s**) large amphibious tropical
  reptile
  crocodiles *n* ▷ crocodile
crocus *n (pl* **-cuses**) small plant with yellow,
  white, or purple flowers in spring
  crocuses *n* ▷ crocus
croft *n (pl* **-s**) small farm worked by one family
  in Scotland > **crofter** *n (pl* **-s**)
  crofter *n* ▷ croft
  crofters *n* ▷ croft
  crofts *n* ▷ croft
croissant [krwah-son] *n (pl* **-s**) rich flaky
  crescent-shaped roll
  croissants *n* ▷ croissant
cromlech *n (pl* **-s**) (BRIT) circle of prehistoric
  standing stones
  cromlechs *n* ▷ cromlech
crone *n (pl* **-s**) witchlike old woman
  crones *n* ▷ crone
  cronies *n* ▷ crony
crony *n (pl* **-nies**) close friend
crook *n (pl* **-s**) (*Informal*) criminal ▶ *adj* (AUST & NZ)
  (*Slang*) unwell, injured
crooked *adj* bent or twisted > **crookedly** *adv*
  > **crookedness** *n*
  crookedly *adv* ▷ crooked

crookedness n ▷ **crooked**
crooks n ▷ **crook**
croon v (**-s, -ing, -ed**) sing, hum, or speak in a soft low tone
crooned v ▷ **croon**
crooner n (pl **-s**) male singer of sentimental ballads
crooners n ▷ **crooner**
crooning v ▷ **croon**
croons v ▷ **croon**
crop n (pl **-s**) cultivated plant ▶ v (**crops, cropping, cropped**) cut very short > **cropper** n (pl **-s**)
cropped v ▷ **crop**
cropper n ▷ **crop**
croppers n ▷ **crop**
cropping v ▷ **crop**
crops n, v ▷ **crop**
croquet [kroh-kay] n (pl **-s**) game played on a lawn in which balls are hit through hoops
croquets n ▷ **croquet**
croquette [kroh-kett] n (pl **-s**) fried cake of potato, meat, or fish
croquettes n ▷ **croquette**
crosier n (pl **-s**) ▷ **crozier**
crosiers n ▷ **crosier**
cross v (**-es, -ing, -ed**) move or go across (something) ▶ n (pl **-es**) structure, symbol, or mark of two intersecting lines ▶ adj (**-er, -est**) angry, annoyed > **crossly** adv > **crossness** n (pl **-es**)
crossbar n (pl **-s**) horizontal bar across goalposts or on a bicycle
crossbars n ▷ **crossbar**
crossbow n (pl **-s**) weapon consisting of a bow fixed across a wooden stock
crossbows n ▷ **crossbow**
crossbred adj bred from two different types of animal or plant
crossbreed n (pl **-s**) crossbred animal or plant
crossbreeds n ▷ **crossbreed**
crossed v ▷ **cross**
crosser adj ▷ **cross**
crosses v, n ▷ **cross**
crossest adj ▷ **cross**
crossfire n (pl **-s**) gunfire crossing another line of fire
crossfires n ▷ **crossfire**
crossing n (pl **-s**) place where a street may be crossed safely ▶ v ▷ **cross**
crossings n ▷ **crossing**
crossly adv ▷ **cross**
crossness n ▷ **cross**
crossnesses n ▷ **cross**
crossroads n place where roads intersect

crosswise adj, adv across
crossword n (pl **-s**) puzzle in which words suggested by clues are written into a grid of squares
crosswords n ▷ **crossword**
crotch n (pl **-es**) part of the body between the tops of the legs
crotches n ▷ **crotch**
crotchet n (pl **-s**) musical note half the length of a minim
crotchetier adj ▷ **crotchety**
crotchetiest adj ▷ **crotchety**
crotchets n ▷ **crotchet**
crotchety adj (**-tier, -tiest**) (Informal) bad-tempered
crouch v (**-es, -ing, -ed**) bend low with the legs and body close ▶ n (pl **-es**) this position
crouched v ▷ **crouch**
crouches v, n ▷ **crouch**
crouching v ▷ **crouch**
croup[1] [kroop] n (pl **-s**) throat disease of children, with a cough
croup[2] [kroop] n (pl **-s**) hind quarters of a horse
croupier [kroop-ee-ay] n (pl **-s**) person who collects bets and pays out winnings at a gambling table in a casino
croupiers n ▷ **croupier**
croups n ▷ **croup**[1, 2]
crouton n (pl **-s**) small piece of fried or toasted bread served in soup
croutons n ▷ **crouton**
crow[1] n (pl **-s**) large black bird with a harsh call
crow[2] v (**-s, -ing, -ed**) (of a cock) make a shrill squawking sound
crowbar n (pl **-s**) iron bar used as a lever
crowbars n ▷ **crowbar**
crowd n (pl **-s**) large group of people or things ▶ v (**-s, -ing, -ed**) gather together in large numbers
crowded v ▷ **crowd**
crowding v ▷ **crowd**
crowds n, v ▷ **crowd**
crowed v ▷ **crow**[2]
crowing v ▷ **crow**[2]
crown n (pl **-s**) monarch's headdress of gold and jewels ▶ v (**-s, -ing, -ed**) put a crown on the head of (someone) to proclaim him or her monarch
crowned v ▷ **crown**
crowning v ▷ **crown**
crowns n, v ▷ **crown**
crows n ▷ **crow**[1] ▶ v ▷ **crow**[2]
crozier, crosier n (pl **-s**) bishop's hooked staff
croziers n ▷ **crozier**
crucial adj very important > **crucially** adv

crucially adv ▷ **crucial**
crucible n (pl -**s**) pot in which metals are melted
  crucibles n ▷ **crucible**
  crucified v ▷ **crucify**
  crucifies v ▷ **crucify**
crucifix n (pl -**es**) model of Christ on the Cross
  crucifixes n ▷ **crucify**
crucifixion n (pl -**s**) crucifying
  crucifixions n ▷ **crucifixion**
cruciform adj cross-shaped
crucify v (-**fies**, -**fying**, -**fied**) put to death by fastening to a cross
  crucifying v ▷ **crucify**
crude adj (-**r**, -**st**) rough and simple > **crudely** adv > **crudeness** n (pl -**es**) > **crudity** n (pl -**ties**)
  crudely adv ▷ **crude**
  crudeness n ▷ **crude**
  crudenesses n ▷ **crude**
  cruder adj ▷ **crude**
  crudest adj ▷ **crude**
  crudities n ▷ **crude**
  crudity n ▷ **crude**
cruel adj (-**ller**, -**llest**) delighting in others' pain > **cruelly** adv > **cruelty** n (pl -**ties**)
  crueller adj ▷ **cruel**
  cruellest adj ▷ **cruel**
  cruelly adv ▷ **cruel**
  cruelties n ▷ **cruel**
  cruelty n ▷ **cruel**
cruet n (pl -**s**) small container for salt, pepper, etc., at table
  cruets n ▷ **cruet**
cruise n (pl -**s**) sail for pleasure ▶ v (**cruises, cruising, cruised**) sail from place to place for pleasure
  cruised n ▷ **cruise**
cruiser n (pl -**s**) fast warship
  cruisers n ▷ **cruiser**
  cruises n, v ▷ **cruise**
  cruising v ▷ **cruise**
crumb n (pl -**s**) small fragment of bread or other dry food
crumble v (-**bles**, -**bling**, -**bled**) break into fragments ▶ n (pl -**s**) pudding of stewed fruit with a crumbly topping > **crumbly** adj (-**blier**, -**bliest**)
  crumbled v ▷ **crumble**
  crumbles v, n ▷ **crumble**
  crumblier adj ▷ **crumble**
  crumbliest adj ▷ **crumble**
  crumbling v ▷ **crumble**
  crumbly adj ▷ **crumble**
  crumbs n ▷ **crumb**
  crummier adj ▷ **crummy**

  crummiest adj ▷ **crummy**
crummy adj (-**mier**, -**miest**) (Slang) of poor quality
crumpet n (pl -**s**) round soft yeast cake, eaten buttered
  crumpets n ▷ **crumpet**
crumple v (-**ples**, -**pling**, -**pled**) crush, crease > **crumpled** adj
  crumpled v, adj ▷ **crumple**
  crumples v ▷ **crumple**
  crumpling v ▷ **crumple**
crunch v (-**es**, -**ing**, -**ed**) bite or chew with a noisy crushing sound ▶ n (pl -**es**) crunching sound (Informal) > **crunchy** adj (-**chier**, -**chiest**)
  crunched v ▷ **crunch**
  crunches v, n ▷ **crunch**
  crunchier adj ▷ **crunch**
  crunchiest adj ▷ **crunch**
  crunching v ▷ **crunch**
  crunchy adj ▷ **crunch**
crupper n (pl -**s**) strap that passes from the back of a saddle under a horse's tail
  cruppers n ▷ **crupper**
crusade n (pl -**s**) medieval Christian war to recover the Holy Land from the Muslims ▶ v (-**sades**, -**sading**, -**saded**) take part in a crusade
  crusaded v ▷ **crusade**
crusader n (pl -**s**) person who took part in the medieval Christian war to recover the Holy Land from the Muslims
  crusaders n ▷ **crusader**
  crusades n, v ▷ **crusade**
  crusading v ▷ **crusade**
crush v (-**es**, -**ing**, -**ed**) compress so as to injure, break, or crumple ▶ n (pl -**es**) dense crowd
  crushed v ▷ **crush**
  crushes v, n ▷ **crush**
  crushing v ▷ **crush**
crust n (pl -**s**) hard outer part of something, esp. bread ▶ v (-**s**, -**ing**, -**ed**) cover with or form a crust
crustacean n (pl -**s**) hard-shelled, usu. aquatic animal with several pairs of legs, such as the crab or lobster
  crustaceans n ▷ **crustacean**
  crusted v ▷ **crust**
  crustier adj ▷ **crusty**
  crustiest adj ▷ **crusty**
  crusting v ▷ **crust**
  crusts n, v ▷ **crust**
crusty adj (-**tier**, -**tiest**) having a crust
crutch n (pl -**es**) long sticklike support with a rest for the armpit, used by a lame person
  crutches n ▷ **crutch**

crux n (pl -es) crucial or decisive point
  cruxes n ▷ **crux**
cry v (**cries, crying, cried**) shed tears ▶ n (pl
  cries) fit of weeping
  crybabies n ▷ **crybaby**
crybaby n (pl **-babies**) person, esp. a child, who
  cries too readily
  crying v ▷ **cry**
  cryogenic adj ▷ **cryogenics**
cryogenics n branch of physics concerned
  with very low temperatures > **cryogenic** adj
crypt n (pl -s) vault under a church, esp. one
  used as a burial place
cryptic adj obscure in meaning, secret
  > **cryptically** adv
  cryptographer n ▷ **cryptography**
  cryptographers n ▷ **cryptography**
cryptography n art of writing in and
  deciphering codes > **cryptographer** n (pl -s)
  crypts n ▷ **crypt**
crystal n (pl -s) (single grain of) a
  symmetrically shaped solid formed naturally
  by some substances ▶ adj bright and clear
crystalline adj of or like crystal or crystals
  crystallization n ▷ **crystallize**
  crystallizations n ▷ **crystallize**
crystallize v (**-lizes, -lizing, -lized**) make or
  become definite > **crystallization** n (pl -s)
  crystallized v ▷ **crystallize**
  crystallizes v ▷ **crystallize**
  crystallizing v ▷ **crystallize**
  crystals n ▷ **crystal**
cub n (pl -s) young wild animal such as a bear
  or fox ▶ v (**cubs, cubbing, cubbed**) give birth
  to cubs
  cubbed v ▷ **cub**
  cubbing v ▷ **cub**
cubbyhole n (pl -s) small enclosed space or
  room
  cubbyholes n ▷ **cubbyhole**
cube n (pl -s) object with six equal square sides
  ▶ v (**cubes, cubing, cubed**) cut into cubes
  cubed v ▷ **cube**
  cubes n, v ▷ **cube**
cubic adj having three dimensions
cubicle n (pl -s) enclosed part of a large room,
  screened for privacy
  cubicles n ▷ **cubicle**
  cubing v ▷ **cube**
cubism n style of art in which objects are
  represented by geometrical shapes > **cubist**
  adj, n (pl -s)
  cubists n ▷ **cubist**
  cubs n, v ▷ **cub**
cuckold n (pl -s) man whose wife has been

unfaithful ▶ v (**-s, -ing, -ed**) be unfaithful to
(one's husband)
  cuckolded v ▷ **cuckold**
  cuckolding v ▷ **cuckold**
  cuckolds n, v ▷ **cuckold**
cuckoo n (pl -s) migratory bird with a
  characteristic two-note call, which lays its
  eggs in the nests of other birds ▶ adj (Informal)
  insane or foolish
  cuckoos n ▷ **cuckoo**
cucumber n (pl -s) long green-skinned fleshy
  fruit used in salads
  cucumbers n ▷ **cucumber**
cud n (pl -s) partially digested food which
  a ruminant brings back into its mouth to
  chew again
cuddle v (**cuddles, cuddling, cuddled**) ▶ n (pl -s)
  hug > **cuddly** adj (**-lier, -liest**)
  cuddled v ▷ **cuddle**
  cuddles v, n ▷ **cuddle**
  cuddlier adj ▷ **cuddle**
  cuddliest adj ▷ **cuddle**
  cuddling v ▷ **cuddle**
  cuddly adj ▷ **cuddle**
cudgel n (pl -s) short thick stick used as a
  weapon
  cudgels n ▷ **cudgel**
  cuds n ▷ **cud**
cue¹ n (pl -s) signal to an actor or musician to
  begin speaking or playing ▶ v (**cues, cueing,
  cued**) give a cue to
cue² n long tapering stick used in billiards,
  snooker, or pool ▶ v (**cues, cueing, cued**) hit (a
  ball) with a cue
  cued v ▷ **cue¹, ²**
  cueing v ▷ **cue¹, ²**
  cues n, v ▷ **cue¹, ²**
cuff¹ n (pl -s) end of a sleeve
cuff² (BRIT, AUST & NZ) v (**-s, -ing, -ed**) hit with an
  open hand ▶ n (pl -s) blow with an open hand
  cuffed v ▷ **cuff²**
  cuffing v ▷ **cuff²**
  cuffs n ▷ **cuff¹, ²** ▶ v ▷ **cuff²**
cuisine [quiz-zeen] n (pl -s) style of cooking
  cuisines n ▷ **cuisine**
culinary adj of kitchens or cookery
cull v (**-s, -ing, -ed**) choose, gather ▶ n (pl -s)
  culling
  culled v ▷ **cull**
  culling v ▷ **cull**
  culls v, n ▷ **cull**
culminate v (**-nates, -nating, -nated**) reach
  the highest point or climax > **culmination**
  n (pl -s)
  culminated v ▷ **culminate**

culminates *v* ▷ culminate
culminating *v* ▷ culminate
culmination *n* ▷ culminate
culminations *n* ▷ culminate
culottes *pl n* women's knee-length trousers cut to look like a skirt
culpabilities *n* ▷ culpable
culpability *n* ▷ culpable
culpable *adj* deserving blame > **culpability** *n* (*pl* -**ties**)> **culpably** *adv*
culpably *adv* ▷ culpable
culprit *n* (*pl* -**s**) person guilty of an offence or misdeed
culprits *n* ▷ culprit
cult *n* (*pl* -**s**) specific system of worship
cultivate *v* (-**vates**, -**vating**, -**vated**) prepare (land) to grow crops > **cultivation** *n*
cultivated *adj* well-educated ▶ *v* ▷ cultivate
cultivates *v* ▷ cultivate
cultivating *v* ▷ cultivate
cultivation *n* ▷ cultivate
cults *n* ▷ cult
cultural *adj* ▷ culture
culturally *adv* ▷ culture
culture *n* (*pl* -**s**) ideas, customs, and art of a particular society > **cultural** *adj* > **culturally** *adv*
cultured *adj* showing good taste or manners
cultures *n* ▷ culture
culvert *n* (*pl* -**s**) drain under a road or railway
culverts *n* ▷ culvert
cumbersome *adj* awkward because of size or shape
cumin, cummin *n* (*pl* -**s**) sweet-smelling seeds of a Mediterranean plant, used in cooking
cumins *n* ▷ cumin
cummerbund *n* (*pl* -**s**) wide sash worn round the waist
cummerbunds *n* ▷ cummerbund
cummin *n* ▷ cumin
cummins *n* ▷ cumin
cumulative *adj* increasing steadily > **cumulatively** *adv*
cumulatively *adv* ▷ cumulative
cumuli *n* ▷ cumulus
cumulus [kew-myew-luss] *n* (*pl* -**li**) thick white or dark grey cloud
cuneiform [kew-nif-form] *n*, *adj* (written in) an ancient system of writing using wedge-shaped characters
cunjevoi *n* (*pl* -**s**) (AUST) plant of tropical Asia and Australia with small flowers, cultivated for its edible rhizome
cunjevois *n* ▷ cunjevoi
cunning *adj* clever at deceiving ▶ *n* cleverness at deceiving > **cunningly** *adv*
cunningly *adv* ▷ cunning
cup *n* (*pl* -**s**) small bowl-shaped drinking container with a handle ▶ *v* (**cups, cupping, cupped**) form (one's hands) into the shape of a cup > **cupful** *n* (*pl* -**s**)
cupboard *n* (*pl* -**s**) piece of furniture or alcove with a door, for storage
cupboards *n* ▷ cupboard
cupful *n* ▷ cup
cupfuls *n* ▷ cup
cupidity [kew-**pid**-it-ee] *n* greed for money or possessions
cupola [kew-pol-la] *n* (*pl* -**s**) domed roof or ceiling
cupolas *n* ▷ cupola
cupped *v* ▷ cup
cupping *v* ▷ cup
cups *n*, *v* ▷ cup
cur *n* (*pl* -**s**) (*Lit*) mongrel dog
curable *adj* ▷ cure
curaçao [kew-rah-so] *n* orange-flavoured liqueur
curacies *n* ▷ curacy
curacy [kew-rah-see] *n* (*pl* -**cies**) work or position of a curate
curare [kew-**rah**-ree] *n* (*pl* -**s**) poisonous resin of a S American tree, used as a muscle relaxant in medicine
curares *n* ▷ curare
curate *n* (*pl* -**s**) clergyman who assists a parish priest
curates *n* ▷ curate
curative *adj*, *n* (*pl* -**s**) (something) able to cure
curatives *n* ▷ curative
curator *n* (*pl* -**s**) person in charge of a museum or art gallery > **curatorship** *n* (*pl* -**s**)
curators *n* ▷ curator
curatorship *n* ▷ curator
curatorships *n* ▷ curator
curb *n* (*pl* -**s**) something that restrains ▶ *v* (-**s**, -**ing**, -**ed**) control, restrain
curbed *v* ▷ curb
curbing *v* ▷ curb
curbs *n*, *v* ▷ curb
curd *n* (*pl* -**s**) coagulated milk, used to make cheese
curdle *v* (-**dles**, -**dling**, -**dled**) turn into curd, coagulate
curdled *v* ▷ curdle
curdles *v* ▷ curdle
curdling *v* ▷ curdle
curds *n* ▷ curd
cure *v* (**cures, curing, cured**) get rid of (an illness or problem) ▶ *n* (*pl* -**s**) (treatment

causing) curing of an illness or person
> **curable** *adj*
cured *v* ▷ **cure**
cures *v, n* ▷ **cure**
curettage *n* ▷ **curette**
curettages *n* ▷ **curette**
curette *n* (*pl* -s) surgical instrument for
scraping tissue from body cavities ▶ *v*
(**curettes, curetting, curetted**) scrape with a
curette > **curettage** *n* (*pl* -s)
curetted *v* ▷ **curette**
curettes *n, v* ▷ **curette**
curetting *v* ▷ **curette**
curfew *n* (*pl* -s) law ordering people to stay
inside their homes after a specific time at
night
curfews *n* ▷ **curfew**
curie *n* (*pl* -s) standard unit of radioactivity
curies *n* ▷ **curie**
curing *v* ▷ **cure**
curio *n* (*pl* -s) rare or unusual object valued as a
collector's item
curios *n* ▷ **curio**
curiosities *n* ▷ **curiosity**
curiosity *n* eagerness to know or find out
(*pl* -ties)
curiously *adv* ▷ **curious**
curious *adj* eager to learn or know > **curiously**
adv
curl *n* (*pl* -s) curved piece of hair ▶ *v* (-s, -ing,
-ed) make (hair) into curls or (of hair) grow in
curls > **curler** *n* (*pl* -s) > **curly** *adj* (-lier, -liest)
curled *v* ▷ **curl**
curler *n* ▷ **curl**
curlers *n* ▷ **curl**
curlew *n* (*pl* -s) long-billed wading bird
curlews *n* ▷ **curlew**
curlier *adj* ▷ **curl**
curliest *adj* ▷ **curl**
curling *n* game like bowls, played with heavy
stones on ice ▶ *v* ▷ **curl**
curls *n, v* ▷ **curl**
curly *adj* ▷ **curl**
curmudgeon *n* (*pl* -s) bad-tempered person
> **curmudgeonly** *adj*
curmudgeonly *adj* ▷ **curmudgeon**
curmudgeons *n* ▷ **curmudgeon**
currajong *n* (*pl* -s) ▷ **kurrajong**
currajongs *n* ▷ **currajong**
currant *n* (*pl* -s) small dried grape
currants *n* ▷ **currant**
currawong *n* (*pl* -s) Australian songbird
currawongs *n* ▷ **currawong**
currencies *n* ▷ **currency**
currency *n* (*pl* -cies) money in use in a

particular country
current *adj* of the immediate present ▶ *n*
(*pl* -s) flow of water or air in one direction
> **currently** *adv*
currently *adv* ▷ **current**
currents *n* ▷ **current**
curricula *n* ▷ **curriculum**
curriculum *n* (*pl* -la, -lums) all the courses of
study offered by a school or college
curriculums *n* ▷ **curriculum**
curried *v* ▷ **curry**[1,2]
curries *n* ▷ **curry**[1] ▶ *v* ▷ **curry**[1,2]
curry[1] *n* (*pl* -ries) Indian dish of meat or
vegetables in a hot spicy sauce ▶ *v* (-ries,
-rying, -ried) prepare (food) with curry
powder
curry[2] *v* (-ries, -rying, -ried) groom (a horse)
currying *v* ▷ **curry**[1,2]
curs *n* ▷ **cur**
curse *v* (**curses, cursing, cursed**) swear (at) ▶ *n*
(*pl* -s) swearword > **cursed** *adj*
cursed *adj, v* ▷ **curse**
curses *v, n* ▷ **curse**
cursing *v* ▷ **curse**
cursive *adj, n* (*pl* -s) (handwriting) done with
joined letters > **cursively** *adv*
cursively *adv* ▷ **cursive**
cursives *n* ▷ **cursive**
cursor *n* (*pl* -s) movable point of light that
shows a specific position on a visual display
unit
cursorily *adv* ▷ **cursory**
cursoriness *n* ▷ **cursory**
cursors *n* ▷ **cursor**
cursory *adj* quick and superficial > **cursorily**
adv > **cursoriness** *n*
curt *adj* (-er, -est) brief and rather rude > **curtly**
adv > **curtness** *n* (*pl* -es)
curtail *v* (-s, -ing, -ed) cut short > **curtailment**
n (*pl* -s)
curtailed *v* ▷ **curtail**
curtailing *v* ▷ **curtail**
curtailment *n* ▷ **curtail**
curtailments *n* ▷ **curtail**
curtails *v* ▷ **curtail**
curtain *n* (*pl* -s) piece of cloth hung at a
window or opening as a screen ▶ *v* (-s, -ing,
-ed) provide with curtains
curtained *v* ▷ **curtain**
curtaining *v* ▷ **curtain**
curtains *n, v* ▷ **curtain**
curter *adj* ▷ **curt**
curtest *adj* ▷ **curt**
curtly *adv* ▷ **curt**
curtness *n* ▷ **curt**

curtnesses *n* ▷ **curt**
curtsey *n* ▷ **curtsy**
curtseyed *v* ▷ **curtsy**
curtseying *v* ▷ **curtsy**
curtseys *n, v* ▷ **curtsy**
curtsied *v* ▷ **curtsy**
curtsies *n, v* ▷ **curtsy**
curtsy, curtsey *n (pl* -**sies, -seys)** woman's gesture of respect made by bending the knees and bowing the head ▶ *v* (-**sies, -seys, -sying, -sied** *or* -**seying**) (-**seyed**) make a curtsy
curtsying *v* ▷ **curtsy**
curvaceous *adj* (*Informal*) (of a woman) having a shapely body
curvature *n (pl* -**s**) curved shape
curvatures *n* ▷ **curvature**
curve *n (pl* -**s**) continuously bending line with no straight parts ▶ *v* (**curves, curving, curved**) form or move in a curve > **curvy** *adj* (-**vier, -viest**)
curved *v* ▷ **curve**
curves *n, v* ▷ **curve**
curvier *adj* ▷ **curve**
curviest *adj* ▷ **curve**
curvilinear *adj* consisting of or bounded by a curve
curving *v* ▷ **curve**
curvy *adj* ▷ **curve**
cuscus *n (pl* -**ses**) large Australian nocturnal possum
cuscuses *n* ▷ **cuscus**
cushier *adj* ▷ **cushy**
cushiest *adj* ▷ **cushy**
cushion *n (pl* -**s**) bag filled with soft material, to make a seat more comfortable ▶ *v* (-**s, -ing, -ed**) lessen the effects of
cushioned *v* ▷ **cushion**
cushioning *v* ▷ **cushion**
cushions *n, v* ▷ **cushion**
cushy *adj* (**cushier, cushiest**) (*Informal*) easy
cusp *n (pl* -**s**) pointed end, esp. on a tooth
cusps *n* ▷ **cusp**
cuss (*Informal*) *n (pl* -**es**) curse, oath ▶ *v* (-**es, -ing, -ed**) swear (at)
cussed [**kuss**-id] *adj* (*Informal*) obstinate ▶ *v* ▷ **cuss** > **cussedly** *adv* > **cussedness** *n*
cussedly *adv* ▷ **cussed**
cussedness *n* ▷ **cussed**
cusses *n, v* ▷ **cuss**
cussing *v* ▷ **cuss**
custard *n (pl* -**s**) sweet yellow sauce made from milk and eggs
custards *n* ▷ **custard**
custodial *adj* ▷ **custody**

custodian *n (pl* -**s**) person in charge of a public building
custodians *n* ▷ **custodian**
custodies *n* ▷ **custody**
custody *n (pl* -**dies**) protective care > **custodial** *adj*
custom *n (pl* -**s**) long-established activity or action ▶ *pl* duty charged on imports or exports
customarily *adv* ▷ **customary**
customary *adj* usual > **customarily** *adv*
customer *n (pl* **s**) person who buys goods or services
customers *n* ▷ **customer**
customs *n* ▷ **custom**
cut *v* (**cuts, cutting, cut**) open up, penetrate, wound, or divide with a sharp instrument ▶ *n* (*pl* -**s**) stroke or incision made by cutting
cutaneous [kew-**tane**-ee-uss] *adj* of the skin
cute *adj* (**cuter, cutest**) appealing or attractive > **cutely** *adv* > **cuteness** *n*
cutely *adv* ▷ **cute**
cuteness *n* ▷ **cute**
cuter *adj* ▷ **cute**
cutest *adj* ▷ **cute**
cuticle *n (pl* -**s**) skin at the base of a fingernail or toenail
cuticles *n* ▷ **cuticle**
cutlass *n (pl* -**es**) curved one-edged sword formerly used by sailors
cutlasses *n* ▷ **cutlass**
cutler *n (pl* -**s**) maker of cutlery
cutlers *n* ▷ **cutler**
cutlery *n* knives, forks, and spoons
cutlet *n (pl* -**s**) small piece of meat like a chop
cutlets *n* ▷ **cutlet**
cuts *v, n* ▷ **cut**
cutter *n (pl* -**s**) person or tool that cuts
cutters *n* ▷ **cutter**
cutting *n (pl* -**s**) article cut from a newspaper or magazine ▶ *adj* (of a remark) hurtful ▶ *v* ▷ **cut** > **cuttingly** *adv*
cuttingly *adv* ▷ **cutting**
cuttings *n* ▷ **cutting**
cuttlefish *n (pl* **cuttlefish**) squidlike sea mollusc

cuz *n* (**cuzzes**). Like **coz**, cuz is an old word for **cousin**. You need a blank tile for the second Z if you're going to play the plural. Cuz scores 14 points.
cwm *n* (**cwms**). Cwm is a Welsh word for a valley. It's a useful one to remember because it doesn't contain any vowels. Cwm scores 10 points.

cyanide *n (pl* -**s**) extremely poisonous chemical

compound

cyanides *n* ▷ cyanide

cybernetics *n* branch of science in which electronic and mechanical systems are studied and compared to biological systems

cyberspace *n* place said to contain all the data stored in computers

cyclamen [sik-la-men] *n* (*pl* -s) plant with red, pink, or white flowers

cyclamens *n* ▷ cyclamen

cycle *v* (**cycles, cycling, cycled**) ride a bicycle
▶ *n* (*pl* -s) (BRIT, AUST & NZ) bicycle

cycled *v* ▷ cycle

cycles *v*, *n* ▷ cycle

cyclic *adj* ▷ cyclical

cyclical, cyclic *adj* occurring in cycles
> **cyclically** *adv*

cyclically *adv* ▷ cyclical

cycling *v* ▷ cycle

cyclist *n* (*pl* -s) person who rides a bicycle

cyclists *n* ▷ cyclist

cyclone *n* (*pl* -s) violent wind moving round a central area

cyclones *n* ▷ cyclone

cyclotron *n* (*pl* -s) apparatus that accelerates charged particles by means of a strong vertical magnetic field

cyclotrons *n* ▷ cyclotron

cygnet *n* (*pl* -s) young swan

cygnets *n* ▷ cygnet

cylinder *n* (*pl* -s) solid or hollow body with straight sides and circular ends > **cylindrical** *adj*

cylinders *n* ▷ cylinder

cylindrical *adj* ▷ cylinder

cymbal *n* (*pl* -s) percussion instrument consisting of a brass plate which is struck against another or hit with a stick

cymbals *n* ▷ cymbal

cynic [sin-ik] *n* (*pl* -s) person who believes that people always act selfishly > **cynical** *adj* > **cynically** *adv* > **cynicism** *n*

cynical *adj* ▷ cynic

cynically *adv* ▷ cynic

cynicism *n* ▷ cynic

cynics *n* ▷ cynic

cynosure [sin-oh-zyure] *n* (*pl* -s) centre of attention

cynosures *n* ▷ cynosure

cypher *n* (*pl* -s) ▷ cipher

cyphers *n* ▷ cypher

cypress *n* (*pl* -es) evergreen tree with dark green leaves

cypresses *n* ▷ cypress

cyst [sist] *n* (*pl* -s) (abnormal) sac in the body containing fluid or soft matter > **cystic** *adj*

cystic *adj* ▷ cyst

cystitis [siss-tite-iss] *n* inflammation of the bladder

cysts *n* ▷ cyst

cytological *adj* ▷ cytology

cytologically *adv* ▷ cytology

cytologies *n* ▷ cytology

cytologist *n* ▷ cytology

cytologists *n* ▷ cytology

cytology [site-ol-a-jee] *n* (*pl* -**logies**) study of plant and animal cells > **cytological** *adj* > **cytologically** *adv* > **cytologist** *n* (*pl* -s)

czar [zahr] *n* (*pl* -s) ▷ tsar > **czarism** *n* > **czarist** *adj*, *n* (*pl* -s)

czarism *n* ▷ czar

czarist *n* ▷ czar

czarists *n* ▷ czar

czars *n* ▷ czar

Dd

D only starts a handful of two-letter words, but it does form a two-letter word before every vowel except U. There are plenty of good three-letter words beginning with D, particularly those with a Y or W: **day, dye** and **dew** are worth 7 points each, for example.

da *n* (**das**). A da is a Burmese knife. Da scores 3 points.

dab¹ *v* (**-s, -bbing, -bbed**) pat lightly ▸ *n* (*pl* **-s**) small amount of something soft or moist

dab² *n* (*pl* **-s**) small European flatfish with rough scales

dabbed *v* ▷ **dab¹**

dabbing *v* ▷ **dab¹**

dabble *v* (**-les, -ling, -led**) be involved in something superficially > **dabbler** *n* (*pl* **-s**)

dabbled *v* ▷ **dabble**

dabbler *n* ▷ **dabble**

dabblers *n* ▷ **dabble**

dabbles *v* ▷ **dabble**

dabbling *v* ▷ **dabble**

dabs *n* ▷ **dab¹, ²** ▸ *v* ▷ **dab¹**

dace *n* (*pl* **dace**) small European freshwater fish

dachshund *n* (*pl* **-s**) dog with a long body and short legs

dachshunds *n* ▷ **dachshund**

dad *n* (*pl* **-s**) (*Informal*) father

daddies *n* ▷ **daddy**

daddy *n* (*pl* **-dies**) (*Informal*) father

dado [day-doe] *n* (*pl* **-does, -dos**) lower part of an interior wall, below a rail, decorated differently from the upper part

dadoes *n* ▷ **dado**

dados *n* ▷ **dado**

dads *n* ▷ **dad**

daffodil *n* (*pl* **-s**) yellow trumpet-shaped flower that blooms in spring

daffodils *n* ▷ **daffodil**

daft *adj* (**-er, -est**) (*Informal*) foolish or crazy > **daftness** *n* (*pl* **-es**)

dafter *adj* ▷ **daft**

daftest *adj* ▷ **daft**

daftness *n* ▷ **daft**

daftnesses *n* ▷ **daft**

dag (NZ) *n* (*pl* **-s**) dried dung on a sheep's rear (*Informal*) ▸ *v* (**-s, -gging, -gged**) remove the dags from a sheep

dagga *n* (*pl* **-s**) (S AFR) (*Informal*) cannabis

daggas *n* ▷ **dagga**

dagged *v* ▷ **dag**

dagger *n* (*pl* **-s**) short knifelike weapon with a pointed blade

daggers *n* ▷ **dagger**

daggier *adj* ▷ **daggy**

daggiest *adj* ▷ **daggy**

dagging *v* ▷ **dag**

daggy *adj* (**-ggier, -ggiest**) (NZ) (*Informal*) amusing

dags *n, v* ▷ **dag**

daguerreotype [dag-**gair**-oh-type] *n* (*pl* **-s**) type of early photograph produced on chemically treated silver

daguerreotypes *n* ▷ **daguerreotype**

dahlia [day-lya] *n* (*pl* **-s**) brightly coloured garden flower

dahlias *n* ▷ **dahlia**

dailies *n* ▷ **daily**

daily *adj* occurring every day or every weekday ▸ *adv* every day ▸ *n* (*pl* **-lies**) daily newspaper

daintier *adj* ▷ **dainty**

daintiest *adj* ▷ **dainty**

daintily *adv* ▷ **dainty**

dainty *adj* (**-tier, -tiest**) delicate or elegant > **daintily** *adv*

daiquiri [dak-eer-ee] *n* (*pl* **-s**) iced drink containing rum, lime juice, and sugar

daiquiris *n* ▷ **daiquiri**

dairies *n* ▷ **dairy**

dairy *n* (*pl* **-ies**) place for the processing or sale of milk and its products ▸ *adj* of milk or its products

dais [day-iss, dayss] *n* (*pl* **-es**) raised platform in a hall, used by a speaker

daises *n* ▷ **dais**

daisies *n* ▷ **daisy**

daisy *n* (*pl* **-sies**) small wild flower with a

yellow centre and white petals

dak n (**daks**). A dak is an old Indian mail or transport system. This is a good word to know if you have a K on your rack but can't think of a longer word in which to use it. Dak scores 8 points.

dale n (pl **-s**) (esp. in N England) valley
　dales n ▷ **dale**
dalliance n (pl **-s**) flirtation
　dalliances n ▷ **dalliance**
　dallied v ▷ **dally**
　dallies v ▷ **dally**
dally v (**-lies, -lying, -lied**) waste time
　dallying v ▷ **dally**
dalmatian n (pl **-s**) large dog with a white coat and black spots
　dalmatians n ▷ **dalmatian**
dam¹ n (pl **-s**) barrier built across a river to create a lake ▶ v (**dams, damming, dammed**) build a dam across (a river)
dam² n (pl **-s**) mother of an animal such as a sheep or horse
damage v (**-ages, -aging, -aged**) harm, spoil ▶ n (pl **-s**) harm to a person or thing ▶ pl money awarded as compensation for injury or loss
　damaged v ▷ **damage**
　damages v, n ▷ **damage**
　damaging v ▷ **damage**
damask n (pl **-s**) fabric with a pattern woven into it, used for tablecloths etc.
　damasks n ▷ **damask**
dame n (pl **-s**) (CHIEFLY US & CANADIAN) (Slang) woman
　dames n ▷ **dame**
　dammed v ▷ **dam¹**
　damming v ▷ **dam¹**
damn interj (Slang) exclamation of annoyance ▶ adv, adj (also **damned**) (Slang) extreme(ly) ▶ v (**-s, -ing, -ed**) condemn as bad or worthless > **damnation** interj, n (pl **-s**)
damnable adj annoying > **damnably** adv
　damnably adv ▷ **damnable**
　damnation interj, n ▷ **damn**
　damnations n ▷ **damn**
　damned v ▷ **damn**
damning adj proving or suggesting guilt ▶ v ▷ **damn**
　damns v ▷ **damn**
damp adj (**-er, -est**) slightly wet ▶ n (pl **-s**) slight wetness, moisture ▶ v (**-s, -ing, -ed**) (also **dampen**) (**-s, -ing, -ed**) make damp (foll. by **down**) > **damply** adv > **dampness** n
　damped v ▷ **damp**
　dampen v ▷ **dampen**
　dampened v ▷ **dampen**

dampening v ▷ **dampen**
dampens v ▷ **dampen**
damper n (pl **-s**) movable plate to regulate the draught in a fire ▶ adj ▷ **damp**
　dampers n ▷ **damper**
　dampest adj ▷ **damp**
　damping v ▷ **damp**
　damply adv ▷ **damp**
　dampness n ▷ **damp**
　damps v, n ▷ **damp**
　dams n ▷ **dam¹, ²** ▶ v ▷ **dam¹**
damsel n (pl **-s**) (Old-fashioned) young woman
　damsels n ▷ **damsel**
damson n (pl **-s**) small blue-black plumlike fruit
　damsons n ▷ **damson**
dance v (**dances, dancing, danced**) move the feet and body rhythmically in time to music ▶ n (pl **-s**) series of steps and movements in time to music > **dancer** n (pl **-s**)
　danced v ▷ **dance**
　dancer n ▷ **dance**
　dancers n ▷ **dance**
　dances v, n ▷ **dance**
　dancing v ▷ **dance**
dandelion n (pl **-s**) yellow-flowered wild plant
　dandelions n ▷ **dandelion**
dander n (pl **-s**) (Slang) anger
　danders n ▷ **dander**
　dandier adj ▷ **dandy**
　dandies n ▷ **dandy**
　dandiest adj ▷ **dandy**
　dandified adj ▷ **dandy**
dandle v (**-dles, -dling, -dled**) move (a child) up and down on one's knee
　dandled v ▷ **dandle**
　dandles v ▷ **dandle**
　dandling v ▷ **dandle**
dandruff n (pl **-s**) loose scales of dry dead skin shed from the scalp
　dandruffs n ▷ **dandruff**
dandy n (pl **-dies**) man who is overconcerned with the elegance of his appearance ▶ adj (**-dier, -diest**) (Informal) very good > **dandified** adj
danger n (pl **-s**) possibility of being injured or killed > **dangerous** adj > **dangerously** adv
　dangerous adj ▷ **danger**
　dangerously adv ▷ **danger**
　dangers n ▷ **danger**
dangle v (**-gles, -gling, -gled**) hang loosely
　dangled v ▷ **dangle**
　dangles v ▷ **dangle**
　dangling v ▷ **dangle**
dank adj (**-er, -est**) unpleasantly damp and

chilly > **dankly** adv > **dankness** n (pl -es)
danker adj ▷ **dank**
dankest adj ▷ **dank**
dankly adv ▷ **dank**
dankness n ▷ **dank**
danknesses n ▷ **dank**
dapper adj (-er, -est) (of a man) neat in appearance > **dapperly** adv > **dapperness** n (pl -es)
dapperer adj ▷ **dapper**
dapperest adj ▷ **dapper**
dapperly adv ▷ **dapper**
dapperness n ▷ **dapper**
dappernesses n ▷ **dapper**
dappled adj marked with spots of a different colour
dare v (dares, daring, dared) be courageous enough to try (to do something) ▶ n (pl -s) challenge to do something risky
dared v ▷ **dare**
daredevil adj, n (pl -s) recklessly bold (person)
daredevils n ▷ **daredevil**
dares v, n ▷ **dare**
daring adj willing to take risks ▶ n courage to do dangerous things ▶ v ▷ **dare** > **daringly** adv
daringly adv ▷ **daring**
dark adj (-er, -est) having little or no light ▶ n (pl -s) absence of light > **darkly** adv > **darkness** n (pl -es) > **darken** v (-s, -ing, -ed)
darken v ▷ **dark**
darkened v ▷ **dark**
darkening v ▷ **dark**
darkens v ▷ **dark**
darker adj ▷ **dark**
darkest adj ▷ **dark**
darkly adv ▷ **dark**
darkness n ▷ **dark**
darknesses n ▷ **dark**
darkroom n (pl -s) darkened room for processing photographic film
darkrooms n ▷ **darkroom**
darks n ▷ **dark**
darling n (pl -s) much-loved person ▶ adj much-loved
darlings n ▷ **darling**
darn[1] v (-s, -ing, -ed) mend (a garment) with a series of interwoven stitches ▶ n (pl -s) patch of darned work
darn[2] interj, adv, adj, v (-s, -ing, -ed) (Euphemistic) damn
darned v ▷ **darn**[1, 2]
darning v ▷ **darn**[1, 2]
darns v ▷ **darn**[1, 2] ▶ n ▷ **darn**[1]
dart n (pl -s) small narrow pointed missile that is thrown or shot, esp. in the game of

darts ▶ pl game in which darts are thrown at a circular numbered board ▶ v (-s, -ing, -ed) move or direct quickly and suddenly
darted v ▷ **dart**
darting v ▷ **dart**
darts n, v ▷ **dart**
dash v (-es, -ing, -ed) move quickly ▶ n (pl -es) sudden quick movement
dashboard n (pl -s) instrument panel in a vehicle
dashboards n ▷ **dashboard**
dashed v ▷ **dash**
dashes v, n ▷ **dash**
dashing adj stylish and attractive ▶ v ▷ **dash** > **dashingly** adv
dashingly adv ▷ **dashing**
dassie n (pl -s) (S AFR) type of hoofed rodent-like animal (also **hyrax**)
dassies n ▷ **dassie**
dastardliness n ▷ **dastardly**
dastardly adj wicked and cowardly > **dastardliness** n
dasyure [dass-ee-your] n (pl -s) small marsupial of Australia, New Guinea, and adjacent islands
dasyures n ▷ **dasyure**
data n information consisting of observations, measurements, or facts
date[1] n (pl -s) specified day of the month ▶ v (dates, dating, dated) mark with the date
date[2] n (pl -s) dark-brown sweet-tasting fruit of the date palm
dated adj old-fashioned ▶ v ▷ **date**[1]
dates n ▷ **date**[1, 2] ▶ v ▷ **date**[1]
dating v ▷ **date**[1]
dative n (pl -s) (in certain languages) the form of the noun that expresses the indirect object
datives n ▷ **dative**
datum n (pl **data**) single piece of information in the form of a fact or statistic
daub v (-s, -ing, -ed) smear or spread quickly or clumsily
daubed v ▷ **daub**
daubing v ▷ **daub**
daubs v ▷ **daub**
daughter n (pl -s) female child > **daughterly** adj
daughterly adj ▷ **daughter**
daughters n ▷ **daughter**
daunting adj intimidating or worrying > **dauntingly** adv
dauntingly adv ▷ **daunting**
dauntless adj fearless > **dauntlessly** adv > **dauntlessness** n
dauntlessly adv ▷ **dauntless**
dauntlessness n ▷ **dauntless**

dauphin [doe-fan] *n* (*pl* -s) (formerly) eldest son of the king of France
dauphins *n* ▷ **dauphin**
davenport *n* (*pl* -s) (CHIEFLY BRIT) small writing table with drawers
davenports *n* ▷ **davenport**
davit [dav-vit] *n* (*pl* -s) crane, usu. one of a pair, at a ship's side, for lowering and hoisting a lifeboat
davits *n* ▷ **davit**
daw *n* (**daws**). A daw is another name for a **jackdaw**. Daw scores 7 points.
dawdle *v* (-dles, -dling, -dled) walk slowly, lag behind
dawdled *v* ▷ **dawdle**
dawdles *v* ▷ **dawdle**
dawdling *v* ▷ **dawdle**
dawn *n* (*pl* -s) daybreak ▶ *v* (-s, -ing, -ed) begin to grow light
dawned *v* ▷ **dawn**
dawning *v* ▷ **dawn**
dawns *n*, *v* ▷ **dawn**
day *n* (*pl* -s) period of 24 hours
daybreak *n* time in the morning when light first appears
daydream *n* (*pl* -s) pleasant fantasy indulged in while awake ▶ *v* (-s, -ing, -ed) indulge in idle fantasy > **daydreamer** *n* (*pl* -s)
daydreamed *v* ▷ **daydream**
daydreamer *n* ▷ **daydream**
daydreamers *n* ▷ **daydream**
daydreaming *v* ▷ **daydream**
daydreams *n*, *v* ▷ **daydream**
daylight *n* light from the sun
days *n* ▷ **day**
daze *v* (**dazes, dazing, dazed**) stun, by a blow or shock ▶ *n* (*pl* -s) state of confusion or shock
dazed *v* ▷ **daze**
dazes *v*, *n* ▷ **daze**
dazing *v* ▷ **daze**
dazzle *v* (-zles, -zling, -zled) impress greatly ▶ *n* (*pl* -s) bright light that dazzles > **dazzling** *adj* > **dazzlingly** *adv*
dazzled *v* ▷ **dazzle**
dazzles *v*, *n* ▷ **dazzle**
dazzling *v*, *adj* ▷ **dazzle**
dazzlingly *adv* ▷ **dazzle**
de *prep*. De means of or from. This is a useful little word to fit in when trying to form several words at once. De scores 3 points.
deacon *n* (*pl* -s) (CHRISTIANITY) ordained minister ranking immediately below a priest
deacons *n* ▷ **deacon**
dead *adj* (-er, -est) no longer alive ▶ *n* (*pl* -s)

period during which coldness or darkness is most intense ▶ *adv* extremely
deadbeat *n* (*pl* -s) (*Informal*) lazy useless person
deadbeats *n* ▷ **deadbeat**
deaden *v* (-s, -ing, -ed) make less intense
deadened *v* ▷ **deaden**
deadening *v* ▷ **deaden**
deadens *v* ▷ **deaden**
deader *adj* ▷ **dead**
deadest *adj* ▷ **dead**
deadlier *adj* ▷ **deadly**
deadliest *adj* ▷ **deadly**
deadline *n* (*pl* -s) time limit
deadlines *n* ▷ **deadline**
deadliness *n* ▷ **deadly**
deadlock *n* (*pl* -s) point in a dispute at which no agreement can be reached > **deadlocked** *adj*
deadlocked *adj* ▷ **deadlock**
deadlocks *n* ▷ **deadlock**
deadly *adj* (-lier, -liest) likely to cause death ▶ *adv* extremely > **deadliness** *n*
deadpan *adj*, *adv* showing no emotion or expression
deads *n* ▷ **dead**
deaf *adj* (-er, -est) unable to hear > **deafness** *n* (*pl* -es)
deafen *v* (-s, -ing, -ed) make deaf, esp. temporarily
deafened *v* ▷ **deafen**
deafening *v* ▷ **deafen**
deafens *v* ▷ **deafen**
deafer *adj* ▷ **deaf**
deafest *adj* ▷ **deaf**
deafness *n* ▷ **deaf**
deafnesses *n* ▷ **deaf**
deal¹ *n* (*pl* -s) agreement or transaction ▶ *v* (**deals, dealing, dealt**) inflict (a blow) on > **dealer** *n* (*pl* -s)
deal² *n* (*pl* -s) plank of fir or pine wood
dealer *n* ▷ **deal¹**
dealers *n* ▷ **deal¹**
dealing *v* ▷ **deal¹**
dealings *pl n* transactions or business relations
deals *v* ▷ **deal¹** ▶ *n* ▷ **deal¹, ²**
dealt *v* ▷ **deal¹**
dean *n* (*pl* -s) chief administrative official of a college or university faculty
deaneries *n* ▷ **deanery**
deanery *n* (*pl* -eries) office or residence of a dean
deans *n* ▷ **dean**
dear *n* (*pl* -s) someone regarded with affection ▶ *adj* (-er, -est) much-loved > **dearly** *adv*

>**dearness** n (pl -es)
dearer adj ▷ dear
dearest adj ▷ dear
dearly adv ▷ dear
dearness n ▷ dear
dearnesses n ▷ dear
dears n ▷ dear
dearth [dirth] n (pl -s) inadequate amount,
scarcity
dearths n ▷ dearth
death n (pl -s) permanent end of life in a person
or animal
deathly adj, adv like death
deaths n ▷ death
deb n (pl -s) (Informal) debutante
debacle [day-bah-kl] n (pl -s) disastrous failure
debacles n ▷ debacle
debar v (-bars, -barring, -barred) prevent, bar
debarred v ▷ debar
debarring v ▷ debar
debars v ▷ debar
debase v (-bases, -basing, -based) lower in
value, quality, or character >**debasement**
n (pl -s)
debased v ▷ debase
debasement n ▷ debase
debasements n ▷ debase
debases v ▷ debase
debasing v ▷ debase
debatable adj not absolutely certain
>**debatably** adv
debate n (pl -s) discussion ▸ v (-bates, -bating,
-bated) discuss formally
debated v ▷ debate
debates n, v ▷ debate
debating v ▷ debate
debauch [dib-bawch] v (-es, -ing, -ed) make
(someone) bad or corrupt, esp. sexually
>**debauchery** n (pl -eries)
debauched adj immoral, sexually corrupt ▸ v
▷ debauch
debaucheries n ▷ debauch
debauchery n ▷ debauch
debauches v ▷ debauch
debauching v ▷ debauch
debenture n (pl -s) long-term bond bearing
fixed interest, issued by a company or a
government agency
debentures n ▷ debenture
debilitate v (-tates, -tating, -tated) weaken,
make feeble >**debilitation** n
debilitated v ▷ debilitate
debilitates v ▷ debilitate
debilitating v ▷ debilitate
debilitation n ▷ debilitate

debilities n ▷ debility
debility n (pl -ities) weakness, infirmity
debit n (pl -s) acknowledgment of a sum owing
by entry on the left side of an account ▸ v (-s,
-ing, -ed) charge (an account) with a debt
debited v ▷ debit
debiting v ▷ debit
debits n, v ▷ debit
debonair adj (of a man) charming and refined
debouch v (-es, -ing, -ed) move out from a
narrow place to a wider one
debouched v ▷ debouch
debouches v ▷ debouch
debouching v ▷ debouch
debrief v (-s, -ing, -ed) receive a report from
(a soldier, diplomat, etc.) after an event
>**debriefing** n (pl -s)
debriefed v ▷ debrief
debriefing v, n ▷ debrief
debriefings n ▷ debrief
debriefs v ▷ debrief
debris [deb-ree] n fragments of something
destroyed
debs n ▷ deb
debt n (pl -s) something owed, esp. money
>**debtor** n (pl -s)
debtor n ▷ debt
debtors n ▷ debt
debts n ▷ debt
debunk v (-s, -ing, -ed) (Informal) expose the
falseness of
debunked v ▷ debunk
debunking v ▷ debunk
debunks v ▷ debunk
debut [day-byoo] n (pl -s) first public
appearance of a performer
debutante [day-byoo-tont] n (pl -s) young
upper-class woman being formally presented
to society
debutantes n ▷ debutante
debuts n ▷ debut
decade n (pl -s) period of ten years
decadence n (pl -s) deterioration in morality
or culture >**decadent** adj >**decadently** adv
decadences n ▷ decadence
decadent adj ▷ decadence
decadently adv ▷ decadence
decades n ▷ decade
decaffeinated [dee-kaf-fin-ate-id] adj (of
coffee, tea, or cola) with caffeine removed
decagon n (pl -s) geometric figure with ten
faces >**decagonal** adj
decagonal adj ▷ decagon
decagons n ▷ decagon
decahedral adj ▷ decahedron

decahedron [deck-a-**heed**-ron] n (pl -s) solid
figure with ten sides > **decahedral** adj
  decahedrons n ▷ **decahedron**
decamp v (-s, -ing, -ed) depart secretly or
suddenly
  decamped v ▷ **decamp**
  decamping v ▷ **decamp**
  decamps v ▷ **decamp**
decant v (-s, -ing, -ed) pour (a liquid) from one
container to another
  decanted v ▷ **decant**
decanter n (pl -s) stoppered bottle for wine
or spirits
  decanters n ▷ **decanter**
  decanting v ▷ **decant**
  decants v ▷ **decant**
decapitate v (-tates, -tating, -tated) behead
  > **decapitation** n (pl -s)
  decapitated v ▷ **decapitate**
  decapitates v ▷ **decapitate**
  decapitating v ▷ **decapitate**
  decapitation n ▷ **decapitate**
  decapitations n ▷ **decapitate**
  decathlete n ▷ **decathlon**
  decathletes n ▷ **decathlon**
decathlon n (pl -s) athletic contest with ten
events > **decathlete** n (pl -s)
  decathlons n ▷ **decathlon**
decay v (-s, -ing, -ed) become weaker or more
corrupt ▶ n (pl -s) process of decaying
  decayed v ▷ **decay**
  decaying v ▷ **decay**
  decays v, n ▷ **decay**
decease n (pl -s) (Formal) death
  deceases n ▷ **decease**
deceased adj (Formal) dead
deceit n (pl -s) behaviour intended to deceive
  > **deceitful** adj > **deceitfully** adv
  deceitful adj ▷ **deceit**
  deceitfully adv ▷ **deceit**
  deceits n ▷ **deceit**
deceive v (-ceives, -ceiving, -ceived) mislead
by lying > **deceiver** n (pl -s)
  deceived v ▷ **deceive**
  deceiver n ▷ **deceive**
  deceivers n ▷ **deceive**
  deceives v ▷ **deceive**
  deceiving v ▷ **deceive**
decelerate v (-rates, -rating, -rated) slow
down > **deceleration** n (pl -s)
  decelerated v ▷ **decelerate**
  decelerates v ▷ **decelerate**
  decelerating v ▷ **decelerate**
  deceleration n ▷ **decelerate**
  decelerations n ▷ **decelerate**

  decencies n ▷ **decent**
  decency n ▷ **decent**
decent adj (-er, -est) (of a person) polite and
morally acceptable > **decently** adv > **decency**
n (pl -cies)
  decenter adj ▷ **decent**
  decentest adj ▷ **decent**
  decently adv ▷ **decent**
  decentralization n ▷ **decentralize**
decentralize v (-lizes, -lizing, -lized)
reorganize into smaller local units
  > **decentralization** n
  decentralized v ▷ **decentralize**
  decentralizes v ▷ **decentralize**
  decentralizing v ▷ **decentralize**
deception n (pl -s) deceiving
  deceptions n ▷ **deception**
deceptive adj likely or designed to deceive
  > **deceptively** adv > **deceptiveness** n
  deceptively adv ▷ **deceptive**
  deceptiveness n ▷ **deceptive**
decibel n (pl -s) unit for measuring the
intensity of sound
  decibels n ▷ **decibel**
decide v (-cides, -ciding, -cided) (cause to)
reach a decision
decided adj unmistakable ▶ v ▷ **decide**
  > **decidedly** adv
  decidedly adv ▷ **decided**
  decides v ▷ **decide**
  deciding v ▷ **decide**
deciduous adj (of a tree) shedding its leaves
annually
decimal n (pl -s) fraction written in the form
of a dot followed by one or more numbers
  ▶ adj relating to or using powers of ten
  > **decimalization** n > **decimally** adv
  decimalization n ▷ **decimal**
  decimally adv ▷ **decimal**
  decimals n ▷ **decimal**
decimate v (-mates, -mating, -mated) destroy
or kill a large proportion of > **decimation**
n (pl -s)
  decimated v ▷ **decimate**
  decimates v ▷ **decimate**
  decimating v ▷ **decimate**
  decimation n ▷ **decimate**
  decimations n ▷ **decimate**
decipher v (-s, -ing, -ed) work out the
meaning of (something illegible or in code)
  > **decipherable** adj
  decipherable adj ▷ **decipher**
  deciphered v ▷ **decipher**
  deciphering v ▷ **decipher**
  deciphers v ▷ **decipher**

decision n (pl -s) judgment, conclusion, or resolution
  decisions n ▷ decision
decisive adj having a definite influence > **decisively** adv > **decisiveness** n
  decisively adv ▷ decisive
  decisiveness n ▷ decisive
deck n (pl -s) area of a ship that forms a floor
decking n wooden platform in a garden
  decks n ▷ deck
declaim v (-s, -ing, -ed) speak loudly and dramatically > **declamation** n (pl -s) > **declamatory** adj
  declaimed v ▷ declaim
  declaiming v ▷ declaim
  declaims v ▷ declaim
  declamation n ▷ declaim
  declamations n ▷ declaim
  declamatory adj ▷ declaim
  declaration n ▷ declare
  declarations n ▷ declare
  declaratory adj ▷ declare
declare v (-clares, -claring, -clared) state firmly and forcefully > **declaration** n (pl -s) > **declaratory** adj
  declared v ▷ declare
  declares v ▷ declare
  declaring v ▷ declare
declension n (pl -s) (GRAMMAR) changes in the form of nouns, pronouns, or adjectives to show case, number, and gender
  declensions n ▷ declension
decline v (-clines, -clining, -clined) become smaller, weaker, or less important ▶ n (pl -s) gradual weakening or loss
  declined v ▷ decline
  declines v, n ▷ decline
  declining v ▷ decline
  declivities n ▷ declivity
declivity n (pl -ties) downward slope
declutch v (-es, -ing, -ed) disengage the clutch of a motor vehicle
  declutched v ▷ declutch
  declutches v ▷ declutch
  declutching v ▷ declutch
decoct v (-s, -ing, -ed) extract the essence from (a substance) by boiling > **decoction** n (pl -s)
  decocted v ▷ decoct
  decocting v ▷ decoct
  decoction n ▷ decoct
  decoctions n ▷ decoct
  decocts v ▷ decoct
decode v (-codes, -coding, -coded) convert from code into ordinary language > **decoder** n (pl -s)

  decoded v ▷ decode
  decoder n ▷ decode
  decoders n ▷ decode
  decodes v ▷ decode
  decoding v ▷ decode
décolleté [day-kol-tay] adj (of a woman's garment) low-cut
decommission v (-s, -ing, -ed) dismantle (a nuclear reactor, weapon, etc.) which is no longer needed
  decommissioned v ▷ decommission
  decommissioning v ▷ decommission
  decommissions v ▷ decommission
decompose v (-poses, -posing, -posed) be broken down through chemical or bacterial action > **decomposition** n (pl -s)
  decomposed v ▷ decompose
  decomposes v ▷ decompose
  decomposing v ▷ decompose
  decomposition n ▷ decompose
  decompositions n ▷ decompose
decompress v (-presses, -pressing, -pressed) free from pressure > **decompression** n (pl -s)
  decompressed v ▷ decompress
  decompresses v ▷ decompress
  decompressing v ▷ decompress
  decompression n ▷ decompress
  decompressions n ▷ decompress
decongestant n (pl -s) medicine that relieves nasal congestion
  decongestants n ▷ decongestant
decontaminate v (-nates, -nating, -nated) make safe by removing poisons, radioactivity, etc. > **decontamination** n (pl -s)
  decontaminated v ▷ decontaminate
  decontaminates v ▷ decontaminate
  decontaminating v ▷ decontaminate
  decontamination n ▷ decontaminate
  decontaminations n ▷ decontaminate
decor [day-core] n (pl -s) style in which a room or house is decorated
decorate v (-rates, -rating, -rated) make more attractive by adding something ornamental > **decoration** n (pl -s) > **decorative** adj > **decorator** n (pl -s)
  decorated v ▷ decorate
  decorates v ▷ decorate
  decorating v ▷ decorate
  decoration n ▷ decorate
  decorations n ▷ decorate
  decorator n ▷ decorate
  decorators n ▷ decorate
decorous [dek-a-russ] adj polite, calm, and sensible in behaviour > **decorously** adv > **decorousness** n

decorously *adv* ▷ **decorous**
decorousness *n* ▷ **decorous**
decors *n* ▷ **decor**
decorum [dik-**core**-um] *n* (*pl* -**s**) polite and socially correct behaviour
  decorums *n* ▷ **decorum**
decoy *n* (*pl* -**s**) person or thing used to lure someone into danger ▶ *v* (-**s, -ing, -ed**) lure away by means of a trick
  decoyed *v* ▷ **decoy**
  decoying *v* ▷ **decoy**
  decoys *n*, *v* ▷ **decoy**
decrease *v* (-**creases, -creasing, -creased**) make or become less ▶ *n* (*pl* -**s**) lessening, reduction
  decreased *v* ▷ **decrease**
  decreases *v*, *n* ▷ **decrease**
  decreasing *v* ▷ **decrease**
decree *n* (*pl* -**s**) law made by someone in authority ▶ *v* (-**crees, -creeing, -creed**) order by decree
  decreed *v* ▷ **decree**
  decreeing *v* ▷ **decree**
  decrees *n*, *v* ▷ **decree**
decrepit *adj* weakened or worn out by age or long use > **decrepitude** *n* (*pl* -**s**)
  decrepitude *n* ▷ **decrepit**
  decrepitudes *n* ▷ **decrepit**
  decried *v* ▷ **decry**
  decries *v* ▷ **decry**
decry *v* (-**cries, -crying, -cried**) express disapproval of
  decrying *v* ▷ **decry**
dedicate *v* (-**cates, -cating, -cated**) commit (oneself or one's time) wholly to a special purpose or cause > **dedication** *n* (*pl* -**s**)
dedicated *adj* devoted to a particular purpose or cause ▶ *v* ▷ **dedicate**
  dedicates *v* ▷ **dedicate**
  dedicating *v* ▷ **dedicate**
  dedication *n* ▷ **dedicate**
  dedications *n* ▷ **dedicate**
deduce *v* (-**duces, -ducing, -duced**) reach (a conclusion) by reasoning from evidence > **deducible** *adj*
  deduced *v* ▷ **deduce**
  deduces *v* ▷ **deduce**
  deducible *adj* ▷ **deduce**
  deducing *v* ▷ **deduce**
deduct *v* (-**s, -ing, -ed**) subtract
  deducted *v* ▷ **deduct**
  deducting *v* ▷ **deduct**
deduction *n* (*pl* -**s**) deducting > **deductive** *adj*
  deductions *n* ▷ **deduction**
  deductive *adj* ▷ **deduction**

  deducts *v* ▷ **deduct**
deed *n* (*pl* -**s**) something that is done
  deeds *n* ▷ **deed**
deem *v* (-**s, -ing, -ed**) consider, judge
  deemed *v* ▷ **deem**
  deeming *v* ▷ **deem**
  deems *v* ▷ **deem**
deep *adj* (-**er, -est**) extending or situated far down, inwards, backwards, or sideways
  > **deepen** *v* (-**s, -ing, -ed**)
  deepen *v* ▷ **deep**
  deepened *v* ▷ **deep**
  deepening *v* ▷ **deep**
  deepens *v* ▷ **deep**
  deeper *adj* ▷ **deep**
  deepest *adj* ▷ **deep**
deepfreeze *n* (*pl* -**s**) ▷ **freezer**
  deepfreezes *n* ▷ **deepfreeze**
deeply *adv* profoundly or intensely
deer *n* (*pl* deer) large wild animal, the male of which has antlers
deerstalker *n* (*pl* -**s**) cloth hat with peaks at the back and front and earflaps
  deerstalkers *n* ▷ **deerstalker**
deface *v* (-**faces, -facing, -faced**) deliberately spoil the appearance of > **defacement** *n* (*pl* -**s**)
  defaced *v* ▷ **deface**
  defacement *n* ▷ **deface**
  defacements *n* ▷ **deface**
  defaces *v* ▷ **deface**
  defacing *v* ▷ **deface**
  defamation *n* ▷ **defame**
  defamations *n* ▷ **defame**
  defamatory *adj* ▷ **defame**
defame *v* (-**fames, -faming, -famed**) attack the good reputation of > **defamation** *n* (*pl* -**s**)
  > **defamatory** [dif-**fam**-a-tree] *adj*
  defamed *v* ▷ **defame**
  defames *v* ▷ **defame**
  defaming *v* ▷ **defame**
default *n* (*pl* -**s**) failure to do something ▶ *v* (-**s, -ing, -ed**) fail to fulfil an obligation > **defaulter** *n* (*pl* -**s**)
  defaulted *v* ▷ **default**
  defaulter *n* ▷ **default**
  defaulters *n* ▷ **default**
  defaulting *v* ▷ **default**
  defaults *n*, *v* ▷ **default**
defeat *v* (-**s, -ing, -ed**) win a victory over ▶ *n* (*pl* -**s**) defeating
  defeated *v* ▷ **defeat**
  defeating *v* ▷ **defeat**
defeatism *n* ready acceptance or expectation of defeat > **defeatist** *adj*, *n* (*pl* -**s**)
  defeatist *n*, *adj* ▷ **defeatism**

defeatists *n* ▷ defeatism
defeats *v, n* ▷ defeat
defecate *v* (-cates, -cating, -cated) discharge
waste from the body through the anus
> defecation *n* (*pl* -s)
defecated *v* ▷ defecate
defecates *v* ▷ defecate
defecating *v* ▷ defecate
defecation *n* ▷ defecate
defecations *n* ▷ defecate
defect *n* (*pl* -s) imperfection, blemish ▶ *v* (-s,
-ing, -ed) desert one's cause or country to
join the opposing forces > defection *n* (*pl* -s)
> defector *n* (*pl* -s)
defected *v* ▷ defect
defecting *v* ▷ defect
defection *n* ▷ defect
defections *n* ▷ defect
defective *adj* imperfect, faulty
> defectiveness *n*
defectiveness *n* ▷ defective
defector *n* ▷ defect
defectors *n* ▷ defect
defects *n, v* ▷ defect
defence *n* (*pl* -s) resistance against attack
> defenceless *adj*
defenceless *adj* ▷ defence
defences *n* ▷ defence
defend *v* (-s, -ing, -ed) protect from harm or
danger
defendant *n* (*pl* -s) person accused of a crime
defendants *n* ▷ defendant
defended *v* ▷ defend
defender *n* (*pl* -s) person who supports
someone or something in the face of
criticism
defenders *n* ▷ defender
defending *v* ▷ defend
defends *v* ▷ defend
defensibilities *n* ▷ defensible
defensibility *n* ▷ defensible
defensible *adj* capable of being defended
because believed to be right > defensibility
n (*pl* -ities)
defensive *adj* intended for defence
> defensively *adv*
defensively *adv* ▷ defensive
defer[1] *v* (-fers, -ferring, -ferred) delay
(something) until a future time > deferment,
deferral *n* (*pl* -s)
defer[2] *v* (-fers, -ferring, -ferred) (*foll. by* to)
comply with the wishes (of)
deference *n* polite and respectful behaviour
> deferential *adj* > deferentially *adv*
deferential *adj* ▷ deference

deferentially *adv* ▷ deference
deferment *n* ▷ defer[1]
deferments *n* ▷ defer[1]
deferral *n* ▷ defer[1]
deferrals *n* ▷ defer[1]
deferred *v* ▷ defer[1, 2]
deferring *v* ▷ defer[1, 2]
defers *v* ▷ defer[1, 2]
defiance *n* ▷ defy
defiances *n* ▷ defy
defiant *adj* ▷ defy
defiantly *adv* ▷ defy
deficiencies *n* ▷ deficiency
deficiency *n* (*pl* -cies) state of being deficient
deficient *adj* lacking some essential thing or
quality > deficiently *adv*
deficiently *adv* ▷ deficient
deficit *n* (*pl* -s) amount by which a sum of
money is too small
deficits *n* ▷ deficit
defied *v* ▷ defy
defies *v* ▷ defy
defile[1] *v* (-files, -filing, -filed) treat (something
sacred or important) without respect
> defilement *n* (*pl* -s)
defile[2] *n* (*pl* -s) narrow valley or pass
defiled *v* ▷ defile[1]
defilement *n* ▷ defile[1]
defilements *n* ▷ defile[1]
defiles *v* ▷ defile[1] ▶ *n* ▷ defile[1, 2]
defiling *v* ▷ defile[1]
definable *adj* ▷ define
define *v* (-fines, -fining, -fined) state precisely
the meaning of > definable *adj*
defined *v* ▷ define
defines *v* ▷ define
defining *v* ▷ define
definite *adj* firm, clear, and precise > definitely
adv
definitely *adv* ▷ definite
definition *n* (*pl* -s) statement of the meaning
of a word or phrase
definitions *n* ▷ definition
definitive *adj* providing an unquestionable
conclusion > definitively *adv*
definitively *adv* ▷ definitive
deflate *v* (-flates, -flating, -flated) (cause to)
collapse through the release of air
deflated *v* ▷ deflate
deflates *v* ▷ deflate
deflating *v* ▷ deflate
deflation *n* (*pl* -s) (ECONOMICS) reduction in
economic activity resulting in lower output
and investment > deflationary *adj*
deflationary *adj* ▷ deflation

deflations n ▷ **deflation**
deflect v (**-flects, -flecting, -flected**) (cause to) turn aside from a course > **deflection** n (pl **-s**) > **deflector** n (pl **-s**)
deflected v ▷ **deflect**
deflecting v ▷ **deflect**
deflection n ▷ **deflect**
deflections n ▷ **deflect**
deflector n ▷ **deflect**
deflectors n ▷ **deflect**
deflects v ▷ **deflect**
deflower v (**-flowers, -flowering, -flowered**) (Lit) deprive (a woman) of her virginity
deflowered v ▷ **deflower**
deflowering v ▷ **deflower**
deflowers v ▷ **deflower**
defoliant n ▷ **defoliate**
defoliants n ▷ **defoliate**
defoliate v (**-ates, -ating, -ated**) deprive (a plant) of its leaves > **defoliant** n (pl **-s**) > **defoliation** n (pl **-s**)
defoliated v ▷ **defoliate**
defoliates v ▷ **defoliate**
defoliating v ▷ **defoliate**
defoliation n ▷ **defoliate**
defoliations n ▷ **defoliate**
deforestation n (pl **-s**) destruction of all the trees in an area
deforestations n ▷ **deforestation**
deform v (**-s, -ing, -ed**) put out of shape or spoil the appearance of > **deformation** n (pl **-s**) > **deformity** n (pl **-ties**)
deformation n ▷ **deform**
deformations n ▷ **deform**
deformed v ▷ **deform**
deforming v ▷ **deform**
deformities n ▷ **deform**
deformity n ▷ **deform**
deforms v ▷ **deform**
defraud v (**-s, -ing, -ed**) cheat out of money, property, etc.
defrauded v ▷ **defraud**
defrauding v ▷ **defraud**
defrauds v ▷ **defraud**
defray v (**-s, -ing, -ed**) provide money for (costs or expenses)
defrayed v ▷ **defray**
defraying v ▷ **defray**
defrays v ▷ **defray**
defrock v (**-s, -ing, -ed**) deprive (a priest) of priestly status
defrocked v ▷ **defrock**
defrocking v ▷ **defrock**
defrocks v ▷ **defrock**
defrost v (**-s, -ing, -ed**) make or become free

of ice
defrosted v ▷ **defrost**
defrosting v ▷ **defrost**
defrosts v ▷ **defrost**
deft adj quick and skilful in movement > **deftly** adv > **deftness** n (pl **-es**)
deftly adv ▷ **deft**
deftness n ▷ **deft**
deftnesses n ▷ **deft**
defunct adj no longer existing or operative
defuse v (**-fuses, -fusing, -fused**) remove the fuse of (an explosive device)
defused v ▷ **defuse**
defuses v ▷ **defuse**
defusing v ▷ **defuse**
defy v (**-fies, -fying, -fied**) resist openly and boldly > **defiance** n (pl **-s**) > **defiant** adj > **defiantly** adv
defying v ▷ **defy**
degeneracies n ▷ **degeneracy**
degeneracy n (pl **-acies**) degenerate behaviour
degenerate adj having deteriorated to a lower mental, moral, or physical level ▶ n (pl **-s**) degenerate person ▶ v (**-ates, -ating, -ated**) become degenerate > **degeneration** n (pl **-s**)
degenerated v ▷ **degenerate**
degenerates n, v ▷ **degenerate**
degenerating v ▷ **degenerate**
degeneration n ▷ **degenerate**
degenerations n ▷ **degenerate**
degradation n ▷ **degrade**
degradations n ▷ **degrade**
degrade v (**-grades, -grading, -graded**) reduce to dishonour or disgrace (CHEM) > **degradation** n (pl **-s**)
degraded v ▷ **degrade**
degrades v ▷ **degrade**
degrading v ▷ **degrade**
degree n (pl **-s**) stage in a scale of relative amount or intensity
degrees n ▷ **degree**
dehumanization n ▷ **dehumanize**
dehumanizations n ▷ **dehumanize**
dehumanize v (**-izes, -izing, -ized**) deprive of human qualities > **dehumanization** n (pl **-s**)
dehumanized v ▷ **dehumanize**
dehumanizes v ▷ **dehumanize**
dehumanizing v ▷ **dehumanize**
dehydrate v (**-ates, -ating, -ated**) remove water from (food) to preserve it > **dehydration** n (pl **-s**)
dehydrated v ▷ **dehydrate**
dehydrates v ▷ **dehydrate**
dehydrating v ▷ **dehydrate**
dehydration n ▷ **dehydrate**

dehydrations n ▷ dehydrate
deification n ▷ deify
deifications n ▷ deify
deified v ▷ deify
deifies v ▷ deify
deify [day-if-fie] v (-fies, -fying, -fied) treat or
worship as a god > **deification** n (pl -s)
deifying v ▷ deify
deign [dane] v (-s, -ing, -ed) agree (to do
something), but as if doing someone a favour
deigned v ▷ deign
deigning v ▷ deign
deigns v ▷ deign
deities n ▷ deity
deity [dee-it-ee, day-it-ee] n (pl -ties) god or
goddess
dejected adj unhappy > **dejectedly** adv
> **dejection** n (pl -s)
dejectedly adv ▷ dejected
dejection n ▷ dejected
dejections n ▷ dejected
dekko n (pl -s) (BRIT, AUST & NZ) (Slang) look
dekkos n ▷ dekko
delay v (-s, -ing, -ed) put off to a later time ▶ n
(pl -s) act of delaying
delayed v ▷ delay
delaying v ▷ delay
delays v, n ▷ delay
delectable adj delightful, very attractive
delectation n (pl -s) (Formal) great pleasure
delectations n ▷ delectation
delegate n (pl -s) person chosen to represent
others, esp. at a meeting ▶ v (-gates, -gating,
-gated) entrust (duties or powers) to
someone
delegated v ▷ delegate
delegates n, v ▷ delegate
delegating v ▷ delegate
delegation n (pl -s) group chosen to represent
others
delegations n ▷ delegation
delete v (-letes, -leting, -leted) remove
(something written or printed) > **deletion**
n (pl -s)
deleted v ▷ delete
deleterious [del-lit-eer-ee-uss] adj harmful,
injurious
deletes v ▷ delete
deleting v ▷ delete
deletion n ▷ delete
deletions n ▷ deletion
deliberate adj planned in advance, intentional
▶ v (-ates, -ating, -ated) think something
over > **deliberately** adv > **deliberation** n (pl -s)
> **deliberative** adj

deliberated v ▷ deliberate
deliberately adv ▷ deliberate
deliberates v ▷ deliberate
deliberating v ▷ deliberate
deliberation n ▷ deliberate
deliberations n ▷ deliberate
deliberative adj ▷ deliberate
delicacies n ▷ delicacy
delicacy n (pl -cies) being delicate
delicate adj fine or subtle in quality or
workmanship > **delicately** adv
delicately adv ▷ delicate
delicatessen n (pl -s) shop selling imported
or unusual foods, often already cooked or
prepared
delicatessens n ▷ delicatessen
delicious adj very appealing to taste or smell
> **deliciously** adv > **deliciousness** n
deliciously adv ▷ delicious
deliciousness n ▷ delicious
delight n (pl -s) (source of) great pleasure ▶ v
(-s, -ing, -ed) please greatly > **delightful** adj
> **delightfully** adv
delighted v ▷ delight
delightful adj ▷ delight
delightfully adv ▷ delight
delighting v ▷ delight
delights n, v ▷ delight
delimit v (-s, -ing, -ed) mark or lay down the
limits of > **delimitation** n (pl -s)
delimitation n ▷ delimit
delimitations n ▷ delimit
delimited v ▷ delimit
delimiting v ▷ delimit
delimits v ▷ delimit
delineate [dill-lin-ee-ate] v (-ates, -ating, -ated)
show by drawing > **delineation** n (pl -s)
delineated v ▷ delineate
delineates v ▷ delineate
delineating v ▷ delineate
delineation n ▷ delineate
delineations n ▷ delineate
delinquencies n ▷ delinquent
delinquency n ▷ delinquent
delinquent n (pl -s) someone, esp. a young
person, who repeatedly breaks the law ▶ adj
repeatedly breaking the law > **delinquency**
n (pl -cies)
delinquents n ▷ delinquent
delirious adj ▷ delirium
deliriously adv ▷ delirium
delirium n (pl -s) state of excitement and
mental confusion, often with hallucinations
> **delirious** adj > **deliriously** adv
deliriums n ▷ delirium

deliver v (**-s, -ing, -ed**) carry (goods etc.) to a destination
deliverance n (pl **-s**) rescue from captivity or evil
  deliverances n ▷ **deliverance**
  delivered v ▷ **deliver**
  deliveries n ▷ **delivery**
  delivering v ▷ **deliver**
  delivers v ▷ **deliver**
delivery n (pl **-eries**) delivering
dell n (pl **-s**) (CHIEFLY BRIT) small wooded hollow
  dells n ▷ **dell**
delphinium n (pl **-s**) large garden plant with blue flowers
  delphiniums n ▷ **delphinium**
delta n (pl **-s**) fourth letter in the Greek alphabet
  deltas n ▷ **delta**
delude v (**-ludes, -luding, -luded**) deceive
  deluded v ▷ **delude**
  deludes v ▷ **delude**
  deluding v ▷ **delude**
deluge [del-lyooj] n (pl **-s**) great flood ▶ v (**-luges, -luging, -luged**) flood
  deluged v ▷ **deluge**
  deluges n, v ▷ **deluge**
  deluging v ▷ **deluge**
delusion n (pl **-s**) mistaken idea or belief > **delusive** adj
  delusions n ▷ **delusion**
  delusive adj ▷ **delusion**
delve v (**delves, delving, delved**) research deeply (for information)
  delved v ▷ **delve**
  delves v ▷ **delve**
  delving v ▷ **delve**
  demagogic adj ▷ **demagogue**
  demagogies v ▷ **demagogue**
demagogue n (pl **-s**) political agitator who appeals to the prejudice and passions of the mob > **demagogic** adj > **demagogy** n (pl **-gies**)
  demagogues n ▷ **demagogue**
  demagogy n ▷ **demagogue**
demand v (**-s, -ing, -ed**) request forcefully ▶ n (pl **-s**) forceful request
  demanded v ▷ **demand**
demanding adj requiring a lot of time or effort ▶ v ▷ **demand**
  demands v, n ▷ **demand**
demarcation n (pl **-s**) (Formal) establishing limits or boundaries, esp. between the work performed by different trade unions
  demarcations n ▷ **demarcation**
demean v (**-s, -ing, -ed**) do something unworthy of one's status or character

  demeaned v ▷ **demean**
  demeaning v ▷ **demean**
demeanour n (pl **-s**) way a person behaves
  demeanours n ▷ **demeanour**
  demeans v ▷ **demean**
demented adj mad > **dementedly** adv
  dementedly adv ▷ **demented**
dementia [dim-men-sha] n (pl **-s**) state of serious mental deterioration
  dementias n ▷ **dementia**
demerit n (pl **-s**) fault, disadvantage
  demerits n ▷ **demerit**
demesne [dim-mane] n (pl **-s**) land surrounding a house
  demesnes n ▷ **demesne**
demijohn n (pl **-s**) large bottle with a short neck, often encased in wicker
  demijohns n ▷ **demijohn**
  demilitarization n ▷ **demilitarize**
  demilitarizations n ▷ **demilitarize**
demilitarize v (**-izes, -izing, -ized**) remove the military forces from > **demilitarization** n (pl **-s**)
  demilitarized v ▷ **demilitarize**
  demilitarizes v ▷ **demilitarize**
  demilitarizing v ▷ **demilitarize**
demimonde n (pl **-s**) (esp. in the 19th century) class of women considered to be outside respectable society because of promiscuity
  demimondes n ▷ **demimonde**
demise n (pl **-s**) eventual failure (of something successful)
  demises n ▷ **demise**
demo n (pl **-s**) (Informal) demonstration, organized expression of public opinion
demob v (**-mobs, -mobbing, -mobbed**) (BRIT, AUST & NZ) (Informal) demobilize
  demobbed v ▷ **demob**
  demobbing v ▷ **demob**
  demobilization n ▷ **demobilize**
  demobilizations n ▷ **demobilize**
demobilize v (**-lizes, -lizing, -lized**) release from the armed forces > **demobilization** n (pl **-s**)
  demobilized v ▷ **demobilize**
  demobilizes v ▷ **demobilize**
  demobilizing v ▷ **demobilize**
  demobs v ▷ **demob**
  democracies n ▷ **democracy**
democracy n (pl **-cies**) government by the people or their elected representatives
democrat n (pl **-s**) advocate of democracy
democratic adj of democracy > **democratically** adv
  democratically adv ▷ **democratic**

democrats n ▷ democrat
demographer n ▷ demography
demographers n ▷ demography
demographic adj ▷ demography
demographies n ▷ demography
demography n (pl -phies) study of population statistics, such as births and deaths
> **demographer** n (pl -s) > **demographic** adj
demolish v (-es, -ing, -ed) knock down or destroy (a building) > **demolition** n (pl -s)
demolished v ▷ demolish
demolishes v ▷ demolish
demolishing v ▷ demolish
demolition n ▷ demolish
demolitions n ▷ demolish
demon n (pl -s) evil spirit
demoniac adj ▷ demonic
demoniacal adj ▷ demonic
demoniacally adv ▷ demonic
demonic adj evil > **demoniac, demoniacal** adj appearing to be possessed by a devil
> **demoniacally** adv
demonologies n ▷ demonology
demonologist n ▷ demonology
demonologists n ▷ demonology
demonology n (pl -logies) study of demons
> **demonologist** n (pl -s)
demons n ▷ demon
demonstrable adj able to be proved
> **demonstrably** adv
demonstrably adv ▷ demonstrable
demonstrate v (-rates, -rating, -rated) show or prove by reasoning or evidence
demonstrated v ▷ demonstrate
demonstrates v ▷ demonstrate
demonstrating v ▷ demonstrate
demonstration n (pl -s) organized expression of public opinion
demonstrations n ▷ demonstration
demonstrative adj tending to show one's feelings unreservedly > **demonstratively** adv
demonstratively adv ▷ demonstrative
demonstrator n (pl -s) person who demonstrates how a device or machine works
demonstrators n ▷ demonstrator
demoralization n ▷ demoralize
demoralizations n ▷ demoralize
demoralize v (-lizes, -lizing, -lized) undermine the morale of > **demoralization** n (pl -s)
demoralized v ▷ demoralize
demoralizes v ▷ demoralize
demoralizing v ▷ demoralize
demos n ▷ demo
demote v (-motes, -moting, -moted) reduce in status or rank > **demotion** n (pl -s)
demoted v ▷ demote
demotes v ▷ demote
demoting v ▷ demote
demotion n ▷ demote
demotions n ▷ demote
demur v (-murs, -murring, -murred) show reluctance
demure adj (-r, -st) quiet, reserved, and rather shy > **demurely** adv
demurely adv ▷ demure
demurer adj ▷ demure
demurest adj ▷ demure
demurred v ▷ demur
demurring v ▷ demur
demurs v ▷ demur
den n (pl -s) home of a wild animal
denationalization n ▷ denationalize
denationalizations n ▷ denationalize
denationalize v (-lizes, -lizing, -lized) transfer (an industry) from public to private ownership > **denationalization** n (pl -s)
denationalized v ▷ denationalize
denationalizes v ▷ denationalize
denationalizing v ▷ denationalize
denature v (-tures, -turing, -tured) change the nature of
denatured v ▷ denature
denatures v ▷ denature
denaturing v ▷ denature
deniable adj ▷ deny
deniably adv ▷ deny
denial n (pl -s) statement that something is not true
denials n ▷ denial
denied v ▷ deny
denier [den-yer] n (pl -s) unit of weight used to measure the fineness of nylon or silk
deniers n ▷ denier
denies v ▷ deny
denigrate v (-grates, -grating, -grated) criticize unfairly > **denigration** n (pl -s)
denigrated v ▷ denigrate
denigrates v ▷ denigrate
denigrating v ▷ denigrate
denigration n ▷ denigrate
denigrations n ▷ denigrate
denim n (pl -s) hard-wearing cotton fabric, usu. blue ▶ pl jeans made of denim
denims n ▷ denim
denizen n (pl -s) inhabitant
denizens n ▷ denizen
denominate v (-nates, -nating, -nated) give a specific name to
denominated v ▷ denominate

denominates v ▷ **denominate**
denominating v ▷ **denominate**
denomination n (pl -s) group having a
distinctive interpretation of a religious faith
> **denominational** adj
denominational adj ▷ **denomination**
denominations n ▷ **denomination**
denominator n (pl -s) number below the line
in a fraction
denominators n ▷ **denominator**
denotation n ▷ **denote**
denotations n ▷ **denote**
denote v (-notes, -noting, -noted) be a sign of
> **denotation** n (pl -s)
denoted v ▷ **denote**
denotes v ▷ **denote**
denoting v ▷ **denote**
denouement [day-noo-mon] n (pl -s) final
outcome or solution in a play or book
denouements n ▷ **denouement**
denounce v (-ces, -cing, -ced) speak
vehemently against
denounced v ▷ **denounce**
denounces v ▷ **denounce**
denouncing v ▷ **denounce**
dens n ▷ **den**
dense adj (-r, -st) closely packed > **densely** adv
densely adv ▷ **dense**
denser adj ▷ **dense**
densest adj ▷ **dense**
densities n ▷ **density**
density n (pl -ties) degree to which something
is filled or occupied
dent n (pl -s) hollow in the surface of
something, made by hitting it ▶ v (-s, -ing,
-ed) make a dent in
dental adj of teeth or dentistry
dented v ▷ **dent**
dentine [den-teen] n (pl -s) hard dense tissue
forming the bulk of a tooth
dentines n ▷ **dentine**
denting v ▷ **dent**
dentist n (pl -s) person qualified to practise
dentistry
dentistries n ▷ **dentistry**
dentistry n (pl -ries) branch of medicine
concerned with the teeth and gums
dentists n ▷ **dentist**
dents n, v ▷ **dent**
denture n (pl -s) false tooth
dentures n ▷ **denture**
denude v (-nudes, -nuding, -nuded) remove
the covering or protection from
denuded v ▷ **denude**
denudes v ▷ **denude**

denuding v ▷ **denude**
denunciation n (pl -s) open condemnation
denunciations n ▷ **denunciation**
deny v (-nies, -nying, -nied) declare to be
untrue > **deniable** adj > **deniably** adv
denying v ▷ **deny**
deodorant n (pl -s) substance applied to the
body to mask the smell of perspiration
deodorants n ▷ **deodorant**
deodorize v (-izes, -izing, -ized) remove or
disguise the smell of
deodorized v ▷ **deodorize**
deodorizes v ▷ **deodorize**
deodorizing v ▷ **deodorize**
depart v (-s, -ing, -ed) leave > **departed**
> **departure** n (pl -s)
departed adj (Euphemistic) dead ▶ v ▷ **depart**
departing v ▷ **depart**
department n (pl -s) specialized division of a
large organization > **departmental** adj
departmental adj ▷ **department**
departments n ▷ **department**
departs v ▷ **depart**
departure n ▷ **depart**
departures n ▷ **depart**
depend v (-s, -ing, -ed) (foll. by on) put trust
(in) > **dependable** adj > **dependably** adv
> **dependability** n (pl -ities)
dependabilities n ▷ **depend**
dependability n ▷ **depend**
dependable adj ▷ **depend**
dependably adv ▷ **depend**
dependant n (pl -s) person who depends on
another for financial support
dependants n ▷ **dependant**
depended v ▷ **depend**
dependence n (pl -s) state of being dependent
dependences n ▷ **dependence**
dependencies n ▷ **dependency**
dependency n (pl -cies) country controlled by
another country
dependent adj depending on someone or
something > **dependently** adv
dependently adv ▷ **dependent**
depending v ▷ **depend**
depends v ▷ **depend**
depict v (-s, -ing, -ed) produce a picture of
> **depiction** n (pl -s)
depicted v ▷ **depict**
depicting v ▷ **depict**
depiction n ▷ **depict**
depictions n ▷ **depict**
depicts v ▷ **depict**
depilatories n ▷ **depilatory**
depilatory [dip-pill-a-tree] n (pl -tories) ▶ adj

(substance) designed to remove unwanted hair

deplete v (-letes, -leting, -leted) use up > **depletion** n (pl -s)

depleted v ▷ deplete

depletes v ▷ deplete

depleting v ▷ deplete

depletion n ▷ deplete

depletions n ▷ deplete

deplorable adj very bad or unpleasant > **deplorably** adv

deplorably adv ▷ deplorable

deplore v (-lores, -loring, -lored) condemn strongly

deplored v ▷ deplore

deplores v ▷ deplore

deploring v ▷ deplore

deploy v (-s, -ing, -ed) organize (troops or resources) into a position ready for immediate action > **deployment** n (pl -s)

deployed v ▷ deploy

deploying v ▷ deploy

deployment n ▷ deploy

deployments n ▷ deploy

deploys v ▷ deploy

depopulate v (-lates, -lating, -lated) reduce the population of > **depopulation** n (pl -s)

depopulated v ▷ depopulate

depopulates v ▷ depopulate

depopulating v ▷ depopulate

depopulation n ▷ depopulate

depopulations n ▷ depopulate

deport v (-s, -ing, -ed) remove forcibly from a country > **deportation** n (pl -s) > **deportee** n (pl -s)

deportation n ▷ deport

deportations n ▷ deport

deported v ▷ deport

deportee n ▷ deport

deportees n ▷ deport

deporting v ▷ deport

deportment n (pl -s) way in which a person moves or stands

deportments n ▷ deportment

deports v ▷ deport

depose v (-poses, -posing, -posed) remove from an office or position of power

deposed v ▷ depose

deposes v ▷ depose

deposing v ▷ depose

deposit v (-s, -ing, -ed) put down ▶ n (pl -s) sum of money paid into a bank account > **depositor** n (pl -s)

depositaries n ▷ depositary

depositary n (pl -aries) person to whom something is entrusted for safety

deposited v ▷ deposit

depositing v ▷ deposit

deposition n (pl -s) (LAW) sworn statement of a witness used in court in his or her absence

depositions n ▷ deposition

depositor n ▷ deposit

depositories n ▷ deposit

depositors n ▷ deposit

depository n (pl -ories) store for furniture etc.

deposits v, n ▷ deposit

depot [dep-oh] n (pl -s) building where goods or vehicles are kept when not in use

depots n ▷ depot

depraved adj morally bad > **depravity** n (pl -ities)

depravities n ▷ depraved

depravity n ▷ depraved

deprecate v (-cates, -cating, -cated) express disapproval of > **deprecation** n (pl -s) > **deprecatory** adj

deprecated v ▷ deprecate

deprecates v ▷ deprecate

deprecating v ▷ deprecate

deprecation n ▷ deprecate

deprecations n ▷ deprecate

deprecatory adj ▷ deprecate

depreciate v (-ates, -ating, -ated) decline in value or price > **depreciation** n (pl -s)

depreciated v ▷ depreciate

depreciates v ▷ depreciate

depreciating v ▷ depreciate

depreciation n ▷ depreciate

depreciations n ▷ depreciate

depredation n (pl -s) plundering

depredations n ▷ depredation

depress v (-es, -ing, -ed) make sad > **depressing** adj > **depressingly** adv

depressant n (pl -s) ▶ adj (drug) able to reduce nervous activity

depressants n ▷ depressant

depressed v ▷ depress

depresses v ▷ depress

depressing v, adj ▷ depress

depressingly adv ▷ depress

depression n (pl -s) mental state in which a person has feelings of gloom and inadequacy

depressions n ▷ depression

depressive adj tending to cause depression ▶ n (pl -s) person who suffers from depression > **depressively** adv

depressively adv ▷ depressive

depressives n ▷ depressive

deprivation n ▷ deprive

deprivations n ▷ deprive

deprive v (-rives, -riving, -rived) (foll. by of) prevent from (having or enjoying) > **deprivation** n (pl -s)

deprived adj lacking adequate living conditions, education, etc. ▶ v ▷ **deprive**

deprives v ▷ **deprive**

depriving v ▷ **deprive**

depth n (pl -s) distance downwards, backwards, or inwards

depths n ▷ **depth**

deputation n (pl -s) body of people appointed to represent others

deputations n ▷ **deputation**

depute v (-putes, -puting, -puted) appoint (someone) to act on one's behalf

deputed v ▷ **depute**

deputes v ▷ **depute**

deputies n ▷ **deputy**

deputing v ▷ **depute**

deputize v (-izes, -izing, -ized) act as deputy

deputized v ▷ **deputize**

deputizes v ▷ **deputize**

deputizing v ▷ **deputize**

deputy n (pl -ties) person appointed to act on behalf of another

derail v (-s, -ing, -ed) cause (a train) to go off the rails > **derailment** n (pl -s)

derailed v ▷ **derail**

derailing v ▷ **derail**

derailment n ▷ **derail**

derailments n ▷ **derail**

derails v ▷ **derail**

deranged adj insane or uncontrolled > **derangement** n (pl -s)

derangement n ▷ **derange**

derangements n ▷ **derange**

derbies n ▷ **derby**

derby [dah-bee] n (pl -bies) sporting event between teams from the same area ▶ n any of various horse races

deregulate v (-ates, -ating, -ated) remove regulations or controls from > **deregulation** n (pl -s)

deregulated v ▷ **deregulate**

deregulates v ▷ **deregulate**

deregulating v ▷ **deregulate**

deregulation n ▷ **deregulate**

deregulations n ▷ **deregulate**

derelict adj unused and falling into ruins ▶ n (pl -s) social outcast, vagrant

dereliction n (pl -s) state of being abandoned

derelictions n ▷ **dereliction**

derelicts n ▷ **derelict**

deride v (-rides, -riding, -rided) treat with contempt or ridicule > **derision** n (pl -s)

derided v ▷ **deride**

derides v ▷ **deride**

deriding v ▷ **deride**

derision n ▷ **deride**

derisions n ▷ **deride**

derisive adj mocking, scornful > **derisively** adv > **derisiveness** n

derisively adv ▷ **derisive**

derisiveness n ▷ **derisive**

derisory adj too small or inadequate to be considered seriously

derivation n ▷ **derive**

derivations n ▷ **derive**

derivative adj word, idea, etc., derived from another > **derivatively** adv

derivatively adv ▷ **derivative**

derive v (-rives, -riving, -rived) (foll. by from) take or develop (from) > **derivation** n (pl -s)

derived v ▷ **derive**

derives v ▷ **derive**

deriving v ▷ **derive**

dermatitis n inflammation of the skin

dermatologies n ▷ **dermatology**

dermatologist n ▷ **dermatology**

dermatologists n ▷ **dermatology**

dermatology n (pl -ogies) branch of medicine concerned with the skin > **dermatologist** n (pl -s)

derogatorily adv ▷ **derogatory**

derogatory [dir-rog-a-tree] adj intentionally offensive > **derogatorily** adv

derrick n (pl -s) simple crane

derricks n ▷ **derrick**

derv n (pl -s) (BRIT) diesel oil, when used for road transport

dervish n (pl -es) member of a Muslim religious order noted for a frenzied whirling dance

dervishes n ▷ **dervish**

dervs n ▷ **derv**

descant n (pl -s) (MUSIC) tune played or sung above a basic melody

descants n ▷ **descant**

descend v (-s, -ing, -ed) move down (a slope etc.)

descendant n (pl -s) person or animal descended from an individual, race, or species

descendants n ▷ **descendant**

descended v ▷ **descend**

descendent adj descending

descending v ▷ **descend**

descends v ▷ **descend**

descent n (pl -s) descending

descents v ▷ **descent**

describe v (-ribes, -ribing, -ribed) give an account of (something or someone) in words
described v ▷ **describe**
describes v ▷ **describe**
describing v ▷ **describe**
descried v ▷ **descry**
descries v ▷ **descry**
description n (pl -s) statement that describes something or someone > **descriptive** adj > **descriptively** adv > **descriptiveness** n
descriptions n ▷ **description**
descriptive adj ▷ **description**
descriptively adv ▷ **description**
descriptiveness n ▷ **description**
descry v (-scries, -scrying, -scried) catch sight of
descrying v ▷ **descry**
desecrate v (-rates, -rating, -rated) damage or insult (something sacred) > **desecration** n (pl -s)
desecrated v ▷ **desecrate**
desecrates v ▷ **desecrate**
desecrating v ▷ **desecrate**
desecration n ▷ **desecrate**
desecrations n ▷ **desecrate**
desegregate v (-gates, -gating, -gated) end racial segregation in > **desegregation** n (pl -s)
desegregated v ▷ **desegregate**
desegregates v ▷ **desegregate**
desegregating v ▷ **desegregate**
desegregation n ▷ **desegregate**
desegregations n ▷ **desegregate**
deselect v (-s, -ing, -ed) (BRIT) (POLITICS) refuse to select (an MP) for re-election > **deselection** n (pl -s)
deselected v ▷ **deselect**
deselecting v ▷ **deselect**
deselection n ▷ **deselect**
deselections n ▷ **deselect**
deselects v ▷ **deselect**
desert[1] n (pl -s) region with little or no vegetation because of low rainfall
desert[2] v (-s, -ing, -ed) abandon (a person or place) without intending to return > **deserter** n (pl -s) > **desertion** n (pl -s)
deserted v ▷ **desert**[2]
deserter n ▷ **desert**[2]
deserters n ▷ **desert**[2]
deserting v ▷ **desert**[2]
desertion n ▷ **desert**[2]
desertions n ▷ **desert**[2]
deserts n ▷ **desert**[1] ▶ pl n the punishment one deserves ▶ v ▷ **desert**[2]
deserve v (-serves, -serving, -served) be entitled to or worthy of

deserved adj rightfully earned ▶ v ▷ **deserve** > **deservedly** adv
deservedly adv ▷ **deserved**
deserves v ▷ **deserve**
deserving adj worthy of help, praise, or reward ▶ v ▷ **deserve**
deshabille [day-zab-**beel**] n (pl -s) state of being partly dressed
deshabilles n ▷ **deshabille**
desiccate v (-siccates, -siccating, -siccated) remove most of the water from > **desiccation** n (pl -s)
desiccated v ▷ **desiccate**
desiccates v ▷ **desiccate**
desiccating v ▷ **desiccate**
desiccation n ▷ **desiccate**
desiccations n ▷ **desiccate**
design v (-s, -ing, -ed) work out the structure or form of (something), by making a sketch or plans ▶ n (pl -s) preliminary drawing
designate [**dez**-zig-nate] v (-nates, -nating, -nated) give a name to ▶ adj appointed but not yet in office
designated v ▷ **designate**
designates v ▷ **designate**
designating v ▷ **designate**
designation n (pl -s) name
designations v ▷ **designation**
designed v ▷ **design**
designedly [dee-**zine**-id-lee] adv intentionally
designer n (pl -s) person who draws up original sketches or plans from which things are made ▶ adj designed by a well-known designer
designers n ▷ **designer**
designing adj cunning and scheming ▶ v ▷ **design**
designs v, n ▷ **design**
desirabilities n ▷ **desirable**
desirability n ▷ **desirable**
desirable adj worth having > **desirability** n (pl -ities) > **desirably** adv
desirably adv ▷ **desirable**
desire v (-sires, -siring, -sired) want very much ▶ n (pl -s) wish, longing
desired v ▷ **desire**
desires v, n ▷ **desire**
desiring v ▷ **desire**
desist v (-s, -ing, -ed) (foll. by from) stop (doing something)
desisted v ▷ **desist**
desisting v ▷ **desist**
desists v ▷ **desist**
desk n (pl -s) piece of furniture with a writing surface and drawers

desks *n* ▷ **desk**

desktop *adj* (of a computer) small enough to use at a desk

desolate *adj* uninhabited and bleak ▶ *v* (**-lates, -lating, -lated**) deprive of inhabitants > **desolately** *adv* > **desolateness** *n* > **desolation** *n* (*pl* -**s**)

desolated *v* ▷ **desolate**

desolately *adv* ▷ **desolate**

desolateness *n* ▷ **desolate**

desolates *v* ▷ **desolate**

desolating *v* ▷ **desolate**

desolation *n* ▷ **desolate**

desolations *n* ▷ **desolate**

despair *n* (*pl* -**s**) total loss of hope ▶ *v* (**-s, -ing, -ed**) lose hope > **despairingly** *adv*

despaired *v* ▷ **despair**

despairing *v* ▷ **despair**

despairingly *adv* ▷ **despair**

despairs *n, v* ▷ **despair**

despatch *v* (**-es, -ing, -ed**) ▶ *n* (*pl* -**es**) ▷ **dispatch**

despatched *v* ▷ **despatch**

despatches *v, n* ▷ **despatch**

despatching *v* ▷ **despatch**

desperado *n* (*pl* -**does, -dos**) reckless person ready to commit any violent illegal act

desperadoes *v* ▷ **desperado**

desperados *v* ▷ **desperado**

desperate *adj* in despair and reckless > **desperately** *adv* > **desperateness** *n* > **desperation** *n* (*pl* -**s**)

desperately *adv* ▷ **desperate**

desperateness *n* ▷ **desperate**

desperation *n* ▷ **desperate**

desperations *n* ▷ **desperate**

despicable *adj* deserving contempt > **despicably** *adv*

despicably *adv* ▷ **despicable**

despise *v* (**-pises, -pising, -pised**) regard with contempt

despised *v* ▷ **despise**

despises *v* ▷ **despise**

despising *v* ▷ **despise**

despite *prep* in spite of

despoil *v* (**-s, -ing, -ed**) (*Formal*) plunder > **despoliation** *n* (*pl* -**s**)

despoiled *v* ▷ **despoil**

despoiling *v* ▷ **despoil**

despoils *v* ▷ **despoil**

despoliation *n* ▷ **despoil**

despoliations *n* ▷ **despoil**

despondencies *n* ▷ **despondent**

despondency *n* ▷ **despondent**

despondent *adj* unhappy > **despondently** *adv* > **despondency** *n* (*pl* -**cies**)

despondently *adv* ▷ **despondent**

despot *n* (*pl* -**s**) person in power who acts unfairly or cruelly > **despotic** *adj* > **despotically** *adv*

despotic *adj* ▷ **despot**

despotically *adv* ▷ **despot**

despotism *n* (*pl* -**s**) unfair or cruel government or behaviour

despotisms *n* ▷ **despotism**

despots *n* ▷ **despot**

dessert *n* (*pl* -**s**) sweet course served at the end of a meal

desserts *n* ▷ **dessert**

dessertspoon *n* (*pl* -**s**) spoon between a tablespoon and a teaspoon in size

dessertspoons *n* ▷ **dessertspoon**

destination *n* (*pl* -**s**) place to which someone or something is going

destinations *n* ▷ **destination**

destined *adj* certain to be or to do something

destinies *n* ▷ **destiny**

destiny *n* (*pl* -**nies**) future marked out for a person or thing

destitute *adj* having no money or possessions > **destitution** *n*

destitution *n* ▷ **destitute**

destroy *v* (**-s, -ing, -ed**) ruin, demolish

destroyed *v* ▷ **destroy**

destroyer *n* (*pl* -**s**) small heavily armed warship

destroyers *n* ▷ **destroyer**

destroying *v* ▷ **destroy**

destroys *v* ▷ **destroy**

destruction *n* (*pl* -**s**) destroying

destructions *n* ▷ **destruction**

destructive *adj* (capable of) causing destruction > **destructively** *adv* > **destructiveness** *n*

destructively *adv* ▷ **destructive**

destructiveness *n* ▷ **destructive**

desuetude [diss-**syoo**-it-tude] *n* (*pl* -**s**) condition of not being in use

desuetudes *n* ▷ **desuetude**

desultorily *adv* ▷ **desultory**

desultoriness *n* ▷ **desultory**

desultory [**dez**-zl-tree] *adj* jumping from one thing to another, disconnected > **desultorily** *adv* > **desultoriness** *n*

detach *v* (**-es, -ing, -ed**) disengage and separate > **detachable** *adj*

detachable *adj* ▷ **detach**

detached *adj* (BRIT, AUST & S AFR) (of a house) not joined to another house ▶ *v* ▷ **detach**

detaches *v* ▷ **detach**

detaching *v* ▷ **detach**

detachment *n* (*pl* -**s**) lack of emotional

involvement
detachments n ▷ **detachment**
detail n (pl -s) individual piece of information
▶ v (-s, -ing, -ed) list fully
detailed v ▷ **detail**
detailing v ▷ **detail**
details n, v ▷ **detail**
detain v (-s, -ing, -ed) delay (someone)
> **detainee** n (pl -s)
detained v ▷ **detain**
detainee n ▷ **detain**
detainees n ▷ **detain**
detaining v ▷ **detain**
detains v ▷ **detain**
detect v (-s, -ing, -ed) notice > **detectable** adj
> **detection** n (pl -s)
detectable adj ▷ **detect**
detected v ▷ **detect**
detecting v ▷ **detect**
detection n ▷ **detect**
detections n ▷ **detect**
detective n (pl -s) policeman or private agent
who investigates crime
detectives n ▷ **detective**
detector n (pl -s) instrument used to find
something
detectors n ▷ **detector**
detects v ▷ **detect**
detente [day-tont] n (pl -s) easing of tension
between nations
detentes n ▷ **detente**
detention n (pl -s) imprisonment
detentions n ▷ **detention**
deter v (-ters, -terring, -terred) discourage
(someone) from doing something by
instilling fear or doubt
detergent n (pl -s) chemical substance for
washing clothes or dishes
detergents n ▷ **detergent**
deteriorate v (-rates, -rating, -rated) become
worse > **deterioration** n (pl -s)
deteriorated v ▷ **deteriorate**
deteriorates v ▷ **deteriorate**
deteriorating v ▷ **deteriorate**
deterioration n ▷ **deteriorate**
deteriorations n ▷ **deteriorate**
determinant n (pl -s) factor that determines
determinants n ▷ **determinant**
determinate adj definitely limited or fixed
> **determinateness** n
determinateness n ▷ **determinate**
determination n (pl -s) being determined or
resolute
determinations n ▷ **determination**
determine v (-mines, -mining, -mined) settle

(an argument or a question) conclusively
determined adj firmly decided, unable to be
dissuaded ▶ v ▷ **determine** > **determinedly**
adv
determiner n (pl -s) (GRAMMAR) word that
determines the object to which a noun
phrase refers
determiners n ▷ **determiner**
determines v ▷ **determine**
determining v ▷ **determine**
determinism n theory that human choice
is not free, but decided by past events
> **determinist** n (pl -s) adj
determinist n ▷ **determinism**
determinists n ▷ **determinism**
deterred v ▷ **deter**
deterrent n (pl -s) something that deters ▶ adj
tending to deter
deterrents n ▷ **deterrent**
deterring v ▷ **deter**
deters v ▷ **deter**
detest v (-s, -ing, -ed) dislike intensely
> **detestable** adj > **detestably** adv
> **detestation** n (pl -s)
detestable adj ▷ **detest**
detestably adv ▷ **detest**
detestation n ▷ **detest**
detestations n ▷ **detest**
detested v ▷ **detest**
detesting v ▷ **detest**
detests v ▷ **detest**
dethrone v (-rones, -roning, -roned) remove
from a throne or position of power
dethroned v ▷ **dethrone**
dethrones v ▷ **dethrone**
dethroning v ▷ **dethrone**
detonate v (-nates, -nating, -nated) explode
> **detonation** n (pl -s)
detonated v ▷ **detonate**
detonates v ▷ **detonate**
detonating v ▷ **detonate**
detonation n ▷ **detonate**
detonations n ▷ **detonate**
detonator n (pl -s) small amount of explosive,
or a device, used to set off an explosion
detonators n ▷ **detonator**
detour n (pl -s) route that is not the most
direct one
detours n ▷ **detour**
detract v (-s, -ing, -ed) (foll. by **from**) make
(something) seem less good > **detractor** n
(pl -s)
detracted v ▷ **detract**
detracting v ▷ **detract**
detractor n ▷ **detract**

detractors n ▷ **detract**
detracts v ▷ **detract**
detriment n (pl -s) disadvantage or damage
 > **detrimental** adj > **detrimentally** adv
detrimental adj ▷ **detract**
detrimentally adv ▷ **detract**
detriments n ▷ **detract**
detritus [dit-**trite**-uss] n loose mass of stones
 and silt worn away from rocks
deuce [**dyewss**] n (pl -s) (TENNIS) score of forty all
 deuces n ▷ **deuce**

> **deus** n (**di**). Deus is a Latin word for a
> god. Its plural, di, is a very handy word
> to know when trying to form several
> words at once. Di scores 3 points.

deuterium n (pl -s) isotope of hydrogen twice
 as heavy as the normal atom
deuteriums n ▷ **deuterium**

> **dev** n (**devs**). A dev is a Hindu god. Dev
> scores 7 points.

devaluation n ▷ **devalue**
devaluations n ▷ **devalue**
devalue v (-lues, -luing, -lued) reduce the
 exchange value of (a currency) > **devaluation**
 n (pl -s)
devalued v ▷ **devalue**
devalues v ▷ **devalue**
devaluing v ▷ **devalue**
devastate v (-tates, -tating, -tated) destroy
 > **devastation** n (pl -s)
devastated adj shocked and extremely upset
 ▶ v ▷ **devastate**
devastates v ▷ **devastate**
devastating v ▷ **devastate**
devastation n ▷ **devastate**
devastations n ▷ **devastate**
develop v (-s, -ing, -ed) grow or bring to a later,
 more elaborate, or more advanced stage
 > **development** n (pl -s)
developed v ▷ **develop**
developer n (pl -s) person who develops
 property
developers n ▷ **developer**
developing v ▷ **develop**
development n ▷ **develop**
developments n ▷ **develop**
develops v ▷ **develop**
deviance n ▷ **deviant**
deviances n ▷ **deviant**
deviant n (pl -s) ▶ adj (person) deviating from
 what is considered acceptable behaviour
 > **deviance** n (pl -s)
deviants n ▷ **deviant**
deviate v (-ates, -ating, -ated) differ from
 others in belief or thought > **deviation** n (pl -s)

deviated v ▷ **deviate**
deviates v ▷ **deviate**
deviating v ▷ **deviate**
deviation n ▷ **deviate**
deviations n ▷ **deviate**
device n (pl -s) machine or tool used for a
 specific task
devices n ▷ **device**
devil n (pl -s) evil spirit (Informal) ▶ v (-ils, -illing,
 -illed) prepare (food) with a highly flavoured
 spiced mixture
devilish adj cruel or unpleasant ▶ adv (also
 devilishly) (Informal) extremely
devilishly adv ▷ **devilish**
devilled v ▷ **devil**
devilling v ▷ **devil**
devil-may-care adj carefree and cheerful
devilment n (pl -s) mischievous conduct
devilments n ▷ **devilment**
devilries n ▷ **devilry**
devilry n (pl -ries) mischievousness
devils n, v ▷ **devil**
devious adj insincere and dishonest
 > **deviously** adv > **deviousness** n
deviously adv ▷ **devious**
deviousness n ▷ **devious**
devise v (-vises, -vising, -vised) work out
 (something) in one's mind
devised v ▷ **devise**
devises v ▷ **devise**
devising v ▷ **devise**
devoid adj (foll. by **of**) completely lacking (in)
devolution n (pl -s) transfer of authority from a
 central government to regional governments
devolutions n ▷ **devolution**
devolve v (-volves, -volving, -volved) (foll.
 by **on** or **to**) pass (power or duties) or (of
 power or duties) be passed to a successor or
 substitute
devolved v ▷ **devolve**
devolves v ▷ **devolve**
devolving v ▷ **devolve**
devote v (-votes, -voting, -voted) apply or
 dedicate to a particular purpose
devoted adj showing loyalty or devotion ▶ v
 ▷ **devote** > **devotedly** adv
devotedly adv ▷ **devoted**
devotee n (pl -s) person who is very
 enthusiastic about something
devotees n ▷ **devotee**
devotes v ▷ **devote**
devoting v ▷ **devote**
devotion n (pl -s) strong affection for or
 loyalty to someone or something ▶ pl prayers
 > **devotional** adj

devotional adj ▷ devotion
devotions adj ▷ devotion
devour v (-s, -ing, -ed) eat greedily
devoured v ▷ devour
devouring v ▷ devour
devours v ▷ devour
devout adj deeply religious > **devoutly** adv
> **devoutness** n
devoutly adv ▷ devout
devoutness n ▷ devout
dew n (pl -s) drops of water that form on the
ground at night from vapour in the air > **dewy**
adj (-wier, -wiest)
dewier adj ▷ dew
dewiest adj ▷ dew
dewlap n (pl -s) loose fold of skin hanging
under the throat in dogs, cattle, etc.
dewlaps n ▷ dewlap
dews n ▷ dew
dewy adj ▷ dew

> **dex** n (**dexes**). Dex is a slang word for a
> kind of amphetamine. This is an easy
> way to pick up a some points after
> another player has used an X. Dex
> scores 11 points.

dexterities n ▷ dexterity
dexterity n (pl -ities) skill in using one's hands
> **dexterous** adj > **dexterously** adv
dexterous adj ▷ dexterity
dexterously adv ▷ dexterity
dextrose n (pl -s) glucose occurring in fruit,
honey, and the blood of animals
dextroses n ▷ dextrose

> **dey** n (**deys**). A dey is an Ottoman
> governor. Dey scores 7 points.

diabetes [die-a-**beet**-eez] n disorder in which
an abnormal amount of urine containing
an excess of sugar is excreted > **diabetic** n
(pl -**s**) adj
diabetic n ▷ diabetes
diabetics n ▷ diabetes
diabolic adj of the Devil
diabolical adj (Informal) extremely bad
> **diabolically** adv > **diabolicalness** n
diabolically adv ▷ diabolical
diabolicalness n ▷ diabolical
diabolism n witchcraft, devil worship
> **diabolist** n (pl -s)
diabolist n ▷ diabolism
diabolists n ▷ diabolism
diaconate n (pl -s) position or period of office
of a deacon
diaconates n ▷ diaconate
diacritic n (pl -s) sign above or below a
character to indicate phonetic value or stress

diacritics n ▷ diacritic
diadem n (pl -s) (Old-fashioned) crown
diadems n ▷ diadem
diaereses n ▷ diaeresis
diaeresis n (pl -ses) mark (¨) placed over
a vowel to show that it is pronounced
separately from the preceding one, for
example in Noël
diagnosed v ▷ diagnosis
diagnoses n, v ▷ diagnosis
diagnosing v ▷ diagnosis
diagnosis [die-ag-no-siss] n (pl -ses) [-seez]
discovery and identification of diseases from
the examination of symptoms > **diagnose** v
(-noses, -nosing, -nosed) > **diagnostic** adj
diagnostic adj ▷ diagnosis
diagonal adj from corner to corner ▶ n (pl -s)
diagonal line > **diagonally** adv
diagonally adv ▷ diagonal
diagonals n ▷ diagonal
diagram n (pl -s) sketch showing the form or
workings of something > **diagrammatic** adj
diagrammatic adj ▷ diagram
diagrams n ▷ diagram
dial n (pl -s) face of a clock or watch ▶ v (**dials,**
dialling, dialled) operate the dial or buttons
on a telephone in order to contact (a number)
dialect n (pl -s) form of a language spoken in
a particular area > **dialectal** adj > **dialectally**
adv
dialectal adj ▷ dialect
dialectally adv ▷ dialect
dialectic n (pl -s) logical debate by question
and answer to resolve differences between
two views > **dialectical** adj > **dialectically** adv
dialectical adj ▷ dialectic
dialectically adv ▷ dialectic
dialectics n ▷ dialectic
dialects n ▷ dialect
dialled v ▷ dial
dialling v ▷ dial
dialogue n (pl -s) conversation between two
people, esp. in a book, film, or play
dialogues n ▷ dialogue
dials n, v ▷ dial
dialyses n ▷ dialysis
dialysis [die-al-iss-iss] n (pl -ses) (MED) filtering
of blood through a membrane to remove
waste products
diamanté [die-a-man-tee] adj decorated with
artificial jewels or sequins
diameter n (pl -s) (length of) a straight line
through the centre of a circle or sphere
diameters n ▷ diameter
diametric, diametrical adj of a diameter

> **diametrically** *adv*
diametrical *adj* ▷ **diametric**
diametrically *adv* ▷ **diametric**
diamond *n* (*pl* -**s**) exceptionally hard, usu. colourless, precious stone
  diamonds *n* ▷ **diamond**
diaper *n* (*pl* -**s**) (US) nappy
  diapers *n* ▷ **diaper**
diaphanous [die-**af**-fan-ous] *adj* fine and almost transparent > **diaphanously** *adv*
  diaphanously *adv* ▷ **diaphanous**
diaphragm [**die**-a-fram] *n* (*pl* -**s**) muscular partition that separates the abdominal cavity and chest cavity
  diaphragms *n* ▷ **diaphragm**
  diaries *n* ▷ **diary**
  diarist *n* ▷ **diary**
  diarists *n* ▷ **diary**
diarrhoea [die-a-**ree**-a] *n* (*pl* -**s**) frequent discharge of abnormally liquid faeces
  diarrhoeas *n* ▷ **diarrhoea**
diary *n* (*pl* -**ries**) (book for) a record of daily events, appointments, or observations
  > **diarist** *n* (*pl* -**s**)
diatribe *n* (*pl* -**s**) bitter critical attack
  diatribes *n* ▷ **diatribe**
dibble *n* (*pl* -**s**) small hand tool used to make holes in the ground for seeds or plants
  dibbles *n* ▷ **dibble**
dice *n* (*pl* **dice**) small cube each of whose sides has a different number of spots (1 to 6), used in games of chance ▸ *v* (**dices, dicing, diced**) cut (food) into small cubes
  diced *v* ▷ **dice**
  dices *v* ▷ **dice**
dicey *adj* (**dicier, diciest**) (*Informal*) dangerous or risky
  dichotomies *n* ▷ **dichotomy**
dichotomy [die-**kot**-a-mee] *n* (*pl* -**mies**) division into two opposed groups or parts
  dicier *adj* ▷ **dice**
  diciest *adj* ▷ **dice**
  dicing *v* ▷ **dice**
  dickier *adj* ▷ **dicky**[2]
  dickies *n* ▷ **dicky**[1]
  dickiest *adj* ▷ **dicky**[2]
dicky[1] *n* (*pl* **dickies**) false shirt front
dicky[2] *adj* (**dickier, dickiest**) (*Informal*) shaky or weak
dickybird *n* (*pl* -**s**) child's word for a bird
  dickybirds *n* ▷ **dickybird**
  dicta *n* ▷ **dictum**
dictate *v* (-**tes, -ting, -ted**) say aloud for someone else to write down (*foll. by* **to**) ▸ *n* (*pl* -**s**) authoritative command > **dictation**

n (*pl* -**s**)
  dictated *v* ▷ **dictate**
  dictates *v, n* ▷ **dictate**
  dictating *v* ▷ **dictate**
  dictation *n* ▷ **dictate**
  dictations *n* ▷ **dictate**
dictator *n* (*pl* -**s**) ruler who has complete power
  > **dictatorship** *n* (*pl* -**s**)
dictatorial *adj* like a dictator > **dictatorially** *adv*
  dictatorially *adv* ▷ **dictatorial**
  dictators *n* ▷ **dictator**
  dictatorship *n* ▷ **dictator**
  dictatorships *n* ▷ **dictator**
diction *n* (*pl* -**s**) manner of pronouncing words and sounds
  dictionaries *n* ▷ **dictionary**
dictionary *n* (*pl* -**aries**) book consisting of an alphabetical list of words with their meanings
  dictions *n* ▷ **diction**
dictum *n* (*pl* -**tums, -ta**) formal statement
  dictums *n* ▷ **dictum**
  did *v* ▷ **do**
didactic *adj* intended to instruct > **didactically** *adv*
  didactically *adv* ▷ **didactic**
diddle *v* (-**dles, -dling, -dled**) (*Informal*) swindle
  diddled *v* ▷ **diddle**
  diddles *v* ▷ **diddle**
  diddling *v* ▷ **diddle**
didgeridoo *n* (*pl* -**s**) Australian musical instrument made from a long hollow piece of wood
  didgeridoos *n* ▷ **didgeridoo**
didn't did not
die[1] *v* (**dies, dying, died**) (of a person, animal, or plant) cease all biological activity permanently
die[2] *n* (*pl* -**s**) shaped block used to cut or form metal
  died *v* ▷ **die**[1]
diehard *n* (*pl* -**s**) person who resists change
  diehards *n* ▷ **diehard**
  diereses *n* ▷ **dieresis**
dieresis [die-**air**-iss-iss] *n* (*pl* -**ses**) [-seez] ▷ **diaeresis**
  dies *v* ▷ **die**[1] ▸ *n* ▷ **die**[2]
diesel *n* (*pl* -**s**) diesel engine
  diesels *n* ▷ **diesel**
diet[1] *n* (*pl* -**s**) food that a person or animal regularly eats ▸ *v* (-**s, -ing, -ed**) follow a special diet so as to lose weight ▸ *adj* (of food) suitable for a weight-reduction diet > **dietary** *adj* > **dieter** *n* (*pl* -**s**)

diet² n (pl **-s**) parliament of some countries
   dietary adj ▷ **diet**
   dieted v ▷ **diet**
   dieter n ▷ **diet**
   dieters n ▷ **diet**
dietetic adj prepared for special dietary requirements
dietetics n study of diet and nutrition
dietician n (pl **-s**) person who specializes in dietetics
   dieticians n ▷ **dietician**
   dieting v ▷ **diet**
   diets v ▷ **diet¹** ▶ n ▷ **diet¹, ²**
differ v (**-s, -ing, -ed**) be unlike
   differed v ▷ **differ**
difference n (pl **-s**) state of being unlike
   differences n ▷ **difference**
different adj unlike > **differently** adv
differential adj of or using a difference ▶ n (pl **-s**) factor that differentiates between two comparable things > **differentially** adv
   differentially adv ▷ **differential**
   differentials n ▷ **differential**
differentiate v, v (**-te, -ting, -ted**) perceive or show the difference (between) > **differentiation** n (pl **-s**)
   differentiated v ▷ **differentiate**
   differentiates v ▷ **differentiate**
   differentiating v ▷ **differentiate**
   differentiation n ▷ **differentiate**
   differentiations n ▷ **differentiate**
   differently n ▷ **different**
   differing v ▷ **differ**
   differs v ▷ **differ**
difficult adj requiring effort or skill to do or understand > **difficultly** adv > **difficulty** n (pl **-ties**)
   difficulties n ▷ **difficult**
   difficultly adv ▷ **difficult**
   difficulty n ▷ **difficult**
   diffidence n ▷ **diffident**
   diffidences n ▷ **diffident**
diffident adj lacking self-confidence > **diffidence** n (pl **-s**) > **diffidently** adv
   diffidently adv ▷ **diffident**
diffraction n (pl **-s**) (PHYSICS) deviation in the direction of a wave at the edge of an obstacle in its path
   diffractions n ▷ **diffraction**
diffuse v (**-fuses, -fusing, -fused**) spread over a wide area ▶ adj widely spread > **diffusely** adv > **diffuseness** n > **diffusion** n (pl **-s**)
   diffused v ▷ **diffuse**
   diffusely adv ▷ **diffuse**
   diffuseness n ▷ **diffuse**

diffuses v ▷ **diffuse**
diffusing v ▷ **diffuse**
diffusion n ▷ **diffuse**
diffusions n ▷ **diffuse**
dig v (**digs, digging, dug**) cut into, break up, and turn over or remove (earth), esp. with a spade ▶ n (pl **-s**) digging ▶ pl (pl **-s**) (BRIT, AUST & S AFR) (Informal) lodgings
digest v (**-s, -ing, -ed**) subject to a process of digestion ▶ n (pl **-s**) shortened version of a book, report, or article > **digestible** adj > **digestibility** n > **digestive** adj > **digestively** adv
   digested v ▷ **digest**
   digestibility n ▷ **digest**
   digestible adj ▷ **digest**
   digesting v ▷ **digest**
digestion n (pl **-s**) (body's system for) breaking down food into easily absorbed substances
   digestions n ▷ **digestion**
   digestive adj ▷ **digest**
   digestively adv ▷ **digest**
   digests v, n ▷ **digest**
digger n (pl **-s**) machine used for digging
   diggers n ▷ **digger**
   digging v ▷ **dig**
   diggings n ▷ **dig**
digit [dij-it] n (pl **-s**) finger or toe
digital adj displaying information as numbers rather than with hands and a dial > **digitally** adv
digitalis n drug made from foxglove leaves, used as a heart stimulant
   digitally adv ▷ **digital**
   digits n ▷ **digit**
   dignified n ▷ **dignify**
   dignifies n ▷ **dignify**
dignify v (**-s, -ing, -ed**) add distinction to
   dignifying v ▷ **dignify**
   dignitaries n ▷ **dignitary**
dignitary n (pl **-aries**) person of high official position
   dignities n ▷ **dignity**
dignity n (pl **-ties**) serious, calm, and controlled behaviour or manner
digress v (**-es, -ing, -ed**) depart from the main subject in speech or writing > **digression** n (pl **-s**)
   digressed v ▷ **digress**
   digresses v ▷ **digress**
   digressing v ▷ **digress**
   digression n ▷ **digress**
   digressions n ▷ **digress**
   digs v, n ▷ **dig**
dike n (pl **-s**) ▷ **dyke**

dikes n ▷ dike
dilapidated adj (of a building) having fallen into ruin > **dilapidation** n (pl -s)
dilapidation n ▷ dilapidated
dilapidations n ▷ dilapidated
dilatation n ▷ dilate
dilatations n ▷ dilate
dilate v (-lates, -lating, -lated) make or become wider or larger > **dilation, dilatation** n (pl -s)
dilated v ▷ dilate
dilates v ▷ dilate
dilating v ▷ dilate
dilation n ▷ dilate
dilations n ▷ dilate
dilatorily adv ▷ dilatory
dilatoriness n ▷ dilatory
dilatory [dill-a-tree] adj tending or intended to waste time > **dilatorily** adv > **dilatoriness** n
dilemma n (pl -s) situation offering a choice between two equally undesirable alternatives
dilemmas n ▷ dilemma
dilettante [dill-it-**tan**-tee] n (pl -**tantes**, -**tanti**) person whose interest in a subject is superficial rather than serious > **dilettantism** n
dilettantes n ▷ dilettante
dilettanti n ▷ dilettante
dilettantism n ▷ dilettante
diligence n ▷ diligent
diligent adj careful and persevering in carrying out duties > **diligently** adv > **diligence** n
diligently adv ▷ diligent
dill n (pl -s) sweet-smelling herb
dills n ▷ dill
dilute v (-lutes, -luting, -luted) make (a liquid) less concentrated, esp. by adding water > **dilution** n (pl -s)
diluted v ▷ dilute
dilutes v ▷ dilute
diluting v ▷ dilute
dilution n ▷ dilute
dilutions n ▷ dilute
diluvial, diluvian adj of a flood, esp. the great Flood described in the Old Testament
diluvian adj ▷ diluvial
dim adj (dimmer, dimmest) badly lit ▶ v (dims, dimming, dimmed) make or become dim > **dimly** adv > **dimness** n
dime n (pl -s) coin of the US and Canada, worth ten cents
dimension n (pl -s) measurement of the size of something in a particular direction
dimensions n ▷ dimension

dimes n ▷ dime
diminish v (-es, -ing, -ed) make or become smaller, fewer, or less > **diminution** n (pl -s)
diminished v ▷ diminish
diminishes v ▷ diminish
diminishing v ▷ diminish
diminuendo n (pl -s) (MUSIC) gradual decrease in loudness
diminuendos n ▷ diminuendo
diminution n ▷ diminish
diminutions n ▷ diminish
diminutive adj very small ▶ n (pl -s) word or affix which implies smallness or unimportance > **diminutively** adv > **diminutiveness** n
diminutively adv ▷ diminutive
diminutiveness n ▷ diminutive
diminutives n ▷ diminutive
dimly adv ▷ dim
dimmed v ▷ dim
dimmer n (pl -s) device for dimming an electric light ▶ adj ▷ dim
dimmers n ▷ dimmer
dimmest adj ▷ dim
dimming v ▷ dim
dimness n ▷ dim
dimple n (pl -s) small natural dent, esp. in the cheeks or chin ▶ v (-ples, -pling, -pled) produce dimples by smiling
dimpled v ▷ dimple
dimples n, v ▷ dimple
dimpling v ▷ dimple
dims v ▷ dim
din n (pl -s) loud unpleasant confused noise ▶ v (dins, dinning, dinned) (foll. by into) instil (something) into someone by constant repetition
dinar [dee-nahr] n (pl -s) monetary unit of various Balkan, Middle Eastern, and North African countries
dinars n ▷ dinar
dine v (dines, dining, dined) eat dinner
dined v ▷ dine
diner n (pl -s) person eating a meal
diners n ▷ diner
dines v ▷ dine
ding n (pl -s) (AUST DATED & NZ) (Informal) small dent in a vehicle
dinghies n ▷ dinghy
dinghy [ding-ee] n (pl -ghies) small boat, powered by sails, oars, or a motor
dingier adj ▷ dingy
dingiest adj ▷ dingy
dinginess n ▷ dingy
dingo n (pl -goes) Australian wild dog

dingoes n ▷ dingo
dings n ▷ ding
dingy [din-jee] adj (-gier, -giest) (BRIT, AUST & NZ) dull and drab > **dinginess** n
dining v ▷ dine
dinkier adj ▷ dinky
dinkiest adj ▷ dinky
dinkum adj (AUST & NZ) (Informal) genuine or right
dinky adj (-kier, -kiest) (BRIT, AUST & NZ) (Informal) small and neat
dinned v ▷ din
dinner n (pl -s) main meal of the day, eaten either in the evening or at midday
dinners n ▷ dinner
dinning v ▷ din
dinosaur n (pl -s) type of extinct prehistoric reptile, many of which were of gigantic size
dinosaurs n ▷ dinosaur
dins n, v ▷ din
dint n (pl -s) means
dints n ▷ dint
diocesan adj ▷ diocese
diocese [die-a-siss] n (pl -s) district over which a bishop has control > **diocesan** adj
dioceses n ▷ diocese
diode n (pl -s) semiconductor device for converting alternating current to direct current
diodes n ▷ diode
dioptre [die-op-ter] n (pl -s) unit for measuring the refractive power of a lens
dioptres n ▷ dioptre
dioxide n (pl -s) oxide containing two oxygen atoms per molecule
dioxides n ▷ dioxide
dip v (dips, dipping, dipped) plunge quickly or briefly into a liquid ▶ n (pl -s) dipping
diphtheria [dif-theer-ya] n (pl -s) contagious disease producing fever and difficulty in breathing and swallowing
diphtherias n ▷ diphtheria
diphthong n (pl -s) union of two vowel sounds in a single compound sound
diphthongs n ▷ diphthong
diploma n (pl -s) qualification awarded by a college on successful completion of a course
diplomacies n ▷ diplomacy
diplomacy n (pl -macies) conduct of the relations between nations by peaceful means
diplomas n ▷ diploma
diplomat n (pl -s) official engaged in diplomacy
diplomatic adj of diplomacy > **diplomatically** adv

diplomatically adv ▷ diplomatic
diplomats n ▷ diplomat
dipped v ▷ dip
dipper n (pl -s) ladle used for dipping
dippers n ▷ dipper
dipping v ▷ dip
diprotodont [die-pro-toe-dont] n (pl -s) marsupial with fewer than three upper incisor teeth on each side of the jaw
diprotodonts n ▷ diprotodont
dips v, n ▷ dip
dipsomania n (pl -s) compulsive craving for alcohol > **dipsomaniac** n (pl -s) adj
dipsomaniac n, adj ▷ dipsomania
dipsomaniacs n ▷ dipsomania
dipsomanias n ▷ dipsomania
diptych [dip-tik] n (pl -s) painting on two hinged panels
diptychs n ▷ diptych
dire adj (-er, -est) disastrous, urgent, or terrible > **direly** adv > **direness** n (pl -es)
direct adj (of a route) shortest, straight ▶ adv in a direct manner ▶ v (-s, -ing, -ed) lead and organize > **directness** n
directed v ▷ direct
directing v ▷ direct
direction n (pl -s) course or line along which a person or thing moves, points, or lies ▶ pl instructions for doing something or for reaching a place > **directional** adj
directional adj ▷ direction
directions n ▷ direction
directive n (pl -s) instruction, order
directives n ▷ directive
directly adv in a direct manner ▶ conj as soon as
directness n ▷ direct
director n (pl -s) person or thing that directs or controls > **directorial** adj > **directorship** n (pl -s)
directorate n (pl -s) board of directors
directorates n ▷ directorate
directorial adj ▷ director
directories n ▷ directory
directors n ▷ director
directorship n ▷ director
directorships n ▷ director
directory n (pl -ries) book listing names, addresses, and telephone numbers
directs v ▷ direct
direly adv ▷ dire
direness n ▷ dire
direnesses n ▷ dire
direr adj ▷ dire
direst adj ▷ dire

dirge n (pl -s) slow sad song of mourning
  dirges n ▷ dirge
dirigible [dir-rij-jib-bl] adj able to be steered ▶ n
  (pl -s) airship
  dirigibles n ▷ dirigible
dirk n (pl -s) dagger, formerly worn by Scottish
  Highlanders
  dirks n ▷ dirk
dirndl n (pl -s) full gathered skirt originating
  from Tyrolean peasant wear
  dirndls n ▷ dirndl
dirt n (pl -s) unclean substance, filth
  dirtied v ▷ dirty
  dirtier adj ▷ dirty
  dirties v ▷ dirty
  dirtiest adj ▷ dirty
  dirtily adv ▷ dirty
  dirtiness n ▷ dirty
  dirts n ▷ dirt
dirty adj (**dirtier, dirtiest**) covered or marked
  with dirt ▶ v (**dirties, dirtying, dirtied**) make
  dirty > **dirtily** adv > **dirtiness** n
  dirtying v ▷ dirty
  disabilities n ▷ disability
disability n (pl -ties) condition of being
  disabled
disable v (-bles, -bling, -bled) make ineffective,
  unfit, or incapable > **disablement** n
disabled adj lacking a physical power, such as
  the ability to walk ▶ v ▷ disable
  disablement n ▷ disable
  disables v ▷ disable
  disabling v ▷ disable
disabuse v (-buses, -busing, -bused) (foll. by of)
  rid (someone) of a mistaken idea
  disabused v ▷ disabuse
  disabuses v ▷ disabuse
  disabusing v ▷ disabuse
disadvantage n (pl -s) unfavourable or
  harmful circumstance > **disadvantageous**
  adj > **disadvantageously** adv
  > **disadvantageousness** n
disadvantaged adj socially or economically
  deprived
  disadvantageous adj ▷ disadvantage
  disadvantageously adv ▷ disadvantage
  disadvantageousness n ▷ disadvantage
  disadvantages n ▷ disadvantage
disaffected adj having lost loyalty to or
  affection for someone or something
  > **disaffectedly** adv > **disaffection** n (pl -s)
  disaffectedly adv ▷ disaffected
  disaffection n ▷ disaffected
  disaffections n ▷ disaffected
disagree v (-grees, -greeing, -greed) argue

or have different opinions > **disagreement**
  n (pl -s)
disagreeable adj unpleasant
  > **disagreeableness** n > **disagreeably** adv
  disagreeableness n ▷ disagreeable
  disagreeably adv ▷ disagreeable
  disagreed v ▷ disagree
  disagreeing v ▷ disagree
  disagreement n ▷ disagree
  disagreements n ▷ disagree
  disagrees v ▷ disagree
disallow v (-s, -ing, -ed) reject as untrue or
  invalid
  disallowed v ▷ disallow
  disallowing v ▷ disallow
  disallows v ▷ disallow
disappear v (-s, -ing, -ed) cease to be visible
  > **disappearance** n (pl -s)
  disappearance n ▷ disappear
  disappearances n ▷ disappear
  disappeared v ▷ disappear
  disappearing v ▷ disappear
  disappears v ▷ disappear
disappoint v (-s, -ing, -ed) fail to meet the
  expectations or hopes of > **disappointingly**
  adv
  disappointed v ▷ disappoint
  disappointing v ▷ disappoint
  disappointingly adv ▷ disappoint
disappointment n (pl -s) feeling of being
  disappointed
  disappointments n ▷ disappointment
  disappoints v ▷ disappoint
disapprobation n (pl -s) disapproval
  disapprobations n ▷ disapprobation
  disapproval n ▷ disapprove
  disapprovals n ▷ disapprove
disapprove v (-proves, -proving, -proved) (foll.
  by of) consider wrong or bad > **disapproval**
  n (pl -s)
  disapproved v ▷ disapprove
  disapproves v ▷ disapprove
  disapproving v ▷ disapprove
disarm v (-s, -ing, -ed) deprive of weapons
  > **disarmament** n (pl -s)
  disarmament n ▷ disarm
  disarmaments n ▷ disarm
  disarmed v ▷ disarm
disarming adj removing hostility or suspicion
  ▶ v ▷ disarm > **disarmingly** adv
  disarmingly adv ▷ disarming
  disarms v ▷ disarm
disarrange v (-ranges, -ranging, -ranged)
  throw into disorder
  disarranged v ▷ disarrange

disarranges v ▷ **disarrange**
disarranging v ▷ **disarrange**
disarray n (pl **-s**) confusion and lack of
discipline
 disarrays n ▷ **disarray**
disaster n (pl **-s**) occurrence that causes great
distress or destruction > **disastrous** adj
 > **disastrously** adv
 disasters n ▷ **disaster**
 disastrous adj ▷ **disaster**
 disastrously adv ▷ **disaster**
disavow v (**-s, -ing, -ed**) deny connection with
or responsibility for > **disavowal** n (pl **-s**)
 disavowal n ▷ **disavow**
 disavowals n ▷ **disavow**
 disavowed v ▷ **disavow**
 disavowing v ▷ **disavow**
 disavows v ▷ **disavow**
disband v (**-s, -ing, -ed**) (cause to) cease to
function as a group
 disbanded v ▷ **disband**
 disbanding v ▷ **disband**
 disbands v ▷ **disband**
 disbelief n ▷ **disbelieve**
disbelieve v (**-lieves, -lieving, -lieved**) reject as
false (foll. by **in**) > **disbelief** n
 disbelieved v ▷ **disbelieve**
 disbelieves v ▷ **disbelieve**
 disbelieving v ▷ **disbelieve**
disburse v (**-burses, -bursing, -bursed**) pay out
 > **disbursement** n (pl **-s**)
 disbursed v ▷ **disburse**
 disbursement n ▷ **disburse**
 disbursements n ▷ **disburse**
 disburses v ▷ **disburse**
 disbursing v ▷ **disburse**
disc n (pl **-s**) flat circular object ▷ **disk**
discard v (**-s, -ing, -ed**) get rid of (something or
someone) as useless or undesirable
 discarded v ▷ **discard**
 discarding v ▷ **discard**
 discards v ▷ **discard**
discern v (**-s, -ing, -ed**) see or be aware
of (something) clearly > **discernible** adj
 > **discernibly** adv > **discernment** n (pl **-s**)
 discerned v ▷ **discern**
 discernible adj ▷ **discern**
 discernibly adv ▷ **discern**
discerning adj having good judgment ▶ v
 ▷ **discern**
 discernment n ▷ **discern**
 discernments n ▷ **discern**
 discerns v ▷ **discern**
discharge v (**-charges, -charging, -charged**)
release, allow to go ▶ n (pl **-s**) substance that

comes out from a place
 discharged v ▷ **discharge**
 discharges v, n ▷ **discharge**
 discharging v ▷ **discharge**
disciple [diss-**sipe**-pl] n (pl **-s**) follower of the
doctrines of a teacher, esp. Jesus Christ
 disciples n ▷ **disciple**
disciplinarian n (pl **-s**) person who practises
strict discipline
 disciplinarians n ▷ **disciplinarian**
 disciplinary adj ▷ **discipline**
discipline n (pl **-s**) practice of imposing strict
rules of behaviour ▶ v (**-plines, -plining,
-plined**) attempt to improve the behaviour
of (oneself or another) by training or rules
 > **disciplinary** adj
disciplined adj able to behave and work in a
controlled way ▶ v ▷ **discipline**
 disciplines n, v ▷ **discipline**
 disciplining v ▷ **discipline**
 disclaimed v ▷ **disclaimer**
disclaimer n (pl **-s**) statement denying
responsibility > **disclaim** v (**-s, -ing, -ed**)
 disclaimers n ▷ **disclaimer**
 disclaiming v ▷ **disclaimer**
 disclaims v ▷ **disclaimer**
disclose v (**-closes, -closing, -closed**) make
known > **disclosure** n (pl **-s**)
 disclosed v ▷ **disclose**
 discloses v ▷ **disclose**
 disclosing v ▷ **disclose**
 disclosure n ▷ **disclose**
 disclosures n ▷ **disclose**
disco n (pl **-s**) nightclub where people dance to
amplified pop records
 discoloration n ▷ **discolour**
 discolorations n ▷ **discolour**
discolour v (**-s, -ing, -ed**) change in colour, fade
 > **discoloration** n (pl **-s**)
 discoloured v ▷ **discolour**
 discolouring v ▷ **discolour**
 discolours v ▷ **discolour**
discomfit v (**-s, -ing, -ed**) make uneasy or
confused > **discomfiture** n (pl **-s**)
 discomfited v ▷ **discomfit**
 discomfiting v ▷ **discomfit**
 discomfits v ▷ **discomfit**
 discomfiture n ▷ **discomfit**
 discomfitures n ▷ **discomfit**
discomfort n (pl **-s**) inconvenience, distress,
or mild pain
 discomforts n ▷ **discomfort**
discommode v (**-modes, -moding, -moded**)
cause inconvenience to
 discommoded v ▷ **discommode**

discommodes v ▷ discommode
discommoding v ▷ discommode
disconcert v (-s, -ing, -ed) embarrass or upset
disconcerted v ▷ disconcert
disconcerting v ▷ disconcert
disconcerts v ▷ disconcert
disconnect v (-s, -ing, -ed) undo or break the connection between (two things) > **disconnection** n (pl -s)
disconnected adj (of speech or ideas) not logically connected ▶ v ▷ **disconnect**
disconnecting v ▷ disconnect
disconnection n ▷ disconnect
disconnections n ▷ disconnect
disconnects v ▷ disconnect
disconsolate adj sad beyond comfort > **disconsolately** adv
disconsolately adv ▷ disconsolate
discontent n (pl -s) lack of contentment > **discontented** adj > **discontentedly** adv
discontented adj ▷ discontent
discontentedly adv ▷ discontent
discontents n ▷ discontent
discontinue v (-nues, -nuing, -nued) come or bring to an end
discontinued v ▷ discontinue
discontinues v ▷ discontinue
discontinuing v ▷ discontinue
discontinuities n ▷ discontinuous
discontinuity n ▷ discontinuous
discontinuous adj characterized by interruptions > **discontinuity** n (pl -nuities)
discord n (pl -s) lack of agreement or harmony between people > **discordant** adj > **discordantly** adv > **discordance** n (pl -s)
discordance n ▷ discord
discordances n ▷ discord
discordant adj ▷ discord
discordantly adv ▷ discord
discords n ▷ discord
discos n ▷ disco
discotheque n (pl -s) ▷ disco
discotheques n ▷ discotheque
discount v (-s, -ing, -ed) take no account of (something) because it is considered to be unreliable, prejudiced, or irrelevant ▶ n (pl -s) deduction from the full price of something
discounted v ▷ discount
discounting v ▷ discount
discounts v, n ▷ discount
discourage v (-rages, -raging, -raged) deprive of the will to persist in something > **discouragement** n (pl -s)
discouraged v ▷ discourage
discouragement n ▷ discourage

discouragements n ▷ discourage
discourages v ▷ discourage
discouraging v ▷ discourage
discourse n (pl -s) conversation ▶ v (-ses, -sing, -sed) (foll. by on) speak or write (about) at length
discoursed v ▷ discourse
discourses n, v ▷ discourse
discoursing v ▷ discourse
discourteous adj showing bad manners > **discourteously** adv > **discourtesy** n (pl -esies)
discourteously adv ▷ discourteous
discourtesies n ▷ discourteous
discourtesy n ▷ discourteous
discover v (-s, -ing, -ed) be the first to find or to find out about > **discoverer** n (pl -s)
discovered v ▷ discover
discoverer n ▷ discover
discoverers n ▷ discover
discoveries n ▷ discovery
discovering v ▷ discover
discovers v ▷ discover
discovery n (pl -eries) discovering
discredit v (-s, -ing, -ed) damage the reputation of ▶ n (pl -s) damage to someone's reputation
discreditable adj bringing shame
discredited v ▷ discredit
discrediting v ▷ discredit
discredits v, n ▷ discredit
discreet adj (-er, -est) careful to avoid embarrassment, esp. by keeping confidences secret > **discreetly** adv > **discreetness** n (pl -es)
discreeter adj ▷ discreet
discreetest adj ▷ discreet
discreetly adv ▷ discreet
discreetness n ▷ discreet
discreetnesses n ▷ discreet
discrepancies n ▷ discrepancy
discrepancy n (pl -cies) conflict or variation between facts, figures, or claims
discrete adj (-r, -st) separate, distinct > **discretely** adv > **discreteness** n (pl -es)
discretely adv ▷ discrete
discreteness n ▷ discrete
discretenesses n ▷ discrete
discreter adj ▷ discrete
discretest adj ▷ discrete
discretion n (pl -s) quality of behaving in a discreet way > **discretionary** adj
discretionary adj ▷ discretion
discretions n ▷ discretion
discriminate v (-nates, -nating, -nated) (foll. by against or in favour of) single

out (a particular person or group) for
worse or better treatment than others
> **discrimination** n (pl -s)
discriminated v ▷ **discriminate**
discriminates v ▷ **discriminate**
discriminating adj showing good taste and
judgment ▶ v ▷ **discriminate**
discrimination n ▷ **discriminate**
discriminations n ▷ **discriminate**
discriminatory adj based on prejudice
discs n ▷ **disc**
discursive adj passing from one topic to
another > **discursively** adv > **discursiveness** n
discursively adv ▷ **discursive**
discursiveness n ▷ **discursive**
discus n (pl -es) heavy disc-shaped object
thrown in sports competitions
discuses n ▷ **discus**
discuss v (-es, -ing, -ed) consider (something)
by talking it over > **discussion** n (pl -s)
discussed v ▷ **discuss**
discusses v ▷ **discuss**
discussing v ▷ **discuss**
discussion n ▷ **discuss**
discussions n ▷ **discuss**
disdain n feeling of superiority and dislike ▶ v
(-s, -ing, -ed) refuse with disdain > **disdainful**
adj > **disdainfully** adv
disdained v ▷ **disdain**
disdainful adj ▷ **disdain**
disdainfully adv ▷ **disdain**
disdaining v ▷ **disdain**
disdains v ▷ **disdain**
disease n (pl -s) illness, sickness > **diseased** adj
diseased n ▷ **disease**
diseases n ▷ **disease**
disembark v (-s, -ing, -ed) get off a ship,
aircraft, or bus > **disembarkation** n (pl -s)
disembarkation n ▷ **disembark**
disembarkations n ▷ **disembark**
disembarked v ▷ **disembark**
disembarking v ▷ **disembark**
disembarks v ▷ **disembark**
disembodied adj lacking a body
disembowel v (-els, -elling, -elled) remove the
entrails of
disembowelled v ▷ **disembowel**
disembowelling v ▷ **disembowel**
disembowels v ▷ **disembowel**
disenchanted adj disappointed and
disillusioned > **disenchantment** n (pl -s)
disenchantment n ▷ **disenchant**
disenchantments n ▷ **disenchant**
disenfranchise, disfranchise v (-ises,
-ising, -ised) deprive (someone) of the right

to vote or of other rights of citizenship
> **disenfranchisement** n (pl -s)
disenfranchised v ▷ **disenfranchise**
disenfranchisement n ▷ **disenfranchise**
disenfranchisements n ▷ **disenfranchise**
disenfranchises v ▷ **disenfranchise**
disenfranchising v ▷ **disenfranchise**
disengage v (-gages, -gaging, -gaged) release
from a connection > **disengagement** n (pl -s)
disengaged v ▷ **disengage**
disengagement n ▷ **disengage**
disengagements n ▷ **disengage**
disengages v ▷ **disengage**
disengaging v ▷ **disengage**
disentangle v (-tangles, -tangling, -tangled)
release from entanglement or confusion
disentangled v ▷ **disentangle**
disentangles v ▷ **disentangle**
disentangling v ▷ **disentangle**
disfavour n (pl -s) disapproval or dislike
disfavours n ▷ **disfavour**
disfigure v (-gures, -guring, -gured) spoil the
appearance of > **disfigurement** n (pl -s)
disfigured v ▷ **disfigure**
disfigurement n ▷ **disfigure**
disfigurements n ▷ **disfigure**
disfigures v ▷ **disfigure**
disfiguring v ▷ **disfigure**
disfranchise v (-ises, -ising, -ised)
▷ **disenfranchise**
disfranchised v ▷ **disfranchise**
disfranchises v ▷ **disfranchise**
disfranchising v ▷ **disfranchise**
disgorge v (-gorges, -gorging, -gorged) empty
out, discharge
disgorged v ▷ **disgorge**
disgorges v ▷ **disgorge**
disgorging v ▷ **disgorge**
disgrace n (pl -s) condition of shame, loss of
reputation, or dishonour ▶ v (-graces,
-gracing, -graced) bring shame upon (oneself
or others) > **disgraceful** adj > **disgracefully**
adv
disgraced v ▷ **disgrace**
disgraceful adj ▷ **disgrace**
disgracefully adv ▷ **disgrace**
disgraces n, v ▷ **disgrace**
disgracing v ▷ **disgrace**
disgruntled adj sulky or discontented
> **disgruntlement** n
disgruntlement n ▷ **disgruntled**
disguise v (-guises, -guising, -guised) change
the appearance or manner in order to conceal
the identity of (someone or something)
▶ n (pl -s) mask, costume, or manner that

disguises
disguised v ▷ disguise
disguises v, n ▷ disguise
disguising v ▷ disguise
disgust n (pl -s) great loathing or distaste ▶ v (-s, -ing, -ed) sicken, fill with loathing
disgusted v ▷ disgust
disgusting v ▷ disgust
disgusts v ▷ disgust
dish n (pl -es) shallow container used for holding or serving food
dishabille [diss-a-beel] n (pl -s) ▷ **deshabille**
dishabilles n ▷ dishabille
dishcloth n (pl -s) cloth for washing dishes
dishcloths n ▷ dishcloth
dishearten v (-s, -ing, -ed) weaken or destroy the hope, courage, or enthusiasm of
disheartened v ▷ dishearten
disheartening v ▷ dishearten
disheartens v ▷ dishearten
dishes n ▷ dish
dishevelled adj (of a person's hair, clothes, or general appearance) disordered and untidy
dishonest adj not honest or fair > **dishonestly** adv > **dishonesty** n (pl -ties)
dishonesties n ▷ dishonest
dishonestly adv ▷ dishonest
dishonesty n ▷ dishonest
dishonour v (-s, -ing, -ed) treat with disrespect ▶ n (pl -s) lack of respect > **dishonourable** adj > **dishonourably** adv
dishonourable adj ▷ dishonour
dishonourably adv ▷ dishonour
dishonoured v ▷ dishonour
dishonouring v ▷ dishonour
dishonours v, n ▷ dishonour
disillusion v (-s, -ing, -ed) destroy the illusions or false ideas of (also **disillusionment**) ▶ n (pl -s) state of being disillusioned
disillusioned v ▷ disillusion
disillusioning v ▷ disillusion
disillusionment n ▷ disillusion
disillusionments n ▷ disillusion
disillusions v, n ▷ disillusion
disincentive n (pl -s) something that acts as a deterrent
disincentives n ▷ disincentive
disinclination n ▷ disinclined
disinclinations n ▷ disinclined
disinclined adj unwilling, reluctant > **disinclination** n (pl -s)
disinfect v (-s, -ing, -ed) rid of harmful germs, chemically > **disinfection** n (pl -s)
disinfectant n (pl -s) substance that destroys harmful germs

disinfectants n ▷ disinfectant
disinfected v ▷ disinfect
disinfecting v ▷ disinfect
disinfection n ▷ disinfect
disinfections n ▷ disinfect
disinfects v ▷ disinfect
disinformation n false information intended to mislead
disingenuous adj not sincere > **disingenuously** adv > **disingenuousness** n
disingenuously adv ▷ disingenuous
disingenuousness n ▷ disingenuous
disinherit v (-s, -ing, -ed) (LAW) deprive (an heir) of inheritance > **disinheritance** n (pl -s)
disinheritance n ▷ disinherit
disinheritances n ▷ disinherit
disinherited v ▷ disinherit
disinheriting v ▷ disinherit
disinherits v ▷ disinherit
disintegrate v (-rates, -rating, -rated) break up > **disintegration** n (pl -s)
disintegrated v ▷ disintegrate
disintegrates v ▷ disintegrate
disintegrating v ▷ disintegrate
disintegration n ▷ disintegrate
disintegrations n ▷ disintegrate
disinter v (-ters, -terring, -terred) dig up
disinterest n ▷ disinterested
disinterested adj free from bias or involvement > **disinterest** n > **disinterestedly** adv > **disinterestedness** n
disinterestedly adv ▷ disinterested
disinterestedness n ▷ disinterested
disinterred v ▷ disinter
disinterring v ▷ disinter
disinters v ▷ disinter
disjointed adj having no coherence, disconnected > **disjointedly** adv
disjointedly adv ▷ disjointed
disk n (pl -s) (COMPUTERS) storage device, consisting of a stack of plates coated with a magnetic layer, which rotates rapidly as a single unit
disks n ▷ disk
dislike v (-likes, -liking, -liked) consider unpleasant or disagreeable ▶ n (pl -s) feeling of not liking something or someone
disliked v ▷ dislike
dislikes v, n ▷ dislike
disliking v ▷ dislike
dislocate v (-cates, -cating, -cated) displace (a bone or joint) from its normal position > **dislocation** n (pl -s)
dislocated v ▷ dislocate
dislocates v ▷ dislocate

dislocating v ▷ **dislocate**
dislocation n ▷ **dislocate**
dislocations n ▷ **dislocate**
dislodge v (**-lodges, -lodging, -lodged**) remove (something) from a previously fixed position
dislodged v ▷ **dislodge**
dislodges v ▷ **dislodge**
dislodging v ▷ **dislodge**
disloyal adj not loyal, deserting one's allegiance > **disloyalty** n (pl **-ties**)
disloyalties n ▷ **disloyalty**
dismal adj gloomy and depressing > **dismally** adv > **dismalness** n
dismally adv ▷ **dismal**
dismalness n ▷ **dismal**
dismantle v (**-mantles, -mantling, -mantled**) take apart piece by piece
dismantled v ▷ **dismantle**
dismantles v ▷ **dismantle**
dismantling v ▷ **dismantle**
dismay v (**-s, -ing, -ed**) fill with alarm or depression ▸ n (pl **-s**) alarm mixed with sadness
dismayed v ▷ **dismay**
dismaying v ▷ **dismay**
dismays v, n ▷ **dismay**
dismember v (**-s, -ing, -ed**) remove the limbs of > **dismemberment** n (pl **-s**)
dismembered v ▷ **dismember**
dismembering v ▷ **dismember**
dismemberment n ▷ **dismember**
dismemberments n ▷ **dismember**
dismembers v ▷ **dismember**
dismiss v (**-es, -ing, -ed**) remove (an employee) from a job > **dismissal** n (pl **-s**)
dismissal n ▷ **dismiss**
dismissals n ▷ **dismiss**
dismissed v ▷ **dismiss**
dismisses v ▷ **dismiss**
dismissing v ▷ **dismiss**
dismissive adj scornful, contemptuous
dismount v (**-s, -ing, -ed**) get off a horse or bicycle
dismounted v ▷ **dismount**
dismounting v ▷ **dismount**
dismounts v ▷ **dismount**
disobedience n ▷ **disobey**
disobedient adj ▷ **disobey**
disobediently adv ▷ **disobey**
disobey v (**-s, -ing, -ed**) neglect or refuse to obey > **disobedient** adj > **disobediently** adv > **disobedience** n
disobeyed v ▷ **disobey**
disobeying v ▷ **disobey**
disobeys v ▷ **disobey**

disobliging adj unwilling to help
disorder n (pl **-s**) state of untidiness and disorganization
disordered adj untidy
disorderliness n ▷ **disorderly**
disorderly adj untidy and disorganized > **disorderliness** n
disorders n ▷ **disorder**
disorganization n ▷ **disorganize**
disorganizations n ▷ **disorganize**
disorganize v (**-nizes, -nizing, -nized**) disrupt the arrangement or system of > **disorganization** n (pl **-s**)
disorganized v ▷ **disorganize**
disorganizes v ▷ **disorganize**
disorganizing v ▷ **disorganize**
disorientate, disorient v (**-tates, -tating, -tated, -s, -ing, -ed**) cause (someone) to lose his or her bearings > **disorientation** n (pl **-s**)
disorientated v ▷ **disorientate**
disorientates v ▷ **disorientate**
disorientating v ▷ **disorientate**
disorientation n ▷ **disorientate**
disorientations n ▷ **disorientate**
disoriented v ▷ **disorientate**
disorienting v ▷ **disorientate**
disorients v ▷ **disorientate**
disown v (**-s, -ing, -ed**) deny any connection with (someone)
disowned v ▷ **disown**
disowning v ▷ **disown**
disowns v ▷ **disown**
disparage v (**-rages, -raging, -raged**) speak contemptuously of > **disparagement** n (pl **-s**)
disparaged v ▷ **disparage**
disparagement n ▷ **disparage**
disparagements n ▷ **disparage**
disparages v ▷ **disparage**
disparaging v ▷ **disparage**
disparate adj completely different > **disparately** adv > **disparateness** n > **disparity** n (pl **-ities**)
disparately adv ▷ **disparate**
disparateness n ▷ **disparate**
disparities n ▷ **disparate**
disparity n ▷ **disparate**
dispassionate adj not influenced by emotion > **dispassionately** adv
dispassionately adv ▷ **dispassionate**
dispatch v (**-es, -ing, -ed**) send off to a destination or to perform a task ▸ n (pl **-es**) official communication or report, sent in haste
dispatched v ▷ **dispatch**
dispatches v, n ▷ **dispatch**

dispatching v ▷ dispatch
dispel v (-pels, -pelling, -pelled) destroy or remove
dispelled v ▷ dispel
dispelling v ▷ dispel
dispels v ▷ dispel
dispensability n ▷ dispensable
dispensable adj not essential > **dispensability** n
dispensaries n ▷ dispensary
dispensary n (pl -saries) place where medicine is dispensed
dispensation n (pl -s) dispensing
dispensations n ▷ dispensation
dispense v (-penses, -pensing, -pensed) distribute in portions > **dispenser** n (pl -s)
dispensed v ▷ dispense
dispenser n ▷ dispense
dispensers n ▷ dispense
dispenses v ▷ dispense
dispensing v ▷ dispense
dispersal n ▷ disperse
dispersals n ▷ disperse
disperse v (-perses, -persing, -persed) scatter over a wide area > **dispersal, dispersion** n (pl -s)
dispersed v ▷ disperse
disperses v ▷ disperse
dispersing v ▷ disperse
dispersion n ▷ disperse
dispersions n ▷ disperse
dispirit v (-s, -ing, -ed) make downhearted
dispirited v ▷ dispirit
dispiriting v ▷ dispirit
dispirits v ▷ dispirit
displace v (-places, -placing, -placed) move from the usual location > **displacement** n (pl -s)
displaced v ▷ displace
displacement n ▷ displace
displacements n ▷ displace
displaces v ▷ displace
displacing v ▷ displace
display v (-s, -ing, -ed) make visible or noticeable ▶ n (pl -s) displaying
displayed v ▷ display
displaying v ▷ display
displays v, n ▷ display
displease v (-ses, -sing, -sed) annoy or upset > **displeasure** n (pl -s)
displeased v ▷ displease
displeases v ▷ displease
displeasing v ▷ displease
displeasure n ▷ displease
displeasures n ▷ displease

disport v (-s, -ing, -ed) indulge oneself in pleasure
disported v ▷ disport
disporting v ▷ disport
disports v ▷ disport
disposability n ▷ disposable
disposable adj designed to be thrown away after use > **disposability** n
disposal n (pl -s) getting rid of something
disposals n ▷ disposal
dispose v (-poses, -posing, -posed) place in a certain order
disposed adj willing or eager ▶ v ▷ dispose
disposes v ▷ dispose
disposing v ▷ dispose
disposition n (pl -s) person's usual temperament
dispositions n ▷ disposition
dispossess v (-es, -ing, -ed) (foll. by of) deprive (someone) of (a possession) > **dispossession** n (pl -s)
dispossessed v ▷ dispossess
dispossesses v ▷ dispossess
dispossessing v ▷ dispossess
dispossession n ▷ dispossess
dispossessions n ▷ dispossess
disproportion n (pl -s) lack of proportion or equality
disproportionate adj out of proportion > **disproportionately** adv
disproportionately adv ▷ disproportionate
disproportions n ▷ disproportion
disprove v (-proves, -proving, -proved) show (an assertion or claim) to be incorrect
disproved v ▷ disprove
disproves v ▷ disprove
disproving v ▷ disprove
dispute n (pl -s) disagreement, argument ▶ v (-putes, -puting, -puted) argue about (something)
disputed v ▷ dispute
disputes n, v ▷ dispute
disputing v ▷ dispute
disqualification n ▷ disqualify
disqualifications n ▷ disqualify
disqualified v ▷ disqualify
disqualifies v ▷ disqualify
disqualify v (-fies, -fying, -fied) stop (someone) officially from taking part in something for wrongdoing > **disqualification** n (pl -s)
disqualifying v ▷ disqualify
disquiet n (pl -s) feeling of anxiety ▶ v (-s, -ing, -ed) make (someone) anxious > **disquietude** n (pl -s)

disquieted v ▷ disquiet
disquieting v ▷ disquiet
disquiets v, n ▷ disquiet
disquietude n ▷ disquiet
disquietudes n ▷ disquiet
disregard v (-s, -ing, -ed) give little or no attention to ▶ n (pl -s) lack of attention or respect
disregarded v ▷ disregard
disregarding v ▷ disregard
disregards v, n ▷ disregard
disrepair n (pl -s) condition of being worn out or in poor working order
disrepairs n ▷ disrepair
disreputable adj having or causing a bad reputation > **disreputably** adv
disreputably adv ▷ disreputable
disrepute n (pl -s) loss or lack of good reputation
disreputes n ▷ disrepute
disrespect n (pl -s) lack of respect > **disrespectful** adj > **disrespectfully** adv
disrespectful adj ▷ disrespect
disrespectfully adv ▷ disrespect
disrespects n ▷ disrespect
disrobe v (-robes, -robing, -robed) undress
disrobed v ▷ disrobe
disrobes v ▷ disrobe
disrobing v ▷ disrobe
disrupt v (-s, -ing, -ed) interrupt the progress of > **disruption** n (pl -s) > **disruptive** adj
disrupted v ▷ disrupt
disrupting v ▷ disrupt
disruption n ▷ disrupt
disruptions n ▷ disrupt
disruptive adj ▷ disrupt
disrupts v ▷ disrupt
dissatisfaction n ▷ dissatisfied
dissatisfactions n ▷ dissatisfied
dissatisfied adj not pleased or contented > **dissatisfaction** n (pl -s)
dissect v (-s, -ing, -ed) cut open (a corpse) to examine it > **dissection** n (pl -s)
dissected v ▷ dissect
dissecting v ▷ dissect
dissection n ▷ dissect
dissections n ▷ dissect
dissects v ▷ dissect
dissemble v (-bles, -bling, -bled) conceal one's real motives or emotions by pretence
dissembled v ▷ dissemble
dissembles v ▷ dissemble
dissembling v ▷ dissemble
disseminate v (-nates, -nating, -nated) spread (information) > **dissemination** n (pl -s)

disseminated v ▷ disseminate
disseminates v ▷ disseminate
disseminating v ▷ disseminate
dissemination n ▷ disseminate
disseminations n ▷ disseminate
dissension n ▷ dissent
dissensions n ▷ dissent
dissent v (-s, -ing, -ed) disagree ▶ n (pl -s) disagreement > **dissension** n (pl -s) > **dissenter** n (pl -s)
dissented v ▷ dissent
dissenter n ▷ dissent
dissenters n ▷ dissent
dissenting v ▷ dissent
dissents v ▷ dissent
dissertation n (pl -s) written thesis, usu. required for a higher university degree
dissertations n ▷ dissertation
disservice n (pl -s) harmful action
disservices n ▷ disservice
dissidence n ▷ dissident
dissidences n ▷ dissident
dissident n (pl -s) person who disagrees with and criticizes the government ▶ adj disagreeing with the government > **dissidence** n (pl -s)
dissidents n ▷ dissident
dissimilar adj not alike, different > **dissimilarity** n (pl -ities)
dissimilarities n ▷ dissimilar
dissimilarity n ▷ dissimilar
dissimulate v (-lates, -lating, -lated) conceal one's real feelings by pretence > **dissimulation** n (pl -s)
dissimulated v ▷ dissimulate
dissimulates v ▷ dissimulate
dissimulating v ▷ dissimulate
dissimulation n ▷ dissimulate
dissimulations n ▷ dissimulate
dissipate v (-pates, -pating, -pated) waste or squander > **dissipation** n (pl -s)
dissipated adj showing signs of overindulgence in alcohol and other physical pleasures ▶ v ▷ dissipate
dissipates v ▷ dissipate
dissipating v ▷ dissipate
dissipation n ▷ dissipate
dissipations n ▷ dissipate
dissociate v (-ciates, -ciating, -ciated) regard or treat as separate > **dissociation** n (pl -s)
dissociated v ▷ dissociate
dissociates v ▷ dissociate
dissociating v ▷ dissociate
dissociation n ▷ dissociate
dissociations n ▷ dissociate

dissolute *adj* leading an immoral life
> **dissolutely** *adv* > **dissoluteness** *n*
  dissolutely *adv* ▷ **dissolute**
  dissoluteness *n* ▷ **dissolute**
dissolution *n* (*pl* -s) official breaking up of
  an organization or institution, such as
  Parliament
  dissolutions *n* ▷ **dissolution**
dissolve *v* (-solves, -solving, -solved) (cause to)
  become liquid
  dissolved *v* ▷ **dissolve**
  dissolves *v* ▷ **dissolve**
  dissolving *v* ▷ **dissolve**
dissonance *n* (*pl* -s) lack of agreement or
  harmony > **dissonant** *adj*
  dissonances *n* ▷ **dissonance**
  dissonant *adj* ▷ **dissonance**
dissuade *v* (-suades, -suading, -suaded)
  deter (someone) by persuasion from doing
  something > **dissuasion** *n* (*pl* -s)
  dissuaded *v* ▷ **dissuade**
  dissuades *v* ▷ **dissuade**
  dissuading *v* ▷ **dissuade**
  dissuasion *n* ▷ **dissuade**
  dissuasions *n* ▷ **dissuade**
distaff *n* (*pl* -s) rod on which wool etc. is
  wound for spinning
  distaffs *n* ▷ **distaff**
distance *n* (*pl* -s) space between two points
  distances *n* ▷ **distance**
distant *adj* far apart > **distantly** *adv*
  distantly *adv* ▷ **distant**
distaste *n* (*pl* -s) dislike, disgust
distasteful *adj* unpleasant, offensive
  > **distastefulness** *n*
  distastefulness *n* ▷ **distasteful**
  distastes *n* ▷ **distaste**
distemper[1] *n* (*pl* -s) highly contagious viral
  disease of dogs
distemper[2] *n* (*pl* -s) paint mixed with water,
  glue, etc., used for painting walls
  distempers *n* ▷ **distemper**[1, 2]
distend *v* (-s, -ing, -ed) (of part of the body)
  swell > **distension** *n* (*pl* -s)
  distended *v* ▷ **distend**
  distending *v* ▷ **distend**
  distends *v* ▷ **distend**
  distension *n* ▷ **distend**
  distensions *n* ▷ **distend**
distil *v* (-tils, -tilling, -tilled) subject to or
  obtain by distillation
  distillate *n* ▷ **distillation**
  distillates *n* ▷ **distillation**
distillation *n* (*pl* -s) process of evaporating
  a liquid and condensing its vapour (*also*

distillate) (*pl* -s)
  distillations *n* ▷ **distillation**
  distilled *v* ▷ **distil**
distiller *n* (*pl* -s) person or company that
  makes strong alcoholic drink, esp. whisky
  distilleries *n* ▷ **distillery**
  distillers *n* ▷ **distiller**
distillery *n* (*pl* -leries) place where a strong
  alcoholic drink, esp. whisky, is made
  distilling *v* ▷ **distil**
  distils *v* ▷ **distil**
distinct *adj* (-er, -est) not the same > **distinctly**
  adv > **distinctness** *n* (*pl* -es)
  distincter *adj* ▷ **distinct**
  distinctest *adj* ▷ **distinct**
distinction *n* (*pl* -s) act of distinguishing
  distinctions *n* ▷ **distinction**
distinctive *adj* easily recognizable
  > **distinctively** *adv* > **distinctiveness** *n*
  distinctively *adv* ▷ **distinctive**
  distinctiveness *n* ▷ **distinctive**
  distinctly *adv* ▷ **distinct**
  distinctness *n* ▷ **distinct**
  distinctnesses *n* ▷ **distinct**
distinguish *v* (-es, -ing, -ed) (*usu. foll. by*
  between) make, show, or recognize a
  difference (between) > **distinguishable** *adj*
  distinguishable *adj* ▷ **distinguish**
distinguished *adj* dignified in appearance ▶ *v*
  ▷ **distinguish**
  distinguishes *v* ▷ **distinguish**
  distinguishing *v* ▷ **distinguish**
distort *v* (-s, -ing, -ed) misrepresent (the truth
  or facts) > **distortion** *n* (*pl* -s)
  distorted *v* ▷ **distort**
  distorting *v* ▷ **distort**
  distortion *n* ▷ **distort**
  distortions *n* ▷ **distort**
  distorts *v* ▷ **distort**
distract *v* (-s, -ing, -ed) draw the attention
  of (a person) away from something
  > **distraction** *n* (*pl* -s)
distracted *adj* unable to concentrate,
  preoccupied ▶ *v* ▷ **distract** > **distractedly** *adv*
  distractedly *adv* ▷ **distracted**
  distracting *v* ▷ **distract**
  distraction *n* ▷ **distract**
  distractions *n* ▷ **distract**
  distracts *v* ▷ **distract**
distrait [diss-**tray**] *adj* absent-minded or
  preoccupied
distraught [diss-**trawt**] *adj* extremely anxious
  or agitated
distress *n* (*pl* -es) extreme unhappiness ▶ *v*
  (-es, -ing, -ed) upset badly > **distressing** *adj*

> **distressingly** *adv*
distressed *adj* extremely upset ▶ *v* ▷ **distress**
  distresses *n*, *v* ▷ **distress**
  distressing *v*, *adj* ▷ **distress**
  distressingly *adv* ▷ **distress**
distribute *v* (**-butes**, **-buting**, **-buted**) hand out
  or deliver > **distributive** *adj* > **distributively**
  adv
  distributed *v* ▷ **distribute**
  distributes *v* ▷ **distribute**
  distributing *v* ▷ **distribute**
distribution *n* (*pl* **-s**) distributing
  distributions *n* ▷ **distribution**
  distributive *adj* ▷ **distribute**
  distributively *adv* ▷ **distribute**
distributor *n* (*pl* **-s**) wholesaler who
  distributes goods to retailers in a specific
  area
  distributors *n* ▷ **distributor**
district *n* (*pl* **-s**) area of land regarded as an
  administrative or geographical unit
  districts *n* ▷ **district**
distrust *v* (**-s**, **-ing**, **-ed**) regard as
  untrustworthy ▶ *n* (*pl* **-s**) feeling of suspicion
  or doubt > **distrustful** *adj*
  distrusted *v* ▷ **distrust**
  distrustful *adj* ▷ **distrust**
  distrusting *v* ▷ **distrust**
  distrusts *v*, *n* ▷ **distrust**
disturb *v* (**-s**, **-ing**, **-ed**) intrude on
  > **disturbance** *n* (*pl* **-s**) > **disturbing** *adj*
  > **disturbingly** *adv*
  disturbance *n* ▷ **disturb**
  disturbances *n* ▷ **disturb**
disturbed *adj* (PSYCHIATRY) emotionally upset or
  maladjusted ▶ *v* ▷ **disturb**
  disturbing *v*, *adj* ▷ **disturb**
  disturbingly *adv* ▷ **disturb**
  disturbs *v* ▷ **disturb**
disunite *v* (**-nites**, **-niting**, **-nited**) cause
  disagreement among > **disunity** *n* (*pl* **-ities**)
  disunited *v* ▷ **disunite**
  disunites *v* ▷ **disunite**
  disunities *n* ▷ **disunite**
  disuniting *v* ▷ **disunite**
  disunity *n* ▷ **disunite**
disuse *n* (*pl* **-s**) state of being no longer used
  > **disused** *adj*
  disused *adj* ▷ **disuse**
  disuses *n* ▷ **disuse**
ditch *n* (*pl* **-es**) narrow channel dug in the earth
  for drainage or irrigation ▶ *v* (**-es**, **-ing**, **-ed**)
  (*Slang*) abandon
  ditched *v* ▷ **ditch**
  ditches *n*, *v* ▷ **ditch**

ditching *v* ▷ **ditch**
dither *v* (**-s**, **-ing**, **-ed**) be uncertain or
  indecisive ▶ *n* (*pl* **-s**) state of indecision or
  agitation > **ditherer** *n* (*pl* **-s**) > **dithery** *adj*
  > **ditheriness** *n*
  dithered *v* ▷ **dither**
  ditheriness *n* ▷ **dither**
  dithering *v* ▷ **dither**
  dithers *v*, *n* ▷ **dither**
  dithery *adj* ▷ **dither**
  ditties *n* ▷ **ditty**
ditto *n* (*pl* **-tos**) the same ▶ *adv* in the same way
  dittos *n* ▷ **ditto**
ditty *n* (*pl* **-ties**) short simple poem or song
diuretic [die-yoor-**et**-ik] *n* (*pl* **-s**) drug that
  increases the flow of urine
  diuretics *n* ▷ **diuretic**
diurnal [die-**urn**-al] *adj* happening during the
  day or daily > **diurnally** *adv*
  diurnally *adv* ▷ **diurnal**
diva *n* (*pl* **-s**) distinguished female singer
divan *n* (*pl* **-s**) low backless bed
  divans *n* ▷ **divan**
  divas *n* ▷ **diva**
dive *v* (**dives**, **diving**, **dived**) plunge headfirst
  into water (*foll. by* **in** *or* **into**) ▶ *n* (*pl* **-s**) diving
  dived *v* ▷ **dive**
diver *n* (*pl* **-s**) person who works or explores
  underwater
diverge *v* (**-verges**, **-verging**, **-verged**) separate
  and go in different directions > **divergence** *n*
  (*pl* **-s**) > **divergent** *adj*
  diverged *v* ▷ **diverge**
  divergence *n* ▷ **diverge**
  divergences *n* ▷ **diverge**
  divergent *adj* ▷ **diverge**
  diverges *v* ▷ **diverge**
  diverging *v* ▷ **diverge**
divers *adj* (*Old-fashioned*) various ▶ *n* ▷ **diver**
diverse *adj* having variety, assorted
  > **diversely** *adv* > **diversify** *v* (**-fies**, **-fying**,
  -fied) > **diversification** *n* (*pl* **-s**)
  diversely *adv* ▷ **diverse**
  diversification *n* ▷ **diverse**
  diversifications *n* ▷ **diverse**
  diversified *v* ▷ **diverse**
  diversifies *v* ▷ **diverse**
  diversify *v* ▷ **diverse**
  diversifying *v* ▷ **diverse**
diversion *n* (*pl* **-s**) official detour used by traffic
  when a main route is closed > **diversionary**
  adj
  diversionary *adj* ▷ **diversion**
  diversions *n* ▷ **diversion**
  diversities *n* ▷ **diversity**

diversity n (pl -**ties**) quality of being different or varied

divert v (-**s**, -**ing**, -**ed**) change the direction of
diverted v ▷ divert
diverting v ▷ divert
diverts v ▷ divert
dives v, n ▷ dive

divest v (-**s**, -**ing**, -**ed**) strip (of clothes)
divested v ▷ divest
divesting v ▷ divest
divests v ▷ divest

divide v (-**vides**, -**viding**, -**vided**) separate into parts ▶ n (pl -**s**) division, split
divided v ▷ divide

dividend n (pl -**s**) sum of money representing part of the profit made, paid by a company to its shareholders
dividends n ▷ dividend

divider n (pl -**s**) screen used to divide a room into separate areas ▶ pl compasses with two pointed arms, used for measuring or dividing lines
dividers n ▷ divider
divides v, n ▷ divide
dividing v ▷ divide

divination n (pl -**s**) art of discovering future events, as though by supernatural powers
divinations n ▷ divine

divine adj (-**r**, -**st**) of God or a god ▶ v (-**nes**, -**ning**, -**ned**) discover (something) by intuition or guessing > **divinely** adv
divined v ▷ divine
divinely adv ▷ divine
diviner adj ▷ divine
divines v ▷ divine
divinest adj ▷ divine
diving v ▷ dive
divining v ▷ divine
divinities n ▷ divinity

divinity n study of religion (pl -**ties**)
divisibility n ▷ divisible
divisible adj > **divisibility** n
division n (pl -**s**) dividing, sharing out
divisional adj of a division in an organization > **divisionally** adv
divisionally adv ▷ divisional
divisions n ▷ division

divisive adj tending to cause disagreement > **divisively** adv > **divisiveness** n
divisively adv ▷ divisive
divisiveness n ▷ divisive

divisor n (pl -**s**) number to be divided into another number
divisors n ▷ divisor

divorce n (pl -**s**) legal ending of a marriage ▶ v

(-**ces**, -**cing**, -**ced**) legally end one's marriage (to)
divorcé n ▷ divorcée
divorced v ▷ divorce

divorcée, masc **divorcé** n (pl -**s**) person who is divorced
divorcées n ▷ divorcée
divorces n, v ▷ divorce
divorcés n ▷ divorcée
divorcing v ▷ divorce

divulge v (-**ges**, -**ging**, -**ged**) make known, disclose > **divulgence** n (pl -**s**)
divulged v ▷ divulge
divulgence n ▷ divulge
divulgences n ▷ divulge
divulges v ▷ divulge
divulging v ▷ divulge

dizzied v ▷ dizzy
dizzier adj ▷ dizzy
dizzies v ▷ dizzy
dizziest adj ▷ dizzy
dizzily adv ▷ dizzy
dizziness n ▷ dizzy

dizzy adj (-**zier**, -**ziest**) having or causing a whirling sensation ▶ v (-**zies**, -**zying**, -**zied**) make dizzy > **dizzily** adv > **dizziness** n
dizzying v ▷ dizzy

do v (**does**, **doing**, **did**, **done**) perform or complete (a deed or action) ▶ n (pl **dos**, **do's**) (Informal) party, celebration

docile adj (-**r**, -**st**) (of a person or animal) easily controlled > **docilely** adv > **docility** n (pl -**ties**)
docilely adv ▷ docile
dociler adj ▷ docile
docilest adj ▷ docile
docilities n ▷ docile
docility n ▷ docile

dock¹ n (pl -**s**) enclosed area of water where ships are loaded, unloaded, or repaired ▶ v (-**s**, -**ing**, -**ed**) bring or be brought into dock

dock² v (**docks**, **docking**, **docked**) deduct money from (a person's wages)

dock³ n (pl -**s**) enclosed space in a court of law where the accused person sits or stands

dock⁴ n (pl -**s**) weed with broad leaves
docked v ▷ dock

docker n (pl -**s**) (BRIT) person employed to load and unload ships
dockers n ▷ docker

docket n (pl **dockets**) label on a package or other delivery, stating contents, delivery instructions, etc.
dockets n ▷ docket
docking v ▷ dock
docks n ▷ dock¹, ³, ⁴ ▶ v ▷ dock¹, ²

dockyard n (pl -s) place where ships are built or repaired
  dockyards n ▷ dockyard
doctor n (pl -s) person licensed to practise medicine ▶ v (-s, -ing, -ed) alter in order to deceive > **doctoral** adj
  doctoral adj ▷ doctor
doctorate n (pl -s) highest academic degree in any field of knowledge
  doctorates n ▷ doctorate
  doctored v ▷ doctor
  doctoring v ▷ doctor
  doctors n, v ▷ doctor
doctrinaire adj stubbornly insistent on the application of a theory without regard to practicality
doctrinal adj of doctrines > **doctrinally** adv
  doctrinally adv ▷ doctrinal
doctrine n (pl -s) body of teachings of a religious, political, or philosophical group
  doctrines n ▷ doctrine
document n (pl -s) piece of paper providing an official record of something ▶ v (-s, -ing, -ed) record or report (something) in detail > **documentation** n (pl -s)
  documentaries n ▷ documentary
documentary n (pl -ries) film or television programme presenting the facts about a particular subject ▶ adj (of evidence) based on documents
  documentation n ▷ document
  documentations n ▷ document
  documented v ▷ document
  documenting v ▷ document
  documents n, v ▷ document
dodder v (-s, -ing, -ed) move unsteadily > **doddery** adj (-rier, -riest)
  doddered v ▷ dodder
  dodderier adj ▷ dodder
  dodderiest adj ▷ dodder
  doddering v ▷ dodder
  dodders v ▷ dodder
  doddery adj ▷ dodder
dodecagon [doe-**deck**-a-gon] n (pl -s) geometric figure with twelve sides
  dodecagons n ▷ dodecagon
dodge v (dodges, dodging, dodged) avoid (a blow, being seen, etc.) by moving suddenly ▶ n (pl -s) cunning or deceitful trick
  dodged v ▷ dodge
dodger n (pl -s) person who evades a responsibility or duty
  dodgers n ▷ dodger
  dodges v, n ▷ dodge
  dodgier adj ▷ dodgy

  dodgiest adj ▷ dodgy
  dodging v ▷ dodge
dodgy adj (-gier, -giest) (Informal) dangerous, risky
dodo n (pl -s, -es) large flightless extinct bird
  dodoes n ▷ dodo
  dodos n ▷ dodo
doe n (pl -s) female deer, hare, or rabbit
  does n ▷ doe ▶ v ▷ do
doesn't does not
doff v (-s, -ing, -ed) take off or lift (one's hat) in polite greeting
  doffed v ▷ doff
  doffing v ▷ doff
  doffs v ▷ doff
dog n (pl -s) domesticated four-legged mammal of many different breeds ▶ v (dogs, dogging, dogged) follow (someone) closely
dogcart n (pl -s) light horse-drawn two-wheeled cart
  dogcarts n ▷ dogcart
doge [doje] n (pl -s) (formerly) chief magistrate of Venice or Genoa
dogeared adj (of a book) having pages folded down at the corner
  doges n ▷ doge
dogfight n (pl -s) close-quarters combat between fighter aircraft
  dogfights n ▷ dogfight
dogfish n (pl -es) small shark
  dogfishes n ▷ dogfish
dogged [dog-gid] adj obstinately determined ▶ v ▷ dog > **doggedly** adv > **doggedness** n (pl -es)
  doggedly adv ▷ dogged
  doggedness n ▷ dogged
  doggednesses n ▷ dogged
doggerel n (pl -s) poorly written poetry, usu. comic
  doggerels n ▷ doggerel
  doggie n ▷ doggy
  doggies n ▷ doggy
  dogging v ▷ dog
doggo adv (Informal) in hiding and keeping quiet
doggy, doggie n (pl -gies) child's word for a dog
doghouse n (pl -s) (us) kennel
  doghouses n ▷ doghouse
dogleg n (pl -s) sharp bend
  doglegs n ▷ dogleg
dogma n (pl -s) doctrine or system of doctrines proclaimed by authority as true > **dogmatic** adj habitually stating one's opinions forcefully or arrogantly > **dogmatically** adv

>**dogmatism** n

dogmas n ▷ **dogma**

dogs n, v ▷ **dog**

dogsbodies n ▷ **dogsbody**

dogsbody n (pl -**bodies**) (Informal) person who carries out boring tasks for others

doh interj. Doh is a sound people make when things go wrong. Doh scores 7 points.

doilies n ▷ **doily**

doily n (pl -**lies**) decorative lacy paper mat, laid on a plate

doing v ▷ **do**

doldrums pl n depressed state of mind

dole n (pl -**s**) (BRIT, AUST & NZ) (Informal) money received from the state while unemployed ▶ v (**doles, doling, doled**) (foll. by **out**) distribute in small quantities

doled v ▷ **dole**

doleful adj dreary, unhappy > **dolefully** adv >**dolefulness** n

dolefully adv ▷ **doleful**

dolefulness n ▷ **doleful**

doles v, n ▷ **dole**

doling v ▷ **dole**

doll n (pl -**s**) small model of a human being, used as a toy

dollar n (pl -**s**) standard monetary unit of many countries

dollars n ▷ **dollar**

dollies n ▷ **dolly**

dollop n (pl -**s**) (Informal) lump (of food)

dollops n ▷ **dollop**

dolls n ▷ **doll**

dolly n (pl -**lies**) child's word for a doll

dolmen n (pl -**s**) prehistoric monument consisting of a horizontal stone supported by vertical stones

dolmens n ▷ **dolmen**

dolomite n (pl -**s**) mineral consisting of calcium magnesium carbonate

dolomites n ▷ **dolomite**

dolorous adj sad, mournful > **dolorously** adv

dolorously adv ▷ **dolorous**

dolphin n (pl -**s**) sea mammal of the whale family, with a beaklike snout

dolphinaria n ▷ **dolphinarium**

dolphinarium n (pl -**ariums, -aria**) aquarium for dolphins

dolphinariums n ▷ **dolphinarium**

dolphins n ▷ **dolphin**

dolt n (pl -**s**) stupid person > **doltish** adj >**doltishness** n

doltish adj ▷ **dolt**

doltishness n ▷ **dolt**

dolts n ▷ **dolt**

domain n (pl -**s**) field of knowledge or activity

domains n ▷ **domain**

dome n (pl -**s**) rounded roof built on a circular base > **domed** adj

domes n ▷ **dome**

domestic adj of one's own country or a specific country ▶ n (pl -**s**) person whose job is to do housework in someone else's house >**domestically** adv > **domesticity** n

domestically adv ▷ **domestic**

domesticate v (-**cates, -cating, -cated**) bring or keep (a wild animal or plant) under control or cultivation > **domestication** n (pl -**s**)

domesticated v ▷ **domesticate**

domesticates v ▷ **domesticate**

domesticating v ▷ **domesticate**

domestication n ▷ **domesticate**

domestications n ▷ **domesticate**

domesticity n ▷ **domestic**

domestics n ▷ **domestic**

domicile [dom-miss-ile] n (pl -**s**) place where one lives

domiciles n ▷ **domicile**

dominance n ▷ **dominant**

dominances n ▷ **dominant**

dominant adj having authority or influence >**dominance** n (pl -**s**)

dominate v (-**nates, -nating, -nated**) control or govern > **domination** n (pl -**s**)

dominated v ▷ **dominate**

dominates v ▷ **dominate**

dominating v ▷ **dominate**

domination n ▷ **dominate**

dominations n ▷ **dominate**

domineering adj forceful and arrogant

dominion n (pl -**s**) control or authority

dominions n ▷ **dominion**

domino n (pl -**noes**) small rectangular block marked with dots, used in dominoes ▶ pl game in which dominoes with matching halves are laid together

dominoes n ▷ **domino**

don[1] v (**dons, donning, donned**) put on (clothing)

don[2] n (pl -**s**) (BRIT) member of the teaching staff at a university or college

donate v (-**nates, -nating, -nated**) give, esp. to a charity or organization

donated v ▷ **donate**

donates v ▷ **donate**

donating v ▷ **donate**

donation n (pl -**s**) donating

donations n ▷ **donation**

done v ▷ **do**

donga [dong-ga] *n* (*pl* **-s**) (S AFR, AUST & NZ) steep-sided gully created by soil erosion
  dongas *n* ▷ **donga**
donkey *n* (*pl* **-s**) long-eared member of the horse family
  donkeys *n* ▷ **donkey**
donkeywork *n* (*pl* **-s**) tedious hard work
  donkeyworks *n* ▷ **donkeywork**
  donned *v* ▷ **don¹**
  donning *v* ▷ **don¹**
donnish *adj* serious and academic > **donnishness** *n* (*pl* **-es**)
  donnishness *n* ▷ **donnish**
  donnishnesses *n* ▷ **donnish**
donor *n* (*pl* **-s**) (MED) person who gives blood or organs for use in the treatment of another person
  donors *n* ▷ **donor**
  dons *v* ▷ **don¹** ▶ *n* ▷ **don²**
doodle *v* (**-dles, -dling, -dled**) scribble or draw aimlessly ▶ *n* (*pl* **-s**) shape or picture drawn aimlessly
  doodled *v* ▷ **doodle**
  doodles *v*, *n* ▷ **doodle**
  doodling *v* ▷ **doodle**
doom *n* (*pl* **-s**) death or a terrible fate ▶ *v* (**-s, -ing, -ed**) destine or condemn to death or a terrible fate
  doomed *v* ▷ **doom**
  dooming *v* ▷ **doom**
  dooms *n*, *v* ▷ **doom**
doomsday *n* (*pl* **-s**) (CHRISTIANITY) day on which the Last Judgment will occur
  doomsdays *n* ▷ **doomday**
door *n* (*pl* **-s**) hinged or sliding panel for closing the entrance to a building, room, etc.
doormat *n* (*pl* **-s**) mat for wiping dirt from shoes before going indoors
  doormats *n* ▷ **doormat**
  doors *n* ▷ **door**
doorway *n* (*pl* **-s**) opening into a building or room
  doorways *n* ▷ **doorway**
dope *n* (*pl* **-s**) (Slang) illegal drug, usu. cannabis ▶ *v* (**dopes, doping, doped**) give a drug to, esp. in order to improve performance in a race
  doped *v* ▷ **dope**
  dopes *n*, *v* ▷ **dope**
dopey, dopy (**dopier, dopiest**) *adj* half-asleep, drowsy
  dopier *adj* ▷ **dopey**
  dopiest *adj* ▷ **dopey**
  doping *v* ▷ **dope**
  dopy *adj* ▷ **dopey**
  dorb *n* ▷ **dorba**

dorba *n* (*pl* **-s**) (AUST) (Slang) stupid, inept, or clumsy person (*also* **dorb**) (*pl* **-s**)
  dorbas *n* ▷ **dorba**
  dorbs *n* ▷ **dorba**
  dories *n* ▷ **dory**
dork *n* (*pl* **-s**) (Slang) stupid person
  dorks *n* ▷ **dork**
  dormancy *n* ▷ **dormant**
dormant *adj* temporarily quiet, inactive, or not being used > **dormancy** *n*
dormer *n* (*pl* **-s**) window that sticks out from a sloping roof
  dormers *n* ▷ **dormer**
  dormice *n* ▷ **dormouse**
  dormitories *n* ▷ **dormitory**
dormitory *n* (*pl* **-ries**) large room, esp. at a school, containing several beds
dormouse *n* (*pl* **-mice**) small mouselike rodent with a furry tail
dorp *n* (*pl* **-s**) (S AFR) small town
  dorps *n* ▷ **dorp**
dorsal *adj* of or on the back
dory *n* (*pl* **-ries**) spiny-finned edible sea fish
  dos *n* ▷ **do**
  do's *n* ▷ **do**
dosage *n* (*pl* **-s**) size of a dose
  dosages *n* ▷ **dosage**
dose *n* (*pl* **-s**) specific quantity of a medicine taken at one time ▶ *v* (**doses, dosing, dosed**) give a dose to
  dosed *v* ▷ **dose**
  doses *n*, *v* ▷ **dose**
  dosing *v* ▷ **dose**
doss *v* (**-es, -ing, -ed**) (Slang) sleep in an uncomfortable place
  dossed *v* ▷ **doss**
  dosses *v* ▷ **doss**
dosshouse *n* (*pl* **-s**) (BRIT & S AFR) (Slang) cheap lodging house for homeless people
  dosshouses *n* ▷ **dosshouse**
dossier [doss-ee-ay] *n* (*pl* **-s**) collection of documents about a subject or person
  dossiers *n* ▷ **dossier**
  dossing *v* ▷ **doss**
dot *n* (*pl* **-s**) small round mark ▶ *v* (**dots, dotting, dotted**) mark with a dot
dotage *n* (*pl* **-s**) weakness as a result of old age
  dotages *n* ▷ **dotage**
dotcom *n* (*pl* **-s**) company that does most of its business on the Internet
  dotcoms *n* ▷ **dotcom**
dote *v* (**dotes, doting, doted**) love to an excessive degree
  doted *v* ▷ **dote**
  dotes *v* ▷ **dote**

doting v ▷ **dote**
dots n, v ▷ **dot**
dotted v ▷ **dot**
dottier adj ▷ **dotty**
dottiest adj ▷ **dotty**
dottily adv ▷ **dotty**
dottiness n ▷ **dotty**
dottinesses n ▷ **dotty**
dotting v ▷ **dot**
dotty adj (**-ttier, -ttiest**) (Slang) rather eccentric > **dottily** adv > **dottiness** n (pl **-es**)
double adj as much again in number, amount, size, etc. ▶ adv twice over ▶ n (pl **-s**) twice the number, amount, size, etc. ▶ pl game between two pairs of players ▶ v (**-bles, -bling, -bled**) make or become twice as much or as many > **doubly** adv
doubled v ▷ **double**
doubles n, v ▷ **double**
doublet [**dub-lit**] n (pl **-s**) (HIST) man's close-fitting jacket, with or without sleeves
doublets n ▷ **doublet**
doubling v ▷ **double**
doubloon n (pl **-s**) former Spanish gold coin
doubloons n ▷ **doubloon**
doubly adv ▷ **double**
doubt n (pl **-s**) uncertainty about the truth, facts, or existence of something ▶ v (**-s, -ing, -ed**) question the truth of > **doubter** n (pl **-s**)
doubted v ▷ **doubt**
doubter n ▷ **doubt**
doubters n ▷ **doubt**
doubtful adj unlikely > **doubtfully** adv
doubtfully adv ▷ **doubtful**
doubting v ▷ **doubt**
doubtless adv probably or certainly > **doubtlessly** adv
doubtlessly adv ▷ **doubtless**
doubts n, v ▷ **doubt**
douche [**doosh**] n (pl **-s**) (instrument for applying) a stream of water directed onto or into the body for cleansing or medical purposes ▶ v (**-es, -ing, -ed**) cleanse or treat by means of a douche
douched v ▷ **douche**
douches n, v ▷ **douche**
douching v ▷ **douche**
dough n (pl **-s**) thick mixture of flour and water or milk, used for making bread etc.
doughnut n (pl **-s**) small cake of sweetened dough fried in deep fat
doughnuts n ▷ **doughnut**
doughs n ▷ **dough**
doughtier adj ▷ **doughty**
doughtiest adj ▷ **doughty**

doughtily adv ▷ **doughty**
doughtiness n ▷ **doughty**
doughtinesses n ▷ **doughty**
doughty [**dowt-ee**] adj (**-tier, -tiest**) (Old-fashioned) brave and determined > **doughtily** adv > **doughtiness** n (pl **-es**)
dour [**doo-er**] adj (**-er, -est**) sullen and unfriendly > **dourly** adv > **dourness** n (pl **-es**)
dourer adj ▷ **dour**
dourest adj ▷ **dour**
dourly adv ▷ **dour**
dourness n ▷ **dour**
dournesses n ▷ **dour**
douse [rhymes with **mouse**] v (**-ses, -sing, -sed**) drench with water or other liquid
doused v ▷ **douse**
douses v ▷ **douse**
dousing v ▷ **douse**
dove n (pl **-s**) bird with a heavy body, small head, and short legs
dovecot n ▷ **dovecote**
dovecote, dovecot n (pl **-s**) structure for housing pigeons
dovecotes n ▷ **dovecote**
dovecots n ▷ **dovecote**
doves n ▷ **dove**
dovetail n (pl **-s**) joint containing wedge-shaped tenons ▶ v (**-s, -ing, -ed**) fit together neatly
dovetailed v ▷ **dovetail**
dovetailing v ▷ **dovetail**
dovetails v ▷ **dovetail**
dow n (**dows**). A dow is an Arab ship. Dow scores 7 points.
dowager n (pl **-s**) widow possessing property or a title obtained from her husband
dowagers n ▷ **dowager**
dowdier adj ▷ **dowdy**
dowdiest adj ▷ **dowdy**
dowdily adv ▷ **dowdy**
dowdiness n ▷ **dowdy**
dowdy adj (**-dier, -diest**) dull and old-fashioned > **dowdily** adv > **dowdiness** n
dowel n (pl **-s**) wooden or metal peg that fits into two corresponding holes to join two adjacent parts
dowels n ▷ **dowel**
dower n (pl **-s**) life interest in a part of her husband's estate allotted to a widow by law
dowers n ▷ **dower**
down[1] prep, adv indicating movement to or position in a lower place ▶ adv indicating completion of an action, lessening of intensity, etc. ▶ adj depressed, unhappy ▶ v (**-s, -ing, -ed**) (Informal) drink quickly

down² n (pl **-s**) soft fine feathers > **downiness** n > **downy** adj (**-nier, -niest**)

downbeat adj (*Informal*) gloomy

downcast adj sad, dejected

downed v ▷ **down¹**

downfall n (pl **-s**) (cause of) a sudden loss of position or reputation

downfalls n ▷ **downfall**

downgrade v (**-grades, -grading, -graded**) reduce in importance or value

downgraded v ▷ **downgrade**

downgrades v ▷ **downgrade**

downgrading v ▷ **downgrade**

downhearted adj sad and discouraged > **downheartedly** adv

downheartedly adv ▷ **downhearted**

downhill adj going or sloping down ▶ adv towards the bottom of a hill

downier adj ▷ **down²**

downiest adj ▷ **down²**

downiness n ▷ **down²**

downing v ▷ **down¹**

download v (**-s, -ing, -ed**) transfer (data) from the memory of one computer to that of another, especially over the Internet ▶ n (pl **-s**) file transferred in such a way

downloaded v ▷ **download**

downloading v ▷ **download**

downloads v, n ▷ **download**

downpour n (pl **-s**) heavy fall of rain

downpours n ▷ **downpour**

downright adj, adv extreme(ly)

downs pl n low grassy hills, esp. in S England ▶ v ▷ **down¹** ▶ n ▷ **down²**

downstairs adv to or on a lower floor ▶ n lower or ground floor

downtrodden adj oppressed and lacking the will to resist

downward adj, adv (descending) from a higher to a lower level, condition, or position

downwards adv from a higher to a lower level, condition, or position

downy adj ▷ **down²**

dowries n ▷ **dowry**

dowry n (pl **-ries**) property brought by a woman to her husband at marriage

dowse [rhymes with **cows**] v (**-ses, -sing, -sed**) search for underground water or minerals using a divining rod

dowsed v ▷ **dowse**

dowses v ▷ **dowse**

dowsing v ▷ **dowse**

doxologies n ▷ **doxology**

doxology n (pl **-gies**) short hymn of praise to God

doy n (**doys**). Doy is a dialect word for a beloved person. Doy scores 7 points.

doyen [**doy-en**] n (pl **-s**) senior member of a group, profession, or society > **doyenne** [**doy-en**] ▶ n fem

doyenne n ▷ **doyen**

doyennes n ▷ **doyen**

doyens n ▷ **doyen**

doze v (**dozes, dozing, dozed**) sleep lightly or briefly ▶ n (pl **-s**) short sleep

dozed v ▷ **doze**

dozen adj, n (pl **-s**) twelve > **dozenth** adj

dozens n ▷ **dozen**

dozenth adj ▷ **dozen**

dozes v, n ▷ **doze**

dozier adj ▷ **dozy**

doziest adj ▷ **dozy**

dozily adv ▷ **dozy**

doziness n ▷ **dozy**

dozing v ▷ **doze**

dozy adj (**dozier, doziest**) feeling sleepy > **dozily** adv > **doziness** adv

drab adj (**drabber, drabbest**) dull and dreary > **drably** adv > **drabness** n (pl **-es**)

drabber adj ▷ **drab**

drabbest adj ▷ **drab**

drably adv ▷ **drab**

drabness n ▷ **drab**

drabnesses n ▷ **drab**

drachm [**dram**] n (pl **-s**) (BRIT) one eighth of a fluid ounce

drachma n (pl **-mas, -mae**) former monetary unit of Greece

drachmae n ▷ **drachma**

drachmas n ▷ **drachma**

drachms n ▷ **drachm**

draconian adj severe, harsh

draft n (pl **-s**) plan, sketch, or drawing of something (US & AUST) ▶ v (**-s, -ing, -ed**) draw up an outline or plan of

drafted v ▷ **draft**

drafting v ▷ **draft**

drafts n, v ▷ **draft**

drag v (**-s, -gging, -gged**) pull with force, esp. along the ground (foll. by **on** or **out**) ▶ n (pl **-s**) person or thing that slows up progress

dragged v ▷ **drag**

dragging v ▷ **drag**

dragnet n (pl **-s**) net used to scour the bottom of a pond or river to search for something

dragnets n ▷ **dragnet**

dragon n (pl **-s**) mythical fire-breathing monster like a huge lizard

dragonflies n ▷ **dragonfly**

dragonfly n (pl **-flies**) brightly coloured insect

with a long slender body and two pairs of wings

dragons *n* ▷ dragon

dragoon *n* (*pl* **-s**) heavily armed cavalryman ▶ *v* (**-s, -ing, -ed**) coerce, force

dragooned *v* ▷ dragoon

dragooning *v* ▷ dragoon

dragoons *n, v* ▷ dragoon

drags *v, n* ▷ drag

drain *n* (*pl* **-s**) pipe or channel that carries off water or sewage ▶ *v* (**-s, -ing, -ed**) draw off or remove liquid from

drainage *n* (*pl* **-s**) system of drains

drainages *n* ▷ drainage

drained *v* ▷ drain

draining *v* ▷ drain

drains *n, v* ▷ drain

drake *n* (*pl* **-s**) male duck

drakes *n* ▷ drake

dram *n* (*pl* **-s**) small amount of a strong alcoholic drink, esp. whisky

drama *n* (*pl* **-s**) serious play for theatre, television, or radio

dramas *n* ▷ drama

dramatic *adj* of or like drama > **dramatically** *adv*

dramatically *adv* ▷ dramatic

dramatist *n* (*pl* **-s**) person who writes plays

dramatists *n* ▷ dramatist

dramatization *n* ▷ dramatize

dramatizations *n* ▷ dramatize

dramatize *v* (**-tizes, -tizing, -tized**) rewrite (a book) in the form of a play > **dramatization** *n* (*pl* **-s**)

dramatized *v* ▷ dramatize

dramatizes *v* ▷ dramatize

dramatizing *v* ▷ dramatize

drams *n* ▷ dram

drank *v* ▷ drink

drape *v* (**drapes, draping, draped**) cover with material, usu. in folds ▶ *n* (*pl* **-s**) (AUST, US & CANADIAN) piece of cloth hung at a window or opening as a screen

draped *v* ▷ drape

draper *n* (*pl* **-s**) (BRIT) person who sells fabrics and sewing materials

draperies *n* ▷ drapery

drapers *n* ▷ draper

drapery *n* (*pl* **-peries**) fabric or clothing arranged and draped

drapes *v, n* ▷ drape

draping *v* ▷ drape

drastic *adj* strong and severe > **drastically** *adv*

drastically *adv* ▷ drastic

draught *n* (*pl* **-s**) current of cold air, esp. in an enclosed space ▶ *pl* game for two players using a chessboard and twelve draughts each ▶ *adj* (of an animal) used for pulling heavy loads

draughtier *adj* ▷ draughty

draughtiest *adj* ▷ draughty

draughtiness *n* ▷ draughty

draughts *n* ▷ draught

draughtsman *n* (*pl* **-men**) person employed to prepare detailed scale drawings of machinery, buildings, etc. > **draughtsmanship** *n*

draughtsmanship *n* ▷ draughtsman

draughtsmen *n* ▷ draughtsman

draughty *adj* (**-tier, -tiest**) exposed to draughts of air > **draughtiness** *n*

draw *v* (**draws, drawing, drew, drawn**) sketch (a figure, picture, etc.) with a pencil or pen ▶ *n* (*pl* **-s**) raffle or lottery

drawback *n* (*pl* **-s**) disadvantage

drawbacks *n* ▷ drawback

drawbridge *n* (*pl* **-s**) bridge that may be raised to prevent access or to enable vessels to pass

drawbridges *n* ▷ drawbridge

drawer *n* (*pl* **-s**) sliding box-shaped part of a piece of furniture, used for storage ▶ *pl* (Old-fashioned) undergarment worn on the lower part of the body

drawers *n* ▷ drawer

drawing *n* (*pl* **-s**) picture or plan made by means of lines on a surface ▶ *v* ▷ draw

drawl *v* (**-s, -ing, -ed**) speak slowly, with long vowel sounds ▶ *n* (*pl* **drawls**) drawling manner of speech

drawled *v* ▷ drawl

drawling *v* ▷ drawl

drawls *v* ▷ drawl

drawls *n* ▷ drawl

drawn *v* ▷ draw ▶ *adj* haggard, tired, or tense in appearance

draws *n, v* ▷ draw

drawstring *n* (*pl* **-s**) cord run through a hem around an opening, so that when it is pulled tighter, the opening closes

drawstrings *n* ▷ drawstring

dray *n* (*pl* **-s**) low cart used for carrying heavy loads

drays *n* ▷ dray

dread *v* (**-s, -ing, -ed**) anticipate with apprehension or fear ▶ *n* (*pl* **-s**) great fear

dreaded *v* ▷ dread

dreadful *adj* very disagreeable or shocking > **dreadfully** *adv*

dreadfully *adv* ▷ dreadful

dreading *v* ▷ dread

dreadlocks *pl n* hair worn in the Rastafarian style of tightly twisted strands
   dreads *v, n* ▷ **dread**
dream *n* (*pl* -**s**) imagined series of events experienced in the mind while asleep (*Informal*) ▶ *v* (-**s, -ing, -ed** *or* -**t**) see imaginary pictures in the mind while asleep (*often foll. by* **of** *or* **about**) (*foll. by* **of**) ▶ *adj* ideal > **dreamer** *n* (*pl* -**s**)
   dreamed *v* ▷ **dream**
   dreamer *n* ▷ **dream**
   dreamers *n* ▷ **dream**
   dreamier *adj* ▷ **dreamy**
   dreamiest *adj* ▷ **dreamy**
   dreamily *adv* ▷ **dreamy**
   dreaminess *n* ▷ **dreamy**
   dreaminesses *n* ▷ **dreamy**
   dreaming *v* ▷ **dream**
   dreams *n, v* ▷ **dream**
   dreamt *v* ▷ **dream**
dreamy *adj* (-**mier, -miest**) vague or impractical > **dreamily** *adv* > **dreaminess** *n* (*pl* -**es**)
   drearier *adj* ▷ **dreary**
   dreariest *adj* ▷ **dreary**
   drearily *adv* ▷ **dreary**
   dreariness *n* ▷ **dreary**
dreary *adj* (**drearier, dreariest**) dull, boring > **drearily** *adv* > **dreariness** *n*
dredge[1] *v* (**dredges, dredging, dredged**) clear or search (a river bed or harbour) by removing silt or mud
dredge[2] *v* (**dredges, dredging, dredged**) sprinkle (food) with flour etc.
   dredged *v* ▷ **dredge[1, 2]**
dredger *n* (*pl* -**s**) boat fitted with machinery for dredging
   dredgers *n* ▷ **dredger**
   dredges *v* ▷ **dredge[1, 2]**
   dredging *v* ▷ **dredge[1, 2]**
dregs *pl n* solid particles that settle at the bottom of some liquids
drench *v* (-**es, -ing, -ed**) make completely wet
   drenched *v* ▷ **drench**
   drenches *v* ▷ **drench**
   drenching *v* ▷ **drench**
dress *n* (*pl* -**es**) one-piece garment for a woman or girl, consisting of a skirt and bodice and sometimes sleeves ▶ *v* (-**es, -ing, -ed**) put clothes on
dressage [dress-ahzh] *n* (*pl* -**s**) training of a horse to perform manoeuvres in response to the rider's body signals
   dressages *n* ▷ **dressage**
   dressed *v* ▷ **dress**

dresser[1] *n* (*pl* -**s**) piece of furniture with shelves and with cupboards, for storing or displaying dishes
dresser[2] *n* (*pl* -**s**) (THEATRE) person employed to assist actors with their costumes
   dressers *n* ▷ **dresser[1, 2]**
   dresses *n, v* ▷ **dress**
   dressier *adj* ▷ **dressy**
   dressiest *adj* ▷ **dressy**
   dressiness *n* ▷ **dressy**
   dressinesses *n* ▷ **dressy**
dressing *n* (*pl* -**s**) sauce for salad ▶ *v* ▷ **dress**
   dressings *n* ▷ **dressing**
dressmaker *n* (*pl* -**s**) person who makes women's clothes > **dressmaking** *n*
   dressmakers *n* ▷ **dressmaker**
   dressmaking *n* ▷ **dressmaker**
dressy *adj* (-**ssier, -ssiest**) (of clothes) elegant > **dressiness** *n* (*pl* -**es**)
   drew *v* ▷ **draw**
drey *n* (*pl* -**s**) squirrel's nest
   dreys *n* ▷ **drey**
dribble *v* (-**les, -ling, -led**) (allow to) flow in drops ▶ *n* (*pl* -**s**) small quantity of liquid falling in drops > **dribbler** *n* (*pl* -**s**)
   dribbled *v* ▷ **dribble**
   dribbler *n* ▷ **dribble**
   dribblers *n* ▷ **dribble**
   dribbles *v, n* ▷ **dribble**
   dribbling *v* ▷ **dribble**
   dried *v* ▷ **dry**
   drier[1] *adj* ▷ **dry**
   drier[2] *n* (*pl* -**s**) ▷ **dryer**
   driers *n* ▷ **drier[2]**
   dries *v* ▷ **dry**
   driest *adj* ▷ **dry**
drift *v* (-**s, -ing, -ed**) be carried along by currents of air or water ▶ *n* (*pl* -**s**) something piled up by the wind or current, such as a snowdrift
   drifted *v* ▷ **drift**
drifter *n* (*pl* -**s**) person who moves aimlessly from place to place or job to job
   drifters *n* ▷ **drifter**
   drifting *v* ▷ **drift**
   drifts *v, n* ▷ **drift**
driftwood *n* (*pl* -**s**) wood floating on or washed ashore by the sea
   driftwoods *n* ▷ **driftwood**
drill[1] *n* (*pl* -**s**) tool or machine for boring holes ▶ *v* (-**s, -ing, -ed**) bore a hole in (something) with or as if with a drill
drill[2] *n* (*pl* -**s**) machine for sowing seed in rows
drill[3] *n* (*pl* -**s**) hard-wearing cotton cloth
   drilled *v* ▷ **drill[1]**

drilling v ▷ **drill**[1]
drills n ▷ **drill**[1, 2, 3] ▶ v ▷ **drill**[1]
drily adv ▷ **dry**
drink v (**drinks, drinking, drank, drunk**)
swallow (a liquid) ▶ n (pl -**s**) (portion of) a
liquid suitable for drinking > **drinkable** adj
> **drinker** n (pl -**s**)
drinkable adj ▷ **drink**
drinker n ▷ **drink**
drinkers n ▷ **drink**
drinking v ▷ **drink**
drinks v, n ▷ **drink**
drip v (**drips, dripping, dripped**) (let) fall in
drops ▶ n (pl -**s**) falling of drops of liquid
dripped v ▷ **drip**
dripping n (pl -**s**) fat that comes from meat
while it is being roasted or fried ▶ v ▷ **drip**
drippings n ▷ **dripping**
drips v, n ▷ **drip**
drive v (**drives, driving, drove, driven**) guide
the movement of (a vehicle) ▶ n (pl -**s**) journey
by car, van, etc.; path for vehicles (also
driveway) (pl -**s**)
drivel n (pl -**s**) foolish talk ▶ v (-**els, -elling,
-elled**) speak foolishly
drivelled v ▷ **drivel**
drivelling v ▷ **drivel**
drivels v, n ▷ **drivel**
driven v ▷ **drive**
driver n (pl -**s**) person who drives a vehicle
drivers n ▷ **driver**
drives v, n ▷ **drive**
driveway n ▷ **drive**
driveways n ▷ **drive**
driving v ▷ **drive**
drizzle n (pl -**s**) very light rain ▶ v (-**zles, -zling,
-zled**) rain lightly > **drizzly** adj
drizzled v ▷ **drizzle**
drizzles n, v ▷ **drizzle**
drizzling v ▷ **drizzle**
drizzly adj ▷ **drizzle**
droll adj (-**er, -est**) quaintly amusing > **drolly**
adv > **drollery** n (pl -**ries**) > **drollness** n (pl -**es**)
droller adj ▷ **droll**
drolleries n ▷ **droll**
drollery n ▷ **droll**
drollest adj ▷ **droll**
drollness n ▷ **droll**
drollnesses n ▷ **droll**
drolly adv ▷ **droll**
dromedaries n ▷ **dromedary**
dromedary [drom-mid-er-ee] n (pl -**daries**)
camel with a single hump
drone[1] n (pl -**s**) male bee
drone[2] v (**drones, droned, droning**) ▶ n (pl -**s**)

(make) a monotonous low dull sound
droned v ▷ **drone**[2]
drones n ▷ **drone**[1, 2] ▶ v ▷ **drone**[2]
drongo n (pl -**gos**) tropical songbird with a
glossy black plumage, a forked tail, and a
stout bill
drongos n ▷ **drongo**
droning v ▷ **drone**[2]
drool v (-**s, -ing, -ed**) (foll. by **over**) show
excessive enthusiasm (for)
drooled v ▷ **drool**
drooling v ▷ **drool**
drools v ▷ **drool**
droop v (-**s, -ing, -ed**) hang downwards loosely
> **droopy** adj (-**pier, -piest**)
drooped v ▷ **droop**
droopier adj ▷ **droop**
droopiest adj ▷ **droop**
drooping v ▷ **droop**
droops v ▷ **droop**
droopy adj ▷ **droop**
drop v (-**s, -pping, -pped**) (allow to) fall
vertically ▶ n (pl -**s**) small quantity of liquid
forming a round shape ▶ pl liquid medication
applied in small drops > **droplet** n (pl -**s**)
droplet n ▷ **drop**
droplets n ▷ **drop**
dropout n (pl -**s**) person who rejects
conventional society
dropouts n ▷ **dropout**
dropped v ▷ **drop**
dropping v ▷ **drop**
droppings pl n faeces of certain animals, such
as rabbits or birds
drops v, n ▷ **drop**
dropsical adj ▷ **dropsy**
dropsies n ▷ **dropsy**
dropsy n (pl -**sies**) illness in which watery fluid
collects in the body > **dropsical** adj
dross n (pl -**es**) scum formed on the surfaces of
molten metals
drosses n ▷ **dross**
drought n (pl -**s**) prolonged shortage of rainfall
droughts n ▷ **drought**
drove[1] v ▷ **drive**
drove[2] n (pl -**s**) very large group, esp. of people
drover n (pl -**s**) person who drives sheep or
cattle
drovers n ▷ **drover**
droves n ▷ **drove**[2]
drown v (-**s, -ing, -ed**) die or kill by immersion
in liquid
drowned v ▷ **drown**
drowning v ▷ **drown**
drowns v ▷ **drown**

drowse v (-ses, -sing, -sed) be sleepy, dull, or sluggish > **drowsy** adj (-sier, -siest) > **drowsily** adv > **drowsiness** n (pl -es)
  drowsed v ▷ drowse
  drowses v ▷ drowse
  drowsier adj ▷ drowse
  drowsiest adj ▷ drowse
  drowsily adv ▷ drowse
  drowsiness n ▷ drowse
  drowsinesses n ▷ drowse
  drowsing v ▷ drowse
  drowsy adj ▷ drowse
drubbing n (pl -s) utter defeat in a contest etc.
  drubbings n ▷ drubbing
drudge n (pl -s) person who works hard at uninteresting tasks > **drudgery** n (pl -eries)
  drudgeries n ▷ drudge
  drudgery n ▷ drudge
  drudges n ▷ drudge
drug n (pl -s) substance used in the treatment or prevention of disease ▶ v (**drugs, drugging, drugged**) give a drug to (a person or animal) to cause sleepiness or unconsciousness
  drugged v ▷ drug
  drugging v ▷ drug
  drugs v, n ▷ drug
drugstore n (pl -s) (US) pharmacy where a wide range of goods are available
  drugstores n ▷ drugstore
druid n (pl -s) member of an ancient order of Celtic priests > **druidic, druidical** adj
  druidic adj ▷ druid
  druidical adj ▷ druid
  druids adj ▷ druid
drum n (pl -s) percussion instrument sounded by striking a membrane stretched across the opening of a hollow cylinder ▶ v (**drums, drumming, drummed**) play (music) on a drum
  drummed v ▷ drum
drummer n (pl -s) person who plays a drum or drums
  drummers n ▷ drummer
  drumming v ▷ drum
  drums n, v ▷ drum
drumstick n (pl -s) stick used for playing a drum
  drumsticks n ▷ drumstick
  drunk v ▷ drink ▶ adj (-er, -est) intoxicated with alcohol to the extent of losing control over normal functions ▶ n (pl -s) person who is drunk or who frequently gets drunk
drunkard n (pl -s) person who frequently gets drunk
  drunkards n ▷ drunkard

drunken adj drunk or frequently drunk > **drunkenly** adv > **drunkenness** n (pl -es)
  drunkenly adv ▷ drunken
  drunkenness n ▷ drunken
  drunkennesses n ▷ drunken
  drunker adj ▷ drunk
  drunkest adj ▷ drunk
  drunks n ▷ drunk
dry adj (drier, driest or dryer, dryest) lacking moisture ▶ v (**dries, drying, dried**) make or become dry > **drily, dryly** adv > **dryness** n (pl -es)
dryad n (pl -s) wood nymph
  dryads n ▷ dryad
dryer, drier n (pl -s) apparatus for removing moisture
  dryer adj ▷ dry
  dryers n ▷ dryer
  dryest adj ▷ dry
  drying v ▷ dry
  dryly adv ▷ dry
  dryness n ▷ dry
  drynesses n ▷ dry

> **dso** n (**dsos**). Dso is one of several spelling for a Tibetan animal bred from yaks and cattle. The other forms are **dzo, zho** and **zo**, and it's worth remembering all of them. Dso scores 4 points.

dual adj having two parts, functions, or aspects > **duality** n (pl -ities) > **dually** adv
  dualities n ▷ dual
  duality n ▷ dual
  dually adv ▷ dual
dub[1] v (**dubs, dubbing, dubbed**) give (a person or place) a name or nickname
dub[2] v (**dubs, dubbing, dubbed**) provide (a film) with a new soundtrack, esp. in a different language
  dubbed v ▷ dub[1, 2]
dubbin n (pl -s) (BRIT) thick grease applied to leather to soften and waterproof it
  dubbing v ▷ dub[1, 2]
  dubbins n ▷ dubbin
  dubieties n ▷ dubious
  dubiety n ▷ dubious
dubious [dew-bee-uss] adj feeling or causing doubt > **dubiously** adv > **dubiousness** n > **dubiety** [dew-by-it-ee] n (pl -ities)
  dubiously adv ▷ dubious
  dubiousness n ▷ dubious
  dubs v ▷ dub[1, 2]
ducal [duke-al] adj of a duke
ducat [duck-it] n (pl -s) former European gold or silver coin

ducats n ▷ **ducat**

duchess n (pl **-es**) woman who holds the rank of duke

duchesse n (pl **-s**) (NZ) dressing table with a mirror

duchesses n ▷ **duchess, duchesse**

duchies n ▷ **duchy**

duchy n (pl **duchies**) territory of a duke or duchess

duck¹ n (pl **-s**) water bird with short legs, webbed feet, and a broad blunt bill

duck² v (**-s, -ing, -ed**) move (the head or body) quickly downwards, to avoid being seen or to dodge a blow

ducked v ▷ **duck²**

ducking v ▷ **duck²**

duckling n (pl **-s**) baby duck

ducklings n ▷ **duckling**

ducks n ▷ **duck¹** ▶ v ▷ **duck²**

duct n (pl **-s**) tube, pipe, or channel through which liquid or gas is conveyed

ductile adj (of a metal) able to be shaped into sheets or wires

ducts n ▷ **duct**

dud (Informal) n (pl **-s**) ineffectual person or thing ▶ adj bad or useless

dude n (pl **-s**) (US) (Informal) man

dudes n ▷ **dude**

dudgeon n (pl **-s**) anger, resentment

dudgeons n ▷ **dudgeon**

duds n ▷ **dud**

due adj expected or scheduled to be present or arrive ▶ n (pl **-s**) something that is owed or required ▶ pl charges for membership of a club or organization ▶ adv directly or exactly

duel n (pl **-s**) formal fight with deadly weapons between two people, to settle a quarrel ▶ v (**-s, -lling, -lled**) fight in a duel > **duellist** n (pl **-s**)

duelled v ▷ **duel**

duelling v ▷ **duel**

duellist n ▷ **duel**

duellists n ▷ **duel**

duels n, v ▷ **duel**

dues n ▷ **due**

duet n (pl **-s**) piece of music for two performers

duets n ▷ **duet**

duff adj (**-er, -est**) (CHIEFLY BRIT) broken or useless

duffel, duffle n (pl **-s**) heavy woollen cloth

duffels n ▷ **duffel**

duffer n (pl **-s**) (Informal) dull or incompetent person ▶ adj ▷ **duff**

duffers n ▷ **duffer**

duffest adj ▷ **duff**

duffle n ▷ **duffel**

duffles n ▷ **duffel**

dug¹ v ▷ **dig**

dug² n (pl **-s**) teat or udder

dugite [doo-gyte] n (pl **-s**) medium-sized Australian venomous snake

dugites n ▷ **dugite**

dugong n (pl **-s**) whalelike mammal of tropical waters

dugongs n ▷ **dugong**

dugout n (pl **-s**) (BRIT) (at a sports ground) covered bench where managers and substitutes sit

dugouts n ▷ **dugout**

dugs n ▷ **dug²**

duke n (pl **-s**) nobleman of the highest rank > **dukedom** n (pl **-s**)

dukedom n ▷ **duke**

dukedoms n ▷ **duke**

dukes n ▷ **duke**

dulcet [dull-sit] adj (of a sound) soothing or pleasant

dulcimer n (pl **-s**) tuned percussion instrument consisting of a set of strings stretched over a sounding board and struck with hammers

dulcimers n ▷ **dulcimer**

dull adj (**-er, -est**) not interesting ▶ v (**-s, -ing, -ed**) make or become dull > **dullness** n (pl **-es**) > **dully** adv

dullard n (pl **-s**) dull or stupid person

dullards n ▷ **dullard**

dulled v ▷ **dull**

duller adj ▷ **dull**

dullest adj ▷ **dull**

dulling v ▷ **dull**

dullness n ▷ **dull**

dullnesses n ▷ **dull**

dulls v ▷ **dull**

dully adv ▷ **dull**

duly adv in a proper manner

dumb adj (**dumber, dumbest**) lacking the power to speak > **dumbly** adv > **dumbness** n

dumbbell n (pl **-s**) short bar with a heavy ball or disc at each end, used for physical exercise

dumbbells n ▷ **dumbbell**

dumber adj ▷ **dumb**

dumbest adj ▷ **dumb**

dumbfounded adj speechless with astonishment

dumbly adv ▷ **dumb**

dumbness n ▷ **dumb**

dumdum n (pl **-s**) soft-nosed bullet that expands on impact and causes serious wounds

dumdums n ▷ **dumdum**

dummies n ▷ **dummy**

dummy *n* (*pl* **-mies**) figure representing the human form, used for displaying clothes etc. ▶ *adj* imitation, substitute

dump *v* (**-s, -ing, -ed**) drop or let fall in a careless manner ▶ *n* (*pl* **-s**) place where waste materials are left
dumped *v* ▷ **dump**
dumpier *adj* ▷ **dumpy**
dumpiest *adj* ▷ **dumpy**
dumpily *adv* ▷ **dumpy**
dumpiness *n* ▷ **dumpy**
dumping *v* ▷ **dump**

dumpling *n* (*pl* **-s**) small ball of dough cooked and served with stew
dumplings *n* ▷ **dumpling**
dumps *v*, *n* ▷ **dump**

dumpy *adj* (**dumpier, dumpiest**) short and plump > **dumpily** *adv* > **dumpiness** *n*

dun (**dunner, dunnest**) *adj* brownish-grey

dunce *n* (*pl* **-s**) person who is stupid or slow to learn
dunces *n* ▷ **dunce**

dunderhead *n* (*pl* **-s**) slow-witted person
dunderheads *n* ▷ **dunderhead**

dune *n* (*pl* **-s**) mound or ridge of drifted sand
dunes *n* ▷ **dune**

dung *n* (*pl* **-s**) faeces from animals such as cattle

dungarees *pl n* trousers with a bib attached

dungeon *n* (*pl* **-s**) underground prison cell
dungeons *n* ▷ **dungeon**
dungs *n* ▷ **dung**

dunk *v* (**-s, -ing, -ed**) dip (a biscuit or bread) in a drink or soup before eating it
dunked *v* ▷ **dunk**
dunking *v* ▷ **dunk**
dunks *v* ▷ **dunk**
dunner *adj* ▷ **dun**
dunnest *adj* ▷ **dun**
dunnies *n* ▷ **dunny**

dunny *n* (*pl* **-nies**) (AUST & OLD-FASHIONED NZ) (*Informal*) toilet

duo *n* (*pl* **-s**) pair of performers
duodena *n* ▷ **duodenum**
duodenal *adj* ▷ **duodenum**

duodenum [dew-oh-**deen**-um] *n* (*pl* **-na, -nums**) first part of the small intestine, just below the stomach > **duodenal** *adj*
duodenums *n* ▷ **duodenum**
duos *n* ▷ **duo**

dupe *v* (**dupes, duping, duped**) deceive or cheat ▶ *n* (*pl* **-s**) person who is easily deceived
duped *v* ▷ **dupe**
dupes *v*, *n* ▷ **dupe**
duping *v* ▷ **dupe**

duple *adj* (MUSIC) having two beats in a bar

duplex *n* (*pl* **-es**) (CHIEFLY US) apartment on two floors
duplexes *n* ▷ **duplex**

duplicate *adj* copied exactly from an original ▶ *n* (*pl* **-s**) exact copy ▶ *v* (**-cates, -cating, -cated**) make an exact copy of > **duplication** *n* (*pl* **-s**) > **duplicator** *n* (*pl* **-s**)
duplicated *v* ▷ **duplicate**
duplicates *n*, *v* ▷ **duplicate**
duplicating *v* ▷ **duplicate**
duplication *n* ▷ **duplicate**
duplications *n* ▷ **duplicate**
duplicator *n* ▷ **duplicate**
duplicators *n* ▷ **duplicate**
duplicities *n* ▷ **duplicity**

duplicity *n* (*pl* **-ities**) deceitful behaviour
durability *n* ▷ **durable**

durable *adj* long-lasting > **durability** *n* > **durably** *adv*

durables *pl n* goods that require infrequent replacement
durably *adv* ▷ **durable**

duration *n* (*pl* **-s**) length of time that something lasts
durations *n* ▷ **duration**

duress *n* compulsion by use of force or threats

during *prep* throughout or within the limit of (a period of time)

dusk *n* (*pl* **-s**) time just before nightfall, when it is almost dark
duskier *adj* ▷ **dusky**
duskiest *adj* ▷ **dusky**
duskily *adv* ▷ **dusky**
duskiness *n* ▷ **dusky**
dusks *n* ▷ **dusk**

dusky *adj* (**duskier, duskiest**) dark in colour > **duskily** *adv* > **duskiness** *n*

dust *n* (*pl* **-s**) small dry particles of earth, sand, or dirt ▶ *v* (**-s, -ing, -ed**) remove dust from (furniture) by wiping

dustbin *n* (*pl* **-s**) large container for household rubbish
dustbins *n* ▷ **dustbin**
dusted *v* ▷ **dust**

duster *n* (*pl* **-s**) cloth used for dusting
dusters *n* ▷ **duster**
dustier *adj* ▷ **dusty**
dustiest *adj* ▷ **dusty**
dusting *v* ▷ **dust**

dustman *n* (*pl* **-men**) (BRIT) man whose job is to collect household rubbish
dustmen *n* ▷ **dustman**

dustpan *n* (*pl* **-s**) short-handled shovel into which dust is swept from floors

dustpans *n* ▷ dustpan
dusts *n, v* ▷ dust
dusty *adj* (**dustier, dustiest**) covered with dust
dutiability *n* ▷ dutiable
dutiable *adj* (of goods) requiring payment of duty > **dutiability** *n*
duties *n* ▷ duty
dutiful *adj* doing what is expected > **dutifully** *adv*
dutifully *adv* ▷ dutiful
duty *n* (*pl* -**ties**) work or a task performed as part of one's job
duvet [doo-vay] *n* (*pl* -**s**) kind of quilt used in bed instead of a top sheet and blankets
duvets *n* ▷ duvet

> **dux** *n* (**duces**). A dux is the top pupil in a school. This is a handy word to have ready if someone else has played a word containing X. Dux scores 11 points.

dwang *n* (*pl* -**s**) (NZ & S AFR) short piece of wood inserted in a timber-framed wall
dwangs *n* ▷ dwang
dwarf *n* (*pl* **dwarfs, dwarves**) person who is smaller than average ▸ *adj* (of an animal or plant) much smaller than the usual size for the species ▸ *v* (**dwarfs, dwarfing** *or* **dwarfed**) cause (someone or something) to seem small by being much larger
dwarfed *v* ▷ dwarf
dwarfing *v* ▷ dwarf
dwarfs *n, v* ▷ dwarf
dwarves *n* ▷ dwarf
dwell *v* (**dwells, dwelling, dwelt** *or* **dwelled**) live, reside
dwelled *v* ▷ dwell
dweller *n* (*pl* -**s**) person who lives in a specified place
dwellers *n* ▷ dweller
dwelling *n* (*pl* -**s**) place of residence ▸ *v* ▷ dwell
dwellings *n* ▷ dwelling
dwells *v* ▷ dwell
dwelt *v* ▷ dwell
dwindle *v* (-**dles, -dling, -dled**) grow less in size, strength, or number
dwindled *v* ▷ dwindle
dwindles *v* ▷ dwindle
dwindling *v* ▷ dwindle
dye *n* (*pl* -**s**) colouring substance ▸ *v* (**dyes, dyeing, dyed**) colour (hair or fabric) by applying a dye > **dyer** *n* (*pl* -**s**)
dyed *v* ▷ dye
dyeing *v* ▷ dye

dyer *n* ▷ dye
dyers *n* ▷ dye
dyes *n, v* ▷ dye
dying *v* ▷ die¹
dyke *n* (*pl* -**s**) wall built to prevent flooding
dykes *n* ▷ dyke
dynamic *adj* full of energy, ambition, and new ideas > **dynamically** *adv*
dynamically *adv* ▷ dynamic
dynamics *n* branch of mechanics concerned with the forces that change or produce the motions of bodies ▸ *pl* forces that produce change in a system
dynamism *n* great energy and enthusiasm
dynamite *n* (*pl* -**s**) explosive made of nitroglycerine ▸ *v* (-**mites, -miting, -mited**) blow (something) up with dynamite
dynamited *v* ▷ dynamite
dynamites *n, v* ▷ dynamite
dynamiting *v* ▷ dynamite
dynamo *n* (*pl* -**s**) device for converting mechanical energy into electrical energy
dynamos *n* ▷ dynamo
dynastic *adj* ▷ dynasty
dynasties *n* ▷ dynasty
dynasty *n* (*pl* -**ties**) sequence of hereditary rulers > **dynastic** *adj*
dysenteries *n* ▷ dysentery
dysentery *n* (*pl* -**teries**) infection of the intestine causing severe diarrhoea
dysfunction *n* (*pl* -**s**) (MED) disturbance or abnormality in the function of an organ or part > **dysfunctional** *adj* > **dysfunctionally** *adv*
dysfunctional *adj* ▷ dysfunction
dysfunctionally *adv* ▷ dysfunction
dysfunctions *n* ▷ dysfunction
dyslexia *n* (*pl* -**s**) disorder causing impaired ability to read > **dyslexic** *adj*
dyslexias *n* ▷ dyslexia
dyslexic *adj* ▷ dyslexia
dysmenorrhoea *n* (*pl* -**s**) painful menstruation
dysmenorrhoeas *n* ▷ dysmenorrhoea
dyspepsia *n* (*pl* -**s**) indigestion > **dyspeptic** *adj*
dyspepsias *n* ▷ dyspepsia
dyspeptic *adj* ▷ dyspepsia
dystrophic *adj* ▷ dystrophy
dystrophies *n* ▷ dystrophy
dystrophy [diss-trof-fee] *n* (*pl* -**phies**) wasting disorder > **dystrophic** *adj*

dzho *n* (**dzhos**). A dzho is one of several ways of spelling the name of a Tibetan animal bred from yaks and cattle. This spelling is less useful than the others (**dso, dzo, zho** and **zo**) because it has four letters rather than two or three. It is, however, a very useful word to know when someone else has played zho, as you can use D to hook another word onto zho, or just to take advantage of the Z already on the board. Dzho scores 17 points.

dzo *n* (**dzos**). Dzo is one of several spelling for a Tibetan animal bred from yaks and cattle. The other forms are **dso, dzho, zho** and **zo**, and it's worth remembering all of them. Dzo scores 13 points.

Ee

E is the most common tile in the game and, while it is only worth one point, as the most frequent letter in English it is extremely useful. Many words contain two or more Es, so, unlike many tiles, it's good to have several Es on your rack. Keep in mind three-letter words formed by two Es either side of a consonant, like **eye**, **ewe** and **eve** (6 points each), and **eke** (7). E can also be handy for getting rid of double consonants: think of words like **egg** or **ebb** (each 5 points). E also combines well with K: as well as **eke**, we have **elk** and **eek** (both 7), and **ewk** (10). If you have an X on your rack, E offers you all kinds of options: just think of all the words that begin with ex-, like **exhaust** (17), which will give you a 50-point bonus if you use all of your tiles to form it. And don't forget **ex** itself, a nice little word that earns you 9 points.

ea *n* (**eas**). Ea is a dialect word for a river. This word won't earn you many points, but it does provide many opportunities to play longer words that form ea in the process. Ea scores 2 points.

each *adj, pron* every (one) taken separately

eager *adj* (**-er, -est**) showing or feeling great desire, keen > **eagerly** *adv* > **eagerness** *n* (*pl* **-es**)
 eagerer *adj* ▷ **eager**
 eagerest *adj* ▷ **eager**
 eagerly *adv* ▷ **eager**
 eagerness *n* ▷ **eager**
 eagernesses *n* ▷ **eager**

eagle *n* (*pl* **-s**) large bird of prey with keen eyesight
 eagles *n* ▷ **eagle**

eaglet *n* (*pl* **-s**) young eagle
 eaglets *n* ▷ **eaglet**

ear[1] *n* (*pl* **-s**) organ of hearing, esp. the external part of it

ear[2] *n* (*pl* **-s**) head of corn

earache *n* (*pl* **-s**) pain in the ear
 earaches *n* ▷ **earache**

earbash *v* (**-es, -ing, -ed**) (AUST & NZ) (*Informal*) talk incessantly > **earbashing** *n* (*pl* **-s**)
 earbashed *n* ▷ **earbash**
 earbashes *n* ▷ **earbash**
 earbashing *v, n* ▷ **earbash**
 earbashings *n* ▷ **earbash**

eardrum *n* (*pl* **-s**) thin piece of skin inside the ear which enables one to hear sounds
 eardrums *n* ▷ **eardrum**

earl *n* (*pl* **-s**) British nobleman ranking next below a marquess > **earldom** *n* (*pl* **-s**)
 earldom *n* ▷ **earl**
 earldoms *n* ▷ **earl**

earlier *adj, adv* ▷ **early**

earliest *adj, adv* ▷ **early**

 earls *n* ▷ **earl**

early *adj, adv* (**-ier, -iest**) before the expected or usual time

earmark *v* (**-s, -ing, -ed**) set (something) aside for a specific purpose
 earmarked *v* ▷ **earmark**
 earmarking *v* ▷ **earmark**
 earmarks *v* ▷ **earmark**

earn *v* (**-s, -ing, -ed**) obtain by work or merit
 earned *v* ▷ **earn**

earnest[1] *adj* serious and sincere > **earnestly** *adv*

earnest[2] *n* (*pl* **-s**) part payment given in advance, esp. to confirm a contract
 earnests *n* ▷ **earnest**[2]
 earning *v* ▷ **earn**

earnings *pl n* money earned
 earns *v* ▷ **earn**

earphone *n* (*pl* **-s**) receiver for a radio etc., held to or put in the ear
 earphones *n* ▷ **earphone**

earring *n* (*pl* **-s**) ornament for the lobe of the ear
 earrings *n* ▷ **earring**
 ears *n* ▷ **ear**[1, 2]

earshot *n* (*pl* **-s**) hearing range
 earshots *n* ▷ **earshot**

earth *n* (*pl* **-s**) land, the ground ▶ *v* (**-s, -ing, -ed**)

connect (a circuit) to earth
earthed *v* ▷ **earth**
earthen *adj* made of baked clay or earth
earthenware *n* (*pl* -s) pottery made of baked
clay
  earthenwares *n* ▷ **earthenwares**
  earthier *adj* ▷ **earthy**
  earthiest *adj* ▷ **earthy**
  earthing *v* ▷ **earth**
earthly *adj* conceivable or possible
earthquake *n* (*pl* -s) violent vibration of the
earth's surface
  earthquakes *n* ▷ **earthquake**
  earths *n*, *v* ▷ **earth**
earthwork *n* (*pl* -s) fortification made of earth
  earthworks *n* ▷ **earthwork**
earthworm *n* (*pl* -s) worm which burrows in
the soil
  earthworms *n* ▷ **earthworm**
earthy *adj* (-thier, -thiest) coarse or crude
earwig *n* (*pl* -s) small insect with a pincer-like
tail
  earwigs *n* ▷ **earwig**
ease *n* (*pl* -ses) freedom from difficulty,
discomfort, or worry ▶ *v* (-ses, -sing, -sed)
give bodily or mental ease to
  eased *v* ▷ **ease**
easel *n* (*pl* -s) frame to support an artist's
canvas or a blackboard
  easels *n* ▷ **easel**
  eases *n*, *v* ▷ **ease**
  easier *adj* ▷ **easy**
  easily *adv* ▷ **easy**
  easiest *adj* ▷ **easy**
  easiness *n* ▷ **easy**
  easinesses *n* ▷ **easy**
  easing *v* ▷ **ease**
east *n* (*pl* -s) (direction towards) the part of
the horizon where the sun rises ▶ *adj* to or
in the east ▶ *adv* in, to, or towards the east
> **easterly** *adj* > **eastern** *adj* > **eastward** *adj*,
adv > **eastwards** *adv*
  easterly *adj* ▷ **east**
  eastern *adj* ▷ **east**
  easts *n* ▷ **east**
  eastward *adj*, *adv* ▷ **east**
  eastwards *adv* ▷ **east**
easy *adj* (-ier, -iest) not needing much work or
effort > **easily** *adv* > **easiness** *n* (*pl* -s)
eat *v* (eats, eating, ate, eaten) take (food) into
the mouth and swallow it
eatable *adj* fit or suitable for eating
  eaten *v* ▷ **eat**
  eating *v* ▷ **eat**
  eats *v* ▷ **eat**

eaves *pl n* overhanging edges of a roof
eavesdrop *v* (-s, -pping, -pped) listen secretly
to a private conversation > **eavesdropper** *n*
(*pl* -s) > **eavesdropping** *n* (*pl* -s)
  eavesdropped *v* ▷ **eavesdrop**
  eavesdropper *n* ▷ **eavesdrop**
  eavesdroppers *n* ▷ **eavesdrop**
  eavesdropping *v*, *n* ▷ **eavesdrop**
  eavesdroppings *n* ▷ **eavesdrop**
  eavesdrops *v* ▷ **eavesdrop**
ebb *v* (-s, -ing, -ed) (of tide water) flow back ▶ *n*
(*pl* -s) flowing back of the tide
  ebbed *v* ▷ **ebb**
  ebbing *v* ▷ **ebb**
  ebbs *v*, *n* ▷ **ebb**
  ebonies *n* ▷ **ebony**
ebony *n* (*pl* -ies) hard black wood ▶ *adj* deep
black
  ebullience *n* ▷ **ebullient**
  ebulliences *n* ▷ **ebullient**
ebullient *adj* full of enthusiasm or excitement
> **ebullience** *n* (*pl* -s)
eccentric *adj* odd or unconventional ▶ *n* (*pl*
-s) eccentric person > **eccentrically** *adv*
> **eccentricity** *n* (*pl* -ies)
  eccentrically *adv* ▷ **eccentric**
  eccentricities *n* ▷ **eccentric**
  eccentricity *n* ▷ **eccentric**
  eccentrics *n* ▷ **eccentric**
ecclesiastic *n* (*pl* -s) member of the clergy ▶ *adj*
(*also* **ecclesiastical**) of the Christian Church
or clergy
  ecclesiastical *adj* ▷ **ecclesiastic**
  ecclesiastics *n* ▷ **ecclesiastic**

> **ech** *v* (**echs, eching, eched**). Ech is
> an old word that Shakespeare uses,
> and means **eke**. It's a good one to
> have ready if you have C and H but no
> obvious place to play them. Ech scores
> 8 points.

echelon [esh-a-lon] *n* (*pl* -s) level of power or
responsibility
  echelons *n* ▷ **echelon**
echidna [ik-kid-na] *n* (*pl* -nas, -nae) [-nee]
Australian spiny egg-laying mammal
  echidnae *n* ▷ **echidna**
  echidnas *n* ▷ **echidna**
echo *n* (*pl* -es) repetition of sounds by
reflection of sound waves off a surface ▶ *v*
(-es, -ing, -ed) repeat or be repeated as an
echo
  echoed *v* ▷ **echo**
  echoes *v*, *n* ▷ **echo**
  echoing *v* ▷ **echo**
éclair *n* (*pl* -s) finger-shaped pastry filled with

cream and covered with chocolate
éclairs *n* ▷ **éclair**
éclat [ake-**lah**] *n* brilliant success
eclectic *adj* selecting from various styles,
ideas, or sources > **eclecticism** *n* (*pl* **-s**)
eclecticism *n* ▷ **eclectic**
eclecticisms *n* ▷ **eclectic**
eclipse *n* (*pl* **-es**) temporary obscuring of one
star or planet by another ▶ *v* (**-ses, -sing, -sed**)
surpass or outclass
eclipsed *v* ▷ **eclipse**
eclipses *v* ▷ **eclipse**
eclipsing *v* ▷ **eclipse**
ecliptic *n* (*pl* **-s**) apparent path of the sun
ecliptics *n* ▷ **ecliptic**
ecological *adj* of ecology > **ecologically** *adv*
ecologically *adv* ▷ **ecological**
ecologist *n* ▷ **ecology**
ecologists *n* ▷ **ecology**
ecology *n* study of the relationships between
living things and their environment
> **ecologist** *n* (*pl* **-s**)
economic *adj* of economics
economical *adj* not wasteful, thrifty
> **economically** *adv*
economically *adv* ▷ **economical**
economics *n* social science concerned with
the production and consumption of goods
and services
economies *n* ▷ **economy**
economist *n* (*pl* **-s**) specialist in economics
economists *n* ▷ **economist**
economize *v* (**-izes, -izing, -ized**) reduce
expense or waste
economized *v* ▷ **economize**
economizes *v* ▷ **economize**
economizing *v* ▷ **economize**
economy *n* (*pl* **-ies**) system of interrelationship
of money, industry, and employment in a
country
ecosystem *n* (*pl* **-s**) system involving
interactions between a community and its
environment
ecosystems *n* ▷ **ecosystem**
ecru *adj* pale creamy-brown
ecstasies *n* ▷ **ecstasy**
ecstasy *n* (*pl* **-ies**) state of intense delight
> **ecstatic** *adj* > **ecstatically** *adv*
ecstatic *adj* ▷ **ecstasy**
ecstatically *adv* ▷ **ecstasy**
ectoplasm *n* (*pl* **-s**) (SPIRITUALISM) substance
that supposedly is emitted from the body of a
medium during a trance
ectoplasms *n* ▷ **ectoplasm**
ecumenical *adj* of the Christian Church

throughout the world, esp. with regard to
its unity
eczema [**ek**-sim-a] *n* (*pl* **s**) skin disease causing
intense itching
eczemas *n* ▷ **eczema**
eddied *v* ▷ **eddy**
eddies *n*, *v* ▷ **eddy**
eddy *n* (*pl* **eddies**) circular movement of air,
water, etc. ▶ *v* (**eddies, eddying, eddied**) move
with a circular motion
eddying *v* ▷ **eddy**
edelweiss [**ade**-el-vice] *n* (*pl* **-es**) alpine plant
with white flowers
edelweisses *n* ▷ **edelweiss**
edge *n* (*pl* **-s**) border or line where something
ends or begins ▶ *v* (**edges, edging, edged**)
provide an edge or border for
edged *v* ▷ **edge**
edges *n*, *v* ▷ **edge**
edgeways *adv* with the edge forwards or
uppermost
edgier *adj* ▷ **edgy**
edgiest *adj* ▷ **edgy**
edging *v* ▷ **edge** ▶ *n* (*pl* **-s**) anything placed
along an edge to finish it
edgings *n* ▷ **edging**
edgy *adj* (**edgier, edgiest**) nervous or irritable
edibilities *n* ▷ **edible**
edibility *n* ▷ **edible**
edible *adj* fit to be eaten > **edibility** *n* (*pl* **-ties**)
edict [**ee**-dikt] *n* (*pl* **-s**) order issued by an
authority
edicts *n* ▷ **edict**
edification *n* ▷ **edify**
edifications *n* ▷ **edify**
edifice [**ed**-if-iss] *n* (*pl* **-s**) large building
edifices *n* ▷ **edifice**
edified *v* ▷ **edify**
edifies *v* ▷ **edify**
edify [**ed**-if-fie] *v* (**-fies, -fying, -fied**) improve
morally by instruction > **edification** *n* (*pl* **-s**)
edifying *v* ▷ **edify**
edit *v* (**-s, -ing, -ed**) prepare (a book, film, etc.)
for publication or broadcast
edited *v* ▷ **edit**
editing *v* ▷ **edit**
edition *n* (*pl* **-s**) number of copies of a new
publication printed at one time
editions *n* ▷ **edition**
editor *n* (*pl* **-s**) person who edits
editorial *n* (*pl* **-s**) newspaper article stating
the opinion of the editor ▶ *adj* of editing or
editors
editorials *n* ▷ **editorial**
editors *n* ▷ **editor**

edits v ▷ edit
educate v (-tes, -ting, -ted) teach > **education**
n (pl -s) > **educational** adj > **educationally** adv
educated v ▷ educate
educates v ▷ educate
educating v ▷ educate
educational adj ▷ educate
educationalist n (pl -s) expert in the theory
of education
educationalists n ▷ educationalist
educationally adv ▷ educate
educations n ▷ educate
educative adj educating

> **ee** n (een). Ee is a Scots word for eye.
> While this word won't earn you a big
> score on its own, it can be very useful
> when you're trying to form several
> words at once. Ee scores 2 points.
> **eek** interj. Eek is a noise that people
> make when they are startled or
> frightened. Eek scores 7 points.

eel n (pl -s) snakelike fish
eels n ▷ eel
eerie adj (-ier, -iest) uncannily frightening or
disturbing > **eerily** adv
eerier adj ▷ eerie
eeriest adj ▷ eerie
eerily adv ▷ eerie

> **ef** n (efs). Ef is the letter F, and is a handy
> word to know when you want to play
> a longer word parallel to a word that's
> already on the board. Ef scores 5 points.

efface v (-ces, -cing, -ced) remove by rubbing
> **effacement** n (pl -s)
effaced v ▷ efface
effacement n ▷ efface
effacements n ▷ efface
effaces v ▷ efface
effacing v ▷ efface
effect n (pl -s) change or result caused by
someone or something ▶ pl personal
belongings ▶ v (-s, -ing, -ed) cause to happen,
accomplish
effected v ▷ effect
effecting v ▷ effect
effective adj producing a desired result
> **effectively** adv
effectively adv ▷ effective
effects n, v ▷ effect
effectual adj producing the intended result
> **effectually** adv
effectually adv ▷ effectual
effeminacies n ▷ effeminate
effeminacy n ▷ effeminate
effeminate adj (of a man) displaying

characteristics thought to be typical of a
woman > **effeminacy** n (pl -ies)
effervescence n ▷ effervescent
effervescences n ▷ effervescent
effervescent adj (of a liquid) giving off bubbles
of gas > **effervescence** n (pl -s)
effete [if-feet] adj powerless, feeble
efficacies n ▷ efficacious
efficacious adj producing the intended result
> **efficacy** n (pl -ies)
efficacy n ▷ efficacious
efficiencies n ▷ efficient
efficiency n ▷ efficient
efficient adj functioning effectively with little
waste of effort > **efficiently** adv > **efficiency**
n (pl -ies)
efficiently adv ▷ efficient
effigies n ▷ effigy
effigy [ef-fij-ee] n (pl -ies) image or likeness of
a person
efflorescence n (pl -s) flowering
efflorescences n ▷ efflorescence
effluent n (pl -s) liquid discharged as waste
effluents n ▷ effluent
effluvia n ▷ effluvium
effluvium n (pl -via) unpleasant smell, as of
decaying matter or gaseous waste
effort n (pl -s) physical or mental exertion
> **effortless** adj
effortless adj ▷ effort
efforts n ▷ effort
effronteries n ▷ effrontery
effrontery n (pl -ies) brazen impudence
effusion n (pl -s) unrestrained outburst
effusions n ▷ effusion
effusive adj openly emotional, demonstrative
> **effusively** adv
effusively adv ▷ effusive
egalitarian adj upholding the equality of all
people ▶ n (pl -s) person who holds egalitarian
beliefs > **egalitarianism** n (pl -s)
egalitarianism n ▷ egalitarian
egalitarianisms n ▷ egalitarian
egalitarians n ▷ egalitarian
egg[1] n (pl -s) oval or round object laid by
the females of birds and other creatures,
containing a developing embryo
egg[2] v (-s, -ing, -ed) encourage or incite, esp.
to do wrong
egged v ▷ egg[2]
egghead n (pl -s) (Informal) intellectual person
eggheads n ▷ egghead
egging v ▷ egg[2]
eggplant n (pl -s) (US, CANADIAN, AUST & NZ)
aubergine

eggplants *n* ▷ **eggplant**

eggs *n*, *v* ▷ **egg**[1,2]

ego *n* (*pl* -s) the conscious mind of an individual

egocentric *adj* self-centred

egoism, egotism *n* excessive concern for one's own interests > **egoist, egotist** *n* (*pl* -s) > **egoistic, egotistic** *adj*

egoist *n* ▷ **egoism**

egoistic *adj* ▷ **egoism**

egoists *n* ▷ **egoism**

egos *n* ▷ **ego**

egotist *n* ▷ **egoism**

egotistic *adj* ▷ **egoism**

egotists *n* ▷ **egoism**

egregious [ig-**greej**-uss] *adj* outstandingly bad

egress [ee-gress] *n* (*pl* -es) departure

egresses *n* ▷ **egress**

egret [ee-grit] *n* (*pl* -s) lesser white heron

egrets *n* ▷ **egret**

eider *n* (*pl* -s) Arctic duck

eiderdown *n* (*pl* -s) quilt (orig. stuffed with eider feathers)

eiderdowns *n* ▷ **eiderdown**

eiders *n* ▷ **eider**

eight *adj, n* (*pl* -s) one more than seven

eighteen *adj, n* (*pl* -s) eight and ten > **eighteenth** *adj, n* (*pl* -s)

eighteens *n* ▷ **eighteen**

eighteenth *adj, n* ▷ **eighteen**

eighteenths *n* ▷ **eighteen**

eighth *adj, n* (*pl* -s) (of) number eight in a series

eighths *n* ▷ **eighth**

eighties *n* ▷ **eighty**

eightieth *n* ▷ **eighty**

eightieths *n* ▷ **eighty**

eights *n* ▷ **eight**

eighty *adj, n* (*pl* -ies) eight times ten > **eightieth** *adj, n* (*pl* -s)

eisteddfod [ice-sted-fod] *n* (*pl* -s) Welsh festival with competitions in music and other performing arts

eisteddfods *n* ▷ **eisteddfod**

either *adj, pron* one or the other (of two) ▶ *conj* used preceding two or more possibilities joined by *or* ▶ *adv* likewise

ejaculate *v* (-tes, -ting, -ted) eject (semen) > **ejaculation** *n* (*pl* -s)

ejaculated *v* ▷ **ejaculate**

ejaculates *v* ▷ **ejaculate**

ejaculating *v* ▷ **ejaculate**

ejaculation *n* ▷ **ejaculate**

ejaculations *n* ▷ **ejaculate**

eject *v* (-s, -ing, -ed) force out, expel > **ejection** *n* (*pl* -s) > **ejector** *n* (*pl* -s)

ejected *v* ▷ **eject**

ejecting *v* ▷ **eject**

ejection *n* ▷ **eject**

ejections *n* ▷ **eject**

ejector *n* ▷ **eject**

ejectors *n* ▷ **eject**

ejects *v* ▷ **eject**

eke *v* (ekes, eking, eked) (*usu. foll. by* **out**) make (a living) with difficulty

eked *v* ▷ **eke**

ekes *v* ▷ **eke**

eking *v* ▷ **eke**

elaborate *adj* with a lot of fine detail ▶ *v* (-tes, -ting, -ted) expand upon > **elaboration** *n* (*pl* -s)

elaborated *v* ▷ **elaborate**

elaborates *v* ▷ **elaborate**

elaborating *v* ▷ **elaborate**

elaboration *n* ▷ **elaborate**

elaborations *n* ▷ **elaborate**

élan [ale-an] *n* (*pl* -s) style and vigour

eland [eel-and] *n* (*pl* -s) large antelope of southern Africa

elands *n* ▷ **eland**

élans *n* ▷ **élan**

elapse *v* (-ses, -sing, -sed) (of time) pass by

elapsed *v* ▷ **elapse**

elapses *v* ▷ **elapse**

elapsing *v* ▷ **elapse**

elastic *adj* resuming normal shape after distortion ▶ *n* (*pl* -s) tape or fabric containing interwoven strands of flexible rubber > **elasticity** *n* (*pl* -ies)

elasticities *n* ▷ **elastic**

elasticity *n* ▷ **elastic**

elastics *n* ▷ **elastic**

elate *v* (-tes, -ting, -ted) make extremely happy and excited > **elation** *n* (*pl* -s)

elated *v* ▷ **elate**

elates *v* ▷ **elate**

elating *v* ▷ **elate**

elation *n* ▷ **elate**

elations *n* ▷ **elate**

elbow *n* (*pl* -s) joint between the upper arm and the forearm ▶ *v* (-s, -ing, -ed) shove or strike with the elbow

elbowed *v* ▷ **elbow**

elbowing *v* ▷ **elbow**

elbows *n*, *v* ▷ **elbow**

elder[1] *adj* older ▶ *n* (*pl* -s) older person

elder[2] *n* (*pl* -s) small tree with white flowers and black berries

elderly *adj* (fairly) old

elders *n* ▷ **elder**[1,2]

eldest *adj* oldest

eldritch adj (SCOT) weird, uncanny
elect v (-s, -ing, -ed) choose by voting ▶ adj appointed but not yet in office
 elected v ▷ **elect**
 electing v ▷ **elect**
election n (pl -s) choosing of representatives by voting
electioneering n (pl -s) active participation in a political campaign
 electioneerings n ▷ **electioneering**
 elections n ▷ **election**
elective adj chosen by election
elector n (pl -s) someone who has the right to vote in an election > **electoral** adj
 electoral adj ▷ **elector**
electorate n (pl -s) people who have the right to vote
 electorates n ▷ **electorate**
 electors n ▷ **elector**
electric adj produced by, transmitting, or powered by electricity
electrical adj using or concerning electricity
electrician n (pl -s) person trained to install and repair electrical equipment
 electricians n ▷ **electrician**
 electricities n ▷ **electricity**
electricity n (pl -ies) form of energy associated with stationary or moving electrons or other charged particles
electrics pl n (BRIT) electric appliances
 electrification n ▷ **electrify**
 electrifications n ▷ **electrify**
 electrified v ▷ **electrify**
 electrifies v ▷ **electrify**
electrify v (-fies, -fying, -fied) adapt for operation by electric power > **electrification** n
 electrifying v ▷ **electrify**
electrocute v (-tes, -ting, -ted) kill or injure by electricity > **electrocution** n (pl -s)
 electrocuted v ▷ **electrocute**
 electrocutes v ▷ **electrocute**
 electrocuting v ▷ **electrocute**
 electrocution n ▷ **electrocute**
 electrocutions n ▷ **electrocute**
electrode n (pl -s) conductor through which an electric current enters or leaves a battery, vacuum tube, etc
 electrodes n ▷ **electrode**
electrodynamics n branch of physics concerned with the interactions between electrical and mechanical forces
 electrolyses n ▷ **electrolysis**
electrolysis [ill-lek-**troll**-iss-iss] n (pl -ses) conduction of electricity by an electrolyte,

esp. to induce chemical change
electrolyte n (pl -s) solution or molten substance that conducts electricity
 > **electrolytic** adj
 electrolytes n ▷ **electrolyte**
 electrolytic adj ▷ **electrolyte**
electromagnet n (pl -s) magnet containing a coil of wire through which an electric current is passed
electromagnetic adj of or operated by an electomagnet
 electromagnets n ▷ **electromagnet**
electron n (pl -s) elementary particle in all atoms that has a negative electrical charge
electronic adj (of a device) dependent on the action of electrons
electronics n technology concerned with the development of electronic devices and circuits
 electrons n ▷ **electron**
electronvolt n (pl -s) unit of energy used in nuclear physics
 electronvolts n ▷ **electronvolt**
electroplate v (-tes, -ting, -ted) coat with silver etc. by electrolysis
 electroplated v ▷ **electroplate**
 electroplates v ▷ **electroplate**
 electroplating v ▷ **electroplate**
 elects v ▷ **elect**
 elegance n ▷ **elegant**
 elegances n ▷ **elegant**
elegant adj pleasing or graceful in dress, style, or design > **elegance** n (pl -s)
elegiac adj mournful or plaintive
 elegies n ▷ **elegy**
elegy [**el**-lij-ee] n (pl -ies) mournful poem, esp. a lament for the dead
element n (pl -s) component part ▶ pl basic principles of something
elemental adj of primitive natural forces or passions
elementary adj simple and straightforward
 elements n ▷ **element**
elephant n (pl -s) huge four-footed thick-skinned animal with ivory tusks and a long trunk
elephantiasis [el-lee-fan-**tie**-a-siss] n disease with hardening of the skin and enlargement of the legs etc.
elephantine adj unwieldy, clumsy
 elephants n ▷ **elephant**
elevate v (-ates, -ating, -ated) raise in rank or status
 elevated v ▷ **elevate**
 elevates v ▷ **elevate**

elevating *v* ▷ **elevate**
elevation *n* (*pl* -s) raising
elevator *n* (*pl* -s) (AUST, US & CANADIAN) lift for carrying people
  elevators *n* ▷ **elevator**
eleven *adj*, *n* (*pl* -s) one more than ten
  elevens *n* ▷ **eleven**
elevenses *n* (BRIT & S AFR) (*Informal*) mid-morning snack
eleventh *adj*, *n* (*pl* -s) (of) number eleven in a series
  elevenths *n* ▷ **eleventh**
elf *n* (*pl* **elves**) (in folklore) small mischievous fairy
elfin *adj* small and delicate
elicit *v* (-s, -ing, -ed) bring about (a response or reaction)
  elicited *v* ▷ **elicit**
  eliciting *v* ▷ **elicit**
  elicits *v* ▷ **elicit**
elide *v* (-des, -ding, -ded) omit (a vowel or syllable) from a spoken word > **elision** *n* (*pl* -s)
  elided *v* ▷ **elide**
  elides *v* ▷ **elide**
  eliding *v* ▷ **elide**
  eligibilities *n* ▷ **eligible**
  eligibility *n* ▷ **eligible**
eligible *adj* meeting the requirements or qualifications needed > **eligibility** *n* (*pl* -ties)
eliminate *v* (-tes, -ting, -ted) get rid of > **elimination** *n* (*pl* -s)
  eliminated *v* ▷ **eliminate**
  eliminates *v* ▷ **eliminate**
  eliminating *v* ▷ **eliminate**
  elimination *n* ▷ **eliminate**
  eliminations *n* ▷ **eliminate**
  elision *n* ▷ **elide**
  elisions *n* ▷ **elide**
elite [ill-**eet**] *n* (*pl* -s) most powerful, rich, or gifted members of a group
  elites *n* ▷ **elite**
elitism *n* (*pl* -s) belief that society should be governed by a small group of superior people > **elitist** *n*, *adj* (*pl* -s)
  elitisms *n* ▷ **elitism**
  elitists *n* ▷ **elitist**
elixir [ill-**ix**-er] *n* (*pl* -s) imaginary liquid that can prolong life or turn base metals into gold
  elixirs *n* ▷ **elixir**
elk *n* (*pl* -s) large deer of N Europe and Asia
  elks *n* ▷ **elk**
ellipse *n* (*pl* -ses) oval shape
  ellipses *n* ▷ **ellipse, ellipsis**
ellipsis *n* (*pl* -ses) omission of letters or words in a sentence

elliptical *adj* oval-shaped
elm *n* (*pl* -s) tree with serrated leaves
  elms *n* ▷ **elm**
elocution *n* (*pl* -s) art of speaking clearly in public
  elocutions *n* ▷ **elocation**
elongate [eel-**long**-gate] *v* (-tes, -ting, -ted) make or become longer > **elongation** *n* (*pl* -s)
  elongated *v* ▷ **elongate**
  elongates *v* ▷ **elongate**
  elongating *v* ▷ **elongate**
  elongation *n* ▷ **elongate**
  elongations *n* ▷ **elongate**
elope *v* (-s, -ing, -ed) (of two people) run away secretly to get married > **elopement** *n* (*pl* -s)
  eloped *v* ▷ **elope**
  elopement *n* ▷ **elope**
  elopements *n* ▷ **elope**
  elopes *v* ▷ **elope**
  eloping *v* ▷ **elope**
eloquence *n* (*pl* -s) fluent powerful use of language > **eloquent** *adj* > **eloquently** *adv*
  eloquencies *n* ▷ **eloquence**
  eloquent *adj* ▷ **eloquence**
  eloquently *adv* ▷ **eloquence**
else *adv* in addition or more
elsewhere *adv* in or to another place
elucidate *v* (-tes, -ting, -ted) make (something difficult) clear > **elucidation** *n* (*pl* -s)
  elucidated *v* ▷ **elucidate**
  elucidates *v* ▷ **elucidate**
  elucidating *v* ▷ **elucidate**
  elucidation *n* ▷ **elucidate**
  elucidations *n* ▷ **elucidate**
elude *v* (-s, -ing, -ed) escape from by cleverness or quickness
  eluded *v* ▷ **elude**
  eludes *v* ▷ **elude**
  eluding *v* ▷ **elude**
elusive *adj* difficult to catch or remember
elver *n* (*pl* -s) young eel
  elvers *n* ▷ **elver**
  elves *n* ▷ **elf**
emaciated [im-**mace**-ee-ate-id] *adj* abnormally thin > **emaciation** *n* (*pl* -s)
  emaciation *n* ▷ **emaciated**
  emaciations *n* ▷ **emaciated**
emanate [em-a-nate] *v* (-tes, -ting, -ted) issue, proceed from a source > **emanation** *n* (*pl* -s)
  emanated *v* ▷ **emanate**
  emanates *v* ▷ **emanate**
  emanating *v* ▷ **emanate**
  emanation *n* ▷ **emanate**
  emanations *n* ▷ **emanate**
emancipate *v* (-tes, -ting, -ted) free

from social, political, or legal restraints
> **emancipation** n (pl **-s**)
emancipated v ▷ emancipate
emancipates v ▷ emancipate
emancipating v ▷ emancipate
emancipation n ▷ emancipate
emancipations n ▷ emancipate
emasculate v (**-tes, -ting, -ted**) deprive of
power > **emasculation** n (pl **-s**)
emasculated v ▷ emasculate
emasculates v ▷ emasculate
emasculating v ▷ emasculate
emasculation n ▷ emasculate
emasculations n ▷ emasculate
embalm v (**-s, -ing, -ed**) preserve (a corpse)
from decay by the use of chemicals etc.
embalmed v ▷ embalm
embalming v ▷ embalm
embalms v ▷ embalm
embankment n (pl **-s**) man-made ridge that
carries a road or railway or holds back water
embankments n ▷ embankment
embargo n (pl **-oes**) order by a government
prohibiting trade with a country ▶ v (**-oes,
-oing, -oed**) put an embargo on
embargoed v ▷ embargo
embargoes n, v ▷ embargo
embargoing v ▷ embargo
embark v (**-s, -ing, -ed**) board a ship or aircraft
(foll. by **on**) > **embarkation** n (**-s**)
embarkation n ▷ embark
embarkations n ▷ embark
embarked v ▷ embark
embarking v ▷ embark
embarks v ▷ embark
embarrass v (**-es, -ing, -ed**) cause to feel self-
conscious or ashamed > **embarrassed** adj
> **embarrassing** adj > **embarrassment** n (pl **-s**)
embarrassed v, adj ▷ embarrass
embarrasses v ▷ embarrass
embarrassing v, adj ▷ embarrass
embarrassment n ▷ embarrass
embarrassments n ▷ embarrass
embassies n ▷ embassy
embassy n (pl **-ies**) offices or official residence
of an ambassador
embattled adj having a lot of difficulties
embed v (**-s, -dding, -dded**) fix firmly in
something solid
embedded adj (of a journalist) assigned
to accompany an active military unit ▶ v
▷ embed
embedding v ▷ embed
embeds v ▷ embed
embellish v (**-es, -ing, -ed**) decorate

> **embellishment** n (pl **-s**)
embellished v ▷ embellish
embellishes v ▷ embellish
embellishing v ▷ embellish
embellishment n ▷ embellish
embellishments n ▷ embellish
ember n (pl **-s**) glowing piece of wood or coal
in a dying fire
embers n ▷ ember
embezzle v (**-s, -ing, -ed**) steal money that has
been entrusted to one > **embezzlement** n (pl
-s) > **embezzler** n (pl **-s**)
embezzled v ▷ embezzle
embezzlement n ▷ embezzle
embezzlements n ▷ embezzle
embezzler n ▷ embezzle
embezzlers n ▷ embezzle
embezzles v ▷ embezzle
embezzling v ▷ embezzle
embittered adj feeling anger as a result of
misfortune
emblazon v (**-s, -ing, -ed**) decorate with bright
colours
emblazoned v ▷ emblazon
emblazoning v ▷ emblazon
emblazons v ▷ emblazon
emblem n (pl **-s**) object or design that
symbolizes a quality, type, or group
> **emblematic** adj
emblematic adj ▷ emblem
emblems n ▷ emblem
embodied v ▷ embody
embodies v ▷ embody
embodiment n ▷ embody
embodiments n ▷ embody
embody v (**-dies, -dying, -died**) be an example
or expression of > **embodiment** n (pl **-s**)
embodying v ▷ embody
embolden v (**-s, -ing, -ed**) encourage
(someone)
emboldened v ▷ embolden
emboldening v ▷ embolden
emboldens v ▷ embolden
embolism n (pl **-s**) blocking of a blood vessel by
a blood clot or air bubble
embolisms n ▷ embolism
embossed adj (of a design or pattern)
standing out from a surface
embrace v (**-ces, -cing, -ced**) clasp in the arms,
hug ▶ n (pl **-s**) act of embracing
embraced v ▷ embrace
embraces v, n ▷ embrace
embracing v ▷ embrace
embrasure n (pl **-s**) door or window having
splayed sides so that the opening is larger

on the inside
embrasures *n* ▷ **embrasure**
embrocation *n* (*pl* -s) lotion for rubbing into
the skin to relieve pain
embrocations *n* ▷ **embrocation**
embroider *v* (-s, -ing, -ed) decorate with
needlework > **embroidery** *n* (*pl* -ies)
embroidered *v* ▷ **embroider**
embroideries *n* ▷ **embroider**
embroidering *v* ▷ **embroider**
embroiders *v* ▷ **embroider**
embroidery *n* ▷ **embroider**
embroil *v* (-s, -ing, -ed) involve (a person) in
problems
embroiled *v* ▷ **embroil**
embroiling *v* ▷ **embroil**
embroils *v* ▷ **embroil**
embryo [em-bree-oh] *n* (*pl* -s) unborn
creature in the early stages of development
> **embryology** *n* (*pl* -ies)
embryologies *n* ▷ **embryo**
embryology *n* ▷ **embryo**
embryonic *adj* at an early stage
embryos *n* ▷ **embryo**
emend *v* (-s, -ing, -ed) remove errors from
> **emendation** *n* (*pl* **emendations**)
emendation *n* ▷ **emend**
emendations *n* ▷ **emend**
emended *v* ▷ **emend**
emending *v* ▷ **emend**
emends *v* ▷ **emend**
emerald *n* (*pl* -s) bright green precious stone
▶ *adj* bright green
emeralds *n* ▷ **emerald**
emerge *v* (-ges, -ging, -ged) come into view
> **emergence** *n* (*pl* -s) > **emergent** *adj*
emerged *v* ▷ **emerge**
emergence *n* ▷ **emerge**
emergences *n* ▷ **emerge**
emergencies *n* ▷ **emergency**
emergency *n* (*pl* -ies) sudden unforeseen
occurrence needing immediate action
emergent *adj* ▷ **emerge**
emerges *v* ▷ **emerge**
emerging *v* ▷ **emerge**
emeries *n* ▷ **emery**
emeritus [im-mer-rit-uss] *adj* retired, but
retaining an honorary title
emery *n* (*pl* -ies) hard mineral used for
smoothing and polishing
emetic [im-met-ik] *n* (*pl* -s) substance that
causes vomiting ▶ *adj* causing vomiting
emetics *n* ▷ **emetic**
emigrant *n* ▷ **emigrate**
emigrants *n* ▷ **emigrate**

emigrate *v* (-tes, -ting, -ted) go and settle
in another country > **emigrant** *n* (*pl* -s)
> **emigration** *n* (*pl* -s)
emigrated *v* ▷ **emigrate**
emigrates *v* ▷ **emigrate**
emigrating *v* ▷ **emigrate**
emigration *n* ▷ **emigrate**
emigrations *n* ▷ **emigrate**
émigré [em-mig-gray] *n* (*pl* -s) someone who
has left his native country for political
reasons
émigrés *n* ▷ **émigré**
eminence *n* (*pl* -s) position of superiority or
fame
eminences *n* ▷ **eminence**
eminent *adj* distinguished, well-known
> **eminently** *adv*
eminently *adv* ▷ **eminent**
emir [em-meer] *n* (*pl* -s) Muslim ruler
emirate *n* (*pl* -s) country ruled by an emir
emirates *n* ▷ **emirate**
emirs *n* ▷ **emir**
emissaries *n* ▷ **emissary**
emissary *n* (*pl* -ies) agent sent on a mission by
a government
emission *n* ▷ **emit**
emissions ▷ **emit**
emit *v* (-s, -tting, -tted) give out (heat, light, or
a smell) > **emission** *n* (*pl* -s)
emits *v* ▷ **emit**
emitted *v* ▷ **emit**
emitting *v* ▷ **emit**
emollient *adj* softening, soothing ▶ *n* (*pl* -s)
substance which softens or soothes the skin
emollients *n* ▷ **emollient**
emolument *n* (*pl* -s) (*formal*) fees or wages from
employment
emoluments *n* ▷ **emolument**
emoticon [i-mote-i-kon] *n* (*pl* -s) (COMPUTERS)
▷ **smiley**
emoticons *n* ▷ **emoticon**
emotion *n* (*pl* -s) strong feeling
emotional *adj* readily affected by or appealing
to the emotions > **emotionally** *adv*
emotionally *adv* ▷ **emotional**
emotions *n* ▷ **emotion**
emotive *adj* tending to arouse emotion
empathies *n* ▷ **empathy**
empathy *n* (*pl* -ies) ability to understand
someone else's feelings as if they were one's
own
emperor *n* (*pl* -s) ruler of an empire > **empress**
n fem (*pl* -es)
emperors *n* ▷ **emperor**
emphases *n* ▷ **emphasis**

emphasis *n* (*pl* **-ses**) special importance or
significance > **emphasize** *v* (**-s, -ing, -ed**)
emphasize *v* ▷ **emphasis**
emphasized *v* ▷ **emphasis**
emphasizes *v* ▷ **emphasis**
emphasizing *v* ▷ **emphasis**
emphatic *adj* showing emphasis
> **emphatically** *adv*
emphatically *adv* ▷ **emphatic**
emphysema [em-fiss-**see**-ma] *n* (*pl* **-s**)
condition in which the air sacs of the lungs
are grossly enlarged, causing breathlessness
emphysemas *n* ▷ **emphysema**
empire *n* (*pl* **-s**) group of territories under the
rule of one state or person
empires *n* ▷ **empire**
empirical *adj* relying on experiment or
experience, not on theory > **empirically** *adv*
empirically *adv* ▷ **empirical**
empiricism *n* (*pl* **-s**) doctrine that all
knowledge derives from experience
> **empiricist** *n* (*pl* **-s**)
empiricisms *n* ▷ **empiricism**
empiricist *n* ▷ **empiricism**
empiricists *n* ▷ **empiricism**
emplacement *n* (*pl* **-s**) prepared position for
a gun
emplacements *n* ▷ **emplacement**
employ *v* (**-s, -ing, -ed**) hire (a person) ▶ *n* (*pl* **-s**)
state of being employed > **employee** *n* (*pl* **-s**)
employed *v* ▷ **employ**
employee *n* ▷ **employ**
employees *n* ▷ **employ**
employer *n* (*pl* **-s**) person or organization that
employs someone
employers *n* ▷ **employer**
employing *v* ▷ **employ**
employment *n* (*pl* **-s**) state of being employed
employments *n* ▷ **employment**
employs *v, n* ▷ **employ**
emporia *n* ▷ **emporium**
emporium *n* (*pl* **-riums, -ria**) (*Old-fashioned*)
large general shop
emporiums *n* ▷ **emporia**
empower *v* (**-s, -ing, -ed**) enable, authorize
empowered *v* ▷ **empower**
empowering *v* ▷ **empower**
empowers *v* ▷ **empower**
empress *n* ▷ **emperor**
empresses *n* ▷ **emperor**
emptied *v* ▷ **empty**
emptier *adj* ▷ **empty**
empties *pl n* empty boxes, bottles, etc. ▶ *v*
▷ **empty**
emptiest *adj* ▷ **empty**

emptiness *n* ▷ **empty**
emptinesses *n* ▷ **empty**
empty *adj* (**-ier, -iest**) containing nothing ▶ *v*
(**-ies, -ying, -ied**) make or become empty
> **emptiness** *n* (*pl* **-es**)
emptying *v* ▷ **empty**
emu *n* (*pl* **-s**) large Australian flightless bird
with long legs
emulate *v* (**-tes, -ting, -ted**) attempt to equal
or surpass by imitating > **emulation** *n* (*pl* **-s**)
emulated *v* ▷ **emulate**
emulates *v* ▷ **emulate**
emulating *v* ▷ **emulate**
emulation *n* ▷ **emulate**
emulations *n* ▷ **emulate**
emulsified *v* ▷ **emulsify**
emulsifier *n* ▷ **emulsify**
emulsifiers *n* ▷ **emulsify**
emulsifies *v* ▷ **emulsify**
emulsify *v* (**-fies, -fying, -fied**) (of two liquids)
join together or join (two liquids) together
> **emulsifier** *n* (*pl* **-s**)
emulsifying *v* ▷ **emulsify**
emulsion *n* (*pl* **-s**) light-sensitive coating on
photographic film ▶ *v* (**-s, -ing, -ed**) paint with
emulsion paint
emulsioned *v* ▷ **emulsion**
emulsioning *v* ▷ **emulsion**
emulsions *n, v* ▷ **emulsion**
emus *n* ▷ **emu**
enable *v* (**-les, -ling, -led**) provide (a person)
with the means, opportunity, or authority
(to do something)
enabled *v* ▷ **enable**
enables *v* ▷ **enable**
enabling *v* ▷ **enable**
enact *v* (**-s, -ing, -ed**) establish by law
> **enactment** *n* (*pl* **-s**)
enacted *v* ▷ **enact**
enacting *v* ▷ **enact**
enactment *n* ▷ **enact**
enactments *n* ▷ **enact**
enacts *v* ▷ **enact**
enamel *n* (*pl* **-s**) glasslike coating applied to
metal etc. to preserve the surface ▶ *v* (**-s,
-lling, -lled**) cover with enamel
enamelled *v* ▷ **enamel**
enamelling *v* ▷ **enamel**
enamels *n, v* ▷ **enamel**
enamoured *adj* inspired with love
encamp *v* (**-s, -ing, -ed**) set up in a camp
> **encampment** *n* (*pl* **-s**)
encamped *v* ▷ **encamp**
encamping *v* ▷ **encamp**
encampment *n* ▷ **encamp**

encampments *n* ▷ **encamp**
encamps *v* ▷ **encamp**
encapsulate *v* (-tes, -ting, -ted) summarize
encapsulated *v* ▷ **encapsulate**
encapsulates *v* ▷ **encapsulate**
encapsulating *v* ▷ **encapsulate**
encephalitis [en-sef-a-**lite**-iss] *n* (*pl* -es)
inflammation of the brain
encephalitises *n* ▷ **encephalitis**
enchant *v* (-s, -ing, -ed) delight and fascinate
▷ **enchantment** *n* (*pl* -s) ▷ **enchanter** *n* (*pl* -s)
▷ **enchantress** *n fem* (*pl* -es)
enchanted *v* ▷ **enchant**
enchanter *n* ▷ **enchant**
enchanters *n* ▷ **enchant**
enchanting *v* ▷ **enchant**
enchantment *n* ▷ **enchant**
enchantments *n* ▷ **enchant**
enchantress *n* ▷ **enchant**
enchantresses *n* ▷ **enchant**
enchants *v* ▷ **enchant**
encircle *v* (-s, -ling, -led) form a circle around
▷ **encirclement** *n* (*pl* -s)
encircled *v* ▷ **encircle**
encirclement *n* ▷ **encircle**
encirclements *n* ▷ **encircle**
encircles *v* ▷ **encircle**
encircling *v* ▷ **encircle**
enclave *n* (*pl* -s) part of a country entirely
surrounded by foreign territory
enclaves *n* ▷ **enclave**
enclose *v* (-s, -sing, -sed) surround completely
▷ **enclosure** *n* (*pl* -s)
enclosed *v* ▷ **enclose**
encloses *v* ▷ **enclose**
enclosing *v* ▷ **enclose**
enclosure *n* ▷ **enclose**
enclosures *n* ▷ **enclose**
encomia *n* ▷ **encomium**
encomium *n* (*pl* -miums, -mia) formal
expression of praise
encomiums *n* ▷ **encomiums**
encompass *v* (-es, -ing, -ed) surround
encompassed *v* ▷ **encompass**
encompasses *v* ▷ **encompass**
encompassing *v* ▷ **encompass**
encore *interj* again, once more ▶ *n* (*pl* -s) extra
performance due to enthusiastic demand
encores *n* ▷ **encore**
encounter *v* (-s, -ing, -ed) meet unexpectedly
▶ *n* (*pl* -s) unexpected meeting
encountered *v* ▷ **encounter**
encountering *v* ▷ **encounter**
encounters *v, n* ▷ **encounter**
encourage *v* (-ges, -ging, -ged) inspire with

confidence ▷ **encouragement** *n* (*pl* -s)
encouraged *v* ▷ **encourage**
encouragement *n* ▷ **encourage**
encouragements *n* ▷ **encourage**
encourages *v* ▷ **encourage**
encouraging *v* ▷ **encourage**
encroach *v* (-es, -ing, -ed) intrude gradually
on a person's rights or land ▷ **encroachment**
n (*pl* -s)
encroached *v* ▷ **encroach**
encroaches *v* ▷ **encroach**
encroaching *v* ▷ **encroach**
encroachment *n* ▷ **encroach**
encroachments *n* ▷ **encroach**
encrust *v* (-s, -ing, -ed) cover with a layer of
something
encrusted *v* ▷ **encrust**
encrusting *v* ▷ **encrust**
encrusts *v* ▷ **encrust**
encumber *v* (-s, -ing, -ed) hinder or impede
encumbered *v* ▷ **encumber**
encumbering *v* ▷ **encumber**
encumbers *v* ▷ **encumber**
encumbrance *n* (*pl* -s) something that
impedes or is burdensome
encumbrances *n* ▷ **encumbrance**
encyclical [en-**sik**-lik-kl] *n* (*pl* -s) letter sent by
the Pope to all bishops
encyclicals *n* ▷ **encyclical**
encyclopaedia *n* ▷ **encyclopedia**
encyclopaedias *n* ▷ **encyclopedia**
encyclopaedic *adj* ▷ **encyclopedia**
encyclopedia, encyclopaedia *n* (*pl* -s) book
or set of books containing facts about
many subjects, usu. in alphabetical order
▷ **encyclopedic, encyclopaedic** *adj*
encyclopedias *n* ▷ **encyclopedia**
encyclopedic *adj* ▷ **encyclopedia**
end *n* (*pl* -s) furthest point or part ▶ *v* (-s, -ing,
-ed) bring or come to a finish ▷ **ending** *n* (*pl* -s)
▷ **endless** *adj*
endanger *v* (-s, -ing, -ed) put in danger
endangered *v* ▷ **endanger**
endangering *v* ▷ **endanger**
endangers *v* ▷ **endanger**
endear *v* (-s, -ing, -ed) cause to be liked
▷ **endearing** *adj*
endeared *v* ▷ **endear**
endearing *v, adj* ▷ **endear**
endearment *n* (*pl* -s) affectionate word or
phrase
endearments *n* ▷ **endearment**
endears *v* ▷ **endear**
endeavour *v* (-s, -ing, -ed) try ▶ *n* (*pl* -s) effort
endeavoured *v* ▷ **endeavour**

endeavouring v ▷ **endeavour**
endeavours v, n ▷ **endeavour**
ended v ▷ **end**
endemic adj present within a localized area or peculiar to a particular group of people
ending v, n ▷ **end**
endings n ▷ **end**
endive n (pl **-s**) curly-leaved plant used in salads
endives n ▷ **endive**
endless adj ▷ **end**
endocrine adj relating to the glands which secrete hormones directly into the bloodstream
endogenous [en-**dodge**-in-uss] adj originating from within
endorse v (-ses, -sing, -sed) give approval to > **endorsement** n (pl **-s**)
endorsed v ▷ **endorse**
endorsement n ▷ **endorse**
endorsements n ▷ **endorse**
endorses v ▷ **endorse**
endorsing v ▷ **endorse**
endow v (-s, -ing, -ed) provide permanent income for > **endowment** n (pl **-s**)
endowed v ▷ **endow**
endowing v ▷ **endow**
endowment v ▷ **endow**
endowments v ▷ **endow**
endows v ▷ **endow**
ends n, v ▷ **end**
endurable adj ▷ **endure**
endurance n (pl **-s**) act or power of enduring
endurances n ▷ **endurance**
endure v (-res, -ring, -red) bear (hardship) patiently > **endurable** adj
endured v ▷ **endure**
endures v ▷ **endure**
enduring v ▷ **endure**
endways adv having the end forwards or upwards
enema [en-im-a] n (pl **-s**) medicine injected into the rectum to empty the bowels
enemas n ▷ **enema**
enemies n ▷ **enemy**
enemy n (pl **-ies**) hostile person or nation, opponent
energetic adj ▷ **energy**
energetically adv ▷ **energy**
energies n ▷ **energy**
energize v (-izes, -izing, -ized) give vigour to
energized v ▷ **energize**
energizes v ▷ **energize**
energizing v ▷ **energize**
energy n (pl **-ies**) capacity for intense activity

> **energetic** adj > **energetically** adv
enervate v (-tes, -ting, -ted) deprive of strength or vitality > **enervation** n (pl **-s**)
enervated v ▷ **enervate**
enervates v ▷ **enervate**
enervating v ▷ **enervate**
enervation n ▷ **enervate**
enervations n ▷ **enervate**
enfeeble v (-les, -ling, -led) weaken
enfeebled v ▷ **enfeeble**
enfeebles v ▷ **enfeeble**
enfeebling v ▷ **enfeeble**
enfold v (-s, -ing, -ed) cover by wrapping something around
enfolded v ▷ **enfold**
enfolding v ▷ **enfold**
enfolds v ▷ **enfold**
enforce v (-ces, -cing, -ced) impose obedience (to a law etc.) > **enforceable** adj > **enforcement** n (pl **-s**)
enforced v ▷ **enforce**
enforcement n ▷ **enforce**
enforcements n ▷ **enforce**
enforces v ▷ **enforce**
enforcing v ▷ **enforce**
enfranchise v (-ses, -sing, -sed) grant (a person) the right to vote > **enfranchisement** n (pl **-s**)
enfranchised v ▷ **enfranchise**
enfranchisement n ▷ **enfranchise**
enfranchisements n ▷ **enfranchise**
enfranchises v ▷ **enfranchise**
enfranchising v ▷ **enfranchise**
engage v (-ges, -ging, -ged) take part, participate > **engagement** n (pl **-s**)
engaged adj pledged to be married ▶ v ▷ **engage**
engagement n ▷ **engage**
engagements n ▷ **engage**
engages v ▷ **engage**
engaging adj charming ▶ v ▷ **engage**
engender v (-s, -ing, -ed) produce, cause to occur
engendered v ▷ **engender**
engendering v ▷ **engender**
engenders v ▷ **engender**
engine n (pl **-s**) any machine which converts energy into mechanical work
engineer n (pl **-s**) person trained in any branch of engineering ▶ v (-s, -ing, -ed) plan in a clever manner
engineered v ▷ **engineer**
engineering v ▷ **engineer** ▶ n (pl **-s**) profession of applying scientific principles to the design and construction of engines, cars, buildings,

or machines

engineerings *n* ▷ engineering

engineers *n*, *v* ▷ engineer

engines *n* ▷ engine

English *n* (*pl* -es) official language of Britain, Ireland, Australia, New Zealand, South Africa, Canada, the US, and several other countries ▶ *adj* relating to England

Englishes *n* ▷ English

engrave *v* (-ves, -ving, -ved) carve (a design) onto a hard surface > **engraver** *n* (*pl* -s)

engraved *v* ▷ engrave

engraver *n* ▷ engrave

engravers *n* ▷ engrave

engraves *v* ▷ engrave

engraving *v* ▷ engrave ▶ *n* (*pl* -s) print made from an engraved plate

engravings *n* ▷ engraving

engross [en-groce] *v* (-es, -ing, -ed) occupy the attention of (a person) completely

engrossed *v* ▷ engross

engrosses *v* ▷ engross

engrossing *v* ▷ engross

engulf *v* (-s, -ing, -ed) cover or surround completely

engulfed *v* ▷ engulf

engulfing *v* ▷ engulf

engulfs *v* ▷ engulf

enhance *v* (-s, -ing, -ed) increase in quality, value, or attractiveness > **enhancement** *n* (*pl* -s)

enhanced *v* ▷ enhance

enhancement *n* ▷ enhance

enhancements *n* ▷ enhance

enhances *v* ▷ enhance

enhancing *v* ▷ enhance

enigma *n* (*pl* -s) puzzling thing or person > **enigmatic** *adj* > **enigmatically** *adv*

enigmas *n* ▷ enigma

enigmatic *adj* ▷ enigma

enigmatically *adv* ▷ enigma

enjoin *v* (-s, -ing, -ed) order (someone) to do something

enjoined *v* ▷ enjoin

enjoining *v* ▷ enjoin

enjoins *v* ▷ enjoin

enjoy *v* (-s, -ing, -ed) take joy in > **enjoyable** *adj* > **enjoyment** *n* (*pl* -s)

enjoyable *adj* ▷ enjoy

enjoyed *v* ▷ enjoy

enjoying *v* ▷ enjoy

enjoyment *n* ▷ enjoy

enjoyments *n* ▷ enjoy

enjoys *v* ▷ enjoy

enlarge *v* (-ges, -ging, -ged) make or grow larger (*foll. by* on) > **enlargement** *n* (*pl* -s)

enlarged *v* ▷ enlarge

enlargement *n* ▷ enlarge

enlargements *n* ▷ enlarge

enlarges *v* ▷ enlarge

enlarging *v* ▷ enlarge

enlighten *v* (-s, -ing, -ed) give information to > **enlightenment** *n* (*pl* -s)

enlightened *v* ▷ enlighten

enlightening *v* ▷ enlighten

enlightenment *n* ▷ enlighten

enlightenments *n* ▷ enlighten

enlightens *v* ▷ enlighten

enlist *v* (-s, -ing, -ed) enter the armed forces > **enlistment** *n* (*pl* -s)

enlisted *v* ▷ enlist

enlisting *v* ▷ enlist

enlistment *n* ▷ enlist

enlistments *n* ▷ enlist

enlists *v* ▷ enlist

enliven *v* (-s, -ing, -ed) make lively or cheerful

enlivened *v* ▷ enliven

enlivening *v* ▷ enliven

enlivens *v* ▷ enliven

enmeshed *adj* deeply involved

enmities *n* ▷ enmity

enmity *n* (*pl* -ies) ill will, hatred

ennoble *v* (-s, -ing, -ed) make noble, elevate

ennobled *v* ▷ ennoble

ennobles *v* ▷ ennoble

ennobling *v* ▷ ennoble

ennui [on-nwee] *n* (*pl* -s) boredom, dissatisfaction

ennuis *n* ▷ ennui

enormities *n* ▷ enormity

enormity *n* (*pl* -ies) great wickedness

enormous *adj* very big, vast

enough *adj* as much or as many as necessary ▶ *pron* sufficient quantity ▶ *adv* sufficiently

enquire *v* (-res, -ring, -red) ▷ inquire > **enquiry** *n* (*pl* -ies)

enquired *v* ▷ enquire

enquires *v* ▷ enquire

enquiries *n* ▷ enquire

enquiring *v* ▷ enquire

enquiry *n* ▷ enquire

enraptured *adj* filled with delight and fascination

enrich *v* (-es, -ing, -ed) improve in quality

enriched *v* ▷ enrich

enriches *v* ▷ enrich

enriching *v* ▷ enrich

enrol *v* (-s, -lling, -lled) (cause to) become a member > **enrolment** *n* (*pl* -s)

enrolled v ▷ enrol
enrolling v ▷ enrol
enrolment n ▷ enrol
enrolments n ▷ enrol
enrols v ▷ enrol
ensconce v (-ces, -cing, -ced) settle firmly or comfortably
ensconced v ▷ ensconce
ensconces v ▷ ensconce
ensconcing v ▷ ensconce
ensemble [on-som-bl] n (pl -s) all the parts of something taken together
ensembles n ▷ ensemble
enshrine v (-nes, -ning, -ned) cherish or treasure
enshrined v ▷ enshrine
enshrines v ▷ enshrine
enshrining v ▷ enshrine
ensign n (pl -s) naval flag
ensigns n ▷ ensign
enslave v (-ves, -ving, -ved) make a slave of (someone) > **enslavement** n (pl -s)
enslaved v ▷ enslave
enslavement n ▷ enslave
enslavements n ▷ enslave
enslaves v ▷ enslave
enslaving v ▷ enslave
ensnare v (-res, -ring, -red) catch in or as if in a snare
ensnared v ▷ ensnare
ensnares v ▷ ensnare
ensnaring v ▷ ensnare
ensue v (-sues, -suing, -sued) come next, result
ensued v ▷ ensue
ensues v ▷ ensue
ensuing v ▷ ensue
ensure v (-re, -ring, -red) make certain or sure
ensured v ▷ ensure
ensures v ▷ ensure
ensuring v ▷ ensure
entail v (-s, -ing, -ed) bring about or impose inevitably
entailed v ▷ entail
entailing v ▷ entail
entails v ▷ entail
entangle v (-les, -ling, -led) catch or involve in or as if in a tangle > **entanglement** n (pl -s)
entangled v ▷ entangle
entanglement n ▷ entangle
entanglements n ▷ entangle
entangles v ▷ entangle
entangling v ▷ entangle
entente [on-tont] n (pl -s) friendly understanding between nations
ententes n ▷ entente

enter v (-s, -ing, -ed) come or go in
entered v ▷ enter
enteric [en-ter-ik] adj intestinal
entering v ▷ enter
enteritis [en-ter-rite-iss] n (pl -es) inflammation of the intestine, causing diarrhoea
enteritises n ▷ enteritis
enterprise n (pl -s) company or firm
enterprises n ▷ enterprise
enterprising adj full of boldness and initiative
enters v ▷ enter
entertain v (-s, -ing, -ed) amuse > **entertainer** n (pl -s) > **entertainment** n (pl -s)
entertained v ▷ entertain
entertainer n ▷ entertain
entertainers n ▷ entertain
entertaining v ▷ entertain
entertainment n ▷ entertain
entertainments n ▷ entertain
entertains v ▷ entertain
enthral [en-thrawl] v (-s, -lling, -lled) hold the attention of > **enthralling** adj
enthralled v ▷ enthral
enthralling v, adj ▷ enthral
enthrals v ▷ enthral
enthuse v (-s, -ing, -ed) (cause to) show enthusiasm
enthused v ▷ enthuse
enthuses v ▷ enthuse
enthusiasm n (pl -s) ardent interest, eagerness
enthusiasms n ▷ enthusiasm
enthusiast n (pl -s) ardent supporter of something > **enthusiastic** adj > **enthusiastically** adv
enthusiastic adj ▷ enthusiast
enthusiastically adv ▷ enthusiast
enthusiasts n ▷ enthusiast
enthusing v ▷ enthuse
entice v (-ces, -cing, -ced) attract by exciting hope or desire, tempt > **enticement** n (pl -s)
enticed v ▷ entice
enticement n ▷ entice
enticements n ▷ entice
entices v ▷ entice
enticing v ▷ entice
entire adj including every detail, part, or aspect of something > **entirely** adv > **entirety** n (pl -ties)
entirely adv ▷ entire
entireties n ▷ entire
entirety n ▷ entire
entities n ▷ entity
entitle v (-les, -ling, -led) give a right to > **entitlement** n (pl -s)

entitled v ▷ entitle
entitlement n ▷ entitle
entitlements n ▷ entitle
entitles v ▷ entitle
entitling v ▷ entitle
entity n (pl **-ties**) separate distinct thing
entomological adj ▷ entomology
entomologies n ▷ entomology
entomologist n ▷ entomology
entomologists n ▷ entomology
entomology n (pl **-ies**) study of insects
> **entomological** adj > **entomologist** n (pl **-s**)
entourage [on-toor-ahzh] n (pl **-s**) group of
people who assist an important person
entourages n ▷ entourage
entrails pl n intestines
entrance[1] n (pl **-s**) way into a place
entrance[2] v (**-s, -ing, -ed**) delight
entranced v ▷ entrance[2]
entrances n ▷ entrance[1] ▶ v ▷ entrance[2]
entrancing v ▷ entrance[2]
entrant n (pl **-s**) person who enters a
university, contest, etc.
entrants n ▷ entrant
entreat v (**-s, -ing, -ed**) ask earnestly
entreated v ▷ entreat
entreaties n ▷ entreaty
entreating v ▷ entreat
entreats v ▷ entreat
entreaty n (pl **-ties**) earnest request
entrée [on-tray] n (pl **-s**) dish served before a
main course
entrées n ▷ entrée
entrench v (**-es, -ing, -ed**) establish firmly
> **entrenchment** n (pl **-s**)
entrenched v ▷ entrench
entrenches v ▷ entrench
entrenching v ▷ entrench
entrenchment n ▷ entrench
entrenchments n ▷ entrench
entrepreneur n (pl **-s**) business person
who attempts to make a profit by risk and
initiative
entrepreneurs n ▷ entrepreneur
entries n ▷ entry
entropies n ▷ entropy
entropy [en-trop-ee] n (pl **-ies**) lack of
organization
entrust v (**-s, -ing, -ed**) put into the care or
protection of
entrusted v ▷ entrust
entrusting v ▷ entrust
entrusts v ▷ entrust
entry n (pl **-ies**) entrance
entwine v (**-s, -ing, -ed**) twist together or
around
entwined v ▷ entwine
entwines v ▷ entwine
entwining v ▷ entwine
enumerate v (**-tes, -ting, -ted**) name one by
one > **enumeration** n (pl **-s**)
enumerated v ▷ enumerate
enumerates v ▷ enumerate
enumerating v ▷ enumerate
enumeration n ▷ enumerate
enumerations n ▷ enumerate
enuncation n ▷ enunciate
enunciate v (**-tes, -ting, -ted**) pronounce
clearly > **enunciation** n (pl **-s**)
enunciated v ▷ enunciate
enunciates v ▷ enunciate
enunciating v ▷ enunciate
enunciation n ▷ enunciate
enunciations n ▷ enunciate
envelop v (**-s, -ing, -ed**) wrap up, enclose
> **envelopment** n (pl **-s**)
envelope n (pl **-s**) folded gummed paper cover
for a letter
enveloped v ▷ envelop
envelopes n ▷ envelope
enveloping v ▷ envelop
envelopment n ▷ envelop
envelopments n ▷ envelop
envelops v ▷ envelop
enviable adj arousing envy, fortunate
envied v ▷ envy
envies n, v ▷ envy
envious adj full of envy
environment [en-vire-on-ment] n (pl **-s**)
external conditions and surroundings
in which people, animals, or plants live
> **environmental** adj
environmental adj ▷ environment
environmentalist n (pl **-s**) person concerned
with the protection of the natural
environment
environmentalists n ▷ environmentalist
environments n ▷ environment
environs pl n surrounding area, esp. of a town
envisage v (**-ges, -ging, -ged**) conceive of as a
possibility
envisaged v ▷ envisage
envisages v ▷ envisage
envisaging v ▷ envisage
envoy n (pl **-s**) messenger
envoys n ▷ envoy
envy n (pl **-ies**) feeling of discontent aroused by
another's good fortune ▶ v (**-ies, -ying, -ied**)
grudge (another's good fortune, success, or
qualities)

envying v ▷ **envy**

enzyme n (pl -s) any of a group of complex proteins that act as catalysts in specific biochemical reactions

enzymes n ▷ **enzyme**

eolithic adj of the early part of the Stone Age

epaulette n (pl -s) shoulder ornament on a uniform

epaulettes n ▷ **epaulette**

ephemeral adj short-lived

epic n (pl -s) long poem, book, or film about heroic events or actions ▶ adj very impressive or ambitious

epicentre n (pl -s) point on the earth's surface immediately above the origin of an earthquake

epicentres n ▷ **epicentre**

epics n ▷ **epic**

epicure n (pl -s) person who enjoys good food and drink

epicurean adj devoted to sensual pleasures, esp. food and drink ▶ n (pl -s) epicure

epicureans n ▷ **epicurean**

epicures n ▷ **epicure**

epidemic n (pl -s) widespread occurrence of a disease

epidemics n ▷ **epidemic**

epidermis n (pl -ses) outer layer of the skin

epidermises n ▷ **epidermis**

epidural [ep-pid-**dure**-al] adj, n (pl -s) (of) spinal anaesthetic injected to relieve pain during childbirth

epidurals n ▷ **epidural**

epiglottis n (pl -ses) thin flap that covers the opening of the larynx during swallowing

epiglottises n ▷ **epiglottis**

epigram n (pl -s) short witty remark or poem > **epigrammatic** adj

epigrammatic adj ▷ **epigram**

epigrams n ▷ **epigram**

epigraph n (pl -s) quotation at the start of a book

epigraphs n ▷ **epigraph**

epilepsies n ▷ **epilepsy**

epilepsy n (pl -ies) disorder of the nervous system causing loss of consciousness and sometimes convulsions

epileptic adj of or having epilepsy ▶ n (pl -s) person who has epilepsy

epileptics n ▷ **epileptic**

epilogue n (pl -s) short speech or poem at the end of a literary work, esp. a play

epilogues n ▷ **epilogue**

epiphanies n ▷ **epiphany**

epiphany n (pl -ies) a moment of great or sudden realization

episcopal [ip-**piss**-kop-al] adj of or governed by bishops

episcopalian adj advocating Church government by bishops ▶ n (pl -s) advocate of such Church government

episcopalians n ▷ **episcopalian**

episode n (pl -s) incident in a series of incidents

episodes n ▷ **episode**

episodic adj occurring at irregular intervals

epistemological adj ▷ **epistemology**

epistemologies n ▷ **epistemology**

epistemology [ip-iss-stem-ol-a-jee] n (pl -ies) study of the source, nature, and limitations of knowledge > **epistemological** adj

epistle n (pl -s) letter, esp. of an apostle > **epistolary** adj

epistles n ▷ **epistle**

epistolary adj ▷ **epistle**

epitaph n (pl -s) commemorative inscription on a tomb

epitaphs n ▷ **epitaph**

epithet n (pl -s) descriptive word or name

epithets n ▷ **epithet**

epitome [ip-pit-a-mee] n (pl -s) typical example

epitomes n ▷ **epitome**

epitomize v (-izes, -izing, -ized) be the epitome of

epitomized v ▷ **epitomize**

epitomizes v ▷ **epitomize**

epitomizing v ▷ **epitomize**

epoch [ee-pok] n (pl -s) period of notable events

epochs n ▷ **epoch**

eponymous [ip-**pon**-im-uss] adj after whom a book, play, etc. is named

equable [ek-wab-bl] adj even-tempered > **equably** adv

equably adv ▷ **equable**

equal adj identical in size, quantity, degree, etc. ▶ n (pl -s) person or thing equal to another ▶ v (-s, -lling, -lled) be equal to > **equally** adv

equalities n ▷ **equality**

equality n (pl -ies) state of being equal

equalization n ▷ **equalize**

equalizations n ▷ **equalize**

equalize v (-lizes, -lizing, -lized) make or become equal > **equalization** n (pl -s)

equalized v ▷ **equalize**

equalizes v ▷ **equalize**

equalizing v ▷ **equalize**

equalled v ▷ **equal**

equalling v ▷ **equal**

equally adv ▷ **equal**

equals n, v ▷ **equal**

equanimities *n* ▷ **equanimity**

equanimity *n* (*pl* -**ies**) calmness of mind

equate *v* (-**tes**, -**ting**, -**ted**) make or regard as equivalent

equated *v* ▷ **equate**

equates *v* ▷ **equate**

equating *v* ▷ **equate**

equation *n* (*pl* -**s**) mathematical statement that two expressions are equal

equations *n* ▷ **equation**

equator *n* (*pl* -**s**) imaginary circle round the earth, equidistant from the poles > **equatorial** *adj*

equatorial *adj* ▷ **equator**

equators *n* ▷ **equator**

equerries *n* ▷ **equerry**

equerry [ek-kwer-ee] *n* (*pl* -**ies**) (BRIT) officer who acts as an attendant to a member of a royal family

equestrian *adj* of horses and riding

equidistant *adj* equally distant

equilateral *adj* having equal sides

equilibria *n* ▷ **equilibriums**

equilibrium *n* (*pl* -**ria**) steadiness or stability

equine *adj* of or like a horse

equinoctial *adj* ▷ **equinox**

equinox *n* (*pl* -**es**) time of year when day and night are of equal length > **equinoctial** *adj*

equinoxes *n* ▷ **equinox**

equip *v* (-**s**, -**pping**, -**pped**) provide with supplies, components, etc.

equipment *n* (*pl* -**s**) set of tools or devices used for a particular purpose

equipments *n* ▷ **equipment**

equipoise *n* (*pl* -**s**) perfect balance

equipoises *n* ▷ **equipoise**

equipped *v* ▷ **equip**

equipping *v* ▷ **equip**

equips *v* ▷ **equips**

equitable *adj* fair and reasonable > **equitably** *adv*

equitably *adv* ▷ **equitable**

equities *n* ▷ **equity**

equity *n* (*pl* -**ties**) fairness ▶ *pl* interest of ordinary shareholders in a company

equivalence *n* ▷ **equivalent**

equivalences *n* ▷ **equivalent**

equivalent *adj* equal in value ▶ *n* (*pl* -**s**) something that is equivalent > **equivalence** *n* (*pl* -**s**)

equivalents *n* ▷ **equivalent**

equivocal *adj* ambiguous > **equivocally** *adv*

equivocally *adv* ▷ **equivocal**

equivocate *v* (-**tes**, -**ting**, -**ted**) use vague or ambiguous language to mislead people

> **equivocation** *n* (*pl* -**s**)

equivocated *v* ▷ **equivocate**

equivocates *v* ▷ **equivocate**

equivocating *v* ▷ **equivocate**

equivocation *n* ▷ **equivocate**

equivocations *n* ▷ **equivocate**

era *n* (*pl* -**s**) period of time considered as distinctive

eradicate *v* (-**tes**, -**ting**, -**ted**) destroy completely > **eradication** *n* (*pl* -**s**)

eradicated *v* ▷ **eradicate**

eradicates *v* ▷ **eradicate**

eradicating *v* ▷ **eradicate**

eradication *n* ▷ **eradicate**

eradications *n* ▷ **eradicate**

eras *n* ▷ **era**

erase *v* (-**ses**, -**sing**, -**sed**) rub out

erased *v* ▷ **erase**

eraser *n* (*pl* -**s**) object for erasing something written

erasers *n* ▷ **eraser**

erases *v* ▷ **erase**

erasing *v* ▷ **erase**

erasure *n* (*pl* -**s**) erasing

erasures *n* ▷ **erasure**

ere *prep, conj* (*Poetic*) before

erect *v* (-**s**, -**ing**, -**ed**) build ▶ *adj* upright > **erection** *n* (*pl* -**s**)

erected *v* ▷ **erect**

erectile *adj* capable of becoming erect from sexual excitement

erecting *v* ▷ **erect**

erection *n* ▷ **erect**

erections *n* ▷ **erect**

erects *v* ▷ **erect**

erg *n* (*pl* -**s**) unit of work or energy

ergonomic *adj* ▷ **ergonomics**

ergonomics *n* (*pl* study of the relationship between workers and their environment > **ergonomic** *adj*

ergot *n* (*pl* -**s**) fungal disease of cereal

ergots *n* ▷ **ergot**

ergs *n* ▷ **erg**

ermine *n* (*pl* -**s**) stoat in northern regions

ermines *n* ▷ **ermine**

erode *v* (-**s**, -**ing**, -**ed**) wear away > **erosion** *n* (*pl* -**s**)

eroded *v* ▷ **erode**

erodes *v* ▷ **erode**

eroding *v* ▷ **erode**

erogenous [ir-roj-in-uss] *adj* sensitive to sexual stimulation

erosion *n* ▷ **erode**

erosions *n* ▷ **erode**

erotic *adj* relating to sexual pleasure or desire

> **eroticism** *n* (*pl* **-s**)

erotica *n* sexual literature or art

  eroticism *n* ▷ **erotic**

  eroticisms *n* ▷ **erotic**

err *v* (**-s, -ing, -ed**) make a mistake

errand *n* (*pl* **-s**) short trip to do something for someone

  errands *n* ▷ **errand**

errant *adj* behaving in a manner considered to be unacceptable

  errata *n* ▷ **erratum**

erratic *adj* irregular or unpredictable

> **erratically** *adv*

  erratically *adv* ▷ **erratic**

erratum *n* (*pl* **-ta**) error in writing or printing

  erred *v* ▷ **err**

  erring *v* ▷ **err**

erroneous *adj* incorrect, mistaken

error *n* (*pl* **-s**) mistake, inaccuracy, or misjudgment

  errors *n* ▷ **error**

  errs *v* ▷ **err**

ersatz [air-zats] *adj* made in imitation

erstwhile *adj* former

erudite *adj* having great academic knowledge

> **erudition** *n* (*pl* **-s**)

  erudition *v* ▷ **erudite**

  eruditions *n* ▷ **erudite**

erupt *v* (**-s, -ing, -ed**) eject (steam, water, or volcanic material) violently > **eruption** *n* (*pl* **-s**)

  erupted *v* ▷ **erupt**

  erupting *v* ▷ **erupt**

  eruption *n* ▷ **erupt**

  eruptions *n* ▷ **erupt**

  erupts *v* ▷ **erupt**

erysipelas [err-riss-**sip**-pel-ass] *n* (*pl* **-es**) acute skin infection causing purplish patches

  erysipelases *n* ▷ **erysipelas**

  es *n* (**eses**). Es is the letter S. This is a useful word when you want to play a high-scoring word that will touch words already on the board. Es scores 2 points.

escalate *v* (**-tes, -ting, -ted**) increase in extent or intensity > **escalation** *n* (*pl* **-s**)

  escalated *v* ▷ **escalate**

  escalates *v* ▷ **escalate**

  escalating *v* ▷ **escalate**

  escalation *n* ▷ **escalate**

  escalations *n* ▷ **escalate**

escalator *n* (*pl* **-s**) moving staircase

  escalators *n* ▷ **escalator**

escalope [ess-kal-lop] *n* (*pl* **-s**) thin slice of meat, esp. veal

  escalopes *n* ▷ **escalope**

escapade *n* (*pl* **-s**) mischievous adventure

  escapades *n* ▷ **escapade**

escape *v* (**-pes, -ping, -ped**) get free (of) ▶ *n* (*pl* **-s**) act of escaping

  escaped *v* ▷ **escape**

escapee *n* (*pl* **-s**) person who has escaped

  escapees *n* ▷ **escapee**

  escapes *v*, *n* ▷ **escape**

  escaping *v* ▷ **escape**

escapism *n* (*pl* **-s**) taking refuge in fantasy to avoid unpleasant reality

  escapisms *n* ▷ **escapism**

  escapologies *n* ▷ **escapologist**

escapologist *n* (*pl* **-s**) entertainer who specializes in freeing himself from confinement > **escapology** *n* (*pl* **-ies**)

  escapologists *n* ▷ **escapologist**

  escapology *n* ▷ **escapologist**

escarpment *n* (*pl* **-s**) steep face of a ridge or mountain

  escarpments *n* ▷ **escarpment**

eschew [iss-chew] *v* (**-s, -ing, -ed**) abstain from, avoid

  eschewed *v* ▷ **eschew**

  eschewing *v* ▷ **eschew**

  eschews *v* ▷ **eschew**

escort *n* (*pl* **-s**) people or vehicles accompanying another person for protection or as an honour ▶ *v* (**-s, -ing, -ed**) act as an escort to

  escorted *v* ▷ **escort**

  escorting *v* ▷ **escort**

  escorts *n*, *v* ▷ **escort**

escudo [ess-**kyoo**-doe] *n* (*pl* **-dos**) former monetary unit of Portugal

  escudos *n* ▷ **escudo**

escutcheon *n* (*pl* **-s**) shield with a coat of arms

  escutcheons *n* ▷ **escutcheon**

esoteric [ee-so-**ter**-rik] *adj* understood by only a small number of people with special knowledge

espadrille [ess-pad-drill] *n* (*pl* **-s**) light canvas shoe with a braided cord sole

  espadrilles *n* ▷ **espadrille**

espalier [ess-pal-yer] *n* (*pl* **-s**) shrub or fruit tree trained to grow flat

  espaliers *n* ▷ **espalier**

esparto *n* (*pl* **-s**) grass of S Europe and N Africa used for making rope etc.

  espartos *n* ▷ **esparto**

especial *adj* (*Formal*) special

especially *adv* particularly

  espied *v* ▷ **espy**

  espies *v* ▷ **espy**

espionage [ess-pyon-ahzh] n (pl -s) spying
 espionages n ▷ **espionage**
esplanade n (pl -s) wide open road used as a
 public promenade
 esplanades n ▷ **esplanade**
 espousal n ▷ **espouse**
 espousals n ▷ **espouse**
espouse v (-ses, -sing, -sed) adopt or give
 support to (a cause etc.) > **espousal** n (pl -s)
 espoused v ▷ **espouse**
 espouses v ▷ **espouse**
 espousing v ▷ **espouse**
espresso n (pl -s) strong coffee made by forcing
 steam or boiling water through ground
 coffee beans
 espressos n ▷ **espresso**
esprit [ess-pree] n (pl -s) spirit, liveliness, or wit
 esprits n ▷ **esprit**
espy v (-ies, -ying, -ied) catch sight of
 espying v ▷ **espy**
esquire n (pl -s) courtesy title placed after a
 man's name
 esquires n ▷ **esquire**
essay n (pl -s) short literary composition ▶ v
 (-s, -ing, -ed) attempt > **essayist** n (pl -s)
 essayed v ▷ **essay**
 essaying v ▷ **essay**
 essayist n ▷ **essay**
 essayists n ▷ **essay**
 essays n, v ▷ **essay**
essence n (pl -s) most important feature of a
 thing which determines its identity
 essences n ▷ **essence**
essential adj vitally important ▶ n (pl -s)
 something fundamental or indispensable
 > **essentially** adv
 essentially adv ▷ **essential**
 essentials n ▷ **essential**
establish v (-es, -ing, -ed) set up on a
 permanent basis
 established v ▷ **establish**
 establishes v ▷ **establish**
 establishing v ▷ **establish**
establishment n (pl -s) act of establishing
 establishments n ▷ **establishment**
estate n (pl -s) landed property
 estates n ▷ **estate**
esteem n (pl -s) high regard ▶ v (-s, -ing, -ed)
 think highly of
 esteemed v ▷ **esteem**
 esteeming v ▷ **esteem**
 esteems n, v ▷ **esteem**
ester n (pl -s) (CHEM) compound produced by
 the reaction between an acid and an alcohol
 esters n ▷ **ester**

estimable adj worthy of respect
estimate v (-tes, -ting, -ted) calculate roughly
 ▶ n (pl -s) approximate calculation
 estimated v ▷ **estimate**
 estimates v, n ▷ **estimate**
 estimating v ▷ **estimate**
estimation n (pl -s) considered opinion
 estimations n ▷ **estimation**
estranged adj no longer living with one's
 spouse > **estrangement** n (pl -s)
 estrangement n ▷ **estranged**
 estrangements n ▷ **estranged**
 estuaries n ▷ **estuary**
estuary n (pl --ies) mouth of a river
etch v (-es, -ing, -ed) wear away or cut the
 surface of (metal, glass, etc.) with acid
 > **etching** n (pl -s)
 etched v ▷ **etch**
 etches v ▷ **etch**
 etching v, n ▷ **etch**
eternal adj without beginning or end
 > **eternally** adv
 eternally adv ▷ **eternal**
 eternities n ▷ **eternity**
eternity n (pl -ies) infinite time
ether n (pl -s) colourless sweet-smelling liquid
 used as an anaesthetic
ethereal [eth-eer-ee-al] adj extremely delicate
 ethers n ▷ **ether**
ethic n (pl -s) moral principle > **ethical** adj
 > **ethically** adv
 ethical adj ▷ **ethic**
 ethically adv ▷ **ethic**
 ethics n ▷ **ethic**
ethnic adj relating to a people or group that
 shares a culture, religion, or language
 ethnological adj ▷ **ethnology**
 ethnologies n ▷ **ethnology**
 ethnologist n ▷ **ethnology**
 ethnologists n ▷ **ethnology**
ethnology n (pl -ies) study of human races
 > **ethnological** adj > **ethnologist** n (pl -s)
ethos [eeth-oss] n (pl -es) distinctive spirit and
 attitudes of a people, culture, etc.
 ethoses n ▷ **ethos**
ethyl [eeth-ile] adj of, consisting of, or
 containing the hydrocarbon group C_2H_5
ethylene n (pl -s) poisonous gas used as an
 anaesthetic and as fuel
 ethylenes n ▷ **ethylene**
etiolate [ee-tee-oh-late] v (-tes, -ting, -ted)
 become pale and weak (BOTANY)
 etiolated v ▷ **etiolate**
 etiolates v ▷ **etiolate**
 etiolating v ▷ **etiolate**

etiologies *n* ▷ **etiology**
etiology *n* (*pl* -**ies**) study of the causes of diseases
etiquette *n* (*pl* -**s**) conventional code of conduct
etiquettes *n* ▷ **etiquette**
étude [ay-tewd] *n* (*pl* -**s**) short musical composition for a solo instrument, esp. intended as a technical exercise
études *n* ▷ **étude**
etymological *adj* ▷ **etymology**
etymologies *n* ▷ **etymology**
etymology *n* (*pl* -**gies**) study of the sources and development of words > **etymological** *adj*
eucalypt *n* ▷ **eucalyptus**
eucalypts *n* ▷ **eucalyptus**
eucalyptus, eucalypt *n* (*pl* -**ses**, -**s**) tree, mainly grown in Australia, that provides timber, gum, and medicinal oil from the leaves
eucalyptuses *n* ▷ **eucalyptus**
eugenics [yew-jen-iks] *n* (*pl* study of methods of improving the human race
eulogies *n* ▷ **eulogy**
eulogistic *adj* ▷ **euology**
eulogize *v* (-**s**, -**ing**, -**ed**) praise (a person or thing) highly in speech or writing
eulogized *v* ▷ **eulogize**
eulogizes *v* ▷ **eulogize**
eulogizing *v* ▷ **eulogize**
eulogy *n* (*pl* -**ies**) speech or writing in praise of a person > **eulogistic** *adj*
eunuch *n* (*pl* -**s**) castrated man, esp. (formerly) a guard in a harem
eunuchs *n* ▷ **eunuch**
euphemism *n* (*pl* -**s**) inoffensive word or phrase substituted for one considered offensive or upsetting > **euphemistic** *adj* > **euphemistically** *adv*
euphemisms *n* ▷ **euphemism**
euphemistic ▷ **euphemism**
euphemistically ▷ **euphemism**
euphonies *n* ▷ **euphony**
euphonious *adj* pleasing to the ear
euphonium *n* (*pl* -**s**) brass musical instrument, tenor tuba
euphoniums *n* ▷ **euphonium**
euphony *n* (*pl* -**nies**) pleasing sound
euphoria *n* (*pl* -**s**) sense of elation > **euphoric** *adj*
euphorias *n* ▷ **euphoria**
euphoric *adj* ▷ **euphoria**
eureka [yew-reek-a] *interj* exclamation of triumph at finding something
euro *n* (*pl* -**s**) unit of the single currency of the European Union

euros *n* ▷ **euro**
euthanasia *n* (*pl* -**s**) act of killing someone painlessly, esp. to relieve his or her suffering
euthanasias *n* ▷ **euthanasia**
evacuate *v* (-**tes**, -**ting**, -**ted**) send (someone) away from a place of danger > **evacuation** *n* (*pl* -**s**) > **evacuee** *n* (*pl* -**s**)
evacuated *v* ▷ **evacuate**
evacuates *v* ▷ **evacuate**
evacuating *v* ▷ **evacuate**
evacuation *n* ▷ **evacuate**
evacuations *n* ▷ **evacuate**
evacuee *n* ▷ **evacuate**
evacuees *n* ▷ **evacuate**
evade *v* (-**des**, -**ding**, -**ded**) get away from or avoid > **evasion** *n* (*pl* -**s**)
evaded *v* ▷ **evade**
evades *v* ▷ **evade**
evading *v* ▷ **evade**
evaluate *v* (-**tes**, -**ting**, -**ted**) find or judge the value of > **evaluation** *n* (*pl* -**s**)
evaluated *v* ▷ **evaluate**
evaluates *v* ▷ **evaluate**
evaluating *v* ▷ **evaluate**
evaluation *n* ▷ **evaluate**
evaluations *n* ▷ **evaluate**
evanescence *n* ▷ **evanescent**
evanescences *n* ▷ **evanescent**
evanescent *adj* quickly fading away > **evanescence** *n* (*pl* -**s**)
evangelical *adj* of or according to gospel teaching ▶ *n* (*pl* -**s**) member of an evangelical sect > **evangelicalism** *n* (*pl* -**s**)
evangelicalism *n* ▷ **evangelical**
evangelicalisms *n* ▷ **evangelical**
evangelicals *n* ▷ **evangelical**
evangelism *n* (*pl* -**s**) teaching and spreading of the Christian gospel
evangelisms *n* ▷ **evangelism**
evangelist *n* (*pl* -**s**) writer of one of the four gospels
evangelists *n* ▷ **evangelist**
evangelization *n* ▷ **evangelize**
evangelizations *n* ▷ **evangelize**
evangelize *v* (-**zes**, -**zing**, -**zed**) preach the gospel > **evangelization** *n* (*pl* -**s**)
evangelized *v* ▷ **evangelize**
evangelizes *v* ▷ **evangelize**
evangelizing *v* ▷ **evangelize**
evaporate *v* (-**tes**, -**ing**, -**ted**) change from a liquid or solid to a vapour > **evaporation** *n* (*pl* -**s**)
evaporated *v* ▷ **evaporate**
evaporates *v* ▷ **evaporate**

evaporating v ▷ **evaporate**
evaporation n ▷ **evaporate**
evaporations n ▷ **evaporate**
evasion n ▷ **evade**
evasions n ▷ **evade**
evasive adj not straightforward > **evasively** adv
evasively adv ▷ **evasive**
evasiveness n ▷ **evasive**
eve n (pl -**s**) evening or day before some special event
even (-**er**, -**est**) adj flat or smooth (foll. by **with**) ▶ adv equally ▶ v (-**s**, -**ing**, -**ed**) make even
evened v ▷ **even**
evener adj ▷ **even**
evenest adj ▷ **even**
evening n (pl -**s**) end of the day or early part of the night ▶ adj of or in the evening ▶ v ▷ **even**
evenings n ▷ **evening**
evens v ▷ **even**
evensong n (pl -**s**) evening prayer
evensongs n ▷ **evensong**
event n (pl -**s**) anything that takes place
eventful adj full of exciting incidents
eventing n (pl -**s**) (BRIT, AUST & NZ) riding competitions, usu. involving cross-country, jumping, and dressage
eventings n ▷ **eventing**
events n ▷ **event**
eventual adj ultimate
eventualities n ▷ **eventuality**
eventuality n (pl -**ies**) possible event
eventually adv at the end of a situation or process
ever adv at any time > **everlasting** adj
evergreen adj, n (pl -**s**) (tree or shrub) having leaves throughout the year
evergreens n ▷ **evergreen**
everlasting adj ▷ **ever**
evermore adv for all time to come
every adj each without exception
everybody pron every person
everyday adj usual or ordinary
everyone pron every person
everything pron all things
everywhere adv in all places
eves n ▷ **eve**
evict v (-**s**, -**ing**, -**ed**) legally expel (someone) from his or her home > **eviction** n (pl -**s**)
evicted v ▷ **evict**
evicting v ▷ **evict**
eviction n ▷ **evict**
evictions n ▷ **evict**
evicts v ▷ **evict**
evidence n (pl -**s**) ground for belief ▶ v (-**ces**, -**cing**, -**ced**) demonstrate, prove
evidenced v ▷ **evidence**
evidences n, v ▷ **evidence**
evidencing v ▷ **evidence**
evident adj easily seen or understood > **evidently** adv
evidential adj of, serving as, or based on evidence
evidently adv ▷ **evident**
evil n (pl -**s**) wickedness ▶ adj (-**ller**, -**llest**) harmful > **evilly** adv
evildoer n (pl -**s**) wicked person
evildoers n ▷ **evildoer**
eviller adj ▷ **evil**
evillest adj ▷ **evil**
evilly adv ▷ **evil**
evils n ▷ **evil**
evince v (-**s**, -**ing**, -**ed**) make evident
evinced v ▷ **evince**
evinces v ▷ **evince**
evincing v ▷ **evince**
eviscerate v (-**tes**, -**ting**, -**ted**) disembowel > **evisceration** n (pl -**s**)
eviscerated v ▷ **eviscerate**
eviscerates v ▷ **eviscerate**
eviscerating v ▷ **eviscerate**
evisceration n ▷ **eviscerate**
eviscerations n ▷ **eviscerate**
evocation n ▷ **evoke**
evocations n ▷ **evoke**
evocative adj ▷ **evoke**
evoke v (-**s**, -**ing**, -**ed**) call or summon up (a memory, feeling, etc.) > **evocation** n (pl -**s**) > **evocative** adj
evoked v ▷ **evoke**
evokes v ▷ **evoke**
evoking v ▷ **evoke**
evolution n (pl -**s**) gradual change in the characteristics of living things over successive generations, esp. to a more complex form > **evolutionary** adj
evolutionary n ▷ **evolution**
evolutions n ▷ **evolution**
evolve v (-**kes**, -**king**, -**ked**) develop gradually
evolved v ▷ **evolve**
evolves v ▷ **evolve**
evolving v ▷ **evolve**
ewe n (pl -**s**) female sheep
ewer n (pl -**s**) large jug with a wide mouth
ewers n ▷ **ewer**
ewes n ▷ **ewe**

ewk n (**ewks**). Ewk is a dialect word for **itch**. It's a handy little word and a good one to remember in case you end up with both K and W, as you're very likely to be able to play it from an E already on the board. Ewk scores 10 points.

ex *n* (*pl* **-es**) (*Informal*) former wife or husband

exacerbate [ig-**zass**-er-bate] *v* (**-tes, -ting, -ted**) make (pain, emotion, or a situation) worse > **exacerbation** *n* (*pl* **-s**)

exacerbated *v* ▷ exacerbate

exacerbates *v* ▷ exacerbate

exacerbating *v* ▷ exacerbate

exacerbation *n* ▷ exacerbate

exacerbations *n* ▷ exacerbate

exact *adj* (**-er, -est**) correct and complete in every detail ▶ *v* (**-s, -ing, -ed**) demand (payment or obedience) > **exactness** *n* (*pl* **-es**) > **exactitude** *n* (*pl* **-s**)

exacted *v* ▷ exact

exacter *adj* ▷ exact

exactest *adj* ▷ exact

exacting *adj* making rigorous or excessive demands ▶ *v* ▷ exact

exactitude *n* ▷ exact

exactitudes *n* ▷ exact

exactly *adv* precisely, in every respect

exactness *n* ▷ exact

exactnesses *n* ▷ exact

exacts *v* ▷ exact

exaggerate *v* (**-tes, -ting, -ted**) regard or represent as greater than is true > **exaggeratedly** *adv* > **exaggeration** *n* (*pl* **-s**)

exaggerated *v* ▷ exaggerate

exaggeratedly *adv* ▷ exaggerate

exaggerates *v* ▷ exaggerate

exaggerating *v* ▷ exaggerate

exaggeration *n* ▷ exaggerate

exaggerations *n* ▷ exaggerate

exalt *v* (**-s, -ing, -ed**) praise highly > **exalted** *adj* > **exaltation** *n* (*pl* **-s**)

exaltation *n* ▷ exalt

exaltations *n* ▷ exalt

exalted *v, adj* ▷ exalt

exalting *v* ▷ exalt

exalts *v* ▷ exalt

exam *n* (*pl* **-s**) ▷ examination

examination *n* (*pl* **-s**) examining

examinations *n* ▷ examination

examine *v* (**-nes, -ning, -ned**) look at closely > **examinee** *n* (*pl* **-s**) > **examiner** *n* (*pl* **-s**)

examined *v* ▷ examine

examinee *n* ▷ examine

examinees *n* ▷ examine

examiner *n* ▷ examine

examiners *n* ▷ examine

examines *v* ▷ examine

examining *v* ▷ examine

example *n* (*pl* **-s**) specimen typical of its group

examples *n* ▷ example

exams *n* ▷ exam

exasperate *v* (**-tes, -ting, -ted**) cause great irritation to > **exasperation** *n* (*pl* **-s**)

exasperated *v* ▷ exasperate

exasperates *v* ▷ exasperate

exasperating *v* ▷ exasperate

exasperation *v* ▷ exasperate

exasperations *v* ▷ exasperate

excavate *v* (**-tes, -ting, -ted**) unearth buried objects from (a piece of land) methodically to learn about the past > **excavation** *n* (*pl* **-s**)

excavated *v* ▷ excavate

excavates *v* ▷ excavate

excavating *v* ▷ excavate

excavation *n* ▷ excavate

excavations *n* ▷ excavate

excavator *n* (*pl* **-s**) large machine used for digging

excavators *n* ▷ excavator

exceed *v* (**-s, -ing, -ed**) be greater than

exceeded *v* ▷ exceed

exceeding *v* ▷ exceed

exceedingly *adv* very

exceeds *v* ▷ exceed

excel *v* (**-s, -lling, -lled**) be superior to

excelled *v* ▷ excel

excellence *n* ▷ excellent

excellences *n* ▷ excellent

excellent *adj* exceptionally good > **excellence** *n* (*pl* **-s**)

excelling *v* ▷ excel

excels *v* ▷ excel

except *prep* (*sometimes foll. by* **for**) other than, not including ▶ *v* (**-s, -ing, -ed**) not include

excepted *v* ▷ except

excepting *prep* except ▶ *v* ▷ except

exception *n* (*pl* **-s**) excepting

exceptional *adj* not ordinary

exceptions *n* ▷ exception

excepts *v* ▷ except

excerpt *n* (*pl* **-s**) passage taken from a book, speech, etc.

excerpts *n* ▷ excerpt

excess *n* (*pl* **-es**) state or act of exceeding the permitted limits > **excessive** *adj* > **excessively** *adv*

excesses *n* ▷ excess

excessive *adj* ▷ excess

excessively *adv* ▷ excess

exchange *v* (**-ges, -ging, -ged**) give or receive (something) in return for something else ▶ *n* (*pl* **-s**) act of exchanging > **exchangeable** *adj*

exchangeable *adj* ▷ exchange

exchanged *v* ▷ exchange

exchanges v, n ▷ exchange
exchanging v ▷ exchange
exchequer n (pl -s) (BRIT) government
department in charge of state money
exchequers n ▷ exchequer
excise v (-ses, -sing, -sed) cut out or away
> **excision** n (pl -s)
excised v ▷ excise
excises v ▷ excise
excising v ▷ excise
excision n ▷ excise
excisions n ▷ excise
excitabilities n ▷ excitable
excitability n ▷ excitable
excitable adj easily excited > **excitability** n
(pl -s)
excite v (-s, -ing, -ed) arouse to strong emotion
> **excitement** n (pl -s)
excited v ▷ excite
excitement n ▷ excite
excitements n ▷ excite
excites v ▷ excite
exciting v ▷ excite
exclaim v (-s, -ing, -ed) speak suddenly, cry out
> **exclamation** n > **exclamatory** adj
exclaimed v ▷ exclaim
exclaiming v ▷ exclaim
exclaims v ▷ exclaim
exclamation n ▷ exclaim
exclamations n ▷ exclaim
exclamatory adj ▷ exclaim
exclude v (-s, -ing, -ed) keep out, leave out
> **exclusion** n (pl -s)
excluded v ▷ exclude
excludes v ▷ exclude
excluding v ▷ exclude
exclusion n ▷ exclude
exclusions n ▷ exclude
exclusive adj excluding everything else ▶ n
(pl -s) story reported in only one newspaper
> **exclusively** adv > **exclusivity** n (pl -ies)
> **exclusiveness** n (pl -es)
exclusively adv ▷ exclusive
exclusiveness n ▷ exclusive
exclusivenesses n ▷ exclusive
exclusives n ▷ exclusive
exclusivities n ▷ exclusive
exclusivity n ▷ exclusive
excommunicate v (-tes, -ting, -ted) exclude
from membership and the sacraments of the
Church > **excommunication** n (pl -s)
excommunicated v ▷ excommunicate
excommunicates v ▷ excommunicate
excommunicating v ▷ excommunicate
excommunication n ▷ excommunicate

excommunications n ▷ excommunicate
excoriate v (-tes, -ting, -ted) censure severely
> **excoriation** n (pl -s)
excoriated v ▷ excoriate
excoriates v ▷ excoriate
excoriating v ▷ excoriate
excoriation n ▷ excoriate
excoriations n ▷ excoriate
excrement n (pl -s) waste matter discharged
from the body
excrements n ▷ excrement
excrescence n (pl -s) lump or growth on the
surface of an animal or plant
excrescences n ▷ excrescence
excreta [ik-skree-ta] n excrement
excrete v (-tes, -ting, -ted) discharge (waste
matter) from the body > **excretion** n (pl -s)
> **excretory** adj
excreted v ▷ excrete
excretes v ▷ excrete
excreting v ▷ excrete
excretion n ▷ excrete
excretions n ▷ excrete
excretory adj ▷ excrete
excruciating adj agonizing > **excruciatingly**
adv
excruciatingly adv ▷ excruciating
exculpate v (-tes, -ting, -ted) free from blame
or guilt
exculpated v ▷ exculpate
exculpates v ▷ exculpate
exculpating v ▷ exculpate
excursion n (pl -s) short journey, esp. for
pleasure
excursions n ▷ excursion
excusable adj ▷ excuse
excuse n (pl -s) explanation offered to justify
(a fault etc.) ▶ v (-ses, -sing, -sed) put forward
a reason or justification for (a fault etc.)
> **excusable** adj
excused v ▷ excuse
excuses n, v ▷ excuse
excusing v ▷ excuse
execrable [eks-sik-rab-bl] adj of very poor
quality
execute v (-tes, -ting, -ted) put (a condemned
person) to death > **execution** n (pl -s)
> **executioner** n (pl -s)
executed v ▷ execute
executes v ▷ execute
executing v ▷ execute
execution n ▷ execute
executioner n ▷ execute
executioners n ▷ execute
executions n ▷ execute

executive *n* (*pl* **-s**) person or group in an administrative position ▶ *adj* having the function of carrying out plans, orders, laws, etc.

executives *n* ▷ **executive**

executor *n* (*pl* **-s**) person appointed to perform the instructions of a will

executors *n* ▷ **executor**

executrices *n* ▷ **executrix**

executrix *n* (*pl* **-ixes, -ices**) woman appointed to perform the instructions of a will

executrixes *n* ▷ **executrix**

exegeses *n* ▷ **exegesis**

exegesis [eks-sij-**jee**-siss] *n* (*pl* **-ses**) [-seez] explanation of a text, esp. of the Bible

exemplar *n* (*pl* **-s**) person or thing to be copied, model

exemplars *n* ▷ **exemplar**

exemplary *adj* being a good example

exemplification *n* ▷ **exemplify**

exemplifications *n* ▷ **exemplify**

exemplified *v* ▷ **exemplify**

exemplifies *v* ▷ **exemplify**

exemplify *v* (**-ies, -fying, -ied**) show an example of > **exemplification** *n* (*pl* **-s**)

exemplifying *v* ▷ **exemplify**

exempt *adj* not subject to an obligation etc. ▶ *v* (**-s, -ing, -ed**) release from an obligation etc. > **exemption** *n* (*pl* **-s**)

exempted *v* ▷ **exempt**

exempting *v* ▷ **exempt**

exemption *n* ▷ **exempt**

exemptions *n* ▷ **exempt**

exempts *v* ▷ **exempt**

> **exequy** *n* (**exequies**). An exequy is a funeral rite. This is a great word if you have the tiles for it, combining X and Q. Even better, if you have all the letters for the plural, exequies, and can play it, you'll score an extra 50 points for using all your tiles. Exequy scores 25 points.

exercise *n* (*pl* **-s**) activity to train the body or mind ▶ *v* (**-ses, -sing, -sed**) make use of

exercised *v* ▷ **exercise**

exercises *n*, *v* ▷ **exercise**

exercising *v* ▷ **exercise**

exert *v* (**-s, -ing, -ed**) use (influence, authority, etc.) forcefully or effectively > **exertion** *n* (*pl* **-s**)

exerted *v* ▷ **exert**

exerting *v* ▷ **exert**

exertion *n* ▷ **exert**

exertions *n* ▷ **exert**

exerts *v* ▷ **exert**

exes *n* ▷ **ex**

exeunt [eks-see-unt] (LATIN) they go out: used as a stage direction

exhalation *n* ▷ **exhale**

exhalations *n* ▷ **exhale**

exhale *v* (**-les, -ling, -led**) breathe out > **exhalation** *n* (*pl* **-s**)

exhaled *v* ▷ **exhale**

exhales *v* ▷ **exhale**

exhaling *v* ▷ **exhale**

exhaust *v* (**-s, -ing, -ed**) tire out ▶ *n* (*pl* **-s**) gases ejected from an engine as waste products

exhausted *v* ▷ **exhaust**

exhausting *v* ▷ **exhaust**

exhaustion *n* (*pl* **-s**) extreme tiredness

exhaustions *n* ▷ **exhaustion**

exhaustive *adj* comprehensive > **exhaustively** *adv*

exhaustively *adv* ▷ **exhaustive**

exhausts *v*, *n* ▷ **exhaust**

exhibit *v* (**-s, -ing, -ed**) display to the public ▶ *n* (*pl* **-s**) object exhibited to the public (LAW) > **exhibitor** *n* (*pl* **-s**)

exhibited *v* ▷ **exhibit**

exhibiting *v* ▷ **exhibit**

exhibition *n* (*pl* **-s**) public display of art, skills, etc.

exhibitionism *n* (*pl* **-s**) compulsive desire to draw attention to oneself > **exhibitionist** *n* (*pl* **-s**)

exhibitionisms *n* ▷ **exhibitionism**

exhibitionist *n* ▷ **exhibitionism**

exhibitionists *n* ▷ **exhibitionism**

exhibitions *n* ▷ **exhibition**

exhibitor *n* ▷ **exhibit**

exhibitors *n* ▷ **exhibit**

exhibits *v*, *n* ▷ **exhibit**

exhilarate *v* (**-tes, -ting, -ted**) make lively and cheerful > **exhilaration** *n* (*pl* **-s**)

exhilarated *v* ▷ **exhilarate**

exhilarates *v* ▷ **exhilarate**

exhilarating *v* ▷ **exhilarate**

exhilaration *n* ▷ **exhilarate**

exhilarations *n* ▷ **exhilarate**

exhort *v* (**-s, -ing, -ed**) urge earnestly > **exhortation** *n* (*pl* **-s**)

exhortation *n* ▷ **exhort**

exhortations *n* ▷ **exhort**

exhorted *v* ▷ **exhort**

exhorting *v* ▷ **exhort**

exhorts *v* ▷ **exhort**

exhumation *n* ▷ **exhume**

exhumations *n* ▷ **exhume**

exhume [ig-**zyume**] *v* (**-mes, -ming, -med**) dig up (something buried, esp. a corpse) > **exhumation** *n* (*pl* **-s**)

exhumed v ▷ exhume
exhumes v ▷ exhume
exhuming v ▷ exhume
exigencies n ▷ exigency
exigency n (pl -cies) urgent demand or need
> exigent adj
exigent adj ▷ exigency
exiguous adj scanty or meagre
exile n (pl -s) prolonged, usu. enforced, absence
from one's country ▶ v (-les, -ling, -led) expel
from one's country
exiled v ▷ exile
exiles n ▷ exile
exiles n, v ▷ exile
exiling v ▷ exile
exist v (-s, -ing, -ed) have being or reality
> existence n (pl -s) > existent adj
existed v ▷ exist
existence n ▷ exist
existences n ▷ exist
existent adj ▷ exist
existential adj of or relating to existence, esp.
human existence
existentialism n (pl -s) philosophical
movement stressing the personal experience
and responsibility of the individual, who
is seen as a free agent > existentialist adj,
n (pl -s)
existentialisms n ▷ existentialism
existentialist adj, n ▷ existentialism
existentialists n ▷ existentialism
existing v ▷ exist
exists v ▷ exist
exit n (pl -s) way out ▶ v (-s, -ing, -ed) go out
exited v ▷ exit
exiting v ▷ exit
exits n, v ▷ exit

exo adj. Exo is an informal Australian
way of saying excellent. This is a great
little word as it allows you to combine
X with two of the most common tiles
in the game, E and O. Exo scores 10
points.

exocrine adj relating to a gland, such as the
sweat gland, that secretes externally through
a duct
exodus [eks-so-duss] n (pl -es) departure of a
large number of people
exoduses n ▷ exodus
exonerate v (-tes, -ting, -ted) free from blame
or a criminal charge > exoneration n (pl -s)
exonerates v ▷ exonerate
exonerated v ▷ exonerate
exonerating v ▷ exonerate
exoneration v ▷ exonerate

exonerations v ▷ exonerate
exorbitant adj (of prices, demands, etc.)
excessive, immoderate > exorbitantly adv
exorbitantly adv ▷ exorbitant
exorcism n ▷ exorcize
exorcisms n ▷ exorcize
exorcist n ▷ exorcize
exorcists n ▷ exorcize
exorcize v (-zes, -zing, -zed) expel (evil spirits)
by prayers and religious rites > exorcism n (pl
-s) > exorcist n (pl -s)
exorcized v ▷ exorcize
exorcizes v ▷ exorcize
exorcizing v ▷ exorcize
exotic adj having a strange allure or beauty ▶ n
(pl -s) non-native plant > exotically adv
exotica pl n (collection of) exotic objects
exotically adv ▷ exotic
exotics n ▷ exotic
expand v (-s, -ing, -ed) make or become larger
(foll. by on) > expansion n (pl -s)
expanded v ▷ expand
expanding v ▷ expand
expands v ▷ expand
expanse n (pl -s) uninterrupted wide area
expanses n ▷ expanse
expansion n ▷ expand
expansions n ▷ expand
expansive adj wide or extensive
expat adj, n (pl -s) short for expatriate
expatiate [iks-pay-shee-ate] v (-tes, -ting, -ted)
(foll. by on) speak or write at great length (on)
expatiated v ▷ expatiate
expatiates v ▷ expatiate
expatiating v ▷ expatiate
expatriate [eks-pat-ree-it] adj living outside
one's native country ▶ n (pl -s) person
living outside his or her native country
> expatriation n (pl -s)
expatriates n ▷ expatriate
expatriation n ▷ expatriate
expatriations n ▷ expatriate
expats n ▷ expat
expect v (-s, -ing, -ed) regard as probable
expectancies n ▷ expectancy
expectancy n (pl -ies) something expected on
the basis of an average
expectant adj expecting or hopeful
> expectantly adv
expectantly adv ▷ expectant
expectation n (pl -s) act or state of expecting
expectations n ▷ expectation
expected v ▷ expect
expecting v ▷ expect
expectorant n (pl -s) medicine that helps

to bring up phlegm from the respiratory
passages
expectorants n ▷ **expectorant**
expectorate v (-tes, -ting, -ted) spit out
(phlegm etc.) > **expectoration** n (pl -s)
expectorated v ▷ **expectorate**
expectorates v ▷ **expectorate**
expectorating v ▷ **expectorate**
expectoration n ▷ **expectorate**
expectorations n ▷ **expectorate**
expects v ▷ **expect**
expediencies n ▷ **expedient**
expediency n ▷ **expedient**
expedient n (pl -s) something that achieves
a particular purpose ▶ adj suitable to the
circumstances, appropriate > **expediency**
n (pl -ies)
expedients n ▷ **expedient**
expedite v (-s, -ing, -ed) hasten the progress of
expedited v ▷ **expedite**
expedites v ▷ **expedite**
expediting v ▷ **expedite**
expedition n (pl -s) organized journey, esp. for
exploration
expeditionary adj relating to an expedition,
esp. a military one
expeditions n ▷ **expedition**
expeditious adj done quickly and efficiently
expel v (-s, -lling, -lled) drive out with force
> **expulsion** n (pl -s)
expelled v ▷ **expel**
expelling v ▷ **expel**
expels v ▷ **expel**
expend v (-s, -ing, -ed) spend, use up
expendable adj able to be sacrificed to achieve
an objective
expended v ▷ **expend**
expending v ▷ **expend**
expenditure n (pl -s) something expended,
esp. money
expenditures n ▷ **expenditure**
expends v ▷ **expend**
expense n (pl -s) cost ▶ pl charges, outlay
incurred
expenses n ▷ **expense**
expensive adj high-priced
experience n (pl -s) direct personal
participation ▶ v (-ces, -cing, -ced)
participate in
experienced v ▷ **experience** ▶ adj skilful from
extensive participation
experiences n, v ▷ **experience**
experiencing v ▷ **experience**
experiment n (pl experiments) test to provide
evidence to prove or disprove a theory

▶ v (-s, -ing, -ed) carry out an experiment
> **experimental** adj > **experimentally** adv
> **experimentation** n (pl -s)
experimental adj ▷ **experiment**
experimentally adv ▷ **experiment**
experimentation n ▷ **experiment**
experimentations n ▷ **experiment**
experimented v ▷ **experiment**
experimenting v ▷ **experiment**
experiments n, v ▷ **experiment**
expert n (pl -s) person with extensive skill or
knowledge in a particular field ▶ adj skilful or
knowledgeable
expertise [eks-per-**teez**] n (pl -s) special skill or
knowledge
expertises n ▷ **expertise**
experts n ▷ **expert**
expiate v (-tes, -ting, -ted) make amends for
> **expiation** n (pl -s)
expiated v ▷ **expiate**
expiates v ▷ **expiate**
expiating v ▷ **expiate**
expiation n ▷ **expiate**
expiations n ▷ **expiate**
expiration n ▷ **expire**
expirations n ▷ **expire**
expire v (-res, -ring, -red) finish or run out (Lit)
> **expiration** n (pl -s)
expired v ▷ **expire**
expires v ▷ **expire**
expiries n ▷ **expiry**
expiring v ▷ **expire**
expiry n (pl -ies) end, esp. of a contract period
explain v (-s, -ing, -ed) make clear and
intelligible > **explanation** n (pl -s)
> **explanatory** adj
explained v ▷ **explain**
explaining v ▷ **explain**
explains v ▷ **explain**
explanation n ▷ **explain**
explanations n ▷ **explain**
explanatory adj ▷ **explain**
expletive n (pl -s) swearword
expletives n ▷ **expletive**
explicable adj able to be explained
explicate v (-tes, -ting, -ted) (Formal) explain
> **explication** n (pl -s)
explicated v ▷ **explicate**
explicates v ▷ **explicate**
explicating v ▷ **explicate**
explication n ▷ **explicate**
explications n ▷ **explicate**
explicit adj precisely and clearly expressed
> **explicitly** adv
explicitly adv ▷ **explicit**

explode v (**-des, -ding, -ded**) burst with great violence, blow up > **explosion** n (pl **-s**)
exploded v ▷ **explode**
explodes v ▷ **explode**
exploding v ▷ **explode**
exploit v (pl **-s**) take advantage of for one's own purposes ▶ n (pl **-s**) notable feat or deed > **exploitation** n (pl **-s**) > **exploiter** n (pl **-s**)
exploitation n ▷ **exploit**
exploitations n ▷ **exploit**
exploited v ▷ **exploit**
exploiter n ▷ **exploit**
exploiters n ▷ **exploit**
exploiting v ▷ **exploit**
exploits v, n ▷ **exploit**
exploration n ▷ **explore**
explorations n ▷ **explore**
exploratory adj ▷ **explore**
explore v (**-res, -ring, -red**) investigate > **exploration** n (pl **-s**) > **exploratory** adj > **explorer** n (pl **-s**)
explored v ▷ **explore**
explorer n ▷ **explore**
explorers n ▷ **explore**
explores v ▷ **explore**
exploring v ▷ **explore**
explosion n ▷ **explode**
explosions n ▷ **explode**
explosive adj tending to explode ▶ n (pl **-s**) substance that causes explosions
explosives n ▷ **explosive**
expo n (pl **-s**) (Informal) exposition, large public exhibition
exponent n (pl **-s**) person who advocates an idea, cause, etc.
exponential adj (Informal) very rapid > **exponentially** adv
exponentially adv ▷ **exponential**
exponents n ▷ **exponent**
export n (pl **-s**) selling or shipping of goods to a foreign country ▶ v (**-s, -ing, -ed**) sell or ship (goods) to a foreign country > **exporter** n (pl **-s**)
exported v ▷ **export**
exporter n ▷ **export**
exporters n ▷ **export**
exporting v ▷ **export**
exports n, v ▷ **export**
expos n ▷ **expo**
expose v (**-ses, -sing, -sed**) uncover or reveal > **exposure** n (pl **-s**) exposing
exposé [iks-**pose**-ay] n (pl **-s**) bringing of a crime, scandal, etc. to public notice
exposed v ▷ **expose**
exposes v ▷ **expose**

exposés n ▷ **exposé**
exposing v ▷ **expose**
exposition n ▷ **expound**
expositions n ▷ **expound**
expostulate v (**-tes, -ting, -ted**) (foll. by **with**) reason (with), esp. to dissuade
expostulated v ▷ **expostulate**
expostulates v ▷ **expostulate**
expostulating v ▷ **expostulate**
exposure n ▷ **expose**
exposures n ▷ **expose**
expound v (**-s, -ing, -ed**) explain in detail > **exposition** n (pl **-s**) explanation
expounded v ▷ **expound**
expounding v ▷ **expound**
expounds v ▷ **expound**
express v (**-es, -ing, -ed**) put into words ▶ adj explicitly stated ▶ n (pl **-es**) fast train or bus stopping at only a few stations ▶ adv by express delivery
expressed v ▷ **express**
expresses v, n ▷ **express**
expressing v ▷ **express**
expression n (pl **-s**) expressing > **expressionless** adj > **expressive** adj
expressionism n (pl **-s**) early 20th-century artistic movement which sought to express emotions rather than represent the physical world > **expressionist** adj, n (pl **-s**)
expressionisms n ▷ **expressionism**
expressionist adj, n ▷ **expressionism**
expressionists n ▷ **expressionism**
expressionless adj ▷ **expression**
expressions n ▷ **expression**
expressive adj ▷ **expression**
expropriate v (**-tes, -ting, -ted**) deprive an owner of (property) > **expropriation** n (pl **-s**)
expropriated v ▷ **expropriate**
expropriates v ▷ **expropriate**
expropriating v ▷ **expropriate**
expropriation n ▷ **expropriate**
expropriations n ▷ **expropriate**
expulsion n ▷ **expel**
expulsions n ▷ **expel**
expunge v (**-ges, -ging, -ged**) delete, erase, blot out
expunged v ▷ **expunge**
expunges v ▷ **expunge**
expunging v ▷ **expunge**
expurgate v (**-tes, -ting, -ted**) remove objectionable parts from (a book etc.)
expurgated v ▷ **expurgate**
expurgates v ▷ **expurgate**
expurgating v ▷ **expurgate**
exquisite adj of extreme beauty or delicacy

> **exquisitely** *adv*
exquisitely *adv* ▷ **exquisite**
extant *adj* still existing
extemporize *v* (-zes, -zing, -zed) speak, perform, or compose without preparation
extemporized *v* ▷ **extemporize**
extemporizes *v* ▷ **extemporize**
extemporizing *v* ▷ **extemporize**
extend *v* (-s, -ing, -ed) draw out or be drawn out, stretch (*foll. by* **to**) > **extendable** *adj*
extendable *adj* ▷ **extend**
extended *v* ▷ **extend**
extending *v* ▷ **extend**
extends *v* ▷ **extend**
extension *n* (*pl* -s) room or rooms added to an existing building
extensions *n* ▷ **extension**
extensive *adj* having a large extent, widespread
extensor *n* (*pl* -s) muscle that extends a part of the body
extensors *n* ▷ **extensor**
extent *n* (*pl* -s) range over which something extends, area
extents *n* ▷ **extent**
extenuate *v* (-tes, -ting, -ted) make (an offence or fault) less blameworthy
> **extenuation** *n* (*pl* -s)
extenuated *v* ▷ **extenuate**
extenuates *v* ▷ **extenuate**
extenuating *v* ▷ **extenuate**
extenuation *n* ▷ **extenuate**
extenuations *n* ▷ **extenuate**
exterior *n* (*pl* -s) part or surface on the outside ▶ *adj* of, on, or coming from the outside
exteriors *n* ▷ **exterior**
exterminate *v* (-tes, -ting, -ted) destroy (animals or people) completely
> **extermination** *n* (*pl* -s) > **exterminator** *n* (*pl* -s)
exterminated *v* ▷ **exterminate**
exterminates *v* ▷ **exterminate**
exterminating *v* ▷ **exterminate**
extermination *n* ▷ **exterminate**
exterminations *n* ▷ **exterminate**
exterminator *n* ▷ **exterminate**
exterminators *n* ▷ **exterminate**
external *adj* of, situated on, or coming from the outside > **externally** *adv*
externally *adv* ▷ **external**
extinct *adj* having died out > **extinction** *n* (*pl* -s)
extinction *n* ▷ **extinct**
extinctions *n* ▷ **extinct**
extinguish *v* (-es, -ing, -ed) put out (a fire or light)

extinguished *v* ▷ **extinguish**
extinguisher *n* (*pl* -s) device for extinguishing a fire or light
extinguishers *n* ▷ **extinguisher**
extinguishes *v* ▷ **extinguish**
extinguishing *v* ▷ **extinguish**
extirpate *v* (-tes, -ting, -ted) destroy utterly
extirpated *v* ▷ **extirpate**
extirpates *v* ▷ **extirpate**
extirpating *v* ▷ **extirpate**
extol *v* (-s, -lling, -lled) praise highly
extolled *v* ▷ **extol**
extolling *v* ▷ **extol**
extols *v* ▷ **extol**
extort *v* (-s, -ing, -ed) get (something) by force or threats > **extortion** *n* (*pl* -s)
extorted *v* ▷ **extort**
extorting *v* ▷ **extort**
extortion *n* ▷ **extort**
extortionate *adj* (of prices) excessive
extortions *n* ▷ **extort**
extorts *v* ▷ **extort**
extra *adj* more than is usual, expected or needed ▶ *n* (*pl* -s) additional person or thing ▶ *adv* unusually or exceptionally
extract *v* (-s, -ing, -ed) pull out by force ▶ *n* (*pl* -s) something extracted, such as a passage from a book etc. > **extraction** *n* (*pl* -s) > **extractor** (*pl* -s) *n*
extracted *v* ▷ **extract**
extracting *v* ▷ **extract**
extraction *n* ▷ **extract**
extractions *n* ▷ **extract**
extractor *n* ▷ **extract**
extractors *n* ▷ **extract**
extracts *n*, *v* ▷ **extract**
extradite *v* (-tes, -ting, -ted) send (an accused person) back to his or her own country for trial > **extradition** *n* (*pl* -s)
extradited *v* ▷ **extradite**
extradites *v* ▷ **extradite**
extraditing *v* ▷ **extradite**
extradition *n* ▷ **extradite**
extraditions *n* ▷ **extradite**
extramural *adj* connected with but outside the normal courses of a university or college
extraneous [iks-**train**-ee-uss] *adj* irrelevant
extraordinarily *adv* ▷ **extraordinary**
extraordinary *adj* very unusual
> **extraordinarily** *adv*
extrapolate *v* (-tes, -ting, -ted) infer (something not known) from the known facts (MATHS) > **extrapolation** *n* (*pl* -s)
extrapolated *v* ▷ **extrapolate**

extrapolates v ▷ extrapolate
extrapolating v ▷ extrapolate
extrapolation n ▷ extrapolate
extrapolations n ▷ extrapolate
extras n ▷ extra
extrasensory adj beyond the normal range of the senses
extravagance n ▷ extravagant
extravagances n ▷ extravagant
extravagant adj spending money excessively > **extravagance** n (pl -s)
extravaganza n (pl -s) elaborate and lavish entertainment, display, etc.
extravaganzas n ▷ extravaganza
extreme adj of a high or the highest degree or intensity ▶ n (pl -s) either of the two limits of a scale or range > **extremely** adv
extremely adv ▷ extreme
extremes n ▷ extreme
extremist n (pl -s) person who favours immoderate methods ▶ adj holding extreme opinions
extremists n ▷ extremist
extremities n ▷ extremity
extremity n (pl -ies) farthest point
extricate v (-tes, -ting, -ted) free from complication or difficulty > **extrication** n (pl -s)
extricated v ▷ extricate
extricates v ▷ extricate
extricating v ▷ extricate
extrication n ▷ extricate
extrications n ▷ extricate
extrovert adj lively and outgoing ▶ n (pl -s) extrovert person
extroverts n ▷ extrovert
extrude v (-des, -ding, -ded) squeeze or force out > **extrusion** n (pl -s)
extruded v ▷ extrude
extrudes v ▷ extrude
extruding v ▷ extrude
extrusion n ▷ extrude
extrusions n ▷ extrude
exuberance n ▷ exuberant
exuberances n ▷ exuberant
exuberant adj high-spirited > **exuberance** n (pl -s)
exude v (-s, -ing, -ed) (of a liquid or smell) seep or flow out slowly and steadily

exuded v ▷ exude
exudes v ▷ exude
exuding v ▷ exude
exult v (-s, -ing, -ed) be joyful or jubilant > **exultation** n (pl -s) > **exultant** adj
exultant adj ▷ exult
exultation n ▷ exult
exultations n ▷ exult
exulted v ▷ exult
exulting v ▷ exult
exults v ▷ exult
eye n (pl -s) organ of sight ▶ v (-s, eyeing or eying, eyed) look at carefully or warily > **eyeless** adj
eyeball n (pl -s) ball-shaped part of the eye
eyeballs n ▷ eyeball
eyebrow n (pl -s) line of hair on the bony ridge above the eye
eyebrows n ▷ eyebrow
eyed v ▷ eye
eyeglass n (pl -es) lens for aiding defective vision
eyeglasses n ▷ eyeglass
eyeing v ▷ eye
eyelash n (pl -es) short hair that grows out from the eyelid
eyelashes n ▷ eyelash
eyeless adj ▷ eye
eyelet n (pl -s) small hole for a lace or cord to be passed through
eyelets n ▷ eyelet
eyelid n (pl -s) fold of skin that covers the eye when it is closed
eyelids n ▷ eyelid
eyeliner n (pl -s) cosmetic used to outline the eyes
eyeliners n ▷ eyeliner
eyes n, v ▷ eye
eyesight n (pl -s) ability to see
eyesights n ▷ eyesight
eyesore n (pl -s) ugly object
eyesores n ▷ eyesore
eyewitness n (pl -es) person who was present at an event and can describe what happened
eyewitnesses n ▷ eyewitness
eying v ▷ eye
eyrie n (pl -s) nest of an eagle
eyries n ▷ eyrie

Ff

F can be an awkward letter in Scrabble: there are only two two-letter words beginning with F, for example (**fa** and **fy**). But if you're aware of this, you won't waste time trying to think of other two-letter words. There are also quite a few words that combine F with X or Z, allowing high scores particularly if you can hit a bonus square with them. **Fax, fix** and **fox** are good examples (13 points each), and don't forgets **fez** (15). If you have a blank tile, you can use it for the second Z in **fuzz** (15) or **fuzzy** (19). **Fey, fly** and **fry** can also be useful (9 each).

fa n (**fas**). Fa is the musical note F. This word isn't going to win you a game on its own, but it's useful when you're trying to form several words at once. Fa scores 5 points.

fab adj Fab is a short form of **fabulous**. Fab scores 8 points.

fable n (pl -**s**) story with a moral

fabled adj made famous in legend

fables n ▷ fable

fabric n (pl -**s**) knitted or woven cloth

fabricate v (-**tes, -ting, -ted**) make up (a story or lie) > **fabrication** n (pl -**s**)

fabricated v ▷ fabricate

fabricates v ▷ fabricate

fabricating v ▷ fabricate

fabrication n ▷ fabricate

fabrications n ▷ fabricate

fabrics n ▷ fabric

fabulous adj (Informal) excellent > **fabulously** adv

fabulously adv ▷ fabulous

facade [fas-**sahd**] n (pl -**s**) front of a building

facades n ▷ facade

face n (pl -**s**) front of the head ▶ v (-**ces, -cing, -ced**) look or turn towards

faced v ▷ face

faceless adj impersonal, anonymous

faces n, v ▷ face

facet n (pl -**s**) aspect

facetious [fas-**see**-shuss] adj funny or trying to be funny, esp. at inappropriate times

facets n ▷ facet

facia n (pl -**ciae**) ▷ fascia

faciae n ▷ fascia

facial adj of the face ▶ n (pl -**s**) beauty treatment for the face

facials n ▷ facial

facile [**fas**-sile] adj (of a remark, argument, etc.) superficial and showing lack of real thought

facilitate v (-**tes, -ting, -ted**) make easy > **facilitation** n (pl -**s**)

facilitated v ▷ facilitate

facilitates v ▷ facilitate

facilitating v ▷ facilitate

facilitation n ▷ facilitate

facilitations n ▷ facilitate

facilities n ▷ facility

facility n (pl -**ties**) skill ▶ pl means or equipment for an activity

facing v ▷ face

facing n (pl -**s**) lining or covering for decoration or reinforcement ▶ pl contrasting collar and cuffs on a jacket

facings n ▷ facing

facsimile [fak-**sim**-ill-ee] n (pl -**s**) exact copy

facsimiles n ▷ facsimile

fact n (pl -**s**) event or thing known to have happened or existed > **factual** adj

faction n (pl -**s**) (dissenting) minority group within a larger body

factions n ▷ faction

factious adj of or producing factions

factitious adj artificial

factor n (pl -**s**) element contributing to a result

factorial n (pl -**s**) product of all the integers from one to a given number

factorials n ▷ factorial

factories n ▷ factory

factorize v (-**zes, -zing, -zed**) calculate the factors of (a number)

factorized v ▷ factorize

factorizes v ▷ factorize

factorizing v ▷ factorize

factors *n* ▷ **factor**
factory *n* (*pl* -**ies**) building where goods are
manufactured
factotum *n* (*pl* -**s**) person employed to do all
sorts of work
factotums *n* ▷ **factotum**
facts *n* ▷ **fact**
factual *adj* ▷ **fact**
faculties *n* ▷ **faculty**
faculty *n* (*pl* -**ties**) physical or mental ability
fad *n* (*pl* -**s**) short-lived fashion > **faddy** (-**ddier**,
-**ddiest**), **faddish** *adj*
faddier *adj* ▷ **fad**
faddiest *adj* ▷ **fad**
faddish *adj* ▷ **fad**
faddy *adj* ▷ **fad**
fade *v* (-**des**, -**ding**, -**ded**) (cause to) lose
brightness, colour, or strength
faded *v* ▷ **fade**
fades *v* ▷ **fade**
fading *v* ▷ **fade**
fads *n* ▷ **fad**
faecal *adj* ▷ **faeces**
faeces [fee-seez] *pl n* waste matter discharged
from the anus > **faecal** [fee-kl] ▶ *adj*
fag¹ *n* (*pl* -**s**) (*Informal*) boring task (BRIT) ▶ *v* (-**gs**,
-**gging**, -**gged**) (BRIT) do menial chores in a
public school
fag² *n* (BRIT) (*Slang*) cigarette
fagged *v* ▷ **fag¹**
fagging *v* ▷ **fag¹**
faggot *n* (*pl* -**s**) (BRIT, AUST & NZ) ball of chopped
liver, herbs, and bread
faggots *n* ▷ **faggot**
fags *n*, *v* ▷ **fag¹, ²**
faïence [fie-ence] *n* (*pl* -**s**) tin-glazed
earthenware
faïences *n* ▷ **faïence**
fail *v* (-**s**, -**ing**, -**ed**) be unsuccessful ▶ *n* (*pl* -**s**)
instance of not passing an exam or test
failed *v* ▷ **fail**
failing *n* (*pl* -**s**) weak point ▶ *prep* in the
absence of ▶ *v* ▷ **fail**
failings *n* ▷ **failing**
fails *v*, *n* ▷ **fail**
failure *n* (*pl* -**s**) act or instance of failing
failures *n* ▷ **failure**
fain *adv* (*Obs*) gladly
faint *adj* lacking clarity, brightness, or
volume ▶ *v* (-**s**, -**ing**, -**ed**) lose consciousness
temporarily ▶ *n* (*pl* -**s**) temporary loss of
consciousness
fainted *v* ▷ **faint**
fainting *v* ▷ **faint**
faints *v*, *n* ▷ **faint**

fair¹ *adj* (-**er**, -**est**) unbiased and reasonable
▶ *adv* fairly > **fairness** *n* (*pl* -**s**)
fair² *n* (*pl* -**s**) travelling entertainment with
sideshows, rides, and amusements
fairer *adj* ▷ **fair¹**
fairest *adj* ▷ **fair¹**
fairground *n* (*pl* -**s**) open space used for a fair
fairgrounds *n* ▷ **fairground**
fairies *n* ▷ **fairy**
fairly *adv* moderately
fairness *n* ▷ **fair¹**
fairnesses *n* ▷ **fair¹**
fairs *n* ▷ **fair¹, ²**
fairway *n* (*pl* -**s**) (GOLF) smooth area between
the tee and the green
fairways *n* ▷ **fairway**
fairy *n* (*pl* -**ries**) imaginary small creature with
magic powers > **fairyland** *n* (*pl* -**s**)
fairyland *n* ▷ **fairy**
fairylands *n* ▷ **fairy**
faith *n* (*pl* -**s**) strong belief, esp. without proof
faithful *adj* loyal > **faithfully** *adv*
faithfully *adv* ▷ **faithful**
faithless *adj* disloyal or dishonest
faiths *n* ▷ **faith**
fake *v* (-**kes**, -**king**, -**ked**) cause something not
genuine to appear real or more valuable by
fraud ▶ *n* (*pl* -**s**) person, thing, or act that is
not genuine ▶ *adj* not genuine
faked *v* ▷ **fake**
fakes *v*, *n* ▷ **fake**
faking *v* ▷ **fake**
fakir [fay-keer] *n* (*pl* -**s**) Muslim who spurns
worldly possessions
fakirs *n* ▷ **fakir**
falcon *n* (*pl* -**s**) small bird of prey
falconer *n* ▷ **falconry**
falconers *n* ▷ **falconry**
falconries *n* ▷ **falconry**
falconry *n* (*pl* -**ries**) art of training falcons
> **falconer** *n* (*pl* -**s**)
falcons *n* ▷ **falcon**
fall *v* (-**s**, -**ing**, **fell**, **fallen**) drop from a higher to
a lower place through the force of gravity ▶ *n*
(*pl* -**s**) falling
fallacies *n* ▷ **fallacy**
fallacious *adj* ▷ **fallacy**
fallacy *n* (*pl* -**cies**) false belief > **fallacious** *adj*
fallen *v* ▷ **fall**
fallibilities *n* ▷ **fallible**
fallibility *n* ▷ **fallible**
fallible *adj* (of a person) liable to make
mistakes > **fallibility** *n* (*pl* -**ties**)
falling *v* ▷ **fall**
fallout *n* (*pl* -**s**) radioactive particles spread as

a result of a nuclear explosion
fallouts n ▷ **fallout**
fallow adj (of land) ploughed but left unseeded to regain fertility
falls v, n ▷ **fall**
false adj (-r, -st) not true or correct > **falsely** adv > **falseness** n (pl -es) > **falsity** n (pl -ties)
falsehood n (pl -s) quality of being untrue
falsehoods n ▷ **falsehood**
falsely adv ▷ **false**
falseness n ▷ **false**
falsenesses n ▷ **false**
falser adj ▷ **false**
falsest adj ▷ **false**
falsetto n (pl -tos) voice pitched higher than one's natural range
falsettos n ▷ **falsetto**
falsification n ▷ **falsify**
falsifications n ▷ **falsify**
falsified v ▷ **falsify**
falsifies v ▷ **falsify**
falsify v (-fies, -fying, -fied) alter fraudulently > **falsification** n (pl -s)
falsifying v ▷ **falsify**
falsities n ▷ **false**
falsity n ▷ **false**
falter v (-s, -ing, -ed) be hesitant, weak, or unsure
faltered v ▷ **falter**
faltering v ▷ **falter**
falters v ▷ **falter**
fame n (pl -s) state of being widely known or recognized
famed adj famous
famed adj ▷ **fame**
fames n ▷ **fame**
familial adj ▷ **family**
familiar adj well-known ▶ n (pl -s) demon supposed to attend a witch > **familiarly** adv > **familiarity** n (pl -ties)
familiarities n ▷ **familiarity**
familiarity n ▷ **familiarity**
familiarize (-zes, -zing, -zed) v acquaint fully with a particular subject > **familiarization** n (pl -s)
familiarization n ▷ **familiarize**
familiarizations n ▷ **familiarize**
familiarized v ▷ **familiarize**
familiarizes v ▷ **familiarize**
familiarizing v ▷ **familiarize**
familiarly adv ▷ **familiar**
familiars n ▷ **familiar**
families n ▷ **family**
family n (pl -lies) group of parents and their children ▶ adj suitable for parents and

children together > **familial** adj
famine n (pl -s) severe shortage of food
famines n ▷ **famine**
famished adj very hungry
famous adj very well-known
famously adv (Informal) excellently
fan[1] n (pl -s) hand-held or mechanical object used to create a current of air for ventilation or cooling ▶ v (-s, -nning, -nned) blow or cool with a fan
fan[2] n (pl -s) (Informal) devotee of a pop star, sport, or hobby
fanatic n (pl -s) person who is excessively enthusiastic about something > **fanatical** adj > **fanatically** adv > **fanaticism** n (pl -s)
fanatical adj ▷ **fanatic**
fanatically adv ▷ **fanatic**
fanaticism n ▷ **fanatic**
fanaticisms n ▷ **fanatic**
fanatics n ▷ **fanatic**
fanbase n (pl -s) body of admirers of a particular pop singer, sports team, etc
fanbases n ▷ **fanbase**
fancied v ▷ **fancy**
fancier adj ▷ **fancy**
fancies n, v ▷ **fancy**
fanciest adj ▷ **fancy**
fanciful adj not based on fact > **fancifully** adv
fancifully adv ▷ **fanciful**
fancy adj (-cier, -ciest) elaborate, not plain ▶ n (pl -cies) sudden irrational liking or desire ▶ v (-cies, -cying, -cied) (Informal) be sexually attracted to
fancy-free adj not in love
fancying v ▷ **fancy**
fandango n (pl -os) lively Spanish dance
fandangos n ▷ **fandango**
fanfare n (pl -s) short loud tune played on brass instruments
fanfares n ▷ **fanfare**
fang n (pl -s) snake's tooth which injects poison
fangs n ▷ **fang**
fanned n ▷ **fan**
fanning n ▷ **fan**
fans n, v ▷ **fan**
fantail n (pl -s) small New Zealand bird with a tail like a fan
fantails n ▷ **fantail**
fantasia n (pl -s) musical composition of an improvised nature
fantasias n ▷ **fantasia**
fantasies n ▷ **fantasy**
fantasize v (-zes, -zing, -zed) indulge in daydreams

fantasized *v* ▷ fantasize
fantasizes *v* ▷ fantasize
fantasizing *v* ▷ fantasize
fantastic *adj* (*Informal*) very good
>fantastically *adv*
fantastically *adv* ▷ fantastic
fantasy *n* (*pl* -sies) far-fetched notion
far *adv* (farther *or* further, farthest *or* furthest)
at, to, or from a great distance ▶ *adj* remote in
space or time
farad *n* (*pl* -s) unit of electrical capacitance
farads *n* ▷ farad
farce *n* (*pl* -s) boisterous comedy
farces *n* ▷ farce
farcical *adj* ludicrous >farcically *adv*
farcically *adv* ▷ farcical
fare *n* (*pl* -s) charge for a passenger's journey
▶ *v* (-res, -ring, -red) get on (as specified)
fared *v* ▷ fare
fares *n, v* ▷ fare
farewell *interj* goodbye ▶ *n* (*pl* -s) act of saying
goodbye and leaving ▶ *v* (-s, -ing, -ed) (NZ) say
goodbye
farewelled *v* ▷ farewell
farewelling *v* ▷ farewell
farewells *n, v* ▷ farewell
farinaceous *adj* containing starch or having a
starchy texture
faring *v* ▷ fare
farm *n* (*pl* -s) area of land for growing crops or
rearing livestock ▶ *v* (-s, -ing, -ed) cultivate
(land) >farmhouse *n* (*pl* -s) >farmyard *n* (*pl* -s)
farmed *v* ▷ farm
farmer *n* (*pl* -s) person who owns or runs a
farm
farmers *n* ▷ farmer
farmhouse *n* ▷ farm
farmhouses *n* ▷ farm
farming *v* ▷ farm
farms *n, v* ▷ farm
farmstead *n* (*pl* -s) farm and its buildings
farmsteads *n* ▷ farmstead
farmyard *n* ▷ farm
farmyards *n* ▷ farm
farrago [far-rah-go] *n* (*pl* -gos, -goes) jumbled
mixture of things
farragoes *n* ▷ farrago
farragos *n* ▷ farrago
farrier *n* (*pl* -s) person who shoes horses
farriers *n* ▷ farrier
farrow *n* (*pl* -s) litter of piglets ▶ *v* (-s, -ing, -ed)
(of a sow) give birth
farrowed *v* ▷ farrow
farrowing *v* ▷ farrow
farrows *n, v* ▷ farrow

farther, farthest *adv, adj* ▷ far
farthing *n* (*pl* -s) former British coin
equivalent to a quarter of a penny
farthings *n* ▷ farthing
fascia [fay-shya] *n* (*pl* -ciae, -cias) outer surface
of a dashboard
fasciae *n* ▷ fascia
fascias *n* ▷ fascia
fascinate *v* (-tes, -ting, -ted) attract
and interest strongly >fascinating *adj*
>fascination *n* (*pl* -s)
fascinated *v* ▷ fascinate
fascinates *v* ▷ fascinate
fascinating *v, adj* ▷ fascinate
fascination *n* ▷ fascinate
fascinations *n* ▷ fascinate
fascism [fash-iz-zum] *n* (*pl* -s) right-wing
totalitarian political system characterized
by state control and extreme nationalism
>fascist *adj, n* (*pl* -s)
fascisms *n* ▷ fascism
fascist *n* ▷ fascism
fascists *n* ▷ fascist
fashion *n* (*pl* -s) style in clothes, hairstyle, etc.,
popular at a particular time ▶ *v* (-s, -ing, -ed)
form or make into a particular shape
fashionable *adj* currently popular
>fashionably *adv*
fashionably *adv* ▷ fashionable
fashioned *v* ▷ fashion
fashioning *v* ▷ fashion
fashions *n, v* ▷ fashion
fast[1] *adj* (-er, -est) (capable of) acting or
moving quickly ▶ *adv* quickly
fast[2] *v* (-s, -ing, -ed) go without food, esp. for
religious reasons ▶ *n* (*pl* -s) period of fasting
fasted *v* ▷ fast[2]
fasten *v* (-s, -ing, -ed) make or become firmly
fixed or joined
fastened *v* ▷ fasten
fastener *n* (*pl* -s) device that fastens
fasteners *n* ▷ fastener
fastening *v* ▷ fasten ▶ *n* (*pl* -s) device that
fastens
fastenings *n* ▷ fastening
fastens *v* ▷ fasten
faster *adj* ▷ fast[1]
fastest *adj* ▷ fast[1]
fastidious *adj* very fussy about details
>fastidiously *adv* >fastidiousness *n*
fastidiously *adv* ▷ fastidious
fastidiousness *n* ▷ fastidious
fastidiousnesses *n* ▷ fastidious
fasting *v* ▷ fast[2]
fastness *n* (*pl* -es) fortress, safe place

fastnesses *n* ▷ fastness
fasts *v*, *n* ▷ fast²
fat *adj* (-**er**, -**est**) having excess flesh on the body ▶ *n* (*pl* -**s**) extra flesh on the body > **fatness** *n* (*pl* -**es**)
fatal *adj* causing death or ruin > **fatally** *adv*
fatalism *n* (*pl* -**s**) belief that all events are predetermined and people are powerless to change their destinies > **fatalist** *n* (*pl* -**s**) > **fatalistic** *adj*
fatalisms *n* ▷ fatalism
fatalist *n* ▷ fatalism
fatalistic *adj* ▷ fatalism
fatalists *n* ▷ fatalism
fatalities *n* ▷ fatality
fatality *n* (*pl* -**ties**) death caused by an accident or disaster
fatally *adv* ▷ fatal
fate *n* (*pl* -**s**) power supposed to predetermine events
fated *adj* destined
fateful *adj* having important, usu. disastrous, consequences
fates *n* ▷ fate
fathead *n* (*pl* -**s**) (*Informal*) stupid person > **fat-headed** *adj*
fatheaded *adj* ▷ fathead
fatheads *n* ▷ fathead
father *n* (*pl* -**s**) male parent ▶ *v* (-**s**, -**ing**, -**ed**) be the father of (offspring) > **fatherhood** *n* (*pl* -**s**) > **fatherless** *adj* > **fatherly** *adj*
fathered *v* ▷ father
fatherhood *n* ▷ father
fatherhoods *n* ▷ fatherhood
fathering *v* ▷ father
fatherland *n* one's native country
fatherlands *n* ▷ fatherland
fatherless *adj* ▷ father
fatherly *adj* ▷ father
fathers *n*, *v* ▷ father
fathom *n* (*pl* -**s**) unit of length, used in navigation, equal to six feet (1.83 metres) ▶ *v* (-**s**, -**ing**, -**ed**) understand > **fathomable** *adj*
fathomable *adj* ▷ fathom
fathomed *v* ▷ fathom
fathoming *v* ▷ fathom
fathomless *adj* too deep or difficult to fathom
fathoms *n*, *v* ▷ fathom
fatigue [fat-**eeg**] *n* (*pl* -**s**) extreme physical or mental tiredness ▶ *v* (-**gues**, -**guing**, -**gued**) tire out
fatigued *v* ▷ fatigue
fatigues *v*, *n* ▷ fatigue
fatiguing *v* ▷ fatigue
fatness *n* ▷ fat

fatnesses *n* ▷ fat
fats *n* ▷ fat
fatten *v* (-**s**, -**ing**, -**ed**) (cause to) become fat
fattened *v* ▷ fatten
fattening *v* ▷ fatten
fattens *v* ▷ fatten
fattier *adj* ▷ fatty
fattiest *adj* ▷ fatty
fatty *adj* (-**ier**, -**iest**) containing fat
fatuities *n* ▷ fatuous
fatuity *n* ▷ fatuous
fatuous *adj* foolish > **fatuously** *adv* > **fatuity** *n* (*pl* -**s**)
fatuously *adv* ▷ fatuous
faucet [**faw**-set] *n* (*pl* -**s**) (US) tap
faucets *n* ▷ faucet
fault *n* (*pl* -**s**) responsibility for something wrong ▶ *v* (-**s**, -**ing**, -**ed**) criticize or blame > **faulty** *adj* (-**tier**, -**tiest**) > **faultless** *adj* > **faultlessly** *adv*
faulted *v* ▷ fault
faultier *adj* ▷ fault
faultiest *adj* ▷ fault
faulting *v* ▷ fault
faultless *adj* ▷ fault
faultlessly *adv* ▷ fault
faults *v* ▷ fault
faulty *n* ▷ fault
faun *n* (*pl* -**s**) (in Roman legend) creature with a human face and torso and a goat's horns and legs
fauna *n* (*pl* -**as**, -**ae**) animals of a given place or time
faunae *n* ▷ fauna
faunas *n* ▷ fauna
fauns *n* ▷ faun
favour *n* (*pl* -**s**) approving attitude ▶ *v* (-**s**, -**ing**, -**ed**) prefer
favourable *adj* encouraging or advantageous > **favourably** *adv*
favourably *adv* ▷ favourable
favoured *v* ▷ favour
favouring *v* ▷ favour
favourite *adj* most liked ▶ *n* (*pl* -**s**) preferred person or thing
favourites *n* ▷ favourite
favouritism *n* (*pl* -**s**) practice of giving special treatment to a person or group
favouritisms *n* ▷ favouritism
favours *n*, *v* ▷ favour

> **faw** *n* (**faws**). A faw is a gypsy. This is a good word for taking advantage of a nearby bonus square. Faw scores 9 points.

fawn¹ *n* (*pl* -**s**) young deer ▶ *adj* light yellowish-brown

fawn² v (**-s, -ing, -ed**) (*foll. by* **on**) seek attention from (someone) by insincere flattery

fawned v ▷ **fawn²**

fawning v ▷ **fawn²**

fawns n, v ▷ **fawn¹, ²**

fax n (*pl* **-es**) electronic system for sending facsimiles of documents by telephone ▶ v (**-xes, -xing, -xed**) send (a document) by this system

faxed n ▷ **fax**

faxes n, v ▷ **fax**

faxing v ▷ **fax**

> **fay** n (**fays**). A fay is a fairy. This is a fairly high-scoring short word that can be helpful in a tight game. Fay scores 9 points.

fealties n ▷ **fealty**

fealty n (*pl* **-ies**) (in feudal society) subordinate's loyalty to his ruler or lord

fear n (*pl* **-s**) distress or alarm caused by impending danger or pain ▶ v (**-s, -ing, -ed**) be afraid of (something or someone) > **fearless** *adj* > **fearlessly** *adv*

feared v ▷ **fear**

fearful *adj* feeling fear (*Informal*) > **fearfully** *adv*

fearfully *adv* ▷ **fearful**

fearing v ▷ **fear**

fearless n ▷ **fear**

fearlessly *adv* ▷ **fear**

fears n, v ▷ **fear**

fearsome *adj* terrifying

feasibilities n ▷ **feasible**

feasibility n ▷ **feasible**

feasible *adj* able to be done, possible > **feasibly** *adv* > **feasibility** n (*pl* **-s**)

feasibly *adv* ▷ **feasible**

feast n (*pl* **-s**) lavish meal ▶ v (**-s, -ing, -ed**) eat a feast

feasted v ▷ **feast**

feasting v ▷ **feast**

feasts n, v ▷ **feast**

feat n (*pl* **-s**) remarkable, skilful, or daring action

feather n (*pl* **-s**) one of the barbed shafts forming the plumage of birds ▶ v (**-s, -ing, -ed**) fit or cover with feathers > **feathered** *adj* > **feathery** *adj* (**-rier, -riest**)

feathered v, *adj* ▷ **feather**

featherier *adj* ▷ **feather**

featheriest *adj* ▷ **feather**

feathering v ▷ **feather**

feathers n, v ▷ **feather**

featherweight n (*pl* **-s**) boxer weighing up to

126lb (professional) or 57kg (amateur)

featherweights n ▷ **featherweight**

feathery *adj* ▷ **feather**

feats n ▷ **feat**

feature n (*pl* **-s**) part of the face, such as the eyes ▶ v (**-res, -ring, -red**) have as a feature or be a feature in > **featureless** *adj*

featured v ▷ **feature**

featureless *adj* ▷ **feature**

features n, v ▷ **feature**

featuring v ▷ **feature**

febrile [**fee**-brile] *adj* feverish

feckless *adj* ineffectual or irresponsible

fecund *adj* fertile > **fecundity** n (*pl* **-ties**)

fecundities n ▷ **fecund**

fecundity n ▷ **fecund**

fed v ▷ **feed**

federal *adj* of a system in which power is divided between one central government and several regional governments > **federalism** n (*pl* **-s**) > **federalist** n (*pl* **-s**)

federalism n ▷ **federal**

federalisms n ▷ **federal**

federalist n ▷ **federal**

federalists n ▷ **federal**

federate v (**-tes, -ting, -ted**) unite in a federation

federated v ▷ **federate**

federates v ▷ **federate**

federating v ▷ **federate**

federation n (*pl* **-s**) union of several states, provinces, etc.

federations n ▷ **federation**

fedora [fid-**or**-a] n (*pl* **-s**) man's soft hat with a brim

fedoras n ▷ **fedora**

fee n (*pl* **-s**) charge paid to be allowed to do something

feeble *adj* (**-r, -st**) lacking physical or mental power > **feebleness** n (*pl* **-es**) > **feebly** *adv*

feebleminded *adj* unable to think or understand effectively

feebleness n ▷ **feeble**

feeblenesses n ▷ **feeble**

feebler *adj* ▷ **feeble**

feeblest *adj* ▷ **feeble**

feebly *adv* ▷ **feeble**

feed v (**-s, -ing, fed**) give food to ▶ n (*pl* **-s**) act of feeding

feedback n (*pl* **-s**) information received in response to something done

feedbacks n ▷ **feedback**

feeder n (*pl* **-s**) road or railway line linking outlying areas to the main traffic network

feeders n ▷ **feeder**

feeding v ▷ **feed**
  feeds v, n ▷ **feed**
feel v (**-s, -ing, felt**) have a physical or emotional sensation of ▶ n (pl **-s**) act of feeling
  feeler n (pl **-s**) organ of touch in some animals
  feelers n ▷ **feeler**
feeling n (pl **-s**) emotional reaction
  feelings n ▷ **feeling** ▶ v ▷ **feel**
  feels v, n ▷ **feel**
  fees n ▷ **fee**
  feet n ▷ **foot**
feign [fane] v (**-s, -ing, -ed**) pretend
  feigned v ▷ **feign**
  feigning v ▷ **feign**
  feigns v ▷ **feign**
feint[1] [faint] n (pl **-s**) sham attack or blow meant to distract an opponent ▶ v (**-s, -ing, -ed**) make a feint
feint[2] [faint] n (pl **-s**) narrow lines on ruled paper
  feinted v ▷ **feint**[1]
  feinting v ▷ **feint**[1]
  feints n, v ▷ **feint**[1, 2]
feldspar n (pl **-s**) hard mineral that is the main constituent of igneous rocks
  feldspars n ▷ **feldspar**
felicitations pl n congratulations
  felicities n ▷ **felicity**
  felicitous adj ▷ **felicity**
felicity n (pl **-ties**) happiness > **felicitous** adj
feline adj of cats ▶ n (pl **-s**) member of the cat family
  felines n ▷ **feline**
  fell[1] v ▷ **fall**
fell[2] v (**-s, -ing, -ed**) cut down (a tree)
fell[3] adj (**-er, -est**) deadly
fell[4] n (pl **-s**) (SCOT & N ENGLISH) mountain, hill, or moor
  felled v ▷ **fell**[2]
  feller adj ▷ **fell**[3]
  fellest adj ▷ **fell**[3]
  felling v ▷ **fell**[2]
felloe n (pl **-oes**) (segment of) the rim of a wheel
  felloes n ▷ **felloe**
fellow n (pl **-s**) man or boy ▶ adj in the same group or condition
  fellows n ▷ **fellow**
fellowship n (pl **-s**) sharing of aims or interests
  fellowships n ▷ **fellowship**
  fells v, n ▷ **fell**[2, 4]
felon n (pl **-s**) (CRIMINAL LAW) (formerly) person guilty of a felony
  felonies n ▷ **felony**

felonious adj ▷ **felony**
  felons n ▷ **felon**
felony n (pl **-nies**) serious crime > **felonious** adj
felspar n (pl **-s**) ▷ **feldspar**
  felspars n ▷ **felspar**
  felt[1] v ▷ **feel**
felt[2] n (pl **-s**) matted fabric made by bonding fibres by pressure
  felts n ▷ **felt**[2]
female adj of the sex which bears offspring ▶ n (pl **-s**) female person or animal
  females n ▷ **female**
feminine adj having qualities traditionally regarded as suitable for, or typical of, women > **femininity** n (pl **-ties**)
  femininities n ▷ **feminine**
  femininity n ▷ **feminine**
feminism n (pl **-s**) advocacy of equal rights for women > **feminist** adj, n (pl **-s**)
  feminisms n ▷ **feminism**
  feminist n ▷ **feminism**
  feminists n ▷ **feminism**
femoral adj of the thigh
femur [fee-mer] n (pl **-s**) thighbone
  femurs n ▷ **femur**
fen n (pl **-s**) (BRIT) low-lying flat marshy land
fence n (pl **-s**) barrier of posts linked by wire or wood, enclosing an area ▶ v (**-ces, -cing, -ced**) enclose with or as if with a fence
  fenced v ▷ **fence**
  fencer n ▷ **fencing**
  fencers n ▷ **fencing**
  fences n, v ▷ **fence**
fencing n (pl **-s**) sport of fighting with swords ▶ v ▷ **fence** > **fencer** n (pl **-s**)
  fencings n ▷ **fencing**
fend v (**-s, -ing, -ed**) provide (for oneself)
  fended v ▷ **fend**
fender n (pl **-s**) low metal frame in front of a fireplace
  fenders n ▷ **fender**
  fending v ▷ **fend**
  fends v ▷ **fend**
fennel n (pl **-s**) fragrant plant whose seeds, leaves, and root are used in cookery
  fennels n ▷ **fennel**
  fens n ▷ **fen**
fenugreek n (pl **-s**) Mediterranean plant grown for its heavily scented seeds
  fenugreeks n ▷ **fenugreek**
feral adj wild
ferment n (pl **-s**) commotion, unrest ▶ v (**-s, -ing, -ed**) undergo or cause to undergo fermentation
fermentation n (pl **-s**) reaction in which

an organic molecule splits into simpler substances, esp. the conversion of sugar to alcohol

fermentations *n* ▷ **fermentation**
fermented *n* ▷ **ferment**
fermenting *v* ▷ **ferment**
ferments *n*, *v* ▷ **ferment**
fern *n* (*pl* **-s**) flowerless plant with fine fronds
ferns *n* ▷ **fern**
ferocious *adj* savagely fierce or cruel > **ferocity** *n* (*pl* **-ties**)
ferocities *n* ▷ **ferocious**
ferocity *n* ▷ **ferocious**
ferret *n* (*pl* **-s**) tamed polecat used to catch rabbits or rats ▶ *v* (**-s, -ing, -ed**) hunt with ferrets
ferreted *v* ▷ **ferret**
ferreting *v* ▷ **ferret**
ferrets *n*, *v* ▷ **ferret**
ferric, ferrous *adj* of or containing iron
ferried *v* ▷ **ferry**
ferries *n*, *v* ▷ **ferry**
ferrous *adj* ▷ **ferric**
ferry *n* (*pl* **-rries**) boat for transporting people and vehicles ▶ *v* (**-rries, -rrying, -rried**) carry by ferry > **ferryman** *n* (*pl* **-men**)
ferrying *v* ▷ **ferry**
ferryman *n* ▷ **ferry**
ferrymen *n* ▷ **ferry**
fertile *adj* capable of producing young, crops, or vegetation > **fertility** *n* (*pl* **-ties**)
fertilities *n* ▷ **fertile**
fertility *n* ▷ **fertile**
fertilization *n* ▷ **fertilize**
fertilizations *n* ▷ **fertilize**
fertilize *v* (**-zes, -zing, -zed**) provide (an animal or plant) with sperm or pollen to bring about fertilization > **fertilization** *n* (*pl* **-s**)
fertilized *v* ▷ **fertilize**
fertilizer *n* (*pl* **-s**) substance added to the soil to increase its productivity
fertilizers *n* ▷ **fertilizer**
fertilizes *v* ▷ **fertilize**
fertilizing *v* ▷ **fertilize**
fervent, fervid *adj* intensely passionate and sincere > **fervently** *adv*
fervently *adv* ▷ **fervent**
fervid *adj* ▷ **fervent**
fervour *n* (*pl* **-s**) intensity of feeling
fervours *n* ▷ **fervour**
fescue *n* (*pl* **-s**) pasture and lawn grass with stiff narrow leaves
fescues *n* ▷ **fescue**
fester *v* (**-s, -ing, -ed**) grow worse and increasingly hostile

festered *v* ▷ **fester**
festering *v* ▷ **fester**
festers *v* ▷ **fester**
festival *n* (*pl* **-s**) organized series of special events or performances
festivals *n* ▷ **festival**
festive *adj* of or like a celebration
festivities *n* ▷ **festivity**
festivity *n* (*pl* **-ties**) happy celebration ▶ *pl* celebrations
festoon *v* (**-s, -ing, -ed**) hang decorations in loops
festooned *v* ▷ **festoon**
festooning *v* ▷ **festoon**
festoons *v* ▷ **festoon**
feta *n* (*pl* **-as**) white salty Greek cheese
fetal *adj* ▷ **fetus**
fetas *n* ▷ **feta**
fetch *v* (**-es, -ing, -ed**) go after and bring back (*Informal*)
fetched *v* ▷ **fetch**
fetches *v* ▷ **fetch**
fetching *v* ▷ **fetch** ▶ *adj* attractive
fete [fate] *n* (*pl* **-s**) gala, bazaar, etc., usu. held outdoors ▶ *v* (**-tes, -ting, -ted**) honour or entertain regally
feted *v* ▷ **fete**
fetes *n*, *v* ▷ **fete**
fetid *adj* (**-er, -est**) stinking
fetider *adj* ▷ **fetid**
fetidest *adj* ▷ **fetid**
feting *v* ▷ **fete**
fetish *n* (*pl* **-es**) form of behaviour in which sexual pleasure is derived from looking at or handling an inanimate object > **fetishism** *n* (*pl* **-s**) > **fetishist** (*pl* **-s**) *n*
fetishes *n* ▷ **fetish**
fetishism *n* ▷ **fetish**
fetishisms *n* ▷ **fetish**
fetishist *n* ▷ **fetish**
fetishists *n* ▷ **fetish**
fetlock *n* (*pl* **-s**) projection behind and above a horse's hoof
fetlocks *n* ▷ **fetlock**
fetter *n* (*pl* **-s**) chain or shackle for the foot ▶ *pl* restrictions ▶ *v* (**-s, -ing, -ed**) restrict
fettered *v* ▷ **fetter**
fettering *v* ▷ **fetter**
fetters *n*, *v* ▷ **fetter**
fettle *n* (*pl* **-s**) state of health or spirits
fettles *n* ▷ **fettle**
fetus [fee-tuss] *n* (*pl* **-tuses**) embryo of a mammal in the later stages of development > **fetal** *adj*
fetuses *n* ▷ **fetus**

feu *n* (*pl* **-s**) (in Scotland) right of use of land in return for a fixed annual payment

feud *n* (*pl* **-s**) long bitter hostility between two people or groups ▶ *v* (**-s, -ing, -ed**) carry on a feud

feudal *adj* of or like feudalism

feudalism *n* (*pl* **-s**) medieval system in which people held land from a lord, and in return worked and fought for him

  feudalisms *n* ▷ feudalism

  feuded *v* ▷ feud

  feuding *v* ▷ feud

  feuds *n, v* ▷ feud

  feus *n* ▷ feu

fever *n* (*pl* **-s**) (illness causing) high body temperature > **fevered** *adj*

  fevered *adj* ▷ fever

feverish *adj* suffering from fever > **feverishly** *adv*

  feverishly *adv* ▷ feverish

  fevers *n* ▷ fever

few *adj* (**-er, -est**) not many

  fewer *adj* ▷ few

  fewest *adj* ▷ few

fey *adj* (**-er, -est**) whimsically strange

  feyer *adj* ▷ fey

  feyest *adj* ▷ fey

fez *n* (*pl* **fezzes**) brimless tasselled cap, orig. from Turkey

  fezzes *n* ▷ fez

fiancé [fee-on-say] *n* (*pl* **-cés**) man engaged to be married > **fiancée** *n fem* (*pl* **-cées**)

  fiancée *n* ▷ fiancé

  fiancées *n* ▷ fiancé

  fiancés *n* ▷ fiancé

fiasco *n* (*pl* **-cos, -coes**) ridiculous or humiliating failure

  fiascoes *n* ▷ fiasco

  fiascos *n* ▷ fiasco

fiat [fee-at] *n* (*pl* **-s**) arbitrary order

  fiats *n* ▷ fiat

fib *n* (*pl* **-s**) trivial lie ▶ *v* (**-s, -bbing, -bbed**) tell a lie > **fibber** *n* (*pl* **-s**)

  fibbed *v* ▷ fib

  fibber *n* ▷ fib

  fibbers *n* ▷ fib

  fibbing *v* ▷ fib

fibre *n* (*pl* **-s**) thread that can be spun into yarn > **fibrous** *adj*

fibreglass *n* (*pl* **-es**) material made of fine glass fibres

  fibreglasses *n* ▷ fibreglass

  fibres *n* ▷ fibre

fibro *n* (*pl* **-ros**) (AUST) mixture of cement and asbestos fibre, used in sheets for building

(*also* **fibrocement**)

fibroid [fibe-royd] *n* (*pl* **-s**) benign tumour composed of fibrous connective tissue

  fibroids *n* ▷ fibroid

  fibros *n* ▷ fibro

  fibrosites *n* ▷ fibrositis

fibrositis [fibe-roh-**site**-iss] *n* (*pl* **-es**) inflammation of the tissues of muscle sheaths

  fibrous *adj* ▷ fibre

  fibs *n, v* ▷ fib

fibula *n* (*pl* **-lae, -las**) slender outer bone of the lower leg

  fibulae *n* ▷ fibula

  fibulas *n* ▷ fibula

fiche [feesh] *n* (*pl* **-s**) sheet of film for storing publications in miniaturized form

  fiches *n* ▷ fiche

fickle *adj* changeable, inconstant > **fickleness** *n* (*pl* **-ess**)

  fickleness *n* ▷ fickle

  ficklenesses *n* ▷ fickle

fiction *n* (*pl* **-s**) literary works of the imagination, such as novels > **fictional** *adj*

  fictional *adj* ▷ fiction

fictionalize *v* (**-zes, -zing, -zed**) turn into fiction

  fictionalized *v* ▷ fictionalize

  fictionalizes *v* ▷ fictionalize

  fictionalizing *v* ▷ fictionalize

  fictions *n* ▷ fiction

fictitious *adj* not genuine

fiddle *n* (*pl* **-s**) violin (*Informal*) ▶ *v* (**-les, -ling, -led**) play the violin

  fiddled *v* ▷ fiddle

  fiddles *n, v* ▷ fiddle

fiddlesticks *interj* expression of annoyance or disagreement

  fiddlier *adj* ▷ fiddly

  fiddliest *adj* ▷ fiddly

  fiddling *v* ▷ fiddle ▶ *adj* trivial

fiddly *adj* (**-lier, -liest**) awkward to do or use

  fidelities *n* ▷ fidelity

fidelity *n* (*pl* **-ies**) faithfulness

fidget *v* (**-s, -ing, -ed**) move about restlessly ▶ *n* (*pl* **-s**) person who fidgets ▶ *pl* restlessness > **fidgety** *adj* (**-tier, -tiest**)

  fidgeted *v* ▷ fidget

  fidgetier *adj* ▷ fidget

  fidgetiest *adj* ▷ fidget

  fidgeting *v* ▷ fidget

  fidgets *v, n* ▷ fidget

  fidgety *adj* ▷ fidget

  fiduciaries *n* ▷ fiduciary

fiduciary [fid-**yew**-she-er-ee] (LAW) *n* (*pl* **-ies**) person bound to act for someone else's benefit, as a trustee ▶ *adj* of a trust or trustee

fief [feef] *n* (*pl* -s) (HIST) land granted by a lord in return for war service
  fiefs *n* ▷ **fief**

field *n* (*pl* -s) enclosed piece of agricultural land ▶ *v* (-s, -ing, -ed) (SPORT) catch and return (a ball)
  fielded *v* ▷ **field**

fielder *n* (*pl* -s) (SPORT) player whose task is to field the ball
  fielders *n* ▷ **fielder**

fieldfare *n* (*pl* -s) type of large Old World thrush
  fieldfares *n* ▷ **fieldfare**
  fielding *v* ▷ **field**
  fields *n*, *v* ▷ **field**

fieldwork *n* (*pl* -s) investigation made in the field as opposed to the classroom or the laboratory
  fieldworks *n* ▷ **fieldwork**

fiend [feend] *n* (*pl* -s) evil spirit (*Informal*) > **fiendish** *adj* > **fiendishly** *adv*
  fiendish *adj* ▷ **fiend**
  fiendishly *adv* ▷ **fiend**
  fiends *n* ▷ **fiend**

fierce *adj* (-r, -st) wild or aggressive > **fiercely** *adv* > **fierceness** *n* (*pl* -es)
  fiercely *adv* ▷ **fierce**
  fierceness *n* ▷ **fierce**
  fiercenesses *n* ▷ **fierce**
  fiercer *adj* ▷ **fierce**
  fiercest *adj* ▷ **fierce**
  fierier *adj* ▷ **fiery**
  fieriest *adj* ▷ **fiery**

fiery *adj* (-rier, -riest) consisting of or like fire

fiesta *n* (*pl* -s) religious festival, carnival
  fiestas *n* ▷ **fiesta**

fife *n* (*pl* -s) small high-pitched flute
  fifes *n* ▷ **fife**

fifteen *adj*, *n* (*pl* -s) five and ten > **fifteenth** *adj*, *n* (*pl* -s)
  fifteens *n* ▷ **fifteen**
fifteenth *adj*, *n* ▷ **fifteen**
  fifteenths *n* ▷ **fifteenth**

fifth *adj*, *n* (*pl* -s) (of) number five in a series
  fifths *n* ▷ **fifth**
  fifties *n* ▷ **fifty**
fiftieth *adj*, *n* ▷ **fifty**
  fiftieths *n* ▷ **fifty**

fifty *adj*, *n* (*pl* -ties) five times ten > **fiftieth** *adj*, *n* (*pl* -s)

fig *n* (*pl* -s) soft pear-shaped fruit

fight *v* (-s, -ing, fought) struggle (against) in battle or physical combat ▶ *n* (*pl* -s) aggressive conflict between two (groups of) people

fighter *n* (*pl* -s) boxer
  fighters *n* ▷ **fighter**
  fighting *v* ▷ **fight**
  fights *n*, *v* ▷ **fight**

figment *n* (*pl* -s) something imagined
  figments *n* ▷ **figment**
  figs *n* ▷ **fig**

figurative *adj* (of language) abstract, imaginative, or symbolic > **figuratively** *adv*
  figuratively *adv* ▷ **figurative**

figure *n* (*pl* -s) numerical symbol (MATHS) ▶ *v* (-res, -ring, -red) consider, conclude
  figured *v* ▷ **figure**

figurehead *n* (*pl* -s) nominal leader
  figureheads *n* ▷ **figurehead**
  figures *n*, *v* ▷ **figure**

figurine *n* (*pl* -s) statuette
  figurines *n* ▷ **figurine**
  figuring *v* ▷ **figure**

filament *n* (*pl* -s) fine wire in a light bulb that gives out light
  filaments *n* ▷ **filament**

filbert *n* (*pl* -s) hazelnut
  filberts *n* ▷ **filbert**

filch *v* (-es, -ing, -ed) steal (small amounts)
  filched *v* ▷ **filch**
  filches *v* ▷ **filch**
  filching *v* ▷ **filch**

file¹ *n* (*pl* -s) box or folder used to keep documents in order ▶ *v* (-les, -ling, -led) place (a document) in a file

file² *n* (*pl* -s) tool with a roughened blade for smoothing or shaping ▶ *v* (-les, -ling, -led) shape or smooth with a file
  filed *v* ▷ **file¹, ²**
  files *n*, *v* ▷ **file¹, ²**

filial *adj* of or befitting a son or daughter

filibuster *n* (*pl* -s) obstruction of legislation by making long speeches ▶ *v* (-s, -ing, -ed) obstruct (legislation) with such delaying tactics
  filibustered *v* ▷ **filibuster**
  filibustering *v* ▷ **filibuster**
  filibusters *n*, *v* ▷ **filibuster**

filigree *n* (*pl* -s) delicate ornamental work of gold or silver wire ▶ *adj* made of filigree
  filigrees *n* ▷ **filigree**
  filing *v* ▷ **file¹, ²**

filings *pl n* shavings removed by a file

fill *v* (-s, -ing, -ed) make or become full
  filled *v* ▷ **fill**

filler *n* (*pl* -s) substance that fills a gap or increases bulk
  fillers *n* ▷ **filler**

fillet *n* (*pl* -s) boneless piece of meat or fish ▶ *v*

(**-s, -ing, -ed**) remove the bones from
filleted v ▷ **fillet**
filleting v ▷ **fillet**
fillets n, v ▷ **fillet**
fillies n ▷ **filly**
filling n (pl **-s**) substance that fills a gap
or cavity, esp. in a tooth ▶ adj (of food)
substantial and satisfying ▶ v ▷ **fill**
fillings n ▷ **filling**
fillip n (pl **-s**) something that adds stimulation
or enjoyment
fillips n ▷ **fillip**
fills v ▷ **fill**
filly n (pl **-lies**) young female horse
film n (pl **-s**) sequence of images projected on
a screen, creating the illusion of movement
▶ v (**-s, -ing, -ed**) photograph with a movie or
video camera ▶ adj connected with films or
the cinema
filmed v ▷ **film**
filmier adj ▷ **filmy**
filmiest adj ▷ **filmy**
filming v ▷ **film**
films n, v ▷ **film**
filmy adj (**-mier, -miest**) very thin, delicate
filter n (pl **-s**) material or device permitting
fluid to pass but retaining solid particles
▶ v (**-s, -ing, -ed**) remove impurities from (a
substance) with a filter
filtered v ▷ **filter**
filtering v ▷ **filter**
filters n, v ▷ **filter**
filth n (pl **-s**) disgusting dirt > **filthy** adj (**-thier,
-thiest**) > **filthiness** n (pl **-es**)
filthier adj ▷ **filth**
filthiest adj ▷ **filth**
filthiness n ▷ **filth**
filthinesses n ▷ **filth**
filths n ▷ **filth**
filthy adj ▷ **filth**
filtrate n (pl **-s**) filtered gas or liquid ▶ v (**-tes,
-ting, -ted**) remove impurities with a filter
> **filtration** n (pl **-s**)
filtrated v ▷ **filtrate**
filtrates n, v ▷ **filtrate**
filtrating v ▷ **filtrate**
filtration n ▷ **filtrate**
filtrations n ▷ **filtrate**
fin n (pl **-s**) projection from a fish's body
enabling it to balance and swim
finagle [fin-**nay**-gl] v (**-les, -ling, -led**) get or
achieve by craftiness or trickery
finagled v ▷ **finagle**
finagles v ▷ **finagle**
finagling v ▷ **finagle**

final adj at the end ▶ n (pl **-s**) deciding contest
between winners of previous rounds
in a competition ▶ pl (BRIT & S AFR) last
examinations in an educational course
> **finally** adv > **finality** n (pl **-ties**)
finale [fin-**nah**-lee] (pl **-s**) n concluding part of a
dramatic performance or musical work
finales n ▷ **finale**
finalist n (pl **-s**) competitor in a final
finalists n ▷ **finalist**
finalities n ▷ **final**
finality n ▷ **final**
finalize v (**-zes, -zing, -zed**) put into final form
finalized v ▷ **finalize**
finalizes v ▷ **finalize**
finalizing v ▷ **finalize**
finally adv ▷ **final**
finals n ▷ **final**
finance v (**-ces, -cing, -ced**) provide or obtain
funds for ▶ n (pl **-s**) management of money,
loans, or credits ▶ pl money resources
> **financial** adj > **financially** adv
financed v ▷ **finance**
finances v, n ▷ **finance**
financial adj ▷ **finance**
financially adv ▷ **finance**
financier n (pl **-s**) person involved in large-
scale financial business
financiers n ▷ **financier**
financing v ▷ **finance**
finch n (pl **-es**) small songbird with a short
strong beak
finches n ▷ **finch**
find v (**-s, -ing, found**) discover by chance ▶ n (pl
-s) person or thing found, esp. when valuable
> **finder** n (pl **-s**)
finder n ▷ **find**
finders n ▷ **find**
finding n (pl **-s**) conclusion from an
investigation ▶ v ▷ **find**
findings n ▷ **finding**
finds v, n ▷ **find**
fine[1] adj (**-r, -st**) very good > **finely** adv
> **fineness** n (pl **-es**)
fine[2] n (pl **-s**) payment imposed as a penalty ▶ v
(**-nes, -ning, -ned**) impose a fine on
fined v ▷ **fine**[2]
finely adv ▷ **fine**[1]
fineness n ▷ **fine**[1]
finenesses n ▷ **fine**[1]
finer adj ▷ **fine**[1]
fineries n ▷ **finery**
finery n (pl **-ries**) showy clothing
fines n, v ▷ **fine**[1, 2]
finesse [fin-**ness**] n (pl **-s**) delicate skill

finesses *n* ▷ **finesse**
finest *adj* ▷ **fine**[1]
finger *n* (*pl* **-s**) one of the four long jointed parts of the hand ▶ *v* (**-s, -ing, -ed**) touch or handle with the fingers
fingerboard *n* part of a stringed instrument against which the strings are pressed
fingerboards *n* ▷ **fingerboard**
fingered *v* ▷ **finger**
fingering *n* technique of using the fingers in playing a musical instrument ▶ *v* ▷ **finger**
fingerprint *n* (*pl* **-s**) impression of the ridges on the tip of the finger ▶ *v* take the fingerprints of (someone)
fingerprints *n* ▷ **fingerprint**
fingers *n, v* ▷ **finger**
finickier *adj* ▷ **finicky**
finickiest *adj* ▷ **finicky**
finicky *adj* (**-ckier, -ckiest**) excessively particular, fussy
fining *v* ▷ **fine**
finish *v* (**-es, -ing, -ed**) bring to an end, stop ▶ *n* (*pl* **-es**) end, last part
finished *v* ▷ **finish**
finishes *v, n* ▷ **finish**
finishing *v* ▷ **finish**
finite *adj* having limits in space, time, or size
fins *n* ▷ **fin**
fiord *n* (*pl* **-s**) ▷ **fjord**
fiords *n* ▷ **fiord**
fir *n* (*pl* **-s**) pyramid-shaped tree with needle-like leaves and erect cones
fire *n* (*pl* **-s**) state of combustion producing heat, flames, and smoke ▶ *v* (**-res, -ring, -red**) operate (a weapon) so that a bullet or missile is released
firearm *n* (*pl* **-s**) rifle, pistol, or shotgun
firearms *n* ▷ **firearms**
firebrand *n* (*pl* **-s**) person who causes unrest
firebrands *n* ▷ **firebrand**
firebreak *n* strip of cleared land to stop the advance of a fire
firebreaks *n* ▷ **firebreak**
fired *v* ▷ **fire**
firedamp *n* (*pl* **-s**) explosive gas, composed mainly of methane, formed in mines
firedamps *n* ▷ **firedamp**
firefighter *n* (*pl* **-s**) member of a fire brigade
firefighters *n* ▷ **firefighter**
fireflies *n* ▷ **firefly**
firefly *n* (*pl* **-flies**) beetle that glows in the dark
fireguard *n* (*pl* **-s**) protective grating in front of a fire
fireguards *n* ▷ **fireguard**
fireplace *n* (*pl* **-s**) recess in a room for a fire

fireplaces *n* ▷ **fireplace**
fires *n, v* ▷ **fire**
firewall *n* (*pl* **-s**) (COMPUTERS) computer that prevents unauthorized access to a computer network from the Internet
firewalls *n* ▷ **firewall**
firework *n* (*pl* **-s**) device containing chemicals that is ignited to produce spectacular explosions and coloured sparks ▶ *pl* show of fireworks
fireworks *n* ▷ **firework**
firing *v* ▷ **fire**
firm[1] *adj* (**-er, -est**) not soft or yielding ▶ *adv* in an unyielding manner ▶ *v* (**-s, -ing, -ed**) make or become firm > **firmly** *adv* > **firmness** *n* (*pl* **-es**)
firm[2] *n* (*pl* **-s**) business company
firmament *n* (*pl* **-s**) (*Lit*) sky or the heavens
firmaments *n* ▷ **firmament**
firmed *v* ▷ **firm**[1]
firmer *adj* ▷ **firm**[1]
firmest *adj* ▷ **firm**[1]
firming *v* ▷ **firm**[1]
firmly *adv* ▷ **firm**[1]
firmness *n* ▷ **firm**[1]
firmnesses *n* ▷ **firm**[1]
firms *v, n* ▷ **firm**[1, 2]
firs *n* ▷ **fir**
first *adj* earliest in time or order ▶ *n* (*pl* **-s**) person or thing coming before all others ▶ *adv* before anything else > **firstly** *adv*
firsthand *adj, adv* (obtained) directly from the original source
firstly *adv* ▷ **first**
firsts *n* ▷ **first**
firth *n* (*pl* **-s**) narrow inlet of the sea, esp. in Scotland
firths *n* ▷ **firth**
fiscal *adj* of government finances, esp. taxes
fish *n* (*pl* **fish, fishes**) cold-blooded vertebrate with gills, that lives in water ▶ *v* (**-es, -ing, -ed**) try to catch fish
fished *v* ▷ **fish**
fisheries *n* ▷ **fishery**
fisherman *n* (*pl* **-men**) person who catches fish for a living or for pleasure
fishermen *n* ▷ **fisherman**
fishery *n* (*pl* **-ries**) area of the sea used for fishing
fishes *n, v* ▷ **fish**
fishfinger *n* (*pl* **-s**) oblong piece of fish covered in breadcrumbs
fishfingers *n* ▷ **fishfinger**
fishier *adj* ▷ **fishy**
fishiest *adj* ▷ **fishy**

fishing *v* ▷ **fish**
fishmeal *n* (*pl* -**s**) dried ground fish used as animal feed or fertilizer
fishmeals *n* ▷ **fishmeal**
fishmonger *n* (*pl* -**s**) seller of fish
fishmongers *n* ▷ **fishmonger**
fishnet *n* (*pl* -**s**) open mesh fabric resembling netting
fishnets *n* ▷ **fishnet**
fishplate *n* (*pl* -**s**) metal plate holding rails together
fishplates *n* ▷ **fishplate**
fishwife *n* (*pl* -**wives**) coarse scolding woman
fishwives *n* ▷ **fishwife**
fishy *adj* (-**shier, -shiest**) of or like fish
fissile *adj* capable of undergoing nuclear fission
fission *n* (*pl* -**s**) splitting > **fissionable** *adj*
fissionable *adj* ▷ **fission**
fissions *n* ▷ **fission**
fissure [fish-er] *n* (*pl* -**s**) long narrow cleft or crack
fissures *n* ▷ **fissure**
fist *n* (*pl* -**s**) clenched hand
fisticuffs *pl n* fighting with the fists
fists *n* ▷ **fist**
fit¹ *v* (-**s, -tting, -tted**) be appropriate or suitable for ▶ *adj* appropriate ▶ *n* (-**tter, -ttest**) (*pl* -**s**) way in which something fits > **fitness** *n* (*pl* -**es**)
fit² *n* (*pl* -**s**) sudden attack or convulsion, such as an epileptic seizure
fitful *adj* occurring in irregular spells > **fitfully** *adv*
fitfully *adv* ▷ **fitful**
fitment *n* (*pl* -**s**) detachable part of the furnishings of a room
fitments *n* ▷ **fitment**
fitness *n* ▷ **fit¹**
fitnesses *n* ▷ **fit¹**
fits *v, n* ▷ **fit¹, ²**
fitted *v* ▷ **fit¹**
fitter *n* (*pl* -**s**) person skilled in the installation and adjustment of machinery ▶ *adj* ▷ **fit¹**
fitters *n* ▷ **fitter**
fittest *adj* ▷ **fit¹**
fitting *adj* appropriate, suitable ▶ *n* (*pl* -**s**) accessory or part ▶ *pl* furnishings and accessories in a building ▶ *v* ▷ **fit**
fittings *n* ▷ **fitting**
five *adj, n* (*pl* -**s**) one more than four
fiver *n* (*pl* -**s**) (*Informal*) five-pound note
fivers *n* ▷ **fiver**
fives *n* ball game resembling squash but played with bats or the hands ▶ *n* ▷ **five**

fix *v* (-**xes, -xing, -xed**) make or become firm, stable, or secure ▶ *n* (*pl* -**es**) (*Informal*) difficult situation > **fixed** *adj* > **fixedly** *adv* steadily
fixated *adj* obsessed
fixation *n* (*pl* -**s**) obsessive interest in something
fixations *n* ▷ **fixation**
fixative *n* (*pl* -**s**) liquid used to preserve or hold things in place
fixatives *n* ▷ **fixative**
fixed *v, adj* ▷ **fix**
fixedly *adv* ▷ **fix**
fixer *n* (*pl* -**s**) solution used to make a photographic image permanent
fixers *n* ▷ **fixer**
fixes *v, n* ▷ **fix**
fixing *v* ▷ **fix**
fixture *n* (*pl* -**s**) permanently fitted piece of household equipment
fixtures *n* ▷ **fixture**
fizz *v* (-**es, -ing, -ed**) make a hissing or bubbling noise ▶ *n* (*pl* -**es**) hissing or bubbling noise > **fizzy** *adj* (-**zzier, -zziest**)
fizzed *v* ▷ **fizz**
fizzes *v* ▷ **fizz**
fizzier *adj* ▷ **fizz**
fizziest *adj* ▷ **fizz**
fizzing *v* ▷ **fizz**
fizzle *v* (-**les, -ling, -led**) make a weak hissing or bubbling sound
fizzled *v* ▷ **fizzle**
fizzles *v* ▷ **fizzle**
fizzling *v* ▷ **fizzle**
fizzy *adj* ▷ **fizz**
fjord [fee-ord] *n* (*pl* -**s**) long narrow inlet of the sea between cliffs, esp. in Norway
fjords *n* ▷ **fjord**
flab *n* (*pl* -**s**) (*Informal*) unsightly body fat
flabbergasted *adj* completely astonished
flabbier *adj* ▷ **flabby**
flabbiest *adj* ▷ **flabby**
flabby *adj* (-**bbier, -bbiest**) having flabby flesh
flabs *n* ▷ **flab**
flaccid [flas-sid] *adj* (-**er, -est**) soft and limp > **flaccidity** *n* (*pl* -**ties**)
flaccider *adj* ▷ **flaccid**
flaccidest *adj* ▷ **flaccid**
flaccidities *n* ▷ **flaccid**
flaccidity *n* ▷ **flaccid**
flag¹ *n* (*pl* -**s**) piece of cloth attached to a pole as an emblem or signal ▶ *v* (-**s, -gging, -gged**) mark with a flag or sticker
flag² *v* (-**s, -gging, -gged**) lose enthusiasm or vigour
flag³, flagstone (*pl* -**s**) *n* flat paving-stone

flagellant n (pl -s) person who whips himself or herself
  flagellants n ▷ flagellant
flagellate [flaj-a-late] v (-tes, -ting, -ted) whip, esp. in religious penance or for sexual pleasure > **flagellation** n (pl -s)
  flagellated v ▷ flagellate
  flagellates v ▷ flagellate
  flagellating v ▷ flagellate
  flagellation n ▷ flagellate
  flagellations n ▷ flagellate
flageolet [flaj-a-**let**] n (pl -s) small instrument like a recorder
  flageolets n ▷ flageolet
flagged adj paved with flagstones ▶ v ▷ flag¹, ²
  flagged v ▷ flag¹, ²
  flagging v ▷ flag¹, ²
flagon n (pl -s) wide bottle for wine or cider
  flagons n ▷ flagon
flagpole, flagstaff (pl -s) n pole for a flag
  flagpoles n ▷ flagpole
flagrant [**flayg**-rant] adj openly outrageous > **flagrantly** adv
  flagrantly adv ▷ flagrant
  flags v, n ▷ flag¹, ², ³
flagship n (pl -s) admiral's ship
  flagships n ▷ flagship
  flagstaff n ▷ flagpole
  flagstaffs n ▷ flagpole
  flagstone n ▷ flag³
  flagstones n ▷ flag³
flail v (-s, -ing, -ed) wave about wildly ▶ n (pl -s) tool formerly used for threshing grain by hand
  flailed v ▷ flail
  flailing v ▷ flail
  flails v, n ▷ flail
flair n (pl -s) natural ability
  flairs n ▷ flair
flak n (pl -s) anti-aircraft fire
flake¹ n (pl -s) small thin piece, esp. chipped off something ▶ v (-kes, -king, -ked) peel off in flakes > **flaky** adj (-kier, -kiest)
flake² n (pl -s) (in Australia) the commercial name for the meat of the gummy shark
  flaked v ▷ flake
  flakes v, n ▷ flake¹, ²
  flakier adj ▷ flaky
  flakiest adj ▷ flaky
  flaking v ▷ flake
  flaks n ▷ flak
  flaky adj ▷ flake¹
flambé [**flahm**-bay] v (-bés, -béing, -béed) cook or serve (food) in flaming brandy
  flambéed v ▷ flambé

  flambéing v ▷ flambé
  flambés v ▷ flambé
  flamboyances n ▷ flamboyant
flamboyant adj behaving in a very noticeable, extravagant way > **flamboyance** n (pl -s)
  flamboyance n ▷ flamboyant
flame n (pl -s) luminous burning gas coming from burning material ▶ v (-mes, -ming, -med) burn brightly
  flamed v ▷ flame
flamenco n (pl -cos) rhythmical Spanish dance accompanied by a guitar and vocalist
  flamencos n ▷ flamenco
  flames n, v ▷ flame
  flaming v ▷ flame
flamingo n (pl -gos, -goes) large pink wading bird with a long neck and legs
  flamingoes n ▷ flamingo
  flamingos n ▷ flamingo
  flammabilities n ▷ flammable
  flammability n ▷ flammable
flammable adj easily set on fire > **flammability** n (pl -ties)
flan n (pl -s) open sweet or savoury tart
flange n (pl -s) projecting rim or collar
  flanges n ▷ flange
flank n (pl -s) part of the side between the hips and ribs ▶ v (-s, -ing, -ed) be at or move along the side of
  flanked v ▷ flank
  flanking v ▷ flank
  flanks n, v ▷ flank
flannel n (pl -s) (BRIT) small piece of cloth for washing the face ▶ pl trousers made of flannel ▶ v (-s, -nelling, -nelled) (Informal) talk evasively
flannelette n (pl -s) cotton imitation of flannel
  flannelettes n ▷ flannelette
  flannelled v ▷ flannel
  flannelling v ▷ flannel
  flannels n, v ▷ flannel
  flans n ▷ flan
flap v (-s, -pping, -pped) move back and forwards or up and down ▶ n (pl -s) action or sound of flapping
flapjack n (pl -s) chewy biscuit made with oats
  flapjacks n ▷ flapjack
  flapped v ▷ flap
  flapping v ▷ flap
  flaps v, n ▷ flap
flare v (-res, -ring, -red) blaze with a sudden unsteady flame ▶ n (pl -s) sudden unsteady flame ▶ pl flared trousers
flared adj (of a skirt or trousers) becoming wider towards the hem ▶ v ▷ flare

flares v, n ▷ flare
flaring v ▷ flare
flash n (pl **-es**) sudden burst of light or flame ▶ v
(**-es, -ing, -ed**) (cause to) burst into flame
flashback n (pl **-s**) scene in a book, play, or film,
that shows earlier events
flashbacks n ▷ flashback
flashed v ▷ flash
flasher n (pl **-s**) (Slang) man who exposes
himself indecently
flashers n ▷ flasher
flashes n, v ▷ flash
flashier adj ▷ flashy
flashiest adj ▷ flashy
flashing n (pl **-s**) watertight material used to
cover joins in a roof ▶ v ▷ **flash**
flashings n ▷ flashing
flashlight n (pl **-s**) (US) torch
flashlights n ▷ flashlight
flashy adj (**-shier, -shiest**) vulgarly showy
flask n (pl **-s**) ▷ **vacuum flask** flat bottle for
carrying alcoholic drink in the pocket
flasks n ▷ flask
flat¹ adj (**-tter, -ttest**) level and horizontal
▶ adv in or into a flat position ▶ n (pl **-s**)
(MUSIC) symbol lowering the pitch of a note
by a semitone > **flatly** adv > **flatness** n (pl **-es**)
> **flatten** v (**-s, -ing, -ed**)
flat² n (pl **-s**) set of rooms for living in which are
part of a larger building ▶ v (**-s, -tting, -tted**)
(AUST & NZ) live in a flat
flatfish n (pl **-fish, -fishes**) sea fish, such as the
sole, which has a flat body
flatfishes n ▷ flatfish
flatlet n (pl **-s**) (BRIT, AUST & S AFR) small flat
flatlets n ▷ flatlet
flatly adv ▷ flat¹
flatmate n (pl **-s**) person with whom one
shares a flat
flatmates n ▷ flatmate
flatness n ▷ flat¹
flatnesses n ▷ flat¹
flat-pack adj (of furniture, etc.) supplied in
pieces in a flat box for assembly by the buyer
flats n, v ▷ flat¹, ²
flatted v ▷ flat²
flatten v ▷ flat¹
flattened v ▷ flat¹
flattening v ▷ flat¹
flatter¹ v (**-s, -ing, -ed**) praise insincerely
> **flatterer** n (pl **-s**) > **flattery** n (pl **-ries**)
flatter² adj ▷ flat¹
flattered v ▷ flatter¹
flatterer n ▷ flatter
flatterers n ▷ flatter

flatteries n ▷ flatter
flattering v ▷ flatter¹
flatters v ▷ flatter¹
flattery n ▷ flatter
flattest adj ▷ flat¹
flattie n (pl **-s**) (NZ & S AFR) (Informal) flat tyre
flatties n ▷ flattie
flatting v ▷ flat²
flatulence n ▷ flatulent
flatulences n ▷ flatulent
flatulent adj suffering from or caused by too
much gas in the intestines > **flatulence** n
(pl **-s**)
flaunt v (**-s, -ing, -ed**) display (oneself or one's
possessions) arrogantly
flaunted v ▷ flaunt
flaunting v ▷ flaunt
flaunts v ▷ flaunt
flautist n (pl **-s**) flute player
flautists n ▷ flautist
flavour n (pl **-s**) distinctive taste ▶ v (**-s, -ing,
-ed**) give flavour to > **flavourless** adj
flavoured v ▷ flavour
flavouring n (pl **-s**) substance used to flavour
food ▶ v ▷ **flavour**
flavourings n ▷ flavouring
flavourless adj ▷ flavour
flavours n, v ▷ flavour
flaw n (pl **-s**) imperfection or blemish > **flawed**
adj > **flawless** adj
flawed adj ▷ flaw
flawless adj ▷ flaw
flaws n ▷ flaw
flax n (pl **-es**) plant grown for its stem fibres
and seeds
flaxen adj (of hair) pale yellow
flaxes n ▷ flax
flay v (**-s, -ing, -ed**) strip the skin off
flayed v ▷ flay
flaying v ▷ flay
flays v ▷ flay
flea n (pl **-s**) small wingless jumping
bloodsucking insect
fleapit n (pl **-s**) (Informal) shabby cinema or
theatre
fleapits n ▷ fleapit
fleas n ▷ flea
fleck n (pl **-s**) small mark, streak, or speck ▶ v
(**-s, -ing, -ed**) speckle
flecked n ▷ fleck
flecking v ▷ fleck
flecks n, v ▷ fleck
fled v ▷ flee
fledged adj (of young birds) able to fly
fledgelings n ▷ fledgling

fledgling, fledgeling (*pl* -s) *n* young bird ▶ *adj* new or inexperienced
  fledglings *n* ▷ **fledgling**
flee *v* (-**lees**, -**leeing**, **fled**) run away (from)
fleece *n* (*pl* -s) sheep's coat of wool ▶ *v* (-**ces**, -**cing**, -**ced**) defraud or overcharge
  fleeced *v* ▷ **fleece**
  fleeces *n, v* ▷ **fleece**
  fleecier *adj* ▷ **fleecy**
  fleeciest *adj* ▷ **fleecy**
  fleecing *v* ▷ **fleece**
fleecy *adj* (-**cier**, -**ciest**) made of or like fleece
  fleeing *v* ▷ **flee**
  flees *v* ▷ **flee**
fleet[1] *n* (*pl* -s) number of warships organized as a unit
fleet[2] *adj* swift in movement
fleeting *adj* rapid and soon passing
  > **fleetingly** *adv*
  fleetingly *adv* ▷ **fleeting**
  fleets *n* ▷ **fleet**
flesh *n* (*pl* -es) soft part of a human or animal body (*Informal*)
  fleshes *n* ▷ **flesh**
  fleshier *adj* ▷ **fleshy**
  fleshiest *adj* ▷ **fleshy**
fleshly *adj* carnal
fleshy *adj* (-**shier**, -**shiest**) plump
  flew *v* ▷ **fly**[1]
flex *n* (*pl* -xes) flexible insulated electric cable ▶ *v* (-**xes**, -**xing**, -**xed**) bend
  flexed *v* ▷ **flex**
  flexes *n, v* ▷ **flex**
  flexibility *n* ▷ **flexible**
flexible *adj* easily bent > **flexibly** *adv*
  > **flexibility** *n* (*pl* -**ties**)
  flexibilities *n* ▷ **flexible**
  flexibly *adv* ▷ **flexible**
  flexing *v* ▷ **flex**
flexitime, flextime *n* (*pl* -s) system permitting variation in starting and finishing times of work
  flexitimes *n* ▷ **flexitime**
  flextimes *n* ▷ **flexitime**
flick *v* (-**s**, -**ing**, -**ed**) touch or move with the finger or hand in a quick movement ▶ *n* (*pl* -s) tap or quick stroke ▶ *pl* (*Slang*) the cinema
  flicked *v* ▷ **flick**
flicker *v* (-**s**, -**ing**, -**ed**) shine unsteadily or intermittently ▶ *n* (*pl* -s) unsteady brief light
  flickered *v* ▷ **flicker**
  flickering *v* ▷ **flicker**
  flickers *v, n* ▷ **flicker**
  flicking *v* ▷ **flick**
  flicks *v, n* ▷ **flick**

flier[1] *adj* ▷ **fly**[3]
flier[2] *n* ▷ **flyer**
  fliers *n* ▷ **flyer**
  flies *v, n* ▷ **fly**[1, 2]
  fliest *adj* ▷ **fly**[3]
flight[1] *n* (*pl* -s) journey by air
flight[2] *n* (*pl* -s) act of running away
  flightier *adj* ▷ **flighty**
  flightiest *adj* ▷ **flighty**
flightless *adj* (of certain birds or insects) unable to fly
  flights *n* ▷ **flight**[1, 2]
flighty *adj* (-**tier**, -**tiest**) frivolous and fickle
  flimsier *adj* ▷ **flimsy**
  flimsiest *adj* ▷ **flimsy**
  flimsily *adv* ▷ **flimsy**
  flimsiness *n* ▷ **flimsy**
  flimsinesses *n* ▷ **flimsy**
flimsy *adj* (-**sier**, -**siest**) not strong or substantial > **flimsily** *adv* > **flimsiness** *n* (*pl* -**es**)
flinch *v* (-**es**, -**ing**, -**ed**) draw back or wince, as from pain
  flinched *v* ▷ **flinch**
  flinches *v* ▷ **flinch**
  flinching *v* ▷ **flinch**
fling *v* (-**s**, -**ing**, **flung**) throw, send, or move forcefully or hurriedly ▶ *n* (*pl* -s) spell of self-indulgent enjoyment
  flinging *v* ▷ **fling**
  flings *v, n* ▷ **fling**
flint *n* (*pl* -s) hard grey stone
  flintier *adj* ▷ **flinty**
  flintiest *adj* ▷ **flinty**
  flints *n* ▷ **flint**
flinty (-**tier**, -**tiest**) *adj* cruel
flip *v* (-**s**, -**pping**, -**pped**) throw (something small or light) carelessly ▶ *adj* (*Informal*) flippant
  flippancies *n* ▷ **flippant**
  flippancy *n* ▷ **flippant**
flippant *adj* treating serious things lightly
  > **flippancy** *n* (*pl* -**cies**)
  flipped *v* ▷ **flip**
flipper (*pl* -s) *n* limb of a sea animal adapted for swimming
  flippers *n* ▷ **flipper**
  flipping *v* ▷ **flip**
  flips *v* ▷ **flip**
flirt *v* (-**s**, -**ing**, -**ed**) behave as if sexually attracted to someone ▶ *n* (*pl* -s) person who flirts > **flirtation** *n* (*pl* -s) > **flirtatious** *adj*
  flirtation *n* ▷ **flirt**
  flirtations *n* ▷ **flirt**
  flirtatious *adj* ▷ **flirt**

flirted v ▷ **flirt**
flirting v ▷ **flirt**
flirts v, n ▷ **flirt**
flit v (**-s, -tting, -tted**) move lightly and rapidly
▶ n (pl **-s**) act of flitting
flits v, n ▷ **flit**
flitted v ▷ **flit**
flitting v ▷ **flit**
float v (**-s, -ing, -ed**) rest on the surface of a
liquid ▶ n (pl **-s**) light object used to help
someone or something float
floated v ▷ **float**
floating adj moving about, changing ▶ v
▷ **float**
floats v, n ▷ **float**
flock[1] n (pl **-s**) number of animals of one kind
together ▶ v (**-s, -ing, -ed**) gather in a crowd
flock[2] n (pl **-s**) wool or cotton waste used as
stuffing ▶ adj (of wallpaper) with a velvety
raised pattern
flocked v ▷ **flock**[1]
flocking v ▷ **flock**[1]
flocks n, v ▷ **flock**[1, 2]
floe n (pl **-s**) sheet of floating ice
floes n ▷ **floe**
flog v (**-s, -gging, -gged**) beat with a whip or
stick > **flogging** n (pl **-s**)
flogged v ▷ **flog**
flogging v, n ▷ **flog**
floggings n ▷ **flog**
flogs v ▷ **flog**
flood n (pl **-s**) overflow of water onto a
normally dry area ▶ v (**-s, -ing, -ed**) cover or
become covered with water
flooded v ▷ **flood**
floodgate n (pl **-s**) gate used to control the
flow of water
floodgates n ▷ **floodgate**
flooding v ▷ **flood**
floodlight n (pl **-s**) lamp that casts a broad
intense beam of light ▶ v (**-lights, -lighting,
-lit**) illuminate by floodlight
floodlighting v ▷ **floodlight**
floodlights n, v ▷ **floodlight**
floodlit v ▷ **floodlight**
floods n, v ▷ **flood**
floor n (pl **-s**) lower surface of a room ▶ v (**-s,
-ing, -ed**) knock down
floored adj covered with a floor ▶ v ▷ **floor**
flooring n (pl **-s**) material for floors ▶ v ▷ **floor**
floorings n ▷ **flooring**
floors n, v ▷ **floor**
floozies n ▷ **floozy**
floozy n (pl **-zies**) (Old-fashioned slang)
disreputable woman

flop v (**-s, -pping, -pped**) bend, fall, or collapse
loosely or carelessly ▶ n (pl **-s**) failure
flopped v ▷ **flop**
floppier adj ▷ **floppy**
floppies n ▷ **floppy**
floppiest adj ▷ **floppy**
flopping v ▷ **flop**
floppy adj (**-ppier, -ppiest**) hanging
downwards, loose ▶ n (pl **-ppies**) (COMPUTERS)
a flexible magnetic disk that stores
information
flops v, n ▷ **flop**
flora n (pl **-s**) plants of a given place or time
floral adj consisting of or decorated with
flowers
floras n ▷ **flora**
floret n (pl **-s**) small flower forming part of a
composite flower head
florets n ▷ **floret**
floribunda n (pl **-s**) type of rose whose flowers
grow in large clusters
floribundas n ▷ **floribunda**
florid adj (**-er, -est**) with a red or flushed
complexion
florider adj ▷ **florid**
floridest adj ▷ **florid**
florin n (pl **-s**) former British and Australian
coin
florins n ▷ **florin**
florist n (pl **-s**) seller of flowers
florists n ▷ **florist**
floss n (pl **-es**) fine silky fibres
flosses n ▷ **floss**
flotation n (pl **-s**) launching or financing of a
business enterprise
flotations n ▷ **flotation**
flotilla n (pl **-s**) small fleet or fleet of small ships
flotillas n ▷ **flotilla**
flotsam n (pl **-s**) floating wreckage
flotsams n ▷ **flotsam**
flounce[1] v (**-ces, -cing, -ced**) go with emphatic
movements ▶ n (pl **-s**) flouncing movement
flounce[2] n (pl **-s**) ornamental frill on a garment
flounced v ▷ **flounce**
flounces v, n ▷ **flounce**[1, 2]
flouncing v ▷ **flounce**
flounder[1] v (**-s, -ing, -ed**) move with difficulty,
as in mud
flounder[2] n (pl **-s**) edible flatfish
floundered v ▷ **flounder**
floundering v ▷ **flounder**
flounders v, n ▷ **flounder**[1, 2]
flour n (pl **-s**) powder made by grinding grain,
esp. wheat ▶ v (**-s, -ing, -ed**) sprinkle with
flour > **floury** adj (**-rier, -riest**)

floured v ▷ **flour**
flourier adj ▷ **flour**
flouriest adj ▷ **flour**
flouring v ▷ **flour**
flourish v (**-es, -ing, -ed**) be active, successful, or widespread ▶ n (pl **-es**) dramatic waving motion > **flourishing** adj
flourished v ▷ **flourish**
flourishes v, n ▷ **flourish**
flourishing n, adj ▷ **flourish**
flours n, v ▷ **flour**
floury adj ▷ **flour**
flout v (**-s, -ing, -ed**) deliberately disobey (a rule, law, etc.)
flouted v ▷ **flout**
flouting v ▷ **flout**
flouts v ▷ **flout**
flow v (**-s, -ing, -ed**) (of liquid) move in a stream ▶ n (pl **-s**) act, rate, or manner of flowing
flowed v ▷ **flow**
flower n (pl **-s**) part of a plant that produces seeds ▶ v (**-s, -ing, -ed**) produce flowers, bloom
flowerbed n (pl **-s**) piece of ground for growing flowers
flowerbeds n ▷ **flowerbed**
flowered adj decorated with a floral design ▶ v ▷ **flower**
flowerier adj ▷ **flowery**
floweriest adj ▷ **flowery**
flowering v ▷ **flower**
flowers n, v ▷ **flower**
flowery adj (**-rier, -riest**) decorated with a floral design
flowing v ▷ **flow**
flown v ▷ **fly¹**
flows v, n ▷ **flow**
flu n (pl **flus**) ▷ **influenza**
fluctuate v (**-tes, -ting, -ted**) change frequently and erratically > **fluctuation** n (pl **-s**)
fluctuated v ▷ **fluctuate**
fluctuates v ▷ **fluctuate**
fluctuating v ▷ **fluctuate**
fluctuation n ▷ **fluctuate**
fluctuations n ▷ **fluctuate**
flue n (pl **-s**) passage or pipe for smoke or hot air
fluencies n ▷ **fluent**
fluency n ▷ **fluent**
fluent adj able to speak or write with ease > **fluently** adv > **fluency** n (pl **-cies**)
fluently adv ▷ **fluent**
flues n ▷ **flue**
fluff n (pl **-s**) soft fibres ▶ v (**-s, -ing, -ed**) make

or become soft and puffy > **fluffy** adj (**-ffier, -ffiest**)
fluffed v ▷ **fluff**
fluffier adj ▷ **fluff**
fluffiest adj ▷ **fluff**
fluffing v ▷ **fluff**
fluffs n, v ▷ **fluff**
fluffy adj ▷ **fluff**
fluid n (pl **-s**) substance able to flow and change its shape; a liquid or a gas ▶ adj able to flow or change shape easily > **fluidity** n (pl **-ies**)
fluidities n ▷ **fluid**
fluidity n ▷ **fluid**
fluids n ▷ **fluid**
fluke¹ n (pl **-s**) accidental stroke of luck
fluke² (pl **-s**) n flat triangular point of an anchor
fluke³ (pl **-s**) n parasitic worm
flukes n ▷ **fluke¹, ², ³**
flume n (pl **-s**) narrow sloping channel for water
flumes n ▷ **flume**
flummox v (**-xes, -xing, -xed**) puzzle or confuse
flummoxed v ▷ **flummox**
flummoxes v ▷ **flummox**
flummoxing v ▷ **flummox**
flung v ▷ **fling**
flunk v (**flunks, flunking, flunked**) (US, AUST, NZ & S AFR) (Informal) fail
flunked v ▷ **flunk**
flunkey n ▷ **flunky**
flunkeys n ▷ **flunky**
flunkies n ▷ **flunky**
flunking v ▷ **flunk**
flunks v ▷ **flunk**
flunky, flunkey n (pl **-kies, -keys**) servile person
fluoresce v (**-ces, -cing, -ced**) exhibit fluorescence
fluoresced v ▷ **fluoresce**
fluorescence n (pl **-s**) emission of light from a substance bombarded by particles, such as electrons, or by radiation
fluorescences n ▷ **fluorescence**
fluorescent adj of or resembling fluorescence
fluoresces v ▷ **fluoresce**
fluorescing v ▷ **fluoresce**
fluoridate v (**-tes, -ting, -ted**) add fluoride to (water) as protection against tooth decay > **fluoridation** n (pl **-s**)
fluoridated v ▷ **fluoridate**
fluoridates v ▷ **fluoridate**
fluoridating v ▷ **fluoridate**
fluoridation n ▷ **fluoridate**
fluoridations n ▷ **fluoridate**

fluoride *n* (*pl* **-s**) compound containing fluorine
  fluorides *n* ▷ **fluoride**
fluorine *n* (*pl* **-s**) (CHEM) toxic yellow gas, most reactive of all the elements
  fluorines *n* ▷ **fluorine**
  flurried *v* ▷ **flurry**
  flurries *n, v* ▷ **flurry**
flurry *n* (*pl* **-rries**) sudden commotion ▶ *v* (**-rries, -rrying, -rried**) confuse
  flus *n* ▷ **flu**
flush[1] *v* (**-es, -ing, -ed**) blush or cause to blush ▶ *n* (*pl* **-es**) blush
flush[2] *adj* level with the surrounding surface
flush[3] *v* (**-es, -ing, -ed**) drive out of a hiding place
flush[4] *n* (*pl* **-es**) (in card games) hand all of one suit
  flushed *v* ▷ **flush**[1, 3]
  flushes *v, n* ▷ **flush**[1, 3, 4]
  flushing *v* ▷ **flush**[1, 3]
fluster *v* (**-s, -ing, -ed**) make nervous or upset ▶ *n* (*pl* **-s**) nervous or upset state
  flustered *v* ▷ **fluster**
  flustering *v* ▷ **fluster**
  flusters *v, n* ▷ **fluster**
flute *n* (*pl* **-s**) wind instrument consisting of a tube with sound holes and a mouth hole in the side
fluted *adj* having decorative grooves
  flutes *n* ▷ **flute**
flutter *v* (**-s, -ing, -ed**) wave rapidly ▶ *n* (*pl* **-s**) flapping movement
  fluttered *v* ▷ **flutter**
  fluttering *v* ▷ **flutter**
  flutters *v, n* ▷ **flutter**
fluvial *adj* of rivers
flux *n* (*pl* **-es**) constant change or instability
  fluxes *n* ▷ **flux**
fly[1] *v* (**flying, flew, flown**) move through the air on wings or in an aircraft ▶ *n* (*pl* **flies**) (*often pl* (BRIT) fastening at the front of trousers ▶ *pl* space above a stage, used for storage
fly[2] *n* (*pl* **flies**) two-winged insect
fly[3] *adj* (**flier, fliest**) (*Slang*) sharp and cunning
flycatcher *n* (*pl* **-s**) small insect-eating songbird
  flycatchers *n* ▷ **flycatcher**
flyer, flier (*pl* **-s**) *n* small advertising leaflet
  flyers *n* ▷ **flyer**
flying *adj* hurried and brief ▶ *v* ▷ **fly**
flyleaf *n* (*pl* **-leaves**) blank leaf at the beginning or end of a book
  flyleaves *n* ▷ **flyleaf**
flyover *n* (*pl* **-s**) road passing over another by a bridge
  flyovers *n* ▷ **flyover**
flypaper *n* (*pl* **-s**) paper with a sticky poisonous coating, used to kill flies
  flypapers *n* ▷ **flypaper**
flyweight *n* (*pl* **-s**) boxer weighing up to 112lb (professional) or 51kg (amateur)
  flyweights *n* ▷ **flyweight**
flywheel (*pl* **-s**) *n* heavy wheel regulating the speed of a machine
  flywheels *n* ▷ **flywheel**
foal *n* (*pl* **-s**) young of a horse or related animal ▶ *v* (**-s, -ing, -ed**) give birth to a foal
  foaled *v* ▷ **foal**
  foaling *v* ▷ **foal**
  foals *n, v* ▷ **foal**
foam *n* (*pl* **-s**) mass of small bubbles on a liquid ▶ *v* (**-s, -ing, -ed**) produce foam > **foamy** *adj* (**-ier, -iest**)
  foamed *v* ▷ **foam**
  foamier *adj* ▷ **foam**
  foamiest *adj* ▷ **foam**
  foaming *v* ▷ **foam**
  foams *n, v* ▷ **foam**
  foamy *adj* ▷ **foam**
fob *n* (*pl* **-s**) short watch chain
  fobs *n* ▷ **fob**
focal *adj* of or at a focus
  foci *n* ▷ **focus**
fo'c's'le *n* (*pl* **fo'c's'les**) ▷ **forecastle**
  fo'c's'les *n* ▷ **fo'c's'le**
focus *n* (*pl* **-cuses, -ci**) [-sye] point at which light or sound waves converge ▶ *v* (**-cuses, -cusing, -cused** *or* **-cusses, -cussing, -cussed**) bring or come into focus
  focused *v* ▷ **focus**
  focuses *n, v* ▷ **focus**
  focusing *v* ▷ **focus**
  focussed *v* ▷ **focus**
  focussing ▷ **focus**
fodder *n* (*pl* **-s**) feed for livestock
  fodders *n* ▷ **fodder**
foe *n* (*pl* **foes**) enemy, opponent
  foes *n* ▷ **foe**
foetid *adj* (**-er, -est**) ▷ **fetid**
  foetider *adj* ▷ **foetid**
  foetidest *adj* ▷ **foetid**
foetus *n* (*pl* **-tuses**) ▷ **fetus**
  foetuses *n* ▷ **foetus**
fog *n* (*pl* **-s**) mass of condensed water vapour in the lower air, often greatly reducing visibility ▶ *v* (**-s, fogging, fogged**) cover with steam > **foggy** *adj* (**-ggier, -ggiest**)
fogey, fogy *n* (*pl* **-geys, -gies**) old-fashioned person

fogeys n ▷ **fogey**
fogged v ▷ **fog**
foggier adj ▷ **fog**
foggiest adj ▷ **fog**
fogging v ▷ **fog**
foggy adj ▷ **fog**
foghorn n (pl -s) large horn sounded to warn
ships in fog
foghorns n ▷ **foghorn**
fogies n ▷ **fogey**
fogs n ▷ **fog**
fogy n ▷ **fogey**
foible n (pl -s) minor weakness or slight
peculiarity
foibles n ▷ **foible**
foil[1] v (-s, -ing, -ed) ruin (someone's plan)
foil[2] n (pl -s) metal in a thin sheet, esp. for
wrapping food
foil[3] n (pl -s) light slender flexible sword tipped
with a button
foiled v ▷ **foil**
foiling v ▷ **foil**
foils v, n ▷ **foil**[1, 2, 3]
foist v (-s, -ing, -ed) (foll. by **on** or **upon**) force
or impose on
foisted v ▷ **foist**
foisting v ▷ **foist**
foists v ▷ **foist**
fold[1] v (-s, -ing, -ed) bend so that one part
covers another ▶ n (pl -s) folded piece or part
fold[2] n (pl -s) (BRIT, AUST & S AFR) enclosure for
sheep
folded v ▷ **fold**
folder n (pl -s) piece of folded cardboard for
holding loose papers
folders n ▷ **folder**
folding v ▷ **fold**
folds v, n ▷ **fold**[1, 2]
foliage n (pl -s) leaves
foliages n ▷ **foliage**
foliation n (pl -s) process of producing leaves
foliations n ▷ **foliation**
folio n (pl -lios) sheet of paper folded in half to
make two leaves of a book
folios n ▷ **folio**
folk n (pl -s) people in general ▶ pl relatives
folklore n (pl -s) traditional beliefs and stories
of a people
folklores n ▷ **folklore**
folks n ▷ **folk**
folksier adj ▷ **folksy**
folksiest adj ▷ **folksy**
folksy adj (-sier, -siest) simple and
unpretentious
follicle n (pl -s) small cavity in the body, esp.

one from which a hair grows
follicles n ▷ **follicle**
follies n ▷ **folly**
follow v (-s, -ing, -ed) go or come after
followed v ▷ **follow**
follower n (pl -s) disciple or supporter
followers n ▷ **follower**
following adj about to be mentioned ▶ n (pl
-s) group of supporters ▶ prep as a result of
▶ v ▷ **follow**
followings n ▷ **following**
follows v ▷ **follow**
folly n (pl -llies) foolishness
foment [foam-**ent**] v (-s, -ing, -ed) encourage or
stir up (trouble)
fomented v ▷ **foment**
fomenting v ▷ **foment**
foments v ▷ **foment**
fond adj (-er, -est) tender, loving > **fondly** adv
> **fondness** n (pl -es)
fondant n (pl -s) (sweet made from) flavoured
paste of sugar and water
fondants n ▷ **fondant**
fonder adj ▷ **fond**
fondest adj ▷ **fond**
fondle v (-les, -ling, -led) caress
fondled v ▷ **fondle**
fondles v ▷ **fondle**
fondling v ▷ **fondle**
fondly adv ▷ **fond**
fondness n ▷ **fond**
fondnesses n ▷ **fond**
fondue n (pl -dues) Swiss dish of a hot melted
cheese sauce into which pieces of bread are
dipped
fondues n ▷ **fondue**
font[1] n (pl -s) bowl in a church for baptismal
water
font[2] (pl -s) n set of printing type of one style
and size
fontanelle n (pl -s) soft membranous gap
between the bones of a baby's skull
fontanelles n ▷ **fontanelle**
fonts n ▷ **font**[1, 2]
food n (pl -dies) what one eats, solid
nourishment
foodie n (pl -s) (Informal) gourmet
foodies n ▷ **foodie**
foods n ▷ **food**
foodstuff n (pl -s) substance used as food
foodstuffs n ▷ **foodstuff**
fool[1] n (pl -s) person lacking sense or judgment
(HIST) ▶ v (-s, -ing, -ed) deceive (someone)
fool[2] (pl -s) n dessert of puréed fruit mixed
with cream

fooled v ▷ **fool**
fooleries n ▷ **foolery**
foolery n (pl -ries) foolish behaviour
foolhardiness n ▷ **foolhardy**
foolhardinesses n ▷ **foolhardy**
foolhardy adj recklessly adventurous
> **foolhardiness** n (pl -es)
fooling v ▷ **fool**
foolish adj (-er, -est) unwise, silly, or absurd
> **foolishly** adv > **foolishness** n (pl -es)
foolisher adj ▷ **foolish**
foolishest adj ▷ **foolish**
foolishly adv ▷ **foolish**
foolishness n ▷ **foolish**
foolishnesses n ▷ **foolish**
foolproof adj unable to fail
fools n, v ▷ **fool**[1, 2]
foolscap n (pl -s) size of paper, 34.3 × 43.2
centimetres
foolscaps n ▷ **foolscap**
foot n (pl **feet**) part of the leg below the ankle
footage n (pl -s) amount of film used
footages n ▷ **footage**
football n (pl -s) game played by two teams of
eleven players kicking a ball in an attempt to
score goals > **footballer** n (pl -s)
footballer n ▷ **football**
footballers n ▷ **footballs**
footballs n ▷ **football**
footbridge n (pl -s) bridge for pedestrians
footbridges n ▷ **footbridge**
footfall n (pl -s) sound of a footstep
footfalls n ▷ **footfall**
foothills pl n hills at the foot of a mountain
foothold n (pl -s) secure position from which
progress may be made
footholds n ▷ **foothold**
footing n (pl -s) basis or foundation
footings n ▷ **footing**
footlight n light at the front of a stage
footlights pl n ▷ **footlight**
footling adj (CHIEFLY BRIT) (Informal) trivial
footloose adj free from ties
footman n (pl -men) male servant in uniform
footmen n ▷ **footman**
footnote n note printed at the foot of a page
footnotes n ▷ **footnote**
footpath n (pl -s) narrow path for walkers only
footpaths n ▷ **footpath**
footplate n (pl -s) platform in the cab of a
locomotive for the driver
footplates n ▷ **footplate**
footprint n (pl -s) mark left by a foot
footprints n ▷ **footprint**
footsie n (pl -s) (Informal) flirtation involving

the touching together of feet
footsies n ▷ **footsie**
footstep n step in walking
footsteps n ▷ **footstep**
footstool n (pl -s) low stool used to rest the
feet on while sitting
footstools n ▷ **footstool**
footwear n (pl -s) anything worn to cover
the feet
footwears n ▷ **footwear**
footwork n (pl -s) skilful use of the feet, as in
sport or dancing
footworks n ▷ **footwork**
fop n (pl -s) man excessively concerned
with fashion > **foppery** n (pl -ies) > **foppish**
adj
fopperies n ▷ **fop**
foppery n ▷ **fop**
foppish n ▷ **fop**
fops n ▷ **fop**
for prep indicating a person intended to
benefit from or receive something, span of
time or distance, person or thing represented
by someone, etc. ▶ conj because
forage v (-ges, -ging, -ged) search about (for)
▶ n (pl -s) food for cattle or horses
foraged v ▷ **forage**
forages v, n ▷ **forage**
foraging v ▷ **forage**
foray n (pl -s) brief raid or attack
forays n ▷ **foray**
forbade v ▷ **forbid**
forbear v (-s, -ing, **forbore**, **forborne**) cease or
refrain (from doing something)
forbearance n (pl -s) tolerance, patience
forbearances n ▷ **forbearance**
forbearing v ▷ **forbear**
forbears v ▷ **forbear**
forbid v (-s, -dding, **forbade**, **forbidden**)
prohibit, refuse to allow > **forbidden** adj
forbidden v, adj ▷ **forbid**
forbidding adj severe, threatening ▶ v ▷ **forbid**
forbids v ▷ **forbid**
forbore v ▷ **forbear**
forborne v ▷ **forbear**
force n (pl -s) strength or power ▶ v (-ces, -cing,
-ced) compel, make (someone) do something
forced adj compulsory ▶ v ▷ **force**
forceful adj emphatic and confident
> **forcefully** adv
forceps pl n surgical pincers
forces n, v ▷ **force**
forcible adj involving physical force or violence
> **forcibly** adv
forcibly adv ▷ **forcible**

forcing v ▷ **force**
ford n (pl -s) shallow place where a river may be crossed ▶ v (-s, -ing, -ed) cross (a river) at a ford
forded v ▷ **ford**
fording v ▷ **ford**
fords n, v ▷ **ford**
fore adj in, at, or towards the front ▶ n (pl -s) front part
forearm[1] n (pl -s) arm from the wrist to the elbow
forearm[2] v (-s, -ing, -ed) prepare beforehand
forearmed v ▷ **forearm**[2]
forearming v ▷ **forearm**[2]
forearms n, v ▷ **forearm**[1, 2]
forebear n (pl -s) ancestor
forebears n ▷ **forebear**
foreboding n (pl -s) feeling that something bad is about to happen
forebodings n ▷ **foreboding**
forecast v (-casts, -casting, -cast or -casted) predict (weather, events, etc.) ▶ n (pl -s) prediction
forecasted v ▷ **forecast**
forecasting v ▷ **forecast**
forecastle [foke-sl] n (pl -s) raised front part of a ship
forecastles n ▷ **forecastle**
forecasts v, n ▷ **forecast**
foreclose v (-ses, -sing, -sed) take possession of (property bought with borrowed money which has not been repaid) > **foreclosure** n (pl -s)
foreclosed v ▷ **foreclose**
forecloses v ▷ **foreclose**
foreclosing v ▷ **foreclose**
foreclosure n ▷ **foreclose**
foreclosures n ▷ **foreclose**
forecourt n (pl -s) courtyard or open space in front of a building
forecourts n ▷ **forecourt**
forefather n (pl -s) ancestor
forefathers n ▷ **forefather**
forefinger n (pl -s) finger next to the thumb
forefingers n ▷ **forefinger**
forefront n (pl -s) most active or prominent position
forefronts n ▷ **forefront**
foregather v (-s, -ing, -ed) meet together or assemble
foregathered v ▷ **foregather**
foregathering v ▷ **foregather**
foregathers v ▷ **foregather**
forego v (-goes, -going, -went, -gone) ▷ **forgo**
foregoes v ▷ **forego**

foregoing adj going before, preceding ▶ v ▷ **forego**
foregone v ▷ **forego**
foreground n (pl -s) part of a view, esp. in a picture, nearest the observer
foregrounds n ▷ **foreground**
forehand n (pl -s) (TENNIS ETC.) stroke played with the palm of the hand facing forward
forehands n ▷ **forehand**
forehead n (pl -s) part of the face above the eyebrows
foreheads n ▷ **forehead**
foreign adj not of, or in, one's own country > **foreigner** n (pl -s)
foreigner n ▷ **foreign**
foreigners n ▷ **foreign**
foreleg n (pl -s) either of the front legs of an animal
forelegs n ▷ **foreleg**
forelock n (pl -s) lock of hair over the forehead
forelocks n ▷ **forelock**
foreman n (pl -men) person in charge of a group of workers
foremast n (pl -s) mast nearest the bow of a ship
foremasts n ▷ **foremast**
foremen n ▷ **foreman**
foremost adj, adv first in time, place, or importance
forename n (pl -s) first name
forenames n ▷ **forename**
forenoon n (pl -s) (CHIEFLY US & CANADIAN) morning
forenoons n ▷ **forenoon**
forensic adj used in or connected with courts of law
foreplay n (pl -s) sexual stimulation before intercourse
foreplays n ▷ **foreplay**
forerunner n (pl -s) person or thing that goes before, precursor
forerunners n ▷ **forerunner**
fores n ▷ **fore**
foresail n (pl -s) main sail on the foremast of a ship
foresails n ▷ **foresail**
foresaw v ▷ **foresee**
foresee v (-sees, -seeing, -saw, -seen) see or know beforehand > **foreseeable** adj
foreseeable adj ▷ **foresee**
foreseeing v ▷ **foresee**
foreseen v ▷ **foresee**
foresees v ▷ **foresee**
foreshadow v (-s, -ing, -ed) show or indicate beforehand

foreshadowed v ▷ **foreshadow**
foreshadowing v ▷ **foreshadow**
foreshadows v ▷ **foreshadow**
foreshore n (pl -s) part of the shore between
high- and low-tide marks
foreshores n ▷ **foreshore**
foreshorten v (-s, -ing, -ed) represent (an
object) in a picture as shorter than it really is,
in accordance with perspective
foreshortened v ▷ **foreshorten**
foreshortening v ▷ **foreshorten**
foreshortens v ▷ **foreshorten**
foresight n (pl -s) ability to anticipate and
provide for future needs
foresights n ▷ **foresight**
foreskin n (pl -s) fold of skin covering the tip
of the penis
foreskins n ▷ **foreskin**
forest n (pl -s) large area with a thick growth of
trees > **forested** adj
forestall v (-s, -ing, -ed) prevent or guard
against in advance
forestalled v ▷ **forestall**
forestalling v ▷ **forestall**
forestalls v ▷ **forestall**
forested adj ▷ **forest**
forester n (pl -s) person skilled in forestry
forester n ▷ **foresters**
forestries n ▷ **forestry**
forestry n (pl -ries) science of planting and
caring for trees
forests n ▷ **forest**
foretaste n (pl -s) early limited experience of
something to come
foretastes n ▷ **foretaste**
foretell v (-s, f -ing, -told) tell or indicate
beforehand
foretelling v ▷ **foretell**
foretells v ▷ **foretell**
forethought n (pl -s) thoughtful planning for
future events
forethoughts n ▷ **forethought**
foretold v ▷ **foretell**
forever adv without end
forewarn v (-s, -ing, -ed) warn beforehand
forewarned v ▷ **forewarn**
forewarning v ▷ **forewarn**
forewarns v ▷ **forewarn**
forewent v ▷ **forego**
foreword n (pl -s) introduction to a book
forewords n ▷ **foreword**
forfeit [for-fit] n (pl -s) thing lost or given up
as a penalty for a fault or mistake ▶ v (-s,
-ing, -ed) lose as a forfeit ▶ adj lost as a forfeit
> **forfeiture** n (pl -s)

forfeited v ▷ **forfeit**
forfeiting v ▷ **forfeit**
forfeits n, v ▷ **forfeit**
forfeiture n ▷ **forfeit**
forfeitures n ▷ **forfeit**
forgave v ▷ **forgive**
forge[1] n (pl -s) place where metal is worked,
smithy ▶ v (-ges, -ging, -ged) make a
fraudulent imitation of (something)
forge[2] v (-ges, -ging, -ged) advance steadily
forged n ▷ **forge**[1, 2]
forger n (pl -s) person who makes an illegal
copy of something
forgeries n ▷ **forgery**
forgers n ▷ **forger**
forgery n (pl -ries) illegal copy of something
forges v, n ▷ **forge**[1, 2]
forget v (-s, -getting, -got, -gotten) fail to
remember
forgetful adj tending to forget > **forgetfulness**
n (pl -es)
forgetfulness n ▷ **forgetful**
forgetfulnesses n ▷ **forgetful**
forgets v ▷ **forget**
forgetting v ▷ **forget**
forging v ▷ **forge**[1, 2]
forgive v (-giving, -gave, -given) cease to
blame or hold resentment against, pardon
> **forgiveness** n (pl -es)
forgiven v ▷ **forgive**
forgiveness n ▷ **forgive**
forgivenesses n ▷ **forgive**
forgiving v ▷ **forgive**
forgo v (-goes, -going, -went, -gone) do
without or give up
forgoes v ▷ **forgo**
forgoing v ▷ **forgo**
forgone v ▷ **forgo**
forgot v ▷ **forget**
forgotten v ▷ **forget**
fork n (pl -s) tool for eating food, with prongs
and a handle ▶ v (-s, -ing, -ed) pick up, dig, etc.
with a fork > **forked** adj
forked v, adj ▷ **fork**
forking v ▷ **fork**
forks n, v ▷ **fork**
forlorn adj lonely and unhappy > **forlornly** adv
forlornly adv ▷ **forlorn**
form n (pl -s) shape or appearance ▶ v (-s, -ing,
-ed) give a (particular) shape to or take a
(particular) shape > **formless** adj
formal adj of or characterized by established
conventions of ceremony and behaviour
> **formally** adv
formaldehyde [for-**mal**-de-hide] n (pl -s)

colourless pungent gas used to make
formalin
formaldehydes *n* ▷ **formaldehyde**
formalin *n* (*pl* **-s**) solution of formaldehyde in
water, used as a disinfectant or a preservative
for biological specimens
formalins *n* ▷ **formalin**
formalities *n* ▷ **formality**
formality *n* (*pl* **-ties**) requirement of custom
or etiquette
formalize *v* (**-zes, -zing, -zed**) make official
or formal
formalized *v* ▷ **formalize**
formalizes *v* ▷ **formalize**
formalizing *v* ▷ **formalize**
formally *adv* ▷ **formal**
format *n* (*pl* **-s**) style in which something is
arranged ▶ *v* (**-s, -matting, -matted**) arrange
in a format
formation *n* (*pl* **-s**) forming
formations *n* ▷ **formation**
formative *adj* of or relating to development
formats *n, v* ▷ **format**
formatted *v* ▷ **format**
formatting *v* ▷ **format**
formed *v* ▷ **form**
former *adj* of an earlier time, previous
> **formerly** *adv*
formerly *adv* ▷ **former**
formidable *adj* frightening because difficult
to overcome or manage > **formidably** *adv*
formidably *adv* ▷ **formidable**
forming *v* ▷ **form**
formless *adj* ▷ **form**
forms *n, v* ▷ **form**
formula *n* (*pl* **-las, -lae**) group of numbers,
letters, or symbols expressing a scientific or
mathematical rule > **formulaic** *adj*
formulae *n* ▷ **formula**
formulaic *adj* ▷ **formula**
formulas *n* ▷ **formula**
formulate *v* (**-tes, -ting, -ted**) plan or describe
precisely and clearly > **formulation** *n* (*pl* **-s**)
formulated *v* ▷ **formulate**
formulates *v* ▷ **formulate**
formulating *v* ▷ **formulates**
formulation *n* ▷ **formulate**
formulations *n* ▷ **formulate**
fornicate *v* (**-tes, -ting, -ted**) have sexual
intercourse without being married
> **fornication** *n* (*pl* **-s**) > **fornicator** *n* (*pl* **-s**)
fornicated *v* ▷ **fornicate**
fornicates *v* ▷ **fornicate**
fornicating *v* ▷ **fornicate**
fornication *n* ▷ **fornicate**

fornications *n* ▷ **fornicate**
fornicator *n* ▷ **fornicate**
fornicators *n* ▷ **fornicate**
forsake *v* (**-sakes, -saking, -sook, -saken**)
withdraw support or friendship from
forsaken *v* ▷ **forsake**
forsakes *v* ▷ **forsake**
forsaking *v* ▷ **forsake**
forsook *v* ▷ **forsake**
forsooth *adv* (*Obs*) indeed
forswear *v* (**-s, -swearing, -swore, -sworn**)
renounce or reject
forswearing *v* ▷ **forswear**
forswears *v* ▷ **forswear**
forswore *v* ▷ **forswear**
forsworn *v* ▷ **forswear**
forsythia [for-**syth**-ee-a] *n* (*pl* **-as**) shrub with
yellow flowers in spring
forsythias *n* ▷ **forsythia**
fort *n* (*pl* **-s**) fortified building or place
forte[1] [for-tay] *n* (*pl* **-s**) thing at which a person
excels
forte[2] [for-tay] *adv* (MUSIC) loudly
fortes *n* ▷ **forte**
forth *adv* forwards, out, or away
forthcoming *adj* about to appear or happen
forthright *adj* direct and outspoken
forthwith *adv* at once
forties *n* ▷ **forty**
fortieth *adj, n* ▷ **forty**
fortieths *n* ▷ **forty**
fortifications *n* ▷ **fortify**
fortified *v* ▷ **fortify**
fortifies *v* ▷ **fortify**
fortify *v* (**-fies, -fying, -fied**) make (a
place) defensible, as by building walls
> **fortification** *n* (*pl* **-s**)
fortification *n* ▷ **fortify**
fortifying *v* ▷ **fortify**
fortissimo *adv* (MUSIC) very loudly
fortitude *n* (*pl* **-s**) courage in adversity or pain
fortitudes *n* ▷ **fortitude**
fortnight *n* (*pl* **-s**) two weeks > **fortnightly**
adv, adj
fortnightly *adv, adj* ▷ **fortnight**
fortnights *n* ▷ **fortnight**
fortress *n* (*pl* **-es**) large fort or fortified town
fortresses *n* ▷ **fortress**
forts *n* ▷ **fort**
fortuitous [for-**tyew**-it-uss] *adj* happening by
(lucky) chance > **fortuitously** *adv*
fortuitously *adv* ▷ **fortuitous**
fortunate *adj* having good luck > **fortunately**
adv
fortunately *adv* ▷ **fortunate**

fortune n (pl -s) luck, esp. when favourable ▶ pl person's destiny
  fortunes n ▷ **fortune**
forty adj, n (pl -ties) four times ten > **fortieth** adj, n (pl -s)
forum n (pl -ums) meeting or medium for open discussion or debate
  forums n ▷ **forum**
forward adj directed or moving ahead ▶ n (pl -s) attacking player in various team games, such as soccer or hockey ▶ adv forwards ▶ v (-s, -ing, -ed) send (a letter etc.) on to an ultimate destination
  forwarded v ▷ **forward**
  forwarding v ▷ **forward**
forwards adv towards or at a place further ahead in space or time ▶ n, v ▷ **forward**
fossick v (-s, -ing, -ed) (AUST & NZ) search, esp. for gold or precious stones
  fossicked v ▷ **fossick**
  fossicking v ▷ **fossick**
  fossicks v ▷ **fossick**
fossil n (pl -s) hardened remains of a prehistoric animal or plant preserved in rock
fossilize v (-zes, -zing, -zed) turn into a fossil
  fossilized v ▷ **fossilize**
  fossilizes v ▷ **fossilize**
  fossilizing v ▷ **fossilize**
  fossils n ▷ **fossil**
foster v (-s, -ing, -ed) promote the growth or development of ▶ adj of or involved in fostering a child
  fostered v ▷ **foster**
  fostering v ▷ **foster**
  fosters v ▷ **foster**
  fought v ▷ **fight**
foul adj (-er, -est) loathsome or offensive ▶ n (pl -s) (SPORT) violation of the rules ▶ v (-s, -ing, -ed) make dirty or polluted
  fouled v ▷ **foul**
  fouler adj ▷ **foul**
  foulest adj ▷ **foul**
  fouling v ▷ **foul**
foulmouthed adj habitually using foul language
  fouls n, v ▷ **foul**
found[1] v ▷ **find**
found[2] v (-s, -ing, -ed) establish or bring into being (foll. by on or upon) > **founder** n (pl -s)
found[3] v (-s, -ing, -ed) cast (metal or glass) by melting and setting in a mould
foundation n (pl -s) basis or base
  foundations n ▷ **foundation**
  founded v ▷ **found**[2,3]
  founder[1] n ▷ **found**[2]

founder[2] v (-s, -ing, -ed) break down or fail
  foundered v ▷ **founder**
  foundering v ▷ **founder**
  founders[1] n ▷ **found**[2]
  founders[2] v ▷ **founder**
  founding v ▷ **found**[2,3]
foundling n (pl -s) (CHIEFLY BRIT) abandoned baby
  foundlings n ▷ **foundling**
  foundries n ▷ **foundry**
foundry n (pl -dries) place where metal is melted and cast
  founds v ▷ **found**[2,3]
fount[1] n (pl -s) (Lit) fountain
fount[2] (pl -s) n set of printing type of one style and size
fountain n (pl -s) jet of water
fountainhead n (pl -s) original source
  fountainheads n ▷ **fountainhead**
  fountains n ▷ **fountain**
  founts n ▷ **fount**[1,2]
four adj, n (pl -s) one more than three
  fours n ▷ **four**
foursome n group of four people
  foursomes n (pl -s) ▷ **foursome**
fourteen adj, n (pl -s) four and ten > **fourteenth** adj, n (pl -s)
  fourteens n ▷ **fourteen**
fourteenth adj, n ▷ **fourteen**
  fourteenths n ▷ **fourteen**
fourth adj, n (pl -s) (of) number four in a series ▶ n quarter
  fourths n ▷ **fourth**
fowl n (pl -s) domestic cock or hen
  fowls n ▷ **fowl**
fox n (pl -es) reddish-brown bushy-tailed animal of the dog family ▶ v (-s, -ing, -ed) (Informal) perplex or deceive
  foxed v ▷ **fox**
  foxes n, v ▷ **fox**
foxglove n (pl -s) tall plant with purple or white flowers
  foxgloves n ▷ **foxglove**
foxhole n (pl -s) (MIL) small pit dug for protection
  foxholes n ▷ **foxhole**
foxhound n (pl -s) dog bred for hunting foxes
  foxhounds n ▷ **foxhound**
  foxier adj ▷ **foxy**
  foxiest adj ▷ **foxy**
  foxing v ▷ **fox**
foxtrot n (pl -s) ballroom dance with slow and quick steps
  foxtrots n ▷ **foxtrot**
foxy adj (-xier, -xiest) of or like a fox, esp. in

craftiness

foy *n* (**foys**). Foy is an old dialect word meaning a farewell meal or gift. This unusual word can be useful when there is little space to form longer words. Foy scores 9 points.

foyer [foy-ay] *n* (*pl* -**s**) entrance hall in a theatre, cinema, or hotel
  foyers *n* ▷ **foyer**
fracas [frak-ah] *n* (*pl* -**es**) noisy quarrel
  fracases *n* ▷ **fracas**
fraction *n* (*pl* -**s**) numerical quantity that is not a whole number > **fractional** *adj*
  > **fractionally** *adv*
  fractional *adj* ▷ **fraction**
  fractionally *adv* ▷ **fraction**
  fractions *n* ▷ **fraction**
fractious *adj* easily upset and angered
fracture *n* (*pl* -**s**) breaking, esp. of a bone ▶ *v*
  (-**res, -ring, -red**) break
  fractured *v* ▷ **fracture**
  fractures *n, v* ▷ **fracture**
  fracturing *v* ▷ **fracture**
fragile *adj* easily broken or damaged > **fragility**
  n (*pl* -**lities**)
  fragilities *n* ▷ **fragile**
  fragility *n* ▷ **fragile**
fragment *n* (*pl* -**s**) piece broken off ▶ *v* (-**s, -ing,**
  -**ed**) break into pieces > **fragmentary** *adj*
  > **fragmentation** *n* (*pl* -**s**)
  fragmentary *adj* ▷ **fragment**
  fragmentation *n* ▷ **fragment**
  fragmentations *n* ▷ **fragment**
  fragmented *v* ▷ **fragment**
  fragmenting *v* ▷ **fragment**
  fragments *n, v* ▷ **fragment**
fragrance *n* (*pl* -**s**) pleasant smell
  fragrances *n* ▷ **fragrance**
fragrant *adj* sweet-smelling
frail *adj* (-**er, -est**) physically weak
  frailer *adj* ▷ **frail**
  frailest *adj* ▷ **frail**
  frailities *n* ▷ **fraility**
frailty *n* (*pl* -**ties**) physical or moral weakness
frame *n* (*pl* -**s**) structure giving shape or
  support ▶ *v* (-**mes, -ming, -med**) put together,
  construct
  framed *v* ▷ **frame**
  frames *n, v* ▷ **frame**
framework *n* (*pl* -**s**) supporting structure
  frameworks *n* ▷ **framework**
  framing *v* ▷ **frame**
franc *n* (*pl* -**s**) monetary unit of Switzerland, various African countries, and formerly of France and Belgium

franchise *n* (*pl* -**s**) right to vote
  franchises *n* ▷ **franchise**
francium *n* (*pl* -**s**) (CHEM) radioactive metallic element
  franciums *n* ▷ **francium**
  francs *n* ▷ **franc**
frangipani [fran-jee-pah-nee] *n* (*pl* -**nis**) Australian evergreen tree with large yellow fragrant flowers
  frangipanis *n* ▷ **frangipani**
frank *adj* (-**er, -est**) honest and straightforward in speech or attitude ▶ *n* (*pl* -**s**) official mark on a letter permitting delivery ▶ *v* (-**s, -ing, -ed**) put such a mark on (a letter) > **frankly** *adv*
  > **frankness** *n* (*pl* -**es**)
  franked *v* ▷ **frank**
  franker *adj* ▷ **frank**
  frankest *adj* ▷ **frank**
frankfurter *n* (*pl* -**s**) smoked sausage
  frankfurters *n* ▷ **frankfurter**
frankincense *n* (*pl* -**es**) aromatic gum resin burned as incense
  frankincenses *n* ▷ **frankincense**
  franking *v* ▷ **frank**
  frankly *adv* ▷ **frank**
  frankness *n* ▷ **frank**
  franknesses *n* ▷ **frank**
  franks *n, v* ▷ **frank**
frantic *adj* distracted with rage, grief, joy, etc.
  > **frantically** *adv*
  frantically *adv* ▷ **frantic**
fraternal *adj* of a brother, brotherly
  > **fraternally** *adv*
fraternity *n* (*pl* -**ties**) group of people with shared interests, aims, etc. (US)
fraternize *v* associate on friendly terms
  > **fraternization** *n*
fratricide *n* (*pl* -**s**) crime of killing one's brother
  fratricides *n* ▷ **fratricide**
frau [rhymes with **how**] *n* (*pl* **fraus, frauen**) married German woman
fraud *n* (*pl* -**s**) (criminal) deception, swindle
  > **fraudulent** *adj* > **fraudulence** *n* (*pl* -**s**)
  frauds *n* ▷ **fraud**
  fraudulence *n* ▷ **fraud**
  fraudulences *n* ▷ **fraud**
  fraudulent *adj* ▷ **fraud**
  frauen *n* ▷ **frau**
fraught [frawt] *adj* (-**er, -est**) tense or anxious
  fraughter *adj* ▷ **fraught**
  fraughtest *adj* ▷ **fraught**
fräulein [froy-line] *n* (*pl* -**leins, -lein**) unmarried German woman
  fräuleins *n* ▷ **fräulein**
  fraus *n* ▷ **frau**

fray[1] *n* (*pl* **-s**) (BRIT, AUST & NZ) noisy quarrel or conflict

fray[2] *v* (**-s, -ing, -ed**) make or become ragged at the edge
  frayed *v* ▷ **fray**[2]
  fraying *v* ▷ **fray**[2]
  frays *n*, *v* ▷ **fray**[1, 2]

frazzle *n* (*pl* **-s**) (*Informal*) exhausted state
  frazzles *n* ▷ **frazzle**

freak *n* (*pl* **-s**) abnormal person or thing ▶ *adj* abnormal > **freakish** *adj*
  freakish *adj* ▷ **freak**
  freaks *n* ▷ **freak**

freckle *n* (*pl* **-s**) small brown spot on the skin
freckled *adj* marked with freckles
  freckles *n* ▷ **freckle**

free *adj* (**freer, freest**) able to act at will, not compelled or restrained ▶ *v* (**frees, freeing, freed**) release, liberate > **freely** *adv*
  freed *v* ▷ **free**

freedom *n* (*pl* **-s**) being free
  freedoms *n* ▷ **freedom**

freehand *adj* drawn without guiding instruments

freehold *n* (*pl* **-s**) tenure of land for life without restrictions > **freeholder** *n* (*pl* **-s**)
  freeholder *n* ▷ **freehold**
  freeholders *n* ▷ **freehold**
  freeholds *n* ▷ **freehold**
  freeing *v* ▷ **free**

freelance *adj*, *n* (*pl* **-s**) (of) a self-employed person doing specific pieces of work for various employers
  freelances *n* ▷ **freelance**

freeloader *n* (*pl* **-s**) (*Slang*) habitual scrounger
  freeloaders *n* ▷ **freeloader**
  freely *adv* ▷ **free**

freemason *n* (*pl* **-s**) member of a secret fraternity pledged to help each other
  freemasons *n* ▷ **freemason**
  freer *adj* ▷ **free**
  frees *v* ▷ **free**

freesia *n* (*pl* **-s**) plant with fragrant tubular flowers
  freesias *n* ▷ **freesia**
  freest *adj* ▷ **free**

freeway *n* (*pl* **-s**) (US & AUST) motorway
  freeways *n* ▷ **freeway**

freewheel *v* (**-s, -ing, -ed**) travel downhill on a bicycle without pedalling
  freewheeled *v* ▷ **freewheel**
  freewheeling *v* ▷ **freewheel**
  freewheels *v* ▷ **freewheel**

freeze *v* (**-zes, -zing, froze, frozen**) change from a liquid to a solid by the reduction of temperature, as water to ice ▶ *n* period of very cold weather

freezer *n* (*pl* **-s**) insulated cabinet for cold-storage of perishable foods
  freezers *n* ▷ **freezer**
  freezes *v* ▷ **freeze**

freezing *adj* (*Informal*) very cold ▶ *v* ▷ **freeze**

freight [frate] *n* (*pl* **-s**) commercial transport of goods ▶ *v* (**-s, -ing, -ed**) send by freight
  freighted *v* ▷ **freight**

freighter *n* (*pl* **-s**) ship or aircraft for transporting goods
  freighters *n* ▷ **freighter**
  freighting *v* ▷ **freight**
  freights *n*, *v* ▷ **freight**

frenetic [frin-**net**-ik] *adj* uncontrolled, excited > **frenetically** *adv*
  frenetically *adv* ▷ **frenetic**
  frenzied *adj* ▷ **frenzy**
  frenziedly *adv* ▷ **frenzy**
  frenzies *n* ▷ **frenzy**

frenzy *n* (*pl* **-zies**) violent mental derangement > **frenzied** *adj* > **frenziedly** *adv*
  frequencies *n* ▷ **frequency**

frequency *n* (*pl* **-cies**) rate of occurrence

frequent *adj* happening often ▶ *v* (**-s, -ing, -ed**) visit habitually > **frequently** *adv*
  frequented *v* ▷ **frequent**
  frequenting *v* ▷ **frequent**
  frequently *adv* ▷ **frequent**
  frequents *v* ▷ **frequent**

fresco *n* (*pl* **-coes, -cos**) watercolour painting done on wet plaster on a wall
  frescoes *n* ▷ **fresco**
  frescos *n* ▷ **fresco**

fresh *adj* (**-er, -est**) newly made, acquired, etc. > **freshly** *adv* > **freshness** *n* (*pl* **-es**)

freshen *v* (**-s, -ing, -ed**) make or become fresh or fresher
  freshened *v* ▷ **freshen**
  freshening *v* ▷ **freshen**
  freshens *v* ▷ **freshen**

fresher *n* (*pl* **-s**) first-year student ▶ *adj* ▷ **fresh**
  freshers *n* ▷ **fresher**
  freshest *adj* ▷ **fresh**
  freshly *adv* ▷ **fresh**

freshman *n* (*pl* **-men**) (BRIT & US) first-year student
  freshmen *n* ▷ **freshman**
  freshness *n* ▷ **fresh**
  freshnesses *n* ▷ **fresh**

fret[1] *v* (**-s, -tting, -tted**) be worried

fret[2] *n* (*pl* **-s**) small bar on the fingerboard of a guitar etc.

fretful *adj* irritable

frets *n* ▷ **fret**[1,2]
fretsaw *n* (*pl* -s) fine saw with a narrow blade, used for fretwork
  fretsaws *n* ▷ **fretsaw**
  fretted *v* ▷ **fret**[1]
  fretting *v* ▷ **fret**[1]
fretwork *n* (*pl* -s) decorative carving in wood
  fretworks *n* ▷ **fretwork**
friable *adj* easily crumbled
friar *n* (*pl* -s) member of a male Roman Catholic religious order
  friaries *n* ▷ **friary**
  friars *n* ▷ **friar**
friary *n* (*pl* -ries) house of friars
fricassee *n* (*pl* -s) stewed meat served in a thick white sauce
  fricassees *n* ▷ **fricassee**
friction *n* (*pl* -s) resistance met with by a body moving over another > **frictional** *adj*
  frictional *adj* ▷ **friction**
  frictions *n* ▷ **friction**
fridge *n* (*pl* -s) apparatus in which food and drinks are kept cool
  fridges *n* ▷ **fridge**
  fried *v* ▷ **fry**[1]
friend *n* (*pl* -s) person whom one knows well and likes > **friendless** *adj* > **friendship** *n* (*pl* -s)
  friendless *adj* ▷ **friend**
  friendlier *adj* ▷ **friendly**
  friendlies *n* ▷ **friendly**
  friendliest *adj* ▷ **friendly**
  friendliness *n* ▷ **friendly**
  friendlinesses *n* ▷ **friendly**
friendly *adj* (-lier, -liest) showing or expressing liking ▶ *n* (*pl* -lies) (SPORT) match played for its own sake and not as part of a competition > **friendliness** *n* (*pl* -es)
  friends *n* ▷ **friend**
  friendship *n* ▷ **friend**
  friendships *n* ▷ **friend**
  fries *v*, *n* ▷ **fry**[1]
Friesian [free-zhan] *n* (*pl* -s) breed of black-and-white dairy cattle
  Friesians *n* ▷ **Friesian**
frieze [freeze] *n* (*pl* -s) ornamental band on a wall
  friezes *n* ▷ **frieze**
frigate [frig-it] *n* (*pl* -s) medium-sized fast warship
  frigates *n* ▷ **frigate**
fright *n* (*pl* -s) sudden fear or alarm
frighten *v* (-s, -ing, -ed) scare or terrify
  > **frightening** *adj*
  frightened *v* ▷ **frighten**
  frightened *v* ▷ **frighten**

frightening *v*, *adj* ▷ **frighten**
frightful *adj* horrifying (*Informal*) > **frightfully** *adv*
  frightfully *adv* ▷ **frightful**
  frights *n* ▷ **fright**
frigid [frij-id] *adj* (of a woman) sexually unresponsive > **frigidity** *n* (*pl* -ties)
  frigidities *n* ▷ **frigid**
  frigidity *n* ▷ **frigid**
frill *n* (*pl* -s) gathered strip of fabric attached at one edge ▶ *pl* superfluous decorations or details > **frilled** *adj* > **frilly** *adj* (-ier, -iest)
  frilled *adj* ▷ **frill**
  frillier *adj* ▷ **frill**
  frilliest *adj* ▷ **frill**
  frills *n* ▷ **frill**
  frilly *adj* ▷ **frill**
fringe *n* (*pl* -es) hair cut short and hanging over the forehead ▶ *v* (-ges, -ging, -ged) decorate with a fringe ▶ *adj* (of theatre) unofficial or unconventional > **fringed** *adj*
  fringed *v*, *adj* ▷ **fringe**
  fringes *n*, *v* ▷ **fringe**
  fringing *v* ▷ **fringe**
  fripperies *n* ▷ **frippery**
frippery *n* (*pl* -ries) useless ornamentation
frisk *v* (-s, -ing, -ed) move or leap playfully
  frisked *v* ▷ **frisk**
  friskier *adj* ▷ **frisky**
  friskiest *adj* ▷ **frisky**
  frisking *v* ▷ **frisk**
  frisks *v* ▷ **frisk**
frisky *adj* (-kier, -kiest) lively or high-spirited
frisson [frees-sonn] *n* (*pl* -s) shiver of fear or excitement
  frissons *n* ▷ **frisson**
fritter *n* (*pl* -s) piece of food fried in batter
  fritters *n* ▷ **fritter**
  frivolities *n* ▷ **frivolous**
  frivolity *n* ▷ **frivolous**
frivolous *adj* not serious or sensible > **frivolity** *n* (*pl* -ties)
frizz *v* (-es, -ing, -ed) form (hair) into stiff wiry curls > **frizzy** *adj* (-zzier, -zziest)
  frizzed *v* ▷ **frizz**
  frizzes *v* ▷ **frizz**
  frizzier *adj* ▷ **frizz**
  frizziest *adj* ▷ **frizz**
  frizzing *v* ▷ **frizz**
frizzle *v* (-les, -ling, -led) cook or heat until crisp and shrivelled
  frizzled *v* ▷ **frizzle**
  frizzles *v* ▷ **frizzle**
  frizzling *v* ▷ **frizzle**
  frizzy *adj* ▷ **frizz**

frock n (pl -s) dress
  frocks n ▷ frock
frog n (pl -s) smooth-skinned tailless
  amphibian with long back legs used for
  jumping
frogman n (pl -men) swimmer with a rubber
  suit and breathing equipment for working
  underwater
  frogmen n ▷ frogman
  frogs n ▷ frog
frogspawn n (pl -s) jelly-like substance
  containing frog's eggs
  frogspawns n ▷ frogspawn
frolic v (-lics, -licking, -licked) run and play
  in a lively way ▶ n (pl -s) lively and merry
  behaviour
  frolicked v ▷ frolic
  frolicking v ▷ frolic
  frolics v, n ▷ frolic
frolicsome adj playful
from prep indicating the point of departure,
  source, distance, cause, change of state, etc.
frond n (pl -s) long leaf or leaflike part of a fern,
  palm, or seaweed
  fronds n ▷ frond
front n (pl -s) fore part ▶ adj of or at the front ▶ v
  (-s, -ing, -ed) face (onto) > **frontal** adj
frontage n (pl -s) facade of a building
  frontages n ▷ frontage
  frontal adj ▷ front
  fronted v ▷ front
frontier n (pl -s) area of a country bordering
  on another
  frontiers n ▷ frontier
  fronting v ▷ front
frontispiece n (pl -s) illustration facing the
  title page of a book
  frontispieces n ▷ frontispiece
frontrunner (pl -s) n (Informal) person regarded
  as most likely to win a race, election, etc.
  frontrunners n ▷ frontrunner
  fronts n, v ▷ front
frost n (pl -s) white frozen dew or mist ▶ v (-s,
  -ing, -ed) become covered with frost
frostbite n destruction of tissue, esp. of the
  fingers or ears, by cold (pl -s) > **frostbitten** adj
  frostbites n ▷ frostbite
  frostbitten adj ▷ frostbite
frosted v ▷ frost ▶ adj (of glass) having a rough
  surface to make it opaque
  frostier adj ▷ frosty
  frostiest adj ▷ frosty
  frostily adv ▷ frosty
  frostiness n ▷ frosty
  frostinesses n ▷ frosty

frosting v ▷ frost ▶ n (pl -s) (CHIEFLY US) sugar
  icing
  frostings n ▷ frosting
  frosts n, v ▷ frost
frosty adj (-tier, -tiest) characterized or
  covered by frost > **frostily** adv > **frostiness**
  n (pl -es)
froth n (pl -s) mass of small bubbles ▶ v (-s, -ing,
  -ed) foam > **frothy** adj (-thier, -thiest)
  frothed v ▷ froth
  frothier adj ▷ froth
  frothiest adj ▷ froth
  frothing v ▷ froth
  froths n, v ▷ froth
  frothy adj ▷ froth
  frowiest adj ▷ frowzy
frown v (-s, -ing, -ed) wrinkle one's brows in
  worry, anger, or thought ▶ n (pl -s) frowning
  expression
  frowned v ▷ frown
  frowning v ▷ frown
  frowns v, n ▷ frown
  frowsier adj ▷ frowzy
  frowsiest adj ▷ frowzy
  frowstier adj ▷ frowsty
  frowstiest adj ▷ frowsty
frowsty adj (-ier, -iest) (BRIT) stale or musty
  frowzier adj ▷ frowzy
frowzy, frowsy adj (-zier, -ziest) dirty or
  unkempt
  froze v ▷ freeze
  frozen v ▷ freeze
frugal adj thrifty, sparing > **frugally** adv
  > **frugality** n (pl -ties)
  frugalities n ▷ frugal
  frugality n ▷ frugal
  frugally adv ▷ frugal
fruit n (pl -s) part of a plant containing seeds,
  esp. if edible ▶ v (-s, -ing, -ed) bear fruit
  fruited v ▷ fruit
fruiterer n (pl -s) person who sells fruit
  fruiterers n ▷ fruiterer
fruitful adj useful or productive > **fruitfully** adv
  fruitfully adv ▷ fruitful
  fruitier adj ▷ fruity
  fruitiest adj ▷ fruity
  fruiting v ▷ fruit
fruition [froo-ish-on] n (pl -s) fulfilment of
  something worked for or desired
  fruitions n ▷ fruition
fruitless adj useless or unproductive
  > **fruitlessly** adv
  fruitlessly adv ▷ fruitless
  fruits n, v ▷ fruit
fruity adj (-tier, -tiest) of or like fruit

frump *n* (*pl* -s) dowdy woman > **frumpy** *adj*
(-pier, -piest)
  frumpier *adj* ▷ **frump**
  frumpiest *adj* ▷ **frump**
  frumps *n* ▷ **frump**
  frumpy *adj* ▷ **frump**
frustrate *v* (-tes, -ting, -ted) upset or
anger > **frustrated** *adj* > **frustrating** *adj*
> **frustration** *n* (*pl* -s)
  frustrated *v, adj* ▷ **frustrate**
  frustrates *v* ▷ **frustrate**
  frustrating *v, adj* ▷ **frustrate**
  frustration *n* ▷ **frustrate**
  frustrations *n* ▷ **frustrate**
fry[1] *v* (-ries, -rying, -ried) cook or be cooked in
fat or oil ▸ *n* (*pl* **fries**) potato chip
fry[2] *pl n* young fishes
  frying *v* ▷ **fry**
fuchsia [fyew-sha] *n* (*pl* -s) ornamental shrub
with hanging flowers
  fuchsias *n* ▷ **fuchsia**
fuddle *v* (-les, -ling, -led) cause to be
intoxicated or confused > **fuddled** *adj*
  fuddled *v, adj* ▷ **fuddle**
  fuddles *v* ▷ **fuddle**
  fuddling *v* ▷ **fuddle**
fudge[1] *n* (*pl* -s) soft caramel-like sweet
fudge[2] *v* (-ges, -ging, -ged) avoid making a
firm statement or decision
  fudged *v* ▷ **fudge**[2]
  fudges *n, v* ▷ **fudge**[1, 2]
  fudging *v* ▷ **fudge**[2]
fuel *n* (*pl* -s) substance burned or treated to
produce heat or power ▸ *v* (-s, -lling, -lled)
provide with fuel
  fuelled *v* ▷ **fuel**
  fuelling *v* ▷ **fuel**
  fuels *n, v* ▷ **fuel**
fug *n* (*pl* -s) hot stale atmosphere > **fuggy** *adj*
(-ggier, -ggiest)
  fuggier *adj* ▷ **fug**
  fuggiest *adj* ▷ **fug**
  fuggy *adj* ▷ **fug**
fugitive [fyew-jit-iv] *n* (*pl* -s) person who flees,
esp. from arrest or pursuit ▸ *adj* fleeing
  fugitives *n* ▷ **fugitive**
  fugs *n* ▷ **fug**
fugue [fyewg] *n* (*pl* -s) musical composition in
which a theme is repeated in different parts
  fugues *n* ▷ **fugue**
  fulcra *n* ▷ **fulcrum**
fulcrum *n* (*pl* -crums, -cra) pivot about which
a lever turns
  fulcrums *n* ▷ **fulcrum**
fulfil *v* (-s, -lling, -lled) bring about the

achievement of (a desire or promise)
> **fulfilment** *n* (*pl* -s)
  fulfilled *n* ▷ **fulfil**
  fulfilling *v* ▷ **fulfil**
  fulfilment *n* ▷ **fulfil**
  fulfilments *n* ▷ **fulfil**
  fulfils *v* ▷ **fulfil**
full *adj* (-er, -est) containing as much or as
many as possible ▸ *adv* completely > **fully** *adv*
> **fullness** *n* (*pl* -es)
  fuller *adj* ▷ **full**
  fullest *adj* ▷ **full**
  fullness *n* ▷ **full**
  fullnesses *n* ▷ **full**
  fully *adv* ▷ **full**
fulmar *n* (*pl* -s) Arctic sea bird
  fulmars *n* ▷ **fulmar**
fulminate *v* (-tes, -ting, -ted) (*foll. by* **against**)
criticize or denounce angrily
  fulminated *v* ▷ **fulminate**
  fulminates *v* ▷ **fulminate**
  fulminating *v* ▷ **fulminate**
fulsome *adj* distastefully excessive or
insincere
fumble *v* (-les, -ling, -led) handle awkwardly
▸ *n* (*pl* -s) act of fumbling
  fumbled *v* ▷ **fumble**
  fumbles *n, v* ▷ **fumble**
  fumbling *v* ▷ **fumble**
fume *v* (-s, -ing, -ed) be very angry ▸ *pl n*
pungent smoke or vapour
  fumed *v* ▷ **fume**
  fumes *v, n* ▷ **fume**
fumigate [fyew-mig-gate] *v* (-tes, -ting, -ted)
disinfect with fumes > **fumigation** *n* (*pl* -s)
  fumigated *v* ▷ **fumigate**
  fumigates *v* ▷ **fumigate**
  fumigating *v* ▷ **fumigate**
  fumigation *n* ▷ **fumigate**
  fumigations *n* ▷ **fuminate**
  fuming *v* ▷ **fume**
fun *n* (*pl* -s) enjoyment or amusement
function *n* (*pl* -s) purpose something exists for
▸ *v* (-s, -ing, -ed) operate or work (*foll. by* **as**)
functional *adj* of or as a function
> **functionally** *adv*
  functionally *adv* ▷ **functional**
  functionaries *n* ▷ **functionary**
functionary *n* (*pl* -ries) official
  functioned *v* ▷ **function**
  functioning *v* ▷ **function**
  functions *n, v* ▷ **function**
fund *n* (*pl* -s) stock of money for a special
purpose ▸ *pl* money resources ▸ *v* (-s, -ing,
-ed) provide money to > **funding** *n* (*pl* -s)

fundamental *adj* essential or primary ▶ *n* (*pl* -s) basic rule or fact > **fundamentally** *adv*

fundamentalism *n* (*pl* -s) literal or strict interpretation of a religion > **fundamentalist** *adj*, *n* (*pl* -s)

fundamentalisms *n* ▷ **fundamentalism**

fundamentalist *adj*, *n* ▷ **fundamentalism**

fundamentalists *n* ▷ **fundamentalism**

fundamentally *adv* ▷ **fundamental**

fundamentals *n* ▷ **fundamental**

funded *v* ▷ **fund**

fundi *n* (*pl* -dis) (S AFR) expert or boffin

funding *v*, *n* ▷ **fund**

fundings *n* ▷ **fund**

fundis *n* ▷ **fundi**

funds *n*, *v* ▷ **fund**

funeral *n* (*pl* -s) ceremony of burying or cremating a dead person

funerals *n* ▷ **funeral**

funerary *adj* of or for a funeral

funereal [fyew-**neer**-ee-al] *adj* gloomy or sombre

funfair *n* (*pl* -s) entertainment with machines to ride on and stalls

funfairs *n* ▷ **funfair**

fungal *adj* ▷ **fungus**

fungi *n* ▷ **fungus**

fungicide *n* (*pl* -s) substance that destroys fungi

fungicides *n* ▷ **fungicides**

fungous *adj* ▷ **fungus**

fungus *n* (*pl* -gi, -guses) plant without leaves, flowers, or roots, such as a mushroom or mould > **fungal, fungous** *adj*

funguses *n* ▷ **fungus**

funicular *n* (*pl* -s) cable railway on a mountainside or cliff

funiculars *n* ▷ **funicular**

funk¹ *n* (*pl* -s) style of dance music with a strong beat

funk² (*Informal*) *n* nervous or fearful state ▶ *v* (-s, -ing, -ed) avoid (doing something) through fear

funked *v* ▷ **funk**

funkier *adj* ▷ **funky**

funkiest *adj* ▷ **funky**

funking *v* ▷ **funk**

funks *n*, *v* ▷ **funk**¹, ²

funky *adj* (-kier, -kiest) (of music) having a strong beat

funnel *n* (*pl* -s) cone-shaped tube for pouring liquids into a narrow opening ▶ *v* (-s, -lling, -lled) (cause to) move through or as if through a funnel

funnelled *v* ▷ **funnel**

funnelling *v* ▷ **funnel**

funnels *n*, *v* ▷ **funnel**

funnier *adj* ▷ **funny**

funniest *adj* ▷ **funny**

funnily *adv* ▷ **funny**

funny *adj* (-nnier, -nniest) comical, humorous > **funnily** *adv*

funs *n* ▷ **fun**

fur *n* (*pl* -s) soft hair of a mammal ▶ *v* (-s, -rring, -rred) cover or become covered with fur > **furry** (-rrier, -rriest) ▶ *adj*

furbish *v* (-es, -ing, -ed) smarten up

furbished *v* ▷ **furbish**

furbishes *v* ▷ **furbish**

furbishing *v* ▷ **furbish**

furies *n* ▷ **fury**

furious *adj* very angry > **furiously** *adv*

furiously *adv* ▷ **furious**

furl *v* (-s, -ing, -ed) roll up and fasten (a sail, umbrella, or flag)

furled *v* ▷ **furl**

furling *v* ▷ **furl**

furlong *n* (*pl* -s) unit of length equal to 220 yards (201.168 metres)

furlongs *n* ▷ **furlongs**

furlough [fur-loh] *n* (*pl* -s) leave of absence

furloughs *n* ▷ **furlough**

furls *v* ▷ **furl**

furnace *n* (*pl* -s) enclosed chamber containing a very hot fire

furnaces *n* ▷ **furnace**

furnish *v* (-es, -ing, -ed) provide (a house or room) with furniture

furnished *v* ▷ **furnish**

furnishes *v* ▷ **furnish**

furnishing *v* ▷ **furnish**

furnishings *pl n* furniture, carpets, and fittings

furniture *n* (*pl* -s) large movable articles such as chairs and wardrobes

furnitures *n* ▷ **furniture**

furore [fyew-ror-ee] *n* (*pl* -s) very excited or angry reaction

furores *n* ▷ **furore**

furred *v* ▷ **fur**

furrier *n* (*pl* -s) dealer in furs ▶ *adj* ▷ **fur**

furriers *n* ▷ **furrier**

furriest *adj* ▷ **fur**

furring *v* ▷ **fur**

furrow *n* (*pl* -s) trench made by a plough ▶ *v* (-s, -ing, -ed) make or become wrinkled

furrowed *v* ▷ **furrow**

furrowing *v* ▷ **furrow**

furrows *n*, *v* ▷ **furrow**

furry *adj* ▷ **fur**

furrying v ▷ **flurry**

furs n, v ▷ **fur**

further adv in addition ▶ adj additional ▶ v (-s, -ing, -ed) assist the progress of > **furtherance** n (pl -s)

furtherance n ▷ **further**

furtherances n ▷ **further**

furthered v ▷ **further**

furthering v ▷ **further**

furthermore adv besides

furthermost adj most distant

furthers v ▷ **further**

furthest adv to the greatest distance or extent ▶ adj most distant

furtive adj sly and secretive > **furtively** adv

furtively adv ▷ **furtive**

fury n (pl -ries) wild anger

furze n (pl -s) gorse

furzes n ▷ **furze**

fuse¹ n (pl -s) cord containing an explosive for detonating a bomb

fuse² n (pl -s) safety device for electric circuits, containing a wire that melts and breaks the connection when the circuit is overloaded ▶ v (-ses, -sing, -sed) (cause to) fail as a result of a blown fuse

fused v ▷ **fuse**

fuselage [fyew-zill-lahzh] n (pl -s) body of an aircraft

fuselages n ▷ **fuselage**

fuses v, n ▷ **fuse**

fusilier [fyew-zill-**leer**] n (pl -s) soldier of certain regiments

fusiliers n ▷ **fusilier**

fusillade [fyew-zill-**lade**] n (pl -s) continuous discharge of firearms

fusillades n ▷ **fusillade**

fusing v ▷ **fuse**

fusion n (pl -s) melting ▶ adj of a style of cooking that combines traditional Western techniques and ingredients with those used in Eastern cuisine

fusions n ▷ **fusion**

fuss n (pl -es) needless activity or worry ▶ v (-es, -ing, -ed) make a fuss

fussed v ▷ **fuss**

fusses n, v ▷ **fuss**

fussier adj ▷ **fussy**

fussiest adj ▷ **fussy**

fussily adv ▷ **fussy**

fussiness n ▷ **fussy**

fussinesses n ▷ **fussy**

fussing v ▷ **fuss**

fussy adj (-ssier, -ssiest) inclined to fuss > **fussily** adv > **fussiness** n (pl -es)

fustier adj ▷ **fusty**

fustiest adj ▷ **fusty**

fustiness n ▷ **fusty**

fustinesses n ▷ **fusty**

fusty adj (-tier, -tiest) stale-smelling > **fustiness** n (pl -es)

futile adj unsuccessful or useless > **futility** n (pl -ties)

futilities n ▷ **futile**

futility n ▷ **futile**

futon [**foo**-tonn] n (pl -s) Japanese-style bed

futons n ▷ **futon**

future n (pl -s) time to come ▶ adj yet to come or be

futures n ▷ **future**

futuristic adj of a design appearing to belong to some future time

fuzz¹ n (pl -es) mass of fine or curly hairs or fibres

fuzz² n (Slang) police

fuzzes n ▷ **fuzz¹**

fuzzier adj ▷ **fuzzy**

fuzziest adj ▷ **fuzzy**

fuzzily adv ▷ **fuzzy**

fuzziness n ▷ **fuzzy**

fuzzinesses n ▷ **fuzzy**

fuzzy adj (-zzier, -zziest) of, like, or covered with fuzz > **fuzzily** adv > **fuzziness** n (pl -es)

fy interj. Fy is an old word that people said when they were disgusted or dismayed. This very unusual word can be really useful when you're trying to form words in more than one direction. Fy scores 8 points.

Gg

Only three two-letter words begin with G (**gi**, **go** and **gu**). Knowing these will save you worrying about other possibilities. There are quite a few short words beginning with G that use Y, which can prove very useful. These include **gay**, **gey**, **goy** and **guy** (7 points each), as well as **gym** and **gyp** (9 points each).

gab *n* (*pl* **-s**) ▶ *v* (**-s, -ing, -ed**) (*Informal*) talk or chatter
gababouts *n* ▷ **gadabout**
gabardine, gaberdine *n* (*pl* **-s**) strong twill cloth used esp. for raincoats
gabardines *n* ▷ **gabardine**
gabbed *v* ▷ **gab**
gabbier *adj* ▷ **gabby**
gabbiest *adj* ▷ **gabby**
gabbing *v* ▷ **gab**
gabble *v* (**-s, -ing, -ed**) speak rapidly and indistinctly ▶ *n* (*pl* **-s**) rapid indistinct speech
gabbled *v* ▷ **gabble**
gabbles *v, n* ▷ **gabble**
gabbling *v* ▷ **gabble**
gabby *adj* (**-bbier, -bbiest**) (*Informal*) talkative
gable *n* (*pl* **-s**) triangular upper part of a wall between sloping roofs > **gabled** *adj*
gabled *adj* ▷ **gable**
gables *n* ▷ **gable**
gabs *n, v* ▷ **gab**
gad *v* (**-s, -dding, -dded**) go around in search of pleasure
gadabout *n* (*pl* **-s**) pleasure-seeker
gadded *v* ▷ **gad**
gadding *v* ▷ **gad**
gadflies *n* ▷ **gadfly**
gadfly *n* (*pl* **-flies**) fly that bites cattle
gadget *n* (*pl* **-s**) small mechanical device or appliance
gadgetries *n* ▷ **gadgetry**
gadgetry *n* (*pl* **-ries**) gadgets
gadgets *n* ▷ **gadget**
gads *v* ▷ **gad**
gaff *n* (*pl* **-s**) stick with an iron hook for landing large fish
gaffe *n* (*pl* **-s**) social blunder
gaffer *n* (*pl* **-s**) (BRIT) (*Informal*) foreman or boss

gaffers *n* ▷ **gaffer**
gaffes *n* ▷ **gaffe**
gaffs *n* ▷ **gaff**
gag¹ *v* (**-s, -gging, -gged**) choke or retch ▶ *n* (*pl* **-s**) cloth etc. put into or tied across the mouth
gag² *n* (*pl* **-s**) (*Informal*) joke
gaga [gah-gah] *adj* (*Slang*) senile
gagged *v* ▷ **gag¹**
gagging *v* ▷ **gag¹**
gaggle *n* (*pl* **-s**) (*Informal*) disorderly crowd
gaggles *n* ▷ **gaggle**
gags *v, n* ▷ **gag¹, ²**
gaieties *n* ▷ **gaiety**
gaiety *n* (*pl* **-ties**) cheerfulness
gaily *adv* merrily
gain *v* (**-s, -ing, -ed**) acquire or obtain ▶ *n* (*pl* **-s**) profit or advantage
gained *v* ▷ **gain**
gainful *adj* useful or profitable > **gainfully** *adv*
gainfully *adv* ▷ **gainful**
gaining *v* ▷ **gain**
gains *v, n* ▷ **gain**
gainsaid *v* ▷ **gainsay**
gainsay *v* (**-s, -ing, -said**) deny or contradict
gainsaying *v* ▷ **gainsay**
gainsays *v* ▷ **gainsay**
gait *n* (*pl* **-s**) manner of walking
gaiter *n* (*pl* **-s**) cloth or leather covering for the lower leg
gaiters *n* ▷ **gaiter**
gaits *n* ▷ **gait**
gala [gah-la] *n* (*pl* **-s**) festival
galactic *adj* ▷ **galaxy**
galas *n* ▷ **gala**
galaxies *n* ▷ **galaxy**
galaxy *n* (*pl* **-xies**) system of stars > **galactic** *adj*
gale *n* (*pl* **-s**) strong wind
gales *n* ▷ **gale**

gall¹ [gawl] *n* (*pl* **-s**) (*Informal*) impudence
gall² [gawl] *v* (**-s, -ing, -ed**) annoy
gall³ [gawl] *n* (*pl* **-s**) abnormal outgrowth on a tree or plant
gallant *adj* (**-er, -est**) brave and noble > **gallantly** *adv*
  gallanter *adj* ▷ **gallant**
  gallantest *adj* ▷ **gallant**
  gallantly *adv* ▷ **gallant**
  gallantries *n* ▷ **gallantry**
gallantry *n* (*pl* **-tries**) showy, attentive treatment of women
  galled *v* ▷ **gall²**
galleon *n* (*pl* **-s**) large three-masted sailing ship of the 15th-17th centuries
  galleons *n* ▷ **galleon**
  galleries *n* ▷ **gallery**
gallery *n* (*pl* **-ries**) room or building for displaying works of art
galley *n* (*pl* **-s**) kitchen of a ship or aircraft
  galleys *n* ▷ **galley**
  galling *v* ▷ **gall²**
gallium *n* (*pl* **-iums**) (CHEM) soft grey metallic element used in semiconductors
  galliums *n* ▷ **gallium**
gallivant *v* (**-s, -ing, -ed**) go about in search of pleasure
  gallivanted *v* ▷ **gallivant**
  gallivanting *v* ▷ **gallivant**
  gallivants *v* ▷ **gallivant**
gallon *n* (*pl* **-s**) liquid measure of eight pints, equal to 4.55 litres
  gallons *n* ▷ **gallon**
gallop *n* (*pl* **-s**) horse's fastest pace ▶ *v* (**-s, -ing, -ed**) go or ride at a gallop
  galloped *v* ▷ **gallop**
  galloping *v* ▷ **gallop**
  gallops *n, v* ▷ **gallop**
gallows *n* (*pl* **-ses**) wooden structure used for hanging criminals
  gallowses *n* ▷ **gallows**
  galls *v, n* ▷ **gall¹, ², ³**
gallstone *n* (*pl* **-s**) hard mass formed in the gall bladder or its ducts
  gallstones *n* ▷ **gallstone**
galore *adv* in abundance
galoshes *pl n* (BRIT, AUST & NZ) waterproof overshoes
galumph *v* (**-s, -ing, -ed**) (BRIT, AUST & NZ) (*Informal*) leap or move about clumsily
  galumphed *v* ▷ **galumph**
  galumphing *v* ▷ **galumph**
  galumphs *v* ▷ **galumph**
galvanic *adj* of or producing an electric current generated by chemical means

galvanize *v* (**-zes, -zing, -zed**) stimulate into action
  galvanized *v* ▷ **galvanize**
  galvanizes *v* ▷ **galvanize**
  galvanizing *v* ▷ **galvanize**
gambit *n* (*pl* **-s**) opening line or move intended to secure an advantage (CHESS)
  gambits *n* ▷ **gambit**
gamble *v* (**-les, -ling, -led**) play games of chance to win money ▶ *n* (*pl* **-s**) risky undertaking > **gambler** *n* (*pl* **-s**) > **gambling** *n* (*pl* **-s**)
  gambled *v* ▷ **gamble**
  gambler *n* ▷ **gamble**
  gamblers *n* ▷ **gamble**
  gambles *v, n* ▷ **gamble**
  gambling *v, n* ▷ **gamble**
  gamblings *n* ▷ **gamble**
gamboge [gam-boje] *n* (*pl* **-s**) gum resin used as a yellow pigment and purgative
  gamboges *n* ▷ **gamboge**
gambol *v* (**-s, -bolling, -bolled**) jump about playfully, frolic ▶ *n* (*pl* **-s**) frolic
  gambolled *v* ▷ **gambol**
  gambolling *v* ▷ **gambol**
  gambols *v, n* ▷ **gambol**
game¹ *n* (*pl* **-s**) amusement or pastime ▶ *v* (**-mes, -ming, -med**) gamble ▶ *adj* (**-er, -est**) brave > **gamely** *adv*
game² *adj* (**-er, -est**) (BRIT, AUST & NZ) lame, crippled
  gamed *v* ▷ **game¹**
gamekeeper *n* (*pl* **-s**) (BRIT, AUST & S AFR) person employed to breed game and prevent poaching
  gamekeepers *n* ▷ **gamekeeper**
  gamely *adv* ▷ **game¹**
gamer *n* person who plays computer games ▶ *adj* ▷ **game¹, ²**
  gamers *n* ▷ **gamer**
  games *n, v* ▷ **game¹**
gamesmanship *n* (**-s**) art of winning by cunning practices without actually cheating
  gamesmanships *n* ▷ **gamesmanship**
  gamest *adj* ▷ **game¹, ²**
gamete *n* (*pl* **-s**) (BIOL) reproductive cell
  gametes *n* ▷ **gamete**
gamine [gam-een] *n* (*pl* **-s**) slim boyish young woman
  gamines *n* ▷ **gamine**
gaming *n* gambling ▶ *v* ▷ **game¹**
gamma *n* (*pl* **-s**) third letter of the Greek alphabet
  gammas *n* ▷ **gamma**
  gammier *adj* ▷ **gammy**

gammiest adj ▷ gammy
gammon n (pl -**s**) cured or smoked ham
gammons n ▷ gammon
gammy adj (-**mier, -miest**) ▷ game²
gamut n (pl -**s**) whole range or scale (of music, emotions, etc.)
gamuts n ▷ gamut
gander n (pl -**s**) male goose
ganders n ▷ gander
gang n (pl -**s**) (criminal) group
gangland n (pl -**s**) criminal underworld
ganglands n ▷ gangland
gangling adj lanky and awkward
ganglion n (pl -**s**) group of nerve cells
ganglions n ▷ ganglion
gangplank n (pl -**s**) portable bridge for boarding or leaving a ship
gangplanks n ▷ gangplank
gangrene n (pl -**s**) decay of body tissue as a result of disease or injury > **gangrenous** adj
gangrenes n ▷ gangrene
gangs n ▷ gang
gangster n (pl -**s**) member of a criminal gang
gangsters n ▷ gangster
gangway n (pl -**s**) passage between rows of seats
gangways n ▷ gangway
gannet n (pl -**s**) large sea bird
gannets n ▷ gannet
gantries n ▷ gantry
gantry n (pl -**ries**) structure supporting something such as a crane or rocket
gaol [jayl] n (pl -**s**) ▷ jail
gaols n ▷ gaol
gap n (pl -**s**) break or opening > **gappy** adj (-**pier, -ppiest**)
gape v (-**pes, -ping, -ped**) stare in wonder > **gaping** adj
gaped v ▷ gape
gapes v ▷ gape
gaping v, adj ▷ gape
gappier adj ▷ gap
gappiest adj ▷ gap
gappy adj ▷ gap
gaps n ▷ gap
garage n (pl -**s**) building used to house cars ▶ v (-**ges, -ging, -ged**) put or keep a car in a garage
garaged v ▷ garage
garages n, v ▷ garage
garaging v ▷ garage
garb n (pl -**s**) clothes ▶ v (-**s, -ing, -ed**) clothe
garbage n (pl -**s**) rubbish
garbages n ▷ garbage
garbed v ▷ garb
garbing v ▷ garb

garbled adj (of a story etc.) jumbled and confused
garbs n, v ▷ garb
garden n (pl -**s**) piece of land for growing flowers, fruit, or vegetables ▶ pl ornamental park ▶ v (-**s, -ing, -ed**) cultivate a garden > **gardener** n (pl -**s**) > **gardening** n (pl -**s**)
gardened v ▷ garden
gardenia [gar-**deen**-ya] n (pl -**s**) large fragrant white waxy flower
gardenias n ▷ gardenia
gardening v ▷ garden
gardens n, v ▷ garden
garfish n (pl -**fishes**) freshwater fish with a long body and very long toothed jaws
garfishes n ▷ garfish
gargantuan adj huge
gargle v (-**les, -ling, -led**) wash the throat with (a liquid) by breathing out slowly through the liquid ▶ n (pl -**s**) liquid used for gargling
gargled v ▷ gargle
gargles v, n ▷ gargle
gargling v ▷ gargle
gargoyle n (pl -**s**) waterspout carved in the form of a grotesque face, esp. on a church
gargoyles n ▷ gargoyle
garish adj crudely bright or colourful > **garishly** adv > **garishness** n (pl -**es**)
garishly adv ▷ garish
garishness n ▷ garish
garishnesses n ▷ garish
garland n (pl -**s**) wreath of flowers worn or hung as a decoration ▶ v (-**s, -ing, -ed**) decorate with garlands
garlanded v ▷ garland
garlanding v ▷ garland
garlands n, v ▷ garland
garlic n (pl -**s**) pungent bulb of a plant of the onion family, used in cooking
garlics n ▷ garlic
garment n (pl -**s**) article of clothing ▶ pl clothes
garments n ▷ garment
garner v (-**s, -ing, -ed**) collect or store
garnered v ▷ garner
garnering v ▷ garner
garners v ▷ garner
garnet n (pl -**s**) red semiprecious stone
garnets n ▷ garnet
garnish v (-**es, -ing, -ed**) decorate (food) ▶ n (pl -**es**) decoration for food
garnished v ▷ garnish
garnishes v, n ▷ garnish
garnishing v ▷ garnish
garotte n ▷ garrotte
garotted v ▷ garrotte

garottes *n*, *v* ▷ garrotte
garotting *v* ▷ garrotte
garret *n* (*pl* -s) attic in a house
  garrets *n* ▷ garret
garrison *n* (*pl* -s) troops stationed in a town or fort ▶ *v* (-s, -ing, -ed) station troops in
  garrisoned *v* ▷ garrison
  garrisoning *v* ▷ garrison
  garrisons *n*, *v* ▷ garrison
garrotte, garotte *n* (*pl* -s) Spanish method of execution by strangling ▶ *v* (-tes, -ting, -ted) kill by this method
  garrotted *v* ▷ garrotte
  garrottes *n*, *v* ▷ garrotte
  garrotting *v* ▷ garrotte
garrulous *adj* talkative
garter *n* (*pl* -s) band worn round the leg to hold up a sock or stocking
  garters *n* ▷ garter
gas *n* (*pl* **gases, gasses**) airlike substance that is not liquid or solid ▶ *v* (**gases, gasses, gassing, gassed**) poison or render unconscious with gas
gasbag *n* (*pl* -s) (*Informal*) person who talks too much
  gasbags *n* ▷ gasbag
gaseous *adj* of or like gas
  gases *n*, *v* ▷ gas
gash *v* (-es, -ing, -ed) make a long deep cut in ▶ *n* (*pl* -es) long deep cut
  gashed *v* ▷ gash
  gashes *v*, *n* ▷ gash
  gashing *v* ▷ gash
gasholder, gasometer [gas-**som**-it-er] (*pl* -s) *n* large tank for storing gas
  gasholders *n* ▷ gasholder
gasket *n* (*pl* -s) piece of rubber etc. placed between the faces of a metal joint to act as a seal
  gaskets *n* ▷ gasket
gasoline *n* (*pl* -s) (*US*) petrol
  gasolines *n* ▷ gasoline
  gasometers *n* ▷ gasholder
gasp *v* (-s, -ing, -ed) draw in breath sharply or with difficulty ▶ *n* (*pl* -s) convulsive intake of breath
  gasped *v* ▷ gasp
  gasping *v* ▷ gasp
  gasps *v*, *n* ▷ gasp
  gassed *v* ▷ gas
  gasses *n*, *v* ▷ gas
  gassier *adj* ▷ gassy
  gassiest *adj* ▷ gassy
  gassing *v* ▷ gas
gassy *adj* (-ssier, -ssiest) filled with gas

gastric *adj* of the stomach
gastritis *n* (*pl* -tes) inflammation of the stomach lining
  gastritises *n* ▷ gastritis
gastroenteritis *n* inflammation of the stomach and intestines
  gastronomies *n* ▷ gastronomy
gastronomy *n* (*pl* -mies) art of good eating > **gastronomic** *adj*
gastropod *n* (*pl* -s) mollusc, such as a snail, with a single flattened muscular foot
  gastropods *n* ▷ gastropod
gate *n* (*pl* -s) movable barrier, usu. hinged, in a wall or fence
gâteau [gat-toe] *n* (*pl* -teaux) [-toes] rich elaborate cake
  gâteaux *n* ▷ gâteau
gatecrash *v* (-es, -ing, -ed) enter (a party) uninvited
  gatecrashed *v* ▷ gatecrash
  gatecrashes *v* ▷ gatecrash
  gatecrashing *v* ▷ gatecrash
gatehouse *n* (*pl* -s) building at or above a gateway
  gatehouses *n* ▷ gatehouse
  gates *n* ▷ gate
gateway *n* (*pl* -s) entrance with a gate
  gateways *n* ▷ gateway
gather *v* (-s, -ing, -ed) assemble
  gathered *v* ▷ gather
gathering *n* (*pl* -s) assembly ▶ *v* ▷ gather
  gatherings *n* ▷ gathering
gathers *pl n* gathered folds in material ▶ *v* ▷ gather
gauche [gohsh] *adj* (-r, -st) socially awkward > **gaucheness** *n* (*pl* -es)
  gaucheness *n* ▷ gauche
  gauchenesses *n* ▷ gauche
  gaucher *adj* ▷ gauche
  gauchest *adj* ▷ gauche
gaucho [gow-choh] *n* (*pl* -hos) S American cowboy
  gauchos *n* ▷ gaucho
  gaudier *adj* ▷ gaudy
  gaudiest *adj* ▷ gaudy
  gaudily *adv* ▷ gaudy
  gaudiness *n* ▷ gaudy
  gaudinesses *n* ▷ gaudy
gaudy *adj* (-dier, -diest) vulgarly bright or colourful > **gaudily** *adv* > **gaudiness** *n* (*pl* -es)
gauge [gayj] *v* (-ges, -ging, -ged) estimate or judge ▶ *n* (*pl* -s) measuring instrument
  gauged *v* ▷ gauge
  gauges *v*, *n* ▷ gauge
  gauging *v* ▷ gauge

gaunt *adj* (**-er, -est**) lean and haggard
> **gauntness** *n* (*pl* **-es**)
gaunter *adj* ▷ **gaunt**
gauntest *adj* ▷ **gaunt**
gauntlet *n* (*pl* **-s**) heavy glove with a long cuff
gauntlets *n* ▷ **gauntlet**
gauntness *n* ▷ **gaunt**
gauntnesses *n* ▷ **gaunt**
gauze *n* (*pl* **-s**) transparent loosely-woven fabric, often used for surgical dressings
> **gauzy** *adj* (**-zier, -ziest**)
gauzes *n* ▷ **gauze**
gauzier *adj* ▷ **gauze**
gauziest *adj* ▷ **gauze**
gauzy *adj* ▷ **gauze**
gave *v* ▷ **give**
gavel [gav-el] *n* (*pl* **-s**) small hammer banged on a table by a judge, auctioneer, or chairman to call for attention
gavels *n* ▷ **gavel**
gavotte *n* (*pl* **-s**) old formal dance
gavottes *n* ▷ **gavotte**
gawk *v* (**-s, -ing, -ed**) stare stupidly
gawked *v* ▷ **gawk**
gawkier *adj* ▷ **gawky**
gawkiest *adj* ▷ **gawky**
gawkiness *n* ▷ **gawky**
gawkinesses *n* ▷ **gawky**
gawking *v* ▷ **gawk**
gawks *v* ▷ **gawk**
gawky *adj* (**-kier, -kiest**) clumsy or awkward
> **gawkiness** *n* (*pl* **-es**)
gawp *v* (**-s, -ing, -ed**) (*Slang*) stare stupidly
gawped *v* ▷ **gawp**
gawping *v* ▷ **gawp**
gawps *v* ▷ **gawp**
gay *adj* (**-er, -est**) homosexual ▶ *n* (*pl* **-s**) homosexual
gayer *adj* ▷ **gay**
gayest *adj* ▷ **gay**
gayness *n* (*pl* **-es**) homosexuality
gaynesses *n* ▷ **gayness**
gays *n* ▷ **gay**
gaze *v* (**-zes, -zing, -zed**) look fixedly ▶ *n* (*pl* **-s**) fixed look
gazebo [gaz-zee-boh] *n* (*pl* **-bos, -boes**) summerhouse with a good view
gazeboes *n* ▷ **gazebo**
gazebos *n* ▷ **gazebo**
gazed *v* ▷ **gaze**
gazelle *n* (*pl* **-s**) small graceful antelope
gazelles *n* ▷ **gazelle**
gazes *v, n* ▷ **gaze**
gazette *n* (*pl* **-s**) official publication containing announcements

gazetteer *n* (part of) a book that lists and describes places
gazetteers *n* ▷ **gazetteer**
gazettes *n* ▷ **gazette**
gazillion *n* (*pl* **-s**) (*Informal*) extremely large, unspecified amount
gazillionaire *n* (*Informal*) enormously rich person
gazillionaires *n* ▷ **gazillionaire**
gazillions *n* ▷ **gazillion**
gazing *v* ▷ **gaze**
gazump *v* (**-s, -ing, -ed**) (BRIT & AUST) raise the price of a property after verbally agreeing it with (a prospective buyer)
gazumped *v* ▷ **gazump**
gazumping *v* ▷ **gazump**
gazumps *v* ▷ **gazump**
gear *n* (*pl* **-s**) set of toothed wheels connecting with another or with a rack to change the direction or speed of transmitted motion ▶ *v* (**-s, -ing, -ed**) prepare or organize for something
gearbox *n* (*pl* **-es**) case enclosing a set of gears in a motor vehicle
gearboxes *n* ▷ **gearbox**
geared *v* ▷ **gear**
gearing *v* ▷ **gear**
gears *n, v* ▷ **gear**
gecko *n* (*pl* **-kos, -koes**) small tropical lizard
geckoes *n* ▷ **gecko**
geckos *n* ▷ **gecko**
geebung [gee-bung] *n* (*pl* **-s**) Australian tree or shrub with an edible but tasteless fruit
geebungs *n* ▷ **geebung**
geek *n* (*pl* **-s**) (*Informal*) boring, unattractive person > **geeky** *adj* (**-kier, -kiest**)
geekier *adj* ▷ **geek**
geekiest *adj* ▷ **geek**
geeks *n* ▷ **geek**
geeky *adj* ▷ **geek**
geelbek *n* (*pl* **-s**) (S AFR) edible marine fish
geelbeks *n* ▷ **geelbek**
geese *n* ▷ **goose**
geezer *n* (*pl* **-s**) (BRIT, AUST & NZ) (*Informal*) man
geezers *n* ▷ **geezer**
geisha [gay-sha] *n* (*pl* **-sha, -shas**) (in Japan) professional female companion for men
geishas *n* ▷ **geisha**
gel [jell] *n* (*pl* **-s**) jelly-like substance, esp. one used to secure a hairstyle ▶ *v* (**-s, gelling, gelled**) form a gel
gelatine [jel-at-teen], **gelatin** *n* (*pl* **-s**) substance made by boiling animal bones
gelatines *n* ▷ **gelatine**
gelatinous [jel-**at**-in-uss] *adj* of or like jelly

geld v (**gelds, gelding, gelded**) castrate
  gelded v ▷ **geld**
gelding n (pl -**s**) castrated horse ▸ v ▷ **geld**
  geldings n ▷ **gelding**
  gelds v ▷ **geld**
gelignite n (pl -**s**) type of dynamite used for
  blasting
  gelignites v ▷ **gelignite**
  gelled v ▷ **gell**
  gelling v ▷ **gell**
  gels n, v ▷ **gel**
gem n (pl -**s**) precious stone or jewel
gemfish (pl -**fishes**) n Australian food fish with
  a delicate flavour
  gemfishes n ▷ **gemfish**
  gems n ▷ **gem**
gen n (pl -**s**) (Informal) information
gendarme [zhohn-darm] n (pl -**s**) member of
  the French police force
  gendarmes n ▷ **gendarme**
gender n (pl -**s**) state of being male or female
  genders n ▷ **gender**
gene [jean] n (pl -**s**) part of a cell which
  determines inherited characteristics
  genealogical adj ▷ **genealogy**
  genealogies n ▷ **genealogy**
  genealogist n ▷ **genealogy**
  genealogists n ▷ **genealogy**
genealogy [jean-ee-**al**-a-gee] n (pl -**gies**) (study
  of) the history and descent of a family or
  families > **genealogical** adj > **genealogist**
  n (pl -**s**)
  genera [jen-er-a] ▷ **genus**
general adj common or widespread ▸ n (pl -**s**)
  very senior army officer > **generally** adv
  generalities n ▷ **generality**
generality n (pl -**ties**) general principle
  generalization n ▷ **generalize**
  generalizations n ▷ **generalize**
generalize v (-**zes, -zing, -zed**) draw general
  conclusions > **generalization** n (pl -**s**)
  generalized v ▷ **generalize**
  generalizes v ▷ **generalize**
  generalizing v ▷ **generalize**
  generally adv ▷ **general**
  generals n ▷ **general**
generate v (-**tes, -ting, -ted**) produce or bring
  into being
  generated v ▷ **generate**
  generates v ▷ **generate**
  generating v ▷ **generate**
generation n (pl -**s**) all the people born about
  the same time
  generations n ▷ **generation**
generative adj capable of producing

generator n (pl -**s**) machine for converting
  mechanical energy into electrical energy
  generators n ▷ **generator**
generic [jin-**ner**-ik] adj of a class, group, or
  genus > **generically** adv
  generically adv ▷ **generic**
  generosities n ▷ **generous**
  generosity n ▷ **generous**
generous adj free in giving > **generously** adv
  > **generosity** n (pl -**ties**)
  generously adv ▷ **generous**
  genes n ▷ **gene**
  geneses n ▷ **genesis**
genesis [jen-iss-iss] n (pl -**ses**) [-iss-eez]
  beginning or origin
genetic [jin-**net**-tik] adj of genes or genetics
  geneticist n ▷ **genetics**
  geneticists n ▷ **genetics**
genetics n study of heredity and variation in
  organisms > **geneticist** n (pl -**s**)
genial [jean-ee-al] adj cheerful and friendly
  > **genially** adv > **geniality** n (pl -**ties**)
  genialities n ▷ **genial**
  geniality n ▷ **genial**
  genially adv ▷ **genial**
genie [jean-ee] n (pl -**s**) (in fairy tales) servant
  who appears by magic and grants wishes
  genies n ▷ **genie**
genital adj of the sexual organs or
  reproduction
  genitalia n ▷ **genitals**
genitals, genitalia [jen-it-**ail**-ya] pl n external
  sexual organs
genitive n (pl -**s**) grammatical case indicating
  possession or association
  genitives n ▷ **genitive**
genius [jean-yuss] n (pl -**es**) (person with)
  exceptional ability in a particular field
  geniuses n ▷ **genius**
genocide [jen-no-side] n (pl -**s**) murder of a race
  of people
  genocides n ▷ **genocide**
genre [zhohn-ra] n (pl -**s**) style of literary,
  musical, or artistic work
  genres n ▷ **genre**
  gens n ▷ **gen**
gent n (pl -**s**) (BRIT, AUST & NZ) (Informal)
  gentleman
genteel adj (-**er, -est**) affectedly proper and
  polite > **genteelly** adv
  genteeler adj ▷ **genteel**
  genteelest adj ▷ **genteel**
  genteelly adv ▷ **genteel**
gentian [jen-shun] n (pl -**s**) mountain plant
  with deep blue flowers

gentians *n* ▷ gentian
gentile *adj*, *n* (*pl* -s) non-Jewish (person)
gentiles *n* ▷ gentile
gentle *adj* (-r, -st) mild or kindly > **gentleness** *n*
(*pl* -es) > **gently** *adv*
gentleman *n* (*pl* -men) polite well-bred man
> **gentlemanly** *adj* > **gentlewoman** *n fem* (*pl*
-women)
gentlemanly *adj* ▷ gentleman
gentlemen *n* ▷ gentleman
gentleness *n* ▷ gentle
gentlenesses *n* ▷ gentle
gentler *adj* ▷ gentle
gentlest *adj* ▷ gentle
gentlewoman *n* ▷ gentleman
gentlewomen *n* ▷ gentleman
gently *adv* ▷ gentle
gentries *n* ▷ gentry
gentries *n* ▷ gentry
gentrification *n* (*pl* -s) taking-over of a
traditionally working-class area by middle-
class incomers
> **gentrify** *v* (-fies, -fying, -fied)
gentrifications *n* ▷ gentrification
gentrified *v* ▷ gentrification
gentrifies *v* ▷ gentrification
gentrifying *v* ▷ gentrification
gentry *n* (*pl* -ies) people just below the nobility
in social rank
gents *n* men's public toilet ▶ *n* ▷ gent
genuflect *v* (-s, -ing, -ed) bend the knee
as a sign of reverence or deference
> **genuflection, genuflexion** *n* (*pl* -s)
genuflected *v* ▷ genuflect
genuflecting *v* ▷ genuflect
genuflection *n* ▷ genuflect
genuflections *n* ▷ genuflect
genuflects *v* ▷ genuflect
genuflexion *n* ▷ genuflect
genuflexions *n* ▷ genuflect
genuine *adj* not fake, authentic > **genuinely**
adv > **genuineness** *n* (-es)
genuinely *adv* ▷ genuine
genuineness *n* ▷ genuine
genuinenesses *n* ▷ genuine
genus [jean-uss] *n* (*pl* **genera**) group into which
a family of animals or plants is divided
geocentric *adj* having the earth as a centre
geographer *n* ▷ geography
geographers *n* ▷ geography
geographic *adj* ▷ geography
geographical *adj* ▷ geography
geographically *adv* ▷ geography
geographies *n* ▷ geography
geography *n* (*pl* -phies) study of the earth's

physical features, climate, population,
etc. > **geographer** *n* (*pl* -s) > **geographical,
geographic** *adj* > **geographically** *adv*
geological *adj* ▷ geology
geologically *adv* ▷ geology
geologies *n* ▷ geology
geologist *n* ▷ geology
geologists *n* ▷ geology
geology *n* (*pl* -gies) study of the earth's origin,
structure, and composition
> **geological** *adj* > **geologically** *adv*
> **geologist** *n* (*pl* -s)
geometric *adj* ▷ geometry
geometrical *adj* ▷ geometry
geometrically *adv* ▷ geometry
geometries *n* ▷ geometry
geometry *n* (*pl* -tries) branch of mathematics
dealing with points, lines, curves, and
surfaces > **geometric, geometrical** *adj*
> **geometrically** *adv*
geostationary *adj* (of a satellite) orbiting
so as to remain over the same point of the
earth's surface
geothermal *adj* of or using the heat in the
earth's interior
geranium *n* (*pl* -s) cultivated plant with red,
pink, or white flowers
geraniums *n* ▷ geranium
gerbil [jer-bill] *n* (*pl* -s) burrowing desert rodent
of Asia and Africa
gerbils *n* ▷ gerbil
geriatric *adj*, *n* (*pl* -s) old (person)
geriatrics *n* (*pl* branch of medicine dealing
with old age and its diseases
▶ *n* ▷ **geriatric**
germ *n* (*pl* -s) microbe, esp. one causing
disease
germane *adj* relevant to
germanium *n* (*pl* -s) (CHEM) brittle grey
element that is a semiconductor
germaniums *n* ▷ germanium
germinal *adj* of or in the earliest stage of
development
germinate *v* (-tes, -ting, -ted) (cause to)
sprout or begin to grow
> **germination** *n* (*pl* -s)
germinated *v* ▷ germinate
germinates *v* ▷ germinate
germinating *v* ▷ germinate
germination *n* ▷ germinate
germinations *n* ▷ germinate
germs *n* ▷ germ
gerrymandering *n* (*pl* -s) alteration of voting
constituencies in order to give an unfair
advantage to one party

gerrymanderings n ▷ **gerrymandering**
gerund [jer-rund] n (pl -s) noun formed from a verb
gerunds n ▷ **gerund**
gestation n (pl -s) (period of) carrying of young in the womb between conception and birth
gestations n ▷ **gestation**
gesticulate v (-tes, -ting, -ted) make expressive movements with the hands and arms > **gesticulation** n (pl -s)
gesticulated v ▷ **gesticulate**
gesticulates v ▷ **gesticulate**
gesticulating v ▷ **gesticulate**
gesticulation n ▷ **gesticulate**
gesticulations n ▷ **gesticulate**
gesture n (pl -s) movement to convey meaning ▶ v (-res, -ring, -red) gesticulate
gestured v ▷ **gesture**
gestures n, v ▷ **gesture**
gesturing v ▷ **gesture**
get v (-s, -tting, got) obtain or receive
getaway adj, n (pl -s) (used in) escape
getaways n ▷ **getaway**
gets v ▷ **get**
getting v ▷ **get**

> **gey** adv. Gey is a Scots word meaning **very.** If you have a G and a Y, it's highly likley that there will be an E you can use somewhere on the board. Gey scores 7 points.

geyser [geez-er] n (pl -s) spring that discharges steam and hot water (BRIT & S AFR)
geysers n ▷ **geyser**
ghastlier adj ▷ **ghastly**
ghastliest adj ▷ **ghastly**
ghastliness n ▷ **ghastly**
ghastlinesses n ▷ **ghastly**
ghastly adj (-lier, -liest) (Informal) unpleasant > **ghastliness** n (pl -es)
ghat n (pl -s) (in India) steps leading down to a river
ghats n ▷ **ghat**
ghee [gee] n (pl -s) (in Indian cookery) clarified butter
ghees n ▷ **ghee**
gherkin n (pl -s) small pickled cucumber
gherkins n ▷ **gherkin**
ghetto n (pl -ttos, -ttoes) slum area inhabited by a deprived minority
ghettoblaster n (Informal) large portable cassette recorder or CD player
ghettoblasters n ▷ **ghettoblaster**
ghettoes n ▷ **ghetto**
ghettos n ▷ **ghetto**

ghillie n (pl -s) ▷ **gillie**
ghillies n ▷ **ghillie**
ghost n (pl -s) disembodied spirit of a dead person ▶ v (-s, -ing, -ed) ghostwrite > **ghostly** adj (-ier, -iest)
ghosted v ▷ **ghost**
ghosting v ▷ **ghost**
ghostlier adj ▷ **ghost**
ghostliest adj ▷ **ghost**
ghostly adj ▷ **ghost**
ghosts n, v ▷ **ghost**
ghostwriter n (pl -s) writer of a book or article on behalf of another person who is credited as the author
ghostwriters n ▷ **ghostwriter**
ghoul [gool] n (pl -s) person with morbid interests > **ghoulish** adj
ghoulish adj ▷ **ghoul**
ghouls n ▷ **ghoul**

> **gi** n. A gi is a suit worn by judo or karate practitioners. Gi is one of only three two-letter words beginning with G, and so is worth knowing. Gi scores 3 points.

giant n (pl -s) mythical being of superhuman size ▶ adj huge
giants n ▷ **giant**
gibber[1] [jib-ber] v (-s, -ing, -ed) speak or utter rapidly and unintelligibly
gibber[2] [gib-ber] n (pl -s) (AUST) boulder
gibbered v ▷ **gibber**[1]
gibbering v ▷ **gibber**[1]
gibberish n rapid unintelligible talk
gibbers n, v ▷ **gibber**[1,2]
gibbet [jib-bit] n (pl -s) gallows for displaying executed criminals
gibbets n ▷ **gibbet**
gibbon [gib-bon] n (pl -s) agile tree-dwelling ape of S Asia
gibbons n ▷ **gibbon**
gibbous adj (of the moon) more than half but less than fully illuminated
gibe [jibe] v, n (pl -s) ▷ **jibe**[1]
gibes n ▷ **gibe**
giblets [jib-lets] pl n gizzard, liver, heart, and neck of a fowl
gidday, g'day interj (AUST & NZ) expression of greeting
giddier adj ▷ **giddy**
giddiest adj ▷ **giddy**
giddily adv ▷ **giddy**
giddiness n ▷ **giddy**
giddinesses n ▷ **giddy**
giddy adj (-ddier, -ddiest) having or causing a feeling of dizziness > **giddily** adv > **giddiness**

n (*pl* **-es**)

gift *n* (*pl* **-s**) present ▶ *v* (**-s, -ing, -ed**) make a present of

gifted *adj* talented ▶ *v* ▷ **gift**

  gifting *v* ▷ **gift**

  gifts *n, v* ▷ **gift**

gig¹ *n* (*pl* **-s**) single performance by pop or jazz musicians ▶ *v* (**-s, -gging, -gged**) play a gig or gigs

gig² (*pl* **-s**) *n* light two-wheeled horse-drawn carriage

gigantic *adj* enormous

  gigged *v* ▷ **gig¹**

  gigging *v* ▷ **gig¹**

giggle *v* (**-les, -ling, -led**) laugh nervously or foolishly ▶ *n* (*pl* **-s**) such a laugh > **giggly** *adj* (**-lier, -liest**)

  giggled *v* ▷ **giggle**

  giggles *v, n* ▷ **giggle**

  gigglier *adj* ▷ **giggle**

  giggliest *adj* ▷ **giggle**

  giggling *v* ▷ **giggle**

  giggly *adj* ▷ **giggle**

gigolo [jig-a-lo] *n* (*pl* **-los**) man paid by an older woman to be her escort or lover

  gigolos *n* ▷ **gigolo**

gigot *n* (*pl* **-s**) (CHIEFLY BRIT) leg of lamb or mutton

  gigots *n* ▷ **gigot**

  gigs *n, v* ▷ **gig¹, ²**

gild *v* (**-s, -ing, -ed** *or* **gilt**) put a thin layer of gold on

  gilded *v* ▷ **gild**

  gilding *v* ▷ **gild**

  gilds *v* ▷ **gild**

gill [jill] *n* (*pl* **-s**) liquid measure of quarter of a pint, equal to 0.142 litres

gillie *n* (*pl* **-s**) (in Scotland) attendant for hunting or fishing

  gillies *n* ▷ **gillie**

gills [gillz] *pl n* breathing organs in fish and other water creatures ▶ *n* ▷ **gill**

gilt *adj* covered with a thin layer of gold ▶ *n* (*pl* **-s**) thin layer of gold used as decoration ▶ *v* ▷ **gild**

  gilts *n* ▷ **gilt**

gimbals *pl n* set of pivoted rings which allow nautical instruments to remain horizontal at sea

gimcrack [jim-krak] *adj* showy but cheap

gimlet [gim-let] *n* (*pl* **-s**) small tool with a screwlike tip for boring holes in wood

  gimlets *n* ▷ **gimlet**

gimmick *n* (*pl* **-s**) something designed to attract attention or publicity > **gimmickry** *n*

(*pl* **-ries**) > **gimmicky** *adj* (**-ier, -iest**)

  gimmickier *adj* ▷ **gimmick**

  gimmickiest *adj* ▷ **gimmick**

  gimmickries *n* ▷ **gimmick**

  gimmickry *n* ▷ **gimmick**

  gimmicks *n* ▷ **gimmick**

  gimmicky *adj* ▷ **gimmick**

gin¹ *n* (*pl* **-s**) spirit flavoured with juniper berries

gin² *n* (*pl* **-s**) wire noose used to trap small animals

gin³ *n* (*pl* **-s**) (AUST) (*Offens*) Aboriginal woman

ginger *n* (*pl* **-s**) root of a tropical plant, used as a spice > **gingery** *adj*

gingerbread *n* (*pl* **-s**) moist cake flavoured with ginger

  gingerbreads *n* ▷ **gingerbread**

gingerly *adv* cautiously

  gingers *n* ▷ **ginger**

  gingery *adj* ▷ **ginger**

gingham *n* (*pl* **-s**) cotton cloth, usu. checked or striped

  ginghams *n* ▷ **gingham**

gingivitis [jin-jiv-**vite**-iss] *n* (*pl* **-tes**) inflammation of the gums

  gingivitises *n* ▷ **gingivitis**

ginkgo [gink-go] *n* (*pl* **-goes**) ornamental Chinese tree

  ginkgoes *n* ▷ **ginkgo**

  gins *n* ▷ **gin¹, ², ³**

ginseng [jin-seng] *n* (*pl* **-s**) (root of) a plant believed to have tonic and energy-giving properties

  ginsengs *n* ▷ **ginseng**

  gipsies *n* ▷ **gipsy**

  gipsy *n* (*pl* **-sies**) ▷ **gypsy**

giraffe *n* (*pl* **-s**) African ruminant mammal with a spotted yellow skin and long neck and legs

  giraffes *n* ▷ **giraffe**

gird *v* (**-s, girding, girded** *or* **girt**) put a belt round

  girded *v* ▷ **gird**

girder *n* (*pl* **-s**) large metal beam

  girders *n* ▷ **girder**

  girding *v* ▷ **gird**

girdle¹ *n* (*pl* **-s**) woman's elastic corset ▶ *v* (**-les, -ling, -led**) surround or encircle

girdle² *n* (*pl* **-s**) (SCOT) griddle

  girdled *v* ▷ **girdle¹**

  girdles *v, n* ▷ **girdle¹, ²**

  girdling *v* ▷ **girdle¹**

  girds *v* ▷ **gird**

girl *n* (*pl* **-s**) female child (*Informal*) > **girlhood** *n* > **girlish** *adj*

girlfriend *n* (*pl* -s) girl or woman with whom a person is romantically or sexually involved
  girlfriends *n* ▷ **girlfriend**
  girlhood *n* ▷ **girl**
  girlhoods *n* ▷ **girl**
girlie, girly *adj* (*Informal*) featuring photographs of naked or scantily clad women
  girlish *adj* ▷ **girl**
  girls *n* ▷ **girl**
  girly *n* ▷ **girlie**
giro [jire-oh] *n* (*pl* -os) (in some countries) system of transferring money within a post office or bank directly from one account to another
  giros *n* ▷ **giro**
  girt *v* ▷ **gird**
girth *n* (*pl* -s) measurement round something
  girths *n* ▷ **girth**
gist [jist] *n* (*pl* -s) substance or main point of a matter
  gists *n* ▷ **gist**
give *v* (-s, giving, gave, given) present (something) to another person ▶ *n* (*pl* -s) resilience or elasticity
giveaway *n* (*pl* -s) something that reveals hidden feelings or intentions ▶ *adj* very cheap or free
  giveaways *n* ▷ **giveaway**
  given *v* ▷ **give**
  gives *v*, *n* ▷ **give**
  giving *v* ▷ **give**
gizzard *n* (*pl* -s) part of a bird's stomach
  gizzards *n* ▷ **gizzard**

> **gju** *n* (**gjus**). A gju (also spelt **gu**) is a kind of violin from Shetland. This unusual term is a great little word, especially when there's not much space on the board. Gju scores 11 points.

glacé [glass-say] *adj* preserved in a thick sugary syrup
glacial *adj* of ice or glaciers
glaciated *adj* covered with or affected by glaciers > **glaciation** *n* (*pl* -s)
  glaciation *n* ▷ **glaciated**
  glaciations *n* ▷ **glaciated**
glacier *n* (*pl* -s) slow-moving mass of ice formed by accumulated snow
  glaciers *n* ▷ **glacier**
glad *adj* (-dder, -ddest) pleased and happy > **gladly** *adv* > **gladness** *n* (*pl* -es)
gladden *v* (-s, -ing, -ed) make glad
  gladdened *v* ▷ **gladden**
  gladdening *v* ▷ **gladden**

gladdens *v* ▷ **gladden**
gladder *adj* ▷ **glad**
gladdest *adj* ▷ **glad**
glade *n* (*pl* -s) open space in a forest
  glades *n* ▷ **glade**
gladiator *n* (*pl* -s) (in ancient Rome) man trained to fight in arenas to provide entertainment
  gladiators *n* ▷ **gladiator**
  gladioli *n* ▷ **gladiolus**
gladiolus *n* (*pl* -lus, -li, -luses) garden plant with sword-shaped leaves
  gladioluses *n* ▷ **gladiolus**
  gladly *adv* ▷ **glad**
  gladness *n* ▷ **glad**
  gladnesses *n* ▷ **glad**
gladwrap ® (AUST, NZ & S AFR) *n* (*pl* -wraps) thin polythene material for wrapping food ▶ *v* (-wraps, -wrapping, -wrapped) wrap in gladwrap
  gladwrapped *v* ▷ **gladwrap**
  gladwrapping *v* ▷ **gladwrap**
  gladwraps *n*, *v* ▷ **gladwrap**
  glamorize *v* ▷ **glamorous**
  glamorized *v* ▷ **glamorous**
  glamorizes *v* ▷ **glamorous**
  glamorizing *v* ▷ **glamorous**
glamorous *adj* alluring > **glamorize** *v* (-zes, -zing, -zed)
glamour *n* (*pl* -s) alluring charm or fascination
  glamours *n* ▷ **glamour**
glance *v* (-ces, -cing, -ced) look rapidly or briefly ▶ *n* (*pl* -s) brief look
  glanced *v* ▷ **glance**
  glances *v*, *n* ▷ **glance**
glancing *adj* hitting at an oblique angle ▶ *v* ▷ **glance**
gland *n* (*pl* -s) organ that produces and secretes substances in the body > **glandular** *adj*
  glands *n* ▷ **gland**
  glandular *adj* ▷ **gland**
glare *v* (-res, -ring, -red) stare angrily ▶ *n* (*pl* -s) angry stare
  glared *v* ▷ **glare**
  glares *v*, *n* ▷ **glare**
glaring *adj* conspicuous ▶ *v* ▷ **glare** > **glaringly** *adv*
  glaringly *adv* ▷ **glaring**
glass *n* (*pl* -es) hard brittle, usu. transparent substance consisting of metal silicates or similar compounds ▶ *pl* spectacles
  glasses *n* ▷ **glass**
glasshouse *n* greenhouse
  glasshouses *n* ▷ **glasshouse**

glassier *adj* ▷ **glassy**
glassiest *adj* ▷ **glassy**
glassy *adj* (**-ssier, -ssiest**) like glass
glaucoma *n* (*pl* **-s**) eye disease
  glaucomas *n* ▷ **glaucoma**
glaze *v* (**-zes, -zing, -zed**) fit or cover with glass
▶ *n* (*pl* **-s**) transparent coating
  glazed *v* ▷ **glaze**
  glazes *v*, *n* ▷ **glaze**
glazier (*pl* **-s**) *n* person who fits windows
with glass
  glaziers *n* ▷ **glazier**
  glazing *v* ▷ **glaze**
gleam *n* (*pl* **-s**) small beam or glow of light ▶ *v*
(**-s, -ing, -ed**) emit a gleam > **gleaming** *adj*
  gleamed *v* ▷ **gleam**
  gleaming *v*, *adj* ▷ **gleam**
  gleams *n*, *v* ▷ **gleam**
glean *v* (**-s, -ing, -ed**) gather (facts etc.) bit by
bit > **gleaner** *n* (*pl* **-s**)
  gleaned *v* ▷ **glean**
  gleaner *n* ▷ **glean**
  gleaners *n* ▷ **glean**
  gleaning *v* ▷ **glean**
  gleans *v* ▷ **glean**
glee *n* (*pl* **-s**) triumph and delight > **gleeful** *adj*
> **gleefully** *adv*
  gleeful *adj* ▷ **glee**
  gleefully *adv* ▷ **glee**
  glees *n* ▷ **glee**
glen *n* (*pl* **-s**) deep narrow valley, esp. in
Scotland
  glens *n* ▷ **glen**
glib *adj* (**-bber, -bbest**) fluent but insincere or
superficial > **glibly** *adv* > **glibness** *n* (*pl* **-es**)
  glibber *adj* ▷ **glib**
  glibbest *adj* ▷ **glib**
  glibly *adv* ▷ **glib**
  glibness *n* ▷ **glib**
  glibnesses *n* ▷ **glib**
glide *v* (**-des, -ding, -ded**) move easily and
smoothly ▶ *n* (*pl* **-s**) smooth easy movement
  glided *v* ▷ **glide**
glider *n* (AUST) flying phalanger
  gliders *n* ▷ **glider**
  glides *n* ▷ **glide**
gliding *n* sport of flying gliders ▶ *v* ▷ **glide**
glimmer *v* (**-s, -ing, -ed**) shine faintly, flicker
▶ *n* (*pl* **-s**) faint gleam
  glimmered *v* ▷ **glimmer**
  glimmering *v* ▷ **glimmer**
  glimmers *v*, *n* ▷ **glimmer**
glimpse *n* (*pl* **-s**) brief or incomplete view ▶ *v*
(**-ses, -sing, -sed**) catch a glimpse of
  glimpsed *v* ▷ **glimpse**

glimpses *n*, *v* ▷ **glimpse**
glimpsing *v* ▷ **glimpse**
glint *v* (**-s, -ing, -ed**) gleam brightly ▶ *n* (*pl* **-s**)
bright gleam
  glinted *v* ▷ **glint**
  glinting *v* ▷ **glint**
  glints *v*, *n* ▷ **glint**
glissando *n* (*pl* **-dos**) (MUSIC) slide between
two notes in which all intermediate notes
are played
  glissandos *n* ▷ **glissando**
glisten *v* (**-s, -ing, -ed**) gleam by reflecting light
  glistened *v* ▷ **glisten**
  glistening *v* ▷ **glisten**
  glistens *v* ▷ **glisten**
glitch *n* (*pl* **-es**) small problem that stops
something from working properly
  glitches *n* ▷ **glitch**
glitter *v* (**-s, -ing, -ed**) shine with bright flashes
▶ *n* (*pl* **-s**) sparkle or brilliance
  glittered *v* ▷ **glitter**
  glittering *v* ▷ **glitter**
  glitters *v*, *n* ▷ **glitter**
gloaming *n* (*pl* **-s**) (SCOT) (*poetic*) twilight
  gloamings *n* ▷ **gloaming**
gloat *v* (**-s, -ing, -ed**) regard one's own good
fortune or the misfortune of others with
smug or malicious pleasure
  gloated *v* ▷ **gloat**
  gloating *v* ▷ **gloat**
  gloats *v* ▷ **gloat**
glob *n* (*pl* **-s**) rounded mass of thick fluid
global *adj* worldwide > **globally** *adv*
globalization *n* (*pl* **-s**) process by which
a company, etc., expands to operate
internationally
  globalizations *n* ▷ **globalization**
  globally *adv* ▷ **global**
globe *n* (*pl* **globes**) sphere with a map of the
earth on it
  globes *n* ▷ **globe**
globetrotter *n* habitual worldwide traveller
> **globetrotting** *adj*, *n* (*pl* **-s**)
  globetrotters *n* ▷ **globetrotter**
  globetrotting *n* ▷ **globetrotter**
  globetrottings *n* ▷ **globetrotter**
  globs *n* ▷ **glob**
  globular *adj* ▷ **globule**
globule *n* (*pl* **-s**) small round drop > **globular** *adj*
  globules *n* ▷ **globule**
glockenspiel *n* (*pl* **-s**) percussion instrument
consisting of small metal bars played with
hammers
  glockenspiels *n* ▷ **glockenspiel**
gloom *n* (*pl* **glooms**) melancholy or depression

> **gloomy** *adj* (-mier, -miest) > **gloomily** *adv*
gloomier *adj* ▷ **gloom**
gloomiest *adj* ▷ **gloom**
gloomily *adv* ▷ **gloom**
glooms *n* ▷ **gloom**
gloomy *adj* ▷ **gloom**
gloried *v* ▷ **glory**
glories *n*, *v* ▷ **glory**
glorification *n* ▷ **glorify**
glorifications *n* ▷ **glorify**
glorified *v* ▷ **glorify**
glorifies *v* ▷ **glorify**
glorify *v* (-fies, -fying, -fied) make (something) seem more worthy than it is > **glorification** *n* (*pl* -s)
glorifying *v* ▷ **glorify**
glorious *adj* brilliantly beautiful > **gloriously** *adv*
gloriously *adv* ▷ **glorious**
glory *n* (*pl* -ries) praise or honour ▶ *v* (-ries, -rying, -ried) (*foll. by* **in**) triumph or exalt
glorying *v* ▷ **glory**
gloss[1] *n* (*pl* -es) surface shine or lustre
gloss[2] *n* (*pl* -es) explanatory comment added to the text of a book ▶ *v* (-es, -ing, -ed) add glosses to
glossaries *n* ▷ **glossary**
glossary *n* (*pl* -ries) list of special or technical words with definitions
glossed *v* ▷ **gloss**[2]
glosses *n*, *v* ▷ **gloss**[1, 2]
glossier *adj* ▷ **glossy**
glossiest *adj* ▷ **glossy**
glossily *adv* ▷ **glossy**
glossiness *n* ▷ **glossy**
glossinesses *n* ▷ **glossy**
glossing *v* ▷ **gloss**[2]
glossy *adj* (-ssier, -ssiest) smooth and shiny > **glossily** *adv* > **glossiness** *n* (*pl* -es)
glottal *adj* of the glottis
glottides *n* ▷ **glottis**
glottis *n* (*pl* -tises, -tides) vocal cords and the space between them
glottises *n* ▷ **glottis**
glove *n* (*pl* -s) covering for the hand with individual sheaths for each finger and the thumb
gloved *adj* covered by a glove or gloves
gloves *n* ▷ **glove**
glow *v* (-s, -ing, -ed) emit light and heat without flames ▶ *n* (*pl* -s) glowing light
glowed *v* ▷ **glow**
glower [rhymes with **power**] *v* (-s, -ing, -ed) ▶ *n* (*pl* -s) scowl
glowered *v* ▷ **glower**

glowering *v* ▷ **glower**
glowers *v*, *n* ▷ **glower**
glowing *v* ▷ **glow**
glows *v*, *n* ▷ **glow**
glowworm *n* (*pl* -s) insect giving out a green light
glowworms *n* ▷ **glowworm**
gloxinia *n* (*pl* -s) tropical plant with large bell-shaped flowers
gloxinias *n* ▷ **gloxinia**
glucose *n* (*pl* -s) kind of sugar found in fruit
glucoses *n* ▷ **glucose**
glue *n* (*pl* **glues**) natural or synthetic sticky substance used as an adhesive ▶ *v* (**glues, gluing** *or* **glueing, glued**) fasten with glue > **gluey** *adj*
glued *v* ▷ **glue**
glueing *v* ▷ **glue**
glues *n*, *v* ▷ **glue**
gluey *adj* ▷ **glue**
gluier *adj* ▷ **glue**
gluiest *adj* ▷ **glue**
gluing *v* ▷ **glue**
glum *adj* (-mmer, -mmest) sullen or gloomy > **glumly** *adv*
glumly *adv* ▷ **glum**
glummer *adj* ▷ **glum**
glummest *adj* ▷ **glum**
glut *n* (*pl* -s) excessive supply ▶ *v* (-s, -tting, -tted) oversupply
gluten [gloo-ten] *n* (*pl* -s) protein found in cereal grain
glutens *n* ▷ **gluten**
glutinous [gloo-tin-uss] *adj* sticky or gluey
gluts *n*, *v* ▷ **glut**
glutted *v* ▷ **glut**
glutting *v* ▷ **glut**
glutton *n* (*pl* -s) greedy person > **gluttonous** *adj* > **gluttony** *n* (*pl* -nies)
gluttonies *n* ▷ **glutton**
gluttonous *adj* ▷ **glutton**
gluttons *n* ▷ **glutton**
gluttony *n* ▷ **glutton**
glycerine, glycerin *n* (*pl* -s) colourless sweet liquid used widely in chemistry and industry
glycerines *n* ▷ **glycerine**
glycerins *n* ▷ **glycerine**
glycerol [gliss-ser-ol] *n* (*pl* -s) ▷ **glycerine**
glycerols *n* ▷ **glycerol**
gnarled *adj* rough, twisted, and knobbly
gnash *v* (-es, -ing, -ed) grind (the teeth) together in anger or pain
gnashed *v* ▷ **gnash**
gnashes *v* ▷ **gnash**
gnashing *v* ▷ **gnash**

gnat *n* (*pl* **-s**) small biting two-winged fly
  gnats *n* ▷ **gnat**
gnaw *v* (**-s, -ing, -ed** *or* **gnawn**) bite or chew
  steadily
  gnawed *v* ▷ **gnaw**
  gnaws *v* ▷ **gnaw**
gneiss *n* (*pl* **-es**) coarse-grained metamorphic
  rock
  gneisses *n* ▷ **gneiss**
gnome *n* (*pl* **-s**) imaginary creature like a little
  old man
  gnomes *n* ▷ **gnome**
gnomic [no-mik] *adj* of pithy sayings
gnu [noo] *n* (*pl* **-s**) oxlike S African antelope
  gnus *n* ▷ **gnu**
go *v* (**going, went, gone**) move to or from a
  place (*pl* **gos**) ▸ *n* attempt
goad *v* (**-s, -ing, -ed**) provoke (someone) to
  take some kind of action, usu. in anger ▸ *n* (*pl*
  -s) spur or provocation
  goaded *v* ▷ **goad**
  goading *v* ▷ **goad**
  goads *v*, *n* ▷ **goad**
goal *n* (*pl* **-s**) (SPORT) posts through which
  the ball or puck has to be propelled to
  score
goalie *n* (*pl* **-s**) (*Informal*) goalkeeper
  goalies *n* ▷ **goalie**
goalkeeper *n* (*pl* **-s**) player whose task is to
  stop shots entering the goal
  goalkeepers *n* ▷ **goalkeeper**
goalpost (*pl* **-s**) *n* one of the two posts marking
  the limit of a goal
  goalposts *n* ▷ **goalpost**
  goals *n* ▷ **goal**
goanna *n* (*pl* **-s**) large Australian lizard
  goannas *n* ▷ **goanna**
goat *n* (*pl* **-s**) sure-footed ruminant animal
  with horns
goatee *n* (*pl* **-s**) pointed tuftlike beard
  goatees *n* ▷ **goatee**
  goats *n* ▷ **goat**
gob *n* (*pl* **-s**) lump of a soft substance (BRIT,
  AUST & NZ)
gobbet *n* (*pl* **-s**) lump, esp. of food
  gobbets *n* ▷ **gobbet**
gobble¹ *v* (**-les, -ling, -led**) eat hastily and
  greedily
gobble² *n* (*pl* **-s**) rapid gurgling cry of the
  male turkey ▸ *v* (**-les, -ling, -led**) make this
  noise
  gobbled *v* ▷ **gobble¹·²**
  gobbledegooks *n* ▷ **gobbledegook**
  gobbledygooks *n* ▷ **gobbledegook**
  gobbles *v*, *n* ▷ **gobble¹·²**

gobbledegook, gobbledygook *n* (*pl* **-s**)
  unintelligible (official) language or jargon
  gobbling *v* ▷ **gobble¹·²**
  gobies *n* ▷ **goby**
goblet *n* (*pl* **-s**) drinking cup without handles
  goblets *n* ▷ **goblet**
goblin *n* (*pl* **-s**) (in folklore) small malevolent
  creature
  goblins *n* ▷ **goblin**
  gobs *n* ▷ **gob**
goby *n* (*pl* **-by, -bies**) small spiny-finned
  fish
god *n* (*pl* **-s**) spirit or being worshipped as
  having supernatural power
  > **godlike** *adj*
godchild *n* (*pl* **-s**) child for whom a person
  stands as godparent
  > **goddaughter** *n* (*pl* **-s**)
  > **godson** *n* (*pl* **-s**)
  goddaughter *n* ▷ **godchild**
  goddaughters *n* ▷ **godchild**
goddess *n fem* (*pl* **-es**) female god
  goddesses *n* ▷ **goddess**
godetia *n* (*pl* **-s**) plant with showy flowers
  godetias *n* ▷ **godetia**
godfather *n* (*pl* **-s**) male godparent
  > **godmother** *n* (*pl* **-s**)
  godfathers *n* ▷ **godfather**
godforsaken *adj* desolate or dismal
  godlier *adj* ▷ **godly**
  godliest *adj* ▷ **godly**
  godlike *adj* ▷ **god**
  godliness *n* ▷ **godly**
  godlinesses *n* ▷ **godly**
godly *adj* (**-lier, -liest**) devout or pious
  > **godliness** *n* (*pl* **-es**)
  godmother *n* ▷ **godfather**
  godmothers *n* ▷ **godfather**
godparent *n* (*pl* **-s**) person who promises at
  a child's baptism to bring the child up as a
  Christian
  godparents *n* ▷ **godparent**
  gods *n* ▷ **god**
godsend *n* (*pl* **-s**) something unexpected but
  welcome
  godsends *n* ▷ **godsend**
  godson *n* ▷ **godchild**
  godsons *n* ▷ **godchild**
gogga *n* (*pl* **-s**) (S AFR) (*Informal*) any small insect
  goggas *n* ▷ **gogga**
goggle *v* (**-les, -ling, -led**) (of the eyes) bulge
  goggled *v* ▷ **goggle**
goggles *pl n* protective spectacles ▸ *v* ▷ **goggle**
  goggling *v* ▷ **goggle**
going *n* (*pl* **-s**) condition of the ground for

walking or riding over ▸ *adj* thriving ▸ *v* ▷ **go**
goings *n* ▷ **going**
goitre [**goy**-ter] *n* (*pl* -**s**) swelling of the thyroid gland in the neck
  goitres *n* ▷ **goitre**
gold *n* (*pl* -**s**) yellow precious metal ▸ *adj* made of gold
goldcrest *n* (*pl* -**s**) small bird with a yellow crown
  goldcrests *n* ▷ **goldcrest**
golden *adj* made of gold
goldfinch *n* (*pl* -**es**) kind of finch, the male of which has yellow-and-black wings
  goldfinches *n* ▷ **goldfinch**
goldfish *n* (*pl* -**es**) orange fish kept in ponds or aquariums
  goldfishes *n* ▷ **goldfish**
  golds *n* ▷ **gold**
golf *n* (*pl* -**s**) outdoor game in which a ball is struck with clubs into a series of holes ▸ *v* (-**s**, -**ing**, -**ed**) play golf > **golfer** *n* (*pl* -**s**)
  golfed *v* ▷ **golf**
  golfer *n* ▷ **golf**
  golfers *n* ▷ **golf**
  golfing *v* ▷ **golf**
  golfs *n*, *v* ▷ **golf**
golliwog *n* (*pl* -**s**) soft black-faced doll
  golliwogs *n* ▷ **golliwog**
gonad *n* (*pl* -**s**) organ producing reproductive cells, such as a testicle or ovary
  gonads *n* ▷ **gonad**
gondola *n* (*pl* -**s**) long narrow boat used in Venice
  gondolas *n* ▷ **gondola**
gondolier *n* (*pl* -**s**) person who propels a gondola
  gondoliers *n* ▷ **gondoliers**
  gone *v* ▷ **go**
goner *n* (*pl* -**s**) (*Informal*) person or thing beyond help or recovery
  goners *n* ▷ **goner**
gong *n* (*pl* -**s**) rimmed metal disc that produces a note when struck
  gongs *n* ▷ **gong**
gonorrhoea [gon-or-**ree**-a] *n* (*pl* -**s**) venereal disease with a discharge from the genitals
  gonorrhoeas *n* ▷ **gonorrhoea**
good *adj* (**better**, **best**) giving pleasure ▸ *n* benefit ▸ *pl* merchandise > **goodness** *n* (*pl* -**es**)
goodbye *interj*, *n* (*pl* -**s**) expression used on parting
  goodbyes *n* ▷ **goodbye**
  goodies *n* ▷ **goody**
goodly *adj* considerable
  goodness *n* ▷ **good**

goodnesses *n* ▷ **good**
goodwill *n* (*pl* -**s**) kindly feeling
  goodwills *n* ▷ **goodwill**
goody *n* (*pl* -**dies**) (*Informal*) hero in a book or film
gooey *adj* (**gooier**, **gooiest**) (*Informal*) sticky and soft
goof (*Informal*) *n* (*pl* -**s**) mistake ▸ *v* (-**s**, -**ing**, -**ed**) make a mistake
  goofed *v* ▷ **goof**
  goofing *v* ▷ **goof**
  goofs *n*, *v* ▷ **goof**
  googlies *n* ▷ **googly**
googly *n* (*pl* -**lies**) (CRICKET) ball that spins unexpectedly from off to leg on the bounce
  gooier *adj* ▷ **gooey**
  gooiest *adj* ▷ **gooey**
goon *n* (*pl* -**s**) (*Informal*) stupid person
  goons *n* ▷ **goon**
goose *n* (*pl* **geese**) web-footed bird like a large duck
  gooseberries *n* ▷ **gooseberry**
gooseberry *n* (*pl* -**ries**) edible yellowy-green berry
gopher [**go**-fer] *n* (*pl* -**s**) American burrowing rodent
  gophers *n* ▷ **gopher**
gore¹ *n* (*pl* -**s**) blood from a wound
gore² *v* (-**res**, -**ring**, -**red**) pierce with horns
  gored *v* ▷ **gore²**
  gores *n*, *v* ▷ **gore¹, ²**
gorge *n* (*pl* -**s**) deep narrow valley ▸ *v* (-**ges**, -**ging**, -**ged**) eat greedily
  gorged *v* ▷ **gorge**
gorgeous *adj* strikingly beautiful or attractive (*Informal*) > **gorgeously** *adv*
  gorgeously *adv* ▷ **gorgeous**
  gorges *n*, *v* ▷ **gorge**
  gorging *v* ▷ **gorge**
gorgon *n* (*pl* -**s**) terrifying or repulsive woman
  gorgons *n* ▷ **gorgon**
  gorier *adj* ▷ **gory**
  goriest *adj* ▷ **gory**
gorilla *n* (*pl* -**s**) largest of the apes, found in Africa
  gorillas *n* ▷ **gorilla**
  goring *v* ▷ **gore²**
gormless *adj* (*Informal*) stupid
gorse *n* (*pl* -**s**) prickly yellow-flowered shrub
  gorses *n* ▷ **gorse**
gory *adj* (-**rier**, -**riest**) horrific or bloodthirsty
  gos *n* ▷ **go**
goshawk *n* (*pl* -**s**) large hawk
  goshawks *n* ▷ **goshawk**
gosling *n* (*pl* -**s**) young goose

goslings _n_ ▷ **gosling**

gospel _n_ (_pl_ -**s**) any of the first four books of the New Testament

gospels _n_ ▷ **gospel**

gossamer _n_ (_pl_ -**s**) very fine fabric

gossamers _n_ ▷ **gossamer**

gossip _n_ (_pl_ -**s**) idle talk, esp. about other people ▶ _v_ (-**s, -ing, -ed**) engage in gossip ▷ **gossipy** _adj_ (-**ier, -iest**)

gossiped _v_ ▷ **gossip**

gossipier _adj_ ▷ **gossip**

gossipiest _adj_ ▷ **gossip**

gossiping _v_ ▷ **gossip**

gossips _n, v_ ▷ **gossip**

gossipy _adj_ ▷ **gossip**

got _v_ ▷ **get**

gouache _n_ (_pl_ -**s**) (painting using) watercolours mixed with glue

gouaches _n_ ▷ **gouache**

gouge [gowj] _v_ (-**ges, -ging, -ged**) scoop or force out ▶ _n_ (_pl_ -**s**) hole or groove

gouged _v_ ▷ **gouge**

gouges _v, n_ ▷ **gouge**

gouging _v_ ▷ **gouge**

goulash [goo-lash] _n_ (_pl_ -**es**) rich stew seasoned with paprika

goulashes _n_ ▷ **goulash**

gourd [goord] _n_ (_pl_ -**s**) fleshy fruit of a climbing plant

gourds _n_ ▷ **gourd**

gourmand [goor-mand] _n_ (_pl_ -**s**) person who is very keen on food and drink

gourmands _n_ ▷ **gourmand**

gourmet [goor-may] _n_ (_pl_ -**s**) connoisseur of food and drink

gourmets _n_ ▷ **gourmet**

gout [gowt] _n_ (_pl_ -**s**) disease causing inflammation of the joints

gouts _n_ ▷ **gout**

govern _v_ (-**s, -ing, -ed**) rule, direct, or control ▷ **governable** _adj_

governable _adj_ ▷ **govern**

governance _n_ (_pl_ -**s**) governing

governances _n_ ▷ **governance**

governed _v_ ▷ **govern**

governess _n_ (_pl_ -**es**) woman teacher in a private household

governesses _n_ ▷ **governess**

governing _v_ ▷ **govern**

government _n_ (_pl_ -**s**) executive policy-making body of a state ▷ **governmental** _adj_

governmental _adj_ ▷ **government**

governments _n_ ▷ **government**

governor _n_ (_pl_ -**s**) official governing a province or state

governors _n_ ▷ **governor**

governs _v_ ▷ **govern**

gown _n_ (_pl_ -**s**) woman's long formal dress

gowns _n_ ▷ **gown**

goy _n_ (_pl_ -**yim, -ys**) (_Slang_) Jewish word for a non-Jew

goyim _n_ ▷ **goy**

goys _n_ ▷ **goy**

> **gox** _n_ (**goxes**). Gox is a short word meaning gaseous oxygen. This unusual word can come in very useful, especially if you can use it to hit a bonus square. Gox scores 11 points.
> **goy** _n_ (**goyim**) or (**goys**). Goy is a Yiddish word for someone who isn't Jewish. For a short word, this earns you a reasonable number of points, and the two plural forms can come in useful too. Goy scores 7 points.

grab _v_ (-**s, -bbing, -bbed**) grasp suddenly, snatch ▶ _n_ sudden snatch

grabbed _v_ ▷ **grab**

grabbing _v_ ▷ **grab**

grabs _v_ ▷ **grab**

grace _n_ (_pl_ -**s**) beauty and elegance ▶ _v_ (-**ces, -cing, -ced**) add grace to ▷ **graceful** _adj_ ▷ **gracefully** _adv_ ▷ **graceless** _adj_

graced _v_ ▷ **grace**

graceful _adj_ ▷ **grace**

gracefully _adv_ ▷ **grace**

graceless _adj_ ▷ **grace**

graces _n, v_ ▷ **grace**

gracing _v_ ▷ **grace**

gracious _adj_ kind and courteous ▷ **graciously** _adv_

graciously _adv_ ▷ **gracious**

gradation _n_ (_pl_ -**s**) (stage in) a series of degrees or steps

gradations _n_ ▷ **gradation**

grade _n_ (_pl_ -**s**) place on a scale of quality, rank, or size ▶ _v_ (-**des, -ding, -ded**) arrange in grades

graded _v_ ▷ **grade**

grades _n, v_ ▷ **grade**

gradient _n_ (_pl_ -**s**) (degree of) slope

gradients _n_ ▷ **gradient**

grading _v_ ▷ **grade**

gradual _adj_ occurring, developing, or moving in small stages ▷ **gradually** _adv_

gradually _adv_ ▷ **gradual**

graduate _v_ (-**tes, -ting, -ted**) receive a degree or diploma ▶ _n_ (_pl_ -**s**) holder of a degree ▷ **graduation** _n_ (_pl_ -**s**)

graduated v ▷ **graduate**
graduates v, n ▷ **graduate**
graduating v ▷ **graduate**
graduation n ▷ **graduate**
graduations n ▷ **graduate**
graffiti [graf-**fee**-tee] pl n words or drawings scribbled or sprayed on walls etc.
graft[1] n (pl -s) surgical transplant of skin or tissue ▶ v (-s, -ing, -ed) transplant (living tissue) surgically
graft[2] (BRIT) (Informal) n hard work ▶ v work hard > **grafter** n (pl -s)
grafted v ▷ **graft**[1, 2]
grafter n ▷ **graft**
grafters n ▷ **graft**
grafting v ▷ **graft**[1, 2]
grafts n, v ▷ **graft**[1, 2]
grain n (pl -s) seedlike fruit of a cereal plant > **grainy** adj (-ier, -iest)
grainier adj ▷ **grain**
grainiest adj ▷ **grain**
grains n ▷ **grain**
grainy adj ▷ **grain**
gram, gramme n (pl -s) metric unit of mass equal to one thousandth of a kilogram
grammar n (pl -s) branch of linguistics dealing with the form, function, and order of words > **grammarian** n (pl -s)
grammarian n ▷ **grammar**
grammarians n ▷ **grammar**
grammars n ▷ **grammar**
grammatical adj according to the rules of grammar > **grammatically** adv
grammatically adv ▷ **grammatical**
gramophone n (pl -s) old-fashioned type of record player
gramophones n ▷ **gramophone**
grampus n (pl -es) dolphin-like mammal
grampuses n ▷ **grampus**
grams n ▷ **gram**
gran n (pl -s) (BRIT, AUST & NZ) (Informal) grandmother
granaries n ▷ **granary**
granary n (pl -ries) storehouse for grain
grand adj large or impressive, imposing ▶ n (pl -s) (Slang) thousand pounds or dollars
grandchild n (pl -children) child of one's child
grandchildren n ▷ **grandchild**
granddaughter n (pl -s) female grandchild
granddaughters n ▷ **granddaughter**
grandee n (pl -s) person of high station
grandees n ▷ **grandee**
grandeur n (pl -s) magnificence
grandeurs n ▷ **grandeur**
grandfather n (pl -s) male grandparent

grandfathers n ▷ **grandfather**
grandiloquences n ▷ **grandiloquent**
grandiloquent adj using pompous language > **grandiloquence** n (pl -s)
grandiloquence n ▷ **grandiloquent**
grandiose adj imposing > **grandiosity** n (pl -ties)
grandiosities n ▷ **grandiose**
grandiosity n ▷ **grandiose**
grandmother n (pl -s) female grandparent
grandmothers n ▷ **grandmother**
grandparent n (pl -s) parent of one's parent
grandparents n ▷ **grandparent**
grands n ▷ **grand**
grandson n (pl -s) male grandchild
grandsons n ▷ **grandson**
grandstand n (pl -s) terraced block of seats giving the best view at a sports ground
grandstands n ▷ **grandstand**
grange n (pl -s) (BRIT) country house with farm buildings
granges n ▷ **grange**
granite [gran-nit] n (pl -s) very hard igneous rock often used in building
granites n ▷ **granite**
grannies n ▷ **granny**
granny, grannie n (pl -nies) (Informal) grandmother
grans n ▷ **gran**
grant v (-s, -ing, -ed) consent to fulfil (a request) ▶ n (pl -s) sum of money provided by a government for a specific purpose, such as education
granted v ▷ **grant**
granting v ▷ **grant**
grants v, n ▷ **grant**
granular adj of or like grains
granulated adj (of sugar) in the form of coarse grains
granule n (pl -s) small grain
granules n ▷ **granule**
grape n (pl -s) small juicy green or purple berry, eaten raw or used to produce wine, raisins, currants, or sultanas
grapefruit n (pl -s) large round yellow citrus fruit
grapefruits n ▷ **grapefruit**
grapes n ▷ **grape**
grapevine n (pl -s) grape-bearing vine
grapevines n ▷ **grapevine**
graph n (pl -s) drawing showing the relation of different numbers or quantities plotted against a set of axes
graphic adj vividly descriptive > **graphically** adv

graphically *adv* ▷ **graphic**
graphics *pl n* diagrams, graphs, etc., esp. as used on a television programme or computer screen
graphite *n* (*pl* -s) soft black form of carbon, used in pencil leads
  graphites *n* ▷ **graphite**
  graphologies *n* ▷ **graphology**
  graphologist *n* ▷ **graphology**
  graphologists *n* ▷ **graphology**
graphology *n* (*pl* -gies) study of handwriting > **graphologist** *n* (*pl* -s)
  graphs *n* ▷ **graph**
grapnel *n* (*pl* -s) device with several hooks, used to grasp or secure things
  grapnels *n* ▷ **grapnel**
grapple *v* (-les, -ling, -led) try to cope with (something difficult)
  grappled *v* ▷ **grapple**
  grapples *v* ▷ **grapple**
  grappling *v* ▷ **grapple**
grasp *v* (-s, -ing, -ed) grip something firmly ▶ *n* (*pl* -s) grip or clasp
  grasped *v* ▷ **grasp**
grasping *adj* greedy or avaricious ▶ *v* ▷ **grasp**
  grasps *v, n* ▷ **grasp**
grass *n* (*pl* -es) common type of plant with jointed stems and long narrow leaves, including cereals and bamboo ▶ *v* (-es, -ing, -ed) cover with grass > **grassy** *adj* (-ssier, -ssiest)
  grassed *v* ▷ **grass**
  grasses *n, v* ▷ **grass**
grasshopper *n* (*pl* -s) jumping insect with long hind legs
  grasshoppers *n* ▷ **grasshopper**
  grassier *adj* ▷ **grass**
  grassiest *adj* ▷ **grass**
  grassing *v* ▷ **grass**
grassroots *adj* of the ordinary members of a group, rather than its leaders
  grassy *adj* ▷ **grass**
grate¹ *v* (-tes, -ting, -ted) rub into small bits on a rough surface > **grater** *n* (*pl* -s)
grate² *n* (*pl* -s) framework of metal bars for holding fuel in a fireplace
  grated *v* ▷ **grate**¹
grateful *adj* feeling or showing gratitude > **gratefully** *adv*
  gratefully *adv* ▷ **grateful**
  grater *n* ▷ **grate**¹
  graters *n* ▷ **grate**¹
  grates *v, n* ▷ **grate**¹, ²
  gratification *n* ▷ **gratify**
  gratifications *n* ▷ **gratify**

gratified *v* ▷ **gratify**
gratifies *v* ▷ **gratify**
gratify *v* (-fies, -fying, -fied) satisfy or please > **gratification** *n* (*pl* -s)
  gratifying *v* ▷ **gratify**
grating *n* (*pl* -s) framework of metal bars covering an opening ▶ *adj* harsh or rasping ▶ *v* ▷ **grate**¹
  gratings *n* ▷ **grating**
gratis *adv, adj* free, for nothing
gratitude *n* (*pl* -s) feeling of being thankful for a favour or gift
  gratitudes *n* ▷ **gratitude**
  gratuities *n* ▷ **gratuity**
gratuitous *adj* unjustified > **gratuitously** *adv*
  gratuitously *adv* ▷ **gratuitous**
gratuity *n* (*pl* -ies) money given for services rendered, tip
grave¹ *n* (*pl* -s) hole for burying a corpse
grave² *adj* causing concern > **gravely** *adv*
grave³ [rhymes with **halve**] *n* (*pl* -s) accent (`) over a vowel to indicate a special pronunciation
gravel *n* (*pl* -s) mixture of small stones and coarse sand
gravelled *adj* covered with gravel
  gravellier *adj* ▷ **gravelly**
  gravelliest *adj* ▷ **gravelly**
gravelly *adj* (-llier, -lliest) covered with gravel
  gravels *n* ▷ **gravel**
  gravely *adv* ▷ **grave**²
graven *adj* carved or engraved
  graves *n* ▷ **grave**¹, ³
gravestone *n* (*pl* -s) stone marking a grave
  gravestones *n* ▷ **gravestone**
graveyard *n* (*pl* -s) cemetery
  graveyards *n* ▷ **graveyard**
gravid [grav-id] *adj* (MED) pregnant
  gravies *n* ▷ **gravy**
gravitate *v* (-tes, -ting, -ted) be influenced or drawn towards > **gravitation** *n* (*pl* -s) > **gravitational** *adj*
  gravitated *v* ▷ **gravitate**
  gravitates *v* ▷ **gravitate**
  gravitating *v* ▷ **gravitate**
  gravitation *n* ▷ **gravitate**
  gravitational *adj* ▷ **gravitate**
  gravitations *n* ▷ **gravitate**
  gravities *n* ▷ **gravity**
gravity *n* (*pl* -ties) force of attraction of one object for another, esp. of objects to the earth
gravy *n* (*pl* -vies) juices from meat in cooking
  grawing *v* ▷ **gnaw**
  grawn *v* ▷ **gnaw**
gray *adj* (-er, -est) (CHIEFLY US) grey

grayer *adj* ▷ gray
grayest *adj* ▷ gray
grayling *n* (*pl* -s) fish of the salmon family
graylings *n* ▷ grayling
graze[1] *v* (-zes, -zing, -zed) feed on grass
graze[2] *v* (-zes, -zing, -zed) scratch or scrape the skin ▶ *n* (*pl* -s) slight scratch or scrape
grazed *v* ▷ graze[1, 2]
grazes *v, n* ▷ graze[1, 2]
grazing *v* ▷ graze[1, 2]
grease *n* (*pl* -s) soft melted animal fat ▶ *v* (-ses, -sing, -sed) apply grease to
greased *v* ▷ grease
greasepaint *n* (*pl* -s) theatrical make-up
greasepaints *n* ▷ greasepaint
greases *n, v* ▷ grease
greasier *adj* ▷ greasy
greasiest *adj* ▷ greasy
greasiness *n* ▷ greasy
greasinesses *n* ▷ greasy
greasing *v* ▷ grease
greasy *adj* (-sier, -siest) covered with or containing grease > **greasiness** *n* (*pl* -s)
great *adj* (-er, -est) large in size or number (*Informal*) > **greatly** *adv* > **greatness** *n* (*pl* -es)
greatcoat *n* (*pl* -s) heavy overcoat
greatcoats *n* ▷ greatcoat
greater *adj* ▷ great
greatest *adj* ▷ great
greatly *adv* ▷ great
greatness *n* ▷ great
greatnesses *n* ▷ great
greave *n* (*pl* -s) piece of armour for the shin
greaves *n* ▷ greave
grebe *n* (*pl* -s) diving water bird
grebes *n* ▷ grebe
greed *n* (*pl* -s) excessive desire for food, wealth, etc. > **greedy** *adj* (-dier, -diest) > **greedily** *adv* > **greediness** *n* (*pl* -es)
greedier *adj* ▷ greed
greediest *adj* ▷ greed
greedily *adv* ▷ greed
greediness *n* ▷ greed
greedinesses *n* ▷ greed
greeds *n* ▷ greed
greedy *adj* ▷ greed
green *adj* (-er, -est) of a colour between blue and yellow ▶ *n* (*pl* -s) colour between blue and yellow ▶ *pl* green vegetables ▶ *v* (-s, -ing, -ed) make or become green > **greenness** *n* (*pl* -es) > **greenish, greeny** *adj*
greened *v* ▷ green
greener *adj* ▷ green
greeneries *n* ▷ greenery
greenery *n* (*pl* -ries) vegetation

greenest *adj* ▷ green
greenfinch *n* (*pl* -es) European finch with dull green plumage in the male
greenfinches *n* ▷ greenfinch
greenflies *n* ▷ greenfly
greenfly *n* (*pl* -flies) green aphid, a common garden pest
greengage *n* (*pl* -s) sweet green plum
greengages *n* ▷ greengage
greengrocer *n* (*pl* -s) (BRIT) shopkeeper selling vegetables and fruit
greengrocer *n* ▷ greengrocers
greenhorn *n* (*pl* -s) (CHIEFLY US) novice
greenhorns *n* ▷ greenhorn
greenhouse *n* (*pl* -s) glass building for rearing plants
greenhouses *n* ▷ greenhouse
greening *v* ▷ green
greenish *adj* ▷ green
greenness *n* ▷ green
greennesses *n* ▷ green
greens *n, v* ▷ green
greenshank (*pl* -s) *n* large European sandpiper
greenshanks *n* ▷ greenshanks
greenstone *n* (*pl* -s) (NZ) type of green jade used for Maori ornaments
greenstones *n* ▷ greenstone
greeny *adj* ▷ green
greet *v* (-s, -ing, -ed) meet with expressions of welcome > **greeting** *n* (*pl* -s)
greeted *v* ▷ greet
greeting *v, n* ▷ greet
greetings *n* ▷ greet
greets *v* ▷ greet
gregarious *adj* fond of company
gremlin *n* (*pl* -s) imaginary being blamed for mechanical malfunctions
gremlins *n* ▷ gremlin
grenade *n* (*pl* -s) small bomb thrown by hand or fired from a rifle
grenades *n* ▷ grenade
grenadier *n* (*pl* -s) soldier of a regiment formerly trained to throw grenades
grenadiers *n* ▷ grenadier
grenadine [gren-a-deen] *n* (*pl* -s) syrup made from pomegranates
grenadines *n* ▷ grenadine
grevillea *n* (*pl* -s) any of various Australian evergreen trees and shrubs
grevilleas *n* ▷ grevillea
grew *v* ▷ grow
grey *adj* (-er, -est) of a colour between black and white ▶ *n* (*pl* -s) grey colour
greyer *adj* ▷ grey
greyest *adj* ▷ grey

greyhound *n* (*pl* **-s**) swift slender dog used in racing
  greyhounds *n* ▷ **greyhound**
greying *adj* (of hair) turning grey > **greyish** *adj* > **greyness** *n* (*pl* **-es**)
  greyish *adj* ▷ **grey**
  greyness *n* ▷ **grey**
  greynesses *n* ▷ **grey**
  greys *n* ▷ **grey**
grid *n* (*pl* **-s**) network of horizontal and vertical lines, bars, etc.
griddle *n* (*pl* **-s**) flat iron plate for cooking
  griddles *n* ▷ **griddle**
gridiron *n* (*pl* **-s**) frame of metal bars for grilling food
  gridirons *n* ▷ **gridiron**
gridlock *n* (*pl* **-s**) situation where traffic is not moving > **gridlocked** *adj*
  gridlocked *adj* ▷ **gridlock**
  gridlocks *n* ▷ **gridlock**
  grids *n* ▷ **grid**
grief *n* (*pl* **-s**) deep sadness
  griefs *n* ▷ **grief**
grievance (*pl* **-s**) *n* real or imaginary cause for complaint
  grievances *n* ▷ **grievances**
grieve *v* (**-ves, -ving, -ved**) (cause to) feel grief
  grieved *v* ▷ **grieve**
  grieves *v* ▷ **grieve**
  grieving *adj* ▷ **grieve**
grievous *adj* very severe or painful
griffin *n* (*pl* **-s**) mythical monster with an eagle's head and wings and a lion's body
  griffins *n* ▷ **griffin**
grill *n* (*pl* **-s**) device on a cooker that radiates heat downwards ▶ *v* (**-s, -ing, -ed**) cook under a grill
grille, grill *n* (*pl* **-s**) grating over an opening
  grilled *v* ▷ **grill**
  grilles *n* ▷ **grille**
grilling *n* (*pl* **-s**) relentless questioning ▶ *v* ▷ **grill**
  grillings *n* ▷ **grilling**
  grills[1] *n, v* ▷ **grill**
  grills[2] *n* ▷ **grille**
grilse [grillss] *n* (*pl* **-s**) salmon on its first return from the sea to fresh water
  grilses *n* ▷ **grilse**
grim *adj* (**-mmer, -mmest**) stern > **grimly** *adv* > **grimness** *n* (*pl* **-es**)
grimace *n* (*pl* **-s**) ugly or distorted facial expression of pain, disgust, etc. ▶ *v* (**-ces, -cing, -ced**) make a grimace
  grimaced *v* ▷ **grimace**
  grimaces *n, v* ▷ **grimace**

grimacing *v* ▷ **grimace**
grime *n* (*pl* **-s**) ingrained dirt ▶ *v* (**-mes, -ming, -med**) make very dirty > **grimy** *adj* (**-mier, -miest**)
  grimed *v* ▷ **grime**
  grimes *n, v* ▷ **grime**
  grimier *adj* ▷ **grime**
  grimiest *adj* ▷ **grime**
  griming *v* ▷ **grime**
  grimly *adv* ▷ **grim**
  grimmer *adj* ▷ **grim**
  grimmest *adj* ▷ **grim**
  grimness *n* ▷ **grim**
  grimnesses *n* ▷ **grim**
  grimy *adj* ▷ **grime**
grin *v* (**-s, -nning, -nned**) smile broadly, showing the teeth ▶ *n* (**-s**) broad smile
grind *v* (**-s, -ing, ground**) crush or rub to a powder ▶ *n* (*pl* **-s**) (*Informal*) hard work
  grinding *v* ▷ **grind**
  grinds *v, n* ▷ **grind**
grindstone *n* (*pl* **-s**) stone used for grinding
  grindstones *n* ▷ **grindstone**
  grinned *v* ▷ **grin**
  grinning *v* ▷ **grin**
  grins *v, n* ▷ **grin**
grip *n* (*pl* **-s**) firm hold or grasp (us) ▶ *v* (**-s, -pping, -pped**) grasp or hold tightly > **gripping** *adj*
gripe *v* (**-pes, -ping, -ped**) (*Informal*) complain persistently ▶ *n* (*pl* **-s**) (*Informal*) complaint
  griped *v* ▷ **gripe**
  gripes *v, n* ▷ **gripe**
  griping *v* ▷ **gripe**
  gripped *v* ▷ **grip**
  gripping *v, adj* ▷ **grip**
  grips *n, v* ▷ **grip**
  grislier *adj* ▷ **grisly**
  grisliest *adj* ▷ **grisly**
grisly *adj* (**-lier, -liest**) horrifying or ghastly
grist *n* (*pl* **-s**) grain for grinding
gristle *n* (*pl* **-s**) tough stringy animal tissue found in meat > **gristly** *adj* (**-lier, -liest**)
  gristles *n* ▷ **gristle**
  gristlier *adj* ▷ **gristle**
  gristliest *adj* ▷ **gristle**
  gristly *adj* ▷ **gristle**
  grists *n* ▷ **grist**
grit *n* (*pl* **-s**) rough particles of sand ▶ *pl* coarsely ground grain ▶ *v* (**-s, -tting, -tted**) spread grit on (an icy road etc.) > **gritty** *adj* (**-ttier, -ttiest**) > **grittiness** *n* (*pl* **-es**)
  grits *v* ▷ **grit**
  gritted *v* ▷ **grit**
  grittier *adj* ▷ **grit**

grittiest *adj* ▷ **grit**
grittiness *n* ▷ **grit**
grittinesses *n* ▷ **grit**
gritting *v* ▷ **grit**
gritty *adj* ▷ **grit**
grizzle *v* (**-les, -ling, -led**) (BRIT, AUST & NZ) (*Informal*) whine or complain
grizzled *adj* grey-haired ▶ *v* ▷ **grizzle**
grizzles *v* ▷ **grizzle**
grizzlies *n* ▷ **grizzly**
grizzling *v* ▷ **grizzle**
grizzly *n* (*pl* **-lies**) large American bear
groan *n* (*pl* **-s**) deep sound of grief or pain ▶ *v* (**-s, -ing, -ed**) utter a groan
groaned *v* ▷ **groan**
groaning *v* ▷ **groan**
groans *n, v* ▷ **groan**
groat *n* (*pl* **-s**) (HIST) fourpenny piece
groats *n* ▷ **groat**
grocer *n* (*pl* **-s**) shopkeeper selling foodstuffs
groceries *n* ▷ **grocery**
grocers *n* ▷ **grocer**
grocery *n* (*pl* **-ceries**) business or premises of a grocer ▶ *pl* goods sold by a grocer
grog *n* (*pl* **-s**) (BRIT, AUST & NZ) spirit, usu. rum, and water
groggier *adj* ▷ **groggy**
groggiest *adj* ▷ **groggy**
groggy *adj* (**-ggier, -ggiest**) (*Informal*) faint, shaky, or dizzy
grogs *n* ▷ **grog**
groin *n* (*pl* **-s**) place where the legs join the abdomen
groins *n* ▷ **groin**
grommet *n* (*pl* **-s**) ring or eyelet
grommets *n* ▷ **grommet**
groom *n* (*pl* **-s**) person who looks after horses ▶ *v* (**-s, -ing, -ed**) make or keep one's clothes and appearance neat and tidy
groomed *v* ▷ **groom**
grooming *v* ▷ **groom**
grooms *n, v* ▷ **groom**
groove *n* (*pl* **-s**) long narrow channel in a surface
grooves *n* ▷ **groove**
grope *v* (**-pes, -ping, -ped**) feel about or search uncertainly > **groping** *n* (*pl* **-s**)
groped *v* ▷ **grope**
gropes *v* ▷ **grope**
groping *v, n* ▷ **grope**
gropings *n* ▷ **grope**
gross *adj* flagrant ▶ *n* (*pl* **-es**) twelve dozen ▶ *v* (**-es, -ing, -ed**) make as total revenue before deductions > **grossly** *adv* > **grossness** *n* (*pl* **-es**)
grossed *v* ▷ **gross**

grosses *n, v* ▷ **gross**
grossing *v* ▷ **gross**
grossly *adv* ▷ **gross**
grossness *n* ▷ **gross**
grossnesses *n* ▷ **gross**
grotesque [grow-**tesk**] *adj* (**-quer, -quest**) strangely distorted ▶ *n* (*pl* **-s**) grotesque person or thing > **grotesquely** *adv*
grotesquely *adv* ▷ **grotesque**
grotesquer *adj* ▷ **grotesque**
grotesques *n* ▷ **grotesque**
grotesquest *adj* ▷ **grotesque**
grottier *adj* ▷ **grotty**
grottiest *adj* ▷ **grotty**
grotto *n* (*pl* **-ttoes, -ttos**) small picturesque cave
grottoes *n* ▷ **grotto**
grottos *n* ▷ **grotto**
grotty *adj* (**-ttier, -ttiest**) (*Informal*) nasty or in bad condition
grouch (*Informal*) *v* (**-es, -ing, -ed**) grumble or complain ▶ *n* (*pl* **-es**) person who is always complaining > **grouchy** *adj* (**-chier, -chiest**)
grouched *v* ▷ **grouch**
grouches *v, n* ▷ **grouch**
grouchier *adj* ▷ **grouch**
grouchiest *adj* ▷ **grouch**
grouching *v* ▷ **grouch**
grouchy *adj* ▷ **grouch**
ground[1] *n* (*pl* **-s**) surface of the earth ▶ *pl* enclosed land round a house ▶ *v* (**-s, -ing, -ed**) base or establish
ground[2] *v* ▷ **grind**
groundbreaking *adj* innovative
grounded *v* ▷ **ground**[1]
grounding *n* (*pl* **-s**) basic knowledge of a subject ▶ *v* ▷ **ground**[1]
groundings *n* ▷ **grounding**
groundless *adj* without reason
groundnut *n* (*pl* **-s**) peanut
groundnuts *n* ▷ **groundnut**
grounds *n, v* ▷ **ground**[1]
groundsheet *n* (*pl* **-s**) waterproof sheet put on the ground under a tent
groundsheets *n* ▷ **groundsheet**
groundsman *n* (*pl* **-men**) person employed to maintain a sports ground or park
groundsmen *n* ▷ **groundsman**
groundswell *n* (*pl* **-s**) rapidly developing general feeling or opinion
groundswells *n* ▷ **groundswell**
groundwork *n* (*pl* **-s**) preliminary work
groundworks *n* ▷ **groundwork**
group *n* (*pl* **-s**) number of people or things regarded as a unit ▶ *v* (**-s, -ing, -ed**) place or

form into a group
grouped v ▷ **group**
grouping v ▷ **group**
groups n, v ▷ **group**
grouse[1] n (pl -s) stocky game bird
grouse[2] v (-ses, -sing, -sed) grumble or
complain ▶ n (pl -s) complaint
groused v ▷ **grouse**[2]
grouses n, v ▷ **grouse**[1, 2]
grousing v ▷ **grouse**[2]
grout n (pl -s) thin mortar ▶ v (-s, -ing, -ed) fill
up with grout
grouted v ▷ **grout**
grouting v ▷ **grout**
grouts n, v ▷ **grout**
grove n (pl -s) small group of trees
grovel [grov-el] v (-s, -elling, -elled) behave
humbly in order to win a superior's favour
grovelled v ▷ **grovel**
grovelling v ▷ **grovel**
grovels v ▷ **grovel**
groves n ▷ **grove**
grow v (-s, growing, grew, grown) develop
physically
growing v ▷ **grow**
growl v (-s, -ing, -ed) make a low rumbling
sound ▶ n (pl -s) growling sound
growled v ▷ **growl**
growling v ▷ **growl**
growls v, n ▷ **growl**
grown v ▷ **grow**
grownup adj, n (pl -s) adult
grownups n ▷ **grownup**
grows v ▷ **grow**
growth n (pl -s) growing
growths n ▷ **growth**
groyne n (pl -s) wall built out from the shore to
control erosion
groynes n ▷ **groyne**
grub n (pl -s) legless insect larva ▶ v (-s, -bbing,
-bbed) search carefully for something by
digging or by moving things about
grubbed v ▷ **grub**
grubbier adj ▷ **grubby**
grubbiest adj ▷ **grubby**
grubbiness n ▷ **grubby**
grubbinesses n ▷ **grubby**
grubbing v ▷ **grub**
grubby adj (-bbier, -bbiest) dirty > **grubbiness**
n (pl -es)
grubs n, v ▷ **grub**
grudge v (-ges, -ging, -ged) be unwilling to
give or allow ▶ n (pl -s) resentment
grudged v ▷ **grudge**
grudges v, n ▷ **grudge**

grudging v ▷ **grudge**
gruel n (pl -s) thin porridge
gruelling adj exhausting or severe
gruels n ▷ **gruel**
gruesome adj (-er, -est) causing horror and
disgust
gruesomer adj ▷ **gruesome**
gruesomest adj ▷ **gruesome**
gruff adj (-er, -est) rough or surly in manner or
voice > **gruffly** adv > **gruffness** n (pl -es)
gruffer adj ▷ **gruff**
gruffest adj ▷ **gruff**
gruffly adv ▷ **gruff**
gruffness n ▷ **gruff**
gruffnesses n ▷ **gruff**
grumble v (-les, -ling, -led) complain ▶ n (pl -s)
complaint > **grumbler** n (pl -s) > **grumbling**
adj, n (pl -s)
grumbled v ▷ **grumble**
grumbler n ▷ **grumble**
grumblers n ▷ **grumble**
grumbles v, n ▷ **grumble**
grumbling v, n ▷ **grumble**
grumblings n ▷ **grumble**
grumpier adj ▷ **grumpy**
grumpiest adj ▷ **grumpy**
grumpily adv ▷ **grumpy**
grumpiness n ▷ **grumpy**
grumpinesses n ▷ **grumpy**
grumpy adj (-pier, -piest) bad-tempered
> **grumpily** adv > **grumpiness** n (pl -es)
grunge n (pl -s) style of rock music with a fuzzy
guitar sound
grunges n ▷ **grunge**
grunt v (-s, -ing, -ed) make a low short gruff
sound, like a pig ▶ n (pl -s) pig's sound
grunted v ▷ **grunt**
grunting v ▷ **grunt**
grunts v, n ▷ **grunt**
gryphon n (pl -s) ▷ **griffin**
gryphons n ▷ **gryphon**

> **gu** n (**gus**). A gu (also spelt **gju**) is a
> kind of violin from Shetland. This is
> one of only three two-letter words
> beginning with G, and so is a good one
> to remember. Gu scores 3 points.

guano [gwah-no] n (pl -nos) dried sea-bird
manure, used as fertilizer
guanos n ▷ **guano**
guarantee n (pl -s) formal assurance, esp. in
writing, that a product will meet certain
standards ▶ v (-s, -teeing, -teed) give a
guarantee
guaranteed v ▷ **guarantee**
guaranteeing v ▷ **guarantee**

guarantees *n*, *v* ▷ **guarantee**
guarantor *n* (*pl* **-s**) person who gives or is bound by a guarantee
guarantors *n* ▷ **guarantor**
guard *v* (**-s, -ing, -ed**) watch over to protect or to prevent escape ▶ *n* (*pl* **-s**) person or group that guards ▶ (**G-**) *pl* regiment with ceremonial duties
guarded *adj* cautious or noncommittal ▶ *v* ▷ **guard** > **guardedly** *adv*
guardedly *adv* ▷ **guarded**
guardian *n* (*pl* **-s**) keeper or protector > **guardianship** *n* (*pl* **-s**)
guardians *n* ▷ **guardian**
guardianship *n* ▷ **guardian**
guardianships *n* ▷ **guardian**
guarding *v* ▷ **guard**
guards *v*, *n* ▷ **guard**
guardsman *n* (*pl* **-s**) member of the Guards
guardsmen *n* ▷ **guardsman**
guava [gwah-va] *n* (*pl* **-s**) yellow-skinned tropical American fruit
guavas *n* ▷ **guava**
gudgeon *n* (*pl* **-s**) small freshwater fish
gudgeons *n* ▷ **gudgeon**
guerillas *n* ▷ **guerrilla**
guerrilla, guerilla *n* (*pl* **-s**) member of an unofficial armed force fighting regular forces
guerrillas *n* ▷ **guerrilla**
guess *v* (**-es, -ing, -ed**) estimate or draw a conclusion without proper knowledge ▶ *n* (*pl* **-es**) estimate or conclusion reached by guessing
guessed *v* ▷ **guess**
guesses *v*, *n* ▷ **guess**
guessing *v* ▷ **guess**
guesswork *n* (*pl* **-s**) process or results of guessing
guessworks *n* ▷ **guesswork**
guest *n* (*pl* **-s**) person entertained at another's house or at another's expense ▶ *v* (**-s, -ing, -ed**) appear as a visiting player or performer
guested *v* ▷ **guest**
guesthouse *n* (*pl* **-s**) boarding house
guesthouses *n* ▷ **guesthouse**
guesting *v* ▷ **guest**
guests *n*, *v* ▷ **guest**
guff *n* (*pl* **-s**) (BRIT, AUST & NZ) (*Slang*) nonsense
guffaw *n* (*pl* **-s**) crude noisy laugh ▶ *v* (**-s, -ing, -ed**) laugh in this way
guffawed *v* ▷ **guffaw**
guffawing *v* ▷ **guffaw**
guffaws *n*, *v* ▷ **guffaw**
guffs *n* ▷ **guff**
guidance *n* (*pl* **-s**) leadership, instruction, or advice
guidances *n* ▷ **guidance**
guide *n* (*pl* **-s**) person who conducts tour expeditions ▶ *v* (**-s, -ing, -ed**) act as a guide for
guided *v* ▷ **guide**
guideline *n* set principle for doing something
guidelines *n* ▷ **guideline**
guides *n*, *v* ▷ **guide**
guiding *v* ▷ **guide**
guild *n* (*pl* **-s**) organization or club
guilder *n* (*pl* **-s**) former monetary unit of the Netherlands
guilders *n* ▷ **guilder**
guilds *n* ▷ **guild**
guile [gile] *n* (*pl* **-s**) cunning or deceit > **guileful** *adj* > **guileless** *adj*
guileful *adj* ▷ **guile**
guileless *adj* ▷ **guile**
guiles *n* ▷ **guile**
guillemot [gil-lee-mot] *n* (*pl* **-s**) black-and-white diving sea bird of N hemisphere
guillemots *n* ▷ **guillemot**
guillotine *n* (*pl* **-s**) machine for beheading people ▶ *v* (**-s, -ing, -ed**) behead by guillotine
guillotined *v* ▷ **guillotine**
guillotines *n*, *v* ▷ **guillotine**
guillotining *v* ▷ **guillotine**
guilt *n* (*pl* **-s**) fact or state of having done wrong
guiltier *adj* ▷ **guilty**
guiltiest *adj* ▷ **guilty**
guiltily *adv* ▷ **guilty**
guiltless *adj* innocent
guilts *n* ▷ **guilt**
guilty *adj* (**-tier, -tiest**) responsible for an offence or misdeed > **guiltily** *adv*
guinea *n* (*pl* **-s**) former British monetary unit worth 21 shillings (1.05 pounds)
guineas *n* ▷ **guinea**
guise [rhymes with **size**] *n* (*pl* **-s**) false appearance
guises *n* ▷ **guise**
guitar *n* (*pl* **-s**) stringed instrument with a flat back and a long neck, played by plucking or strumming > **guitarist** *n*
guitarist *n* ▷ **guitar**
guitarists *n* ▷ **guitar**
guitars *n* ▷ **guitar**
gulch *n* (*pl* **-es**) (US) deep narrow valley
gulches *n* ▷ **gulch**
gulf *n* (*pl* **-s**) large deep bay
gulfs *n* ▷ **gulf**
gull *n* (*pl* **-s**) long-winged sea bird
gullet *n* (*pl* **-s**) muscular tube through which food passes from the mouth to the stomach
gullets *n* ▷ **gullet**

gullibilities n ▷ gullible
gullibility n ▷ gullible
gullible adj easily tricked > **gullibility** n (pl -ties)
gullies n ▷ gully
gulls n ▷ gull
gully n (pl -llies) channel cut by running water
gulp v (-s, -ing, -ed) swallow hastily ▶ n (pl -s)
gulping
gulped v ▷ gulp
gulping v ▷ gulp
gulps v, n ▷ gulp
gum¹ n (pl -s) firm flesh in which the teeth are set
gum² n (pl -s) sticky substance obtained from certain trees ▶ v (-s, -mming, -mmed) stick with gum
gumboot n (pl -s) (CHIEFLY BRIT) Wellington boot
gumboots n ▷ gumboot
gumdrop n (pl -s) hard jelly-like sweet
gumdrops n ▷ gumdrop
gummed v ▷ gum²
gummier adj ▷ gummy¹, ²
gummiest adj ▷ gummy¹, ²
gumming v ▷ gum²
gummy¹ adj (-mmier, -mmiest) toothless
gummy² adj (-mmier, -mmiest) sticky
gumption n (pl -s) (Informal) resourcefulness
gumptions n ▷ gumption
gums n ▷ gum¹, ²
gun n (pl -s) weapon with a metal tube from which missiles are fired by explosion ▶ v (-s, -nning, -nned) cause (an engine) to run at high speed
gunboat n (pl -s) small warship
gunboats n ▷ gunboat
gunge n (pl -s) (Informal) sticky unpleasant substance > **gungy** adj (-gier, -giest)
gunges n ▷ gunge
gungier adj ▷ gung
gungiest adj ▷ gung
gungy adj ▷ gung
gunman n (pl -men) armed criminal
gunmen n ▷ gunman
gunmetal n (pl -s) alloy of copper, tin, and zinc ▶ adj dark grey
gunmetals n ▷ gunmetal
gunned v ▷ gun
gunnel n ▷ gunwale
gunnels n ▷ gunwale
gunner n (pl -s) artillery soldier
gunneries n ▷ gunnery
gunners n ▷ gunner
gunnery n (pl -ries) use or science of large guns
gunnies n ▷ gunny

gunning v ▷ gun
gunny n (pl -ies) strong coarse fabric used for sacks
gunpowder n (pl -s) explosive mixture of potassium nitrate, sulphur, and charcoal
gunpowders n ▷ gunpowder
gunrunner n ▷ gunrunning
gunrunners n ▷ gunrunning
gunrunning n (pl -s) smuggling of guns and ammunition > **gunrunner** n (pl -s)
gunrunnings n ▷ gunrunning
guns n, v ▷ gun
gunshot n (pl -s) shot or range of a gun
gunshots n ▷ gunshot
gunwale, gunnel [gun-nel] n (pl -s) top of a ship's side
gunwales n ▷ gunwale
gunyah n (pl -s) (AUST) hut or shelter in the bush
gunyahs n ▷ gunyah
guppies n ▷ guppy
guppy n (pl -ppies) small colourful aquarium fish
gurgle v (-les, -ling, -led) ▶ n (pl -s) (make) a bubbling noise
gurgled v ▷ gurgle
gurgles v, n ▷ gurgle
gurgling v ▷ gurgle
guru n (pl -s) Hindu or Sikh religious teacher or leader
gurus n ▷ guru
gush v (-es, -ing, -ed) flow out suddenly and profusely ▶ n (pl -es) sudden copious flow
gushed v ▷ gush
gusher n (pl -s) spurting oil well
gushers n ▷ gusher
gushes v, n ▷ gush
gushing v ▷ gush
gusset n (pl -s) piece of material sewn into a garment to strengthen it
gussets n ▷ gusset
gust n (pl -s) sudden blast of wind ▶ v (-s, -ing, -ed) blow in gusts > **gusty** adj (-tier, -tiest)
gusted v ▷ gust
gustier adj ▷ gust
gustiest adj ▷ gust
gusting v ▷ gust
gusto n (pl -tos) enjoyment or zest
gustos n ▷ gusto
gusts n, v ▷ gust
gusty adj ▷ gust
gut n (pl -s) intestine (Informal) ▷ **catgut** ▶ pl internal organs ▶ v (-s, -tting, -tted) remove the guts from ▶ adj basic or instinctive
guts n ▷ gut
gutsier adj ▷ gutsy

gutsiest adj ▷ **gutsy**
gutsy adj (**-sier, -siest**) (Informal) courageous
gutted adj (BRIT, AUST & NZ) (Informal) disappointed and upset ▶ v ▷ **gut**
gutter n (pl **-s**) shallow channel for carrying away water from a roof or roadside ▶ v (**-s, -ing, -ed**) (of a candle) burn unsteadily, with wax running down the sides
guttered v ▷ **gutter**
guttering n material for gutters ▶ v ▷ **gutter**
gutters n, v ▷ **gutter**
guttersnipe n (pl **-s**) (BRIT) neglected slum child
guttersnipes n ▷ **guttersnipe**
gutting v ▷ **gut**
guttural adj (of a sound) produced at the back of the throat
guy[1] n (pl **-s**) (Informal) man or boy
guy[2] n (pl **-s**) rope or chain to steady or secure something
guys n ▷ **guy**[1, 2]
guzzle v (**-les, -ling, -led**) eat or drink greedily
guzzled v ▷ **guzzle**
guzzles v ▷ **guzzle**
guzzling v ▷ **guzzle**
gybe [jibe] v (**-bes, -bing, -bed**) (of a fore-and-aft sail) swing suddenly from one side to the other
gybed v ▷ **gybe**
gybes v ▷ **gybe**
gybing v ▷ **gybe**
gym n (pl **-s**) gymnasium
gymkhana [jim-kah-na] n (pl **-s**) horse-riding competition
gymkhanas n ▷ **gymkhana**
gymnasium n (pl **-s**) large room with equipment for physical training
gymnasiums n ▷ **gymnasium**
gymnast n (pl **-s**) expert in gymnastics
gymnastic n ▷ **gymnastics**
gymnastics pl n exercises to develop strength and agility > **gymnastic** adj
gymnasts n ▷ **gymnast**

gyms n ▷ **gym**
gynaecological adj ▷ **gynaecology**
gynaecologies n ▷ **gynaecology**
gynaecologist n ▷ **gynaecology**
gynaecologists n ▷ **gynaecology**
gynaecology [guy-nee-**kol**-la-jee] n (pl **-ies**) branch of medicine dealing with diseases and conditions specific to women > **gynaecological** adj > **gynaecologist** n (pl **-s**)

gyp n (**gyps, gypping, gyped**). Gyp is a slang word meaning to cheat or swindle. This word and its inflections can be very useful when there is a word ending in Y on the board. Gyp scores 9 points.

gypsies n ▷ **gypsy**
gypsophila n (pl **-s**) garden plant with small white flowers
gypsophilas n ▷ **gypsophila**
gypsum n (pl **-s**) chalklike mineral used to make plaster of Paris
gypsums n ▷ **gypsum**
gypsy n (pl **-sies**) member of a travelling people found throughout Europe
gyrate [jire-**rate**] v (**-tes, -ting, -ted**) rotate or spiral about a point or axis > **gyration** n (pl **-s**)
gyrated v ▷ **gyrate**
gyrates v ▷ **gyrate**
gyrating v ▷ **gyrate**
gyration n ▷ **gyrate**
gyrations n ▷ **gyrate**
gyratory adj gyrating
gyrocompass n (pl **-es**) compass using a gyroscope
gyrocompasses n ▷ **gyrocompass**
gyroscope [jire-oh-skohp] n (pl **-s**) disc rotating on an axis that can turn in any direction, so the disc maintains the same position regardless of the movement of the surrounding structure > **gyroscopic** adj
gyroscopes n ▷ **gyroscope**
gyroscopic adj ▷ **gyroscope**

Hh

H forms a two-letter word in front of every vowel except U (and you can make **uh** with U), making it a versatile tile when you want to form words in more than one direction. As H is worth 4 points on its own, you can earn some very high scores by doing this: even **ha, he, hi** and **ho** will give 5 points each. There are lots of good short words beginning with H, like **haw, hew, how, hay, hey** and **hoy** (9 each).

ha *interj*. Ha is a sound people make to express triumph or surprise. This gives a reasonable score for a two-letter word, and is a good one to form when making a longer word in another direction at the same time. Ha scores 5 points.

haberdasher *n* (*pl* -s) (BRIT, AUST & NZ) dealer in small articles used for sewing
> **haberdashery** *n* (*pl* -ries)
  haberdasheries *n* ▷ **haberdasher**
  haberdashers *n* ▷ **haberdasher**
  haberdashery *n* ▷ **haberdasher**
habit *n* (*pl* -s) established way of behaving
habitable *adj* fit to be lived in
habitat *n* (*pl* -s) natural home of an animal or plant
habitation *n* (*pl* -s) (occupation of) a dwelling place
  habitations *n* ▷ **habitation**
  habitats *n* ▷ **habitat**
  habits *n* ▷ **habit**
habitual *adj* done regularly and repeatedly
> **habitually** *adv*
  habitually *adv* ▷ **habitual**
habituate *v* (-tes, -ting, -ted) accustom
> **habituation** *n* (*pl* -s)
  habituated *v* ▷ **habituate**
  habituates *v* ▷ **habituate**
  habituating *v* ▷ **habituate**
  habituation *n* ▷ **habituate**
  habituations *n* ▷ **habituate**
habitué [hab-**it**-yew-ay] *n* (*pl* -s) frequent visitor to a place
  habitués *n* ▷ **habitué**
hacienda [hass-ee-**end**-a] *n* (*pl* -s) ranch or large estate in Latin America
  haciendas *n* ▷ **hacienda**
hack¹ *v* (-s, -ing, -ed) cut or chop violently (BRIT

, & NZ) (*Informal*)
hack² *n* (*pl* -s) (inferior) writer or journalist
  hacked *v* ▷ **hack¹**
hacker *n* (*pl* -s) (*Slang*) computer enthusiast, esp. one who breaks into the computer system of a company or government
  hackers *n* ▷ **hacker**
  hacking *v* ▷ **hack¹**
hackles *pl n* hairs on the neck and back of an animal
hackney *n* (*pl* -s) (BRIT) taxi
hackneyed *adj* (of a word or phrase) unoriginal and overused
  hackneys *n* ▷ **hackney**
  hacks *v* ▷ **hack¹** ▶ *n* ▷ **hack²**
hacksaw *n* (*pl* -s) small saw for cutting metal
  hacksaws *n* ▷ **hacksaw**
  had *v* ▷ **have**
haddock *n* (*pl* -s) edible sea fish of N Atlantic
  haddocks *n* ▷ **haddock**
  hadj *n* (*pl* -es) ▷ **hajj**
  hadjes *n* ▷ **hadj**
  haematologies *n* ▷ **haematology**
haematology *n* (*pl* -gies) study of blood and its diseases
haemoglobin [hee-moh-**globe**-in] *n* (*pl* -s) protein found in red blood cells which carries oxygen
  haemoglobins *n* ▷ **haemoglobin**
haemophilia [hee-moh-**fill**-lee-a] *n* (*pl* -s) hereditary illness in which the blood does not clot > **haemophiliac** *n* (*pl* -s)
  haemophiliac *n* ▷ **haemophilia**
  haemophiliacs *n* ▷ **haemophilia**
  haemophilias *n* ▷ **haemophilia**
haemorrhage [hem-or-ij] *n* (*pl* -ges) heavy bleeding ▶ *v* (-ges, -ging, -ged) bleed heavily
  haemorrhaged *v* ▷ **haemorrhage**
  haemorrhages *n*, *v* ▷ **haemorrhage**

haemorrhaging *v* ▷ **haemorrhage**
haemorrhoids [hem-or-oydz] *pl n* swollen
veins in the anus (*also* **piles**)
hafnium *n* (*pl* -s) (CHEM) metallic element
found in zirconium ores
hafniums *n* ▷ **hafnium**
haft *n* (*pl* -s) handle of an axe, knife, or dagger
hafts *n* ▷ **haft**
hag *n* (*pl* -s) ugly old woman
haggard *adj* looking tired and ill
haggis *n* (*pl* -es) Scottish dish made from
sheep's offal, oatmeal, suet, and seasonings,
boiled in a bag made from the sheep's
stomach
haggises *n* ▷ **haggis**
haggle *v* (-les, -ling, -led) bargain or wrangle
over a price
haggled *v* ▷ **haggle**
haggles *v* ▷ **haggle**
haggling *v* ▷ **haggle**
hagiographies *n* ▷ **hagiography**
hagiography *n* (*pl* -phies) writing about the
lives of the saints
hags *n* ▷ **hag**
hail[1] *n* (*pl* -s) (shower of) small pellets of ice
▶ *v* (-s, -ing, -ed) fall as or like hail > **hailstone**
n (*pl* -s)
hail[2] *v* (-s, -ing, -ed) call out to, greet
hailed *v* ▷ **hail**[1, 2]
hailing *v* ▷ **hail**[1, 2]
hails *v* ▷ **hail**[1, 2] ▶ *n* ▷ **hail**[1]
hailstone *n* ▷ **hail**[1]
hailstones *n* ▷ **hail**[1]
hair *n* (*pl* hairs) threadlike growth on the skin
hairclip *n* (*pl* -s) small bent metal hairpin
hairclips *n* ▷ **hairclip**
hairdo *n* (*pl* -s) (*Informal*) hairstyle
hairdos *n* ▷ **hairdo**
hairdresser *n* (*pl* -s) person who cuts and
styles hair
hairdressers *n* ▷ **hairdresser**
hairgrip *n* (BRIT) (*pl* -s) ▷ **hairclip**
hairgrips *n* ▷ **hairgrip**
hairier *adj* ▷ **hairy**
hairiest *adj* ▷ **hairy**
hairiness *n* ▷ **hairy**
hairinesses *n* ▷ **hairy**
hairline *n* (*pl* -s) edge of hair at the top of the
forehead ▶ *adj* very fine or narrow
hairlines *n* ▷ **hairline**
hairpin *n* (*pl* -s) U-shaped wire used to hold the
hair in place
hairpins *n* ▷ **hairpin**
hairs *n* ▷ **hair**
hairsplitting *n* (*pl* -s) ▶ *adj* making petty

distinctions
hairsplittings *n* ▷ **hairsplitting**
hairstyle *n* (*pl* -s) cut and arrangement of a
person's hair
hairstyles *n* ▷ **hairstyle**
hairy *adj* (-rier, -riest) covered with hair
> **hairiness** *n* (*pl* -es)

> **haj** *n*. Haj is the same as **hajj**. This is
> a very useful word, especially when
> there isn't much space on the board.
> Remember that this spelling doesn't
> have a plural form. Haj scores 13 points.

hajj *n* (*pl* -es) pilgrimage a Muslim makes to
Mecca
hajjes *n* ▷ **hajj**
haka *n* (*pl* -s) (NZ) ceremonial Maori dance with
chanting
hakas *n* ▷ **haka**
hake *n* (*pl* hakes) edible sea fish of N
hemisphere (AUST) ▷ **barracouta**
hakea [hah-kee-a] *n* (*pl* -s) Australian tree or
shrub with hard woody fruit
hakeas *n* ▷ **hakea**
hakes *n* ▷ **hake**
halal *n* (*pl* -s) meat from animals slaughtered
according to Muslim law
halals *n* ▷ **halal**
halberd *n* (*pl* -s) (HIST) spear with an axe blade
halberds *n* ▷ **halberd**
halcyon [hal-see-on] *adj* peaceful and happy
hale *adj* (-ler, -lest) healthy, robust
haler *adj* ▷ **hale**
halest *adj* ▷ **hale**
half *n* (*pl* -lves) either of two equal parts ▶ *adj*
denoting one of two equal parts ▶ *adv* to the
extent of half
halfhearted *adj* unenthusiastic
halflife *n* (*pl* -ves) time taken for half the atoms
in radioactive material to decay
halflives *n* ▷ **halflife**
halfpennies *n* ▷ **halfpenny**
halfpenny [hayp-nee] *n* (*pl* -nnies) former
British coin worth half an old penny
halftime *n* (*pl* -s) (SPORT) short rest period
between two halves of a game
halftimes *n* ▷ **halftime**
halftone *n* (*pl* -s) illustration showing lights
and shadows by means of very small dots
halftones *n* ▷ **halftone**
halfway *adv*, *adj* at or to half the distance
halfwit *n* (*pl* -s) foolish or stupid person
halfwits *n* ▷ **halfwit**
halibut *n* (*pl* halibuts) large edible flatfish of
N Atlantic
halibuts *n* ▷ **halibut**

halitosis *n* (*pl* -**ises**) unpleasant-smelling breath
　halitosises *n* ▷ **halitosis**
hall *n* (*pl* -**s**) (*also* **hallway**) entrance passage
hallelujah [hal-ee-loo-ya] *interj* exclamation of praise to God
hallmark *n* (*pl* -**s**) typical feature ▶ *v* (-**s, -ing, -ed**) stamp with a hallmark
　hallmarked *v* ▷ **hallmark**
　hallmarking *v* ▷ **hallmark**
　hallmarks *n, v* ▷ **hallmark**
　hallo *interj* ▷ **hello**
hallowed *adj* regarded as holy
Halloween, Hallowe'en *n* (*pl* -**s**) October 31, celebrated by children by dressing up as ghosts, witches, etc.
　Halloweens *n* ▷ **Halloween**
　halls *n* ▷ **hall**
hallucinate *v* (-**tes, -ting, -ted**) seem to see something that is not really there
　> **hallucination** *n* (*pl* -**s**) > **hallucinatory** *adj*
　hallucinated *v* ▷ **hallucinate**
　hallucinates *v* ▷ **hallucinate**
　hallucinating *v* ▷ **hallucinate**
　hallucination *n* ▷ **hallucinate**
　hallucinations *n* ▷ **hallucinate**
　hallucinatory *adj* ▷ **hallucinate**
hallucinogen *n* (*pl* -**s**) drug that causes hallucinations > **hallucinogenic** *adj*
　hallucinogenic *adj* ▷ **hallucinogen**
　hallucinogens *n* ▷ **hallucinogen**
halo [hay-loh] *n* (*pl* -**loes, -los**) ring of light round the head of a sacred figure
　haloes *n* ▷ **halo**
halogen [hal-oh-jen] *n* (*pl* -**s**) (CHEM) any of a group of nonmetallic elements including chlorine and iodine
　halogens *n* ▷ **halogen**
　halos *n* ▷ **halo**
halt *v* (-**s, -ing, -ed**) come or bring to a stop ▶ *n* (*pl* -**s**) temporary stop
　halted *v* ▷ **halt**
halter *n* (*pl* -**s**) strap round a horse's head with a rope to lead it with
halterneck *n* (*pl* -**s**) woman's top or dress with a strap fastened at the back of the neck
　halternecks *n* ▷ **halterneck**
　halters *n* ▷ **halter**
halting *adj* hesitant, uncertain ▶ *v* ▷ **halt**
　halts *v, n* ▷ **halt**
halve *v* (-**ves, -ving, -ved**) divide in half
　halved *v* ▷ **halve**
　halves *v* ▷ **halve** ▶ *n* ▷ **half**
　halving *v* ▷ **halve**
halyard *n* (*pl* -**s**) rope for raising a ship's sail or flag
　halyards *n* ▷ **halyard**
ham[1] *n* (*pl* -**s**) smoked or salted meat from a pig's thigh
ham[2] (*Informal*) *n* (*pl* -**s**) amateur radio operator ▶ *v* (-**s, -mming, -mmed**) overact
hamburger *n* (*pl* -**s**) minced beef shaped into a flat disc, cooked and usu. served in a bread roll
　hamburgers *n* ▷ **hamburger**
hamlet *n* (*pl* -**s**) small village
　hamlets *n* ▷ **hamlet**
　hammed *v* ▷ **ham**[2]
hammer *n* (*pl* -**s**) tool with a heavy metal head and a wooden handle, used to drive in nails etc. ▶ *v* (-**s, -ing, -ed**) hit (as if) with a hammer
　hammered *v* ▷ **hammer**
hammerhead *n* (*pl* -**s**) shark with a wide flattened head
　hammerheads *n* ▷ **hammerhead**
　hammering *v* ▷ **hammer**
　hammers *n, v* ▷ **hammer**
　hamming *v* ▷ **ham**[2]
hammock *n* (*pl* -**s**) hanging bed made of canvas or net
　hammocks *n* ▷ **hammock**
hamper[1] *v* (-**s, -ing, -ed**) make it difficult for (someone or something) to move or progress
hamper[2] *n* (*pl* -**s**) large basket with a lid
　hampered *v* ▷ **hamper**[1]
　hampering *v* ▷ **hamper**[1]
　hampers *v, n* ▷ **hamper**[1, 2]
　hams *n, v* ▷ **ham**[1, 2]
hamster *n* (*pl* -**s**) small rodent with a short tail and cheek pouches
　hamsters *n* ▷ **hamster**
hamstring *n* (*pl* -**s**) tendon at the back of the knee ▶ *v* (-**s, -ing, -rung**) make it difficult for (someone) to take any action
　hamstringing *v* ▷ **hamstring**
　hamstrings *n, v* ▷ **hamstring**
　hamstrung *v* ▷ **hamstring**
hand *n* (*pl* -**s**) part of the body at the end of the arm, consisting of a palm, four fingers, and a thumb ▶ *v* (-**s, -ing, -ed**) pass, give
handbag *n* (*pl* -**s**) woman's small bag for carrying personal articles in
　handbags *n* ▷ **handbag**
handbill *n* (*pl* -**s**) small printed notice
　handbills *n* ▷ **handbill**
handbook *n* (*pl* -**s**) small reference or instruction book
　handbooks *n* ▷ **handbook**
handcuff *n* (*pl* -**s**) one of a linked pair of metal rings designed to be locked round a

prisoner's wrists by the police ▶ *v* (**-s, -ing, -ed**) put handcuffs on
handcuffed *v* ▷ **handcuff**
handcuffing *v* ▷ **handcuff**
handcuffs *n, v* ▷ **handcuff**
handed *v* ▷ **hand**
handful *n* (*pl* **-s**) amount that can be held in the hand
handfuls *n* ▷ **handful**
handheld *adj* (*of a film camera*) held rather than mounted, as in close-up action shots ▶ *n* (*pl* **-s**) computer that can be held in the hand
handhelds *n* ▷ **handheld**
handicap *n* (*pl* **-s**) physical or mental disability ▶ *v* (**-s, -pping, -pped**) make it difficult for (someone) to do something
handicapped *v* ▷ **handicap**
handicapping *v* ▷ **handicap**
handicaps *n, v* ▷ **handicap**
handicraft *n* (*pl* **-s**) objects made by hand
handicrafts *n* ▷ **handicraft**
handier *adj* ▷ **handy**
handiest *adj* ▷ **handy**
handily *adv* ▷ **handy**
handing *v* ▷ **hand**
handiwork *n* (*pl* **-s**) result of someone's work or activity
handiworks *n* ▷ **handiwork**
handkerchief *n* (*pl* **-s**) small square of fabric used to wipe the nose
handkerchiefs *n* ▷ **handkerchief**
handle *n* (*pl* **-s**) part of an object that is held so that it can be used ▶ *v* (**-les, -ling, -led**) hold, feel, or move with the hands
handlebars *pl n* curved metal bar used to steer a cycle
handled *v* ▷ **handle**
handler *n* (*pl* **-s**) person who controls an animal
handlers *n* ▷ **handler**
handles *n, v* ▷ **handle**
handling *v* ▷ **handle**
handout *n* (*pl* **-s**) clothing, food, or money given to a needy person
handouts *n* ▷ **handout**
hands *n, v* ▷ **hand**
handsome *adj* (esp. of a man) good-looking
handstand *n* (*pl* **-s**) act of supporting the body on the hands in an upside-down position
handstands *n* ▷ **handstand**
handwriting *n* (*pl* **-s**) (style of) writing by hand
handwritings *n* ▷ **handwriting**
handy *adj* (**-dier, -diest**) convenient, useful
> **handily** *adv*
handyman *n* (*pl* **-men**) man who is good at

making or repairing things
handymen *n* ▷ **handyman**
hang *v* (**-s, -ing, hung** *or* **hanged**) attach or be attached at the top with the lower part free
hangar *n* (*pl* **-s**) large shed for storing aircraft
hangars *n* ▷ **hangar**
hangdog *adj* guilty, ashamed
hanged *v* ▷ **hang**
hanger *n* (*pl* **-s**) curved piece of wood, wire, or plastic, with a hook, for hanging up clothes (*also* **coat hanger**)
hangers *n* ▷ **hanger**
hangi *n* (*pl* **-gi, -gis**) (NZ) Maori oven consisting of a hole in the ground filled with hot stones
hanging *v* ▷ **hang**
hangis *n* ▷ **hangi**
hangman *n* (*pl* **-men**) man who executes people by hanging
hangmen *n* ▷ **hangman**
hangover *n* (*pl* **-s**) headache and nausea as a result of drinking too much alcohol
hangovers *n* ▷ **hangover**
hangs *v* ▷ **hang**
hangup *n* (*pl* **-s**) (*Informal*) emotional or psychological problem
hangups *n* ▷ **hangup**
hank *n* (*pl* **-s**) coil, esp. of yarn
hanker *v* (**-s, -ing, -ed**) (*foll. by* **after** *or* **for**) desire intensely
hankered *v* ▷ **hanker**
hankering *v* ▷ **hanker**
hankers *v* ▷ **hanker**
hankie *n* ▷ **hanky**
hankies *n* ▷ **hanky**
hanks *n* ▷ **hank**
hanky, hankie *n* (*pl* **hankies**) (*Informal*) handkerchief
haphazard *adj* not organized or planned
> **haphazardly** *adv*
haphazardly *adv* ▷ **haphazard**
hapless *adj* unlucky
happen *v* (**-s, -ing, -ed**) take place, occur
happened *v* ▷ **happen**
happening *n* (*pl* **-s**) event, occurrence ▶ *v* ▷ **happen**
happenings *n* ▷ **happening**
happens *v* ▷ **happen**
happier *adj* ▷ **happy**
happiest *adj* ▷ **happy**
happily *adv* ▷ **happy**
happiness *n* ▷ **happy**
happinesses *n* ▷ **happiness**
happy *adj* (**-ppier, -ppiest**) feeling or causing joy > **happily** *adv* > **happiness** *n* (*pl* **-es**)
harangue *v* (**-gues, -guing, -gued**) address

angrily or forcefully ▶ *n* (*pl* **-gues**) angry or forceful speech
  harangued *v* ▷ **harangue**
  harangues *v*, *n* ▷ **harangue**
  haranguing *v* ▷ **harangue**
harass *v* (**-es, -ing, -ssed**) annoy or trouble constantly > **harassed** *adj* > **harassment** *n* (*pl* **-s**)
  harassed *v*, *adj* ▷ **harass**
  harasses *v* ▷ **harass**
  harassing *v* ▷ **harass**
  harassment *n* ▷ **harrass**
  harassments *n* ▷ **harassment**
harbinger [har-binj-a] *n* (*pl* **-s**) someone or something that announces the approach of something
  harbingers *n* ▷ **harbinger**
harbour *n* (*pl* **-s**) sheltered port ▶ *v* (**-s, -ing, -ed**) maintain secretly in the mind
  harboured *v* ▷ **harbour**
  harbouring *v* ▷ **harbour**
  harbours *n*, *v* ▷ **harbour**
hard *adj* firm, solid, or rigid ▶ *adv* with great energy or effort > **harden** *v* (**-s, -ing, -ed**) > **hardness** *n* (*pl* **-es**)
hardboard *n* (*pl* ▷ **-s**) thin stiff board made of compressed sawdust and wood chips
  hardboards *n* ▷ **hardboard**
  harden *v* ▷ **hard**
  hardened *v* ▷ **hard**
  hardening *v* ▷ **hard**
  hardens *v* ▷ **hard**
hardfill *n* (*pl* **-s**) (NZ & S AFR) stone waste material used for landscaping
  hardfills *n* ▷ **hardfill**
hardheaded *adj* shrewd, practical
hardhearted *adj* unsympathetic, uncaring
  hardier *adj* ▷ **hardy**
  hardiest *adj* ▷ **hardy**
  hardiness *n* ▷ **hardy**
  hardinesses *n* ▷ **hardy**
hardly *adv* scarcely or not at all
  hardness *n* ▷ **hard**
  hardnesses *n* ▷ **hard**
hardship *n* (*pl* **-s**) suffering
  hardships *n* ▷ **hardship**
hardware *n* (*pl* **-s**) metal tools or implements
  hardwares *n* ▷ **hardware**
hardwood *n* (*pl* **-s**) wood of a broadleaved tree such as oak or ash
  hardwoods *n* ▷ **hardwood**
hardy *adj* (**-dier, -diest**) able to stand difficult conditions > **hardiness** *n* (*pl* **-es**)
hare *n* (*pl* **-s**) animal like a large rabbit, with longer ears and legs ▶ *v* (**-res, -ring, -red**) (*usu.*

foll. by **off**) run (away) quickly
harebell *n* (*pl* **-s**) blue bell-shaped flower
  harebells *n* ▷ **harebell**
harebrained *adj* foolish or impractical
  hared *v* ▷ **hare**
harelip *n* (*pl* **-s**) slight split in the upper lip
  harelips *n* ▷ **harelip**
harem *n* (*pl* **-s**) (apartments of) a Muslim man's wives and concubines
  harems *n* ▷ **harem**
  hares *v*, *n* ▷ **hare**
  haring *v* ▷ **hare**
hark *v* (**-s, -ing, -ed**) (*Old-fashioned*) listen
  harked *v* ▷ **hark**
  harking *v* ▷ **hark**
  harks *v* ▷ **hark**
harlequin *n* (*pl* **-s**) stock comic character with a diamond-patterned costume and mask ▶ *adj* in many colours
  harlequins *n* ▷ **harlequin**
harlot *n* (*pl* **-s**) (*Lit*) prostitute
  harlots *n* ▷ **harlot**
harm *v* (**-s, -ing, -ed**) injure physically, mentally, or morally ▶ *n* (*pl* **-s**) physical, mental, or moral injury > **harmful** *adj* > **harmless** *adj*
  harmed *v* ▷ **harm**
  harmful *adj* ▷ **harm**
  harming *v* ▷ **harm**
  harmless *adj* ▷ **harm**
harmonic *adj* of harmony
harmonica *n* (*pl* **-s**) small wind instrument played by sucking and blowing
  harmonicas *n* ▷ **harmonica**
harmonics *n* science of musical sounds
  harmonies *n* ▷ **harmony**
  harmonious *adj* ▷ **harmony**
  harmoniously *adv* ▷ **harmony**
harmonium *n* (*pl* **-s**) keyboard instrument like a small organ
  harmoniums *n* ▷ **harmonium**
  harmonization *v* ▷ **harmonize**
  harmonizations *v* ▷ **harmonize**
harmonize *v* (**-zes, -zing, -zed**) blend well together > **harmonization** *n* (*pl* **-s**)
  harmonized *v* ▷ **harmonize**
  harmonizes *v* ▷ **harmonize**
  harmonizing *v* ▷ **harmonize**
harmony *n* (*pl* **-nies**) peaceful agreement and cooperation > **harmonious** *adj* > **harmoniously** *adv*
  harms *v*, *n* ▷ **harm**
harness *n* (*pl* **-es**) arrangement of straps for attaching a horse to a cart or plough ▶ *v* (**-es, -ing, -ed**) put a harness on

harnessed v ▷ **harness**
harnesses n, v ▷ **harness**
harnessing v ▷ **harness**
harp n (pl -s) large triangular stringed instrument played with the fingers > **harpist** n (pl -s)
harpies n ▷ **harpy**
harpist n ▷ **harp**
harpists n ▷ **harp**
harpoon n (pl -s) barbed spear attached to a rope used for hunting whales ▶ v (-s, -ing, -ed) spear with a harpoon
harpooned v ▷ **harpoon**
harpooning v ▷ **harpoon**
harpoons n, v ▷ **harpoon**
harps n ▷ **harp**
harpsichord n (pl -s) stringed keyboard instrument
harpsichords n ▷ **harpsichord**
harpy n (pl -pies) nasty or bad-tempered woman
harridan n (pl -s) nagging or vicious woman
harridans n ▷ **harridan**
harried v ▷ **harry**
harrier n (pl -s) cross-country runner
harriers n ▷ **harrier**
harries v ▷ **harry**
harrow n (pl -s) implement used to break up lumps of soil ▶ v (-s, -ing, -ed) draw a harrow over
harrowed v ▷ **harrow**
harrowing adj very distressing ▶ v ▷ **harrow**
harrows n, v ▷ **harrow**
harry v (-rries, -rrying, -rried) keep asking (someone) to do something, pester
harrying v ▷ **harry**
harsh adj severe and difficult to cope with > **harshly** adv > **harshness** n (pl -es)
harshly adv ▷ **harsh**
harshness n ▷ **harsh**
harshnesses n ▷ **harsh**
hart n (pl -s) adult male deer
harts n ▷ **hart**
harvest n (pl -s) (season for) the gathering of crops ▶ v (-s, -ing, -ed) gather (a ripened crop) > **harvester** n (pl -s)
harvested v ▷ **harvest**
harvester n ▷ **harvest**
harvesters n ▷ **harvest**
harvesting v ▷ **harvest**
harvests n, v ▷ **harvest**
has v ▷ **have**
hash[1] n (pl -es) dish of diced cooked meat and vegetables reheated
hash[2] n (pl -es) (Informal) hashish

hashes n ▷ **hash**[1, 2]
hashish [hash-eesh] n (pl -es) drug made from the cannabis plant, smoked for its intoxicating effects
hashishes n ▷ **hashish**
hasp n (pl -s) clasp that fits over a staple and is secured by a bolt or padlock, used as a fastening
hasps n ▷ **hasp**
hassle (Informal) n (pl -s) trouble, bother ▶ v (-les, -ling, -led) bother or annoy
hassled v ▷ **hassle**
hassles n, v ▷ **hassle**
hassling v ▷ **hassle**
hassock n (pl -s) cushion for kneeling on in church
hassocks n ▷ **hassock**
haste n (pl -s) (excessive) quickness
hasten v (-s, -ing, -ed) (cause to) hurry
hastened v ▷ **hasten**
hastening n ▷ **hasten**
hastens n ▷ **hasten**
hastes n ▷ **haste**
hastier adj ▷ **hasty**
hastiest adj ▷ **hasty**
hastily adv ▷ **hasty**
hasty adj (-tier, -tiest) (too) quick > **hastily** adv
hat n (pl -s) covering for the head, often with a brim, usu. worn to give protection from the weather
hatch[1] v (-es, -ing, -ed) (cause to) emerge from an egg
hatch[2] n (pl -es) hinged door covering an opening in a floor or wall
hatchback n (pl -s) car with a lifting door at the back
hatchbacks n ▷ **hatchback**
hatched v ▷ **hatch**[1]
hatches v ▷ **hatch**[1] ▶ n ▷ **hatch**[2]
hatchet n (pl -s) small axe
hatchets n ▷ **hatchet**
hatching v ▷ **hatch**[1]
hatchway n (pl -s) opening in the deck of a ship
hatchways n ▷ **hatchway**
hate v (-tes, -ting, -ted) dislike intensely ▶ n (pl -s) intense dislike > **hater** n (pl -s)
hated v ▷ **hate**
hateful adj causing or deserving hate
hater n ▷ **hate**
haters n ▷ **hate**
hates v, n ▷ **hate**
hating v ▷ **hate**
hatred n (pl -s) intense dislike
hatreds n ▷ **hatred**

hats *n* ▷ hat
haughtier *adj* ▷ haughty
haughtiest *adj* ▷ haughty
haughtily *adv* ▷ haughty
haughtiness *n* ▷ haughty
haughtinesses *n* ▷ haughty
haughty *adj* (-tier, -tiest) proud, arrogant
> **haughtily** *adv* > **haughtiness** *n* (*pl* -es)
haul *v* (-s, -ing, -ed) pull or drag with effort ▶ *n*
(*pl* -s) amount gained by effort or theft
haulage *n* (*pl* -s) (charge for) transporting
goods
haulages *n* ▷ haulage
hauled *v* ▷ haul
haulier *n* (*pl* -s) firm or person that transports
goods by road
hauliers *n* ▷ haulier
hauling *v* ▷ haul
hauls *v, n* ▷ haul
haunch *n* (*pl* -es) human hip or fleshy
hindquarter of an animal
haunches *n* ▷ haunch
haunt *v* (-s, -ing, -ed) visit in the form of a
ghost ▶ *n* (*pl* -s) place visited frequently
haunted *adj* frequented by ghosts ▶ *v* ▷ **haunt**
haunting *adj* memorably beautiful or sad ▶ *v*
▷ **haunt**
haunts *v, n* ▷ haunt
hauteur [oat-ur] *n* (*pl* -s) haughtiness
hauteurs *n* ▷ hauteur
have *v* (**has, having, had**) possess, hold
haven *n* (*pl* -s) place of safety
havens *n* ▷ haven
haversack *n* (*pl* -s) canvas bag carried on the
back or shoulder
haversacks *n* ▷ haversack
having *v* ▷ have
havoc *n* (*pl* -s) disorder and confusion
havocs *n* ▷ havoc
haw *n* (*pl* -s) hawthorn berry
hawk¹ *n* (*pl* -s) bird of prey with a short hooked
bill and very good eyesight > **hawkish,
hawklike** *adj*
hawk² *v* (-s, -ing, -ed) offer (goods) for sale in
the street or door-to-door > **hawker** *n* (*pl* -s)
hawk³ *v* (-s, -ing, -ed) cough noisily
hawked *v* ▷ hawk²,³
hawker *n* ▷ hawk²
hawkers *n* ▷ hawk²
hawk-eyed *adj* having very good eyesight
hawking *v* ▷ hawk²,³
hawkish *adj* ▷ hawk¹
hawks *n* ▷ hawk¹ ▶ *v* ▷ hawk²,³
hawlike *adj* ▷ hawk¹
haws *n* ▷ haw

hawser *n* (*pl* -s) large rope used on a ship
hawsers *n* ▷ hawser
hawthorn *n* (*pl* -s) thorny shrub or tree
hawthorns *n* ▷ hawthorn
hay *n* (*pl* **hays**) grass cut and dried as fodder
hays *n* ▷ hay
haystack *n* (*pl* -s) large pile of stored hay
haystacks *n* ▷ haystack
haywire *adj* (*Informal*) not functioning properly
hazard *n* (*pl* -s) something that could be
dangerous ▶ *v* (-s, -ing, -ed) put in danger
> **hazardous** *adj*
hazarded *v* ▷ hazard
hazarding *v* ▷ hazard
hazardous *adj* ▷ hazard
hazards *n, v* ▷ hazard
haze *n* (*pl* -s) mist, often caused by heat
hazel *n* (*pl* -s) small tree producing edible nuts
▶ *adj* (of eyes) greenish-brown > **hazelnut**
n (*pl* -s)
hazelnut *n* ▷ hazel
hazelnuts *n* ▷ hazel
hazels *n* ▷ hazel
hazes *n* ▷ haze
hazier *adj* ▷ hazy
haziest *adj* ▷ hazy
hazy *adj* (-zier, -ziest) not clear, misty
he *pron* refers to: male person or animal ▶ *n* (*pl*
-s) male person or animal
head *n* (*pl* -s) upper or front part of the body,
containing the sense organs and the brain
▶ *adj* chief, principal ▶ *v* (-s, -ing, -ed) be at the
top or front of
headache *n* (*pl* -s) continuous pain in the head
headaches *n* ▷ headache
headboard *n* (*pl* -s) vertical board at the top
end of a bed
headboards *n* ▷ headboard
headdress *n* (*pl* -s) decorative head covering
headdresses *n* ▷ headdress
headed *v* ▷ head
header *n* (*pl* -s) striking a ball with the head
headers *n* ▷ header
headhunt *v* (-s, -ing, -ed) (of a company)
approach and offer a job to (a person working
for a rival company) > **headhunter** *n* (*pl* -s)
headhunted *v* ▷ headhunt
headhunter *n* ▷ headhunt
headhunters *n* ▷ headhunt
headhunting *v* ▷ headhunt
headhunts *v* ▷ headhunt
headier *adj* ▷ heady
headiest *adj* ▷ heady
heading *n* (*pl* -s) title written or printed at the
top of a page ▶ *v* ▷ head

headings *n* ▷ **heading**

headland *n* (*pl* -s) area of land jutting out into the sea

  headlands *n* ▷ **headland**

headlight *n* (*pl* -s) powerful light on the front of a vehicle

  headlights *n* ▷ **headlight**

headline *n* (*pl* -s) title at the top of a newspaper article, esp. on the front page

  headlines *n* ▷ **headline** ▶ *pl n* main points of a news broadcast

headlong *adv, adj* with the head first

headphones *pl n* two small loudspeakers held against the ears

headquarters *pl n* centre from which operations are directed

heads *adv* (*Informal*) with the side of a coin which has a portrait of a head on it uppermost ▶ *n, v* ▷ **head**

headstone *n* (*pl* -s) memorial stone on a grave

  headstones *n* ▷ **headstone**

headstrong *adj* self-willed, obstinate

headway *n* (*pl* -s) progress

  headways *n* ▷ **headway**

headwind *n* (*pl* -s) wind blowing against the course of an aircraft or ship

  headwinds *n* ▷ **headwind**

heady *adj* (-**dier**, -**diest**) intoxicating or exciting

heal *v* (-**s**, -**ing**, -**ed**) make or become well > **healer** *n* (*pl* -s)

  healed *v* ▷ **heal**

  healer *n* ▷ **heal**

  healers *n* ▷ **heal**

  healing *v* ▷ **heal**

  heals *v* ▷ **heal**

health *n* (*pl* -s) normal (good) condition of someone's body

  healthier *adj* ▷ **healthy**

  healthiest *adj* ▷ **healthy**

  healthily *adv* ▷ **healthy**

  healths *n* ▷ **health**

healthy *adj* (-**thier**, -**thiest**) having good health > **healthily** *adv*

heap *n* (*pl* -s) pile of things one on top of another ▶ *v* (-**s**, -**ing**, -**ed**) gather into a pile

  heaped *v* ▷ **heap**

  heaping *v* ▷ **heap**

  heaps *n, v* ▷ **heap**

hear *v* (-**s**, -**ing**, **heard**) perceive (a sound) by ear > **hearer** *n* (*pl* -s)

  heard *v* ▷ **hear**

  hearer *n* ▷ **hear**

  hearers *n* ▷ **hear**

hearing *n* (*pl* -s) ability to hear ▶ *v* ▷ **hear**

hearings *n* ▷ **hearing**

  hears *v* ▷ **hear**

hearsay *n* (*pl* -s) gossip, rumour

  hearsays *n* ▷ **hearsay**

hearse *n* (*pl* -s) funeral car used to carry a coffin

  hearses *n* ▷ **hearse**

heart *n* (*pl* -s) organ that pumps blood round the body

heartache *n* (*pl* -s) intense anguish

  heartaches *n* ▷ **heartache**

heartbeat *n* (*pl* -s) one complete pulsation of the heart

  heartbeats *n* ▷ **heartbeat**

heartbreak *n* (*pl* -s) intense grief

  heartbreaks *n* ▷ **heartbreak**

heartburn *n* (*pl* -s) burning sensation in the chest caused by indigestion

  heartburns *n* ▷ **heartburn**

hearten *v* (-**s**, -**ing**, -**ed**) encourage, make cheerful

  heartened *v* ▷ **hearten**

  heartening *v* ▷ **hearten**

  heartens *v* ▷ **hearten**

heartfelt *adj* felt sincerely or strongly

hearth *n* (*pl* -s) floor of a fireplace

  hearths *n* ▷ **hearth**

  heartier *adj* ▷ **hearty**

  heartiest *adj* ▷ **hearty**

  heartily *adv* ▷ **hearty**

heartless *adj* cruel, unkind

heartrending *adj* causing great sorrow

  hearts *n* ▷ **heart**

heartthrob *n* (*pl* -s) (*Slang*) very attractive man, esp. a film or pop star

  heartthrobs *n* ▷ **heartthrob**

hearty *adj* (-**tier**, -**tiest**) substantial, nourishing > **heartily** *adv*

heat *v* (-**s**, -**ing**, -**ed**) make or become hot ▶ *n* (*pl* -s) state of being hot > **heater** *n* (*pl* -s)

  heated *v* ▷ **heat** ▶ *adj* angry and excited > **heatedly** *adv*

  heatedly *adv* ▷ **heated**

  heater *n* ▷ **heat**

  heaters *n* ▷ **heat**

heath *n* (*pl* -s) (BRIT) area of open uncultivated land

heathen *adj, n* (*pl* -s) (of) a person who does not believe in an established religion

  heathens *n* ▷ **heathen**

heather *n* (*pl* -s) low-growing plant with small purple, pinkish, or white flowers, growing on heaths and mountains

  heathers *n* ▷ **heather**

  heaths *n* ▷ **heath**

  heating *v* ▷ **heat**

heats v, n ▷ **heat**
heave v (**-ves, -ving, -ved**) lift with effort ▶ n
(pl **-s**) heaving
heaved v ▷ **heave**
heaven n (pl **-s**) place believed to be the home
of God, where good people go when they die
heavenly adj of or like heaven
heavens n ▷ **heaven**
heaves v, n ▷ **heave**
heavier adj ▷ **heavy**
heaviest adj ▷ **heavy**
heavily adv ▷ **heavy**
heaviness n ▷ **heavy**
heavinesses n ▷ **heavy**
heaving v ▷ **heave**
heavy adj (**-vier, -viest**) of great weight
> **heavily** adv > **heaviness** n (pl **-es**)
heavyweight n (pl **-s**) boxer weighing over
175lb (professional) or 81kg (amateur)
heavyweights n ▷ **heavyweight**
heckle v (**-les, -ling, -led**) interrupt (a public
speaker) with comments, questions, or
taunts > **heckler** n (pl **-s**)
heckled v ▷ **heckle**
heckler n ▷ **heckle**
hecklers n ▷ **heckle**
heckles v ▷ **heckle**
heckling v ▷ **heckle**
hectare n (pl **-s**) one hundred ares or 10 000
square metres (2.471 acres)
hectares n ▷ **hectare**
hectic adj rushed or busy
hector v (**-s, -ing, -ed**) bully
hectored v ▷ **hector**
hectoring v ▷ **hector**
hectors v ▷ **hector**
hedge n (pl **-s**) row of bushes forming a barrier
or boundary ▶ v (**-ges, -ging, -ged**) be evasive
or noncommittal
hedged v ▷ **hedge**
hedgehog n (pl **-s**) small mammal with a
protective covering of spines
hedgehogs n ▷ **hedgehog**
hedgerow n (pl **-s**) bushes forming a hedge
hedgerows n ▷ **hedgerow**
hedges n, v ▷ **hedge**
hedging v ▷ **hedge**
hedonism n (pl **-s**) doctrine that pleasure is the
most important thing in life > **hedonist** n (pl
-s) > **hedonistic** adj
hedonisms n ▷ **hedonism**
hedonist n ▷ **hedonism**
hedonistic n ▷ **hedonism**
hedonists n ▷ **hedonism**
heed n (pl **-s**) careful attention ▶ v (**-s, -ing, -ed**)

pay careful attention to
heeded v ▷ **heed**
heeding v ▷ **heed**
heedless adj taking no notice of
heeds v, n ▷ **heed**
heel[1] n (pl **-s**) back part of the foot ▶ v (**-s, -ing,
-ed**) repair the heel of (a shoe)
heel[2] v (**-s, -ing, -ed**) (foll. by **over**) lean to
one side
heeled v ▷ **heel**[1, 2]
heeler n (pl **-s**) (AUST & NZ) dog that herds cattle
by biting at their heels
heelers n ▷ **heeler**
heeling v ▷ **heel**[1, 2]
heels n ▷ **heel**[1] ▶ v ▷ **heel**[1, 2]
heftier adj ▷ **hefty**
heftiest adj ▷ **hefty**
hefty adj (**-tier, -tiest**) large, heavy, or strong
hegemonies n ▷ **hegemony**
hegemony [hig-**em**-on-ee] n (pl **-nies**) political
domination
hegira n (pl **-s**) Mohammed's flight from Mecca
to Medina in 622 AD
hegiras n ▷ **hegira**
heifer [**hef**-fer] n (pl **-s**) young cow
heifers n ▷ **heifer**
height n (pl **-s**) distance from base to top
heighten v (**-s, -ing, -ed**) make or become
higher or more intense
heightened v ▷ **heighten**
heightening v ▷ **heighten**
heightens v ▷ **heighten**
heights n ▷ **height**
heinous adj evil and shocking
heir n (pl **-s**) person entitled to inherit property
or rank > **heiress** n fem (pl **-es**)
heiresses n ▷ **heiress**
heirloom n (pl **-s**) object that has belonged to a
family for generations
heirlooms n ▷ **heirloom**
heirs n ▷ **heir**
held v ▷ **hold**[1]
helical adj spiral
helices n ▷ **helix**
helicopter n (pl **-s**) aircraft lifted and propelled
by rotating overhead blades
helicopters n ▷ **helicopter**
heliotrope n (pl **-s**) plant with purple flowers
▶ adj light purple
heliotropes n ▷ **heliotrope**
heliport n (pl **-s**) airport for helicopters
heliports n ▷ **heliport**
helium [**heel**-ee-um] n (pl **-s**) (CHEM) very light
colourless odourless gas
heliums n ▷ **helium**

helix [heel-iks] *n* (*pl* -**ices**, -**ixes**) spiral
  helixes *n* ▷ **helix**
hell *n* (*pl* -**s**) place believed to be where wicked
  people go when they die > **hellish** *adj*
hellbent *adj* (*foll. by* **on**) intent
  hellish *adj* ▷ **hell**
hello *interj* expression of greeting or surprise
  hells *n* ▷ **hell**
helm *n* (*pl* -**s**) tiller or wheel for steering a ship
helmet *n* (*pl* -**s**) hard hat worn for protection
  helmets *n* ▷ **helmet**
  helms *n* ▷ **helm**
help *v* (-**s**, -**ing**, -**ed**) make something easier,
  better, or quicker for (someone) ▶ *n* (*pl*
  -**s**) assistance or support > **helper** *n* (*pl* -**s**)
  > **helpful** *adj*
  helped *v* ▷ **help**
  helper *n* ▷ **help**
  helpers *n* ▷ **help**
  helpful *adj* ▷ **help**
helping *n* (*pl* -**s**) single portion of food ▶ *v*
  ▷ **help**
  helpings *n* ▷ **helping**
helpless *adj* weak or incapable > **helplessly** *adv*
  helplessly *adv* ▷ **helpless**
helpline *n* (*pl* -**s**) telephone line set aside for
  callers to contact an organization for help
  with a problem
  helplines *n* ▷ **helpline**
helpmate *n* (*pl* -**s**) companion and helper, esp.
  a husband or wife
  helpmates *n* ▷ **helpmate**
  helps *v*, *n* ▷ **help**
hem *n* (*pl* -**s**) bottom edge of a garment, folded
  under and stitched down ▶ *v* (-**s**, -**mming**,
  -**mmed**) provide with a hem
hemisphere *n* (*pl* -**s**) half of a sphere, esp. the
  earth > **hemispherical** *adj*
  hemispheres *n* ▷ **hemisphere**
hemline *n* (*pl* -**s**) level to which the hem of a
  skirt hangs
  hemlines *n* ▷ **hemline**
hemlock *n* (*pl* -**s**) poison made from a plant
  with spotted stems and small white flowers
  hemlocks *n* ▷ **hemlock**
  hemmed *v* ▷ **hem**
  hemming *v* ▷ **hem**
hemp *n* (*pl* -**s**) (*also* **cannabis**) Asian plant with
  tough fibres
  hemps *n* ▷ **hemp**
  hems *n*, *v* ▷ **hem**
hen *n* (*pl* -**s**) female domestic fowl
hence *conj* for this reason ▶ *adv* from this time
henceforth *adv* from now on
henchman *n* (*pl* -**men**) person employed by

someone powerful to carry out orders
  henchmen *n* ▷ **henchman**
henna *n* (*pl* -**s**) reddish dye made from a shrub
  or tree ▶ *v* (-**s**, -**ing**, -**ed**) dye (the hair) with
  henna
  hennaed *v* ▷ **henna**
  hennaing *v* ▷ **henna**
  hennas *n*, *v* ▷ **henna**
henpecked *adj* (of a man) dominated by his
  wife
  henries *n* ▷ **henry**
henry *n* (*pl* -**ries**, -**rys**) unit of electrical
  inductance
  henrys *n* ▷ **henry**
  hens *n* ▷ **hen**
hepatitis *n* (*pl* -**es**) inflammation of the liver
  hepatitises *n* ▷ **hepatitis**
heptagon *n* (*pl* -**s**) geometric figure with
  seven sides
  heptagons *n* ▷ **heptagon**
heptathlon *n* (*pl* -**s**) athletic contest for
  women, involving seven events
  heptathlons *n* ▷ **heptathlon**
her *pron* refers to a female person or animal or
  anything personified as feminine when the
  object of a sentence or clause ▶ *adj* belonging
  to her
herald *n* (*pl* -**s**) person who announces
  important news ▶ *v* (-**s**, -**ing**, -**ed**) signal the
  approach of
  heralded *v* ▷ **herald**
  heraldic *adj* ▷ **heraldry**
  heralding *v* ▷ **herald**
  heraldries *n* ▷ **heraldry**
heraldry *n* (*pl* -**ries**) study of coats of arms and
  family trees > **heraldic** *adj*
  heralds *n*, *v* ▷ **herald**
herb *n* (*pl* -**s**) plant used for flavouring in
  cookery, and in medicine > **herbal** *adj*
herbaceous *adj* (of a plant) soft-stemmed
  herbal *adj* ▷ **herb**
herbalist *n* (*pl* -**s**) person who grows or
  specializes in the use of medicinal herbs
  herbalists *n* ▷ **herbalist**
herbicide *n* (*pl* -**s**) chemical used to destroy
  plants, esp. weeds
  herbicides *n* ▷ **herbicide**
herbivore *n* (*pl* -**s**) animal that eats only plants
  > **herbivorous** [her-biv-or-uss] ▶ *adj*
  herbivores *n* ▷ **herbivore**
  herbivorous *adj* ▷ **herbivore**
  herbs *n* ▷ **herb**
herculean [her-kew-lee-an] *adj* requiring great
  strength or effort
herd *n* (*pl* -**s**) group of animals feeding and

living together ▶ v (-s, -ing, -ed) collect into a herd
herded v ▷ **herd**
herding v ▷ **herd**
herds n, v ▷ **herd**
herdsman n (pl -men) man who looks after a herd of animals
herdsmen n ▷ **herd**
here adv in, at, or to this place or point
hereabouts adv near here
hereafter adv after this point or time
hereby adv by means of or as a result of this
hereditary adj passed on genetically from one generation to another
heredities n ▷ **heredity**
heredity [hir-**red**-it-ee] n (pl -ties) passing on of characteristics from one generation to another
herein adv in this place, matter, or document
heresies n ▷ **heresy**
heresy [**herr**-iss-ee] n (pl -sies) opinion contrary to accepted opinion or belief
heretic [**herr**-it-ik] n (pl -s) person who holds unorthodox opinions > **heretical** [hir-**ret**-ik-al] ▶ adj
heretical n ▷ **heretic**
heretics n ▷ **heretic**
herewith adv with this
heritage n (pl -s) something inherited
heritages n ▷ **heritage**
hermaphrodite [her-**maf**-roe-dite] n (pl -s) animal, plant, or person with both male and female reproductive organs
hermaphrodites n ▷ **hermaphrodite**
hermetic adj sealed so as to be airtight > **hermetically** adv
hermetically adv ▷ **hermetic**
hermit n (pl -s) person living in solitude, esp. for religious reasons
hermitage n (pl -s) home of a hermit
hermitages n ▷ **hermitage**
hermits n ▷ **hermit**
hernia n (pl -s) protrusion of an organ or part through the lining of the surrounding body cavity
hernias n ▷ **hernia**
hero n (pl -es) principal character in a film, book, etc. > **heroine** n fem (pl -s) > **heroism** [**herr**-oh-izz-um] n (pl -s)
heroes n ▷ **hero**
heroic adj courageous > **heroically** adv
heroically adv ▷ **heroic**
heroics pl n extravagant behaviour
heroin n (pl -s) highly addictive drug derived from morphine

heroine n ▷ **hero**
heroines n ▷ **hero**
heroins n ▷ **heroin**
heroism n ▷ **hero**
heroisms n ▷ **hero**
heron n (pl -s) long-legged wading bird
herons n ▷ **heron**
herpes [**her**-peez] n (pl -es) any of several inflammatory skin diseases, including shingles and cold sores
herpeses n ▷ **herpes**
herring n (pl -s) important food fish of northern seas
herringbone n (pl -s) pattern of zigzag lines
herringbones n ▷ **herringbone**
herrings n ▷ **herring**
hertz n (pl -es) (PHYSICS) unit of frequency
hertzes n ▷ **hertz**
hes n ▷ **he**
hesitancies n ▷ **hesitant**
hesitancy n ▷ **hesitant**
hesitant adj undecided or wavering > **hesitantly** adv > **hesitancy** n (pl -cies)
hesitantly adv ▷ **hesitant**
hesitate v (-tes, -ting, -ted) be slow or uncertain in doing something > **hesitation** n (pl -s)
hesitated v ▷ **hesitate**
hesitates v ▷ **hesitate**
hesitating v ▷ **hesitate**
hesitation n ▷ **hesitate**
hesitations n ▷ **hesitate**
hessian n (pl -s) coarse jute fabric
hessians n ▷ **hessian**
heterodox adj differing from accepted doctrines or beliefs > **heterodoxy** n (pl -xies)
heterodoxies n ▷ **heterodox**
heterodoxy n ▷ **heterodox**
heterogeneities n ▷ **heterogeneous**
heterogeneity n ▷ **heterogeneous**
heterogeneous [het-er-oh-**jean**-ee-uss] adj composed of diverse elements > **heterogeneity** n (pl -ties)
heterosexual n (pl -s) person sexually attracted to members of the opposite sex ▶ adj > **heterosexuality** n (pl -ties)
heterosexualities n ▷ **heterosexual**
heterosexuality n ▷ **heterosexual**
heterosexuals n ▷ **heterosexual**
heuristic [hew-**rist**-ik] adj involving learning by investigation
hew v (-s, -ing, -ed or **hewn**) cut with an axe
hewed v ▷ **hew**
hewing v ▷ **hew**
hewn v ▷ **hew**

hews v ▷ **hew**

■ **hex** n hexes. A hex is a curse or spell. This is a really useful word to remember when you have an X, as there is likely to be an E or H on the board already.

hexagon n (pl -s) geometrical figure with six sides > **hexagonal** adj

hexagonal adj ▷ **hexagon**

hexagons n ▷ **hexagon**

hey interj expression of surprise or for catching attention

heyday n (pl -s) time of greatest success, prime

heydays n ▷ **heyday**

■ **hi** interj. Hi is an informal word for hello. This everyday word is worth keeping in mind when you want to form a word adjacent to a parallel word below or above. Hi scores 5 points.

hiatus [hie-**ay**-tuss] n (pl -**tuses, -tus**) pause or interruption in continuity

hiatuses n ▷ **hiatus**

hibernate v (-**tes, -ting, -ted**) (of an animal) pass the winter as if in a deep sleep > **hibernation** n (pl -s)

hibernated v ▷ **hibernate**

hibernates v ▷ **hibernate**

hibernating v ▷ **hibernate**

hibernation n ▷ **hibernate**

hibernations n ▷ **hibernate**

hibiscus n (pl -**cuses**) tropical plant with large brightly coloured flowers

hibiscuses n ▷ **hibiscus**

hiccough n, v ▷ **hiccup**

hiccoughed v ▷ **hiccup**

hiccoughing v ▷ **hiccup**

hiccoughs n, v ▷ **hiccup**

hiccup, hiccough n (pl -s) spasm of the breathing organs with a sharp coughlike sound (Informal) ▶ v (-**s, -pping, -pped**) make a hiccup

hiccupped v ▷ **hiccup**

hiccupping v ▷ **hiccup**

hiccups n, v ▷ **hiccup**

hick n (pl -s) (US, AUST & NZ) (Informal) unsophisticated country person

hickories n ▷ **hickory**

hickory n (pl -**ries**) N American nut-bearing tree

hicks n ▷ **hick**

hid v ▷ **hide¹**

hidden v ▷ **hide¹**

hide¹ v (-**des, -ding, hid, hidden**) put (oneself or an object) somewhere difficult to see or find ▶ n (pl -s) place of concealment, esp. for a bird-watcher

hide² n (pl -s) skin of an animal

hidebound adj unwilling to accept new ideas

hideous [hid-ee-uss] adj ugly, revolting > **hideously** adv

hideously adv ▷ **hideous**

hideout n (pl -s) place to hide in

hideouts n ▷ **hideout**

hides v ▷ **hide¹** ▶ n ▷ **hide¹, ²**

hiding n (pl -s) (Slang) severe beating ▶ v ▷ **hide¹**

hidings n ▷ **hiding**

hierarchical adj ▷ **hierarchy**

hierarchies n ▷ **hierarchy**

hierarchy [**hire**-ark-ee] n (pl -**chies**) system of people or things arranged in a graded order > **hierarchical** adj

hieroglyphic [hire-oh-**gliff**-ik] adj of a form of writing using picture symbols, as used in ancient Egypt ▶ n (pl -s) symbol that is difficult to decipher (also **hieroglyph**)

hieroglyphics n ▷ **hieroglyphic**

high adj (-**er, -est**) of a great height ▶ adv at or to a high level > **highly** adv

highbrow adj, n (pl -s) intellectual and serious (person)

highbrows n ▷ **highbrow**

higher adj ▷ **high**

highest adj ▷ **high**

highlands pl n area of high ground

highlight n (pl -s) outstanding part or feature ▶ v (-**s, -ing, -ed**) give emphasis to

highlighted v ▷ **highlight**

highlighting v ▷ **highlight**

highlights n, v ▷ **highlight**

highly adv ▷ **high**

highway n (pl -s) (US, AUST & NZ) main road

highwayman n (pl -**men**) (formerly) robber, usu. on horseback, who robbed travellers at gunpoint

highwaymen n ▷ **highwayman**

highways n ▷ **highway**

hijack v (-**s, -ing, -ed**) seize control of (an aircraft or other vehicle) while travelling > **hijacker** n (pl -s)

hijacked v ▷ **hijack**

hijacker n ▷ **hijack**

hijackers n ▷ **hijack**

hijacking v ▷ **hijack**

hijacks v ▷ **hijack**

hike n (pl -s) long walk in the country, esp. for pleasure ▶ v (-**kes, -king, -ked**) go for a long walk > **hiker** n (pl -s)

hiked v ▷ **hike**

hiker n ▷ **hike**

hikers n ▷ **hike**

hikes *n, v* ▷ hike
hiking *v* ▷ hike
hilarious *adj* very funny > **hilariously** *adv*
> **hilarity** *n* (*pl* -ties)
hilariously *adv* ▷ hilarious
hilarities *n* ▷ hilarious
hilarity *n* ▷ hilarious
hill *n* (*pl* -s) raised part of the earth's surface,
less high than a mountain > **hilly** *adj* (-lier,
-liest)
hillbillies *n* ▷ hillbilly
hillbilly *n* (*pl* -llies) (us) unsophisticated
country person
hillier *adj* ▷ hill
hilliest *adj* ▷ hill
hillock *n* (*pl* -s) small hill
hillocks *n* ▷ hillock
hills *n* ▷ hill
hilly *adj* ▷ hill
hilt *n* (*pl* -s) handle of a sword or knife
hilts *n* ▷ hilt
him *pron* refers to a male person or animal
when the object of a sentence or clause
hind¹ *adj* (-er, -most) situated at the back
hind² *n* (*pl* -s) female deer
hinder *adj* ▷ hind¹ ▶ *v* (-s, -ing, -ed) get in the
way of > **hindrance** *n* (*pl* -s)
hindered *v* ▷ hinder
hindering *v* ▷ hinder
hinders *v* ▷ hinder
hindmost *adj* ▷ hind¹
hindrance *n* ▷ hinder
hindrances *n* ▷ hinder
hinds *n* ▷ hind²
hinge *n* (*pl* -s) device for holding together two
parts so that one can swing freely ▶ *v* (-ges,
-ging, -ged) (*foll. by* **on**) depend (on)
hinged *v* ▷ hinge
hinges *n, v* ▷ hinge
hinging *v* ▷ hinge
hint *n* (*pl* -s) indirect suggestion ▶ *v* (-s, -ing,
-ed) suggest indirectly
hinted *v* ▷ hint
hinterland *n* (*pl* -s) land lying behind a coast or
near a city, esp. a port
hinterlands *n* ▷ hinterland
hinting *v* ▷ hint
hints *n, v* ▷ hint
hip¹ *n* (*pl* -s) either side of the body between
the pelvis and the thigh
hip² *n* (*pl* -s) rosehip
hippie *adj, n* (*pl* -s) ▷ hippy
hippies *n* ▷ hippie
hippo *n* (*pl* -ppos) (*Informal*) hippopotamus
hippodrome *n* (*pl* -s) music hall, variety

theatre, or circus
hippodromes *n* ▷ hippodrome
hippopotami *n* ▷ hippopotamus
hippopotamus *n* (*pl* -muses, -mi) large African
mammal with thick wrinkled skin, living
near rivers
hippopotamuses *n* ▷ hippopotamus
hippos *n* ▷ hippo
hippy *adj, n* (*pl* -ppies) (esp. in the 1960s) (of)
a person whose behaviour and dress imply a
rejection of conventional values
hips *n* ▷ hip¹, ²
hire *v* (-res, -ring, -red) pay to have temporary
use of ▶ *n* (*pl* -s) hiring
hired *v* ▷ hire
hireling *n* (*pl* -s) person who works only for
wages
hirelings *n* ▷ hireling
hires *v, n* ▷ hire
hiring *v* ▷ hire
hirsute [her-suit] *adj* hairy
his *pron, adj* (something) belonging to him
hiss *n* (*pl* -es) sound like that of a long s (as an
expression of contempt) ▶ *v* (-es, -ing, -ed)
utter a hiss
hissed *v* ▷ hiss
hisses *n, v* ▷ hiss
hissing *v* ▷ hiss
histamine [hiss-ta-meen] *n* (*pl* -s) substance
released by the body tissues in allergic
reactions
histamines *n* ▷ histamine
histogram *n* (*pl* -s) statistical graph in which
the frequency of values is represented by
vertical bars of varying heights and widths
histograms *n* ▷ histogram
histologies *n* ▷ histology
histology *n* (*pl* -gies) study of the tissues of an
animal or plant
historian *n* (*pl* -s) writer of history
historians *n* ▷ historian
historic *adj* famous or significant in history
historical *adj* occurring in the past
> **historically** *adv*
historically *adv* ▷ historical
histories *n* ▷ history
history *n* (*pl* -ries) (record or account of) past
events and developments
histrionic *adj* excessively dramatic
histrionics *pl n* excessively dramatic
behaviour
hit *v* (-s, -tting, hit) strike, touch forcefully ▶ *n*
(*pl* -s) hitting ▶ *adj* sometimes successful and
sometimes not
hitch *n* (*pl* -es) minor problem ▶ *v* (-es, -ing, -ed)

(*Informal*) obtain (a lift) by hitchhiking
hitched v ▷ **hitch**
hitches n, v ▷ **hitch**
hitchhike v (-**kes, -king, -ked**) travel by
obtaining free lifts > **hitchhiker** n (pl -**s**)
hitchhiked n ▷ **hitchhike**
hitchhiker n ▷ **hitchhike**
hitchhikers n ▷ **hitchhike**
hitchhikes n ▷ **hitchhike**
hitchhiking n ▷ **hitchhike**
hitching v ▷ **hitch**
hither adv (*Old-fashioned*) to or towards this
place
hitherto adv until this time
hits n, v ▷ **hit**
hitting v ▷ **hit**
hive n (pl -**s**) ▷ **beehive**
hives n ▷ **hive**

> **hm** or **hmm** *interj*. This is a noise that
> people make when they are thinking
> or considering something. Both forms
> of this word are useful because neither
> contains a vowel, which is great if
> you have no vowels on your rack. Hm
> scores 5 points, while hmm scores 8.
> **ho** *interj*. Ho is a noise people make
> when they laugh. This little word is
> useful when you want to go in two
> directions at once. It's also worth
> remembering that ho is oh backwards:
> if you can't use one, you might be able
> to use the other. Ho scores 5 points.

hoard n (pl -**s**) store hidden away for future
use ▶ v (-**s, -ing, -ed**) save or store > **hoarder**
n (pl -**s**)
hoarded v ▷ **hoard**
hoarder n ▷ **hoard**
hoarders n ▷ **hoard**
hoarding n (pl -**s**) large board for displaying
advertisements ▶ v ▷ **hoard**
hoardings n ▷ **hoarding**
hoards n, v ▷ **hoard**
hoarfrost n (pl -**s**) white ground frost
hoarfrosts n ▷ **hoarfrost**
hoarier adj ▷ **hoary**
hoariest adj ▷ **hoary**
hoarse adj (-**ser, -sest**) (of a voice) rough and
unclear > **hoarsely** adv > **hoarseness** n (pl -**es**)
hoarsely adv ▷ **hoarse**
hoarseness n ▷ **hoarse**
hoarsenesses n ▷ **hoarse**
hoarsest adj ▷ **hoarse**
hoarsest adj ▷ **hoarse**
hoary adj (-**rier, -riest**) grey or white(-haired)
hoax n (pl -**es**) deception or trick ▶ v (-**es, -ing,**

-**ed**) deceive or play a trick upon > **hoaxer** n
hoaxed v ▷ **hoax**
hoaxer n ▷ **hoax**
hoaxers n ▷ **hoax**
hoaxes n, v ▷ **hoax**
hoaxing v ▷ **hoax**
hob n (pl -**s**) (BRIT) flat top part of a cooker, or
a separate flat surface, containing gas or
electric rings for cooking on
hobbies n ▷ **hobby**
hobble v (-**les, -ling, -led**) walk lamely
hobbled v ▷ **hobble**
hobbles v ▷ **hobble**
hobbling v ▷ **hobble**
hobby n (pl -**bbies**) activity pursued in one's
spare time
hobbyhorse n (pl -**s**) favourite topic
hobbyhorses n ▷ **hobbyhorse**
hobgoblin n (pl -**s**) mischievous goblin
hobgoblins n ▷ **hobgoblin**
hobnob v (-**s, -nobbing, -nobbed**) (*foll. by* **with**)
be on friendly terms (with)
hobnobbed v ▷ **hobnob**
hobnobbing v ▷ **hobnob**
hobnobs v ▷ **hobnob**
hobo n (pl -**s**) (US, AUST & NZ) tramp or vagrant
hobos n ▷ **hobo**
hobs n ▷ **hob**
hock¹ n (pl -**s**) joint in the back leg of an animal
such as a horse that corresponds to the
human ankle
hock² n (pl -**s**) white German wine
hock³ v (-**s, -ing, -ed**) (*Informal*) pawn
hocked v ▷ **hock**
hockey n (pl -**s**) team game played on a field
with a ball and curved sticks
hockeys n ▷ **hockey**
hocking v ▷ **hock**
hocks n ▷ **hock¹, ²** ▶ v ▷ **hock³**
hod n (pl -**s**) open wooden box attached to a
pole, for carrying bricks or mortar
hods n ▷ **hod**
hoe n (pl -**s**) long-handled tool used for
loosening soil or weeding ▶ v (-**oes, -oeing,**
-**oed**) scrape or weed with a hoe
hoed v ▷ **hoe**
hoeing v ▷ **hoe**
hoes n, v ▷ **hoe**
hog n (pl -**s**) castrated male pig (*Informal*) ▶ v
(-**s, -gging, -gged**) (*Informal*) take more than
one's share of
hogged v ▷ **hog**
hogging v ▷ **hog**
hogmanay n (pl -**s**) (in Scotland) New Year's
Eve

hogmanays n ▷ **hogmanay**
hogs n, v ▷ **hog**
hogshead n (pl -s) large cask
  hogsheads n ▷ **hogshead**
hogwash n (pl -es) (Informal) nonsense
  hogwashes n ▷ **hogwash**
hoick v (-s, -ing, -ed) raise abruptly and sharply
  hoicked v ▷ **hoick**
  hoicking v ▷ **hoick**
  hoicks v ▷ **hoick**
hoist v (-s, -ing, -ed) raise or lift up ▶ n (pl -s) device for lifting things
  hoisted v ▷ **hoist**
  hoisting v ▷ **hoist**
  hoists v, n ▷ **hoist**
hold¹ v (-s, -ing, held) keep or support in or with the hands or arms ▶ n (pl -s) act or way of holding > **holder** n (pl -s)
hold² n (pl -s) cargo compartment in a ship or aircraft
holdall n (pl -s) large strong travelling bag
  holdalls n ▷ **holdall**
  holder n ▷ **hold¹**
  holders n ▷ **hold¹**
holding n (pl -s) property, such as land or stocks and shares ▶ v ▷ **hold¹**
  holds n ▷ **hold¹, ²** ▶ v ▷ **hold¹**
holdup n (pl -s) armed robbery
  holdups n ▷ **holdup**
hole n (pl -s) area hollowed out in a solid ▶ v (-les, -ling, -led) make holes in
  holed v ▷ **hole**
  holes n, v ▷ **hole**
holiday n (pl -s) time spent away from home for rest or recreation
  holidays n ▷ **holiday**
  holier adj ▷ **holy**
  holiest adj ▷ **holy**
holiness n (pl -es) state of being holy
  holinesses n ▷ **holiness**
  holing v ▷ **hole**
  holisms n ▷ **holism**
holistic adj considering the complete person, physically and mentally, in the treatment of an illness > **holism** n (pl -s)
  hollies n ▷ **holly**
  holloganism n ▷ **hooligan**
hollow adj having a hole or space inside ▶ n (pl -s) cavity or space ▶ v (-s, -ing, -ed) form a hollow in
  hollowed v ▷ **hollow**
  hollowing v ▷ **hollow**
  hollows n, v ▷ **hollow**
holly n (pl -llies) evergreen tree with prickly leaves and red berries

hollyhock n (pl -s) tall garden plant with spikes of colourful flowers
  hollyhocks n ▷ **hollyhock**
holocaust n (pl -s) destruction or loss of life on a massive scale
  holocausts n ▷ **holocaust**
hologram n (pl -s) three-dimensional photographic image
  holograms n ▷ **hologram**
holograph n (pl -s) document handwritten by the author
  holographs n ▷ **holograph**
holster n (pl -s) leather case for a pistol, hung from a belt
  holsters n ▷ **holster**
holy adj (-lier, -liest) of God or a god
homage n (pl -s) show of respect or honour towards someone or something
  homages n ▷ **homage**
home n (pl -s) place where one lives ▶ adj of one's home, birthplace, or native country (SPORT) ▶ adv to or at home ▶ v (-mes, -ming, -med) (foll. by **in** or **in on**) direct towards (a point or target) > **homeward** adj, adv > **homewards** adv
  homed v ▷ **home**
homeland n (pl -s) country from which a person's ancestors came
  homelands n ▷ **homeland**
homeless adj having nowhere to live ▶ pl n people who have nowhere to live > **homelessness** n (pl -es)
  homelessness n ▷ **homeless**
  homelessnesses n ▷ **homeless**
  homelier adj ▷ **homely**
  homeliest adj ▷ **homely**
homely adj (-lier, -liest) simple, ordinary, and comfortable
homemade adj made at home or on the premises
homeopath n (pl -s) person who practises homeopathy > **homeopathic** adj
  homeopathic adj ▷ **homeopath**
  homeopathies n ▷ **homeopath**
  homeopaths n ▷ **homeopath**
homeopathy [home-ee-op-ath-ee] n (pl -thies) treatment of disease by small doses of a drug that produces symptoms of the disease in healthy people
  homes n, v ▷ **home**
homesick adj sad because missing one's home and family > **homesickness** n (pl -es)
  homesickness n ▷ **homesick**
  homesicknesses n ▷ **homesick**
homeward adj, adv ▷ **home**

homewards *adv* ▷ **home**
homework *n* (*pl* -**s**) school work done at home
homeworks *n* ▷ **homework**
homicidal *adj* ▷ **homicide**
homicide *n* (*pl* -**s**) killing of a human being
 > **homicidal** *adj*
homicides *n* ▷ **homicide**
homilies *n* ▷ **homliy**
homily *n* (*pl* -**lies**) speech telling people how
 they should behave
homing *v* ▷ **home**
hominid *n* (*pl* -**s**) man or any extinct forerunner
 of man
hominids *n* ▷ **hominid**
homogeneities *n* ▷ **homogeneous**
homogeneity *n* ▷ **homogeneous**
homogeneous [home-oh-**jean**-ee-uss] *adj*
 formed of similar parts > **homogeneity** *n*
 (*pl* -**ties**)
homogenize *v* (-**zes**, -**zing**, -**zed**) break up
 fat globules in (milk or cream) to distribute
 them evenly
homogenized *v* ▷ **homogenize**
homogenizes *v* ▷ **homogenize**
homogenizing *v* ▷ **homogenize**
homograph *n* (*pl* -**s**) word spelt the same as
 another, but with a different meaning
homographs *n* ▷ **homograph**
homologous [hom-ol-log-uss] *adj* having a
 related or similar position or structure
homonym *n* (*pl* -**s**) word spelt or pronounced
 the same as another, but with a different
 meaning
homonyms *n* ▷ **homonym**
homophobia *n* (*pl* -**s**) hatred or fear of
 homosexuals > **homophobic** *adj*
homophobias *n* ▷ **homophobia**
homophobic *adj* ▷ **homophobia**
homophone *n* (*pl* -**s**) word pronounced
 the same as another, but with a different
 meaning or spelling
homophones *n* ▷ **homophone**
homosexual *n* (*pl* -**s**) ▶ *adj* (person) sexually
 attracted to members of the same sex
 > **homosexuality** *n* (*pl* -**ties**)
homosexualities *n* ▷ **homosexual**
homosexuality *n* ▷ **homosexual**
homosexuals *n* ▷ **homosexual**
hone *v* (-**nes**, -**ning**, -**ned**) sharpen
honed *v* ▷ **hone**
hones *v* ▷ **hone**
honest *adj* (-**er**, -**est**) truthful and moral
 > **honestly** *adv*
honester *adj* ▷ **honest**
honestest *adj* ▷ **honest**

honesties *n* ▷ **honesty**
honestly *adv* ▷ **honest**
honesty *n* (*pl* -**ties**) quality of being honest
honey *n* (*pl* -**s**) sweet edible sticky substance
 made by bees from nectar
honeycomb *n* (*pl* -**s**) waxy structure of six-
 sided cells in which honey is stored by bees
 in a beehive
honeycombs *n* ▷ **honeycomb**
honeymoon *n* (*pl* -**s**) holiday taken by a newly
 married couple
honeymoons *n* ▷ **honeymoon**
honeys *n* ▷ **honey**
honeysuckle *n* (*pl* -**s**) climbing shrub with
 sweet-smelling flowers
honeysuckles *n* ▷ **honeysuckle**
hongi [hong-jee] *n* (*pl* -**s**) (NZ) Maori greeting in
 which people touch noses
hongis *n* ▷ **hongi**
honing *v* ▷ **hone**
honk *n* (*pl* -**s**) sound made by a car horn ▶ *v* (-**s**,
 -**ing**, -**ed**) (cause to) make this sound
honked *v* ▷ **honk**
honking *v* ▷ **honk**
honks *n*, *v* ▷ **honk**
honorary *adj* held or given only as an honour
honorific *adj* showing respect
honour *n* (*pl* -**s**) sense of honesty and fairness
 ▶ *v* (-**s**, -**ing**, -**ed**) give praise and attention to
honourable *adj* worthy of respect or esteem
 > **honourably** *adv*
honourably *adv* ▷ **honourable**
honoured *v* ▷ **honour**
honouring *v* ▷ **honour**
honours *n*, *v* ▷ **honour** ▶ *pl n* university degree
 of a higher standard than an ordinary degree
hood¹ *n* (*pl* -**s**) head covering, often attached to
 a coat or jacket
hood² *n* (*pl* -**s**) (CHIEFLY US) (*Slang*) hoodlum
hooded *adj* (of a garment) having a hood
hoodlum *n* (*pl* -**s**) (*Slang*) violent criminal,
 gangster
hoodlums *n* ▷ **hoodlum**
hoodoo *n* (*pl* -**s**) (cause of) bad luck
hoodoos *n* ▷ **hoodoo**
hoods *n* ▷ **hood¹, ²**
hoodwink *v* (-**s**, -**ing**, -**ed**) trick, deceive
hoodwinked *v* ▷ **hoodwink**
hoodwinking *v* ▷ **hoodwink**
hoodwinks *v* ▷ **hoodwink**
hoof *n* (*pl* **hooves**, **hoofs**) horny covering of the
 foot of a horse, deer, etc.
hoofs *n* ▷ **hoof**
hook *n* (*pl* -**s**) curved piece of metal, plastic,
 etc., used to hang, hold, or pull something

▸ v (**-s, -ing, -ed**) fasten or catch (as if) with a hook
hookah n (pl **-s**) oriental pipe in which smoke is drawn through water and a long tube
   hookahs n ▷ **hookah**
hooked adj bent like a hook ▸ v ▷ **hook**
hooker n (pl **-s**) (CHIEFLY US) (Slang) prostitute
   hookers n ▷ **hooher**
   hooking v ▷ **hook**
   hooks n, v ▷ **hook**
hookup n (pl **-s**) linking of radio or television stations
   hookups n ▷ **hookup**
hookworm n (pl **-s**) blood-sucking worm with hooked mouthparts
   hookworms n ▷ **hookworm**
hooligan n (pl **-s**) rowdy young person
   > **hooliganism** n (pl **-s**)
   hooliganisms n ▷ **hooligan**
   hooligans n ▷ **hooligan**
hoon n (pl **-s**) (AUST & NZ) (Slang) loutish youth who drives irresponsibly
   hoons n ▷ **hoon**
hoop n (pl **-s**) rigid circular band, used esp. as a child's toy or for animals to jump through in the circus
hoopla n (pl **-s**) fairground game in which hoops are thrown over objects in an attempt to win them
   hooplas n ▷ **hoopla**
   hoops n ▷ **hoop**
   hooray interj ▷ **hurrah**
hoot n (pl **-s**) sound of a car horn ▸ v (**-s, -ing, -ed**) sound (a car horn)
   hooted v ▷ **hoot**
hooter n (pl **-s**) device that hoots
   hooters n ▷ **hooter**
   hooting v ▷ **hoot**
   hoots n, v ▷ **hoot**
hoover n ® (pl **-s**) vacuum cleaner ▸ v (**-s, -ing, -ed**) clean with a vacuum cleaner
   hoovered v ▷ **hoover**
   hoovering v ▷ **hoover**
   hoovers n, v ▷ **hoover**
   hooves n ▷ **hoof**
hop[1] v (**-s, -pping, -pped**) jump on one foot ▸ n (pl **-s**) instance of hopping
hop[2] n (pl **-s**) (often pl) climbing plant, the dried flowers of which are used to make beer
hope v (**-pes, -ping, -ped**) want (something) to happen or be true ▸ n (pl **-s**) expectation of something desired > **hopeless** adj
   hoped v ▷ **hope**
hopeful adj having, expressing, or inspiring hope ▸ n (pl **-s**) person considered to be on the brink of success
   hopefully adv in a hopeful manner
   hopefully adj ▷ **hopeful**
   hopefuls n ▷ **hopeful**
   hopeless adj ▷ **hope**
   hopes v, n ▷ **hope**
   hoping v ▷ **hope**
   hopped v ▷ **hop**[1]
hopper n (pl **-s**) container for storing substances such as grain or sand
   hoppers n ▷ **hopper**
   hopping v ▷ **hop**[1]
   hops n ▷ **hop**[1, 2] ▸ v ▷ **hop**[1]
hopscotch n (pl **-es**) children's game of hopping in a pattern drawn on the ground
   hopscotches n ▷ **hopscotch**
horde n (pl **-s**) large crowd
   hordes n ▷ **horde**
horizon n (pl **-s**) apparent line that divides the earth and the sky
   horizons n ▷ **horizon** ▸ pl n limits of scope, interest, or knowledge
horizontal adj parallel to the horizon, level, flat > **horizontally** adv
   horizontally adv ▷ **horizontal**
   hormonal adj ▷ **hormone**
hormone n (pl **-s**) substance secreted by certain glands which stimulates certain organs of the body > **hormonal** adj
   hormones n ▷ **hormone**
horn n (pl **-s**) one of a pair of bony growths sticking out of the heads of cattle, sheep, etc. > **horned** adj
hornbeam n (pl **-s**) tree with smooth grey bark
   hornbeams n ▷ **hornbeam**
hornbill n (pl **-s**) bird with a bony growth on its large beak
   hornbills n ▷ **hornbill**
hornblende n (pl **-s**) mineral containing aluminium, calcium, sodium, magnesium, and iron
   hornblendes n ▷ **hornblende**
   horned adj ▷ **horn**
hornet n (pl **-s**) large wasp with a severe sting
   hornets n ▷ **hornet**
hornpipe n (pl **-s**) (music for) a solo dance, traditionally performed by sailors
   hornpipes n ▷ **hornpipe**
   horns n ▷ **horn**
horny adj (**-nier, -niest**) of or like horn
horoscope n (pl **-s**) prediction of a person's future based on the positions of the planets, sun, and moon at his or her birth
   horoscopes n ▷ **horoscope**
horrendous adj very unpleasant and shocking

horrible *adj* disagreeable, unpleasant
> **horribly** *adv*
horribly *adv* ▷ **horrible**
horrid *adj* disagreeable, unpleasant
horrific *adj* causing horror
horrified *v* ▷ **horrify**
horrifies *v* ▷ **horrify**
horrify *v* (-fies, -fying, -fied) cause to feel horror or shock
horrifying *v* ▷ **horrify**
horror *n* (*pl* -s) (thing or person causing) terror or hatred
horrors *n* ▷ **horror**
horse *n* (*pl* -s) large animal with hooves, a mane, and a tail, used for riding and pulling carts etc.
horseflies *n* ▷ **horsefly**
horsefly *n* (*pl* -flies) large bloodsucking fly
horsehair *n* (*pl* -s) hair from the tail or mane of a horse
horsehairs *n* ▷ **horsehair**
horseman *n* (*pl* -men) person riding a horse
horsemen *n* ▷ **horseman**
horseplay *n* (*pl* -s) rough or rowdy play
horseplays *n* ▷ **horseplay**
horsepower *n* (*pl* -s) unit of power (equivalent to 745.7 watts), used to measure the power of an engine
horsepowers *n* ▷ **horsepower**
horseradish *n* (*pl* -es) strong-tasting root of a plant, usu. made into a sauce
horseradishes *n* ▷ **horseradish**
horses *n* ▷ **horse**
horseshoe *n* (*pl* -s) protective U-shaped piece of iron nailed to a horse's hoof, regarded as a symbol of good luck
horseshoes *n* ▷ **horseshoe**
horsewoman *n* (*pl* -men) woman riding a horse
horsewomen *n* ▷ **horsewoman**
horsey, horsy *adj* (-sier, -siest) very keen on horses
horsier *adj* ▷ **horsey**
horsiest *adj* ▷ **horsey**
horsy *adj* ▷ **horsey**
horticultural *adj* ▷ **horticulture**
horticulturalist *n* ▷ **horticulture**
horticulturalists *n* ▷ **horticulture**
horticulture *n* (*pl* -s) art or science of cultivating gardens > **horticultural** *adj*
> **horticulturalist, horticulturist** *n* (*pl* -s)
horticultures *n* ▷ **horticulture**
horticulturist *n* ▷ **horticulture**
horticulturists *n* ▷ **horticulture**
hosanna *interj* exclamation of praise to God

hose[1] *n* (*pl* -s) flexible pipe for conveying liquid
▶ *v* (-ses, -sing, -sed) water with a hose
hose[2] *n* (*pl* -s) stockings, socks, and tights
hosed *v* ▷ **hose**[1]
hoses *n*, *v* ▷ **hose**[1, 2] ▶ *v* ▷ **hose**[1]
hosieries *n* ▷ **hosiery**
hosiery *n* (*pl* -ries) stockings, socks, and tights collectively
hosing *v* ▷ **hose**[1]
hospice [hoss-piss] *n* (*pl* -s) nursing home for the terminally ill
hospices *n* ▷ **hospice**
hospitable *adj* welcoming to strangers or guests
hospital *n* (*pl* -s) place where people who are ill are looked after and treated
hospitalities *n* ▷ **hospitality**
hospitalities *n* ▷ **hospitality**
hospitality *n* (*pl* -ties) kindness in welcoming strangers or guests
hospitalization *n* ▷ **hospitalize**
hospitalizations *n* ▷ **hospitalize**
hospitalize *v* (-izes, -izing, -ized) send or admit to hospital > **hospitalization** *n* (*pl* -s)
hospitalized *v* ▷ **hospitalize**
hospitalizes *v* ▷ **hospitalize**
hospitalizing *v* ▷ **hospitalize**
hospitals *n* ▷ **hospital**
host[1] *n* (*pl* -s) man who entertains guests, esp. in his own home ▶ *v* (-s, -ing, -ed) be the host of
host[2] *n* (*pl* -s) large number
hostage *n* (*pl* -s) person who is illegally held prisoner until certain demands are met by other people
hostages *n* ▷ **hostage**
hosted *v* ▷ **host**[1]
hostel *n* (*pl* -s) building providing accommodation at a low cost for a specific group of people such as students, travellers, homeless people, etc.
hostelries *n* ▷ **hostelry**
hostelry *n* (*pl* -ries) (Old-fashioned or facetious) inn, pub
hostels *n* ▷ **hostel**
hostess *n* (*pl* -es) woman who entertains guests, esp. in her own home
hostesses *n* ▷ **hostess**
hostile *adj* unfriendly
hostilities *n* ▷ **hostility** ▶ *pl n* acts of warfare
hostility *n* (*pl* -ties) unfriendly and aggressive feelings or behaviour
hosting *v* ▷ **host**[1]
hosts *n* ▷ **host**[1, 2] ▶ *v* ▷ **host**[1]
hot *adj* (-tter, -ttest) having a high

temperature in trouble > **hotly** *adv*
hotbed *n* (*pl* **-s**) any place encouraging a particular activity
  hotbeds *n* ▷ **hotbed**
hotchpotch *n* (*pl* **-es**) jumbled mixture
  hotchpotches *n* ▷ **hotchpotch**
hotel *n* (*pl* **-s**) commercial establishment providing lodging and meals
hotelier *n* (*pl* **-s**) owner or manager of a hotel
  hoteliers *n* ▷ **hotelier**
  hotels *n* ▷ **hotel**
hotfoot *adv* (*Informal*) quickly and eagerly
hotheaded *adj* rash, having a hot temper
hothouse *n* (*pl* **-s**) greenhouse
  hothouses *n* ▷ **hothouse**
hotline *n* (*pl* **-s**) direct telephone link for emergency use
  hotlines *n* ▷ **hotline**
  hotly *adv* ▷ **hot**
hotplate *n* (*pl* **-s**) heated metal surface on an electric cooker
  hotplates *n* ▷ **hotplate**
  hotter *adj* ▷ **hot**
  hottest *adj* ▷ **hot**
hound *n* (*pl* **-s**) hunting dog ▶ *v* (**-s, -ing, -ed**) pursue relentlessly
  hounded *v* ▷ **hound**
  hounding *v* ▷ **hound**
  hounds *n*, *v* ▷ **hound**
hour *n* (*pl* **-s**) twenty-fourth part of a day, sixty minutes
hourglass *n* (*pl* **-es**) device with two glass compartments, containing a quantity of sand that takes an hour to trickle from the top section to the bottom one
  hourglasses *n* ▷ **hourglass**
houri *n* (*pl* **-s**) (ISLAM) any of the nymphs of paradise
  houris *n* ▷ **houri**
hourly *adj*, *adv* (happening) every hour
hours *pl n* period regularly appointed for work or business ▶ *n* ▷ **hour**
house *n* (*pl* **-s**) building used as a home ▶ *v* (**-ses, -sing, -sed**) give accommodation to
houseboat *n* (*pl* **-s**) stationary boat used as a home
  houseboats *n* ▷ **houseboat**
housebreaker *n* (*pl* **-s**) burglar
  housebreakers *n* ▷ **housebreaker**
housecoat *n* (*pl* **-s**) woman's long loose coat-shaped garment for wearing at home
  housecoats *n* ▷ **housecoat**
  housed *v* ▷ **house**
household *n* (*pl* **-s**) all the people living in a house

householder *n* (*pl* **-s**) person who owns or rents a house
  householders *n* ▷ **householder**
  households *n* ▷ **household**
housekeeper *n* (*pl* **-s**) person employed to run someone else's household
  housekeepers *n* ▷ **housekeeper**
housekeeping *n* (*pl* **-s**) (money for) running a household
  housekeepings *n* ▷ **housekeeping**
housemaid *n* (*pl* **-s**) female servant employed to do housework
  housemaids *n* ▷ **housemaid**
  houses *n*, *v* ▷ **house**
housewarming *n* (*pl* **-s**) party to celebrate moving into a new home
  housewarmings *n* ▷ **housewarming**
housewife *n* (*pl* **-wives**) woman who runs her own household and does not have a job
  housewives *n* ▷ **housewife**
housework *n* (*pl* **-s**) work of running a home, such as cleaning, cooking, and shopping
  houseworks *n* ▷ **housework**
housing *n* (*pl* **-s**) (providing of) houses ▶ *v* ▷ **house**
  housings *n* ▷ **housing**
hovea *n* (*pl* **-s**) Australian plant with purple flowers
  hoveas *n* ▷ **hovea**
hovel *n* (*pl* **-s**) small dirty house or hut
  hovels *n* ▷ **hovel**
hover *v* (**-s, -ing, -red**) (of a bird etc.) remain suspended in one place in the air
hovercraft *n* (*pl* **-s**) vehicle which can travel over both land and sea on a cushion of air
  hovercrafts *n* ▷ **hovercraft**
  hovered *v* ▷ **hover**
  hovering *v* ▷ **hover**
  hovers *v* ▷ **hover**
how *adv* in what way, by what means
howdah *n* (*pl* **-s**) canopied seat on an elephant's back
  howdahs *n* ▷ **howdah**
however *adv* nevertheless
howitzer *n* (*pl* **-s**) large gun firing shells at a steep angle
  howitzers *n* ▷ **howitzer**
howl *n* (*pl* **-s**) loud wailing cry ▶ *v* (**-s, -ing, -ed**) utter a howl
  howled *v* ▷ **howl**
howler *n* (*pl* **-s**) (*Informal*) stupid mistake
  howlers *n* ▷ **howler**
  howling *v* ▷ **howl**
  howls *n*, *v* ▷ **howl**
hoyden *n* (*pl* **-s**) (*Old-fashioned*) wild or

boisterous girl
hoydens n ▷ **hoyden**

hox v (**hoxes, hoxing, hoxed**). This is a word found in Shakespeare's plays, and means to cut a horse's hamstring. This unusual word is a handy one to remember if you draw an X. Hox scores 12 points.

hub n (pl -**s**) centre of a wheel, through which the axle passes
  hubbies n ▷ **hubby**
hubbub n (pl -**s**) confused noise of many voices
  hubbubs n ▷ **hubbub**
hubby n (pl -**bbies**) (Informal) husband
hubris [hew-briss] n (pl -**es**) (Formal) pride, arrogance
  hubrises ▷ **hubris**
  hubs n ▷ **hub**
huckster n (pl -**s**) person using aggressive methods of selling
  hucksters n ▷ **huckster**
huddle v (-**les, -ling, -led**) hunch (oneself) through cold or fear ▶ n (pl -**s**) small group
  huddled v ▷ **huddle**
  huddles n, v ▷ **huddle**
  huddling v ▷ **huddle**
hue n (pl -**s**) colour, shade
  hues n ▷ **hue**
huff n (pl -**s**) passing mood of anger or resentment ▶ v (-**s, -ing, -ed**) blow or puff heavily > **huffy** adj (-**fier, -ffiest**) > **huffily** adv
  huffed v ▷ **huff**
  huffier adj ▷ **huff**
  huffiest adj ▷ **huff**
  huffily adv ▷ **huff**
  huffing v ▷ **huff**
  huffs n, v ▷ **huff**
  huffy adj ▷ **huff**
hug v (-**s, -gging, -gged**) clasp tightly in the arms, usu. with affection ▶ n (pl -**s**) tight or fond embrace
huge adj (-**r, -st**) very big > **hugely** adv
  huger adj ▷ **huge**
  hugest adj ▷ **huge**
  hugged v ▷ **hug**
  hugging v ▷ **hug**
  hugs n, v ▷ **hug**
huh interj exclamation of derision, bewilderment, or inquiry
hui [hoo-ee] n (pl **huies**) (NZ) meeting of Maori people
  huies n ▷ **hui**
hula n (pl -**s**) swaying Hawaiian dance
  hulas n ▷ **hula**
hulk n (pl -**s**) body of an abandoned ship

hulking adj bulky, unwieldy
  hulks n ▷ **hulk**
hull n (pl -**s**) main body of a boat ▶ v (-**s, -ing, -ed**) remove the hulls from
hullabaloo n (pl -**loos**) loud confused noise or clamour
  hullabaloos n ▷ **hullabaloo**
  hulled v ▷ **hull**
  hulling v ▷ **hull**
  hulls n, v ▷ **hull**
hum v (-**s, -mming, -mmed**) make a low continuous vibrating sound ▶ n (pl -**s**) humming sound
human adj of or typical of people ▶ n (pl -**s**) human being
humane adj (-**r, -st**) kind or merciful > **humanely** adv
  humanely adv ▷ **humane**
  humaner adj ▷ **humane**
  humanest adj ▷ **humane**
humanism n (pl -**s**) belief in human effort rather than religion > **humanist** n (pl -**s**)
  humanisms n ▷ **humanism**
  humanist n ▷ **humanism**
  humanists n ▷ **humanism**
humanitarian adj, n (pl -**s**) (person) having the interests of humankind at heart
  humanitarians n ▷ **humanitarian**
  humanities n ▷ **humanity** ▶ pl n study of literature, philosophy, and the arts
humanity n (pl -**ties**) human race
humanize v (-**zes, -zing, -zed**) make human or humane
  humanized v ▷ **humanize**
  humanizes v ▷ **humanize**
  humanizing v ▷ **humanize**
humankind n (pl -**s**) human race
  humankinds n ▷ **humankind**
humanly adv by human powers or means
  humans n ▷ **human**
humble adj (-**r, -st**) conscious of one's failings ▶ v (-**les, -ling, -led**) cause to feel humble, humiliate > **humbly** adv
  humbled v ▷ **humble**
  humbler adj ▷ **humble**
  humbles v ▷ **humble**
  humblest adj ▷ **humble**
  humbling v ▷ **humble**
  humbly adv ▷ **humble**
humbug n (pl -**s**) (BRIT) hard striped peppermint sweet
  humbugs n ▷ **humbug**
humdinger n (pl -**s**) (Slang) excellent person or thing
  humdingers n ▷ **humdinger**

humdrum *adj* ordinary, dull
humeri *n* ▷ humerus
humerus [**hew**-mer-uss] *n* (*pl* -**meri**) [-mer-rye]
bone from the shoulder to the elbow
humid *adj* (-**er**, -**est**) damp and hot > **humidity**
n (*pl* -**ties**) > **humidify** *v* (-**fies**, -**fying**, -**fied**)
humider *adj* ▷ humid
humidest *adj* ▷ humid
humidified *v* ▷ humid
humidifier *n* (*pl* -**s**) device for increasing the
amount of water vapour in the air in a room
humidifiers *n* ▷ humidifier
humidifies *v* ▷ humid
humidifying *v* ▷ humidify
humidities *n* ▷ humid
humidity *n* ▷ humid
humiliate *v* (-**tes**, -**ting**, -**ted**) lower the
dignity or hurt the pride of > **humiliating** *adj*
> **humiliation** *n* (*pl* -**s**)
humiliated *v* ▷ humiliate
humiliates *v* ▷ humiliate
humiliating *v*, *adj* ▷ humiliate
humiliation *n* ▷ humiliate
humiliations *n* ▷ humiliate
humilities *n* ▷ humility
humility *n* (*pl* **humilities**) quality of being
humble
hummed *v* ▷ hum
humming *v* ▷ hum
hummingbird *n* (*pl* -**s**) very small American
bird whose powerful wings make a humming
noise as they vibrate
hummingbirds *n* ▷ hummingbird
hummock *n* (*pl* -**s**) very small hill
hummocks *n* ▷ hummock
humorist *n* (*pl* -**s**) writer or entertainer who
uses humour in his or her work
humorists *n* ▷ humorist
humorous *adj* ▷ humour
humorously *adj* ▷ humour
humour *n* (*pl* -**s**) ability to say or perceive
things that are amusing ▶ *v* (-**s**,
-**ing**, -**ed**) (*Slang*) carry or heave
be kind and indulgent to > **humorous** *adj*
> **humorously** *adv*
humoured *v* ▷ humour
humouring *v* ▷ humour
humours *n*, *v* ▷ humour
hump *n* (*pl* -**s**) raised piece of ground ▶ *v* (-**s**,
-**ing**, -**ed**) (*Slang*) carry or heave
humped *v* ▷ hump
humping *v* ▷ hump
humps *n*, *v* ▷ hump
hums *v*, *n* ▷ hum
humus [**hew**-muss] *n* (*pl* -**es**) decomposing
vegetable and animal mould in the soil

humuses *n* ▷ humus
hunch *n* (*pl* -**es**) feeling or suspicion not
based on facts ▶ *v* (-**es**, -**ing**, -**ed**) draw (one's
shoulders) up or together
hunchback *n* (*pl* -**s**) (*Offens*) person with an
abnormal curvature of the spine
hunchbacks *n* ▷ hunchback
hunched *v* ▷ hunch
hunches *n*, *v* ▷ hunch
hunching *v* ▷ hunch
hundred *adj* ten times ten ▶ *n* (*pl* -**s**) (*often pl*)
large but unspecified number > **hundredth**
adj, *n* (*pl* -**s**)
hundreds *n* ▷ hundred
hundredth *n* ▷ hundred
hundredths *n* ▷ hundred
hundredweight *n* (*pl* -**s**) (BRIT) unit of weight
of 112 pounds (50.8 kilograms)
hundredweights *n* ▷ hundredweight
hung *v* ▷ hang ▶ *adj* (of a parliament or jury)
with no side having a clear majority
hunger *n* (*pl* -**s**) discomfort or weakness from
lack of food ▶ *v* (-**s**, -**ing**, -**ed**) (*foll. by* **for**) want
very much
hungered *v* ▷ hunger
hungering *v* ▷ hunger
hungers *n*, *v* ▷ hunger
hungrier *adj* ▷ hungry
hungriest *adj* ▷ hungry
hungrily *adv* ▷ hungry
hungry *adj* (-**rier**, -**riest**) desiring food (*foll. by*
for) > **hungrily** *adv*
hunk *n* (*pl* -**s**) large piece
hunks *n* ▷ hunk
hunt *v* (-**s**, -**ing**, -**ed**) seek out and kill (wild
animals) for food or sport ▶ *n* (*pl* -**s**) hunting
huntaway *n* (*pl* -**s**) (NZ) sheepdog trained to
drive sheep by barking
huntaways *n* ▷ huntaway
hunted *v* ▷ hunt
hunter *n* (*pl* -**s**) person or animal that hunts
wild animals for food or sport
hunters *n* ▷ hunter
hunting *v* ▷ hunt
hunts *v*, *n* ▷ hunt
huntsman *n* (*pl* -**men**) man who hunts wild
animals, esp. foxes
huntsmen *n* ▷ huntsman
hurdle *n* (*pl* -**s**) (SPORT) light barrier for jumping
over in some races ▶ *v* (-**les**, -**ling**, -**led**) jump
over (something) > **hurdler** *n* (*pl* -**s**)
hurdled *v* ▷ hurdle
hurdler *n* ▷ hurdle
hurdlers *n* ▷ hurdle
hurdles *n*, *v* ▷ hurdle ▶ *pl n* race involving

hurdles
hurdling v ▷ **hurdle**
hurl v (-s, -ing, -ed) throw or utter forcefully
hurled v ▷ **hurl**
hurley n ▷ **hurling**
hurleys n ▷ **hurling**
hurling, hurley n (pl -s) Irish game like hockey
▶ v ▷ **hurl**
hurlings n ▷ **hurling**
hurls v ▷ **hurl**
hurrah, hurray interj exclamation of joy or
applause
hurricane n (pl -s) very strong, often
destructive, wind or storm
hurricanes n ▷ **hurricane**
hurried v ▷ **hurry**
hurriedly adv ▷ **hurry**
hurries v, n ▷ **hurry**
hurry v (-ries, -rying, -ried) (cause to) move or
act very quickly ▶ n (pl -ries) doing something
quickly or the need to do something quickly
> **hurriedly** adv
hurrying v ▷ **hurry**
hurt v (-s, -ing, hurt) cause physical or
mental pain to ▶ n (pl -s) physical or mental
pain
hurtful adj unkind
hurting v ▷ **hurt**
hurtle v (-les, -ling, -led) move quickly or
violently
hurtled v ▷ **hurtle**
hurtles v ▷ **hurtle**
hurtling v ▷ **hurtle**
hurts v, n ▷ **hurt**
husband n (pl -s) woman's partner in marriage
▶ v (-s, -ing, -ed) use economically
husbanded v ▷ **husband**
husbanding v ▷ **husband**
husbandries n ▷ **husbandry**
husbandry n (pl -ries) farming
husbands n, v ▷ **husband**
hush v (-es, -ing, -ed) make or be silent ▶ n (pl
-es) stillness or silence
hushed v ▷ **hush**
hushes v, n ▷ **hush**
hushing v ▷ **hush**
husk n (pl -s) outer covering of certain seeds
and fruits ▶ v (-s, -ing, -ed) remove the husk
from
husked v ▷ **husk**
huskier adj ▷ **husky**[1]
huskies n ▷ **husky**[2]
huskiest adj ▷ **husky**[1]
huskily adv ▷ **husky**[1]
husking v ▷ **husk**

husks n, v ▷ **husk**
husky[1] adj (-kier, -kiest) slightly hoarse
> **huskily** adv
husky[2] n (pl -kies) Arctic sledge dog with thick
hair and a curled tail
hussar [hoo-**zar**] n (pl -s) (HIST) lightly armed
cavalry soldier
hussars n ▷ **hussar**
hussies n ▷ **hussy**
hussy n (pl -sies) immodest or promiscuous
woman
hustings pl n political campaigns and
speeches before an election
hustle v (-les, -ling, -led) push about, jostle ▶ n
(pl -les) lively activity or bustle
hustled v ▷ **hustle**
hustles v, n ▷ **hustle**
hustling v ▷ **hustle**
hut n (pl -s) small house, shelter, or shed
hutch n (pl -es) cage for pet rabbits etc.
hutches n ▷ **hutch**
huts n ▷ **hut**
hyacinth n (pl -s) sweet-smelling spring flower
that grows from a bulb
hyacinths n ▷ **hyacinth**
hyaena n (pl -s) ▷ **hyena**
hyaenas n ▷ **hyaena**
hybrid n (pl -s) offspring of two plants or
animals of different species ▶ adj of mixed
origin
hybrids n ▷ **hybrid**
hydra n (pl -s) mythical many-headed water
serpent
hydrangea n (pl -s) ornamental shrub with
clusters of pink, blue, or white flowers
hydrangeas n ▷ **hydrangea**
hydrant n (pl -s) outlet from a water main with
a nozzle for a hose
hydrants n ▷ **hydrant**
hydras n ▷ **hydra**
hydrate n (pl -tes) chemical compound of
water with another substance
hydrates n ▷ **hydrate**
hydraulic adj operated by pressure forced
through a pipe by a liquid such as water or oil
hydraulically adv ▷ **hydraulics**
hydraulics n study of the mechanical
properties of fluids as they apply to practical
engineering > **hydraulically** adv
hydro[1] n (pl -s) hotel offering facilities for
hydropathy
hydro[2] adj ▷ **hydroelectric**
hydrocarbon n (pl -s) compound of hydrogen
and carbon
hydrocarbons n ▷ **hydrocarbon**

hydroelectric *adj* of the generation of electricity by water pressure

hydrofoil *n* (*pl* -s) fast light boat with its hull raised out of the water on one or more pairs of fins

hydrofoils *n* ▷ hydrofoil

hydrogen *n* (*pl* -s) (CHEM) light flammable colourless gas that combines with oxygen to form water

hydrogens *n* ▷ hydrogen

hydrolyses *n* ▷ hydrolysis

hydrolysis [hie-drol-iss-iss] *n* (*pl* -yses) decomposition of a chemical compound reacting with water

hydrometer [hie-drom-it-er] *n* (*pl* -s) instrument for measuring the density of a liquid

hydrometers *n* ▷ hydrometer

hydropathies *n* ▷ hydropathy

hydropathy *n* (*pl* -thies) method of treating disease by the use of large quantities of water both internally and externally

hydrophobia *n* (*pl* -s) rabies

hydrophobias *n* ▷ hydrophobia

hydroplane *n* (*pl* -s) light motorboat that skims the water

hydroplanes *n* ▷ hydroplane

hydroponics *n* method of growing plants in water rather than soil

hydros *n* ▷ hydro[1]

hydrotherapies *n* ▷ hydrotherapy

hydrotherapy *n* (*pl* -pies) (MED) treatment of certain diseases by exercise in water

hyena *n* (*pl* -s) scavenging doglike mammal of Africa and S Asia

hyenas *n* ▷ hyena

hygiene *n* (*pl* -s) principles and practice of health and cleanliness > **hygienic** *adj* > **hygienically** *adv*

hygienic *adj* ▷ hygiene

hygienically *adj* ▷ hygiene

hymen *n* (*pl* -s) membrane partly covering the opening of a girl's vagina, which breaks before puberty or at the first occurrence of sexual intercourse

hymens *n* ▷ hymen

hymn *n* (*pl* -s) Christian song of praise sung to God or a saint

hymnal *n* (*pl* -s) book of hymns (*also* **hymn book**)

hymnals *n* ▷ hymnal

hymns *n* ▷ hymn

hype *n* (*pl* -s) intensive or exaggerated publicity or sales promotion ▶ *v* (**-pes, -ping, -ped**) promote (a product) using intensive or exaggerated publicity

hyped *v* ▷ hype

hyper *adj* (*Informal*) overactive or overexcited

hyperbola [hie-per-bol-a] *n* (*pl* -s) (GEOM) curve produced when a cone is cut by a plane at a steeper angle to its base than its side

hyperbolas *n* ▷ hyperbola

hyperbole [hie-per-bol-ee] *n* (*pl* -s) deliberate exaggeration for effect > **hyperbolic** *adj*

hyperboles *n* ▷ hyperbole

hyperbolic *adj* ▷ hyperbole

hyperlink (COMPUTERS) *n* (*pl* -s) link from a hypertext file that gives users instant access to related material in another file ▶ *v* (**-s, -ing, -ed**) link (files) in this way

hyperlinked *v* ▷ hyperlink

hyperlinking *v* ▷ hyperlink

hyperlinks *v*, *n* ▷ hyperlink

hypermarket *n* (*pl* -s) huge self-service store

hypermarkets *n* ▷ hypermarket

hypersensitive *adj* extremely sensitive to certain drugs, extremes of temperature, etc.

hypersonic *adj* having a speed of at least five times the speed of sound

hypertension *n* (*pl* -s) very high blood pressure

hypertensions *n* ▷ hypertension

hypertensions *n* ▷ hypertension

hypertext *n* (*pl* -s) computer software and hardware that allows users to store and view text and move between related items easily

hypertexts *n* ▷ hypertext

hypes *n*, *v* ▷ hype

hyphen *n* (*pl* -s) punctuation mark (-) indicating that two words or syllables are connected

hyphenated *adj* (of two words or syllables) having a hyphen between them > **hyphenation** *n* (*pl* -s)

hyphenation *n* ▷ hyphenated

hyphenations *n* ▷ hyphenated

hyphens *n* ▷ hyphen

hyping *v* ▷ hype

hypnoses *n* ▷ hypnosis

hypnosis *n* (*pl* -noses) artificially induced state of relaxation in which the mind is more than usually receptive to suggestion

hypnotic *adj* of or (as if) producing hypnosis

hypnotism *n* (*pl* -s) inducing hypnosis in someone > **hypnotist** *n* (*pl* -s) > **hypnotize** *v* (**-tizes, -tizing, -tized**)

hypnotisms *n* ▷ hypnotism

hypnotist *n* ▷ hypnotism

hypnotists *n* ▷ hypnotism

hypnotize *v* ▷ hypnotism

hypnotized v ▷ hypnotism
hypnotizes v ▷ hypnotism
hypnotizing v ▷ hypnotism
hypoallergenic adj (of cosmetics) not likely to cause an allergic reaction
hypochondria n (pl -s) undue preoccupation with one's health > **hypochondriac** n (pl -s)
hypochondriac n ▷ hypochondria
hypochondriacs n ▷ hypochondria
hypochondrias n ▷ hypochondria
hypocrisies n ▷ hypocrisy
hypocrisy [hip-**ok**-rass-ee] n (pl -**sies**) (instance of) pretence of having standards or beliefs that are contrary to one's real character or actual behaviour
hypocrite [hip-oh-krit] n (pl -s) person who pretends to be what he or she is not > **hypocritical** adj > **hypocritically** adv
hypocrites n ▷ hypocrite
hypocritical adj ▷ hypocrite
hypocritically adv ▷ hypocrite
hypodermic adj, n (pl -s) (denoting) a syringe or needle used to inject a drug beneath the skin
hypodermics n ▷ hypodermic
hypotension n (pl -s) very low blood pressure
hypotenuse [hie-**pot**-a-news] n (pl -s) side of a right-angled triangle opposite the right angle
hypotenuses n ▷ hypotenuse
hypothermia n (pl -s) condition in which a person's body temperature is dangerously low as a result of prolonged exposure to severe cold
hypothermias n ▷ hypothermia
hypotheses n ▷ hypothesis
hypothesis [hie-**poth**-iss-iss] n (pl -**ses**) [-seez] suggested but unproved explanation of something
hypothetical adj based on assumption rather than fact or reality > **hypothetically** adv
hypothetically adj ▷ hypothetical
hyraces n ▷ hyrax
hyrax n (pl -**raxes** or -**races**) type of hoofed rodent-like animal of Africa and Asia
hyraxes n ▷ hyrax
hysterectomies n ▷ hysterectomy
hysterectomy n (pl -**mies**) surgical removal of the womb
hysteria n (pl -s) state of uncontrolled excitement, anger, or panic > **hysterical** adj > **hysterically** adv
hysterias n ▷ hysteria
hysterical adj ▷ hysteria
hysterically adj ▷ hysteria
hysterics pl n attack of hysteria

I i

The letter I can prove a difficult tile to use effectively in Scrabble. It's one of the most common tiles in the game, so you often end up with two or more on your rack, but it can be hard to get rid of. Where I does come in very useful, though, is in the number of everyday short words that can be formed from it, which are very helpful when you need to form short words in addition to the main word that you want to play. These words include **in, is, it** (2 points each), **id** (3) and **if** (5). Other handy words are **icy** (8), **ivy** (9) and **imp** (7). Don't forget the three-letter words that use K: **ilk, ink** and **irk** (7 each).

ibex [ibe-eks] n (pl -es) wild goat of N with large backward-curving horns
　ibexes n ▷ **ibex**
ibis [ibe-iss] n (pl -es) large wading bird with long legs
　ibises n ▷ **ibis**
ice n (pl -s) frozen water ▶ v (-ces, -cing, -ced) (foll. by **up** or **over**) become covered with ice
iceberg n (pl -s) large floating mass of ice
　icebergs n ▷ **iceberg**
icebox n (pl -es) (US) refrigerator
　iceboxes n ▷ **icebox**
icecap n (pl -s) mass of ice permanently covering an area
　icecaps n ▷ **icecap**
iced adj covered with icing ▶ v ▷ **ice**
　ices v, n ▷ **ice**
　ich pron. Ich is an old dialect form of I. This is a useful little word that is worth remembering because of its unusual combination of letters and relatively high score. Ich scores 8 points.
ichthyologies n ▷ **ichthyology**
ichthyology [ik-thi-ol-a-jee] n (pl -gies) scientific study of fish
icicle n (pl -s) tapering spike of ice hanging where water has dripped
　icicles n ▷ **icicle**
　icier adj ▷ **icy**
　iciest adj ▷ **icy**
　icily adv ▷ **icy**
　iciness n ▷ **icy**
　icinesses n ▷ **icy**
icing v ▷ **ice** ▶ n (pl -s) mixture of sugar and water etc., used to cover and decorate cakes
　icings n ▷ **icing**
　ick interj. Ick is something that people

say when they encounter something unpleasant or disgusting. Ick is a good word to remember because, in addition to being useful when there's little space, it's one of the highest-scoring three-letter word beginning with I. Ick scores 9 points.
icon n (pl -s) picture of Christ or another religious figure, regarded as holy in the Orthodox Church
iconoclast n (pl -s) person who attacks established ideas or principles > **iconoclastic** adj
　iconoclastic adj ▷ **iconoclastic**
　iconoclasts n ▷ **iconoclast**
　icons n ▷ **icon**
icy adj (-cier, -ciest) very cold > **icily** adv > **iciness** n (pl -es)
id n (pl -s) (PSYCHOANALYSIS) the mind's instinctive unconscious energies
　ide n (ides). An ide is a kind of fish. This combination of letters is a good one to keep in mind because it is both a suffix that can be added to words already on the board and a word in its own right. Ide scores 4 points.
idea n (pl -s) plan or thought formed in the mind
ideal adj most suitable ▶ n (pl -s) conception of something that is perfect > **idealist** n (pl -s) > **idealistic** adj > **ideally** adv
idealism n (pl -s) tendency to seek perfection in everything
　idealisms n ▷ **idealism**
　idealist n ▷ **ideal**
　idealistic adj ▷ **ideal**
　idealists n ▷ **ideal**

idealization *n* ▷ idealize
idealizations *n* ▷ idealize
idealize *v* (-izes, -izing, -ized) regard or portray as perfect or nearly perfect > **idealization** *n* (*pl* -s)
idealized *n* ▷ idealize
idealizes *n* ▷ idealize
idealizing *n* ▷ idealize
ideally *adv* ▷ ideal
ideals *n* ▷ ideal
ideas *n* ▷ idea
idem *pron, adj* (LATIN) the same: used to refer to an article, chapter, or book already quoted
identical *adj* exactly the same > **identically** *adv*
identically *adv* ▷ identical
identifiable *adj* ▷ identify
identification *n* ▷ identify
identifications *n* ▷ identify
identified *v* ▷ identify
identifies *v* ▷ identify
identify *v* (-fies, -fying, -fied) prove or recognize as being a certain person or thing > **identifiable** *adj* > **identification** *n* (*pl* -s)
identifying *v* ▷ identify
identities *n* ▷ identity
identity *n* (*pl* -ties) state of being a specified person or thing
ideological *adj* ▷ ideology
ideologies *n* ▷ ideology
ideologist *n* ▷ ideology
ideologists *n* ▷ ideology
ideology *n* (*pl* -gies) body of ideas and beliefs of a group, nation, etc. > **ideological** *adj* > **ideologist** *n* (*pl* -s)
idiocies *n* ▷ idiocy
idiocy *n* (*pl* -cies) utter stupidity
idiom *n* (*pl* -s) group of words which when used together have a different meaning from the words individually > **idiomatic** *adj* > **idiomatically** *adv*
idiomatic *adj* ▷ idiom
idiomatically *adv* ▷ idiom
idioms *n* ▷ idiom
idiosyncrasies *n* ▷ idiosyncrasy
idiosyncrasy *n* (*pl* -sies) personal peculiarity of mind, habit, or behaviour
idiot *n* (*pl* -s) foolish or stupid person > **idiotic** *adj* > **idiotically** *adv*
idiotic *adj* ▷ idiot
idiotically *adv* ▷ idiot
idiots *n* ▷ idiot
idle *adj* not doing anything ▶ *v* (-les, -ling, -led) (*usu. foll. by* **away**) spend (time) doing very little > **idleness** *n* (*pl* -s) > **idler** *n* (*pl* -s) > **idly** *adv*

idled *v* ▷ idle
idleness *n* ▷ idle
idlenesses *n* ▷ idle
idler *n* ▷ idle
idlers *n* ▷ idle
idles *v* ▷ idle
idling *v* ▷ idle
idly *adj* ▷ idle
idol *n* (*pl* -s) object of excessive devotion
idolatries *n* ▷ idolatry
idolatrous *adj* ▷ idolatry
idolatry *n* (*pl* -ries) worship of idols > **idolatrous** *adj*
idolize *v* (-izes, -izing, -ized) love or admire excessively
idolized *v* ▷ idolize
idolizes *v* ▷ idolize
idolizing *v* ▷ idolize
idols *n* ▷ idol
ids *n* ▷ id
idyll [id-ill] *n* (*pl* -s) scene or time of great peace and happiness > **idyllic** *adj* > **idyllically** *adv*
idyllic *adj* ▷ idyll
idyllically *adj* ▷ idyll
idylls *n* ▷ idyll
if *conj* on the condition or supposition that ▶ *n* (*pl* -s) uncertainty or doubt

> **iff** *conj*. Iff is a word used in logic to mean if and only if. This word is worth remembering: not only can it come in handy when there isn't much space on the board, but it's also one of the highest-scoring three-letter word beginning with I. Iff scores 9 points.

iffy *adj* (*Informal*) doubtful, uncertain
ifs *n* ▷ if
igloo *n* (*pl* -loos) dome-shaped Inuit house made of snow and ice
igloos *n* ▷ igloo
igneous [ig-nee-uss] *adj* (of rock) formed as molten rock cools and hardens
ignite *v* (-tes, -ting, -ted) catch fire or set fire to
ignited *v* ▷ ignite
ignites *v* ▷ ignite
igniting *v* ▷ ignite
ignition *n* (*pl* -s) system that ignites the fuel-and-air mixture to start an engine
ignitions *n* ▷ ignition
ignoble *adj* dishonourable
ignominies *n* ▷ ignominy
ignominious *adj* ▷ ignominy
ignominiously *adj* ▷ ignominy
ignominy [ig-nom-in-ee] *n* (*pl* -nies) humiliating disgrace > **ignominious** *adj* > **ignominiously** *adv*

ignoramus *n* (*pl* **-muses**) ignorant person
  ignoramuses *n* ▷ **ignoramus**
  ignorance *n* ▷ **ignorant**
  ignorances *n* ▷ **ignorance**
ignorant *adj* lacking knowledge > **ignorance**
  n (*pl* **-s**)
ignore *v* (**-res, -ring, -red**) refuse to notice,
  disregard deliberately
  ignored *v* ▷ **ignore**
  ignores *v* ▷ **ignore**
  ignoring *v* ▷ **ignore**
iguana *n* (*pl* **-s**) large tropical American lizard
  iguanas *n* ▷ **iguana**
ileum *n* (*pl* **-s**) lowest part of the small
  intestine
  ileums *n* ▷ **ileum**
ilk *n* (*pl* **-s**) type
  ilks *n* ▷ **ilk**
ill *adj* not in good health ▶ *n* (*pl* **-s**) evil, harm
  ▶ *adv* badly > **illness** *n* (*pl* **-s**)
illegal *adj* against the law > **illegally** *adv*
  > **illegality** *n* (*pl* **-ties**)
  illegalities *n* ▷ **illegal**
  illegality *n* ▷ **illegal**
  illegally *adv* ▷ **illegal**
illegible *adj* unable to be read or deciphered
  illegitimacies *n* ▷ **illegitimate**
  illegitimacy *n* ▷ **illegitimate**
illegitimate *adj* born of parents not married to
  each other > **illegitimacy** *n* (*pl* **-s**)
illicit *adj* illegal
  illiteracies *n* ▷ **illiterate**
  illiteracy *n* ▷ **illiterate**
illiterate *n* (*pl* **-s**) ▶ *adj* (person) unable to read
  or write > **illiteracy** *n* (*pl* **-s**)
  illiterates *n* ▷ **illiterate**
  illness *n* ▷ **ill**
  illnesses *n* ▷ **ill**
illogical *adj* unreasonable > **illogicality** *n* (*pl*
  -lities)
  illogicalities *adj* ▷ **illogical**
  illogicality *adj* ▷ **illogical**
  ills *n* ▷ **ill**
illuminate *v* (**-tes, -ting, -ted**) light up
  > **illumination** *n* (*pl* **-s**) > **illuminating** *adj*
  illuminated *v* ▷ **illuminate**
  illuminates *v* ▷ **illuminate**
  illuminating *adj, v* ▷ **illuminate**
  illumination *n* ▷ **illuminate**
  illuminations *n* ▷ **illuminate**
illusion *n* (*pl* **-s**) deceptive appearance or belief
illusionist *n* (*pl* **-s**) conjuror
  illusionists *n* ▷ **illusionist**
  illusions *n* ▷ **illusion**
illusory *adj* seeming to be true, but actually

false
illustrate *v* (**-tes, -ting, -ted**) explain by use
  of examples > **illustrative** *adj* > **illustrator**
  n (*pl* **-s**)
  illustrated *v* ▷ **illustrate**
  illustrates *v* ▷ **illustrate**
  illustrating *v* ▷ **illustrate**
illustration *n* (*pl* **-s**) picture or diagram
  illustrations *n* ▷ **illustrate**
  illustrative *adj* ▷ **illustrate**
  illustrator *n* ▷ **illustrate**
  illustrators *n* ▷ **illustrate**
illustrious *adj* famous and distinguished
image *n* (*pl* **-s**) mental picture of someone or
  something
  imageries *n* ▷ **imagery**
imagery *n* (*pl* **-ries**) images collectively, esp.
  in the arts
  images *n* ▷ **image**
  imaginable *adj* ▷ **imagine**
imaginary *adj* existing only in the
  imagination
imagination *n* (*pl* **-s**) ability to make mental
  images of things that may not exist in real life
  imaginations *n* ▷ **imagination**
imaginative *adj* having or showing a lot of
  creative mental ability > **imaginatively** *adv*
  imaginatively *adv* ▷ **imaginative**
imagine *v* (**-nes, -ning, -ned**) form a mental
  image of > **imaginable** *adj*
  imagined *v* ▷ **imagine**
  imagines *v* ▷ **imagine** ▶ *n* ▷ **imago**
  imagining *v* ▷ **imagine**
imago [im-**may**-go] *n* (*pl* **-goes, -gines**) [im-**maj**-
  in-ees] sexually mature adult insect
  imagoes *n* ▷ **imago**
imam *n* (*pl* **-s**) leader of prayers in a mosque
  imams *n* ▷ **imam**
imbalance *n* (*pl* **-s**) lack of balance or
  proportion
  imbalances *n* ▷ **imbalance**
imbecile [**imb**-ess-eel] *n* (*pl* **-s**) stupid person
  ▶ *adj* (*also* **imbecilic**) stupid or senseless
  > **imbecility** *n* (*pl* **-ties**)
  imbeciles *n* ▷ **imbecile**
  imbecilic *adj* ▷ **imbecile**
  imbecilities *n* ▷ **imbecile**
  imbecility *n* ▷ **imbecile**
imbibe *v* (**-bes, -bing, -bed**) drink (alcoholic
  drinks)
  imbibed *v* ▷ **imbibe**
  imbibes *v* ▷ **imbibe**
  imbibing *v* ▷ **imbibe**
imbroglio [imb-**role**-ee-oh] *n* (*pl* **-ios**) confusing
  and complicated situation

imbroglios *n* ▷ imbroglio
imbue *v* (**-ues, -uing, -ued**) (*usu. foll. by* **with**) fill or inspire with (ideals or principles)
  imbued *v* ▷ imbue
  imbues *v* ▷ imbue
  imbuing *v* ▷ imbue
imitate *v* (**-tes, -ting, -ted**) take as a model > **imitative** *adj* > **imitator** *n* (*pl* **-s**)
  imitated *v* ▷ imitate
  imitates *v* ▷ imitate
  imitating *v* ▷ imitate
imitation *n* (*pl* **-s**) copy of an original
  imitations *n* ▷ imitation
  imitative *adj* ▷ imitate
  imitator *n* ▷ imitate
  imitators *n* ▷ imitate
immaculate *adj* completely clean or tidy > **immaculately** *adv*
  immaculately *adv* ▷ immaculate
  immanence *n* ▷ immanent
  immanences *n* ▷ immanent
immanent *adj* present within and throughout something > **immanence** *n* (*pl* **-s**)
immaterial *adj* not important, not relevant
immature *adj* not fully developed > **immaturity** *n* (*pl* **-ties**)
  immaturities *n* ▷ immature
  immaturity *n* ▷ immature
  immediacies *n* ▷ immediate
  immediacy *n* ▷ immediate
immediate *adj* occurring at once > **immediately** *adv* > **immediacy** *n* (*pl* **-cies**)
  immediately *adv* ▷ immediate
immemorial *adj* longer than anyone can remember
immense *adj* extremely large > **immensity** *n* (*pl* **-ties**)
immensely *adv* to a very great degree
  immensities *n* ▷ immense
  immensity *n* ▷ immense
immerse *v* (**-ses, -sing, -sed**) involve deeply, engross > **immersion** *n* (*pl* **-s**)
  immersed *v* ▷ immerse
  immerses *v* ▷ immerse
  immersing *v* ▷ immerse
  immersion *n* ▷ immerse
  immersions *n* ▷ immerse
  immigrant *n* ▷ immigration
  immigrants *n* ▷ immigration
immigration *n* (*pl* **-s**) coming to a foreign country in order to settle there > **immigrant** *n* (*pl* **-s**)
  immigrations *n* ▷ immigration
  imminence *n* ▷ imminent
  imminences *n* ▷ imminent

imminent *adj* about to happen > **imminently** *adv* > **imminence** *n* (*pl* **-s**)
  imminently *adv* ▷ imminent
immobile *adj* not moving > **immobility** *n* (*pl* **-ties**)
  immobilities *adj* ▷ immobile
  immobility *adj* ▷ immobile
immobilize *v* (**-izes, -izing, -ized**) make unable to move or work
  immobilized *v* ▷ immobilize
  immobilizes *v* ▷ immobilize
  immobilizing *v* ▷ immobilize
immoderate *adj* excessive or unreasonable
immolate *v* (**-tes, -ting, -ted**) kill as a sacrifice > **immolation** *n* (*pl* **-s**)
  immolated *v* ▷ immolate
  immolates *v* ▷ immolate
  immolating *v* ▷ immolate
  immolation *n* ▷ immolate
  immolations *n* ▷ immolate
immoral *adj* morally wrong, corrupt > **immorality** *n* (*pl* **-ties**)
  immoralities *n* ▷ immoral
  immorality *n* ▷ immoral
immortal *adj* living forever ▶ *n* (*pl* **-s**) person whose fame will last for all time > **immortality** *n* (*pl* **-s**) > **immortalize** *v* (**-lizes, -lizing, -lized**)
  immortalities *n* ▷ immortal
  immortality *n* ▷ immortal
  immortalized *v* ▷ immortal
  immortalizes *v* ▷ immortal
  immortalizing *v* ▷ immortal
  immortals *n* ▷ immortal
immune *adj* protected against a specific disease
  immunities *n* ▷ immunity
immunity *n* (*pl* **-ties**) ability to resist disease
  immunization *n* ▷ immunize
  immunizations *n* ▷ immunize
immunize *v* (**-izes, -izing, -ized**) make immune to a disease > **immunization** *n* (*pl* **-s**)
  immunized *v* ▷ immunize
  immunizes *v* ▷ immunize
  immunizing *v* ▷ immunize
  immunodeficiencies *n* ▷ immunodeficiency
immunodeficiency *n* (*pl* **-cies**) deficiency in or breakdown of a person's ability to fight diseases
  immunological *adj* ▷ immunology
  immunologies *n* ▷ immunology
  immunologist *n* ▷ immunology
  immunologists *n* ▷ immunology
immunology *n* (*pl* **-gies**) branch of medicine concerned with the study of immunity

> **immunological** adj > **immunologist** n (pl -**s**)
immutabilities n ▷ **immutable**
immutability n ▷ **immutable**
immutable [im-**mute**-a-bl] adj unchangeable
> **immutability** n (pl -**ties**)
imp n (pl -**s**) (in folklore) mischievous small creature with magical powers
impact n (pl -**s**) strong effect ▶ v (-**s**, -**ing**, -**ed**) press firmly into something
impacted v ▷ **impact**
impacting v ▷ **impact**
impacts n, v ▷ **impact**
impair v (-**s**, -**ing**, -**ed**) weaken or damage
> **impairment** n (pl -**s**)
impaired v ▷ **impair**
impairing v ▷ **impair**
impairment n ▷ **impair**
impairments n ▷ **impair**
impairs v ▷ **impair**
impala [imp-**ah**-la] n (pl -**s**) southern African antelope
impalas n ▷ **impala**
impale v (-**les**, -**ling**, -**led**) pierce with a sharp object
impaled v ▷ **impale**
impales v ▷ **impale**
impaling v ▷ **impale**
impalpable adj difficult to define or understand
impart v (-**s**, -**ing**, -**ed**) communicate (information)
imparted v ▷ **impart**
impartial adj not favouring one side or the other > **impartially** adv > **impartiality** n (pl -**ties**)
impartialities n ▷ **impartial**
impartiality n ▷ **impartial**
impartially adv ▷ **impartial**
imparting v ▷ **impart**
imparts v ▷ **impart**
impassable adj (of a road etc.) impossible to travel through or over
impasse [am-**pass**] n (pl -**s**) situation in which progress is impossible
impasses n ▷ **impasse**
impassioned adj full of emotion
impassive adj showing no emotion, calm
impatience n ▷ **impatient**
impatiences n ▷ **impatient**
impatient adj irritable at any delay or difficulty > **impatiently** adv > **impatience** n (pl -**s**)
impatiently adv ▷ **impatient**
impeach v (-**es**, -**ing**, -**ed**) charge with a serious crime against the state > **impeachment** n

(pl -**s**)
impeached v ▷ **impeach**
impeaches v ▷ **impeach**
impeaching v ▷ **impeach**
impeachment n ▷ **impeach**
impeachments n ▷ **impeach**
impeccable adj without fault, excellent
> **impeccably** adv
impeccably adv ▷ **impeccable**
impecunious adj penniless, poor
impedance [imp-**eed**-anss] n (pl -**s**) (ELECTRICITY) measure of the opposition to the flow of an alternating current
impedances n ▷ **impedance**
impede v (-**des**, -**ding**, -**ded**) hinder in action or progress
impeded v ▷ **impede**
impedes v ▷ **impede**
impediment n (pl -**s**) something that makes action, speech, or progress difficult
impedimenta pl n objects impeding progress, esp. baggage or equipment
impediments n ▷ **impediment**
impeding v ▷ **impede**
impel v (-**s**, -**lling**, -**lled**) push or force (someone) to do something
impelled v ▷ **impel**
impelling v ▷ **impel**
impels v ▷ **impel**
impending adj (esp. of something bad) about to happen
impenetrable adj impossible to get through
imperative adj extremely urgent, vital ▶ n (pl -**s**) (GRAMMAR) imperative mood
imperatives n ▷ **imperative**
imperceptible adj too slight or gradual to be noticed > **imperceptibly** adv
imperceptibly adv ▷ **imperceptible**
imperfect adj having faults or mistakes ▶ n (pl -**s**) (GRAMMAR) imperfect tense > **imperfection** n (pl -**s**)
imperfection n ▷ **imperfect**
imperfections n ▷ **imperfect**
imperfects n ▷ **imperfect**
imperial adj of or like an empire or emperor
imperialism n (pl -**s**) rule by one country over many others > **imperialist** adj, n (pl -**s**)
imperialisms n ▷ **imperialism**
imperialist adj, n ▷ **imperial**
imperialists n ▷ **imperialist**
imperil v (-**s**, -**lling**, -**lled**) put in danger
imperilled v ▷ **imperil**
imperilling v ▷ **imperil**
imperils v ▷ **imperil**
imperious adj proud and domineering

impersonal *adj* not relating to any particular person, objective > **impersonality** *n* (*pl* -ties)
impersonalities *n* ▷ impersonal
impersonality *n* ▷ impersonal
impersonate *v* (-tes, -ting, -ted) pretend to be (another person) > **impersonation** *n* (*pl* -s)
> **impersonator** *n* (*pl* -s)
impersonated *v* ▷ impersonate
impersonates *v* ▷ impersonate
impersonating *v* ▷ impersonate
impersonation *n* ▷ impersonate
impersonations *n* ▷ impersonate
impersonator *n* ▷ impersonate
impersonators *n* ▷ impersonate
impertinence *n* ▷ impertinent
impertinences *n* ▷ impertinent
impertinent *adj* disrespectful or rude
> **impertinently** *adv* > **impertinence** *n* (*pl* -s)
impertinently *adv* ▷ impertinent
imperturbable *adj* calm, not excitable
impervious *adj* (*foll. by* **to**) not letting (water etc.) through
impetigo [imp-it-**tie**-go] *n* (*pl* -s) contagious skin disease
impetigos *n* ▷ impetigo
impetuosities *n* ▷ impetuous
impetuosity *n* ▷ impetuous
impetuous *adj* done or acting without thought, rash > **impetuously** *adv*
> **impetuosity** *n* (*pl* -ties)
impetuously *adv* ▷ impetuous
impetus [imp-it-uss] *n* (*pl* -es) incentive, impulse
impetuses *n* ▷ impetus
impinge *v* (-ges, -ging, -ged) (*foll. by* **on**) affect or restrict
impinged *v* ▷ impinge
impinges *v* ▷ impinge
impinging *v* ▷ impinge
impious [imp-ee-uss] *adj* showing a lack of respect or reverence
impish *adj* mischievous
implacabilities *n* ▷ implacable
implacability *n* ▷ implacable
implacable *adj* not prepared to be appeased, unyielding > **implacably** *adv* > **implacability** *n* (*pl* -ties)
implacably *adv* ▷ implacably
implant *n* (*pl* -s) (MED) something put into someone's body, usu. by surgical operation
▶ *v* (-s, -ing, -ed) put (something) into someone's body, usu. by surgical operation
> **implantation** *n* (*pl* -s)
implantation *n* ▷ implant
implantations *n* ▷ implant

implanted *v* ▷ implant
implanting *v* ▷ implant
implants *n, v* ▷ implant
implement *v* (-s, -ing, -ed) carry out (instructions etc.) ▶ *n* (*pl* -s) tool, instrument
> **implementation** *n* (*pl* -s)
implementation *n* ▷ implement
implementations *n* ▷ implement
implemented *v* ▷ implement
implementing *v* ▷ implement
implements *v, n* ▷ implement
implicate *v* (-tes, -ting, -ted) show to be involved, esp. in a crime
implicated *v* ▷ implicate
implicates *v* ▷ implicate
implicating *v* ▷ implicate
implication *n* (*pl* -s) something implied
implications *n* ▷ implication
implicit *adj* expressed indirectly > **implicitly** *adv*
implicitly *adv* ▷ implicit
implied *v* ▷ imply
implies *v* ▷ imply
implore *v* (-res, -ring, -red) beg earnestly
implored *v* ▷ implore
implores *v* ▷ implore
imploring *v* ▷ implore
imply *v* (-lies, -lying, -lied) indicate by hinting, suggest
implying *v* ▷ imply
impolitic *adj* unwise or inadvisable
imponderable *n* (*pl* -s) ▶ *adj* (something) impossible to assess
imponderables *n* ▷ imponderable
import *v* (-s, -ing, -ed) bring in (goods) from another country ▶ *n* (*pl* -s) something imported > **importation** *n* (*pl* -s) > **importer** *n* (*pl* -s)
importance *n* ▷ important
importances *n* ▷ important
important *adj* of great significance or value
> **importance** *n* (*pl* -s)
importation *n* ▷ import
importations *n* ▷ import
imported *v* ▷ import
importer *n* ▷ import
importers *n* ▷ import
importing *v* ▷ import
imports *v, n* ▷ import
importunate *adj* persistent or demanding
importune *v* (-nes, -ning, -ned) harass with persistent requests > **importunity** *n* (*pl* -ties)
importuned *v* ▷ importune
importunes *v* ▷ importune
importuning *v* ▷ importune

importunities *n* ▷ **importune**
importunity *n* ▷ **importune**
impose *v* (**-ses, -sing, -sed**) force the acceptance of
imposed *v* ▷ **impose**
imposes *v* ▷ **impose**
imposing *adj* grand, impressive ▶ *v* ▷ **impose**
imposition *n* (*pl* **-s**) unreasonable demand
impositions *n* ▷ **imposition**
impossibilities *n* ▷ **impossible**
impossibility *n* ▷ **impossible**
impossible *adj* not able to be done or to happen > **impossibly** *adv* > **impossibility** *n* (*pl* **-ties**)
impossibly *adv* ▷ **impossible**
imposter, impostor *n* (*pl* **-s**) person who cheats or swindles by pretending to be someone else
imposters *n* ▷ **imposter**
impostor *n* ▷ **imposter**
impostors *n* ▷ **imposter**
impotence *n* ▷ **impotent**
impotences *n* ▷ **impotent**
impotent [imp-a-tent] *adj* powerless > **impotence** *n* (*pl* **-s**) > **impotently** *adv*
impotently *adv* ▷ **impotent**
impound *v* (**-s, -ing, -ed**) take legal possession of, confiscate
impounded *v* ▷ **impound**
impounding *v* ▷ **impound**
impounds *v* ▷ **impound**
impoverish *v* (**-es, -ing, -ed**) make poor or weak > **impoverishment** *n* (*pl* **-s**)
impoverished *v* ▷ **impoverish**
impoverishes *v* ▷ **impoverish**
impoverishing *v* ▷ **impoverish**
impoverishment *n* ▷ **impoverish**
impoverishments *n* ▷ **impoverish**
impracticable *adj* incapable of being put into practice
impractical *adj* not sensible
imprecation *n* (*pl* **-s**) curse
imprecations *n* ▷ **imprecation**
impregnabilities *n* ▷ **impregnable**
impregnability *n* ▷ **impregnable**
impregnable *adj* impossible to break into > **impregnability** *n* (*pl* **-ties**)
impregnate *v* (**-tes, -ting, -ted**) saturate, spread all through > **impregnation** *n* (*pl* **-s**)
impregnated *v* ▷ **impregnate**
impregnates *v* ▷ **impregnate**
impregnating *v* ▷ **impregnate**
impregnation *n* ▷ **impregnate**
impregnations *n* ▷ **impregnate**
impresario *n* (*pl* **-s**) person who runs theatre performances, concerts, etc.
impresarios *n* ▷ **impresario**
impress *v* (**-es, -ing, -ed**) affect strongly, usu. favourably
impressed *v* ▷ **impress**
impresses *v* ▷ **impress**
impressing *v* ▷ **impress**
impression *n* (*pl* **-s**) effect, esp. a strong or favourable one
impressionable *adj* easily impressed or influenced
impressionism *n* (*pl* **-s**) art style that gives a general effect or mood rather than form or structure > **impressionist** *n* (*pl* **-s**) > **impressionistic** *adj*
impressionisms *n* ▷ **impressionism**
impressionist *n* ▷ **impressionism**
impressionistic *adj* ▷ **impressionism**
impressionists *n* ▷ **impressionism**
impressions *n* ▷ **impression**
impressive *adj* making a strong impression, esp. through size, importance, or quality
imprimatur [imp-rim-**ah**-ter] *n* (*pl* **-s**) official approval to print a book
imprimaturs *n* ▷ **imprimatur**
imprint *n* (*pl* **-s**) mark made by printing or stamping ▶ *v* (**-s, -ing, -ed**) produce (a mark) by printing or stamping
imprinted *v* ▷ **imprint**
imprinting *v* ▷ **imprint**
imprints *n*, *v* ▷ **imprint**
imprison *v* (**-s, -ing, -ed**) put in prison > **imprisonment** *n* (*pl* **-s**)
imprisoned *v* ▷ **imprison**
imprisoning *v* ▷ **imprison**
imprisonment *n* ▷ **imprison**
imprisonments *n* ▷ **imprisonment**
imprisons *v* ▷ **imprison**
improbabilities *n* ▷ **improbable**
improbability *n* ▷ **improbable**
improbable *adj* not likely to be true or to happen > **improbability** *n* (*pl* **-ties**)
impromptu *adj* without planning or preparation
improper *adj* indecent
improprieties *n* ▷ **impropriety**
impropriety [imp-roe-**pry**-a-tee] *n* (*pl* **-ties**) unsuitable or slightly improper behaviour
improve *v* (**-ves, -ving, -ved**) make or become better > **improvement** *n* (*pl* **-s**)
improved *v* ▷ **improve**
improvement *n* ▷ **improvement**
improvements *n* ▷ **improvement**
improves *v* ▷ **improve**
improvidence *n* ▷ **improvident**

improvidences *n* ▷ **improvident**
improvident *adj* not planning for future needs
> **improvidence** *n* (*pl* -s)
improving *v* ▷ **improve**
improvisation *n* ▷ **improvise**
improvisations *n* ▷ **improvise**
improvise *v* (-ises, -sing, -sed) make use
of whatever materials are available
> **improvisation** *n* (*pl* -s)
improvised *v* ▷ **improvise**
improvises *v* ▷ **improvise**
improvising *v* ▷ **improvise**
imps *n* ▷ **imp**
impudence *n* ▷ **impudent**
impudences *n* ▷ **impudent**
impudent *adj* cheeky, disrespectful
> **impudently** *adv* > **impudence** *n* (*pl* -s)
impudently *adv* ▷ **impudently**
impugn [imp-yoon] *v* (-s, -ing, -ed) challenge
the truth or validity of
impugned *v* ▷ **impugn**
impugning *v* ▷ **impugn**
impugns *v* ▷ **impugn**
impulse *n* (*pl* -s) sudden urge to do something
> **impulsive** *adj* acting or done without
careful consideration > **impulsively** *adv*
impulses *n* ▷ **impulse**
impulsive *adj* ▷ **impulse**
impulsively *adv* ▷ **impulse**
impunities *n* ▷ **impunity**
impunity [imp-yoon-it-ee] *n* (*pl* -ties) without
punishment
impure *adj* having dirty or unwanted
substances mixed in > **impurity** *n* (*pl* -ties)
impurities *n* ▷ **impure**
impurity *n* ▷ **impure**
imputation *n* ▷ **impute**
imputations *n* ▷ **impute**
impute *v* (-tes, -ting, -ted) attribute
responsibility to > **imputation** *n* (*pl* -s)
imputed *v* ▷ **impute**
imputes *v* ▷ **impute**
imputing *v* ▷ **impute**
in *prep* indicating position inside, state or
situation, etc. ▶ *adv* indicating position
inside, entry into, etc. ▶ *adj* fashionable
inabilities *n* ▷ **inability**
inability *n* (*pl* -ties) lack of means or skill to do
something
inaccuracies *n* ▷ **inaccurate**
inaccuracy *n* ▷ **inaccurate**
inaccurate *adj* not correct > **inaccuracy** *n*
(*pl* -cies)
inadequacies *n* ▷ **inadequate**
inadequacy *n* ▷ **inadequate**

inadequate *adj* not enough > **inadequacy** *n*
(*pl* -cies)
inadvertent *adj* unintentional
> **inadvertently** *adv*
inadvertently *adv* ▷ **inadvertent**
inalienable *adj* not able to be taken away
inane *adj* senseless, silly > **inanity** *n* (*pl* -ties)
inanimate *adj* not living
inanities *n* ▷ **inane**
inanity *n* ▷ **inane**
inappropriate *adj* not suitable
inarticulate *adj* unable to express oneself
clearly or well
inaugural *adj* ▷ **inaugurate**
inaugurate *v* (-tes, -ting, -ted) open or begin
the use of, esp. with ceremony > **inaugural**
adj > **inauguration** *n* (*pl* -s)
inaugurated *v* ▷ **inaugurate**
inaugurates *v* ▷ **inaugurate**
inaugurating *v* ▷ **inaugurate**
inauguration *n* ▷ **inaugurate**
inaugurations *n* ▷ **inaugurate**
inauspicious *adj* unlucky, likely to have an
unfavourable outcome
inboard *adj* (of a boat's engine) inside the hull
inborn *adj* existing from birth, natural
inbred *adj* produced as a result of inbreeding
inbreeding *n* (*pl* -s) breeding of animals or
people that are closely related
inbreedings *n* ▷ **inbreeding**
inbuilt *adj* present from the start
incalculable *adj* too great to be estimated
incandescence *n* ▷ **incandescent**
incandescences *n* ▷ **incandescent**
incandescent *adj* glowing with heat
> **incandescence** *n* (*pl* -s)
incantation *n* (*pl* -s) ritual chanting of magic
words or sounds
incantations *n* ▷ **incantation**
incapable *adj* (*foll. by* **of**) unable (to do
something)
incapacitate *v* (-tates, -tating, -tated) deprive
of strength or ability > **incapacity** *n* (*pl* -ties)
incapacitated *v* ▷ **incapacitate**
incapacitates *v* ▷ **incapacitate**
incapacitating *v* ▷ **incapacitate**
incapacities *n* ▷ **incapacitate**
incapacity *n* ▷ **incapacitate**
incarcerate *v* (-tes, -ting, -ted) imprison
> **incarceration** *n* (*pl* -s)
incarcerated *v* ▷ **incarcerate**
incarcerates *v* ▷ **incarcerate**
incarcerating *v* ▷ **incarcerate**
incarceration *n* ▷ **incarcerate**
incarcerations *n* ▷ **incarcerate**

incarnate *adj* in human form > **incarnation** *n* (*pl* -**s**)
  incarnation *n* ▷ **incarnate**
  incarnations *n* ▷ **incarnate**
  incendiaries *n* ▷ **incendiary**
incendiary [in-**send**-ya-ree] *adj* (of a bomb, attack, etc.) designed to cause fires ▸ *n* (*pl* -**ries**) bomb designed to cause fires
incense[1] *v* (-**ses**, -**sing**, -**sed**) make very angry
incense[2] *n* (*pl* **incenses**) substance that gives off a sweet perfume when burned
  incensed *v* ▷ **incense**[1]
  incenses *v* ▷ **incense**[1] ▸ *n* ▷ **incense**[2]
  incensing *v* ▷ **incense**[1]
incentive *n* (*pl* -**s**) something that encourages effort or action
  incentives *n* ▷ **incentive**
inception *n* (*pl* -**s**) beginning
  inceptions *n* ▷ **inception**
incessant *adj* never stopping > **incessantly** *adv*
  incessantly *adv* ▷ **incessant**
incest *n* (*pl* -**s**) sexual intercourse between two people too closely related to marry > **incestuous** *adj*
  incests *n* ▷ **incest**
  incestuous *adj* ▷ **incest**
inch *n* (*pl* -**es**) unit of length equal to one twelfth of a foot or 2.54 centimetres ▸ *v* (-**ches**, -**ching**, -**ched**) move slowly and gradually
  inched *v* ▷ **inch**
  inches *v*, *n* ▷ **inch**
  inching *v* ▷ **inch**
inchoate [in-**koe**-ate] *adj* just begun and not yet properly developed
incidence *n* (*pl* -**s**) extent or frequency of occurrence
  incidences *n* ▷ **incidence**
incident *n* (*pl* -**s**) something that happens
incidental *adj* occurring in connection with or resulting from something more important > **incidentally** *adv*
  incidentally *adv* ▷ **incidental**
  incidents *n* ▷ **incident**
incinerate *v* (-**tes**, -**ting**, -**ted**) burn to ashes > **incineration** *n* (*pl* -**s**)
  incinerated *v* ▷ **incinerate**
  incinerates *v* ▷ **incinerate**
  incinerating *v* ▷ **incinerate**
  incineration *n* ▷ **incinerate**
  incinerations *n* ▷ **incineration**
incinerator *n* (*pl* -**s**) furnace for burning rubbish
  incinerators *n* ▷ **incinerator**
incipient *adj* just starting to appear or happen

incise *v* (-**ses**, -**sing**, -**sed**) cut into with a sharp tool > **incision** *n* (*pl* -**s**)
  incised *v* ▷ **incise**
  incises *v* ▷ **incise**
  incising *v* ▷ **incise**
  incision *n* ▷ **incise**
  incisions *n* ▷ **incise**
incisive *adj* direct and forceful
incisor *n* (*pl* -**s**) front tooth, used for biting into food
  incisors *n* ▷ **incisor**
incite *v* (-**tes**, -**ting**, -**ted**) stir up, provoke > **incitement** *n* (*pl* -**s**)
  incited *v* ▷ **incite**
  incitement *n* ▷ **incite**
  incitements *n* ▷ **incite**
  incites *v* ▷ **incite**
  inciting *v* ▷ **incite**
  incivilities *n* ▷ **incivility**
incivility *n* (*pl* -**ties**) rudeness or a rude remark
inclement *adj* (of weather) stormy or severe
inclination *n* (*pl* -**s**) liking, tendency, or preference
  inclinations *n* ▷ **inclination**
incline *v* (-**nes**, -**ning**, -**ned**) lean, slope ▸ *n* (*pl* -**s**) slope
  inclined *v* ▷ **incline**
  inclines *v*, *n* ▷ **incline**
  inclining *v* ▷ **incline**
include *v* (-**des**, -**ding**, -**ded**) have as part of the whole > **inclusion** *n* (*pl* -**s**)
  included *v* ▷ **include**
  includes *v* ▷ **include**
  including *v* ▷ **include**
  inclusion *n* ▷ **include**
  inclusions *n* ▷ **include**
inclusive *adj* including everything (specified) > **inclusively** *adv*
  inclusively *adv* ▷ **inclusive**
incognito [in-kog-**nee**-toe] *adj*, *adv* having adopted a false identity ▸ *n* (*pl* -**tos**) false identity
  incognitos *n* ▷ **incognito**
  incoherence *n* ▷ **incoherent**
  incoherences *n* ▷ **incoherent**
incoherent *adj* unclear and impossible to understand > **incoherence** *n* (*pl* -**s**) > **incoherently** *adv*
  incoherently *adv* ▷ **incoherent**
income *n* (*pl* -**s**) amount of money earned from work, investments, etc.
  incomes *n* ▷ **income**
incoming *adj* coming in
incommode *v* (-**des**, -**ding**, -**ded**) cause inconvenience to

incommoded v ▷ incommode
incommodes v ▷ incommode
incommoding v ▷ incommode
incommunicado adj, adv deprived of communication with other people
incomparable adj beyond comparison, unequalled > **incomparably** adv
incomparably adv ▷ incomparable
incompatibilities n ▷ incompatible
incompatibility n ▷ incompatible
incompatible adj inconsistent or conflicting > **incompatibility** n (pl -ties)
incompetence n ▷ incompetent
incompetences n ▷ incompetent
incompetent adj not having the necessary ability or skill to do something > **incompetence** n (pl -s)
inconceivable adj extremely unlikely, unimaginable
inconclusive adj not giving a final decision or result
incongruities n ▷ incongruous
incongruity n ▷ incongruous
incongruous adj inappropriate or out of place > **incongruously** adv > **incongruity** n (pl -ties)
incongruously adv ▷ incongruous
inconsequential adj unimportant, insignificant
inconsiderable adj fairly large
inconstant adj liable to change one's loyalties or opinions
incontinence n ▷ incontinent
incontinences n ▷ incontinent
incontinent adj unable to control one's bladder or bowels > **incontinence** n (pl -s)
incontrovertible adj impossible to deny or disprove
inconvenience n (pl -s) trouble or difficulty ▶ v (-ces, -ncing, -nced) cause trouble or difficulty to > **inconvenient** adj
inconvenienced v ▷ inconvenience
inconveniences n, v ▷ inconvenience
inconveniencing v ▷ inconvenience
inconvenient adj ▷ inconvenience
incorporate v (-tes, -ting, -ted) include or be included as part of a larger unit
incorporated v ▷ incorporate
incorporates v ▷ incorporate
incorporating v ▷ incorporate
incorporeal adj without material form
incorrigible adj beyond correction or reform
incorruptible adj too honest to be bribed or corrupted
increase v (-ses, -sing, -sed) make or become greater in size, number, etc. ▶ n (pl -s) rise in

number, size, etc. > **increasingly** adv
increased v ▷ increase
increases v, n ▷ increase
increasing v ▷ increase
increasingly adv ▷ increase
incredible adj hard to believe or imagine > **incredibly** adv
incredibly adv ▷ incredible
incredulities n ▷ incredulous
incredulity n ▷ incredulous
incredulous adj not willing to believe something > **incredulity** n (pl -ties)
increment n (pl -s) increase in money or value, esp. a regular salary increase > **incremental** adj
incremental adj ▷ increment
increments n ▷ increment
incriminate v (-tes, -ting, -ted) make (someone) seem guilty of a crime > **incriminating** adj
incriminated v ▷ incriminate
incriminates v ▷ incriminate
incriminating v, adj ▷ incriminate
incubate [in-cube-ate] v (-tes, -ting, -ted) (of a bird) hatch (eggs) by sitting on them > **incubation** n (pl -s)
incubated v ▷ incubate
incubates v ▷ incubate
incubating v ▷ incubate
incubation n ▷ incubate
incubations n ▷ incubate
incubator n (pl -s) heated enclosed apparatus for rearing premature babies
incubators n ▷ incubator
incubi n ▷ incubus
incubus [in-cube-uss] n (pl -bi, -buses) (in folklore) demon believed to have sex with sleeping women
incubuses n ▷ incubus
inculcate v (-tes, -ting, -ted) fix in someone's mind by constant repetition > **inculcation** n (pl -s)
inculcated v ▷ inculcate
inculcates v ▷ inculcate
inculcating v ▷ inculcate
inculcation n ▷ inculcate
inculcations n ▷ inculcate
incumbencies n ▷ incumbent
incumbency n ▷ incumbent
incumbent n (pl -s) person holding a particular office or position ▶ adj it is the duty of > **incumbency** n (pl -cies)
incumbents n ▷ incumbent
incur v (-s, -rring, -rred) cause (something unpleasant) to happen

incurable *adj* not able to be cured > **incurably** *adv*
  incurably *adv* ▷ incurable
incurious *adj* showing no curiosity or interest
  incurred *v* ▷ incur
  incurring *v* ▷ incur
  incurs *v* ▷ incur
incursion *n* (*pl* -s) sudden brief invasion
  incursions *n* ▷ incursion
indebted *adj* owing gratitude for help or favours > **indebtedness** *n* (*pl* -es)
  indebtedness *n* ▷ indebted
  indebtednesses *n* ▷ indebted
  indecencies *n* ▷ indecent
  indecency *n* ▷ indecent
indecent *adj* morally or sexually offensive > **indecently** *adv* > **indecency** *n* (*pl* -cies)
  indecently *adv* ▷ indecent
indecipherable *adj* impossible to read
indeed *adv* really, certainly ▶ *interj* expression of indignation or surprise
indefatigable *adj* never getting tired > **indefatigably** *adv*
  indefatigably *adv* ▷ indefatigable
indefensible *adj* unable to be justified
indefinite *adj* without exact limits > **indefinitely** *adv*
  indefinitely *adv* ▷ indefinite
indelible *adj* impossible to erase or remove > **indelibly** *adv*
  indelibly *adv* ▷ indelible
indelicate *adj* offensive or embarrassing
  indemnified *v* ▷ indemnify
  indemnifies *v* ▷ indemnify
indemnify *v* (-fies, -fying, -fied) secure against loss, damage, or liability
  indemnifying *v* ▷ indemnify
  indemnities *v* ▷ indemnity
indemnity *n* (*pl* -ties) insurance against loss or damage
indent *v* (-s, -ing, -ed) start (a line of writing) further from the margin than the other lines
indentation *n* (*pl* -s) dent in a surface or edge
  indentations *n* ▷ indentation
  indented *v* ▷ indent
  indenting *v* ▷ indent
  indents *v* ▷ indent
indenture *n* (*pl* -s) contract, esp. one binding an apprentice to his or her employer
  indentures *n* ▷ indenture
  independence *n* ▷ independent
  independences *n* ▷ independent
independent *adj* free from the control or influence of others ▶ *n* (*pl* -s) politician who does not represent any political party

  > **independently** *adv* > **independence** *n* (*pl* -s)
  independently *adsv* ▷ independent
  independents *n* ▷ independent
indescribable *adj* too intense or extreme for words > **indescribably** *adv*
  indescribably *adv* ▷ indescribable
  indeterminacies *n* ▷ indeterminate
  indeterminacy *n* ▷ indeterminate
indeterminate *adj* uncertain in extent, amount, or nature > **indeterminacy** *n* (*pl* -cies)
index *n* (*pl* -dices) [in-diss-eez] alphabetical list of names or subjects dealt with in a book ▶ *v* (-dexes, -dexing, -dexed) provide (a book) with an index
  indexed *v* ▷ index
  indexes *v* ▷ index
  indexing *v* ▷ index
indicate *v* (-tes, -ting, -ted) be a sign or symptom of > **indication** *n* (*pl* -s)
  indicated *v* ▷ indicate
  indicates *v* ▷ indicate
  indicating *v* ▷ indicate
  indication *n* ▷ indicate
  indications *n* ▷ indicate
indicative *adj* (foll. by of) suggesting ▶ *n* (*pl* -s) (GRAMMAR) indicative mood
  indicatives *n* ▷ indicative
indicator *n* (*pl* -s) something acting as a sign or indication
  indicators *n* ▷ indicator
  indices *n* ▷ index
indict [in-dite] *v* (-s, -ing, -ed) formally charge with a crime > **indictable** *adj* > **indictment** *n* (*pl* -s)
  indictable *adj* ▷ indict
  indicted *v* ▷ indict
  indicting *v* ▷ indict
  indictment *n* ▷ indict
  indictments *n* ▷ indict
  indicts *v* ▷ indict
indie *adj* (Informal) (of rock music) released by an independent record company
  indifference *n* ▷ indifferent
  indifferences *n* ▷ indifferent
indifferent *adj* showing no interest or concern > **indifference** *n* (*pl* -s) > **indifferently** *adv*
  indifferently *adv* ▷ indifferent
  indigence *n* ▷ indigent
  indigences *n* ▷ indigent
indigenous [in-dij-in-uss] *adj* born in or natural to a country
indigent *adj* extremely poor > **indigence** *n* (*pl* -s)
  indigestible *adj* ▷ indigestion
indigestion *n* (*pl* -s) (discomfort or pain

caused by) difficulty in digesting food
> **indigestible** *adj*
indigestions *n* ▷ **indigestion**
indignant *adj* feeling or showing indignation
> **indignantly** *adv*
indignantly *adv* ▷ **indignant**
indignation *n* (*pl* -s) anger at something
unfair or wrong
indignations *n* ▷ **indignation**
indignities *n* ▷ **indignity**
indignity *n* (*pl* -ties) embarrassing or
humiliating treatment
indigo *adj* deep violet-blue ▶ *n* (*pl* -s) dye of
this colour
indigos *n* ▷ **indigo**
indirect *adj* done or caused by someone or
something else
indiscreet *adj* incautious or tactless
in revealing secrets > **indiscreetly** *adv*
> **indiscretion** *n* (*pl* -s)
indiscreetly *adv* ▷ **indiscreet**
indiscretion *n* ▷ **indiscreet**
indiscretions *n* ▷ **indiscreet**
indiscriminate *adj* showing lack of careful
thought
indispensable *adj* absolutely essential
indisposed *adj* unwell, ill > **indisposition** *n*
(*pl* -s)
indisposition *n* ▷ **indisposed**
indispositions *n* ▷ **indisposed**
indisputable *adj* beyond doubt > **indisputably**
adv
indisputably *adv* ▷ **indisputable**
indissoluble *adj* permanent
indium *n* (*pl* -s) (CHEM) soft silvery-white
metallic element
indiums *n* ▷ **indium**
individual *adj* characteristic of or meant for a
single person or thing ▶ *n* (*pl* -s) single person
or thing > **individually** *adv* > **individuality**
n (*pl* -ties)
individualism *n* (*pl* -s) principle of living one's
life in one's own way > **individualist** *n* (*pl* -s)
> **individualistic** *adj*
individualisms *n* ▷ **individualism**
individualist *n* ▷ **individualism**
individualistic *adj* ▷ **individualism**
individualists *n* ▷ **individualism**
individualities *n* ▷ **individual**
individuality *n* ▷ **individual**
individually *adv* ▷ **individual**
individuals *n* ▷ **individual**
indoctrinate *v* (-tes, -ting, -ted) teach
(someone) to accept a doctrine or belief
uncritically > **indoctrination** *n* (*pl* -s)

indoctrinated *v* ▷ **indoctrinate**
indoctrinates *v* ▷ **indoctrinate**
indoctrinating *v* ▷ **indoctrinate**
indoctrination *n* ▷ **indoctrinate**
indoctrinations *n* ▷ **indoctrinate**
indolence *n* ▷ **indolent**
indolences *n* ▷ **indolent**
indolent *adj* lazy > **indolence** *n* (*pl* -s)
indomitable *adj* too strong to be defeated or
discouraged > **indomitably** *adv*
indomitably *adv* ▷ **indomitable**
indoor *adj* inside a building > **indoors** *adv*
indoors *adv* ▷ **indoor**
indubitable *adj* beyond doubt, certain
> **indubitably** *adv*
indubitably *adv* ▷ **indubitable**
induce *v* (-ces, -cing, -ced) persuade or
influence
induced *v* ▷ **induce**
inducement *n* (*pl* -s) something used to
persuade someone to do something
inducements *n* ▷ **inducement**
induces *v* ▷ **induce**
inducing *v* ▷ **induce**
induct *v* (-s, -ing, -ed) formally install
(someone, esp. a clergyman) in office
inductance *n* (*pl* -s) property of an electric
circuit creating voltage by a change of
current
inductances *n* ▷ **inductance**
inducted *v* ▷ **induct**
inducting *v* ▷ **induct**
induction *n* (*pl* -s) reasoning process by
which general conclusions are drawn from
particular instances > **inductive** *adj*
inductions *n* ▷ **induction**
inductive *adj* ▷ **induction**
inducts *v* ▷ **induct**
indulge *v* (-ges, -ging, -ged) allow oneself
pleasure > **indulgent** *adj* > **indulgently** *adv*
indulged *v* ▷ **indulge**
indulgence *n* (*pl* -s) something allowed
because it gives pleasure
indulgences *n* ▷ **indulgence**
indulgent *adj* ▷ **indulge**
indulgently *adj* ▷ **indulge**
indulges *v* ▷ **indulge**
indulging *v* ▷ **indulge**
industrial *adj* of, used in, or employed in
industry
industrialization *n* ▷ **industrialize**
industrializations *n* ▷ **industrialize**
industrialize *v* (-izes, -izing, -ized) develop
large-scale industry in (a country or region)
> **industrialization** *n* (*pl* -s)

industrialized v ▷ **industrialize**
industrializes v ▷ **industrialize**
industrializing v ▷ **industrialize**
industries n ▷ **industry**
industrious adj ▷ **industry**
industry n (pl -**tries**) manufacture of goods
> **industrious** adj hard-working
inebriate n (pl -**s**) ▶ adj (person who is)
habitually drunk
inebriated adj drunk > **inebriation** n (pl -**s**)
inebriates n ▷ **inebriate**
inebriation n ▷ **inebriated**
inebriations n ▷ **inebriated**
inedible adj not fit to be eaten
ineffable adj too great for words > **ineffably**
adv
ineffably adv ▷ **ineffable**
ineffectual adj having very little effect
ineligible adj not qualified for or entitled to
something
ineluctable adj impossible to avoid
inept adj clumsy, lacking skill > **ineptitude**
n (pl -**s**)
ineptitude n ▷ **inept**
ineptitudes n ▷ **inept**
inequitable adj unfair
ineradicable adj impossible to remove
inert adj without the power of motion or
resistance > **inertness** n (pl -**es**)
inertia n (pl -**s**) feeling of unwillingness to do
anything
inertias n ▷ **inertia**
inertness n ▷ **inert**
inertnesses n ▷ **inert**
inescapable adj unavoidable
inestimable adj too great to be estimated
> **inestimably** adv
inestimably adv ▷ **inestimable**
inevitabilities n ▷ **inevitable**
inevitability n ▷ **inevitable**
inevitable adj unavoidable, sure to happen
> **inevitably** adv > **inevitability** n (pl -**ties**)
inevitably adv ▷ **inevitable**
inexorable adj unable to be prevented from
continuing or progressing > **inexorably** adv
inexorably adv ▷ **inexorable**
inexpert adj lacking skill
inexplicable adj impossible to explain
> **inexplicably** adv
inexplicably adv ▷ **inexplicable**
inextricable adj impossible to escape from
infallibilities adv ▷ **infallible**
infallibility adv ▷ **infallible**
infallible adj never wrong > **infallibly** adv
> **infallibility** n (pl -**ties**)

infallibly adv ▷ **infallible**
infamies n ▷ **infamous**
infamous [in-fam-uss] adj well-known for
something bad > **infamously** adv > **infamy**
n (pl -**mies**)
infamously adv ▷ **infamous**
infamy n ▷ **infamous**
infancies n ▷ **infancy**
infancy n (pl -**cies**) early childhood
infant n (pl -**s**) very young child
infanticide n (pl -**s**) murder of an infant
infanticides n ▷ **infanticide**
infantile adj childish
infantries n ▷ **infantry**
infantry n (pl -**ries**) soldiers who fight on foot
infants n ▷ **infant**
infatuated adj feeling intense unreasoning
passion
infatuation n (pl -**s**) intense unreasoning
passion
infatuations n ▷ **infatuation**
infect v (-**s**, -**ing**, -**ed**) affect with a disease
> **infection** n (pl -**s**)
infected v ▷ **infect**
infecting v ▷ **infect**
infection n ▷ **infect**
infections n ▷ **infect**
infectious adj (of a disease) spreading without
actual contact
infects v ▷ **infect**
infer v (-**s**, -**rring**, -**rred**) work out from
evidence > **inference** n (pl -**s**)
inference n ▷ **infer**
inferences n ▷ **infer**
inferior adj lower in quality, position, or status
▶ n (pl -**s**) person of lower position or status
> **inferiority** n (pl -**ties**)
inferiorities n ▷ **inferior**
inferiority n ▷ **inferior**
inferiors n ▷ **inferior**
infernal adj of hell (Informal) > **infernally** adv
infernally adv ▷ **infernal**
inferno n (pl -**s**) intense raging fire
infernos n ▷ **inferno**
inferred v ▷ **infer**
inferring v ▷ **infer**
infers v ▷ **infer**
infertile adj unable to produce offspring
> **infertility** n (pl -**ties**)
infertilities n ▷ **infertile**
infertility n ▷ **infertile**
infest v (-**s**, -**ing**, -**ed**) inhabit or overrun in
unpleasantly large numbers > **infestation**
n (pl -**s**)
infestation n ▷ **infest**

infestations *n* ▷ infest
infested *v* ▷ infest
infesting *v* ▷ infest
infests *v* ▷ infest
infidel *n* (*pl* -s) person with no religion
infidelities *n* ▷ infidelity
infidelity *n* (*pl* -ties) (act of) sexual
unfaithfulness to one's husband, wife, or lover
infidels *n* ▷ infidel
infighting *n* (*pl* -s) quarrelling within a group
infightings *n* ▷ infighting
infiltrate *v* (-tes, -ting, -ted) enter gradually
and secretly > **infiltration** *n* (*pl* -s) > **infiltrator**
n (*pl* -s)
infiltrated *v* ▷ infiltrate
infiltrates *v* ▷ infiltrate
infiltrating *v* ▷ infiltrate
infiltration *n* ▷ infiltrate
infiltrations *n* ▷ infiltrate
infiltrator *n* ▷ infiltrate
infiltrators *n* ▷ infiltrate
infinite [in-fin-it] *adj* without any limit or end
> **infinitely** *adv*
infinitely *adv* ▷ infinite
infinitesimal *adj* extremely small
infinities *n* ▷ infinity
infinitive *n* (*pl* -s) (GRAMMAR) form of a verb not
showing tense, person, or number
infinitives *n* ▷ infinitive
infinity *n* (*pl* -ties) endless space, time, or
number
infirm *adj* physically or mentally weak
> **infirmity** *n* (*pl* -ties)
infirmaries *n* ▷ infirmary
infirmary *n* (*pl* -ries) hospital
infirmities *n* ▷ infirm
infirmity *n* ▷ infirm
inflame *v* (-mes, -ming, -med) make angry
or excited
inflamed *adj* (of part of the body) red, swollen,
and painful because of infection ▶ *v* ▷ **inflame**
> **inflammation** *n* (*pl* -s)
inflames *v* ▷ inflame
inflaming *v* ▷ inflame
inflammable *adj* easily set on fire
inflammation *n* ▷ inflamed
inflammations *n* ▷ inflamed
inflammatory *adj* likely to provoke anger
inflatable *adj* able to be inflated ▶ *n* (*pl* -s)
plastic or rubber object which can be inflated
inflatables *n* ▷ inflatable
inflate *v* (-tes, -ting, -ted) expand by filling
with air or gas
inflated *v* ▷ inflate
inflates *v* ▷ inflate

inflating *v* ▷ inflate
inflation *n* (*pl* -s) inflating > **inflationary** *adj*
inflationary *adj* ▷ inflationary
inflations *n* ▷ inflation
inflection, inflexion *n* (*pl* -s) change in the
pitch of the voice
inflections *n* ▷ inflection
inflexibilities *n* ▷ inflexible
inflexibility *n* ▷ inflexible
inflexible *adj* unwilling to be persuaded,
obstinate > **inflexibly** *adv* > **inflexibility** *n*
(*pl* -ties)
inflexibly *n* ▷ inflexibly
inflexion *n* ▷ inflection
inflexions *n* ▷ inflection
inflict *v* (-s, -ing, -ed) impose (something
unpleasant) on > **infliction** *n* (*pl* -s)
inflicted *v* ▷ inflict
inflicting *v* ▷ inflict
infliction *n* ▷ inflict
inflictions *n* ▷ inflict
inflicts *v* ▷ inflict
inflorescence *n* (*pl* -s) (BOTANY) arrangement of
flowers on a stem
inflorescences *n* ▷ inflorescence
influence *n* (*pl* -s) effect of one person or thing
on another ▶ *v* (-ces, -cing, -ced) have an
effect on > **influential** *adj*
influenced *v* ▷ influence
influences *n, v* ▷ influence
influencing *v* ▷ influence
influential *adj* ▷ influence
influenza *n* (*pl* -s) contagious viral disease
causing headaches, muscle pains, and fever
influenzas *n* ▷ influenza
influx *n* (*pl* -es) arrival or entry of many people
or things
influxes *n* ▷ influx
info *n* (*pl* -s) (*Informal*) information
inform *v* (-s, -ing, -ed) tell
informal *adj* relaxed and friendly > **informally**
adv > **informality** *n* (*pl* -s)
informalities *n* ▷ informal
informality *n* ▷ informal
informally *adv* ▷ informal
informant *n* (*pl* -s) person who gives
information
informants *n* ▷ informant
information *n* (*pl* -s) knowledge or facts
informations *n* ▷ information
informative *adj* giving useful information
informed *v* ▷ inform
informer *n* (*pl* -s) person who informs to the
police
informers *n* ▷ informer

informing v ▷ inform
informs v ▷ inform
infos n ▷ info
infrared adj of or using rays below the red end
of the visible spectrum
infrastructure n (pl -s) basic facilities,
services, and equipment needed for a
country or organization to function properly
infrastructures n ▷ infrastructure
infringe v (-ges, -ging, -ged) break (a law or
agreement) > **infringement** n (pl -s)
infringed v ▷ infringe
infringement n ▷ infringe
infringements n ▷ infringe
infringes v ▷ infringe
infringing v ▷ infringe
infuriate v (-tes, -ting, -ted) make very angry
infuriated v ▷ infuriate
infuriates v ▷ infuriate
infuriating v ▷ infuriate
infuse v (-ses, -sing, -sed) fill (with an emotion
or quality) > **infusion** n (pl -s) infusing
infused v ▷ infuse
infuses v ▷ infuse
infusing v ▷ infuse
infusion n ▷ infuse
infusions n ▷ infuse
ingenious [in-**jean**-ee-uss] adj showing
cleverness and originality > **ingeniously** adv
> **ingenuity** [in-jen-**new**-it-ee] n (pl -**ties**)
ingeniously adv ▷ ingenious
ingénue [**an**-jay-new] n (pl -s) naive young
woman, esp. as a role played by an actress
ingénues n ▷ ingénue
ingenuities n ▷ ingenious
ingenuity n ▷ ingenious
ingenuous [in-jen-**new**-uss] adj unsophisticated
and trusting > **ingenuously** adv
ingenuously adv ▷ ingenuously
ingest v (-s, -ing, -ed) take (food or liquid) into
the body > **ingestion** n (pl -s)
ingested v ▷ ingest
ingesting v ▷ ingest
ingestion n ▷ ingest
ingestions n ▷ ingest
ingests v ▷ ingest
inglorious adj dishonourable, shameful
ingot n (pl -s) oblong block of cast metal
ingots n ▷ ingot
ingrained adj firmly fixed
ingratiate v (-iates, -iating, -iated) try to
make (oneself) popular with someone
> **ingratiating** adj > **ingratiatingly** adv
ingratiated v ▷ ingratiate
ingratiates v ▷ ingratiate

ingratiating v, adj ▷ ingratiate
ingratiatingly adv ▷ ingratiatingly
ingredient n (pl -s) component of a mixture or
compound
ingredients n ▷ ingredient
ingress n (pl -es) act or right of entering
ingresses n ▷ ingress
ingrowing adj (of a toenail) growing
abnormally into the flesh
inhabit v (-s, -ing, -ed) live in > **inhabitable** adj
> **inhabitant** n (pl -s)
inhabitable adj ▷ inhabitable
inhabitant n ▷ inhabit
inhabitants n ▷ inhabit
inhabited v ▷ inhabit
inhabiting v ▷ inhabit
inhabits v ▷ inhabit
inhalant n (pl -s) medical preparation inhaled
to help breathing problems
inhalants n ▷ inhalant
inhalations n ▷ inhalation
inhale v (-les, -ling, -led) breathe in (air, smoke,
etc.) > **inhalation** n (pl -s)
inhaled v ▷ inhale
inhaler n (pl -s) container for an inhalant
inhalers n ▷ inhaler
inhales v ▷ inhale
inhaling v ▷ inhale
inherent adj existing as an inseparable part
> **inherently** adv
inherently adv ▷ inherent
inherit v (-s, -ing, -ed) receive (money etc.)
from someone who has died > **inheritance** n
(pl -s) > **inheritor** n (pl -s)
inheritance n ▷ inherit
inheritances n ▷ inherit
inherited v ▷ inherit
inheriting v ▷ inherit
inheritor n ▷ inherit
inheritors n ▷ inherit
inherits v ▷ inherit
inhibit v (-s, -ing, -ed) restrain (an impulse or
desire) > **inhibited** adj
inhibited v, adj ▷ inhibit
inhibiting v ▷ inhibit
inhibition n (pl -s) feeling of fear or
embarrassment that stops one from
behaving naturally
inhibitions n ▷ inhibition
inhibits v ▷ inhibit
inhospitable adj not welcoming, unfriendly
inhuman adj cruel or brutal
inhumane adj cruel or brutal > **inhumanity**
n (pl -**ties**)
inhumanities n ▷ inhumane

inhumanity *n* ▷ **inhumane**
inimical *adj* unfavourable or hostile
inimitable *adj* impossible to imitate, unique
  iniquities *n* ▷ **iniquity**
  iniquitous *adj* ▷ **iniquity**
iniquity *n* (*pl* **-ties**) injustice or wickedness
  > **iniquitous** *adj*
initial *adj* first, at the beginning ▶ *n* (*pl* **-s**) first
  letter, esp. of a person's name ▶ *v* (**-s, -lling,**
  -lled) sign with one's initials > **initially** *adv*
  initialled *v* ▷ **initial**
  initialling *v* ▷ **initial**
  initially *adv* ▷ **initial**
  initials *n*, *v* ▷ **initial**
initiate *v* (**-tes, -ting, -ted**) begin or set
  going ▶ *n* (*pl* **-s**) recently initiated person
  > **initiation** *n* (*pl* **-s**) > **initiator** *n* (*pl* **-s**)
  initiated *v* ▷ **initiate**
initiates *v*, *n* ▷ **initiate**
  initiating *v* ▷ **initiate**
  initiation *n* ▷ **initiation**
  initiations *n* ▷ **initiation**
initiative *n* (*pl* **-ves**) first step, commencing
  move
  initiatives *n* ▷ **initiative**
  initiator *n* ▷ **initiation**
  initiators *n* ▷ **initiation**
inject *v* (**-s, -ing, -ed**) put (a fluid) into the body
  with a syringe > **injection** *n* (*pl* **-s**)
  injected *v* ▷ **inject**
  injecting *v* ▷ **inject**
  injection *n* ▷ **inject**
  injections *n* ▷ **inject**
  injects *v* ▷ **inject**
injudicious *adj* showing poor judgment,
  unwise
injunction *n* (*pl* **-s**) court order not to do
  something
  injunctions *n* ▷ **injunction**
injure *v* (**-res, -ring, -red**) hurt physically or
  mentally > **injury** *n* (*pl* **-ries**) > **injurious** *adj*
  injured *v* ▷ **injure**
  injures *v* ▷ **injure**
  injuries *n* ▷ **injure**
  injuring *v* ▷ **injure**
  injurious *adj* ▷ **injure**
  injury *n* ▷ **injure**
injustice *n* (*pl* **-s**) unfairness
  injustices *n* ▷ **injustice**
ink *n* (*pl* **-s**) coloured liquid used for writing or
  printing ▶ *v* (**-s, -ing, -ed**) (*foll. by* **in**) mark in
  ink (something already marked in pencil)
  inked *v* ▷ **ink**
  inking *v* ▷ **ink**
inkling *n* (*pl* **-s**) slight idea or suspicion

inklings *n* ▷ **inkling**
  inks *v*, *n* ▷ **ink**
inky *adj* dark or black
inlaid *adj* set in another material so that the
  surface is smooth
inland *adj*, *adv* in or towards the interior of a
  country, away from the sea
inlay *n* (*pl* **-s**) inlaid substance or pattern
  inlays *n* ▷ **inlay**
inlet *n* (*pl* **-s**) narrow strip of water extending
  from the sea into the land
  inlets *n* ▷ **inlet**
inmate *n* (*pl* **-s**) person living in an institution
  such as a prison
  inmates *n* ▷ **inmate**
inmost *adj* innermost
inn *n* (*pl* **-s**) pub or small hotel, esp. in the
  country > **innkeeper** *n* (*pl* **-s**)
innards *pl n* (*Informal*) internal organs
innate *adj* being part of someone's nature,
  inborn
inner *adj* happening or located inside
innermost *adj* furthest inside
innings *n* (SPORT) player's or side's turn of
  batting
  innkeeper *n* ▷ **inn**
  innkeepers *n* ▷ **inn**
  innocence *n* ▷ **innocent**
  innocences *n* ▷ **innocent**
innocent *adj* not guilty of a crime ▶ *n* (*pl* **-s**)
  innocent person, esp. a child > **innocently** *adv*
  > **innocence** *n* (*pl* **-s**)
  innocently *adv* ▷ **innocent**
  innocents *n* ▷ **innocent**
innocuous *adj* not harmful > **innocuously** *adv*
  innocuously *adv* ▷ **innocuous**
  innovated *v* ▷ **innovation**
  innovates *v* ▷ **innovation**
  innovating *v* ▷ **innovation**
innovation *n* (*pl* **-s**) new idea or method
  > **innovate** *v* (**-tes, -ting, -ted**) > **innovative**
  adj > **innovator** *n* (*pl* **-s**)
  innovations *n* ▷ **innovation**
  innovative *adj* ▷ **innovation**
  innovator *n* ▷ **innovation**
  innovators *n* ▷ **innovation**
  inns *n* ▷ **inn**
innuendo *n* (*pl* **-does**) (remark making) an
  indirect reference to something rude or
  unpleasant
  innuendoes *n* ▷ **innuendo**
innumerable *adj* too many to be counted
  innumeracies *n* ▷ **innumerate**
  innumeracy *n* ▷ **innumerate**
innumerate *adj* having no understanding

of mathematics or science > **innumeracy** *n*
(*pl* -**cies**)

inoculate *v* (-**tes, -ting, -ted**) protect
against disease by injecting with a vaccine
> **inoculation** *n* (*pl* -**s**)
 inoculated *v* ▷ **inoculate**
 inoculates *v* ▷ **inoculate**
 inoculating *v* ▷ **inoculate**
 inoculation *n* ▷ **inoculate**
 inoculations *n* ▷ **inoculate**

inoperable *adj* (of a tumour or cancer) unable
to be surgically removed

inopportune *adj* badly timed, unsuitable

inordinate *adj* excessive

inorganic *adj* not having the characteristics of
living organisms

inpatient *n* (*pl* -**s**) patient who stays in a
hospital for treatment
 inpatients *n* ▷ **inpatient**

input *n* (*pl* -**s**) resources put into a project etc.
▶ *v* (-**s, -tting, -put**) enter (data) in a computer
 inputs *v, n* ▷ **input**
 inputting *v, n* ▷ **input**

inquest *n* (*pl* -**s**) official inquiry into a sudden
death
 inquests *n* ▷ **inquest**

inquire *v* (-**res, -ring, -red**) seek information or
ask (about) > **inquirer** *n* (*pl* -**s**)
 inquired *v* ▷ **inquire**
 inquirer *n* ▷ **inquire**
 inquirers *n* ▷ **inquire**
 inquires *v* ▷ **inquire**
 inquiries *n* ▷ **inquiry**
 inquiring *v* ▷ **inquire**

inquiry *n* (*pl* -**ries**) question

inquisition *n* (*pl* -**s**) thorough investigation
> **inquisitor** *n* (*pl* -**s**) > **inquisitorial** *adj*
 inquisitions *n* ▷ **inquisition**

inquisitive *adj* excessively curious about
other people's affairs > **inquisitively** *adv*
 inquisitively *adv* ▷ **inquisitive**
 inquisitor *n* ▷ **inquisition**
 inquisitorial *adj* ▷ **inquisition**
 inquisitors *n* ▷ **inquisition**

inquorate *adj* without enough people present
to make a quorum

inroads *pl n* start affecting or reducing

insalubrious *adj* unpleasant, unhealthy, or
sordid

insane *adj* mentally ill > **insanely** *adv*
> **insanity** *n* (*pl* -**ties**)
 insanely *adv* ▷ **insane**

insanitary *adj* dirty or unhealthy
 insanities *n* ▷ **insane**
 insanity *n* ▷ **insane**

insatiable [in-**saysh**-a-bl] *adj* unable to be
satisfied

inscribe *v* (-**bes, -bing, -bed**) write or carve
words on
 inscribed *v* ▷ **inscribe**
 inscribes *v* ▷ **inscribe**
 inscribing *v* ▷ **inscribe**

inscription *n* (*pl* -**s**) words inscribed
 inscriptions *n* ▷ **inscription**

inscrutable *adj* mysterious, enigmatic
> **inscrutably** *adv*
 inscrutably *adv* ▷ **inscrutable**

insect *n* (*pl* -**s**) small animal with six legs and
usu. wings, such as an ant or fly

insecticide *n* (*pl* -**s**) substance for killing
insects
 insecticides *n* ▷ **insecticide**

insectivorous *adj* insect-eating
 insects *n* ▷ **insect**

insecure *adj* anxious, not confident
 inseminated *v* ▷ **insemination**
 inseminates *v* ▷ **insemination**
 inseminating *v* ▷ **insemination**

insemination *n* (*pl* -**s**) putting semen into a
woman's or female animal's body to try to
make her pregnant > **inseminate** *v* (-**tes,
-ting, -ted**)
 inseminations *n* ▷ **insemination**

insensate *adj* without sensation, unconscious

insensible *adj* unconscious, without feeling

insensitive *adj* unaware of or ignoring other
people's feelings > **insensitivity** *n* (*pl* -**ties**)
 insensitivities *n* ▷ **insensitive**
 insensitivity *n* ▷ **insensitive**

inseparable *adj* (of two people) spending
most of the time together

insert *v* (-**s, -ing, -ed**) put inside or include ▶ *n*
(*pl* -**s**) something inserted > **insertion** *n* (*pl* -**s**)
 inserted *v* ▷ **insert**
 inserting *v* ▷ **insert**
 insertion *n* ▷ **insert**
 insertions *n* ▷ **insert**
 inserts *v, n* ▷ **insert**

inset *n* (*pl* -**s**) small picture inserted within a
larger one
 insets *n* ▷ **inset**

inshore *adj* close to the shore ▶ *adj, adv*
towards the shore

inside *prep* in or to the interior of ▶ *adj* on or
of the inside ▶ *adv* on, in, or to the inside,
indoors ▶ *n* (*pl* -**s**) inner side, surface, or part

insider *n* (*pl* -**s**) member of a group who has
privileged knowledge about it
 insiders *n* ▷ **insider**
 insides *n* ▷ **inside** ▶ *pl n* (*Informal*) stomach

and bowels
insidious adj subtle or unseen but dangerous
> **insidiously** adv
insidiously adv ▷ **insidious**
insight n (pl -s) deep understanding
insights n ▷ **insight**
insignia n (pl -s) badge or emblem of honour
or office
insignias n ▷ **insignia**
insignificance n ▷ **insignificant**
insignificances n ▷ **insignificant**
insignificant adj not important
> **insignificance** n (pl -s)
insincere adj showing false feelings, not
genuine > **insincerely** adv > **insincerity** n
(pl -ties)
insincerely adv ▷ **insincerely**
insincerities n ▷ **insincere**
insincerity n ▷ **insincere**
insinuate v (-tes, -ting, -ted) suggest
indirectly > **insinuation** n (pl -s)
insinuated v ▷ **insinuate**
insinuates v ▷ **insinuate**
insinuating v ▷ **insinuate**
insinuation n ▷ **insinuate**
insinuations n ▷ **insinuate**
insipid adj lacking interest, spirit, or flavour
insist v (-s, -ing, -ed) demand or state firmly
> **insistent** adj making persistent demands
> **insistently** adv > **insistence** n (pl -s)
insisted v ▷ **insist**
insistence n ▷ **insist**
insistences n ▷ **insist**
insistent adj ▷ **insist**
insistently adv ▷ **insist**
insisting v ▷ **insist**
insists v ▷ **insist**
insole n (pl -s) inner sole of a shoe or boot
insolence n ▷ **insolent**
insolences n ▷ **insolent**
insolent adj rude and disrespectful
> **insolence** n (pl -s) > **insolently** adv
insolently adv ▷ **insolent**
insoles n ▷ **insole**
insoluble adj incapable of being solved
insolvencies n ▷ **insolvent**
insolvency n ▷ **insolvent**
insolvent adj unable to pay one's debts
> **insolvency** n (pl -cies)
insomnia n (pl -s) inability to sleep
> **insomniac** n (pl -s)
insomniac n ▷ **insomnia**
insomniacs n ▷ **insomnia**
insomnias n ▷ **insomnia**
insouciance n ▷ **insouciant**

insouciances n ▷ **insouciant**
insouciant adj carefree and unconcerned
> **insouciance** n (pl -s)
inspect v (-s, -ing, -ed) check closely or
officially > **inspection** n (pl -s)
inspected v ▷ **inspect**
inspecting v ▷ **inspect**
inspection n ▷ **inspect**
inspections n ▷ **inspect**
inspector n (pl -s) person who inspects
inspectors n ▷ **inspector**
inspects v ▷ **inspect**
inspiration n (pl -s) creative influence or
stimulus > **inspirational** adj
inspirational adj ▷ **inspiration**
inspirations n ▷ **inspiration**
inspire v (-res, -ring, -red) fill with enthusiasm,
stimulate
inspired v ▷ **inspire**
inspires v ▷ **inspire**
inspiring v ▷ **inspire**
instabilities n ▷ **instability**
instability n (pl -ties) lack of steadiness or
reliability
install v (-lls, -lling, -lled) put in and prepare
(equipment) for use
installation n (pl -s) installing
installations n ▷ **installation**
installed v ▷ **install**
installing v ▷ **install**
installs v ▷ **install**
instalment n (pl -s) any of the portions of a
thing presented or a debt paid in successive
parts
instalments n ▷ **instalment**
instance n (pl -s) particular example ▶ v (-ces,
-cing, -ced) mention as an example
instanced v ▷ **instance**
instances n, v ▷ **instance**
instancing v ▷ **instance**
instant n (pl -s) very brief time ▶ adj happening
at once > **instantly** adv
instantaneous adj happening at once
> **instantaneously** adv
instantaneously adv ▷ **instantaneous**
instantly adv ▷ **instant**
instants n ▷ **instant**
instead adv as a replacement or substitute
instep n (pl -s) part of the foot forming the arch
between the ankle and toes
insteps n ▷ **instep**
instigate v (-tes, -ting, -ted) cause to happen
> **instigation** n (pl -s) > **instigator** n (pl -s)
instigated v ▷ **instigate**
instigates v ▷ **instigate**

instigating v ▷ instigate
instigation n ▷ instigate
instigations n ▷ instigate
instigator n ▷ instigate
instigators n ▷ instigate
instil v (-s, -lling, -lled) introduce (an idea etc.) gradually into someone's mind
instilled v ▷ instil
instilling v ▷ instil
instils v ▷ instil
instinct n (pl -s) inborn tendency to behave in a certain way > **instinctive** adj > **instinctively** adv
instinctive adj ▷ instinct
instinctively adv ▷ instinct
instincts n ▷ instinct
institute n (pl -s) organization set up for a specific purpose, esp. research or teaching ▶ v (-tutes, -tuting, -tuted) start or establish
instituted v ▷ institute
institutes n, v ▷ institute
instituting v ▷ institute
institution n (pl -s) large important organization such as a university or bank > **institutional** adj > **institutionalize** v (-izes, -izing, -ized)
institutional adj ▷ institution
institutionalize v ▷ institution
institutionalized v ▷ institution
institutionalizes v ▷ institution
institutionalizing n ▷ institution
institutions n ▷ institution
instruct v (-s, -ing, -ed) order to do something > **instructor** n (pl -s)
instructed v ▷ instruct
instructing v ▷ instruct
instruction n (pl -s) order to do something
instructions n ▷ instruction ▶ pl n information on how to do or use something
instructive adj informative or helpful
instructor n ▷ instruct
instructors n ▷ instruct
instructs v ▷ instruct
instrument n (pl -s) tool used for particular work
instrumental adj (foll. by in) having an important function (in)
instrumentalist n (pl -s) player of a musical instrument
instrumentalists n ▷ instrumentalist
instrumentation n (pl -s) set of instruments in a car etc.
instrumentations n ▷ instrumentation
instruments n ▷ instrument
insubordinate adj not submissive to

authority > **insubordination** n (pl -s)
insubordination n ▷ insubordinate
insubordinations n ▷ insubordinate
insufferable adj unbearable
insular adj not open to new ideas, narrow-minded > **insularity** n (pl -ties)
insularities n ▷ insular
insularity n ▷ insular
insulate v (-tes, -ting, -ted) prevent or reduce the transfer of electricity, heat, or sound by surrounding or lining with a nonconducting material > **insulation** n (pl -s) > **insulator** n (pl -s)
insulated v ▷ insulate
insulates v ▷ insulate
insulating v ▷ insulate
insulation n ▷ insulate
insulations n ▷ insulate
insulator n ▷ insulate
insulators n ▷ insulate
insulin n (pl -s) hormone produced in the pancreas that controls the amount of sugar in the blood
insulins n ▷ insulin
insult v (-s, -ing, -ed) behave rudely to, offend ▶ n (pl -s) insulting remark or action > **insulting** adj
insulted v ▷ insult
insulting v, adj ▷ insult
insults v, n ▷ insult
insuperable adj impossible to overcome
insupportable adj impossible to tolerate
insurance n (pl -ces) agreement by which one makes regular payments to a company who pay an agreed sum if damage, loss, or death occurs
insurances n ▷ insurance
insure v (-res, -ring, -red) protect by insurance
insured v ▷ insure
insures v ▷ insure
insurgent n (pl -s) ▶ adj (person) in revolt against an established authority
insurgents n ▷ insurgent
insuring v ▷ insure
insurrection n (pl -s) rebellion
insurrections n ▷ insurrection
intact adj not changed or damaged in any way
intaglio [in-**tah**-lee-oh] n (pl -s) (gem carved with) an engraved design
intaglios n ▷ intaglio
intake n (pl -kes) amount or number taken in
intakes n ▷ intake
integer n (pl -s) positive or negative whole number or zero
integers n ▷ integer

integral *adj* being an essential part of a whole ▶ *n* (*pl* -s) (MATHS) sum of a large number of very small quantities
  integrals *n* ▷ **integral**
integrate *v* (-tes, -ting, -ted) combine into a whole > **integration** *n* (*pl* -s)
  integrated *v* ▷ **integrate**
  integrates *v* ▷ **integrate**
  integrating *v* ▷ **integrate**
  integration *n* ▷ **integrate**
  integrations *n* ▷ **integrate**
  integrities *n* ▷ **integrity**
integrity *n* (*pl* -ties) quality of having high moral principles
intellect *n* (*pl* -s) power of thinking and reasoning
  intellects *n* ▷ **intellect**
intellectual *adj* of or appealing to the intellect ▶ *n* (*pl* -s) intellectual person > **intellectually** *adv*
  intellectually *adv* ▷ **intellectual**
  intellectuals *n* ▷ **intellectual**
intelligence *n* (*pl* -s) quality of being intelligent
  intelligences *n* ▷ **intelligence**
intelligent *adj* able to understand, learn, and think things out quickly > **intelligently** *adv*
  intelligently *adv* ▷ **intelligent**
intelligentsia *n* (*pl* -s) intellectual or cultured people in a society
  intelligentsias *n* ▷ **intelligentsia**
  intelligibilities *n* ▷ **intelligibile**
  intelligibility *n* ▷ **intelligibile**
intelligible *adj* able to be understood > **intelligibility** *n* (*pl* -ties)
  intemperance *n* ▷ **intemperate**
  intemperances *n* ▷ **intemperate**
intemperate *adj* unrestrained, uncontrolled > **intemperance** *n* (*pl* -s)
intend *v* (-s, -ing, -ed) propose or plan (to do something)
  intended *v* ▷ **intend**
  intending *v* ▷ **intend**
  intends *v* ▷ **intend**
intense *adj* of great strength or degree > **intensity** *n* (*pl* -ties)
  intensification *n* ▷ **intensify**
  intensifications *n* ▷ **intensify**
  intensified *v* ▷ **intensify**
  intensifies *v* ▷ **intensify**
intensify *v* (-fies, -fying, -fied) make or become more intense > **intensification** *n* (*pl* -s)
  intensifying *v* ▷ **intensify**
  intensities *n* ▷ **intense**
  intensity *n* ▷ **intense**

intensive *adj* using or needing concentrated effort or resources > **intensively** *adv*
  intensively *adv* ▷ **intensive**
intent *n* (*pl* -s) intention ▶ *adj* paying close attention > **intently** *adv* > **intentness** *n* (*pl* -s)
intention *n* (*pl* -s) something intended
intentional *adj* planned in advance, deliberate > **intentionally** *adv*
  intentionally *adv* ▷ **intentional**
  intentions *n* ▷ **intention**
  intently *adv* ▷ **intent**
  intentness *n* ▷ **intent**
  intentnesses *n* ▷ **intent**
  intents *n* ▷ **intent**
inter [in-**ter**] *v* (-s, -rring, -rred) bury (a corpse) > **interment** *n* (*pl* -s)
interact *v* (-s, -ing, -ed) act on or in close relation with each other > **interaction** *n* (*pl* -s) > **interactive** *adj*
  interacted *v* ▷ **interact**
  interacting *v* ▷ **interact**
  interaction *n* ▷ **interact**
  interactions *n* ▷ **interact**
  interactive *adj* ▷ **interact**
  interacts *v* ▷ **interact**
  interbred *v* ▷ **interbreed**
interbreed *v* (-s, -ing, -bred) breed within a related group
  interbreeding *v* ▷ **interbreed**
  interbreeds *v* ▷ **interbreed**
intercede *v* (-des, -ding, -ded) try to end a dispute between two people or groups > **intercession** *n* (*pl* -s)
  interceded *v* ▷ **intercede**
  intercedes *v* ▷ **intercede**
  interceding *v* ▷ **intercede**
intercept *v* (-s, -ing, -ed) seize or stop in transit > **interception** *n* (*pl* -s)
  intercepted *v* ▷ **intercept**
  intercepting *v* ▷ **intercept**
  interception *n* ▷ **intercept**
  interceptions *n* ▷ **intercept**
  intercepts *v* ▷ **intercept**
  intercession *n* ▷ **intercede**
  intercessions *n* ▷ **intercede**
interchange *v* (-ges, -ging, -ged) (cause to) exchange places ▶ *n* (*pl* -ges) motorway junction > **interchangeable** *adj*
  interchangeable *adj* ▷ **interchange**
  interchanged *v* ▷ **interchange**
  interchanges *v*, *n* ▷ **interchange**
  interchanging *v* ▷ **interchange**
intercom *n* (*pl* -s) internal communication system with loudspeakers
  intercoms *n* ▷ **intercom**

intercontinental *adj* travelling between or linking continents

intercourse *n* (*pl* -s) sexual intercourse
 intercourses *n* ▷ intercourse
 interdict *n* ▷ interdiction

interdiction, interdict *n* (*pl* -s) formal order forbidding something
 interdictions *n* ▷ interdiction
 interdicts *n* ▷ interdiction

interdisciplinary *adj* involving more than one branch of learning

interest *n* (*pl* -s) desire to know or hear more about something ▶ *v* (**-s, -ing, -ed**) arouse the interest of > **interesting** *adj* > **interestingly** *adv*

interested *adj* feeling or showing interest ▶ *v* ▷ interest
 interesting *v, adj* ▷ interest
 interestingly *adv* ▷ interest
 interests *n, v* ▷ interest

interface *n* (*pl* -s) area where two things interact or link
 interfaces *n* ▷ interface

interfere *v* (**-res, -ring, -red**) try to influence other people's affairs where one is not involved or wanted > **interfering** *adj* > **interference** *n* (*pl* -s) interfering
 interfered *v* ▷ interfere
 interference *n* ▷ interfere
 interference *n* ▷ interfere
 interferes *v* ▷ interfere
 interfering *v, adj* ▷ interfere

interferon *n* (*pl* -s) protein that stops the development of an invading virus
 interferons *n* ▷ interferon

interim *adj* temporary or provisional

interior *n* (*pl* -s) inside ▶ *adj* inside, inner
 interiors *n* ▷ interior

interject *v* (**-s, -ing, -ed**) make (a remark) suddenly or as an interruption > **interjection** *n* (*pl* -s)
 interjected *v* ▷ interject
 interjecting *v* ▷ interject
 interjection *n* ▷ interject
 interjections *n* ▷ interject
 interjects *v* ▷ interject

interlace *v* (**-ces, -cing, -ced**) join together as if by weaving
 interlaced *v* ▷ interlace
 interlaces *v* ▷ interlace
 interlacing *v* ▷ interlace

interlink *v* (**-s, -ing, -ed**) connect together
 interlinked *v* ▷ interlink
 interlinking *v* ▷ interlink
 interlinks *v* ▷ interlink

interlock *v* (**-s, -ing, -ed**) join firmly together
 interlocked *v* ▷ interlock
 interlocking *v* ▷ interlock
 interlocks *v* ▷ interlock

interlocutor [in-ter-**lok**-yew-ter] *n* (*pl* -s) person who takes part in a conversation
 interlocutors *n* ▷ interlocutor

interloper [in-ter-**lope**-er] *n* (*pl* -s) person in a place or situation where he or she has no right to be
 interlopers *n* ▷ interloper

interlude *n* (*pl* -s) short rest or break in an activity or event
 interludes *n* ▷ interlude

intermarriage *n* ▷ intermarry
 intermarriages *n* ▷ intermarry
 intermarried *v* ▷ intermarry
 intermarries *v* ▷ intermarry

intermarry *v* (**-rries, -rrying, -rried**) (of families, races, or religions) become linked by marriage > **intermarriage** *n* (*pl* -s)
 intermarrying *v* ▷ intermarry
 intermediaries *n* ▷ intermediary

intermediary *n* (*pl* -ries) person trying to create agreement between others

intermediate *adj* coming between two points or extremes
 interment *n* ▷ inter
 interments *n* ▷ inter

intermezzo [in-ter-**met**-so] *n* (*pl* -s) short piece of music, esp. one performed between the acts of an opera
 intermezzos *n* ▷ intermezzo

interminable *adj* seemingly endless because boring > **interminably** *adv*
 interminably *adv* ▷ interminable

intermingle *v* (**-les, -ling, -led**) mix together
 intermingled *v* ▷ intermingle
 intermingles *v* ▷ intermingle
 intermingling *v* ▷ intermingle

intermission *n* (*pl* -s) interval between parts of a play, film, etc.
 intermissions *n* ▷ intermission

intermittent *adj* occurring at intervals > **intermittently** *adv*
 intermittently *adv* ▷ intermittent

intern *v* (**-s, -ing, -ed**) imprison, esp. during a war ▶ *n* (*pl* -s) trainee doctor in a hospital > **internment** *n* (*pl* -s)
 internment *n* (*pl* -s)

internal *adj* of or on the inside > **internally** *adv*
 internally *adv* ▷ internal

international *adj* of or involving two or more countries ▶ *n* (*pl* -s) game or match between teams of different countries > **internationally** *adv*

internationally *adv* ▷ international
internationals *n* ▷ international
internecine *adj* mutually destructive
interned *v* ▷ intern
internee *n* (*pl* -s) person who is interned
internees *n* ▷ internee
interning *v* ▷ intern
internment *n* ▷ intern
internments *n* ▷ intern
interns *v*, *n* ▷ intern
interplanetary *adj* of or linking planets
interplay *n* (*pl* -s) action and reaction of two
things upon each other
interplays *n* ▷ interplay
interpolate [in-ter-pole-ate] *v* (-**tes, -ting,
-ted**) insert (a comment or passage) into (a
conversation or text) > **interpolation** *n* (*pl* -s)
interpolated *v* ▷ interpolate
interpolates *v* ▷ interpolate
interpolating *v* ▷ interpolate
interpolation *n* ▷ interpolate
interpolations *n* ▷ interpolate
interpose *v* (-**ses, -sing, -sed**) insert between
or among things
interposed *v* ▷ interpose
interposes *v* ▷ interpose
interposing *v* ▷ interpose
interpret *v* (-**s, -ing, -ed**) explain the meaning
of > **interpretation** *n* (*pl* -s)
interpretation *n* ▷ interpret
interpretations *n* ▷ interpret
interpreted *v* ▷ interpret
interpreter *n* (*pl* -s) person who translates
orally from one language into another
interpreters *n* ▷ interpreter
interpreting *v* ▷ interpret
interprets *v* ▷ interpret
interred *v* ▷ inter
interregna *n* ▷ interregnum
interregnum *n* (*pl* -nums, -na) interval
between reigns
interregnums *n* ▷ interregnum
interring *v* ▷ inter
interrogate *v* (-**tes, -ting, -ted**) question
closely > **interrogation** *n* (*pl* -s)
interrogated *v* ▷ interrogate
interrogates *v* ▷ interrogate
interrogating *v* ▷ interrogate
interrogation *n* ▷ interrogate
interrogations *n* ▷ interrogate
interrogative *adj* questioning ▸ *n* (*pl* -s) word
used in asking a question, such as *how* or *why*
> **interrogator** *n* (*pl* -s)
interrogatives *n* ▷ interrogative
interrogator *n* ▷ interrogative

interrogators *n* ▷ interrogative
interrupt *v* (-**s, -ing, -ed**) break into (a
conversation etc.) > **interruption** *n* (*pl* -s)
interrupted *v* ▷ interrupt
interrupting *v* ▷ interrupt
interruption *n* ▷ interrupt
interruptions *n* ▷ interrupt
interrupts *v* ▷ interrupt
inters *v* ▷ inter
intersect *v* (-**s, -ing, -ed**) (of roads) meet and
cross > **intersection** *n* (*pl* -s)
intersected *v* ▷ intersect
intersecting *v* ▷ intersect
intersection *n* ▷ intersect
intersections *n* ▷ intersect
intersects *v* ▷ intersect
interspersed *adj* scattered (among, between,
or on)
interstellar *adj* between or among stars
interstice [in-ter-stiss] *n* (*pl* -ces) small crack or
gap between things
interstices *n* ▷ interstice
intertwine *v* (-**nes, -ning, -ned**) twist together
intertwined *v* ▷ intertwine
intertwines *v* ▷ intertwine
intertwining *v* ▷ intertwine
interval *n* (*pl* -s) time between two particular
moments or events
intervals *n* ▷ interval
intervene *v* (-**nes, -ning, -ned**) involve oneself
in a situation, esp. to prevent conflict
> **intervention** *n* (*pl* -s)
intervened *v* ▷ intervene
intervenes *v* ▷ intervene
intervening *v* ▷ intervene
intervention *n* ▷ intervene
interventions *n* ▷ intervene
interview *n* (*pl* -s) formal discussion, esp.
between a job-seeker and an employer ▸ *v*
(-**s, -ing, -ed**) conduct an interview with
> **interviewee** *n* (*pl* -s) > **interviewer** *n* (*pl* -s)
interviewed *v* ▷ interview
interviewee *n* ▷ interview
interviewees *n* ▷ interview
interviewer *n* ▷ interview
interviewers *n* ▷ interview
interviewing *v* ▷ interview
interviews *n*, *v* ▷ interview
interweave *v* (-**ves, -ving, -wove, -woven**)
weave together
interweaves *v* ▷ interweave
interweaving *v* ▷ interweave
interwove *v* ▷ interweave
interwoven *v* ▷ interweave
intestacies *n* ▷ intestate

intestacy n ▷ intestate
intestate adj not having made a will
> intestacy n (pl -cies)
intestinal adj ▷ intestine
intestinally adv ▷ intestine
intestine n (pl -s) (often pl lower part of the
alimentary canal between the stomach and
the anus > intestinal adj > intestinally adv
intestines n ▷ intestine
intimacies n ▷ intimate¹
intimacy n ▷ intimate¹
intimate¹ adj having a close personal
relationship ▶ n (pl -s) close friend
> intimately adv > intimacy n (pl -cies)
intimate² v (-tes, -ting, -ted) hint at or suggest
> intimation n (pl -s)
intimated v ▷ intimate²
intimately adv ▷ intimate¹
intimates n ▷ intimate¹ ▶ v ▷ intimate²
intimating v ▷ intimate²
intimation n ▷ intimate²
intimations n ▷ intimate²
intimidate v (-tes, -ting, -ted) subdue
or influence by fear > intimidating adj
> intimidation n (pl -s)
intimidated v ▷ intimidate
intimidates v ▷ intimidate
intimidating v, adj ▷ intimidate
intimidation n ▷ intimidate
intimidations n ▷ intimidate
into prep indicating motion towards the centre,
result of a change, division, etc.
intolerable adj more than can be endured
> intolerably adv
intolerably adv ▷ intolerable
intolerance n ▷ intolerant
intolerances n ▷ intolerant
intolerant adj refusing to accept practices
and beliefs different from one's own
> intolerance n (pl -s)
intonation n (pl -s) sound pattern produced by
variations in the voice
intonations n ▷ intonation
intone v (-nes, -ning, -ned) speak or recite in
an unvarying tone of voice
intoned v ▷ intone
intones v ▷ intone
intoning v ▷ intone
intoxicant n (pl -s) intoxicating drink
intoxicants n ▷ intoxicant
intoxicate v (-tes, -ting, -ted) make drunk
intoxicated v ▷ intoxicate
intoxicates v ▷ intoxicate
intoxicating v ▷ intoxicate
intoxication n (pl -s) state of being drunk

intoxications n ▷ intoxication
intractable adj (of a person) difficult to control
intranet n (pl -s) (COMPUTERS) internal network
that makes use of Internet technology
intranets n ▷ intranet
intransigence n ▷ intransigent
intransigences n ▷ intransigent
intransigent adj refusing to change one's
attitude > intransigence n (pl -s)
intransitive adj (of a verb) not taking a direct
object
intrauterine adj within the womb
intravenous [in-tra-vee-nuss] adj into a vein
> intravenously adv
intravenously adv ▷ intravenously
intrepid adj fearless, bold > intrepidity n (pl
-ties)
intrepidities n ▷ intrepid
intrepidity n ▷ intrepid
intricacies n ▷ intricate
intricacy n ▷ intricate
intricate adj involved or complicated
> intricately adv > intricacy n (pl -cies)
intricately adv ▷ intricate
intrigue v (-gues, -guing, -gued) make
interested or curious ▶ n (pl -gues) secret
plotting > intriguing adj
intrigued v ▷ intrigue
intrigues v, n ▷ intrigue
intriguing v, adj ▷ intrigue
intrinsic adj essential to the basic nature of
something > intrinsically adv
intrinsically adv ▷ intrinsic
introduce v (-ces, -cing, -ced) present
(someone) by name (to another person)
introduced v ▷ introduce
introduces v ▷ introduce
introducing v ▷ introduce
introduction n (pl -s) presentation of one
person to another > introductory adj
introductions n ▷ introduction
introductory adj ▷ introduction
introspection n (pl -s) examination of one's
own thoughts and feelings > introspective adj
introspections n ▷ introspection
introspective adj ▷ introspection
introversion n ▷ introvert
introversions n ▷ introvert
introvert n (pl -s) person concerned more
with his or her thoughts and feelings than
with the outside world > introverted adj
> introversion n (pl -s)
introverted adj ▷ introvert
introverts n ▷ introvert
intrude v (-des, -ding, -ded) come in or join

in without being invited > **intrusion** n (pl -s)
> **intrusive** adj
intruded v ▷ **intrude**
intruder n (pl -s) person who enters a place
without permission
  intruders n ▷ **intruder**
  intrudes v ▷ **intrude**
  intruding v ▷ **intrude**
  intrusion n ▷ **intrude**
  intrusions n ▷ **intrude**
  intrusive adj ▷ **intrude**
intuition n (pl -s) instinctive knowledge
or insight without conscious reasoning
> **intuitive** adj > **intuitively** adv
  intuitions n ▷ **intuition**
  intuitive adj ▷ **intuition**
  intuitively adv ▷ **intuition**
inundate v (-tes, -ting, -ted) flood
> **inundation** n (pl -s)
  inundated v ▷ **inundate**
  inundates v ▷ **inundate**
  inundating v ▷ **inundate**
  inundation n ▷ **inundate**
  inundations n ▷ **inundate**
inured adj accustomed, esp. to hardship or
danger
invade v (-des, -ding, -ded) enter (a country) by
military force > **invader** n (pl -s)
  invaded v ▷ **invade**
  invader n ▷ **invade**
  invaders n ▷ **invade**
  invades v ▷ **invade**
  invading v ▷ **invade**
invalid[1] adj, n (pl -s) disabled or chronically ill
(person) ▶ v (-s, -ing, -ed) (often foll. by **out**)
dismiss from active service because of illness
or injury > **invalidity** n (pl -ties)
invalid[2] adj having no legal force
invalidate v (-tes, -ting, -ted) make or show
to be invalid
  invalidated v ▷ **invalidate**
  invalidates v ▷ **invalidate**
  invalidating v ▷ **invalidate**
  invalided v ▷ **invalid**[1]
  invaliding v ▷ **invalid**[1]
  invalidities n ▷ **invalid**[1]
  invalidity n ▷ **invalid**[1]
  invalids n, v ▷ **invalid**[1]
invaluable adj of very great value or worth
invasion n (pl -s) invading
  invasions n ▷ **invasion**
invective n (pl -s) abusive speech or writing
  invectives n ▷ **invective**
inveigh [in-vay] v (-s, -ing, -ed) (foll. by **against**)
criticize strongly

  inveighed v ▷ **inveigh**
  inveighing v ▷ **inveigh**
  inveighs v ▷ **inveigh**
inveigle v (-les, -ling, -led) coax by cunning
or trickery
  inveigled v ▷ **inveigle**
  inveigles v ▷ **inveigle**
  inveigling v ▷ **inveigle**
invent v (-s, -ing, -ed) think up or create
(something new)
  invented v ▷ **invent**
  inventing v ▷ **invent**
invention n (pl -s) something invented
inventive adj creative and resourceful
> **inventiveness** n (pl -s) > **inventor** n (pl -s)
  inventiveness n ▷ **inventive**
  inventivenesses n ▷ **inventive**
  inventor n ▷ **inventive**
  inventories v ▷ **inventory**
  inventors n ▷ **inventive**
inventory n (pl -ries) detailed list of goods or
furnishings
  invents v ▷ **invent**
inverse adj reversed in effect, sequence,
direction, etc. > **inversely** adv
  inversely adv ▷ **inverse**
  inversion n ▷ **invert**
  inversions n ▷ **invert**
invert v (-s, -ing, -ed) turn upside down or
inside out > **inversion** n (pl -s)
invertebrate n (pl -s) animal with no
backbone
  invertebrates n ▷ **invertebrate**
  inverted v ▷ **invert**
  inverting v ▷ **invert**
  inverts v ▷ **invert**
invest v (-s, -ing, -ed) spend (money, time, etc.)
on something with the expectation of profit
  invested v ▷ **invest**
investigate v (-tes, -ting, -ted) inquire
into, examine > **investigation** n (pl -s)
> **investigative** adj > **investigator** n (pl -s)
  investigated v ▷ **investigate**
  investigates v ▷ **investigate**
  investigating v ▷ **investigate**
  investigation n ▷ **investigate**
  investigations n ▷ **investigate**
  investigative adj ▷ **investigate**
  investigator n ▷ **investigate**
  investigators n ▷ **investigate**
  investing v ▷ **invest**
investiture n (pl -s) formal installation of a
person in an office or rank
  investitures n ▷ **investiture**
investment n (pl -s) money invested

> **investor** n (pl -s)
investments n ▷ investment
investor n ▷ investment
investors n ▷ investment
invests v ▷ invest
inveterate adj firmly established in a habit or condition
invidious adj likely to cause resentment
invigilate v (-tes, -ting, -ted) supervise people sitting an examination > **invigilator** n (pl -s)
invigilated v ▷ invigilate
invigilates v ▷ invigilate
invigilating v ▷ invigilate
invigilation n ▷ invigilate
invigilations n ▷ invigilate
invigilator n ▷ invigilate
invigilators n ▷ invigilate
invigorate v (-tes, -ting, -ted) give energy to, refresh
invigorated v ▷ invigorate
invigorates v ▷ invigorate
invigorating v ▷ invigorate
invincibilities n ▷ invincibile
invincibility n ▷ invincibile
invincible adj impossible to defeat
> **invincibility** n (pl -ties)
inviolable adj unable to be broken or violated
inviolate adj unharmed, unaffected
invisibilities n ▷ invisible
invisibility adv ▷ invisible
invisible adj not able to be seen > **invisibly** adv
> **invisibility** n (pl -ties)
invisibly adv ▷ invisible
invitation n ▷ invite
invitations n ▷ invite
invite v (-tes, -ting, -ted) request the company of ▶ n (pl -s) (Informal) invitation > **invitation** n (pl -s)
invited v ▷ invite
invites v, n ▷ invite
inviting adj tempting, attractive ▶ v ▷ invite
invocation n ▷ invoke
invocations n ▷ invoke
invoice v (-ces, -cing, -ced) ▶ n (pl -s) (present with) a bill for goods or services supplied
invoiced v ▷ invoice
invoices n, v ▷ invoice
invoicing v ▷ invoice
invoke v (-kes, -king, -ked) put (a law or penalty) into operation > **invocation** n (pl -s)
invoked v ▷ invoke
invokes v ▷ invoke
invoking v ▷ invoke
involuntarily adv ▷ involuntary
involuntary adj not done consciously, unintentional > **involuntarily** adv
involve v (-lves, -lving, -lved) include as a necessary part > **involved** adj complicated
> **involvement** n (pl -s)
involved v, adj ▷ involve
involvement n ▷ involve
involvements n ▷ involve
involves v ▷ involve
involving v ▷ involve
invulnerable adj not able to be wounded or harmed
inward adj directed towards the middle ▶ adv (also **inwards**) towards the inside or middle
> **inwardly** adv
inwardly adv ▷ inward
inwards adv ▷ inward

io n (**ios**). An io a cry of joy or grief. While io doesn't earn many points, it's useful when you want to form words in more than one direction: I and O are two of the most common tiles in the game, so there's a good chance that you'll be able to use io when forming a word in another direction. Io scores 2 points.

iodine n (pl -s) (CHEM) bluish-black element used in medicine and photography
iodines n ▷ iodine
iodize v (-izes, -izing, -ized) treat with iodine
iodized n ▷ iodize
iodizes n ▷ iodize
iodizing n ▷ iodize
ion n (pl -s) electrically charged atom > **ionic** adj
ionic adj ▷ ion
ionization n ▷ ionize
ionizations n ▷ ionize
ionize v (-izes, -izing, -ized) change into ions
> **ionization** n (pl -s)
ionized v ▷ ionize
ionizes v ▷ ionize
ionizing v ▷ ionize
ionosphere n (pl -s) region of ionized air in the upper atmosphere that reflects radio waves
ionospheres n ▷ ionosphere
ions n ▷ ion
iota n (pl -s) very small amount
iotas n ▷ iota
irascibilities n ▷ irascible
irascibility n ▷ irascible
irascible adj easily angered > **irascibility** n (pl -ties)
irate adj very angry
ire n (pl -s) (Lit) anger
ires n ▷ ire
iridescence n ▷ iridescent

iridescences *n* ▷ **iridescent**

iridescent *adj* having shimmering changing colours like a rainbow > **iridescence** *n* (*pl* -s)

iridium *n* (*pl* -s) (CHEM) very hard corrosion-resistant metal

iridiums *n* ▷ **iridium**

iris *n* (*pl* -ses) coloured circular membrane of the eye containing the pupil

irises *n* ▷ **iris**

irk *v* (-s, -ing, -ed) irritate, annoy

irked *v* ▷ **irk**

irking *v* ▷ **irk**

irks *v* ▷ **irk**

irksome *adj* irritating, annoying

iron *n* (*pl* -s) strong silvery-white metallic element, widely used for structural and engineering purposes ▶ *adj* made of iron ▶ *v* (-s, -ing, -ed) smooth (clothes or fabric) with an iron

ironbark *n* (*pl* -s) Australian eucalyptus with hard rough bark

ironbarks *n* ▷ **ironbark**

ironed *v* ▷ **iron**

ironic, ironical *adj* using irony > **ironically** *adv*

ironical *adj* ▷ **ironic**

ironically *adv* ▷ **ironic**

ironies *n* ▷ **irony**

ironing *n* (*pl* -s) clothes to be ironed ▶ *v* ▷ **iron**

ironings *n* ▷ **ironing**

ironmonger *n* (*pl* -s) shopkeeper or shop dealing in hardware > **ironmongery** *n* (*pl* -ries)

ironmongeries *n* ▷ **ironmonger**

ironmongers *n* ▷ **ironmonger**

ironmongery *n* ▷ **ironmonger**

irons *n*, *v* ▷ **iron** ▶ *pl n* chains, restraints

ironstone *n* (*pl* -s) rock consisting mainly of iron ore

ironstones *n* ▷ **ironstone**

irony *n* (*pl* -nies) mildly sarcastic use of words to imply the opposite of what is said

irradiate *v* (-tes, -ting, -ted) subject to or treat with radiation > **irradiation** *n* (*pl* -s)

irradiated *v* ▷ **irradiate**

irradiates *v* ▷ **irradiate**

irradiating *v* ▷ **irradiate**

irradiation *n* ▷ **irradiate**

irradiations *n* ▷ **irradiate**

irrational *adj* not based on or not using logical reasoning

irredeemable *adj* not able to be reformed or corrected

irreducible *adj* impossible to put in a simpler form

irrefutable *adj* impossible to deny or disprove

irregular *adj* not regular or even > **irregularly** *adv* > **irregularity** *n* (*pl* -ties)

irregularities *n* ▷ **irregular**

irregularity *n* ▷ **irregular**

irregularly *adv* ▷ **irregular**

irrelevance *n* ▷ **irrelevant**

irrelevances *n* ▷ **irrelevant**

irrelevant *adj* not connected with the matter in hand > **irrelevantly** *adv* > **irrelevance** *n* (*pl* -s)

irrelevantly *adv* ▷ **irrelevant**

irreparable *adj* not able to be repaired or put right > **irreparably** *adv*

irreparably *adv* ▷ **irreparable**

irreplaceable *adj* impossible to replace

irreproachable *adj* blameless, faultless

irresistible *adj* too attractive or strong to resist > **irresistibly** *adv*

irresistibly *adv* ▷ **irresistible**

irresponsibilities *n* ▷ **irresponsible**

irresponsibility *n* ▷ **irresponsible**

irresponsible *adj* not showing or not done with due care for the consequences of one's actions or attitudes > **irresponsibility** *n* (*pl* -ties)

irreverence *n* ▷ **irreverent**

irreverences *n* ▷ **irreverent**

irreverent *adj* not showing due respect > **irreverence** *n* (*pl* -s)

irreversible *adj* not able to be reversed or put right again > **irreversibly** *adv*

irreversibly *adv* ▷ **irreversible**

irrevocable *adj* not possible to change or undo > **irrevocably** *adv*

irrevocably *adv* ▷ **irrevocable**

irrigate *v* (-tes, -ting, -ted) supply (land) with water by artificial channels or pipes > **irrigation** *n* (*pl* -s)

irrigated *v* ▷ **irrigate**

irrigates *v* ▷ **irrigate**

irrigating *v* ▷ **irrigate**

irrigation *n* ▷ **irrigate**

irrigations *n* ▷ **irrigate**

irritable *adj* easily annoyed > **irritably** *adv*

irritably *adv* ▷ **irritable**

irritant *n* (*pl* -s) ▶ *adj* (person or thing) causing irritation

irritants *n* ▷ **irritant**

irritate *v* (-tes, -ting, -ted) annoy, anger > **irritation** *n* (*pl* -s)

irritated *v* ▷ **irritate**

irritates *v* ▷ **irritate**

irritating *v* ▷ **irritate**

irritation *n* ▷ **irritate**

irritations *n* ▷ **irritate**

is v ▷ **be**

ish n (**ishes**). An ish is a word for an issue in Scots law. If you have I, S and H on your rack, remember that as well as adding **ish** to the end of many words, you can also play those letters as a word in its own right. Ish scores 6 points.

isinglass [ize-ing-glass] n (pl -**es**) kind of gelatine obtained from some freshwater fish
isinglasses n ▷ **isinglass**
island n (pl -**s**) piece of land surrounded by water
islander n (pl -**s**) person who lives on an island
islanders n ▷ **islander**
islands n ▷ **island**
isle n (pl -**s**) (Poetic) island
isles n ▷ **isle**
islet n small island
islets n ▷ **islet**

ism n (**isms**). An ism is an informal word for a belief or doctrine. While **ism** can be added to the ends of many words as a suffix, it's worth remembering as a word in its own right. Ism scores 5 points.

isobar [ice-oh-bar] n (pl -**s**) line on a map connecting places of equal atmospheric pressure
isobars n ▷ **isobar**
isolate v (-**tes**, -**ting**, -**ted**) place apart or alone > **isolation** n (pl -**s**)
isolated v ▷ **isolate**
isolates v ▷ **isolate**
isolating v ▷ **isolate**
isolation n ▷ **isolate**
isolationism n (pl -**s**) policy of not participating in international affairs > **isolationist** n (pl -**s**) adj
isolationisms n ▷ **isolationism**
isolationist n, adj ▷ **isolationism**
isolationists n ▷ **isolationsim**
isolations n ▷ **isolate**
isomer [ice-oh-mer] n (pl -**s**) substance whose molecules contain the same atoms as another but in a different arrangement
isomers n ▷ **isomer**
isometric adj relating to muscular contraction without shortening of the muscle
isometrics pl n isometric exercises
isotherm [ice-oh-therm] n (pl -**s**) line on a map connecting points of equal temperature
isotherms n ▷ **isotherm**
isotope [ice-oh-tope] n (pl -**s**) one of two or

more atoms with the same number of protons in the nucleus but a different number of neutrons
isotopes n ▷ **isotope**
issue n (pl -**s**) topic of interest or discussion ▶ v (-**ssues**, -**ssuing**, -**ssued**) make (a statement etc.) publicly
issued v ▷ **issue**
issues n, v ▷ **issue**
issuing v ▷ **issue**
isthmus [iss-muss] n (pl -**muses**) narrow strip of land connecting two areas of land
isthmuses n ▷ **isthmus**
it pron refers to a nonhuman, animal, plant, or inanimate object > **its** adj, pron belonging to it
italic adj (of printing type) sloping to the right
italicize v (-**izes**, -**izing**, -**ized**) put in italics
italicized v ▷ **italicize**
italicizes v ▷ **italicize**
italicizing v ▷ **italicize**
italics pl n this type, used for emphasis
itch n (pl -**es**) skin irritation causing a desire to scratch ▶ v (-**es**, -**ing**, -**ed**) have an itch > **itchy** adj
itched v ▷ **itch**
itches n, v ▷ **itch**
itching v ▷ **itch**
itchy adj ▷ **itch**
item n (pl -**s**) single thing in a list or collection > **itemize** v (-**izes**, -**izing**, -**ized**) make a list of
itemized n ▷ **item**
itemizes n ▷ **item**
itemizing n ▷ **item**
items n ▷ **item**
iterate v (-**tes**, -**ting**, -**ted**) repeat > **iteration** n (pl -**s**)
iterated v ▷ **iterate**
iterates v ▷ **iterate**
iterating v ▷ **iterate**
iteration n ▷ **iterate**
iterations n ▷ **iterate**
itinerant adj travelling from place to place
itineraries n ▷ **itinerary**
itinerary n (pl -**aries**) detailed plan of a journey
itself pron ▷ **it**
ivies n ▷ **ivy**
ivories n ▷ **ivory**
ivory n (pl -**ries**) hard white bony substance forming the tusks of elephants ▶ adj yellowish-white
ivy n (pl -**vies**) evergreen climbing plant
iwi [ee-wee] n (pl -**s**) (NZ) Maori tribe
iwis n ▷ **iwi**

Jj

J is one of the best tiles to have in Scrabble, as it is worth 8 points on its own. J also forms a number of words with X and Z, allowing you to earn some huge scores if you get the right tiles to go with it. Even better, some of these words are seven letters in length, so the right combination of tiles will give you a 50-point bonus if you are lucky enough to have it on your rack. On the other hand, J isn't the easiest tile to use when forming words in different directions. There's only one two-letter word that begins with J **jo**. If you remember this, however, you won't waste time trying to think of others. As J has such a high value, look out for double- and triple-letter squares when playing it. There are plenty of good three-letter words starting with J: **jab** (12 points), **jam** (12), **jar** (10), **jaw** (13), **jay** (13), **jet** (10), **jib** (12), **jig** (11), **job** (12), **jog** (11), **jot** (10), **joy** (13), **jug** (11) and **jut** (10). In addition to these, there are other fantastic words beginning with J. **Jazz** (19) is very useful – you'll need a blank tile for the second Z, but if you can form it, you may also be able to play **jazzes** (21) or **jazzy** (23). **Jinx** (18) is also handy, and don't forget **jukebox** (27), which can be formed from **box** or **ox** if someone has played those.

jab v (**-s, -bbing, -bbed**) poke sharply ▶ n (pl **-s**)
  jabbed v ▷ jab
jabber v (**-s, -ing, -ed**) talk rapidly or
  incoherently
  jabbered v ▷ jabber
  jabbering v ▷ jabber
  jabbers v ▷ jabber
  jabbing v ▷ jab
jabiru n (pl **-s**) large white-and-black
  Australian stork
  jabirus n ▷ jabiru
  jabs v, n ▷ jab
jacaranda n (pl **-s**) tropical tree with sweet-
  smelling wood
  jacarandas n ▷ jacaranda
jack n (pl **-s**) device for raising a motor vehicle
  or other heavy object
  jacks n ▷ jack
jackal n (pl **-s**) doglike wild animal of Africa
  and Asia
  jackals n ▷ jackal
jackaroo, jackeroo n (pl **-roos**) (AUST) trainee
  on a sheep station
  jackaroos n ▷ jackaroo
jackass n (pl **-es**) fool
  jackasses n ▷ jackass
jackboot n (pl **-s**) high military boot

jackboots n ▷ jackboot
jackdaw n (pl **-s**) black-and-grey Eurasian bird
  of the crow family
  jackdaws n ▷ jackdaw
  jackeroo n ▷ jackaroo
  jackeroos n ▷ jackaroo
jacket n (pl **-s**) short coat
  jackets n ▷ jacket
jackknife v (**-s, -fing, -fed**) (of an articulated
  truck) go out of control so that the trailer
  swings round at a sharp angle to the cab ▶ n
  (pl **-knives**) large clasp knife
  jackknifed v ▷ jackknife
  jackknifes v ▷ jackknife
  jackknifing v ▷ jackknife
  jackknives n ▷ jackknife
jackpot n (pl **-s**) largest prize that may be won
  in a game
  jackpots n ▷ jackpot
jacuzzi [jak-oo-zee] n ® (pl **-s**) circular bath with
  a device that swirls the water
  jacuzzis n ▷ jacuzzi
jade n (pl **-s**) ornamental semiprecious stone,
  usu. dark green ▶ adj bluish-green
jaded adj tired and unenthusiastic
  jades n ▷ jade
jagged [jag-gid] adj having an uneven edge

with sharp points

jaguar n (pl **-s**) large S American spotted cat
   jaguars n ▷ **jaguar**

jail n (pl **-s**) prison ▶ v (**-s, -ing, -ed**) send to
   prison > **jailer** n (pl **-s**)

jailbird n (pl **-s**) (Informal) person who has often
   been in prison
   jailbirds n ▷ **jailbird**
   jailed v ▷ **jail**
   jailer n ▷ **jail**
   jailers n ▷ **jail**
   jailing v ▷ **jail**
   jails n, v ▷ **jail**
   jalopies n ▷ **jalopy**

jalopy [jal-**lop**-ee] n (pl **-pies**) (Informal) old car

jam[1] v (**-s, -mming, -mmed**) pack tightly into a
   place ▶ n (pl **-s**) hold-up of traffic

jam[2] n (pl **-s**) food made from fruit boiled with
   sugar

jamb n (pl **-s**) side post of a door or window
   frame

jamboree n (pl **-s**) large gathering or
   celebration
   jamborees n ▷ **jamboree**
   jambs n ▷ **jamb**
   jammed v ▷ **jam**[1]
   jamming v ▷ **jam**[1]
   jams v ▷ **jam**[1] ▶ n ▷ **jam**[1, 2]

jandal n (pl **-s**) (NZ) sandal with a strap between
   the toes
   jandals n ▷ **jandal**

jangle v (**-les, -ling, -led**) (cause to) make a
   harsh ringing noise
   jangled v ▷ **jangle**
   jangles v ▷ **jangle**
   jangling v ▷ **jangle**

janitor n (pl **-s**) caretaker of a school or other
   building
   janitors n ▷ **janitor**

> **janizar** or **janizary** n (**janizars,
> janizaries**). A janizar was an elite
> soldier in the armies of the Ottoman
> Empire. This is a very useful word,
> and will earn you a 50-point bonus if
> you are able to use all your letters in
> playing it. Also, if janizar is already on
> the board, you have an opportunity to
> earn a good score by adding an S, Y or
> IES. Janizar scores 23 points.

japan n (pl **-s**) very hard varnish, usu. black ▶ v
   (**-s, -nning, -nned**) cover with this varnish
   japanned v ▷ **japan**
   japanning v ▷ **japan**
   japans n, v ▷ **japan**

jape n (pl **-s**) (Old-fashioned) joke or prank

japes n ▷ **jape**

japonica n (pl **-s**) shrub with red flowers
   japonicas n ▷ **japonica**

jar[1] n (pl **-s**) wide-mouthed container, usu.
   round and made of glass

jar[2] v (**-s, -rring, -rred**) have a disturbing or
   unpleasant effect ▶ n (pl **-s**) jolt or shock

jargon n (pl **-s**) specialized technical language
   of a particular subject
   jargons n ▷ **jargon**

jarrah n (pl **-s**) Australian eucalypt yielding
   valuable timber
   jarrahs n ▷ **jarrah**
   jarred v ▷ **jar**[2]
   jarring v ▷ **jar**[2]
   jars v ▷ **jar**[2] ▶ n ▷ **jar**[1, 2]

jasmine n (pl **-s**) shrub with sweet-smelling
   yellow or white flowers
   jasmines n ▷ **jasmine**

jasper n (pl **-s**) red, yellow, dark green, or brown
   variety of quartz
   jaspers n ▷ **jasper**

jaundice n (pl **-s**) disease marked by
   yellowness of the skin

jaundiced adj (of an attitude or opinion) bitter
   or cynical
   jaundices n ▷ **jaundice**

jaunt n (pl **-s**) short journey for pleasure
   jauntier adj ▷ **jaunty**
   jauntiest adj ▷ **jaunty**
   jauntily adv ▷ **jaunty**
   jaunts n ▷ **jaunt**

jaunty adj (**-tier, -tiest**) sprightly and cheerful
   > **jauntily** adv

javelin n (pl **-s**) light spear thrown in sports
   competitions
   javelins n ▷ **javelin**

jaw n (pl **-s**) one of the bones in which the teeth
   are set ▶ v (**-s, -ing, -ed**) (Slang) talk lengthily

> **jawbox** n (**jawboxes**). Jawbox is a
> Scots word for a sink. Watch out for
> opportunities to form this if someone
> else has played either jaw or box, and
> if jawbox itself is on the board; you can
> earn 27 points just by making it plural
> with es. Jawbox scores 25 points.

jawed v ▷ **jaw**
jawing v ▷ **jaw**
jaws n, v ▷ **jaw** ▶ pl n mouth
jay n (pl **-s**) bird with a pinkish body and blue-
   and-black wings
   jays n ▷ **jay**

jaywalker n (pl **-s**) person who crosses the
   road in a careless or dangerous manner
   > **jaywalking** n (pl **-s**)

jaywalkers *n* ▷ **jaywalker**
jaywalking *n* ▷ **jaywalker**
jaywalkings *n* ▷ **jaywalker**

jazy *n* (**jazies**). Jazy is an old word for a wig. This is a marvellous word, combining J and Z. If you get this combination and have either an A or a Y, look for the missing letter on the board, as it's highly likely to be there. Jazy scores 23 points.

jazz *n* (*pl* -**es**) kind of music with an exciting rhythm, usu. involving improvisation
jazzes *n* ▷ **jazz**
jazzier *adj* ▷ **jazzy**
jazziest *adj* ▷ **jazzy**
jazzy *adj* (-**zier**, -**ziest**) flashy or showy
jealous *adj* fearful of losing a partner or possession to a rival > **jealously** *adv*
> **jealousy** *n* (*pl* -**sies**)
jealousies *n* ▷ **jealous**
jealously *adv* ▷ **jealous**
jealousy *n* ▷ **jealous**
jeans *pl n* casual denim trousers
jeer *v* (-**s**, -**ing**, -**ed**) scoff or deride ▶ *n* (*pl* -**s**) cry of derision
jeered *v* ▷ **jeer**
jeering *v* ▷ **jeer**
jeers *v*, *n* ▷ **jeer**
jejune *adj* simple or naive
jell *v* (-**s**, -**ing**, -**ed**) form into a jelly-like substance
jelled *v* ▷ **jell**
jellied *adj* prepared in a jelly
jelling *v* ▷ **jell**
jells *v* ▷ **jell**
jellies *n* ▷ **jelly**
jelly *n* (*pl* -**lies**) soft food made of liquid set with gelatine
jellyfish *n* (*pl* **jellyfish**) small jelly-like sea animal
jemmies *n* ▷ **jemmy**
jemmy *n* (*pl* -**mmies**) short steel crowbar used by burglars
jennies *n* ▷ **jenny**
jenny *n* (*pl* -**nnies**) female ass or wren
jeopardies *n* ▷ **jeopardy**
jeopardize *v* (-**izes**, -**izing**, -**ized**) place in danger
jeopardized *n* ▷ **jeopardy**
jeopardizes *n* ▷ **jeopardy**
jeopardizing *n* ▷ **jeopardy**
jeopardy *n* (*pl* -**dies**) danger
jerboa *n* (*pl* -**s**) small mouselike rodent with long hind legs
jerboas *n* ▷ **jerboa**

jerk *v* (-**s**, -**ing**, -**ed**) move or throw abruptly ▶ *n* (*pl* -**s**) sharp or abruptly stopped movement
jerked *v* ▷ **jerk**
jerkily *adv* ▷ **jerky**
jerkin *n* (*pl* -**s**) sleeveless jacket
jerkiness *n* ▷ **jerky**
jerkinesses *n* ▷ **jerky**
jerking *v* ▷ **jerk**
jerkins *n* ▷ **jerkin**
jerks *v*, *n* ▷ **jerk**
jerky *adj* sudden or abrupt > **jerkily** *adv*
> **jerkiness** *n* (*pl* -**s**)

jerque *v* (**jerques, jerquing, jerqued**), *n* (**jerquer, jerquers, jerquing, jerquings**). Jerque means to search a ship for smuggled goods. If you have all the tiles for jerques, jerquer or jerqued, you'll get a 50-point bonus for using all your letters, which will give you a fantastic score. Jerque scores 22 points.

jersey *n* (*pl* -**s**) knitted jumper
jerseys *n* ▷ **jersey**
jest *n* (*pl* -**s**) ▶ *v* (-**s**, -**ing**, -**ed**) joke
jested *v* ▷ **jest**
jester *n* (*pl* -**s**) (HIST) professional clown at court
jesters *n* ▷ **jester**
jesting *v* ▷ **jest**
jests *n*, *v* ▷ **jest**
jet¹ *n* (*pl* -**s**) aircraft driven by jet propulsion ▶ *v* (-**s, jetting, jetted**) fly by jet aircraft
jet² *n* (*pl* -**s**) hard black mineral
jetboat *n* (*pl* -**s**) motorboat propelled by a jet of water
jetboats *n* ▷ **jetboat**
jets *n* ▷ **jet¹, ²** ▶ *v* ▷ **jet¹**
jetsam *n* (*pl* -**s**) goods thrown overboard to lighten a ship
jetsams *n* ▷ **jetsam**
jetted *v* ▷ **jet¹**
jetties *n* ▷ **jetty**
jetting *v* ▷ **jet¹**
jettison *v* (-**s**, -**ing**, -**ed**) abandon
jettisoned *v* ▷ **jettison**
jettisoning *v* ▷ **jettison**
jettisons *v* ▷ **jettison**
jetty *n* (*pl* -**ties**) small pier

jeu *n* (**jeux**). Jeu is the French word for **game** or **play**. The plural form, **jeux**, is a great little word, using both J and X particularly if you can play it on a double- or triple-word square. Jeux scores 18 points.

jewel *n* (*pl* -**s**) precious stone
jeweller *n* (*pl* -**s**) dealer in jewels
jewelleries *n* ▷ **jewellery**

jewellers *n* ▷ jeweller
jewellery *n* (*pl* -s) objects decorated with precious stones
jewels *n* ▷ jewel
jewfish *n* (*pl* jewfish) (AUST) freshwater catfish

jezail *n* (**jezails**). A jezail is a kind of heavy Afghan musket. This word is potentially a very high scorer, as its plural uses seven tiles. If you can play all of these at once, you'll earn the 50-point bonus for a total of 73 points! Jezail scores 22 points.

jib¹ *n* (*pl* -s) triangular sail set in front of a mast
jib² *v* (**-s, -bbing, -bbed**) (of a horse, person, etc.) stop and refuse to go on
jib³ *n* (*pl* -s) projecting arm of a crane or derrick
jibbed *v* ▷ jib²
jibbing *v* ▷ jib²
jibe¹ *n* (*pl* -s) ▶ *v* (**-jibes, -jibing, -jibed**) taunt or jeer
jibed *v* ▷ jibe¹
jibes *n*, *v* ▷ jibe¹
jibing *v* ▷ jibe¹
jibs *n* ▷ jib¹, ³ ▶ *v* ▷ jib²
jiffies *n* ▷ jiffy
jiffy *n* (*pl* -**ffies**) (*Informal*) very short period of time
jig *n* (*pl* -s) type of lively dance ▶ *v* (**-s, -gging, -gged**) make jerky up-and-down movements
jigged *v* ▷ jig
jigging *v* ▷ jig
jiggle *v* (**-ggles, -ggling, -ggled**) move up and down with short jerky movements
jiggled *v* ▷ jiggle
jiggles *v* ▷ jiggle
jiggling *v* ▷ jiggle
jigs *n*, *v* ▷ jig
jigsaw *n* (*pl* -s) (*also* **jigsaw puzzle**) picture cut into interlocking pieces, which the user tries to fit together again
jigsaws *n* ▷ jigsaw
jihad *n* (*pl* -s) Islamic holy war against unbelievers
jihads *n* ▷ jihad
jilt *v* (**-s, -ing, -ed**) leave or reject (one's lover)
jilted *v* ▷ jilt
jilting *v* ▷ jilt
jilts *v* ▷ jilt
jingle *n* (*pl* -s) catchy verse or song used in a radio or television advert ▶ *v* (**-les, -ling, -led**) (cause to) make a gentle ringing sound
jingled *v* ▷ jingle
jingles *n*, *v* ▷ jingle
jingling *v* ▷ jingle
jingoism *n* (*pl* -s) aggressive nationalism

▷ **jingoistic** *adj*
jingoisms *n* ▷ jingoism
jingoistic *adj* ▷ jingoism
jinks *pl n* boisterous merrymaking
jinn *n* ▷ jinni
jinni *n* (*pl* jinn) spirit in Muslim mythology
jinx *n* (*pl* -**es**) person or thing bringing bad luck
▶ *v* (**-xes, -xing, -xed**) be or put a jinx on
jinxed *v* ▷ jinx
jinxes *n*, *v* ▷ jinx
jinxing *v* ▷ jinx
jitters *pl n* worried nervousness
jittery *adj* nervous
jive *n* (*pl* -s) lively dance of the 1940s and '50s
▶ *v* (**-ves, -ving, -ved**) dance the jive
jived *v* ▷ jive
jives *n*, *v* ▷ jive
jiving *v* ▷ jive

jiz *n* (**jizes**). Jiz is an old word for a wig. This is a very useful word for when you find yourself with J and Z but nothing else that looks promising: there will almost certainly be an I on the board around which you can form jiz. Jiz scores 19 points.

jizz *n* (**jizzes**). A jizz is the combination of characteristics used to identify a bird or plant species. A blank tile is required to form jizz because it contains two Zs. If **jiz** is already on the board, a blank or a blank and ES will earn you 19 or 21 points. Jizz scores 19 points.

jo *n* (**joes**). Jo is a Scots word for a sweetheart. This is the only two-letter word that starts with J, and is worth remembering for that reason. It's also a good word to form when playing in more than one direction at once. Jo scores 9 points.

job *n* (*pl* -s) occupation or paid employment
jobbing *adj* doing individual jobs for payment
jobless *adj*, *pl n* unemployed (people)
jobs *n* ▷ job
jockey *n* (*pl* -s) (professional) rider of racehorses ▶ *v* (**-ys, -ying, -yed**) manoeuvre to obtain an advantage
jockeyed *v* ▷ jockey
jockeying *v* ▷ jockey
jockeys *n*, *v* ▷ jockey
jockstrap *n* (*pl* -s) belt with a pouch to support the genitals, worn by male athletes
jockstraps *n* ▷ jockstrap
jocose [joke-**kohss**] *adj* playful or humorous
jocular *adj* fond of joking ▷ **jocularity** *n* (*pl*

-ties) > **jocularly** adv
jocularities n ▷ **jocular**
jocularity n ▷ **jocular**
jocularly adv ▷ **jocular**
jocund [jok-kund] adj (Lit) merry or cheerful
jodhpurs pl n riding trousers, loose-fitting above the knee but tight below
joey n (pl -ys) (AUST) young kangaroo
joeys n ▷ **joey**
jog v (-s, -gging, -gged) run at a gentle pace, esp. for exercise ▶ n (pl -s) slow run > **jogger** n (pl -s) > **jogging** n (pl -s)
jogged v ▷ **jog**
jogger n ▷ **jog**
joggers n ▷ **jog**
jogging n, v ▷ **jog**
joggings n ▷ **jog**
joggle v (-les, -ling, -led) shake or move jerkily
joggled v ▷ **joggle**
joggles v ▷ **joggle**
joggling v ▷ **joggle**
jogs n, v ▷ **jog**
join v (-s, -ing, -ed) become a member (of) ▶ n (pl -s) place where two things are joined
joined v ▷ **join**
joiner n (pl -s) maker of finished woodwork
joineries n ▷ **joinery**
joiners n ▷ **joiner**
joinery n (pl -ries) joiner's work
joining v ▷ **join**
joins n, v ▷ **join**
joint adj shared by two or more ▶ n (pl -s) place where bones meet but can move ▶ v (-s, -ing, -ed) divide meat into joints > **jointed** adj > **jointly** adv
jointed v, adj ▷ **joint**
jointing v ▷ **joint**
jointly adv ▷ **joint**
joints n, v ▷ **joint**
joist n (pl -s) horizontal beam that helps support a floor or ceiling
joists n ▷ **joist**
jojoba [hoe-hoe-ba] n (pl -s) shrub of SW North America whose seeds yield oil used in cosmetics
jojobas n ▷ **jojoba**
joke n (pl -s) thing said or done to cause laughter ▶ v (-kes, -king, -ked) make jokes > **jokey** adj > **jokingly** adv
joked v ▷ **joke**
joker n (pl -s) person who jokes
jokers n ▷ **joker**
jokes n, v ▷ **joke**
jokey adj ▷ **joke**
joking v ▷ **joke**

jokingly adv ▷ **joke**
jollied v ▷ **jolly**
jollier adj ▷ **jolly**
jollies v ▷ **jolly**
jolliest adj ▷ **jolly**
jollities n ▷ **jolly**
jollity n ▷ **jolly**
jolly adj (-llier, -lliest) (of a person) happy and cheerful ▶ v (-lies, -lying, -lied) try to keep (someone) cheerful by flattery or coaxing > **jollity** n (pl -ties)
jollification n (pl -s) merrymaking
jollifications n ▷ **jolly**
jollying v ▷ **jolly**
jolt n (pl -s) unpleasant surprise or shock ▶ v (-s, -ing, -ed) surprise or shock
jolted v ▷ **jolt**
jolting v ▷ **jolt**
jolts n, v ▷ **jolt**
jonquil n (pl -s) fragrant narcissus
jonquils n ▷ **jonquil**
josh v (-es, -ing, -ed) (CHIEFLY US) (Slang) tease
joshed v ▷ **josh**
joshes v ▷ **josh**
joshing v ▷ **josh**
jostle v (-les, -ling, -led) knock or push against
jostled v ▷ **jostle**
jostles v ▷ **jostle**
jostling v ▷ **jostle**
jot v (-s, -tting, -tted) write briefly ▶ n (pl -s) very small amount
jotted v ▷ **jot**
jotting v ▷ **jot**
jotter n (pl -s) notebook
jotters n ▷ **jotter**
jottings pl n notes jotted down
jots v, n ▷ **jot**
joule [jool] n (pl -s) (PHYSICS) unit of work or energy
joules n ▷ **joule**
journal n (pl -s) daily newspaper or magazine
journalese n (pl -s) superficial style of writing, found in some newspapers
journaleses n ▷ **journalese**
journalism n (pl -s) writing in or editing of newspapers and magazines > **journalist** n (pl -s) > **journalistic** adj
journalisms n ▷ **journalism**
journalist n ▷ **journalism**
journalistic adj ▷ **journalism**
journalists n ▷ **journalism**
journals n ▷ **journal**
journey n (pl -s) act or process of travelling from one place to another ▶ v (-s, -ing, -ed) travel

journeyed v ▷ journey
journeying v ▷ journey
journeyman n (pl -men) qualified craftsman employed by another
journeymen n ▷ journeyman
journeys n, v ▷ journey
joust (HIST) n (pl -s) combat with lances between two mounted knights ▶ v (-s, -ing, -ed) fight on horseback using lances
jousted v ▷ joust
jousting v ▷ joust
jousts n, v ▷ joust
jovial adj happy and cheerful > **jovially** adv > **joviality** n (pl -ties)
jovialities n ▷ jovial
joviality n ▷ jovial
jovially adv ▷ jovial
jowl[1] n (pl -s) lower jaw
jowl[2] n (pl -s) fatty flesh hanging from the lower jaw
jowls n ▷ jowl[1, 2] ▶ pl n cheeks
joy n (pl -s) feeling of great delight or pleasure > **joyful** adj > **joyless** adj
joyful adj ▷ joy
joyless adj ▷ joy
joyous adj extremely happy and enthusiastic
joyride n ▷ joyriding
joyrider n ▷ joyriding
joyriders n ▷ joyriding
joyrides n ▷ joyriding
joyriding n (pl -s) driving for pleasure, esp. in a stolen car > **joyride** n (pl -s) > **joyrider** n (pl -s)
joyridings n ▷ joyriding
joystick n (pl -s) control device for an aircraft or computer
joysticks n ▷ joystick
joys n ▷ joy
jubilant adj feeling or expressing great joy > **jubilantly** adv > **jubilation** n (pl -s)
jubilantly adv ▷ jubilant
jubilation n ▷ jubilant
jubilations n ▷ jubilant
jubilee n (pl -s) special anniversary, esp. 25th (**silver jubilee**) or 50th (**golden jubilee**)
jubilees n ▷ jubilee
judder v (-s, -ing, -ed) vibrate violently ▶ n (pl -s) violent vibration
juddered v ▷ judder
juddering v ▷ judder
judders v, n ▷ judder
judge n (pl -s) public official who tries cases and passes sentence in a court of law ▶ v (-dges, -dging, -dged) act as a judge
judged v ▷ judge
judgement n ▷ judgment

judgements n ▷ judgment
judgemental adj ▷ judgment
judges n, v ▷ judge
judging v ▷ judge
judgment, judgement n (pl -s) opinion reached after careful thought > **judgmental, judgemental** adj
judgmental adj ▷ judgment
judgments n ▷ judgment
judicial adj of or by a court or judge > **judicially** adv
judicially adv ▷ judicial
judiciary n (pl -ries) system of courts and judges
judiciaries n ▷ judiciary
judicious adj well-judged and sensible > **judiciously** adv
judiciously adv ▷ judicious
judo n sport in which two opponents try to throw each other to the ground
jug n (pl -s) container for liquids, with a handle and small spout
juggernaut n (pl -s) (BRIT) large heavy truck
juggernauts n ▷ juggernaut
juggle v (-les, -ling, -led) throw and catch (several objects) so that most are in the air at the same time > **juggler** n (pl -s)
juggled v ▷ juggle
juggler n ▷ juggle
jugglers n ▷ juggle
juggles v ▷ juggle
juggling v ▷ juggle
jugs n ▷ jug
jugular n (pl -s) one of three large veins of the neck that return blood from the head to the heart
jugulars n ▷ jugular
juice n (pl -s) liquid part of vegetables, fruit, or meat
juices n ▷ juice
juicier adj ▷ juicy
juiciest adj ▷ juicy
juicy adj (-cier, -ciest) full of juice
jujitsu n (pl -s) Japanese art of wrestling and self-defence
jujitsus n ▷ jujitsu
juju n (pl -s) W African magic charm or fetish
jujus n ▷ juju
jukebox n (pl -es) coin-operated machine on which records, CDs, or videos can be played
jukeboxes n ▷ jukebox
julep n (pl -s) sweet alcoholic drink
juleps n ▷ julep
jumble n (pl -s) confused heap or state ▶ v (-les, -ling, -led) mix in a disordered way

jumbled v ▷ jumble
jumbles n, v ▷ jumble
jumbling v ▷ jumble
jumbo adj (Informal) very large ▶ n (pl -s) (also **jumbo jet**) large jet airliner
jumbos n ▷ jumbo
jumbuck n (pl -s) (AUST) (Old-fashioned slang) sheep
jumbucks n ▷ jumbuck
jump v (-s, -ing, -ed) leap or spring into the air using the leg muscles ▶ n (pl -s) act of jumping
jumped v ▷ jump
jumper n (pl -s) sweater or pullover
jumpers n ▷ jumper
jumpier adj ▷ jumpy
jumpiest adj ▷ jumpy
jumping v ▷ jump
jumps v, n ▷ jump
jumpy adj (-pier, -piest) nervous
junction n (pl -s) place where routes, railway lines, or roads meet
junctions n ▷ junction
juncture n (pl -s) point in time, esp. a critical one
junctures n ▷ juncture
jungle n (pl -s) tropical forest of dense tangled vegetation
jungles n ▷ jungle
junior adj of lower standing ▶ n (pl -s) junior person
juniors n ▷ junior
juniper n (pl -s) evergreen shrub with purple berries
junipers n ▷ juniper
junk¹ n (pl -s) discarded or useless objects
junk² n (pl -s) flat-bottomed Chinese sailing boat
junket n (pl -s) excursion by public officials paid for from public funds
junkets n ▷ junket
junkie, junky n (pl -kies) (Slang) drug addict
junkies n ▷ junkie
junks n ▷ junk¹, ²
junky n ▷ junkie
junta n (pl -s) group of military officers holding power in a country, esp. after a coup
juntas n ▷ junta
juridical adj of law or the administration of justice
juries n ▷ jury
jurisdiction n (pl -s) right or power to administer justice and apply laws

jurisdictions n ▷ jurisdiction
jurisprudence n (pl -s) science or philosophy of law
jurisprudences n ▷ jurisprudence
jurist n (pl -s) expert in law
jurists n ▷ jurist
juror n (pl -s) member of a jury
jurors n ▷ juror
jury n (pl -ries) group of people sworn to deliver a verdict in a court of law
just adv very recently ▶ adj fair or impartial in action or judgment > **justly** adv > **justness** n (pl -s)
justice n (pl -s) quality of being just
justices n ▷ justice
justifiable adj ▷ justify
justifiably adv ▷ justify
justification n ▷ justify
justifications n ▷ justify
justified v ▷ justify
justifies v ▷ justify
justify v (-fies, -fying, -fied) prove right or reasonable > **justifiable** adj > **justifiably** adv > **justification** n (pl -s)
justifying v ▷ justify
justly adv ▷ just
justness n ▷ just
justnesses n ▷ just
jut v (-s, -tting, -tted) project or stick out
jute n (pl -s) plant fibre, used for rope, canvas, etc.
jutes n ▷ jute
juts v ▷ jut
jutted v ▷ jut
jutting v ▷ jut
juvenilia pl n works produced in an author's youth
juvenile adj young ▶ n (pl -s) young person or child
juveniles n ▷ juvenile
juxtapose v (-ses, -sing, -sed) put side by side > **juxtaposition** n (pl -s)
juxtaposed v ▷ juxtapose
juxtaposes v ▷ juxtapose
juxtaposing v ▷ juxtapose
juxtaposition n ▷ juxtapose
juxtapositions n ▷ juxtapose

jynx n (**jynxes**). A jynx is a kind of woodpecker. This unusual word is unique in combining J, Y and Z without using any vowels. Jynx scores 21 points.

Kk

Worth 5 points, K is a valuable tile to have in your rack. However, it's not the most useful tile for the short words that you need when forming words in different directions at the same time. There are only three two-letter words beginning with K: **ka, ko** and **ky.** Remembering these will stop you wasting time trying to think of others. There aren't very many three-letter words either, but remember **kak** (11 points), **keg** (8), **ken** (7), **key** (10), **kid** (8), **kin** (7), **kip** (9) and **kit (7).**

ka n (**kas**). A ka is a supernatural being in ancient Egyptian mythology. This is worth remembering as, along with **ko** and **ky,** it's one of only three two-letter words starting with K. Ka scores 6 points.

kaftan n (pl -s) long loose Eastern garment
kaftans n ▷ kaftan
kaiser [kize-er] n (pl -s) (HIST) German or Austro-Hungarian emperor
kaisers n ▷ kaiser
kak n (pl S AFR) (Slang) faeces
kalashnikov n (pl -s) Russian-made automatic rifle
kalashnikovs n ▷ kalashnikov
kale n (pl -s) cabbage with crinkled leaves
kales n ▷ kale
kaleidoscope n (pl -s) tube-shaped toy containing loose coloured pieces reflected by mirrors so that intricate patterns form when the tube is twisted > **kaleidoscopic** adj
kaleidoscopes n ▷ kaleidoscope
kaleidoscopic adj ▷ kaleidoscope
kamikaze [kam-mee-**kah**-zee] n (pl -s) (in World War II) Japanese pilot who performed a suicide mission ▸ adj (of an action) undertaken in the knowledge that it will kill or injure the person performing it
kamikazes n ▷ kamikaze
kangaroo n (pl -s) Australian marsupial which moves by jumping with its powerful hind legs
kangaroos n ▷ kangaroo
kaolin n (pl -s) fine white clay used to make porcelain and in some medicines
kaolins n ▷ kaolin
kapok n (pl -s) fluffy fibre from a tropical tree, used to stuff cushions etc.

kapoks n ▷ kapok
kaput [kap-**poot**] adj (Informal) ruined or broken
karaoke n (pl -s) form of entertainment in which people sing over a prerecorded backing tape
karaokes n ▷ karaoke
karate n (pl -s) Japanese system of unarmed combat using blows with the feet, hands, elbows, and legs
karates n ▷ karate
karma n (pl -s) (BUDDHISM, HINDUISM) person's actions affecting his or her fate in the next reincarnation
karmas n ▷ karma
karri n (pl -s) Australian eucalypt
karris n ▷ karri
katipo n (pl -s) small poisonous New Zealand spider
katipos n ▷ katipo
kayak n (pl -s) Inuit canoe made of sealskins stretched over a frame
kayaks n ▷ kayak
kebab n (pl -s) dish of small pieces of meat grilled on skewers
kebabs n ▷ kebab
kedgeree n (pl -s) dish of fish with rice and eggs
kedgerees n ▷ kedgeree
keel n (pl -s) main lengthways timber or steel support along the base of a ship
keels n ▷ keel
keen[1] adj (-er, -est) eager or enthusiastic > **keenly** adv > **keenness** n
keen[2] v (-s, -ing, -ed) wail over the dead
keened v ▷ keen[2]
keener adj ▷ keen[1]
keenest adj ▷ keen[1]
keening v ▷ keen[2]

keenly *adv* ▷ **keen¹**
keenness *n* ▷ **keen¹**
keens *v* ▷ **keen²**
keep *v* (**-s, -ing, kept**) have or retain possession of ▶ *n* (**-s**) cost of food and everyday expenses
keeper *n* (**-s**) person who looks after animals in a zoo ▶ *n* ▷ **keeper**
keeping *v* ▷ **keep** ▶ *n* (**-s**) care or charge ▶ *n* ▷ **keeping** ▶ *v* ▷ **keep** ▶ *n* ▷ **keep** > **keepsake** *n* (**-s**) gift treasured for the sake of the giver
keepsakes *n* ▷ **keepsake**
keg *n* (*pl* **-s**) small metal beer barrel
kegs *n* ▷ **keg**
kelp *n* (*pl* **-s**) large brown seaweed
kelpie *n* (*pl* **-s**) Australian sheepdog with a smooth coat and upright ears
kelpies *n* ▷ **kelpie**
kelps *n* ▷ **kelp**
kelvin *n* (*pl* **-s**) SI unit of temperature
kelvins *n* ▷ **kelvin**
ken *v* (**-s, -nning, -nned** *or* **kent**) (SCOT) know
kenning *v* ▷ **ken**
kenned *v* ▷ **ken**
kendo *n* (*pl* **-s**) Japanese sport of fencing using wooden staves
kendos *n* ▷ **kendo**
kennel *n* (*pl* **-s**) hutlike shelter for a dog
kennels *n* ▷ **kennel**
kens *v* ▷ **ken**
kent *v* ▷ **ken**
kept *v* ▷ **keep**
keratin *n* (*pl* **-s**) fibrous protein found in the hair and nails
keratins *n* ▷ **keratin**
kerb *n* (*pl* **-s**) edging to a footpath
kerbs *n* ▷ **kerb**
kerchief *n* (*pl* **-s**) piece of cloth worn over the head or round the neck
kerchiefs *n* ▷ **kerchief**
kerfuffle *n* (*pl* **-s**) (*Informal*) commotion or disorder
kerfuffles *n* ▷ **kerfuffle**
kernel *n* (*pl* **-s**) seed of a nut, cereal, or fruit stone
kernels *n* ▷ **kernel**
kerosene *n* (*pl* **-s**) (US, CANADIAN, AUST & NZ) liquid mixture distilled from petroleum and used as a fuel or solvent
kerosenes *n* ▷ **kerosene**
kestrel *n* (*pl* **-s**) type of small falcon
kestrels *n* ▷ **kestrel**
ketch *n* (*pl* **-es**) two-masted sailing ship
ketches *n* ▷ **ketch**
ketchup *n* (*pl* **-s**) thick cold sauce, usu. made of tomatoes

ketchups *n* ▷ **ketchup**
kettle *n* (*pl* **-s**) container with a spout and handle used for boiling water
kettledrum *n* (*pl* **-s**) large bowl-shaped metal drum
kettledrums *n* ▷ **kettledrum**
kettles *n* ▷ **kettle**
key *n* (*pl* **-s**) device for operating a lock by moving a bolt ▶ *adj* of great importance ▶ *v* (**-s, -ing, -ed**) enter (text) using a keyboard
keyboard *n* (*pl* **-s**) set of keys on a piano, computer, etc. ▶ *v* (**-s, -ing, -ed**) enter (text) using a keyboard
keyboarded *v* ▷ **keyboard**
keyboarding *v* ▷ **keyboard**
keyboards *n*, *v* ▷ **keyboard**
keyed *v* ▷ **key**
keyhole *n* (*pl* **-s**) opening for inserting a key into a lock
keyholes *n* ▷ **keyhole**
keying *v* ▷ **key**
keynote *n* (*pl* **-s**) dominant idea of a speech etc.
keynotes *n* ▷ **keynote**
keys *n*, *v* ▷ **key**
keystone *n* (*pl* **-s**) most important part of a process, organization, etc.
keystones *n* ▷ **keystone**

> **kex** *n* (**kexes**). A kex is a hollow-stemmed plant. This is a great three-letter word, combining K with X. If you have these letters on your rack, you can be confident that there will be, or will soon be, an E on the board, around which you can form kex. Kex scores 14 points.

khaki *adj* dull yellowish-brown ▶ *n* (*pl* **-s**) hard-wearing fabric of this colour used for military uniforms
khakis *n* ▷ **khaki**

> **khi** *n* (**khis**). Khi is a letter of the Greek alphabet, also spelt **chi**. This is one of the higher-scoring three-letter words starting with K, and so is worth remembering. Khi scores 10 points.

kibbutz *n* (*pl* **-im**) communal farm or factory in Israel
kibbutzim *n* ▷ **kibbutz**
kick *v* (**-s, -ing, -ed**) drive, push, or strike with the foot ▶ *n* (*pl* **kicks**) thrust or blow with the foot
kickback (*Informal*) *n* (*pl* **-s**) money paid illegally for favours done
kickbacks *n* ▷ **kickback**
kicked *v* ▷ **kick**

kicking *n, v* ▷ **kick**
kicks *n, v* ▷ **kick**
kid¹ *n* (*pl* -s) (*Informal*) child
kid² *v* (-s, -dding, -dded) (*Informal*) tease or deceive (someone)
  kidded *v* ▷ **kid²**
  kidding *v* ▷ **kid²**
kidnap *v* (-s, -pping, -pped) seize and hold (a person) to ransom > **kidnapper** *n* (*pl* -s)
  kidnapped *n* ▷ **kidnap**
  kidnapper *n* ▷ **kidnap**
  kidnappers *n* ▷ **kidnap**
  kidnapping *n* ▷ **kidnap**
  kidnaps *n* ▷ **kidnap**
kidney *n* (*pl* **kidneys**) either of the pair of organs that filter waste products from the blood to produce urine
  kidneys *n* ▷ **kidney**
  kids *n* ▷ **kid¹** ▶ *v* ▷ **kid²**
kill *v* (-s, -ing, -ed) cause the death of (*Informal*) ▶ *n* (*pl* -s) act of killing > **killer** *n* (*pl* **killers**)
  killed *v* ▷ **kill**
  killer *n* ▷ **kill**
  killers *n* ▷ **kill**
killing (*Informal*) *adj* very tiring ▶ *n* (*pl* -s) sudden financial success ▶ *v* ▷ **kill**
  killings *n* ▷ **killing**
killjoy *n* (*pl* -s) person who spoils others' pleasure
  killjoys *n* ▷ **killjoy**
  kills *v, n* ▷ **kill**
kiln *n* (*pl* -s) oven for baking, drying, or processing pottery, bricks, etc.
  kilns *n* ▷ **kiln**
kilobyte *n* (*pl* -s) (COMPUTERS) 1024 units of information
  kilobytes *n* ▷ **kilobyte**
kilogram, kilogramme *n* (*pl* -s) one thousand grams
  kilogrammes *n* ▷ **kilogram**
  kilograms *n* ▷ **kilogram**
kilohertz *n* (*pl* -es) one thousand hertz
  kilohertzes *n* ▷ **kilohertz**
kilometre *n* (*pl* -s) one thousand metres
  kilometres *n* ▷ **kilometre**
kilowatt *n* (*pl* -s) (ELECTRICITY) one thousand watts
  kilowatts *n* ▷ **kilowatt**
kilt *n* (*pl* -s) knee-length pleated tartan skirt worn orig. by Scottish Highlanders > **kilted** *adj*
  kilted *n* ▷ **kilt**
  kilts *n* ▷ **kilt**
kimono *n* (*pl* -s) loose wide-sleeved Japanese robe, fastened with a sash

kimonos *n* ▷ **kimono**
kin, kinsfolk *n* person's relatives collectively > **kinship** (*pl* -s) ▶ *n*
kind¹ *adj* (-er, -est) considerate, friendly, and helpful > **kindness** *n* (*pl* -es) > **kindliness** *n* (*pl* -es) > **kind-hearted** *adj*
kind² *n* (*pl* -s) class or group with common characteristics
  kinder *adj* ▷ **kind¹**
kindergarten *n* (*pl* -s) class or school for children under six years old
  kindergartens *n* ▷ **kindergarten**
  kindest *adj* ▷ **kind¹**
  kindhearted *adj* ▷ **kind¹**
  kindies *n* ▷ **kindy**
  kindliness *n* (*pl* -es) ▷ **kind¹**
  kindlinesses *n* ▷ **kind¹**
kindle *v* (-les, -ling, -led) set (a fire) alight
  kindled *v* ▷ **kindle**
  kindles *v* ▷ **kindle**
kindling *n* (*pl* -s) dry wood or straw for starting fires ▶ *v* ▷ **kindle**
kindly *adj* having a warm-hearted nature ▶ *adv* in a considerate way
kindness *n* (*pl* -es) ▷ **kind¹**
  kindnesses *n* ▷ **kind¹**
  kinds *n* ▷ **kind²**
kindred *adj* having similar qualities ▶ *n* (*pl* -s) ▷ **kin**
kindy, kindie *n* (*pl* -dies) (AUST & NZ) (*Informal*) kindergarten
kinetic [kin-**net**-ik] *adj* relating to or caused by motion
king *n* (*pl* **kings**) male ruler of a monarchy > **kingship** *n* (*pl* -s)
kingdom *n* (*pl* -s) state ruled by a king or queen
  kingdoms *n* ▷ **kingdom**
  kings *n* ▷ **king**
kingship *n* (*pl* -s) ▷ **king**
  kingships *n* ▷ **king**
kingfisher *n* (*pl* -s) small bird, often with a bright-coloured plumage, that dives for fish
  kingfishers *n* ▷ **kingfisher**
kingpin *n* (*pl* -s) most important person in an organization
  kingpins *n* ▷ **kingpin**
kink *n* (*pl* -s) twist or bend in rope, wire, hair, etc.
  kinks *n* ▷ **kink**
kinky *adj* (*Slang*) given to unusual sexual practices
  kinships *n* ▷ **kinship**
kiosk *n* (*pl* -s) small booth selling drinks, cigarettes, newspapers, etc.
  kiosks *n* ▷ **kiosk**

kip (*Informal*) *n* (*pl* -s) sleep ▶ *v* (-s, -pping, -pped) sleep
  kipped *v* ▷ **kip**
kipper *n* (*pl* -s) cleaned, salted, and smoked herring
  kippers *n* ▷ **kipper**
  kipping *v* ▷ **kip**
  kips *v* ▷ **kip**
kirk *n* (*pl* -s) (SCOT) church
  kirks *n* ▷ **kirk**
kismet *n* (*pl* -s) fate or destiny
  kismets *n* ▷ **kismet**
kiss *v* (-es, -ing, -ed) touch with the lips in affection or greeting ▶ *n* (*pl* -es) touch with the lips
kissagram *n* (*pl* -s) greetings service in which a messenger kisses the person celebrating
  kissagrams *n* ▷ **kissagram**
  kissed *v* ▷ **kiss**
kisser *n* (*pl* -s) (*Slang*) mouth or face
  kissers *n* ▷ **kisser**
  kisses *v*, *n* ▷ **kiss**
  kissing *v* ▷ **kiss**
kist *n* (*pl* -s) (S AFR) large wooden chest
  kists *n* ▷ **kist**
kit *n* (*pl* -s) outfit or equipment for a specific purpose
kitbag *n* (*pl* -s) bag for a soldier's or traveller's belongings
  kitbags *n* ▷ **kitbag**
  kits *n* ▷ **kit**
kitset *n* (*pl* -s) (NZ) unassembled pieces for constructing a piece of furniture
kitchen *n* (*pl* -s) room used for cooking
kitchenette *n* (*pl* -s) small kitchen
  kitchenettes *n* ▷ **kitchetenette**
  kitchens *n* ▷ **kitchen**
  kitches *n* ▷ **kitch**
kite *n* (*pl* -s) light frame covered with a thin material flown on a string in the wind
  kites *n* ▷ **kite**
kith *n* (*pl* -s) friends and relatives
  kiths *n* ▷ **kith**
kitsch *n* (*pl* -es) art or literature with popular sentimental appeal
kitten *n* (*pl* -s) young cat
kittenish *adj* lively and flirtatious
  kittens *n* ▷ **kitten**
  kitties *n* ▷ **kitty**
kittiwake *n* (*pl* -s) type of seagull
  kittiwakes *n* ▷ **kittiwake**
kitty *n* (*pl* -ties) communal fund
kiwi *n* (*pl* -s) New Zealand flightless bird with a long beak and no tail
  kiwis *n* ▷ **kiwi**

klaxon *n* (*pl* -s) loud horn used on emergency vehicles as a warning signal
  klaxons *n* ▷ **klaxon**
kleptomania *n* (*pl* -s) compulsive tendency to steal > **kleptomaniac** *n* (*pl* -s)
kleptomaniac *n* (*pl* -s) ▷ **kleptomania**
  kleptomaniacs *n* ▷ **kleptomania**
kloof *n* (*pl* **kloofs**) (S AFR) mountain pass or gorge
  kloofs *n* ▷ **kloof**
knack *n* (*pl* **knacks**) skilful way of doing something
  knacks *n* ▷ **knack**
knacker *n* (*pl* -s) (BRIT) buyer of old horses for killing
knackered *adj* (*Slang*) extremely tired
  knackers *n* ▷ **knacker**
knapsack *n* (*pl* -s) soldier's or traveller's bag worn strapped on the back
  knapsacks *n* ▷ **knapsack**
knave *n* (*pl* -s) jack at cards (*Obs*)
  knaves *n* ▷ **knave**
knead *v* (-s, -ing, -ed) work (dough) into a smooth mixture with the hands
  kneaded *v* ▷ **knead**
  kneading *v* ▷ **knead**
  kneads *v* ▷ **knead**
knee *n* (*pl* **knees**) joint between thigh and lower leg ▶ *v* (-s, -ing, -d) strike or push with the knee
kneecap *n* (*pl* **kneecaps**) bone in front of the knee ▶ *v* (-pping, -pped) shoot in the kneecap
  kneed *v* ▷ **knee**
  kneeing *v* ▷ **knee**
kneejerk *adj* (of a reply or reaction) automatic and predictable
kneel *v* (-s, -ing, -ed *or* **knelt**) fall or rest on one's knees
  kneeled, knelt *v* ▷ **kneel**
  kneeling *v* ▷ **kneel**
  kneels *v* ▷ **kneel**
  knees *n*, *v* ▷ **knee**
knell *n* (*pl* -s) sound of a bell, esp. at a funeral or death
  knells *n* ▷ **knell**
  knelt *v* ▷ **kneel**
  knew *v* ▷ **know**
knickerbockers *pl n* loose-fitting short trousers gathered in at the knee
knickers *pl n* woman's or girl's undergarment covering the lower trunk and having legs or legholes
knife *n* (*pl* **knives**) cutting tool or weapon consisting of a sharp-edged blade with a handle ▶ *v* (-s, -ing, -ed) cut or stab with a

knife
knifed v ▷ knife
knifes v ▷ knife
knifing v ▷ knife
knight n (pl -s) man who has been given a knighthood ▶ v (-s, -ing, -ed) award a knighthood to > **knightly** adj > **knighthood** n (pl -s) honorary title given to a man by the British sovereign
knighted v ▷ knight
knighthoods n ▷ knighthood
knighting v ▷ knight
knights n, v ▷ knight
knit v (-s, -tting, -tted or knit) make (a garment) by interlocking a series of loops in wool or other yarn > **knitting** n (pl -s)
knits v ▷ knit
knitted v ▷ knit
knitting v ▷ knit
knittings n ▷ knit
knitwear n (pl -s) knitted clothes, such as sweaters
knitwears n ▷ knitwear
knives n ▷ knife
knob n (pl -s) rounded projection, such as a switch on a radio
knobblier adj ▷ knobbly
knobbliest adj ▷ knobbly
knobbly adj (-lier, -liest) covered with small bumps
knobkerrie n (pl -s) (S AFR) club with a rounded end
knobkerries n ▷ knobkerrie
knobs n ▷ knob
knock v (-s, -ing, -ed) give a blow or push to ▶ n (pl -s) blow or rap
knockabout adj (of comedy) boisterous
knockdown adj (of a price) very low
knocked v ▷ knock
knocker n (pl -s) metal fitting for knocking on a door
knockers n ▷ knocker
knocking v ▷ knock
knockout n (pl -s) blow that renders an opponent unconscious
knockouts n ▷ knockout
knocks v, n ▷ knock
knoll n (pl -s) small rounded hill
knolls n ▷ knoll
knot n (pl -s) fastening made by looping and pulling tight strands of string, cord, or rope ▶ v (-s, -tting, -tted) tie with or into a knot
knots n ▷ knot
knotted n ▷ knot

knotting n ▷ knot
knotty adj full of knots
know v (-s, -ing, knew, known) be or feel certain of the truth of (information etc.) > **knowable** adj
knowing v ▷ know ▶ adj suggesting secret knowledge
knowingly adv deliberately
knowhow n (pl -s) (Informal) ingenuity, aptitude, or skill
knowhows n ▷ know-how
knowledgable n ▷ knowledgeable
knowledge n (pl -s) facts or experiences known by a person
knowledgeable, knowledgable adj intelligent or well-informed
knowledges n ▷ knowledge
known v ▷ know
knows v ▷ know
knuckle n (pl -s) bone at the finger joint
knuckles n ▷ knuckle

ko n (kos). A ko is a Maori digging-stick. This is worth remembering as, along with ka and ky, it's one of only three two-letter words starting with K. Ko scores 6 points.

koala n (pl -s) tree-dwelling Australian marsupial with dense grey fur
koalas n ▷ koala
kohl n (pl -s) cosmetic powder used to darken the edges of the eyelids
kohls n ▷ kohls
kookaburra n (pl -s) large Australian kingfisher with a cackling cry
kookaburras n ▷ kookaburra
koori n (pl -s) Australian Aborigine
kooris n ▷ koori
kopje, koppie n (pl -s) (S AFR) small hill
kopjes n ▷ kopje
kosher [koh-sher] adj conforming to Jewish religious law, esp. (of food) to Jewish dietary law ▶ n (pl -s) kosher food
koshers n ▷ kosher
kowhai n (pl -s) New Zealand tree with clusters of yellow flowers
kowhais n ▷ kowhai

kow n (kows). A kow is a Scots word for a bunch of twigs. Kow is relatively high-scoring for a three-letter word, and so can be a good one to form when playing in more than one direction. Kow scores 10 points.

kowtow v (-s, -ing, -ed) be servile (towards)
kowtowed v ▷ kowtow

kowtowing v ▷ kowtow

kowtows v ▷ kowtow

kraal n (pl -s) S African village surrounded by a strong fence

kraals n ▷ kraal

krill n small shrimplike sea creature(s)

krypton n (pl -s) (CHEM) colourless gas present in the atmosphere and used in fluorescent lights

kryptons n ▷ krypton

kudos n (pl -es) fame or credit

kudoses n ▷ kudoses

kugel [koog-el] n (pl -s) (S AFR) rich, fashion-conscious, materialistic young woman

kugels n ▷ kugel

kumara n (pl -s) (NZ) tropical root vegetable with yellow flesh

kumaras n ▷ kumara

kumquat [kumm-kwott] n (pl -s) citrus fruit resembling a tiny orange

kumquats n ▷ kumquat

kurrajong n (pl -s) Australian tree or shrub with tough fibrous bark

kurrajongs n ▷ kurrajong

ky or **kye** n. Ky is a Scots word for **cows.** If you are playing a longer word beginning with K, you may be able to use ky to tag onto a word on the board that ends in Y. Ky scores 9 points.

kyu n (**kyus**). A kyu is a beginner's grade in judo. The unusual combination of letters makes this a useful word to have when you have an unpromising set of letters on your rack. Kyu scores 10 points.

Ll

L can be a difficult letter to use well, especially when you need to play short words. Just three two-letter words begin with L: **la, li** and **lo**. Knowing this will save you valuable time in a game, especially when you are trying to fit words into a crowded board. There aren't a great number of three-letter words either, but don't forget common words like **lab** (5 points), **law** (6), **lay** (6), **low** (6) and **lye** (6). Try to remember the three-letter words that combine L with X: **lax, lex, lox** and **lux** (10 points each). These are particularly useful towards the end of a game if you have an X but little opportunity to play it.

la *n* (**las**). In music, la is the sixth note of a major scale. La is also spelt **lah**. La scores 2 points.
label *n* (*pl* **-s**) piece of card or other material fixed to an object to show its ownership, destination, etc. ▶ *v* (**-s, -lling, -lled**) give a label to
  labels *n* ▷ **label**
labia *pl n* (*sing* **-bium**) four liplike folds of skin forming part of the female genitals
labial [lay-bee-al] *adj* of the lips
  labium *n* ▷ **labia**
labor *n* (*pl* **-s**) (US & AUST) ▷ **labour**
  laboratories *n* ▷ **laboratory**
laboratory *n* (*pl* **-ies**) building or room designed for scientific research or for the teaching of practical science
laborious *adj* involving great prolonged effort > **laboriously** *adv*
  laboriously *adv* ▷ **laborious**
  labors *n* ▷ **labor**
labour, (US & AUST) **labor** *n* (*pl* **-s**) physical work or exertion ▶ *v* (**-s, -ing, -ed**) work hard
laboured *adj* uttered or done with difficulty
  ▶ *v* ▷ **labour**
labourer *n* (*pl* **-s**) person who labours, esp. someone doing manual work for wages
  labourers *n* ▷ **labourer**
  labouring *v* ▷ **labour**
  labours *n, v* ▷ **labour**
labrador *n* (*pl* **-s**) large retriever dog with a usu. gold or black coat
  labradors *n* ▷ **labrador**
laburnum *n* (*pl* **-s**) ornamental tree with yellow hanging flowers
  laburnums *n* ▷ **laburnum**
labyrinth [lab-er-inth] *n* (*pl* **-s**) complicated

network of passages > **labyrinthine** *adj*
  labyrinthine *adj* ▷ **labyrinth**
  labyrinths *n* ▷ **labyrinth**
lace *n* (*pl* **-s**) delicate decorative fabric made from threads woven into an open weblike pattern ▶ *v* (**-ces, -cing, -ced**) fasten with laces
  laced *v* ▷ **lace**
  laces *n, v* ▷ **lace**
  lacing *v* ▷ **lace**
lacerate [lass-er-rate] *v* (**-tes, -ting, -ted**) tear (flesh) > **laceration** *n* (*pl* **-s**)
  lacerated *v* ▷ **lacerate**
  lacerates *v* ▷ **lacerate**
  lacerating *v* ▷ **lacerate**
  lacerations *v* ▷ **lacerate**
lachrymose *adj* tearful
lack *n* (*pl* **-s**) shortage or absence of something needed or wanted ▶ *v* (**-s, -ing, -ed**) need or be short of (something)
lackadaisical *adj* lazy and careless in a dreamy way
  lacked *v* ▷ **lack**
lackey *n* (*pl* **-s**) servile follower
  lackeys *n* ▷ **lackey**
  lacking *v* ▷ **lack**
lacklustre *adj* lacking brilliance or vitality
laconic *adj* using only a few words, terse > **laconically** *adv*
  laconically *adv* ▷ **laconic**
lacquer *n* (*pl* **-s**) hard varnish for wood or metal
  lacquers *n* ▷ **lacquer**
lacrimal *adj* of tears or the glands which produce them
lacrosse *n* (*pl* **-s**) sport in which teams catch

and throw a ball using long sticks with a pouched net at the end, in an attempt to score goals

lacks *n, v* ▷ **lack**

lactation *n* (*pl* -**s**) secretion of milk by female mammals to feed young

lactations *n* ▷ **lactation**

lactic *adj* of or derived from milk

lactose *n* (*pl* -**s**) white crystalline sugar found in milk

lactoses *n* ▷ **lactose**

lacuna [lak-**kew**-na] *n* (*pl* -**e**) gap or missing part, esp. in a document or series

lacy *adj* fine, like lace

lad *n* (*pl* -**s**) boy or young man

lads *n* ▷ **lad**

ladder *n* (*pl* -**s**) frame of two poles connected by horizontal steps used for climbing ▶ *v* (-**s**, -**ing**, -**ed**) have or cause to have such a line of undone stitches

laddered *v* ▷ **ladder**

laddering *v* ▷ **ladder**

ladders *n, v* ▷ **ladder**

laden *adj* loaded

ladle *n* (*pl* -**s**) spoon with a long handle and a large bowl, used for serving soup etc. ▶ *v* (-**les**, -**ling**, -**led**) serve out

ladled *v* ▷ **ladle**

ladles *n, v* ▷ **ladle**

ladling *v* ▷ **ladle**

lady *n* (*pl* -**dies**) woman regarded as having characteristics of good breeding or high rank

ladybird *n* (*pl* -**s**) small red beetle with black spots

ladybirds *n* ▷ **ladybird**

ladykiller *n* (*pl* -**s**) (*Informal*) man who is or thinks he is irresistible to women

ladykillers *n* ▷ **ladykiller**

ladylike *adj* polite and dignified

lag¹ *v* (-**s**, -**gging**, -**gged**) go too slowly, fall behind ▶ *n* (*pl* -**s**) delay between events

lag² *v* (-**s**, -**gging**, -**gged**) wrap (a boiler, pipes, etc.) with insulating material

lag³ *n* (*pl* -**s**) (BRIT, AUST & NZ) (*Slang*) convict

laggard *n* (*pl* -**s**) person who lags behind

laggards *n* ▷ **laggard**

lagging *n* (*pl* -**s**) insulating material ▶ *v* ▷ **lag¹,²**

laggings *n* ▷ **lagging**

lager *n* (*pl* -**s**) light-bodied beer

lagers *n* ▷ **lager**

lagoon *n* (*pl* -**s**) body of water cut off from the open sea by coral reefs or sand bars

lagoons *n* ▷ **lagoon**

lags *n* ▷ **lag¹,³**

laid *v* ▷ **lay¹**

lain *v* ▷ **lie²**

lair *n* (*pl* -**s**) resting place of an animal

lairs *n* ▷ **lair**

laird *n* (*pl* -**s**) Scottish landowner

lairds *n* ▷ **laird**

laity [**lay**-it-ee] *n* (*pl* -**ties**) people who are not members of the clergy

laities *n* ▷ **laity**

lake¹ *n* (*pl* -**s**) expanse of water entirely surrounded by land > **lakeside** *n* (*pl* -**s**)

lake² *n* (*pl* -**s**) red pigment

lakes *n* ▷ **lake¹,²**

lakesides *n* ▷ **lake¹**

lama *n* (*pl* -**s**) Buddhist priest in Tibet or Mongolia

lamas *n* ▷ **lama**

lamb *n* (*pl* -**s**) young sheep ▶ *v* (-**s**, -**ing**, -**ed**) (of sheep) give birth to a lamb or lambs > **lambskin** *n* (*pl* -**s**) > **lambswool** *n* (*pl* -**s**)

lambast, lambaste *v* (-**s**, -**ing**, -**ed**) beat or thrash

lambasted *v* ▷ **lambast**

lambasting *v* ▷ **lambast**

lambasts *v* ▷ **lambast**

lambed *v* ▷ **lamb**

lambent *adj* (*Lit*) (of a flame) flickering softly

lambing *v* ▷ **lamb**

lambs *n, v* ▷ **lamb**

lambskin *n* ▷ **lamb**

lambswool *v* ▷ **lamb**

lame *adj* (-**er**, -**est**) having an injured or disabled leg or foot ▶ *v* (-**mes**, -**ming**, -**med**) make lame > **lamely** *adv* > **lameness** *n* (*pl* -**s**)

lamé [**lah**-may] *n* (*pl* -**s**) ▶ *adj* (fabric) interwoven with gold or silver thread

lamed *v* ▷ **lame**

lamely *adv* ▷ **lame**

lamenesses *n* ▷ **lame**

lament *v* (-**s**, -**ing**, -**ed**) feel or express sorrow (for) ▶ *n* (*pl* -**s**) passionate expression of grief > **lamentation** *n* (*pl* -**s**)

lamentable *adj* very disappointing

lamentations *v* ▷ **lament**

lamented *adj* grieved for ▶ *v* ▷ **lament**

lamenting *v* ▷ **lament**

laments *v, n* ▷ **lament**

lamer *adj* ▷ **lame**

lames *v* ▷ **lame**

lamés *n* ▷ **lamé**

lamest *adj* ▷ **lame**

laminate *v* (-**tes**, -**ting**, -**ted**) make (a sheet of material) by sticking together thin sheets ▶ *n* (*pl* -**s**) laminated sheet > **laminated** *adj*

laminated *v, adj* ▷ **laminate**

laminates *v, n* ▷ **laminate**

laminating v ▷ laminate
laming v ▷ lame
lamington n (pl -s) (AUST & NZ) sponge cake coated with a sweet coating
lamingtons n ▷ lamington
lamp n (pl -s) device which produces light from electricity, oil, or gas > **lampshade** (pl -s) ▸ n
lamppost n (pl -s) post supporting a lamp in the street
lampposts n ▷ lamppost
lamps n ▷ lamp
lampoon n (pl -s) humorous satire ridiculing someone ▸ v (-s, -ing, -ed) satirize or ridicule
lampooned v ▷ lampoon
lampooning v ▷ lampoon
lampoons n, v ▷ lampoon
lamprey n (pl -s) eel-like fish with a round sucking mouth
lampreys n ▷ lamprey
lampshades n ▷ lamp
lance n (pl -s) long spear used by a mounted soldier ▸ v (-ces, -cing, -ced) pierce (a boil or abscess) with a lancet
lanced v ▷ lance
lancer n (pl -s) formerly, cavalry soldier armed with a lance
lancers n ▷ lancer
lances n, v ▷ lance
lancing v ▷ lance
lancet n (pl -s) pointed two-edged surgical knife
lancets n ▷ lancet
land n (pl -s) solid part of the earth's surface ▸ v (-s, -ing, -ed) come or bring to earth after a flight, jump, or fall > **landless** adj
landau [lan-daw] n (pl -s) four-wheeled carriage with two folding hoods
landaus n ▷ landau
landed adj possessing or consisting of lands ▸ v ▷ land
landfall n (pl -s) ship's first landing after a voyage
landfalls n ▷ landfall
landing n (pl -s) floor area at the top of a flight of stairs ▸ v ▷ land
landings n ▷ landing
landlocked adj completely surrounded by land
lands n, v ▷ land
landlady n (pl -dies) woman who rents out land, houses, etc.
landladies n ▷ landlady
landless v ▷ land
landlord n (pl -s) man who rents out land, houses, etc.
landlords n ▷ landlord

landlubber n (pl -s) person who is not experienced at sea
landlubbers n ▷ landlubber
landmark n (pl -s) prominent object in or feature of a landscape
landmarks n ▷ landmark
landscape n (pl -s) extensive piece of inland scenery seen from one place ▸ v (-pes, -ping, -ped) improve natural features of (a piece of land)
landscaped v ▷ landscape
landscapes n, v ▷ landscape
landscaping v ▷ landscape
landslide (also **landslip**) n (pl -s) falling of soil, rock, etc. down the side of a mountain
landslides n ▷ landslide
landslip n ▷ landslide
landslips n ▷ landslide ▸ adj nearest to or facing the land ▸ adv (also **landwards**) towards land
landwards adv ▷ landward
lane n (pl -s) narrow road
lanes n ▷ lane
language n (pl -s) system of sounds, symbols, etc. for communicating thought
languages n ▷ language
languid adj lacking energy or enthusiasm > **languidly** adv
languidly adv ▷ languid
languish v (-es, -ing, -ed) suffer neglect or hardship
languished v ▷ languish
languishes v ▷ languish
languishing v ▷ languish
languor [lang-ger] n (pl -s) state of dreamy relaxation > **languorous** adj
languorous n ▷ languor
languors n ▷ languor
lank adj (-er, -est) (of hair) straight and limp
lanker adj ▷ lank
lankest adj ▷ lank
lankier adj ▷ lanky
lankiest adj ▷ lanky
lanky adj (-kier, -kiest) ungracefully tall and thin
lanolin n (pl -s) grease from sheep's wool used in ointments etc.
lanolins n ▷ lanolin
lantana [lan-tay-na] n (pl -s) shrub with orange or yellow flowers, considered a weed in Australia
lantanas n ▷ lantana
lantern n (pl -s) light in a transparent protective case
lanterns n ▷ lantern

lanthanum *n* (*pl* **-s**) (CHEM) silvery-white metallic element
  lanthanums *n* ▷ **lanthanum**
lanyard *n* (*pl* **-s**) cord worn round the neck to hold a knife or whistle
  lanyards *n* ▷ **lanyard**
lap¹ *n* (*pl* **-s**) part between the waist and knees of a person when sitting
lap² *n* (*pl* **-s**) single circuit of a racecourse or track ▶ *v* (**-s, -pping, -pped**) overtake an opponent so as to be one or more circuits ahead
lap³ *v* (**-s, -pping, -pped**) (of waves) beat softly against (a shore etc.)
lapel [lap-**pel**] *n* (*pl* **-s**) part of the front of a coat or jacket folded back towards the shoulders
  lapels *n* ▷ **lapel**
lapidary *adj* of or relating to stones
  lapped *v* ▷ **lap²,³**
  lapping *v* ▷ **lap²,³**
  laps *n* ▷ **lap¹,²** ▶ *v* ▷ **lap²,³**
lapse *n* (*pl* **-s**) temporary drop in a standard, esp. through forgetfulness or carelessness ▶ *v* (**-ses, -sing, -sed**) drop in standard > **lapsed** *adj*
  lapsed *v* ▷ **lapse**
  lapses *n*, *v* ▷ **lapse**
  lapsing *v* ▷ **lapse**
laptop *adj* (*of a computer*) small enough to fit on a user's lap ▶ *n* (*pl* **-s**) computer small enough to fit on a user's lap
  laptops *n* ▷ **laptop**
lapwing *n* (*pl* **-s**) plover with a tuft of feathers on the head
  lapwings *n* ▷ **lapwing**
larboard *adj*, *n* (*pl* **-s**) (*Old-fashioned*) port (side of a ship)
  larboards *n* ▷ **larboard**
  larcenies *n* ▷ **larceny**
larceny *n* (*pl* **-nies**) (LAW) theft
larch *n* (*pl* **-es**) deciduous coniferous tree
  larches *n* ▷ **larch**
lard *n* (*pl* **-s**) soft white fat obtained from a pig ▶ *v* (**-s, -ing, -ed**) insert strips of bacon in (meat) before cooking
  larded *v* ▷ **lard**
larder *n* (*pl* **-s**) storeroom for food
  larders *n* ▷ **larder**
  larding *v* ▷ **lard**
  lards *n*, *v* ▷ **lard**
large *adj* (**-r, -st**) great in size, number, or extent > **largely** *adv* > **largish** *adj*
  largely *adv* ▷ **large**
  larger *adj* ▷ **large**
  largess *n* (*pl* **-es**) ▷ **largesse**
largesse, largess [lar-**jess**] *n* (*pl* **-(es)**) generous

giving, esp. of money
  largesses *n* ▷ **largesse**
  largest *adj* ▷ **large**
  largish *adj* ▷ **large**
largo *n* (*pl* **-s**) ▶ *adv* (MUSIC) (piece to be played) in a slow and dignified manner
  largos *n* ▷ **largo**
lariat *n* (*pl* **-s**) lasso
  lariats *n* ▷ **lariat**
lark¹ *n* (*pl* **-s**) small brown songbird, skylark
lark² *n* (*pl* **-s**) (*Informal*) harmless piece of mischief or fun
  larks *n* ▷ **lark¹,²**
larkspur *n* (*pl* **-s**) plant with spikes of blue, pink, or white flowers with spurs
  larkspurs *n* ▷ **larkspur**
larrikin *n* (*pl* **-s**) (AUST & NZ) (*Old-fashioned slang*) mischievous or unruly person
  larrikins *n* ▷ **larrikin**
larva *n* (*pl* **-e**) insect in an immature stage, often resembling a worm > **larval** *adj*
  larval *adj* ▷ **larva**
  larynges *n* ▷ **larynx**
  laryngeal *adj* ▷ **larynx**
laryngitis *n* (*pl* **-ses**) inflammation of the larynx
  laryngitises *n* ▷ **laryngitis**
larynx *n* (*pl* **-nges**) part of the throat containing the vocal cords > **laryngeal** *adj*
lasagne, lasagna [laz-**zan**-ya] *n* (*pl* **-s**) pasta in wide flat sheets
  lasagnas *n* ▷ **lasagne**
  lasagnes *n* ▷ **lasagne**
lascivious [lass-**iv**-ee-uss] *adj* showing or producing sexual desire > **lasciviously** *adv*
  lasciviously *adv* ▷ **lascivious**
laser [**lay**-zer] *n* (*pl* **-s**) device that produces a very narrow intense beam of light, used for cutting very hard materials and in surgery etc.
  lasers *n* ▷ **laser**
lash¹ *n* (*pl* **-es**) eyelash ▶ *v* (**-es, -ing, -ed**) hit with a whip
lash² *v* (**-es, -ing, -ed**) fasten or bind tightly with cord etc.
  lashed *v* ▷ **lash¹,²**
  lashes *n* ▷ **lash¹** ▶ *v* ▷ **lash¹,²**
  lashing *v* ▷ **lash¹,²**
lashings *pl n* (*Old-fashioned*) large amounts
lass, lassie *n* (*pl* **-es, -s**) (SCOT & N ENGLISH) girl
  lasses *n* ▷ **lass**
  lassies *n* ▷ **lass**
lassitude *n* (*pl* **-s**) physical or mental weariness
  lassitudes *n* ▷ **lassitude**
lasso [lass-**oo**] *n* (*pl* **-s, -es**) rope with a noose for

catching cattle and horses ▶ v (**-s, -ing, -ed**) catch with a lasso
    lassoed v ▷ **lasso**
    lassoes n ▷ **lasso**
    lassoing v ▷ **lasso**
    lassos n, v ▷ **lasso**
last¹ adj, adv coming at the end or after all others ▶ adj only remaining ▶ n (pl **-s**) last person or thing > **lastly** adv
last² v (**-s, -ing, -ed**) continue > **lasting** adj
last³ n (pl **-s**) model of a foot on which shoes and boots are made or repaired
    lasted v ▷ **last²**
lasting v, adj ▷ **last²**
    lastly adv ▷ **last¹**
    lasts n ▷ **last¹,³** ▶ v ▷ **last²**
latch n (pl **-es**) fastening for a door with a bar and lever ▶ v (**-es, -ing, -ed**) fasten with a latch
    latched v ▷ **latch**
    latches n, v ▷ **latch**
    latching v ▷ **latch**
late adj (**-r, -st**) after the normal or expected time ▶ adv after the normal or expected time > **lateness** n (pl **-es**)
lately adv in recent times
    latencies n ▷ **latent**
    lateness n ▷ **late**
    latenesses n ▷ **late**
latent adj hidden and not yet developed > **latency** n (pl **-cies**)
    later adj ▷ **late**
lateral [lat-ter-al] adj of or relating to the side or sides > **laterally** adv
    latest adj ▷ **late**
latex n (pl **-es**) milky fluid found in some plants, esp. the rubber tree, used in making rubber
    latexes n ▷ **latex**
lath n (pl **-s**) thin strip of wood used to support plaster, tiles, etc.
    laths n ▷ **lath**
lathe n (pl **-s**) machine for turning wood or metal while it is being shaped
    lathes n ▷ **lathe**
lather n (pl **-s**) froth of soap and water ▶ v (**-s, -ing, -ed**) make frothy
    lathered v ▷ **lather**
    lathering v ▷ **lather**
    lathers n, v ▷ **lather**
lathery adj (**-rier, -riest**) frothy
    latherier adj ▷ **lathery**
    latheriest adj ▷ **lathery**
latitude n (pl **-s**) angular distance measured in degrees N or S of the equator
    latitudes n ▷ **latitude**
latrine n (pl **-s**) toilet in a barracks or camp

    latrines n ▷ **latrine**
latter adj second of two > **latterly** adv
latter-day adj modern
    latterly adv ▷ **latter**
lattice [lat-iss] n (pl **-s**) framework of intersecting strips of wood, metal, etc. > **latticed** adj
    latticed adj ▷ **lattice**
    lattices n ▷ **lattice**
laud v (**-s, -ing, -ed**) praise or glorify > **laudably** adv
laudable adj praiseworthy
    laudably adv ▷ **laudable**
laudanum [lawd-a-num] n (pl **-s**) opium-based sedative
    laudanums n ▷ **laudanum**
laudatory adj praising or glorifying
    lauded v ▷ **laud**
    lauding v ▷ **laud**
    lauds v ▷ **laud**
laugh v (**-s, -ing, -ed**) make inarticulate sounds with the voice expressing amusement, merriment, or scorn ▶ n (pl **-s**) act or instance of laughing
    laughable adj ▷ **laugh**
    laughed v ▷ **laugh**
    laughing v ▷ **laugh**
    laughs v, n ▷ **laugh**
laughter n (pl **-s**) sound or action of laughing
    laughters n ▷ **laughter**
launch¹ v (**-es, -ing, -ed**) put (a ship or boat) into the water, esp. for the first time ▶ n (pl **-es**) launching > **launcher** n (pl **-s**)
launch² n (pl **-s**) open motorboat
    launched v ▷ **launch¹**
    launchers n ▷ **launch¹**
    launches v ▷ **launch¹** ▶ n ▷ **launch¹,²**
    launches n ▷ **launch¹**
    launching v ▷ **launch¹**
launder v (**-s, -ing, -ed**) wash and iron (clothes and linen)
launderette n ® (pl **-s**) shop with coin-operated washing and drying machines
    laundered v ▷ **launder**
    launderettes n ▷ **launderette**
    laundering v ▷ **launder**
    launders v ▷ **launder**
laundry n (pl **-ries**) clothes etc. for washing or which have recently been washed
    laundries n ▷ **laundry**
laureate [lor-ee-at] adj (of a poet) appointed to the court of Britain
laurel n (pl **-s**) glossy-leaved shrub, bay tree ▶ pl wreath of laurel, an emblem of victory or merit

laurels n ▷ laurel

lava n (pl -e) molten rock thrown out by volcanoes, which hardens as it cools

lavae n ▷ lava

lavatory n (pl -ries) toilet

lavatories n ▷ lavatory

lavender n (pl -s) shrub with fragrant flowers ▶ adj bluish-purple

lavenders n ▷ lavender

lavish adj great in quantity or richness ▶ v (-es, -ing, -ed) give or spend generously > **lavishly** adv

lavished v ▷ lavish

lavishes v ▷ lavish

lavishing v ▷ lavish

lavishly adv ▷ lavish

law n (pl -s) rule binding on a community > **lawfully** adv > **lawlessness** n (pl -es) > **law-breaker** n (pl -s)

lawful adj allowed by law

lawfully adv ▷ law

lawless adj breaking the law, esp. in a violent way

lawlessness n ▷ law

lawlessnesses n ▷ law

lawn[1] n (pl -s) area of tended and mown grass

lawn[2] n (pl -s) fine linen or cotton fabric

lawns n ▷ lawn[1,2]

laws n ▷ law

lawsuit n (pl -s) court case brought by one person or group against another

lawsuits n ▷ lawsuit

lawyer n (pl -s) professionally qualified legal expert

lawyers n ▷ lawyer

lax adj not strict > **laxity** n (pl -ties)

laxative n (pl -s) ▶ adj (medicine) inducing the emptying of the bowels

laxatives n ▷ laxative

laxities n ▷ lax

laxity n ▷ lax

lay[1] v (-s, -ing, laid) cause to lie

lay[2] v ▷ lie[2]

lay[3] adj of or involving people who are not clergymen

lay[4] n (pl -s) short narrative poem designed to be sung

layabout n (pl -s) lazy person

layabouts n ▷ layabout

layer n (pl -s) single thickness of some substance, as a cover or coating on a surface ▶ v (-s, -ing, -ed) form a layer > **layered** adj

layered v, adj ▷ layer

layering v ▷ layer

layers n, v ▷ layer

layette n (pl -s) clothes for a newborn baby

layettes n ▷ layette

laying v ▷ lay[1]

layman n (pl -men) person who is not a member of the clergy

laymen n ▷ layman

layout n (pl -s) arrangement, esp. of matter for printing or of a building

layouts n ▷ layout

lays v ▷ lay[1] ▶ n ▷ lay[4]

laze v (-s, -ing, -ed) be idle or lazy ▶ n (pl -s) time spent lazing

lazed v ▷ laze

lazes v, n ▷ laze

lazily adv ▷ lazy

laziness adv ▷ lazy

lazinesses adv ▷ lazy

lazing v ▷ laze

lazy adj (-zier, -ziest) not inclined to work or exert oneself > **lazily** adv > **laziness** n (pl -s)

lea n (pl -s) (Poetic) meadow

leas n ▷ lea

leach v (-es, -ing, -ed) remove or be removed from a substance by a liquid passing through it

leached v ▷ leach

leaches v ▷ leach

leaching v ▷ leach

lead[1] v (-s, -ing, led) guide or conduct ▶ n (pl -s) first or most prominent place ▶ adj acting as a leader or lead

lead[2] n (pl -s) soft heavy grey metal

leaded adj (of windows) made from many small panes of glass held together by lead strips

leaden adj heavy or sluggish

leader n (pl -s) person who leads > **leadership** n (pl -s)

leaders n ▷ leader

leaderships n ▷ leader

leading adj principal

leads n ▷ lead[1,2] ▶ v ▷ lead[1]

leaf n (pl leaves) flat usu. green blade attached to the stem of a plant > **leafy** (-fier, -fiest) ▶ adj > **leafless** adj

leafier adj ▷ leaf

leafiest adj ▷ leaf

leafless adj ▷ leaf

leaflet n (pl -s) sheet of printed matter for distribution

leaflets n ▷ leaflet

leafy adj ▷ leaf

league[1] n (pl -s) association promoting the interests of its members

league[2] n (Obs) measure of distance, about

three miles
leagues *n* ▷ **league**[1,2]
leak *n* (*pl* -**s**) hole or defect that allows the
escape or entrance of liquid, gas, radiation,
etc. ▶ *v* (-**s**, -**ing**, -**ed**) let liquid etc. in or out
> **leaky** (-**kier**, -**kiest**) ▶ *adj*
leakage *n* (*pl* -**s**) act or instance of leaking
  leakages *n* ▷ **leakage**
  leaked *v* ▷ **leak**
  leakier *adj* ▷ **leak**
  leakiest *adj* ▷ **leak**
  leaking *v* ▷ **leak**
  leaks *n*, *v* ▷ **leak**
  leaky *adj* (-**kier**, -**kiest**) ▷ **leak**
lean[1] *v* (-**ing**, -**ed** *or* **leant**) rest against
lean[2] *adj* (-**er**, -**est**) thin but healthy-looking ▶ *n*
  (*pl* -**s**) lean part of meat > **leanness** *n* (*pl* -**es**)
  leaner *adj* ▷ **lean**
  leanest *adj* ▷ **lean**
leaning *n* (*pl* -**s**) tendency ▶ *v* ▷ **lean**[1]
  leanings *n* ▷ **leaning**
  leanness *n* ▷ **lean**[2]
  leannesses *n* ▷ **lean**[2]
  leans *v*, *n* ▷ **lean**[1]
  leant *n* ▷ **lean**[1]
leap *v* (-**s**, -**ing**, **leapt** *or* -**ed**) make a sudden
  powerful jump ▶ *n* (*pl* -**s**) sudden powerful
  jump
  leaped *v* ▷ **leap**
leapfrog *n* (*pl* -**s**) game in which a player vaults
  over another bending down
  leapfrogs *n* ▷ **leapfrog**
  leaping *v* ▷ **leap**
  leaps *v*, *n* ▷ **leap**
  leapt *v* ▷ **leap**
learn *v* (-**s**, -**ing**, -**ed** *or* **learnt**) gain skill or
  knowledge by study, practice, or teaching
  > **learner** *n* (*pl* -**s**)
learned *adj* erudite, deeply read
  learner *n* ▷ **learn**
  learners *n* ▷ **learn**
learning *n* (*pl* -**s**) knowledge got by study ▶ *v*
  ▷ **learn**
  learnings *n* ▷ **learning**
lease *n* (*pl* -**s**) contract by which land or
  property is rented for a stated time by the
  owner to a tenant ▶ *v* (-**ses**, -**sing**, -**sed**) let or
  rent by lease > **leaseholder** *n* (*pl* -**s**)
leasehold *n*, *adj* (land or property) held on
  lease
  leaseholder *n* ▷ **lease**
  leaseholders *n* ▷ **lease**
  leaseholds *n* ▷ **leasehold**
  leased *v* ▷ **lease**
  leases *n*, *v* ▷ **lease**

leash *n* (*pl* -**es**) lead for a dog
  leashes *n* ▷ **leash**
  leasing *v* ▷ **lease**
least *adj* ▷ **little** smallest ▶ *n* smallest one ▶ *adv*
  in the smallest degree
leather *n* (*pl* -**s**) material made from specially
  treated animal skins ▶ *adj* made of leather ▶ *v*
  (-**s**, -**ing**, -**ed**) beat or thrash
  leathered *v* ▷ **leather**
  leatherier *adj* ▷ **leathery**
  leatheriest *adj* ▷ **leathery**
  leathering *v* ▷ **leather**
  leathers *n*, *v* ▷ **leather**
leathery *adj* (-**rier**, -**riest**) like leather, tough
leave[1] *v* (-**s**, -**ing**, **left**) go away from
leave[2] *n* (*pl* -**s**) permission to be absent from
  work or duty
leaven [lev-ven] *n* substance that causes
  dough to rise ▶ *v* (-**s**, -**ing**, -**ed**) raise with
  leaven
  leavens *v* ▷ **leaven**
  leavening *v* ▷ **leaven**
  leavened *v* ▷ **leaven**
  leaves *v* ▷ **leave**
  leaving *v* ▷ **leave**
lecher *n* (*pl* -**s**) man who has or shows
  excessive sexual desire > **lechery** *n* (*pl* -**ries**)
  lecheries *n* ▷ **lechery**
lecherous [letch-er-uss] *adj* (of a man) having
  or showing excessive sexual desire
  lechers *n* ▷ **lecher**
lectern *n* (*pl* -**s**) sloping reading desk, esp. in
  a church
  lecterns *n* ▷ **lectern**
lecture *n* (*pl* -**s**) informative talk to an audience
  on a subject ▶ *v* (-**s**, -**ing**, -**ed**) give a talk
  lectured *v* ▷ **lecture**
lecturer *n* (*pl* -**s**) person who lectures, esp. in a
  university or college
  lecturers *n* ▷ **lecturer**
  lectures *n*, *v* ▷ **lecture**
lectureship *n* (*pl* -**s**) appointment as a lecturer
  lectureships *n* ▷ **lectureship**
  lecturing *v* ▷ **lecture**
ledge *n* (*pl* -**s**) narrow shelf sticking out from
  a wall
ledger *n* (*pl* -**s**) book of debit and credit
  accounts of a firm
  ledgers *n* ▷ **ledger**
  ledges *n* ▷ **ledge**
lee *n* (*pl* -**s**) sheltered part or side ▶ *adv* towards
  this side
leech *n* (*pl* -**es**) species of bloodsucking worm
  leeches *n* ▷ **leech**
leek *n* (*pl* -**s**) vegetable of the onion family with

a long bulb and thick stem
leeks *n* ▷ **leek**
leer *v* (**-s, -ing, -ed**) look or grin at in a sneering or suggestive manner ▶ *n* (*pl* **-s**) sneering or suggestive look or grin
  leered *v* ▷ **leer**
  leerier *adj* ▷ **leery**
  leeriest *adj* ▷ **leery**
  leering *v* ▷ **leer**
  leers *v, n* ▷ **leer**
leery *adj* (*Informal*) (**-rier, -riest**) suspicious or wary (of)
lees *pl n* sediment of wine ▶ *n* ▷ **lee**
leeward *adj, n* (*pl* **-s**) (on) the lee side
  leewards *n* ▷ **leeward**
leeway *n* (*pl* **-s**) room for free movement within limits
  leeways *n* ▷ **leeway**
left[1] *adj* of the side that faces west when the front faces north ▶ *adv* on or towards the left ▶ *n* (*pl* **-s**) left hand or part
left[2] *v* ▷ **leave**[1]
leftist *n* (*pl* **-s**) ▶ *adj* (person) of the political left
  leftists *n* ▷ **leftist**
leftover *n* (*pl* **-s**) unused portion of food or material
  leftovers *n* ▷ **leftover**
  lefts *n* ▷ **left**[1]
leg *n* (*pl* **-s**) one of the limbs on which a person or animal walks, runs, or stands
  legacies *n* ▷ **legacy**
legacy *n* (*pl* **-cies**) thing left in a will
legal *adj* established or permitted by law > **legally** *adv* > **legality** *n* (*pl* **-ties**) > **legalization** *n* (*pl* **-s**)
  legalities *n* ▷ **legal**
  legality *n* ▷ **legal**
  legalization *n* ▷ **legal**
  legalizations *n* ▷ **legal**
legalize *v* (**-zes, -zing, -zed**) make legal
  legalized *adv* ▷ **legalize**
  legalizes *adv* ▷ **legalize**
  legalizing *adv* ▷ **legalize**
  legally *adv* ▷ **legal**
legate *n* (*pl* **-s**) messenger or representative, esp. from the Pope
legatee *n* (*pl* **-s**) recipient of a legacy
  legatees *n* ▷ **legatee**
  legates *n* ▷ **legate**
legation *n* (*pl* **-s**) diplomatic minister and his staff
  legations *n* ▷ **legation**
legato [leg-ah-toe] *n* (*pl* **-s**), *adv* (MUSIC) (piece to be played) smoothly
  legatos *n* ▷ **legato**

legend *n* (*pl* **-s**) traditional story or myth
legendary *adj* famous
  legends *n* ▷ **legend**
legerdemain [lej-er-de-**main**] *n* (*pl* **-s**) sleight of hand
  legerdemains *n* ▷ **legerdemain**
  leggier *adj* ▷ **leggy**
  leggiest *adj* ▷ **leggy**
leggings *pl n* covering of leather or other material for the legs
leggy *adj* (**-gier, -giest**) having long legs
  legibilities *n* ▷ **legible**
  legibility *n* ▷ **legible**
legible *adj* easily read > **legibility** *n* (*pl* **-ties**) > **legibly** *adv*
  legibly *adv* ▷ **legible**
legion *n* (*pl* **-s**) large military force > **legionary** *adj, n* (*pl* **-ries**)
  legionaries *n* ▷ **legion**
  legionary *adj, n* ▷ **legion**
legionnaire *n* (*pl* **-s**) member of a legion
  legionnaires *n* ▷ **legionnaire**
  legions *n* ▷ **legion**
legislate *v* (**-tes, -ting, -ted**) make laws > **legislative** *adj*
  legislated *v* ▷ **legislate**
  legislates *v* ▷ **legislate**
  legislating *v* ▷ **legislate**
legislation *n* (*pl* **-s**) legislating
  legislations *n* ▷ **legislation**
  legislative *v* ▷ **legislate**
legislator *n* (*pl* **-s**) maker of laws
  legislators *n* ▷ **legislator**
legislature *n* (*pl* **-s**) body of people that makes, amends, or repeals laws
  legislatures *n* ▷ **legislature**
  legitimacies *n* ▷ **legitimate**
  legitimacy *n* ▷ **legitimate**
legitimate *adj* authorized by or in accordance with law ▶ *v* (**-tes, -ting, -ted**) make legitimate > **legitimacy** *n* (*pl* **-cies**) > **legitimately** *adv*
  legitimated *v* ▷ **legitimate**
  legitimately *adv* ▷ **legitimate**
  legitimates *v* ▷ **legitimate**
  legitimating *v* ▷ **legitimate**
legitimize *v* (**-zes, -zing, -zed**) make legitimate, legalize > **legitimization** *n* (*pl* **-s**)
  legitimization *n* ▷ **legitimize**
  legitimizations *n* ▷ **legitimize**
  legitimized *v* ▷ **legitimize**
  legitimizes *v* ▷ **legitimize**
  legitimizing *v* ▷ **legitimize**
legless *adj* without legs
  legs *n* ▷ **leg**

leguaan [leg-oo-ahn] *n* (*pl* **-s**) large S African lizard
  leguaans *n* ▷ **leguaan**
legume *n* (*pl* **-s**) pod of a plant of the pea or bean family ▶ *pl* peas or beans
  legumes *n* ▷ **legume**
leguminous *adj* (of plants) pod-bearing
lei *n* (*pl* **-s**) (in Hawaii) garland of flowers
  leis *n* ▷ **lei**
leisure *n* (*pl* **-s**) time for relaxation or hobbies
leisured *adj* with plenty of spare time
leisurely *adj* deliberate, unhurried ▶ *adv* slowly
  leisures *n* ▷ **leisure**
leitmotif [lite-mote-eef] *n* (*pl* **-s**) (MUSIC) recurring theme associated with a person, situation, or thought
  leitmotifs *n* ▷ **leitmotif**
lekker *adj* (S AFR) (*Slang*) attractive or nice
lemming *n* (*pl* **-s**) rodent of arctic regions, reputed to run into the sea and drown during mass migrations
  lemmings *n* ▷ **lemming**
lemon *n* (*pl* **-s**) yellow oval fruit that grows on trees ▶ *adj* pale-yellow
lemonade *n* (*pl* **-s**) lemon-flavoured soft drink, often fizzy
  lemonades *n* ▷ **lemonade**
  lemons *n* ▷ **lemon**
lemur *n* (*pl* **-s**) nocturnal animal like a small monkey, found in Madagascar
  lemurs *n* ▷ **lemur**
lend *v* (**-s, -ing, lent**) give the temporary use of > **lender** *n* (*pl* **-s**)
  lending *v* ▷ **lend**
  lender *n* ▷ **lend**
  lenders *n* ▷ **lend**
  lends *v* ▷ **lend**
length *n* (*pl* **-s**) extent or measurement from end to end > **lengthily** *adv* > **lengthways, lengthwise** *adj, adv*
lengthen *v* (**-s, -ing, -ed**) make or become longer
  lengthened *v* ▷ **lengthen**
  lengthening *v* ▷ **lengthen**
  lengthens *v* ▷ **lengthen**
  lengthier *adj* ▷ **length**
  lengthiest *adj* ▷ **length**
  lengthily *adv* ▷ **length**
  lengths *n* ▷ **length**
  lengthways *adj, adv* ▷ **length**
  lengthwise *adj, adv* ▷ **lengthen**
lengthy *adj* (**-thier, -thiest**) very long or tiresome
  leniencies *n* ▷ **lenient**
  leniency *n* ▷ **lenient**

lenient [lee-nee-ent] *adj* tolerant, not strict or severe > **leniency** *n* (*pl* **-cies**) > **leniently** *adv*
  leniently *adv* ▷ **lenient**
lens *n* (*pl* **-es**) piece of glass or similar material with one or both sides curved, used to bring together or spread light rays in cameras, spectacles, telescopes, etc.
  lenses *n* ▷ **lens**
  lent *v* ▷ **lend**
lentil *n* (*pl* **-s**) edible seed of a leguminous Asian plant
  lentils *n* ▷ **lentil**
lento *n* (*pl* **-tos**), *adv* (MUSIC) (piece to be played) slowly
  lentos *n* ▷ **lento**
  Lents *n* ▷ **Lent**
leonine *adj* like a lion
leopard *n* (*pl* **-s**) large spotted carnivorous animal of the cat family
  leopards *n* ▷ **leopard**
leotard *n* (*pl* **-s**) tight-fitting garment covering the upper body, worn for dancing or exercise
  leotards *n* ▷ **leotard**
leper *n* (*pl* **-s**) person suffering from leprosy
  lepers *n* ▷ **leper**
lepidoptera *pl n* order of insects with four wings covered with fine gossamer scales, as moths and butterflies
lepidopterist *n* (*pl* **-s**) person who studies or collects butterflies or moths
  lepidopterists *n* ▷ **lepidopterist**
leprechaun *n* (*pl* **-s**) mischievous elf of Irish folklore
  leprechauns *n* ▷ **leprechaun**
leprosy *n* (*pl* **-sies**) disease attacking the nerves and skin, resulting in loss of feeling in the affected parts > **leprous** *adj*
  leprosies *n* ▷ **leprosy**
  leprous *adj* ▷ **leprosy**
lesbian *n* (*pl* **-s**) homosexual woman ▶ *adj* of homosexual women > **lesbianism** *n* (*pl* **-s**)
  lesbians *n* ▷ **lesbian**
  lesbianisms *n* ▷ **lesbian**
lesion *n* (*pl* **-s**) structural change in an organ of the body caused by illness or injury
  lesions *n* ▷ **lesion**
less *adj* smaller in extent, degree, or duration ▷ **little** ▶ *pron* smaller part or quantity ▶ *adv* to a smaller extent or degree ▶ *prep* after deducting, minus
lessee *n* (*pl* **-s**) person to whom a lease is granted
  lessees *n* ▷ **lessee**
lessen *v* (**-s, -ing, -ed**) make or become smaller or not as much

lessened v ▷ **lessen**
lessening v ▷ **lessen**
lessens v ▷ **lessen**
lesser adj not as great in quantity, size, or worth
lesson n (pl -s) single period of instruction in a subject
lessons n ▷ **lesson**
lest conj so as to prevent any possibility that
let¹ v (-s, -tting, let) allow, enable, or cause
let² n (pl -s) (TENNIS) minor infringement or obstruction of the ball requiring a replay of the point
letdown n (pl -s) disappointment
letdowns n ▷ **letdown**
lets v ▷ **let¹** ▶ n ▷ **let²**
lethal adj deadly
lethargic adj ▷ **lethargy**
lethargically adv ▷ **lethargy**
lethargies n ▷ **lethargy**
lethargy n (pl -gies) sluggishness or dullness > **lethargic** adj > **lethargically** adv
letter n (pl -s) written message, usu. sent by post ▶ pl literary knowledge or ability > **lettering** n (pl -s)
lettered adj learned
letterhead n (pl -s) printed heading on stationery giving the sender's name and address
letterheads n ▷ **letterhead**
lettering n ▷ **letter**
letterings n ▷ **letter**
letters n ▷ **letter**
letting v ▷ **let¹**
lettuce n (pl -s) plant with large green leaves used in salads
lettuces n ▷ **lettuce**
leucocyte [loo-koh-site] n (pl -s) white blood cell
leucocytes n ▷ **leucocyte**
leukaemia [loo-kee-mee-a] n (pl -s) disease caused by uncontrolled overproduction of white blood cells
leukaemias n ▷ **leukaemia**
levee n (pl -s) (US) natural or artificial river embankment
levees n ▷ **levee**
level adj (-llest, -ller) horizontal ▶ v (-s, -lling, -lled, -ller) make even or horizontal ▶ n (pl -s) horizontal line or surface
levelled v ▷ **level**
leveller v ▷ **level**
levellest adj ▷ **level**
levelling v ▷ **level**
levels v, n ▷ **level**
lever n (pl -s) handle used to operate

machinery ▶ v (-s, -ing, -ed) prise or move with a lever
leverage n (pl -s) action or power of a lever
leverages n ▷ **leverage**
levered v ▷ **lever**
levering v ▷ **lever**
levers n, v ▷ **lever**
leveret [lev-ver-it] n (pl -s) young hare
leverets n ▷ **leveret**
leviathan [lev-vie-ath-an] n (pl -s) sea monster
leviathans n ▷ **leviathan**
levitate v (-tes, -ting, -ted) rise or cause to rise into the air
levitated v ▷ **levitate**
levitates v ▷ **levitate**
levitating v ▷ **levitate**
levitation n (pl -s) raising of a solid body into the air supernaturally
levitations n ▷ **levitation**
levities n ▷ **levity**
levity n (pl -ties) inclination to make a joke of serious matters
levy [lev-vee] v (-vies, -ing, -vied) impose and collect (a tax) ▶ n (pl -vies) imposition or collection of taxes
levied v ▷ **levy**
levies v, n ▷ **levy**
levying v ▷ **levy**
lewd adj (-er, -est) lustful or indecent > **lewdly** adv > **lewdness** n (pl -es)
lewder adj ▷ **lewd**
lewdest adj ▷ **lewd**
lewdly adv ▷ **lewd**
lewdness n ▷ **lewd**
lewdnesses n ▷ **lewd**

> **lex** n (**leges**). A lex is a system or body of laws. This is a really handy word when you have L and X, as there is likely to be an E available on the board. Lex scores 10 points.

lexical adj relating to the vocabulary of a language
lexicographer n (pl -s) writer of dictionaries
lexicographers n ▷ **lexicographer**
lexicography n ▷ **lexicon**
lexicographies n ▷ **lexicon**
lexicon n (pl -s) dictionary > **lexicography** n (pl -phies)
lexicons n ▷ **lexicon**

> **li** n (**lis**). The li is a Chinese unit of length. This low-scoring word is worth knowing for when you want to form words in more than one direction at the same time. Li scores 2 points.

liability n (pl -ties) hindrance or disadvantage

liable *adj* legally obliged or responsible
liaise *v* (-ses, -sing, -sed) establish and maintain communication (with)
liaised *v* ▷ liaise
liaises *v* ▷ liaise
liaising *v* ▷ liaise
liaison *n* (*pl* -s) communication and contact between groups
liaisons *n* ▷ liaison
liana *n* (*pl* -s) climbing plant in tropical forests
lianas *n* ▷ liana
liar *n* (*pl* -s) person who tells lies
liars *n* ▷ liar
libation [lie-bay-shun] *n* (*pl* -s) drink poured as an offering to the gods
libations *n* ▷ libation
libel *n* (*pl* -s) published statement falsely damaging a person's reputation ▶ *v* (-s, -lling, -lled) falsely damage the reputation of (someone) > libellous *adj*
libelled *v* ▷ libel
libelling *v* ▷ libel
libellous *adj* ▷ libel
libels *n, v* ▷ libel
liberal *adj* having social and political views that favour progress and reform ▶ *n* (*pl* -s) person who has liberal ideas or opinions > liberally *adv* > liberalization *n* (*pl* -s)
liberalism *n* (*pl* -s) belief in democratic reforms and individual freedom
liberalisms *n* ▷ liberalism
liberalities *n* ▷ liberality
liberality *n* (*pl* -ties) generosity
liberalization *n* ▷ liberal
liberalizations *n* ▷ liberal
liberalize *v* (-zes, -zing, -zed) make (laws, a country, etc.) less restrictive
liberalized *v* ▷ liberalize
liberalizes *v* ▷ liberalize
liberalizing *v* ▷ liberalize
liberally *adv* ▷ liberal
liberals *n* ▷ liberal
liberate *v* (-tes, -ting, -ted) set free > liberation *n* (*pl* -s) > liberator *n* (*pl* -s)
liberated *v* ▷ liberate
liberates *v* ▷ liberate
liberating *v* ▷ liberate
liberation *n* ▷ liberate
liberations *n* ▷ liberate
liberator *n* ▷ liberate
liberators *n* ▷ liberate
libertarian *n* (*pl* -s) believer in freedom of thought and action ▶ *adj* having such a belief
libertarians *n* ▷ libertarian
libertine [lib-er-teen] *n* (*pl* -s) morally dissolute person
libertines *n* ▷ libertine
liberties *n* ▷ liberty
liberty *n* (*pl* -ties) freedom
libidinous *adj* lustful
libido [lib-ee-doe] *n* (*pl* -s) psychic energy
libidos *n* ▷ libido
librarian *n* (*pl* -s) keeper of or worker in a library > librarianship *n* (*pl* -s)
librarians *n* ▷ librarian
librarianship *n* ▷ librarian
librarianships *n* ▷ librarian
libraries *n* ▷ library
library *n* (*pl* -ries) room or building where books are kept
libretti *n* ▷ libretto
librettist *n* ▷ libretto
librettists *n* ▷ libretto
libretto *n* (*pl* -ttos, -tti) words of an opera > librettist *n* (*pl* -s)
librettos *n* ▷ libretto
lice *n* ▷ louse
licence *n* (*pl* -s) document giving official permission to do something
licences *n* ▷ licence
license *v* (-ses, -sing, -sed) grant a licence to > licensed *adj*
licensed *v, adj* ▷ license
licensee *n* (*pl* -s) holder of a licence, esp. to sell alcohol
licensees *n* ▷ licensee
licenses *v* ▷ license
licensing *v* ▷ license
licentiate *n* (*pl* -s) person licensed as competent to practise a profession
licentiates *n* ▷ licentiate
licentious *adj* sexually unrestrained or promiscuous
lichen *n* (*pl* -s) small flowerless plant forming a crust on rocks, trees, etc.
lichens *n* ▷ lichen
licit *adj* lawful, permitted
lick *v* (-s, -ing, -ed) pass the tongue over ▶ *n* (*pl* -s) licking
licked *v* ▷ lick
licking *v* ▷ lick
licks *v, n* ▷ lick
licorice *n* (*pl* -s) ▷ liquorice
licorices *n* ▷ licorice
lid *n* (*pl* -s) movable cover
lids *n* ▷ lid
lido [lee-doe] *n* (*pl* -s) open-air centre for swimming and water sports
lidos *n* ▷ lido
lie¹ *v* (-s, lying, lied) make a deliberately false

statement ▸ n (pl -s) deliberate falsehood
lie² v (-s, lying, lay, lain) place oneself or be in a horizontal position ▸ n (pl -s) way something lies
　lied¹ v ▷ **lie¹**
lied² [leed] n (pl **lieder**) (MUSIC) setting for voice and piano of a romantic poem
liege [leej] adj bound to give or receive feudal service ▸ n (pl -s) lord
　lieges n ▷ **liege**
lien n (pl -s) (LAW) right to hold another's property until a debt is paid
　liens n ▷ **lien**
　lies v, n ▷ **lie¹,²**
lieutenant [lef-ten-ant] n (pl -s) junior officer in the army or navy
　lieutenants n ▷ **lieutenant**
life n (pl **lives**) state of living beings, characterized by growth, reproduction, and response to stimuli > **lifelike** adj
lifeboat n (pl -s) boat used for rescuing people at sea
　lifeboats adj ▷ **lifeboat**
　lifeless adj dead
　lifelike adj ▷ **life**
lifeline n (pl -s) means of contact or support
　lifelines n ▷ **lifeline**
　lifelong adj lasting all of a person's life
lifestyle n (pl -s) particular attitudes, habits, etc.
　lifestyles n ▷ **lifestyle**
lifetime n (pl -s) length of time a person is alive
　lifetimes n ▷ **lifetime**
lift v (lifts, lifting, lifted) move upwards in position, status, volume, etc. ▸ n (pl **lifts**) cage raised and lowered in a vertical shaft to transport people or goods
liftoff n moment a rocket leaves the ground
　lifts v ▷ **lift**
　lifting v ▷ **lift**
　lifted v ▷ **lift**
　lifts n ▷ **lift**
ligament n (pl -s) band of tissue joining bones
　ligaments n ▷ **ligament**
ligature n (pl -s) link, bond, or tie
　ligatures n ▷ **ligature**
light¹ n (pl -s) electromagnetic radiation by which things are visible ▸ pl traffic lights ▸ adj bright ▸ v (-s, -ing, lit) ignite
light² adj (-er, -est) not heavy, weighing relatively little ▸ adv with little equipment or luggage ▸ v (-s, -ing, -ed, lit) (esp. of birds) settle after flight > **lightly** adv > **lightness** n (pl -s)
　lighted v ▷ **light²**

lighten¹ v (-s, -ing, -ed) make less dark
lighten² v (-s, -ing, -ed) make less heavy or burdensome
　lightened v ▷ **lighten¹,²**
　lightening v ▷ **lighten¹,²**
　lightens v ▷ **lighten¹,²**
　lighter adj ▷ **light²**
　lightest adj ▷ **light²**
lighthouse n (pl -s) tower with a light to guide ships
　lighthouses n ▷ **lighthouse**
lighting n (pl -s) apparatus for and use of artificial light in theatres, films, etc. ▸ v ▷ **light¹,²**
　lightings n ▷ **lighting**
lighter¹ n (pl -s) device for lighting cigarettes etc.
lighter² n (pl -s) flat-bottomed boat for unloading ships
　lighters n ▷ **lighter¹,²**
　lightly adv ▷ **light²**
　lightness n ▷ **light²**
　lightnesses n ▷ **light²**
lightning n (pl -s) visible discharge of electricity in the atmosphere ▸ adj fast and sudden
　lightnings n ▷ **lightning**
lights pl n lungs of animals as animal food ▸ n ▷ **light¹** ▸ v ▷ **light¹,²**
lightweight n (pl -s) ▸ adj (person) of little importance
　lightweights n ▷ **lightweight**
　ligneous adj of or like wood
lignite [lig-nite] n (pl -s) woody textured rock used as fuel
　lignites n ▷ **lignite**
like¹ prep, conj adj, pron indicating similarity, comparison, etc.
like² v (-s, -ing, -ed) find enjoyable > **likeable, likable** adj > **liking** n fondness
　liked v ▷ **like**
liken v (-s, -ing, -ed) compare
　likelier adj ▷ **likely**
　likeliest adj ▷ **likely**
likelihood n (pl -s) probability
　likelihoods n ▷ **likelihood**
likely adj (-lier, -liest) tending or inclined ▸ adv probably
　likened v ▷ **liken**
likeness n resemblance
　likening v ▷ **liken**
　likens v ▷ **liken**
　likes v ▷ **like**
likewise adv similarly
　liking v ▷ **like**

lilac n (pl -s) shrub with pale mauve or white flowers ▶ adj light-purple
  lilacs n ▷ **lilac**
lilt n (pl -s) pleasing musical quality in speaking > **lilting** adj
  lilting adj ▷ **lilt**
  lilts n ▷ **lilt**
lily n (pl -lies) plant which grows from a bulb and has large, often white, flowers
limb n (pl -s) arm, leg, or wing
  limbs n ▷ **limb**
limber adj pliant or supple
limbo n (pl -s) West Indian dance in which dancers lean backwards to pass under a bar
  limbos n ▷ **limbo**
lime¹ n (pl -s) calcium compound used as a fertilizer or in making cement
lime² n (pl -s) small green citrus fruit
lime³ n (pl -s) deciduous tree with heart-shaped leaves and fragrant flowers
limelight n (pl -s) glare of publicity
  limelights n ▷ **lime**
limerick [lim-mer-ik] n (pl -s) humorous verse of five lines
  limericks n ▷ **limerick**
  limes n ▷ **lime**¹,²,³
limestone n (pl -s) sedimentary rock used in building
  limestones n ▷ **limestone**
limey n (pl -s) (US) (Slang) British person
  limeys n ▷ **limey**
limit n (pl -s) ultimate extent, degree, or amount of something ▶ v (-s, -ing, -ed) restrict or confine > **limitation** n (pl -s) > **limitless** adj
  limitation n ▷ **limit**
  limitations n ▷ **limit**
  limited v ▷ **limit**
  limiting v ▷ **limit**
  limitless v ▷ **limit**
  limits n, v ▷ **limit**
limousine n (pl -s) large luxurious car
  limousines n ▷ **limousine**
limp¹ v (-s, -ing, -ed) walk with an uneven step ▶ n (pl -s) limping walk
limp² (-er, -est) adj without firmness or stiffness > **limply** adv
  limped v ▷ **limp**¹
  limper adj ▷ **limp**²
  limpest adj ▷ **limp**²
  limping v ▷ **limp**¹
  limply adv ▷ **limp**²
  limps v, n ▷ **limp**¹
limpet n (pl -s) shellfish which sticks tightly to rocks

  limpets n ▷ **limpet**
limpid adj clear or transparent > **limpidity** n (pl -ties)
  limpidities n ▷ **limpid**
  limpidity n ▷ **limpid**
linchpin, lynchpin n (pl -s) pin to hold a wheel on its axle
  linchpins n ▷ **linchpin**
linctus n (pl -es) syrupy cough medicine
  linctuses n ▷ **linctus**
linden n (pl -s) ▷ **lime**³
  lindens n ▷ **linden**
line¹ n (pl -s) long narrow mark ▶ pl words of a theatrical part ▶ v (-s, -ing, -ed) mark with lines
line² v (-s, -ning, -ned) give a lining to
  lined v ▷ **line**¹,²
  lines n, v ▷ **line**¹,²
  lining v ▷ **line**¹,²
lineage [lin-ee-ij] n (pl -s) descent from an ancestor
  lineages n ▷ **lineage**
lineament n (pl -s) facial feature
  lineaments n ▷ **lineament**
linear [lin-ee-er] adj of or in lines
linen n (pl -s) cloth or thread made from flax
  linens n ▷ **linen**
liner¹ n (pl -s) large passenger ship or aircraft
liner² n something used as a lining
  liners n ▷ **liner**¹,²
linesman n (pl -men) (in some sports) an official who helps the referee or umpire
  linesmen n ▷ **linesman**
ling¹ n slender food fish
ling² n (pl lings) heather
linger v (-s, -ing, -ed) delay or prolong departure
  lingered v ▷ **linger**
lingerie [lan-zher-ee] n (pl -s) women's underwear or nightwear
  lingeries n ▷ **lingerie**
  lingering v ▷ **linger**
  lingers v ▷ **linger**
lingo n (pl -s) (Informal) foreign or unfamiliar language or jargon
  lingos n ▷ **lingo**
  lings n ▷ **ling**²
lingual adj of the tongue
linguist n (pl -s) person skilled in foreign languages
linguistic adj of languages
linguistics n (pl -s) scientific study of language
  linguists n ▷ **linguist**
liniment n (pl -s) medicated liquid rubbed on the skin to relieve pain or stiffness

liniments *n* ▷ liniment

lining *n* (*pl* -s) layer of cloth attached to the inside of a garment etc.

linings *n* ▷ lining

link *n* (*pl* -s) any of the rings forming a chain ▶ *v* (-s, -ing, -ed) connect with or as if with links > **linkage** *n* (*pl* -s)

linkage *n* ▷ link

linkages *n* ▷ link

linked *v* ▷ link

linking *v* ▷ link

links *pl n* golf course, esp. one by the sea

links *n*, *v* ▷ link

linnet *n* (*pl* -s) songbird of the finch family

linnets *n* ▷ linnet

linoleum *n* (*pl* -s) floor covering of hessian or jute with a smooth decorative coating of powdered cork

linoleums *n* ▷ linoleum

linseed *n* (*pl* -s) seed of the flax plant

linseeds *n* ▷ linseeds

lint *n* (*pl* -s) soft material for dressing a wound

lintel *n* (*pl* -s) horizontal beam at the top of a door or window

lintels *n* ▷ lintel

lints *n* ▷ lint

lion *n* (*pl* -s) large animal of the cat family, the male of which has a shaggy mane > **lioness** *n fem*

lioness *n* ▷ lion

lions *n* ▷ lion

lip *n* (*pl* -s) either of the fleshy edges of the mouth

lips *n* ▷ lip

lipstick *n* (*pl* -s) cosmetic in stick form, for colouring the lips

liquefy *v* (-fies, -fying, -fied) make or become liquid > **liquefaction** *n* (*pl* -s)

liquefaction *n* ▷ liquefy

liquefactions *n* ▷ liquefy

liquefied *v* ▷ liquefy

liquefies *v* ▷ liquefy

liquefying *v* ▷ liquefy

liqueur [lik-cure] *n* (*pl* -s) flavoured and sweetened alcoholic spirit

liqueurs *n* ▷ liqueur

liquid *n* (*pl* -s) substance in a physical state which can change shape but not size ▶ *adj* of or being a liquid

liquidate *v* (-tes, -ting, -ted) pay (a debt) > **liquidation** *n* (*pl* -s)

liquidated *v* ▷ liquidate

liquidates *v* ▷ liquidate

liquidating *v* ▷ liquidate

liquidation *n* ▷ liquidate

liquidations *n* ▷ liquidate

liquidities *n* ▷ liquidity

liquidator *n* (*pl* -s) official appointed to liquidate a business

liquidators *n* ▷ liquidator

liquidity *n* (*pl* -ties) state of being able to meet financial obligations ▶ *v* (-zes, -zing, -zed) make or become liquid

liquidized *v* ▷ liquidize

liquidizer *n* (*pl* -s) kitchen appliance that liquidizes food

liquidizers *v* ▷ liquidizer

liquidizes *v* ▷ liquidize

liquidizing *v* ▷ liquidize

liquids *n* ▷ liquid

liquor *n* (*pl* -s) alcoholic drink, esp. spirits

liquors *n* ▷ liquor

liquorice [lik-ker-iss] *n* (*pl* -s) black substance used in medicine and as a sweet

liquorices *n* ▷ liquorice

lira *n* (*pl* -re, -ras) monetary unit of Turkey and formerly of Italy

liras *n* ▷ lira

lire *n* ▷ lira

lisle [rhymes with **mile**] *n* (*pl* -s) strong fine cotton thread or fabric

lisles *n* ▷ lisle

lisp *n* (*pl* -s) speech defect in which *s* and *z* are pronounced *th* ▶ *v* (-s, -ing, -ed) speak or utter with a lisp

lisped *v* ▷ lisp

lisping *v* ▷ lisp

lisps *n*, *v* ▷ lisp

lissom, lissome *adj* supple, agile

lissome *adj* ▷ lissom

list[1] *n* (*pl* -s) item-by-item record of names or things, usu. written one below another ▶ *v* (-s, -ing, -ed) make a list of

list[2] *v* (-s, -ing, -ed) (of a ship) lean to one side ▶ *n* (*pl* -s) leaning to one side

listed *v* ▷ list[1,2]

listing *v* ▷ list[1,2]

lists *n*, *v* ▷ list[1,2]

listen *v* (-s, -ing, -ed) concentrate on hearing something > **listener** *n* (*pl* -s)

listened *v* ▷ listen

listener *n* ▷ listen

listeners *n* ▷ listen

listening *v* ▷ listen

listens *v* ▷ listen

listeriosis *n* (*pl* -ses) dangerous form of food poisoning

listerioses *n* ▷ listeriosis

listless *adj* lacking interest or energy > **listlessly** *adv*

listlessly *adv* ▷ listless
lit *v* ▷ light[1,2]
litanies *n* ▷ litany
litany *n* (*pl* -nies) prayer with responses from the congregation
literacies *n* ▷ literacy
literacy *n* (*pl* -cies) ability to read and write
literal *adj* according to the explicit meaning of a word or text, not figurative > **literally** *adv*
literally *adv* ▷ literal
literary *adj* of or knowledgeable about literature
literate *adj* able to read and write
literati *pl n* literary people
literature *n* (*pl* -s) written works such as novels, plays, and poetry
literatures *n* ▷ literature
lithe *adj* (-ther, -thest) flexible or supple, pliant
lither *adj* ▷ lithe
lithest *adj* ▷ lithe
lithium *n* (*pl* -s) (CHEM) chemical element, the lightest known metal
lithograph *n* (*pl* -s) print made by lithography
lithographer *n* ▷ lithography
lithographers *n* ▷ lithography
lithographic *adj* ▷ lithography
lithographied *v* ▷ lithography
lithographies *n*, *v* ▷ lithography
lithographs *n* ▷ lithograph
lithography [lith-og-ra-fee] *n* (*pl* -phies) method of printing from a metal or stone surface in which the printing areas are made receptive to ink ▶ *v* (-phies, -ying, -phied) reproduce by lithography > **lithographer** *n* (*pl* -s) > **lithographic** *adj*
lithographying *v* ▷ lithography
litigant *n* (*pl* -s) person involved in a lawsuit
litigants *n* ▷ litigant
litigate *v* (-tes, -ting, -ted) bring or contest a law suit
litigated *v* ▷ litigate
litigates *v* ▷ litigate
litigating *v* ▷ litigate
litigation *n* (*pl* -s) legal action
litigations *n* ▷ litigation
litigious [lit-ij-uss] *adj* frequently going to law
litmus *n* (*pl* -es) blue dye turned red by acids and restored to blue by alkalis
litmuses *n* ▷ litmus
litotes [lie-toe-teez] *n* ironical understatement used for effect
litre *n* (*pl* -s) unit of liquid measure equal to 1000 cubic centimetres or 1.76 pints
litres *n* ▷ litre
litter *n* (*pl* -s) untidy rubbish dropped in public

places ▶ *v* (-s, -ing, -ed) strew with litter
littered *v* ▷ litter
littering *v* ▷ litter
litters *n*, *v* ▷ litter
little *adj* small or smaller than average ▶ *adv* not a lot ▶ *n* small amount, extent, or duration
littoral *adj* of or by the seashore ▶ *n* (*pl* -s) coastal district
littorals *n* ▷ littoral
liturgical *n* ▷ liturgy
liturgies *n* ▷ liturgy
liturgy *n* (*pl* -gies) prescribed form of public worship > **liturgical** *adj*
live[1] *v* (-s, -ing, -ed) be alive
live[2] *adj* living, alive ▶ *adv* in the form of a live performance > **liveliness** *n* (*pl* -es)
lived *v* ▷ live[1]
liveliness *n* ▷ live[2]
livelinesses *n* ▷ live[2]
lively *adj* full of life or vigour
livelihood *n* (*pl* livelihoods) occupation or employment
livelihoods *n* ▷ livelihood
lively *adj* full of life or vigour
liver[1] *n* (*pl* -s) organ secreting bile
liver[2] *n* (*pl* -s) person who lives in a specified way
liveried *adj* ▷ livery
liverish *adj* having a disorder of the liver
livers *n* ▷ liver[1,2]
livery *n* (*pl* -ries) distinctive dress, esp. of a servant or servants > **liveried** *adj*
lives *v* ▷ live[1] ▶ *n* ▷ life
livestock *n* (*pl* -s) farm animals
livestocks *n* ▷ livestock
livid *adj* (*Informal*) (-er, -est) angry or furious
livider *adj* ▷ livid
lividest *adj* ▷ livid
living *adj* possessing life, not dead or inanimate ▶ *n* (*pl* -s) condition of being alive ▶ *v* ▷ live
livings *n* ▷ living
lizard *n* (*pl* -s) four-footed reptile with a long body and tail
lizards *n* ▷ lizard
llama *n* (*pl* -s) woolly animal of the camel family used as a beast of burden in S America
llamas *n* ▷ llama

> **lo** *interj*. Lo is a command that means look! Along with **la** and **li**, lo is one of just three two-letter words that begin with L. Lo scores 2 points.

loach *n* (*pl* -es) carplike freshwater fish
loaches *n* ▷ loach

load *n* (*pl* **-s**) burden or weight ▸ *pl* (*Informal*) lots ▸ *v* (**-s, -ing, -ed**) put a load on or into
loaded *adj* (of a question) containing a hidden trap or implication
  loaded *v, adj* ▷ **load**
  loads *n, v* ▷ **load**
  loading *v* ▷ **load**
loaf¹ *n* (*pl* **loaves**) shaped mass of baked bread
loaf² *v* (**-s, -ing, -ed**) idle, loiter > **loafer** *n* (*pl* **-s**)
  loafed *v* ▷ **loaf²**
  loafer *n* ▷ **loaf²**
  loafers *n* ▷ **loaf²**
  loafing *v* ▷ **loaf²**
  loafs *v* ▷ **loaf²**
loam *n* (*pl* **-s**) fertile soil
  loams *n* ▷ **loam**
loan *n* (*pl* **-s**) money lent at interest ▸ *v* (**-s, -ing, -ed**) lend
  loaned *v* ▷ **loan**
  loaning *v* ▷ **loan**
  loans *n, v* ▷ **loan**
loath, loth [rhymes with **both**] *adj* unwilling or reluctant (to)
loathe *v* (**-s, -thing, -thed**) hate, be disgusted by > **loathing** *n* (*pl* **-s**) > **loathsome** *adj*
  loathed *v* ▷ **loathe**
  loathes *v* ▷ **loathe**
  loathing *v, n* ▷ **loathe**
  loathings *n* ▷ **loathe**
  loathsome *adj* ▷ **loathe**
  loaves *n* ▷ **loaf¹**
lob (SPORT) *n* (*pl* **-s**) ball struck or thrown in a high arc ▸ *v* (**-s, -bbing, -bbed**) strike or throw (a ball) in a high arc
  lobbed *v* ▷ **lob**
  lobbied *v* ▷ **lobby**
  lobbies *n, v* ▷ **lobby**
  lobbing *v* ▷ **lob**
lobby *n* (*pl* **-bies**) corridor into which rooms open ▸ *v* (**-bies, -ing, -bied**) try to influence (legislators) in the formulation of policy > **lobbyist** *n*
  lobbying *v* ▷ **lobby**
lobe *n* (*pl* **-s**) rounded projection > **lobed** *adj*
  lobed *n* ▷ **lobe**
lobelia *n* (*pl* **-s**) garden plant with blue, red, or white flowers
  lobelias *n* ▷ **lobelia**
  lobes *n* ▷ **lobe**
lobola [law-bawl-a] *n* (*pl* **-s**) (S AFR) (in African custom) price paid by a bridegroom's family to his bride's family
  lobolas *n* ▷ **lobola**
lobotomy *n* (*pl* **-mies**) surgical incision into a lobe of the brain to treat mental disorders

  lobotomies *n* ▷ **lobotomy**
  lobs *n, v* ▷ **lob**
lobster *n* (*pl* **-s**) shellfish with a long tail and claws, which turns red when boiled
  lobsters *n* ▷ **lobster**
local *adj* of or existing in a particular place ▸ *n* (*pl* **-s**) person belonging to a particular district > **locally** *adv*
locale [loh-**kahl**] *n* (*pl* **-s**) scene of an event
  localities *n* ▷ **locality**
locality *n* (*pl* **-ties**) neighbourhood or area
localize *v* (**-zes, -zing, -zed**) restrict to a particular place
  localized *v* ▷ **localize**
  localizes *v* ▷ **localize**
  localizing *v* ▷ **localize**
  locally *adv* ▷ **local**
  locals *n* ▷ **local**
locate *v* (**-s, -ing, -ed**) discover the whereabouts of
  located *v* ▷ **locate**
  locates *v* ▷ **locate**
  locating *v* ▷ **locate**
location *n* (*pl* **-s**) site or position
  locations *n* ▷ **location**
loch *n* (*pl* **-s**) (SCOT) lake
  lochs *n* ▷ **loch**
  loci *n* ▷ **locus**
lock¹ *n* (*pl* **-s**) appliance for fastening a door, case, etc. ▸ *v* (**-s, -ing, -ed**) fasten or become fastened securely
lock² *n* (*pl* **-s**) strand of hair
  locked *v* ▷ **lock¹**
locker *n* (*pl* **-s**) small cupboard with a lock
  lockers *n* ▷ **locker**
locket *n* (*pl* **-s**) small hinged pendant for a portrait etc.
  lockets *n* ▷ **locket**
  locking *v* ▷ **lock¹**
lockjaw *n* (*pl* **-s**) tetanus
  lockjaws *n* ▷ **lockjaw**
locomotion *n* (*pl* **-s**) action or power of moving
  locomotions *n* ▷ **locomotion**
locomotive *n* (*pl* **-s**) self-propelled engine for pulling trains ▸ *adj* of locomotion
  locomotives *n* ▷ **locomotive**
lockout *n* (*pl* **-s**) closing of a workplace by an employer to force workers to accept terms
  lockouts *n* ▷ **lockout**
  locks *n* ▷ **lock¹,²** ▸ *v* ▷ **lock¹**
locksmith *n* (*pl* **-s**) person who makes and mends locks
  locksmiths *n* ▷ **locksmith**
lockup *n* (*pl* **-s**) prison
  lockups *n* ▷ **lockup**

locum n (pl -s) temporary stand-in for a doctor or clergyman
  locums n ▷ locum
locus [loh-kuss] n (pl -ci) [loh-sigh] area or place where something happens
locust n (pl -s) destructive African insect that flies in swarms and eats crops
  locusts n ▷ locust
lode n (pl -s) vein of ore
  lodes n ▷ lode
lodestar n (pl -s) star used in navigation or astronomy as a point of reference
  lodestars n ▷ lodestar
lodestone n (pl -s) magnetic iron ore
  lodestones n ▷ lodestone
lodge n (pl -s) (CHIEFLY BRIT) gatekeeper's house ▶ v (-dges, -dging, -dged) live in another's house at a fixed charge > **lodger** n (pl -s)
  lodged v ▷ lodge
  lodger n ▷ lodge
  lodgers n ▷ lodge
  lodges n, v ▷ lodge
lodging n (pl -s) temporary residence ▶ pl rented room or rooms in another person's house ▶ v ▷ lodge
  lodgings n ▷ lodging
loft n (pl -s) space between the top storey and roof of a building ▶ v (-s, -ing, -ed) (SPORT) strike, throw, or kick (a ball) high into the air
  lofted v ▷ loft
  loftier adj ▷ lofty
  loftiest adj ▷ lofty
loftily adv haughtily
  lofting v ▷ loft
  lofts n, v ▷ loft
lofty adj (-tier, -tiest) of great height
log[1] n (pl -s) portion of a felled tree stripped of branches ▶ v (-s, -gging, -gged) saw logs from a tree
  log[2] n ▷ logarithm
loganberry n (pl -rries) purplish-red fruit, similar to a raspberry
  loganberries n ▷ loganberry
logarithm n (pl -s) one of a series of arithmetical functions used to make certain calculations easier
  logarithms n ▷ logarithm
logbook n (pl -s) book recording the details about a car or a ship's journeys
  logbooks n ▷ logbook
  logged v ▷ log[1]
loggerheads pl n quarrelling, disputing
loggia [loj-ya] n (pl -s) covered gallery at the side of a building
  loggias n ▷ loggia

logging n (pl -s) work of cutting and transporting logs ▶ v ▷ log[1]
  loggings n ▷ logging
logic n (pl -s) philosophy of reasoning > **logically** adv > **logician** n (pl -s)
logical adj of logic
  logically adv ▷ logic
  logician n ▷ logic
  logicians n ▷ logic
  logics n ▷ logic
  logistical adj ▷ logistics
logistics n detailed planning and organization of a large, esp. military, operation
  > **logistical, logistic** adj
logo [loh-go] n (pl -s) emblem used by a company or other organization
  logos n ▷ logo
  logs n ▷ log[1]
loin n (pl -s) part of the body between the ribs and the hips
loincloth n (pl -s) piece of cloth covering the loins only
  loincloths n ▷ loincloth
  loins n ▷ loin
loiter v (-s, -ing, -ed) stand or wait aimlessly or idly
  loitered v ▷ loiter
  loitering v ▷ loiter
  loiters v ▷ loiter
loll v (-s, -ing, -ed) lounge lazily
  lolled v ▷ loll
  lollies n ▷ lolly
  lolling v ▷ loll
lollipop n (pl -s) boiled sweet on a small wooden stick
  lollipops n ▷ lollipop
  lolls v ▷ loll
lolly n (pl -llies) (Informal) lollipop or ice lolly
lone adj solitary > **lonesome** adj lonely
  loneliness n ▷ lonely
  lonelinesses n ▷ lonely
lonely adj sad because alone > **loneliness** n (pl -s)
loner n (pl -s) (Informal) person who prefers to be alone
  loners n ▷ -s
  lonesome adj ▷ lone
long[1] adj (-er, -est) having length, esp. great length, in space or time ▶ adv for an extensive period
long[2] v (-s, -ing, -ed) have a strong desire (for)
  longed v ▷ long[2]
  longer adj ▷ long[1]
  longest adj ▷ long[1]
  longevities n ▷ longevity

longevity [lon-**jev**-it-ee] *n* (*pl* -**ties**) long life
longhand *n* (*pl* -**s**) ordinary writing, not
shorthand or typing
  longhands *n* ▷ **longhand**
longing *n* (*pl* -**s**) yearning ▶ *v* ▷ **long²**
  > **longingly** *adv*
  longingly *adv* ▷ **longing**
  longings *n* ▷ **longing**
longitude *n* (*pl* -**s**) distance east or west from a
standard meridian
  longitudes *n* ▷ **longitude**
longitudinal *adj* of length or longitude
  longs *v* ▷ **long²**
longshoreman *n* (*pl* -**men**) (us) docker
  longshoremen *n* ▷ **longshoreman**
loo *n* (*pl* -**s**) (*Informal*) toilet
  loos *n* ▷ **loo**
loofah *n* (*pl* -**s**) sponge made from the dried
pod of a gourd
  loofahs *n* ▷ **loofah**
look *v* (-**s**, -**ing**, -**ed**) direct the eyes or attention
(towards) ▶ *n* (*pl* -**s**) instance of looking
lookalike *n* (*pl* -**s**) person who is the double
of another
  lookalikes *n* ▷ **lookalike**
  looked *v* ▷ **look**
  looking *v* ▷ **look**
lookout *n* (*pl* -**s**) guard
  lookouts *n* ▷ **lookout**
  looks *v*, *n* ▷ **look**
loom¹ *n* (*pl* -**s**) machine for weaving cloth
loom² *v* (-**s**, -**ing**, -**ed**) appear dimly
  loomed *v* ▷ **loom²**
  looming *v* ▷ **loom²**
  looms *n* ▷ **loom¹** ▶ *v* **loom²**
  loonies *n* ▷ **loony**
loony (*Slang*) *adj* (-**nier**, -**niest**) foolish or insane
▶ *n* (*pl* -**nies**) foolish or insane person
loop *n* (*pl* -**s**) rounded shape made by a curved
line or rope crossing itself ▶ *v* (-**s**, -**ing**, -**ed**)
form or fasten with a loop
  looped *v* ▷ **loop**
loophole *n* (*pl* -**s**) means of evading a rule
without breaking it
  loopholes *n* ▷ **loophole**
  looping *v* ▷ **loop**
  loops *n*, *v* ▷ **loop**
loose *adj* (-**r**, -**est**) not tight, fastened, fixed, or
tense ▶ *adv* in a loose manner ▶ *v* (-**s**, -**sing**,
-**sed**) free > **loosely** *adv* > **looseness** *n* (*pl* -**s**)
  loosed *v* ▷ **loose**
  loosely *adv* ▷ **loose**
loosen *v* (-**s**, -**ing**, -**ed**) make loose
  loosened *v* ▷ **loosen**
  looseness *n* ▷ **loose**

  loosenesses *n* ▷ **loose**
  loosening *v* ▷ **loosen**
  loosens *v* ▷ **loosen**
  looser *adj* ▷ **loose**
  looses *v* ▷ **loose**
  loosest *adj* ▷ **loose**
  loosing *v* ▷ **loose**
loot *n*, *v* (-**s**, -**ing**, -**ed**) plunder ▶ *n* (*pl* -**s**)
(*Informal*) money > **looter** *n* (*pl* -**s**) > **looting**
n (*pl* -**s**)
  looted *v* ▷ **loot**
  looter *n* ▷ **loot**
  looters *n* ▷ **loot**
  looting *v*, *n* ▷ **loot**
  lootings *n* ▷ **loot**
  loots *v*, *n* ▷ **loot**
lop *v* (-**s**, -**ping**, -**pped**) cut away twigs and
branches
lope *v* (-**s**, -**ing**, -**ed**) run with long easy strides
  loped *v* ▷ **lope**
  lopes *v* ▷ **lope**
  loping *v* ▷ **lope**
lopsided *adj* greater in height, weight, or size
on one side
loquacious *adj* talkative > **loquacity** *n* (*pl* -**ties**)
  loquacities *n* ▷ **loquacity**
lord *n* (*pl* -**s**) person with power over others,
such as a monarch or master
  lordlier *adj* ▷ **lordly**
  lordliest *adj* ▷ **lordly**
lordly *adj* (-**lier**, -**liest**) imperious, proud
  lords *n* ▷ **lord**
lore *n* (*pl* -**s**) body of traditions on a subject
  lores *n* ▷ **lore**
lorgnette [lor-**nyet**] *n* (*pl* -**s**) pair of spectacles
mounted on a long handle
  lorgnettes *n* ▷ **lorgnette**
  lorries *n* ▷ **lorry**
lorikeet *n* (*pl* -**s**) small brightly coloured
Australian parrot
  lorikeets *n* ▷ **lorikeet**
lorry *n* (*pl* -**rries**) (BRIT & S AFR) large vehicle for
transporting loads by road
lose *v* (-**s**, -**sing**, **lost**) come to be without, esp.
by accident or carelessness
loser *n* (*pl* -**s**) person or thing that loses
  losers *n* ▷ **loser**
  loses *v* ▷ **lose**
  losing *v* ▷ **lose**
loss *n* (*pl* -**es**) losing
  losses *n* ▷ **loss**
  lost *v* ▷ **lose** ▶ *adj* unable to find one's way
lot *pron* great number ▶ *n* (*pl* -**s**) collection of
people or things
  lots *n* ▷ **lot**

loth *adj* ▷ **loath**
lotion *n* (*pl* -s) medical or cosmetic liquid for use on the skin
  lotions *n* ▷ **lotion**
lottery *n* (*pl* -ries) method of raising money by selling tickets that win prizes by chance
lotto *n* (*pl* -s) game of chance like bingo
  lottos *n* ▷ **lotto**
lotus *n* (*pl* -es) legendary plant whose fruit induces forgetfulness
  lotuses *n* ▷ **lotus**
loud *adj* (-er, -est) relatively great in volume > **loudly** *adv* > **loudness** *n* (*pl* -es)
  louder *adj* ▷ **loud**
  loudest *adj* ▷ **loud**
  loudly *adv* ▷ **loud**
  loudness *n* ▷ **loud**
  loudnesses *n* ▷ **loud**
loudspeaker *n* (*pl* -s) instrument for converting electrical signals into sound
  loudspeakers *n* ▷ **loudspeaker**
lough *n* (*pl* -s) (IRISH) loch
  loughs *n* ▷ **lough**
lounge *n* (*pl* -s) living room in a private house ▶ *v* (-s, -ging, -ged) sit, lie, or stand in a relaxed manner
  lounged *v* ▷ **lounge**
  lounges *n*, *v* ▷ **lounge**
  lounging *v* ▷ **lounge**
lour *v* (-s, -ing, -ed) ▷ **lower²**
  loured *v* ▷ **lour**
  louring *v* ▷ **lour**
  lours *v* ▷ **lour**
louse *n* (*pl* lice, louses) wingless parasitic insect
  louses *n* ▷ **louse**
  lousier *adj* ▷ **lousy**
  lousiest *adj* ▷ **lousy**
lousy *adj* (-sier, -siest) (*Slang*) mean or unpleasant
lout *n* (*pl* -s) crude, oafish, or aggressive person > **loutish** *adj*
  loutish *adj* ▷ **lout**
  louts *n* ▷ **lout**
louvre [loo-ver] *n* (*pl* -s) one of a set of parallel slats slanted to admit air but not rain > **louvred** *adj*
  louvred *adj* ▷ **louvre**
  louvres *n* ▷ **louvre**
love *v* (-s, -ving, -ved) have a great affection for ▶ *n* (*pl* -s) great affection > **lovable, loveable** *adj* > **loveless** *adj* > **lovemaking** *n* (*pl* -s)
  lovable *adj* ▷ **love**
  loveable *adj* ▷ **love**
lovebird *n* (*pl* -s) small parrot

lovebirds *n* ▷ **lovebird**
loved *v* ▷ **love**
loveless *adj* ▷ **love**
lovelier *adj* ▷ **lovely**
loveliest *adj* ▷ **lovely**
lovelorn *adj* miserable because of unhappiness in love
lovely *adj* (-lier, -liest) very attractive
  lovemaking *n* ▷ **love**
  lovemakings *n* ▷ **love**
lover *n* (*pl* -s) person having a sexual relationship outside marriage
  lovers *n* ▷ **lover**
  loves *v*, *n* ▷ **love**
loving *adj* affectionate, tender ▶ *v* ▷ **love** > **lovingly** *adv*
  lovingly *adv* ▷ **loving**
low¹ *adj* not tall, high, or elevated ▶ *adv* in or to a low position, level, or degree ▶ *n* (*pl* -s) low position, level, or degree > **lowland** *n* (*pl* -s)
low² *n* (*pl* -s) cry of cattle, moo ▶ *v* (-s, -ing, -ed) moo
lowbrow *n* (*pl* -s) ▶ *adj* (person) with nonintellectual tastes and interests
  lowbrows *n* ▷ **lowbrow**
lowdown *n* (*pl* -s) (*Informal*) inside information
  lowdowns *n* ▷ **lowdown**
  lowed *v* ▷ **low²**
lower¹ *adj* (-est) below one or more other things ▶ *v* (-s, -ing, -ed) cause or allow to move down
lower², lour *v* (of the sky or weather) look gloomy or threatening
  lowered *v* ▷ **lower¹,²**
  lowering *v* ▷ **lower¹,²**
  lowers *v* ▷ **lower¹,²**
  lowest *adj* ▷ **lower**
  lowing *v* ▷ **low²**
lowland *n* (*pl* -s) low-lying country
  lowlands *n* ▷ **lowland**
  lowlier *adj* ▷ **lowly**
  lowliest *adj* ▷ **lowly**
  lowliness *n* ▷ **lowly**
  lowlinesses *n* ▷ **lowly**
lowly *adj* (-lier, -liest) modest, humble > **lowliness** *n* (*pl* -s)
  lows *n* ▷ **low¹,²** ▶ *v* ▷ **low²**

> **lox** *n* (**loxes**). Lox is a kind of smoked salmon. This is a good word if you get have an X and L in the late stages of the game: there's likely to be a usable O on the board already. Lox scores 10 points.

loyal *adj* (-ler, -lest) faithful to one's friends, country, or government > **loyally** *adv* > **loyalty** *n* (*pl* -ties) > **loyalist** *n* (*pl* -s)

loyalist *n* ▷ loyal
loyalists *n* ▷ loyal
loyaller *adj* ▷ loyal
loyallest *adj* ▷ loyal
loyally *adv* ▷ loyal
loyalties *n* ▷ loyal
loyalty *n* ▷ loyal
lozenge *n* (*pl* -s) medicated tablet held in the mouth until it dissolves
lozenges *n* ▷ lozenge
lubricate [loo-brik-ate] *v* (-tes, -ting, -ted) oil or grease to lessen friction > **lubrication** *n* (*pl* -s)
lubricant *n* (*pl* -s) lubricating substance, such as oil
  lubricants *n* ▷ lubricant
  lubricated *v* ▷ lubricate
  lubricates *v* ▷ lubricate
  lubricating *v* ▷ lubricate
  lubrication *n* ▷ lubricate
  lubrications *n* ▷ lubricate
lubricious *adj* (*Lit*) lewd
lucerne *n* (*pl* -s) fodder plant like clover, alfalfa
  lucernes *n* ▷ lucerne
lucid *adj* clear and easily understood > **lucidly** *adv* > **lucidity** *n* (*pl* -ties)
  lucidities *n* ▷ lucid
  lucidity *n* ▷ lucid
  lucidly *adv* ▷ lucid
luck *n* (*pl* -s) fortune, good or bad
luckily *adv* fortunately
luckless *adj* having bad luck
lucrative *adj* very profitable
lucre [loo-ker] *n* (*pl* -s) (*Facetious*) money
lucks *n* having bad luck
lucky *adj* having or bringing good luck
luderick *n* (*pl* -s) Australian fish, usu. black or dark brown in colour
  ludericks *n* ▷ luderick
ludicrous *adj* absurd or ridiculous > **ludicrously** *adv*
  ludicrously *adv* ▷ ludicrous
ludo *n* (*pl* -s) game played with dice and counters on a board
lug[1] *v* (-s, -gging, -gged) carry or drag with great effort
lug[2] *n* (*pl* -s) projection serving as a handle
luggage *n* (*pl* -s) traveller's cases, bags, etc.
luggages *n* projection serving as a handle ▷ luggage
lugs *v* ▷ lug[1] ▶ *n* ▷ lug[2]
lugubrious *adj* mournful, gloomy > **lugubriously** *adv*
  lugubriously *adv* ▷ lugubrious
lugworm *n* (*pl* -s) large worm used as bait
  lugworms *n* ▷ lugworm

lukewarm *adj* moderately warm, tepid
lull *v* (-s, -ing, -ed) soothe (someone) by soft sounds or motions ▶ *n* (*pl* -s) brief time of quiet in a storm etc.
  lullabies *n* ▷ lullaby
lullaby *n* (*pl* -bies) quiet song to send a child to sleep
  lulled *v* ▷ lull
  lulling *v* ▷ lull
  lulls *v*, *n* ▷ lull
lumbago [lum-bay-go] *n* (*pl* -s) pain in the lower back
  lumbagos *n* ▷ lumbago
lumbar *adj* relating to the lower back
lumber[1] *n* (*pl* -s) (BRIT) unwanted disused household articles ▶ *v* (-s, -ing, -ed) (*Informal*) burden with something unpleasant
lumber[2] *v* move heavily and awkwardly > **lumbering** *adj*
  lumbered *v* ▷ lumber[1,2]
  lumbering *v* ▷ lumber[1,2] ▶ *adj* ▷ lumber[2]
lumberjack *n* (*pl* -s) (US) man who fells trees and prepares logs for transport
  lumberjacks *n* ▷ lumberjack
  lumbers *n*[1] ▶ *v* ▷ lumber[1,2]
luminary *n* (*pl* -s) famous person
luminescence *n* (*pl* -s) emission of light at low temperatures by any process other than burning
  luminescences *n* ▷ luminescence
  luminescent *adj* ▷ luminous
  luminosities *n* ▷ luminous
  luminosity *n* ▷ luminous
luminous *adj* reflecting or giving off light > **luminosity** *n* (*pl* -s) > **luminescent** *adj*
lump[1] *n* (*pl* -s) shapeless piece or mass ▶ *v* (-s, -ing, -ed) consider as a single group > **lumpy** *adj* (-pier, -piest)
lump[2] *v* (*Informal*) tolerate or put up with it
  lumped *v* ▷ lump[1,2]
  lumpier *adj* ▷ lump[1]
  lumpiest *adj* ▷ lump[1]
  lumping *v* ▷ lump[1,2]
  lumps *n*, *v* ▷ lump[1,2]
  lumpy *adj* ▷ lump[1]
lunar *adj* relating to the moon
  lunacies *n* ▷ lunacy
lunatic *adj* foolish and irresponsible ▶ *n* (*pl* -s) foolish or annoying person > **lunacy** *n* (*pl* -cies)
  lunatics *n* ▷ lunatic
lunch *n* (*pl* lunches) meal taken in the middle of the day ▶ *v* (-es, -ing, -ed) eat lunch
  lunched *v* ▷ lunch
luncheon *n* (*pl* -s) formal lunch

luncheons *n* ▷ **luncheon**
lunches *n*, *v* ▷ **lunch**
 lunching *v* ▷ **lunch**
lung *n* (*pl* -**s**) organ that allows an animal or bird to breathe air: humans have two lungs in the chest
lungfish *n* freshwater bony fish with an air-breathing lung of South America and Australia
 lungs *n* ▷ **lung**
lunge *n* (*pl* -**s**) sudden forward motion ▶ *v* (-**s**, -**ging**, -**ged**) move with or make a lunge
 lunged *v* ▷ **lunge**
 lunges *n*, *v* ▷ **lunge**
 lunging *v* ▷ **lunge**
lupin *n* (*pl* -**s**) garden plant with tall spikes of flowers
 lupins *n* ▷ **lupin**
lupine *adj* like a wolf
lurch *v* (-**es**, -**ing**, -**ed**) tilt or lean suddenly to one side ▶ *n* (*pl* -**es**) lurching movement
 lurched *v* ▷ **lurch**
lurcher *n* (*pl* -**s**) crossbred dog trained to hunt silently
 lurchers *n* ▷ **lurcher**
 lurches *v*, *n* ▷ **lurch**
 lurching *v* ▷ **lurch**
lure *v* (-**s**, -**red**, -**ring**) tempt or attract by the promise of reward ▶ *n* (*pl* -**s**) person or thing that lures
 lured *v* ▷ **lure**
 lures *v*, *n* ▷ **lure**
 luring *v* ▷ **lure**
lurid *adj* (-**er**, -**est**) vivid in shocking detail, sensational > **luridly** *adv*
 lurider *adj* ▷ **lurid**
 luridest *adj* ▷ **lurid**
 luridly *adv* ▷ **lurid**
 luring *v* ▷ **lure**
lurk *v* (-**s**, -**ing**, -**ed**) lie hidden or move stealthily, esp. for sinister purposes
 lurked *v* ▷ **lurk**
 lurking *v* ▷ **lurk**
 lurks *v* ▷ **lurk**
luscious [lush-uss] *adj* extremely pleasurable to taste or smell
lush¹ *adj* (-**er**, -**est**) (of grass etc.) growing thickly and healthily
lush² *n* (*pl* -**es**) (*Slang*) alcoholic
 lusher *adj* ▷ **lush¹**
 lushes *n* ▷ **lush²**
 lushest *adj* ▷ **lush¹**
lust *n* (*pl* -**s**) strong sexual desire ▶ *v* (-**s**, -**ing**, -**ed**) have passionate desire (for) > **lustful** *adj* > **lusty** *adj* vigorous, healthy > **lustily** *adv*

lusted *v* ▷ **lust**
lustful *adj* ▷ **lust**
lustier *adj* ▷ **lusty**
lustiest *adj* ▷ **lusty**
lustily *adv* ▷ **lust**
lusting *v* ▷ **lust**
lustre *n* (*pl* -**s**) gloss, sheen
 lustres *n* ▷ **lustre**
lustrous *adj* shining, luminous
lusts *n*, *v* ▷ **lust**
lusty *adj* (-**tier**, -**tiest**) vigorous, healthy
lute *n* (*pl* -**s**) ancient guitar-like musical instrument with a body shaped like a half pear
 lutes *n* ▷ **lute**

> **lux** *n* (**lux**). A lux is a unit of illumination. This is a great word to know when you have an X but little opportunity to play it. Lux scores 10 points.

luxuriant *adj* rich and abundant > **luxuriance** *n* (*pl* -**ces**) > **luxuriantly** *adv*
 luxuriance *n* ▷ **luxuriant**
 luxuriances *n* ▷ **luxuriant**
 luxuriantly *adv* ▷ **luxuriant**
luxuriate *v* (-**tes**, -**ting**, -**ted**) take self-indulgent pleasure (in)
 luxuriated *v* ▷ **luxuriate**
 luxuriates *v* ▷ **luxuriate**
 luxuriating *v* ▷ **luxuriate**
luxurious *adj* full of luxury, sumptuous > **luxuriously** *adv*
 luxuriously *adv* ▷ **luxurious**
luxury *n* (*pl* -**ries**) enjoyment of rich, very comfortable living ▶ *adj* of or providing luxury

> **luz** *n* (**luzzes**). In traditional Jewish writings, the luz was a bone that was supposed to be indestructible. This very unusual word is very useful, especially if you have a Z at the end of a game when there is little opportunity to use it in a longer word. Luz scores 12 points.

lychee [lie-**chee**] *n* (*pl* -**s**) Chinese fruit with a whitish juicy pulp
 lychees *n* ▷ **lychee**
lye *n* (*pl* -**s**) caustic solution obtained by leaching wood ash
 lyes *n* ▷ **lye**
 lying *v* ▷ **lie¹,²**
lymph *n* (*pl* -**s**) colourless bodily fluid consisting mainly of white blood cells > **lymphatic** *adj*
 lymphatic *adj* ▷ **lymph**
lymphocyte *n* (*pl* -**s**) type of white blood cell
 lymphocytes *n* ▷ **lymphocyte**

lymphs *n* ▷ **lymph**
lynch *v* (**-es, -ing, -ed**) put to death without
a trial
  lynched *v* ▷ **lynch**
  lynches *v* ▷ **lynch**
  lynching *v* ▷ **lynch**
  lynchpin *n* ▷ **lynchpin**
  lynchpins *n* ▷ **lynchpin**
lynx *n* (*pl* **-es**) animal of the cat family with
tufted ears and a short tail
  lynxes *n* ▷ **lynx**

lyre *n* (*pl* **-s**) ancient musical instrument like a
U-shaped harp
  lyres *n* ▷ **lyre**
lyric *adj* (of poetry) expressing personal
emotion in songlike style ▶ *n* (*pl* **-s**) short
poem in a songlike style > **lyrical** *adj* lyric
  lyrical *n* ▷ **lyric**
lyricist *n* (*pl* **-s**) person who writes the words of
songs or musicals
  lyricists *n* ▷ **lyricist**
  lyrics *n* ▷ **lyric**

Mm

M is a very useful letter when you need to form short words as it starts a two-letter word with every vowel, as well as with Y and with another M. Remembering this allows you to use M effectively when you're forming a word parallel to, and in contact with, a word that is already on the board. M also combines well with X and Z, so there is a lot of potential for high-scoring words. Keep **max, mix** and **mux** (12 points each) in mind, as well as **miz** and **muz** (14 each). It's also worth remembering the three-letter words ending in W: **maw, mew** and **mow** (8 points each).

ma n (pl -s) (Informal) mother
  mas n ▷ **ma**
mac n (pl -s) (BRIT) (Informal) mackintosh
  macs n ▷ **mac**
macabre [mak-**kahb**-ra] adj strange and horrible, gruesome
macadam n (pl -s) road surface of pressed layers of small broken stones
  macadams n ▷ **macadam**
macadamia n (pl -s) Australian tree with edible nuts
  macadamias n ▷ **macadamia**
macaroni n (pl -s) pasta in short tube shapes
  macaronis n ▷ **macaroni**
macaroon n (pl -s) small biscuit or cake made with ground almonds
  macaroons n ▷ **macaroon**
macaw n (pl -s) large tropical American parrot
  macaws n ▷ **macaw**
mace¹ n (pl -s) ceremonial staff of office
mace² n (pl -s) spice made from the dried husk of the nutmeg
  maces n ▷ **mace¹,²**
macerate [**mass**-er-ate] v (-tes, -ting, -ted) soften by soaking > **maceration** n (pl -s)
  macerated v ▷ **macerate**
  macerates v ▷ **macerate**
  macerating v ▷ **macerate**
  maceration n ▷ **macerate**
  macerations n ▷ **macerate**
machete [mash-**ett**-ee] n (pl -s) broad heavy knife used for cutting or as a weapon
  machetes n ▷ **machete**
machinations [mak-in-**nay**-shunz] pl n cunning plots and ploys
machine n (pl -s) apparatus, usu. powered by electricity, designed to perform a particular

task ▶ v (-nes, -ning, -ned) make or produce by machine
  machined v ▷ **machine**
machinegun v (-s, -nning, -nned) fire at with such a gun
  machinegunned v ▷ **machinegun**
  machinegunning v ▷ **machinegun**
  machineguns v ▷ **machinegun**
  machineries n ▷ **machinery**
machinery n (pl -ries) machines or machine parts collectively
  machines n, v ▷ **machine**
  machining v ▷ **machine**
machinist n (pl -s) person who operates a machine
  machinists n ▷ **machinist**
machismo [mak-**izz**-moh] n (pl -s) exaggerated or strong masculinity
  machismos n ▷ **machismo**
macho [**match**-oh] adj strongly or exaggeratedly masculine
mackerel n edible sea fish
mackintosh n (pl -es) waterproof raincoat of rubberized cloth
  mackintoshes n ▷ **mackintosh**
macramé [mak-**rah**-mee] n (pl -s) ornamental work of knotted cord
  macramés n ▷ **macramé**
macrobiotics n dietary system advocating whole grains and vegetables grown without chemical additives > **macrobiotic** adj
  macrobiotic adj ▷ **macrobiotics**
macrocosm n (pl -s) the universe
  macrocosms n ▷ **macrocosm**
mad adj (**madder, maddest**) mentally deranged, insane > **madly** adv > **madness** n (pl -es) > **madman** n (pl -men) > **madwoman**

n (pl -**women**)
madam n (pl **madams**) polite form of address
to a woman
madams n ▷ **madam**
madame [mad-**dam**] n (pl **mesdames**) [may-
dam] French title equivalent to Mrs
madcap adj foolish or reckless
madden v (-**s**, -**ed**, -**ing**) infuriate or irritate
> **maddening** adj
maddened v ▷ **madden**
maddening v ▷ **madden** ▶ adj ▷ **madden**
maddens v ▷ **madden**
madder n (pl -**s**) climbing plant ▶ adj ▷ **mad**
maddest adj ▷ **mad**
made v ▷ **make**
madeira [mad-**deer**-a] n (pl -**s**) fortified white
wine
madeiras n ▷ **madeira**
mademoiselle [mad-mwah-**zel**, maid-mwah-
zel] n (pl -**s**) French title equivalent to Miss
mademoiselles n ▷ **mademoiselle**
madonna n (pl -**s**) the Virgin Mary
madly adv ▷ **mad**
madman n ▷ **mad**
madmen n ▷ **mad**
madness n ▷ **mad**
madnesses n ▷ **madness**
madonnas n ▷ **madonna**
madrigal n (pl -**s**) 16th–17th -century part song
for unaccompanied voices
madrigals n ▷ **madrigal**
madwoman n ▷ **mad**
madwomen n ▷ **mad**
maelstrom [**male**-strom] n (pl -**s**) great
whirlpool
maelstroms n ▷ **maelstrom**
maestri n ▷ **maestro**
maestro [**my**-stroh] n (pl -**tri**, -**tros**) outstanding
musician or conductor
maestros n ▷ **maestro**
mafia n (pl -**s**) international secret criminal
organization
mafias n ▷ **mafia**
mafiosi n ▷ **mafioso**
mafioso n (pl -**sos**, -**si**) member of the Mafia
mafiosos n ▷ **mafioso**
magazine n (pl -**s**) periodical publication with
articles by different writers
magazines n ▷ **magazine**
magenta [maj-**jen**-ta] adj deep purplish-red
maggot n (pl -**s**) larva of an insect > **maggoty**
adj
maggots n ▷ **maggot**
maggoty adj ▷ **maggot**
magi [**maje**-eye] pl n wise men from the East

who came to worship the infant Jesus
magic n (pl -**s**) supposed art of invoking
supernatural powers to influence events
▶ adj (also **magical**) of, using, or like magic
> **magically** adv
magical adj ▷ **magic**
magically adv ▷ **magic**
magician n (pl -**s**) conjuror
magicians n ▷ **magician**
magics n ▷ **magic**
magisterial adj commanding or authoritative
magistrate n (pl -**s**) public officer
administering the law
magistrates n ▷ **magistrate**
magma n (pl -**s**) molten rock inside the earth's
crust
magmas n ▷ **magma**
magnanimous adj noble and generous
> **magnanimously** adv > **magnanimity** n
(pl -**ties**)
magnanimities n ▷ **magnanimous**
magnanimity n ▷ **magnanimous**
magnanimously n ▷ **magnanimous**
magnate n (pl -**s**) influential or wealthy
person, esp. in industry
magnates n ▷ **magnate**
magnesia n (pl -**s**) white tasteless substance
used as an antacid and a laxative;
magnesium oxide
magnesias n ▷ **magnesia**
magnesium n (pl -**s**) (CHEM) silvery-white
metallic element
magnesiums n ▷ **magnesium**
magnet n (pl -**s**) piece of iron or steel capable
of attracting iron and pointing north when
suspended
magnetic adj having the properties of a
magnet > **magnetically** adv
magnetically adv ▷ **magnetic**
magnetism n (pl -**s**) magnetic property
magnetisms n ▷ **magnetism**
magnetize v (-**zes**, -**zed**, -**zing**) make into a
magnet
magnetized v ▷ **magnetize**
magnetizes v ▷ **magnetize**
magnetizing v ▷ **magnetize**
magnets n ▷ **magnet**
magneto [mag-**nee**-toe] n (pl -**s**) apparatus for
ignition in an internal-combustion engine
magnificent adj splendid or impressive
> **magnificently** adv > **magnificence** n (pl -**s**)
magnificence n ▷ **magnificent**
magnificences n ▷ **magnificent**
magnificently adv ▷ **magnificent**
magnify v (-**fies**, -**ing**, -**fied**) increase in

apparent size, as with a lens > **magnification** *n* (*pl* **-s**)

magnification *n* ▷ **magnify**

magnifications *n* ▷ **magnify**

magnified *v* ▷ **magnify**

magnifies *v* ▷ **magnify**

magnifying *v* ▷ **magnify**

magnitude *n* (*pl* **-s**) relative importance or size

magnitudes *n* ▷ **magnitude**

magnolia *n* (*pl* **-s**) shrub or tree with showy white or pink flowers

magnolias *n* ▷ **magnolia**

magnum *n* (*pl* **s**) large wine bottle holding about 1.5 litres

magnums *n* ▷ **magnum**

magpie *n* (*pl* **-s**) black-and-white bird

magpies *n* ▷ **magpie**

maharajah *n* (*pl* **-s**) former title of some Indian princes > **maharani** *n fem* (*pl* **-s**)

maharajahs *n* ▷ **maharajah**

maharani *n* ▷ **maharajah**

maharanis *n* ▷ **maharajah**

mahogany *n* (*pl* **-nies**) hard reddish-brown wood of several tropical trees

mahoganies *n* ▷ **mahogany**

mahout [ma-howt] *n* (*pl* **s**) (in India and the East Indies) elephant driver or keeper

mahouts *n* ▷ **mahout**

maid (*also* **maidservant**) *n* (*pl* **-s**) female servant

maiden *n* (*pl* **-s**) (*Lit*) young unmarried woman ▶ *adj* unmarried

maidenhair *n* (*pl* **-s**) fern with delicate fronds

maidenhairs *n* ▷ **maidenhair**

maidenhead *n* (*pl* **-s**) virginity

maidenheads *n* ▷ **maidenhead**

maidenly *adj* modest

maidens *n* ▷ **maiden**

maids *n* ▷ **maid**

maidservant *n* ▷ **maid**

maidservants *n* ▷ **maid**

mail¹ *n* (*pl* **-s**) letters and packages transported and delivered by the post office ▶ *v* (**-s, -ing, -ed**) send by mail

mail² *n* (*pl* **-s**) flexible armour of interlaced rings or links

mailbox *n* (*pl* **-es**) (US, CANADIAN & AUST) box into which letters and parcels are delivered

mailboxes *n* ▷ **mailbox**

mailed *v* ▷ **mail¹**

mailing *v* ▷ **mail¹**

mails *n* ▷ **mail¹,²** ▶ *v* ▷ **mail²**

mailshot *n* (*pl* **-s**) (BRIT) posting of advertising material to many selected people at once

mailshots *n* ▷ **mailshot**

maim *v* (**-s, -ing, -ed**) cripple or mutilate

maimed *v* ▷ **maim**

maiming *v* ▷ **maim**

maims *v* ▷ **maim**

main *adj* chief or principal ▶ *n* (*pl* **-s**) principal pipe or line carrying water, gas, or electricity

mainframe *n* (*pl* **-s**) ▶ *adj* (COMPUTERS) (denoting) a high-speed general-purpose computer

mainframes *n* ▷ **mainframe**

mainland *n* (*pl* **-s**) stretch of land which forms the main part of a country

mainlands *n* ▷ **mainland**

mainly *adv* for the most part, chiefly

mainmast *n* (*pl* **-s**) chief mast of a ship

mainmasts *n* ▷ **mainmast**

mains *n* ▷ **main**

mainsail *n* (*pl* **-s**) largest sail on a mainmast

mainsails *n* ▷ **mainsail**

mainspring *n* (*pl* **-s**) chief cause or motive

mainsprings *n* ▷ **mainspring**

mainstay *n* (*pl* **-s**) chief support

mainstays *n* ▷ **mainstay**

mainstream *adj* (of) a prevailing cultural trend

maintain *v* (**-s, -ing, -ed**) continue or keep in existence

maintained *v* ▷ **maintain**

maintaining *v* ▷ **maintain**

maintains *v* ▷ **maintain**

maintenance *n* (*pl* **-s**) maintaining

maintenances *n* ▷ **maintenance**

maisonette *n* (*pl* **-s**) (BRIT) flat with more than one floor

maisonettes *n* ▷ **maisonette**

maize *n* (*pl* **-s**) type of corn with spikes of yellow grains

maizes *n* ▷ **maize**

majesty *n* (*pl* **-ties**) stateliness or grandeur > **majestic** *adj* > **majestically** *adv*

majestic *adj* ▷ **majesty**

majestically *adv* ▷ **majesty**

majesties *n* ▷ **majesty**

major *adj* greater in number, quality, or extent ▶ *n* (*pl* **-s**) middle-ranking army officer ▶ *v* (**-s, -ing, -ed**) (*foll. by* **in**) (US, CANADIAN, S AFR, AUST & NZ) do one's principal study in (a particular subject)

majordomo *n* (*pl* **-s**) chief steward of a great household

majordomos *n* ▷ **majordomo**

majored *v* ▷ **major**

majoring *v* ▷ **major**

majorities *n* ▷ **majority**

majority *n* (*pl* **-ties**) greater number

majors *n, v* ▷ **major**
make *v* (**-kes, -king, made**) create, construct, or establish ▶ *n* (*pl* **-s**) brand, type, or style
maker *n* (*pl* **-s**) > **makeweight** *n* (*pl* **-s**) something unimportant added to make up a lack
maker *n* ▷ **make**
makers *n* ▷ **make**
makes *n, v* ▷ **make**
makeshift *adj* serving as a temporary substitute
makeup *n* (*pl* **-s**) cosmetics
makeups *n* ▷ **makeup**
making *v* ▷ **make** ▶ *n* (*pl* **-s**) creation or production
makings *n* ▷ **making**
malachite [mal-a-kite] *n* (*pl* **-s**) green mineral
malachites *n* ▷ **malachite**
maladjusted *adj* (PSYCHOL) unable to meet the demands of society > **maladjustment** *n* (*pl* **-s**)
maladjustment *n* ▷ **maladjusted**
maladjustments *n* ▷ **maladjusted**
maladministration *n* (*pl* **-s**) inefficient or dishonest administration
maladministrations *n* ▷ **maladministration**
maladroit *adj* clumsy or awkward
malady *n* (*pl* **-dies**) disease or illness
maladies *n* ▷ **malady**
malaise [mal-laze] *n* (*pl* **-s**) vague feeling of unease, illness, or depression
malaises *n* ▷ **malaise**
malapropism *n* (*pl* **-s**) comical misuse of a word by confusion with one which sounds similar, e.g. *I am not under the affluence of alcohol*
malapropisms *n* ▷ **malapropism**
malaria *n* (*pl* **-s**) infectious disease caused by the bite of some mosquitoes > **malarial** *adj*
malarias *n* ▷ **malaria**
malarial *adj* ▷ **malaria**
malcontent *n* (*pl* **-s**) discontented person
malcontents *n* ▷ **malcontent**
male *adj* of the sex which can fertilize female reproductive cells ▶ *n* (*pl* **males**) male person or animal
males *n* ▷ **male**
malediction [mal-lid-dik-shun] *n* (*pl* **-s**) curse
maledictions *n* ▷ **malediction**
malefactor [mal-if-act-or] *n* (*pl* **-s**) criminal or wrongdoer
malefactors *n* ▷ **malefactor**
malevolent [mal-lev-a-lent] *adj* wishing evil to others > **malevolently** *adv* > **malevolence** *n* (*pl* **-s**)
malevolence *n* ▷ **malevolent**

malevolences *n* ▷ **malevolent**
malevolently *adv* ▷ **malevolent**
malfeasance [mal-fee-zanss] *n* (*pl* **-s**) misconduct, esp. by a public official
malfeasances *n* ▷ **malfeasance**
malformed *adj* misshapen or deformed
> **malformation** *n* (*pl* **-s**)
malformation *n* ▷ **malformed**
malformations *n* ▷ **malformed**
malfunction *v* (**-s, -ing, -ed**) function imperfectly or fail to function ▶ *n* (*pl* **-s**) defective functioning or failure to function
malfunctioned *v* ▷ **malfunction**
malfunctioning *v* ▷ **malfunction**
malfunctions *v, n* ▷ **malfunction**
malice [mal-iss] *n* (*pl* **-s**) desire to cause harm to others > **malicious** *adj* > **maliciously** *adv*
malices *n* ▷ **malice**
malicious *adj* ▷ **malice**
maliciously *adj* ▷ **malice**
malign [mal-line] *v* (**-s, -ing, -ed**) slander or defame ▶ *adj* evil in influence or effect
> **malignity** *n* (*pl* **-nities**) evil disposition
malignancies *n* ▷ **malignant**
malignancy *n* ▷ **malignant**
malignant [mal-lig-nant] *adj* seeking to harm others > **malignancy** *n* (*pl* **-cies**)
maligned *v* ▷ **malign**
maligning *v* ▷ **malign**
malignities *n* ▷ **malign**
malignity *n* ▷ **malign**
maligns *v* ▷ **malign**
malinger *v* (**-s, -ing, -ed**) feign illness to avoid work > **malingerer** *n* (*pl* **-s**)
malingered *v* ▷ **malinger**
malingerer *n* ▷ **malinger**
malingering *v* ▷ **malinger**
malingerers *n* ▷ **malinger**
malingers *v* ▷ **malinger**
mall [mawl] *n* (*pl* **-s**) street or shopping area closed to vehicles
mallard *n* wild duck
malleable [mal-lee-a-bl] *adj* capable of being hammered or pressed into shape
> **malleability** *n* (*pl* **-ties**)
malleability *n* ▷ **malleable**
malleabilities *n* ▷ **malleable**
mallee *n* (*pl* **-s**) (AUST) low-growing eucalypt in dry regions
mallees *n* ▷ **mallee**
mallet *n* (*pl* **-s**) (wooden) hammer
mallets *n* ▷ **mallet**
mallow *n* (*pl* **-s**) plant with pink or purple flowers
mallows *n* ▷ **mallow**

malls *n* ▷ **mall**
malnutrition *n* (*pl* -**s**) inadequate nutrition
　malnutritions *n* ▷ **malnutrition**
malodorous [mal-**lode**-or-uss] *adj* bad-smelling
malpractice *n* (*pl* -**s**) immoral, illegal, or
　unethical professional conduct
　malpractices *n* ▷ **malpractice**
malt *n* (*pl* -**s**) grain, such as barley, prepared for
　use in making beer or whisky
　malts *n* ▷ **malt**
maltreat *v* (-**s, -ing, -ed**) treat badly
　> **maltreatment** *n* (*pl* -**s**)
　maltreated *v* ▷ **maltreat**
　maltreating *v* ▷ **maltreat**
　maltreatment *n* ▷ **maltreat**
　maltreatments *n* ▷ **maltreat**
　maltreats *v* ▷ **maltreat**
mama *n* (*pl* -**s**) (*Old-fashioned*) mother
　mamas *n* ▷ **mama**
mamba *n* (*pl* -**s**) deadly S African snake
　mambas *n* ▷ **mamba**
mamma *n* (*pl* -**s**) ▷ **mama**
　mammas *n* ▷ **mamma**
mammal *n* (*pl* -**s**) animal of the type that
　suckles its young > **mammalian** *adj*
　mammalian *adj* ▷ **mammal**
　mammals *n* ▷ **mammal**
mammary *adj* of the breasts or milk-
　producing glands
mammon *n* (*pl* -**s**) wealth regarded as a source
　of evil
　mammons *n* ▷ **mammon**
mammoth *n* (*pl* -**s**) extinct elephant-like
　mammal ▶ *adj* colossal
　mammoths *n* ▷ **mammoth**
man *n* (*pl* **men**) adult male ▶ *v* (-**s, -nning,**
　-nned) supply with sufficient people for
　operation or defence > **manhood** *n* (*pl* -**s**)
mana *n* (*pl* -**s**) (NZ) authority, influence
manacle [**man**-a-kl] *n* (*pl* -**s**) handcuff or fetter
　▶ *v* (-**les, -ling, -led**) handcuff or fetter
　manacled *v* ▷ **manacle**
　manacling *v* ▷ **manacle**
　manacles *n, v* ▷ **manacle**
manage *v* (-**ges, -ging, -ged**) succeed in doing
　> **manageable** *adj* > **management** *n* (*pl* -**s**)
　managers collectively
　manageable *adj* ▷ **manage**
　managed *v* ▷ **manage**
　managing *v* ▷ **manage**
　management *n* ▷ **manage**
　managements *n* ▷ **manage**
　manages *v* ▷ **manage**
manager *n* (*pl* -**s**) person in charge of a
　business, institution, actor, sports team, etc.

　> **managerial** *adj*
manageress *n* (*pl* -**es**) woman in charge of a
　business, institution, actor, sports team, etc.
　manageresses *n* ▷ **manager**
　managerial *adj* ▷ **manager**
　managers *n* ▷ **manager**
　manas *n* ▷ **mana**
manatee *n* (*pl* -**s**) large tropical plant-eating
　aquatic mammal
　manatees *n* ▷ **manatee**
mandarin *n* (*pl* -**s**) high-ranking government
　official
　mandarins *n* ▷ **mandarin**
mandate *n* (*pl* -**s**) official or authoritative
　command ▶ *v* (-**tes, -ting, -ted**) give authority
　to
　mandated *v* ▷ **mandate**
　mandates *n, v* ▷ **mandate**
　mandating *v* ▷ **mandate**
mandatory *adj* compulsory
mandible *n* (*pl* -**s**) lower jawbone or jawlike
　part
　mandibles *n* ▷ **mandible**
mandolin *n* (*pl* **s**) musical instrument with
　four pairs of strings
　mandolins *n* ▷ **mandolin**
mandrake *n* (*pl* -**s**) plant with a forked root,
　formerly used as a narcotic
　mandrakes *n* ▷ **mandrake**
mandrel *n* (*pl* -**s**) shaft on which work is held
　in a lathe
　mandrels *n* ▷ **mandrel**
mandrill *n* (*pl* -**s**) large blue-faced baboon
　mandrills *n* ▷ **mandrill**
mane *n* (*pl* -**s**) long hair on the neck of a horse,
　lion, etc.
　manes *n* ▷ **mane**
manful *adj* determined and brave > **manfully**
　adv
　manfully *adv* ▷ **manful**
manganese *n* (*pl* -**s**) (CHEM) brittle greyish-
　white metallic element
　manganeses *n* ▷ **manganese**
mange *n* (*pl* -**s**) skin disease of domestic
　animals
　manges *n* ▷ **mange**
mangelwurzel *n* (*pl* -**s**) variety of beet used as
　cattle food
　mangelwurzels *n* ▷ **mangelwurzel**
manger *n* (*pl* -**s**) eating trough in a stable or
　barn
　mangers *n* ▷ **manger**
mangetout [mawnzh-**too**] *n* (*pl* -**s**) variety of
　pea with an edible pod
　mangetouts *n* ▷ **mangetout**

mangier *adj* ▷ **mangy**
mangiest *adj* ▷ **mangy**
mangle[1] *v* (**-les, -ling, -led**) destroy by crushing and twisting
mangle[2] *n* (*pl* **-s**) machine with rollers for squeezing water from washed clothes ▶ *v* (**-les, -ling, -led**) put through a mangle
mangled *v* ▷ **mangle**[1,2]
mangling *v* ▷ **mangle**[1,2]
mangles *v* ▷ **mangle**[1,2] ▶ *n* ▷ **mangle**[2]
mango *n* (*pl* **-goes, -gos**) tropical fruit with sweet juicy yellow flesh
mangoes *n* ▷ **mango**
mangos *n* ▷ **mango**
mangrove *n* (*pl* **-s**) tropical tree with exposed roots, which grows beside water
mangroves *n* ▷ **mangrove**
mangy *adj* (**-gier, -giest**) having mange
manhandle *v* (**-les, -ling, -led**) treat roughly
manhandled *v* ▷ **manhandle**
manhandling *v* ▷ **manhandle**
manhandles *v* ▷ **manhandle**
manhole *n* (*pl* **-s**) hole with a cover, through which a person can enter a drain or sewer
manholes *n* ▷ **manhole**
manhood *n* ▷ **man**
manhoods *n* ▷ **man**
mania *n* (*pl* **-s**) extreme enthusiasm
> **maniacal** [man-**eye**-a-kl] ▶ *adj*
maniac *n* (*pl* **-s**) mad person
maniacal *adj* ▷ **mania**
maniacs *n* ▷ **mania**
manias *n* ▷ **mania**
manic *adj* affected by mania
manicure *n* (*pl* **-s**) cosmetic care of the fingernails and hands ▶ *v* (**-res, -ring, -red**) care for (the fingernails and hands) in this way > **manicurist** *n* (*pl* **-s**)
manicured *v* ▷ **manicure**
manicures *n, v* ▷ **manicure**
manicuring *v* ▷ **manicure**
manicurist *n* ▷ **manicure**
manicurists *n* ▷ **manicure**
manifest *adj* easily noticed, obvious ▶ *v* (**-s, -ing, -ed**) show plainly ▶ *n* (*pl* **-s**) list of cargo or passengers for customs > **manifestation** *n* (*pl* **-s**)
manifestation *n* ▷ **manifest**
manifestations *n* ▷ **manifest**
manifested *v* ▷ **manifest**
manifesting *v, n* ▷ **manifest**
manifesto *n* (*pl* **-tos, -toes**) declaration of policy as issued by a political party
manifestoes *n* ▷ **manifesto**
manifestos *n* ▷ **manifesto**

manifests *v* ▷ **manifest**
manifold *adj* numerous and varied ▶ *n* (*pl* **-s**) pipe with several outlets, esp. in an internal-combustion engine
manifolds *n* ▷ **manifold**
manikin *n* (*pl* **-s**) little man or dwarf
manikins *n* ▷ **manikin**
manila, manilla *n* (*pl* **-s**) strong brown paper used for envelopes
manilas *n* ▷ **manila**
manillas *n* ▷ **manila**
manipulate *v* (**-tes, -ting, -ted**) handle skilfully > **manipulation** *n* (*pl* **-s**) > **manipulative** *adj* > **manipulator** *n* (*pl* **-s**)
manipulated *v* ▷ **manipulate**
manipulates *v* ▷ **manipulate**
manipulating *v* ▷ **manipulate**
manipulation *n* ▷ **manipulate**
manipulations *n* ▷ **manipulate**
manipulative *adj* ▷ **manipulate**
manipulator *n* ▷ **manipulate**
manipulators *n* ▷ **manipulate**
mankind *n* (*pl* **-s**) human beings collectively
mankinds *n* ▷ **mankind**
manlier *adj* ▷ **manly**
manliest *adj* ▷ **manly**
manliness *n* ▷ **manly**
manlinesses *n* ▷ **manly**
manly *adj* (**-lier, -liest**) (possessing qualities) appropriate to a man > **manliness** *n* (*pl* **-s**)
manna *n* (*pl* **-s**) (BIBLE) miraculous food which sustained the Israelites in the wilderness
mannas *n* ▷ **manna**
manned *v* ▷ **man**
mannequin *n* (*pl* **-s**) woman who models clothes at a fashion show
mannequins *n* ▷ **mannequin**
manner *n* (*pl* **-s**) way a thing happens or is done > **mannered** *adj* affected
mannered *adj* ▷ **manner**
mannerism *n* (*pl* **-s**) person's distinctive habit or trait
mannerisms *n* ▷ **manner**
manners *n* ▷ **manner**
mannikin *n* (*pl* **-s**) ▷ **manikin**
mannikins *n* ▷ **mannikin**
manning *v* ▷ **man**
mannish *adj* (of a woman) like a man
manoeuvre [man-**noo**-ver] *n* (*pl* **-s**) skilful movement military or naval exercises ▶ *v* (**-res, -ring, -red**) manipulate or contrive skilfully or cunningly > **manoeuvrable** *adj*
manoeuvred *v* ▷ **manoeuvre**
manoeuvres *n, v* ▷ **manoeuvre**
manoeuvring *v* ▷ **manoeuvre**

manor n (pl -s) (BRIT) large country house and its lands > **manorial** adj
  manorial adj ▷ **manor**
  manors n ▷ **manor**
manpower n (pl -s) available number of workers
  manpowers n ▷ **manpower**
manqué [mong-kay] adj would-be
  mans v ▷ **man**
manse n (pl -s) house provided for a minister in some religious denominations
  manses n ▷ **manse**
manservant n (pl **menservants**) male servant, esp. a valet
mansion n (pl -s) large house
  mansions n ▷ **mansion**
manslaughter n (pl -s) unlawful but unintentional killing of a person
  manslaughters n ▷ **manslaughter**
mantel n (pl -s) structure round a fireplace
mantelpiece n (pl -es) shelf above a fireplace
  mantelpieces n ▷ **mantelpiece**
  mantels n ▷ **mantel**
mantilla n (pl -s) (in Spain) a lace scarf covering a woman's head and shoulders
  mantillas n ▷ **mantilla**
mantis n (pl -ses, -tes) carnivorous insect like a grasshopper
  mantes n ▷ **mantis**
  mantises n ▷ **mantis**
mantle n (pl -s) loose cloak
  mantles n ▷ **mantle**
mantra n (pl -s) (HINDUISM, BUDDHISM) any sacred word or syllable used as an object of concentration
  mantras n ▷ **mantra**
manual adj of or done with the hands ▶ n (pl -s) handbook > **manually** adv
  manually adv ▷ **manual**
  manuals n ▷ **manual**
manufacture v (-res, -ring, -red) process or make (goods) on a large scale using machinery ▶ n (pl -s) process of manufacturing goods
  manufactured v ▷ **manufacture**
manufacturer n (pl -s) company that manufactures goods
  manufacturers n ▷ **manufacturer**
  manufactures v, n ▷ **manufacture**
  manufacturing v ▷ **manufacture**
manure n (pl -s) animal excrement used as a fertilizer
  manures n ▷ **manure**
manuscript n (pl -s) book or document, orig. one written by hand

manuscripts n ▷ **manuscript**
many adj (**more, most**) numerous ▶ n large number
map n (pl -s) representation of the earth's surface or some part of it, showing geographical features ▶ v (-s, -pping, -pped) make a map of
maple n (pl -s) tree with broad leaves, a variety of which (**sugar maple**) yields sugar
  maples n ▷ **maple**
  mapped v ▷ **map**
  mapping v ▷ **map**
  maps n, v ▷ **map**
mar v (-s, -rring, -rred) spoil or impair
marabou n (pl -s) large black-and-white African stork
  marabous n ▷ **marabou**
maraca [mar-rak-a] n (pl -s) shaken percussion instrument made from a gourd containing dried seeds etc.
  maracas n ▷ **maraca**
marae n (pl -s) (NZ) enclosed space in front of a Maori meeting house
  maraes n ▷ **marae**
marathon n (pl -s) long-distance race of 26 miles 385 yards (42.195 kilometres)
  marathons n ▷ **marathon**
  marauder n ▷ **marauding**
  marauders n ▷ **marauder**
marauding adj wandering or raiding in search of plunder > **marauder** n (pl -s)
marble n (pl -s) kind of limestone with a mottled appearance, which can be highly polished > **marbled** adj having a mottled appearance like marble
  marbled n ▷ **marble**
  marbles n ▷ **marble**
march¹ v (-es, -ing, -ed) walk with a military step ▶ n (pl -es) action of marching > **marcher** n (pl -s)
march² n (pl -s) border or frontier
  marched v ▷ **march¹**
  marches v ▷ **march¹** ▶ n ▷ **march¹,²**
  marching v ▷ **march¹**
marchioness [marsh-on-ness] n (pl -es) woman holding the rank of marquis
  marchionesses n ▷ **marchioness**
mare n (pl -s) female horse or zebra
  mares n ▷ **mare**
margarine n (pl -s) butter substitute made from animal or vegetable fats
  margarines n ▷ **margarine**
marge n (pl -s) (Informal) margarine
  marges n ▷ **marge**
margin n (pl -s) edge or border > **marginal** adj

insignificant, unimportant > **marginally** adv
marginal adj ▷ **margin**
marginalize v (**-zes, -zing, -zed**) make or treat as insignificant
marginalized v ▷ **marginalize**
marginalizes v ▷ **marginalize**
marginalizing v ▷ **marginalize**
margins n ▷ **margin**
marguerite n (pl **-s**) large daisy
marguerites n ▷ **marguerite**
marigold n (pl **-s**) plant with yellow or orange flowers
marigolds n ▷ **marigold**
marijuana [mar-ree-**wah**-na] n (pl **-s**) dried flowers and leaves of the cannabis plant, used as a drug, esp. in cigarettes
marijuanas n ▷ **marijuana**
marina n (pl **-s**) harbour for yachts and other pleasure boats
marinas n ▷ **marina**
marinade n (pl **-s**) seasoned liquid in which fish or meat is soaked before cooking ▶ v (**-des, -ding, -ded**) ▷ **marinate**
marinaded v ▷ **marinade**
marinades n, v ▷ **marinade**
marinading v ▷ **marinade**
marinate v (**-tes, -ting, -ted**) soak in marinade
marinated v ▷ **marinate**
marinates v ▷ **marinate**
marinating v ▷ **marinate**
marine adj of the sea or shipping ▶ n (pl **-s**) (esp. in Britain and the US) soldier trained for land and sea combat
mariner n (pl **-s**) sailor
mariners n ▷ **mariner**
marines n ▷ **marine**
marionette n (pl **-s**) puppet worked with strings
marionettes n ▷ **marionette**
marital adj relating to marriage
maritime adj relating to shipping
marjoram n (pl **-s**) aromatic herb used for seasoning food and in salads
marjorams n ▷ **marjoram**
mark[1] n (pl **-s**) line, dot, scar, etc. visible on a surface ▶ v (**-s, -ing, -ed**) make a mark on > **marked** adj noticeable > **markedly** adv > **marker** n (pl **-s**)
mark[2] n ▷ **Deutschmark**
marked v, adj ▷ **mark**[1]
markedly adv ▷ **mark**[1]
marker n ▷ **mark**[1]
markers n ▷ **mark**
marking v ▷ **mark**[1]
marks n ▷ **mark**[1,2] ▶ v ▷ **mark**[1]

market n (pl **-s**) assembly or place for buying and selling ▶ v (**-s, -ing, -ed**) offer or produce for sale > **marketable** adj
marketable adj ▷ **market**
marketing n (pl **-s**) part of a business that controls the way that goods or services are sold
marketings n ▷ **marketing**
marketplace n (pl **-s**) market
marketplaces n ▷ **marketplace**
markets n, v ▷ **market**
marksman n (pl **-men**) person skilled at shooting > **marksmanship** n (pl **-s**)
marksmanship n ▷ **marksman**
marksmanships n ▷ **marksman**
marksmen n ▷ **marksman**
marl n (pl **-s**) soil formed of clay and lime, used as fertilizer
marls n ▷ **marl**
marlin n large food and game fish of warm and tropical seas, with a very long upper jaw
marlinespike, marlinspike n (pl **-s**) pointed hook used to separate strands of rope
marlinespikes n ▷ **marlinespike**
marlinspikes n ▷ **marlinspike**
marmalade n (pl **-s**) jam made from citrus fruits
marmalades n ▷ **marmalade**
marmoreal adj of or like marble
marmoset n (pl **-s**) small bushy-tailed monkey
marmosets n ▷ **marmoset**
marmot n (pl **-s**) burrowing rodent
marmots n ▷ **marmot**
maroon[1] adj reddish-purple
maroon[2] v (**-s, -ing, -ed**) abandon ashore, esp. on an island
marooned v ▷ **maroon**
marooning v ▷ **maroon**
maroons v ▷ **maroon**
marquee n (pl **-s**) large tent used for a party or exhibition
marquees n ▷ **marquee**
marquess [mar-kwiss] n (pl **-es**) (BRIT) nobleman of the rank below a duke
marquesses n ▷ **marquess**
marquetry n (pl **-ries**) ornamental inlaid work of wood
marquetries n ▷ **marquetry**
marquis n (pl **-es**) (in some European countries) nobleman of the rank above a count
marquises n ▷ **marquis**
marred v ▷ **mar**
marriage n (pl **-s**) state of being married > **marriageable** adj

marriageable *adj* ▷ **marriage**
marriages *n* ▷ **marriage**
married *v* ▷ **marry**
marries *v* ▷ **marry**
marring *v* ▷ **mar**
marrow *n* (*pl* -s) fatty substance inside bones
marrows *n* ▷ **marrow**
marry *v* (-ries, -ing, -ried) take as a husband or wife
marrying *v* ▷ **marry**
mars *v* ▷ **mar**
marsala [mar-**sah**-la] *n* (*pl* -s) dark sweet wine
marsh *n* (*pl* -es) low-lying wet land > **marshy** *adj* (-shier, -shiest)
marshal *n* (*pl* -s) officer of the highest rank ▶ *v* (-s, -shalling, -shalled) arrange in order
marshalled *v* ▷ **marshal**
marshalling *v* ▷ **marshal**
marshals *n*, *v* ▷ **marshal**
marshes *n* ▷ **marsh**
marshier *adj* ▷ **marsh**
marshiest *adj* ▷ **marsh**
marshmallow *n* (*pl* -s) spongy pink or white sweet
marshmallows *n* ▷ **marshmallow**
marshy *n* ▷ **marsh**
marsupial [mar-**soop**-ee-al] *n* (*pl* -s) animal that carries its young in a pouch, such as a kangaroo
marsupials *n* ▷ **marsupial**
mart *n* (*pl* -s) market
marts *n* ▷ **mart**
marten *n* (*pl* -s) weasel-like animal
martens *n* ▷ **marten**
martial *adj* of war, warlike
martian [**marsh**-an] *adj* of Mars ▶ *n* (*pl* -s) supposed inhabitant of Mars
martians *n* ▷ **martian**
martin *n* (*pl* -s) bird with a slightly forked tail
martins *n* ▷ **martin**
martinet *n* (*pl* -s) person who maintains strict discipline
martinets *n* ▷ **martinet**
martini *n* (*pl* -s) cocktail of vermouth and gin
martinis *n* ▷ **martini**
martyr *n* (*pl* -s) person who dies or suffers for his or her beliefs ▶ *v* (-s, -ing, -ed) make a martyr of > **martyrdom** *n* (*pl* -s)
martyrdom *n* ▷ **martyr**
martyrdoms *n* ▷ **martyr**
martyred *v* ▷ **martyr**
martyring *v* ▷ **martyr**
martyrs *n*, *v* ▷ **martyr**
marvel *v* (-s, -velling, -velled) be filled with wonder ▶ *n* wonderful thing

marvelled *v* ▷ **marvel**
marvelling *v* ▷ **marvel**
marvellous *adj* amazing
marvels *v* ▷ **marvel**
marzipan *n* (*pl* -s) paste of ground almonds, sugar, and egg whites
marzipans *n* ▷ **marzipan**
mascara *n* (*pl* -s) cosmetic for darkening the eyelashes
mascaras *n* ▷ **mascara**
mascot *n* (*pl* -s) person, animal, or thing supposed to bring good luck
mascots *n* ▷ **mascot**
masculine *adj* relating to males > **masculinity** *n* (*pl* -ties)
masculinities *n* ▷ **masculine**
masculinity *n* ▷ **masculine**
mash *n* (*pl* -es) (*Informal*) mashed potatoes ▶ *v* (-es, -ing, -ed) crush into a soft mass
mashed *v* ▷ **mash**
mashes *n*, *v* ▷ **mash**
mashing *v* ▷ **mash**
mask *n* (*pl* -s) covering for the face, as a disguise or protection ▶ *v* (-s, -ing, -ed) cover with a mask
masked *v* ▷ **mask**
masking *v* ▷ **mask**
masks *n*, *v* ▷ **mask**
masochism [**mass**-oh-kiz-zum] *n* (*pl* -s) condition in which (sexual) pleasure is obtained from feeling pain or from being humiliated > **masochist** *n* (*pl* -s) > **masochistic** *adj*
masochist *n* ▷ **masochism**
masochistic *n* ▷ **masochism**
masochists *n* ▷ **masochism**
mason *n* (*pl* -s) person who works with stone
masonic *adj* of Freemasonry
masonry *n* (*pl* -ries) stonework
masonries *n* (*pl* -ries) stonework
masons *n* ▷ **mason**
masque [**mask**] *n* (*pl* -s) (HIST) 16th–17th-century form of dramatic entertainment
masques *n* ▷ **masque**
masquerade [mask-er-**aid**] *n* (*pl* -s) deceptive show or pretence ▶ *v* (-des, -ding, -ded) pretend to be someone or something else
masqueraded *v* ▷ **masquerade**
masquerades *n*, *v* ▷ **masquerade**
masquerading *v* ▷ **masquerade**
mass *n* (*pl* -es) coherent body of matter ▶ *adj* large-scale ▶ *v* (-es, -ing, -ed) form into a mass
massacre [**mass**-a-ker] *n* (*pl* -s) indiscriminate killing of large numbers of people ▶ *v* (-res, -ring, -red) kill in large numbers

massacred v ▷ massacre
massacres n, v ▷ massacre
massacring v ▷ massacre
massage [mass-ahzh] n (pl -s) rubbing and kneading of parts of the body to reduce pain or stiffness ▶ v (-ges, -ging, -ged) give a massage to
massaged v ▷ massage
massages n, v ▷ massage
massaging v ▷ massage
massed v ▷ mass
masses n, v ▷ mass
masseur, fem **masseuse** n (pl -s) person who gives massages
masseurs n ▷ masseur
masseuse n ▷ masseuses
massing v ▷ mass
massive adj large and heavy
massif [mass-seef] n (pl -s) connected group of mountains
massifs n ▷ massif
mast[1] n (pl -s) tall pole for supporting something, esp. a ship's sails
mast[2] n (pl -s) fruit of the beech, oak, etc., used as pig fodder
masts n ▷ mast[1,2]
mastectomies n ▷ mastectomy
mastectomy [mass-**tek**-tom-ee] n (pl -mies) surgical removal of a breast
master n (pl -s) person in control, such as an employer or an owner of slaves or animals ▶ adj overall or controlling ▶ v (-s, -ing, -ed) acquire knowledge of or skill in
mastered v ▷ master
masterful adj domineering
masteries n ▷ mastery
mastering v ▷ master
masterly adj showing great skill
mastermind v plan and direct (a complex task) n person who plans and directs a complex task
masterpiece n outstanding work of art
masters n, v ▷ master
mastery n (pl -ries) expertise
mastic n (pl -s) gum obtained from certain trees
mastics n ▷ mastic
masticate v (-tes, -ting, -ted) chew > **mastication** n (pl -s)
masticated v ▷ masticate
masticates v ▷ masticate
masticating v ▷ masticate
mastication n ▷ masticate
mastications n ▷ masticate
mastiff n (pl -s) large dog

mastiffs n ▷ mastiff
mastitis n (pl -tises) inflammation of a breast or udder
mastitises n ▷ mastitis
mastodon n (pl -s) extinct elephant-like mammal
mastodons n ▷ mastodon
mastoid n (pl -s) projection of the bone behind the ear
mastoids n ▷ mastoid
masturbate v (-tes, -ting, -ted) fondle the genitals (of) > **masturbation** n (pl -s)
masturbated v ▷ masturbate
masturbates v ▷ masturbate
masturbating v ▷ masturbate
masturbation n ▷ masturbate
masturbations n ▷ masturbate
mat n (pl -s) piece of fabric used as a floor covering or to protect a surface ▶ v (-s, -tting, -tted) tangle or become tangled into a dense mass
matador n (pl -s) man who kills the bull in bullfights
matadors n ▷ matador
match[1] n (pl -es) contest in a game or sport ▶ v (-es, -ing, -ed) be exactly like, equal to, or in harmony with
match[2] n small stick with a tip which ignites when scraped on a rough surface > **matchbox** n (pl -es)
matchbox n ▷ match[2]
matchboxes n ▷ match[2]
matched v ▷ match[1]
matches v ▷ match[1] ▶ n ▷ match[1,2]
matching v ▷ match[1]
matchless adj unequalled
matchmaker n (pl -s) person who schemes to bring about a marriage > **matchmaking** n (pl -s) adj
matchmakers n ▷ matchmaker
matchmaking n ▷ matchmaker
matchmakings n ▷ matchmaker
matchstick n (pl -s) wooden part of a match ▶ adj (of drawn figures) thin and straight
matchsticks n ▷ matchstick
matchwood n (pl -s) small splinters
matchwoods n ▷ matchwood
mate[1] n (pl -s) (Informal) friend ▶ v (-tes, -ting, -ted) pair (animals) or (of animals) be paired for reproduction
mate[2] n (pl -s) checkmate ▶ v (-tes, -ting, -ted) (CHESS) checkmate
mated v ▷ mate[1,2]
mates n, v ▷ mate[1,2]
mating v ▷ mate[1,2]

material *n* (*pl* -**s**) substance of which a thing is made ▶ *adj* of matter or substance > **materialist** *adj*, *n* > **materialistic** *adj*
materialism *n* (*pl* -**s**) excessive interest in or desire for money and possessions
  materialisms *n* ▷ materialism
  materialist *adj*, *n* (*pl* -**s**) ▷ material
  materialistic *adj* ▷ material
  materialists *n* ▷ material
materialize *v* (-**zes**, -**zing**, -**zed**) actually happen > **materialization** *n* (*pl* -**s**)
  materialization *n* ▷ materialize
  materializations *n* ▷ materialize
  materialized *v* ▷ materialize
  materializes *v* ▷ materialize
  materializing *v* ▷ materialize
materially *adv* considerably
  materials *n* ▷ material
maternal *adj* of a mother ▶ *adj* of or for pregnant women
  maternities *n* ▷ maternity
maternity *n* (*pl* -**ties**) motherhood
matey *adj* (-**tier**, -**tiest**) (BRIT) (*Informal*) friendly or intimate
mathematics *n* science of number, quantity, shape, and space > **mathematical** *adj* > **mathematically** *adv* > **mathematician** *n* (*pl* -**s**)
  mathematical *adj* ▷ mathematics
  mathematically *adv* ▷ mathematics
  mathematician *n* ▷ mathematics
  mathematicians *n* ▷ mathematics
maths *n* (*Informal*) mathematics
  matier *adj* ▷ matey
  matiest *adj* ▷ matey
matilda *n* (*pl* -**s**) (AUST HIST) swagman's bundle of belongings
  matildas *n* ▷ matilda
matinée [mat-in-nay] *n* (*pl* -**s**) afternoon performance in a theatre or cinema
  matinées *n* ▷ matinée
matins *pl n* early morning service in various Christian Churches
matriarch [mate-ree-ark] *n* (*pl* -**s**) female head of a tribe or family > **matriarchal** *adj*
  matriarchal *n* ▷ matriarch
  matriarchies *n* ▷ matriarchy
  matriarchs *n* ▷ matriarch
matriarchy *n* (*pl* -**chies**) society governed by a female, in which descent is traced through the female line
  matrices *n* ▷ matrix
matricide *n* (*pl* -**s**) crime of killing one's mother
  matricides *n* ▷ matricide
matriculate *v* (-**tes**, -**ting**, -**ted**) enrol or

be enrolled in a college or university
  > **matriculation** *n* (*pl* -**s**)
  matriculated *v* ▷ matriculate
  matriculates *v* ▷ matriculate
  matriculating *v* ▷ matriculate
  matriculation *n* ▷ matriculate
  matriculations *n* ▷ matriculate
  matrimonial *adj* ▷ matrimony
  matrimonies *n* ▷ matrimony
matrimony *n* (*pl* -**nies**) marriage
  > **matrimonial** *adj*
matrix [may-trix] *n* (*pl* -**trices**) substance or situation in which something originates, takes form, or is enclosed
matron *n* (*pl* -**s**) staid or dignified married woman > **matronly** *adj*
  matrons *n* ▷ matron
  mats *n*, *v* ▷ mat
matt *adj* dull, not shiny
  matted *v* ▷ mat
matter *n* (*pl* -**s**) substance of which something is made ▶ *v* (-**s**, -**ing**, -**ed**) be of importance
  mattered *v* ▷ matter
  mattering *v* ▷ matter
  matters *n*, *v* ▷ matter
  matting *v* ▷ mat
mattock *n* (*pl* -**s**) large pick with one of its blade ends flattened for loosening soil
  mattocks *n* ▷ mattock
mattress *n* (*pl* -**es**) large stuffed flat case, often with springs, used on or as a bed
  mattresses *n* ▷ mattress
mature *adj* fully developed or grown-up ▶ *v* (-**res**, -**ring**, -**red**) make or become mature > **maturation** *n* (*pl* -**s**)
  maturation *n* ▷ mature
  maturations *n* ▷ mature
  matured *v* ▷ mature
  matures *v* ▷ mature
  maturing *v* ▷ mature
  maturities *n* ▷ maturity
maturity *n* (*pl* -**ties**) state of being mature
maudlin *adj* foolishly or tearfully sentimental
maul *v* (-**s**, -**ing**, -**ed**) handle roughly
  mauled *v* ▷ maul
  mauling *v* ▷ maul
  mauls *v* ▷ maul
maunder *v* (-**s**, -**ing**, -**ed**) talk or act aimlessly or idly
  maundered *v* ▷ maunder
  maundering *v* ▷ maunder
  maunders *v* ▷ maunder
mausoleum [maw-so-lee-um] *n* (*pl* -**s**) stately tomb
  mausoleums *n* ▷ mausoleum

mauve adj (-r, -est) pale purple
  mauver adj ▷ **mauve**
  mauvest adj ▷ **mauve**
maverick n (pl -s) ▶ adj independent and unorthodox (person)
  mavericks n ▷ **maverick**
maw n (pl -s) animal's mouth, throat, or stomach
  maws n ▷ **maw**
mawkish adj foolishly sentimental
  max n (maxes). Max is a short form of **maximum**. This is a useful word, particularly if you find yourself with an X toward the end of the game, with limited opportunity to play it. Max scores 12 points.
maxim n (pl -s) general truth or principle
  maxima n ▷ **maximum**
  maximal adj ▷ **maxim**
  maxims n ▷ **maxim**
maximum adj, n (pl -s, -ma) greatest possible (amount or number) > **maximal** adj
maximize v (-zes, -zing, -zed) increase to a maximum
  maximized v ▷ **maximize**
  maximizes v ▷ **maximize**
  maximizing v ▷ **maximize**
  maximums n ▷ **maximum**
may¹ v (past tense **might**) used as an auxiliary to express possibility, permission, opportunity, etc.
  may² n (pl -s) ▷ **hawthorn**
  mays n ▷ **may²**
maybe adv perhaps, possibly
mayday n (pl -s) international radio distress signal
  maydays n ▷ **mayday**
  mayflies n ▷ **mayfly**
mayfly n (pl -lies) short-lived aquatic insect
mayhem n (pl -s) violent destruction or confusion
  mayhems n ▷ **mayhem**
mayonnaise n (pl -s) creamy sauce of egg yolks, oil, and vinegar
  mayonnaises n ▷ **mayonnaise**
mayor n (pl -s) head of a municipality
  mayoralties n ▷ **mayoralty**
  mayoralty n (pl -ies) (term of) office of a mayor
mayoress n (pl -es) mayor's wife
  mayoresses n ▷ **mayoress**
  mayors n ▷ **mayor**
maypole n (pl -s) pole set up for dancing round on the first day of May to celebrate spring
  maypoles n ▷ **maypole**
maze n (pl -s) complex network of paths or lines designed to puzzle
  mazes n ▷ **maze**
mazurka n (pl -s) lively Polish dance
  mazurkas n ▷ **mazurka**
me pron ▷ **I**
mead n (pl -s) alcoholic drink made from honey
  meads n ▷ **mead**
meadow n (pl -s) piece of grassland
  meadows n ▷ **meadow**
meadowsweet n (pl -s) plant with dense heads of small fragrant flowers
  meadowseets n ▷ **meadowsweet**
meagre adj scanty or insufficient
meal¹ n (pl -s) occasion when food is served and eaten
meal² n (pl -s) grain ground to powder > **mealy** -lier, -liest) ▶ adj
mealie n (pl -s) (S AFR) maize
  mealier adj ▷ **meal²**
  mealies n ▷ **mealie**
  mealiest adj ▷ **meal²**
  meals n ▷ **meal¹,²**
  mealy adj ▷ **meal²**
mealymouthed adj not outspoken enough
mean¹ v (-s, -ing, meant) intend to convey or express > **meaningful** adj > **meaningless** adj
mean² adj (-er, -est) miserly, ungenerous, or petty > **meanly** adv > **meanness** n (pl -es)
mean³ n (pl -s) middle point between two extremes ▶ pl method by which something is done ▶ adj intermediate in size or quantity
  meaner adj ▷ **mean²**
  meanest adj ▷ **mean²**
meaning n (pl -s) sense, significance
  meaningful adj ▷ **mean¹**
  meaningless adj ▷ **mean¹**
  meanings n ▷ **meaning**
  meanly adv ▷ **mean²**
  meanness n ▷ **mean²**
  meannesses n ▷ **mean²**
  means v ▷ **mean¹** ▶ n ▷ **mean³**
meander [mee-and-er] v (-s, -ing, -ed) follow a winding course ▶ n (pl -s) winding course
  meandered v ▷ **meander**
  meandering v ▷ **meander**
  meanders v, n ▷ **meander**
meantime n (pl -s) intervening period ▶ adv meanwhile
  meantimes n ▷ **meantime**
meanwhile adv during the intervening period
measles n infectious disease producing red spots
measly adj (Informal) meagre
measure n (pl -s) size or quantity ▶ v (-res, -ring, -red) determine the size or quantity of

> **measurable** *adj*
measurable *adj* ▷ **measure**
measured *adj* slow and steady ▶ *v* ▷ **measure**
measurement *n* (*pl* -s) measuring
measures *n*, *v* ▷ **measure**
measuring *v* ▷ **measure**
meat *n* (*pl* -s) animal flesh as food
meatier *adj* ▷ **meaty**
meatiest *adj* ▷ **meaty**
meats *n* ▷ **meat**
meaty *adj* (-tier, -tiest) (tasting) of or like meat
mechanic *n* (*pl* -s) person skilled in repairing
or operating machinery
mechanical *adj* of or done by machines
> **mechanically** *adv*
mechanically *adv* ▷ **mechanical**
mechanics *n* scientific study of motion and
force ▷ **mechanic**
mechanism *n* (*pl* -s) way a machine works
mechanisms *n* ▷ **mechanism**
mechanization *n* ▷ **mechanize**
mechanizations *n* ▷ **mechanism**
mechanize *v* (-zes, -zing, -zed) equip with
machinery > **mechanization** *n* (*pl* -s)
mechanized *v* ▷ **mechanize**
mechanizes *v* ▷ **mechanize**
mechanizing *v* ▷ **mechanize**
medal *n* (*pl* -s) piece of metal with an
inscription etc., given as a reward or
memento
medallion *n* (*pl* -s) disc-shaped ornament
worn on a chain round the neck
medallions *n* ▷ **medallion**
medallist *n* (*pl* -s) winner of a medal
medallists *n* ▷ **medallist**
medals *n* ▷ **medal**
meddle *v* (-les, -ling, -led) interfere annoyingly
> **meddler** *n* (*pl* -s) > **meddlesome** *adj*
meddled *v* ▷ **meddle**
meddler *n* ▷ **meddle**
meddlers *n* ▷ **meddle**
meddles *v* ▷ **meddle**
meddlesome *adj* ▷ **meddle**
meddling *v* ▷ **meddle**
media *n* (*pl* -iae) ▷ **medium** the mass media
collectively
mediae *n* ▷ **media**
mediaeval *adj* ▷ **medieval**
medial *adj* of or in the middle
median *adj*, *n* (*pl* -s) middle (point or line)
medians *n* ▷ **median**
mediate *v* (-tes, -ting, -ted) intervene
in a dispute to bring about agreement
> **mediation** *n* (*pl* -s) > **mediator** *n* (*pl* -s)
mediated *v* ▷ **mediate**

mediates *v* ▷ **mediate**
mediating *v* ▷ **mediate**
mediation *n* ▷ **mediate**
mediations *n* ▷ **mediate**
mediator *n* ▷ **mediate**
mediators *n* ▷ **mediate**
medic *n* (*pl* -s) (*Informal*) doctor or medical
student
medics *n* ▷ **medic**
medical *adj* of the science of medicine
▶ *n* (*pl* -s) (*Informal*) medical examination
> **medically** *adv*
medically *adv* ▷ **medical**
medicals *n* ▷ **medical**
medicate *v* (-tes, -ting, -ted) treat with a
medicinal substance
medicated *v* ▷ **medicate**
medicates *v* ▷ **medicate**
medicating *v* ▷ **medicate**
medication *n* (*pl* -s) (treatment with) a
medicinal substance
medications *n* ▷ **medication**
medicine *n* (*pl* -s) substance used to treat
disease
medicinal [med-**diss**-in-al] *adj* having
therapeutic properties
medicines *n* ▷ **medicine**
medieval [med-ee-**eve**-al] *adj* of the Middle
Ages
mediocre [mee-dee-**oak**-er] *adj* average in
quality > **mediocrity** [mee-dee-**ok**-rit-ee] ▶ *n*
(*pl* -ties)
mediocrities *n* ▷ **mediocre**
mediocrity *n* ▷ **mediocre**
meditate *v* (-tes, -ting, -ted) reflect deeply,
esp. on spiritual matters > **meditation** *n*
(*pl* -s) > **meditative** *adj* > **meditatively** *adv*
> **meditator** *n* (*pl* -s)
meditated *v* ▷ **meditate**
meditates *v* ▷ **meditate**
meditating *v* ▷ **meditate**
meditation *n* ▷ **meditate**
meditations *n* ▷ **meditate**
meditative *adj* ▷ **meditate**
meditatively *adv* ▷ **meditate**
meditator *n* ▷ **meditate**
meditators *n* ▷ **meditate**
medium *adj* midway between extremes,
average ▶ *n* (*pl* -dia, -diums) middle state,
degree, or condition
mediums *n* ▷ **medium**
medlar *n* (*pl* -s) apple-like fruit of a small tree,
eaten when it begins to decay
medlars *n* ▷ **medlar**
medley *n* (*pl* -s) miscellaneous mixture

medleys n ▷ medley
medulla [mid-**dull**-la] n (pl -**las**, -**lae**) marrow, pith, or inner tissue
  medullae n ▷ medulla
  medullas n ▷ medulla
meek adj (-**er**, -**est**) submissive or humble > **meekly** adv > **meekness** n (pl -**es**)
  meeker adj ▷ meek
  meekest adj ▷ meek
  meekly adv ▷ meek
  meekness n ▷ meek
  meeknesses n ▷ meek
meerkat n (pl -**s**) S African mongoose
  meerkats n ▷ meerkat
meerschaum [**meer**-shum] n (pl -**s**) white substance like clay
  meerschaums n ▷ meerschaum
meet[1] v (-**s**, **meeting**, **met**) come together (with) ▶ n (pl -**s**) meeting, esp. a sports meeting
meet[2] adj (-**er**, -**est**) (Obs) fit or suitable
  meeter adj ▷ meet[2]
  meetest adj ▷ meet[2]
meeting n (pl -**s**) coming together ▶ v ▷ meet[1]
  meets v, n ▷ meek[1]
megabyte n (pl -**s**) (COMPUTERS) 2^{20} or 1 048 576 bytes
  megabytes n ▷ megabyte
megahertz n one million hertz
megalith n (pl -**s**) great stone, esp. as part of a prehistoric monument > **megalithic** adj
  megalithic adj ▷ megalith
  megaliths n ▷ megalith
megalomania n (pl -**s**) craving for or mental delusions of power > **megalomaniac** adj, n (pl -**s**)
  megalomaniac n ▷ megalomania
  megalomaniacs n ▷ megalomania
  megalomanias n ▷ megalomania
megaphone n (pl -**s**) cone-shaped instrument used to amplify the voice
  megaphones n ▷ megaphone
megapode n (pl -**s**) bird of Australia, New Guinea, and adjacent islands
  megapodes n ▷ megapode
megaton n (pl -**s**) explosive power equal to that of one million tons of TNT
  megatons n ▷ megaton
melaleuca [mel-a-**loo**-ka] n (pl -**s**) Australian shrub or tree with a white trunk and black branches
  melaleucas n ▷ melaleuca
melancholia [mel-an-**kole**-lee-a] n (pl -**s**) state of depression
  melancholias n ▷ melancholia

melancholic adj ▷ melancholy
melancholies n ▷ melancholy
melancholy [**mel**-an-kol-lee] n (pl -**lies**) sadness or gloom ▶ adj sad or gloomy > **melancholic** adj, n (pl -**s**)
melange [may-**lahnzh**] n (pl -**s**) mixture
  melanges n ▷ melange
melanin n (pl -**s**) dark pigment found in the hair, skin, and eyes of humans and animals
  melanins n ▷ melanin
mêlée [**mel**-lay] n (pl -**s**) noisy confused fight or crowd
  mêlées n ▷ mêlée
mellifluous [mel-**lif**-flew-uss] adj (of sound) smooth and sweet
mellow adj soft, not harsh ▶ v (-**s**, -**ing**, -**ed**) make or become mellow
  mellowed v ▷ mellow
  mellowing v ▷ mellow
  mellows v ▷ mellow
melodic [mel-**lod**-ik] adj of melody
melodious [mel-**lode**-ee-uss] adj pleasing to the ear
melodrama n (pl -**s**) play full of extravagant action and emotion > **melodramatic** adj
  melodramas n ▷ melodrama
  melodramatic adj ▷ melodrama
melody n (pl -**dies**) series of musical notes which make a tune
melon n (pl -**s**) large round juicy fruit with a hard rind
  melons n ▷ melon
melt v (-**s**, -**ing**, -**ed**) (cause to) become liquid by heat
meltdown n (pl -**s**) (in a nuclear reactor) melting of the fuel rods, with the possible release of radiation
  meltdowns n ▷ meltdown
  melted v ▷ melt
  melting v ▷ melt
  melts v ▷ melt
member n (pl -**s**) individual making up a body or society > **membership** n (pl -**s**)
  members n ▷ member
  membership n ▷ member
  memberships n ▷ member
membrane n (pl -**s**) thin flexible tissue in a plant or animal body > **membranous** adj
  membranes n ▷ membrane
  membranous adj ▷ membrane
memento n (pl -**tos**, -**toes**) thing serving to remind, souvenir
  mementoes n ▷ memento
  mementos n ▷ memento
memo n (pl -**s**) ▷ memorandum

memos *n* ▷ memo
memoir [mem-wahr] *n* (*pl* -s) biography or historical account based on personal knowledge ▶ *pl* collection of these
memoirs *n* ▷ memoir
memorable *adj* worth remembering, noteworthy > **memorably** *adv*
memorably *adv* ▷ memorable
memoranda *n* ▷ memorandum
memorandum *n* (*pl* -dums, -da) written record or communication within a business
memorandums *n* ▷ memorandum
memorial *n* (*pl* -s) something serving to commemorate a person or thing ▶ *adj* serving as a memorial
memorials *n* ▷ memorandum
memorize *v* (-zes, -zing, -zed) commit to memory
memorized *v* ▷ memorize
memorizes *v* ▷ memorize
memorizing *v* ▷ memorize
memory *n* (*pl* -ries) ability to remember
men *n* ▷ man
menace *n* (*pl* -s) threat ▶ *v* (-ces, -cing, -ced) threaten, endanger > **menacing** *adj*
menaced *v* ▷ menace
menaces *n*, *v* ▷ menace
menacing *v*, *adj* ▷ menace
ménage [may-nahzh] *n* (*pl* -s) household
ménages *n* ▷ ménage
menagerie [min-naj-er-ee] *n* (*pl* -s) collection of wild animals for exhibition
menageries *n* ▷ menagerie
mend *v* (-s, -ing, -ed) repair or patch ▶ *n* (*pl* -s) mended area
mendacious *adj* ▷ mendacity
mendacities *n* ▷ mendacity
mendacity *n* (*pl* -ties) (tendency to) untruthfulness > **mendacious** *adj*
mended *v* ▷ mend
mendicant *adj* begging ▶ *n* (*pl* -s) beggar
mendicants *n* ▷ mendicant
mending *v* ▷ mend
mends *v*, *n* ▷ mend
menhir [men-hear] *n* (*pl* -s) single upright prehistoric stone
menhirs *n* ▷ menhir
menial [mean-nee-al] *adj* involving boring work of low status ▶ *n* (*pl* -s) person with a menial job
menials *n* ▷ menial
meningitis [men-in-jite-iss] *n* (*pl* -es) inflammation of the membranes of the brain
meningitises *n* ▷ meningitis
meniscus *n* (*pl* -ci) curved surface of a liquid

menisci *n* ▷ meniscus
menopausal *adj* ▷ menopause
menopause *n* (*pl* -s) time when a woman's menstrual cycle ceases > **menopausal** *adj*
menopauses *n* ▷ menopause
menservants *n* ▷ manservant
menstruation *n* (*pl* -s) approximately monthly discharge of blood and cellular debris from the womb of a nonpregnant woman > **menstruate** *v* (-tes, -ting, -ted) > **menstrual** *adj*
menstrual *adj* ▷ menstruation
menstruated *v* ▷ menstruation
menstruates *v* ▷ menstruation
menstruating *v* ▷ menstruation
menstruations *n* ▷ menstruation
mensuration *n* (*pl* -s) measuring, esp. in geometry
mensurations *n* ▷ mensuration
mental *adj* of, in, or done by the mind > **mentally** *adv*
mentalities *n* ▷ mentality
mentality *n* (*pl* -ties) way of thinking
mentally *adv* ▷ mental
menthol *n* (*pl* -s) organic compound found in peppermint, used medicinally
menthols *n* ▷ menthol
mention *v* (-s, -ing, -ed) refer to briefly ▶ *n* (*pl* -s) brief reference to a person or thing
mentioned *v* ▷ mention
mentioning *v* ▷ mention
mentions *v*, *n* ▷ mention
mentor *n* (*pl* -s) adviser or guide
mentors *n* ▷ mentor
menu *n* (*pl* -s) list of dishes to be served, or from which to order
menus *n* ▷ menu
mercantile *adj* of trade or traders
mercenaries *n* ▷ mercenary
mercenary *adj* influenced by greed ▶ *n* (*pl* -ries) hired soldier
merchandises *n* ▷ merchandise
merchandise *n* (*pl* -s) commodities
merchant *n* (*pl* -s) person engaged in trade, wholesale trader
merchantman *n* (*pl* -men) trading ship
merchantmen *n* ▷ merchantman
merchants *n* ▷ merchant
merciful *adj* compassionate
merciless *adj* ▷ mercy
mercurial *adj* lively, changeable
mercuries *n* ▷ mercury
mercury *n* (*pl* -ries) (CHEM) silvery liquid metal
mercy *n* (*pl* -cies) compassionate treatment of an offender or enemy who is in one's power

> **merciless** adj

mere¹ adj (-r, -st) nothing more than > **merely** adv

mere² n (pl -s) (BRIT) (Obs) lake

merely adv ▷ **mere¹**

merer adj ▷ **mere¹**

meres n ▷ **mere²**

merest adj ▷ **mere¹**

meretricious adj superficially or garishly attractive but of no real value

merganser [mer-**gan**-ser] n (pl -s) large crested diving duck

mergansers n ▷ **merganser**

merge v (-ges, -ging, -ged) combine or blend

merged v ▷ **merge**

merger n (pl -s) combination of business firms into one

merges v ▷ **merge**

merging v ▷ **merge**

mergers n ▷ **merger**

meridian n (pl -s) imaginary circle of the earth passing through both poles

meridians n ▷ **meridian**

meringue [mer-**rang**] n (pl -s) baked mixture of egg whites and sugar

meringues n ▷ **meringue**

merino n (pl -s) breed of sheep with fine soft wool

merinos n ▷ **merino**

merit n (pl -s) excellence or worth ▶ pl admirable qualities ▶ v (-s, -ing, -ed) deserve

merited v ▷ **merit**

meriting v ▷ **merit**

meritocracies n ▷ **meritocracy**

meritocracy [mer-it-**tok**-rass-ee] n (pl -s) rule by people of superior talent or intellect

meritorious adj deserving praise

merits n, v ▷ **merit**

merlin n (pl -s) small falcon

merlins n ▷ **merlin**

mermaid n (pl -s) imaginary sea creature with the upper part of a woman and the lower part of a fish

mermaids n ▷ **mermaid**

merrier adj ▷ **merry**

merriest adj ▷ **merry**

merrily adv ▷ **merry**

merriment n ▷ **merry**

merriments n ▷ **merry**

merry adj (-rrier, -rriest) cheerful or jolly > **merrily** adv > **merriment** n (pl -s)

merrymaking n (pl -s) noisy, cheerful celebrations or fun

merrymakings n ▷ **merrymaking**

mesdames n ▷ **madame**

mesdemoiselles n ▷ **mademoiselle**

mesh n (pl -es) network or net ▶ v (-es, -ing, -ed) (of gear teeth) engage

meshed v ▷ **mesh**

meshes n, v ▷ **mesh**

meshing v ▷ **mesh**

mesmerize v (-zes, -zing, -zed) hold spellbound

mesmerized v ▷ **mesmerize**

mesmerizes v ▷ **mesmerize**

mesmerizing v ▷ **mesmerize**

meson [**mee**-zon] n (pl -s) elementary atomic particle

mesons n ▷ **meson**

mess n (pl -es) untidy or dirty confusion ▶ v (-es, -ing, -ed) muddle or dirty

message n (pl -s) communication sent

messages n ▷ **message**

messaging n (pl -s) sending and receiving of textual communications by mobile phone

messagings n ▷ **message**

messed v ▷ **mess**

messeigneurs n ▷ **monseigneur**

messenger n (pl -s) bearer of a message

messengers n ▷ **messenger**

messes n, v ▷ **mess**

messiah n (pl -s) promised deliverer > **messianic** adj

messiahs n ▷ **messiah**

messianic adj ▷ **messiah**

messier adj ▷ **messy**

messiest adj ▷ **messy**

messieurs n ▷ **monsieur**

messily adv ▷ **messy**

messing v ▷ **mess**

messy adj (-ssier, -ssiest) dirty, confused, or untidy > **messily** adv

met v ▷ **meet¹**

metabolic adj ▷ **metabolism**

metabolism [met-**tab**-oh-liz-zum] n (pl -s) chemical processes of a living body > **metabolic** adj

metabolisms n ▷ **metabolism**

metabolize v (-zes, -zing, -zed) produce or be produced by metabolism

metabolized v ▷ **metabolize**

metabolizes v ▷ **metabolize**

metabolizing v ▷ **metabolize**

metal n (pl -s) chemical element, such as iron or copper, that is malleable and capable of conducting heat and electricity > **metallic** adj

metallic adj ▷ **metal**

metallurgical adj ▷ **metallurgy**

metallurgist n ▷ **metallurgy**

metallurgists n ▷ **metallurgy**

metallurgy n (pl -**gies**) scientific study of the structure, properties, extraction, and refining of metals > **metallurgical** adj > **metallurgist** n (pl -**s**)
metals n ▷ **metal**
metamorphic adj (of rocks) changed in texture or structure by heat and pressure
metamorphose v (-**ses, -sing, -sed**) transform
metamorphosed v ▷ **metamorphose**
metamorphoses n, v ▷ **metamorphosis**
metamorphosing v ▷ **metamorphose**
metamorphosis [met-a-**more**-foss-is] n (pl -**ses**) [-foss-eez] change of form or character
metaphor n (pl -**s**) figure of speech in which a term is applied to something it does not literally denote in order to imply a resemblance > **metaphorical** adj > **metaphorically** adv
metaphorically adv ▷ **metaphor**
metaphors n ▷ **metaphor**
metaphysical adj ▷ **metaphysics**
metaphysics n branch of philosophy concerned with being and knowing > **metaphysical** adj
mete v (-**tes, -ting, -ted**) (usu. with **out**) deal out as punishment
meted v ▷ **mete**
meteor n (pl -**s**) small fast-moving heavenly body, visible as a streak of incandescence if it enters the earth's atmosphere
meteoric [meet-ee-**or**-rik] adj of a meteor
meteorite n (pl -**s**) meteor that has fallen to earth
meteorites n ▷ **meteorite**
meteorological adj ▷ **meteorology**
meteorologies n ▷ **meteorology**
meteorologist n ▷ **meteorology**
meteorologists n ▷ **meteorology**
meteorology n (pl -**gies**) study of the earth's atmosphere, esp. for weather forecasting > **meteorological** adj > **meteorologist** n (pl -**s**)
meteors n ▷ **meteor**
meter n (pl -**s**) instrument for measuring and recording something, such as the consumption of gas or electricity ▶ v (-**s, -ing, -ed**) measure by meter
meters n, v ▷ **meter**
metes v ▷ **mete**
meting v ▷ **mete**
methane n (pl -**s**) colourless inflammable gas
methanes n ▷ **methane**
methanol n (pl -**s**) colourless poisonous liquid used as a solvent and fuel (also **methyl alcohol**)
methanols n ▷ **methanol**

methinks v (past tense **methought**) (Obs) it seems to me
method n (pl -**s**) way or manner
methodical adj orderly > **methodically** adv
methodically adv ▷ **methodical**
methodism n ▷ **methodist**
methodisms n ▷ **methodist**
methodist n (pl -**s**) member of any of the Protestant churches originated by John Wesley and his followers ▶ adj of methodists or their Church > **methodism** n (pl -**s**)
methodists n ▷ **methodist**
methodologies n ▷ **methodology**
methodology n (pl -**gies**) particular method or procedure
methods n ▷ **method**
meths n (Informal) methylated spirits
methyl n (pl -**s**) (compound containing) a saturated hydrocarbon group of atoms
methyls n ▷ **methyl**
meticulous adj very careful about details > **meticulously** adv
meticulously adv ▷ **meticulous**
métier [met-ee-**ay**] n (pl -**s**) profession or trade
métiers n ▷ **métier**
metonymies n ▷ **metonymy**
metonymy [mit-**on**-im-ee] n (pl -**mies**) figure of speech in which one thing is replaced by another associated with it, such as 'the Crown' for 'the queen'
metre n (pl -**s**) basic unit of length equal to about 1.094 yards (100 centimetres)
metres n ▷ **metre**
metric adj of the decimal system of weights and measures based on the metre
metrical adj of measurement
metrication n (pl -**s**) conversion to the metric system
metrications n ▷ **metrication**
metronome n (pl -**s**) instrument which marks musical time by means of a ticking pendulum
metronomes n ▷ **metronome**
metropolis [mit-**trop**-oh-liss] n (pl -**es**) chief city of a country or region
metropolises n ▷ **metropolis**
metropolitan adj of a metropolis
metrosexual adj, n (pl -**s**) (of) a heterosexual man who is preoccupied with his appearance
metrosexuals n ▷ **metrosexual**
mettle n (pl -**s**) courage or spirit
mettles n ▷ **mettle**
mew n (pl -**s**) cry of a cat ▶ v (-**s, -ing, -ed**) utter this cry
mewed v ▷ **mew**
mewing v ▷ **mew**

mews *n*, *v* ▷ **mew**

> **mezquit** *n* (**mezquit**). A mezquit is a small spiny tree or shrub. With its combination of Q and Z, mezquit is a very high-scoring word. As it contains seven letters, mezquit can earn you a bonus of 50 points if you manage to use all the letters on your rack to form it. Mezquit scores 28 points.

mezzanine [mez-zan-een] *n* (*pl* -**s**) intermediate storey, esp. between the ground and first floor

mezzanines *n* ▷ **mezzanine**

mezzotint [met-so-tint] *n* (*pl* -**s**) method of engraving by scraping the roughened surface of a metal plate

mezzotints *n* ▷ **mezzotint**

> **mi** *n* (**mis**). Mi is the third degree of a major scale in music. This isn't a high-scoring word, but can be very helpful when you want to form words in more than one direction. Mi scores 4 points.

miaow [mee-ow] *n* (*pl* -**s**) ▸ *v* (-**s**, -**ing**, -**wed**) ▷ **mew**

miaowed *v* ▷ **miaow**

miaowing *v* ▷ **miaow**

miaows *v*, *n* ▷ **miaow**

miasma [mee-azz-ma] *n* (*pl* -**mata**) unwholesome or foreboding atmosphere

miasmata *n* ▷ **miasma**

mica [my-ka] *n* (*pl* -**s**) glasslike mineral used as an electrical insulator

micas *n* ▷ **mica**

mice *n* ▷ **mouse**

microbe *n* (*pl* -**s**) minute organism, esp. one causing disease > **microbial** *adj*

microbes *n* ▷ **microbe**

microbial *adj* ▷ **microbe**

microchip *n* (*pl* -**s**) small wafer of silicon containing electronic circuits

microchips *n* ▷ **microchip**

microcomputer *n* (*pl* -**s**) computer with a central processing unit contained in one or more silicon chips

microcomputers *n* ▷ **microcomputer**

microcosm *n* (*pl* -**s**) miniature representation of something

microcosms *n* ▷ **microcosm**

microfiche [my-kroh-feesh] *n* (*pl* -**s**) microfilm in sheet form

microfiches *n* ▷ **microfiche**

microfilm *n* (*pl* -**s**) miniaturized recording of books or documents on a roll of film

microfilms *n* ▷ **microfilm**

microlight *n* (*pl* -**s**) very small light private aircraft with large wings

microlights *n* ▷ **microlight**

micrometer [my-krom-it-er] *n* (*pl* -**s**) instrument for measuring very small distances or angles

micrometers *n* ▷ **micrometer**

micron [my-kron] *n* (*pl* -**s**) one millionth of a metre

microns *n* ▷ **micron**

microorganism *n* (*pl* -**ms**) organism of microscopic size

microorganisms *n* ▷ **microorganism**

microphone *n* (*pl* -**s**) instrument for amplifying or transmitting sounds

microphones *n* ▷ **microphone**

microprocessor *n* (*pl* -**s**) integrated circuit acting as the central processing unit in a small computer

microprocessors *n* ▷ **microprocessor**

microscope *n* (*pl* -**s**) instrument with lens(es) which produces a magnified image of a very small object > **microscopic** *adj* too small to be seen except with a microscope > **microscopically** *adv*

microscopes *n* ▷ **microscope**

microscopic *adj* ▷ **microscope**

microscopically *adv* ▷ **microscope**

microscopies *n* ▷ **microscopy**

microscopy *n* (*pl* -**pies**) use of a microscope

microsurgeries *n* ▷ **microsurgery**

microsurgery *n* (*pl* -**ries**) intricate surgery using a special microscope and miniature precision instruments

microwave *n* (*pl* -**s**) electromagnetic wave with a wavelength of a few centimetres, used in radar and cooking ▸ *v* (-**ves**, -**ving**, -**ved**) cook in a microwave oven

microwaved *v* ▷ **microwave**

microwaves *n*, *v* ▷ **microwave**

microwaving *v* ▷ **microwave**

mid *adj* intermediate, middle

midday *n* (*pl* -**s**) noon

middays *n* ▷ **midday**

midden *n* (*pl* -**s**) (BRIT & AUST) dunghill or rubbish heap

middens *n* ▷ **midden**

middle *adj* equidistant from two extremes ▸ *n* (*pl* -**s**) middle point or part

middleman *n* (*pl* -**men**) trader who buys from the producer and sells to the consumer

middlemen *n* ▷ **middleman**

middles *n* ▷ **middle**

middleweight *n* (*pl* -**s**) boxer weighing up to 160lb (professional) or 75kg (amateur)

middleweights *n* ▷ **middleweight**

middling *adj* mediocre

midge *n* (*pl* -s) small mosquito-like insect
midges *n* ▷ midge

midget *n* (*pl* -s) very small person or thing
midgets *n* ▷ midget

midland *n* (*pl* -s) (BRIT, AUST & US) middle part
of a country
midlands *n* ▷ midland

midnight *n* (*pl* -s) twelve o'clock at night
midnights *n* ▷ midnight

midriff *n* (*pl* -s) middle part of the body
midriffs *n* ▷ midriff

midshipman *n* (*pl* -men) naval officer of the
lowest commissioned rank
midshipmen *n* ▷ midshipman

midsummer *n* (*pl* -s) middle of summer
midsummers *n* ▷ midsummer

midway *adj*, *adv* halfway

midwife *n* (*pl* -wives) trained person who
assists at childbirth > midwifery *n* (*pl* -ries)
midwiferies *n* ▷ midwife
midwifery *n* ▷ midwife
midwives *n* ▷ midwife

midwinter *n* (*pl* -s) middle or depth of winter
midwinters *n* ▷ midwinter

mien [mean] *n* (*pl* -s) (*Lit*) person's bearing,
demeanour, or appearance
miens *n* ▷ mien

miffed *adj* (*Informal*) offended or upset
might¹ ▷ may

might² *n* (*pl* -s) power or strength
mightier *adj* ▷ mighty
mightiest *adj* ▷ mighty
mightily *adv* ▷ mighty

mighty *adj* (-tier, -tiest) powerful ▶ *adv* (US &
AUST) (*Informal*) very > mightily *adv*

migraine [mee-grain] *n* (*pl* -s) severe headache,
often with nausea and visual disturbances
migraines *n* ▷ migraine

migrant *n* (*pl* -s) person or animal that moves
from one place to another ▶ *adj* moving from
one place to another
migrants *n* ▷ migrant

migrate *v* (-tes, -ting, -ted) move from one
place to settle in another > migration *n* (*pl* -s)
migrated *v* ▷ migrate
migrates *v* ▷ migrate
migrating *v* ▷ migrate
migration *n* ▷ migrate
migrations *n* ▷ migrate

migratory *adj* (of an animal) migrating every
year

mike *n* (*pl* -s) (*Informal*) microphone
mikes *n* ▷ mike

milch *adj* (CHIEFLY BRIT) (of a cow) giving milk

mild *adj* (-er, -est) not strongly flavoured
> mildly *adv* > mildness *n* (*pl* -es)
milder *adj* ▷ mild
mildest *adj* ▷ mild

mildew *n* (*pl* -s) destructive fungus on plants
or things exposed to damp > mildewed *adj*
mildewed *adj* ▷ mildew
mildews *n* ▷ mildew
mildly *adv* ▷ mild
mildness *n* ▷ mild
mildnesses *n* ▷ mild

mile *n* (*pl* -s) unit of length equal to 1760 yards
or 1.609 kilometres

mileage *n* (*pl* -s) distance travelled in miles
mileages *n* ▷ mileage

mileometer *n* (*pl* -s) (BRIT) device that records
the number of miles a vehicle has travelled
mileometers *n* ▷ mileometer
miles *n* ▷ mile

milestone *n* (*pl* -s) significant event
milestones *n* ▷ milestone

milieu [meal-yer] *n* (*pl* milieux, milieus) [meal-
yerz] environment or surroundings
milieus *n* ▷ milieu
milieux *n* ▷ milieu

militancies *n* ▷ militant
militancy *n* ▷ militant

militant *adj* aggressive or vigorous in support
of a cause > militancy *n* (*pl* -cies)
militants *n* ▷ militant
militaries *n* ▷ military

militarism *n* (*pl* -s) belief in the use of military
force and methods
militarisms *n* ▷ militarism
militarist *n* ▷ military
militarists *n* ▷ military
militarized *adj* ▷ military

military *adj* of or for soldiers, armies, or war
▶ *n* (*pl* -ries) armed services > militarist *n* (*pl*
-s) > militarized *adj*

militate *v* (-tes, -ting, -ted) (*usu.* with against
or for) have a strong influence or effect
militated *v* ▷ militate
militates *v* ▷ militate
militating *v* ▷ militate

militia [mill-ish-a] *n* (*pl* -s) military force of
trained citizens for use in emergency only
militias *n* ▷ militia

milk *n* (*pl* -s) white fluid produced by female
mammals to feed their young ▶ *v* (-s, -ing, -ed)
draw milk from > milky *adj* (-kier, -kiest)
milked *v* ▷ milk
milkier *adj* ▷ milk
milkiest *adj* ▷ milk
milking *v* ▷ milk

milkmaid n (pl -s) (esp. in former times) woman who milks cows
  milkmaids n ▷ **milkmaid**
milkman n (pl -men) (BRIT, AUST & NZ) man who delivers milk to people's houses
  milkmen n ▷ **milkman**
  milks n, v ▷ **milk**
milkshake n (pl -s) frothy flavoured cold milk drink
  milkshakes n ▷ **milkshake**
milksop n (pl -s) feeble man
  milksops n ▷ **milk**
  milky adj ▷ **milk**
mill n (pl -s) factory ▶ v (-s, -ing, -ed) grind, press, or process in or as if in a mill
  milled v ▷ **mill**
millennium n (pl -nnia, -nniums) period of a thousand years
  millennia n ▷ **mill**
  millenniums n ▷ **mill**
miller n (pl -s) person who works in a mill
  millers n ▷ **miller**
millet n (pl -s) type of cereal grass
  millets n ▷ **millet**
millibar n (pl -s) unit of atmospheric pressure
  millibars n ▷ **millibar**
millimetre n (pl -s) thousandth part of a metre
  millimetres n ▷ **millimetre**
milliner n (pl -s) maker or seller of women's hats > **millinery** n (pl -ries)
  millineries n ▷ **milliner**
  milliners n ▷ **milliner**
  millinery n ▷ **milliner**
  milling v ▷ **mill**
million n (pl -s) one thousand thousands > **millionth** adj, n (pl -s)
millionaire n (pl -s) person who owns at least a million pounds, dollars, etc.
  millionaires n ▷ **millionaire**
  millions n ▷ **million**
  millionths n ▷ **million**
millipede n (pl -s) small animal with a jointed body and many pairs of legs
  millipedes n ▷ **millipede**
  mills n, v ▷ **mill**
millstone n (pl -s) flat circular stone for grinding corn
  millstones n ▷ **millstone**
millwheel n (pl -s) waterwheel that drives a mill
  millwheels n ▷ **millwheel**
milometer n (pl -s) (BRIT) ▷ **mileometer**
  milometers n ▷ **milometer**
milt n (pl -s) sperm of fish
  milts n ▷ **milt**

mime n (pl -s) acting without the use of words ▶ v (-mes, -ming, -med) act in mime
  mimed v ▷ **mime**
  mimes n, v ▷ **mime**
  miming v ▷ **mime**
mimic v (-ics, -icking, -icked) imitate (a person or manner), esp. for satirical effect ▶ n (pl -s) person or animal that is good at mimicking > **mimicry** n (pl -ries)
  mimicked v ▷ **mimic**
  mimicking v ▷ **mimic**
  mimicry n ▷ **mimic**
  mimics n, v ▷ **mimic**
  mina n ▷ **myna**
  minas n ▷ **myna**
minaret n (pl -s) tall slender tower of a mosque
  minarets n ▷ **minaret**
mince v (-ces, -cing, -ced) cut or grind into very small pieces ▶ n (pl -s) minced meat
  minced v ▷ **mince**
mincemeat n (pl -s) sweet mixture of dried fruit and spices
  mincemeats n ▷ **mincemeat**
mincer n (pl -s) machine for mincing meat
  mincers n ▷ **mince**
  minces v, n ▷ **mince**
mincing adj affected in manner ▶ v ▷ **mince**
mind n (pl -s) thinking faculties ▶ v (-s, -ing, -ed) take offence at
minded adj having an inclination as specified ▶ v ▷ **mind**
minder n (pl -s) (Informal) aide or bodyguard
  minders n ▷ **minder**
mindful adj heedful
  minding v ▷ **mind**
mindless adj stupid
  minds n, v ▷ **mind**
mine[1] pron belonging to me
mine[2] n (pl -s) deep hole for digging out coal, ores, etc. ▶ v (-nes, -ning, -ned) dig for minerals
  mined v ▷ **mine**
minefield n (pl -s) area of land or water containing mines
  minefields n ▷ **minefield**
miner n (pl -s) person who works in a mine
mineral n (pl -s) naturally occurring inorganic substance, such as metal ▶ adj of, containing, or like minerals
  mineralogies n ▷ **mineralogy**
mineralogy [min-er-al-a-jee] n (pl -gies) study of minerals
  minerals n ▷ **mineral**
  miners n ▷ **miner**
  mines n, v ▷ **mine**

minestrone [min-ness-**strone**-ee] *n* (*pl* -**s**) soup containing vegetables and pasta
  minestrones *n* ▷ **minestrone**
minesweeper *n* (*pl* -**s**) ship for clearing away mines
  minesweepers *n* ▷ **minesweeper**
  mining *v* ▷ **mine**
minger *n* (*pl* -**s**) (BRIT) (*Informal*) unattractive person
  mingers *n* ▷ **minger**
  mingier *adj* ▷ **mingy**
  mingiest *adj* ▷ **mingy**
minging *adj* (BRIT) (*Informal*) unattractive or unpleasant
mingle *v* (-**les**, -**ling**, -**led**) mix or blend
  mingled *v* ▷ **mingle**
  mingles *v* ▷ **mingle**
  mingling *v* ▷ **mingle**
mingy *adj* (-**gier**, -**giest**) (*Informal*) miserly
mini *n* (*pl* -**s**) ▶ *adj* (-**ier**, -**iest**) (something) small or miniature
  minier *adj* ▷ **mini**
  miniest *adj* ▷ **mini**
  minis *n* ▷ **mini**
miniature *n* (*pl* -**s**) small portrait, model, or copy ▶ *adj* small-scale > **miniaturist** *n* (*pl* -**s**)
  miniatures *n* ▷ **miniature**
  miniaturist *n* ▷ **miniature**
  miniaturists *n* ▷ **miniature**
miniaturize *v* (-**zes**, -**zing**, -**zed**) make to a very small scale
  miniaturized *v* ▷ **miniaturize**
  miniaturizes *v* ▷ **miniaturize**
  miniaturizing *v* ▷ **miniaturize**
minibar *n* (*pl* -**s**) selection of drinks and confectionery provided in a hotel room
minibus *n* (*pl* -**es**) small bus
  minibuses *n* ▷ **minibus**
minicab *n* (*pl* -**s**) (BRIT) ordinary car used as a taxi
  minicabs *n* ▷ **minicab**
minicomputer *n* (*pl* -**s**) computer smaller than a mainframe but more powerful than a microcomputer
  minicomputers *n* ▷ **minicomputer**
minidisc *n* (*pl* -**s**) small recordable compact disc
  minidiscs *n* ▷ **minidisc**
minim *n* (*pl* -**s**) (MUSIC) note half the length of a semibreve
  minima *n* ▷ **minimum**
minimal *adj* minimum
minimize *v* (-**zes**, -**zing**, -**zed**) reduce to a minimum
  minimized *v* ▷ **minimize**

  minimizes *v* ▷ **minimize**
  minimizing *v* ▷ **minimize**
  minims *n* ▷ **minim**
minimum *adj*, *n* (*pl* -**mums**, -**ma**) least possible (amount or number)
  minimums *n* ▷ **minimum**
minion *n* (*pl* -**s**) servile assistant
  minions *n* ▷ **minion**
miniseries *n* (*pl* -**ries**) TV programme shown in several parts, often on consecutive days
  miniseries *n* ▷ **miniseries**
minister *n* (*pl* -**s**) head of a government department ▶ *v* (-**s**, -**ing**, -**ed**) (*foll. by* **to**) attend to the needs of > **ministerial** *adj*
  ministered *v* ▷ **minister**
  ministerial *adj* ▷ **minister**
  ministering *v* ▷ **minister**
  ministers *n*, *v* ▷ **minister**
ministration *n* (*pl* -**s**) giving of help
  ministrations *n* ▷ **ministration**
  ministries *n* ▷ **ministry**
ministry *n* (*pl* -**tries**) profession or duties of a clergyman
mink *n* stoatlike animal
minnow *n* (*pl* -**s**) small freshwater fish
  minnows *n* ▷ **minnow**
minor *adj* lesser ▶ *n* (*pl* -**s**) person regarded legally as a child
  minorities *n* ▷ **minority**
minority *n* (*pl* -**ties**) lesser number
  minors *n* ▷ **minor**
minster *n* (*pl* -**s**) (BRIT) cathedral or large church
  minsters *n* ▷ **minster**
minstrel *n* (*pl* -**s**) medieval singer or musician
  minstrels *n* ▷ **minstrel**
mint¹ *n* (*pl* -**s**) plant with aromatic leaves used for seasoning and flavouring
mint² *n* place where money is coined ▶ *v* (-**s**, -**ing**, -**ed**) make (coins)
  minted *v* ▷ **mint²**
  minting *v* ▷ **mint²**
  mints *n* ▷ **mint¹,²** ▶ *v* ▷ ²
minuet [min-new-**wet**] *n* (*pl* -**s**) stately dance
  minuets *n* ▷ **minuet**
minus *prep*, *adj* indicating subtraction ▶ *adj* less than zero ▶ *n* (*pl* -**es**) sign (-) denoting subtraction or a number less than zero
  minuses *n* ▷ **minus**
minuscule [min-niss-skyool] *adj* very small
minute¹ [min-it] *n* (*pl* -**s**) 60th part of an hour or degree ▶ *pl* record of the proceedings of a meeting ▶ *v* (-**tes**, -**ting**, -**ted**) record in the minutes
minute² [my-newt] *adj* (-**r**, -**st**) very small
  > **minutely** *adv*

minuted v ▷ minute¹
minutely adv ▷ minute²
minuter adj ▷ minute²
minutes n, v ▷ minute¹
minutest adj ▷ minute²
minutiae [my-**new**-shee-eye] pl n trifling or precise details
minuting v ▷ minute¹
minx n (pl -es) bold or flirtatious girl
minxes n ▷ minx
miracle n (pl -s) wonderful supernatural event > **miraculous** adj > **miraculously** adv
miracles n ▷ miracle
miraculous adj ▷ miracle
miraculously adv ▷ miracle
mirage [mir-**rahzh**] n (pl -s) optical illusion, esp. one caused by hot air
mirages n ▷ mirage
mire n (pl -s) swampy ground
mires n ▷ mire
mirror n (pl -s) coated glass surface for reflecting images ▶ v (-s, -ing, -ed) reflect in or as if in a mirror
mirrored v ▷ mirror
mirroring v ▷ mirror
mirrors n, v ▷ mirror
mirth n (pl -s) laughter, merriment, or gaiety > **mirthful** adj > **mirthless** adj
mirthful adv ▷ mirth
mirthless adj ▷ mirth
mirths n ▷ mirth
misadventure n (pl -s) unlucky chance
misadventures n ▷ misadventure
misanthrope [**miz**-zan-thrope] n (pl -s) person who dislikes people in general > **misanthropic** [miz-zan-**throp**-ik] ▶ adj > **misanthropy** [miz-**zan**-throp-ee] ▶ n (pl -pies)
misanthropes n ▷ misanthrope
misanthropies n ▷ misanthrope
misanthropic adj ▷ misanthrope
misanthropy n ▷ misanthrope
misapprehend v (-s, -ing, -ed) missunderstand > **misapprehension** n (pl -s)
misapprehended v ▷ misapprehend
misapprehending v ▷ misapprehend
misapprehends v ▷ misapprehend
misapprehension n ▷ misapprehend
misapprehensions n ▷ misapprehend
misappropriate v (-tes, -ting, -ted) take and use (money) dishonestly > **misappropriation** n (pl -s)
misappropriated v ▷ misappropriate
misappropriates v ▷ misappropriate
misappropriating v ▷ misappropriate
misappropriation n ▷ misappropriate

misappropriations n ▷ misappropriate
miscarriage n (pl -s) spontaneous premature expulsion of a fetus from the womb
miscarriages n ▷ miscarriage
miscarried v ▷ miscarry
miscarries v ▷ miscarry
miscarry v (-ries, -rying, -ried) have a miscarriage
miscarrying v ▷ miscarry
miscast v (-s, -ing, -cast) cast (a role or actor) in (a play or film) inappropriately
miscasting v ▷ miscast
miscasts v ▷ miscast
miscegenation [miss-ij-in-**nay**-shun] n (pl -s) interbreeding of races
miscegenations n ▷ miscegenation
miscellaneous [miss-sell-**lane**-ee-uss] adj mixed or assorted
miscellanies n ▷ miscellany
miscellany [miss-**sell**-a-nee] n (pl -nies) mixed assortment
mischance n (pl -es) unlucky event
mischances n ▷ mischance
mischief n (pl -s) annoying but not malicious behaviour
mischiefs n ▷ mischief
mischievous adj full of mischief > **mischievously** adv
mischievously adv ▷ mischievous
miscible [miss-**sib**-bl] adj able to be mixed
misconception n (pl -s) wrong idea or belief
misconceptions n ▷ misconception
misconduct n (pl -s) immoral or unethical behaviour
misconducts n ▷ misconduct
miscreant [miss-**kree**-ant] n (pl -s) wrongdoer
miscreants n ▷ miscreant
misdeed n (pl -s) wrongful act
misdeeds n ▷ misdeed
misdemeanour n (pl -s) minor wrongdoing
misdemeanours n ▷ misdemeanour
miser n (pl -s) person who hoards money and hates spending it > **miserly** adj
miserable adj very unhappy, wretched
miseries adj ▷ misery
miserly adj ▷ miser
misers n ▷ miser
misery n (pl -ries) great unhappiness
misfire v (-res, -ring, -red) (of a firearm or engine) fail to fire correctly
misfired v ▷ misfire
misfires v ▷ misfire
misfiring v ▷ misfire
misfit n (pl -s) person not suited to his or her social environment

misfits n ▷ **misfit**
misfortune n (pl -s) (piece of) bad luck
   misfortunes n ▷ **misfortune**
misgiving n (pl -s) feeling of fear or doubt
   misgivings n ▷ **misgiving**
misguided adj mistaken or unwise
mishandle v (-les, -ling, -led) handle badly or
   inefficiently
   mishandled v ▷ **mishandle**
   mishandles v ▷ **mishandle**
   mishandling v ▷ **mishandle**
mishap n (pl -s) minor accident
   mishaps n ▷ **mishap**
misinform v (-s, -ing, -ed) give incorrect
   information to > **misinformation** n (pl -s)
   misinformation n ▷ **misinform**
   misinformations n ▷ **misinform**
   misinformed v ▷ **misinform**
   misinforming v ▷ **misinform**
   misinforms v ▷ **misinform**
misjudge v (-ges, -ging, -ged) judge wrongly
   or unfairly > **misjudgment, misjudgement**
   n (pl -s)
   misjudged v ▷ **misjudge**
   misjudgement n ▷ **misjudge**
   misjudges v ▷ **misjudge**
   misjudging v ▷ **misjudge**
   misjudgment n ▷ **misjudge**
   mislaid v ▷ **mislay**
mislay v (-s, -ing, -laid) lose (something)
   temporarily
   mislaying v ▷ **mislay**
   mislays v ▷ **mislay**
mislead v (-s, -ing, -led) give false or confusing
   information to > **misleading** adj
   misleading v, adj ▷ **mislead**
   misleads v ▷ **mislead**
   misled v ▷ **mislead**
mismanage v (-ges, -ging, -ged) organize or
   run (something) badly > **mismanagement**
   n (pl -s)
   mismanaged v ▷ **mismanage**
   mismanagement n ▷ **mismanage**
   mismanagements n ▷ **mismanage**
   mismanages v ▷ **mismanage**
   mismanaging v ▷ **mismanage**
misnomer [miss-no-mer] n (pl -s) incorrect or
   unsuitable name
   misnomers n ▷ **misnomer**
misogyny [miss-oj-in-ee] n (pl -nies) hatred of
   women > **misogynist** n (pl -s)
   misogynies n ▷ **misogyny**
   misogynist n ▷ **misogyny**
   misogynists n ▷ **misogyny**
misplace v (-ces, -cing, -ced) mislay

misplaced v ▷ **misplace**
misplaces v ▷ **misplace**
misplacing v ▷ **misplace**
misprint n (pl -s) printing error
   misprints n ▷ **misprint**
misrepresent v (-s, -ing, -ed) represent
   wrongly or inaccurately
   misrepresented v ▷ **misrepresent**
   misrepresenting v ▷ **misrepresent**
   misrepresents v ▷ **misrepresent**
miss v (-es, -ing, -ed) fail to notice, hear,
   hit, reach, find, or catch ▶ n (pl -es) fact or
   instance of missing
   missed v ▷ **miss**
   misses v, n ▷ **miss**
missing adj lost or absent ▶ v ▷ **miss**
missal n (pl -s) book containing the prayers
   and rites of the Mass
   missals n ▷ **missal**
misshapen adj badly shaped, deformed
missile n (pl -s) object or weapon thrown,
   shot, or launched at a target
   missiles n ▷ **missile**
mission n (pl -s) specific task or duty
   missionaries n ▷ **mission**
missionary n (pl -ries) person sent abroad to
   do religious and social work
   missions n ▷ **mission**
missive n (pl -s) letter
   missives n ▷ **missive**
misspent adj wasted or misused
mist n (pl -s) thin fog
   mists n ▷ **mist**
mistake n (pl -s) error or blunder ▶ v (-takes,
   -taking, -took, -taken) misunderstand
   mistaken v ▷ **mistake**
   mistakes n, v ▷ **mistake**
   mistaking v ▷ **mistake**
mister n (pl -s) an informal form of address
   for a man
   misters n ▷ **mister**
   mistier adj ▷ **misty**
   mistiest adj ▷ **misty**
mistletoe n (pl -s) evergreen plant with white
   berries growing as a parasite on trees
   mistletoes n ▷ **mistletoe**
   mistook v ▷ **mistake**
mistral n (pl -s) strong dry northerly wind of
   S France
   mistrals n ▷ **mistral**
mistress n (pl -es) woman who has a
   continuing sexual relationship with a
   married man
   mistresses n ▷ **mistress**
mistrial n (pl -s) (LAW) trial made void because

of some error
mistrials n ▷ **mistrial**
mistrust v (**-s, -ing, -ed**) have doubts or suspicions about ▶ n (pl **-s**) lack of trust > **mistrustful** adj
mistrusted v ▷ **mistrust**
mistrustful adj ▷ **mistrust**
mistrusting v ▷ **mistrust**
mistrusts v, n ▷ **mistrust**
misty adj full of mist
misunderstand v (**-stands, -standing, -stood**) fail to understand properly > **misunderstanding** n (pl **-s**)
misunderstanding v, n ▷ **misunderstand**
misunderstandings n ▷ **misunderstand**
misunderstands v ▷ **misunderstand**
misunderstood v ▷ **misunderstand**
misuse n (pl **-s**) incorrect, improper, or careless use ▶ v (**-ses, -sing, -sed**) use wrongly
misused v ▷ **misuse**
misuses n, v ▷ **misuse**
misusing v ▷ **misuse**
mite n (pl **-s**) very small spider-like animal
mites n ▷ **mite**
mitigate v (**-tes, -ting, -ted**) make less severe > **mitigation** n (pl **-s**)
mitigated v ▷ **mitigate**
mitigating v ▷ **mitigate**
mitigates v ▷ **mitigate**
mitigation n ▷ **mitigate**
mitigations n ▷ **mitigate**
mitre [my-ter] n (pl **-s**) bishop's pointed headdress ▶ v (**-res, -ring, -red**) join with a mitre joint
mitred v ▷ **mitre**
mitres n, v ▷ **mitre**
mitring v ▷ **mitre**
mitt n (pl **-s**) baseball catcher's glove
mitts n ▷ **mitt**
mitten n (pl **-s**) glove with one section for the thumb and one for the four fingers together
mittens n ▷ **mitten**
mix v (**-es, -ing, -ed**) combine or blend into one mass ▶ n (pl **-es**) mixture > **mixed** adj > **mixup** n (pl **-s**) > **mixer** n (pl **-s**)
mixed v, adj ▷ **mix**
mixer n ▷ **mix**
mixers n ▷ **mix**
mixes v, n ▷ **mix**
mixing v ▷ **mix**
mixture n (pl **-s**) something mixed
mixtures n ▷ **mixture**
mixup n ▷ **mix**
mixups n ▷ **mix**
miz n (**mizzes**). Miz is an informal short form of **misery.** This is a useful word, giving a high score for three letters. Remember that you'll need a blank tile for the second Z if you want to form the plural. Miz scores 14 points.
mizzenmast n (pl **-s**) (on a vessel with three or more masts) third mast from the bow
mizzenmasts n ▷ **mizzenmast**
mm interj. Mm is a sound that people make to express satisfaction. This two-letter word with no vowels can be very handy when forming several words at once. Mm scores 6 points.
mnemonic [nim-on-ik] n (pl **-s**) ▶ adj (something, such as a rhyme) intended to help the memory
mnemonics n ▷ **mnemonic**
mo n (**mos**). Mo is an informal short form of **moment.** This word can come in handy when you are trying to play words in more than one direction at once. Mo scores 4 points.
moa n (pl **-s**) large extinct flightless New Zealand bird
moas n ▷ **moa**
moan n (pl **-s**) low cry of pain ▶ v (**-s, -ing, -ed**) make or utter with a moan
moaned v ▷ **moan**
moaning v ▷ **moan**
moans n, v ▷ **moan**
moat n (pl **-s**) deep wide ditch, esp. round a castle
moats n ▷ **moat**
mob n (pl **-s**) disorderly crowd ▶ v (**-s, -bbing, -bbed**) surround in a mob to acclaim or attack
mobbed v ▷ **mob**
mobbing v ▷ **mob**
mobs n, v ▷ **mob**
mobile adj able to move ▶ n (pl **-s**) hanging structure designed to move in air currents > **mobility** n (pl **-ties**)
mobiles n ▷ **mobile**
mobilities n ▷ **mobile**
mobility n ▷ **mobile**
mobilization n ▷ **mobilize**
mobilizations n ▷ **mobilize**
mobilize v (**-zes, -zing, -zed**) (of the armed services) prepare for active service > **mobilization** n (pl **-s**)
mobilized v ▷ **mobilize**
mobilizes v ▷ **mobilize**
mobilizing v ▷ **mobilize**
moccasin n (pl **-s**) soft leather shoe
moccasins n ▷ **moccasin**
mocha [mock-a] n (pl **-s**) kind of strong dark

coffee

mochas *n* ▷ mocha

mock *v* (**-s, -ing, -ed**) make fun of ▶ *adj* sham or imitation

mocked *v* ▷ mock

mockeries *n* ▷ mockery

mockery *n* (*pl* -ries) derision

mocking *v* ▷ mock

mockingbird *n* (*pl* -s) N American bird which imitates other birds' songs

mockingbirds *n* ▷ mockingbird

mocks *pl n* (*Informal*) (in England and Wales) practice exams taken before public exams ▶ *v* ▷ mock

mock-up *n* (*pl* -s) full-scale model for test or study

mock-ups *n* ▷ mock-up

mode *n* (*pl* -s) method or manner

modes *n* ▷ mode

model *n* (*pl* -s) (miniature) representation ▶ *v* (**-s, -elling, -elled**) make a model of

modelled *n* ▷ model

modelling *n* ▷ model

models *n* ▷ model

modem [mode-em] *n* (*pl* -s) device for connecting two computers by a telephone line

modems *n* ▷ modem

moderate *adj* not extreme ▶ *n* (*pl* -s) person of moderate views ▶ *v* (**-tes, -ting, -ted**) make or become less violent or extreme > **moderately** *adv* > **moderation** (*pl* -s) *n*

moderated *v* ▷ moderate

moderately *adv* ▷ moderate

moderates *n, v* ▷ moderate

moderating *v* ▷ moderate

moderation *n* ▷ moderate

moderations *n* ▷ moderate

moderator *n* (*pl* -s) (Presbyterian Church) minister appointed to preside over a Church court, general assembly, etc.

moderators *n* ▷ moderate

modern *adj* (**-er, -est**) of present or recent times > **modernity** *n* (*pl* -ties)

moderner *adj* ▷ modern

modernest *adj* ▷ modern

modernism *n* (*pl* -s) (support of) modern tendencies, thoughts, or styles > **modernist** *adj, n* (*pl* -s)

modernism *n* ▷ modern

modernisms *n* ▷ modern

modernist *n* ▷ modern

modernists *n* ▷ modern

modernities *n* ▷ modern

modernity *n* ▷ modern

modernization *n* ▷ modernize

modernizations *n* ▷ modernize

modernize *v* (**-izes, -izing, -ized**) bring up to date > **modernization** *n* (*pl* -s)

modest *adj* (**-er, -est**) not vain or boastful > **modestly** *adv* > **modesty** *n* (*pl* -s)

modester *adj* ▷ modest

modestest *adj* ▷ modest

modesties *n* ▷ modest

modestly *adv* ▷ modest

modesty *n* ▷ modest

modicum *n* (*pl* -s) small quantity

modicums *n* ▷ modicum

modify *v* (**-fies, -fying, -fied**) change slightly > **modification** *n* (*pl* -s)

modified *v* ▷ modify

modifier *n* (*pl* -s) word that qualifies the sense of another

modifiers *n* ▷ modifier

modish [mode-ish] *adj* in fashion

modulate *v* (**-tes, -ting, -ted**) vary in tone > **modulation** *n* (*pl* -s) > **modulator** *n* (*pl* -s)

modulated *v* ▷ modulate

modulates *v* ▷ modulate

modulating *v* ▷ modulate

modulation *n* ▷ modulate

modulations *n* ▷ modulate

module *n* (*pl* -s) self-contained unit, section, or component with a specific function

modules *n* ▷ module

mogul [moh-gl] *n* (*pl* -s) important or powerful person

moguls *n* ▷ mogul

mohair *n* (*pl* -s) fine hair of the Angora goat

mohairs *n* ▷ mohair

mohican *n* (*pl* -s) punk hairstyle with shaved sides and a stiff central strip of hair, often brightly coloured

mohicans *n* ▷ mohican

moieties *n* ▷ moieties

moiety [moy-it-ee] *n* (*pl* -ties) half

moist *adj* (**-er, -est**) slightly wet

moisten *v* (**-s, -ing, -ed**) make or become moist

moistened *v* ▷ moisten

moistening *v* ▷ moisten

moistens *v* ▷ moisten

moister *adj* ▷ moist

moistest *adj* ▷ moist

moisture *n* (*pl* -s) liquid diffused as vapour or condensed in drops

moistures *n* ▷ moisture

moisturize *v* (**-zes, -zing, -zed**) add moisture to (the skin etc.)

moisturized *v* ▷ moisten

moisturizes *v* ▷ moisten

moisturizing v ▷ moisten
molar n (pl -s) large back tooth used for grinding
   molars n ▷ molar
molasses n dark syrup, a by-product of sugar refining
mole¹ n (pl -s) small dark raised spot on the skin
mole² n (pl -s) small burrowing mammal
mole³ n (pl -s) unit of amount of substance
mole⁴ n (pl -s) breakwater
molecule [mol-lik-kyool] n (pl -s) simplest freely existing chemical unit, composed of two or more atoms > molecular [mol-**lek**-yew-lar] ▶ adj
   molecular adj ▷ molecule
   molecules n ▷ molecule
   moles n ▷ mole¹,²,³,⁴
molest v (-s, -ing, -ed) interfere with sexually > molester n (pl -s) > molestation n (pl -s)
   molested v ▷ molest
   molester n ▷ molest
   molesters n ▷ molest
   molesting v ▷ molest
   molests v ▷ molest
moll n (pl -s) (Slang) gangster's female accomplice
   mollified v ▷ mollify
   mollifies v ▷ mollify
mollify v (-fies, -fying, -fied) pacify or soothe
   mollifying v ▷ mollify
   molls n ▷ moll
mollusc n (pl -s) soft-bodied, usu. hard-shelled, animal, such as a snail or oyster
   molluscs n ▷ mollusc
mollycoddle v (-les, -ling, -led) pamper
   mollycoddled v ▷ mollycoddle
   mollycoddles v ▷ mollycoddle
   mollycoddling v ▷ mollycoddle
molten adj liquefied or melted
molybdenum [mol-**lib**-din-um] n (pl -s) (CHEM) hard silvery-white metallic element
   molybdenums n ▷ molybdenum
moment n (pl -s) short space of time
   momenta n ▷ momentum
   momentarily adv ▷ momentary
momentary adj lasting only a moment > momentarily adv
momentous [moh-**men**-tuss] adj of great significance
   moments n ▷ moment
momentum n (pl -ta) impetus of a moving body
monarch n (pl -s) sovereign ruler of a state > monarchical adj

monarchical adj ▷ monarch
monarchies n ▷ monarchy
monarchist n (pl -s) supporter of monarchy
   monarchists n ▷ monarchist
   monarchs n ▷ monarch
monarchy n (pl -chies) government by or a state ruled by a sovereign
   monasteries n ▷ monastery
monastery n (pl -ries) residence of a community of monks > monasticism n (pl -s)
monastic adj of monks, nuns, or monasteries
   monasticism n ▷ monastery
   monasticisms n ▷ monastery
monetarism n (pl -s) theory that inflation is caused by an increase in the money supply > monetarist n (pl -s) adj
   monetarisms n ▷ monetarism
   monetarist n, adj ▷ monetarism
   monetarists n ▷ monetarism
monetary adj of money or currency
money n (pl -s) medium of exchange, coins or banknotes > moneyed, monied adj rich
   moneyed adj ▷ money
   moneys n ▷ money
mongoose n (pl -s) stoatlike mammal of Asia and Africa that kills snakes
   mongooses n ▷ money
mongrel n (pl -s) animal, esp. a dog, of mixed breed ▶ adj of mixed breed or origin
   mongrels n ▷ mongrel
   monied adj ▷ money
monitor n (pl -s) person or device that checks, controls, warns, or keeps a record of something ▶ v (-s, -ing, -ed) watch and check on
   monitored v ▷ monitor
   monitoring v ▷ monitor
   monitors n, v ▷ monitor
monk n (pl -s) member of an all-male religious community bound by vows > monkish adj
monkey n (pl -s) long-tailed primate ▶ v (-s, -ing, -ed) (usu. foll. by about or around) meddle or fool
   monkeyed v ▷ monkey
   monkeying v ▷ monkey
   monkeys n, v ▷ monkey
   monkish adj ▷ monk
   monks n ▷ monk
monochrome adj (PHOTOG) black-and-white
monocle n (pl -s) eyeglass for one eye only
   monocles n ▷ monocle
   monogamies n ▷ monogamy
monogamy n (pl -mies) custom of being married to one person at a time
monogram n (pl -s) design of combined

letters, esp. a person's initials
monograms n ▷ monogram
monograph n (pl -**s**) book or paper on a single subject
monographs n ▷ monograph
monolith n (pl -**s**) large upright block of stone > **monolithic** adj
monolithic n ▷ monolith
monoliths n ▷ monolith
monologue n (pl -**s**) long speech by one person
monologues n ▷ monologue
monomania n (pl -**s**) obsession with one thing > **monomaniac** n, adj
monomaniac adj ▷ monomania
monomanias n ▷ monomania
monoplane n (pl -**s**) aeroplane with one pair of wings
monoplanes n ▷ monoplane
monopolies n ▷ monopoly
monopolize v (-**zes**, -**zing**, -**zed**) have or take exclusive possession of
monopolized v ▷ monopoly
monopolizes v ▷ monopoly
monopolizing v ▷ monopoly
monopoly n (pl -**lies**) exclusive possession of or right to do something
monorail n (pl -**s**) single-rail railway
monorails n ▷ monorail
monotheism n (pl -**s**) belief in only one God > **monotheistic** adj
monotheisms n ▷ monorail
monotheistic adj ▷ monotheism
monotone n (pl -**s**) unvaried pitch in speech or sound > **monotony** n (pl -**s**)
monotones n ▷ monotone
monotonies n ▷ monotone
monotonous adj tedious due to lack of variety > **monotonously** adv
monotonously adv ▷ monotous
monseigneur [mon-sen-**nyur**] n (pl **messeigneurs**) [may-sen-**nyur**] title of French prelates
monsieur [muss-**syur**] n (pl **messieurs**) [may-**syur**] French title of address equivalent to sir or Mr
monsignor n (pl -**s**) (RC CHURCH) title attached to certain offices
monsignors n ▷ monsignor
monsoon n (pl -**s**) seasonal wind of SE Asia
monsoons n ▷ monsoon
monster n (pl -**s**) imaginary, usu. frightening, beast ▸ adj huge
monsters n ▷ monster
monstrance n (pl -**ces**) (RC CHURCH) container in which the consecrated Host is exposed for

adoration
monstrances n ▷ monstrance
monstrocities n ▷ monstrosity
monstrosity n (pl -**ties**) large ugly thing
monstrous adj unnatural or ugly > **monstrously** adv
monstrously adv ▷ monstrous
montage [mon-**tahzh**] n (pl -**s**) (making of) a picture composed from pieces of others
montages n ▷ montage
month n (pl -**s**) one of the twelve divisions of the calendar year
monthlies n ▷ month
monthly adj happening or payable once a month ▸ adv once a month ▸ n (pl -**lies**) monthly magazine
months n ▷ month
monument n (pl -**s**) something, esp. a building or statue, that commemorates something
monumental adj large, impressive, or lasting > **monumentally** adv
monumentally adv ▷ monumental
monuments n ▷ monument
moo n (pl -**s**) long deep cry of a cow ▸ v (-**s**, -**ing**, -**ed**) make this noise
mooed v ▷ moo
mooing v ▷ moo
moos n, v ▷ moo
mooch v (-**es**, -**ing**, -**ed**) (Slang) loiter about aimlessly
mooched v ▷ mooch
mooches v ▷ mooch
mooching v ▷ mooch
mood[1] n (pl -**s**) temporary (gloomy) state of mind
mood[2] n (GRAMMAR) form of a verb indicating whether it expresses a fact, wish, supposition, or command
moodier adj ▷ moody
moodiest adj ▷ moody
moodily adv ▷ moody
moods n ▷ mood[1,2]
moody adj (-**dier**, -**iest**) sullen or gloomy > **moodily** adv
moon n (pl -**s**) natural satellite of the earth ▸ v (-**s**, -**ing**, -**ed**) (foll. by **about** or **around**) be idle in a listless or dreamy way
mooned v ▷ moon
mooning v ▷ moon
moonlight n (pl -**s**) light from the moon ▸ v (-**s**, -**ing**, -**ed**) (Informal) work at a secondary job, esp. illegally
moonlighted v ▷ moonlight
moonlighting v ▷ moonlight
moonlights n, v ▷ moonlight

moons *n, v* ▷ **moon**
moonshine *n* (*pl* **-s**) (US & CANADIAN) illicitly distilled whisky
 moonshines *n* ▷ **moonshine**
moonstone *n* (*pl* **-s**) translucent semiprecious stone
 moonstones *n* ▷ **moonstone**
moonstruck *adj* slightly mad or odd
moor[1] *n* (*pl* **-s**) (BRIT) tract of open uncultivated ground covered with grass and heather
moor[2] *v* (**-s, -ing, -ed**) secure (a ship) with ropes etc. > **mooring** *n* (*pl* **-s**)
 moored *v* ▷ **moor**[2]
moorhen *n* (*pl* **-s**) small black water bird
 moorhens *n* ▷ **moorhen**
 mooring *v, n* ▷ **moor**[2]
 moors *n* ▷ **moor**[1] ▶ *v* ▷ **moor**[2]
moose *n* large N American deer
moot *adj* (**-er, -est**) debatable ▶ *v* (**-s, -ing, -ed**) bring up for discussion
 mooted *v* ▷ **moot**
 mooter *adj* ▷ **moot**
 mootest *adj* ▷ **moot**
 mooting *v* ▷ **moot**
 moots *v* ▷ **moot**
mop *n* (*pl* **-s**) long stick with twists of cotton or a sponge on the end, used for cleaning ▶ *v* (**-s, -pping, -pped**) clean or soak up with or as if with a mop
mope *v* (**-pes, -ping, -ped**) be gloomy and apathetic
moped *n* (*pl* **-s**) light motorized cycle ▶ *v* ▷ **mope**
 mopeds *v* ▷ **mope**
 mopes *v* ▷ **mope**
 moping *v* ▷ **mope**
mopoke *n* (*pl* **-s**) small spotted owl of Australia and New Zealand
 mopokes *n* ▷ **mopoke**
 mopped *v* ▷ **mop**
 mopping *v* ▷ **mop**
 mops *n, v* ▷ **mop**
moraine *n* (*pl* **-s**) accumulated mass of debris deposited by a glacier
 moraines *n* ▷ **moraine**
moral *adj* concerned with right and wrong conduct ▶ *n* (*pl* **-s**) lesson to be obtained from a story or event > **morally** *adv*
morale [mor-**rahl**] *n* (*pl* **-s**) degree of confidence or hope of a person or group
 morales *n* ▷ **morale**
moralist *n* (*pl* **-s**) person with a strong sense of right and wrong
 moralists *n* ▷ **moralist**
 moralities *n* ▷ **morality**

morality *n* (*pl* **-ties**) good moral conduct
moralize *v* (**-zes, -zing, -zed**) make moral pronouncements
 moralized *v* ▷ **moralize**
 moralizes *v* ▷ **moralize**
 moralizing *v* ▷ **moralize**
 morally *adv* ▷ **moral**
 morals *n* ▷ **moral**
morass *n* (*pl* **-es**) marsh
 morasses *n* ▷ **morass**
 moratoria *n* ▷ **moratorium**
moratorium *n* (*pl* **-ria, -riums**) legally authorized ban or delay
 moratoriums *n* ▷ **moratorium**
moray *n* (*pl* **-s**) large voracious eel
 morays *n* ▷ **moray**
morbid *adj* unduly interested in death or unpleasant events
mordant *adj* sarcastic or scathing ▶ *n* (*pl* **-s**) substance used to fix dyes
 mordants *n* ▷ **mordant**
more *adj* greater in amount or degree ▷ **much, many** ▶ *adv* to a greater extent ▶ *pron* greater or additional amount or number
moreover *adv* in addition to what has already been said
mores [**more**-rayz] *pl n* customs and conventions embodying the fundamental values of a community
morgue *n* (*pl* **-s**) mortuary
 morgues *n* ▷ **morgue**
moribund *adj* without force or vitality
morn *n* (*pl* **morns**) (*Poetic*) morning
 morns *n* ▷ **morn**
morning *n* (*pl* **-s**) part of the day before noon
 mornings *n* ▷ **morning**
morocco *n* (*pl* **-s**) goatskin leather
 moroccos *n* ▷ **morocco**
moron *n* (*pl* **-s**) (*Informal*) foolish or stupid person > **moronic** *adj*
 moronic *adj* ▷ **moron**
 morons *n* ▷ **moron**
morose [mor-**rohss**] *adj* (**-r, -st**) sullen or moody
 moroser *adj* ▷ **morose**
 morosest *adj* ▷ **morose**
 morphia *n* ▷ **morphine**
 morphines *n* ▷ **morphine**
morphine, morphia *n* (*pl* **-s**) drug extracted from opium, used as an anaesthetic and sedative
 morphological *adj* ▷ **morphology**
 morphologies *n* ▷ **morphology**
morphology *n* (*pl* **-gies**) science of forms and structures of organisms or words > **morphological** *adj*

morrow n (pl -s) (Poetic) next day
　morrows n ▷ morrow
morse n (pl -s) clasp or fastening
morsel n (pl -s) small piece, esp. of food
　morsels n ▷ morsel
　morses n ▷ morse
mortal adj subject to death ▶ n (pl -s) human
　being > **mortally** adv
　mortalities n ▷ mortal
mortality n (pl -ties) state of being mortal
　mortally adj ▷ mortal
　mortals n ▷ mortal
mortar n (pl -s) small cannon with a short
　range
mortarboard n (pl -s) black square academic
　cap
　mortarboards n ▷ mortarboard
　mortars n ▷ mortar
mortgage n (pl -s) conditional pledging of
　property, esp. a house, as security for the
　repayment of a loan ▶ v (-ges, -ging, -ged)
　pledge (property) as security thus
　mortgaged v ▷ mortgage
mortgagee n (pl -s) creditor in a mortgage
　mortgagees n ▷ mortgagee
　mortgages n, v ▷ mortgage
　mortgaging v ▷ mortgage
mortgagor n (pl -s) debtor in a mortgage
　mortgagors n ▷ mortgagor
mortice, mortise [more-tiss] n (pl -s) hole in
　a piece of wood or stone shaped to receive a
　matching projection on another piece
　mortices n ▷ mortice
　mortification n ▷ mortify
　mortifications n ▷ mortify
　mortified v ▷ mortify
　mortifies v ▷ mortify
mortify v (-fies, -fying, -fied) humiliate
　> **mortification** n (pl -s)
　mortifying v ▷ mortify
　mortise n ▷ mortice
　mortises n ▷ mortice
　mortuaries n ▷ mortuary
mortuary n (pl -aries) building where corpses
　are kept before burial or cremation
mosaic [mow-**zay**-ik] n (pl -s) design or
　decoration using small pieces of coloured
　stone or glass
　mosaics n ▷ mosaic
mosque n (pl -s) Muslim temple
　mosques n ▷ mosque
mosquito n (pl -toes, -tos) blood-sucking
　flying insect
　mosquitoes n ▷ mosquito
　mosquitos n ▷ mosquito

moss n (pl -es) small flowerless plant growing
　in masses on moist surfaces > **mossy** adj
　(-ssier, -ssiest)
　mosses n ▷ moss
　mossier adj ▷ moss
　mossiest adj ▷ moss
　mossy adj (-ssier, -ssiest) ▷ moss
most n greatest number or degree ▶ adj
　greatest in number or degree ▷ **much, many**
　▶ adv in the greatest degree
mostly adv for the most part, generally
motel n (pl -s) roadside hotel for motorists
　motels n ▷ motel
motet n (pl -s) short sacred choral song
　motets n ▷ motet
moth n (pl -s) nocturnal insect like a butterfly
mothball n (pl -s) small ball of camphor or
　naphthalene used to repel moths from stored
　clothes ▶ v (-ed, -ing, -ed) store (something
　operational) for future use
　mothballed v ▷ moth
　mothballing v ▷ moth
　mothballs n, v ▷ moth
　moths n ▷ moth
mother n (pl -s) female parent ▶ adj native
　or inborn ▶ v (-s, -ing, -ed) look after as a
　mother > **motherhood** n (pl -s) > **motherly** adj
　> **motherless** adj
　mothered v ▷ mother
　motherhood n ▷ mother
　motherhoods n ▷ mother
　mothering v ▷ mother
　motherless adj ▷ mother
　motherly adj ▷ mother
　mothers n, v ▷ mother
　mothers-in-law n ▷ mother-in-law
motif [moh-**teef**] n (pl -s) (recurring) theme
　or design
　motifs n ▷ motif
motion n (pl -s) process, action, or way of
　moving ▶ v (-s, -ing, -ed) direct (someone)
　by gesture
　motioned v ▷ motion
　motioning v ▷ motion
motionless adj not moving
　motions n, v ▷ motion
motivate v (-tes, -ting, -ted) give incentive to
　> **motivation** n (pl -s)
　motivated v ▷ motivate
　motivates v ▷ motivate
　motivating v ▷ motivate
　motivation n ▷ motivate
　motivations n ▷ motivate
motive n (pl -s) reason for a course of action
　▶ adj causing motion

motives *n* ▷ **motive**
motley *adj* miscellaneous
motocross *n* (*pl* **-es**) motorcycle race over a rough course
motocrosses *n* ▷ **motocross**
motor *n* (*pl* **-s**) engine, esp. of a vehicle ▶ *v* (**-s, -ing, -ed**) travel by car ▷ **motorized** *adj* equipped with a motor or motor transport ▷ **motorbike** *n* (*pl* **-s**) ▷ **motorboat** *n* (*pl* **-s**) ▷ **motorcar** *n* (*pl* **-s**) ▷ **motorcycle** *n* (*pl* **-s**) ▷ **motorcyclist** *n* (*pl* **-s**)
motorbike *n* ▷ **motor**
motorbikes *n* ▷ **motor**
motorboat *n* ▷ **motor**
motorboats *n* ▷ **motor**
motorcar *n* ▷ **motor**
motorcars *n* ▷ **motor**
motorcycle *n* ▷ **motor**
motorcycles *n* ▷ **motor**
motorcyclist *n* ▷ **motor**
motorcyclists *n* ▷ **motor**
motored *v* ▷ **motor**
motoring *v* ▷ **motor**
motorist *n* (*pl* **-s**) driver of a car
motorists *n* ▷ **motorist**
motorized *adj* ▷ **motor**
motors *n*, *v* ▷ **motor**
motorway *n* (*pl* **-s**) main road for fast-moving traffic
motorways *n* ▷ **motorway**
mottled *adj* marked with blotches
motto *n* (*pl* **-ttoes, -ttos**) saying expressing an ideal or rule of conduct
mottoes *n* ▷ **motto**
mottos *n* ▷ **motto**
mould[1] *n* (*pl* **-s**) hollow container in which metal etc. is cast ▶ *v* (**-s, -ing, -ed**) shape
mould[2] *n* (*pl* **-s**) fungal growth caused by dampness
mould[3] *n* (*pl* **-s**) loose soil
moulded *v* ▷ **mould**[1]
moulder *v* (**-s, -ing, -ed**) decay into dust
mouldered *v* ▷ **moulder**
mouldering *v* ▷ **moulder**
moulders *v* ▷ **moulder**
mouldier *adj* ▷ **mouldy**
mouldiest *adj* ▷ **mouldy**
moulding *n* (*pl* **-s**) moulded ornamental edging ▶ *v* ▷ **mould**[1]
moulds *n* ▷ **mould**[1,2,3] ▶ *v* ▷ **mould**[1]
mouldy *adj* (**-dier, -diest**) stale or musty; dull or boring
moult *v* (**-s, -ing, -ed**) shed feathers, hair, or skin to make way for new growth ▶ *n* (*pl* **-s**) process of moulting

moulted *v* ▷ **moult**
moulting *v* ▷ **moult**
moults *v*, *n* ▷ **moult**
mound *n* (*pl* **-s**) heap, esp. of earth or stones
mounds *n* ▷ **mound**
mount *v* (**-s, -ing, -ed**) climb or ascend ▶ *n* (*pl* **-s**) backing or support on which something is fixed
mountain *n* (*pl* **-s**) hill of great size ▷ **mountainous** *adj* full of mountains *n* (*pl* **-s**) person who climbs mountains ▷ **mountaineering** *n* (*pl* **-s**)
mountaineering *n* ▷ **mountaineer**
mountaineerings *n* ▷ **mountaineer**
mountaineers *n* ▷ **mountaineer**
mountains *n* ▷ **mountain**
mountebank *n* (*pl* **-s**) charlatan or fake
mountebanks *n* ▷ **mountebank**
mounted *v* ▷ **mount**
mounting *v* ▷ **mount**
mounts *v*, *n* ▷ **mount**
mourn *v* (**-s, -ing, -ed**) feel or express sorrow for (a dead person or lost thing)
mourned *v* ▷ **mourn**
mourner *n* (*pl* **mourners**) person attending a funeral
mourners *n* ▷ **mourner**
mournful *adj* (**-ler, -lest**) sad or dismal ▷ **mournfully** *adv*
mournfuller *adj* ▷ **mournful**
mournfullest *adj* ▷ **mournful**
mournfully *adv* ▷ **mournful**
mourning *n* (*pl* **-s**) grieving ▶ *v* ▷ **mourn**
mournings *n* ▷ **mourning**
mourns *v* ▷ **mourn**
mouse *n* (*pl* **mice**) small long-tailed rodent
mouser *n* (*pl* **-s**) cat used to catch mice
mousers *n* ▷ **mouser**
mousse *n* (*pl* **-s**) dish of flavoured cream whipped and set
mousses *n* ▷ **mousse**
moustache *n* (*pl* **-s**) hair on the upper lip
moustaches *n* ▷ **moustache**
mousy *adj* like a mouse, esp. in hair colour
mouth *n* (*pl* **-s**) opening in the head for eating and issuing sounds ▶ *v* (**-s, -ing, -ed**) form (words) with the lips without speaking
mouthed *v* ▷ **mouth**
mouthful *n* (*pl* **-s**) amount of food or drink put into the mouth at any one time when eating or drinking
mouthfuls *n* ▷ **mouthful**
mouthing *v* ▷ **mouth**
mouthpiece *n* (*pl* **-s**) part of a telephone into which a person speaks

mouthpieces *n* ▷ **mouthpiece**
mouths *n*, *v* ▷ **mouth**
move *v* (-ves, -ving, -ved) change in place or position ▶ *n* (*pl* -s) moving > **movable,** **moveable** *adj*
movement *n* (*pl* -s) action or process of moving
movements *n* ▷ **movement**
moved *v* ▷ **move**
moves *v*, *n* ▷ **move**
movie *n* (*pl* -s) (*Informal*) cinema film
movies *n* ▷ **movie**
moving *v* ▷ **move**
mow *v* (-s, -ing, -ed *or* **mown**) cut (grass or crops)
mowed *v* ▷ **mow**
mower *n* (*pl* -s) machine for cutting grass
mowers *n* ▷ **mower**
mowing *v* ▷ **mow**
mown *v* ▷ **mow**
mows *v* ▷ **mow**

moz *n* (**mozes**). Moz is an old Australian slang word for a jinx or hex. This is an unusual word that is worth remembering as it can be very useful if you have a Z but little chance to play it on a crowded board. Moz scores 14 points.

mozzarella [mot-sa-**rel**-la] *n* (*pl* -s) moist white cheese originally made in Italy from buffalo milk
mozzarellas *n* ▷ **mozzarella**

mu *n* (**mus**). Mu is the 12th letter in the Greek alphabet. This is a useful word to remember: it won't score you many points on its own, but it can be very helpful on a crowded board when you need to form words in different directions. Mu scores 4 points.

much *adj* (**more, most**) large amount or degree of ▶ *n* large amount or degree ▶ *adv* (**more, most**) to a great degree
mucilage [**mew**-sill-ij] *n* (*pl* -s) gum or glue
mucilages *n* ▷ **mucilage**
muck *n* (*pl* -s) dirt, filth > **mucky** *adj*
mucks *n* ▷ **mucks**
mucky *adj* ▷ **mucks**
mucus [**mew**-kuss] *n* (*pl* -s) slimy secretion of the mucous membranes
mucuses *n* ▷ **mucus**
mud *n* (*pl* -s) wet soft earth > **muddy** *adj*
muddier *adj* ▷ **mud**
muddiest *adj* ▷ **mud**
muddy *adj* (-ddier, -ddiest) ▷ **mud**
mudguard *n* (*pl* -s) cover over a wheel to prevent mud or water being thrown up by it
mudguards *n* ▷ **mudguard**
muds *n* ▷ **mud**
muddle *v* (-les, -ling, -led) (*often foll. by* **up**) confuse ▶ *n* (*pl* -s) state of confusion
muddled *v* ▷ **muddle**
muddles *v*, *n* ▷ **muddle**
muddling *v* ▷ **muddle**
muesli [**mewz**-lee] *n* (*pl* -s) mixture of grain, nuts, and dried fruit, eaten with milk
mueslis *n* ▷ **muesli**
muezzin [moo-**ezz**-in] *n* (*pl* -s) official who summons Muslims to prayer
muezzins *n* ▷ **muezzin**
muff¹ *n* (*pl* -s) tube-shaped covering to keep the hands warm
muff² *v* (-s, -ing, -ed) bungle (an action)
muffed *v* ▷ **muff**
muffin *n* (*pl* -s) light round flat yeast cake
muffing *v* ▷ **muff**
muffins *n* ▷ **muffin**
muffs *n* ▷ **muff¹** ▶ *v* ▷ **muff²**
muffle *v* (-les, -ling, -led) wrap up for warmth or to deaden sound
muffled *v* ▷ **muffle**
muffler *n* (*pl* -s) (BRIT) scarf
mufflers *n* ▷ **muffle**
muffles *v* ▷ **muffle**
muffling *v* ▷ **muffle**
mufti *n* (*pl* -s) civilian clothes worn by a person who usually wears a uniform
muftis *n* ▷ **mufti**
mug¹ *n* (*pl* -s) large drinking cup
mug² *n* (*pl* -s) (*Slang*) face ▶ *v* (-s, -gging, -gged) (*Informal*) attack in order to rob > **mugger** *n* (*pl* -s)
mug³ *v* (-s, -gging, -gged) (*foll. by* **up**) (*Informal*) study hard
mugged *v* ▷ **mug²·³**
mugger *v* ▷ **mug²**
muggers *v* ▷ **mug²**
muggier *adj* ▷ **muggy**
muggiest *adj* ▷ **muggy**
mugging *v* ▷ **mug²·³**
muggins *n* (*Informal*) stupid or gullible person
muggy *adj* (-ggier, -ggiest) (of weather) damp and stifling
mugs *n* ▷ **mug¹·²**
mulatto [mew-**lat**-toe] *n* (*pl* -tos, -toes) child of one Black and one White parent
mulattoes *adj* ▷ **mulatto**
mulattos *adj* ▷ **mulatto**
mulberries *n* ▷ **mulberry**
mulberry *n* (*pl* -rries) tree whose leaves are used to feed silkworms

mulch *n* (*pl* **-es**) mixture of wet straw, leaves, etc., used to protect the roots of plants ▸ *v* (**-es, -ing, -ed**) cover (land) with mulch
mulched *v* ▷ **mulch**
mulches *n, v* ▷ **mulch**
mulching *v* ▷ **mulch**
mule¹ *n* (*pl* **-s**) offspring of a horse and a donkey > **mulish** *adj* obstinate
mule² *n* backless shoe or slipper
mules *n* ▷ **mule¹,²**
mulga *n* (*pl* **-s**) Australian acacia shrub growing in desert regions
mulgas *n* ▷ **mulga**
mulish *adj* ▷ **mule¹**
mull *v* (**-s, -ing, -ed**) think (over) or ponder > **mulled** *adj* (of wine or ale) flavoured with sugar and spices and served hot
mullah *n* (*pl* **-s**) Muslim scholar, teacher, or religious leader
mullahs *n* ▷ **mullah**
mulled *v, adj* ▷ **mull**
mullet¹ *n* (*pl* **-s**) edible sea fish
mullet² *n* (*pl* **-s**) haircut in which the hair is short at the top and sides and long at the back
mullets *n* ▷ **mullet¹,²**
mulling *v* ▷ **mull**
mulls *v* ▷ **mull**
mulligatawnies *n* ▷ **mulligatawny**
mulligatawny *n* (*pl* **-nies**) soup made with curry powder
mullion *n* (*pl* **-s**) vertical dividing bar in a window > **mullioned** *adj*
mullioned *adj* ▷ **mullion**
mullions *n* ▷ **mullion**
mulloway *n* (*pl* **-s**) large Australian sea fish, valued for sport and food
mulloways *n* ▷ **mulloway**
multifarious [mull-tee-**fare**-ee-uss] *adj* having many various parts
multiple *adj* having many parts ▸ *n* (*pl* **-s**) quantity which contains another an exact number of times
multiples *n* ▷ **multiple**
multiplex *n* (*pl* **-es**) purpose-built complex containing several cinemas and usu. restaurants and bars ▸ *adj* having many elements, complex
multiplexes *n* ▷ **multiplex**
multiplicities *n* ▷ **multiplicity**
multiplicity *n* (*pl* **-ties**) large number or great variety
multiply *v* (**-lies, -lying, -lied**) (cause to) increase in number, quantity, or degree > **multiplication** *n* (*pl* **-s**)

multiplicand *n* (*pl* **-s**) (MATHS) number to be multiplied
multiplicands *n* ▷ **multiplicand**
multiplication *n* ▷ **multiply**
multiplications *n* ▷ **multiply**
multiplied *v* ▷ **multiply**
multiplies *v* ▷ **multiply**
multiplying *v* ▷ **multiply**
multipurpose *adj* having many uses
multitude *n* (*pl* **-s**) great number
multitudes *n* ▷ **multitude**
multitudinous *adj* very numerous
mum *n* (*pl* **-s**) (*Informal*) mother
mums *n* ▷ **mum**
mumble *v* (**-les, -ling, -led**) speak indistinctly, mutter
mumbled *v* ▷ **mumble**
mumbles *v* ▷ **mumble**
mumbling *v* ▷ **mumble**
mummer *n* (*pl* **-s**) actor in a traditional English folk play or mime
mummers *n* ▷ **mummer**
mummies *n* ▷ **mummer**
mummified *adj* (of a body) preserved as a mummy
mummy¹ *n* (*pl* **-mmies**) body embalmed and wrapped for burial in ancient Egypt
mummy² *n* (*pl* **-mmies**) ▷ **mother**
mumps *n* infectious disease with swelling in the glands of the neck
munch *v* (**-es, -ing, -ed**) chew noisily and steadily
munched *v* ▷ **munch**
munches *v* ▷ **munch**
munching *v* ▷ **munch**
mundane *adj* everyday
municipal *adj* relating to a city or town
municipalities *n* ▷ **municipality**
municipality *n* (*pl* **-ties**) city or town with local self-government
munificence *n* ▷ **munificent**
munificences *n* ▷ **munificent**
munificent [mew-**niff**-fiss-sent] *adj* very generous > **munificence** *n* (*pl* **-s**)
muniments *pl n* title deeds or similar documents
munitions *pl n* military stores
munted *adj* (NZ) (*Slang*) destroyed or ruined
mural *n* (*pl* **-s**) painting on a wall
murals *n* ▷ **mural**
murder *n* (*pl* **-s**) unlawful intentional killing of a human being ▸ *v* (**-s, -ing, -ed**) kill in this way > **murderer, murderess** *n* (*pl* **-s**) > **murderous** *adj*
murdered *v* ▷ **murder**

murderer n ▷ murder
murderers n ▷ murder
murderess n ▷ murder
murderesses n ▷ murder
murdering v ▷ murder
murderous adj ▷ murder
murders v, n ▷ murder
murk n (pl -s) thick darkness
murkier adj ▷ murky
murkiest adj ▷ murky
murks n ▷ murk
murky adj (-kier, -kiest) dark or gloomy
murmur v (-s, -ing, -ed) speak or say in a quiet
  indistinct way ▶ n (pl -s) continuous low
  indistinct sound
murmured v ▷ murmur
murmuring v ▷ murmur
murmurs v, n ▷ murmur
muscle n (pl -s) tissue in the body which
  produces movement by contracting
muscles n ▷ muscle
muscular adj with well-developed muscles
muse v (-ses, -sing, -sed) ponder quietly
mused v ▷ muse
musing v ▷ muse
muses v ▷ muse
museum n (pl -s) building where natural,
  artistic, historical, or scientific objects are
  exhibited and preserved
museums n ▷ museum
mush n (pl -es) soft pulpy mass > **mushy** adj
  (-shier, -shiest)
mushes n ▷ mush
mushier adj ▷ mush
mushiest adj ▷ mush
mushroom n (pl -s) edible fungus with a stem
  and cap ▶ v (-s, -ing, -ed) grow rapidly
mushroomed v ▷ mushroom
mushrooming v ▷ mushroom
mushrooms n, v ▷ mushroom
mushy (-shier, -shiest) adj ▷ mush
music n (pl -s) art form using a melodious
  and harmonious combination of notes ▶ n
  (pl -s) play or film with songs and dancing
  > **musician** n (pl -s)
musical adj of or like music > **musically** adv
musically adv ▷ musical
musician n ▷ music
musicians n ▷ music
musicologies n ▷ musicology
musicologist n ▷ musicology
musicologists n ▷ musicology
musicology n (pl -gies) scientific study of
  music > **musicologist** n (pl -s)
musics n ▷ music

musk n (pl -s) scent obtained from a gland
  of the musk deer or produced synthetically
  > **musky** adj (-kier, -kiest)
musket n (pl -s) (HIST) long-barrelled gun
  > **musketeer** n (pl -s)
musketeer n ▷ musket
musketeers n ▷ musket
musketries n ▷ musketry
musketry n (pl -ries) (use of) muskets
muskets n ▷ musket
muskier adj ▷ musk
muskiest adj ▷ musk
muskrat n (pl -s) N American beaver-like
  rodent
muskrats n ▷ muskrat
musks n ▷ musk
musky adj (-kier, -kiest) ▷ musk
muslin n (pl -s) fine cotton fabric
muslins n ▷ muslin
mussel n (pl -s) edible shellfish with a dark
  hinged shell
mussels n ▷ mussel
must[1] v used as an auxiliary to express
  obligation, certainty, or resolution ▶ n (pl -s)
  essential or necessary thing
must[2] n (pl -s) newly pressed grape juice
musts n ▷ must[1,2]
mustang n (pl -s) wild horse of SW USA
mustangs n ▷ mustang
mustard n (pl -s) paste made from the
  powdered seeds of a plant, used as a
  condiment
mustards n ▷ mustard
muster v (-s, -ing, -ed) assemble ▶ n (pl -s)
  assembly of military personnel
mustered v ▷ muster
mustering v ▷ muster
musters v, n ▷ muster
mustier adj ▷ musty
mustiest adj ▷ musty
mustiness n ▷ musty
mustinesses n ▷ musty
musty adj (mustier, mustiest) smelling
  mouldy and stale > **mustiness** n (pl -es)
mutabilities n ▷ mutable
mutability n ▷ mutable
mutable [mew-tab-bl] adj liable to change
  > **mutability** n (pl -ties)
mutant n (pl -s) mutated animal, plant, etc.
mutants n ▷ mutant
mutate v (-tes, -ting, -ted) (cause to) undergo
  mutation
mutated v ▷ mutate
mutates v ▷ mutate
mutating v ▷ mutate

mutation n (pl -s) (genetic) change
   mutations n ▷ **mutation**
mute adj (-r, -st) silent ▶ n (pl -s) person who is
   unable to speak > **mutely** adv
muted adj (of sound or colour) softened
   mutely adv ▷ **mute**
   muter adj ▷ **mute**
   mutes n ▷ **mute**
   mutest adj ▷ **mute**
muti [moo-ti] n (pl -s) (S AFR) (Informal) medicine,
   esp. herbal medicine
   mutis n ▷ **muti**
mutilate [mew-till-ate] v (-tes, -ting, -ted)
   deprive of a limb or other part > **mutilation**
   n (pl -s)
   mutilated v ▷ **mutilate**
   mutilates v ▷ **mutilate**
   mutilating v ▷ **mutilate**
   mutilation n ▷ **mutilate**
   mutilations n ▷ **mutilate**
   mutineer n ▷ **mutiny**
   mutineers n ▷ **mutiny**
   mutinied v ▷ **mutiny**
   mutinies v ▷ **mutiny**
   mutinous n ▷ **mutiny**
mutiny [mew-tin-ee] n (pl -nies) rebellion
   against authority, esp. by soldiers or sailors
   ▶ v (-nies, -nying, -nied) commit mutiny
   > **mutineer** n (pl -s) > **mutinous** adj
   mutinying n ▷ **mutiny**
mutt n (pl -s) (Slang) mongrel dog
   mutts n ▷ **mutt**
mutter v (-s, -ing, -ed) utter or speak
   indistinctly ▶ n (pl -s) muttered sound or
   grumble
   muttered v ▷ **mutter**
   muttering v ▷ **mutter**
   mutters v, n ▷ **mutter**
mutton n (pl -s) flesh of sheep, used as food
   muttons n ▷ **mutton**
mutual [mew-chew-al] adj felt or expressed
   by each of two people about the other
   > **mutually** adv
   mutually adv ▷ **mutual**

> **mux** v (muxes, muxing, muxed). Mux
> is an old American word meaning
> to make a mess of something. This
> word is very useful not only because
> it contains an X, but because its verb
> forms can enable you to clear your rack
> of unpromising letters. Mux scores
> 12 points.
> **muzjik** n (muzjiks). A muzjik is a
> Russian peasant. This is a great high-
> scoring word, combining Z, J and K. If

> you can play the plural using all of your
> tiles, you'll get a bonus of 50 points.
> Muzjik scores 28 points.

muzzle n (pl -s) animal's mouth and nose ▶ v
   (-les, -ling, -led) prevent from being heard
   or noticed
   muzzled v ▷ **muzzle**
   muzzles n, v ▷ **muzzle**
   muzzling v ▷ **muzzle**
muzzy adj (-zzier, -zziest) confused or muddled
my adj belonging to me
myall n (pl -s) Australian acacia with hard
   scented wood
   myalls n ▷ **myall**
mycology n (pl -gies) study of fungi
   mycologies n ▷ **mycology**
myna, mynah, mina n (pl -s) Asian bird which
   can mimic human speech
   mynah n ▷ **myna**
   mynahs n ▷ **myna**
   mynas n ▷ **myna**
myopia [my-oh-pee-a] n (pl -s) short-
   sightedness > **myopic** [my-op-ik] ▶ adj
   myopias n ▷ **myopia**
   myopic adj ▷ **myopia**
myriad [mir-ree-ad] adj innumerable ▶ n (pl -s)
   large indefinite number
   myriads n ▷ **myriad**
myrrh [mur] n (pl -s) aromatic gum used in
   perfume, incense, and medicine
   myrrhs n ▷ **myrrh**
myrtle [mur-tl] n (pl -s) flowering evergreen
   shrub
   myrtles n ▷ **myrtle**
   myself pron ▷ **I**
   mysteries n ▷ **mystery**
   mysterious adj ▷ **mystery**
   mysteriously adv ▷ **mystery**
mystery n (pl -ries) strange or inexplicable
   event or phenomenon > **mysterious** adj
   > **mysteriously** adv
mystic n (pl -s) person who seeks spiritual
   knowledge ▶ adj mystical > **mysticism** n (pl -s)
mystical adj having a spiritual or religious
   significance beyond human understanding
   mysticism n ▷ **mystic**
   mysticisms n ▷ **mystic**
   mystics n ▷ **mystic**
   mystification v ▷ **mystify**
   mystifications v ▷ **mystify**
   mystified v ▷ **mystify**
   mystifies v ▷ **mystify**
mystify v (-fies, -fying, -fied) bewilder or
   puzzle > **mystification** n (pl -s)
   mystifying v ▷ **mystify**

mystique [miss-**steek**] *n* (*pl* **-s**) aura of mystery
or power
mystiques *n* ▷ **mystique**
myth *n* (*pl* **-s**) tale with supernatural
characters, usu. of how the world and
mankind began > **mythical, mythic** *adj*
mythic *adj* ▷ **myth**
mythical *adj* ▷ **myth**

mythological *adj* ▷ **mythology**
mythologies *n* ▷ **mythology**
mythology *n* (*pl* **-gies**) myths collectively
> **mythological** *adj*
myths *n* ▷ **myth**
myxomatoses *n* ▷ **myxomatosis**
myxomatosis [mix-a-mat-**oh**-siss] *n* (*pl* **-ses**)
contagious fatal viral disease of rabbits

Nn

Along with R and T, N is one of the most common consonants in Scrabble. As you'll often have it on your rack, it's well worth learning what N can do in different situations. N is useful when you need short words, as it begins two-letter words with every vowel except I, and with Y as well. There are plenty of three-letter words starting with N, but there aren't many high-scoring ones. Remember words like **nab** (5 points), **nag** (4), **nap** (5), **nay** (6), **new** (6), **nib** (5), **nob** (5), **nod** (4) and **now** (6).

na *interj.* Na is a Scots word for **no** or **not**. This word can be very convenient when you need to form words in different directions. Na scores 2 points.

naan *n (pl -s)* ▷ nan bread
  naans *n* ▷ **naan**
naartjie [nahr-chee] *n (pl -s)* (S AFR) tangerine
  naartjies *n* ▷ **naartjie**
nab *v (-s, -bbing, -bbed)* (*Informal*) arrest (someone)
  nabbed *v* ▷ **nab**
  nabbing *v* ▷ **nab**
  nabs *v* ▷ **nab**
nadir *n (pl -s)* point in the sky opposite the zenith
  nadirs *n* ▷ **nadir**
  naevi *n* ▷ **naevus**
naevus [nee-vuss] *n (pl -vi)* birthmark or mole
naff *adj (-er, -est)* (BRIT) (*Slang*) lacking quality or taste
  naffer *adj* ▷ **naff**
  naffest *adj* ▷ **naff**
nag[1] *v (-s, -gging, -gged)* scold or find fault constantly ▶ *n (pl -s)* person who nags
  > **nagging** *adj, n (pl -s)*
nag[2] *n (pl -s)* (*Informal*) old horse
  nagged *v* ▷ **nag**[1]
  nagging *v, adj n* ▷ **nag**[1]
  naggings *n* ▷ **nag**[1]
  nags *v* ▷ **nag**[1] ▶ *n* ▷ **nag**[1,2]
naiad [nye-ad] *n (pl -s)* (GREEK MYTH) nymph living in a lake or river
  naiads *n* ▷ **naiad**
nail *n (pl -s)* pointed piece of metal with a head, hit with a hammer to join two objects together ▶ *v (-s, -ing, -ed)* attach (something) with nails

nailed *v* ▷ **nail**
nailing *v* ▷ **nail**
nails *n, v* ▷ **nail**
naive [nye-eev] *adj (-r, -st)* innocent and gullible > **naively** *adv* > **naivety** [nye-eev-tee] *n (pl -ties)*, **naïveté** *(pl -s)*
naively *adv* ▷ **naive**
naiver *adj* ▷ **naive**
naivest *adj* ▷ **naive**
naïveté *n* ▷ **naive**
naïvetés *n* ▷ **naive**
naiveties *n* ▷ **naive**
naivety *n* ▷ **naive**
naked *adj (-er, -est)* without clothes
  > **nakedness** *n (pl -es)*
  nakeder *adj* ▷ **naked**
  nakedest *adj* ▷ **naked**
  nakedness *n* ▷ **naked**
  nakednesses *n* ▷ **naked**
name *n (pl -s)* word by which a person or thing is known ▶ *v (-mes, -ming, -med)* give a name to
  named *v* ▷ **name**
nameless *adj* without a name
namely *adv* that is to say
  names *n, v* ▷ **name**
namesake *n (pl -s)* person with the same name as another
  namesakes *n* ▷ **namely**
  naming *v* ▷ **name**
  nannies *n* ▷ **nanny**
nanny *n (pl -nnies)* woman whose job is looking after young children
nap[1] *n (pl -s)* short sleep ▶ *v (-s, -pping, -pped)* have a short sleep
nap[2] *n (pl -s)* raised fibres of velvet or similar cloth

nap³ n (pl **-s**) card game similar to whist
napalm n (pl **-s**) highly inflammable jellied
petrol, used in bombs
  napalms n ▷ **napalm**
nape n (pl **-s**) back of the neck
  napes n ▷ **nape**
naphtha n (pl **-s**) liquid mixture distilled from
coal tar or petroleum, used as a solvent and
in petrol
naphthalene n (pl **-s**) white crystalline
product distilled from coal tar or petroleum,
used in disinfectants, mothballs, and
explosives
  naphthalenes n ▷ **naphthalene**
  naphthas n ▷ **naphtha**
napkin n (pl **-s**) piece of cloth or paper for
wiping the mouth or protecting the clothes
while eating
  napkins n ▷ **napkin**
  napped v ▷ **nap¹**
  nappies n ▷ **nappy**
  napping v ▷ **nap¹**
nappy n (pl **-ppies**) piece of absorbent material
fastened round a baby's lower torso to absorb
urine and faeces
  naps n ▷ **nap** ▶ v ▷ **nap¹**
narcissism n (pl **-s**) exceptional interest in or
admiration for oneself > **narcissistic** adj
  narcissisms n ▷ **narcissism**
  narcissistic adj ▷ **narcissism**
  narcissi n ▷ **narcissus**
narcissus n (pl **-cissi**) yellow, orange, or white
flower related to the daffodil
  narcoses n ▷ **narcosis**
narcosis n (pl **-s**) effect of a narcotic
narcotic n (pl **-s**) ▶ adj (of) a drug, such as
morphine or opium, which produces
numbness and drowsiness, used medicinally
but addictive
  narcotics n ▷ **narcotic**
nark (Slang) v (**-s, -ing, -ed**) annoy ▶ n (pl **-s**)
informer or spy
  narked v ▷ **nark**
  narkier adj ▷ **narky**
  narkiest adj ▷ **narky**
  narking v ▷ **nark**
  narks v, n ▷ **nark**
narky adj (Slang) (**-kier, -kiest**) irritable or
complaining
narrate v (**-tes, -ting, -ted**) tell (a story)
> **narration** n (pl **-s**) > **narrator** n (pl **-s**)
  narrated v ▷ **narrate**
  narrates v ▷ **narrate**
  narrating v ▷ **narrate**
  narration n ▷ **narrate**

  narrations n ▷ **narrate**
narrative n (pl **-s**) account, story
  narratives n ▷ **narrative**
  narrator n ▷ **narrate**
  narrators n ▷ **narrate**
narrow adj (**-er, -est**) small in breadth in
comparison to length ▶ v (**-s, -ing, -ed**)
make or become narrow > **narrowly** adv
> **narrowness** n (pl **-es**)
  narrowed v ▷ **narrow**
  narrower adj ▷ **narrow**
  narrowest adj ▷ **narrow**
  narrowing v ▷ **narrow**
  narrowly adv ▷ **narrow**
  narrowness n ▷ **narrow**
  narrownesses n ▷ **narrow**
  narrows v ▷ **narrow** ▶ pl n narrow part of a
strait, river, or current
narwhal n (pl **-s**) arctic whale with a long
spiral tusk
  narwhals n ▷ **narwhal**
nasal adj of the nose > **nasally** adv
  nasally adv ▷ **nasal**
nascent adj starting to grow or develop
  nastier adj ▷ **nasty**
  nastiest adj ▷ **nasty**
  nastily adv ▷ **nasty**
  nastiness n ▷ **nasty**
  nastinesses n ▷ **nasty**
nasturtium n (pl **-s**) plant with yellow, red, or
orange trumpet-shaped flowers
  nasturtiums n ▷ **nasturtium**
nasty adj (**-tier, -tiest**) unpleasant > **nastily** adv
> **nastiness** n (pl **-es**)
natal adj of or relating to birth
nation n (pl **nations**) people of one or more
cultures or races organized as a single state
  nations n ▷ **nation**
national adj characteristic of a particular
nation ▶ n (pl **-s**) citizen of a nation
> **nationally** adv
nationalism n (pl **-s**) policy of national
independence > **nationalist** n (pl **-s**) adj
  nationalisms n ▷ **nationalism**
  nationalist n ▷ **nationalism**
  nationalists n ▷ **nationalism**
  nationalities n ▷ **nationality**
nationality n (pl **-ties**) fact of being a citizen of
a particular nation
  nationalization n ▷ **nationalize**
  nationalizations n ▷ **nationalize**
nationalize v (**-izes, -izing, -ized**) put (an
industry or a company) under state control
> **nationalization** n (pl **-s**)
  nationalized v ▷ **nationalize**

nationalizes v ▷ nationalize
nationalizing v ▷ nationalize
nationally adv ▷ national
nationals n ▷ national
native adj relating to a place where a person was born ▶ n (pl -s) person born in a specified place
natives n ▷ native
nativities n ▷ nativity
nativity n (pl -ties) birth or origin
natter (Informal) v (-s, -ing, -ed) talk idly or chatter ▶ n (pl -s) long idle chat
nattered v ▷ natter
nattering v ▷ natter
natters v, n ▷ natter
nattier adj ▷ natty
nattiest adj ▷ natty
natty adj (-ttier, -ttiest) (Informal) smart and spruce
natural adj normal or to be expected ▶ n (pl -s) person with an inborn talent or skill
naturalism n (pl -s) movement in art and literature advocating detailed realism
> **naturalistic** adj
naturalisms n ▷ naturalism
naturalist n (pl -s) student of natural history
naturalistic n ▷ naturalism
naturalists n ▷ naturalist
naturalization n ▷ naturalize
naturalizations n ▷ naturalize
naturalize v (-izes, -izing, -ized) give citizenship to (a person born in another country) > **naturalization** n (pl -s)
naturalized v ▷ naturalize
naturalizes v ▷ naturalize
naturalizing v ▷ naturalize
naturally adv of course
naturals n ▷ natural
nature n (pl -s) whole system of the existence, forces, and events of the physical world that are not controlled by human beings
natures n ▷ nature
naturism n (pl -s) nudism > **naturist** n (pl -s)
naturisms n ▷ naturism
naturist n ▷ naturism
naturists n ▷ naturism
naught n (pl -s) (Lit) nothing
naughtier adj ▷ naughty
naughtiest adj ▷ naughty
naughtily adv ▷ naughty
naughtiness n ▷ naughty
naughtinesses n ▷ naughty
naughts n ▷ naught
naughty adj (-tier, -tiest) disobedient or mischievous > **naughtily** adv > **naughtiness**

n (pl -es)
nausea [naw-zee-a] n (pl -s) feeling of being about to vomit
nauseas n ▷ nausea
nauseate v (-tes, -ting, -ted) make (someone) feel sick
nauseated v ▷ nauseate
nauseates v ▷ nauseate
nauseating v ▷ nauseate
nauseous adj as if about to vomit
nautical adj of the sea or ships
nautili n ▷ nautilus
nautilus n (pl -luses, -li) shellfish with many tentacles
nautiluses n ▷ nautilus
naval adj ▷ navy
nave n (pl -s) long central part of a church
navel n (pl -s) hollow in the middle of the abdomen where the umbilical cord was attached
navels n ▷ navel
naves n ▷ nave
navies n ▷ navy
navigable adj wide, deep, or safe enough to be sailed through
navigate v (-tes, -ting, -ted) direct or plot the path or position of a ship, aircraft, or car
> **navigation** n (pl -s) > **navigator** n (pl -s)
navigated v ▷ navigate
navigates v ▷ navigate
navigating v ▷ navigate
navigation n ▷ navigate
navigations n ▷ navigate
navigator n ▷ navigate
navigators n ▷ navigate
navvies n ▷ navvy
navvy n (pl -vvies) (BRIT) labourer employed on a road or a building site
navy n (pl -vies) branch of a country's armed services comprising warships with their crews and organization
nay interj (Obs) no

> **ne** adv. Ne is an old word meaning **not**. This handy little word can be very helpful when you are trying to form several words at once. Ne scores 2 points.

neanderthal [nee-ann-der-tahl] adj of a type of primitive man that lived in Europe before 12 000 BC
near prep, adv adj (-er, -est) indicating a place or time not far away ▶ adj almost being the thing specified ▶ v (-s, -ing, -ed) draw close (to) > **nearness** n (pl -es)
nearby adj not far away

neared v ▷ near
nearer adj ▷ near
nearest adj ▷ near
nearing v ▷ near
nearly adv almost
nearness n ▷ near
nearnesses n ▷ near
nears v ▷ near
nearside n (pl -s) side of a vehicle that is nearer the kerb
nearsides n ▷ nearside
neat adj (-er, -est) tidy and clean > **neatly** adv > **neatness** n (pl -es)
neater adj ▷ neat
neatest adj ▷ neat
neatly adv ▷ neat
neatness n ▷ neat
neatnesses n ▷ neat
nebula n (pl -lae) (ASTRONOMY) hazy cloud of particles and gases > **nebulous** adj vague and unclear
nebulae n ▷ nebula
nebulous adj ▷ nebula
necessarily adv ▷ necessary
necessary adj needed to obtain the desired result > **necessarily** adv
necessitate v (-tes, -ting, -ted) compel or require
necessitated v ▷ necessitate
necessitates v ▷ necessitate
necessitating v ▷ necessitate
necessities n ▷ necessity
necessity n (pl -ties) circumstances that inevitably require a certain result
neck n (pl -s) part of the body joining the head to the shoulders ▶ v (-s, -ing, -ed) (Slang) kiss and cuddle
necked v ▷ neck
neckerchief n (pl -s) piece of cloth worn tied round the neck
neckerchiefs n ▷ neckerchief
necking v ▷ neck
necklace n (pl -s) decorative piece of jewellery worn around the neck
necklaces n ▷ necklace
necks n, v ▷ neck
necromancies n ▷ necromancy
necromancy n (pl -cies) communication with the dead
necropolis [neck-rop-pol-liss] n (pl -ses) cemetery
necropolises n ▷ necropolis
nectar n (pl -s) sweet liquid collected from flowers by bees
nectars n ▷ nectar

nectarine n (pl -s) smooth-skinned peach
nectarines n ▷ nectarine
née [nay] prep indicating the maiden name of a married woman
need v (-s, -ing, -ed) require or be in want of ▶ n (pl -s) condition of lacking something
needed v ▷ need
needful adj necessary or required
needier adj ▷ needy
neediest adj ▷ needy
needing v ▷ need
needle n (pl -s) thin pointed piece of metal with an eye through which thread is passed for sewing ▶ v (-les, -ling, -led) (Informal) goad or provoke
needled v ▷ needle
needles n, v ▷ needle
needless adj unnecessary
needlework n (pl -s) sewing and embroidery
needleworks n ▷ needlework
needling v ▷ needle
needs v, n ▷ need ▶ adv (preceded or foll. by **must**) necessarily
needy adj (-dier, -diest) poor, in need of financial support
nefarious [nif-**fair**-ee-uss] adj wicked
negate v (-tes, -ting, -ted) invalidate > **negation** n (pl -s)
negated v ▷ negate
negates v ▷ negate
negating v ▷ negate
negation n ▷ negate
negations n ▷ negate
negative adj expressing a denial or refusal ▶ n (pl -s) negative word or statement
negatives n ▷ negative
neglect v (-s, -ing, -ed) take no care of ▶ n (pl -s) neglecting or being neglected > **neglectful** adj
neglected v ▷ neglect
neglectful adj ▷ neglect
neglecting v ▷ neglect
neglects v, n ▷ neglect
negligee [neg-lee-zhay] n (pl -s) woman's lightweight usu. lace-trimmed dressing gown
negligees n ▷ negligee
negligence n (pl -s) neglect or carelessness > **negligent** adj > **negligently** adv
negligences n ▷ negligence
negligent adj ▷ negligence
negligently adv ▷ negligence
negligible adj so small or unimportant as to be not worth considering
negotiable adj ▷ negotiate

negotiate v (-**tes, -ting, -ted**) discuss in order to reach (an agreement) > **negotiation** n (pl -s) > **negotiator** n (pl -s) > **negotiable** adj
negotiated v ▷ **negotiate**
negotiates v ▷ **negotiate**
negotiating v ▷ **negotiate**
negotiation n ▷ **negotiate**
negotiations n ▷ **negotiate**
negotiator n ▷ **negotiate**
negotiators n ▷ **negotiate**
neigh n (pl -s) loud high-pitched sound made by a horse ▶ v (-**s, -ing, -ed**) make this sound
neighed v ▷ **neigh**
neighing v ▷ **neigh**
neighs n, v ▷ **neigh**
neighbour n (pl -s) person who lives or is situated near another
neighbourhood n (pl -s) district
neighbourhoods n ▷ **neighbourhood**
neighbouring adj situated nearby
neighbourly adj kind, friendly, and helpful
neighbours n ▷ **neighbour**
neither adj, pron not one nor the other ▶ conj not
nemeses n ▷ **nemesis**
nemesis [nem-miss-iss] n (pl -ses) retribution or vengeance
neo- combining form new, recent, or a modern form of
neolith n (pl -s) stone implement from the Neolithic age
neoliths n ▷ **neolith**
neologism [nee-ol-a-jiz-zum] n (pl -s) newly-coined word or an established word used in a new sense
neologisms n ▷ **neologism**
neon n (pl -s) (CHEM) colourless odourless gaseous element used in illuminated signs and lights
neons n ▷ **neon**
neophyte n (pl -s) beginner or novice
neophytes n ▷ **neophyte**
nephew n (pl -s) son of one's sister or brother
nephews n ▷ **nephew**
nephritis [nif-frite-tiss] n (pl -tises) inflammation of a kidney
nephritises n ▷ **nephritis**
nepotism [nep-a-tiz-zum] n (pl -s) favouritism in business shown to relatives and friends
nepotisms n ▷ **nepotism**
nerd n (pl -s) (Slang) boring person obsessed with a particular subject
nerds n ▷ **nerd**
nerve n (pl -s) cordlike bundle of fibres that conducts impulses between the brain and

other parts of the body
nerveless adj numb, without feeling
nerves n ▷ **nerve** ▶ pl n anxiety or tension
nervier adj ▷ **nervy**
nerviest adj ▷ **nervy**
nervous adj apprehensive or worried > **nervously** adv > **nervousness** n (pl -es)
nervously adv ▷ **nervous**
nervousness n ▷ **nervous**
nervousnesses n ▷ **nervous**
nervy adj (-**vier, -viest**) excitable or nervous
nest n (pl -s) place or structure in which birds or certain animals lay eggs or give birth to young ▶ v (-**s, -ing, -ed**) make or inhabit a nest
nested v ▷ **nest**
nesting v ▷ **nest**
nests v, n ▷ **nest**
nestle v (-**les, -ling, -led**) snuggle
nestled v ▷ **nestle**
nestles v ▷ **nestle**
nestling n (pl -s) bird too young to leave the nest ▶ v ▷ **nestle**
nestlings n ▷ **nestling**
net[1] n (pl -s) fabric of meshes of string, thread, or wire with many openings ▶ v (-**s, -tting, -tted**) catch (a fish or animal) in a net
net[2], **nett** adj left after all deductions ▶ v (-**s, -tting, -tted**) yield or earn as a clear profit
netball n (pl -s) team game in which a ball has to be thrown through a net hanging from a ring at the top of a pole
netballs n ▷ **netball**
nether adj lower
nets v ▷ **net**[1, 2]
nets n ▷ **net**[1]
nett adj ▷ **net**[2]
netted v ▷ **net**[1, 2]
netting v ▷ **net**[1, 2] ▶ n (pl -s) material made of net
nettings n ▷ **netting**
nettle n (pl -s) plant with stinging hairs on the leaves
nettled adj irritated or annoyed
nettles n ▷ **nettle**
network n (pl -s) system of intersecting lines, roads, etc.
networks n ▷ **network**
neural adj of a nerve or the nervous system
neuralgia n (pl -s) severe pain along a nerve
neuralgias n ▷ **neuralgia**
neuritis [nyoor-rite-tiss] n (pl -tises) inflammation of a nerve or nerves
neuritises n ▷ **neuritis**
neurologies n ▷ **neurology**
neurologist n ▷ **neurology**

neurologists *n* ▷ **neurology**

neurology *n* (*pl* -**gies**) scientific study of the nervous system > **neurologist** *n* (*pl* -**s**)

neuroses *n* ▷ **neurosis**

neurosis *n* (*pl* -**ses**) mental disorder producing hysteria, anxiety, depression, or obsessive behaviour

neurotic *adj* emotionally unstable ▶ *n* (*pl* -**s**) neurotic person

neurotics *n* ▷ **neurotic**

neuter *adj* belonging to a particular class of grammatical inflections in some languages ▶ *v* (-**s, -ing, -ed**) castrate (an animal)

neutered *v* ▷ **neuter**

neutering *v* ▷ **neuter**

neuters *v* ▷ **neuter**

neutral *adj* taking neither side in a war or dispute ▶ *n* (*pl* -**s**) neutral person or nation > **neutrality** *n* (*pl* -**ties**)

neutralities *n* ▷ **neutral**

neutrality *n* ▷ **neutral**

neutralize *v* (-**izes, -izing, -ized**) make ineffective or neutral

neutralized *v* ▷ **neutralize**

neutralizes *v* ▷ **neutralize**

neutralizing *v* ▷ **neutralize**

neutrals *n* ▷ **neutral**

neutrino [new-**tree**-no] *n* (*pl* -**nos**) elementary particle with no mass or electrical charge

neutrinos *n* ▷ **neutrino**

neutron *n* (*pl* -**s**) electrically neutral elementary particle of about the same mass as a proton

neutrons *n* ▷ **neutron**

never *adv* at no time

nevertheless *adv* in spite of that

new *adj* (-**er, -est**) not existing before (*foll. by* **to**) ▶ *adv* recently

newbie (*Informal*) *n* (*pl* -**s**) person new to a job, club, etc

newbies *n* ▷ **newbie**

newborn *adj* recently or just born

newcomer *n* (*pl* -**s**) recent arrival or participant

newcomers *n* ▷ **newcomer**

newel *n* (*pl* -**s**) post at the top or bottom of a flight of stairs that supports the handrail

newels *n* ▷ **newel**

newer *adj* ▷ **new**

newest *adj* ▷ **new**

newfangled *adj* objectionably or unnecessarily modern

newlyweds *pl n* recently married couple

newness *n* (*pl* -**es**) novelty

newnesses *n* ▷ **newness**

news *n* important or interesting new happenings

newsagent *n* (*pl* -**s**) (BRIT) shopkeeper who sells newspapers and magazines

newsagents *n* ▷ **newsagent**

newscaster *n* ▷ **newsreader**

newscasters *n* ▷ **newsreader**

newsflash *n* (*pl* -**es**) brief important news item, which interrupts a radio or television programme

newsflashes *n* ▷ **newsflash**

newsier *adj* ▷ **newsy**

newsiest *adj* ▷ **newsy**

newsletter *n* (*pl* -**s**) bulletin issued periodically to members of a group

newsletters *n* ▷ **newsletter**

newspaper *n* (*pl* -**s**) weekly or daily publication containing news

newspapers *n* ▷ **newspaper**

newsprint *n* (*pl* -**s**) inexpensive paper used for newspapers

newsprints *n* ▷ **newsprint**

newsreader, newscaster *n* (*pl* -**s**) person who reads the news on the television or radio

newsreaders *n* ▷ **newsreader**

newsreel *n* (*pl* -**s**) short film giving news

newsreels *n* ▷ **newsreel**

newsroom *n* (*pl* -**s**) room where news is received and prepared for publication or broadcasting

newsrooms *n* ▷ **newsroom**

newsworthy *adj* sufficiently interesting to be reported as news

newsy *adj* (-**sier, -siest**) full of news

newt *n* (*pl* -**s**) small amphibious creature with a long slender body and tail

newton *n* (*pl* -**s**) unit of force

newtons *n* ▷ **newton**

newts *n* ▷ **newt**

next *adj, adv* immediately following

nexus *n* (*pl* **nexus**) connection or link

nib *n* (*pl* -**s**) writing point of a pen

nibble *v* (-**les, -ling, -led**) take little bites (of) ▶ *n* (*pl* -**les**) little bite

nibbled *v* ▷ **nibble**

nibbles *v, n* ▷ **nibble**

nibbling *v* ▷ **nibble**

nibs *n* (*pl* ▷ **nib**

nibses *n* ▷ **nibs**

nice *adj* (-**r, -st**) pleasant > **nicely** *adv* > **niceness** *n* (*pl* -**es**)

nicely *adv* ▷ **nice**

niceness *n* ▷ **nice**

nicenesses *n* ▷ **nice**

nicer *adj* ▷ **nice**

nicest *adj* ▷ **nice**
niceties *n* ▷ **nicety**
nicety *n* (*pl* **-ties**) subtle point
niche [neesh] *n* (*pl* **-s**) hollow area in a wall
niches *n* ▷ **niche**
nick *v* (**-s, -ing, -ed**) make a small cut in ▶ *n* (*pl* **-s**) small cut
nicked *v* ▷ **nick**
nickel *n* (*pl* **-s**) (CHEM) silvery-white metal often used in alloys
nickelodeon *n* (*pl* **-s**) (US) early type of jukebox
nickelodeons *n* ▷ **nickelodeon**
nickels *n* ▷ **nickel**
nicking *v* ▷ **nick**
nickname *n* (*pl* **-s**) familiar name given to a person or place ▶ *v* (**-mes, -ming, -med**) call by a nickname
nicknamed *v* ▷ **nickname**
nicknames *n, v* ▷ **nickname**
nicknaming *v* ▷ **nickname**
nicks *v, n* ▷ **nick**
nicotine *n* (*pl* **-s**) poisonous substance found in tobacco
nicotines *n* ▷ **nicotine**
niece *n* (*pl* **-s**) daughter of one's sister or brother
nieces *n* ▷ **niece**
niftier *adj* ▷ **nifty**
niftiest *adj* ▷ **nifty**
nifty *adj* (**-tier, -tiest**) (*Informal*) neat or smart
niggard *n* ▷ **niggardly**
niggardly *adj* stingy ▶ **niggard** *n* (*pl* **-s**) stingy person
niggards *n* ▷ **niggardly**
niggle *v* (**-les, -ling, -led**) worry slightly ▶ *n* (*pl* **-s**) small worry or doubt
niggled *v* ▷ **niggle**
niggles *v, n* ▷ **niggle**
niggling *v* ▷ **niggle**
nigh *adv, prep* (*Lit*) near
night *n* (*pl* **-s**) time of darkness between sunset and sunrise
nightcap *n* (*pl* **-s**) drink taken just before bedtime
nightcaps *n* ▷ **nightcap**
nightclub *n* (*pl* **-s**) establishment for dancing, music, etc., open late at night
nightclubs *n* ▷ **nightclub**
nightdress *n* (*pl* **-es**) woman's loose dress worn in bed
nightdresses *n* ▷ **nightdress**
nightfall *n* (*pl* **-s**) approach of darkness
nightfalls *n* ▷ **nightfall**
nightie *n* (*pl* **-s**) (*Informal*) nightdress
nighties *n* ▷ **nightie**

nightingale *n* (*pl* **-s**) small bird with a musical song usu. heard at night
nightingales *n* ▷ **nightingale**
nightjar *n* (*pl* **-s**) nocturnal bird with a harsh cry
nightjars *n* ▷ **nightjar**
nightlife *n* (*pl* **-s**) entertainment and social activities available at night in a town or city
nightlifes *n* ▷ **nightlife**
nightly *adj, adv* (happening) each night
nightmare *n* (*pl* **-s**) very bad dream
nightmares *n* ▷ **nightmare**
nights *n* ▷ **night**
nightshade *n* (*pl* **-s**) plant with bell-shaped flowers which are often poisonous
nightshades *n* ▷ **nightshade**
nightshirt *n* (*pl* **-s**) long loose shirt worn in bed
nightshirts *n* ▷ **nightshirt**
nihilism [nye-ill-liz-zum] *n* (*pl* **-s**) rejection of all established authority and institutions > **nihilist** *n* (*pl* **-s**) > **nihilistic** *adj*
nihilisms *n* ▷ **nihilism**
nihilist *n* ▷ **nihilism**
nihilistic *adj* ▷ **nihilism**
nihilists *n* ▷ **nihilism**
nil *n* (*pl* **-s**) nothing, zero
nils *n* ▷ **nil**
nimbi *n* ▷ **nimbus**
nimble *adj* (**-r, -st**) agile and quick > **nimbly** *adv*
nimbler *adj* ▷ **nimble**
nimblest *adj* ▷ **nimble**
nimbly *adv* ▷ **nimble**
nimbus *n* (*pl* **-bi, -buses**) dark grey rain cloud
nimbuses *n* ▷ **nimbus**
nincompoop *n* (*pl* **-s**) (*Informal*) stupid person
nincompoops *n* ▷ **nincompoop**
nine *adj, n* (*pl* **-s**) one more than eight
ninepins *n* game of skittles
nines *n* ▷ **nine**
nineteen *adj, n* (*pl* **-s**) ten and nine > **nineteenth** *adj, n* (*pl* **-s**)
nineteens *n* ▷ **nineteen**
nineteenth *adj, n* ▷ **nineteen**
nineteenths *n* ▷ **nineteen**
nineties *n* ▷ **ninety**
ninetieth *adj, n* ▷ **ninety**
ninetieths *n* ▷ **ninety**
ninety *adj, n* (*pl* **-ties**) ten times nine > **ninetieth** *adj, n* (*pl* **-s**)
ninth *adj, n* (*pl* **-s**) (of) number nine in a series
ninths *n* ▷ **ninth**
niobium *n* (*pl* **-s**) (CHEM) white superconductive metallic element
niobiums *n* ▷ **niobium**
nip¹ *v* (**-s, -pping, -pped**) (*Informal*) hurry ▶ *n* (*pl*

-s) pinch or light bite

nip² n (pl **nips**) small alcoholic drink
nipped v ▷ **nip¹**
nipper n (pl **-s**) (BRIT, AUST & NZ) (Informal) small child
nippers n ▷ **nipper**
nippier adj ▷ **nippy**
nippiest adj ▷ **nippy**
nipping v ▷ **nip¹**
nipple n (pl **-s**) projection in the centre of a breast
nipples n ▷ **nipple**
nippy adj (Informal) (**-pier, -piest**) frosty or chilly
nips v ▷ **nip¹** ▶ n ▷ **nip¹, ²**
nirvana [near-**vah**-na] n (pl **-s**) (BUDDHISM) (HINDUISM) absolute spiritual enlightenment and bliss
nirvanas n ▷ **nirvana**
nit n (pl **-s**) egg or larva of a louse (Informal)
▷ **nitwit**
nitrate n (pl **-s**) compound of nitric acid, used as a fertilizer
nitrates n ▷ **nitrate**
nitric, nitrous, nitrogenous adj of or containing nitrogen
nitrogen [nite-roj-jen] n (pl **-s**) (CHEM) colourless odourless gas that forms four fifths of the air
nitrogenous n ▷ **nitric**
nitrogens n ▷ **nitrogen**
nitroglycerin n ▷ **nitroglycerine**
nitroglycerine, nitroglycerin n (pl **-s**) explosive liquid
nitroglycerines n ▷ **nitroglycerine**
nitroglycerins n ▷ **nitroglycerine**
nitrous adj ▷ **nitric**
nits n ▷ **nit**
nitwit n (pl **-s**) (Informal) stupid person
nitwits n ▷ **nitwit**

> **nix** n (**nixes**). A nix is a water sprite in Germanic mythology. This is a handy little word, combining X with two of the most common tiles in the game. If you have an X on your rack, look out for opportunities on the board to play this as there's most likely an N or I available. Nix scores 10 points.

no interj expresses denial, disagreement, or refusal ▶ adj not any, not a ▶ adv not at all ▶ n (pl **noes, nos**) answer or vote of 'no'
nob n (pl **-s**) (CHIEFLY BRIT) (Slang) person of wealth or social distinction
nobs n ▷ **nob**
nobble v (**-les, -ling, -led**) (BRIT) (Slang) attract the attention of (someone) in order to talk to him or her

nobbled v ▷ **nobble**
nobbles v ▷ **nobble**
nobbling v ▷ **nobble**
nobelium n (pl **-s**) (CHEM) artificially-produced radioactive element
nobeliums n ▷ **nobelium**
nobilities n ▷ **nobility**
nobility n (pl **-ties**) quality of being noble
> **nobleman, noblewoman** n (pl **-men**)
noble adj (**-r, -st**) showing or having high moral qualities ▶ n (pl **-s**) member of the nobility
> **nobly** adv
nobleman n ▷ **nobility**
noblemen n ▷ **nobility**
nobler adj ▷ **noble**
nobles n ▷ **noble**
noblest adj ▷ **noble**
noblewoman n ▷ **nobility**
noblewomen n ▷ **nobility**
nobly adv ▷ **noble**
nobodies n ▷ **nobody**
nobody pron no person ▶ n (pl **-dies**) person of no importance
nocturnal adj of the night
nocturne n (pl **-s**) short dreamy piece of music
nocturnes n ▷ **nocturne**
nod v (**-s, -dding, -dded**) lower and raise (one's head) briefly in agreement or greeting ▶ n (pl **-s**) act of nodding
nodded v ▷ **nod**
nodding v ▷ **nod**
noddle n (pl **s**) (CHIEFLY BRIT) (Informal) the head
noddles n ▷ **noddle**
node n (pl **-s**) point on a plant stem from which leaves grow
nodes n ▷ **node**
nods v, n ▷ **nod**
nodule n (pl **-s**) small knot or lump
nodules n ▷ **nodule**
noel n (pl **-s**) Christmas carol
noels n ▷ **noel**
noes n ▷ **no**
noggin n (pl **-s**) (Informal) head
noggins n ▷ **noggin**
noise n (pl **-s**) sound, usu. a loud or disturbing one > **noiseless** adj
noiseless adj ▷ **noise**
noises n ▷ **noise**
noisier adj ▷ **noisy**
noisiest adj ▷ **noisy**
noisily adv ▷ **noisy**
noisy adj (**-sier, -siest**) making a lot of noise
> **noisily** adv
noisome adj (of smells) offensive
nomad n (pl **-s**) member of a tribe with no fixed

dwelling place, wanderer > **nomadic** adj
nomadic adj ▷ nomad
nomads n ▷ nomad
nomenclature n (pl -s) system of names used in a particular subject
nomenclatures n ▷ nomenclature
nominal adj in name only > **nominally** adv
nominally adv ▷ nominal
nominate v (-tes, -ting, -ted) suggest as a candidate > **nomination** n (pl -s)
nominated v ▷ nominate
nominates v ▷ nominate
nominating v ▷ nominate
nomination n ▷ nominate
nominations n ▷ nominate
nominative n (pl -s) form of a noun indicating the subject of a verb
nominatives n ▷ nominative
nominee n (pl -s) candidate
nominees n ▷ nominee
non- prefix indicating: negation
nonagenarian n (pl -s) person aged between ninety and ninety-nine
nonagenarians n ▷ nonagenarian
nonaggression n (pl -s) policy of not attacking other countries
nonaggressions n ▷ nonaggression
nonagon n (pl -s) geometric figure with nine sides
nonagons n ▷ nonagon
nonalcoholic adj containing no alcohol
nonaligned adj (of a country) not part of a major alliance or power bloc
nonce n (pl -s) for the present
nonces n ▷ nonce
nonchalance n ▷ nonchalant
nonchalances n ▷ nonchalant
nonchalant adj casually unconcerned or indifferent > **nonchalantly** adv > **nonchalance** n (pl -s)
nonchalantly adv ▷ nonchalant
noncombatant n (pl -s) member of the armed forces whose duties do not include fighting
noncombatants n ▷ noncombatant
noncommittal adj not committing oneself to any particular opinion
nonconductor n (pl -s) substance that is a poor conductor of heat, electricity, or sound
nonconductors n ▷ nonconductor
nonconformist n (pl -s) person who does not conform to generally accepted patterns of behaviour or thought (N-) ▶ adj (of behaviour or ideas) not conforming to accepted patterns > **nonconformity** n (pl -ties)
nonconformists n ▷ nonconformist

nonconformities n ▷ nonconformist
nonconformity n ▷ nonconformist
noncontributory adj (BRIT) denoting a pension scheme for employees, the premiums of which are paid entirely by the employer
nondescript adj lacking outstanding features
none pron not any
nonentities n ▷ nonentity
nonentity [non-**enn**-tit-tee] n (pl -ties) insignificant person or thing
nonetheless adv despite that, however
nonevent n (pl -s) disappointing or insignificant occurrence
nonevents n ▷ nonevent
nonflammable adj not easily set on fire
nonintervention n (pl refusal to intervene in the affairs of others
nonpareil [non-par-**rail**] n (pl -s) person or thing that is unsurpassed
nonpareils n ▷ nonpareil
nonpayment n (pl -s) failure to pay money owed
nonpayments n ▷ nonpayment
nonplussed adj perplexed
nonsense n (pl -s) something that has or makes no sense > **nonsensical** adj
nonsenses n ▷ nonsense
nonsensical adj ▷ nonsense
nonstandard adj denoting language that is not regarded as correct by educated native speakers
nonstarter n (pl -s) person or idea that has little chance of success
nonstarters n ▷ nonstarter
nonstick adj coated with a substance that food will not stick to when cooked
nonstop adj, adv without a stop
nontoxic adj not poisonous
noodles pl n long thin strips of pasta
nook n (pl -s) sheltered place
nooks n ▷ nook
noon n (pl -s) twelve o'clock midday
noonday adj happening at noon
noons n ▷ noon
noose n (pl -s) loop in the end of a rope, tied with a slipknot
nooses n ▷ noose
nor conj and not
norm n (pl -s) standard that is regarded as normal
normal adj usual, regular, or typical > **normally** adv > **normality** n (pl -ties) > **normalize** v (-izes, -izing, -ized)
normalities n ▷ normal

normality *n* ▷ **normal**
normalized *v* ▷ **normal**
normalizes *v* ▷ **normal**
normalizing *v* ▷ **normal**
normally *adv* ▷ **normal**
norms *n* ▷ **norm**
north *n* (*pl* -**s**) direction towards the North
Pole, opposite south ▶ *adj* to or in the north
▶ *adv* in, to, or towards the north > **northerly**
adj > **northern** *adj* > **northward** *adj, adv*
> **northwards** *adv*
northerly *adj* ▷ **north**
northern *adj* ▷ **north**
northerner *n* (*pl* -**s**) person from the north of a
country or area
northerners *n* ▷ **northerner**
norths *n* ▷ **north**
northward *adj, adv* ▷ **north**
northwards *adv* ▷ **north**
nos *n* ▷ **no**
nose *n* (*pl* -**s**) organ of smell, used also in
breathing ▶ *v* (-**ses, -sing, -sed**) move forward
slowly and carefully
nosed *v* ▷ **nose**
nosegay *n* (*pl* -**s**) small bunch of flowers
nosegays *n* ▷ **nosegay**
noses *n, v* ▷ **nose**
nosey, nosy *adj* (*Informal*) (-**sier, -siest**) prying
or inquisitive > **nosiness** *n* (*pl* -**es**)
nosier *adj* ▷ **nosey**
nosiest *adj* ▷ **nosey**
nosiness *n* ▷ **nosey**
nosinesses *n* ▷ **nosey**
nosing *v* ▷ **nose**
nosh *n* (*pl* -**es**) (BRIT, AUST & NZ) (*Slang*) food ▶ *v*
(-**shes, -shing, -shed**) eat
noshed *v* ▷ **nosh**
noshes *n, v* ▷ **nosh**
noshing *v* ▷ **nosh**
nostalgia *n* (*pl* -**s**) sentimental longing for the
past > **nostalgic** *adj*
nostalgias *n* ▷ **nostalgia**
nostalgic *adj* ▷ **nostalgia**
nostril *n* (*pl* -**s**) one of the two openings at the
end of the nose
nostrils *n* ▷ **nostril**
nostrum *n* (*pl* -**s**) quack medicine
nostrums *n* ▷ **nostrum**
nosy *adj* (-**sier, -siest**) ▷ **nosey**
not *adv* expressing negation, refusal, or denial
notable *adj* worthy of being noted,
remarkable ▶ *n* (*pl* -**s**) person of distinction
> **notably** *adv*
notabilities *n* ▷ **notability**
notability *n* (*pl* -**ties**)

notables *n* ▷ **notable**
notably *adv* ▷ **notable**
notaries *n* ▷ **notary**
notary *n* (*pl* -**ries**) person authorized to
witness the signing of legal documents
notation *n* (*pl* -**s**) representation of numbers or
quantities in a system by a series of symbols
notations *n* ▷ **notation**
notch *n* (*pl* -**es**) V-shaped cut ▶ *v* (-**ches, -ching,
-ched**) make a notch in (*foll. by* **up**)
notched *v* ▷ **notch**
notches *n, v* ▷ **notch**
notching *v* ▷ **notch**
note *n* (*pl* -**s**) short letter ▶ *v* (-**tes, -ting, -ted**)
notice, pay attention to
notebook *n* (*pl* -**s**) book for writing in
notebooks *n* ▷ **notebook**
noted *v* ▷ **note** ▶ *adj* well-known
notes *n, v* ▷ **note**
noteworthy *adj* worth noting, remarkable
nothing *pron* not anything ▶ *adv* not at all
nothingness *n* (*pl* -**es**) nonexistence
nothingnesses *n* ▷ **nothingness**
notice *n* (*pl* -**s**) observation or attention ▶ *v*
(-**ces, -cing, -ced**) observe, become aware of
noticeable *adj* easily seen or detected,
appreciable
noticed *v* ▷ **notice**
notices *n, v* ▷ **notice**
noticing *v* ▷ **notice**
notifiable *adj* having to be reported to the
authorities
notification *n* ▷ **notify**
notifications *n* ▷ **notify**
notified *v* ▷ **notify**
notifies *v* ▷ **notify**
notify *v* (-**fies, -fying, -fied**) inform
> **notification** *n* (*pl* -**s**)
notifying *v* ▷ **notify**
noting *v* ▷ **note**
notion *n* (*pl* -**s**) idea or opinion
notional *adj* speculative, imaginary, or unreal
notions *n* ▷ **notion**
notorieties *n* ▷ **notorious**
notoriety *n* ▷ **notorious**
notorious *adj* well known for something bad
> **notoriously** *adv* > **notoriety** *n* (*pl* -**ties**)
notoriously *adv* ▷ **notorious**
notwithstanding *prep* in spite of
nougat *n* (*pl* -**s**) chewy sweet containing nuts
and fruit
nougats *n* ▷ **nougat**
nought *n* (*pl* -**s**) figure o
noughties *pl n* (*Informal*) decade from 2000
to 2009

noughts *n* ▷ **nought**
noun *n* (*pl* **-s**) word that refers to a person, place, or thing
nouns *n* ▷ **noun**
nourish *v* (**-shes, -shing, -shed**) feed
> **nourishment** *n* (*pl* **-s**)
nourished *v* ▷ **nourish**
nourishes *v* ▷ **nourish**
nourishing *adj* providing the food necessary for life and growth ▶ *v* ▷ **nourish**
nourishment *n* ▷ **nourish**
nourishments *n* ▷ **nourish**
nova *n* (*pl* **-vae, -vas**) star that suddenly becomes brighter and then gradually decreases to its original brightness
novae *n* ▷ **nova**
novas *n* ▷ **nova**
novel[1] *n* (*pl* **-s**) long fictitious story in book form
novel[2] *adj* fresh, new, or original > **novelist** *n* (*pl* **-s**) writer of novels
novelists *n* ▷ **novelist**
novella *n* (*pl* **-s, -llae**) short novel
novellae *n* ▷ **novella**
novellas *n* ▷ **novella**
novels *n* ▷ **novel**[1]
novelties *n* ▷ **novelty**
novelty *n* (*pl* **-ties**) newness
novena [no-**vee**-na] *n* (*pl* **-s**) (RC CHURCH) set of prayers or services on nine consecutive days
novenas *n* ▷ **novena**
novice *n* (*pl* **-s**) beginner
novices *n* ▷ **novice**
now *adv* at or for the present time ▶ *conj* seeing that, since
nowadays *adv* in these times
nowhere *adv* not anywhere

nox *n* (**noxes**). In chemistry, nox is short for nitrogen oxide. This is an unusual word which can come in useful in the later stages of the game when there isn't much space left, or when you have an X but can't form a longer word with it. Nox scores 10 points.

noxious *adj* poisonous or harmful
nozzle *n* (*pl* **-s**) projecting spout through which fluid is discharged
nozzles *n* ▷ **nozzle**

nth *adv*. In mathematics, nth represents an unspecified ordinal number. Nth is a good word to remember for awkward situations on the board, as it's one of very few three-letter words that doesn't contain a vowel. Nth scores 6 points.

nu *n* nus. Nu is the 13th letter in the Greek alphabet. This word is worth remembering, as it can be really useful when you want to form short words in the process of playing a longer one. Nu scores 2 points.

nuance [**new**-ahnss] *n* (*pl* **-s**) subtle difference in colour, meaning, or tone
nuances *n* ▷ **nuance**
nub *n* (*pl* **-s**) point or gist (of a story etc.)
nubs *n* ▷ **nub**
nubile [**new**-bile] *adj* (of a young woman) sexually attractive
nuclear *adj* of nuclear weapons or energy
nuclei *n* ▷ **nucleus**
nucleus *n* (*pl* **-clei**) centre, esp. of an atom or cell
nude *adj* (**-r, -st**) naked ▶ *n* (*pl* **-s**) naked figure in painting, sculpture, or photography > **nudity** *n* (*pl* **-ties**)
nuder *adj* ▷ **nude**
nudes *n* ▷ **nude**
nudest *adj* ▷ **nude**
nudge *v* (**-dges, -dging, -dged**) push gently, esp. with the elbow ▶ *n* (*pl* **-s**) gentle push or touch
nudged *v* ▷ **nudge**
nudges *v, n* ▷ **nudge**
nudging *v* ▷ **nudge**
nudism *n* (*pl* **-s**) practice of not wearing clothes > **nudist** *n* (*pl* **-s**)
nudisms *n* ▷ **nudism**
nudist *n* ▷ **nudism**
nudists *n* ▷ **nudism**
nudities *n* ▷ **nude**
nudity *n* ▷ **nude**
nugatory [**new**-gat-tree] *adj* of little value
nugget *n* (*pl* **-s**) small lump of gold in its natural state ▶ *v* (**-s, -tting, -tted**) (NZ & S AFR) polish footwear
nuggets *n, v* ▷ **nugget**
nuggetted *v* ▷ **nugget**
nuggetting *v* ▷ **nugget**
nuisance *n* (*pl* **-s**) something or someone that causes annoyance or bother
nuisances *n* ▷ **nuisance**
nuke (*Slang*) *v* (**-kes, -king, -ked**) attack with nuclear weapons ▶ *n* (*pl* **-s**) nuclear weapon
nuked *v* ▷ **nuke**
nukes *v, n* ▷ **nuke**
nuking *v* ▷ **nuke**
null *adj* not legally valid > **nullity** *n* (*pl* **-s**)
nullified *v* ▷ **nullify**
nullifies *v* ▷ **nullify**

nullify v (**-fies, -fying, -fied**) make ineffective
  nullifying v ▷ **nullify**
  nullities n ▷ **null**
  nullity n ▷ **null**
numb adj (**-er, -est**) without feeling, as
  through cold, shock, or fear ▶ v (**-s, -ing, -ed**)
  make numb > **numbly** adv > **numbness** n
  (pl **-es**)
numbat n (pl **-s**) small Australian marsupial
  with a long snout and tongue
  numbats n ▷ **numbat**
  numbed v ▷ **numb**
  number¹ adj ▷ **numb**
number² n (pl **-s**) sum or quantity ▶ v (**-s, -ing,
  -ed**) count
  numbered v ▷ **number**
  numbering v ▷ **number**
numberless adj too many to be counted
numberplate n (pl **-s**) plate on a car showing
  the registration number
  numberplates n ▷ **numberplate**
  numbers n, v ▷ **number**
  numbest adj ▷ **numb**
  numbing v ▷ **numb**
  numbly adv ▷ **numb**
  numbness n ▷ **numb**
  numbnesses n ▷ **numb**
  numbs v ▷ **numb**
numbskull n (pl **-s**) stupid person
  numbskulls n ▷ **numbskull**
  numeracies n ▷ **numerate**
  numeracy n ▷ **numerate**
numeral n (pl **-s**) word or symbol used to
  express a sum or quantity
  numerals n ▷ **numeral**
numerate adj able to do basic arithmetic
  > **numeracy** n (pl **-cies**)
numeration n (pl **-s**) act or process of
  numbering or counting
  numerations n ▷ **numeration**
numerator n (pl **-s**) (MATHS) number above the
  line in a fraction
  numerators n ▷ **numerator**
numerical adj measured or expressed in
  numbers > **numerically** adv
  numerically adv ▷ **numerical**
numerous adj existing or happening in large
  numbers
numismatist n (pl **-s**) coin collector
  numismatists n ▷ **numismatist**
numskull n (pl **-s**) ▷ **numbskull**
  numskulls n ▷ **numskull**
nun n (pl **-s**) female member of a religious order
nuncio n (pl **-s**) (RC CHURCH) pope's ambassador
  nuncios n ▷ **nuncio**

  nunneries n ▷ **nunnery**
nunnery n (pl **-ries**) convent
  nuns n ▷ **nun**
nuptial adj relating to marriage
nuptials pl n wedding
nurse n (pl **-s**) person employed to look after
  sick people, usu. in a hospital ▶ v (**-ses, -sing,
  -sed**) look after (a sick person)
  nursed v ▷ **nurse**
  nurseries n ▷ **nursery**
nursery n (pl **-ries**) room where children sleep
  or play
nurseryman n (pl **-men**) person who raises
  plants for sale
  nurserymen n ▷ **nurseryman**
  nurses n, v ▷ **nurse**
  nursing v ▷ **nurse**
nurture n (pl **-s**) act or process of promoting
  the development of a child or young plant ▶ v
  (**-res, -ring, -red**) promote or encourage the
  development of
  nurtured v ▷ **nurture**
  nurtures n, v ▷ **nurture**
  nurturing v ▷ **nurture**
nut n (pl **-s**) fruit consisting of a hard shell and
  a kernel
nutcracker n (pl **-s**) device for cracking the
  shells of nuts
  nutcrackers n ▷ **nutcracker**
nuthatch n (pl **-es**) small songbird
  nuthatches n ▷ **nuthatch**
nutmeg n (pl **-s**) spice made from the seed of a
  tropical tree
  nutmeg n ▷ **nutmeg**
nutria n (pl **-s**) fur of the coypu
  nutrias n ▷ **nutria**
nutrient n (pl **-s**) substance that provides
  nourishment
  nutrients n ▷ **nutrient**
nutriment n (pl **-s**) food or nourishment
  required by all living things to grow and stay
  healthy
  nutriments n ▷ **nutriment**
nutrition n (pl **-s**) process of taking in and
  absorbing nutrients > **nutritional** adj
  nutritional adj ▷ **nutrition**
  nutritions n ▷ **nutrition**
nutritious, nutritive adj nourishing
  nutritive adj ▷ **nutritious**
  nuts n ▷ **nut**
nutter n (pl **-s**) (BRIT) (Slang) insane person
  nutters n ▷ **nutter**
  nuttier adj ▷ **nutty**
  nuttiest adj ▷ **nutty**
nutty adj (**-ttier, -ttiest**) containing or

resembling nuts

nuzzle *v* (**-les, -ling, -led**) push or rub gently with the nose or snout

nuzzled *v* ▷ **nuzzle**

nuzzles *v* ▷ **nuzzle**

nuzzling *v* ▷ **nuzzle**

ny *adj, adv.* Ny is an old spelling of **nigh.** This word can be useful when you're forming one word adjacent to another, and so need to form two-letter words where the two words meet. Ny is also unusual in that it doesn't contain a vowel. Ny scores 5 points.

nylon *n* (*pl* **-s**) synthetic material used for clothing etc.

nylons *n* ▷ **nylon** ▶ *pl n* stockings made of nylon

nymph *n* (*pl* **-s**) mythical spirit of nature, represented as a beautiful young woman

nymphs *n* ▷ **nymph**

nymphet *n* (*pl* **-s**) sexually precocious young girl

nymphets *n* ▷ **nymphet**

Oo

With eight Os in the bag, you're likely to have at least one on your rack during a game. There are plenty of good two-letter words starting with O. It's worth knowing that O will form a two-letter word in front of every other vowel except A, as well as in front of Y. O also combines well with X, with **ox** (9 points) as the obvious starting point, and several words that refer to **oxygen** (17), including **oxo** (10) and **oxy** (13). Don't forget the short everyday words that begin with O. While **on** and **or** (2 each) won't earn you many points, they can be very helpful when you are trying to score in more than one direction at a time. **Of** and **oh** (5 each) can also prove very useful.

oaf n (pl -**s**) stupid or clumsy person > **oafish** adj
  oafish adj ▷ **oaf**
  oafs n ▷ **oaf**
oak n (pl -**s**) deciduous forest tree > **oaken** adj
  oaken adj ▷ **oak**
  oaks n ▷ **oak**
oakum n (pl -**s**) fibre obtained by unravelling old rope
  oakums n ▷ **oakum**
oar n (pl -**s**) pole with a broad blade, used for rowing a boat
  oars n ▷ **oar**
oasis n (pl -**ses**) fertile area in a desert
  oases n ▷ **oasis**
oast n (pl -**s**) (CHIEFLY BRIT) oven for drying hops
  oasts n ▷ **oast**
oat n (pl -**s**) hard cereal grown as food ▶ pl grain of this cereal
oath n (pl -**s**) solemn promise, esp. to be truthful in court
  oaths n ▷ **oath**
oatmeal adj pale brownish-cream
  oats n ▷ **oat**
obbligato [ob-lig-**gah**-toe] n (pl -**os**) (MUSIC) essential part or accompaniment
  obbligatos n ▷ **obbligato**
  obduracies n ▷ **obdurate**
  obduracy n ▷ **obdurate**
obdurate adj hardhearted or stubborn > **obduracy** n (pl -**cies**)
  obedience n ▷ **obedient**
  obediences n ▷ **obedient**
obedient adj obeying or willing to obey > **obedience** n (pl -**s**) > **obediently** adv
  obediently adv ▷ **obedient**
obeisance [oh-**bay**-sanss] n (pl -**s**) attitude of respect

  obeisances n ▷ **obeisance**
obelisk [**ob**-bill-isk] n (pl -**s**) four-sided stone column tapering to a pyramid at the top
  obelisks n ▷ **obelisk**
obese [oh-**beess**] adj (-**r**, -**st**) very fat > **obesity** n (pl -**ties**)
  obeser adj ▷ **obese**
  obesest adj ▷ **obese**
  obesities n ▷ **obese**
  obesity n ▷ **obese**
obey v (-**s**, -**ing**, -**ed**) carry out instructions or orders
  obeyed v ▷ **obey**
  obeying v ▷ **obey**
  obeys v ▷ **obey**
obfuscate v (-**tes**, -**ting**, -**ted**) make (something) confusing
  obfuscated v ▷ **obfuscate**
  obfuscates v ▷ **obfuscate**
  obfuscating v ▷ **obfuscate**
  obituaries n ▷ **obituary**
  obituarist n ▷ **obituary**
  obituarists n ▷ **obituary**
obituary n (pl -**ies**) announcement of someone's death, esp. in a newspaper > **obituarist** n (pl -**s**)
object[1] n (pl -**s**) physical thing
object[2] v (-**s**, -**ing**, -**ed**) express disapproval > **objection** n (pl -**s**) > **objector** n (pl -**s**)
  objected v ▷ **object**[2]
  objecting v ▷ **object**[2]
  objection n ▷ **object**[2]
objectionable adj unpleasant
  objections n ▷ **object**[2]
objective n (pl -**s**) aim or purpose ▶ adj not

biased > **objectively** *adv* > **objectivity** *n* (*pl* -ties)
objectively *adv* ▷ **objective**
objectives *n* ▷ **objective**
objectivities *n* ▷ **objective**
objectivity *n* ▷ **objective**
objector *n* ▷ **object**²
objectors *n* ▷ **object**²
objects *n, v* ▷ **object**¹,²
oblation *n* (*pl* -s) religious offering
oblations *n* ▷ **oblation**
obligated *adj* obliged to do something
obligation *n* (*pl* -s) duty
obligations *n* ▷ **obligation**
obligatory *adj* required by a rule or law
oblige *v* (-ges, -ging, -ged) compel (someone) morally or by law to do something
obliged *v* ▷ **oblige**
obliges *v* ▷ **oblige**
obliging *adj* ready to help other people ▶ *v* ▷ **oblige** > **obligingly** *adv*
obligingly *adv* ▷ **oblige**
oblique [oh-**bleak**] *adj* (-r, -st) slanting ▶ *n* (*pl* -s) the symbol (/) > **obliquely** *adv*
obliquely *adv* ▷ **oblique**
obliquer *adj* ▷ **oblique**
obliques *n* ▷ **oblique**
obliquest *adj* ▷ **oblique**
obliterate *v* (-tes, -ting, -ted) wipe out, destroy > **obliteration** *n* (*pl* -s)
obliterated *v* ▷ **obliterate**
obliterates *v* ▷ **obliterate**
obliterating *v* ▷ **obliterate**
obliteration *n* ▷ **obliterate**
obliterations *n* ▷ **obliterate**
oblivion *n* (*pl* -s) state of being forgotten
oblivions *n* ▷ **oblivion**
oblivious *adj* unaware
oblong *adj* having two long sides, two short sides, and four right angles ▶ *n* (*pl* -s) oblong figure
oblongs *n* ▷ **oblong**
obloquies *n* ▷ **obloquy**
obloquy [ob-**lock**-wee] *n* (*pl* -**quies**) verbal abuse
obnoxious *adj* offensive
oboe *n* (*pl* -s) double-reeded woodwind instrument > **oboist** *n* (*pl* -s)
oboes *n* ▷ **oboe**
oboist *n* ▷ **oboe**
oboists *n* ▷ **oboe**
obscene *adj* (-r, -st) portraying sex offensively > **obscenity** *n* (*pl* -ies)
obscener *adj* ▷ **obscene**
obscenest *adj* ▷ **obscene**
obscenities *n* ▷ **obscene**

obscenity *n* ▷ **obscene**
obscure *adj* (-r, -st) not well known ▶ *v* (-res, -ring, -red) make (something) obscure > **obscurity** *n* (*pl* -ties)
obscured *v* ▷ **obscure**
obscurer *adj* ▷ **obscure**
obscures *v* ▷ **obscure**
obscurest *adj* ▷ **obscure**
obscuring *v* ▷ **obscure**
obscurities *n* ▷ **obscure**
obscurity *n* ▷ **obscure**
obsequies [**ob**-sick-weez] *pl n* funeral rites
obsequious [ob-**seek**-wee-uss] *adj* overattentive in order to gain favour > **obsequiousness** *n*
obsequiousness *n* ▷ **obsequious**
observe *v* (-ves, -ving, -ved) see or notice > **observable** *adj*
observable *adj* ▷ **observe**
observance *n* (*pl* -s) observing of a custom
observances *n* ▷ **observance**
observant *adj* quick to notice things
observation *n* (*pl* -s) action or habit of observing
observations *n* ▷ **observation**
observatories *n* ▷ **observatory**
observatory *n* (*pl* -ries) building equipped for studying the weather and the stars
observed *v* ▷ **observe**
observer *n* (*pl* -s) person who observes, esp. one who watches someone or something carefully
observers *n* ▷ **observer**
observes *v* ▷ **observe**
observing *v* ▷ **observe**
obsess *v* (-es, -ing, -ed) preoccupy (someone) compulsively > **obsessed** *adj* > **obsessive** *adj* > **obsession** *n* (*pl* -s)
obsessed *v, adj* ▷ **obsess**
obsesses *v* ▷ **obsess**
obsessing *v* ▷ **obsess**
obsession *n* ▷ **obsess**
obsessions *n* ▷ **obsess**
obsessive *adj* ▷ **obsess**
obsidian *n* (*pl* -s) dark glassy volcanic rock
obsidians *n* ▷ **obsidian**
obsolescence *n* ▷ **obsolescent**
obsolescences *n* ▷ **obsolescent**
obsolescent *adj* becoming obsolete > **obsolescence** *n* (*pl* -s)
obsolete *adj* no longer in use
obstacle *n* (*pl* -s) something that makes progress difficult
obstacles *n* ▷ **obstacle**
obstetric *adj* ▷ **obstetrics**

obstetrician *n* ▷ obstetrics
obstetricians *n* ▷ obstetrics
obstetrics *n* branch of medicine concerned
with pregnancy and childbirth > **obstetric** *adj*
> **obstetrician** *n* (*pl* -s)
obstinacy *n* ▷ obstinate
obstinacies *n* ▷ obstinate
obstinate *adj* stubborn > **obstinately** *adv*
> **obstinacy** *n* (*pl* -cies)
obstinately *adv* ▷ obstinate
obstreperous *adj* unruly, noisy
obstruct *v* (-s, -ing, -ed) block with an obstacle
> **obstruction** *n* (*pl* -s) > **obstructive** *adj*
obstructed *v* ▷ obstruct
obstructing *v* ▷ obstruct
obstruction *n* ▷ obstruct
obstructions *n* ▷ obstruct
obstructive *adj* ▷ obstruct
obstructs *v* ▷ obstruct
obtain *v* (-s, -ing, -ed) acquire intentionally
> **obtainable** *adj*
obtainable *adj* ▷ obtain
obtained *v* ▷ obtain
obtaining *v* ▷ obtain
obtains *v* ▷ obtain
obtrude *v* (-des, -ding, -ded) push oneself or
one's ideas on others
obtruded *v* ▷ obtrude
obtrudes *v* ▷ obtrude
obtruding *v* ▷ obtrude
obtuse *adj* (-r, -st) mentally slow > **obtuseness**
n (*pl* -es)
obtuseness *n* ▷ obtuse
obtusenesses *n* ▷ obtuse
obtuser *adj* ▷ obtuse
obtusest *adj* ▷ obtuse
obtrusive *adj* unpleasantly noticeable
> **obtrusively** *adv*
obtrusively *adv* ▷ obstrusive
obverse *n* (*pl* -s) opposite way of looking at
an idea
obverses *n* ▷ obverse
obviate *v* (-tes, -ting, -ted) make unnecessary
obviated *v* ▷ obviate
obviates *v* ▷ obviate
obviating *v* ▷ obviate
obvious *adj* easy to see or understand, evident
> **obviously** *adv*
obviously *adv* ▷ obvious
ocarina *n* (*pl* -s) small oval wind instrument
ocarinas *n* ▷ ocarina
occasion *n* (*pl* -s) time at which a particular
thing happens ▶ *v* (-s, -ing, -ed) cause
occasional *adj* happening sometimes
> **occasionally** *adv*

occasionally *adv* ▷ occasional
occasioned *v* ▷ occasion
occasioning *v* ▷ occasion
occasions *n*, *v* ▷ occasion
occident *n* (*pl* occidents) (*Lit*) west
> **occidental** *adj*
occidental *adj* ▷ occident
occidents *n* ▷ occident
occiput [ox-sip-put] *n* (*pl* -s) back of the head
occiputs *n* ▷ occiput
occlude *v* (-des, -ding, -ded) obstruct
> **occlusion** *n* (*pl* -s)
occluded *v* ▷ occlude
occludes *v* ▷ occlude
occluding *v* ▷ occlude
occlusion *n* ▷ occlude
occlusions *n* ▷ occlude
occult *adj* relating to the supernatural
occupancies *n* ▷ occupancy
occupancy *n* (*pl* -cies) (length of) a person's
stay in a specified place
occupant *n* (*pl* -s) person occupying a
specified place
occupants *n* ▷ occupant
occupation *n* (*pl* -s) profession > **occupational**
adj
occupational *adj* ▷ occupation
occupations *n* ▷ occupation
occupied *v* ▷ occupy
occupier *n* ▷ occupy
occupiers *n* ▷ occupy
occupies *v* ▷ occupy
occupy *v* (-pies, -pying, -pied) live or work in (a
building) > **occupier** *n* (*pl* -s)
occur *v* (-s, -rring, -rred) happen
occurrence *n* (*pl* -s) something that occurs
occurrences *n* ▷ occurrence
occurred *v* ▷ occur
occurring *v* ▷ occur
occurs *v* ▷ occur
ocean *n* (*pl* -s) vast area of sea between
continents > **oceanic** *adj*
oceanic *adj* ▷ ocean
oceanographies *n* ▷ oceanography
oceanography *n* (*pl* -phies) scientific study of
the oceans
oceans *n* ▷ ocean
ocelot [oss-ill-lot] *n* (*pl* -s) American wild cat
with a spotted coat
ocelots *n* ▷ ocelot
oche [ok-kee] *n* (*pl* -s) (DARTS) mark on the floor
behind which a player must stand
oches *n* ▷ oche
ochre [oak-er] *adj*, *n* (*pl* -s) brownish-yellow
(earth)

ochres *n* ▷ **ochre**
octagon *n* (*pl* **-s**) geometric figure with eight sides > **octagonal** *adj*
octagonal *adj* ▷ **octagon**
octagons *n* ▷ **octagon**
octahedra *n* ▷ **octahedron**
octahedron [ok-ta-**heed**-ron] *n* (*pl* **-drons, -dra**) three-dimensional geometric figure with eight faces
octahedrons *n* ▷ **octahedra**
octane *n* (*pl* **-s**) hydrocarbon found in petrol
octanes *n* ▷ **octane**
octave *n* (*pl* **-s**) (MUSIC) (interval between the first and) eighth note of a scale
octaves *n* ▷ **octave**
octet *n* (*pl* **-s**) group of eight performers
octets *n* ▷ **octet**
octogenarian *n* (*pl* **-s**) person aged between eighty and eighty-nine
octogenarians *n* ▷ **octogenarian**
octopus *n* (*pl* **-es**) sea creature with a soft body and eight tentacles
octopuses *n* ▷ **octopus**
ocular *adj* relating to the eyes or sight
odd (**-er, -est**) *adj* unusual
odder *adj* ▷ **odd**
oddest *adj* ▷ **odd**
oddities *n* ▷ **oddity**
oddity *n* (*pl* **-ties**) odd person or thing
oddments *pl n* things left over
oddness *n* (*pl* **-es**) quality of being odd
oddnesses *n* ▷ **oddness**
odds *pl n* (ratio showing) the probability of something happening
ode *n* (*pl* **-s**) lyric poem, usu. addressed to a particular subject
odes *n* ▷ **ode**
odious *adj* offensive
odium [oh-dee-um] *n* (*pl* **-s**) widespread dislike
odiums *n* ▷ **odium**
odorous *adj* ▷ **odour**
odour *n* (*pl* **-s**) particular smell > **odorous** *adj* > **odourless** *adj*
odourless *adj* ▷ **odour**
odours *n* ▷ **odour**
odyssey [**odd**-iss-ee] *n* (*pl* **-s**) long eventful journey
odysseys *n* ▷ **odyssey**

> **oe** *n* (**oes**). Oe is a Scots word for a grandchild. This is a good word to remember, as it combines two of the most common letters in the game without using any consonants. Oe scores 2 points.

oedema [id-**deem**-a] *n* (*pl* **-mata**) (MED)
abnormal swelling
oedemata *n* ▷ **oedema**
oesophagi *n* ▷ **oesophagus**
oesophagus [ee-**soff**-a-guss] *n* (*pl* **-gi**) passage between the mouth and stomach
oestrogen [ee-stra-jen] *n* (*pl* **-s**) female hormone that controls the reproductive cycle
oestrogens *n* ▷ **oestrogen**
of *prep* belonging to
off *prep* away from ▶ *adv* away ▶ *adj* not operating ▶ *n* (*pl* **-s**) (CRICKET) side of the field to which the batsman's feet point
offal *n* (*pl* **-s**) edible organs of an animal, such as liver or kidneys
offals *n* ▷ **offal**
offcut *n* (*pl* **-s**) piece remaining after the required parts have been cut out
offcuts *n* ▷ **offcut**
offend *v* (**-s, -ing, -ed**) hurt the feelings of, insult
offence *n* (*pl* **-s**) (cause of) hurt feelings or annoyance
offences *n* ▷ **offence**
offended *v* ▷ **offend**
offender *n* (*pl* **-s**) person who commits a crime
offenders *n* ▷ **offender**
offending *v* ▷ **offend**
offends *v* ▷ **offend**
offensive *adj* disagreeable ▶ *n* (*pl* **-s**) position or action of attack
offensives *n* ▷ **offensive**
offer *v* (**-s, -ing, -ed**) present (something) for acceptance or rejection ▶ *n* (*pl* **-s**) instance of offering something
offering *n* (*pl* **-s**) thing offered
offered *v* ▷ **offer**
offering *v* ▷ **offer**
offerings *n* ▷ **offering**
offers *v, n* ▷ **offer**
offertories *n* ▷ **offertory**
offertory *n* (**-ries**) (CHRISTIANITY) offering of the bread and wine for Communion
offhand *adj* casual, curt ▶ *adv* without preparation
office *n* (*pl* **-s**) room or building where people work at desks
officer *n* (*pl* **-s**) person in authority in the armed services
officers *n* ▷ **officer**
offices *n* ▷ **office**
official *adj* of a position of authority ▶ *n* (*pl* **-s**) person who holds a position of authority > **officially** *adv*
officialdom *n* (*pl* **-s**) officials collectively
officialdoms *n* ▷ **officialdom**

officially *adv* ▷ **official**
officials *n* ▷ **official**
officiate *v* (**-tes, -ting, -ted**) act in an official role
officiated *v* ▷ **officiate**
officiates *v* ▷ **officiate**
officiating *v* ▷ **officiate**
officious *adj* interfering unnecessarily
offing *n* (*pl* **-s**) area of the sea visible from the shore
offings *n* ▷ **offing**
offs *n* ▷ **off**
offset *v* (**-sets, -setting, -set**) cancel out, compensate for
offsets *v* ▷ **offset**
offsetting *v* ▷ **offset**
offshoot *n* (*pl* **-s**) something developed from something else
offshoots *n* ▷ **offshoot**
offside *adj, adv* (SPORT) (positioned) illegally ahead of the ball
offspring *n* (*pl* **-s**) child
offsprings *n* ▷ **offspring**
oft *adv* (*Poetic*) often
often *adv* frequently, much of the time
ogle *v* (**-les, -ling, -led**) stare at (someone) lustfully
ogled *v* ▷ **ogle**
ogles *v* ▷ **ogle**
ogling *v* ▷ **ogle**
ogre *n* (*pl* **-s**) giant that eats human flesh
ogres *n* ▷ **ogre**
oh *interj* exclamation of surprise, pain, etc.
ohm *n* (*pl* **-s**) unit of electrical resistance
ohms *n* ▷ **ohm**

> **oi** *interj.* Oi is something people shout to attract attention. This is a good word to remember, as it combines two of the most common letters in the game without using any consonants. Oi scores 2 points.

oil *n* (*pl* **-s**) viscous liquid, insoluble in water and usu. flammable ▷ **petroleum** ▶ *pl* oil-based paints used in art ▶ *v* (**-s, -ing, -ed**) lubricate (a machine) with oil > **oily** *adj* (**-lier, -liest**)
oiled *v* ▷ **oil**
oilfield *n* (**-s**) area containing oil reserves
oilfields *n* ▷ **oilfield**
oilier *adj* ▷ **oil**
oiliest *adj* ▷ **oil**
oiling *v* ▷ **oil**
oils *n, v* ▷ **oil**
oilskin *n* (*pl* **-s**) (garment made from) waterproof material

oilskins *n* ▷ **oilskin**
oily *adj* ▷ **oil**
ointment *n* (*pl* **-s**) greasy substance used for healing skin or as a cosmetic
ointments *n* ▷ **ointment**
okapi [ok-kah-pee] *n* (*pl* **-s**) African animal related to the giraffe but with a shorter neck
okapis *n* ▷ **okapi**
okra *n* (*pl* **-s**) tropical plant with edible green pods
okras *n* ▷ **okra**
okay (*Informal*) *interj* expression of approval ▶ *v* (**-s, -ing, -ed**) approve (something) ▶ *n* (*pl* **-s**) approval
okayed *v* ▷ **okay**
okaying *v* ▷ **okay**
okays *v, n* ▷ **okay**
old *adj* (**-er, -est**) having lived or existed for a long time
olden *adj* old
older *adj* ▷ **old**
oldest *adj* ▷ **old**
oldie *n* (*pl* **-s**) (*Informal*) old but popular song or film
oldies *n* ▷ **oldie**
oleaginous [ol-lee-**aj**-in-uss] *adj* oily, producing oil
oleander [ol-lee-**ann**-der] *n* (*pl* **-s**) Mediterranean flowering evergreen shrub
oleanders *n* ▷ **oleander**
olfactory *adj* relating to the sense of smell
oligarchic *adj* ▷ **oiligarchy**
oligarchical *adj* ▷ **oligarchy**
oligarchies *n* ▷ **oligarchy**
oligarchy [ol-lee-**gark**-ee] *n* (*pl* **-ies**) government by a small group of people > **oligarchic, oligarchical** *adj*
olive *n* (*pl* **-s**) small green or black fruit used as food or pressed for its oil ▶ *adj* greyish-green
olives *n* ▷ **olive**
ombudsman *n* (*pl* **-men**) official who investigates complaints against government organizations
ombudsmen *n* ▷ **ombudsman**
omelette *n* (*pl* **-s**) dish of eggs beaten and fried
omelettes *n* ▷ **omelette**
omen *n* (*pl* (*pl* **-s**) happening or object thought to foretell success or misfortune
omens *n* ▷ **omen**
ominous *adj* worrying, seeming to foretell misfortune
omit *v* (**-s, -tting, -tted**) leave out > **omission** *n* (*pl* **-s**)
omission *n* ▷ **omit**
omissions *n* ▷ **omit**

omits v ▷ omit

omitted v ▷ omit

omitting v ▷ omit

omnibus n (pl -es) several books or TV or radio programmes made into one

omnibuses n ▷ omnibus

omnipotence n ▷ omnipotent

omnipotences n ▷ omnipotent

omnipotent adj having unlimited power > **omnipotence** n (pl -s)

omnipresence n ▷ omnipresent

omnipresences n ▷ omnipresent

omnipresent adj present everywhere > **omnipresence** n (pl -s)

omniscience n ▷ omniscient

omnisciences n ▷ omniscient

omniscient [om-niss-ee-ent] adj knowing everything > **omniscience** n (pl -s)

omnivore n (pl -s) omnivorous animal

omnivores n ▷ omnivore

omnivorous [om-niv-vor-uss] adj eating food obtained from both animals and plants

on prep indicating position above, attachment, closeness, etc. ▶ adv in operation ▶ adj operating ▶ n (pl -s) (CRICKET) side of the field on which the batsman stands

once adv on one occasion ▶ conj as soon as

oncogene [on-koh-jean] n (pl -s) gene that can cause cancer when abnormally activated

oncogenes n ▷ oncogene

oncoming adj approaching from the front

one adj single, lone ▶ n (pl -s) number or figure 1 ▶ pron any person

oneness n (pl -es) unity

onenesses n ▷ oneness

onerous [own-er-uss] adj (of a task) difficult to carry out

ones n ▷ one

oneself pron ▷ one

ongoing adj in progress, continuing

onion n (pl -s) strongly flavoured edible bulb

onions n ▷ onion

online adj (of a computer) directly controlled by a central processor

onlooker n (pl -s) person who watches without taking part

onlookers n ▷ onlooker

only adj alone of its kind ▶ adv exclusively ▶ conj but

onomatopoeia [on-a-mat-a-pee-a] n (pl -s) use of a word which imitates the sound it represents, such as hiss > **onomatopoeic** adj

onomatopoeias n ▷ onomatopoeia

onomatopoeic adj ▷ onomatopoeia

onset n (pl -s) beginning

onsets n ▷ onset

onslaught n (pl -s) violent attack

onslaughts n ▷ onslaught

onto prep to a position on

ontological adj ▷ ontology

ontologies n ▷ ontology

ontology n (pl -gies) branch of philosophy concerned with existence > **ontological** adj

onus [own-uss] n (pl -es) responsibility or burden

onuses n ▷ onus

onward adj directed or moving forward ▶ adv (also **onwards**) ahead, forward

onwards see ▷ onward

onyx n (pl -es) type of quartz with coloured layers

onyxes n ▷ onyx

oo n (oos). Oo is a Scots word for **wool**. This is a good word to remember, as it combines two of the most common letters in the game without using any consonants. Oo scores two points.

oodles pl n (Informal) great quantities

ooze[1] v (-zes, -zing, -zed) flow slowly ▶ n (pl -s) sluggish flow > **oozy** adj (-zier, -ziest)

ooze[2] n (-s) soft mud at the bottom of a lake or river

oozed v ▷ ooze

oozes v, n ▷ ooze[1, 2]

oozier adj ▷ ooze[1]

ooziest adj ▷ ooze[1]

oozing v ▷ ooze

oozy adj ▷ ooze[1]

opacities n ▷ opaque

opacity n ▷ opaque

opal n (pl -s) iridescent precious stone

opalescent adj iridescent like an opal

opals n ▷ opal

opaque adj (-r, -st) not able to be seen through, not transparent > **opacity** n (-ties)

opaquer adj ▷ opaque

opaquest adj ▷ opaque

open adj (-er, -est) not closed ▶ v (-s, -ing, -ed) (cause to) become open ▶ n (pl -s) (SPORT) competition which all may enter

opened v ▷ open

opener n instrument for opening containers

openest adj ▷ open

opening n (pl -s) opportunity ▶ adj first ▶ v ▷ open

openings n ▷ opening

openly adv without concealment

opens v, n ▷ open

opera[1] n (pl -s) drama in which the text is sung to an orchestral accompaniment > **operatic**

adj
opera² *n* ▷ **opus**
operas *n* ▷ **opera**
operate *v* (**-tes, -ting, -ted**) (cause to) work
> **operator** *n* (*pl* **-s**)
operated *v* ▷ **operate**
operates *v* ▷ **operate**
operatic *adj* ▷ **opera¹**
operating *v* ▷ **operate**
operation *n* (*pl* **-s**) method or procedure of
working
operational *adj* in working order
operations *n* ▷ **operation**
operative *adj* working ▶ *n* (*pl* **-s**) worker with
a special skill
operatives *n* ▷ **operative**
operator *n* ▷ **operate**
operators *n* ▷ **operate**
operetta *n* (*pl* **-s**) light-hearted comic opera
operettas *n* ▷ **operetta**
ophthalmic *adj* relating to the eye
ophthalmologies *n* ▷ **ophthalmology**
ophthalmologist *n* ▷ **ophthalmology**
ophthalmologists *n* ▷ **ophthalmology**
ophthalmology *n* (*pl* **-gies**) study of the eye
and its diseases > **ophthalmologist** *n* (*pl* **-s**)
opiate *n* (*pl* **-s**) narcotic drug containing
opium
opiates *n* ▷ **opiate**
opine *v* (**-nes, -ning, -ned**) (*Old-fashioned*)
express an opinion
opined *v* ▷ **opine**
opines *v* ▷ **opine**
opining *v* ▷ **opine**
opinion *n* (*pl* **-s**) personal belief or judgment
opinionated *adj* having strong opinions
opinions *n* ▷ **opinion**
opium *n* (*pl* **-s**) addictive narcotic drug made
from poppy seeds
opiums *n* ▷ **opium**
opossum *n* (*pl* **-s**) small marsupial of America
or Australasia
opossums *n* ▷ **opossum**
opponent *n* (*pl* **-s**) person one is working
against in a contest, battle, or argument
opponents *n* ▷ **opponent**
opportune *adj* happening at a suitable time
opportunism *n* ▷ **opportunist**
opportunisms , ▷ **opportunist**
opportunist *n* (*pl* **-s**) ▶ *adj* (person) doing
whatever is advantageous without regard for
principles > **opportunism** *n* (*pl* **-s**)
opportunists *n* ▷ **opportunist**
opportunities *n* ▷ **opportunity**
opportunity *n* (*pl* **-ties**) favourable time or

condition
oppose *v* (**-ses, -sing, -sed**) work against
opposed *v* ▷ **oppose**
opposes *v* ▷ **oppose**
opposing *v* ▷ **oppose**
opposition *n* (*pl* **-s**) obstruction or hostility
oppositions *n* ▷ **opposition**
opposite *adj* situated on the other side ▶ *n*
(*pl* **-s**) person or thing that is opposite ▶ *prep*
facing ▶ *adv* on the other side
opposites *n* ▷ **opposite**
oppress *v* (**-es, -ing, -ed**) control by cruelty or
force > **oppression** *n* (*pl* **-s**) > **oppressor** *n* (*pl* **-s**)
oppressed *v* ▷ **oppress**
oppresses *v* ▷ **oppress**
oppressing *v* ▷ **oppress**
oppression *n* ▷ **oppress**
oppressions *n* ▷ **oppress**
oppressive *adj* tyrannical > **oppressively** *adv*
oppressively *adv* ▷ **oppressive**
oppressor *n* ▷ **oppress**
oppressors *n* ▷ **oppress**
opprobrium [op-**probe**-ree-um] *n* (*pl* **-s**) state
of being criticized severely for wrong one
has done
opprobriums *n* ▷ **opprobrium**
opt *v* (**-s, -ing, -ed**) show a preference, choose
opted *v* ▷ **opt**
opting *v* ▷ **opt**
opts *v* ▷ **opt**
optic *adj* relating to the eyes or sight > **optical**
adj
optical *adj* ▷ **optic**
optics *n* science of sight and light
optician *n* (*pl* **-s**) (*also* **ophthalmic optician**)
person qualified to prescribe glasses (*also*
dispensing optician)
opticians *n* ▷ **optician**
optimism *n* (*pl* **-s**) tendency to take the most
hopeful view > **optimist** *n* (*pl* **-s**) > **optimistic**
adj > **optimistically** *adv*
optimisms *n* ▷ **optimism**
optimist *n* ▷ **optimism**
optimistic *adj* ▷ **optimism**
optimistically *adv* ▷ **optimism**
optimists *n* ▷ **optimism**
optima *n* ▷ **optimum**
optimal *adj* ▷ **optimum**
optimize *v* (**-zes, -zing, -zed**) make the most of
optimized *v* ▷ **optimize**
optimizes *v* ▷ **optimize**
optimizing *v* ▷ **optimize**
optimum *n* (*pl* **-ma, -mums**) best possible
conditions ▶ *adj* most favourable > **optimal**
adj

optimums *n* ▷ **optimum**
option *n* (*pl* -**s**) choice
optional *adj* possible but not compulsory
options *n* ▷ **option**
optometries *n* ▷ **optometry**
optometrist *n* (*pl* -**s**) person qualified to
prescribe glasses > **optometry** *n* (-**ries**)
optometrists *n* ▷ **optometrist**
optometry *n* ▷ **optometrist**
opulence *n* ▷ **opulent**
opulences *n* ▷ **opulent**
opulent [op-pew-lent] *adj* having or indicating
wealth > **opulence** *n* (-**s**)
opus *n* (*pl* **opuses, opera**) artistic creation, esp.
a musical work
opuses *n* ▷ **opus**
or *conj* used to join alternatives
oracle *n* (*pl* -**s**) shrine of an ancient god
> **oracular** *adj*
oracles *n* ▷ **oracle**
oracular *adj* ▷ **oracle**
oral *adj* spoken ▶ *n* (*pl* -**s**) spoken examination
> **orally** *adv*
orally *adv* ▷ **oral**
orals *n* ▷ **oral**
orange *n* (*pl* -**s**) reddish-yellow citrus fruit ▶ *adj*
reddish-yellow
orangeade *n* (BRIT) orange-flavoured, usu.
fizzy drink
orangeades *n* ▷ **orangeade**
orangeries *n* ▷ **orangery**
orangery *n* (*pl* -**ries**) greenhouse for growing
orange trees
oranges *n* ▷ **orange**
oration *n* (*pl* -**s**) formal speech
orations *n* ▷ **oration**
orator [or-rat-tor] *n* (*pl* -**s**) skilful public speaker
oratorical *adj* ▷ **oratory**
oratories *n* ▷ **oratory**[1, 2]
oratorio [or-rat-**tor**-ee-oh] *n* (*pl* -**s**) musical
composition for choir and orchestra, usu.
with a religious theme
oratorios *n* ▷ **oratorio**
orators *n* ▷ **orator**
oratory[1] [or-rat-tree] *n* (*pl* -**ries**) art of making
speeches > **oratorical** *adj*
oratory[2] *n* (*pl* -**ries**) small private chapel
orb *n* (*pl* -**s**) ceremonial decorated sphere with
a cross on top, carried by a monarch
orbs *n* ▷ **orb**
orbit *n* (*pl* -**s**) curved path of a planet, satellite,
or spacecraft around another body ▶ *v* (-**s**,
-**ing, -ed**) move in an orbit around > **orbital** *adj*
orbital *adj* ▷ **orbit**
orbited *v* ▷ **orbit**

orbiting *v* ▷ **orbit**
orbits *n*, *v* ▷ **orbit**
orchard *n* (*pl* -**s**) area where fruit trees are
grown
orchards *n* ▷ **orchard**
orchestra *n* (*pl* -**s**) large group of musicians,
esp. playing a variety of instruments (*also*
orchestra pit) > **orchestral** *adj*
orchestral *adj* ▷ **orchestra**
orchestras *n* ▷ **orchestra**
orchestrate *v* (-**tes, -ting, -ted**) arrange
(music) for orchestra > **orchestration** *n* (*pl* -**s**)
orchestrated *v* ▷ **orchestrate**
orchestrates *v* ▷ **orchestrate**
orchestrating *v* ▷ **orchestrate**
orchestration *n* ▷ **orchestrate**
orchestrations *n* ▷ **orchestrate**
orchid *n* (*pl* -**s**) plant with flowers that have
unusual lip-shaped petals
orchids *n* ▷ **orchid**
ordain *v* (-**s, -ing, -ed**) make (someone) a
member of the clergy
ordained *v* ▷ **ordain**
ordaining *v* ▷ **ordain**
ordains *v* ▷ **ordain**
ordeal *n* (*pl* -**s**) painful or difficult experience
ordeals *n* ▷ **ordeal**
order *n* (*pl* -**s**) instruction to be carried out ▶ *v*
(-**s, -ing, -ed**) give an instruction to
orderlies *n* ▷ **orderly**
orderliness *n* ▷ **orderly**
orderlinesses *n* ▷ **orderly**
orderly *adj* well-organized ▶ *n* (*pl* -**lies**) male
hospital attendant > **orderliness** *n* (*pl* -**es**)
ordered *v* ▷ **order**
ordering *v* ▷ **order**
orders *n*, *v* ▷ **order**
ordinance *n* (*pl* -**s**) official rule or order
ordinances *n* ▷ **ordinance**
ordinarily *adv* ▷ **ordinary**
ordinary *adj* usual or normal > **ordinarily** *adv*
ordination *n* (*pl* -**s**) act of making someone a
member of the clergy
ordinations *n* ▷ **ordination**
ordnance *n* (*pl* -**s**) weapons and military
supplies
ordnances *n* ▷ **ordnance**
ordure *n* (*pl* -**s**) excrement
ordures *n* ▷ **ordure**
ore *n* (*pl* -**s**) (rock containing) a mineral which
yields metal
ores *n* ▷ **ore**
oregano [or-rig-**gah**-no] *n* (*pl* -**nos**) sweet-
smelling herb used in cooking
oreganos *n* ▷ **oregano**

organ *n* (*pl* **-s**) part of an animal or plant that has a particular function, such as the heart or lungs

organdie *n* (*pl* **-s**) fine cotton fabric
　organdies *n* ▷ **organdie**

organic *adj* of or produced from animals or plants (CHEM) > **organically** *adv*
　organically *adv* ▷ **organic**

organism *n* (**-s**) any living animal or plant
　organisms *n* ▷ **organism**

organist *n* (*pl* **-s**) organ player
　organists *n* ▷ **organist**

organization *n* (*pl* **-s**) group of people working together > **organizational** *adj*
　organizational *adj* ▷ **organization**
　organizations *n* ▷ **organization**

organize *v* (**-zes**, **-zing**, **-zed**) make arrangements for > **organizer** *n* (*pl* **-s**)
　organized *v* ▷ **organize**
　organizer *n* ▷ **organize**
　organizers *n* ▷ **organize**
　organizes *v* ▷ **organize**
　organizing *v* ▷ **organize**
　organs *n* ▷ **organ**

orgasm *n* (*pl* **-s**) most intense point of sexual pleasure > **orgasmic** *adj*
　orgasmic *adj* ▷ **orgasm**
　orgasms *n* ▷ **orgasm**
　orgiastic *adj* ▷ **orgy**
　orgies *n* ▷ **orgy**

orgy *n* (*pl* **-gies**) party involving promiscuous sexual activity > **orgiastic** *adj*

orient[1], **orientate** *v* (**-s**, **-ing**, **-ed**) position (oneself) according to one's surroundings > **orientation** *n* (*pl* **-s**)

orient[2] *n* (*pl* **-s**) (Lit) east > **oriental** *adj*
　oriental *adj* ▷ **orient**[2]
　orientate *v* ▷ **orient**
　orientated *v* ▷ **orient**
　orientates *v* ▷ **orient**
　orientating *v* ▷ **orient**
　orientation *n* ▷ **orient**
　orientations *n* ▷ **orient**
　oriented *v* ▷ **orient**

orienteering *n* (*pl* **-s**) sport in which competitors hike over a course using a compass and map
　orienteerings *n* ▷ **orienteering**
　orienting *v* ▷ **orient**
　orients *v* ▷ **orient**
　Orients *n* ▷ **Orient**

Orientalist *n* (*pl* **-s**) specialist in the languages and history of the Far East
　Orientalists *n* ▷ **Orientalist**

orifice [or-rif-fiss] *n* (*pl* **-s**) opening or hole

orifices *n* ▷ **orifice**

origami [or-rig-**gah**-mee] *n* (*pl* **-mis**) Japanese decorative art of paper folding
　origamis *n* ▷ **origami**

origin *n* (*pl* **-s**) point from which something develops

original *adj* first or earliest ▶ *n* (*pl* **-s**) first version, from which others are copied > **originality** *n* (*pl* **-ies**) > **originally** *adv*
　originalities *n* ▷ **original**
　originality *n* ▷ **original**
　originally *adv* ▷ **original**
　originals *n* ▷ **original**

originate *v* (**-tes**, **-ting**, **-ted**) come or bring into existence > **origination** *n* (*pl* **-s**) > **originator** *n* (*pl* **-s**)
　originated *v* ▷ **originate**
　originates *v* ▷ **originate**
　originating *v* ▷ **originate**
　origination *n* ▷ **origination**
　originations *n* ▷ **originate**
　originator *n* ▷ **originate**
　originator *n* ▷ **originate**
　origins *n* ▷ **origin**

oriole *n* (*pl* **-s**) tropical or American songbird
　orioles *n* ▷ **oriole**

ormolu *n* (*pl* **-lus**) gold-coloured alloy used for decoration
　ormulus *n* ▷ **ormulu**

ornament *n* (*pl* **-s**) decorative object ▶ *v* (**-s**, **-ing**, **-ed**) decorate > **ornamental** *adj* > **ornamentation** *n* (*pl* **-s**)
　ornamental *adj* ▷ **ornament**
　ornamentation *n* ▷ **ornament**
　ornamentations *n* ▷ **ornament**
　ornamented *v* ▷ **ornament**
　ornamenting *v* ▷ **ornament**
　ornaments *n*, *v* ▷ **ornament**

ornate *adj* highly decorated, elaborate
　ornithological *adj* ▷ **ornithology**
　ornithologies *n* ▷ **ornithology**
　ornithologist *n* ▷ **ornithology**
　ornithologists *n* ▷ **ornithology**

ornithology *n* (*pl* **-gies**) study of birds > **ornithological** *adj* > **ornithologist** *n* (*pl* **-s**)

orphan *n* (*pl* **-s**) child whose parents are dead

orphanage *n* (*pl* **-s**) children's home for orphans
　orphanages *n* ▷ **orphanage**

orphaned *adj* having no living parents
　orphans *n* ▷ **orphan**
　orreries *n* ▷ **orrery**

orrery *n* (*pl* **-ries**) mechanical model of the solar system

orris *n* (*pl* **-es**) kind of iris (*also* **orris root**)

orrises n ▷ orris

orthodontics n (pl branch of dentistry concerned with correcting irregular teeth > **orthodontist** n (pl -s)

orthodontist n ▷ orthodontics

orthodontists n ▷ orhtodontics

orthodox adj conforming to established views > **orthodoxy** n (pl -ies)

orthodoxies n ▷ orthodox

orthodoxy n ▷ orthodox

orthography n (pl -phies) correct spelling

orthographies n ▷ orthography

orthopaedic adj ▷ orthopaedics

orthopaedics n (pl branch of medicine concerned with disorders of the bones or joints > **orthopaedic** adj

oryx n (pl -es) large African antelope

oryxes n ▷ oryx

> **os** n (**ossa**). Os is a technical word for **bone**. This word won't score many points on its own, but will allow you to connect a word beginning with O to one ending in S (e.g. most plurals). Os scores 2 points.

oscillate [oss-ill-late] v (-tes, -ting, -ted) swing back and forth > **oscillation** n (pl -s) > **oscillator** n (pl -s)

oscillated v ▷ oscillate

oscillates v ▷ oscillate

oscillating v ▷ oscillate

oscillation n ▷ oscillate

oscillation n ▷ oscillate

oscillations n ▷ oscillate

oscillator n ▷ oscillate

oscillators n ▷ oscillate

oscilloscope [oss-sill-oh-scope] n (pl -s) instrument that shows the shape of a wave on a cathode-ray tube

oscilloscopes n ▷ oscilloscope

osier [oh-zee-er] n (pl -s) willow tree

osiers n ▷ osier

osmium n (pl -s) (CHEM) heaviest known metallic element

osmiums n ▷ osmium

osmosis n (pl -ses) movement of a liquid through a membrane from a lower to a higher concentration > **osmotic** adj

osmoses n ▷ osmosis

osmotic adj ▷ osmosis

osprey n (pl -s) large fish-eating bird of prey

ospreys n ▷ osprey

ossification n ▷ ossify

ossifications n ▷ ossify

ossified v ▷ ossify

ossifies v ▷ ossify

ossify v (-fies, -fying, -fied) (cause to) become bone, harden > **ossification** n (pl -s)

ossifying v ▷ ossify

ostensible adj apparent, seeming > **ostensibly** adv

ostensibly adv ▷ ostensible

ostentation n (pl -s) pretentious display > **ostentatious** adj > **ostentatiously** adv

ostentations n ▷ ostentation

ostentatious adj ▷ ostentation

ostentatiously adv ▷ ostentation

osteopath n ▷ osteopathy

osteopathies n ▷ osteopathy

osteopaths n ▷ osteopathy

osteopathy n (pl -thies) medical treatment involving manipulation of the joints > **osteopath** n (pl -s)

osteoporosis n (pl -ses) brittleness of the bones, caused by lack of calcium

osteoporoses n ▷ osteoporosis

ostracism n ▷ ostracize

ostracisms n ▷ ostracize

ostracize v (-zes, -zing, -zed) exclude (a person) from a group > **ostracism** n (pl -s)

ostracized v ▷ ostracize

ostracizes v ▷ ostracize

ostracizing v ▷ ostracize

ostrich n (pl -es) large African bird that runs fast but cannot fly

ostriches n ▷ ostrich

other adj remaining in a group of which one or some have been specified ▶ n (pl -s) other person or thing

others n ▷ other

otherwise conj or else, if not ▶ adv differently, in another way

otherworldly adj concerned with spiritual rather than practical matters

otiose [oh-tee-oze] adj not useful

otter n (pl -s) small brown freshwater mammal that eats fish

otters n ▷ otter

ottoman n (pl -mans) storage chest with a padded lid for use as a seat

ottomans n ▷ ottoman

> **ou** n (**ous**). Ou is a South African slang word for a man. This word doesn't score many points, but is very useful when you are trying to form words in more than one direction. Ou scores 2 points.

oubliette [oo-blee-ett] n (pl -s) dungeon entered only by a trapdoor

oubliettes n ▷ oubliette

ouch interj exclamation of sudden pain

ought v used to express: obligation
ounce n (pl -s) unit of weight equal to one sixteenth of a pound (28.4 grams)
  ounces n ▷ ounce
our adj belonging to us
ours pron thing(s) belonging to us
  ourselves pron ▷ we, us
  ousel n (pl -s) ▷ dipper
  ousels n ▷ ousel
oust v (-s, -ing, -ed) force (someone) out, expel
  ousted v ▷ oust
  ousting v ▷ oust
  ousts v ▷ oust
out adv, adj denoting movement or distance away from, a state of being used up or extinguished, public availability, etc. ▶ v (-s, -ing, -ed) (Informal) name (a public figure) as being homosexual
outback n (pl -s) remote bush country of Australia
  outbacks n ▷ outback
outbid v (-bids, -bidding, -bid, -bidden) offer a higher price than
  outbid v ▷ outbid
  outbidden v ▷ outbid
  outbidding v ▷ outbid
  outbids v ▷ outbid
outbreak n (pl -s) sudden occurrence (of something unpleasant)
  outbreaks n ▷ outbreak
outburst n (pl -s) sudden expression of emotion
  outbursts n ▷ outburst
outcast n (pl -s) person rejected by a particular group
  outcasts n ▷ outcast
outclass v (-es, -ing, -ed) surpass in quality
  outclassed v ▷ outclass
  outclasses v ▷ outclass
  outclassing v ▷ outclass
outcome n (pl -s) result
  outcomes n ▷ outcome
  outcries n ▷ outcry
outcrop n (pl -s) part of a rock formation that sticks out of the earth
  outcrops n ▷ outcrop
outcry n (pl -ries) vehement or widespread protest
outdo v (-does, -doing, -did, -done) surpass in performance
  outdid v ▷ outdo
  outdoes v ▷ outdo
  outdoing v ▷ outdo
  outdone v ▷ outdo
  outdoor adj ▷ outdoors

outdoors adv in(to) the open air ▶ n (pl the open air > **outdoor** adj
  outed v ▷ out
outer adj on the outside
outermost adj furthest out
outface v (-ces, -cing, -ced) subdue or disconcert (someone) by staring
  outfaced v ▷ outface
  outfaces v ▷ outface
  outfacing v ▷ outface
outfield n (pl -s) (CRICKET) area far from the pitch
  outfields n ▷ outfield
outfit n (pl -s) matching set of clothes
  outfits n ▷ outfit
outfitter n (pl -s) supplier of men's clothes
  outfitters n ▷ outfitter
outflank v (-s, -ing, -ed) get round the side of (an enemy army)
  outflanked v ▷ outflank
  outflanking v ▷ outflank
  outflanks v ▷ outflank
outgoing adj leaving
outgoings pl n expenses
outgrow v (-grows, -growing, -grew, -grown) become too large or too old for
  outgrew v ▷ outgrow
  outgrowing v ▷ outgrow
  outgrown v ▷ outgrow
  outgrows v ▷ outgrow
outgrowth n natural development
  outgrowths n ▷ outgrowth
outhouse n (pl -s) building near a main building
  outhouses n ▷ outhouse
outing n (pl -s) leisure trip ▶ v ▷ out
  outings n ▷ outing

> **outjinx** v (outjinxes, outjinxing, outjinxed). Outjinx means to outmanoeuvre. If someone else plays **jinx,** you can outjinx them by adding O, U and T! If you can form the whole word using all of your letters, you'll get a 50-point bonus. Outjinx scores 21 points.

outlandish adj extremely unconventional
outlaw n (pl -s) (HIST) criminal deprived of legal protection, bandit ▶ v (-s, -ing, -ed) make illegal (HIST)
  outlawed v ▷ outlaw
  outlawing v ▷ outlaw
  outlaws n, v ▷ outlaw
outlay n (pl -s) expenditure
  outlays n ▷ outlay
outlet n (pl -s) means of expressing emotion
  outlets n ▷ outlet

outline n (pl -s) short general explanation ▸ v (-nes, -ning, -ned) summarize
  outlined v ▷ outline
  outlines n, v ▷ outline
  outlining v ▷ outline
outlook n (pl -s) attitude
  outlooks n ▷ outlook
outlying adj distant from the main area
outmanoeuvre v (-res, -ring, -red) get an advantage over
  outmanoeuvred v ▷ outmanoeuvre
  outmanoeuvres v ▷ outmanoeuvre
  outmanoeuvring v ▷ outmanoeuvre
outmoded adj no longer fashionable or accepted
outnumber v (-s, -ing, -ed) exceed in number
  outnumbered v ▷ outnumber
  outnumbering v ▷ outnumber
  outnumbers v ▷ outnumber
outpatient n (pl -s) patient who does not stay in hospital overnight
  outpatients n ▷ outpatient
outpost n (pl -s) outlying settlement
  outposts n ▷ outpost
outpouring n (pl -s) passionate outburst
  outpourings n ▷ outpouring
output n (pl -s) amount produced ▸ v (-puts, -putting, -putted) (COMPUTERS) produce (data) at the end of a process
  outputted v ▷ output
  outputting v ▷ output
  outputs n, v ▷ output
outrage n (pl -s) great moral indignation ▸ v (-s, -ing, -ed) offend morally
  outraged v ▷ outrage
outrageous adj shocking > **outrageously** adv
  outrageously adv ▷ outrageous
  outrages n, v ▷ outrage
  outraging v ▷ outrage
outré [oo-tray] adj shockingly eccentric
outrider n (pl -s) motorcyclist acting as an escort
  outriders n ▷ outrider
outrigger n (pl -s) stabilizing frame projecting from a boat
  outriggers n ▷ outrigger
outright adj, adv absolute(ly)
outrun v (-runs, -running, -ran, -run) run faster than
  outran v ▷ outrun
  outrun v ▷ outrun
  outrunning v ▷ outrun
  outruns v ▷ outrun
  outs v ▷ out
outset n (pl -s) beginning

outsets n ▷ outset
outshine v (-shines, -shining, -shone) surpass (someone) in excellence
  outshines v ▷ outshine
  outshining v ▷ outshine
  outshone v ▷ outshine
outside prep, adj adv indicating movement to or position on the exterior ▸ adj unlikely ▸ n (pl -s) external area or surface
outsider n (pl -s) person outside a specific group
  outsiders n ▷ outsider
  outsides n ▷ outside
outsize, outsized adj larger than normal
  outsized adj ▷ outsize
outskirts pl n outer areas, esp. of a town
outsmart v (-s, -ing, -ed) (Informal) outwit
  outsmarted v ▷ outsmart
  outsmarting v ▷ outsmart
  outsmarts v ▷ outsmart
outspan v (-s, -nning, -nned) (S AFR) relax
  outspanned v ▷ outspan
  outspanning v ▷ outspan
  outspans v ▷ outspan
outspoken adj tending to say what one thinks
outstanding adj excellent
outstrip v (-s, -pping, -pped) surpass
  outstripped v ▷ outstrip
  outstripping v ▷ outstrip
  outstrips v ▷ outstrip
outtake n (pl -s) unreleased take from a recording session, film, or TV programme
  outtakes n ▷ outtake
outward adj apparent ▸ adv (also **outwards**) away from somewhere > **outwardly** adv
  outwardly adv ▷ outward
outweigh v (-s, -ing, -ed) be more important, significant, or influential than
  outweighed v ▷ outweigh
  outweighing v ▷ outweigh
  outweighs v ▷ outweigh
outwit v (-s, -tting, -tted) get the better of (someone) by cunning
  outwits v ▷ outwit
  outwitted v ▷ outwit
  outwitting v ▷ outwit
ouzel [ooze-el] n (pl -s) ▷ dipper
  ouzels n ▷ ouzel
  ova n ▷ ovum
oval adj egg-shaped ▸ n (pl -s) anything that is oval in shape
  ovals n ▷ oval
  ovarian adj ▷ ovary
  ovaries n ▷ ovary
ovary n (pl -ries) female egg-producing organ

> **ovarian** *adj*
ovation *n* (*pl* -**s**) enthusiastic round of applause
  ovations *n* ▷ **ovation**
oven *n* (*pl* -**s**) heated compartment or container for cooking or for drying or firing ceramics
  ovens *n* ▷ **oven**
over *prep*, *adv* indicating position on the top of, movement to the other side of, amount greater than, etc. ▶ *adj* finished ▶ *n* (*pl* -**s**) (CRICKET) series of six balls bowled from one end
overall *adj*, *adv* in total ▶ *n* (*pl* -**s**) coat-shaped protective garment ▶ *pl* protective garment consisting of trousers with a jacket or bib and braces attached
  overalls *n* ▷ **overall**
overarm *adj*, *adv* (thrown) with the arm above the shoulder
overawe *v* (-**wes**, -**wing**, -**wed**) affect (someone) with an overpowering sense of awe
  overawed *v* ▷ **overawe**
  overawes *v* ▷ **overawe**
  overawing *v* ▷ **overawe**
overbalance *v* (-**ces**, -**cing**, -**ced**) lose balance
  overbalanced *v* ▷ **overbalance**
  overbalances *v* ▷ **overbalance**
  overbalancing *v* ▷ **overbalance**
overbearing *adj* unpleasantly forceful
overblown *adj* excessive
overboard *adv* from a boat into the water
  overcame *v* ▷ **overcome**
overcast *adj* (of the sky) covered by clouds
overcoat *n* (*pl* -**s**) heavy coat
  overcoats *n* ▷ **overcoat**
overcome *v* (-**comes**, -**coming**, -**came**, -**come**) gain control over after an effort
  overcomes *v* ▷ **overcome**
  overcoming *v* ▷ **overcome**
overcrowded *adj* containing more people or things than is desirable
  overdid *v* ▷ **overdo**
overdo *v* (-**does**, -**doing**, -**did**, -**done**) do to excess
  overdoes *v* ▷ **overdo**
  overdoing *v* ▷ **overdo**
  overdone *v* ▷ **overdo**
overdose *n* (*pl* -**s**) excessive dose of a drug ▶ *v* (-**ses**, -**sing**, -**sed**) take an overdose
  overdosed *n* ▷ **overdose**
  overdoses *n*, *v* ▷ **overdose**
  overdosing *v* ▷ **overdose**
overdraft *n* (*pl* -**s**) overdrawing

overdrafts *n* ▷ **overdraft**
overdraw *v* (-**draws**, -**drawing**, -**drew**, -**drawn**) withdraw more money than is in (one's bank account)
  overdrawing *v* ▷ **overdraw**
  overdrawn *v* ▷ **overdraw**
  overdraws *v* ▷ **overdraw**
  overdrew *v* ▷ **overdraw**
overdrawn *adj* having overdrawn one's account
overdrive *n* (*pl* -**s**) very high gear in a motor vehicle
  overdrives *n* ▷ **overdrive**
overdue *adj* still due after the time allowed
overgrown *adj* thickly covered with plants and weeds
overhaul *v* (-**s**, -**ing**, -**ed**) examine and repair ▶ *n* (*pl* -**s**) examination and repair
  overhauled *v* ▷ **overhaul**
  overhauling *v* ▷ **overhaul**
  overhauls *v*, *n* ▷ **overhaul**
overhead *adv*, *adj* above one's head
overheads *pl n* general cost of maintaining a business
overhear *v* (-**hears**, -**hearing**, -**heard**) hear (a speaker or remark) unintentionally or without the speaker's knowledge
  overheard *v* ▷ **overhear**
  overhearing *v* ▷ **overhear**
  overhears *v* ▷ **overhear**
overjoyed *adj* extremely pleased
overkill *n* (*pl* -**s**) treatment that is greater than required
  overkills *n* ▷ **overkill**
overland *adj*, *adv* by land
overlap *v* (-**s**, -**pping**, -**pped**) share part of the same space or period of time (as) ▶ *n* (*pl* -**s**) area overlapping
  overlapped *v* ▷ **overlap**
  overlapping *v* ▷ **overlap**
  overlaps *v*, *n* ▷ **overlap**
overleaf *adv* on the back of the current page
overlook *v* (-**s**, -**ing**, -**ed**) fail to notice
  overlooked *v* ▷ **overlook**
  overlooking *v* ▷ **overlook**
  overlooks *v* ▷ **overlook**
overly *adv* excessively
overnight *adj*, *adv* (taking place) during one night
overpower *v* (-**s**, -**ing**, -**ed**) subdue or overcome (someone)
  overpowered *v* ▷ **overpower**
  overpowering *v* ▷ **overpower**
  overpowers *v* ▷ **overpower**
  overran *v* ▷ **overrun**

overreach v (-es, -ing, -ed) fail by trying to be too clever
overreached v ▷ overreach
overreaches v ▷ overreach
overreaching v ▷ overreach
override v (-rides, -riding, -rode, -ridden) overrule
overridden v ▷ override
overrides v ▷ override
overriding v ▷ override
overrode v ▷ override
overrule v (-les, -ling, -led) reverse the decision of (a person with less power)
overruled v ▷ overrule
overrules v ▷ overrule
overruling v ▷ overrule
overrun v (-runs, -running, -ran, -run) spread over (a place) rapidly
overrunning v ▷ overrun
overruns v ▷ overrun
overs n ▷ over
oversaw v ▷ oversee
overseas adv, adj to, of, or from a distant country
oversee v (-sees, -seeing, -saw, -seen) watch over from a position of authority > **overseer** n (-s)
overseeing v ▷ oversee
overseen v ▷ oversee
overseer n ▷ oversee
overseers n ▷ oversee
oversees v ▷ oversee
overshadow v (-s, -ing, -ed) reduce the significance of (a person or thing) by comparison
overshadowed v ▷ overshadow
overshadowing v ▷ overshadow
overshadows v ▷ overshadow
oversight n (pl -s) mistake caused by not noticing something
oversights n ▷ oversight
overspill n (pl -s) (BRIT) rehousing of people from crowded cities in smaller towns
overspills n ▷ overspill
overstay v (-s, -ing, -ed) stay longer than one's host or hostess would like
overstayed v ▷ overstay
overstayer n (-s) (NZ) person who remains in New Zealand after their permit has expired
overstayers n ▷ overstyer
overstaying v ▷ overstay
overstays v ▷ overstay
overt adj open, not hidden > **overtly** adv
overtly adv ▷ overt
overtake v (-takes, -taking, -took, -taken)

move past (a vehicle or person) travelling in the same direction
overtaken v ▷ overtake
overtakes v ▷ overtake
overtaking v ▷ overtake
overtook v ▷ overtake
overthrew v ▷ overthrow
overthrow v (-throws, -throwing, -threw, -thrown) defeat and replace ▶ n (pl -s) downfall, destruction
overthrowing v ▷ overthrow
overthrown v ▷ overthrow
overthrows v, n ▷ overthrow
overtime n, adv (pl -s) (paid work done) in addition to one's normal working hours
overtimes n ▷ overtime
overtone n (pl -s) additional meaning
overtones n ▷ overtone
overture n (pl -s) (MUSIC) orchestral introduction ▶ pl opening moves in a new relationship
overtures n ▷ overture
overturn v (-s, -ing, -ed) turn upside down
overturned v ▷ overturn
overturning v ▷ overturn
overturns v ▷ overturn
overweight adj weighing more than is healthy
overwhelm v (-s, -ing, -ed) overpower, esp. emotionally > **overwhelming** adj > **overwhelmingly** adv
overwhelmed v ▷ overwhelm
overwhelming v, adj ▷ overwhelm
overwhelmingly adv ▷ overwhelm
overwhelms v ▷ overwhelm
overwrought adj nervous and agitated
ovoid [oh-void] adj egg-shaped
ovulate [ov-yew-late] v (-tes, -ting, -ted) produce or release an egg cell from an ovary > **ovulation** n (-s)
ovulated v ▷ ovulate
ovulates v ▷ ovulate
ovulating v ▷ ovulate
ovulation n ▷ ovulate
ovulations n ▷ ovulate
ovum [oh-vum] n (pl ova) unfertilized egg cell
owe v (owes, owing, owed) be obliged to pay (a sum of money) to (a person)
owed v ▷ owe
owes v ▷ owe
owing v ▷ owe
owl n (pl -s) night bird of prey > **owlish** adj
owlish adj ▷ owl
owls n ▷ owl
own adj used to emphasize possession

▶ v (**-s, -ing, -ed**) possess > **owner** n (pl **-s**)
> **ownership** n (pl **-s**)
owned v ▷ own
owner n ▷ own
owners n ▷ own
ownership n ▷ own
ownerships n ▷ own
owning v ▷ own
owns v ▷ own
ox n (pl **oxen**) castrated bull
oxen n ▷ ox
oxide n (pl **-s**) compound of oxygen and one
other element
oxides n ▷ oxide
oxidize v (**-zes, -zing, -zed**) combine
chemically with oxygen, as in burning or
rusting
oxidized v ▷ oxidize
oxidizes v ▷ oxidize
oxidizing v ▷ oxidize
oxygen n (pl **-s**) (CHEM) gaseous element

essential to life and combustion
oxygenate v (**-tes, -ting, -ted**) add oxygen to
oxygenated v ▷ oxygenate
oxygenates v ▷ oxygenate
oxygenating v ▷ oxygenate
oxygens n ▷ oxygen
oxymora n ▷ oxymoron
oxymoron [ox-see-**more**-on] n (pl **-mora,
-morons**) figure of speech that combines two
apparently contradictory ideas
oxymorons n ▷ oxymoron
oyez interj (HIST) shouted three times by a
public crier, listen
oyster n (pl **-s**) edible shellfish
oystercatcher n (pl **-s**) wading bird with black-
and-white feathers
oystercatchers n ▷ oystercatcher
oysters n ▷ oyster
ozone n (pl **-s**) strong-smelling form of oxygen
ozones n ▷ ozone

Pp

P forms a two-letter word in front of every vowel except U, which makes it very useful for joining a new word to one already on the board. It also forms several three-letter words with X: **pax, pix, pox** (12 points each) and **pyx** (15). You should also remember one of the strangest words in Scrabble – **pH** (7), which is valid because it doesn't start with a capital letter. When you have the letter P on your rack, look for an H on the board, as they may allow you to play a word beginning or ending in PH, adding to your options.

pa n (pl -**s**) (NZ) (formerly) a fortified Maori settlement

pace n (pl -**s**) single step in walking ▶ v (**-ces, -cing, -ced**) walk up and down, esp. in anxiety
  paced v ▷ **pace**

pacemaker n (pl -**s**) electronic device surgically implanted in a person with heart disease to regulate the heartbeat
  pacemakers n ▷ **pacemaker**
  paces n, v ▷ **pace**

pachyderm [pak-ee-durm] n (pl -**s**) thick-skinned animal such as an elephant
  pachyderms n ▷ **pachyderm**
  pacification n ▷ **pacify**
  pacifications n ▷ **pacify**
  pacified v ▷ **pacify**
  pacifies v ▷ **pacify**
  pacifism n ▷ **pacifist**
  pacifisms n ▷ **pacifist**

pacifist n (pl -**s**) person who refuses on principle to take part in war > **pacifism** n (pl -**s**)
  pacifists n ▷ **pacifist**

pacify v (**-fies, -fying, -fied**) soothe, calm > **pacification** n (pl -**s**)
  pacifying v ▷ **pacify**
  pacing v ▷ **pace**

pack v (**-s, -ing, -ed**) put (clothes etc.) together in a suitcase or bag ▶ n (pl -**s**) bag carried on a person's or animal's back
  packed v ▷ **pack**
  packing v ▷ **pack**
  packs v, n ▷ **pack**

package n (pl -**s**) small parcel ▶ v (**-ges, -ging, -ged**) put into a package > **packaging** n (pl -**s**)
  packaged v ▷ **package**

  packages n, v ▷ **package**
  packaging v, n ▷ **package**
  packagings n ▷ **package**

packet n (pl -**s**) small container (and contents)
  packets n ▷ **packet**

packhorse n (pl -**s**) horse used for carrying goods
  packhorses n ▷ **packhorse**

pact n (pl -**s**) formal agreement
  pacts n ▷ **pact**

pad n (pl -**s**) piece of soft material used for protection, support, absorption of liquid, etc. ▶ v (**padding, padded**) protect or fill with soft material
  padded v ▷ **pad**
  paddies n ▷ **paddy**

padding n (pl -**s**) soft material used to pad something ▶ v ▷ **pad**
  paddings n ▷ **padding**

paddle¹ n (pl -**s**) short oar with a broad blade at one or each end ▶ v (**-les, -ling, -led**) move (a canoe etc.) with a paddle

paddle² v (**-les, -ling, -led**) walk barefoot in shallow water
  paddled v ▷ **paddle¹, ²**
  paddles n, v ▷ **paddle¹, ²**
  paddling v ▷ **paddle¹, ²**

paddock n (pl -**s**) small field or enclosure for horses
  paddocks n ▷ **paddock**

paddy n (pl -**ies**) (BRIT) (Informal) fit of temper
  paddymelons n ▷ **pademelon**

pademelon, paddymelon [pad-ee-mel-an] n (pl -**s**) small Australian wallaby
  pademelons n ▷ **pademelon**

padlock n (pl -**s**) detachable lock with a hinged

hoop fastened over a ring on the object to be secured

padlocks n ▷ **padlock**

padre [pah-dray] n (pl -s) chaplain to the armed forces

padres n ▷ **padre**

pads v, n ▷ **pad**

paean [pee-an] n (pl -s) song of triumph or thanksgiving

paeans n ▷ **paean**

paediatrics n branch of medicine concerned with diseases of children > **paediatrician** n

paella [pie-ell-a] n (pl -s) Spanish dish of rice, chicken, shellfish, and vegetables

paellas n ▷ **paella**

pagan n (pl -s) ▶ adj (person) not belonging to one of the world's main religions

pagans n ▷ **pagan**

page[1] n (pl -s) (one side of) a sheet of paper forming a book etc.

page[2] n (also **pageboy**) small boy who attends a bride at her wedding ▶ v (**-ges, -ging, -ged**) summon (someone) by bleeper or loudspeaker, in order to pass on a message

pageant n (pl -s) parade or display of people in costume, usu. illustrating a scene from history > **pageantry** n (pl -ries)

pageantries n ▷ **pageant**

pageantry n ▷ **pageant**

pageants n ▷ **pageant**

paged v ▷ **page**[2]

pages n, v ▷ **page**[1, 2]

pagination n (pl -s) numbering of the pages of a book etc.

paginations n ▷ **pagination**

paging v ▷ **page**[2]

pagoda n (pl -s) pyramid-shaped Asian temple or tower

pagodas n ▷ **pagoda**

paid v ▷ **pay**

pail n (pl -s) (contents of) a bucket

pails n ▷ **pail**

pain n (pl -s) physical or mental suffering ▶ pl trouble, effort > **painful** adj > **painfully** adv > **painless** adj > **painlessly** adv

painful adj ▷ **pain**

painfully adv ▷ **pain**

painkiller n (pl -s) drug that relieves pain

painkillers n ▷ **painkiller**

painless adj ▷ **pain**

painlessly adv ▷ **pain**

pains n ▷ **pain**

painstaking adj extremely thorough and careful

paint n (pl -s) coloured substance, spread on a surface with a brush or roller ▶ v (**-s, -ing, -ed**) colour or coat with paint > **painter** n (pl -s) > **painting** n (pl -s)

painted v ▷ **paint**

painter[1] n ▷ **paint**

painter[2] n (pl -s) rope at the front of a boat, for tying it up

painters n ▷ **paint painter**[2]

painting v, n ▷ **paint**

paintings n ▷ **paint**

paints n, v ▷ **paint**

pair n (pl -s) set of two things matched for use together ▶ v (**-s, -ing, -ed**) group or be grouped in twos

paired v ▷ **pair**

pairing v ▷ **pair**

pairs n, v ▷ **pair**

pakeha [pah-kee-ha] n (pl -s) (NZ) New Zealander who is not of Maori descent

pakehas n ▷ **pakeha**

pal n (pl -s) (Informal) (Old-fashioned in NZ) friend

pals n ▷ **pal**

palace n (pl -s) residence of a king, bishop, etc.

palaces n ▷ **palace**

palaeographies n ▷ **palaeography**

palaeography [pal-ee-og-ra-fee] n (pl -ies) study of ancient manuscripts

palaeolithic [pal-ee-oh-lith-ik] adj of the Old Stone Age

palaeontologies n ▷ **palaeontology**

palaeontology [pal-ee-on-tol-a-jee] n (pl -ies) study of past geological periods and fossils

palagi [pa-lang-gee] n (pl -s) (NZ) Samoan name for a pakeha

palagis n ▷ **palagi**

palatable adj pleasant to taste

palate n (pl -s) roof of the mouth

palates n ▷ **palate**

palatial adj like a palace, magnificent

palaver [pal-lah-ver] n (pl -s) time-wasting fuss

palavers n ▷ **palaver**

pale[1] adj (**-er, -est**) light, whitish ▶ v (**-les, -ling, -led**) become pale

pale[2] n (pl -s) wooden or metal post used in fences

paled v ▷ **pale**

paler adj ▷ **pale**[1]

pales v ▷ **pale**[1, 2]

palest adj ▷ **pale**[1]

paling v ▷ **pale**

palette n (pl -s) artist's flat board for mixing colours on

palettes n ▷ **palette**

palindrome n (pl -s) word or phrase that reads the same backwards as forwards

palindromes *n* ▷ **palindrome**
paling *n* (*pl* -**s**) wooden or metal post used in fences
palings *n* ▷ **paling**
palisade *n* (*pl* -**s**) fence made of wooden posts driven into the ground
palisades *n* ▷ **palisade**
pall¹ *n* (*pl* -**s**) cloth spread over a coffin
pall² *v* (-**s, -ing, -ed**) become boring
pallbearer *n* (*pl* -**s**) person who helps to carry the coffin at a funeral
pallbearers *n* ▷ **pallbearer**
palled *v* ▷ **pall²**
palling *v* ▷ **pall²**
palls *n* ▷ **pall¹** ▶ *v* ▷ **pall²**
palladium *n* (*pl* -**s**) (CHEM) silvery-white element of the platinum metal group
palladiums *n* ▷ **palladium**
pallet¹ *n* (*pl* -**s**) portable platform for storing and moving goods
pallet² *n* straw-filled mattress or bed
pallets *n* ▷ **pallet¹, ²**
palliate *v* (-**tes, -ting, -ted**) lessen the severity of (something) without curing it
palliated *v* ▷ **palliate**
palliates *v* ▷ **palliate**
palliating *v* ▷ **palliate**
palliative *adj* giving temporary or partial relief ▶ *n* (*pl* -**s**) something, for example a drug, that palliates
palliatives *n* ▷ **palliative**
pallid *adj* (-**er, -est**) pale, esp. because ill or weak > **pallor** *n* (*pl* -**s**)
pallider *adj* ▷ **pallid**
pallidest *adj* ▷ **pallid**
pallier *adj* ▷ **pally**
palliest *adj* ▷ **pally**
pallor *n* ▷ **pallid**
pallors *n* ▷ **pallid**
pally *adj* (-**lier, -lliest**) (*Informal*) on friendly terms
palm¹ *n* (*pl* -**s**) inner surface of the hand
palm² *n* (*pl* -**s**) tropical tree with long pointed leaves growing out of the top of a straight trunk
palmist *n* ▷ **palmistry**
palmistries *n* ▷ **palmistry**
palmistry *n* (*pl* -**ries**) fortune-telling from lines on the palm of the hand > **palmist** *n* (*pl* -**s**)
palmists *n* ▷ **palmistry**
palms *n* ▷ **palm¹, ²**
palmtop *adj* (of a computer) small enough to be held in the hand ▶ *n* (*pl* -**s**) computer small enough to be held in the hand
palmtops *n* ▷ **palmtop**

palomino *n* (*pl* -**s**) gold-coloured horse with a white mane and tail
palominos *n* ▷ **palomino**
palpable *adj* obvious > **palpably** *adv*
palpably *adv* ▷ **palpable**
palpate *v* (-**tes, -ting, -ted**) (MED) examine (an area of the body) by touching
palpated *v* ▷ **palpate**
palpates *v* ▷ **palpate**
palpating *v* ▷ **palpate**
palpitate *v* (-**tes, -ting, -ted**) (of the heart) beat rapidly > **palpitation** *n* (*pl* -**s**)
palpitated *v* ▷ **palpitate**
palpitates *v* ▷ **palpitate**
palpitating *v* ▷ **palpitate**
palpitation *n* ▷ **palpitate**
palpitations *v* ▷ **palpitate**
palsied *adj* affected with palsy
palsies *n* ▷ **palsy**
palsy [pawl-zee] *n* (*pl* -**sies**) paralysis
paltrier *adj* ▷ **paltry**
paltriest *adj* ▷ **paltry**
paltry *adj* (-**rier, -riest**) insignificant
pampas *pl n* vast grassy plains in S America
pamper *v* (-**s, -ing, -ed**) treat (someone) with great indulgence, spoil
pampered *v* ▷ **pamper**
pampering *v* ▷ **pamper**
pampers *v* ▷ **pamper**
pamphlet *n* (*pl* -**s**) thin paper-covered booklet
pamphleteer *n* (*pl* -**s**) writer of pamphlets
pamphleteers *n* ▷ **pamphleteer**
pamphlets *n* ▷ **pamphlet**
pan¹ *n* (*pl* -**s**) wide long-handled metal container used in cooking ▶ *v* (-**s, -nning, -nned**) sift gravel from (a river) in a pan to search for gold (*Informal*)
pan² *v* (-**s, -nning, -nned**) (of a film camera) be moved slowly so as to cover a whole scene or follow a moving object
panacea [pan-a-see-a] *n* (*pl* -**s**) remedy for all diseases or problems
panaceas *n* ▷ **panacea**
panache [pan-ash] *n* (*pl* -**s**) confident elegant style
panaches *n* ▷ **panache**
panatella *n* (*pl* -**s**) long slender cigar
panatellas *n* ▷ **panatella**
pancake *n* (*pl* -**s**) thin flat circle of fried batter
pancakes *n* ▷ **pancake**
panchromatic *adj* (PHOTOG) sensitive to light of all colours
pancreas [pang-kree-ass] *n* (*pl* -**es**) large gland behind the stomach that produces insulin and helps digestion > **pancreatic** *adj*

pancreases *n* ▷ pancreas
pancreatic *adj* ▷ pancreas
panda *n* (*pl* -s) large black-and-white bearlike mammal from China
pandas *n* ▷ panda
pandemic *adj* (of a disease) occurring over a wide area
pandemonium *n* (*pl* -s) wild confusion, uproar
pandemoniums *n* ▷ pandemonium
pander[1] *v* (-s, -ing, -ed) (*foll. by* to) indulge (a person his or her desires)
pander[2] *n* (*pl* -s) (*Old-fashioned*) person who procures a sexual partner for someone
pandered *v* ▷ pander
pandering *v* ▷ pander
panders *v, n* ▷ pander[1, 2]
pane *n* (*pl* -s) sheet of glass in a window or door
panes *n* ▷ pane
panegyric [pan-ee-**jire**-ik] *n* (*pl* -s) formal speech or piece of writing in praise of someone or something
panegyrics *n* ▷ panegyric
panel *n* (*pl* -s) flat distinct section of a larger surface, for example in a door ▶ *v* (-s, -lling, -lled) cover or decorate with panels
panelled *v* ▷ panel
panelling *n* (*pl* -s) panels collectively, esp. on a wall ▶ *v* ▷ panel
panellings *n* ▷ panelling
panellist *n* (*pl* -s) member of a panel
panellists *n* ▷ panellist
panels *n* ▷ panel
pang *n* (*pl* -s) sudden sharp feeling of pain or sadness
pangs *n* ▷ pang
pangolin *n* (*pl* -s) animal of tropical countries with a scaly body and a long snout for eating ants and termites (*also* **scaly anteater**)
pangolins *n* ▷ pangolin
panic *n* (*pl* -s) sudden overwhelming fear, often affecting a whole group of people ▶ *v* (-s, -cking, -cked) feel or cause to feel panic > **panicky** *adj* (-ier, -iest)
panicked *v* ▷ panic
panickier *adj* ▷ panic
panickiest *adj* ▷ panic
panicking *v* ▷ panic
panicky *adj* ▷ panic
panics *n, v* ▷ panic
panic-stricken *adj* ▷ panic
pannier *n* (*pl* -s) bag fixed on the back of a cycle
panniers *n* ▷ pannier
panoplies *n* ▷ panoply
panoply *n* (*pl* -ies) magnificent array
panorama *n* (*pl* -s) wide unbroken view of a

scene > **panoramic** *adj*
panoramas *n* ▷ panorama
panoramic *adj* ▷ panorama
pansies *n* ▷ pansy
pansy *n* (*pl* -sies) small garden flower with velvety purple, yellow, or white petals
pant *v* (-s, -ing, -ed) breathe quickly and noisily during or after exertion
pantaloons *pl n* baggy trousers gathered at the ankles
pantechnicon *n* (*pl* -s) large van for furniture removals
pantechnicons *n* ▷ pantechnicon
panted *v* ▷ pant
pantheism *n* (*pl* -s) belief that God is present in everything > **pantheist** *n* (*pl* -s) > **pantheistic** *adj*
pantheisms *n* ▷ pantheism
pantheist *n* ▷ pantheism
pantheistic *adj* ▷ pantheism
pantheists *n* ▷ pantheism
pantheon *n* (*pl* -s) (in ancient Greece and Rome) temple built to honour all the gods
pantheons *n* ▷ pantheon
panther *n* (*pl* -s) leopard, esp. a black one
panthers *n* ▷ panther
panties *pl n* women's underpants
pantile *n* (*pl* -s) roofing tile with an S-shaped cross section
pantiles *n* ▷ pantile
panting *v* ▷ pant
pantomime *n* (*pl* -s) play based on a fairy tale, performed at Christmas time
pantomimes *n* ▷ pantomime
pantries *n* ▷ pantry
pantry *n* (*pl* -ries) small room or cupboard for storing food
pants *v* ▷ pant
pants *pl n* undergarment for the lower part of the body
pap *n* (*pl* -s) soft food for babies or invalids
papacies *n* ▷ papacy
paps *n* ▷ pap
papacy [**pay**-pa-see] *n* (*pl* -cies) position or term of office of a pope
papal *adj* of the pope
paparazzi *n* ▷ paparazzo
paparazzo [pap-a-**rat**-so] *n* (*pl* -razzi) photographer specializing in candid photographs of famous people
papaya [pa-**pie**-ya] *n* (*pl* -s) large sweet West Indian fruit
papayas *n* ▷ papaya
paper *n* (*pl* -s) material made in sheets from wood pulp or other fibres ▶ *pl* personal

documents ▶ v (**-s, -ing, -ed**) cover (walls) with wallpaper

paperback n (pl **-s**) book with covers made of flexible card

  paperbacks n ▷ **paperback**

  papering v ▷ **paper**

  papered v ▷ **paper**

  papers n, v ▷ **paper**

paperweight n (pl **-s**) heavy decorative object placed on top of loose papers

  paperweights n ▷ **paperweight**

paperwork n (pl **-s**) clerical work, such as writing reports and letters

  paperworks n ▷ **paperwork**

papoose n (pl **-s**) Native American child

  papooses n ▷ **papoose**

paprika n (pl **-s**) mild powdered seasoning made from red peppers

  paprikas n ▷ **paprika**

  papyri n ▷ **papyrus**

papyrus [pap-ire-uss] n (pl **-ri, -ruses**) tall water plant

  papyruses n ▷ **papyrus**

par n (pl **-s**) usual or average condition

parable n (pl **-s**) story that illustrates a religious teaching

  parables n ▷ **parable**

parabola [par-**ab**-bol-a] n (pl **-s**) regular curve resembling the course of an object thrown forward and up > **parabolic** adj

  parabolas n ▷ **parabola**

  parabolic adj ▷ **parabola**

paracetamol n (pl **-s**) mild pain-relieving drug

  paracetamols n ▷ **paracetamol**

parachute n (pl **-s**) large fabric canopy that slows the descent of a person or object from an aircraft ▶ v (**-tes, -ting, -ted**) land or drop by parachute > **parachutist** n (pl **-s**)

  parachuted n, v ▷ **parachute**

  parachutes v ▷ **parachute**

  parachuting v ▷ **parachute**

  parachutist n ▷ **parachute**

  parachutists n ▷ **parachute**

parade n (pl **-s**) procession or march ▶ v (**-des, -ding, -ded**) display or flaunt

  paraded v ▷ **parade**

  parades n, v ▷ **parade**

  parading v ▷ **parade**

paradigm [par-a-dime] n (pl **-s**) example or model

  paradigms n ▷ **paradigm**

paradise n (pl **-s**) heaven

  paradises n ▷ **paradise**

paradox n (pl **-xes**) statement that seems self-contradictory but may be true > **paradoxical**

adj > **paradoxically** adv

  paradoxes n ▷ **paradox**

  paradoxical adj ▷ **paradox**

  paradoxically adv ▷ **paradox**

paraffin n (pl **-s**) (BRIT & S AFR) liquid mixture distilled from petroleum and used as a fuel or solvent

  paraffins n ▷ **paraffin**

paragliding n (pl **-s**) cross-country gliding wearing a parachute shaped like wings

  paraglidings n ▷ **paragliding**

paragon n (pl **-s**) model of perfection

  paragons n ▷ **paragon**

paragraph n (pl **-s**) section of a piece of writing starting on a new line

  paragraphs n ▷ **paragraph**

parakeet n (pl **-s**) small long-tailed parrot

  parakeets n ▷ **parakeet**

parallax n (pl **-es**) apparent change in an object's position due to a change in the observer's position

  parallaxes n ▷ **parallax**

parallel adj separated by an equal distance at every point ▶ n (pl **-s**) line separated from another by an equal distance at every point ▶ v (**-s, -ing, -ed**) correspond to

  paralleled n ▷ **parallel**

  paralleling v ▷ **parallel**

  parallels n, v ▷ **parallel**

parallelogram n (pl **-s**) four-sided geometric figure with opposite sides parallel

  parallelograms n ▷ **parallelogram**

paralyse v (**-ses, -sing, -sed**) affect with paralysis

  paralysed v ▷ **paralyse**

  paralyses v ▷ **paralyse** ▶ n ▷ **paralysis**

  paralysing ▷ **paralyse**

paralysis n (pl **-ses**) inability to move or feel, because of damage to the nervous system

paralytic n (pl **-s**) ▶ adj (person) affected with paralysis

  paralytics n ▷ **paralytic**

paramedic n (pl **-s**) person working in support of the medical profession > **paramedical** adj

  paramedical n ▷ **paramedic**

  paramedics n ▷ **paramedic**

parameter [par-am-it-er] n (pl **-s**) limiting factor, boundary

  parameters n ▷ **parameter**

paramilitary adj organized on military lines

paramount adj of the greatest importance

paramour n (pl **-s**) (Old-fashioned) lover, esp. of a person married to someone else

  paramours n ▷ **paramour**

paranoia n (pl **-s**) mental illness causing

delusions of grandeur or persecution (*Informal*) > **paranoid, paranoiac** *adj*, *n* (*pl* -**s**)
paranoiac *adj*, *n* ▷ **paranoia**
paranoiacs *n* ▷ **paranoia**
paranoias *n* ▷ **paranoia**
paranoid *adj*, *n* ▷ **paranoia**
paranoids *n* ▷ **paranoia**
paranormal *adj* beyond scientific explanation
parapet *n* (*pl* -**s**) low wall or railing along the edge of a balcony or roof
parapets *n* ▷ **parapet**
paraphernalia *n* (*pl* -**s**) personal belongings or bits of equipment
paraphernalias *n* ▷ **paraphernalia**
paraphrase *v* (-**ses**, -**sing**, -**sed**) put (a statement or text) into other words
paraphrased *v* ▷ **paraphrase**
paraphrases *v* ▷ **paraphrase**
paraphrasing *v* ▷ **paraphrase**
paraplegia [par-a-**pleej**-ya] *n* (*pl* -**s**) paralysis of the lower half of the body > **paraplegic** *adj*, *n* (*pl* -**s**)
paraplegias *n* ▷ **paraplegia**
paraplegic *adj*, *n* ▷ **paraplegia**
paraplegics *n* ▷ **paraplegia**
parapsychologies *n* ▷ **parapsychology**
parapsychology *n* (*pl* -**gies**) study of mental phenomena such as telepathy
parasite *n* (*pl* -**s**) animal or plant living in or on another > **parasitic** *adj*
parasites *n* ▷ **parasite**
parasitic *adj* ▷ **parasite**
parasol *n* (*pl* -**s**) umbrella-like sunshade
parasols *n* ▷ **parasol**
paratrooper *n* (*pl* -**s**) soldier trained to be dropped by parachute into a battle area > **paratroops** *pl n*
paratroopers *n* ▷ **paratrooper**
paratroops *n* ▷ **paratrooper**
parboil *v* (-**s**, -**ing**, -**ed**) boil until partly cooked
parboiled *v* ▷ **parboil**
parboiling *v* ▷ **parboil**
parboils *v* ▷ **parboil**
parcel *n* (*pl* -**s**) something wrapped up, package ▶ *v* (-**s**, -**lling**, -**lled**) (*often foll. by* **up**) wrap up
parcelled *v* ▷ **parcel**
parcelling *v* ▷ **parcel**
parcels *n*, *v* ▷ **parcel**
parch *v* (-**es**, -**ing**, -**ed**) make very hot and dry
parched *v* ▷ **parch**
parches *v* ▷ **parch**
parching *v* ▷ **parch**
parchment *n* (*pl* -**s**) thick smooth writing material made from animal skin

parchments *n* ▷ **parchment**
pardon *v* (-**s**, -**ing**, -**ed**) forgive, excuse ▶ *n* (*pl* -**s**) forgiveness > **pardonable** *adj*
pardonable *adj* ▷ **pardon**
pardoned *v* ▷ **pardon**
pardoning *v* ▷ **pardon**
pardons *v*, *n* ▷ **pardon**
pare *v* (-**res**, -**ring**, -**red**) cut off the skin or top layer of (*often foll. by* **down**)
pared *v* ▷ **pare**
pares *v* ▷ **pare**
paring *v* ▷ **pare** ▶ *n* (*pl* -**s**) piece pared off
parings *n* ▷ **pareing**
parent *n* (*pl* -**s**) father or mother > **parental** *adj* > **parenthood** *n* (*pl* -**s**)
parentage *n* (*pl* -**s**) ancestry or family
parentages *n* ▷ **parentage**
parental *adj* ▷ **parent**
parenthood *n* ▷ **parent**
parenthoods *n* ▷ **parent**
parenting *n* (*pl* -**s**) activity of bringing up children
parentings *n* ▷ **parenting**
parents *n* ▷ **parent**
parenthesis [par-en-**thiss**-iss] *n* (*pl* -**ses**) word or sentence inserted into a passage, marked off by brackets or dashes ▶ *pl* round brackets, ( ) > **parenthetical** *adj*
parentheses *n* ▷ **parenthesis**
parenthetical *adj* ▷ **parenthesis**
pariah [par-**rye**-a] *n* (*pl* -**s**) social outcast
pariahs *n* ▷ **pariah**
parietal [par-**rye**-it-al] *adj* of the walls of a body cavity such as the skull
parish *n* (*pl* -**es**) area that has its own church and a priest or pastor
parishes *n* ▷ **parish**
parishioner *n* (*pl* -**s**) inhabitant of a parish
parishioners *n* ▷ **parishioner**
parities *n* ▷ **parity**
parity *n* (*pl* -**ties**) equality or equivalence
park *n* (*pl* -**s**) area of open land for recreational use by the public ▶ *v* (-**s**, -**ing**, -**ed**) stop and leave (a vehicle) temporarily
parked *v* ▷ **park**
parking *v* ▷ **park**
parks *n*, *v* ▷ **park**
parka *n* (*pl* -**s**) large waterproof jacket with a hood
parkas *n* ▷ **parka**
parkier *adj* ▷ **parky**
parkiest *adj* ▷ **parky**
parky *adj* (-**kier**, -**kiest**) (BRIT) (*Informal*) (of the weather) chilly
parlance *n* (*pl* -**s**) particular way of speaking,

idiom

parlances *n* ▷ **parlance**

parley *n* (*pl* -s) meeting between leaders or representatives of opposing forces to discuss terms ▶ *v* (-s, -ing, -ed) have a parley

parleyed *v* ▷ **parley**

parleying *v* ▷ **parley**

parleys *n*, *v* ▷ **parley**

parliament *n* (*pl* -s) law-making assembly of a country > **parliamentary** *adj*

parliamentary *adj* ▷ **parliament**

parliaments *n* ▷ **parliament**

parlour *n* (*pl* -s) (*Old-fashioned*) living room for receiving visitors

parlours *n* ▷ **parlour**

parlous *adj* (*Old-fashioned*) dire

parochial *adj* narrow in outlook > **parochialism** *n* (*pl* -s)

parochialism *n* ▷ **parochial**

parochialisms *n* ▷ **parochial**

parodied *v* ▷ **parody**

parodies *n*, *v* ▷ **parody**

parody *n* (*pl* -**dies**) exaggerated and amusing imitation of someone else's style ▶ *v* (-**ies**, -**ying**, -**ied**) make a parody of

parodying *v* ▷ **parody**

parole *n* (*pl* -s) early freeing of a prisoner on condition that he or she behaves well ▶ *v* (-**les**, -**ling**, -**led**) put on parole

paroled *v* ▷ **parole**

paroles *n*, *v* ▷ **parole**

paroling *v* ▷ **parole**

paroxysm *n* (*pl* -s) uncontrollable outburst of rage, delight, etc.

paroxysms *n* ▷ **paroxysm**

parquet [par-kay] *n* (*pl* -s) floor covering made of wooden blocks arranged in a geometric pattern > **parquetry** *n* (*pl* -**ies**)

parquetries *n* ▷ **parquet**

parquetry *n* ▷ **parquet**

parquets *n* ▷ **parquet**

parricide *n* (*pl* -s) crime of killing either of one's parents

parricides *n* ▷ **parricide**

parried *v* ▷ **parry**

parries *v* ▷ **parry**

parrot *n* (*pl* -s) tropical bird with a short hooked beak and an ability to imitate human speech ▶ *v* (-s, -ing, -ed) repeat (someone else's words) without thinking

parroted *v* ▷ **parrot**

parroting *v* ▷ **parrot**

parrots *n*, *v* ▷ **parrot**

parry *v* (-**rries**, -**rrying**, -**rried**) ward off (an attack)

parrying *v* ▷ **parry**

pars *n* ▷ **par**

parse [parz] *v* (-**ses**, -**sing**, -**sed**) analyse (a sentence) in terms of grammar

parsed *v* ▷ **parse**

parses *v* ▷ **parse**

parsing *v* ▷ **parse**

parsimonies *n* ▷ **parsimony**

parsimonious *adj* ▷ **parsimony**

parsimony *n* (*pl* -**nies**) extreme caution in spending money > **parsimonious** *adj*

parsley *n* (*pl* -s) herb used for seasoning and decorating food

parsleys *n* ▷ **parsley**

parsnip *n* (*pl* -s) long tapering cream-coloured root vegetable

parsnips *n* ▷ **parsnip**

parson *n* (*pl* -s) Anglican parish priest

parsons *n* ▷ **parson**

parsonage *n* (*pl* -s) parson's house

parsonages *n* ▷ **parsonage**

part *n* (*pl* -s) one of the pieces that make up a whole ▶ *v* (-s, -ing, -ed) divide or separate

partake *v* (-**takes**, -**taking**, -**took**, -**taken**) (*foll.* by **of**) take (food or drink)

partaken *v* ▷ **partake**

partakes *v* ▷ **partake**

partaking *v* ▷ **partake**

partial *adj* not complete > **partiality** *n* (*pl* -**ties**) > **partially** *adv*

partialities *n* ▷ **partial**

partiality *n* ▷ **partial**

partially *adv* ▷ **partial**

parted *v* ▷ **part**

participate *v* (-**tes**, -**ting**, -**ted**) become actively involved > **participant** *n* (*pl* -s) > **participation** *n* (*pl* -s)

participant *n* ▷ **participate**

participants *n* ▷ **participate**

participated *v* ▷ **participate**

participates *v* ▷ **participate**

participating *v* ▷ **participate**

participation *n* ▷ **participation**

participations *n* ▷ **participations**

participle *n* (*pl* -s) form of a verb used in compound tenses or as an adjective

participles *n* ▷ **participle**

particle *n* (*pl* -s) extremely small piece or amount

particles *n* ▷ **particle**

particular *adj* relating to one person or thing, not general ▶ *n* (*pl* -s) item of information, detail > **particularly** *adv*

particularize *v* (-**zes**, -**zing**, -**zed**) give details about

particularized v ▷ particularize
particularizes v ▷ particularize
particularizing v ▷ particularize
particularly adv ▷ particular
particulars n ▷ particular
parties n ▷ party
parting n (pl -s) occasion when one person leaves another ▶ v ▷ part
partings n ▷ parting
partisan n (pl -s) strong supporter of a party or group ▶ adj prejudiced or one-sided
partisans n ▷ partisan
partition n (pl -s) screen or thin wall that divides a room ▶ v (-s, -ing, -ed) divide with a partition
partitioned v ▷ partition
partitioning v ▷ partition
partitions n, v ▷ partition
partly adv not completely
partner n (pl -s) either member of a couple in a relationship or activity ▶ v (-s, -ing, -ed) be the partner of
partnered v ▷ partner
partnering v ▷ partner
partners n, v ▷ partner
partnership n (pl -s) joint business venture between two or more people
partnerships n ▷ partnership
partook v ▷ partake
partridge n (pl -s) game bird of the grouse family
partridges n ▷ partridge
parts n, v ▷ part
parturition n (pl -s) act of giving birth
party n (pl -ties) social gathering for pleasure
parvenu [par-ven-new] n (pl -s) person newly risen to a position of power or wealth
parvenus n ▷ parvenu
pas n ▷ pa
pascal n (pl -s) unit of pressure
pascals n ▷ pascal
paspalum [pass-**pale**-um] n (pl -s) (AUST & NZ) type of grass with wide leaves
paspalums n ▷ paspalum
pass v (-es, -ing, -ed) go by, past, or through (SPORT) ▶ n (pl -es) successful result in a test or examination
passable adj (just) acceptable
passage n (pl -s) channel or opening providing a way through
passages n ▷ passage
passageway n (pl -s) passage or corridor
passageways n ▷ passageway
passbook n (pl -s) book issued by a bank or building society for keeping a record of

deposits and withdrawals
passbooks n ▷ passbook
passé [pas-say] adj out-of-date
passed v ▷ pass
passenger n (pl -s) person travelling in a vehicle driven by someone else
passengers n ▷ passenger
passes v, n ▷ pass
passim adv (LATIN) everywhere, throughout
passing adj brief or transitory ▶ v ▷ pass
passion n (pl -s) intense sexual love
   > **passionate** adj
passionate adj ▷ passion
passionflower n (pl -s) tropical American plant
passionflowers n ▷ passionflower
passions n ▷ passion
passive adj not playing an active part
   > **passivity** n (pl -ties)
passivities n ▷ passive
passivity n ▷ passive
passport n (pl -s) official document of nationality granting permission to travel abroad
passports n ▷ passport
password n (pl -s) secret word or phrase that ensures admission
passwords n ▷ password
past adj of the time before the present ▶ n (pl -s) period of time before the present ▶ adv by, along ▶ prep beyond
pasta n (pl -s) type of food, such as spaghetti, that is made in different shapes from flour and water
pastas n ▷ pasta
paste n (pl -s) moist soft mixture, such as toothpaste ▶ v (-tes, -ting, -ted) fasten with paste
pasteboard n (pl -s) stiff thick paper
pasteboards n ▷ pasteboard
pasted v ▷ paste
pastel n (pl -s) coloured chalk crayon for drawing ▶ adj pale and delicate in colour
pastels n ▷ pastel
pastes n, v ▷ paste
pasteurize v (-zes, -zing, -zed) sterilize by heating > **pasteurization** n (pl -s)
pasteurization n ▷ pasteurize
pasteurizations n ▷ pasteurize
pasteurized v ▷ pasteurize
pasteurizes v ▷ pasteurize
pasteurizing v ▷ pasteurize
pastiche [pass-**teesh**] n (pl -s) work of art that mixes styles or copies the style of another artist
pastiches n ▷ pastiche

pastier *adj* ▷ **pasty**[1]

pasties *n* ▷ **pasty**[2]

pastiest *adj* ▷ **pasty**[1]

pastille *n* (*pl* **-s**) small fruit-flavoured and sometimes medicated sweet

pastilles *n* ▷ **pastille**

pastime *n* (*pl* **-s**) activity that makes time pass pleasantly

pastimes *n* ▷ **pastime**

pasting *n* (*pl* **-s**) (*Informal*) heavy defeat ▶ *v* ▷ **paste**

pastings *n* ▷ **pasting**

pastor *n* (*pl* **-s**) member of the clergy in charge of a congregation

pastoral *adj* of or depicting country life

pastors *n* ▷ **pastor**

pastrami *n* (*pl* **-s**) highly seasoned smoked beef

pastramis *n* ▷ **pastrami**

pastries *n* ▷ **pastry**

pastry *n* (*pl* **-ries**) baking dough made of flour, fat, and water

pasts *n* ▷ **past**

pasture *n* (*pl* **-s**) grassy land for farm animals to graze on

pastures *n* ▷ **pasture**

pasty[1] [pay-stee] *adj* (**-tier, -tiest**) (of a complexion) pale and unhealthy

pasty[2] [pass-tee] *n* (*pl* **-ties**) round of pastry folded over a savoury filling

pat[1] *v* (**-s, -tting, -tted**) tap lightly ▶ *n* (*pl* **-s**) gentle tap or stroke

pat[2] *adj* quick, ready, or glib

patch *n* (*pl* **-es**) piece of material sewn on a garment ▶ *v* (**-es, -ing, -ed**) mend with a patch

patched *v* ▷ **patch**

patches *n, v* ▷ **patch**

patchier *adj* ▷ **patchy**

patchiest *adj* ▷ **patchy**

patching *v* ▷ **patch**

patchwork *n* (*pl* **-s**) needlework made of pieces of different materials sewn together

patchworks *n* ▷ **patchwork**

patchy *adj* (**-hier, -hiest**) of uneven quality or intensity

pate *n* (*pl* **-s**) (*Old-fashioned*) head

pates *n* ▷ **pate**

pâté [pat-ay] *n* (*pl* **-s**) spread of finely minced liver etc.

pâtés *n* ▷ **pâté**

patella *n* (*pl* **-ae**) kneecap

patellae *n* ▷ **patella**

patent *n* (*pl* **-s**) document giving the exclusive right to make or sell an invention ▶ *adj* open to public inspection ▶ *v* (**-s, -ing, -ed**) obtain a patent for

patented *v* ▷ **patent**

patenting *v* ▷ **patent**

patently *adv* obviously

patents *n, v* ▷ **patent**

paternal *adj* fatherly

paternities *n* ▷ **paternity**

paternity *n* (*pl* **-ties**) fact or state of being a father

paternalism *n* (*pl* **-s**) authority exercised in a way that limits individual responsibility > **paternalistic** *adj*

paternalisms *n* ▷ **paternalism**

paternalistic *adj* ▷ **paternalism**

path *n* (*pl* **-s**) surfaced walk or track

pathname *n* (*pl* **-s**) (COMPUTERS) file name listing the sequence of directories leading to a particular file or directory

pathnames *n* ▷ **pathname**

paths *n* ▷ **path**

pathetic *adj* causing feelings of pity or sadness > **pathetically** *adv*

pathetically *adv* ▷ **pathetic**

pathogen *n* (*pl* **-s**) thing that causes disease > **pathogenic** *adj*

pathogenic *adj* ▷ **pathogen**

pathogens *n* ▷ **pathogen**

pathologies *n* ▷ **pathology**

pathology *n* (*pl* **-gies**) scientific study of diseases > **pathologist** *n* (*pl* **-s**)

pathological *adj* of pathology

pathologist *n* ▷ **pathology**

pathologists *n* ▷ **pathology**

pathos *n* (*pl* **-es**) power of arousing pity or sadness

pathoses *n* ▷ **pathos**

patience *n* (*pl* **-s**) quality of being patient

patiences *n* ▷ **patience**

patient *adj* enduring difficulties or delays calmly ▶ *n* (*pl* **-s**) person receiving medical treatment

patients *n* ▷ **patient**

patina *n* (*pl* **-s**) fine layer on a surface

patinas *n* ▷ **patina**

patio *n* (*pl* **-os**) paved area adjoining a house

patios *n* ▷ **patio**

patois [pat-wah] *n* (*pl* **patois**) [pat-wahz] regional dialect, esp. of French

patriarch *n* (*pl* **-s**) male head of a family or tribe > **patriarchal** *adj*

patriarchal *adj* ▷ **patriarch**

patriarchies *n* ▷ **patriarchy**

patriarchs *n* ▷ **patriarch**

patriarchy *n* (*pl* **-hies**) society in which men have most of the power

patrician n (pl -s) member of the nobility ▶ adj of noble birth
  patricians n ▷ patrician
patricide n (pl -s) crime of killing one's father
  patricides n ▷ patricide
  patrimonies n ▷ patrimony
patrimony n (pl -nies) property inherited from ancestors
patriot n (pl -s) person who loves his or her country and supports its interests > **patriotic** adj > **patriotism** n (pl -s)
  patriotic adj ▷ patriot
  patriotism n ▷ patriot
  patriotisms n ▷ patriot
  patriots n ▷ patriot
patrol n (pl -s) regular circuit by a guard ▶ v (-s, -lling, -lled) go round on guard, or reconnoitring
  patrolled v ▷ patrol
  patrolling v ▷ patrol
  patrols n, v ▷ patrol
patron n (pl -s) person who gives financial support to charities, artists, etc.
patronage n (pl -s) support given by a patron
  patronages n ▷ patronage
patronize v (-zes, -zing, -zed) treat in a condescending way
  patronized v ▷ patronize
  patronizes v ▷ patronize
  patronizing v ▷ patronize
  patrons n ▷ patron
patronymic n (pl -s) name derived from one's father or a male ancestor
  patronymics n ▷ patronymic
  pats v, n ▷ pat[1]
  patted v ▷ pat[1]
patter[1] v (-s, -ing, -ed) make repeated soft tapping sounds ▶ n (pl -s) quick succession of taps
patter[2] n (pl -s) glib rapid speech
  pattered v ▷ patter[1]
  pattering v ▷ patter[1]
  patters v, n ▷ patter[1, 2]
pattern n (pl -s) arrangement of repeated parts or decorative designs
patterned adj decorated with a pattern
  patterns n ▷ pattern
  patties n ▷ patty
  patting v ▷ pat[1]
patty n (pl -tties) small flattened cake of minced food
  paucities n ▷ paucity
paucity n (pl -ties) scarcity
paunch n (pl -es) protruding belly
  paunches n ▷ paunch

pauper n (pl -s) very poor person
  paupers n ▷ pauper
pause v (-ses, -sing, -sed) stop for a time ▶ n (pl -s) stop or rest in speech or action
  paused v ▷ pause
  pauses v, n ▷ pause
  pausing v ▷ pause
pave v (-ves, -ving, -ved) form (a surface) with stone or brick
  paved v ▷ pave
pavement n (pl -s) paved path for pedestrians
  pavements n ▷ pavement
  paves v ▷ pave
  paving v ▷ pave
pavilion n (pl -s) building on a playing field etc.
  pavilions n ▷ pavilion
paw n (pl -s) animal's foot with claws and pads ▶ v (-s, -ing, -ed) scrape with the paw or hoof
  pawed v ▷ paw
  pawing v ▷ paw
  paws n, v ▷ paw
pawn[1] v (-s, -ing, -ed) deposit (an article) as security for money borrowed
pawn[2] n (pl -s) chessman of the lowest value
pawnbroker n (pl -s) lender of money on goods deposited
  pawnbrokers n ▷ pawnbroker
  pawned v ▷ pawn[1]
  pawning v ▷ pawn[1]
  pawns v, n ▷ pawn[1, 2]
pay v (-s, -ing, paid) give money etc. in return for goods or services ▶ n (pl -s) wages or salary
payable adj due to be paid
payee n (pl -s) person to whom money is paid or due
  payees n ▷ payee
  paying v ▷ pay
payload n (pl -s) passengers or cargo of an aircraft
  payloads n ▷ payload
payment n (pl -s) act of paying
  payments n ▷ payment
payola n (pl -s) (CHIEFLY US) (Informal) bribe to get special treatment, esp. to promote a commercial product
pays v, n ▷ pay
  payolas n ▷ payola

> **pax** n (**paxes**). A pax is a period of peace, especially when there is one dominant nation. If you have a P and an X on your rack, there is likely to be an A available on the board. Pax gives a decent score for a three-letter word, so watch out for chances to play it on a bonus square. Pax scores 12 points.

pe *n* (**pes**). Pe is the 17th letter in the Hebrew alphabet. This is a very handy word because it allows you to connect words beginning with P to those ending in E, or vice versa and E is the most common tile in the game. Pe scores 4 points.

pea *n* (*pl* **-s**) climbing plant with seeds growing in pods

peas *n* ▷ **pea**

peace *n* (*pl* **-s**) calm, quietness > **peaceful** *adj* > **peacefully** *adv*

peaceable *adj* inclined towards peace > **peaceably** *adv*

peaceably *adv* ▷ **peaceable**

peaceful *adj* ▷ **peace**

peacefully *adv* ▷ **peace**

peaces *n* ▷ **peace**

peach *n* (*pl* **-es**) soft juicy fruit with a stone and a downy skin ▶ *adj* pinkish-orange

peaches *n* ▷ **peach**

peacock *n* (*pl* **-s**) large male bird with a brilliantly coloured fanlike tail > **peahen** *n fem* (*pl* **-s**)

peacocks *n* ▷ **peacock**

peahen *n* ▷ **peacock**

peahens *n* ▷ **peacock**

peak *n* (*pl* **-s**) pointed top, esp. of a mountain ▶ *v* (**-s, -ing, -ed**) form or reach a peak ▶ *adj* of or at the point of greatest demand > **peaked** *adj*

peaked *adj, v* ▷ **peak**

peakier *adj* ▷ **peaky**

peakiest *adj* ▷ **peaky**

peaking *v* ▷ **peak**

peaks *n, v* ▷ **peak**

peaky *adj* (**-kier, -kiest**) pale and sickly

peal *n* (*pl* **-s**) long loud echoing sound, esp. of bells or thunder ▶ *v* (**-s, -ing, -ed**) sound with a peal or peals

pealed *v* ▷ **peal**

pealing *v* ▷ **peal**

peals *n, v* ▷ **peal**

peanut *n* (*pl* **-s**) pea-shaped nut that ripens underground ▶ *pl* (*Informal*) trifling amount of money

peanuts *n* ▷ **peanut**

pear *n* (*pl* **-s**) sweet juicy fruit with a narrow top and rounded base

pears *n* ▷ **pear**

pearl *n* (*pl* **-s**) hard round shiny object found inside some oyster shells and used as a jewel > **pearly** *adj* (**-lier, -liest**)

pearlier *adj* ▷ **pearl**

pearliest *adj* ▷ **peral**

pearls *n* ▷ **pearl**

pearly *adj* ▷ **pearl**

peasant *n* (*pl* **-s**) person working on the land, esp. in poorer countries or in the past

peasantries *n* ▷ **peasantry**

peasantry *n* (*pl* **-ries**) peasants collectively

peasants *n* ▷ **peasant**

peat *n* (*pl* **-s**) decayed vegetable material found in bogs, used as fertilizer or fuel

peats *n* ▷ **peat**

pebble *n* (*pl* **-s**) small roundish stone > **pebbly** *adj* (**-lier, -liest**)

pebbles *n* ▷ **pebble**

pebblier *adj* ▷ **pebble**

pebbliest *adj* ▷ **pebble**

pebbly *adj* ▷ **pebble**

pecan [pee-kan] *n* (*pl* **-s**) edible nut of a N American tree

pecans *n* ▷ **pecan**

peccadillo *n* (*pl* **-lloes, -llos**) trivial misdeed

peccadilloes *n* ▷ **peccadillo**

peccadillos *n* ▷ **peccadillo**

peck *v* (**-s, -ing, -ed**) strike or pick up with the beak ▶ *n* (*pl* **-s**) pecking movement

pecked *v* ▷ **peck**

pecking *v* ▷ **peck**

peckish *adj* (*Informal*) slightly hungry

pecks *v, n* ▷ **peck**

pecs *pl n* (*Informal*) pectoral muscles

pectin *n* (*pl* **-s**) substance in fruit that makes jam set

pectins *n* ▷ **pectin**

pectoral *adj* of the chest or thorax ▶ *n* (*pl* **-s**) pectoral muscle or fin

pectorals *n* ▷ **pectoral**

peculiar *adj* strange

peculiarities *n* ▷ **peculiarity**

peculiarity *n* (*pl* **-ties**) oddity, eccentricity

pecuniary *adj* relating to, or consisting of, money

pedagogue *n* (*pl* **-s**) schoolteacher, esp. a pedantic one

pedagogues *n* ▷ **pedagogue**

pedal *n* (*pl* **-s**) foot-operated lever used to control a vehicle or machine, or to modify the tone of a musical instrument ▶ *v* (**-s, -lling, -lled**) propel (a bicycle) by using its pedals

pedalled *v* ▷ **pedal**

pedalling *v* ▷ **pedal**

pedals *n* ▷ **pedal**

pedant *n* (*pl* **-s**) person who is excessively concerned with details and rules, esp. in academic work > **pedantic** *adj* > **pedantry** *n* (*pl* **-ries**)

pedantic *adj* ▷ **pedant**

pedantries n ▷ pedant
pedantry n ▷ pedant
pedants n ▷ pedant
peddle v (-les, -ling, -led) sell (goods) from door to door
peddled v ▷ peddle
peddles v ▷ peddle
peddling v ▷ peddle
peddler n (pl -s) person who sells illegal drugs
peddlers n ▷ peddler
pedestal n (pl -s) base supporting a column, statue, etc.
pedestals n ▷ pedestal
pedestrian n (pl -s) person who walks ▶ adj dull, uninspiring
pedestrians n ▷ pedestrian
pedicure n (pl -s) medical or cosmetic treatment of the feet
pedicures n ▷ pedicure
pedigree n (pl -s) register of ancestors, esp. of a purebred animal
pedigrees n ▷ pedigree
pediment n (pl -s) triangular part over a door etc.
pediments n ▷ pediment
pedlar n (pl -s) person who sells goods from door to door
pedlars n ▷ pedlar
pee (Informal) v (-s, -ing, peed) urinate ▶ n (-s) act of urinating
peed v ▷ pee
peeing v ▷ pee
pees v, n ▷ pee
peek v, n (pl -s) peep or glance
peeks n ▷ peek
peel v (-s, -ing, -ed) remove the skin or rind of (a vegetable or fruit) ▶ n (pl -s) rind or skin > **peelings** pl n
peeled v ▷ peel
peeling v ▷ peel
peelings n ▷ peel
peels v, n ▷ peel
peep¹ v (-s, -ing, -ed) look slyly or quickly ▶ n (pl -s) peeping look
peep² v (-s, -ing, -ed) make a small shrill noise ▶ n (-s) small shrill noise
peeped v ▷ peep¹, ²
peeping v ▷ peep¹, ²
peeps v, n ▷ peep¹, ²
peer¹ n (pl -s), fem **peeress** (pl -es) (in Britain) member of the nobility
peer² v (-s, -ing, -ed) look closely and intently
peerage n (BRIT) whole body of peers
peerages n ▷ peerage
peered v ▷ peer²

peeress n ▷ peer
peeresses n ▷ peer
peering v ▷ peer²
peerless adj unequalled, unsurpassed
peers n, v ▷ peer¹, ²
peers v ▷ peer
peering v ▷ peer
peered v ▷ peer
peeved adj (Informal) annoyed
peevish adj fretful or irritable > **peevishly** adv
peevishly adv ▷ peevish
peewee n (pl -s) black-and-white Australian bird
peewees n ▷ peewee
peewit n (pl -s) ▷ lapwing
peewits n ▷ peewit
peg n (pl -s) pin or clip for joining, fastening, marking, etc. ▶ v (-s, -gging, -gged) fasten with pegs
pegged v ▷ peg
pegging v ▷ peg
pegs n, v ▷ peg
peignoir [pay-nwahr] n (pl -s) woman's light dressing gown
peignoirs n ▷ peignoir
pejorative [pij-jor-a-tiv] adj (of words etc.) with an insulting or critical meaning
pelargonium n (pl -s) plant with red, white, purple, or pink flowers
pelargoniums n ▷ pelargonium
pelican n (pl -s) large water bird with a pouch beneath its bill for storing fish
pelicans n ▷ pelican
pellagra n (pl -s) disease caused by lack of vitamin B
pellagras n ▷ pellagra
pellet n (pl -s) small ball of something
pellets n ▷ pellet
pellucid adj very clear
pelmet n (pl -s) ornamental drapery or board, concealing a curtain rail
pelmets n ▷ pelmet
pelt¹ v (-s, -ing, -ed) throw missiles at
pelt² n (pl -s) skin of a fur-bearing animal
pelted v ▷ pelt¹
pelting v ▷ pelt¹
pelts v, n ▷ pelt¹, ²
pelvic adj ▷ pelvis
pelvis n (pl -es) framework of bones at the base of the spine, to which the hips are attached > **pelvic** adj
pelvises n ▷ pelvis
pen¹ n (pl -s) instrument for writing in ink ▶ v (-s, -nning, -nned) write or compose
pen² n small enclosure for domestic animals

▶ *v* (**-s, -nning, -nned**) put or keep in a pen
pen³ *n* (*pl* **-s**) female swan
penal [pee-nal] *adj* of or used in punishment
penalize (**-zes, -zing, -zed**) *v* impose a penalty
on
  penalized *v* ▷ penalize
  penalizes *v* ▷ penalize
  penalizing *v* ▷ penalize
  penalties *n* ▷ penalty
penalty *n* (*pl* **-ties**) punishment for a crime
or offence
penance *n* (*pl* (*pl* **-s**) voluntary self-punishment
to make amends for wrongdoing
  penances *n* ▷ penance
pence *n* (BRIT) ▷ **penny**
penchant [pon-shon] *n* (*pl* **-s**) inclination or
liking
  penchants *n* ▷ penchant
pencil *n* (*pl* **-s**) thin cylindrical instrument
containing graphite, for writing or drawing
▶ *v* (**-s, -lling, -lled**) draw, write, or mark with
a pencil
  pencilled *v* ▷ pencil
  pencilling *v* ▷ pencil
  pencils *n*, *v* ▷ pencil
pendant *n* (*pl* **-s**) ornament worn on a chain
round the neck
  pendants *n* ▷ pendant
pendent *adj* hanging
pending *prep* while waiting for ▶ *adj* not yet
decided or settled
pendulous *adj* hanging, swinging
pendulum *n* (*pl* **-s**) suspended weight
swinging to and fro, esp. as a regulator for
a clock
  pendulums *n* ▷ pendulum
penetrate *v* (**-tes, -ting, -ted**) find or force a
way into or through > **penetration** *n* (*pl* **-s**)
penetrable *adj* capable of being penetrated
  penetrated *v* ▷ penetrate
  penetrates *v* ▷ penetrate
penetrating *adj* (of a sound) loud and
unpleasant ▶ *v* ▷ **penetrate**
  penetration *n* ▷ penetrate
  penetrations *n* ▷ penetrate
penguin *n* (*pl* **-s**) flightless black-and-white
sea bird of the southern hemisphere
  penguins *n* ▷ penguin
penicillin *n* (*pl* **-s**) antibiotic drug effective
against a wide range of diseases and
infections
  penicillins *n* ▷ penicillin
peninsula *n* (*pl* **-s**) strip of land nearly
surrounded by water > **peninsular** *adj*
  penisular *adj* ▷ penisula

  peninsulas *n* ▷ peninsula
penis *n* (*pl* **-es**) organ of copulation and
urination in male mammals
  penises *n* ▷ penis
  penitence *n* ▷ penitent
  penitences *n* ▷ penitent
penitent *adj* feeling sorry for having done
wrong ▶ *n* (*pl* **-s**) someone who is penitent
  > **penitence** *n* (*pl* **-s**)
  penitentiaries *n* ▷ penitentiary
penitentiary *n* (*pl* **-ries**) (US) prison ▶ *adj* (*also*
penitential) relating to penance
  penitents *n* ▷ penitent
penknife *n* (*pl* **-knives**) small knife with
blade(s) that fold into the handle
  penknives *n* ▷ penknife
pennant *n* (*pl* **-s**) long narrow flag
  pennants *n* ▷ pennant
  penned *v* ▷ pen¹, ²
  pennies *n* ▷ penny
penniless *adj* very poor
  penning *v* ▷ pen¹, ²
penny *n* (*pl* **pence, pennies**) British bronze coin
worth one hundredth of a pound
  pens *n* ▷ pen¹, ², ³
pension¹ *n* (*pl* **-s**) regular payment to people
above a certain age, retired employees,
widows, etc. > **pensionable** *adj*
pension² [pon-syon] *n* (*pl* **-s**) boarding house
in Europe
  pensionable *adj* ▷ pension
pensioner *n* (*pl* **-s**) person receiving a pension
  pensioners *n* ▷ pension
  pensions *n* ▷ pension¹, ²
pensive *adj* deeply thoughtful, often with a
tinge of sadness
pentagon *n* (*pl* **-s**) geometric figure with five
sides > **pentagonal** *adj*
  pentagonal *adj* ▷ pentagon
  pentagons *n* ▷ pentagon
pentameter [pen-tam-it-er] *n* (*pl* **-s**) line of
poetry with five metrical feet
  pentameters *n* ▷ pentameter
penthouse *n* (*pl* **-s**) flat built on the roof or top
floor of a building
  penthouses *n* ▷ penthouse
penultimate *adj* second last
penumbra *n* (*pl* **-brae, -bras**) (in an eclipse) the
partially shadowed region which surrounds
the full shadow
  penumbrae *n* ▷ penumbra
  penumbras *n* ▷ penumbra
  penuries *n* ▷ penury
  penurious *adj* ▷ penury
penury *n* (*pl* **-ries**) extreme poverty

> **penurious** *adj*
peonies *n* ▷ peony
peony *n* (*pl* **-nies**) garden plant with showy red, pink, or white flowers
people *pl n* persons generally ▶ *n* (*pl* **-s**) race or nation ▶ *v* (**-les, -ling, -led**) provide with inhabitants
peopled *v* ▷ people
peoples *n*, *v* ▷ people
peopling *v* ▷ people
pep *n* (*pl* **-s**) (*Informal*) high spirits, energy, or enthusiasm
pepper *n* (*pl* **-s**) sharp hot condiment made from the fruit of an East Indian climbing plant ▶ *v* (**-s, -ing, -ed**) season with pepper
peppercorn *n* dried berry of the pepper plant
peppercorns *n* ▷ peppercorn
peppered *v* ▷ pepper
pepperier *adj* ▷ peppery
pepperiest *adj* ▷ peppery
peppering *v* ▷ pepper
peppermint *n* (*pl* **-s**) plant that yields an oil with a strong sharp flavour
peppermints *n* ▷ peppermint
peppers *n*, *v* ▷ pepper
peppery *adj* (**-rier, -riest**) tasting of pepper
peps *n* ▷ pep
peptic *adj* relating to digestion or the digestive juices
per *prep* for each
perambulate *v* (**-tes, -ting, -ted**) (*Old-fashioned*) walk through or about (a place)
> **perambulation** *n* (*pl* **-s**)
perambulated *v* ▷ perambulate
perambulates *v* ▷ perambulate
perambulating *v* ▷ perambulate
perambulation *n* ▷ perambulate
perambulations *n* ▷ perambulate
perambulator *n* (*pl* **-s**) pram
perambulators *n* ▷ perambulator
perceive *v* (**-ves, -ving, -ved**) become aware of (something) through the senses
perceived *v* ▷ perceive
perceives *v* ▷ perceive
perceiving *v* ▷ perceive
perceptible *adj* discernible, recognizable
perception *n* (*pl* **-s**) act of perceiving
> **perceptive** *adj*
perceptions *n* ▷ perception
perceptive *adj* ▷ perception
perch[1] *n* (*pl* **-es**) resting place for a bird ▶ *v* (**-es, -ing, -ed**) alight, rest, or place on or as if on a perch
perch[2] *n* (*pl* **-es**) any of various edible fishes
perchance *adv* (*Old-fashioned*) perhaps

perches *n*, *v* ▷ perch[1, 2]
perching *v* ▷ perch[1, 2]
perched *v* ▷ perch[1, 2]
percipient *adj* quick to notice things, observant
percolate *v* (**-tes, -ting, -ted**) pass or filter through small holes > **percolation** *n*
percolated *v* ▷ percolate
percolates *v* ▷ percolate
percolating *v* ▷ percolate
percolation *n* ▷ percolate
percolations *n* ▷ percolate
percolator *n* (*pl* **-s**) coffeepot in which boiling water is forced through a tube and filters down through coffee
percolators *n* ▷ percolator
percussion *n* (*pl* **-s**) striking of one thing against another
percussions *n* ▷ percussion
perdition *n* (*pl* **-s**) (CHRISTIANITY) spiritual ruin
perditions *n* ▷ perdition
peregrination *n* (*pl* **-s**) (*Obs*) travels, roaming
peregrinations *n* ▷ peregrination
peremptory *adj* authoritative, imperious
perennial *adj* lasting through many years
▶ *n* (*pl* **-s**) plant lasting more than two years
> **perennially** *adv*
perennially *adv* ▷ perennial
perennials *n* ▷ perennial
perfect *adj* (**-er, -est**) having all the essential elements ▶ *n* (*pl* **-s**) (GRAMMAR) perfect tense
▶ *v* (**-s, -ing, -ed**) improve > **perfectly** *adv*
perfected *n* ▷ perfect
perfecter *adj* ▷ perfect
perfectest *adj* ▷ perfect
perfecting *v* ▷ perfect
perfection *n* (*pl* **-s**) state of being perfect
perfectionist *n* (*pl* **-s**) person who demands the highest standards of excellence
> **perfectionism** *n* (*pl* **-s**)
perfectionism *n* ▷ perfectionist
perfectionisms *n* ▷ perfectionist
perfectionists *n* ▷ perfectionist
perfections *n* ▷ perfection
perfectly *adv* ▷ perfect
perfects *n*, *v* ▷ perfect
perfidious *adj* (*Lit*) treacherous, disloyal
> **perfidy** *n* (*pl* **-ies**)
perfidies *n* ▷ perfidious
perfidy *n* ▷ perfidious
perforate *v* (**-es, -ing, -ed**) make holes in
> **perforation** *n* (*pl* **-s**)
perforated *v* ▷ perforate
perforates *v* ▷ perforate
perforating *v* ▷ perforate

perforation n ▷ **perforate**
perforations n ▷ **perforate**
perforce adv of necessity
perform v (**-s, -ing, -ed**) carry out (an action)
> **performance** n (pl **-s**) > **performer** n (pl **-s**)
performance n ▷ **perform**
performances n ▷ **perform**
performed v ▷ **perform**
performer n ▷ **perform**
performers n ▷ **perform**
performing v ▷ **perform**
performs v ▷ **perform**
perfume n (pl **-s**) liquid cosmetic worn for
its pleasant smell ▶ v (**-es, -ing, -ed**) give a
pleasant smell to
perfumed v ▷ **perfume**
perfumeries n ▷ **perfumery**
perfumery n (pl **-ries**) perfumes in general
perfumes n, v ▷ **perfume**
perfuming v ▷ **perfume**
perfunctorily adv ▷ **perfunctory**
perfunctory adj done only as a matter of
routine, superficial > **perfunctorily** adv
pergola n (pl **-s**) arch or framework of trellis
supporting climbing plants
pergolas n ▷ **pergola**
perhaps adv possibly, maybe
pericardia n ▷ **pericardum**
pericardium n (pl **-dia**) membrane enclosing
the heart
perihelia n ▷ **perihelion**
perihelion n (pl **-lia**) point in the orbit of a
planet or comet that is nearest to the sun
peril n (pl **-s**) great danger > **perilous** adj
> **perilously** adv
perilous adj ▷ **peril**
perilously adv ▷ **peril**
perils n ▷ **peril**
perimeter [per-**rim**-it-er] n (pl **-s**) (length of) the
outer edge of an area
perimeters n ▷ **perimeter**
perinatal adj of or in the weeks shortly before
or after birth
period n (pl **-s**) particular portion of time (US)
▶ adj (of furniture, dress, a play, etc.) dating
from or in the style of an earlier time
periodic adj recurring at intervals
periodical n (pl **-s**) magazine issued at regular
intervals ▶ adj periodic
periodicals n ▷ **periodical**
periods n ▷ **period**
peripatetic [per-rip-a-**tet**-ik] adj travelling
about from place to place
peripheral [per-**if**-er-al] adj unimportant, not
central

peripheries n ▷ **periphery**
periphery [per-**if**-er-ee] n (pl **-ries**) boundary
or edge
periscope n (pl **-s**) instrument used, esp. in
submarines, to give a view of objects on a
different level
periscopes n ▷ **periscope**
perish v (**-es, -ing, -ed**) be destroyed or die
perishable adj liable to rot quickly
perished v ▷ **perish**
perishes v ▷ **perish**
perishing adj (Informal) very cold ▶ v ▷ **perish**
peritonea n ▷ **peritoneum**
peritoneum [per-rit-toe-**nee**-um] n (pl **-nea,
-neums**) membrane lining the internal
surface of the abdomen
peritoneums n ▷ **peritoneum**
peritonitis [per-rit-tone-**ite**-iss] n (pl **-tises**)
inflammation of the peritoneum
peritonitises n ▷ **peritonitis**
periwinkle[1] n (pl **-s**) small edible shellfish,
the winkle
periwinkle[2] n (pl **-s**) plant with trailing stems
and blue flowers
periwinkles n ▷ **periwinkle**[1, 2]
perjuries n ▷ **perjury**
perjury n (pl **-ies**) act or crime of lying while
under oath in a court
perk n (pl **-s**) (Informal) incidental benefit
gained from a job, such as a company car
perkier adj ▷ **perk**
perkiest adj ▷ **perk**
perks n ▷ **perk**
perky adj (**-kier, -kiest**) lively or cheerful
perlemoen n (pl **-s**) (S AFR) edible sea creature
with a shell lined with mother of pearl
perlemoens n ▷ **perlemoen**
perm n (pl **-s**) long-lasting curly hairstyle
produced by treating the hair with chemicals
▶ v (**-s, -ing, -ed**) give (hair) a perm
permafrost n (pl **-s**) permanently frozen
ground
permafrosts n ▷ **permafrost**
permanence n ▷ **permanent**
permanences n ▷ **permanent**
permanent adj lasting forever > **permanence**
n (pl **-s**) > **permanently** adv
permanently adv ▷ **permanent**
permeate v (**-tes, -ting, -ted**) pervade or pass
through the whole of (something)
permeable adj able to be permeated, esp.
by liquid
permeated v ▷ **permeate**
permeates v ▷ **permeate**
permeating v ▷ **permeate**

permed v ▷ **perm**
perming v ▷ **perm**
permissible adj ▷ **permit**
permission n (pl -s) authorization to do
something
permissions n ▷ **permission**
permissive adj (excessively) tolerant, esp. in
sexual matters
permit v (-s, -tting, -tted) give permission,
allow ▶ n (pl -s) document giving permission
to do something > **permissible** adj
permits v, n ▷ **permit**
permitted v ▷ **permit**
permitting v ▷ **permit**
perms n, v ▷ **perm**
permutation n (pl -s) any of the ways a
number of things can be arranged or
combined
permutations n ▷ **permutation**
pernicious adj wicked
pernickety adj (Informal) (excessively) fussy
about details
peroration n (pl -s) concluding part of a
speech, usu. summing up the main points
perorations n ▷ **peroration**
peroxide n (pl -s) hydrogen peroxide used as a
hair bleach
peroxides n ▷ **peroxide**
perpendicular adj at right angles to a line or
surface ▶ n (pl -s) line or plane at right angles
to another
perpendiculars n ▷ **perpendicular**
perpetrate v (-tes, -ting, -ted) commit
or be responsible for (a wrongdoing)
> **perpetration** n (pl -s) > **perpetrator** n (pl -s)
perpetrated v ▷ **perpetrate**
perpetrates v ▷ **perpetrate**
perpetrating v ▷ **perpetrate**
perpetration n ▷ **perpetrate**
perpetrations n ▷ **perpetrate**
perpetrator n ▷ **perpetrate**
perpetrators n ▷ **perpetrate**
perpetual adj lasting forever > **perpetually** adv
perpetually adv ▷ **perpetual**
perpetuate v (-tes, -ting, -ted) cause to
continue or be remembered > **perpetuation**
n (pl -s)
perpetuated v ▷ **perpetuate**
perpetuates v ▷ **perpetuate**
perpetuating v ▷ **perpetuate**
perpetuation n ▷
perpetuations n ▷
perplex v (-es, -ing, -ed) puzzle, bewilder
> **perplexity** n (pl -ties)
perplexed v ▷ **perplex**

perplexes v ▷ **perplex**
perplexing v ▷ **perplex**
perplexities n ▷ **perplex**
perplexity n ▷ **perplex**
perquisite n (pl -s) (Formal) ▷ **perk**
perquisites n ▷ **perquisite**
perries n ▷ **perry**
perry n (pl -rries) alcoholic drink made from
fermented pears
persecute v (-tes, -ting, -ted) treat cruelly
because of race, religion, etc. > **persecution** n
(pl -s) > **persecutor** n (pl -s)
persecuted v ▷ **persecute**
persecutes v ▷ **persecute**
persecuting v ▷ **persecute**
persecution n ▷ **persecute**
persecutions n ▷ **persecute**
persecutor n ▷ **persecute**
persecutors n ▷ **persecute**
persevere v (-res, -ring, -red) keep making an
effort despite difficulties > **perseverance**
n (pl -s)
perseverance n ▷ **persevere**
perseverances n ▷ **persevere**
persevered v ▷ **persevere**
perseveres v ▷ **persevere**
persevering v ▷ **persevere**
persimmon n (pl -s) sweet red tropical fruit
persimmons n ▷ **persimmon**
persist v (-s, -ing, -ed) continue to be or
happen, last > **persistent** adj > **persistently**
adv > **persistence** n (pl -s)
persisted v ▷ **persist**
persistence adj ▷ **persist**
persistences adj ▷ **persist**
persistent adj ▷ **persist**
persistently v ▷ **persist**
persisting v ▷ **persist**
persists v ▷ **persist**
person n (pl -s) human being
persons n ▷ **person**
persona [per-soh-na] n (pl -nae) [-nee]
someone's personality as presented to others
personable adj pleasant in appearance and
personality
personae n ▷ **persona**
personage n (pl -s) important person
personages n ▷ **personage**
personal adj individual or private
personalities n ▷ **personality**
personality n (pl -ties) person's distinctive
characteristics
personally adv directly, not by delegation to
others
personification n ▷ **personify**

personifications *n* ▷ personify
personified *v* ▷ personify
personifies *v* ▷ personify
personify *v* (**-fies, -fying, -fied**) give human
characteristics to > **personification** *n* (*pl* **-s**)
personifying *v* ▷ personify
personnel *n* (*pl* **-s**) people employed in an
organization
personnels *n* ▷ personnel
perspective *n* (*pl* **-s**) view of the relative
importance of situations or facts
perspectives *n* ▷ perspective
perspicacious *adj* having quick mental
insight > **perspicacity** *n* (*pl* **-ties**)
perspicacities *n* ▷ perspicacious
perspicacity *n* ▷ perspicacious
perspiration *n* ▷ perspire
perspirations *n* ▷ perspire
perspire *v* (**-res, -ring, -red**) sweat
> **perspiration** *n* (*pl* **-s**)
perspired *v* ▷ perspire
perspires *v* ▷ perspire
perspiring *v* ▷ perspire
persuade *v* (**-des, -ding, -ded**) make (someone)
do something by argument, charm, etc.
> **persuasive** *adj*
persuasion *n* (*pl* **-s**) act of persuading
persuasions *n* ▷ persuasion
persuasive *adj* ▷ persuade
persuaded *v* ▷ persuade
persuades *v* ▷ persuade
persuading *v* ▷ persuade
pert *adj* (**-er, -est**) saucy and cheeky
pertain *v* (**-s, -ing, -ed**) belong or be relevant
(to)
pertained *v* ▷ pertain
pertaining *v* ▷ pertain
pertains *v* ▷ pertain
perter *adj* ▷ pert
pertest *adj* ▷ pert
pertinacious *adj* (*Formal*) very persistent and
determined > **pertinacity** *n* (*pl* **-ties**)
pertinacities *n* ▷ pertinacious
pertinacity *n* ▷ pertinacious
pertinence *n* ▷ pertinent
pertinences *n* ▷ pertinent
pertinent *adj* relevant > **pertinence** *n* (*pl* **-s**)
perturb *v* (**-s, -ing, -ed**) disturb greatly
> **perturbation** *n* (*pl* **-s**)
perturbation *n* ▷ perturb
perturbation *n* ▷ perturb
perturbed *v* ▷ perturb
perturbing *v* ▷ perturb
perturbs *v* ▷ perturb
perusal *n* ▷ peruse

perusals *n* ▷ peruse
peruse *v* (**-ses, -sing, -sed**) read in a careful or
leisurely manner > **perusal** *n* (*pl* **-s**)
perused *v* ▷ peruse
peruses *v* ▷ peruse
perusing *v* ▷ peruse
pervade *v* (**-des, -ding, -ded**) spread right
through (something) > **pervasive** *adj*
pervaded *v* ▷ pervade
pervades *v* ▷ pervade
pervading *v* ▷ pervade
pervasive *adj* ▷ pervade
perverse *adj* (**-r, -st**) deliberately doing
something different from what is thought
normal or proper > **perversely** *adv*
> **perversity** *n* (*pl* **-ties**)
perversely *n* ▷ perverse
perverser *adj* ▷ perverse
perversest *adj* ▷ perverse
perversion *n* (*pl* **-s**) sexual act or desire
considered abnormal
perversions *n* ▷ perversion
perversities *n* ▷ perverse
perversity *n* ▷ perverse
pervert *v* (**-s, -ing, -ed**) use or alter for a wrong
purpose ▸ *n* (*pl* **-s**) person who practises
sexual perversion
perverted *v* ▷ pervert
perverting *v* ▷ pervert
perverts *v*, *n* ▷ pervert
pervious *adj* able to be penetrated, permeable
peseta [pa-**say**-ta] *n* (*pl* **-s**) former monetary
unit of Spain
pesetas *n* ▷ peseta
pessaries *n* ▷ pessary
pessary *n* (*pl* **-ries**) appliance worn in the
vagina, either to prevent conception or to
support the womb
pessimism *n* (*pl* **-s**) tendency to expect the
worst in all things > **pessimist** *n* (*pl* **-s**)
> **pessimistic** *adj* > **pessimistically** *adv*
pessimisms *n* ▷ pessimism
pessimist *n* ▷ pessimism
pessimistic *adj* ▷ pessimism
pessimistically *adv* ▷ pessimism
pessimists *n* ▷ pessimism
pest *n* (*pl* **-s**) annoying person
pesticide *n* (*pl* **-s**) chemical for killing insect
pests
pesticides *n* ▷ pesticide
pester *v* (**-s, -ing, -ed**) annoy or nag continually
pestered *v* ▷ pester
pestering *v* ▷ pester
pesters *v* ▷ pester
pestilence *n* (*pl* **-s**) deadly epidemic disease

pestilences *n* ▷ pestilence
pestilent *adj* annoying, troublesome
 > **pestilential** *adj*
 pestilential *adj* ▷ pestilent
pestle *n* (*pl* -s) club-shaped implement for grinding things to powder in a mortar
 pestles *n* ▷ pestle
 pests *n* ▷ pest
pet *n* (*pl* -s) animal kept for pleasure and companionship ▶ *adj* particularly cherished
 ▶ *v* (-s, -tting, -tted) treat as a pet
petal *n* (*pl* -s) one of the brightly coloured outer parts of a flower > **petalled** *adj*
 petalled *adj* ▷ petal
 petals *n* ▷ petal
petard *n* (*pl* -s) being the victim of one's own schemes
 petards *n* ▷ petard
petite *adj* (of a woman) small and dainty
petition *n* (*pl* -s) formal request, esp. one signed by many people and presented to parliament ▶ *v* (-s, -ing, -ed) present a petition to > **petitioner** *n* (*pl* -s)
 petitioned *v* ▷ petition
 petitioner *n* ▷ petition
 petitioners *n* ▷ petition
 petitioning *v* ▷ petition
 petitions *n, v* ▷ petition
petrel *n* (*pl* -s) sea bird with a hooked bill and tubular nostrils
 petrels *n* ▷ petrel
 petrification *n* ▷ petrify
 petrifications *n* ▷ petrify
 petrified *v* ▷ petrify
 petrifies *v* ▷ petrify
petrify *v* (-fies, -fying, -fied) frighten severely
 > **petrification** *n* (*pl* -s)
petrochemical *n* (*pl* -s) substance, such as acetone, obtained from petroleum
 petrochemicals *n* ▷ petrochemical
petrol *n* (*pl* -s) flammable liquid obtained from petroleum, used as fuel in internal-combustion engines
petroleum *n* (*pl* -s) thick dark oil found underground
 petroleums *n* ▷ petroleums
 petrols *n* ▷ petrol
 pets *n, v* ▷ pet
 petted *v* ▷ pet
petticoat *n* (*pl* -s) woman's skirt-shaped undergarment
 petticoats *n* ▷ petticoat
 pettier *adj* ▷ petty
 pettiest *adj* ▷ petty
pettifogging *adj* excessively concerned with

unimportant detail
 pettiness *n* ▷ petty
 pettinesses *n* ▷ petty
 petting *v* ▷ pet
petty *adj* (-tier, -tiest) unimportant, trivial
 > **pettiness** *n* (*pl* -es)
 petulance *n* ▷ petulant
 petulances *n* ▷ petulant
petulant *adj* childishly irritable or peevish
 > **petulance** *n* (*pl* -s) > **petulantly** *adv*
 petulantly *adv* ▷ petulant
petunia *n* (*pl* -s) garden plant with funnel-shaped flowers
 petunias *n* ▷ petunia
pew *n* (*pl* -s) fixed benchlike seat in a church
 pews *n* ▷ pew
pewter *n* (*pl* -s) greyish metal made of tin and lead
 pewters *n* ▷ pewter
phalanger *n* (*pl* -s) long-tailed Australian tree-dwelling marsupial
 phalangers *n* ▷ phalanger
phalanx *n* (*pl* -es) closely grouped mass of people
 phalanxes *n* ▷ phalanx
 phalli *n* ▷ phallus
 phallic *adj* ▷ phallic
phallus *n* (*pl* -lluses, -lli) penis, esp. as a symbol of reproductive power in primitive rites
 > **phallic** *adj*
 phalluses *n* ▷ phallus
phantasm *n* (*pl* -s) unreal vision, illusion
 > **phantasmal** *adj*
 phantasmal *adj* ▷ phantasm
 phantasms *n* ▷ phantasm
phantasmagoria *n* (*pl* -s) shifting medley of dreamlike figures
 phantasmagorias *n* ▷ phantasmagoria
phantom *n* (*pl* -s) ghost
 phantoms *n* ▷ phantom
pharmaceutical *adj* of pharmacy
 pharmacies *n* ▷ pharmacy
pharmacist *n* (*pl* -s) person qualified to prepare and sell drugs and medicines
 pharmacists *n* ▷ pharmacist
 pharmacological *adj* ▷ pharmacology
 pharmacologies *n* ▷ pharmacology
 pharmacologist *n* ▷ pharmacology
 pharmacologists *n* ▷ pharmacology
pharmacology *n* (*pl* -gies) study of drugs
 > **pharmacological** *adj* > **pharmacologist** *n* (*pl* -s)
pharmacopoeia [far-ma-koh-**pee**-a] *n* (*pl* -s) book with a list of and directions for the use of drugs

pharmacopoeias n ▷ **pharmacopoeia**
pharmacy n (pl **-cies**) preparation and dispensing of drugs and medicines
pharynges n ▷ **pharynx**
pharyngitis [far-rin-**jite**-iss] n (pl **-tes**) inflammation of the pharynx
pharyngitises n ▷ **pharynx**
pharynx [**far**-rinks] n (pl **-nges, -nxes**) cavity forming the back part of the mouth
pharynxes ▷ **pharynx**
phase n (pl **-s**) any distinct or characteristic stage in a development or chain of events
▶ v (**-ses, -sing, -sed**) arrange or carry out in stages or to coincide with something else
phased v ▷ **phase**
phases n, v ▷ **phase**
phasing v ▷ **phase**
pheasant n (pl **-s**) game bird with bright plumage
pheasants n ▷ **pheasant**
phenobarbitone n (pl **-s**) drug inducing sleep or relaxation
phenobarbitones n ▷ **phenobarbitone**
phenol n (pl **-s**) chemical used in disinfectants and antiseptics
phenols n ▷ **phenol**
phenomena n ▷ **phenomenon**
phenomenal adj extraordinary, outstanding > **phenomenally** adv
phenomenally adv ▷ **phenomenal**
phenomenon n (pl **-mena**) anything appearing or observed
phial n (pl **-s**) small bottle for medicine etc.
phials n ▷ **phial**
philadelphus n (pl **-es**) shrub with sweet-scented flowers
philadelphuses n ▷ **philadelphus**
philanderer n (pl **-s**) man who flirts or has many casual love affairs > **philandering** adj, n (pl **-s**)
philanderers n ▷ **philanderer**
philandering n ▷ **philanderer**
philanderings n ▷ **philanderer**
philanthropic adj ▷ **philanthropy**
philanthropies n ▷ **philanthropy**
philanthropist n ▷ **philanthropy**
philanthropists n ▷ **philanthropy**
philanthropy n (pl **-pies**) practice of helping people less well-off than oneself > **philanthropic** adj > **philanthropist** n (pl **-s**)
philatelies n ▷ **philately**
philatelist n ▷ **philately**
philatelists n ▷ **philately**
philately [fill-**lat**-a-lee] n (pl **-lies**) stamp collecting > **philatelist** n (pl **-s**)

philharmonic adj (in names of orchestras etc.) music-loving
philistine adj, n (pl **-s**) boorishly uncultivated (person) > **philistinism** n (pl **-s**)
philistines n ▷ **philistine**
philistinism n ▷ **philistine**
philistinisms n ▷ **philistine**
philological adj ▷ **philology**
philologies n ▷ **philology**
philologist n ▷ **philology**
philologists n ▷ **philology**
philology n (pl **-gies**) science of the structure and development of languages > **philological** adj > **philologist** n (pl **-s**)
philosopher n (pl **-s**) person who studies philosophy
philosophers n ▷ **philosopher**
philosophize v (**-zes, -zing, -zed**) discuss in a philosophical manner
philosophized v ▷ **philosophize**
philosophizes v ▷ **philosophize**
philosophizing v ▷ **philosophize**
philosophic adj ▷ **philosophy**
philosophical adj ▷ **philosophy**
philosophically adv ▷ **philosophy**
philosophies n ▷ **philosophy**
philosophy n (pl **-phies**) study of the meaning of life, knowledge, thought, etc. > **philosophical, philosophic** adj of philosophy > **philosophically** adv
philtre n (pl **-s**) magic drink supposed to arouse love in the person who drinks it
philtres n ▷ **philtre**
phlebitis [fleb-**bite**-iss] n (pl **-es**) inflammation of a vein
phlebitises n ▷ **phlebitis**
phlegm [**flem**] n (pl **-s**) thick yellowish substance formed in the nose and throat during a cold
phlegmatic [fleg-**mat**-ik] adj not easily excited, unemotional > **phlegmatically** adv
phlematically adv ▷ **phlegmatic**
phlegms n ▷ **phlegm**
phlox n (pl phlox, **-xes**) flowering garden plant
phloxes n ▷ **phlox**
phobia n (pl **-s**) intense and unreasoning fear or dislike
phobias n ▷ **phobia**
phoenix n (pl **-es**) legendary bird said to set fire to itself and rise anew from its ashes
phoenixes n ▷ **phoenix**
phone n, v (**-nes, -ning, -ned**) (Informal) telephone
phonecard n (pl **-s**) card used to operate certain public telephones

phonecards *n* ▷ phonecard
phoned *v* ▷ phone
phones *v* ▷ phone
phonetic *adj* of speech sounds > **phonetically**
adv
phonetically *adv* ▷ phonetic
phonetics *n* science of speech sounds
phoney, phony (*Informal*) *adj* (**-nier, -niest**) not
genuine ▶ *n* (*pl* **-neys, -nies**) phoney person
or thing
phoneys *n* ▷ phoney
phonier *adj* ▷ phoney
phonies *n* ▷ phoney
phoniest *adj* ▷ phoney
phoning *v* ▷ phone
phonograph *n* (*pl* **-s**) (US) (*old-fashioned*) record
player
phonographs *n* ▷ phonograph
phony *adj* ▷ phony
phosphorescence *n* (*pl* **-s**) faint glow in the
dark > **phosphorescent** *adj*
phosphorescences *n* ▷ phosphorescence
phosphorescent *adj* ▷ phosphorescence
phosphate *n* (*pl* **-s**) compound of phosphorus
phosphates *n* ▷ phosphate
phosphorus *n* (*pl* **-es**) (CHEM) toxic flammable
nonmetallic element which appears
luminous in the dark
phosphoruses *n* ▷ phosphorus
photo *n* (*pl* **-s**) ▷ photograph
photocopied *v* ▷ photocopy
photocopier *n* ▷ photocopy
photocopiers *n* ▷ photocopy
photocopies *n, v* ▷ photocopy
photocopy *n* (*pl* **-pies**) photographic
reproduction ▶ *v* (**-pies, -pying, -pied**) make a
photocopy of > **photocopier** *n* (*pl* **-s**)
photocopying *v* ▷ photocopy
photoelectric *adj* using or worked by
electricity produced by the action of light
photogenic *adj* always looking attractive in
photographs
photograph *n* (*pl* **-s**) picture made by the
chemical action of light on sensitive film
▶ *v* (**-s, -ing, -ed**) take a photograph of
> **photographic** *adj*
photographed *v* ▷ photograph
photographer *n* (*pl* **-s**) person who takes
photographs, esp. professionally
photographers *n* ▷ photographer
photographic *adj* ▷ photograph
photographing *v* ▷ photograph
photographs *n, v* ▷ photograph
photographies *n* ▷ photography
photography *n* (*pl* **-s**) art of taking

photographs
photos *n* ▷ photo
photostat *n* (*pl* **-s**) copy made by photocopying
machine
photostats *n* ▷ photostat
photosyntheses *n* ▷ photosynthesis
photosynthesis *n* (*pl* **-ses**) process by which
a green plant uses sunlight to build up
carbohydrate reserves
phrase *n* (*pl* **-s**) group of words forming a unit
of meaning, esp. within a sentence ▶ *v* (**-ses,
-sing, -sed**) express in words
phrased *v* ▷ phrase
phrases *n, v* ▷ phrase
phrasing *v* ▷ phrase
phraseologies *n* ▷ phraseology
phraseology *n* (*pl* **-gies**) way in which words
are used
physical *adj* of the body, as contrasted with
the mind or spirit > **physically** *adv*
physically *adv* ▷ physical
physician *n* (*pl* **-s**) doctor of medicine
physicians *n* ▷ physician
physics *n* science of the properties of matter
and energy
physicist *n* (*pl* **-s**) person skilled in or studying
physics
physicists *n* ▷ physicist
physiognomies *n* ▷ physiognomy
physiognomy [fiz-ee-on-om-ee] *n* (*pl* **-mies**)
face
physiological *adj* ▷ physiology
physiologies *n* ▷ physiology
physiologist *n* ▷ physiology
physiologists *n* ▷ physiology
physiology *n* (*pl* **-gies**) science of the normal
function of living things > **physiological** *adj*
> **physiologist** *n* (*pl* **-s**)
physiotherapies *n* ▷ physiotherapy
physiotherapist *n* ▷ physiotherapy
physiotherapists *n* ▷ physiotherapy
physiotherapy *n* (*pl* **-pies**) treatment
of disease or injury by physical means
such as massage, rather than by drugs
> **physiotherapist** *n* (*pl* **-s**)
physique *n* (*pl* **-s**) person's bodily build and
muscular development
physiques *n* ▷ physique
pi *n* (*pl* **-s**) (MATHS) ratio of the circumference of
a circle to its diameter
pis *n* ▷ pi
pianissimo *adv* (MUSIC) very quietly
piano[1] *n* (*pl* **-os**) musical instrument with
strings which are struck by hammers worked
by a keyboard (*also* **pianoforte**) (*pl* **-s**) > **pianist**

n (*pl* -s)
pianist *n* ▷ **piano¹**
pianists *n* ▷ **piano¹**
piano² *adv* (MUSIC) quietly
pianoforte *n* ▷ **piano¹**
pianofortes *n* ▷ **piano¹**
pianos *n* ▷ **piano¹**
piazza *n* (*pl* -s) square or marketplace, esp. in Italy
piazzas *n* ▷ **piazza**
pic *n* (*pl* -s, pix) (*Informal*) photograph or illustration
picador *n* (*pl* -s) mounted bullfighter with a lance
picadors *n* ▷ **picador**
picaresque *adj* denoting a type of fiction in which the hero, a rogue, has a series of adventures
piccalilli *n* (*pl* -s) pickle of vegetables in mustard sauce
piccalillis *n* ▷ **piccalilli**
piccolo *n* (*pl* -os) small flute
piccolos *n* ▷ **piccolo**
pick¹ *v* (-s, -ing, -ed) choose
▶ *n* (*pl* -s) choice
pick² *n* (*pl* -s) tool with a curved iron crossbar and wooden shaft, for breaking up hard ground or rocks
pickaxe *n* (*pl* -s) large pick
pickaxes *n* ▷ **pickaxe**
picked *v* ▷ **pick¹**
picket *n* (*pl* -s) person or group standing outside a workplace to deter would-be workers during a strike ▶ *v* (-s, -ing, -ed) form a picket outside (a workplace)
picketed *v* ▷ **picket**
picketing *v* ▷ **picket**
pickets *n*, *v* ▷ **picket**
picking *v* ▷ **pick¹**
pickings *pl n* money easily acquired
pickle *n* (*pl* -s) food preserved in vinegar or salt water ▶ *v* (-les, -ling, -led) preserve in vinegar or salt water
pickled *adj* (of food) preserved ▶ *n* ▷ **pickle**
pickles *n*, *v* ▷ **pickle**
pickling *v* ▷ **pickle**
pickpocket *n* (*pl* -s) thief who steals from someone's pocket
pickpockets *n* ▷ **pickpocket**
picks *n*, *v* ▷ **pick¹, ²**
picnic *n* (*pl* -s) informal meal out of doors ▶ *v* (-s, -cking, -cked) have a picnic
picknicked *v* ▷ **picnic**
picknicking *v* ▷ **picnic**
picnics *n*, *v* ▷ **picnic**

pics *n* ▷ **pic**
pictorial *adj* of or in painting or pictures
picture *n* (*pl* -s) drawing or painting ▶ *pl* cinema ▶ *v* (-res, -ring, -red) visualize, imagine
pictured *v* ▷ **picture**
pictures *n*, *v* ▷ **picture**
picturesque *adj* (of a place or view) pleasant to look at
picturing *v* ▷ **picture**
piddle *v* (-les, -ling, -led) (*Informal*) urinate
piddled *v* ▷ **piddle**
piddles *v* ▷ **piddle**
piddling *v* ▷ **piddle**
pidgin *n* (*pl* -s) language, not a mother tongue, made up of elements of two or more other languages
pidgins *n* ▷ **pidgin**
pie *n* (*pl* -s) dish of meat, fruit, etc. baked in pastry
pies *n* ▷ **pie**
piebald *adj*, *n* (*pl* -s) (horse) with irregular black-and-white markings
piebalds *n* ▷ **piebald**
piece *n* (*pl* -s) separate bit or part
pieces *n* ▷ **piece**
piecemeal *adv* bit by bit
piecework *n* (*pl* -s) work paid for according to the quantity produced
pieceworks *n* ▷ **piecework**
pied *adj* having markings of two or more colours
pier *n* (*pl* -s) platform on stilts sticking out into the sea
piers *n* ▷ **pier**
pierce *v* (-ces, -cing, -ced) make a hole in or through with a sharp instrument
pierced *v* ▷ **pierce**
pierces *v* ▷ **pierce**
piercing *adj* (of a sound) shrill and high-pitched ▶ *v* ▷ **pierce**
pierrot [pier-roe] *n* (*pl* -s) pantomime clown with a whitened face
pierrots *n* ▷ **pierrot**
pieties *n* ▷ **piety**
piety *n* (*pl* -ties) deep devotion to God and religion
piffle *n* (*pl* -s) (*Informal*) nonsense
piffles *n* ▷ **piffle**
pig *n* (*pl* -s) animal kept and killed for pork, ham, and bacon
pigeon¹ *n* (*pl* -s) bird with a heavy body and short legs, sometimes trained to carry messages
pigeon² *n* (*Informal*) concern or responsibility

pigeonhole *n* (**-s**) compartment for papers in a desk etc. ▸ *v* (**-les, -ling, -led**) classify
  pigeonholed *v* ▷ **pigeonhole**
  pigeonholing *v* ▷ **pigeonhole**
  pigeonholes *n, v* ▷ **pigeonhole**
  pigeons *n* ▷ **pigeon**[1, 2]
  piggeries *n* ▷ **piggery**
piggery *n* (*pl* **-ries**) place for keeping and breeding pigs
  piggier *adj* ▷ **piggy**
  piggiest *adj* ▷ **piggy**
piggish, piggy (**-ggier, -ggiest**) *adj* (*Informal*) dirty
  piggy *adj* ▷ **piggish**
piggyback *n* (*pl* **-s**) ride on someone's shoulders ▸ *adv* carried on someone's shoulders
  piggybacks *n* ▷ **piggyback**
pigment *n* (*pl* **-s**) colouring matter, paint or dye > **pigmentation** *n* (*pl* **-s**)
  pigmentation *n* ▷ **pigment**
  pigmentations *n* ▷ **pigment**
  pigments *n* ▷ **pigment**
  pigmies *n* ▷ **pigmy**
pigmy *n* (*pl* **-mies**) ▷ **pygmy**
  pigs *n* ▷ **pig**
pigtail *n* (*pl* **-s**) plait of hair hanging from the back or either side of the head
  pigtails *n* ▷ **pigtail**
pike[1] *n* (*pl* **-s**) large predatory freshwater fish
pike[2] *n* (*pl* **-s**) (HIST) long-handled spear
  pikes *n* ▷ **pike**[1, 2]
pikelet *n* (*pl* **-s**) (AUST & NZ) small thick pancake
  pikelets *n* ▷ **pikelet**
piker *n* (*pl* **-s**) (AUST & NZ) (*Slang*) shirker
  pikers *n* ▷ **piker**
pilaster *n* (*pl* **-s**) square column, usu. set in a wall
  pilasters *n* ▷ **pilaster**
pilau, pilaf, pilaff *n* (*pl* **-s**) Middle Eastern dish of meat, fish, or poultry boiled with rice, spices, etc.
  pilaffs *n* ▷ **pilaff**
  pilafs *n* ▷ **pilaf**
pilchard *n* (*pl* **-s**) small edible sea fish of the herring family
  pilchards *n* ▷ **pilchard**
pile[1] *n* (*pl* **-s**) number of things lying on top of each other ▸ *v* (**-les, -ling, -led**) collect into a pile
pile[2] *n* (*pl* **-s**) beam driven into the ground, esp. as a foundation for building
pile[3] *n* (*pl* **-s**) fibres of a carpet or a fabric, esp. velvet, that stand up from the weave
  piled *v* ▷ **pile**[1]

piling *v* ▷ **pile**[1]
piles *pl n* swollen veins in the rectum, haemorrhoids ▸ *v, n* ▷ **pile**[1, 2, 3]
pilfer *v* (**-s, -ing, -ed**) steal in small quantities
  pilfered *v* ▷ **pilfer**
  pilfering *v* ▷ **pilfer**
  pilfers *v* ▷ **pilfer**
pilgrim *n* (*pl* **-s**) person who journeys to a holy place > **pilgrimage** *n* (*pl* **-s**)
  pilgrimage *n* ▷ **pilgrim**
  pilgrimages *n* ▷ **pilgrim**
  pilgrims *n* ▷ **pilgrim**
pill *n* (*pl* **-s**) small ball of medicine swallowed whole
  pills *n* ▷ **pill**
pillage *v* (**-ges, -ging, -ged**) steal property by violence in war ▸ *n* (*pl* **-s**) violent seizure of goods, esp. in war
  pillaged *v* ▷ **pillage**
  pillages *v, n* ▷ **pillage**
  pillaging *v* ▷ **pillage**
pillar *n* (*pl* **-s**) upright post, usu. supporting a roof
  pillars *n* ▷ **pillar**
pillion *n* (*pl* **-s**) seat for a passenger behind the rider of a motorcycle
  pillions *n* ▷ **pillion**
  pilloried *v* ▷ **pillory**
  pillories *n, v* ▷ **pillory**
pillory *n* (*pl* **-ries**) (HIST) frame with holes for the head and hands in which an offender was locked and exposed to public abuse ▸ *v* (**-ies, -ying, -ied**) ridicule publicly
pillow *n* (*pl* **-s**) stuffed cloth bag for supporting the head in bed ▸ *v* (**-s, -ing, -ed**) rest as if on a pillow
pillowcase, pillowslip *n* (*pl* **-s**) removable cover for a pillow
  pillowcases *n* ▷ **pillowcase**
  pillowed *v* ▷ **pillow**
  pillowing *v* ▷ **pillow**
  pillows *n, v* ▷ **pillow**
  pillowslip *n* ▷ **pillowcase**
  pillowslips *n* ▷ **pillowcase**
pilot *n* (*pl* **-s**) person qualified to fly an aircraft or spacecraft ▸ *adj* experimental and preliminary ▸ *v* (**-s, -ing, -ed**) act as the pilot of
  piloted *v* ▷ **pilot**
  piloting *v* ▷ **pilot**
  pilots *n, v* ▷ **pilot**
pimento *n* (*pl* **-tos**) mild-tasting red pepper
  pimentos *n* ▷ **pimento**
pimp *n* (*pl* **-s**) man who gets customers for a prostitute in return for a share of his or her earnings ▸ *v* (**-s, -ing, -ed**) act as a pimp

pimped v ▷ pimp
pimpernel n (pl -s) wild plant with small star-shaped flowers
  pimpernels n ▷ pimpernel
  pimping v ▷ pimp
pimple n (pl -s) small pus-filled spot on the skin
  > **pimply** adj (-lier, -liest)
  pimples n ▷ pimple
  pimplier v ▷ pimple
  pimpliest v ▷ pimple
  pimply v ▷ pimple
  pimps n, v ▷ pimp
pin n (pl -s) short thin piece of stiff wire with a point and head, for fastening things ▶ v (-s, pinning, pinned) fasten with a pin
pinafore n (pl -s) apron
  pinafores n ▷ pinafore
pinball n (pl -s) electrically operated table game in which a small ball is shot through various hazards
  pinballs n ▷ pinball
pincers pl n tool consisting of two hinged arms, for gripping
pinch v (-es, -ing, -ed) squeeze between finger and thumb ▶ n (pl -es) act of pinching
pinchbeck n (pl -s) alloy of zinc and copper, used as imitation gold
  pinchbecks n ▷ pinchbeck
  pinched v ▷ pinch
  pinches v, n ▷ pinch
  pinching v ▷ pinch
  pinned v ▷ pin
  pinning v ▷ pin
  pins n, v ▷ pin
pine[1] n (pl -s) evergreen coniferous tree
pine[2] v (-nes, -ning, -ned) (foll. by for) feel great longing (for)
pineapple n (pl -s) large tropical fruit with juicy yellow flesh and a hard skin
  pineapples n ▷ pineapple
  pined v ▷ pine[2]
  pines n, v ▷ pine[1, 2]
ping v (-s, -ing, -ed) ▶ n (pl -s) (make) a short high-pitched sound
  pinged v ▷ ping
  pinging v ▷ ping
  pings v, n ▷ ping
  pining v ▷ pine[2]
pinion[1] n (pl -s) bird's wing ▶ v (-s, -ing, -ed) immobilize (someone) by tying or holding his or her arms
pinion[2] n (pl -s) small cogwheel
  pinioned v ▷ pinion
  pinioning v ▷ pinion
  pinions n, v ▷ pinion[1, 2]

pink n (pl -s) pale reddish colour ▶ adj (-er, -est) of the colour pink ▶ v (-s, -ing, -ed) (of an engine) make a metallic noise because not working properly, knock
  pinked v ▷ pink
  pinker adj ▷ pink
  pinkest adj ▷ pink
  pinking v ▷ pink
  pinks n, v ▷ pink
pinnacle n (pl -s) highest point of fame or success
  pinnacles n ▷ pinnacle
pinotage [pin-no-tajj] n (pl -s) blended red wine of S Africa
  pinotages n ▷ pinotage
pinpoint v (-s, -ing, -ed) locate or identify exactly
  pinpointed v ▷ pinpoint
  pinpointing v ▷ pinpoint
  pinpoints v ▷ pinpoint
pinstripe n (pl -s) very narrow stripe in fabric
  pinstripes n ▷ pinstripe
pint n (pl -s) liquid measure, 1/8 gallon (.568 litre)
  pints n ▷ pint
pioneer n (pl -s) explorer or early settler of a new country ▶ v (-s, -ing, -ed) be the pioneer or leader of
  pioneered v ▷ pioneer
  pioneering v ▷ pioneer
  pioneers n, v ▷ pioneer
pious adj deeply religious, devout
pip[1] n (pl -s) small seed in a fruit
pip[2] n high-pitched sound used as a time signal on radio (Informal)
  pips n ▷ pip[1, 2]
pipe n (pl -s) tube for conveying liquid or gas ▶ pl bagpipes ▶ v (-pes, -ping, -ped) play on a pipe
  piped v ▷ pipe
piper n (pl -s) player on a pipe or bagpipes
  pipers n ▷ piper
piping n (pl -s) system of pipes ▶ v ▷ pipe
  pipings n ▷ piping
pipeline n (pl -s) long pipe for transporting oil, water, etc.
  pipelines n ▷ pipeline
  pipes n, v ▷ pipe
pipette n (pl -s) slender glass tube used to transfer or measure fluids
  pipettes n ▷ pipette
pipi n (pl -s) (AUST) mollusc often used as bait
pipit n (pl -s) small brownish songbird
  pipits n ▷ pipit
pippin n (pl -s) type of eating apple

pippins *n* ▷ pippin
pips *n* ▷ pip[1, 2]
piquancies *n* ▷ piquant
piquancy *n* ▷ piquant
piquant [pee-kant] *adj* having a pleasant spicy taste > **piquancy** *n* (*pl* -**cies**)
pique [peek] *n* (*pl* -**s**) feeling of hurt pride, baffled curiosity, or resentment ▶ *v* (-**ques, -quing, -qued**) hurt the pride of
piqué [pee-kay] *n* (*pl* -**s**) stiff ribbed cotton fabric
piqued *v* ▷ pique
piques *n, v* ▷ pique
piqués *n* ▷ piqué
piquing *v* ▷ pique
piquet [pik-**ket**] *n* (*pl* -**s**) card game for two
piquets *n* ▷ piquet
piracies *n* ▷ pirate
piracy *n* ▷ pirate
piranha *n* (*pl* -**s**) small fierce freshwater fish of tropical America
piranhas *n* ▷ piranha
pirate *n* (*pl* -**s**) sea robber ▶ *v* (-**tes, -ting, -ted**) sell or reproduce (artistic work etc.) illegally > **piracy** *n* (*pl* -**cies**) > **piratical** *adj*
pirated *v* ▷ pirate
pirates *n, v* ▷ pirate
piratical *adj* ▷ pirate
pirating *v* ▷ pirate
pirouette *v, n* (*pl* -**s**) (make) a spinning turn balanced on the toes of one foot
pirouettes *n* ▷ pirouette
pistachio *n* (*pl* -**s**) edible nut of a Mediterranean tree
pistachios *n* ▷ pistachio
piste [peest] *n* (*pl* -**s**) ski slope
pistes *n* ▷ piste
pistil *n* (*pl* -**s**) seed-bearing part of a flower
pistils *n* ▷ pistil
pistol *n* (*pl* -**s**) short-barrelled handgun
pistols *n* ▷ pistol
piston *n* (*pl* -**s**) cylindrical part in an engine that slides to and fro in a cylinder
pistons *n* ▷ piston
pit *n* (*pl* -**s**) deep hole in the ground ▷ **orchestra pit** ▶ *v* (-**s, -tting, -tteds**) mark with small dents or scars
pitch[1] *v* (-**es, -ing, -ed**) throw, hurl ▶ *n* (*pl* -**es**) area marked out for playing sport
pitch[2] *n* dark sticky substance obtained from tar
pitched *v* ▷ pitch[1]
pitches *v, n* ▷ pitch[1]
pitching *v* ▷ pitch[1]
pitchblende *n* (*pl* -**s**) mineral composed largely of uranium oxide, yielding radium
pitchblendes *n* ▷ pitchblende
pitcher *n* (*pl* -**s**) large jug with a narrow neck
pitchers *n* ▷ pitcher
pitchfork *n* (*pl* -**s**) large long-handled fork for lifting hay ▶ *v* (-**s, -ing, -ed**) thrust abruptly or violently
pitchforked *v* ▷ pitchfork
pitchforking *v* ▷ pitchfork
pitchforks *n, v* ▷ pitchfork
piteous, pitiable *adj* arousing pity
pitfall *n* (*pl* -**s**) hidden difficulty or danger
pitfalls *n* ▷ pitfall
pith *n* (*pl* -**s**) soft white lining of the rind of oranges etc.
pithier *adj* ▷ pithy
pithiest *adj* ▷ pithy
piths *n* ▷ pith
pithy *adj* (-**thier, -thiest**) short and full of meaning
pitiable *adj* ▷ piteous
pitied *v* ▷ pity
pities *n, v* ▷ pity
pitiful *adj* arousing pity > **pitifully** *adv*
pitifully *adv* ▷ pitiful
pitiless *adj* feeling no pity or mercy > **pitilessly** *adv*
pitilessly *adv* ▷ pitiless
piton [peet-on] *n* (*pl* -**s**) metal spike used in climbing to secure a rope
pitons *n* ▷ piton
pits *n, v* ▷ pit
pittance *n* (*pl* -**s**) very small amount of money
pittances *n* ▷ pittance
pitted *v* ▷ pit
pitting *v* ▷ pit
pituitaries *n* ▷ pituitary
pituitary *n* (*pl* -**ies**) gland at the base of the brain, that helps to control growth
pity *n* (*pl* -**ties**) sympathy or sorrow for others' suffering ▶ *v* (-**ies, -ying, -ied**) feel pity for
pitying *v* ▷ pity
pivot *n* (*pl* -**s**) central shaft on which something turns ▶ *v* (-**s, -ing, -ed**) provide with or turn on a pivot
pivotal *adj* of crucial importance
pivoted *v* ▷ pivot
pivoting *v* ▷ pivot
pivots *n, v* ▷ pivot
pix *n* (*Informal*) ▷ pic
pixie *n* (*pl* -**s**) (in folklore) fairy
pixies *n* ▷ pixie
pizza *n* (*pl* -**s**) flat disc of dough covered with a wide variety of savoury toppings and baked
pizzas *n* ▷ pizza

pizzazz n (pl **-es**) (*Informal*) attractive combination of energy and style
  pizzazzes n ▷ pizzazz
pizzicato [pit-see-**kah**-toe] adj (MUSIC) played by plucking the string of a violin etc. with the finger
placard n (pl **-s**) notice that is carried or displayed in public
  placards n ▷ placard
placate v (**-tes, -ting, -ted**) make (someone) stop feeling angry or upset > **placatory** adj
  placated v ▷ placate
  placates v ▷ placate
  placating v ▷ placate
  placatory adj ▷ placate
place n (pl **-s**) particular part of an area or space ▶ v (**-ces, -cing, -ced**) put in a particular place
  placed v ▷ place
  places n, v ▷ place
placebo [plas-**see**-bo] n (pl **-bos, -boes**) sugar pill etc. given to an unsuspecting patient instead of an active drug
  placeboes n ▷ placebo
  placebos n ▷ placebo
placenta [plass-**ent**-a] n (pl **-tas, -tae**) organ formed in the womb during pregnancy, providing nutrients for the fetus > **placental** adj
  placentae n ▷ placenta
  placental adj ▷ placenta
  placentas n ▷ placenta
placid adj (**-er, -est**) not easily excited or upset, calm > **placidity** n (pl **-ties**)
  placider adj ▷ placid
  placidest adj ▷ placid
  placidities n ▷ placid
  placidity n ▷ placid
  placing v ▷ place
plagiarize [**play**-jer-ize] v (**-zes, -zing, -zed**) steal ideas, passages, etc. from (someone else's work) and present them as one's own > **plagiarism** n (pl **-s**)
  plagiarism n ▷ plagiarize
  plagiarisms n ▷ plagiarize
  plagiarized v ▷ plagiarize
  plagiarizes v ▷ plagiarize
  plagiarizing v ▷ plagiarize
plague n (pl **-s**) fast-spreading fatal disease ▶ v (**-gues, -guing, -gued**) trouble or annoy continually
  plagued v ▷ plague
  plagues n, v ▷ plague
  plaguing v ▷ plague
plaice n (pl **plaice**) edible European flatfish

plaid n (pl **-s**) long piece of tartan cloth worn as part of Highland dress
  plaids n ▷ plaid
plain (**-er, -est**) adj easy to see or understand ▶ n (pl **-s**) large stretch of level country > **plainly** adv > **plainness** n (pl **-es**)
  plainer adj ▷ plain
  plainest adj ▷ plain
  plainly adj ▷ plain
  plainness n ▷ plain
  plainnesses n ▷ plain
  plains n ▷ plain
plainsong n (pl **-s**) unaccompanied singing, esp. in a medieval church
  plainsongs n ▷ plainsong
plaintiff n (pl **-s**) person who sues in a court of law
  plaintiffs n ▷ plaintiff
plaintive adj sad, mournful > **plaintively** adv
  plaintively adv ▷ plaintive
plait [platt] n (pl **-s**) intertwined length of hair ▶ v (**-s, -ing, -ed**) intertwine separate strands in a pattern
  plaited v ▷ plait
  plaiting v ▷ plait
  plaits n, v ▷ plait
plan n (pl **-s**) way thought out to do or achieve something ▶ v (**-s, -nning, -nned**) arrange beforehand > **planner** n (pl **-s**)
plane¹ n (pl **-s**) aeroplane ▶ adj perfectly flat or level ▶ v (**-nes, -ning, -ned**) glide or skim
plane² n (pl **-s**) tool for smoothing wood ▶ v (**-nes, -ning, -ned**) smooth (wood) with a plane
plane³ n (pl **-s**) tree with broad leaves
  planed v ▷ plane¹, ²
  planes n, v ▷ plane¹, ², ³
planet n (pl **-s**) large body in space that revolves round the sun or another star > **planetary** adj
  planetaria n ▷ planetarium
planetarium n (pl **-iums, -ia**) building where the movements of the stars, planets, etc. are shown by projecting lights on the inside of a dome
  planetariums n ▷ planetarium
  planetary adj ▷ planet
  planets n ▷ planet
plangent adj (of sounds) mournful and resounding
  planing v ▷ plane¹, ²
plank n (pl **-s**) long flat piece of sawn timber
  planks n ▷ plank
plankton n (pl **-s**) minute animals and plants floating in the surface water of a sea or lake

planktons *n* ▷ plankton
planned *v* ▷ plan
planner *n* ▷ plan
planners *n* ▷ plan
planning *v* ▷ plan
plans *n, v* ▷ plan
plant *n (pl -s)* living organism that grows in the ground and has no power to move ▶ *v* (**-s, -ing, -ed**) put in the ground to grow
plantain¹ *n (pl -s)* low-growing wild plant with broad leaves
plantain² *n (-s)* tropical fruit like a green banana
plantains *n* ▷ plantain¹, ²
plantation *n (pl -s)* estate for the cultivation of tea, tobacco, etc.
plantations *n* ▷ plantation
planted *v* ▷ plant
planter *n (pl -s)* owner of a plantation
planters *n* ▷ planter
planting *v* ▷ plant
plants *n, v* ▷ plant
plaque *n (pl -s)* inscribed commemorative stone or metal plate
plaques *n* ▷ plaque
plasma *n (pl -s)* clear liquid part of blood
plasmas *n* ▷ plasma
plaster *n (pl -s)* mixture of lime, sand, etc. for coating walls ▶ *v* (**-s, -ing, -ed**) cover with plaster
plastered *adj (Slang)* drunk ▶ *v* ▷ plaster
plastering *v* ▷ plaster
plasters *n, v* ▷ plaster
plastic *n (pl -s)* synthetic material that can be moulded when soft but sets in a hard long-lasting shape ▶ *adj* made of plastic
plasticities *n* ▷ plasticity
plasticity *n (pl -ties)* ability to be moulded
plastics *n* ▷ plastic
plate *n (pl -s)* shallow dish for holding food ▶ *v* (**-tes, -ting, -ted**) cover with a thin coating of gold, silver, or other metal > **plateful** *n (pl -s)*
plateau *n (pl -teaus, -teaux)* area of level high land
plateaus *n* ▷ plateau
plateaux *n* ▷ plateau
plated *v* ▷ plate
plateful *n* ▷ plate
platefuls *n* ▷ plate
platen *n (pl -s)* roller of a typewriter, against which the paper is held
platens *n* ▷ platen
plates *n, v* ▷ plate
platform *n (pl -s)* raised floor
platforms *n* ▷ platform

plating *v* ▷ plate
platinum *n (pl -s)* (CHEM) valuable silvery-white metal
platinums *n* ▷ platinum
platitude *n (pl -s)* remark that is true but not interesting or original > **platitudinous** *adj*
platitudes *n* ▷ platitude
platitudinous *adj* ▷ platitude
platonic *adj* (of a relationship) friendly or affectionate but not sexual
platoon *n (pl -s)* smaller unit within a company of soldiers
platoons *n* ▷ platoon
platteland *n (pl -s)* (S AFR) rural district
plattelands *n* ▷ plattelands
platter *n (pl -s)* large dish
platters *n* ▷ platter
platypus *n (pl -es)* Australian egg-laying amphibious mammal, with dense fur, webbed feet, and a ducklike bill (*also* **duck-billed platypus**)
platypuses *n* ▷ platypus
plaudits *pl n* expressions of approval
plausible *adj* apparently true or reasonable > **plausibly** *adv* > **plausibility** *n (pl -ties)*
plausibilities *n* ▷ plausible
plausibility *n* ▷ plausible
plausibly *adj* ▷ plausible
play *v* (**-s, -ing, -ed**) occupy oneself in (a game or recreation) ▶ *n (pl -s)* story performed on stage or broadcast
playboy *n (pl -s)* rich man who lives only for pleasure
playboys *n* ▷ playboy
playcentre *n (pl -s)* (NZ & S AFR) centre for preschool children run by parents
playcentres *n* ▷ playcentre
played *v* ▷ play
player *n (pl -s)* person who plays a game or sport
players *n* ▷ player
playful *adj* lively
playgroup *n (pl -s)* regular meeting of very young children for supervised play
playgroups *n* ▷ playgroup
playhouse *n* theatre
playhouses *n* ▷ playhouse
playing *v* ▷ play
plays *v, n* ▷ play
playschool *n (pl -s)* nursery group for young children
playschools *n* ▷ playschool
plaything *n* toy
playthings *n* ▷ plaything
playwright *n* author of plays

playwrights n ▷ **playwright**
plaza n (pl -s) open space or square
  plazas n ▷ **plaza**
plea n (pl -s) serious or urgent request,
entreaty
  pleas n ▷ **plea**
plead v (-s, -ing, -ed) ask urgently or with deep
feeling (LAW)
  pleaded v ▷ **plead**
  pleading v ▷ **plead**
  pleads v ▷ **plead**
pleasant adj (-er, -est) pleasing, enjoyable
  > **pleasantly** adv
  pleasanter adj ▷ **pleasant**
  pleasantest adj ▷ **pleasant**
  pleasantly adv ▷ **pleasant**
  pleasantries n ▷ **pleasantry**
pleasantry n (pl -ries) polite or joking remark
please v (-ses, -sing, -sed) give pleasure or
satisfaction to ▶ adv polite word of request
> **pleased** adj > **pleasing** adj
  pleased v, adj ▷ **please**
  pleasing v, adj ▷ **please**
  pleases v ▷ **please**
pleasurable adj giving pleasure > **pleasurably**
adv
  pleasurably adv ▷ **pleasurable**
pleasure n (pl -s) feeling of happiness and
satisfaction
  pleasures n ▷ **pleasure**
pleat n (pl -s) fold made by doubling material
back on itself ▶ v (-s, -ing, -ed) arrange
(material) in pleats
  pleated v ▷ **pleat**
  pleating v ▷ **pleat**
  pleats n, v ▷ **pleat**
plebeian [pleb-ee-an] adj of the lower social
classes ▶ n (pl -s) (also **pleb**) member of the
lower social classes
  plebeians n ▷ **plebeian**
plebiscite [pleb-iss-ite] n (pl -s) decision by
direct voting of the people of a country
  plebiscites n ▷ **plebiscite**
  plectra n ▷ **plectrum**
plectrum n (pl -rums, -ra) small implement for
plucking the strings of a guitar etc.
  plectrums n ▷ **plectrum**
pledge n (pl -s) solemn promise ▶ v (-ges, -ging,
-ged) promise solemnly
  pledged v ▷ **pledge**
  pledges n, v ▷ **pledge**
  pledging v ▷ **pledge**
plenary adj (of a meeting) attended by all
members
plenipotentiary adj having full powers

▶ n diplomat or representative having full
powers
plenitude n (pl -s) completeness, abundance
  plenitudes n ▷ **plenitude**
plenteous adj plentiful
  plenties n ▷ **plenty**
plenty n (pl -ties) large amount or number
plentiful adj existing in large amounts or
numbers > **plentifully** adv
  plentifully adv ▷ **plentiful**
pleonasm n (pl -s) use of more words than
necessary
  pleonasms n ▷ **pleonasm**
plethora n (pl -s) excess
  plethoras n ▷ **plethora**
  pleurisies n ▷ **pleurisy**
pleurisy n (pl -sies) inflammation of the
membrane covering the lungs
  pliabilities n ▷ **pliable**
  pliability n ▷ **pliable**
pliable adj easily bent > **pliability** n (pl -ties)
  pliancies n ▷ **pliant**
  pliancy n ▷ **pliant**
pliant adj pliable > **pliancy** n (pl -cies)
  plied v ▷ **ply**
  plies v, n ▷ **ply**
pliers pl n tool with hinged arms and jaws for
gripping
plight[1] n (pl -s) difficult or dangerous situation
plight[2] v (-s, -ing, -ed) pledge
  plighted v ▷ **plight**[2]
  plighting v ▷ **plight**[2]
  plights n, v ▷ **plight**[1, 2]
plimsolls pl n (BRIT) rubber-soled canvas shoes
plinth n (pl -s) slab forming the base of a
statue, column, etc.
  plinths n ▷ **plinth**
plod v (-s, -dding, -dded) walk with slow heavy
steps > **plodder** n (pl -s)
  plodded v ▷ **plod**
  plodder n ▷ **plod**
  plodders n ▷ **plod**
  plodding v ▷ **plod**
  plods v ▷ **plod**
plonk[1] v (-s, -ing, -ed) put (something) down
heavily and carelessly
plonk[2] n (pl -s) (Informal) cheap inferior wine
  plonked v ▷ **plonk**[1]
  plonking v ▷ **plonk**[1]
  plonks v, n ▷ **plonk**[1, 2]
plop n (pl -s) sound of an object falling into
water without a splash ▶ v (-s, -pping, -pped)
make this sound
  plopped v ▷ **plop**
  plopping v ▷ **plop**

plops *n, v* ▷ **plop**
plot¹ *n* (*pl* **-s**) secret plan to do something illegal or wrong ▶ *v* (**-s, -tting, -tted**) plan secretly, conspire
plot² *n* (**-s**) small piece of land
   plotted *v* ▷ **plot¹**
   plotting *v* ▷ **plot¹**
   plots *n, v* ▷ **plot¹, ²**
plough *n* (*pl* **-s**) agricultural tool for turning over soil ▶ *v* (**-s, -ing, -ed**) turn over (earth) with a plough > **ploughman** *n* (*pl* **-men**)
   ploughed *v* ▷ **plough**
   ploughing *v* ▷ **plough**
   ploughman *n* ▷ **plough**
   ploughmen *n* ▷ **plough**
   ploughs *n, v* ▷ **plough**
ploughshare *n* (*pl* **-s**) blade of a plough
   ploughshares *n* ▷ **ploughshare**
plover *n* (*pl* **-s**) shore bird with a straight bill and long pointed wings
   plovers *n* ▷ **plover**
ploy *n* (*pl* **-s**) manoeuvre designed to gain an advantage
   ploys *n* ▷ **ploy**
pluck *v* (**-s, -ing, -ed**) pull or pick off ▶ *n* (*pl* **-s**) courage
   plucked *v* ▷ **pluck**
   pluckier *adj* ▷ **plucky**
   pluckiest *adj* ▷ **plucky**
   pluckily *adj* ▷ **plucky**
   plucking *v* ▷ **pluck**
   plucks *v, n* ▷ **pluck**
plucky *adj* (**-kier, -kiest**) brave > **pluckily** *adv*
plug *n* (*pl* **-s**) thing fitting into and filling a hole ▶ *v* (**-s, -gging, -gged**) block or seal (a hole or gap) with a plug
   plugged *v* ▷ **plug**
   plugging *v* ▷ **plug**
   plugs *n, v* ▷ **plug**
plum *n* (*pl* **-s**) oval usu. dark red fruit with a stone in the middle ▶ *adj* dark purplish-red
plumage *n* (*pl* **-s**) bird's feathers
   plumages *n* ▷ **plumage**
plumb *v* (**-s, -ing, -ed**) understand (something obscure) ▶ *adv* exactly
   plumbed *v* ▷ **plumb**
plumber *n* (*pl* **-s**) person who fits and repairs pipes and fixtures for water and drainage systems
   plumbers *n* ▷ **plumber**
plumbing *n* pipes and fixtures used in water and drainage systems ▶ *v* ▷ **plumb**
   plumbs *v* ▷ **plumb**
plume *n* (*pl* **-s**) feather, esp. one worn as an ornament

   plumes *n* ▷ **plume**
plummet *v* (**-s, -ing, -ed**) plunge downward
   plummeted *v* ▷ **plummet**
   plummeting *v* ▷ **plummet**
   plummets *v* ▷ **plummet**
plump¹ *adj* (**-er, -est**) moderately or attractively fat > **plumpness** *n* (*pl* **-es**)
plump² *v* (**-s, -ing, -ed**) sit or fall heavily and suddenly
   plumper *adj* ▷ **plump¹**
   plumpest *adj* ▷ **plump¹**
   plumped *v* ▷ **plump²**
   plumping *v* ▷ **plump²**
   plumpness *n* ▷ **plump**
   plumpnesses *n* ▷ **plump**
   plumps *v* ▷ **plump²**
   plums *n* ▷ **plum**
plunder *v* (**-s, -ing, -ed**) take by force, esp. in time of war ▶ *n* (*pl* **-s**) things plundered, spoils
   plundered *v* ▷ **plunder**
   plundering *v* ▷ **plunder**
   plunders *v, n* ▷ **plunder**
plunge *v* (**-ges, -ging, -ged**) put or throw forcibly or suddenly (into) ▶ *n* (*pl* **-s**) plunging, dive
   plunged *v* ▷ **plunge**
plunger *n* (*pl* **-s**) rubber suction cup used to clear blocked pipes
   plungers *n* ▷ **plunger**
   plunges *v, n* ▷ **plunge**
   plunging *v* ▷ **plunge**
pluperfect *adj, n* (*pl* **-s**) (GRAMMAR) (tense) expressing an action completed before a past time, e.g. *had gone* in *his wife had gone already*
   pluperfects *n* ▷ **pluperfect**
plural *adj* of or consisting of more than one ▶ *n* (*pl* **-s**) word indicating more than one
   plurals *n* ▷ **plural**
pluralism *n* (*pl* **-s**) existence and toleration of a variety of peoples, opinions, etc. in a society > **pluralist** *n* (*pl* **-s**) > **pluralistic** *adj*
   pluralisms *n* ▷ **pluralism**
   pluralist *n* ▷ **pluralism**
   pluralists *n* ▷ **pluralism**
   pluralistic *adj* ▷ **pluralism**
plus *prep, adj* indicating addition ▶ *adj* more than zero ▶ *n* (*pl* **-es**) sign (+) denoting addition
   pluses *n* ▷ **plus**
plush *n* (*pl* **-es**) fabric with long velvety pile ▶ *adj* (**-er, -est**) (*also* **plushy**) (**-ier, -iest**) luxurious
   plusher *adj* ▷ **plush**
   plushest *adj* ▷ **plush**
   plushes *n* ▷ **plush**

plushier *adj* ▷ plush
plushiest *adj* ▷ plush
plutocrat *n* (*pl* -s) person who is powerful because of being very rich > **plutocratic** *adj*
plutocratic *adj* ▷ plutocrat
plutocrats *n* ▷ plutocrat
plutonium *n* (*pl* -s) (CHEM) radioactive metallic element used esp. in nuclear reactors and weapons
plutoniums *n* ▷ plutonium
ply[1] *v* (-ies, -ying, -ied) work at (a job or trade)
ply[2] *n* (*pl* -ies) thickness of wool, fabric, etc.
plying *v* ▷ ply[1]
plywood *n* (*pl* -s) board made of thin layers of wood glued together
plywoods *n* ▷ plywood
pneumatic *adj* worked by or inflated with wind or air
pneumonia *n* (*pl* -s) inflammation of the lungs
pneumonias *n* ▷ pneumonia

> **po** *n* (**pos**). A po is an informal word for a chamber pot. This is a good word to have ready in case you see an opportunity to play a good word beginning with P next to a word ending in O, or vice versa. Po scores 4 points.

poach[1] *v* (-es, -ing, -ed) catch (animals) illegally on someone else's land
poach[2] *v* (-es, -ing, -ed) simmer (food) gently in liquid
poached *v* ▷ poach
poacher *n* (*pl* -s) person who catches animals illegally on someone else's land
poachers *n* ▷ poacher
poaches *v* ▷ poach
poaching *v* ▷ poach
pocket *n* (*pl* -s) small bag sewn into clothing for carrying things ▶ *v* (-s, -ing, -ed) put into one's pocket ▶ *adj* small
pocketed *v* ▷ pocket
pocketing *v* ▷ pocket
pockets *n*, *v* ▷ pocket
pockmarked *adj* (of the skin) marked with hollow scars where diseased spots have been
pod *n* (*pl* -s) long narrow seed case of peas, beans, etc.
podgier *adj* ▷ podgy
podgiest *adj* ▷ podgy
pods *n* ▷ pod
podgy *adj* (-gier, -giest) short and fat
podia *n* ▷ podium
podium *n* (*pl* -diums, -dia) small raised platform for a conductor or speaker
podiums *n* ▷ podium

poem *n* (*pl* -s) imaginative piece of writing in rhythmic lines
poems *n* ▷ poem
poep *n* (*pl* -s) (S AFR) (Slang) emission of gas from the anus
poeps *n* ▷ poep
poesies *n* ▷ poesy
poesy *n* (*pl* -sies) (Obs) poetry
poet *n* (*pl* -s) writer of poems
poetic, poetical *adj* of or like poetry > **poetically** *adv*
poetical *adj* ▷ poetic
poetically *adv* ▷ poetic
poetries *n* ▷ poetry
poetry *n* (*pl* -ries) poems
poets *n* ▷ poet
pogrom *n* (*pl* -s) organized persecution and massacre
pogroms *n* ▷ pogrom
poignancies *n* ▷ poignant
poignancy *n* ▷ poignant
poignant *adj* sharply painful to the feelings > **poignancy** *n* (*pl* -cies)
poinsettia *n* (*pl* -s) Central American shrub widely grown for its clusters of scarlet leaves, which resemble petals
poinsettias *n* ▷ poinsettia
point *n* (*pl* -s) main idea in a discussion, argument, etc. ▶ *v* (-s, -ing, -ed) show the direction or position of something or draw attention to it by extending a finger or other pointed object towards it
pointed *adj* having a sharp end ▶ *v* ▷ point > **pointedly** *adv*
pointedly *adv* ▷ pointed
pointer *n* (*pl* -s) helpful hint
pointers *n* ▷ pointer
pointing *v* ▷ point
pointless *adj* meaningless, irrelevant
points *n*, *v* ▷ point
poise *n* (*pl* -s) calm dignified manner
poised *adj* absolutely ready
poises *n* ▷ poise
poison *n* (*pl* -s) substance that kills or injures when swallowed or absorbed ▶ *v* (-s, -ing, -ed) give poison to > **poisoner** *n* (*pl* -s) > **poisonous** *adj*
poisoned *v* ▷ poison
poisoner *n* ▷ poison
poisoners *n* ▷ poison
poisoning *v* ▷ poison
poisonous *adj* ▷ poison
poisons *n*, *v* ▷ poison
poke *v* (-kes, -king, -ked) jab or prod with one's finger, a stick, etc. ▶ *n* (*pl* -s) poking

poked v ▷ poke
poker[1] n (pl -s) metal rod for stirring a fire
poker[2] n (pl -s) card game in which players bet on the hands dealt
pokers n ▷ poker[1, 2]
pokier adj ▷ poky
pokiest adj ▷ poky
poking v ▷ poke
pokes v, n ▷ poke
poky adj (-kier, -kiest) small and cramped
polar adj of or near either of the earth's poles
polarize v (-zes, -zing, -zed) form or cause to form into groups with directly opposite views > **polarization** n (pl -s)
polarization n ▷ polarize
polarizations n ▷ polarize
polarized v ▷ polarize
polarizes v ▷ polarize
polarizing v ▷ polarize
polder n (pl -s) land reclaimed from the sea, esp. in the Netherlands
polders n ▷ polder
pole[1] n (pl -s) long rounded piece of wood etc.
pole[2] n (pl -s) point furthest north or south on the earth's axis of rotation
poleaxe v (-xes, -xing, -xed) hit or stun with a heavy blow
poleaxed v ▷ poleaxe
poleaxes v ▷ poleaxe
poleaxing v ▷ poleaxe
polecat n (pl -s) small animal of the weasel family
polecats n ▷ polecat
polemic [pol-em-ik] n (pl -s) fierce attack on or defence of a particular opinion, belief, etc. > **polemical** adj
polemical adj ▷ polemic
polemics n ▷ polemic
poles n ▷ pole[1, 2]
police n organized force in a state which keeps law and order ▶ v (-ces, -cing, -ced) control or watch over with police or a similar body
policed v ▷ police
policeman, policewoman n (pl -men, -women) member of a police force
policemen n ▷ policeman
polices v ▷ police
policewomen n ▷ policeman
policies n ▷ policy[1, 2]
policing v ▷ police
policy[1] n (pl -cies) plan of action adopted by a person, group, or state
policy[2] n (pl -cies) document containing an insurance contract
polio n (pl -s) disease affecting the spinal

cord, which often causes paralysis (also **poliomyelitis**)
polios n ▷ polio
polish v (-es, -ing, -ed) make smooth and shiny by rubbing ▶ n (pl -es) substance used for polishing
polished adj accomplished ▶ v ▷ polish
polishing v ▷ polish
polishes v, n ▷ polish
polite adj showing consideration for others in one's manners, speech, etc. > **politely** adv > **politeness** n (pl -es)
politely adv ▷ polite
politeness n ▷ polite
politenesses n ▷ politeness
politic adj wise and likely to prove advantageous
political adj of the state, government, or public administration > **politically** adv
politically adv ▷ political
politician n (pl -s) person actively engaged in politics, esp. a member of parliament
politicians n ▷ politician
politics n winning and using of power to govern society
polka n (pl -s) lively 19th-century dance
polkas n ▷ polka
poll n (pl -s) (also **opinion poll**) questioning of a random sample of people to find out general opinion ▶ v (-s, -ing, -ed) receive (votes)
pollarded adj (of a tree) growing very bushy because its top branches have been cut short
polled v ▷ poll
pollen n (pl -s) fine dust produced by flowers to fertilize other flowers
pollens ▷
pollinate v (-tes, -ting, -ted) fertilize with pollen
pollinated v ▷ pollinate
pollinates v ▷ pollinate
pollinating v ▷ pollinate
polling v ▷ poll
polls n, v ▷ poll
pollster n (pl -s) person who conducts opinion polls
pollsters n ▷ pollster
pollute v (-tes, -ting, -ted) contaminate with something poisonous or harmful > **pollution** n (pl -s)
pollutant n (pl -s) something that pollutes
pollutants n ▷ pollutant
polluted v ▷ pollute
pollutes v ▷ pollute
polluting v ▷ pollute
pollution n ▷ pollute

pollutions *n* ▷ pollute

polo *n* (*pl* -**s**) game like hockey played by teams of players on horseback

polonaise *n* (*pl* -**s**) old stately dance

polonaises *n* ▷ polonaise

polonium *n* (*pl* -**s**) (CHEM) radioactive element that occurs in trace amounts in uranium ores

poloniums *n* ▷ polonium

polos *n* ▷ polo

poltergeist *n* (*pl* -**s**) spirit believed to move furniture and throw objects around

poltergeists *n* ▷ poltergeist

poltroon *n* (*pl* -**s**) (*Obs*) utter coward

poltroons *n* ▷ poltroon

polyandries *n* ▷ polyandry

polyandry *n* (*pl* -**ries**) practice of having more than one husband at the same time

polyanthus *n* (*pl* -**es**) garden primrose

polyanthuses *n* ▷ polyanthus

polychromatic *adj* many-coloured

polyester *n* (*pl* -**s**) synthetic material used to make plastics and textile fibres

polyesters *n* ▷ polyester

polygamies *n* ▷ polygamy

polygamist *n* ▷ polygamy

polygamists *n* ▷ polygamy

polygamous *adj* ▷ polygamy

polygamy [pol-**ig**-a-mee] *n* (*pl* -**mies**) practice of having more than one husband or wife at the same time > **polygamous** *adj* > **polygamist** *n* (*pl* -**s**)

polyglot *adj*, *n* (*pl* -**s**) (person) able to speak or write several languages

polyglots *n* ▷ polyglot

polygon *n* (*pl* -**s**) geometrical figure with three or more angles and sides > **polygonal** *adj*

polygonal *adj* ▷ polygon

polygons *n* ▷ polygon

polyhedra *n* ▷ polyhedron

polyhedron *n* (*pl* -**rons**, -**ra**) solid figure with four or more sides

polyhedrons *n* ▷ polyhedron

polymer *n* (*pl* -**s**) chemical compound with large molecules made of simple molecules of the same kind

polymerize *v* (-**zes**, -**zing**, -**zed**) form into polymers > **polymerization** *n* (*pl* -**s**)

polymerization *n* ▷ polymerize

polymerizations *n* ▷ polymerize

polymerized *v* ▷ polymerize

polymerizes *v* ▷ polymerize

polymerizing *v* ▷ polymerize

polymers *n* ▷ polymer

polyp *n* (*pl* -**s**) small simple sea creature with a hollow cylindrical body

polyps *n* ▷ polyp

polyphonic *adj* (MUSIC) consisting of several melodies played simultaneously

polystyrene *n* (*pl* -**s**) synthetic material used esp. as white rigid foam for packing and insulation

polystyrenes *n* ▷ polystyrene

polytechnic *n* (*pl* -**s**) (in New Zealand and formerly in Britain) college offering courses in many subjects at and below degree level

polytechnics *n* ▷ polytechnic

polytheism *n* (*pl* -**s**) belief in many gods > **polytheistic** *adj*

polytheisms *n* ▷ polytheism

polytheistic *n* ▷ polytheism

polythene *n* (*pl* -**s**) light plastic used for bags etc.

polythenes *n* ▷ polythene

polyunsaturated *adj* of a group of fats that do not form cholesterol in the blood

polyurethane *n* (*pl* -**s**) synthetic material used esp. in paints

polyurethanes *n* ▷ polyurethane

pom *n* (*pl* -**s**) (AUST & NZ) (*Slang*) person from England (*also* **pommy**) (*pl* -**mmies**)

pomander *n* (*pl* -**s**) (container for) a mixture of sweet-smelling petals, herbs, etc.

pomanders *n* ▷ pomander

pomegranate *n* (*pl* -**s**) round tropical fruit with a thick rind containing many seeds in a red pulp

pomegranates *n* ▷ pomegranate

pommel *n* (*pl* -**s**) raised part on the front of a saddle

pommels *n* ▷ pommel

pommies *n* ▷ pom

pommy *n* ▷ pom

poms *n* ▷ pom

pomp *n* (*pl* -**s**) stately display or ceremony

pomps *n* ▷ pomp

pompom *n* (*pl* -**s**) decorative ball of tufted wool, silk, etc.

pompoms *n* ▷ pompom

pomposities *n* ▷ pompous

pomposity *n* ▷ pompous

pompous *adj* foolishly serious and grand, self-important > **pompously** *adv* > **pomposity** *n* (*pl* -**ties**)

pompously *adv* ▷ pompous

poncho *n* (*pl* -**os**) loose circular cloak with a hole for the head

ponchos *n* ▷ poncho

pond *n* (*pl* -**s**) small area of still water

ponds *n* ▷ pond

ponder *v* (-**s**, -**ing**, -**ed**) think thoroughly or

deeply (about)
pondered v ▷ **ponder**
pondering v ▷ **ponder**
ponderous adj serious and dull > **ponderously** adv
ponderously adv ▷ **ponderous**
ponders v ▷ **ponder**
pong v, n (pl -s) (Informal) (give off) a strong unpleasant smell
pongs n ▷ **pong**
ponies n ▷ **pony**
pontiff n (pl -s) the Pope
pontiffs n ▷ **pontiff**
pontificate v (-tes, -ting, -ted) state one's opinions as if they were the only possible correct ones ▶ n (pl -s) period of office of a Pope
pontificated v ▷ **pontificate**
pontificates v, n ▷ **pontificate**
pontificating v ▷ **pontificate**
pontoon[1] n (pl -s) floating platform supporting a temporary bridge
pontoon[2] n (pl -s) gambling card game
pontoons n ▷ **pontoon**[1, 2]
pony n (pl -nies) small horse
ponytail n (pl -s) long hair tied in one bunch at the back of the head
ponytails n ▷ **ponytail**
poodle n (pl -s) dog with curly hair often clipped fancifully
poodles n ▷ **poodle**
pool[1] n (pl -s) small body of still water
pool[2] n (pl -s) shared fund or group of workers or resources ▶ pl (BRIT) ▷ **football pools** ▶ v (-s, -ing, -ed) put in a common fund
pooled v ▷ **pool**[2]
pooling v ▷ **pool**[2]
pools n, v ▷ **pool**[1, 2]
poop n (pl -s) raised part at the back of a sailing ship
poops n ▷ **poop**
poor adj having little money and few possessions
poorlier adj ▷ **poorly**
poorliest adj ▷ **poorly**
poorly adv in a poor manner ▶ adj (-lier, -liest) not in good health
pop[1] v (-s, -pping, -pped) make or cause to make a small explosive sound (Informal) ▶ n small explosive sound (BRIT)
pop[2] n (pl -s) music of general appeal, esp. to young people
pop[3] n (pl -s) (Informal) father
popcorn n (pl -s) grains of maize heated until they puff up and burst

popcorns n ▷ **popcorn**
pope n (pl -s) head of the Roman Catholic Church
popes n ▷ **pope**
poplar n (pl -s) tall slender tree
poplars n ▷ **poplar**
poplin n (pl -s) ribbed cotton material
poplins n ▷ **poplin**
poppadom n (pl -s) thin round crisp Indian bread
poppadoms n ▷ **poppadom**
popped v ▷ **pop**[1]
poppies n ▷ **poppy**
popping v ▷ **pop**[1]
poppy n (pl -ppies) plant with a large red flower
pops n ▷ **pop**
populace n (pl -s) the ordinary people
populaces n ▷ **populace**
popular adj widely liked and admired > **popularly** adv > **popularity** n (pl -ties)
popularize v (-zes, -zing, -zed) make popular
popularized v ▷ **popularize**
popularizes v ▷ **popularize**
popularizing v ▷ **popularize**
popularities n ▷ **popular**
popularity n ▷ **popular**
popularly adv ▷ **popular**
populate v (-tes, -ting, -ted) live in, inhabit
populated v ▷ **populate**
populates v ▷ **populate**
populating v ▷ **populate**
population n (pl -s) all the people who live in a particular place
populations n ▷ **population**
populous adj densely populated
porbeagle n (pl -s) kind of shark
porbeagles n ▷ **porbeagle**
porcelain n (pl -s) fine china
porcelains n ▷ **porcelain**
porch n (pl -es) covered approach to the entrance of a building
porches n ▷ **porch**
porcine adj of or like a pig
porcupine n (pl -s) animal covered with long pointed quills
porcupines n ▷ **porcupine**
pore n (pl -s) tiny opening in the skin or in the surface of a plant
pores n ▷ **pore**
pork n (pl -s) pig meat
porker n (pl -s) pig raised for food
porkers n ▷ **porker**
porks n ▷ **pork**
porn, porno adj, n (pl -s) (Informal)
▷ **pornography, pornographic**

pornographies n ▷ pornography
pornography n (pl **-hies**) writing, films, or pictures designed to be sexually exciting > **pornographic** adj
pornographer n (pl **-s**) producer of pornography
pornographers n ▷ pornographer
pornographic n ▷ pornography
pornos n ▷ porn
porns n ▷ porn
porosities n ▷ porous
porosity n ▷ porous
porous adj allowing liquid to pass through gradually > **porosity** n (pl **-ties**)
porphyries n ▷ porphyry
porphyry [por-fir-ee] n (pl **-ries**) reddish rock with large crystals in it
porpoise n (pl **-s**) fishlike sea mammal
porpoises n ▷ porpoise
porridge n (pl **-s**) breakfast food made of oatmeal cooked in water or milk
porridges n ▷ porridge
port¹ n (pl **-s**) (town with) a harbour
port² n (pl **-s**) left side of a ship or aircraft when facing the front of it
port³ n (pl **-s**) strong sweet wine, usu. red
port⁴ n (pl **-s**) opening in the side of a ship
portabilities n ▷ portable
portability n ▷ portable
portable adj easily carried > **portability** n (pl **-ties**)
portal n (pl **-s**) large imposing doorway or gate
portals n ▷ portal
portcullis n (pl **-es**) grating suspended above a castle gateway, that can be lowered to block the entrance
portcullises n ▷ portcullis
portend v (**-s, -ing, -ed**) be a sign of
portended v ▷ portend
portending v ▷ portend
portends v ▷ portend
portent n (pl **-s**) sign of a future event
portentous adj of great or ominous significance
portents n ▷ portent
porter¹ n (pl **-s**) man who carries luggage
porter² n (pl **-s**) doorman or gatekeeper of a building
porters n ▷ porter¹, ²
portfolio n (pl **-s**) (flat case for carrying) examples of an artist's work
portfolios n ▷ portfolio
porthole n (pl **-s**) small round window in a ship or aircraft
portholes n ▷ porthole

portico n (pl **-coes, -cos**) porch or covered walkway with columns supporting the roof
porticoes n ▷ portico
porticos n ▷ portico
portion n (pl **-s**) part or share
portions n ▷ portion
portlier adj ▷ portly
portliest adj ▷ portly
portly adj (**-lier, -liest**) rather fat
portmanteau n (pl **-eaus, -eaux**) (Old-fashioned) large suitcase that opens into two compartments ▶ adj combining aspects of different things
portmanteaus n ▷ portmanteau
portmanteaux n ▷ portmanteau
portrait n (pl **-s**) picture of a person
portraits n ▷ portrait
portray v (**-s, -ing, -ed**) describe or represent by artistic means, as in writing or film > **portrayal** n (pl **-s**)
portrayal n ▷ portray
portrayals n ▷ portray
portrayed v ▷ portray
portraying v ▷ portray
portrays v ▷ portray
ports n ▷ port¹, ², ³, ⁴
pose v (**-ses, -sing, -sed**) place in or take up a particular position to be photographed or drawn ▶ n (pl **-s**) position while posing
posed v ▷ pose
poser n (pl **-s**) puzzling question
posers n ▷ poser
poses v, n ▷ pose
poseur n (pl **-s**) person who behaves in an affected way to impress others
poseurs n ▷ poseur
posies n ▷ posy
posing v ▷ pose
posh adj (Informal) smart, luxurious
posit [pozz-it] v (**-s, -ing, -ed**) lay down as a basis for argument
posited v ▷ posit
positing v ▷ posit
position n (pl **-s**) place ▶ v (**-s, -ing, -ed**) place
positioned v ▷ position
positioning v ▷ position
positions n, v ▷ position
posits v ▷ posit
positive adj feeling no doubts, certain (MATHS) > **positively** adv
positively adv ▷ positive
positron n (pl **-s**) (PHYSICS) particle with same mass as electron but positive charge
positrons n ▷ positron
posse [poss-ee] n (pl **-s**) (US) group of men

organized to maintain law and order

posses *n* ▷ **posse**

possess *v* (-es, -ing, -ed) have as one's property > **possessor** *n* (*pl* -s)

possessed *v* ▷ **possess**

possesses *v* ▷ **possess**

possessing *v* ▷ **possess**

possession *n* (*pl* -s) state of possessing, ownership ▶ *pl* things a person possesses

possessions *n* ▷ **possession**

possessive *adj* wanting all the attention or love of another person > **possessiveness** *n*

possessiveness *n* ▷ **possessive**

possessor *n* ▷ **possess**

possessors *n* ▷ **possess**

possibilities *n* ▷ **possibility**

possibility *n* ▷ **possible**

possible *adj* able to exist, happen, or be done ▶ *n* (*pl* -s) person or thing that might be suitable or chosen > **possibility** *n* (*pl* -ties)

possibles *n* ▷ **possible**

possibly *adv* perhaps, not necessarily

possum *n* (*pl* -s) ▷ **opossum** (AUST & NZ) ▷ **phalanger**

possums *n* ▷ **possum**

post¹ *n* (*pl* -s) official system of delivering letters and parcels ▶ *v* (-s, -ing, -ed) send by post > **postal** *adj*

post² *n* (*pl* -s) length of wood, concrete, etc. fixed upright to support or mark something ▶ *v* (-s, -ing, -ed) put up (a notice) in a public place

post³ *n* (*pl* -s) job ▶ *v* (-s, -ing, -ed) send (a person) to a new place to work

postage *n* charge for sending a letter or parcel by post

postages *n* ▷ **postage**

postal *adj* ▷ **post¹**

postbag *n* (*pl* -s) postman's bag

postbags *n* ▷ **postbag**

postcard *n* (*pl* -s) card for sending a message by post without an envelope

postcards *n* ▷ **postcard**

postcode *n* system of letters and numbers used to aid the sorting of mail

postcodes *n* ▷ **postcode**

postdate *v* (-tes, -ting, -ted) write a date on (a cheque) that is later than the actual date

postdated *v* ▷ **postdate**

postdates *v* ▷ **postdate**

postdating *v* ▷ **postdate**

posted *v* ▷ **post¹, ², ³**

poster *n* (*pl* -s) large picture or notice stuck on a wall

posterior *n* (*pl* -s) buttocks ▶ *adj* behind, at

the back of

posteriors *n* ▷ **posterior**

posterities *n* ▷ **posterity**

posterity *n* (*pl* -ties) future generations, descendants

postern *n* (*pl* -s) small back door or gate

posterns *n* ▷ **postern**

posters *n* ▷ **poster**

postgraduate *n* (*pl* -s) person with a degree who is studying for a more advanced qualification

postgraduates *n* ▷ **postgraduate**

posthaste *adv* with great speed

posthumous [poss-tume-uss] *adj* occurring after one's death > **posthumously** *adv*

posthumously *adv* ▷ **posthumous**

postie *n* (*pl* -s) (SCOT, AUST & NZ) (*Informal*) postman

posties *n* ▷ **postie**

postilion, postillion *n* (*pl* -s) (HIST) person riding one of a pair of horses drawing a carriage

postilions *n* ▷ **postilion**

postillion *n* ▷ **postilion**

postillions *n* ▷ **postilion**

posting *v* ▷ **post¹, ², ³**

postman, postwoman *n* (*pl* -men, -women) person who collects and delivers post

postmark *n* (*pl* -s) official mark stamped on letters showing place and date of posting

postmarks *n* ▷ **postmark**

postmen *n* ▷ **postman**

postmaster, postmistress *n* (*pl* -s, -es) (in some countries) official in charge of a post office

postmasters *n* ▷ **postmaster**

postmistress *n* ▷ **postmaster**

postmistresses *n* ▷ **postmaster**

postmortem ▶ *n* (*pl* -s) medical examination of a body to establish the cause of death

postmortems *n* ▷ **postmortem**

postnatal *adj* occurring after childbirth

postpone *v* (-nes, -ning, -ned) put off to a later time > **postponement** *n* (*pl* -s)

postponed *v* ▷ **postpone**

postponement *n* ▷ **postpone**

postponements *n* ▷ **postpone**

postpones *v* ▷ **postpone**

postponing *v* ▷ **postpone**

posts *n*, *v* ▷ **post¹, ², ³**

postscript *n* (*pl* -s) passage added at the end of a letter

postscripts *n* ▷ **postscript**

postulant *n* (*pl* -s) candidate for admission to a religious order

postulants *n* ▷ **postulant**
postulate *v* (**-tes, -ting, -ted**) assume to be true as the basis of an argument or theory
postulated *v* ▷ **postulate**
postulates *v* ▷ **postulate**
postulating *v* ▷ **postulate**
posture *n* (*pl* **-s**) position or way in which someone stands, walks, etc. ▶ *v* (**-res, -ring, -red**) behave in an exaggerated way to get attention
postured *v* ▷ **posture**
postures *n, v* ▷ **posture**
posturing *v* ▷ **posture**
postwomen *n* ▷ **postman**
posy *n* (*pl* **-sies**) small bunch of flowers
pot[1] *n* (*pl* **-s**) round deep container ▶ *pl* (*Informal*) large amount ▶ *v* (**-s, -tting, -tted**) plant in a pot
pot[2] *n* (*Slang*) cannabis
potted *adj* grown in a pot ▶ *v* ▷ **pot**[1]
potting *v* ▷ **pot**[1]
pots *n* ▷ **pot**[1]
potable [pote-a-bl] *adj* drinkable
potash *n* (*pl* **-es**) white powdery substance obtained from ashes and used as fertilizer
potashes *n* ▷ **potash**
potassium *n* (*pl* **-s**) (CHEM) silvery metallic element
potassiums *n* ▷ **potassium**
potato ▶ *n* (*pl* **-oes**) roundish starchy vegetable that grows underground
potatoes *n* ▷ **potato**
poteen *n* (*pl* **-s**) (in Ireland) illegally made alcoholic drink
poteens *n* ▷ **poteen**
potencies *n* ▷ **potent**
potency *n* ▷ **potent**
potent *adj* having great power or influence > **potency** *n* (*pl* **-cies**)
potentate *n* (*pl* **-s**) ruler or monarch
potentates *n* ▷ **potentate**
potential *adj* possible but not yet actual ▶ *n* (*pl* **-s**) ability or talent not yet fully used > **potentially** *adv* > **potentiality** *n* (*pl* **-ties**)
potentialities *n* ▷ **potential**
potentiality *n* ▷ **potential**
potentially *adv* ▷ **potential**
potentials *n* ▷ **potential**
pothole *n* (*pl* **-s**) hole in the surface of a road
potholer *n* ▷ **potholing**
potholers *n* ▷ **potholing**
potholes *n* ▷ **pothole**
potholing *n* (*pl* **-s**) sport of exploring underground caves > **potholer** *n* (*pl* **-s**)
potholings *n* ▷ **potholing**

potion *n* (*pl* **-s**) dose of medicine or poison
potions *n* ▷ **potion**
potoroo *n* (*pl* **-s**) Australian leaping rodent
potoroos *n* ▷ **potoroo**
potpourri [po-poor-ee] *n* (*pl* **-s**) fragrant mixture of dried flower petals
potpourris *n* ▷ **potpourri**
pottage *n* (*pl* **-s**) (*Old-fashioned*) thick soup or stew
pottages *n* ▷ **pottage**
potter[1] *n* (*pl* **-s**) person who makes pottery
potter[2] *v* (**-s, -ing, -ed**) be busy in a pleasant but aimless way
pottered *v* ▷ **potter**[2]
potteries *n* ▷ **pottery**
pottering *v* ▷ **potter**[2]
potters *n, v* ▷ **potter**[1, 2]
pottery *n* (*pl* **-ries**) articles made from baked clay
pottier *adj* ▷ **potty**
potties *n* ▷ **potty**[2]
pottiest *adj* ▷ **potty**
potty[1] *adj* (**-ttier, -ttiest**) (*Informal*) crazy or silly
potty[2] *n* (*pl* **-tries**) bowl used by a small child as a toilet
pouch *n* (*pl* **-es**) small bag
pouches *n* ▷ **pouch**
pouf, pouffe [poof] *n* (*pl* **-s**) large solid cushion used as a seat
pouffe *n* ▷ **pouf**
pouffes *n* ▷ **pouf**
poufs *n* ▷ **pouf**
poulterer *n* (*pl* **-s**) (BRIT) person who sells poultry
poulterers *n* ▷ **poulterer**
poultice [pole-tiss] *n* (*pl* **-s**) moist dressing, often heated, applied to inflamed skin
poultices *n* ▷ **poultice**
poultries *n* ▷ **poultry**
poultry *n* (*pl* **-ries**) domestic fowls
pounce *v* (**-ces, -cing, -ced**) spring upon suddenly to attack or capture ▶ *n* (*pl* **-s**) pouncing
pounced *v* ▷ **pounce**
pouncing *v* ▷ **pounce**
pounces *v, n* ▷ **pounce**
pound[1] *n* (*pl* **-s**) monetary unit of Britain and some other countries
pound[2] *v* (**-s, -ing, -ed**) hit heavily and repeatedly
pound[3] *n* (*pl* **-s**) enclosure for stray animals or officially removed vehicles
pounded *v* ▷ **pound**[2]
pounding *v* ▷ **pound**[2]
pounds *n, v* ▷ **pound**[1, 3]

pour v (**-s, -ing, -ed**) flow or cause to flow out in a stream
  poured v ▷ **pour**
  pouring v ▷ **pour**
  pours v ▷ **pour**
pout v (**-s, -ing, -ed**) thrust out one's lips, look sulky ▶ n (pl **-s**) pouting look
  pouted v ▷ **pout**
  pouting v ▷ **pout**
  pouts v, n ▷ **pout**
  poverties n ▷ **poverty**
poverty n (pl **-ties**) state of being without enough food or money
powder n (pl **-s**) substance in the form of tiny loose particles ▶ v (**-s, -ing, -ed**) apply powder to > **powdery** adj (**-rier, -riest**)
powdered adj, v ▷ **powder**
  powderier adj ▷ **powder**
  powderiest adj ▷ **powder**
  powdering v ▷ **powder**
  powders n, v ▷ **powder**
power n (pl **-s**) ability to do or act > **powerful** adj > **powerless** adj
powered adj having or operated by mechanical or electrical power
  powerful adj ▷ **power**
  powerless adj ▷ **power**
  powers n ▷ **power**
powwow n (pl **-s**) (*Informal*) talk or conference
  powwows n ▷ **powwow**
pox n (pl **-es**) disease in which skin pustules form
  poxes n ▷ **pox**

> **poz** adj. Poz is an old-fashioned short form of **positive.** This is a good word for a crowded board towards the end of the game, especially if you can form another word in the process, or form it on a bonus square. Poz scores 24 points.

practicabilities n ▷ **practicable**
practicability n ▷ **practicable**
practicable adj capable of being done successfully > **practicability** n (pl **-ties**)
practical adj involving experience or actual use rather than theory ▶ n (pl **-s**) examination in which something has to be done or made > **practically** adv
  practically adv ▷ **practical**
  practicals n ▷ **practical**
practice n (pl **-s**) something done regularly or habitually
  practices n ▷ **practice**
practise v (**-ses, -sing, -sed**) do repeatedly so as to gain skill

  practised v ▷ **practise**
  practises v ▷ **practise**
  practising v ▷ **practise**
practitioner n (pl **-s**) person who practises a profession
  practitioners n ▷ **practitioner**
pragmatic adj concerned with practical consequences rather than theory > **pragmatism** n (pl **-s**) > **pragmatist** n (pl **-s**)
  pragmatism n ▷ **pragmatic**
  pragmatisms n ▷ **pragmatic**
  pragmatist n ▷ **pragmatic**
  pragmatists n ▷ **pragmatic**
prairie n (pl **-s**) large treeless area of grassland, esp. in N America and Canada
  prairies n ▷ **prairie**
praise v (**-ses, -sing, -sed**) express approval or admiration of (someone or something) ▶ n (pl **-s**) something said or written to show approval or admiration > **praiseworthy** adj
  praised v ▷ **praise**
  praises v, n ▷ **praise**
  praiseworthy adj ▷ **praise**
  praising v ▷ **praise**
praline [prah-leen] n (pl **-s**) sweet made of nuts and caramelized sugar
  pralines n ▷ **praline**
pram n (pl **-s**) four-wheeled carriage for a baby, pushed by hand
  prams n ▷ **pram**
prance v (**-ces, -cing, -ced**) walk with exaggerated bouncing steps
  pranced v ▷ **prance**
  prances v ▷ **prance**
  prancing v ▷ **prance**
prang v, n (pl **-s**) (*Slang*) (have) a crash in a car or aircraft
  prangs n ▷ **prang**
prank n (pl **-s**) mischievous trick
  pranks n ▷ **prank**
prat n (pl **-s**) (BRIT, AUST & NZ) (*Informal*) stupid person
  prats n ▷ **prat**
prattle v (**-les, -ling, -led**) chatter in a childish or foolish way ▶ n (pl **-s**) childish or foolish talk
  prattled v ▷ **prattle**
  prattles v, n ▷ **prattle**
  prattling v ▷ **prattle**
prawn n (pl **-s**) edible shellfish like a large shrimp
  prawns n ▷ **prawn**
praxis n (pl **praxises**) practice as opposed to theory
  praxises n ▷ **praxis**
pray v (**-s, -ing, -ed**) say prayers

prayed v ▷ **pray**

prayer n (pl -s) thanks or appeal addressed to one's God

prayers n ▷ **prayer**

praying v ▷ **pray**

prays v ▷ **pray**

preach v (-es, -ing, -ed) give a talk on a religious theme as part of a church service

preached v ▷ **preach**

preaches v ▷ **preach**

preaching v ▷ **preach**

preacher n (pl -s) person who preaches, esp. in church

preachers n ▷ **preacher**

preamble n (pl -s) introductory part to something said or written

preambles n ▷ **preamble**

prearranged adj arranged beforehand

prebendaries n ▷ **prebendary**

prebendary n (pl -ries) clergyman who is a member of the chapter of a cathedral

precarious adj insecure, unsafe, likely to fall or collapse > **precariously** adv

precariously adv ▷ **precarious**

precaution n (pl -s) action taken in advance to prevent something bad happening > **precautionary** adj

precautionary adj ▷ **precaution**

precautions n ▷ **precaution**

precede v (-des, -ding, -ded) go or be before

preceded v ▷ **precede**

precedence [press-ee-denss] n (pl -s) formal order of rank or position

precedences n ▷ **precedence**

precedent n (pl -s) previous case or occurrence regarded as an example to be followed

precedents n ▷ **precedent**

precedes v ▷ **precede**

preceding v ▷ **precede**

precentor n (pl -s) person who leads the singing in a church

precentors n ▷ **precentor**

precept n (pl -s) rule of behaviour > **preceptive** adj

preceptive adj ▷ **precept**

precepts n ▷ **precept**

precinct n (pl -s) (BRIT, AUST & S AFR) area in a town closed to traffic ▶ pl surrounding region

precincts n ▷ **precinct**

precious adj of great value and importance

precipice n (pl -s) very steep face of cliff or rockface

precipices n ▷ **precipice**

precipitate v (-tes, -ting, -ted) cause to happen suddenly ▶ adj done rashly or hastily

▶ n (pl -s) (CHEM) substance precipitated from a solution > **precipitately** adv > **precipitation** n (pl -s) precipitating

precipitated v, n ▷ **precipitate**

precipitately adv ▷ **precipitate**

precipitates v, n ▷ **precipitate**

precipitating v ▷ **precipitate**

precipitation n ▷ **precipitate**

precipitations n ▷ **precipitate**

precipitous adj sheer

précis [pray-see] n (pl **précis**) short written summary of a longer piece ▶ v (-ses, -sing, -sed) make a précis of

precise adj (-r, -st) exact, accurate in every detail > **precisely** adv > **precision** n (pl -s)

précised v ▷ **précis**

précises v ▷ **précis**

precisely adv ▷ **precise**

preciser adj ▷ **precise**

precisest adj ▷ **precise**

précising v ▷ **précis**

precision n ▷ **precise**

precisions n ▷ **precise**

preclude v (-des, -ding, -ded) make impossible to happen

precluded v ▷ **preclude**

precludes v ▷ **preclude**

precluding v ▷ **preclude**

precocious adj having developed or matured early or too soon > **precocity** n (pl -ties)

precocities n ▷ **precocious**

precocity n ▷ **precocious**

precognition n (pl -s) alleged ability to foretell the future

precognitions n ▷ **precognition**

preconceived adj (of an idea) formed without real experience or reliable information > **preconception** n (pl -s)

preconception n ▷ **preconceived**

preconceptions n ▷ **preconcieve**

precondition n (pl -s) something that must happen or exist before something else can

preconditions n ▷ **precondition**

precursor n (pl -s) something that precedes and is a signal of something else, forerunner

precursors n ▷ **precursor**

predate v (-tes, -ting, -ted) occur at an earlier date than

predated v ▷ **predate**

predates v ▷ **predate**

predating v ▷ **predate**

predator n (pl -s) predatory animal

predators n ▷ **predators**

predatory [pred-a-tree] adj habitually hunting and killing other animals for food

predecease v (-ses, -sing, -sed) die before (someone else)
predeceased v ▷ predecease
predeceases v ▷ predecease
predeceasing v ▷ predecease
predecessor n (pl -s) person who precedes another in an office or position
predecessors n ▷ predecessor
predestination n (pl -s) (THEOLOGY) belief that future events have already been decided by God or fate > **predestined** adj
predestinations n ▷ predestine
predestined adj ▷ predestination
predetermined adj decided in advance
predicament n (pl -s) embarrassing or difficult situation
predicaments n ▷ predicament
predicate n (pl -tes) (GRAMMAR) part of a sentence in which something is said about the subject, e.g. went home in I went home ▶ v (-tes, -ting, -ted) declare or assert
predicated v ▷ predicate
predicates n, v ▷ predicate
predicating v ▷ predicate
predict v (-s, -ing, -ed) tell about in advance, prophesy > **predictable** adj > **prediction** n (pl -s)
predictable adj ▷ predict
predicted v ▷ predict
predicting v ▷ predict
prediction n ▷ predict
predictions n ▷ predict
predictive adj relating to or able to make predictions
predicts v ▷ predict
predilection n (pl -s) (Formal) preference or liking
predilections n ▷ predilection
predispose v (-ses, -sing, -sed) influence (someone) in favour of something > **predisposition** n (pl -s)
predisposed v ▷ predispose
predisposes v ▷ predispose
predisposing v ▷ predispose
predisposition n ▷ predispose
predispositions n ▷ predispose
predominate v (-tes, -ting, -ted) be the main or controlling element > **predominance** n (pl -s) > **predominant** adj > **predominantly** adv
predominance n ▷ predominances
predominances n ▷ predominance
predominant n ▷ predominate
predominantly adv ▷ predominate
predominated v ▷ predominate
predominates v ▷ predominate

predominating v ▷ predominate
preen v (-s, -ing, -ed) (of a bird) clean or trim (feathers) with the beak
preened v ▷ preen
preening v ▷ preen
preens v ▷ preen
prefab n (pl -s) prefabricated house
prefabricated adj (of a building) manufactured in shaped sections for rapid assembly on site
prefabs n ▷ prefab
preface [pref-iss] n (pl -s) introduction to a book ▶ v (-ces, -cing, -ced) serve as an introduction to (a book, speech, etc.) > **prefatory** adj
prefaced v ▷ preface
prefaces n, v ▷ preface
prefacing v ▷ preface
prefatory adj ▷ preface
prefect n (pl -s) senior pupil in a school, with limited power over others
prefects n ▷ prefect
prefecture n (pl -s) office or area of authority of a prefect
prefectures n ▷ prefecture
prefer v (-s, -rring, -rred) like better > **preference** n (pl -s)
preferable adj more desirable > **preferably** adv
preferably adv ▷ preferable
preference n ▷ prefer
preferences n ▷ prefer
preferential adj showing preference
preferment n (pl -s) promotion or advancement
preferments n ▷ preferment
preferred v ▷ prefer
preferring v ▷ prefer
prefers v ▷ prefer
prefigure v (-res, -ring, -red) represent or suggest in advance
prefigured v ▷ prefigure
prefigures v ▷ prefigure
prefiguring v ▷ prefigure
prefix n (pl -es) letter or group of letters put at the beginning of a word to make a new word, such as un- in unhappy ▶ v (-es, -ing, -ed) put as an introduction or prefix (to)
prefixed v ▷ prefix
prefixes n, v ▷ prefix
prefixing v ▷ prefix
pregnacies n ▷ pregnant
pregnancy n ▷ pregnant
pregnant adj carrying a fetus in the womb > **pregnancy** n (pl -cies)
prehensile adj capable of grasping

prehistoric *adj* of the period before written history begins > **prehistory** *n* (*pl* -ries)
prehistories *n* ▷ **prehistoric**
prehistory *n* ▷ **prehistoric**
prejudice *n* (*pl* -s) unreasonable or unfair dislike or preference ▸ *v* (-ces, -cing, -ced) cause (someone) to have a prejudice > **prejudicial** *adj* disadvantageous, harmful
prejudiced *v* ▷ **prejudice**
prejudicial *adj* ▷ **prejudice**
prejudicing *v* ▷ **prejudice**
prejudices *n, v* ▷ **prejudice**
prelate [**prel**-it] *n* (*pl* -s) bishop or other churchman of high rank
prelates *n* ▷ **prelate**
preliminaries *n* ▷ **preliminary**
preliminary *adj* happening before and in preparation, introductory ▸ *n* (*pl* -ries) preliminary remark, contest, etc.
prelude *n* (*pl* -s) introductory movement in music
preludes *n* ▷ **prelude**
premarital *adj* occurring before marriage
premature *adj* happening or done before the normal or expected time > **prematurely** *adv*
prematurely *adv* ▷ **premature**
premeditated *adj* planned in advance > **premeditation** *n* (*pl* -s)
premeditation *n* ▷ **premeditated**
premeditations *n* ▷ **premeditated**
premenstrual *adj* occurring or experienced before a menstrual period
premier *n* (*pl* -s) prime minister ▸ *adj* chief, leading > **premiership** *n* (*pl* -s)
première *n* (*pl* -s) first performance of a play, film, etc.
premières *n* ▷ **première**
premiers *n* ▷ **premier**
premiership *n* ▷ **premier**
premierships *n* ▷ **premier**
premise, premiss *n* (*pl* -s, -es) statement assumed to be true and used as the basis of reasoning
premises *n* ▷ **premise**
premises *pl n* house or other building and its land
premisses *n* ▷ **premise**
premium *n* (*pl* -s) additional sum of money, as on a wage or charge
premiums *n* ▷ **premium**
premonition *n* (*pl* -s) feeling that something unpleasant is going to happen; foreboding > **premonitory** *adj*
premonitions *n* ▷ **premonition**
premonitory *adj* ▷ **premonition**

prenatal *adj* before birth, during pregnancy
preoccupied *v* ▷ **preoccupy**
preoccupies *v* ▷ **preoccupy**
preoccupy *v* (-pied, -pying, -pied) fill the thoughts or attention of (someone) to the exclusion of other things > **preoccupation** *n* (*pl* -s)
preoccupation *n* ▷ **preoccupy**
preoccupations *n* ▷ **preoccupy**
preoccupying *v* ▷ **preoccupy**
preordained *adj* decreed or determined in advance
prep. preparatory
prepacked *adj* sold already wrapped
prepaid *adj* paid for in advance
prepare *v* (-res, -ring, -red) make or get ready
preparation *n* (*pl* -s) preparing
preparations *n* ▷ **preparation**
preparatory [prip-**par**-a-tree] *adj* preparing for
prepared *adj* willing ▸ *v* ▷ **prepare**
prepares *v* ▷ **prepare**
preparing *v* ▷ **prepare**
preponderance *n* (*pl* -s) greater force, amount, or influence > **preponderant** *adj*
preponderances *adj* ▷ **preponderance**
preponderant *adj* ▷ **preponderance**
preposition *n* (*pl* -s) word used before a noun or pronoun to show its relationship with other words, such as *by* in *go by bus* > **prepositional** *adj*
prepositional *n* ▷ **preposition**
prepositions *n* ▷ **preposition**
prepossessing *adj* making a favourable impression, attractive
preposterous *adj* utterly absurd
prepuce [**pree**-pyewss] *n* (*pl* -s) retractable fold of skin covering the tip of the penis, foreskin
prepuces *n* ▷ **prepuce**
prerecorded *adj* recorded in advance to be played or broadcast later
prerequisite *adj, n* (*pl* -s) (something) required before something else is possible
prerequisites *n* ▷ **prerequisite**
prerogative *n* (*pl* -s) special power or privilege
prerogatives *n* ▷ **prerogative**
presage [**press**-ij] *v* (-ges, -ging, -ged) be a sign or warning of
presaged *v* ▷ **presage**
presages *v* ▷ **presage**
presaging *v* ▷ **presage**
presbyteries *n* ▷ **presbytery**
presbytery *n* (*pl* -ies) (PRESBYTERIAN CHURCH) local church court
prescience [**press**-ee-enss] *n* (*pl* -s) knowledge of events before they happen > **prescient** *adj*

presciences n ▷ **prescience**
prescient adj ▷ **prescience**
prescribe v (-bes, -bing, -bed) recommend the use of (a medicine)
prescribed v ▷ **prescribe**
prescribes v ▷ **prescribe**
prescribing v ▷ **prescribe**
prescription n written instructions from a doctor for the making up and use of a medicine
prescriptions n ▷ **prescription**
prescriptive adj laying down rules
presence n (pl -s) fact of being in a specified place
presences n ▷ **presence**
present[1] adj being in a specified place ▶ n (pl -s) present time or tense
present[2] n something given to bring pleasure to another person ▶ v (-s, -ing, -ed) introduce formally or publicly > **presentation** n (pl -s)
presentable adj attractive, neat, fit for people to see
presented n ▷ **present**[2]
presenter n (pl -s) person introducing a TV or radio show
presenters n ▷ **presenter**
presentiment [priz-**zen**-tim-ent] n (pl -s) sense of something unpleasant about to happen
presentiments n ▷ **presentiment**
presenting v ▷ **present**[2]
presently adv soon (US & SCOT)
presents n, v ▷ **present**[1, 2]
preserve v (-ves, -ving, -ved) keep from being damaged, changed, or ended ▶ n (pl -s) area of interest restricted to a particular person or group > **preservation** n (pl -s)
preservation n ▷ **preserve**
preservations n ▷ **preserve**
preservative n (pl -s) chemical that prevents decay
preservatives n ▷ **preservative**
preserved v ▷ **preserve**
preserves v, n ▷ **preserve**
preserving v ▷ **preserve**
preshrunk adj (of fabric or a garment) having been shrunk during manufacture so that further shrinkage will not occur when washed
preside v (-des, -ding, -ded) be in charge, esp. of a meeting
presided v ▷ **preside**
presidencies n ▷ **president**
presidency n ▷ **president**
president n (pl -s) head of state in many countries > **presidential** adj > **presidency** n

(pl -cies)
presidential n ▷ **president**
presidents n ▷ **president**
presides v ▷ **preside**
presiding v ▷ **preside**
press v (-es, -ing, -ed) apply force or weight to ▶ n (pl -es) printing machine
pressed v ▷ **press**
presses v, n ▷ **press**
pressing adj urgent ▶ v ▷ **press**
presses n ▷ **press**
pressure n (pl -s) force produced by pressing
pressures n ▷ **pressure**
prestidigitation n (pl -s) skilful quickness with the hands, conjuring
prestidigitations n ▷ **prestidigitation**
prestige n (pl -s) high status or respect resulting from success or achievements > **prestigious** adj
prestiges n ▷ **prestige**
prestigious adj ▷ **prestige**
presumed v ▷ **presume**
presto adv (MUSIC) very quickly
prestressed adj (of concrete) containing stretched steel wires to strengthen it
presume v (-mes, -ing, -med) suppose to be the case
presumably adv one supposes (that)
presumed v ▷ **presume**
presumes v ▷ **presume**
presuming v ▷ **presume**
presumption (pl -s) n bold insolent behaviour
presumption n ▷ **presumption**
presumptive adj assumed to be true or valid until the contrary is proved
presumptuous adj doing things one has no right to do
presuppose v (-ses, -sing, -sed) need as a previous condition in order to be true > **presupposition** n (pl -s)
presupposed v ▷ **presuppose**
presupposes v ▷ **presuppose**
presupposing v ▷ **presuppose**
presupposition v ▷ **presuppose**
presuppositions v ▷ **presuppose**
pretence n (pl -s) behaviour intended to deceive, pretending
pretences n ▷ **pretence**
pretend v (-s, -ing, -ed) claim or give the appearance of (something untrue) to deceive or in play
pretended v ▷ **pretend**
pretender n (pl -s) person who makes a false or disputed claim to a position of power
pretenders n ▷ **pretender**

pretending *v* ▷ pretend
pretends *v* ▷ pretend
pretension *n* ▷ pretentious
pretensions *n* ▷ pretentious
pretentious *adj* making (unjustified) claims to special merit or importance > **pretension** *n* (*pl* -**s**)
preternatural *adj* beyond what is natural, supernatural
pretext *n* (*pl* -**s**) false reason given to hide the real one
pretexts *n* ▷ pretext
prettier *adj* ▷ pretty
prettiest *adj* ▷ pretty
prettily *adv* ▷ pretty
prettiness *n* ▷ pretty
prettinesses *n* ▷ pretty
pretty *adj* (-**ttier, -ttiest**) pleasing to look at ▶ *adv* fairly, moderately > **prettily** *adv* > **prettiness** *n* (*pl* -**es**)
pretzel *n* (*pl* -**s**) brittle salted biscuit
pretzels *n* ▷ pretzel
prevail *v* (-**s, -ing, -ed**) gain mastery
prevailed *v* ▷ prevail
prevailing *adj* widespread ▶ *v* ▷ prevail
prevails *v* ▷ prevail
prevalence *n* ▷ prevalent
prevalences *n* ▷ prevalent
prevalent *adj* widespread, common > **prevalence** *n* (*pl* -**s**)
prevaricate *v* (-**tes, -ting, -ted**) avoid giving a direct or truthful answer > **prevarication** *n* (*pl* -**s**)
prevaricated *v* ▷ prevaricate
prevaricates *v* ▷ prevaricate
prevaricating *v* ▷ prevaricate
prevarication *n* ▷ prevaricate
prevarications *n* ▷ prevaricate
prevent *v* (-**s, -ing, -ed**) keep from happening or doing > **preventable** *adj* > **prevention** *n* (*pl* -**s**) > **preventive** *adj*, *n* (*pl* -**s**)
preventable *adj* ▷ prevent
prevented *v* ▷ prevent
preventing *v* ▷ prevent
prevention *n* ▷ prevent
preventions *n* ▷ prevent
preventive *adj*, *n* ▷ prevent
preventives *n* ▷ prevent
prevents *v* ▷ prevent
preview *n* (*pl* -**s**) advance showing of a film or exhibition before it is shown to the public
previews *n* ▷ preview
previous *adj* coming or happening before > **previously** *adv*
previously *adv* ▷ previous

prey *n* (*pl* -**s**) animal hunted and killed for food by another animal
preys *n* ▷ prey
price *n* (*pl* -**s**) amount of money for which a thing is bought or sold ▶ *v* (-**ces, -cing, -ced**) fix or ask the price of
priced *v* ▷ price
priceless *adj* very valuable
prices *n*, *v* ▷ price
pricier *adj* ▷ pricey
priciest *adj* ▷ pricey
pricing *v* ▷ price
pricey *adj* (-**cier, -ciest**) (*Informal*) expensive
prick *v* (-**s, -ing, -ed**) pierce lightly with a sharp point ▶ *n* (*pl* -**s**) sudden sharp pain caused by pricking
pricked *v* ▷ prick
pricking *v* ▷ prick
prickle *n* (*pl* -**s**) thorn or spike on a plant ▶ *v* (-**les, -ling, -led**) have a tingling or pricking sensation > **prickly** *adj* (-**lier, -liest**)
prickled *v* ▷ prickle
prickles *n*, *v* ▷ prickle
pricklier *adj* ▷ prickle
prickliest *adj* ▷ prickle
prickling *v* ▷ prickle
prickly *adj* ▷ prickle
pricks *v*, *n* ▷ prick
pride *n* (*pl* -**s**) feeling of pleasure and satisfaction when one has done well
prides *n* ▷ pride
pried *v* ▷ pry
pries *v* ▷ pry
priest *n* (*pl* -**s**) (in the Christian church) a person who can administer the sacraments and preach > **priestess** *n fem* (*pl* -**es**) > **priesthood** *n* (*pl* -**s**) > **priestly** *adj* (-**lier, -liest**)
priestess *n* ▷ priest
priestesses *n* ▷ priest
priesthood *n* ▷ priest
priesthoods *n* ▷ priest
priestlier *adj* ▷ priest
priestliest *adj* ▷ priest
priestly *adj* ▷ priest
priests *n* ▷ priest
prig *n* (*pl* -**s**) self-righteous person who acts as if superior to others > **priggish** *adj* > **priggishness** *n* (*pl* -**s**)
priggish *adj* ▷ prig
priggishness *n* ▷ prig
prigishnesses *n* ▷ prig
prigs *n* ▷ prig
prim *adj* (-**mmer, -mmest**) formal, proper, and rather prudish > **primly** *adv*
primacies *n* ▷ primacy

primacy *n* (*pl* -**ies**) state of being first in rank, grade, etc.
primaeval *adj* ▷ **primeval**
primal *adj* of basic causes or origins
primarily *adv* ▷ **primary**
primary *adj* chief, most important > **primarily** *adv*
primate¹ *n* (*pl* -**s**) member of an order of mammals including monkeys and humans
primate² *n* (*pl* -**s**) archbishop
primates *n* ▷ **primate¹, ²**
prime *adj* main, most important ▸ *n* (*pl* -**s**) time when someone is at his or her best or most vigorous ▸ *v* (-**mes**, -**ming**, -**med**) give (someone) information in advance to prepare them for something
primed *v* ▷ **prime**
primer *n* (*pl* -**s**) special paint applied to bare wood etc. before the main paint
primers *n* ▷ **primer**
primes *n*, *v* ▷ **prime**
priming *v* ▷ **prime**
primeval [prime-**ee**-val] *adj* of the earliest age of the world
primitive *adj* of an early simple stage of development
primly *adv* ▷ **prim**
primmer *adj* ▷ **prim**
primmest *adj* ▷ **prim**
primogeniture *n* (*pl* -**s**) system under which the eldest son inherits all his parents' property
primogenitures *n* ▷ **primogeniture**
primordial *adj* existing at or from the beginning
primrose *n* (*pl* -**s**) pale yellow spring flower
primroses *n* ▷ **primrose**
primula *n* (*pl* -**s**) type of primrose with brightly coloured flowers
primulas *n* ▷ **primula**
prince *n* (*pl* -**s**) male member of a royal family, esp. the son of the king or queen
princelier *adj* ▷ **princely**
princeliest *adj* ▷ **princely**
princely *adj* (-**lier**, -**liest**) of or like a prince
princess *n* (*pl* -**es**) female member of a royal family, esp. the daughter of the king or queen
princes *n* ▷ **prince**
princesses *n* ▷ **princess**
principal *adj* main, most important ▸ *n* (*pl* -**s**) head of a school or college > **principally** *adv*
principalities *n* ▷ **principality**
principality *n* (*pl* -**ties**) territory ruled by a prince
principally *adv* ▷ **principal**

principals *n* ▷ **principal**
principle *n* (*pl* -**s**) moral rule guiding behaviour
principles *n* ▷ **principle**
print *v* (-**s**, -**ing**, -**ed**) reproduce (a newspaper, book, etc.) in large quantities by mechanical or electronic means ▸ *n* (*pl* -**s**) printed words etc. > **printing** *n* (*pl* -**s**)
printed *v* ▷ **print**
printer *n* (*pl* -**s**) person or company engaged in printing
printers *n* ▷ **printer**
printing *n*, *v* ▷ **print**
printings *n* ▷ **print**
prints *v* ▷ **print**
printing *v* ▷ **print**
printed *v* ▷ **print**
prints *n* ▷ **print**
prior¹ *adj* earlier
prior² *n* (*pl* -**s**) head monk in a priory
prioress *n* (*pl* -**es**) deputy head nun in a convent
prioresses *n* ▷ **prioress**
priories *n* ▷ **priory**
priors *n* ▷ **prior²**
priory *n* (*pl* -**ries**) place where certain orders of monks or nuns live
priors *n* ▷ **prior**
priorities *n* ▷ **priority**
priority *n* (*pl* -**ties**) most important thing that must be dealt with first
prise *v* (-**ses**, -**sing**, -**sed**) force open by levering
prised *v* ▷ **prise**
prises *v* ▷ **prise**
prising *v* ▷ **prise**
prism *n* (*pl* -**s**) transparent block usu. with triangular ends and rectangular sides, used to disperse light into a spectrum or refract it in optical instruments
prismatic *adj* of or shaped like a prism
prisms *n* ▷ **prism**
prison *n* (*pl* -**s**) building where criminals and accused people are held
prisons *n* ▷ **prison**
prisoner *n* (*pl* -**s**) person held captive
prisoners *n* ▷ **prisoner**
prissier *adj* ▷ **prissy**
prissiest *adj* ▷ **prissy**
prissily *adv* ▷ **prissy**
prissy *adj* (-**ssier**, -**ssiest**) prim, correct, and easily shocked > **prissily** *adv*
pristine *adj* clean, new, and unused
privacies *n* ▷ **private**
privacy *n* ▷ **private**
private *adj* for the use of one person or group only ▸ *n* (*pl* -**s**) soldier of the lowest rank

> **privately** adv > **privacy** n (pl -**cies**)
privately adv ▷ **private**
privates n ▷ **private**
privateer n (pl -**s**) (HIST) privately owned armed vessel authorized by the government to take part in a war
  privateers n ▷ **privateer**
privation n (pl -**s**) loss or lack of the necessities of life
  privations n ▷ **privation**
  privatization n ▷ **privatize**
  privatizations n ▷ **privatize**
privatize v (-**zes**, -**zing**, -**zed**) sell (a publicly owned company) to individuals or a private company > **privatization** n (pl -**s**)
  privatized v ▷ **privatize**
  privatizes v ▷ **privatize**
  privatizing v ▷ **privatize**
privet n (pl -**s**) bushy evergreen shrub used for hedges
  privets n ▷ **privet**
  privier adj ▷ **privy**
  privies n ▷ **privy**
  priviest adj ▷ **privy**
privilege n (pl -**s**) advantage or favour that only some people have
privileged adj enjoying a special right or immunity
  privileges n ▷ **privilege**
privy adj (-**vier**, -**viest**) sharing knowledge of something secret ▶ n (pl -**ies**) (Obs) toilet, esp. an outside one
prize[1] n (pl -**s**) reward given for success in a competition etc. ▶ adj winning or likely to win a prize
prize[2] v (-**zes**, -**zing**, -**zed**) value highly
prize[3] v ▷ **prise**
  prized v ▷ **prize**
prizefighter n (pl -**s**) boxer who fights for money
  prizefighters n ▷ **prizefighter**
  prizes n, v ▷ **prize**[1, 2]
  prizing v ▷ **prize**[2]
pro[1] adv, prep in favour of
pro[2] n (pl -**s**) (Informal) professional
  probabilities n ▷ **probable**
  probabilitity n ▷ **probable**
probable adj likely to happen or be true
  > **probability** n (pl -**ties**)
probably adv in all likelihood
probate n (pl -**s**) process of proving the validity of a will
  probates n ▷ **probate**
probation n (pl -**s**) system of dealing with law-breakers, esp. juvenile ones, by placing them under supervision
probationer n (pl -**s**) person on probation
  probationers n ▷ **probationer**
  probations n ▷ **probation**
probe v (-**bes**, -**bing**, -**bed**) search into or examine closely ▶ n (pl -**s**) surgical instrument used to examine a wound, cavity, etc.
  probed v ▷ **probe**
  probes v, n ▷ **probe**
  probing v ▷ **probe**
probiotic adj, n (pl -**s**) (of) a bacterium that protects the body from harmful bacteria
  probiotics n ▷ **probiotic**
  probities n ▷ **probity**
probity n (pl -**ties**) honesty, integrity
problem n (pl -**s**) something difficult to deal with or solve > **problematic, problematical** adj
  problematic adj ▷ **problem**
  problematical adj ▷ **problem**
  problems n ▷ **problem**
proboscis [pro-**boss**-iss] n (pl -**scises**) long trunk or snout
  proboscises n ▷ **proboscis**
  procedural adj ▷ **procedure**
procedure n (pl -**s**) way of doing something, esp. the correct or usual one > **procedural** adj
  procedures n ▷ **procedure**
proceed v (-**s**, -**ing**, -**ed**) start or continue doing
  proceeded v ▷ **proceed**
  proceeds pl n money obtained from an event or activity ▶ v ▷ **proceed**
  proceeding v ▷ **proceed**
  proceedings pl n organized or related series of events
process n (pl -**es**) series of actions or changes ▶ v (-**es**, -**ing**, -**ed**) handle or prepare by a special method of manufacture > **processor** n (pl -**s**)
processed adj (of food) treated to prevent it decaying ▶ v ▷ **process**
  processes n, v ▷ **process**
  processing v ▷ **process**
procession n (pl -**s**) line of people or vehicles moving forward together in order
  processions n ▷ **procession**
  processor n ▷ **process**
  processors n ▷ **process**
proclaim v (-**s**, -**ing**, -**ed**) declare publicly > **proclamation** n (pl -**s**)
  proclaimed v ▷ **proclaim**
  proclaiming v ▷ **proclaim**
  proclaims v ▷ **proclaim**
  proclamation n ▷ **proclaim**
  proclamations n ▷ **proclaim**

proclivities *n* ▷ **proclivity**
proclivity *n* (*pl* **-ties**) inclination, tendency
procrastinate *v* (**-tes, -ting, -ted**) put off
taking action, delay > **procrastination** *n* (*pl* **-s**)
  procrastinated *v* ▷ **procrastinate**
  procrastinates *v* ▷ **procrastinate**
  procrastinating *v* ▷ **procrastinate**
  procrastination *n* ▷ **procrastinate**
  procrastinations *n* ▷ **procrastinate**
procreate *v* (**-tes, -ting, -ted**) (*Formal*) produce
offspring > **procreation** *n* (*pl* **-s**)
  procreated *v* ▷ **procreate**
  procreates *v* ▷ **procreate**
  procreating *v* ▷ **procreate**
  procreation *n* ▷ **procreate**
  procreations *n* ▷ **procreate**
procure *v* (**-res, -ring, -red**) get, provide
  > **procurement** *n* (*pl* **-s**)
  procured *v* ▷ **procure**
  procurement *n* ▷ **procure**
  procurements *n* ▷ **procure**
procurer, procuress *n* (*pl* **-s, -es**) person who
obtains people to act as prostitutes
  procurers *n* ▷ **procurer**
  procures *v* ▷ **procure**
  procuress *n* ▷ **procurer**
  procuresses *n* ▷ **procurer**
  procuring *v* ▷ **procure**
prod *v* (**-s, -dding, -dded**) poke with something
pointed ▶ *n* (*pl* **-s**) prodding
  prodded *v* ▷ **prod**
  prodding *v* ▷ **prod**
prodigal *adj* recklessly extravagant, wasteful
  > **prodigality** *n* (*pl* **-s**)
  prodigalities *n* ▷ **prodigal**
  prodigality *n* ▷ **prodigal**
  prodigies *n* ▷ **prodigy**
prodigious *adj* very large, immense
  > **prodigiously** *adv*
  prodigiously *adv* ▷ **prodigious**
prodigy *n* (*pl* **-gies**) person with some
marvellous talent
prods *v, n* ▷ **prod**
produce *v* (**-ces, -cing, -ced**) bring into
existence ▶ *n* (*pl* **-s**) food grown for sale
  produced *v* ▷ **produce**
producer *n* (*pl* **-s**) person with control over the
making of a film, record, etc.
  producers *n* ▷ **producer**
  produces *v, n* ▷ **produce**
  producing *v* ▷ **produce**
product *n* (*pl* **-s**) something produced
production *n* (*pl* **-s**) producing
  productions *n* ▷ **production**
productive *adj* producing large quantities

  > **productivity** *n* (*pl* **-ies**)
  productivities *n* ▷ **productive**
  productivity *n* ▷ **productive**
  products *n* ▷ **product**
profane *adj* showing disrespect for religion
or holy things ▶ *v* (**-nes, -ning, -ned**) treat
(something sacred) irreverently, desecrate
profanation *n* (*pl* **-s**) act of profaning
  profanations *n* ▷ **profanation**
  profaned *v* ▷ **profane**
  profanes *v* ▷ **profane**
  profaning *v* ▷ **profane**
  profanities *n* ▷ **profanity**
profanity *n* (*pl* **-ties**) profane talk or behaviour,
blasphemy
profess *v* (**-es, -ing, -ed**) state or claim
(something as true), sometimes falsely
  > **professed** *adj* supposed
  professed *v, adj* ▷ **profess**
  professes *v* ▷ **profess**
  professing *v* ▷ **profess**
profession *n* (*pl* **-s**) type of work, such as being
a doctor, that needs special training
professional *adj* working in a profession
  ▶ *n* person who works in a profession
  > **professionally** *adv* > **professionalism** *n*
  (*pl* **-s**)
  professionally *adv* ▷ **professional**
  professionalism *n* ▷ **professional**
  professionalisms *n* ▷ **professional**
  professions *n* ▷ **profession**
professor *n* (*pl* **-s**) teacher of the highest
rank in a university > **professorial** *adj*
  > **professorship** *n* (*pl* **-s**)
  professorial *adj* ▷ **professor**
  professors *n* ▷ **professor**
  professorship *n* ▷ **professor**
  professorships *n* ▷ **professor**
proffer *v* (**-s, -ing, -ed**) offer
  proffered *v* ▷ **proffer**
  proffering *v* ▷ **proffer**
  proffers *v* ▷ **proffer**
  proficiencies *n* ▷ **proficient**
  proficiency *n* ▷ **proficient**
proficient *adj* skilled, expert > **proficiency** *n*
  (*pl* **-cies**)
profile *n* (*pl* **-s**) outline, esp. of the face, as seen
from the side
  profiles *n* ▷ **profile**
profit *n* (*pl* **-s**) money gained ▶ *v* (**-s, -ing, -ed**)
gain or benefit
profitable *adj* making profit > **profitably** *adv*
  > **profitability** *n* (*pl* **-ties**)
  profitabilities *n* ▷ **profitable**
  profitability *n* ▷ **profitable**

profitably *adv* ▷ **profitable**
profited *v* ▷ **profit**
profiteer *n* (*pl* -**s**) person who makes
excessive profits at the expense of the public
> **profiteering** *n* (*pl* -**s**)
profiteering *n* ▷ **profiteer**
profiteerings *n* ▷ **profiteer**
profiteers *n* ▷ **profiteer**
profiting *v* ▷ **profit**
profits *n*, *v* ▷ **profit**
profligacies *n* ▷ **profligate**
profligacy *n* ▷ **profligate**
profligate *adj* recklessly extravagant ▶ *n* (*pl* -**s**)
profligate person > **profligacy** *n* (*pl* -**cies**)
profligates *n* ▷ **profligate**
profound *adj* (-**er**, -**est**) showing or needing
great knowledge > **profundity** *n* (*pl* -**ties**)
profounder *adj* ▷ **profound**
profoundest *adj* ▷ **profound**
profundities *n* ▷ **profound**
profundity *n* ▷ **profound**
profuse *adj* plentiful > **profusion** *n* (*pl* -**s**)
profusion *n* ▷ **profuse**
profusions *n* ▷ **profuse**
progenies *n* ▷ **progeny**
progeny [proj-in-ee] *n* (*pl* -**nies**) children
progenitor [pro-jen-it-er] *n* (*pl* -**s**) ancestor
progenitors *n* ▷ **progenitor**
progesterone *n* (*pl* -**s**) hormone which
prepares the womb for pregnancy and
prevents further ovulation
progesterones *n* ▷ **progesterone**
prognoses *n* ▷ **prognosis**
prognosis *n* (*pl* -**noses**) doctor's forecast about
the progress of an illness
prognostication *n* (*pl* -**s**) forecast or
prediction
prognostications *n* ▷ **prognostication**
program *n* (*pl* -**s**) sequence of coded
instructions for a computer ▶ *v* (-**s**, -**mming**,
--**mmed**) arrange (data) so that it can be
processed by a computer > **programmer** *n* (*pl*
-**s**) > **programmable** *adj*
programmable *adj* ▷ **program**
programmed *v* ▷ **program**
programmer *n* ▷ **program**
programmers *n* ▷ **program**
programming *v* ▷ **program**
programs *n*, *v* ▷ **program**
programme *n* (*pl* -**s**) planned series of events
programmes *n* ▷ **programme**
progress *n* (*pl* -**es**) improvement, development
▶ *v* (-**es**, -**ing**, -**ed**) become more advanced or
skilful > **progression** *n* (*pl* -**s**)
progressed *v* ▷ **progress**

progresses *v* ▷ **progress**
progressing *v* ▷ **progress**
progression *n* ▷ **progress**
progressions *n* ▷ **progress**
progressive *adj* favouring political or social
reform > **progressively** *adv*
progressively *adv* ▷ **progressive**
prohibit *v* (-**s**, -**ing**, -**ed**) forbid or prevent from
happening
prohibited *v* ▷ **prohibit**
prohibiting *v* ▷ **prohibit**
prohibition *n* (*pl* -**s**) act of forbidding
prohibitions *n* ▷ **prohibition**
prohibitive *adj* (of prices) too high to be
affordable > **prohibitively** *adv*
prohibitively *adv* ▷ **prohibitive**
prohibits *v* ▷ **prohibit**
project *n* (*pl* **projects**) planned scheme to do or
examine something over a period ▶ *v* (-**s**, -**ing**,
-**ed**) make a forecast based on known data
> **projection** *n* (*pl* -**s**)
projected *v* ▷ **project**
projectile *n* (*pl* -**s**) object thrown as a weapon
or fired from a gun
projectiles *n* ▷ **projectile**
projecting *v* ▷ **project**
projection *n* ▷ **project**
projectionist *n* (*pl* -**s**) person who operates a
projector
projectionists *n* ▷ **projectionist**
projections *n* ▷ **project**
projector *n* (*pl* -**s**) apparatus for projecting
photographic images, films, or slides on a
screen
projectors *n* ▷ **projector**
projects *n*, *v* ▷ **project**
prolapse *n* (*pl* -**s**) slipping down of an internal
organ of the body from its normal position
prolapses *n* ▷ **prolapse**
prole *adj*, *n* (*pl* -**s**) (CHIEFLY BRIT) (*Slang*)
proletarian
proles *n* ▷ **prole**
proletariat [pro-lit-**air**-ee-at] *n* (*pl* -**s**) working
class > **proletarian** *adj*, *n* (*pl* -**s**)
proletarian *n* ▷ **proletariat**
proletarians *n* ▷ **proletariat**
proletariats *n* ▷ **proletariat**
proliferate *v* (-**tes**, -**ting**, -**ted**) grow or
reproduce rapidly > **proliferation** *n* (*pl* -**s**)
proliferated *v* ▷ **proliferate**
proliferates *v* ▷ **proliferate**
proliferating *v* ▷ **proliferate**
proliferation *n* ▷ **proliferate**
proliferations *n* ▷ **proliferate**
prolific *adj* very productive > **prolifically** *adv*

prolifically *adv* ▷ prolific
prolix *adj* (of speech or a piece of writing) overlong and boring
prologue *n* (*pl* -**s**) introduction to a play or book
  prologues *n* ▷ prologue
prolong *v* (-**s**, -**ing**, -**ed**) make (something) last longer > **prolongation** *n* (*pl* -**s**)
  prolongation *n* ▷ prolong
  prolongations *n* ▷ prolong
  prolonged *v* ▷ prolong
  prolonging *v* ▷ prolong
  prolongs *v* ▷ prolong
  prom *n* (*pl* -**s**) ▷ promenade
promenade *n* (*pl* -**s**) (CHIEFLY BRIT) paved walkway along the seafront at a holiday resort ▶ *v* (-**des**, -**ding**, -**ded**) ▶ *n* (*Old-fashioned*) (take) a leisurely walk
  promenaded *v* ▷ promenade
  promenades *n*, *v* ▷ promenade
  promenading *v* ▷ promenade
  prominence *n* ▷ prominent
  prominences *n* ▷ prominent
prominent *adj* very noticeable > **prominently** *adv* > **prominence** *n* (*pl* -**s**)
  prominently *adv* ▷ prominent
  promiscuities *n* ▷ promiscuous
  promiscuity *n* ▷ promiscuous
promiscuous *adj* having many casual sexual relationships > **promiscuity** *n* (*pl* -**ties**)
promise *v* (-**ses**, -**sing**, -**sed**) say that one will definitely do or not do something ▶ *n* (*pl* -**s**) undertaking to do or not to do something
  promised *v* ▷ promise
  promises *v* ▷ promise
promising *adj* likely to succeed or turn out well ▶ *v* ▷ promise
promo *n* (*pl* -**os**) (*Informal*) short film to promote a product
  promontories *n* ▷ promontory
promontory *n* (*pl* -**ries**) point of high land jutting out into the sea
  promos *n* ▷ promo
promote *v* (-**tes**, -**ting**, -**ted**) help to make (something) happen or increase > **promotion** *n* (*pl* -**s**) > **promotional** *adj*
  promoted *v* ▷ promote
promoter *n* (*pl* -**s**) person who organizes or finances an event etc.
  promoters *n* ▷ promoter
  promotes *v* ▷ promote
  promoting *v* ▷ promote
  promotion *n* ▷ promote
  promotional *adj* ▷ promote
  promotions *n* ▷ promote

prompt *v* (-**s**, -**ing**, -**ed**) cause (an action) ▶ *adj* done without delay ▶ *adv* exactly > **promptness** *n* (*pl* -**es**)
  prompted *v* ▷ prompt
prompter, prompt *n* (*pl* -**s**) person offstage who prompts actors
  prompter *n* ▷ prompter
  prompting *v* ▷ prompt
promptly *adv* immediately, without delay
  promptness *n* ▷ prompt
  promptnesses *n* ▷ prompt
  prompts *v*, *n* ▷ prompt
  proms *n* ▷ prom
promulgate *v* (-**tes**, -**ting**, -**ted**) put (a law etc.) into effect by announcing it officially > **promulgation** *n* (*pl* -**s**)
  promulgated *v* ▷ promulgate
  promulgates *v* ▷ promulgate
  promulgating *v* ▷ promulgate
  promulgation *n* ▷ promulgate
  promulgations *n* ▷ promulgate
prone *adj* (-**r**, -**st**) (*foll. by* **to**) likely to do or be affected by (something)
  proner *adj* ▷ prone
  pronest *adj* ▷ prone
prong *n* (*pl* -**s**) one spike of a fork or similar instrument > **pronged** *adj*
  pronged *adj* ▷ prong
  prongs *n* ▷ prong
pronoun *n* (*pl* -**s**) word, such as *she* or *it*, used to replace a noun
  pronouns *n* ▷ pronoun
pronounce *v* (-**ces**, -**cing**, -**ced**) form the sounds of (words or letters), esp. clearly or in a particular way > **pronounceable** *adj*
  pronouncable *adj* ▷ pronounce
pronounced *adj* very noticeable ▶ *v* ▷ pronounce
  pronounces *v* ▷ pronounce
pronouncement *n* (*pl* -**s**) formal announcement
  pronouncements *n* ▷ pronouncement
  pronouncing *v* ▷ pronounce
pronunciation *n* (*pl* -**s**) way in which a word or language is pronounced
  pronunciations *n* ▷ pronunciation
pronto *adv* (*Informal*) at once
proof *n* (*pl* -**s**) evidence that shows that something is true or has happened ▶ *adj* able to withstand
proofread *v* (-**s**, -**ing**, -**read**) read and correct (printer's proofs) > **proofreader** *n* (*pl* -**s**)
  proofreader *n* ▷ proofread
  proofreaders *n* ▷ proofread
  proofreading *v* ▷ proofread

proofreads v ▷ proofread
proofs n ▷ proof
prop[1] v (-s, -pping, -pped) support (something) so that it stays upright or in place ▶ n (pl -s) pole, beam, etc. used as a support
prop[2] n (pl -s) movable object used on the set of a film or play
prop[3] n (pl -s) (Informal) propeller
propaganda n (pl -s) (organized promotion of) information to assist or damage the cause of a government or movement > **propagandist** n (pl -s)
  propagandas n ▷ propaganda
  propagandist n ▷ propaganda
  propagandists n ▷ propaganda
propagate v (-tes, -ting, -ted) spread (information and ideas) > **propagation** n (pl -s)
  propagated v ▷ propagate
  propagates v ▷ propagate
  propagating v ▷ propagate
  propagation n ▷ propagate
  propagations n ▷ propagate
propane n (pl -s) flammable gas found in petroleum and used as a fuel
  propanes n ▷ propane
propel v (-s, -lling, -lled) cause to move forward
propellant n (pl -s) something that provides or causes propulsion
  propellants n ▷ propellant
  propelled v ▷ propel
propeller n (pl -s) revolving shaft with blades for driving a ship or aircraft
  propellers n ▷ propeller
  propelling v ▷ propel
  propels v ▷ propel
  propped v ▷ prop[1]
  propping v ▷ prop[1]
  props v, n ▷ prop[1, 2, 3]
propulsion n (pl -s) method by which something is propelled
  propulsions n ▷ propulsion
  propensities n ▷ propensity
propensity n (pl -ies) natural tendency
proper adj (-er, -est) real or genuine > **properly** adv
  properer adj ▷ proper
  properest adj ▷ proper
  properly adv ▷ proper
  properties n ▷ property
property n (pl -ties) something owned
  prophecies n ▷ prophecy
prophecy n (pl -cies) prediction
  prophesied v ▷ prophesy
  prophesies v ▷ prophesy

prophesy v (-sies, -sying, -sied) foretell
  prophesying v ▷ prophesy
prophet n (pl -s) person supposedly chosen by God to spread His word > **prophetic** adj > **prophetically** adv
  prophetic adj ▷ prophet
  prophetically adv ▷ prophet
  prophets n ▷ prophet
prophylactic n (pl -s) ▶ adj (drug) used to prevent disease
  prophylactics n ▷ prophylactic
propitiate v (-tes, -ting, -ted) appease, win the favour of > **propitiation** n
  propitiated v ▷ propitiate
  propitiates v ▷ propitiate
  propitiating v ▷ propitiate
  propitiation n ▷ propitiate
  propitiations n ▷ propitiate
propitious adj favourable or auspicious
proponent n (pl -s) person who argues in favour of something
  proponents n ▷ proponent
proportion n (pl -s) relative size or extent ▶ pl dimensions or size ▶ v (-s, -ing, -ed) adjust in relative amount or size
proportional, proportionate adj being in proportion > **proportionally, proportionately** adv
  proportionally adv ▷ proportional
  proportionate adj ▷ proportional
  proportionately adv ▷ proportional
  proportioned v ▷ proportion
  proportioning v ▷ proportion
  proportions n, v ▷ proportion
propose v (-ses, -sing, -sed) put forward for consideration > **proposal** n (pl -s)
  proposal n ▷ propose
  proposals n ▷ propose
  proposed v ▷ propose
  proposes v ▷ propose
  proposing v ▷ propose
proposition n (pl -s) offer ▶ v (-s, -ing, -ed) (Informal) ask (someone) to have sexual intercourse
  propositioned v ▷ proposition
  propositioning v ▷ proposition
  propositions n, v ▷ proposition
propound v (-s, -ing, -ed) put forward for consideration
  propounded v ▷ propound
  propounding v ▷ propound
  propounds v ▷ propound
proprietor n (pl -s) owner of a business establishment > **proprietress** n fem (pl -es)
proprietary adj made and distributed under

a trade name
proprieties n ▷ propriety
proprietors n ▷ proprietor
proprietress n ▷ proprietor
proprietresses n ▷ proprietor
propriety n (pl -**ties**) correct conduct
propulsion n ▷ propel
prorogue v (-**gues, -guing, -gued**) suspend
(parliament) without dissolving it
> **prorogation** n (pl -**s**)
prorogation n ▷ prorogue
prorogations n ▷ prorogue
prorogued v ▷ prorogue
prorogues v ▷ prorogue
proroguing v ▷ prorogue
pros n ▷ pro
prosaic [pro-**zay**-ik] adj lacking imagination,
dull > **prosaically** adv
prosaically adv ▷ prosaic
proscenia n ▷ proscenium
proscenium n (pl -**nia, -niums**) arch in a
theatre separating the stage from the
auditorium
prosceniums n ▷ proscenium
proscribe v (-**bes, -bing, -bed**) prohibit, outlaw
> **proscription** n (pl -**s**) > **proscriptive** adj
proscribed v ▷ proscribe
proscribes v ▷ proscribe
proscribing v ▷ proscribe
proscription n ▷ proscribe
proscriptions n ▷ proscribe
proscriptive adj ▷ proscribe
prose n (pl -**s**) ordinary speech or writing in
contrast to poetry
proses n ▷ prose
prosecute v (-**tes, -ting, -ted**) bring a criminal
charge against > **prosecution** n (pl -**s**)
> **prosecutor** n (pl -**s**)
prosecuted v ▷ prosecute
prosecutes v ▷ prosecute
prosecuting v ▷ prosecute
prosecution n ▷ prosecute
prosecutions n ▷ prosecute
prosecutor n ▷ prosecute
prosecutors n ▷ prosecute
proselyte [**pross**-ill-ite] n (pl -**s**) recent convert
proselytes n ▷ proselyte
proselytize [**pross**-ill-it-ize] v (-**zes, -zing, -zed**)
attempt to convert
proselytized v ▷ proselytize
proselytized v ▷ proselytize
proselytizing v ▷ proselytize
prospect n (pl -**s**) something anticipated
(Old-fashioned) ▶ pl probability of future
success ▶ v (-**s, -ing, -ed**) explore, esp. for gold

> **prospector** n (pl -**s**)
prospected v ▷ prospect
prospecting v ▷ prospect
prospective adj future
prospector n ▷ prospect
prospectors n ▷ prospect
prospects n, v ▷ prospect
prospectus n (pl -**es**) booklet giving details of a
university, company, etc.
prospectuses n ▷ prospectus
prosper v (-**s, -ing, -ed**) be successful
> **prosperous** adj
prospered v ▷ prosper
prospering v ▷ prosper
prosperities n ▷ prosperity
prosperity n success and wealth
prosperous adj ▷ prosper
prospers v ▷ prosper
prostate n (pl -**s**) gland in male mammals that
surrounds the neck of the bladder
prostates n ▷ prostate
prostheses n ▷ prosthesis
prosthesis [pross-**theess**-iss] n (pl -**ses**) [-seez]
artificial body part, such as a limb or breast
> **prosthetic** adj
prosthetic adj ▷ prosthesis
prostitute n (pl -**s**) person who offers
sexual intercourse in return for payment
▶ v (-**tes, -ting, -ted**) make a prostitute of
> **prostitution** n (pl -**s**)
prostituted v ▷ prostitute
prostitutes n, v ▷ prostitute
prostituting v ▷ prostitute
prostitution n ▷ prostitute
prostitutions n ▷ prostitute
prostrate adj lying face downwards ▶ v (-**tes,
-ting, -ted**) lie face downwards > **prostration**
n (pl -**s**)
prostrated v ▷ prostrate
prostrates v ▷ prostrate
prostrating v ▷ prostrate
prostration n ▷ prostrate
prostrations n ▷ prostrate
protagonist n (pl -**s**) supporter of a cause
protagonists n ▷ protagonist
protea [pro-**tee**-a] n (pl -**s**) African shrub with
showy flowers
protean [pro-**tee**-an] adj constantly changing
proteas n ▷ protea
protect v (-**s, -ing, -ed**) defend from trouble,
harm, or loss > **protection** n (pl -**s**)
protected v ▷ protect
protecting v ▷ protect
protection n ▷ protect
protectionism n policy of protecting

industries by taxing competing imports
> **protectionist** n (pl -**s**) adj
protectionisms n ▷ **protectionism**
protectionist n ▷ **protectionism**
protectionists n ▷ **protectionism**
protections n ▷ **protect**
protective adj giving protection
protector n (pl -**s**) person or thing that
protects
protectorate n (pl -**s**) territory largely
controlled by a stronger state
protectorates n ▷ **protectorate**
protectors n ▷ **protector**
protects v ▷ **protect**
protégé, fem **protégée** [pro-ti-zhay] n (pl
-**s**) person who is protected and helped by
another
protégés n ▷ **protégé**
protein n (pl -**s**) any of a group of complex
organic compounds that are essential for life
proteins n ▷ **protein**
protest n (pl -**s**) declaration or demonstration
of objection ▶ v (-**s**, -**ing**, -**ed**) object, disagree
protestant n (pl -**s**) one who protests
protestants n ▷ **protestant**
protestation n (pl -**s**) strong declaration
protestations n ▷ **protestation**
protested v ▷ **protest**
protesting v ▷ **protest**
protests n, v ▷ **protest**
protocol n (pl -**s**) rules of behaviour for formal
occasions
protocols n ▷ **protocol**
proton n (pl -**s**) positively charged particle in
the nucleus of an atom
protons n ▷ **proton**
protoplasm n (pl -**s**) substance forming the
living contents of a cell
protoplasms n ▷ **protoplasm**
prototype n (pl -**s**) original or model to be
copied or developed
prototypes n ▷ **prototype**
protozoa n ▷ **protozoan**
protozoan [pro-toe-**zoe**-an] n (pl -**zoa**)
microscopic one-celled creature
protracted adj lengthened or extended
protractor n (pl -**s**) instrument for measuring
angles
protractors n ▷ **protractor**
protrude v (-**des**, -**ding**, -**ded**) stick out, project
> **protrusion** n (pl -**s**)
protruded v ▷ **protrude**
protrudes v ▷ **protrude**
protruding v ▷ **protrude**
protrusion n ▷ **protrude**

protrusions n ▷ **protrude**
protuberance n ▷ **protuberant**
protuberances n ▷ **protuberant**
protuberant adj swelling out, bulging
> **protuberance** n (pl -**s**)
proud adj (-**er**, -**est**) feeling pleasure and
satisfaction > **proudly** adv
prouder adj ▷ **proud**
proudest adj ▷ **proud**
proudly adv ▷ **proud**
prove v (-**ves**, -**ving**, -**ved** or -**ven**) establish the
validity of
proved v ▷ **prove**
proven adj known from experience to work
▶ v ▷ **prove**
provenance [**prov**-in-anss] n (pl -**s**) place of
origin
provenances n ▷ **provenance**
provender n (pl -**s**) (Old-fashioned) fodder
provenders n ▷ **provender**
proverb n (pl -**s**) short saying that expresses a
truth or gives a warning > **proverbial** adj
proverbial adj ▷ **proverb**
proverbs n ▷ **proverb**
proves v ▷ **prove**
provide v (-**des**, -**ding**, -**ded**) make available
> **provider** n (pl -**s**)
provided v ▷ **provide**
providence n (pl -**s**) God or nature seen as a
protective force that arranges people's lives
providences n ▷ **providence**
provident adj thrifty
providential adj lucky
provider n ▷ **provide**
providers n ▷ **provide**
provides v ▷ **provide**
providing v ▷ **provide**
province n (pl -**s**) area governed as a unit of
a country or empire ▶ pl parts of a country
outside the capital
provincial adj of a province or the provinces
▶ n (pl -**s**) unsophisticated person
provincialism n (pl -**s**) narrow-mindedness
and lack of sophistication
provincialisms n ▷ **provincialism**
provincials n ▷ **provincial**
provinces n ▷ **province**
proving v ▷ **prove**
provision n (pl -**s**) act of supplying something
▶ pl food ▶ v (-**s**, -**ing**, -**ed**) supply with food
provisional adj temporary or conditional
> **provisionally** adv
provisionally adv ▷ **provisional**
provisioned v ▷ **provision**
provisioning v ▷ **provision**

provisions *n, v* ▷ provision
proviso [pro-vize-oh] *n (pl* -sos, -soes)
  condition, stipulation
  provisoes *n* ▷ proviso
  provisos *n* ▷ proviso
  provocation *n* ▷ provoke
  provocations *n* ▷ provoke
  provocative *adj* ▷ provoke
provoke *v* (-kes, -king, -ked) deliberately anger
  > provocation *n (pl* -s) > provocative *adj*
  provoked *v* ▷ provoke
  provokes *v* ▷ provoke
  provoking *v* ▷ provoke
provost *n (pl* -s) head of certain university
  colleges in Britain
  provosts *n* ▷ provost
prow *n (pl* -s) bow of a vessel
  prows *n* ▷ prow
prowess *n (pl* -es) superior skill or ability
  prowesses *n* ▷ prowess
prowl *v* (-s, -ing, -ed) move stealthily around a
  place as if in search of prey or plunder ▶ *n (pl*
  -s) prowling
  prowled *v* ▷ prowl
prowler *n (pl* -s) person who moves stealthily
  around a place as if in search of prey or
  plunder
  prowlers *n* ▷ prowler
  prowling *v* ▷ prowl
  prowls *v, n* ▷ prowl
  proxies *n* ▷ proxy
  proximate *n* ▷ proximity
  proximities *n* ▷ proximity
proximity *n (pl* -ties) nearness in space or time
  > proximate *adj*
proxy *n (pl* -xies) person authorized to act on
  behalf of someone else
prude *n (pl* -s) person who is excessively
  modest, prim, or proper > prudish *adj*
  > prudery *n (pl* -ries)
  prudence *n* ▷ prudent
  prudences *n* ▷ prudent
prudent *adj* cautious, discreet, and sensible
  > prudence *n (pl* -s)
prudential *adj* (Old-fashioned) prudent
  prudes *n* ▷ prude
  pruderies *n* ▷ prude
  prudery *n* ▷ prude
  prudish *adj* ▷ prude
prune¹ *n (pl* -s) dried plum
prune² *v* (-nes, -ning, -ned) cut off dead parts
  or excessive branches from (a tree or plant)
  pruned *v* ▷ prune
  prunes *n, v* ▷ prune¹, ²
  pruning *v* ▷ prune

prurience *n* ▷ prurient
  pruriences *n* ▷ prurient
prurient *adj* excessively interested in sexual
  matters > prurience *n (pl* -s)
pry *v* (prys, prying, pried) make an
  impertinent or uninvited inquiry into a
  private matter
  prying *v* ▷ pry
psalm *n (pl* -s) sacred song
psalmist *n (pl* -s) writer of psalms
  psalmists *n* ▷ psalmist
  psalms *n* ▷ psalm
psalter *n (pl* -s) book containing (a version of)
  psalms from the Bible
  psalteries *n* ▷ psalter
psaltery *n (pl* -ries) ancient instrument played
  by plucking strings
  psalters *n* ▷ psalter
  psephologies *n* ▷ psephology
psephology [sef-fol-a-jee] *n (pl* -gies) statistical
  study of elections
pseud *n (pl* -s) (Informal) pretentious person
  pseuds *n* ▷ pseud
pseudonym *n (pl* -s) fictitious name adopted
  esp. by an author > pseudonymous *adj*
  pseudonymous *adj* ▷ pseudonym
  pseudonyms *n* ▷ pseudonym

  psi *n* (**psis**). Psi is the 23rd letter of
  the Greek alphabet. This word can
  be useful if you have a difficult rack,
  especially if you can form another
  word at the same time. Psi scores 5
  points.

psittacosis *n (pl* -ses) disease of parrots that
  can be transmitted to humans
  psittacoses *n* ▷ psittacosis

  pst *interj*. Pst is a sound people make
  when they want to draw someone's
  attention to something without
  making too much noise. This is a useful
  word to remember because it doesn't
  use any vowels, and so can be useful if
  you have no vowels on your rack. Pst
  scores 5 points.

psyche [sye-kee] *n (pl* -s) human mind or soul
psychedelic *adj* denoting a drug that causes
  hallucinations
  psyche *n* ▷ psyche
  psychiatric *adj* ▷ psychiatry
  psychiatries *n* ▷ psychiatry
  psychiatrist *n* ▷ psychiatry
  psychiatrists *n* ▷ psychiatry
psychiatry *n (pl* -ries) branch of medicine
  concerned with mental disorders
  > psychiatric *adj* > psychiatrist *n*

psychic *adj* (*also* **psychical**) having mental powers which cannot be explained by natural laws ▶ *n* (*pl* **-s**) person with psychic powers
psychics *n* ▷ **psychic**
psycho *n* (*pl* **-s**) (*Informal*) psychopath
psychoanalyse *v* ▷ **psychoanalysis**
psychoanalysed *v* ▷ **psychoanalysis**
psychoanalyses *n*, *v* ▷ **psychoanalysis**
psychoanalysing *v* ▷ **psychoanalysis**
psychoanalysis *n* (*pl* **-ses**) method of treating mental and emotional disorders by discussion and analysis of one's thoughts and feelings > **psychoanalyse** *v* (**-ses, -sing, -sed**) > **psychoanalyst** *n* (*pl* **-s**)
psychoanalyst *n* ▷ **psychoanalysis**
psychoanalysts *n* ▷ **psychoanalysis**
psychological *adj* of or affecting the mind > **psychologically** *adv*
psychologically *adv* ▷ **psychological**
psychologies *n* ▷ **psychology**
psychologist *n* ▷ **psychology**
psychologists *n* ▷ **psychology**
psychology *n* (*pl* **-gies**) study of human and animal behaviour > **psychologist** *n* (*pl* **-s**)
psychopath *n* (*pl* **-s**) person afflicted with a personality disorder causing him or her to commit antisocial or violent acts > **psychopathic** *adj*
psychopathic *adj* ▷ **psychopath**
psychopaths *n* ▷ **psychopath**
psychos *n* ▷ **psycho**
psychoses *n* ▷ **psychosis**
psychosis *n* (*pl* **-ses**) severe mental disorder in which the sufferer's contact with reality becomes distorted > **psychotic** *adj*
psychosomatic *adj* (of a physical disorder) thought to have psychological causes
psychotherapeutic *adj* ▷ **psychotherapy**
psychotherapies *n* ▷ **psychotherapy**
psychotherapist *n* ▷ **psychotherapy**
psychotherapists *n* ▷ **psychotherapy**
psychotherapy *n* (*pl* **-pies**) treatment of nervous disorders by psychological methods > **psychotherapeutic** *adj* > **psychotherapist** *n*
psychotic *adj* ▷ **psychosis**
ptarmigan [tar-mig-an] *n* (*pl* **-s**) bird of the grouse family which turns white in winter
ptarmigans *n* ▷ **ptarmigan**
pterodactyl [terr-roe-**dak**-til] *n* (*pl* **-s**) extinct flying reptile with batlike wings
pterodactyls *n* ▷ **pterodactyl**
ptomaine [**toe**-main] *n* (*pl* **-s**) any of a group of poisonous alkaloids found in decaying matter
ptomaines *n* ▷ **ptomaine**

pub *n* (*pl* **-s**) building with a bar licensed to sell alcoholic drinks
pubertal *adj* ▷ **puberty**
puberties *n* ▷ **puberty**
puberty *n* (*pl* **-ties**) beginning of sexual maturity > **pubertal** *adj*
pubic *adj* of the lower abdomen
public *adj* of or concerning the people as a whole ▶ *n* (*pl* **-s**) the community, people in general > **publicly** *adv*
publican *n* (*pl* **-s**) (BRIT, AUST & NZ) person who owns or runs a pub
publicans *n* ▷ **publican**
publication *n* ▷ **publish**
publications *n* ▷ **publish**
publicist *n* (*pl* **-s**) person, esp. a press agent or journalist, who publicizes something
publicists *n* ▷ **publicist**
publicities *n* ▷ **publicity**
publicity *n* (*pl* **-ties**) process or information used to arouse public attention
publicize *v* (**-zes, -zing, -zed**) bring to public attention
publicized *v* ▷ **publicize**
publicizes *v* ▷ **publicize**
publicizing *v* ▷ **publicize**
publicly *adv* ▷ **public**
publics *n* ▷ **public**
publish *v* (**-es, -ing, -ed**) produce and issue (printed matter) for sale > **publication** *n* (*pl* **-s**) > **publisher** *n* (*pl* **-s**)
published *v* ▷ **publish**
publisher *n* ▷ **publish**
publishers *n* ▷ **publish**
publishes *v* ▷ **publish**
publishing *v* ▷ **publish**
pubs *n* ▷ **pub**
puce *adj* (**pucer, pucest**) purplish-brown
pucer *adj* ▷ **puce**
pucest *adj* ▷ **puce**
puck¹ *n* (*pl* **-s**) small rubber disc used in ice hockey
puck² *n* (*pl* **-s**) mischievous or evil spirit > **puckish** *adj*
pucker *v* (**-s, -ing, -ed**) gather into wrinkles ▶ *n* (*pl* **-s**) wrinkle or crease
puckered *v* ▷ **pucker**
puckering *v* ▷ **pucker**
puckers *v*, *n* ▷ **pucker**
puckish *adj* ▷ **puck²**
pucks *n* ▷ **puck¹, ²**
pudding *n* (*pl* **-s**) dessert, esp. a cooked one served hot
puddings *n* ▷ **pudding**
puddle *n* (*pl* **-s**) small pool of water, esp. of rain

puddles *n* ▷ puddle
puerile *adj* silly and childish
puerperal [pew-er-per-al] *adj* concerning the period following childbirth
puff *n* (*pl* -s) (sound of) a short blast of breath, wind, etc. ▶ *v* (-s, -ing, -ed) blow or breathe in short quick draughts > **puffy** *adj* (-ffier, -ffiest)
puffball *n* (*pl* -s) ball-shaped fungus
  puffballs *n* ▷ puffball
  puffed *v* ▷ puff
  puffier *adj* ▷ puff
  puffiest *adj* ▷ puff
puffin *n* (*pl* -s) black-and-white sea bird with a brightly-coloured beak
  puffins *n* ▷ puffin
  puffing *v* ▷ puff
  puffs *n*, *v* ▷ puff
  puffy *adj* ▷ puff
pug *n* (*pl* -s) small snub-nosed dog
  pugs *n* ▷ pug
pugilist [pew-jil-ist] *n* (*pl* -s) boxer > **pugilism** *n* (*pl* -s) > **pugilistic** *adj*
  pugilism *n* ▷ pugilist
  pugilisms *n* ▷ pugilist
  pugilistic *adj* ▷ pugilist
  pugilists *n* ▷ pugilist
pugnacious *adj* ready and eager to fight > **pugnacity** *n* (*pl* -ties)
  pugnacities *n* ▷ pugnacious
  pugnacity *n* ▷ pugnacious
puissance [pwee-sonce] *n* (*pl* -s) showjumping competition that tests a horse's ability to jump large obstacles
  puissances *n* ▷ puissance
puke (*Slang*) *v* (-kes, -king, -ked) vomit ▶ *n* (*pl* -s) act of vomiting
  puked *v* ▷ puke
  pukes *v*, *n* ▷ puke
  puking *v* ▷ puke
pulchritude *n* (*pl* -s) (*Lit*) beauty
  pulchritudes *n* ▷ pulchritude
pull *v* (-s, -ing, -ed) exert force on (an object) to move it towards the source of the force ▶ *n* (*pl* -s) act of pulling
  pulled *v* ▷ pull
pullet *n* (*pl* -s) young hen
  pullets *n* ▷ pullet
pulley *n* (*pl* -s) wheel with a grooved rim in which a belt, chain, or piece of rope runs in order to lift weights by a downward pull
  pulleys *n* ▷ pulley
  pulling *v* ▷ pull
pullover *n* (*pl* -s) sweater that is pulled on over the head
  pullovers *n* ▷ pullover

pulls *v*, *n* ▷ pull
pulmonary *adj* of the lungs
pulp *n* (*pl* -s) soft wet substance made from crushed or beaten matter ▶ *v* (-s, -ing, -ed) reduce to pulp
  pulped *v* ▷ pulp
  pulping *v* ▷ pulp
pulpit *n* (*pl* -s) raised platform for a preacher
  pulpits *n* ▷ pulpit
  pulps *n*, *v* ▷ pulp
pulsar *n* (*pl* -s) small dense star which emits regular bursts of radio waves
  pulsars *n* ▷ pulsar
  pulsate *v* ▷ pulse[1]
  pulsated *v* ▷ pulse[1]
  pulsates *v* ▷ pulse[1]
  pulsating *v* ▷ pulse[1]
  pulsation *n* ▷ pulse[1]
  pulsations *n* ▷ pulse[1]
pulse[1] *n* (*pl* -s) regular beating of blood through the arteries at each heartbeat > **pulsate** *v* (-s, -ing, -ed) throb, quiver > **pulsation** *n* (*pl* -s)
pulse[2] *n* (-s) edible seed of a pod-bearing plant such as a bean or pea
  pulses *n* ▷ pulse[1, 2]
pulverize *v* (-zes, -zing, -zed) reduce to fine pieces
  pulverized *v* ▷ pulverize
  pulverizes *v* ▷ pulverize
  pulverizing *v* ▷ pulverize
puma *n* (*pl* -s) large American wild cat with a greyish-brown coat
  pumas *n* ▷ puma
pumice [pumm-iss] *n* (*pl* -s) light porous stone used for scouring
  pumices *n* ▷ pumice
pummel *v* (-s, -lling, -lled) strike repeatedly with or as if with the fists
  pummelled *v* ▷ pummel
  pummelling *v* ▷ pummel
  pummels *v* ▷ pummel
pump[1] *n* (*pl* -s) machine used to force a liquid or gas to move in a particular direction ▶ *v* (-s, -ing, -ed) raise or drive with a pump
pump[2] *n* (*pl* -s) light flat-soled shoe
  pumped *v* ▷ pump
  pumping *v* ▷ pump
pumpkin *n* (*pl* -s) large round fruit with an orange rind, soft flesh, and many seeds
  pumpkins *n* ▷ pumpkin
  pumps *n*, *v* ▷ pump[1, 2]
pun *n* (*pl* -s) use of words to exploit double meanings for humorous effect ▶ *v* (-s, -nning, -nned) make puns

punch¹ v (**-es, -ing, -ed**) strike at with a clenched fist ▶ n (pl **-es**) blow with a clenched fist (Informal)

punch² n (pl **-es**) tool or machine for shaping, piercing, or engraving ▶ v (**-es, -ing, -ed**) pierce, cut, stamp, shape, or drive with a punch

punch³ n (pl **-es**) drink made from a mixture of wine, spirits, fruit, sugar, and spices
  punched v ▷ **punch¹,²**

punches v, n ▷ **punch**
  punchier adj ▷ **punchy**
  punchiest adj ▷ **punchy**
  punching v ▷ **punch¹,²**

punchy adj (**-chier, -chiest**) forceful

punctilious adj paying great attention to correctness in etiquette

punctual adj arriving or taking place at the correct time > **punctuality** n (pl **-ties**) > **punctually** adv
  punctualities n ▷ **punctual**
  punctuality n ▷ **punctual**
  punctually adv ▷ **punctual**

punctuate v (**-tes, -ting, -ted**) put punctuation marks in
  punctuated v ▷ **punctuate**
  punctuates v ▷ **punctuate**
  punctuating v ▷ **punctuate**

punctuation n (pl **-s**) (use of) marks such as commas, colons, etc. in writing, to assist in making the sense clear
  punctuations n ▷ **punctuation**

puncture n (pl **-s**) small hole made by a sharp object, esp. in a tyre ▶ v (**-res, -ring, -red**) pierce a hole in
  punctured v ▷ **puncture**
  punctures n, v ▷ **puncture**
  puncturing v ▷ **puncture**

pundit n (pl **-s**) expert who speaks publicly on a subject
  pundits n ▷ **pundit**
  pungencies n ▷ **pungent**
  pungency n ▷ **pungent**

pungent adj having a strong sharp bitter flavour > **pungency** n (pl **-cies**)
  punier adj ▷ **puny**
  puniest adj ▷ **puny**

punish v (**-es, -ing, -ed**) cause (someone) to suffer or undergo a penalty for some wrongdoing > **punishment** n (pl **-s**)
  punished v ▷ **punish**
  punishes v ▷ **punish**

punishing adj harsh or difficult ▶ v ▷ **punish**
  punishment n ▷ **punish**
  punishments n ▷ **punish**

punitive [pew-nit-tiv] adj relating to punishment

punk n (pl **-s**) anti-Establishment youth movement and style of rock music of the late 1970s
  punks n ▷ **punk**
  punned v ▷ **pun**

punnet n (pl **-s**) small basket for fruit
  punnets n ▷ **punnet**
  punning v ▷ **pun**
  puns n, v ▷ **pun**

punt¹ n (pl **-s**) open flat-bottomed boat propelled by a pole ▶ v (**-s, -ing, -ed**) travel in a punt

punt² (SPORT) n (pl **-s**) kick of a ball before it touches the ground when dropped from the hands ▶ v (**-s, -ing, -ed**) kick (a ball) in this way

punt³ n (pl **-s**) former monetary unit of the Irish Republic
  punted v ▷ **punt**

punter n (pl **-s**) person who bets
  punters n ▷ **punter**
  punting v ▷ **punt**
  punts n, v ▷ **punt¹,²,³**

puny adj (**-nier, -niest**) small and feeble

pup n (pl **-s**) young of certain animals, such as dogs and seals

pupa n (pl **-pae, -pas**) insect at the stage of development between a larva and an adult
  pupae n ▷ **pupa**
  pupas n ▷ **pupa**

pupil¹ n (pl **-s**) person who is taught by a teacher

pupil² n (pl **-s**) round dark opening in the centre of the eye
  pupils n ▷ **pupil¹,²**

puppet n (pl **-s**) small doll or figure moved by strings or by the operator's hand > **puppeteer** n (pl **-s**)
  puppeteer n ▷ **puppet**
  puppeteers n ▷ **puppet**
  puppets n ▷ **puppet**
  puppies n ▷ **puppy**

puppy n (pl **-ppies**) young dog
  pups n ▷ **pup**

purchase v (**-ses, -sing, -sed**) obtain by payment ▶ n (pl **-s**) thing that is bought > **purchaser** n (pl **-s**)
  purchased v ▷ **purchase**
  purchaser n ▷ **purchase**
  purchasers n ▷ **purchase**
  purchases v, n ▷ **purchase**
  purchasing v ▷ **purchase**

purdah n (pl **-s**) Muslim and Hindu custom of keeping women in seclusion, with clothing that conceals them completely when they go out

purdahs *n* ▷ **purdah**

pure *adj* (**-r, -st**) unmixed, untainted > **purely** *adv* > **purity** *n* (*pl* -**ies**)

purely *adv* ▷ **pure**

purée [pure-ray] *n* (*pl* -**s**) pulp of cooked food ▶ *v* (**-s, -réeing, -réed**) make into a purée

puréed *v* ▷ **purée**

puréeing *v* ▷ **purée**

purées *n*, *v* ▷ **purée**

purer *adj* ▷ **pure**

purest *adj* ▷ **pure**

purgatorial *adj* ▷ **purgatory**

purgatories *n* ▷ **purgatory**

purgatory *n* (*pl* -**ries**) place or state of temporary suffering > **purgatorial** *adj*

purge *v* (**-ges, -ging, -ged**) rid (a thing or place) of (unwanted things or people) ▶ *n* (*pl* -**s**) purging

purgative *n*, *adj* (medicine) designed to cause defecation

purgatives *n* ▷ **purgative**

purged *v* ▷ **purge**

purges *v*, *n* ▷ **purge**

purging *v* ▷ **purge**

purification *n* ▷ **purify**

purifications *n* ▷ **purify**

purified *v* ▷ **purify**

purifies *v* ▷ **purify**

purify *v* (**-fies, -fying, -fied**) make or become pure > **purification** *n* (*pl* -**s**)

purifying *v* ▷ **purify**

purist *n* (*pl* -**s**) person concerned with strict obedience to the traditions of a subject

purists *n* ▷ **purist**

puritan *n* (*pl* -**s**) person with strict moral and religious principles > **puritanical** *adj* > **puritanism** *n* (*pl* -**s**)

puritanical *adj* ▷ **puritan**

puritanism *n* ▷ **puritan**

puritanisms *n* ▷ **puritan**

puritans *n* ▷ **puritan**

purities *n* ▷ **pure**

purity *n* ▷ **pure**

purl *n* (*pl* -**s**) stitch made by knitting a plain stitch backwards ▶ *v* (**-s, -ing, -ed**) knit in purl

purled *v* ▷ **purl**

purlieus [per-lyooz] *pl n* (*Lit*) outskirts

purling *v* ▷ **purl**

purloin *v* (**-s, -ing, -ed**) steal

purloined *v* ▷ **purloin**

purloining *v* ▷ **purloin**

purloins *v* ▷ **purloin**

purls *n*, *v* ▷ **purl**

purple *adj*, *n* (*pl* -**s**) (of) a colour between red and blue

purples *n* ▷ **purple**

purport *v* (**-s, -ing, -ed**) claim (to be or do something) ▶ *n* (*pl* -**s**) apparent meaning, significance

purported *v* ▷ **purport**

purporting *v* ▷ **purport**

purports *v*, *n* ▷ **purport**

purpose *n* (*pl* -**s**) reason for which something is done or exists

purposely *adv* intentionally

purposes *n* ▷ **purpose**

purr *v* (**-s, -ing, -ed**) (of cats) make low vibrant sound, usu. when pleased ▶ *n* (*pl* -**s**) this sound

purred *v* ▷ **purr**

purring *v* ▷ **purr**

purrs *v*, *n* ▷ **purr**

purse *n* (*pl* -**s**) small bag for money (US & NZ) ▶ *v* (**-ses, -sing, -sed**) draw (one's lips) together into a small round shape

pursed *v* ▷ **purse**

purser *n* (*pl* -**s**) ship's officer who keeps the accounts

pursers *n* ▷ **purser**

purses *n*, *v* ▷ **purse**

pursing *v* ▷ **purse**

pursue *v* (**-sues, -suing, -sued**) chase > **pursuer** *n* (*pl* -**s**)

pursued *v* ▷ **pursue**

pursuer *n* ▷ **pursue**

pursuers *n* ▷ **pursue**

pursues *v* ▷ **pursue**

pursuing *v* ▷ **pursue**

pursuit *n* (*pl* -**s**) pursuing

pursuits *n* ▷ **pursuit**

purulent [pure-yoo-lent] *adj* of or containing pus

purvey *v* (**-s, -ing, -ed**) supply (provisions) > **purveyor** *n* (*pl* -**s**)

purveyed *v* ▷ **purvey**

purveying *v* ▷ **purvey**

purveyor *n* ▷ **purvey**

purveyors *n* ▷ **purvey**

purveys *v* ▷ **purvey**

purview *n* (*pl* -**s**) scope or range of activity or outlook

purviews *n* ▷ **purview**

pus *n* (*pl* -**es**) yellowish matter produced by infected tissue

puses *n* ▷ **pus**

push *v* (**-es, -ing, -ed**) move or try to move by steady force (*Informal*) ▶ *n* (*pl* -**es**) act of pushing

pushed v ▷ push
pusher n (pl -s) person who sells illegal drugs
  pushers n ▷ pusher
pushes v, n ▷ push
  pushier adj ▷ pushy
  pushiest adj ▷ pushy
  pushing v ▷ push
pushy adj (-shier, -shiest) too assertive or
  ambitious
pushchair n (pl -s) (BRIT) folding chair on
  wheels for a baby
  pushchairs n ▷ pushchair
pusillanimous adj timid and cowardly
  > **pusillanimity** n (pl -ies)
  pusillanimities n ▷ pusillanimous
  pusillanimity n ▷ pusillanimous
puss, pussy n (pl -es, -ies) (Informal) cat
  pusses n ▷ puss
  pussies n ▷ puss
pussyfoot v (-s, -ing, -ed) (Informal) behave too
  cautiously
  pussyfooted v ▷ pussyfoot
  pussyfooting v ▷ pussyfoot
  pussyfoots v ▷ pussyfoot
pustule n (pl -s) pimple containing pus
  pustules n ▷ pustule
put v (puts, putting, put) cause to be (in a
  position, state, or place) ▶ n (pl -s) throw in
  putting the shot
putative adj reputed, supposed
  putrefied v ▷ putrify
  putrefies v ▷ putrify
putrefy v (-fies, -fying, -fied) rot and produce
  an offensive smell > **putrefaction** n (pl -s)
  putrefaction n ▷ putrefy
  putrefactions n ▷ putrefy
  putrefying v ▷ putrefy
putrescent adj rotting
putrid adj rotten and foul-smelling
  puts v, n ▷ put
putsch n (pl -es) sudden violent attempt to
  remove a government from power
  putsches n ▷ putsch
putt (GOLF) n (pl -s) stroke on the putting green
  to roll the ball into or near the hole ▶ v (-s,
  -ing, -ed) strike (the ball) in this way
  putted n, v ▷ putt
putter n (pl -s) golf club for putting
  putters n ▷ putter

putties n ▷ putty
putting v ▷ put putt
putts v, n ▷ putt
putty n (pl -ies) adhesive used to fix glass into
  frames and fill cracks in woodwork
puzzle v (-les, -ling, -led) perplex and confuse
  or be perplexed or confused ▶ n (pl -s) problem
  that cannot be easily solved > **puzzlement** n
  (pl -s) > **puzzling** adj
  puzzled v ▷ puzzle
  puzzlement n ▷ puzzle
  puzzlements n ▷ puzzle
  puzzles v, n ▷ puzzle
puzzling v, adj ▷ puzzle
  pygmies n ▷ pygmy
pygmy n (pl -ies) something that is a very small
  example of its type ▶ adj (p-) very small
pyjamas pl n loose-fitting trousers and top
  worn in bed
pylon n (pl -s) steel tower-like structure
  supporting electrical cables
  pylons n ▷ pylon
pyramid n (pl -s) solid figure with a flat base
  and triangular sides sloping upwards to a
  point > **pyramidal** adj
  pyramidal adj ▷ pyramid
  pyramids n ▷ pyramid
pyre n (pl -s) pile of wood for burning a corpse
  on
  pyres n ▷ pyre
pyromania n (pl -s) uncontrollable urge to set
  things on fire > **pyromaniac** n (pl -s)
  pyromanias n ▷ pyromania
  pyromaniac n ▷ pyromania
  pyromaniacs n ▷ pyromania
pyrotechnics n art of making fireworks
  > **pyrotechnic** adj
  pyrotechnic adj ▷ pyrotechnics
python n (pl -s) large nonpoisonous snake that
  crushes its prey
  pythons n ▷ python

> **pyx** n (pyxes). A **pyx** is a container used
> for testing the weight of coins. This
> word can also be spelt **pix**. It's a great
> word to know as it earns a good score
> and doesn't use any vowels very helpful
> if you have a difficult rack. Pyx scores
> 15 points.

Qq

With a value of 10 points, Q is one of the best tiles to have on your rack. It can, however, be a difficult letter to use, especially if you don't have a U to play it with. It's therefore a good idea to remember the short words beginning with Q that don't need a U. This is easy, as there's only one two-letter word starting with Q: **qi** (11 points). There are three three-letter words, only one of which needs a U: **qua** (12). The other two are **qat** and **qis** (12 each). If you do have a U, remember **quiz** (22), which is a very useful word. If you have a blank tile for the second Z, you may be able to form its plural or verb inflections: **quizzes** (24), **quizzed** (25) and **quizzing** (26). This is especially worth remembering in case someone else plays quiz. Don't forget **quartz** (24) either.

qat n (**qats**). Qat is a shrub that grows in Africa and Arabia. This is a great word as it combines Q with two of the most common letters in the game, and thus is very handy if there isn't a U on your rack or the board. Qat scores 12 points.

qi n (**qis**). In Chinese medicine, qi is vital energy believed to circulate in the body. This is an exceptionally useful word, as it's the only two-letter word containing Q, and doesn't contain a U. The plural is one of only three three-letter words that begin with Q. As I is one of the more common tiles on the board, it's highly likely that you will be able to play qi if you have a Q. Qi scores 11 points.

qua prep. Qua means in the capacity of. This is the only three-letter word beginning with Q that needs a U, and is useful when you have a U, or there is a U on the board, but don't have any promising tiles to go with it. Qua scores 12 points.

quack¹ v (**-s, -ing, -ed**) (of a duck) utter a harsh guttural sound ▶ n (pl **-s**) sound made by a duck

quack² n (pl **-s**) unqualified person who claims medical knowledge

quacked v ▷ **quack¹**

quacking v ▷ **quack¹**

quacks v ▷ **quack¹** ▶ n ▷ **quack¹, ²**

quad n (pl **-s**) ▷ **quadrangle** ▶ adj ▷ **quadraphonic**

quadrangle n (pl **-s**) (also **quad**) rectangular courtyard with buildings on all four sides > **quadrangular** adj

quadrangles n ▷ **quadrangle**

quadrangular adj ▷ **quadrangle**

quadrant n (pl **-s**) quarter of a circle

quadrants n ▷ **quadrant**

quadraphonic adj (also **quad**) using four independent channels to reproduce or record sound

quadratic (MATHS) n (pl **-s**) equation in which the variable is raised to the power of two, but nowhere raised to a higher power ▶ adj of the second power

quadratics n ▷ **quadratic**

quadrennial adj occurring every four years

quadrilateral adj having four sides ▶ n (pl **-s**) polygon with four sides

quadrilaterals n ▷ **quadrilateral**

quadrille n (pl **-s**) square dance for four couples

quadrilles n ▷ **quadrille**

quadriplegia n (pl **-s**) paralysis of all four limbs

quadriplegias n ▷ **quadriplegia**

quadruped [kwod-roo-ped] n (pl **-s**) any animal with four legs

quadrupeds n ▷ **quadruped**

quadruple v (**-les, -ling, -led**) multiply by four ▶ adj four times as much or as many

quadrupled v ▷ **quadruple**

quadruples v ▷ **quadruple**

quadruplet n (pl **-s**) one of four offspring born

at one birth
quadruplets *n* ▷ **quadruplet**
quadrupling *v* ▷ **quadruple**
quads *n* ▷ **quad**
quaff [kwoff] *v* (**-s, -ing, -ed**) drink heartily or in one draught
quaffed *v* ▷ **quaff**
quaffing *v* ▷ **quaff**
quaffs *v* ▷ **quaff**
quagmire [kwog-mire] *n* (*pl* -**s**) soft wet area of land
quagmires *n* ▷ **quagmire**
quail[1] *n* (*pl* -**s**) small game bird of the partridge family
quail[2] *v* (**-s, -ing, -ed**) shrink back with fear
quailed *v* ▷ **quail**
quailing *v* ▷ **quail**
quails *n* ▷ **quail**[1] ▶ *v* ▷ **quail**[2]
quaint *adj* (**-er, -est**) attractively unusual, esp. in an old-fashioned style > **quaintly** *adv*
quainter *adj* ▷ **quaint**
quaintest *adj* ▷ **quaint**
quaintly *adv* ▷ **quaint**
quake *v* (**-kes, -king, -ked**) shake or tremble with or as if with fear ▶ *n* (*pl* -**s**) (*Informal*) earthquake
quaked *v*, *n* ▷ **quake**
quakes *v* ▷ **quake**
quaking *v* ▷ **quake**
qualification *n* (*pl* -**s**) official record of achievement in a course or examination
qualifications *n* ▷ **qualification**
qualified *v*, *adj* ▷ **qualify**
qualifies *v* ▷ **qualify**
qualify *v* (**-fies, -fying, -fied**) provide or be provided with the abilities necessary for a task, office, or duty > **qualified** *adj*
qualifying *v* ▷ **qualify**
qualitative *adj* of or relating to quality
qualities *n* ▷ **quality**
quality *n* (*pl* -**ties**) degree or standard of excellence ▶ *adj* excellent or superior
qualm [kwahm] *n* (*pl* -**s**) pang of conscience
qualms *n* ▷ **qualm**
quandaries *n* ▷ **quandary**
quandary *n* (*pl* -**ries**) difficult situation or dilemma
quandong [kwon-dong] *n* (*pl* -**s**) small Australian tree with edible fruit and nuts used in preserves
quandongs *n* ▷ **quandong**
quango *n* (*pl* -**s**) (CHIEFLY BRIT) quasi-autonomous nongovernmental organization: any partly independent official body set up by a government

quangos *n* ▷ **quango**
quanta *n* ▷ **quantum**
quantifiable *adj* ▷ **quantify**
quantification *n* ▷ **quantify**
quantifications *n* ▷ **quantify**
quantified *v* ▷ **quantify**
quantifies *v* ▷ **quantify**
quantify *v* (**-fies, -fying, -fied**) discover or express the quantity of > **quantifiable** *adj* > **quantification** *n* (*pl* -**s**)
quantifying *v* ▷ **quantify**
quantitative *adj* of or relating to quantity
quantities *n* ▷ **quantity**
quantity *n* (*pl* -**ties**) specified or definite amount or number
quantum *n* (*pl* -**ta**) desired or required amount, esp. a very small one
quarantine *n* (*pl* -**s**) period of isolation of people or animals to prevent the spread of disease ▶ *v* (**-nes, -ning, -ned**) isolate in or as if in quarantine
quarantined *v* ▷ **quarantine**
quarantines *n*, *v* ▷ **quarantine**
quarantining *v* ▷ **quarantine**
quark *n* (*pl* -**s**) (PHYSICS) subatomic particle thought to be the fundamental unit of matter
quarks *n* ▷ **quark**
quarrel *n* (*pl* -**s**) angry disagreement ▶ *v* (**-s, -lling, -lled**) have a disagreement or dispute > **quarrelsome** *adj*
quarrelled *v* ▷ **quarrel**
quarrelling *v* ▷ **quarrel**
quarrels *n*, *v* ▷ **quarrel**
quarrelsome *adj* ▷ **quarrel**
quarried *v* ▷ **quarry**[1]
quarries *n* ▷ **quarry**[1, 2] ▶ *v* ▷ **quarry**[1]
quarry[1] *n* (*pl* -**rries**) place where stone is dug from the surface of the earth ▶ *v* (**-rries, -rrying, -rried**) extract (stone) from a quarry
quarry[2] *n* (*pl* -**rries**) person or animal that is being hunted
quart *n* (*pl* -**s**) unit of liquid measure equal to two pints (1.136 litres)
quarter *n* (*pl* -**s**) one of four equal parts of something ▶ *v* (**-s, -ing, -ed**) divide into four equal parts
quarterdeck *n* (*pl* -**s**) (NAUT) rear part of the upper deck of a ship
quarterdecks *n* ▷ **quarterdeck**
quartered *v* ▷ **quarter**
quarterfinal *n* (*pl* -**s**) round before the semifinal in a competition
quarterfinals *n* ▷ **quarterfinal**
quartering *v* ▷ **quarter**

quarterlies n ▷ quarterly

quarterly adj occurring, due, or issued at intervals of three months ▶ n (pl -**lies**) magazine issued every three months ▶ adv once every three months

quartermaster n (pl -**s**) military officer responsible for accommodation, food, and equipment

quartermasters n ▷ quartermaster

quarters n, v ▷ quarter

quartet n (pl -**s**) group of four performers

quartets n ▷ quartet

quarto n (pl -**s**) book size in which the sheets are folded into four leaves

quarto n ▷ quarto

quarts n ▷ quart

quartz n (pl -**es**) hard glossy mineral

quartzes n ▷ quartz

quasar [kway-zar] n (pl -**s**) extremely distant starlike object that emits powerful radio waves

quasars n ▷ quasar

quash v (-**shes**, -**shing**, -**shed**) annul or make void

quashed v ▷ quash

quashes v ▷ quash

quashing v ▷ quash

quatrain n (pl -**s**) stanza or poem of four lines

quatrains n ▷ quatrain

quaver v (-**s**, -**ing**, -**ed**) (of a voice) quiver or tremble ▶ n (pl -**s**) (MUSIC) note half the length of a crotchet

quavered v ▷ quaver

quavering v ▷ quaver

quavers v, n ▷ quaver

quay [kee] n (pl -**s**) wharf built parallel to the shore

quays n ▷ quay

queasier adj ▷ queasy

queasiest adj ▷ queasy

queasiness n ▷ queasy

queasinesses n ▷ queasy

queasy adj (-**sier**, -**siest**) having the feeling that one is about to vomit > **queasiness** n (pl -**es**)

queen n (pl -**s**) female sovereign who is the official ruler or head of state > **queenly** adj

queenly adj ▷ queen

queens n ▷ queen

queer adj (-**er**, -**est**) not normal or usual

queerer adj ▷ queer

queerest adj ▷ queer

quell v (-**s**, -**ing**, -**ed**) suppress

quelled v ▷ quell

quelling v ▷ quell

quells v ▷ quell

quench v (-**es**, -**ing**, -**ed**) satisfy (one's thirst)

quenched v ▷ quench

quenches v ▷ quench

quenching v ▷ quench

queried v ▷ query

queries n, v ▷ query

quern n (pl -**s**) stone hand mill for grinding corn

querns n ▷ quern

querulous [kwer-yoo-luss] adj complaining or whining > **querulously** adv

querulously adv ▷ querulous

query n (pl -**ries**) question, esp. one raising doubt ▶ v (-**ries**, -**rying**, -**ried**) express uncertainty, doubt, or an objection concerning (something)

querying v ▷ query

quest n (pl -**s**) long and difficult search ▶ v (-**s**, -**ing**, -**ed**) (foll. by **for** or **after**) go in search of

quested v ▷ quest

questing v ▷ quest

question n (pl -**s**) form of words addressed to a person in order to obtain an answer ▶ v (-**s**, -**ing**, -**ed**) put a question or questions to (a person)

questionable adj of disputable value or authority > **questionably** adv

questionably adv ▷ questionable

questioned v ▷ question

questioning v ▷ question

questionnaire n (pl -**s**) set of questions on a form, used to collect information from people

questionnaires n ▷ questionnaire

questions n, v ▷ question

quests n, v ▷ quest

> **quetzal** or **quezal** n (**quetzals**, **quezales**, **quezals**). The quetzal is a crested bird of Central and South America. This is a great word if you can get the tiles for it, so it's well worth remembering both spellings and the three plural forms. If you can use all your letters to play quetzal or quezals, you'll earn a bonus of 50 points. Quetzal scores 25 points.

queue n (pl -**s**) line of people or vehicles waiting for something ▶ v (**queues**, **queuing** or **queueing**, **queued**) (often foll. by **up**) form or remain in a line while waiting

queued v ▷ queue

queueing v ▷ queue

queues n, v ▷ queue

queuing v ▷ queue

quibble v (-**les**, -**ling**, -**led**) make trivial

objections ▸ *n (pl* **-s**) trivial objection

quibbled *v* ▷ **quibble**

quibbles *v, n* ▷ **quibble**

quibbling *v* ▷ **quibble**

quiche [keesh] *n (pl* -s) savoury flan with an egg custard filling to which vegetables etc. are added

quiches *n* ▷ **quiche**

quick *adj* (-er, -est) speedy, fast ▸ *n (pl* -s) area of sensitive flesh under a nail ▸ *adv (Informal)* in a rapid manner > **quickly** *adv*

quicken *v* (-s, -ing, -ed) make or become faster

quickened *v* ▷ **quicken**

quickening *v* ▷ **quicken**

quickens *v* ▷ **quicken**

quicker *adj* ▷ **quick**

quickest *adj* ▷ **quick**

quicklime *n (pl* -s) white solid used in the manufacture of glass and steel

quicklimes *n* ▷ **quicklime**

quickly *adv* ▷ **quick**

quicks *n* ▷ **quick**

quicksand *n (pl* -s) deep mass of loose wet sand that sucks anything on top of it into it

quicksands *n* ▷ **quicksand**

quicksilver *n (pl* -s) mercury

quicksilvers *n* ▷ **quicksilver**

quickstep *n (pl* -s) fast modern ballroom dance

quicksteps *n* ▷ **quickstep**

quid *n (pl* quid, -s) (BRIT) (*Slang*) pound (sterling)

quids *n* ▷ **quid**

quiescence *n* ▷ **quiescent**

quiescences *n* ▷ **quiescent**

quiescent [kwee-**ess**-ent] *adj* quiet, inactive, or dormant > **quiescence** *n (pl* -s)

quiet *adj* (-er, -est) with little noise ▸ *n (pl* -s) quietness ▸ *v* (-s, -ing, -ed) make or become quiet > **quietly** *adv* > **quietness** *n (pl* -es)

quieted *v* ▷ **quiet**

quieten *v* (-s, -ing, -ed) (*often foll. by* **down**) make or become quiet

quieter *adj* ▷ **quiet**

quietest *adj* ▷ **quiet**

quieting *v* ▷ **quiet**

quietism *n (pl* -s) passivity and calmness of mind towards external events

quietisms *n* ▷ **quietism**

quietly *adv* ▷ **quiet**

quietness *n* ▷ **quiet**

quietnesses *n* ▷ **quiet**

quiets *v, n* ▷ **quiet**

quietude *n* (-s) quietness, peace, or tranquillity

quietudes *n* ▷ **quietude**

quiff *n (pl* -s) tuft of hair brushed up above the forehead

quiffs *n* ▷ **quiff**

quill *n (pl* -s) pen made from the feather of a bird's wing or tail

quills *n* ▷ **quill**

quilt *n (pl* -s) padded covering for a bed

quilted *adj* consisting of two layers of fabric with a layer of soft material between them

quilts *n* ▷ **quilt**

quince *n (pl* -s) acid-tasting pear-shaped fruit

quinces *n* ▷ **quince**

quinine *n (pl* -s) bitter drug used as a tonic and formerly to treat malaria

quinines *n* ▷ **quinine**

quinquennial *adj* occurring every five years

quins *n* ▷ **quin**

quinsies *n* ▷ **quinsy**

quinsy *n (pl* -sies) inflammation of the throat or tonsils

quintessence *n (pl* -s) most perfect representation of a quality or state > **quintessential** *adj*

quintessences *n* ▷ **quintessence**

quintessential *adj* ▷ **quintessence**

quintet *n (pl* -s) group of five performers

quintets *n* ▷ **quintet**

quintuplet *n (pl* -s) one of five offspring born at one birth

quintuplets *n* ▷ **quintuplet**

quinze *n* (**quinzes**). Quinze is a card game. This is a high-scoring word, and if you can use all of your tiles to form the plural, you'll get a 50-points bonus. Quinze scores 24 points.

quip *n (pl* -s) witty saying ▸ *v* (-s, -pping, -pped) make a quip

quipped *v* ▷ **quip**

quipping *v* ▷ **quip**

quips *n, v* ▷ **quip**

quire *n (pl* -s) set of 24 or 25 sheets of paper

quires *n* ▷ **quire**

quirk *n (pl* -s) peculiarity of character > **quirky** *adj* (-kier, -kiest)

quirks *n* ▷ **quirk**

quirky *adj* ▷ **quirk**

quisling *n (pl* -s) traitor who aids an occupying enemy force

quislings *n* ▷ **quisling**

quit *v* (**quits, quitting, quit**) stop (doing something)

quite *adv* somewhat ▸ *interj* expression of agreement

quits *adj* (*Informal*) on an equal footing ▸ *v* ▷ **quit**

quitter *n (pl* -s) person who lacks perseverance

quitters *n* ▷ **quitter**
quitting *v* ▷ **quit**
quiver[1] *v* (**-s, -ing, -ed**) shake with a tremulous movement ▶ *n* (*pl* **-s**) shaking or trembling
quiver[2] *n* (*pl* **-s**) case for arrows
quivered *v* ▷ **quiver**[1]
quivering *v* ▷ **quiver**[1]
quivers *v* ▷ **quiver**[1] ▶ *n* ▷ **quiver**[1, 2]

> **quixote** *n* (**quixotes**). A quixote is an impractically idealistic person. This is a high-scoring word; if you have all the letters to play it, and can place them on the board, you'll score a 50-point bonus for using all of your tiles. Quixote scores 23 points.

quixotic [kwik-**sot**-ik] *adj* romantic and unrealistic > **quixotically** *adv*
quixotically *adv* ▷ **quixotic**
quiz *n* (*pl* **-zzes**) entertainment in which the knowledge of the players is tested by a series of questions ▶ *v* (**-zzes, -zzing, -zzed**) investigate by close questioning
quizzed *v* ▷ **quiz**
quizzes *n*, *v* ▷ **quiz**
quizzical *adj* questioning and mocking > **quizzically** *adv*
quizzically *adv* ▷ **quizzical**
quizzing *v* ▷ **quiz**
quod *n* (*pl* **-s**) (BRIT) (*Slang*) jail
quods *n* ▷ **quod**
quoit *n* (*pl* **-s**) large ring used in the game of

quoits ▶ *pl* game in which quoits are tossed at a stake in the ground in attempts to encircle it
quoits *n* ▷ **quoit**
quokka *n* (*pl* **-s**) small Australian wallaby
quokkas *n* ▷ **quokka**
quorum *n* (*pl* **-s**) minimum number of people required to be present at a meeting before any transactions can take place
quorums *n* ▷ **quorum**
quota *n* (*pl* **-s**) share that is due from, due to, or allocated to a group or person
quotable *adj* ▷ **quote**
quotas *n* ▷ **quota**
quotation *n* (*pl* **-s**) written or spoken passage repeated exactly in a later work, speech, or conversation
quotations *n* ▷ **quotation**
quote *v* (**-tes, -ting, -ted**) repeat (words) exactly from (an earlier work, speech, or conversation) ▶ *n* (*pl* **-s**) (*Informal*) quotation > **quotable** *adj*
quoted *v* ▷ **quote**
quotes *v*, *n* ▷ **quote**
quoth *v* (*Obs*) said
quotidian *adj* daily
quotient *n* (*pl* **-s**) result of the division of one number or quantity by another
quotients *n* ▷ **quotient**
quoting *v* ▷ **quote**

Rr

R is one of the most common consonants in Scrabble, along with N and T. Despite this, however, there is only one two-letter word beginning with R: **re** (2 points). This is worth remembering, as you won't need to waste time trying to think of others. There are some good three-letter words with R, however, some of which are quite unusual: **raj, rax, rex** (10 each), **rez** and **riz** (12 each). Also, don't forget common words like **raw, ray** and **row** (6 each).

rabbi [rab-bye] *n* (*pl* **-s**) Jewish spiritual leader > **rabbinical** *adj*
  rabbinical *adj* ▷ **rabbi**
  rabbis *n* ▷ **rabbi**
rabbit *n* (*pl* **-s**) small burrowing mammal with long ears
  rabbits *n* ▷ **rabbit**
rabble *n* (*pl* **-s**) disorderly crowd of noisy people
  rabbles *n* ▷ **rabble**
rabid *adj* (**-er, -est**) fanatical > **rabidly** *adv*
  rabider *adj* ▷ **rabid**
  rabidest *adj* ▷ **rabid**
  rabidly *adv* ▷ **rabid**
rabies [ray-beez] *n* usu. fatal viral disease transmitted by dogs and certain other animals
raccoon *n* (*pl* **-s**) small N American mammal with a long striped tail
  raccoons *n* ▷ **raccoon**
race[1] *n* (*pl* **-s**) contest of speed ▶ *pl* meeting for horse racing ▶ *v* (**-ces, -cing, -ced**) compete with in a race > **racer** *n* (*pl* **-s**) > **racecourse** *n* (*pl* **-s**) > **racehorse** *n* (*pl* **-s**) > **racetrack** *n* (*pl* **-s**)
race[2] *n* (*pl* **-s**) group of people of common ancestry with distinguishing physical features, such as skin colour > **racial** *adj*
raced *n, v* ▷ **race**[1]
  racecourse *n* ▷ **race**[1]
  racecourses *n* ▷ **race**[1]
  raced *n, v* ▷ **race**[1]
racehorse *n* ▷ **race**[1]
  racehorses *n* ▷ **race**[1]
raceme [rass-eem] *n* (*pl* **-s**) cluster of flowers along a central stem, as in the foxglove
  racemes *n* ▷ **raceme**
racer *n* ▷ **race**[1]
  racers *n* ▷ **race**[1]
  races *n* ▷ **race**[1, 2] ▶ *v* ▷ **race**[1]

racetrack *n* ▷ **race**[1]
racetracks *n* ▷ **race**[1]
racial *adj* ▷ **race**[2]
racialism *n* ▷ **racism**
racialisms *adj, n* ▷ **racism**
racialist *n* ▷ **racism**
racialists *n* ▷ **racism**
racier *adj* ▷ **racy**
raciest *adj* ▷ **racy**
racing *v* ▷ **race**
racism, racialism *n* (*pl* **-s**) hostile attitude or behaviour to members of other races, based on a belief in the innate superiority of one's own race > **racist, racialist** *adj, n* (*pl* **-s**)
  racisms *n* ▷ **racism**
  racist *n* ▷ **racism**
  racists *n* ▷ **racism**
rack *n* (*pl* **-s**) framework for holding particular articles, such as coats or luggage (HIST) ▶ *v* (**-s, -ing, -ed**) cause great suffering to
  racked *v* ▷ **rack**
racket[1] *n* (*pl* **-s**) noisy disturbance
racket[2], **racquet** *n* (**-s**) bat with strings stretched in an oval frame, used in tennis etc.
racketeer *n* (*pl* **-s**) person making illegal profits
  racketeers *n* ▷ **racketeer**
rackets *n* ball game played in a paved walled court ▶ *n* ▷ **racket**[1, 2]
  racking *v* ▷ **rack**
  racks *n, v* ▷ **rack**
raconteur [rak-on-tur] *n* (*pl* **-s**) skilled storyteller
  raconteurs *n* ▷ **raconteur**
  racquet *n* ▷ **racket**[2]
  racquets *n* ▷ **racket**[2]
racy *adj* (**-cier, -ciest**) slightly shocking
radar *n* (*pl* **-s**) device for tracking distant objects by bouncing high-frequency radio

pulses off them
radars n ▷ **radar**
radial adj spreading out from a common
central point
radiance n ▷ **radiant**
radiances n ▷ **radiant**
radiant adj looking happy > **radiance** n (**-s**)
radiate v (**-tes, -ting, -ted**) spread out from
a centre
radiated v ▷ **radiate**
radiates v ▷ **radiate**
radiating v ▷ **radiate**
radiation n (pl **-s**) transmission of energy from
one body to another
radiations n ▷ **radiation**
radiator n (**-s**) (BRIT) arrangement of pipes
containing hot water or steam to heat a
room
radiators n ▷ **radiator**
radical adj fundamental ▶ n (pl **-s**) person
advocating fundamental (political) change
> **radically** adv > **radicalism** n (**-s**)
radicalism n ▷ **radical**
radicalisms n ▷ **radical**
radically adv ▷ **radical**
radicals n ▷ **radical**
radicle n (pl **-s**) small or developing root
radicles n ▷ **radicle**
radii n ▷ **radius**
radio n (pl **-s**) use of electromagnetic waves for
broadcasting, communication, etc. ▶ v (**-s,
-ing, -ed**) transmit (a message) by radio
radioactive adj emitting radiation as a result
of nuclear decay > **radioactivity** n (pl **-ies**)
radioactivities n ▷ **radioactive**
radioactivity n ▷ **radioactive**
radioed v ▷ **radio**
radiographer n ▷ **radiography**
radiographers n ▷ **radiography**
radiographies n ▷ **radiography**
radiography [ray-dee-og-ra-fee] n (pl **-phies**)
production of an image on a film or plate by
radiation > **radiographer** n (pl **-s**)
radioing v ▷ **radio**
radiologies n ▷ **radiology**
radiologist n ▷ **radiology**
radiologists n ▷ **radiology**
radiology [ray-dee-ol-a-jee] n (pl **-gies**) science
of using x-rays in medicine > **radiologist** n
(pl **-s**)
radios n, v ▷ **radio**
radiotherapies n ▷ **radiotherapy**
radiotherapist n ▷ **radiotherapy**
radiotherapists n ▷ **radiotherapy**
radiotherapy n (pl **-pies**) treatment of disease,

esp. cancer, by radiation > **radiotherapist**
n (pl **-s**)
radish n (pl **-es**) small hot-flavoured root
vegetable eaten raw in salads
radishes n ▷ **radish**
radium n (pl **-s**) (CHEM) radioactive metallic
element
radiums n ▷ **radiums**
radius n (pl **radii, radiuses**) (length of)
a straight line from the centre to the
circumference of a circle
radiuses n ▷ **radius**
radon [ray-don] n (pl **-s**) (CHEM) radioactive
gaseous element
radons n ▷ **radon**
raffia n (pl **-s**) prepared palm fibre for weaving
mats etc.
raffias n ▷ **raffia**
raffish adj slightly disreputable
raffle n (pl **-s**) lottery with goods as prizes ▶ v
(**-les, -ling, -led**) offer as a prize in a raffle
raffled v ▷ **raffle**
raffles n, v ▷ **raffle**
raffling v ▷ **raffle**
raft n (pl **-s**) floating platform of logs, planks,
etc.
rafter n (pl **-s**) one of the main beams of a roof
rafters n ▷ **rafter**
rafts n ▷ **raft**
rag[1] n (pl **-s**) fragment of cloth ▶ pl tattered
clothing
rag[2] (BRIT) v (**-s, -gging, -gged**) tease ▶ adj, n (pl
-s) (of) events organized by students to raise
money for charities
rage n (pl **-s**) violent anger or passion ▶ v (**-ges,
-ging, -ged**) speak or act with fury
raged v ▷ **rage**
rages n, v ▷ **rage**
ragamuffin n (pl **-s**) ragged dirty child
ragamuffins n ▷ **ragamuffin**
ragged [rag-gid] adj dressed in shabby or torn
clothes ▶ v ▷ **rag**[2]
ragging v ▷ **rag**[2]
raging v ▷ **rage**
raglan adj (of a sleeve) joined to a garment
by diagonal seams from the neck to the
underarm
ragout [rag-goo] n (pl **-s**) richly seasoned stew
of meat and vegetables
ragouts n ▷ **ragout**
rags n, v ▷ **rag**[1,2]
ragtime n (pl **-s**) style of jazz piano music
ragtimes n ▷ **ragtime**
raid n (pl **-s**) sudden surprise attack or search
▶ v (**-s, -ing, -ed**) make a raid on > **raider** n

(*pl* -**s**)
raided *v* ▷ **raid**
raider *n* ▷ **raid**
raiders *n* ▷ **raid**
raiding *v* ▷ **raid**
raids *n, v* ▷ **raid**
rail[1] *n* (*pl* -**s**) horizontal bar, esp. as part of a fence or track
rail[2] *v* (-**s, -ing, -ed**) (*foll. by* **at** *or* **against**) complain bitterly or loudly
rail[3] *n* (*pl* -**s**) small marsh bird
railed *v* ▷ **rail**[2]
railing *n* (*pl* -**s**) fence made of rails supported by posts ▶ *v* ▷ **rail**[2]
railings *n* ▷ **railing**
railleries *n* ▷ **raillery**
raillery *n* (*pl* -**ies**) teasing or joking
rails *n* ▷ **rail**[1,2,3] ▶ *v* ▷ **rail**[2]
railway *n* (*pl* -**s**) track of iron rails on which trains run
railways *n* ▷ **railway**
raiment *n* (*pl* -**s**) (*Obs*) clothing
raiments *n* ▷ **raiment**
rain *n* (*pl* -**s**) water falling in drops from the clouds ▶ *v* (-**s, -ing, -ed**) fall or pour down as rain > **rainy** *adj* (-**nier, -niest**)
rainbow *n* (*pl* -**s**) arch of colours in the sky
rainbows *n* ▷ **rainbow**
raincoat *n* (*pl* -**s**) water-resistant overcoat
raincoats *n* ▷ **raincoat**
rained *v* ▷ **rain**
rainier *adj* ▷ **rainy**
rainiest *adj* ▷ **rainy**
rainfall *n* (*pl* -**s**) amount of rain
rainfalls *n* ▷ **rainfall**
rainforest *n* (*pl* -**s**) dense forest in tropical and temperate areas
rainforests *n* ▷ **rainforest**
raining *v* ▷ **rain**
rains *n, v* ▷ **rain**
rainy *adj* ▷ **rain**
raise *v* (-**ses, -sing, -sed**) lift up
raised *v* ▷ **raise**
raises *v* ▷ **raise**
raisin *n* (*pl* -**s**) dried grape
raising *v* ▷ **raise**
raisins *n* ▷ **raisin**

raj *n* (**rajes**). Raj is an Indian word for government. This word can be very useful when there isn't much space on the board. If you can't play raj, remember that it's just **jar** backwards you might be able to fit that in somewhere. Raj scores 10 points.

raja, rajah *n* (*pl* -**s**) (HIST) Indian prince or ruler

rajah *n* ▷ **raja**
rajahs *n* ▷ **raja**
rajas *n* ▷ **raja**
rake[1] *n* (*pl* -**s**) tool with a long handle and a crosspiece with teeth, used for smoothing earth or gathering leaves, hay, etc. ▶ *v* (-**kes, -king, -ked**) gather or smooth with a rake
rake[2] *n* (*pl* -**s**) dissolute or immoral man
raked *v* ▷ **rake**[1]
rakes *n, v* ▷ **rake**[1,2] ▶ *v* ▷ **rake**[1]
raking *v* ▷ **rake**[1]
rakish *adj* dashing or jaunty
rallied *v* ▷ **rally**
rallies *n, v* ▷ **rally**
rally *n* (*pl* -**ies**) large gathering of people for a meeting ▶ *v* (-**ies, -ying, -ied**) bring or come together after dispersal or for a common cause
rallying *v* ▷ **rally**
ram *n* (*pl* -**s**) male sheep ▶ *v* (-**s, -mming, -mmed**) strike against with force
ramble *v* (-**les, -ling, -led**) walk without a definite route ▶ *n* (*pl* -**s**) walk, esp. in the country
rambled *v* ▷ **ramble**
rambler *n* (*pl* -**s**) person who rambles
ramblers *n* ▷ **rambler**
rambles *v, n* ▷ **ramble**
rambling *v* ▷ **ramble**
ramekin [ram-ik-in] *n* (*pl* -**s**) small ovenproof dish for a single serving of food
ramekins *n* ▷ **ramekin**
ramifications *pl n* consequences resulting from an action
rammed *v* ▷ **ram**
ramming *v* ▷ **ram**
ramp *n* (*pl* -**s**) slope joining two level surfaces
rampage *v* (-**ges, -ging, -ged**) dash about violently
rampaged *v* ▷ **rampage**
rampages *v* ▷ **rampage**
rampaging *v* ▷ **rampage**
rampant *adj* growing or spreading uncontrollably
rampart *n* (*pl* -**s**) mound or wall for defence
ramparts *n* ▷ **rampart**
ramps *n* ▷ **ramp**
rams *n, v* ▷ **ram**
ramshackle *adj* tumbledown, rickety, or makeshift
ran *v* ▷ **run**
ranch *n* (*pl* -**es**) large cattle farm in the American West > **rancher** *n* (*pl* -**s**)
rancher *n* ▷ **ranch**
ranchers *n* ▷ **ranch**

ranches *n* ▷ **ranch**
rancid *adj* (of butter, bacon, etc.) stale and having an offensive smell > **rancidity** *n* (*pl* -ies)
rancidities *n* ▷ **rancidity**
rancidity *n* ▷ **rancid**
rancorous *adj* ▷ **rancour**
rancour *n* (*pl* -s) deep bitter hate > **rancorous** *adj*
rancours *n* ▷ **rancour**
rand *n* (*pl* -s) monetary unit of S Africa
randier *adj* ▷ **randy**
randiest *adj* ▷ **randy**
random *adj* made or done by chance or without plan
rands *n* ▷ **rand**
randy *adj* (-ier, -iest) (*Informal*) sexually aroused
rang *v* ▷ **ring¹**
range *n* (*pl* -s) limits of effectiveness or variation ▶ *v* (-ges, -ging, -ged) vary between one point and another
ranged *v* ▷ **range**
ranger *n* (*pl* -s) official in charge of a nature reserve etc.
rangers *n* ▷ **ranger**
rangefinder *n* (*pl* -s) instrument for finding how far away an object is
rangefinders *n* ▷ **rangefinder**
ranges *n*, *v* ▷ **range**
rangier *adj* ▷ **rangy**
rangiest *adj* ▷ **rangy**
ranging *v* ▷ **range**
rangy [rain-jee] *adj* (-ier, -iest) having long slender limbs
rank¹ *n* (*pl* -s) relative place or position ▶ *v* (-s, -ing, -ed) have a specific rank or position
rank² *adj* complete or absolute
ranked *v* ▷ **rank**
ranking *v* ▷ **rank**
rankle *v* (-les, -ling, -led) continue to cause resentment or bitterness
rankled *v* ▷ **rankle**
rankles *v* ▷ **rankle**
rankling *v* ▷ **rankle**
ranks *n*, *v* ▷ **rank¹**
ransack *v* (-s, -ing, -ed) search thoroughly
ransacked *v* ▷ **ransack**
ransacking *v* ▷ **ransack**
ransacks *v* ▷ **ransack**
ransom *n* (*pl* -s) money demanded in return for the release of someone who has been kidnapped
ransoms *n* ▷ **ransom**
rant *v* (-s, -ing, -ed) talk in a loud and excited way > **ranter** *n* (*pl* -s)

ranted *v* ▷ **rant**
ranter *n* ▷ **rant**
ranters *n* ▷ **rant**
ranting *v* ▷ **rant**
rants *v* ▷ **rant**
rap *v* (-s, -pping, -pped) hit with a sharp quick blow ▶ *n* (*pl* -s) quick sharp blow > **rapper** *n* (*pl* -s)
rapacious *adj* greedy or grasping > **rapacity** *n* (*pl* -ies)
rapacities *n* ▷ **rapacious**
rapacity *n* ▷ **rapacious**
rape¹ *v* (-pes, -ping, -ped) force to submit to sexual intercourse ▶ *n* (*pl* -s) act of raping > **rapist** *n* (*pl* -s)
rape² *n* (*pl* -s) plant with oil-yielding seeds, also used as fodder
raped *v* ▷ **rape¹**
rapes *v* ▷ **rape¹** ▶ *n* ▷ **rape¹,²**
rapid *adj* (-er, -est) quick, swift > **rapidly** *adv* > **rapidity** *n* (*pl* -ies)
rapider *adj* ▷ **rapid**
rapidest *adj* ▷ **rapid**
rapidities *n* ▷ **rapid**
rapidity *n* ▷ **rapid**
rapidly *adv* ▷ **rapid**
rapids *pl n* part of a river with a fast turbulent current
rapier [ray-pyer] *n* (*pl* -s) fine-bladed sword
rapiers *n* ▷ **rapier**
raping *v* ▷ **rape¹**
rapist *n* ▷ **rape¹**
rapists *n* ▷ **rape¹**
rapped *v* ▷ **rap**
rapper *n* ▷ **rap**
rappers *n* ▷ **rap**
rapping *v* ▷ **rap**
rapport [rap-pore] *n* (*pl* -s) harmony or agreement
rapports *n* ▷ **rapport**
rapprochement [rap-prosh-mong] *n* (*pl* -s) re-establishment of friendly relations, esp. between nations
rapprochements *n* ▷ **rapprochement**
raps *v*, *n* ▷ **rap**
rapt *adj* engrossed or spellbound
rapture *n* (*pl* -s) ecstasy > **rapturous** *adj*
raptures *n* ▷ **rapture**
rapturous *adj* ▷ **rapture**
rare¹ *adj* (-r, -st) uncommon > **rarity** *n* (*pl* -ies)
rare² *adj* (-r, -st) (of meat) lightly cooked
rarebit *n* (*pl* -s) dish of melted cheese on toast
rarebits *n* ▷ **rarebit**
rarefied [rare-if-ide] *adj* highly specialized, exalted

rarely *adv* seldom
rarer *adj* ▷ **rare**[1,2]
rarest *adj* ▷ **rare**[1,2]
raring *adj* enthusiastic, willing, or ready to
rarities *n* ▷ **rare**[1]
rarity *n* ▷ **rare**[1]
rascal *n* (*pl* -s) rogue > **rascally** *adj* (-ier, -iest)
rascalliest *adj* ▷ **rascal**
rascally *adj* ▷ **rascal**
rascals *n* ▷ **rascal**
rash[1] *adj* (-er, -est) hasty, reckless, or incautious > **rashly** *adv*
rash[2] *n* (*pl* -es) eruption of spots or patches on the skin
rasher *n* (*pl* -s) thin slice of bacon ▶ *adj* ▷ **rash**[1]
rashers *n* ▷ **rasher**
rashes *n* ▷ **rash**[2]
rashest *adj* ▷ **rash**[1]
rashly *adv* ▷ **rash**[1]
rasp *n* (*pl* -s) harsh grating noise ▶ *v* (-s, -ing, -ed) speak in a grating voice
raspberries *n* ▷ **raspberry**
raspberry *n* (*pl* -ies) red juicy edible berry (*Informal*)
rasped *v* ▷ **rasp**
rasping *v* ▷ **rasp**
rasps *n*, *v* ▷ **rasp**
rat *n* (*pl* -s) small rodent (*Informal*) ▶ *v* (-s, -tting, -tted) (*Informal*) inform (on)
ratafia [rat-a-**fee**-a] *n* (*pl* -s) liqueur made from fruit
ratafias *n* ▷ **ratafia**
ratatouille [rat-a-**twee**] *n* (*pl* -s) vegetable casserole of tomatoes, aubergines, etc.
ratatouilles *n* ▷ **ratatouille**
ratchet *n* (*pl* -s) set of teeth on a bar or wheel allowing motion in one direction only
ratchets *n* ▷ **ratchet**
rate *n* (*pl* -s) degree of speed or progress ▶ *pl* local tax on business ▶ *v* (-tes, -ting, -ted) consider or value > **ratepayer** *n* (*pl* -s)
rateable *adj* able to be rated
rated *v* ▷ **rate**
ratepayer *n* ▷ **rate**
ratepayers *n* ▷ **rate**
rates *n*, *v* ▷ **rate**
rather *adv* to some extent
ratification *n* ▷ **ratify**
ratifications *n* ▷ **ratify**
ratified *v* ▷ **ratify**
ratifies *v* ▷ **ratify**
ratify *v* (-ies, -ying, -ied) give formal approval to > **ratification** *n* (*pl* -s)
ratifiying *v* ▷ **ratify**
rating *n* (*pl* -s) valuation or assessment ▶ *pl* size of the audience for a TV programme ▶ *v* ▷ **rate**
ratings *n* ▷ **rating**
ratio *n* (*pl* -s) relationship between two numbers or amounts expressed as a proportion
ration *n* (*pl* -s) fixed allowance of food etc. ▶ *v* (-s, -ing, -ed) limit to a certain amount per person
rational *adj* reasonable, sensible > **rationally** *adv* > **rationality** *n* (*pl* -ies)
rationale [rash-a-**nahl**] *n* (*pl* -s) reason for an action or decision
rationales *n* ▷ **rationale**
rationalism *n* (*pl* -s) philosophy that regards reason as the only basis for beliefs or actions > **rationalist** *n* (*pl* -s)
rationalisms *n* ▷ **rationalism**
rationalist *n* ▷ **rationalism**
rationalists *n* ▷ **rationalism**
rationalities *n* ▷ **rational**
rationality *n* ▷ **rational**
rationalize *v* (-zes, -zing, -zed) justify by plausible reasoning > **rationalization** *n* (*pl* -s)
rationalization *n* ▷ **rationalize**
rationalizations *n* ▷ **rationalize**
rationalized *v* ▷ **rationalize**
rationalizes *v* ▷ **rationalize**
rationalizing *v* ▷ **rationalize**
rationally *adv* ▷ **rational**
rationed *v* ▷ **ration**
rationing *v* ▷ **ration**
rations *n*, *v* ▷ **ration**
ratios *n* ▷ **ratio**
rats *n* ▷ **rat**
rattan *n* (*pl* -s) climbing palm with jointed stems used for canes
rattans *n* ▷ **rattan**
ratted *v* ▷ **rat**
rattier *adj* ▷ **ratty**
rattiest *adj* ▷ **ratty**
ratting *v* ▷ **rat**
rattle *v* (-les, -ling, -led) give out a succession of short sharp sounds ▶ *n* (*pl* -s) short sharp sound
rattled *v* ▷ **rattle**
rattlesnake *n* (*pl* -s) poisonous snake with loose horny segments on the tail that make a rattling sound
rattlesnakes *n* ▷ **rattlesnake**
rattles *v*, *n* ▷ **rattle**
rattling *v* ▷ **rattle**
ratty *adj* (-ier, -iest) (BRIT & NZ) (*Informal*) bad-tempered, irritable
raucous *adj* hoarse or harsh

raunchier *adj* ▷ **raunchy**
raunchiest *adj* ▷ **raunchy**
raunchy *adj* (**-chier, -chiest**) (*Slang*) earthy, sexy
ravage *v* (**-ges, -ging, -ged**) cause extensive damage to
ravaged *v* ▷ **ravage**
ravages *pl n* damaging effects ▸ *v* ▷ **ravage**
ravaging *v* ▷ **ravage**
rave *v* (**-ves, -ving, -ved**) talk wildly or with enthusiasm ▸ *n* (*pl* **-s**) (*Slang*) large-scale party with electronic dance music
raved *v* ▷ **rave**
ravel *v* (**-s, -lling, -lled**) tangle or become entangled
ravelled *v* ▷ **ravel**
ravelling *v* ▷ **ravel**
ravels *v* ▷ **ravel**
raven *n* (*pl* **-s**) black bird like a large crow ▸ *adj* (of hair) shiny black
ravens *n* ▷ **raven**
ravenous *adj* very hungry
raves *v*, *n* ▷ **rave**
ravine [rav-**veen**] *n* (*pl* **-s**) narrow steep-sided valley worn by a stream
ravines *n* ▷ **ravine**
raving *adj* delirious ▸ *v* ▷ **rave**
ravioli *pl n* small squares of pasta with a savoury filling
ravish *v* (**-es, -ing, -ed**) enrapture
ravished *v* ▷ **ravish**
ravishes *v* ▷ **ravish**
ravishing *adj*, *v* ▷ **ravish**
raw *adj* (**-er, -est**) uncooked
rawer *adj* ▷ **raw**
rawest *adj* ▷ **raw**
rawhide *n* (*pl* **-s**) untanned hide
rawhides *n* ▷ **rawhide**

> **rax** *v* (**raxes, raxing, raxed**). Rax is a Scots word that means to stretch or extend. This is a good word to have ready when you have an X on your rack, as there is probably an A or R on the board already. The verb forms can also help you to get a better score. Rax scores 10 points.

ray[1] *n* (*pl* **-s**) single line or narrow beam of light
ray[2] *n* (*pl* **-s**) large sea fish with a flat body and a whiplike tail
rays *n* ▷ **ray**[1, 2]
rayon *n* (*pl* **-s**) (fabric made of) a synthetic fibre
rayons *n* ▷ **rayon**
raze *v* (**-zes, -zing, -zed**) destroy (buildings or a town) completely
razed *v* ▷ **raze**
razes *v* ▷ **raze**

razing *v* ▷ **raze**
razor *n* (*pl* **-s**) sharp instrument for shaving
razorbill *n* (*pl* **-s**) sea bird of the North Atlantic with a stout sideways flattened bill
razorbills *n* ▷ **razorbill**
razors *n* ▷ **razor**

> **re** *n* (**res**). Re is a musical note. This is the only two-letter word beginning with R, and so is a good one to remember. Re is very useful as it allows you to connect a word beginning with R to one ending in E, or vice versa and R and E are two of the most common tiles in the game. Re scores 2 points.

reach *v* (**-es, -ing, -ed**) arrive at ▸ *n* (*pl* **-es**) distance that one can reach; stretch of a river > **reachable** *adj*
reachable *adj* ▷ **reach**
reached *v* ▷ **reach**
reaches *v*, *n* ▷ **reach**
reaching *v* ▷ **reach**
react *v* (**-s, -ing, -ed**) act in response (to) (*foll. by* **against**)
reactance *n* (*pl* **-s**) (ELECTRICITY) resistance to the flow of an alternating current caused by the inductance or capacitance of the circuit
reactances *n* ▷ **reactance**
reacted *v* ▷ **react**
reacting *v* ▷ **react**
reaction *n* (*pl* **-s**) physical or emotional response to a stimulus
reactionaries *n* ▷ **reactionary**
reactionary *n*, *adj* (*pl* **-ies**) (person) opposed to change, esp. in politics
reactionary *n* ▷ **reaction**
reactions *n* ▷ **reaction**
reactive *adj* chemically active
reactor *n* (*pl* **-s**) apparatus in which a nuclear reaction is maintained and controlled to produce nuclear energy
reactors *n* ▷ **reactor**
reacts *v* ▷ **react**
read *v* (**-s, -ing, read**) look at and understand or take in (written or printed matter) ▸ *n* matter suitable for reading > **reading** *n* (*pl* **-s**)
readable *adj* enjoyable to read
reader *n* (*pl* **-s**) person who reads
readers *n* ▷ **reader**
readership *n* (*pl* **-s**) readers of a publication collectively
readerships *n* ▷ **readership**
readier *adj* ▷ **ready**
readiest *adj* ▷ **ready**
readily *adv* ▷ **ready**
readiness *n* ▷ **ready**

readinesses n ▷ **ready**
reading n, v ▷ **read**
readings n ▷ **read**
readjust v (**-s, -ing, -ed**) adapt to a new situation > **readjustment** n (pl **-s**)
readjusted v ▷ **readjust**
readjusting v ▷ **readjust**
readjustment n ▷ **readjust**
readjustments n ▷ **readjust**
readjusts v ▷ **readjust**
reads v ▷ **read**
ready adj (**-dier, -diest**) prepared for use or action > **readily** adv > **readiness** n (pl **-es**)
reagent [ree-age-ent] n (pl **-s**) chemical substance that reacts with another, used to detect the presence of the other
reagents n ▷ **reagent**
real adj (**-er, -est**) existing in fact
realism n ▷ **realistic**
realisms n ▷ **realistic**
realist n ▷ **realistic**
realistically adv ▷ **realistic**
realists n ▷ **realistic**
realistic adj seeing and accepting things as they really are, practical > **realistically** adv > **realism** n (pl **-s**) > **realist** n (pl **-s**)
realities n ▷ **reality**
reality n (pl **-ies**) state of things as they are
realize v (**-zes, -zing, -zed**) become aware or grasp the significance of > **realization** n (pl **-s**)
realization n ▷ **realize**
realizations n ▷ **realize**
realized v ▷ **realize**
realizes v ▷ **realize**
realizing v ▷ **realize**
really adv very ▶ interj exclamation of dismay, doubt, or surprise
realm n (pl **-s**) kingdom
realms n ▷ **realm**
ream n (pl **-s**) twenty quires of paper, generally 500 sheets ▶ pl (Informal) large quantity (of written matter)
reams n ▷ **ream**
reap v (**-s, -ing, -ed**) cut and gather (a harvest) > **reaper** n (pl **-s**)
reaped v ▷ **reap**
reaper n ▷ **reap**
reapers n ▷ **reap**
reaping v ▷ **reap**
reappear v (**-s, -ing, -ed**) appear again > **reappearance** n (pl **-s**)
reappearance n ▷ **reappear**
reappearances n ▷ **reappear**
reappeared v ▷ **reappear**
reappearing v ▷ **reappear**

reappears v ▷ **reappear**
reaps v ▷ **reap**
rear[1] n (pl **-s**) back part > **rearmost** adj
rear[2] v (**-s, -ing, -ed**) care for and educate (children)
reared v ▷ **rear**
rearguard n (pl **-s**) troops protecting the rear of an army
rearguards n ▷ **rearguard**
rearing v ▷ **rear**
rearmost adj ▷ **rear**[1]
rearrange v (**-ges, -ging, -ged**) organize differently, alter > **rearrangement** n (pl **-s**)
rearranged v ▷ **rearrange**
rearrangement n ▷ **rearrange**
rearrangements n ▷ **rearrange**
rearranges v ▷ **rearrange**
rearranging v ▷ **rearrange**
rears n ▷ **rear**[1] ▶ v ▷ **rear**[2]
reason n (pl **-s**) cause or motive ▶ v (**-s, -ing, -ed**) think logically in forming conclusions
reasonable adj sensible > **reasonably** adv
reasoned v ▷ **reason**
reasoning v ▷ **reason**
reasons n, v ▷ **reason**
reassess v (**-es, -ing, -ed**) reconsider the value or importance of
reassessed v ▷ **reassess**
reassesses v ▷ **reassess**
reassessing v ▷ **reassess**
reassure v (**-res, -ring, -red**) restore confidence to > **reassurance** n (pl **-s**)
reassurance n ▷ **reassure**
reassurances n ▷ **reassure**
reassured v ▷ **reassure**
reassures v ▷ **reassure**
reassuring v ▷ **reassure**
rebate n (pl **-s**) discount or refund
rebates n ▷ **rebate**
rebel v (**-s, -lling, -lled**) revolt against the ruling power ▶ n (pl **-s**) person who rebels > **rebellious** adj
rebelled v ▷ **rebel**
rebelling v ▷ **rebel**
rebellion n (pl **-s**) organized open resistance to authority
rebellions n ▷ **rebellion**
rebellious adj ▷ **rebel**
rebels v, n ▷ **rebel**
rebore, reboring n (pl **-s**) boring of a cylinder to restore its true shape
rebores n ▷ **rebore**
reboring n ▷ **rebore**
reborings n ▷ **rebore**
rebound v (**-s, -ing, -ed**) spring back

rebounded v ▷ **rebound**
rebounding v ▷ **rebound**
rebounds v ▷ **rebound**
rebuff v (**-s, -ing, -ed**) reject or snub ▶ n (pl **-s**) blunt refusal, snub
rebuffed v ▷ **rebuff**
rebuffing v ▷ **rebuff**
rebuffs v, n ▷ **rebuff**
rebuke v (**-kes, -king, -ked**) scold sternly ▶ n (pl **-s**) stern scolding
rebuked v ▷ **rebuke**
rebukes v, n ▷ **rebuke**
rebuking v ▷ **rebuke**
rebus n (pl **-es**) puzzle consisting of pictures and symbols representing words or syllables
rebuses n ▷ **rebus**
rebut v (**-s, -tting, -tted**) prove that (a claim) is untrue > **rebuttal** n (pl **-s**)
rebuts v ▷ **rebut**
rebuttal n ▷ **rebut**
rebuttals n ▷ **rebut**
rebutted v ▷ **rebut**
rebutting v ▷ **rebut**
recalcitrant adj wilfully disobedient > **recalcitrance** n (pl **-s**)
recalcitrance n ▷ **recalcitrant**
recalcitrances n ▷ **recalcitrant**
recall v (**-s, -ing, -ed**) recollect or remember ▶ n (pl (pl **-s**) ability to remember
recalled v ▷ **recall**
recalling v ▷ **recall**
recalls v, n ▷ **recall**
recant v (**-s, -ing, -ed**) withdraw (a statement or belief) publicly > **recantation** n (pl **-s**)
recantation n ▷ **recant**
recantations n ▷ **recant**
recanted v ▷ **recant**
recanting v ▷ **recant**
recants v ▷ **recant**
recap (Informal) v (**-s, -pping, -pped**) recapitulate ▶ n (pl **-s**) recapitulation
recapitulate v (**-tes, -ting, -ted**) state again briefly, repeat > **recapitulation** n (pl **-s**)
recapitulated v ▷ **recapitulate**
recapitulates v ▷ **recapitulate**
recapitulating v ▷ **recapitulate**
recapitulation n ▷ **recapitulate**
recapitulations n ▷ **recapitulate**
recapped v ▷ **recap**
recapping v ▷ **recap**
recaps v, n ▷ **recap**
recapture v (**-res, -ring, -red**) experience again
recaptured v ▷ **recapture**
recaptures v ▷ **recapture**
recapturing v ▷ **recapture**

recce (CHIEFLY BRIT) (Slang) v (**-s, -ceing, -ced** or **-ceed**) reconnoitre ▶ n (pl **-s**) reconnaissance
recced v ▷ **recce**
recceed v ▷ **recce**
recceing v ▷ **recce**
recces v, n ▷ **recce**
recede v (**-des, -ding, -ded**) move to a more distant place
receded v ▷ **recede**
recedes v ▷ **recede**
receding v ▷ **recede**
receipt n (pl **-s**) written acknowledgment of money or goods received
receipts n ▷ **receipt**
receive v (**-ves, -ving, -ved**) take, accept, or get
received adj generally accepted ▶ v ▷ **receive**
receiver n (pl **-s**) part of telephone that is held to the ear
receivers n ▷ **receiver**
receivership n (pl **-s**) state of being administered by a receiver
receiverships n ▷ **receivership**
receives v ▷ **receive**
receiving v ▷ **receive**
recent adj (**-er, -est**) having happened lately > **recently** adv
recenter adj ▷ **recent**
recentest adj ▷ **recent**
recently adv ▷ **recent**
receptacle n (pl **-s**) object used to contain something
receptacles n ▷ **receptacle**
reception n (pl **-s**) area for receiving guests, clients, etc.
receptionist n (pl **-s**) person who receives guests, clients, etc.
receptionists n ▷ **receptionist**
receptions n ▷ **reception**
receptive adj willing to accept new ideas, suggestions, etc. > **receptivity** n (pl **-ies**)
receptivities n ▷ **receptive**
receptivity n ▷ **receptive**
recess n (pl **-es**) niche or alcove
recessed adj hidden or placed in a recess
recesses n ▷ **recess**
recession n (pl **-s**) period of economic difficulty when little is being bought or sold
recessions n ▷ **recession**
recessive adj receding
recherché [rish-**air**-shay] adj refined or elegant
recidivism n (pl **-s**) habitual relapse into crime > **recidivist** n (pl **-s**)
recidivisms n ▷ **recidivism**
recidivist n ▷ **recidivism**
recidivists n ▷ **recidivism**

recipe n (pl -s) directions for cooking a dish
  recipes n ▷ **recipe**
recipient n (pl -s) person who receives
  something
  recipients n ▷ **recipient**
reciprocal [ris-**sip**-pro-kl] adj mutual
  > **reciprocally** adv
  reciprocally adv ▷ **reciprocal**
reciprocate v (-tes, -ting, -ted) give or feel in
  return > **reciprocation** n (pl -s) > **reciprocity**
  n (pl -s)
  reciprocated v ▷ **reciprocate**
  reciprocates v ▷ **reciprocate**
  reciprocating v ▷ **reciprocate**
  reciprocation n ▷ **reciprocate**
  reciprocations n ▷ **reciprocate**
  reciprocities n ▷ **reciprocate**
  reciprocity n ▷ **reciprocate**
recital n (pl -s) musical performance by a
  soloist or soloists
  recitals n ▷ **recital**
recitation n (pl -s) recital, usu. from memory,
  of poetry or prose
  recitations n ▷ **recitation**
recitative [ress-it-a-**teev**] n (pl -s) speechlike
  style of singing, used esp. for narrative
  passages in opera
  recitatives n ▷ **recitative**
recite v (-tes, -ting, -ted) repeat (a poem etc.)
  aloud to an audience
  recited v ▷ **recite**
  recites v ▷ **recite**
  reciting v ▷ **recite**
reckless adj heedless of danger > **recklessly**
  adv > **recklessness** n (pl -s)
  recklessly adv ▷ **reckless**
  recklessness n ▷ **reckless**
  recklessnesses n ▷ **reckless**
reckon v (-s, -ing, -ed) consider or think
  > **reckoning** n (pl -s)
  reckoned v ▷ **reckon**
  reckoning v, n ▷ **reckon**
  reckonings n ▷ **reckon**
  reckons v ▷ **reckon**
reclaim v (-s, -ing, -ed) regain possession of
  > **reclamation** n (pl -s)
  reclaimed v ▷ **reclaim**
  reclaiming v ▷ **reclaim**
  reclaims v ▷ **reclaim**
  reclamation n ▷ **reclaim**
  reclamations n ▷ **reclaim**
recline v (-nes, -ning, -ned) rest in a leaning
  position > **reclining** adj
  reclined v ▷ **recline**
  reclines v ▷ **recline**

reclining v, adj ▷ **recline**
recluse n (pl -s) person who avoids other
  people > **reclusive** adj
  recluses n ▷ **recluse**
  reclusive adj ▷ **recluse**
  recognition n ▷ **recognize**
  recognitions n ▷ **recognize**
  recognizable adj ▷ **recognize**
recognizance [rik-**og**-nizz-anss] n (pl -s)
  undertaking before a court to observe some
  condition
  recognizances n ▷ **recognizance**
recognize v (-zes, -zing, -zed) identify
  as (a person or thing) already known
  > **recognition** n (pl -s) > **recognizable** adj
  recognized v ▷ **recognize**
  recognizes v ▷ **recognize**
  recognizing v ▷ **recognize**
recoil v (-s, -ing, -ed) jerk or spring back ▶ n (pl
  -s) backward jerk
  recoiled v ▷ **recoil**
  recoiling v ▷ **recoil**
  recoils v, n ▷ **recoil**
recollect v (-s, -ing, -ed) call back to mind,
  remember > **recollection** n (pl -s)
  recollected v ▷ **recollect**
  recollecting v ▷ **recollect**
  recollection n ▷ **recollect**
  recollections n ▷ **recollect**
  recollects v ▷ **recollect**
recommend v (-s, -ing, -ed) advise or counsel
  > **recommendation** n (pl -s)
  recommendation n ▷ **recommend**
  recommendations n ▷ **recommend**
  recommended v ▷ **recommend**
  recommending v ▷ **recommend**
  recommends v ▷ **recommend**
recompense v (-ses, -sing, -sed) pay or reward
  ▶ n (pl -s) compensation
  recompensed v ▷ **recompense**
  recompenses v, n ▷ **recompense**
  recompensing v ▷ **recompense**
reconcile v (-les, -ling, -led) harmonize
  (conflicting beliefs etc.) > **reconciliation**
  n (pl -s)
  reconciled v ▷ **reconcile**
  reconciles v ▷ **reconcile**
  reconciliation n ▷ **reconcile**
  reconciliations n ▷ **reconcile**
  reconciling v ▷ **reconcile**
recondite adj difficult to understand
recondition v (-s, -ing, -ed) restore to good
  condition or working order
  reconditioned v ▷ **recondition**
  reconditioning v ▷ **recondition**

reconditions v ▷ **recondition**
reconnaissance [rik-**kon**-iss-anss] n (pl -**s**)
survey for military or engineering purposes
reconnaissances n ▷ **reconnaissance**
reconnoitre [rek-a-**noy**-ter] v (-**res**, -**ring**, -**red**)
make a reconnaissance of
reconnoitred v ▷ **reconnoitre**
reconnoitres v ▷ **reconnoitre**
reconnoitring v ▷ **reconnoitre**
reconsider v (-**s**, -**ing**, -**ed**) think about again,
consider changing
reconsidered v ▷ **reconsider**
reconsidering v ▷ **reconsider**
reconsiders v ▷ **reconsider**
reconstitute v (-**tes**, -**ting**, -**ted**) reorganize
> **reconstitution** n (pl -**s**)
reconstituted v ▷ **reconstitute**
reconstitutes v ▷ **reconstitute**
reconstituting v ▷ **reconstitute**
reconstitution n ▷ **reconstitute**
reconstitutions n ▷ **reconstitute**
reconstruct v (-**s**, -**ing**, -**ed**) rebuild
> **reconstruction** n (pl -**s**)
reconstructed v ▷ **reconstruct**
reconstructing v ▷ **reconstruct**
reconstruction n ▷ **reconstruct**
reconstructions n ▷ **reconstruct**
reconstructs v ▷ **reconstruct**
record n (pl -**s**) [**rek**-ord] document or other
thing that preserves information ▶ v (-**s**, -**ing**,
-**ed**) [rik-**kord**] put in writing > **recording** n
(pl -**s**)
recorded v ▷ **record**
recorder n (pl -**s**) person or machine that
records, esp. a video, cassette, or tape
recorder
recorders n ▷ **recorder**
recording v ▷ **record**
records n, v ▷ **record**
recount v (-**s**, -**ing**, -**ed**) tell in detail
recounted v ▷ **recount**
recounting v ▷ **recount**
recounts v ▷ **recount**
recoup [rik-**koop**] v (-**s**, -**ing**, -**ed**) regain or
make good (a loss)
recouped v ▷ **recoup**
recouping v ▷ **recoup**
recoups v ▷ **recoup**
recourse n (pl -**s**) source of help
recourses n ▷ **recourse**
recover v (-**s**, -**ing**, -**ed**) become healthy again
> **recovery** n (pl -**ies**) > **recoverable** adj
recoverable adj ▷ **recover**
recovered v ▷ **recover**
recoveries n ▷ **recover**

recovering v ▷ **recover**
recovers v ▷ **recover**
recovery v ▷ **recover**
recreation n (pl -**s**) agreeable or refreshing
occupation, relaxation, or amusement
> **recreational** adj
recreational adj ▷ **recreation**
recreations n ▷ **recreation**
recrimination n (pl -**s**) mutual blame
> **recriminatory** adj
recriminations n ▷ **recrimination**
recriminatory adj ▷ **recrimination**
recruit v (-**s**, -**ing**, -**ed**) enlist (new soldiers,
members, etc.) ▶ n (pl -**s**) newly enlisted
soldier > **recruitment** n (pl -**s**)
recruited v ▷ **recruit**
recruiting v ▷ **recruit**
recruitment n ▷ **recruit**
recruitments n ▷ **recruit**
recruits v, n ▷ **recruit**
recta n ▷ **rectum**
rectangle n (pl -**s**) oblong four-sided figure
with four right angles > **rectangular** adj
rectangles n ▷ **rectangle**
rectangular adj ▷ **rectangle**
rectification n ▷ **rectify**
rectifications n ▷ **rectify**
rectified v ▷ **rectify**
rectifier n ▷ **rectify**
rectifiers n ▷ **rectify**
rectifies v ▷ **rectify**
rectify v (-**ies**, -**ying**, -**ied**) put right, correct
(CHEM) (ELECTRICITY) > **rectification** n (pl -**s**)
rectifying v ▷ **rectify**
rectilinear adj in a straight line
rectitude n (pl -**s**) moral correctness
rectitudes n ▷ **rectitude**
recto n (pl -**os**) right-hand page of a book
rector n (pl -**s**) clergyman in charge of a parish
rectories n ▷ **rectory**
rectors n ▷ **rector**
rectory n (pl -**s**) rector's house
rectos n ▷ **recto**
rectum n (pl -**tums**, -**ta**) final section of the
large intestine
rectums n ▷ **rectum**
recumbent adj lying down
recuperate v (-**tes**, -**ting**, -**ted**) recover from
illness > **recuperation** n (pl -**s**) > **recuperative**
adj
recuperated v ▷ **recuperate**
recuperates v ▷ **recuperate**
recuperating v ▷ **recuperate**
recuperation n ▷ **recuperate**
recuperations n ▷ **recuperate**

recuperative *adj* ▷ **recuperate**
recur *v* (**-s, -rring, -rred**) happen again
> **recurrence** *n* (*pl* -s) repetition > **recurrent**
adj
  recurred *v* ▷ **recur**
  recurrence *n* ▷ **recur**
  recurrences *n* ▷ **recur**
  recurrent *adj* ▷ **recur**
  recurring *v* ▷ **recur**
  recurs *v* ▷ **recur**
recycle *v* (**-les, -ling, -led**) reprocess (used
materials) for further use > **recyclable** *adj*
  recyclable *adj* ▷ **recycle**
  recycled *v* ▷ **recycle**
  recycles *v* ▷ **recycle**
  recycling *v* ▷ **recycle**
red *adj* (**-dder, -ddest**) of a colour varying from
crimson to orange and seen in blood, fire, etc.
▶ *n* (*pl* -s) red colour > **reddish** *adj* > **redness**
n (*pl* -**es**)
redbrick *adj* (of a university in Britain)
founded in the late 19th or early 20th century
redcoat *n* (*pl* -s) (HIST) British soldier
  redcoats *n* ▷ **redcoat**
redcurrant *n* (*pl* -s) small round edible red
berry
  redcurrants *n* ▷ **redcurrant**
redden *v* (**-s, -ing, -ed**) make or become red
  reddened *v* ▷ **redden**
  reddening *v* ▷ **redden**
  reddens *v* ▷ **redden**
  redder *adj* ▷ **red**
  reddest *adj* ▷ **red**
  reddish *adj* ▷ **red**
redeem *v* (**-s, -ing, -ed**) make up for
> **redeemable** *adj* > **redemption** *n* (*pl* -s)
> **redemptive** *adj*
  redeemable *adj* ▷ **reddem**
  redeemed *v* ▷ **redeem**
  redeeming *v* ▷ **redeem**
  redeems *v* ▷ **redeem**
  redemption *adj* ▷ **reddem**
  redemptions *adj* ▷ **reddem**
  redemptive *adj* ▷ **reddem**
redeploy *v* (**-s, -ing, -ed**) assign to a new
position or task > **redeployment** *n* (*pl* -s)
  redeployed *v* ▷ **redeploy**
  redeploying *v* ▷ **redeploy**
  redeployment *n* ▷ **redeploy**
  redeployment *n* ▷ **redeploy**
  redeploys *v* ▷ **redeploy**
redevelop *v* (**-s, -ing, -ed**) rebuild or renovate
(an area or building) > **redevelopment** *n* (*pl* -s)
  redeveloped *v* ▷ **redevelop**
  redeveloping *v* ▷ **redevelop**

  redevelopment *n* ▷ **redevelop**
  redevelopments *n* ▷ **redevelop**
  redevelops *v* ▷ **redevelop**
  redness *n* ▷ **red**
redolent *adj* reminiscent (of)
redouble *v* (**-les, -ling, -led**) increase, multiply,
or intensify
  redoubled *v* ▷ **redouble**
  redoubles *v* ▷ **redouble**
  redoubling *v* ▷ **redouble**
redoubt *n* (*pl* -s) small fort defending a hilltop
or pass
redoubtable *adj* formidable
  redoubts *n* ▷ **redoubt**
redound *v* (**-s, -ing, -ed**) cause advantage or
disadvantage (to)
  redounded *v* ▷ **redound**
  redounding *v* ▷ **redound**
  redounds *v* ▷ **redound**
redox *n* (*pl* -es) chemical reaction in which
one substance is reduced and the other is
oxidized
  redoxes *n* ▷ **redox**
redress *v* (**-es, -ing, -ed**) make amends for ▶ *n*
(*pl* -es) compensation or amends
  redressed *v* ▷ **redress**
  redresses *v*, *n* ▷ **redress**
  redressing *v* ▷ **redress**
  reds *n* ▷ **red**
reduce *v* (**-ces, -cing, -ced**) bring down, lower
> **reducible** *adj* > **reduction** *n* (*pl* -s)
  reduced *v* ▷ **reduce**
  reduces *v* ▷ **reduce**
  reducible *adj* ▷ **reduce**
  reducing *v* ▷ **reduce**
  reduction *n* ▷ **reduce**
  reductions *n* ▷ **reduce**
  redundancies *n* ▷ **redundant**
  redundancy *n* ▷ **redundant**
redundant *adj* (of a worker) no longer needed
> **redundancy** *n* (*pl* -s)
reed *n* (*pl* -s) tall grass that grows in swamps
and shallow water
  reedier *adj* ▷ **reedy**
  reediest *n* ▷ **reedy**
  reeds *n* ▷ **reed**
reedy (**-dier, -diest**) *adj* harsh and thin in tone
reef[1] *n* (*pl* -s) ridge of rock or coral near the
surface of the sea
reef[2] *n* (*pl* -s) part of a sail which can be rolled
up to reduce its area ▶ *v* (**-s, -ing, -ed**) take
in a reef of
  reefed *v* ▷ **reef**[2]
reefer *n* (*pl* -s) short thick jacket worn esp.
by sailors

reefers _n_ ▷ **reefer**
reefing _v_ ▷ **reef**²
reefs _n_ ▷ **reef**¹,² ▶ _v_ ▷ **reef**²
reek _v_ (**-s, -ing, -ed**) smell strongly ▶ _n_ (_pl_ **-s**) strong unpleasant smell
reeked _v_ ▷ **reek**
reeking _v_ ▷ **reek**
reeks _v, n_ ▷ **reek**
reel¹ _n_ (_pl_ **-s**) cylindrical object on which film, tape, thread, or wire is wound
reel² _v_ (**-s, -ing, -ed**) stagger, sway, or whirl
reel³ _n_ (_pl_ **-s**) lively Scottish dance
reeled _v_ ▷ **reel**²
reeling _v_ ▷ **reel**²
reels _n_ ▷ **reel**¹,³ ▶ _v_ ▷ **reel**²
ref _n_ (_pl_ **-s**) (_Informal_) referee in sport
refectories _n_ ▷ **refectory**
refectory _n_ (_pl_ **-ies**) room for meals in a college etc.
refer _v_ (**-s, -rring, -rred**) (_foll. by_ **to**) allude (to)
> **referral** _n_ (_pl_ **-s**)
referee _n_ (_pl_ **-s**) umpire in sports, esp. soccer or boxing ▶ _v_ (**-s, -ing, -eed**) act as referee of
refereed _v_ ▷ **referee**
refereeing _v_ ▷ **referee**
referees _n, v_ ▷ **referee**
reference _n_ (_pl_ **-s**) act of referring
references _n_ ▷ **reference**
referenda _n_ ▷ **referendum**
referendum _n_ (_pl_ **-dums, -da**) direct vote of the electorate on an important question
referendums _n_ ▷ **referendum**
referral _n_ ▷ **refer**
referrals _n_ ▷ **refer**
referred _v_ ▷ **refer**
referring _v_ ▷ **refer**
refers _v_ ▷ **refer**
refill _v_ (**-s, -ing, -ed**) fill again ▶ _n_ (_pl_ **-s**) second or subsequent filling
refilled _v_ ▷ **refill**
refilling _v_ ▷ **refill**
refills _v, n_ ▷ **refill**
refine _v_ (**-nes, -ning, -ned**) purify
refined _adj_ cultured or polite ▶ _v_ ▷ **refine**
refinement _n_ (_pl_ **-s**) improvement or elaboration
refinements _n_ ▷ **refinement**
refineries _n_ ▷ **refinery**
refinery _n_ (_pl_ **-ies**) place where sugar, oil, etc. is refined
refines _v_ ▷ **refine**
refining _v_ ▷ **refine**
reflate _v_ ▷ **reflation**
reflated _v_ ▷ **reflation**
reflates _v_ ▷ **reflation**

reflating _v_ ▷ **reflation**
reflation _n_ (_pl_ **-s**) increase in the supply of money and credit designed to encourage economic activity > **reflate** _v_ (**-tes, -ting, -ted**) > **reflationary** _adj_
reflationary _adj_ ▷ **reflation**
reflations _n_ ▷ **reflation**
reflect _v_ (**-s, -ing, -ed**) throw back, esp. rays of light, heat, etc.
reflected _v_ ▷ **reflect**
reflecting _v_ ▷ **reflect**
reflection _n_ (_pl_ **-s**) act of reflecting
reflections _n_ ▷ **reflect**
reflective _adj_ quiet, contemplative
reflector _n_ (_pl_ **-s**) polished surface for reflecting light etc.
reflectors _n_ ▷ **reflector**
reflects _v_ ▷ **reflect**
reflex _n_ (_pl_ **-es**) involuntary response to a stimulus or situation ▶ _adj_ (of a muscular action) involuntary
reflexes _n_ ▷ **reflex**
reflexive _adj_ (GRAMMAR) denoting a verb whose subject is the same as its object
reflexologies _n_ ▷ **reflexology**
reflexology _n_ (_pl_ **-ies**) foot massage as a therapy in alternative medicine
reform _n_ (_pl_ **-s**) improvement ▶ _v_ (**-s, -ing, -ed**) improve > **reformer** _n_ (_pl_ **-s**)
reformation _n_ (_pl_ **-s**) act or instance of something being reformed
reformations _n_ ▷ **reformation**
reformatories _n_ ▷ **reformatory**
reformatory _n_ (_pl_ **-s**) (formerly) institution for reforming young offenders
reformed _v_ ▷ **reform**
reformer _n_ ▷ **reform**
reformers _n_ ▷ **reform**
reforming _v_ ▷ **reform**
reforms _n, v_ ▷ **reform**
refract _v_ (**-s, -ing, -ed**) change the course of (light etc.) passing from one medium to another > **refraction** _n_ (_pl_ **-s**) > **refractive** _adj_ > **refractor** _n_ (_pl_ **-s**)
refracted _v_ ▷ **refract**
refracting _v_ ▷ **refract**
refraction _n_ ▷ **refract**
refractions _n_ ▷ **refract**
refractive _adj_ ▷ **refract**
refractor _n_ ▷ **refract**
refractors _n_ ▷ **refract**
refractory _adj_ unmanageable or rebellious
refracts _v_ ▷ **refract**
refrain¹ _v_ (**-s, -ing, -ed**) keep oneself from doing
refrain² _n_ (_pl_ **-s**) frequently repeated part of

a song
refrained v ▷ **refrain¹**
refraining v ▷ **refrain¹**
refrains n ▷ **refrain¹, ²** ▶ v ▷ **refrain²**
refresh v (**-es, -ing, -ed**) revive or reinvigorate, as through food, drink, or rest > **refresher** n (pl **-s**)
refreshed v ▷ **refresh**
refresher n ▷ **refresh**
refreshers n ▷ **refresh**
refreshes v ▷ **refresh**
refreshing adj having a reviving effect ▶ v ▷ **refresh**
refreshment n (pl **-s**) something that refreshes, esp. food or drink
refreshments n ▷ **refreshment**
refrigerate v (**-tes, -ting, -ted**) cool or freeze in order to preserve > **refrigeration** n (pl **-s**)
refrigerated v ▷ **refrigerate**
refrigerates v ▷ **refrigerate**
refrigerating v ▷ **refrigerate**
refrigeration n ▷ **refrigerate**
refrigerations n ▷ **refrigerate**
refrigerator n (pl **-s**) ▷ **fridge**
refrigerators n ▷ **refrigerator**
refs n ▷ **ref**
refuge n (pl **-s**) (source of) shelter or protection
refugee n (pl **-s**) person who seeks refuge, esp. in a foreign country
refugees n ▷ **refugee**
refuges n ▷ **refuge**
refulgent adj shining, radiant
refund v (**-s, -ing, -ed**) pay back ▶ n (pl **-s**) return of money
refunded v ▷ **refund**
refunding v ▷ **refund**
refunds v, n ▷ **refund**
refurbish v (**-es, -ing, -ed**) renovate and brighten up
refurbished v ▷ **refurbish**
refurbishes v ▷ **refurbish**
refurbishing v ▷ **refurbish**
refusal n (pl **-s**) denial of anything demanded or offered
refusals n ▷ **refusal**
refuse¹ v (**-ses, -sing, -sed**) decline, deny, or reject
refuse² n (pl **-s**) rubbish or useless matter
refused v ▷ **refuse¹**
refuses v ▷ **refuse¹** ▶ n ▷ **refuse²**
refusing v ▷ **refuse¹**
refute v (**-tes, -ting, -ted**) disprove > **refutation** n (pl **-s**)
refutation n ▷ **refute**
refutations n ▷ **refute**

refuted v ▷ **refute**
refutes v ▷ **refute**
refuting v ▷ **refute**
regain v (**-s, -ing, -ed**) get back or recover
regained v ▷ **regain**
regaining v ▷ **regain**
regains v ▷ **regain**
regal adj of or like a king or queen > **regally** adv
regalia pl n ceremonial emblems of royalty or high office
regale v (**-les, -ling, -led**) entertain (someone) with stories etc.
regaled v ▷ **regale**
regales v ▷ **regale**
regaling v ▷ **regale**
regally adv ▷ **regal**
regard v (**-s, -ing, -ed**) consider ▶ n (pl **-s**) respect or esteem ▶ pl expression of goodwill
regarded v ▷ **regard**
regarding in respect of, concerning v ▷ **regard**
regardless adj heedless ▶ adv in spite of everything
regards v, n ▷ **regard**
regatta n (pl **-s**) meeting for yacht or boat races
regattas n ▷ **regatta**
regenerate v (**-tes, -ting, -ted**) (cause to) undergo spiritual, moral, or physical renewal > **regeneration** n (pl **-s**) > **regenerative** adj
regenerated v ▷ **regenerate**
regenerates v ▷ **regenerate**
regenerating v ▷ **regenerate**
regeneration n ▷ **regenerate**
regenerations n ▷ **regenerate**
regenerative adj ▷ **regenerate**
regencies n ▷ **regency**
regency n (pl **-ies**) status or period of office of a regent
regent n (pl **-s**) ruler of a kingdom during the absence, childhood, or illness of its monarch ▶ adj ruling as a regent
regents n ▷ **regent**
reggae n (pl **-s**) style of Jamaican popular music with a strong beat
reggaes n ▷ **reggae**
regicide n (pl **-s**) killing of a king
regicides n ▷ **regicide**
regime [ray-zheem] n (pl **-s**) system of government
regimen n (pl **-s**) prescribed system of diet etc.
regimens n ▷ **regimen**
regiment n (pl **-s**) organized body of troops as a unit of the army > **regimental** adj > **regimentation** n (pl **-s**)
regimental adj ▷ **regiment**
regimentation n ▷ **regiment**

regimentations *n* ▷ **regiment**
regimented *adj* very strictly controlled
regiments *n* ▷ **regiment**
regimes *n* ▷ **regime**
region *n* (*pl* -s) administrative division of a
country > **regional** *adj*
regional *adj* ▷ **region**
regions *n* ▷ **region**
register *n* (*pl* -s) (book containing) an official
list or record of things ▶ *v* (-s, -ing, -ed)
enter in a register or set down in writing
> **registration** *n* (*pl* -s)
registered *v* ▷ **register**
registering *v* ▷ **register**
registers *n*, *v* ▷ **register**
registrar *n* (*pl* -s) keeper of official records
registrars *n* ▷ **registrar**
registration *n* ▷ **register**
registrations *n* ▷ **registers**
regress *v* (-es, -ing, -ed) revert to a former
worse condition
regressed *v* ▷ **regress**
regresses *v* ▷ **regress**
regressing *v* ▷ **regress**
regression *n* (*pl* -s) act of regressing (PSYCHOL)
> **regressive** *adj*
regressions *n* ▷ **regression**
regressive *adj* ▷ **regression**
regret *v* (-s, -tting, -tted) feel sorry about ▶ *n*
(*pl* -s) feeling of repentance, guilt, or sorrow
> **regretful** *adj* > **regrettable** *adj*
regretful *adj* ▷ **regret**
regrets *v* ▷ **regret**
regrettable *adj* ▷ **regret**
regretted *v* ▷ **regret**
regretting *v* ▷ **regret**
regular *adj* normal, customary, or usual ▶ *n*
(*pl* -s) regular soldier > **regularity** *n* (*pl* -s)
> **regularize** *v* (-zes, -zing, -zed) > **regularly**
adv
regularities *n* ▷ **regular**
regularity *n* ▷ **regular**
regularize *v* ▷ **regular**
regularized *v* ▷ **regular**
regularizes *v* ▷ **regular**
regularizing *v* ▷ **regular**
regularly *adv* ▷ **regular**
regulars *n* ▷ **regular**
regulate *v* (-tes, -ting, -ted) control, esp. by
rules
regulated *v* ▷ **regulate**
regulates *v* ▷ **regulate**
regulating *v* ▷ **regulate**
regulation *n* (*pl* -s) rule
regulations *n* ▷ **regulation**

regulator *n* (*pl* -s) device that automatically
controls pressure, temperature, etc.
regulators *n* ▷ **regulator**
regurgitate *v* (-tes, -ting, -ted) vomit
> **regurgitation** *n* (*pl* -s)
regurgitated *v* ▷ **regurgitate**
regurgitates *v* ▷ **regurgitate**
regurgitating *v* ▷ **regurgitate**
regurgitation *n* ▷ **regurgitate**
regurgitations *n* ▷ **regurgitate**
rehabilitate *v* (-tes, -ting, -ted) help (a
person) to readjust to society after illness,
imprisonment, etc. > **rehabilitation** *n* (*pl* -s)
rehabilitated *v* ▷ **rehabilitate**
rehabilitates *v* ▷ **rehabilitate**
rehabilitating *v* ▷ **rehabilitate**
rehabilitation *n* ▷ **rehabilitate**
rehabilitations *n* ▷ **rehabilitate**
rehash *v* (-es, -ing, -ed) rework or reuse ▶ *n* (*pl*
-es) old ideas presented in a new form
rehashed *v* ▷ **rehash**
rehashes *v*, *n* ▷ **rehash**
rehashing *v* ▷ **rehash**
rehearse *v* (-ses, -sing, -sed) practise (a play,
concert, etc.) > **rehearsal** *n* (*pl* -s)
rehearsal *n* ▷ **rehearse**
rehearsals *n* ▷ **rehearse**
rehearsed *v* ▷ **rehearse**
rehearses *v* ▷ **rehearse**
rehearsing *v* ▷ **rehearse**
rehouse *v* (-ses, -sing, -sed) provide with a
new (and better) home
rehoused *v* ▷ **rehouse**
rehouses *v* ▷ **rehouse**
rehousing *v* ▷ **rehouse**
reign *n* (*pl* -s) period of a sovereign's rule ▶ *v* (-s,
-ing, -ed) rule (a country)
reigned *v* ▷ **reign**
reigning *v* ▷ **reign**
reigns *n*, *v* ▷ **reign**
reimburse *v* (-ses, -sing, -sed) refund, pay back
> **reimbursement** *n* (*pl* -s)
reimbursed *v* ▷ **reimburse**
reimbursement *n* ▷ **reimburse**
reimbursements *n* ▷ **reimburse**
reimburses *v* ▷ **reimburse**
reimbursing *v* ▷ **reimburse**
rein *v* (-s, -ing, -ed) check or manage with reins
reincarnation *n* (*pl* -s) rebirth of a soul in
successive bodies > **reincarnate** *v* (-tes,
-ting, -ted)
reincarnate *v* ▷ **reincarnation**
reincarnated *v* ▷ **reincarnation**
reincarnates *v* ▷ **reincarnation**
reincarnating *v* ▷ **reincarnation**

reincarnations *n* ▷ **reincarnation**
reindeer *n* (*pl* -**deer, -deers**) deer of arctic
regions with large branched antlers
reindeers *n* ▷ **reindeer**
reined *v* ▷ **rein**
reining *v* ▷ **rein**
reinforce *v* (-**ces, -cing, -ced**) strengthen
with new support, material, or force
> **reinforcement** *n* (*pl* -**s**)
reinforced *v* ▷ **reinforce**
reinforcement *n* ▷ **reinforce**
reinforcements *n* ▷ **reinforce**
reinforces *v* ▷ **reinforce**
reinforcing *v* ▷ **reinforce**
reins *pl n* narrow straps attached to a bit to
guide a horse ▶ *v* ▷ **rein**
reinstate *v* (-**tes, -ting, -ted**) restore to a
former position > **reinstatement** *n* (*pl* -**s**)
reinstated *v* ▷ **reinstate**
reinstatement *n* ▷ **reinstate**
reinstatements *n* ▷ **reinstate**
reinstates *v* ▷ **reinstate**
reinstating *v* ▷ **reinstate**
reiterate *v* (-**tes, -ting, -ted**) repeat again and
again > **reiteration** *n* (*pl* -**s**)
reiterated *v* ▷ **reiterate**
reiterates *v* ▷ **reiterate**
reiterating *v* ▷ **reiterate**
reiteration *n* ▷ **reiterate**
reiterations *n* ▷ **reiterate**
reject *v* (-**s, -ing, -ed**) refuse to accept or believe
▶ *n* (*pl* -**s**) person or thing rejected as not up to
standard > **rejection** *n* (*pl* -**s**)
rejected *v* ▷ **reject**
rejecting *v* ▷ **reject**
rejection *n* ▷ **reject**
rejections *n* ▷ **reject**
rejects *v, n* ▷ **reject**
rejig *v* (-**s, -gging, -gged**) re-equip (a factory
or plant)
rejigged *v* ▷ **rejig**
rejigging *v* ▷ **rejig**
rejigs *v* ▷ **rejig**
rejoice *v* (-**ces, -cing, -ced**) feel or express great
happiness
rejoiced *v* ▷ **rejoice**
rejoices *v* ▷ **rejoice**
rejoicing *v* ▷ **rejoice**
rejoin[1] *v* (-**s, -ing, -ed**) join again
rejoin[2] *v* (-**s, -ing, -ed**) reply
rejoinder (*pl* -**s**) *n* answer, retort
rejoinders *n* ▷ **rejoinder**
rejoined *v* ▷ **rejoin**[1, 2]
rejoining *v* ▷ **rejoin**[1, 2]
rejoins *v* ▷ **rejoin**[1, 2]

rejuvenate *v* (-**tes, -ting, -ted**) restore youth or
vitality to > **rejuvenation** *n* (*pl* -**s**)
rejuvenated *v* ▷ **rejuvenate**
rejuvenates *v* ▷ **rejuvenate**
rejuvenating *v* ▷ **rejuvenate**
rejuvenation *n* ▷ **rejuvenate**
rejuvenations *v* ▷ **rejuvenate**
relapse *v* (-**ses, -sing, -sed**) fall back into bad
habits, illness, etc. ▶ *n* (*pl* -**s**) return of bad
habits, illness, etc.
relapsed *v* ▷ **relapse**
relapses *v, n* ▷ **relapse**
relapsing *v* ▷ **relapse**
relate *v* (-**tes, -ting, -ted**) establish a relation
between > **related** *adj*
related *adj, v* ▷ **relate**
relates *v* ▷ **relate**
relating *v* ▷ **relate**
relation *n* (*pl* -**s**) connection between things
▶ *pl* social or political dealings
relations *n* ▷ **relation**
relationship *n* (*pl* -**s**) dealings and feelings
between people or countries
relationships *n* ▷ **relationship**
relative *adj* dependent on relation to
something else, not absolute ▶ *n* (*pl* -**s**) person
connected by blood or marriage > **relatively**
adv
relatively *adv* ▷ **relative**
relatives *n* ▷ **relative**
relativities *n* ▷ **relativity**
relativity *n* (*pl* -**ies**) subject of two theories of
Albert Einstein, dealing with relationships
of space, time, and motion, and acceleration
and gravity
relax *v* (-**es, -ing, -ed**) make or become
looser, less tense, or less rigid > **relaxing** *adj*
> **relaxation** *n* (*pl* -**s**)
relaxation *n* ▷ **relax**
relaxations *n* ▷ **relax**
relaxed *v* ▷ **relax**
relaxes *v* ▷ **relax**
relaxing *v, adj* ▷ **relax**
relay *n* (*pl* -**s**) fresh set of people or animals
relieving others ▶ *v* (-**s, -ing, -ed**) pass on (a
message)
relayed *v* ▷ **relay**
relaying *v* ▷ **relay**
relays *n, v* ▷ **relay**
release *v* (-**ses, -sing, -sed**) set free ▶ *n* (*pl* -**s**)
setting free
released *v* ▷ **release**
releases *v, n* ▷ **release**
releasing *v* ▷ **release**
relegate *v* (-**tes, -ting, -ted**) put in a less

important position > **relegation** n (pl -s)
relegated v ▷ relegate
relegates v ▷ relegate
relegating v ▷ relegate
relegation n ▷ relegate
relegations n ▷ relegate
relent v (-s, -ing, -ed) give up a harsh intention,
become less severe
relented v ▷ relent
relenting v ▷ relent
relentless adj unremitting
relents v ▷ relent
relevance n ▷ relevant
relevances n ▷ relevant
relevant adj to do with the matter in hand
> **relevance** n (pl -s)
reliabilities n ▷ reliable
reliability n ▷ reliable
reliable adj able to be trusted, dependable
> **reliably** adv > **reliability** n (pl -ies)
reliably adv ▷ reliable
reliance n (pl -s) dependence, confidence, or
trust > **reliant** adj
reliances n ▷ reliance
reliant adj ▷ reliance
relic n (pl -s) something that has survived from
the past ▶ pl remains or traces
relics n ▷ relic
relict n (pl -s) (Obs) widow
relicts n ▷ relict
relied v ▷ rely
relief n (pl -s) gladness at the end or removal of
pain, distress, etc.
reliefs n ▷ relief
relies v ▷ rely
relieve v (-ves, -ving, -ved) bring relief to
relieved v ▷ relieve
relieves v ▷ relieve
relieving v ▷ relieve
religion n (pl -s) system of belief in and
worship of a supernatural power or god
religious adj of religion > **religiously** adv
religiously adv ▷ religious
religions n ▷ religion
relinquish v (-es, -ing, -ed) give up or abandon
relinquished v ▷ relinquish
relinquishes v ▷ relinquish
relinquishing v ▷ relinquish
reliquaries n ▷ reliquary
reliquary n (pl -ies) case or shrine for holy relics
relish v (-es, -ing, -ed) enjoy, like very much ▶ n
(pl -es) liking or enjoyment
relished v ▷ relish
relishes v, n ▷ relish
relishing v ▷ relish

relocate v (-tes, -ting, -ted) move to a new
place to live or work > **relocation** n (pl -s)
relocated v ▷ relocate
relocates v ▷ relocate
relocating v ▷ relocate
relocation n ▷ relocate
relocations n ▷ relocate
reluctance n ▷ reluctant
reluctances n ▷ reluctant
reluctant adj unwilling or disinclined
> **reluctantly** adv > **reluctance** n (pl -s)
reluctantly adv ▷ reluctant
rely v (-ies, -ying, -ied) depend (on)
relying v ▷ rely
remain v (-s, -ing, -ed) continue
remainder n (pl -s) part which is left ▶ v (-s,
-ing, -ed) offer (copies of a poorly selling
book) at reduced prices
remaindered v ▷ remainders
remaindering v ▷ remainders
remainders n, v ▷ remainders
remained v ▷ remain
remaining v ▷ remain
remains pl n relics, esp. of ancient buildings
▶ v ▷ remain
remand v (-s, -ing, -ed) send back into custody
or put on bail before trial
remanded v ▷ remand
remanding v ▷ remand
remands v ▷ remand
remark v (-s, -ing, -ed) make a casual comment
(on) ▶ n (pl -s) observation or comment
remarkable adj worthy of note or attention
> **remarkably** adv
remarkably adv ▷ remarkable
remarked v ▷ remark
remarking v ▷ remark
remarks v, n ▷ remark
remedial adj intended to correct a specific
disability, handicap, etc.
remedied v ▷ remedy
remedies n, v ▷ remedy
remedy n (pl -ies) means of curing pain or
disease ▶ v (-ies, -ying, -ied) put right
remedying v ▷ remedy
remember v (-s, -ing, -ed) retain in or recall to
one's memory
remembered v ▷ remember
remembering v ▷ remember
remembers v ▷ remember
remembrance n (pl -s) memory
remembrances n ▷ remembrance
remind v (-s, -ing, -ed) cause to remember
reminded v ▷ remind
reminder n (pl -s) something that recalls the

past
reminders *n* ▷ **reminder**
reminding *v* ▷ **remind**
reminds *v* ▷ **remind**
reminisce *v* (**-ces, -cing, -ced**) talk or write of past times, experiences, etc.
reminisced *v* ▷ **reminisce**
reminiscence *n* (*pl* **-s**) remembering ▶ *pl* memoirs
reminiscences *n* ▷ **reminiscence**
reminiscent *adj* reminding or suggestive (of)
reminisces *v* ▷ **reminisce**
reminiscing *v* ▷ **reminisce**
remiss *adj* negligent or careless
remission *n* (*pl* **-s**) reduction in the length of a prison term
remissions *n* ▷ **remission**
remit *v* (**-s, -tting, -tted**) send (money) for goods, services, etc., esp. by post ▶ *n* (*pl* **-s**) [**ree-mitt**] area of competence or authority
remits *v*, *n* ▷ **remit**
remittance *n* (*pl* **-s**) money sent as payment
remittances *n* ▷ **remittance**
remitted *v* ▷ **remit**
remitting *v* ▷ **remit**
remnant *n* (*pl* **-s**) small piece, esp. of fabric, left over
remnants *n* ▷ **remnant**
remonstrance *n* ▷ **remonstrate**
remonstrances *n* ▷ **remonstrate**
remonstrate *v* (**-tes, -ting, -ted**) argue in protest > **remonstrance** *n* (*pl* **-s**)
remonstrated *v* ▷ **remonstrate**
remonstrates *v* ▷ **remonstrate**
remonstrating *v* ▷ **remonstrate**
remorse *n* (*pl* **-s**) feeling of sorrow and regret for something one did > **remorseful** *adj*
remorseful *adj* ▷ **remorse**
remorseless *adj* pitiless > **remorselessly** *adv*
remorselessly *adv* ▷ **remorseless**
remorses *n* ▷ **remorse**
remote *adj* (**-er, -est**) far away, distant > **remotely** *adv*
remoter *adj* ▷ **remote**
remotest *adj* ▷ **remote**
remotely *adv* ▷ **remote**
remould *v* (**-s, -ing, -ed**) (BRIT) renovate (a worn tyre) ▶ *n* (*pl* **-s**) (BRIT) renovated tyre
remoulded *v* ▷ **remould**
remoulding *v* ▷ **remould**
remoulds *v*, *n* ▷ **remould**
remove *v* (**-ves, -ving, -ved**) take away or off ▶ *n* (*pl* **-s**) degree of difference > **removable** *adj*
removable *adj* ▷ **remove**
removal *n* (*pl* **-s**) removing, esp. changing

residence
removals *n* ▷ **removal**
removed *v* ▷ **remove**
removes *v*, *n* ▷ **remove**
removing *v* ▷ **remove**
remunerate *v* (**-tes, -ting, -ted**) reward or pay > **remunerative** *adj*
remunerated *v* ▷ **remunerate**
remunerates *v* ▷ **remunerate**
remunerating *v* ▷ **remunerate**
remuneration *n* (*pl* **-s**) reward or payment
remunerations *n* ▷ **remuneration**
remunerative *adj* ▷ **remuneration**
renaissance *n* (*pl* **-s**) revival or rebirth
renaissances *n* ▷ **renaissance**
renal [**ree-nal**] *adj* of the kidneys
renascent *adj* becoming active or vigorous again
rend *v* (**-s, -ing, rent**) tear or wrench apart
render *v* (**-s, -ing, -ed**) cause to become
rendered *v* ▷ **render**
rendering *v* ▷ **render**
renders *v* ▷ **render**
rendezvous [**ron**-day-voo] *n* (*pl* **-vous**) appointment ▶ *v* (**-vous, -vousing, -voused**) meet as arranged
rendezvoused *v* ▷ **rendezvous**
rendezvousing *v* ▷ **rendezvous**
rending *v* ▷ **rend**
rendition *n* (*pl* **-s**) performance
renditions *n* ▷ **rendition**
rends *v* ▷ **rend**
renegade *n* (*pl* **-s**) person who deserts a cause
renegades *n* ▷ **renegade**
renege [rin-**nayg**] *v* (**-ges, -ging, -ged**) go back (on a promise etc.)
reneged *v* ▷ **renege**
reneges *v* ▷ **renege**
reneging *v* ▷ **renege**
renew *v* (**-s, -ing, -ed**) begin again > **renewable** *adj* > **renewal** *n* (*pl* **-s**)
renewable *adj* ▷ **renew**
renewal *n* ▷ **renew**
renewals *n* ▷ **renew**
renewed *v* ▷ **renew**
renewing *v* ▷ **renew**
renews *v* ▷ **renew**
rennet *n* (*pl* **-s**) substance for curdling milk to make cheese
rennets *n* ▷ **rennet**
renounce *v* (**-ces, -cing, -ced**) give up (a belief, habit, etc.) voluntarily > **renunciation** *n* (*pl* **-s**)
renounced *v* ▷ **renounce**
renounces *v* ▷ **renounce**
renouncing *v* ▷ **renounce**

renovate v (-tes, -ting, -ted) restore to good condition > **renovation** n (pl -s)
  renovated v ▷ **renovate**
  renovates v ▷ **renovate**
  renovating v ▷ **renovate**
  renovation n ▷ **renovate**
  renovations n ▷ **renovate**
renown n (pl -s) widespread good reputation
renowned adj famous
  renowns n ▷ **renown**
rent[1] v (-s, -ing, -ed) give or have use of in return for regular payments ▶ n (pl -s) regular payment for use of land, a building, machine, etc.
rent[2] n (pl -s) tear or fissure ▶ v ▷ **rend**
rental n (pl -s) sum payable as rent
  rentals n ▷ **rental**
  rented v ▷ **rent**[1]
  renting v ▷ **rent**[1]
  rents v ▷ **rent**[1] ▶ n ▷ **rent**[2]
  renunciation n ▷ **renounce**
  renunciations n ▷ **renounce**
reorganize v (-zes, -zing, -zed) organize in a new and more efficient way > **reorganization** n (pl -s)
  reorganization n ▷ **reorganize**
  reorganizations n ▷ **reorganize**
  reorganized v ▷ **reorganize**
  reorganizes v ▷ **reorganize**
  reorganizing v ▷ **reorganize**
rep[1] n (pl -s) repertory company
  rep[2] n (pl -s) ▷ **representative**
repair[1] v (-s, -ing, -ed) restore to good condition, mend ▶ n (pl -s) act of repairing
repair[2] v (-s, -ing, -ed) go (to)
  repaired v ▷ **repair**[1, 2]
  repairing v ▷ **repair**[1, 2]
  repairs v ▷ **repair**[1, 2] ▶ n ▷ **repair**[1]
reparation n (pl -s) something done or given as compensation
  reparations n ▷ **reparation**
repartee n (pl -s) interchange of witty retorts
  repartees n ▷ **repartee**
repast n (pl -s) meal
  repasts n ▷ **repast**
repatriate v (-tes, -ting, -ted) send (someone) back to his or her own country > **repatriation** n (pl -s)
  repatriated v ▷ **repatriate**
  repatriates v ▷ **repatriate**
  repatriating v ▷ **repatriate**
  repatriation n ▷ **repatriate**
  repatriations n ▷ **repatriate**
repay v (-s, -ing, -paid) pay back, refund > **repayable** adj > **repayment** n (pl -s)

repayable adj ▷ **repay**
repaying v ▷ **repay**
repayment n ▷ **repay**
repayments n ▷ **repay**
repays v ▷ **repay**
repeal v (-s, -ing, -ed) cancel (a law) officially ▶ n (pl -s) act of repealing
  repealed v ▷ **repeal**
  repealing v ▷ **repeal**
  repeals v, n ▷ **repeal**
repeat v (-s, -ing, -ed) say or do again ▶ n (pl -s) act or instance of repeating > **repeatedly** adv
  repeated v ▷ **repeat**
  repeatedly adv ▷ **repeat**
repeater n (pl -s) firearm that may be discharged many times without reloading
  repeaters n ▷ **repeater**
  repeating v ▷ **repeat**
  repeats v, n ▷ **repeat**
repel v (-s, -lling, -lled) be disgusting to
  repelled v ▷ **repel**
repellent adj distasteful ▶ n (pl -s) something that repels, esp. a chemical to repel insects
  repellents n ▷ **repellent**
  repelling v ▷ **repel**
  repels v ▷ **repel**
repent v (-s, -ing, -ed) feel regret for (a deed or omission) > **repentance** n (pl -s) > **repentant** adj
  repentance n ▷ **repent**
  repentances n ▷ **repent**
  repentant adj ▷ **repent**
  repented v ▷ **repent**
  repenting v ▷ **repent**
  repents v ▷ **repent**
repercussions pl n indirect effects, often unpleasant
repertoire n (pl -s) stock of plays, songs, etc. that a player or company can give
  repertoires n ▷ **repertoire**
  repertories n ▷ **repertory**
repertory n (pl -ies) repertoire
repetition n (pl -s) act of repeating
  repetitions n ▷ **repetition**
  repetitious adj ▷ **repetitive**
repetitive, repetitious adj full of repetition
rephrase v (-ses, -sing, -sed) express in different words
  rephrased v ▷ **rephrase**
  rephrases v ▷ **rephrase**
  rephrasing v ▷ **rephrase**
repine v (-nes, -ning, -ned) fret or complain
  repined v ▷ **repine**
  repines v ▷ **repine**
  repining v ▷ **repine**

replace v (-ces, -cing, -ced) substitute for
> **replacement** n (pl -s)
replaced v ▷ **replace**
replacement n ▷ **replace**
replacements n ▷ **replace**
replaces v ▷ **replace**
replacing v ▷ **replace**
replay n (pl -s) immediate reshowing on TV
of an incident in sport, esp. in slow motion
▶ v (-s, -ing, -ed) play (a match, recording,
etc.) again
replayed v ▷ **replay**
replaying v ▷ **replay**
replays n, v ▷ **replay**
replenish v (-es, -ing, -ed) fill up again,
resupply > **replenishment** n (pl -s)
replenished v ▷ **replenish**
replenishes v ▷ **replenish**
replenishing v ▷ **replenish**
replenishment n ▷ **replenish**
replenishments n ▷ **replenish**
replete adj filled or gorged
replica n (pl -s) exact copy
replicas n ▷ **replica**
replicate v (-s, -ing, -ed) make or be a copy of
replicated v ▷ **replicate**
replicates v ▷ **replicate**
replicating v ▷ **replicate**
replied v ▷ **reply**
replies v, n ▷ **reply**
reply v (-ies, -ying, -ied) answer or respond ▶ n
(pl -ies) answer or response
replying v ▷ **reply**
report v (-s, -ing, -ed) give an account of ▶ n (pl
-s) account or statement
reported v ▷ **report**
reportedly adv according to rumour
reporter n (pl -s) person who gathers news for
a newspaper, TV, etc.
reporters n ▷ **reporter**
reporting v ▷ **report**
reports v, n ▷ **report**
repose n (pl -s) peace ▶ v (-ses, -sing, -sed) lie
or lay at rest
reposed v ▷ **repose**
reposes n, v ▷ **repose**
reposing v ▷ **repose**
repositories n ▷ **repository**
repository n (pl -ies) place where valuables are
deposited for safekeeping, store
repossess v (-es, -ing, -ed) (of a lender) take
back property from a customer who is behind
with payments > **repossession** n (pl -s)
repossessed v ▷ **repossess**
repossesses v ▷ **repossess**

repossessing v ▷ **repossess**
repossession n ▷ **repossess**
repossessions n ▷ **repossess**
reprehensible adj open to criticism,
unworthy
represent v (-s, -ing, -ed) act as a delegate or
substitute for > **representation** n (pl -s)
representation n ▷ **represent**
representations n ▷ **represent**
representative n (pl -s) person chosen to
stand for a group ▶ adj typical
representatives n ▷ **representative**
represented v ▷ **represent**
representing v ▷ **represent**
represents v ▷ **represent**
repress v (-es, -ing, -ed) keep (feelings) in
check > **repression** n (pl -s) > **repressive** adj
repressed v ▷ **repress**
represses v ▷ **repress**
repressing v ▷ **repress**
repression n ▷ **repress**
repressions n ▷ **repress**
repressive adj ▷ **repress**
reprieve v (-ves, -ving, -ved) postpone the
execution of (a condemned person) ▶ n (pl
-s) (document granting) postponement or
cancellation of a punishment
reprieved v ▷ **reprieve**
reprieves v, n ▷ **reprieve**
reprieving v ▷ **reprieve**
reprimand v (-s, -ing, -ed) blame (someone)
officially for a fault ▶ n (pl -s) official blame
reprimanded v ▷ **reprimand**
reprimanding v ▷ **reprimand**
reprimands v, n ▷ **reprimand**
reprint v (-s, -ing, -ed) print further copies of (a
book) ▶ n (pl -s) reprinted copy
reprinted v ▷ **reprint**
reprinting v ▷ **reprint**
reprints v, n ▷ **reprint**
reprisal n (pl -s) retaliation
reprisals n ▷ **reprisal**
reproach n, v (-es, -ing, -ed) blame, rebuke
> **reproachful** adj > **reproachfully** adv
reproached v ▷ **reproach**
reproaches v ▷ **reproach**
reproachful adj ▷ **reproach**
reproachfully adv ▷ **reproach**
reproaching v ▷ **reproach**
reprobate adj, n (pl -s) depraved or
disreputable (person)
reprobates n ▷ **reprobate**
reproduce v (-ces, -cing, -ced) produce a copy
of > **reproducible** adj
reproduced v ▷ **reproduce**

reproduces v ▷ reproduce
reproducible adj ▷ reproduce
reproducing v ▷ reproduce
reproduction n (pl -s) process of reproducing > **reproductive** adj
reproductions n ▷ reproduction
reproductive adj ▷ reproduction
reproof n (pl -s) severe blaming of someone for a fault
reproofs n ▷ reproof
reprove v (-ves, -ving, -ved) speak severely to (someone) about a fault
reproved v ▷ reprove
reproves v ▷ reprove
reproving v ▷ reprove
reps n ▷ rep[1, 2]
reptile n (pl -s) cold-blooded egg-laying vertebrate with horny scales or plates, such as a snake or tortoise > **reptilian** adj
reptiles n ▷ reptile
reptilian adj ▷ reptile
republic n (pl -s) form of government in which the people or their elected representatives possess the supreme power
republican n (pl -s) supporter or advocate of a republic > **republicanism** n (pl -s)
republicans n ▷ republican
republicanism n ▷ republican
republicanisms n ▷ republican
republics n ▷ republic
repudiate [rip-**pew**-dee-ate] v (-tes, -ting, -ted) reject the authority or validity of > **repudiation** n (pl -s)
repudiated v ▷ repudiate
repudiates v ▷ repudiate
repudiating v ▷ repudiate
repudiation n ▷ repudiate
repudiations n ▷ repudiate
repugnance n ▷ repugnant
repugnances n ▷ repugnant
repugnant adj offensive or distasteful > **repugnance** n (pl -s)
repulse v (-ses, -sing, -sed) be disgusting to ▶ n (pl -s) driving back
repulsed v ▷ repulse
repulsing v ▷ repulse
repulses v, n ▷ repulse
repulsion n (pl -s) distaste or aversion
repulsions n ▷ repulsion
repulsive adj loathsome, disgusting
reputable adj of good reputation, respectable
reputation n (pl -s) estimation in which a person is held
reputations n ▷ reputation
repute n (pl -s) reputation

reputed adj supposed > **reputedly** adv
reputedly adv ▷ reputed
reputes n ▷ repute
request v (-s, -ing, -ed) ask ▶ n (pl -s) asking
requested v ▷ request
requesting v ▷ request
requests v, n ▷ request
requiem [rek-wee-em] n (pl -s) Mass for the dead
requiems n ▷ requiem
require v (-res, -ring, -red) want or need
required v ▷ require
requirement n (pl -s) essential condition
requirements n ▷ requirement
requires v ▷ require
requiring v ▷ require
requisite [rek-**wizz**-it] adj necessary, essential ▶ n (pl -s) essential thing
requisites n ▷ requisite
requisition v (-s, -ing, -ed) demand (supplies) ▶ n (pl -s) formal demand, such as for materials or supplies
requisitioned v ▷ requisition
requisitioning v ▷ requisition
requisitions v, n ▷ requisition
requite v (-tes, -ting, -ted) return to someone (the same treatment or feeling as received)
requited v ▷ requite
requites v ▷ requite
requiting v ▷ requite
reredos [**rear**-doss] n (pl -es) ornamental screen behind an altar
reredoses n ▷ reredos
resat v ▷ resit
rescind v (-s, -ing, -ed) annul or repeal
rescinded v ▷ rescind
rescinding v ▷ rescind
rescinds v ▷ rescind
rescue v (-cues, -cuing, -cued) deliver from danger or trouble, save ▶ n (pl -s) rescuing > **rescuer** n (pl -s)
rescued v ▷ rescue
rescuer n ▷ rescue
rescuers n ▷ rescue
rescues v, n ▷ rescue
rescuing v ▷ rescue
research n (pl -es) systematic investigation to discover facts or collect information ▶ v (-es, -ing, -ed) carry out investigations > **researcher** n (pl -s)
researched v ▷ research
researcher n ▷ research
researchers n ▷ research
researches n, v ▷ research
researching v ▷ research

resemblance *n* ▷ resemble
resemblances *n* ▷ resemble
resemble *v* (-les, -ling, -led) be or look like
> **resemblance** *n* (*pl* -s)
resembled *v* ▷ resemble
resembles *v* ▷ resemble
resembling *v* ▷ resemble
resent *v* (-s, -ing, -ed) feel bitter about
> **resentful** *adj* > **resentment** *n* (*pl* -s)
resented *v* ▷ resent
resentful *adj* ▷ resent
resenting *v* ▷ resent
resentment *n* ▷ resent
resentments *n* ▷ resent
resents *v* ▷ resent
reservation *n* (*pl* -s) doubt
reservations *n* ▷ reservation
reserve *v* (-ves, -ving, -ved) set aside, keep for
future use ▶ *n* (*pl* -s) something, esp. money
or troops, kept for emergencies (SPORT)
reserved *adj* not showing one's feelings,
lacking friendliness ▶ *v* ▷ **reserve**
reserves *v*, *n* ▷ reserve
reserving *v* ▷ reserve
reservist *n* (*pl* -s) member of a military reserve
reservists *n* ▷ reservist
reservoir *n* (*pl* -s) natural or artificial lake
storing water for community supplies
reservoirs *n* ▷ reservoir
reshuffle *n* (*pl* -s) reorganization ▶ *v* (-s, -ing,
-ed) reorganize
reshuffled *n* ▷ reshuffle
reshuffles *n*, *v* ▷ reshuffle
reshuffling *v* ▷ reshuffle
reside *v* (-des, -ding, -ded) dwell permanently
resided *v* ▷ reside
residence *n* (*pl* -s) home or house
residences *n* ▷ residence
resident *n* (*pl* -s) person who lives in a place
▶ *adj* living in a place
residential *adj* (of part of a town) consisting
mainly of houses
residents *n* ▷ resident
resides *v* ▷ reside
residing *v* ▷ reside
residue *n* (*pl* -s) what is left, remainder
> **residual** *adj*
residual *adj* ▷ residue
residues *n* ▷ residue
resign *v* (-s, -ing, -ed) give up office, a job, etc.
resignation *n* (*pl* -s) resigning
resignations *n* ▷ resignation
resigned *adj* content to endure ▶ *v* ▷ **resign**
resigning *v* ▷ resign
resigns *v* ▷ resign

resilience *n* ▷ resilient
resiliences *n* ▷ resilient
resilient *adj* (of a person) recovering quickly
from a shock etc. > **resilience** *n* (*pl* -s)
resin [rezz-in] *n* (*pl* -s) sticky substance from
plants, esp. pines > **resinous** *adj*
resinous *adj* ▷ resin
resins *n* ▷ resin
resist *v* (-s, -ing, -ed) withstand or oppose
> **resistant** *adj* > **resistible** *adj*
resistance *n* (*pl* -s) act of resisting
resistances *n* ▷ resistance
resistant *adj* ▷ resist
resisted *v* ▷ resist
resistible *adj* ▷ resist
resisting *v* ▷ resist
resistor *n* (*pl* -s) component of an electrical
circuit producing resistance
resistors *n* ▷ resistor
resists *v* ▷ resist
resit *v* (-s, -tting, -sat) take (an exam) again ▶ *n*
(*pl* -s) exam that has to be taken again
resitting *v* ▷ resit
resits *v*, *n* ▷ resit
resolute *adj* firm in purpose > **resolutely** *adv*
resolutely *adv* ▷ resolute
resolution *n* (*pl* -s) firmness of conduct or
character
resolutions *n* ▷ resolution
resolve *v* (-ves, -ving, -ved) decide with an
effort of will
resolved *adj* determined ▶ *v* ▷ **resolve**
resolves *v* ▷ resolve
resolving *v* ▷ resolve
resonance *n* (*pl* -s) echoing, esp. with a deep
sound > **resonant** *adj* > **resonate** *v* (-tes,
-ting, -ted)
resonances *n* ▷ resonance
resonant *adj* ▷ resonance
resonate *v* ▷ resonance
resonated *v* ▷ resonance
resonates *v* ▷ resonance
resonating *v* ▷ resonance
resort *v* (-s, -ing, -ed) have recourse (to) for
help etc. ▶ *n* (*pl* -s) place for holidays
resorted *v* ▷ resort
resorting *v* ▷ resort
resorts *v*, *n* ▷ resort
resound [riz-zownd] *v* (-s, -ing, -ed) echo or ring
with sound
resounded *v* ▷ resound
resounding *adj* echoing ▶ *v* ▷ **resound**
resounds *v* ▷ resound
resource *n* (*pl* -s) thing resorted to for
support ▶ *pl* sources of economic wealth

> **resourceful** adj > **resourcefulness** n
resourceful adj ▷ **resource**
resourcefulness n ▷ **resource**
resources n ▷ **resource**
respect n (pl -**s**) consideration ▶ v (-**s**, -**ing**, -**ed**) treat with esteem > **respecter** n (pl -**s**) > **respectful** adj
respectable adj worthy of respect
> **respectably** adv > **respectability** n (pl -**ies**)
respectabilities n ▷ **respectable**
respectability n ▷ **respectable**
respectably adv ▷ **respectable**
respected v ▷ **respect**
respecter n ▷ **respect**
respecters n ▷ **respect**
respectful adj ▷ **respect**
respecting prep concerning ▶ v ▷ **respect**
respective adj relating separately to each of those in question > **respectively** adv
respectively adv ▷ **respective**
respects n, v ▷ **respect**
respiration [ress-per-**ray**-shun] n (pl -**s**) breathing > **respiratory** adj
respirations n ▷ **respiration**
respirator n apparatus worn over the mouth and breathed through as protection against dust, poison gas, etc., or to provide artificial respiration
respirators n ▷ **respirator**
respiratory adj ▷ **respiration**
respire v (-**res**, -**ring**, -**red**) breathe
respired v ▷ **respire**
respires v ▷ **respire**
respiring v ▷ **respire**
respite n (pl -**s**) pause, interval of rest
respites n ▷ **respite**
resplendence n ▷ **resplendent**
resplendences n ▷ **resplendent**
resplendent adj brilliant or splendid
> **resplendence** n (pl -**s**)
respond v (-**s**, -**ing**, -**ed**) answer
responded v ▷ **respond**
respondent n (pl -**s**) (LAW) defendant
respondents n ▷ **respondent**
responding v ▷ **respond**
responds v ▷ **respond**
response n (pl -**s**) answer
responses n ▷ **response**
responsibilities n ▷ **responsibility**
responsibility n (pl -**ies**) state of being responsible
responsible adj having control and authority
> **responsibly** adv
responsibly adv ▷ **responsible**
responsive adj readily reacting to some

influence > **responsiveness** n
responsiveness n ▷ **responsive**
rest[1] n (pl -**s**) freedom from exertion etc. ▶ v (-**s**, -**ing**, -**ed**) take a rest > **restful** adj > **restless** adj
rest[2] n what is left ▶ v (-**s**, -**ing**, -**ed**) remain, continue to be
restaurant n (pl -**s**) commercial establishment serving meals
restaurants n ▷ **restaurant**
restaurateur [rest-er-a-**tur**] n (pl -**s**) person who owns or runs a restaurant
restaurateurs n ▷ **restaurateur**
rested v ▷ **rest**[1, 2]
restful (-**ler**, -**lest**) adj ▷ **rest**[1]
restfuller adj ▷ **restful**
restfullest adj ▷ **restful**
resting v ▷ **rest**[1, 2]
restitution n (pl -**s**) giving back
restitutions n ▷ **restitution**
restive adj restless or impatient
restless adj ▷ **rest**[1]
restore v (-**res**, -**ring**, -**red**) return (a building, painting, etc.) to its original condition
> **restoration** n (pl -**s**) > **restorer** n (pl -**s**)
restoration n ▷ **restore**
restorations n ▷ **restore**
restorative adj restoring ▶ n (pl -**s**) food or medicine to strengthen etc.
restoratives n ▷ **restorative**
restored v ▷ **restore**
restorer n ▷ **restore**
restorers n ▷ **restore**
restores v ▷ **restore**
restoring v ▷ **restore**
restrain v (-**s**, -**ing**, -**ed**) hold (someone) back from action
restrained adj not displaying emotion ▶ v ▷ **restrain**
restraining v ▷ **restrain**
restrains v ▷ **restrain**
restraint n (pl -**s**) control, esp. self-control
restraints n ▷ **restraint**
restrict v (-**s**, -**ing**, -**ed**) confine to certain limits > **restriction** n (pl -**s**) > **restrictive** adj
restricted v ▷ **restrict**
restricting v ▷ **restrict**
restriction n ▷ **restrict**
restrictions n ▷ **restrict**
restrictive adj ▷ **restrict**
restricts v ▷ **restrict**
restructure v (-**res**, -**ring**, -**red**) organize in a different way
restructured v ▷ **restructure**
restructures v ▷ **restructure**
restructuring v ▷ **restructure**

rests *n, v* ▷ **rest**[1, 2]
result *n* (*pl* -s) outcome or consequence ▶ *v* (-s, -ing, -ed) (*foll. by* **from**) be the outcome or consequence (of) > **resultant** *adj*
resultant *adj* ▷ **result**
resulted *v* ▷ **result**
resulting *v* ▷ **result**
results *n, v* ▷ **result**
resume *v* (-mes, -ming, -med) begin again > **resumption** *n* (*pl* -s)
résumé [rezz-yew-may] *n* (*pl* -s) summary
resumed *v* ▷ **resume**
resumes *v* ▷ **resume**
résumés *n* ▷ **résumé**
resuming *v* ▷ **resume**
resumption *n* ▷ **resume**
resumptions *n* ▷ **resume**
resurgence *n* (*pl* -s) rising again to vigour > **resurgent** *adj*
resurgences *n* ▷ **resurgence**
resurgent *adj* ▷ **resurgence**
resurrect *v* (-s, -ing, -ed) restore to life
resurrected *v* ▷ **resurrect**
resurrecting *v* ▷ **resurrect**
resurrection *n* (*pl* -s) rising again (esp. from the dead)
resurrections *n* ▷ **resurrection**
resurrects *v* ▷ **resurrect**
resuscitate [ris-suss-it-tate] *v* (-tes, -ting, -ted) restore to consciousness > **resuscitation** *n* (*pl* -s)
resuscitated *v* ▷ **resuscitate**
resuscitates *v* ▷ **resuscitate**
resuscitating *v* ▷ **resuscitate**
resuscitation *n* ▷ **resuscitate**
resuscitations *n* ▷ **resuscitate**
retail *n* (*pl* -s) selling of goods individually or in small amounts to the public ▶ *adv* by retail ▶ *v* (-s, -ing, -ed) sell or be sold retail
retailed *v* ▷ **retail**
retailer *n* (*pl* -s) person or company that sells goods to the public
retailers *n* ▷ **retailer**
retailing *v* ▷ **retail**
retails *n, v* ▷ **retail**
retain *v* (-s, -ing, -ed) keep in one's possession
retained *v* ▷ **retain**
retainer *n* (*pl* -s) fee to retain someone's services
retainers *n* ▷ **retainer**
retaining *v* ▷ **retain**
retains *v* ▷ **retain**
retaliate *v* (-tes, -ting, -ted) repay an injury or wrong in kind > **retaliation** *n* (*pl* -s) > **retaliatory** *adj*

retaliated *v* ▷ **retaliate**
retaliates *v* ▷ **retaliate**
retaliating *v* ▷ **retaliate**
retaliation *n* ▷ **retaliate**
retaliations *n* ▷ **retaliate**
retaliatory *adj* ▷ **retaliate**
retard *v* (-s, -ing, -ed) delay or slow (progress or development) > **retardation** *n* (*pl* -s)
retardation *n* ▷ **retard**
retardations *n* ▷ **retard**
retarded *adj* underdeveloped, esp. mentally ▶ *v* ▷ **retard**
retarding *v* ▷ **retard**
retards *v* ▷ **retard**
retch *v* (-es, -ing, -ed) try to vomit
retched *v* ▷ **retch**
retches *v* ▷ **retch**
retching *v* ▷ **retch**
rethink *v* (-s, -ing, -thought) consider again, esp. with a view to changing one's tactics
rethinks *v* ▷ **rethink**
rethinking *v* ▷ **rethink**
rethought *v* ▷ **rethink**
reticence *n* ▷ **reticent**
reticences *n* ▷ **reticent**
reticent *adj* uncommunicative, reserved > **reticence** *n* (*pl* -s)
retina *n* (*pl* -nas, -nae) light-sensitive membrane at the back of the eye
retinae *n* ▷ **retina**
retinas *n* ▷ **retina**
retinue *n* (*pl* -s) band of attendants
retinues *n* ▷ **retinue**
retire *v* (-res, -ring, -red) (cause to) give up office or work, esp. through age > **retirement** *n* (*pl* -s)
retired *adj* having retired from work etc. ▶ *v* ▷ **retire**
retirement *n* ▷ **retire**
retirements *n* ▷ **retire**
retires *v* ▷ **retire**
retiring *adj* shy ▶ *v* ▷ **retire**
retort[1] *v* (-s, -ing, -ed) reply quickly, wittily, or angrily ▶ *n* (*pl* -s) quick, witty, or angry reply
retort[2] *n* (*pl* -s) glass container with a bent neck used for distilling
retorted *v* ▷ **retort**[1]
retorting *v* ▷ **retort**[1]
retorts *v* ▷ **retort**[1] ▶ *n* ▷ **retort**[1,2]
retouch *v* (-es, -ing, -ed) restore or improve by new touches, esp. of paint
retouched *v* ▷ **retouch**
retouches *v* ▷ **retouch**
retouching *v* ▷ **retouch**
retrace *v* (-ces, -cing, -ced) go back over (a

route etc.) again

retraced v ▷ **retrace**

retraces v ▷ **retrace**

retracing v ▷ **retrace**

retract v (-s, -ing, -ed) withdraw (a statement etc.) > **retraction** n (pl -s)

retractable, retractile adj able to be retracted

retracted v ▷ **retract**

retractile adj ▷ **retractable**

retracting v ▷ **retract**

retracts v ▷ **retract**

retraction n ▷ **retract**

retractions n ▷ **retract**

retread v (-s, -ing, -ed) ▶ n (pl -s) ▷ **remould**

retreaded v ▷ **retread**

retreading v ▷ **retread**

retreads v, n ▷ **retread**

retreat v (-s, -ing, -ed) move back from a position, withdraw ▶ n (pl -s) act of or military signal for retiring or withdrawal

retreated v ▷ **retreat**

retreating v ▷ **retreat**

retreats v, n ▷ **retreat**

retrench v (-es, -ing, -ed) reduce expenditure, cut back > **retrenchment** n (pl -s)

retrenched v ▷ **retrench**

retrenches v ▷ **retrench**

retrenching v ▷ **retrench**

retrenchment n ▷ **retrench**

retrenchments n ▷ **retrench**

retrial n (pl -s) second trial of a case or defendant in a court of law

retrials n ▷ **retrial**

retribution n (pl -s) punishment or vengeance for evil deeds > **retributive** adj

retributions n ▷ **retribution**

retributive adj ▷ **retributions**

retrieve v (-ves, -ving, -ved) fetch back again > **retrievable** adj > **retrieval** n (pl -s)

retrievable adj ▷ **retrieve**

retrieval n ▷ **retrieve**

retrievals n ▷ **retrieve**

retrieved v ▷ **retrieve**

retriever n (pl -s) dog trained to retrieve shot game

retrievers n ▷ **retrieve**

retrieves v ▷ **retrieve**

retrieving v ▷ **retrieve**

retroactive adj effective from a date in the past

retrograde adj tending towards an earlier worse condition

retrogressive adj going back to an earlier worse condition > **retrogression** n (pl -s)

retrogression n ▷ **retrogressive**

retrogressions n ▷ **retrogressive**

retrorocket n (pl -s) small rocket engine used to slow a spacecraft

retrorockets n ▷ **retrorocket**

retrospective adj looking back in time ▶ n (pl -s) exhibition of an artist's life's work

retrospectives n ▷ **retrospective**

retroussé [rit-**troo**-say] adj (of a nose) turned upwards

retsina n (pl -s) Greek wine flavoured with resin

retsinas n ▷ **retsina**

return v (-s, -ing, -ed) go or come back ▶ n (pl -s) returning > **returnable** adj

returnable adj ▷ **return**

returned v ▷ **return**

returning v ▷ **return**

returns v, n ▷ **return**

reunion n (pl -s) meeting of people who have been apart

reunions n ▷ **reunion**

reunite v (-tes, -ting, -ted) bring or come together again after a separation

reunited v ▷ **reunite**

reunites v ▷ **reunite**

reuniting v ▷ **reunite**

reuse v (-ses, -sing, -sed) use again > **reusable** adj

reusable adj ▷ **reuse**

reused v ▷ **reuse**

reuses v ▷ **reuse**

reusing v ▷ **reuse**

rev (Informal) n (pl -s) revolution (of an engine) ▶ v (-s, -vving, -vved) (foll. by **up**) increase the speed of revolution of (an engine)

revalue v (-ues, -uing, -ued) adjust the exchange value of (a currency) upwards > **revaluation** n (pl -s)

revaluation n ▷ **revalue**

revaluations n ▷ **revalue**

revalued v ▷ **revalue**

revalues v ▷ **revalue**

revaluing v ▷ **revalue**

revamp v (-s, -ing, -ed) renovate or restore

revamped v ▷ **revamp**

revamping v ▷ **revamp**

revamps v ▷ **revamp**

reveal v (-s, -ing, -ed) make known > **revelation** n (pl -s)

revealed v ▷ **reveal**

revealing v ▷ **reveal**

reveals v ▷ **reveal**

reveille [riv-**val**-ee] n (pl -s) morning bugle call to waken soldiers

reveilles n ▷ **reveille**

revel v (-s, -lling, -lled) take pleasure (in)
  > **reveller** n (pl -s)
  revelation n ▷ **revel**
  revelations n ▷ **revel**
  revelled v ▷ **revel**
  reveller n ▷ **revel**
  revellers n ▷ **revel**
  revelling v ▷ **revel**
  revelries n ▷ **revelry**
revelry n (pl -s) festivity
revels pl n merrymaking ▶ v ▷ **revel**
revenge n (pl -s) retaliation for wrong done
  ▶ v (-ges, -ging, -ged) make retaliation for
  > **revengeful** adj
  revenged v ▷ **revenge**
  revengeful adj ▷ **revenge**
  revenges n, v ▷ **revenge**
  revenging v ▷ **revenge**
revenue n (pl -s) income, esp. of a state
  revenues n ▷ **revenue**
reverberate v (-tes, -ting, -ted) echo or
  resound > **reverberation** n (pl -s)
  reverberated v ▷ **reverberate**
  reverberates v ▷ **reverberate**
  reverberating v ▷ **reverberate**
  reverberation n ▷ **reverberate**
  reverberations n ▷ **reverberate**
revere v (-s, -ing, -ed) be in awe of and respect
  greatly
  revered v ▷ **revere**
reverence n (pl -s) awe mingled with respect
  and esteem
  reverences n ▷ **reverence**
reverent adj showing reverence > **reverently**
  adv
reverential adj marked by reverence
  reverently adv ▷ **reverent**
  reveres v ▷ **revere**
  revering v ▷ **revere**
reverie n (pl -s) absent-minded daydream
  reveries n ▷ **reverie**
revers [riv-veer] n (pl -s) turned back part of a
  garment, such as the lapel
reverse v (-ses, -sing, -sed) turn upside down
  or the other way round ▶ n (pl -s) opposite
  ▶ adj opposite or contrary > **reversal** n (pl -s)
  > **reversible** adj
  reversal n ▷ **reverse**
  reversals n ▷ **reverse**
  reversed v ▷ **reverse**
  reverses v, n ▷ **reverse**
  reversible adj ▷ **reverse**
  reversing v ▷ **reverse**
  reversion n ▷ **revert**
  reversions n ▷ **revert**

revert v (-s, -ing, -ed) return to a former state
  > **reversion** n (pl -s)
  reverted v ▷ **revert**
  reverting v ▷ **revert**
  reverts v ▷ **revert**
review n (pl -s) critical assessment of a book,
  concert, etc. ▶ v (-s, -ing, -ed) hold or write
  a review of
  reviewed v ▷ **review**
reviewer n (pl -s) writer of reviews
  reviewers n ▷ **reviewer**
  reviewing v ▷ **review**
  reviews n, v ▷ **review**
revile v (-les, -ling, -led) be abusively scornful
  of
  reviled v ▷ **revile**
  reviles v ▷ **revile**
  reviling v ▷ **revile**
revise v (-ses, -sing, -sed) change or alter
  > **revision** n (pl -s)
  revised v ▷ **revise**
  revises v ▷ **revise**
  revising v ▷ **revise**
  revision n ▷ **revive**
  revisions n ▷ **revive**
revival n (pl -s) reviving or renewal
  > **revivalism** n (pl -s) > **revivalist** n (pl -s)
  revivalism n ▷ **revival**
  revivalisms n ▷ **revival**
  revivalists n ▷ **revival**
  revivalist n ▷ **revival**
  revivals n ▷ **revival**
revive v (-ves, -ving, -ved) bring or come back
  to life, vigour, use, etc.
  revived v ▷ **revive**
  revives v ▷ **revive**
  reviving v ▷ **revive**
  revocation n ▷ **revoke**
  revocations n ▷ **revoke**
revoke v (-kes, -king, -ked) cancel (a will,
  agreement, etc.) > **revocation** n (pl -s)
  revoked v ▷ **revoke**
  revokes v ▷ **revoke**
  revoking v ▷ **revoke**
revolt n (pl -s) uprising against authority ▶ v
  (-s, -ing, -ed) rise in rebellion
  revolted v ▷ **revolt**
revolting adj disgusting, horrible ▶ v ▷ **revolt**
  revolts n, v ▷ **revolt**
revolution n (pl -s) overthrow of a government
  by the governed
  revolutionaries n ▷ **revolutionary**
revolutionary adj advocating or engaged in
  revolution ▶ n (pl -ies) person advocating or
  engaged in revolution

revolutionize v (-zes, -zing, -zed) change considerably
  revolutionized v ▷ **revolutionize**
  revolutionizes v ▷ **revolutionize**
  revolutionizing v ▷ **revolutionize**
  revolutions n ▷ **revolution**
revolve v (-ves, -ving, -ved) turn round, rotate
  revolved v ▷ **revolve**
revolver n (pl -s) repeating pistol
  revolvers n ▷ **revolver**
  revolves v ▷ **revolve**
  revolving v ▷ **revolve**
  revs n, v ▷ **rev**
revue n (pl -s) theatrical entertainment with topical sketches and songs
  revues n ▷ **revue**
revulsion n (pl -s) strong disgust
  revulsions n ▷ **revulsion**
  revved v ▷ **rev**
  revving v ▷ **rev**
reward n (pl -s) something given in return for a service ▸ v (-s, -ing, -ed) pay or give something to (someone) for a service, information, etc.
  rewarded v ▷ **reward**
  rewarding v ▷ **reward**
  rewards n, v ▷ **reward**
rewind v (-s, -ing, -wound) run (a tape or film) back to an earlier point in order to replay
  rewinding v ▷ **rewind**
  rewinds v ▷ **rewind**
rewire v (-res, -ring, -red) provide (a house, engine, etc.) with new wiring
  rewired v ▷ **rewire**
  rewires v ▷ **rewire**
  rewiring v ▷ **rewire**
  rewound v ▷ **rewind**
rewrite v (-tes, -ting, -wrote, -written) write again in a different way ▸ n (pl -s) something rewritten
  rewrites v, n ▷ **rewrite**
  rewriting v ▷ **rewrite**
  rewritten v ▷ **rewrite**
  rewrote v ▷ **rewrite**

> **rex** n (rexes). Rex is a Latin word for king. This is a very useful word, as it combines X with two of the most common letters on the board, making it one to look for when you get an X. Rex scores 10 points.
> **rez** n (rezes). Rez is a short informal word for reservation. Combining Z with two of the most common tiles on the board, this is one of the first words to think about when you draw a Z and

don't have the letters for a longer word. Rez scores 12 points.

rhapsodic adj ▷ **rhapsody**
rhapsodies n ▷ **rhapsody**
rhapsodize v (-zes, -zing, -zed) speak or write with extravagant enthusiasm
  rhapsodized v ▷ **rhapsodize**
  rhapsodizes v ▷ **rhapsodize**
  rhapsodizing v ▷ **rhapsodize**
rhapsody n (pl -ies) freely structured emotional piece of music > **rhapsodic** adj
rhea [ree-a] n (pl -s) S American three-toed ostrich
  rheas n ▷ **rhea**
rhenium n (pl -s) (CHEM) silvery-white metallic element with a high melting point
  rheniums n ▷ **rhenium**
rheostat n (pl -s) instrument for varying the resistance of an electrical circuit
  rheostats n ▷ **rheostat**
rhesus [ree-suss] n (pl -es) small long-tailed monkey of S Asia
  rhesuses n ▷ **rhesus**
rhetoric n (pl -s) art of effective speaking or writing
rhetorical adj (of a question) not requiring an answer > **rhetorically** adv
  rhetorically adv ▷ **rhetorical**
  rhetorics n ▷ **rhetoric**
rheumatic n, adj (pl -s) (person) affected by rheumatism
  rheumatics n ▷ **rheumatic**
rheumatism n (pl -s) painful inflammation of joints or muscles
  rheumatisms n ▷ **rheumatism**
rheumatoid adj of or like rheumatism
rhinestone n (pl -s) imitation diamond
  rhinestones n ▷ **rhinestone**
rhino n (pl -s) rhinoceros
rhinoceros n (pl -oses, -os) large thick-skinned animal with one or two horns on its nose
  rhinoceroses n ▷ **rhinoceros**
  rhinos n ▷ **rhino**
rhizome n (pl -s) thick underground stem producing new plants
  rhizomes n ▷ **rhizome**

> **rho** n (rhos). Rho is the 17th letter of the Greek alphabet. It's useful to remember words that start with RH, as there are quite a few that can come in useful. If you or someone else plays rho, remember that it could be expanded to **rhodium, rhombus** or **rhomboid**. Rho scores 6 points.

rhodium n (pl -s) (CHEM) hard metallic element

rhodiums *n* ▷ **rhodium**
rhododendron *n* (*pl* -s) evergreen flowering shrub
  rhododendrons *n* ▷ **rhododendron**
  rhombi *n* ▷ **rhombus**
rhomboid *n* (*pl* -s) parallelogram with adjacent sides of unequal length
  rhomboids *n* ▷ **rhomboid**
rhombus *n* (*pl* -buses, -bi) parallelogram with sides of equal length but no right angles, diamond-shaped figure
  rhombuses *n* ▷ **rhombus**
rhubarb *n* (*pl* -s) garden plant of which the fleshy stalks are cooked as fruit
  rhubarbs *n* ▷ **rhubarb**

> **rhy** *n* (**rhys**). Rhy is an alternative spelling of rye. This is a useful word as it doesn't contain a vowel, and so can be helpful when you have a poor combination of tiles on your rack. Rhy scores 9 points.

rhyme *n* (*pl* -s) sameness of the final sounds at the ends of lines of verse, or in words ▶ *v* (-mes, -ming, -med) make a rhyme
  rhymed *v* ▷ **rhyme**
  rhymes *n*, *v* ▷ **rhyme**
  rhyming *v* ▷ **rhyme**
rhythm *n* (*pl* -s) any regular movement or beat > **rhythmic**, **rhythmical** *adj* > **rhythmically** *adv*
  rhythmic *adj* ▷ **rhythm**
  rhythmical *adj* ▷ **rhythm**
  rhythmically *adv* ▷ **rhythm**
  rhythms *n* ▷ **rhythm**
rib¹ *n* (*pl* -s) one of the curved bones forming the framework of the upper part of the body ▶ *v* (-s, -bbing, -bbed) provide or mark with ribs > **ribbed** *adj* > **ribbing** *n* (*pl* -s)
rib² *v* (-s, -bbing, -bbed) (*Informal*) tease or ridicule > **ribbing** *n* (*pl* -s)
ribald *adj* humorously or mockingly rude or obscene > **ribaldry** *n* (*pl* -s)
  ribaldries *n* ▷ **ribald**
  ribaldry *n* ▷ **ribald**
  ribbed *v*, *adj* ▷ **rib¹, ²**
  ribbing *v*, *n* ▷ **rib¹, ²**
  ribbings *n* ▷ **rib¹, ²**
ribbon *n* (*pl* -s) narrow band of fabric used for trimming, tying, etc.
  ribbons *n* ▷ **ribbon**
ribcage *n* (*pl* -s) bony structure of ribs enclosing the lungs
  ribcages *n* ▷ **ribcage**
riboflavin [rye-boe-**flay**-vin] *n* (*pl* -s) form of vitamin B

riboflavins *n* ▷ **riboflavin**
ribs *n*, *v* ▷ **rib¹, ²**
rice *n* (*pl* -s) cereal plant grown on wet ground in warm countries
  rices *n* ▷ **rice**
rich *adj* (-er, -est) owning a lot of money or property, wealthy > **richness** *n* (*pl* -es)
  richer *adj* ▷ **rich**
riches *pl n* wealth
  richest *adj* ▷ **rich**
richly *adv* elaborately
  richness *n* ▷ **rich**
  richnesses *n* ▷ **rich**
rick¹ *n* (*pl* -s) stack of hay etc.
rick² *v*, *n* (-s, -ing, -ed) sprain or wrench
  ricked *v* ▷ **rick²**
  ricketier *adj* ▷ **rickety**
  ricketiest *adj* ▷ **rickety**
rickets *n* disease of children marked by softening of the bones, bow legs, etc., caused by vitamin D deficiency
rickety *adj* (-tier, -tiest) shaky or unstable
  ricking *v* ▷ **rick¹**
  ricks *n* ▷ **rick¹** ▶ *v* ▷ **rick²**
rickshaw *n* (*pl* -s) light two-wheeled man-drawn Asian vehicle
  rickshaws *n* ▷ **rickshaw**
ricochet [rik-osh-ay] *v* (-s, -ing, -ed) (of a bullet) rebound from a solid surface ▶ *n* (*pl* -s) such a rebound
  ricocheted *v* ▷ **ricochet**
  ricocheting *v* ▷ **ricochet**
  ricochets *v*, *n* ▷ **ricochet**
rid *v* (-s, -dding, rid) clear or relieve (of)
ridden *v* ▷ **ride** ▶ *adj* afflicted or affected by the thing specified
  ridding *v* ▷ **rid**
riddle¹ *n* (*pl* -s) question made puzzling to test one's ingenuity
riddle² *v* (-les, -ling, -led) pierce with many holes ▶ *n* (*pl* -s) coarse sieve for gravel etc.
  riddled *v* ▷ **riddle²**
  riddles *n* ▷ **riddle¹, ²** ▶ *v* ▷ **riddle²**
  riddling *v* ▷ **riddle²**
ride *v* (-des, -ding, rode, ridden) sit on and control or propel (a horse, bicycle, etc.) ▶ *n* (*pl* -s) journey on a horse etc., or in a vehicle
rider *n* (*pl* -s) person who rides
  riders *n* ▷ **rider**
  rides *v*, *n* ▷ **ride**
ridge *n* (*pl* -s) long narrow hill > **ridged** *adj*
  ridged *adj* ▷ **ridge**
  ridges *n* ▷ **ridge**
ridicule *n* (*pl* -s) treatment of a person or thing as ridiculous ▶ *v* (-les, -ling, -led) laugh at,

make fun of
ridiculed v ▷ ridicule
ridicules n, v ▷ ridicule
ridiculing v ▷ ridicule
ridiculous adj deserving to be laughed at,
absurd
riding[1] v ▷ ride
riding[2] n (pl -s) (in Canada) parliamentary
constituency
ridings n ▷ riding
rids v ▷ rid
riesling n (pl -s) type of white wine
rieslings n ▷ riesling
rife adj (-r, -st) widespread or common
rifer adj ▷ rife
rifest adj ▷ rife
riff n (pl -s) (JAZZ, ROCK) short repeated melodic
figure
riffle v (-les, -ling, -led) flick through (pages
etc.) quickly
riffled v ▷ riffle
riffles v ▷ riffle
riffling v ▷ riffle
riffraff n (pl -s) rabble, disreputable people
riffraffs n ▷ riffraff
riffs n ▷ riff
rifle[1] n (pl -s) firearm with a long barrel
rifle[2] v (-les, -ling, -led) search and rob
rifled v ▷ rifle[2]
rifles n ▷ rifle[1] ▶ v ▷ rifle[2]
rifling v ▷ rifle[2]
rift n (pl -s) break in friendly relations
rifts n ▷ rift
rig v (-s, -gging, -gged) arrange in a dishonest
way ▶ n (pl -s) apparatus for drilling for oil
and gas
rigged v ▷ rig
rigging n ship's spars and ropes ▶ v ▷ rig
right adj (-er, -est) just ▶ adv properly ▶ n (pl
-s) claim, title, etc. allowed or due ▶ v (-s,
-ing, -ed) bring or come back to a normal
or correct state > **rightly** adv > **rightful** adj
> **rightfully** adv
righted v ▷ right
righteous [rye-chuss] adj upright, godly, or
virtuous > **righteousness** n (pl -s)
righteousness n ▷ righteous
righteousnesses n ▷ righteous
righter adj ▷ right
rightest adj ▷ right
rightful adj ▷ right
rightfully adv ▷ right
righting v ▷ right
rightist n (pl -s) ▶ adj (person) on the political
right

rightists n ▷ rightist
rightly adv ▷ right
rights n, v ▷ right
rigid adj (-er, -est) inflexible or strict > **rigidly**
adv > **rigidity** n (pl -s)
rigider adj ▷ rigid
rigidest adj ▷ rigid
rigidities n ▷ rigid
rigidity n ▷ rigid
rigidly n ▷ rigid
rigmarole n (pl -s) long complicated procedure
rigmaroles n ▷ rigmarole
rigorous adj harsh, severe, or stern
rigour n (pl -s) harshness, severity, or
strictness
rigours n ▷ rigour
rigs v, n ▷ rig
rile v (-les, -ling, -led) anger or annoy
riled v ▷ rile
riles v ▷ rile
riling v ▷ rile
rill n (pl -s) small stream
rills n ▷ rill
rim n (pl -s) edge or border > **rimmed** adj
rime n (pl -s) (Lit) hoarfrost
rimes n ▷ rime
rimmed adj ▷ rim
rims n ▷ rim
rimu n (pl -s) (NZ) New Zealand tree whose
wood is used for building and furniture
rimus n ▷ rimu
rind n (pl -s) tough outer coating of fruits,
cheese, or bacon
rinds n ▷ rind
ring[1] v (-s, -ing, rang, rung) give out a clear
resonant sound, as a bell ▶ n (pl -s) ringing
ring[2] n (pl -s) circle of gold etc., esp. for a finger
▶ v (-s, -ing, -ed) put a ring round
ringed v ▷ ring[2]
ringer n (pl -s) (BRIT, AUST & NZ) (Slang) person or
thing apparently identical to another
ringers n ▷ ringer
ringing v ▷ ring[1, 2]
ringleader n (pl -s) instigator of a mutiny,
riot, etc.
ringleaders n ▷ ringleader
ringlet n (pl -s) curly lock of hair
ringlets n ▷ ringlet
rings n, v ▷ ring[1, 2]
ringside n (pl -s) row of seats nearest a boxing
or circus ring
ringsides n ▷ ringside
ringtail n (pl -s) (AUST) possum with a curling
tail used to grip branches while climbing
ringtails n ▷ ringtail

ringtone n (pl -s) tune played by a mobile phone when it receives a call
  ringtones n ▷ **ringtone**
ringworm n (pl -s) fungal skin disease in circular patches
  ringworms n ▷ **ringworm**
rink n (pl -s) sheet of ice for skating or curling
  rinks n ▷ **rink**
rinse v (-ses, -sing, -sed) remove soap from (washed clothes, hair, etc.) by applying clean water ▶ n (pl -s) rinsing
  rinsed v ▷ **rinse**
  rinses v, n ▷ **rinse**
  rinsing v ▷ **rinse**
riot n (pl -s) disorderly unruly disturbance ▶ v (-s, -ing, -ed) take part in a riot
  rioted v ▷ **riot**
  rioting v ▷ **riot**
riotous adj unrestrained
  riots n, v ▷ **riot**
rip v (-s, -pping, -pped) tear violently (Informal) ▶ n (pl -s) split or tear
riparian [rip-pair-ee-an] adj of or on the banks of a river
ripcord n (pl -s) cord pulled to open a parachute
  ripcords n ▷ **ripcord**
ripe adj (-er, -est) ready to be reaped, eaten, etc.
ripen v (-s, -ing, -ed) grow ripe
  ripened v ▷ **ripen**
  ripening v ▷ **ripen**
  ripens v ▷ **ripen**
  riper adj ▷ **ripe**
  ripest adj ▷ **ripe**
riposte [rip-posst] n (pl -s) verbal retort ▶ v (-tes, -ting, -ted) make a riposte
  riposted v ▷ **riposte**
  ripostes n, v ▷ **riposte**
  riposting v ▷ **riposte**
  ripped v ▷ **rip**
  ripping v ▷ **rip**
ripple n (pl -s) slight wave or ruffling of a surface ▶ v (-les, -ling, -led) flow or form into little waves (on)
  rippled v ▷ **ripple**
  ripples n, v ▷ **ripple**
  rippling v ▷ **ripple**
  rips v, n ▷ **rip**
rise v (-ses, -sing, rose, risen) get up from a lying, sitting, or kneeling position ▶ n (pl -s) rising
  risen v ▷ **rise**
riser n (pl -s) person who rises, esp. from bed
  risers n ▷ **riser**
  rises v, n ▷ **rise**

rising n (pl -s) revolt ▶ adj increasing in rank or maturity ▶ v ▷ **rise**
  risings n ▷ **rising**
risible [riz-zib-bl] adj causing laughter, ridiculous
risk n (pl -s) chance of disaster or loss ▶ v (-s, -ing, -ed) act in spite of the possibility of (injury or loss)
  risked v ▷ **risk**
  riskier adj ▷ **risky**
  riskiest adj ▷ **risky**
  risking v ▷ **risk**
  risks n, v ▷ **risk**
risky adj (-kier, -kiest) full of risk, dangerous
risotto n (pl -s) dish of rice cooked in stock with vegetables, meat, etc.
  risottos n ▷ **risotto**
risqué [risk-ay] adj bordering on indecency
rissole n (pl -s) cake of minced meat, coated with breadcrumbs and fried
  rissoles n ▷ **rissole**
rite n (pl -s) formal practice or custom, esp. religious
  rites n ▷ **rite**
ritual n (pl -s) prescribed order of rites ▶ adj concerning rites > **ritually** adv
ritualistic adj like a ritual
  ritually adv ▷ **ritual**
  rituals n ▷ **ritual**
  ritzier adj ▷ **ritzy**
  ritziest adj ▷ **ritzy**
ritzy adj (-zier, -ziest) (Slang) luxurious or elegant
rival n (pl -s) person or thing that competes with or equals another for favour, success, etc. ▶ adj in the position of a rival ▶ v (-s, -lling, -lled) (try to) equal
  rivalled v ▷ **rival**
  rivalling v ▷ **rival**
  rivalries n ▷ **rivalry**
rivalry n (pl -s) keen competition
  rivals v, n ▷ **rival**
riven adj split apart
river n (pl -s) large natural stream of water
  rivers n ▷ **river**
rivet [riv-vit] n (pl -s) bolt for fastening metal plates, the end being put through holes and then beaten flat ▶ v (-s, -ing, -ed) fasten with rivets
  riveted v ▷ **rivet**
riveting adj very interesting and exciting ▶ v ▷ **rivet**
  rivets n, v ▷ **rivet**
rivulet n (pl -s) small stream
  rivulets n ▷ **rivulet**

riz v. Riz is the past tense of rise in some US dialects. This unusual word can be very useful if you get a Z in the later stages of the game, as you will probably be able to find either I or R on the board already. Riz scores 12 points.

roach n (pl **-es**) Eurasian freshwater fish
 roaches n ▷ roach
road n (pl **-s**) way prepared for passengers, vehicles, etc.
roadblock n (pl **-s**) barricade across a road to stop traffic for inspection etc.
 roadblocks n ▷ roadblock
roadhouse n (pl **-s**) (BRIT, AUST & S AFR) pub or restaurant on a country road
 roadhouses n ▷ roadhouse
roadie n (pl **-s**) (BRIT, AUST & NZ) (Informal) person who transports and sets up equipment for a band
 roadies n ▷ roadie
 roads n ▷ road
roadside n (pl **-s**) ▷ adj by the road
 roadsides n ▷ roadside
roadway n (pl **-s**) the part of a road used by vehicles
 roadways n ▷ roadway
roadworks pl n repairs to a road, esp. blocking part of the road
roadworthy adj (of a vehicle) mechanically sound
roam v (**-s, -ing, -ed**) wander about
 roamed v ▷ roam
 roaming v ▷ roam
 roams v ▷ roam
roan adj (of a horse) having a brown or black coat sprinkled with white hairs ▶ n (pl **-s**) roan horse
 roans n ▷ roan
roar v (**-s, -ing, -ed**) make or utter a loud deep hoarse sound like that of a lion ▶ n (pl **-s**) such a sound
 roared v ▷ roar
 roaring v ▷ roar
 roars v, n ▷ roar
roast v (**-s, -ing, -ed**) cook by dry heat, as in an oven ▶ n (pl **-s**) roasted joint of meat ▶ adj roasted
 roasted v ▷ roast
roasting (Informal) adj extremely hot ▶ n (pl **-s**) severe criticism or scolding ▶ v ▷ roast
 roastings n ▷ roasting
 roasts v, n ▷ roast
rob v (**-s, -bbing, -bbed**) steal from > **robber** n (pl **-s**) > **robbery** n (pl **-ies**)
 robbed v ▷ rob

robber n ▷ rob
robberies n ▷ rob
robbers n ▷ rob
robbery n ▷ rob
robbing v ▷ rob
robe n (pl **-s**) long loose outer garment ▶ v (**-bes, -bing, -bed**) put a robe on
 robed v ▷ robe
 robes v, n ▷ robe
robin n (pl **-s**) small brown bird with a red breast
 robing v ▷ robe
 robins n ▷ robin
robot n (pl **-s**) automated machine, esp. one performing functions in a human manner > **robotic** adj
 robotic adj ▷ robot
robotics n science of designing and using robots
 robots n ▷ robot
 robs v ▷ rob
robust adj (**-er, -est**) very strong and healthy > **robustly** adv > **robustness** n (pl **-s**)
 robuster adj ▷ robust
 robustest adj ▷ robust
 robustly adv ▷ robust
 robustness n ▷ robust
 robustnesses n ▷ robust
roc n (pl **-s**) monstrous bird of Arabian mythology
rock¹ n (pl **-s**) hard mineral substance that makes up part of the earth's crust, stone
rock² v (**-s, -ing, -ed**) (cause to) sway to and fro ▶ n style of pop music with a heavy beat
 rocked v ▷ rock²
rocker n (pl **-s**) rocking chair
 rockeries n ▷ rockery
 rockers n ▷ rocker
rockery n (pl **-ies**) mound of stones in a garden for rock plants
rocket n (pl **-s**) self-propelling device powered by the burning of explosive contents (used as a firework, weapon, etc.) ▶ v (**-s, -ing, -ed**) move fast, esp. upwards, like a rocket
 rocketed v ▷ rocket
 rocketing v ▷ rocket
 rockets n, v ▷ rocket
 rockier adj ▷ rocky¹, rocky²
 rockiest adj ▷ rocky¹, rocky²
 rocking v ▷ rock²
 rocks n ▷ rock¹ ▶ v ▷ rock²
rocky¹ adj (**-ier, -iest**) having many rocks
rocky² adj (**-ier, -iest**) shaky or unstable
rococo [rok-koe-koe] adj (of furniture, architecture, etc.) having much elaborate

decoration in an early 18th-century style

rocs *n* ▷ **roc**

rod *n* (*pl* -s) slender straight bar, stick

rode *v* ▷ **ride**

rodent *n* (*pl* -s) animal with teeth specialized for gnawing, such as a rat, mouse, or squirrel

rodents *n* ▷ **rodent**

rodeo *n* (*pl* -s) display of skill by cowboys, such as bareback riding

rodeos *n* ▷ **rodeo**

rods *n* ▷ **rod**

roe¹ *n* (*pl* -s) mass of eggs in a fish, sometimes eaten as food

roe² *n* (*pl* -s) small species of deer

roentgen [ront-gan] *n* (*pl* -s) unit measuring a radiation dose

roentgens *n* ▷ **roentgen**

roes *n* ▷ **roe¹, ²**

rogue *n* (*pl* -s) dishonest or unprincipled person ▶ *adj* (of a wild beast) having a savage temper and living apart from the herd > **roguish** *adj*

rogues *n* ▷ **rogue**

roguish *adj* ▷ **rogee**

roister *v* (-s, -ing, -ed) make merry noisily or boisterously

roistered *v* ▷ **roister**

roistering *v* ▷ **roister**

roisters *v* ▷ **roister**

> **rok** *n* (roks). Rok is an alternative spelling of **roc**. This uncommon word can be helpful if you have a K without the tiles needed for a longer word. Rok scores 7 points.

role *n* (*pl* -s) task or function

roles *n* ▷ **role**

roll *v* (-s, -ing, -ed) move by turning over and over ▶ *n* (*pl* -s) act of rolling over or from side to side

rolled *v* ▷ **roll**

roller *n* (*pl* -s) rotating cylinder used for smoothing or supporting a thing to be moved, spreading paint, etc.

rollers *n* ▷ **roller**

rollicking *adj* boisterously carefree

rolling *v* ▷ **roll**

rolls *v*, *n* ▷ **roll**

roman *n* roman type or print

romance *n* (*pl* -s) love affair

romances *n* ▷ **romance**

romantic *adj* of or dealing with love ▶ *n* (*pl* -s) romantic person or artist > **romantically** *adv* > **romanticism** *n* (*pl* -s)

romantically *adv* ▷ **romantic**

romanticism *n* ▷ **romantic**

romanticisms *n* ▷ **romantic**

romanticize *v* (-zes, -zing, -zed) describe or regard in an idealized and unrealistic way

romanticized *v* ▷ **romanticize**

romanticizes *v* ▷ **romanticize**

romanticizing *v* ▷ **romanticize**

romantics *n* ▷ **romantic**

romp *v* (-s, -ing, -ed) play wildly and joyfully ▶ *n* (*pl* -s) boisterous activity

romped *v* ▷ **romp**

rompers *pl n* child's overalls

romping *v* ▷ **romp**

romps *v*, *n* ▷ **romp**

rondo *n* (*pl* -s) piece of music with a leading theme continually returned to

rondos *n* ▷ **rondo**

roo *n* (*pl* -s) (AUST) (*Informal*) kangaroo

rood *n* (*pl* -s) (CHRISTIANITY) the Cross

roods *n* ▷ **rood**

roof *n* (*pl* -s) outside upper covering of a building, car, etc. ▶ *v* put a roof on

roofs *n* ▷ **roofs**

rooibos [roy-boss] *n* (*pl* -es) (S AFR) tea prepared from the dried leaves of an African plant

rooiboses *n* ▷ **rooibos**

rook¹ *n* (*pl* -s) Eurasian bird of the crow family

rook² *n* (*pl* -s) chess piece shaped like a castle

rookeries *n* ▷ **rookery**

rookery *n* (*pl* -ies) colony of rooks, penguins, or seals

rookie *n* (*pl* -s) (*Informal*) new recruit

rookies *n* ▷ **rookie**

rooks *n* ▷ **rook**

room *n* (*pl* -s) enclosed area in a building ▶ *pl* lodgings

roomier *adj* ▷ **roomy**

roomiest *adj* ▷ **roomy**

rooms *n* ▷ **room**

roomy *adj* (-ier, -iest) spacious

roos *n* ▷ **roo**

roost *n* (*pl* -s) perch for fowls ▶ *v* (-s, -ing, -ed) perch

roosted *v* ▷ **roost**

rooster *n* (*pl* -s) domestic cock

roosters *n* ▷ **rooster**

roosting *v* ▷ **roost**

roosts *v*, *n* ▷ **roost**

root¹ *n* (*pl* -s) part of a plant that grows down into the earth obtaining nourishment ▶ *pl* person's sense of belonging ▶ *v* (-s, -ing, -ed) establish a root and start to grow

root² *v* (-s, -ing, -ed) dig or burrow

rooted *v* ▷ **root¹, ²**

rooting *v* ▷ **root¹, ²**

rootless *adj* having no sense of belonging

roots *n* ▷ **root¹** ▶ *v* ▷ **root¹, ²**

rope *n* (*pl* **-s**) thick cord

ropes *n* ▷ **rope**

ropey, ropy *adj* (**-pier, -piest**) (BRIT) (*Informal*) inferior or inadequate

ropier *adj* ▷ **ropy**

ropiest *adj* ▷ **ropy**

ropy *adj* ▷ **ropey**

rorqual *n* (*pl* **-s**) toothless whale with a dorsal fin

rorquals *n* ▷ **rorqual**

rort (AUST) (*Informal*) *n* (*pl* **-s**) dishonest scheme ▶ *v* (**-s, -ing, -ed**) take unfair advantage of something

rorted *v* ▷ **rort**

rorting *v* ▷ **rort**

rorts *n, v* ▷ **rort**

rosaries *n* ▷ **rosary**

rosary *n* (*pl* **-ies**) series of prayers

rose¹ *n* (*pl* **-s**) shrub or climbing plant with prickly stems and fragrant flowers ▶ *adj* pink

rose² *v* ▷ **rise**

roseate [roe-zee-ate] *adj* rose-coloured

rosehip *n* (*pl* **-s**) berry-like fruit of a rose plant

rosehips *n* ▷ **rosehip**

rosella *n* (*pl* **-s**) type of Australian parrot

rosellas *n* ▷ **rosella**

rosemaries *n* ▷ **rosemary**

rosemary *n* (*pl* **-ies**) fragrant flowering shrub

roses *n* ▷ **rose¹**

rosette *n* (*pl* **-s**) rose-shaped ornament, esp. a circular bunch of ribbons

rosettes *n* ▷ **rosette**

rosewood *n* (*pl* **-s**) fragrant wood used to make furniture

rosewoods *n* ▷ **rosewood**

rosier *adj* ▷ **rosy**

rosiest *adj* ▷ **rosy**

rosin [rozz-in] *n* (*pl* **-s**) resin used for treating the bows of violins etc.

rosins *n* ▷ **rosin**

roster *n* (*pl* **-s**) list of people and their turns of duty

rosters *n* ▷ **roster**

rostra *n* ▷ **rostrum**

rostrum *n* (*pl* **-trums, -tra**) platform or stage

rostrums *n* ▷ **rostrum**

rosy *adj* (**-sier, -siest**) pink-coloured

rot *v* (**-s, -tting, -tted**) decompose or decay ▶ *n* (*pl* **-s**) decay (*Informal*)

rota *n* (*pl* **-s**) list of people who take it in turn to do a particular task

rotas *n* ▷ **rota**

rotary *adj* revolving

rotate *v* (**-tes, -ting, -ted**) (cause to) move

round a centre or on a pivot > **rotation** *n* (*pl* **-s**)

rotated *v* ▷ **rotate**

rotates *v* ▷ **rotate**

rotating *v* ▷ **rotate**

rotation *n* ▷ **rotate**

rotations *n* ▷ **rotate**

rote *n* (*pl* **-s**) mechanical repetition

rotes *n* ▷ **rote**

rotisserie *n* (*pl* **-s**) rotating spit for cooking meat

rotisseries *n* ▷ **rotisserie**

rotor *n* (*pl* **-s**) revolving portion of a dynamo, motor, or turbine

rotors *n* ▷ **rotor**

rots *v, n* ▷ **rot**

rotted *v* ▷ **rot**

rotten *adj* (**-er, -est**) decaying (*Informal*)

rottener *adj* ▷ **rotten**

rottenest *adj* ▷ **rotten**

rotter *n* (*pl* **-s**) (CHIEFLY BRIT) (*Slang*) despicable person

rotters *n* ▷ **rotter**

rotting *v* ▷ **rot**

rotund [roe-tund] *adj* round and plump > **rotundity** *n* (*pl* **-ies**)

rotunda *n* (*pl* **-s**) circular building or room, esp. with a dome

rotundas *n* ▷ **rotunda**

rotundities *n* ▷ **rotund**

rotundity *n* ▷ **rotund**

rouble [roo-bl] *n* (*pl* **-s**) monetary unit of Russia, Belarus, and Tajikistan

roubles *n* ▷ **rouble**

roué [roo-ay] *n* (*pl* **-s**) man given to immoral living

roués *n* ▷ **roué**

rouge *n* (*pl* **-s**) red cosmetic used to colour the cheeks

rouges *n* ▷ **rouge**

rough *adj* (**-er, -est**) uneven or irregular ▶ *v* (**-s, -ing, -ed**) make rough ▶ *n* (*pl* **-s**) rough state or area > **roughen** *v* (**-s, -ing, -ed**) > **roughly** *adv* > **roughness** *n* (*pl* **-s**)

roughage *n* (*pl* **-s**) indigestible constituents of food which aid digestion

roughages *n* ▷ **roughage**

roughcast *n* (*pl* **-s**) mixture of plaster and small stones for outside walls ▶ *v* (**-s, -ing, -cast**) coat with this

roughcasting *v* ▷ **roughcast**

roughcasts *n, v* ▷ **roughcast**

roughed *v* ▷ **rough**

roughen *v* ▷ **rough**

roughened *v* ▷ **rough**

roughening *v* ▷ **rough**

roughens v ▷ rough
rougher adj ▷ rough
roughest adj ▷ rough
roughhouse n (pl -s) (CHIEFLY US) (Slang) fight
roughhouses n ▷ roughhouse
roughing v ▷ rough
roughly adv ▷ rough
roughness n ▷ rough
roughnesses n ▷ rough
roughs v, n ▷ rough
roughshod adv with total disregard
roulette n (pl -s) gambling game played with a revolving wheel and a ball
roulettes n ▷ roulette
round adj (-er, -est) spherical, cylindrical, circular, or curved ▶ adv, prep indicating an encircling movement, presence on all sides, etc. ▶ v (-s, -ing, -ed) move round ▶ n (pl -s) customary course, as of a milkman
roundabout n (pl -s) road junction at which traffic passes round a central island ▶ adj not straightforward
roundabouts n ▷ roundabout
rounded v ▷ round
roundel n (pl -s) small disc
roundelay n (pl -s) simple song with a refrain
roundelays n ▷ roundelay
roundels n ▷ roundel
rounder adj ▷ round
roundest adj ▷ round
rounders n bat-and-ball team game
rounding v ▷ round
roundly adv thoroughly
rounds v, n ▷ round
rouse[1] [rhymes with **cows**] v (-ses, -sing, -sed) wake up
rouse[2] [rhymes with **mouse**] v (-ses, -sing, -sed) (foll. by **on**) (AUST) scold or rebuke
rouseabout n (pl -s) (AUST & NZ) labourer in a shearing shed
rouseabouts n ▷ rouseabout
roused v ▷ rouse[1, 2]
rouses v ▷ rouse[1, 2]
rousing v ▷ rouse[1, 2]
roustabout n (pl -s) labourer on an oil rig
roustabouts n ▷ roustabout
rout n (pl -s) overwhelming defeat ▶ v (-s, -ing, -ed) defeat and put to flight
route n (pl -s) roads taken to reach a destination
routed v ▷ rout
routes n ▷ route
routine n (pl -s) usual or regular method of procedure ▶ adj ordinary or regular
routines n ▷ routine

routing v ▷ rout
routs n, v ▷ rout
roux [roo] n (pl **roux**) fat and flour cooked together as a basis for sauces
rove v (-ves, -ving, -ved) wander
roved v ▷ rove
rover n (pl -s) wanderer, traveller
rovers n ▷ rover
roves v ▷ rove
roving v ▷ rove
row[1] [rhymes with **go**] n (pl -s) straight line of people or things
row[2] [rhymes with **go**] v (-s, -ing, -ed) propel (a boat) by oars ▶ n (-s) spell of rowing
row[3] [rhymes with **now**] (Informal) n (-s) dispute ▶ v (-s, -ing, -ed) quarrel noisily
rowan n (pl -s) tree producing bright red berries, mountain ash
rowans n ▷ rowan
rowdier adj ▷ rowdy
rowdiest adj ▷ rowdy
rowdies n ▷ rowdy
rowdy adj (-dier, -diest) disorderly, noisy, and rough ▶ n (pl -ies) person like this
rowed v ▷ row[2, 3]
rowel [rhymes with **towel**] n (pl -s) small spiked wheel on a spur
rowels n ▷ rowel
rowing v ▷ row[2, 3]
rowlock [rol-luk] n (pl -s) device on a boat that holds an oar in place
rowlocks n ▷ rowlock
rows n ▷ row[1, 2, 3] ▶ v ▷ row[2, 3]
royal adj (-ler, -lest) of, befitting, or supported by a king or queen ▶ n (pl -s) (Informal) member of a royal family > **royally** adv
royalist n (pl -s) supporter of monarchy
royalists n ▷ royalist
royaller adj ▷ royal
royallest adj ▷ royal
royally adv ▷ royal
royals n ▷ royal
royalties n ▷ royalty
royalty n (pl -ies) royal people
rub v (-s, -bbing, -bbed) apply pressure and friction to (something) with a circular or backwards-and-forwards movement ▶ n (-s) act of rubbing
rubato adv, n (pl -s) (MUSIC) (with) expressive flexibility of tempo
rubatos n ▷ rubato
rubbed v ▷ rub
rubber[1] n (pl -s) strong waterproof elastic material, orig. made from the dried sap of a tropical tree, now usu. synthetic ▶ adj made

of or producing rubber > **rubbery** *adj* (**-rier,
-riest**)
rubber² *n* (*pl* **-s**) match consisting of three
games of bridge, whist, etc.
  rubberier *adj* ▷ **rubber¹**
  rubberiest *adj* ▷ **rubber¹**
rubberneck *v* (**-s, -ing, -ed**) stare with
unthinking curiosity
  rubbernecked *v* ▷ **rubberneck**
  rubbernecking *v* ▷ **rubberneck**
  rubbernecks *v* ▷ **rubberneck**
  rubbers *n* ▷ **rubber¹, ²**
  rubbery *adj* ▷ **rubber¹**
  rubbing *v* ▷ **rub**
rubbish *n* (*pl* **-es**) waste matter > **rubbishy** *adj*
  rubbishes *n* ▷ **rubbish**
  rubbishy *adj* ▷ **rubbish**
rubble *n* (*pl* **-s**) fragments of broken stone,
brick, etc.
  rubbles *n* ▷ **rubble**
rubella *n* (*pl* **-s**) ▷ **German measles**
  rubellas *n* ▷ **rubella**
rubicund *adj* ruddy
rubidium *n* (*pl* **-s**) (CHEM) soft highly reactive
radioactive element
  rubidiums *n* ▷ **rubidium**
  rubies *n* ▷ **ruby**
rubric *n* (*pl* **-s**) heading or explanation inserted
in a text
  rubrics *n* ▷ **rubric**
  rubs *v, n* ▷ **rub**
ruby *n* (*pl* **-ies**) red precious gemstone ▶ *adj*
deep red
ruck¹ *n* (*pl* **-s**) rough crowd of common people
ruck² *n, v* (**-s, -ing, -ed**) wrinkle or crease
  rucked *v* ▷ **ruck²**
  rucking *v* ▷ **ruck²**
  rucks *n* ▷ **ruck¹, ²** ▶ *v* ▷ **ruck²**
rucksack *n* (*pl* **-s**) (BRIT, AUST & S AFR) large pack
carried on the back
  rucksacks *n* ▷ **rucksack**
ructions *pl n* (*Informal*) noisy uproar
rudder *n* (*pl* **-s**) vertical hinged piece at the
stern of a boat or at the rear of an aircraft,
for steering
  rudders *n* ▷ **rudder**
  ruddier *adj* ▷ **ruddy**
  ruddiest *adj* ▷ **ruddy**
ruddy *adj* (**-dier, -diest**) of a fresh healthy red
colour
rude *adj* (**-r, -st**) impolite or insulting > **rudely**
adv > **rudeness** *n* (*pl* **-s**)
  rudely *adv* ▷ **rude**
  rudeness *n* ▷ **rude**
  rudenesses *n* ▷ **rude**

  ruder *adj* ▷ **rude**
  rudest *adj* ▷ **rude**
rudimentary *adj* basic, elementary
rudiments *pl n* simplest and most basic stages
of a subject
rue¹ *v* (**rues, ruing, rued**) feel regret for
rue² *n* (*pl* **-s**) plant with evergreen bitter leaves
rueful *adj* regretful or sorry > **ruefully** *adv*
  ruefully *adv* ▷ **rueful**
  rued *v* ▷ **rue¹**
  rues *v* ▷ **rue¹** ▶ *n* ▷ **rue²**
ruff *n* (*pl* **-s**) starched and frilled collar
ruffian *n* (*pl* **-s**) violent lawless person
  ruffians *n* ▷ **ruffian**
ruffle *v* (**-les, -ling, -led**) disturb the calm of ▶ *n*
(*pl* **-s**) frill or pleat
  ruffled *v* ▷ **ruffle**
  ruffles *v, n* ▷ **ruffle**
  ruffling *v* ▷ **ruffle**
  ruffs *n* ▷ **ruff**
rug *n* (*pl* **-s**) small carpet
  rugbies *n* ▷ **rugby**
rugby *n* (*pl* **-ies**) form of football played with an
oval ball which may be handled by the players
rugged [rug-gid] *adj* rocky or steep
rugger *n* (*pl* **-s**) (CHIEFLY BRIT) (*Informal*) rugby
  ruggers *n* ▷ **rugger**
  rugs *n* ▷ **rug**
ruin *v* (**-s, -ing, -ed**) destroy or spoil completely
▶ *n* (*pl* **-s**) destruction or decay
ruination *n* (*pl* **-s**) act of ruining
  ruinations *n* ▷ **ruination**
  ruined *v* ▷ **ruin**
  ruing *v* ▷ **rue¹**
  ruining *v* ▷ **ruin**
ruinous *adj* causing ruin > **ruinously** *adv*
  ruinously *adv* ▷ **ruinous**
  ruins *v, n* ▷ **ruin**
rule *n* (*pl* **-s**) statement of what is allowed,
for example in a game or procedure ▶ *v* (**-les,
-ling, -led**) govern
  ruled *v* ▷ **rule**
ruler *n* (*pl* **-s**) person who governs
  rulers *n* ▷ **ruler**
  rules *n, v* ▷ **rule**
ruling *n* (*pl* **-s**) formal decision ▶ *v* ▷ **rule**
  rulings *n* ▷ **ruling**
rum *n* (*pl* **-s**) alcoholic drink distilled from
sugar cane
rumba *n* (*pl* **-s**) lively ballroom dance of Cuban
origin
  rumbas *n* ▷ **rumba**
rumble *v* (**-les, -ling, -led**) make a low
continuous noise (BRIT) (*Informal*) ▶ *n* (*pl* **-s**)
deep resonant sound

rumbled v ▷ rumble
rumbles v, n ▷ rumble
  rumbling v ▷ rumble
rumbustious adj boisterous or unruly
ruminate v (-tes, -ting, -ted) chew the cud
ruminant adj, n (pl -s) cud-chewing (animal,
  such as a cow, sheep, or deer)
  ruminants n ▷ ruminant
  ruminated v ▷ ruminate
  ruminates v ▷ ruminate
  ruminating v ▷ ruminate
rumination n (pl -s) quiet meditation and
  reflection > **ruminative** adj
  ruminations n ▷ rumination
  ruminative adj ▷ rumination
rummage v (-ges, -ging, -ged) search untidily
  and at length ▶ n (pl -s) untidy search through
  a collection of things
  rummaged v ▷ rummage
  rummages v, n ▷ rummage
  rummaging v ▷ rummage
  rummies n ▷ rummy
rummy n (pl -ies) card game in which players
  try to collect sets or sequences
rumour n (pl -s) unproved statement
rumoured adj suggested by rumour
  rumours n ▷ rumour
rump n (pl -s) buttocks
rumple v (-les, -ling, -led) make untidy,
  crumpled, or dishevelled
  rumpled v ▷ rumple
  rumples v ▷ rumple
  rumpling v ▷ rumple
  rumps n ▷ rump
rumpus n (pl -es) noisy commotion
  rumpuses n ▷ rumpus
  rums n ▷ rum
run v (runs, running, ran, run) move with a
  more rapid gait than walking ▶ n (pl -s) act or
  spell of running
rune n (pl -s) any character of the earliest
  Germanic alphabet > **runic** adj
  runes n ▷ rune
rung¹ n (pl -s) crossbar on a ladder
  rung² v ▷ ring¹
  rungs n ▷ rung¹
  runic adj ▷ rune
runnel n (pl -s) small brook
  runnels n ▷ runnel
runner n (pl -s) competitor in a race
  runners n ▷ runner
  runnier adj ▷ runny
  runniest adj ▷ runny
running adj continuous ▶ n (pl -s) act of
  moving or flowing quickly ▶ v ▷ run

runnings n ▷ running
runny adj (-nier, -niest) tending to flow
runs v, n ▷ run
runt n (pl -s) smallest animal in a litter
  runts n ▷ runt
runway n (pl -s) hard level roadway where
  aircraft take off and land
  runways n ▷ runway
rupee n (pl -s) monetary unit of India and
  Pakistan
  rupees n ▷ rupee
rupture n (pl -s) breaking, breach ▶ v (-res,
  -ring, -red) break, burst, or sever
  ruptured v ▷ rupture
  ruptures n, v ▷ rupture
  rupturing v ▷ rupture
rural adj in or of the countryside
ruse [rooz] n (pl -s) stratagem or trick
  ruses n ▷ ruse
rush¹ v (-es, -ing, -ed) move or do very quickly
  ▶ n (pl -es) sudden quick or violent movement
  ▶ pl first unedited prints of a scene for a film
  ▶ adj done with speed, hasty
rush² n (pl -es) marsh plant with a slender
  pithy stem
  rushed v ▷ rush¹
  rushes v, n ▷ rush¹, ²
  rushier adj ▷ rushy
  rushiest adj ▷ rushy
  rushing v ▷ rush¹
rushy adj (-shier, -shiest) full of rushes
rusk n (pl -s) hard brown crisp biscuit, used
  esp. for feeding babies
  rusks n ▷ rusk
russet adj reddish-brown ▶ n (pl -s) apple with
  rough reddish-brown skin
  russets n ▷ russet
rust n (pl -s) reddish-brown coating formed on
  iron etc. that has been exposed to moisture
  ▶ adj reddish-brown ▶ v (-s, -ing, -ed) become
  coated with rust
  rusted v ▷ rust
rustic adj of or resembling country people ▶ n
  (pl -s) person from the country
  rustics n ▷ rustic
  rustier adj ▷ rusty
  rustiest adj ▷ rusty
  rusting v ▷ rust
rustle¹ v, n (pl -s) (make) a low whispering
  sound
rustle² v (-les, -ling, -led) (us) steal (cattle)
  rustled v ▷ rustle
rustler n (pl -s) (us) cattle thief
  rustlers n ▷ rustler
  rustles n, v ▷ rustle

rustling *v* ▷ rustle
rusts *n*, *v* ▷ rust
rusty *adj* (**-tier, -tiest**) coated with rust
rut¹ *n* (*pl* **-s**) furrow made by wheels
rut² *n* recurrent period of sexual excitability in male deer ▶ *v* (**-s, -tting, -tted**) be in a period of sexual excitability
ruthenium *n* (*pl* **-s**) (CHEM) rare hard brittle white element
rutheniums *n* ▷ ruthenium
ruthless *adj* pitiless, merciless > **ruthlessly** *adv*

> ruthlessness *n* (*pl* **-es**)
ruthlessly *adv* ▷ ruthless
ruthlessness *n* ▷ ruthless
ruthlessnesses *n* ▷ ruthless
ruts *n* ▷ rut¹, ² ▶ *v* ▷ rut²
rutted *v* ▷ rut²
rutting *v* ▷ rut²
rye *n* (*pl* **-s**) kind of grain used for fodder and bread
ryes *n* ▷ rye

Ss

S begins only four two-letter words, **sh** (5 points), **si, so** and **st** (2 each). These are easy to remember, and it's worth noting that two of them, **sh** and **st**, don't use any vowels. Interestingly, there are quite a few three-letter words beginning with S that don't contain vowels, some of which give good scores. These are **shh** (9), **shy** (9), **sky** (10), **sly** (6), **sny** (6), **spy** (8), **sty** (6), **swy** (9) and **syn** (6). S also forms a number of three-letter words with X. These are easy to remember as they use every vowel except U: **sax, sex, six** and **sox** (10 each). Apart from the two- and three-letter words, don't forget **squeeze** (25), which uses the two highest-scoring tiles in the game.

sabbath *n* (*pl* -**s**) day of worship and rest: Saturday for Jews, Sunday for Christians
 sabbaths *n* ▷ **sabbath**
sabbatical *adj*, *n* (*pl* -**s**) (denoting) leave for study
 sabbaticals *n* ▷ **sabbatical**
sable *n* (*pl* -**s**) dark fur from a small weasel-like Arctic animal ▶ *adj* black
 sables *n* ▷ **sable**
sabot [sab-oh] *n* (*pl* -**s**) wooden shoe traditionally worn by peasants in France
sabotage *n* (*pl* -**s**) intentional damage done to machinery, systems, etc. ▶ *v* (-**ges**, -**ging**, -**ged**) damage intentionally
 sabotaged *v* ▷ **sabotage**
 sabotages *n*, *v* ▷ **sabotage**
 sabotaging *v* ▷ **sabotage**
saboteur *n* (*pl* -**s**) person who commits sabotage
 saboteurs *n* ▷ **saboteur**
 sabots *n* ▷ **sabot**
sabre *n* (*pl* -**s**) curved cavalry sword
 sabres *n* ▷ **sabre**
sac *n* (*pl* -**s**) pouchlike structure in an animal or plant
saccharin *n* (*pl* -**s**) artificial sweetener > **saccharine** *adj* excessively sweet
 saccharine *adj* ▷ **saccharin**
 saccharins *n* ▷ **saccharin**
sacerdotal *adj* of priests
sachet *n* (*pl* -**s**) small envelope or bag containing a single portion
 sachets *n* ▷ **sachet**
sack[1] *n* (*pl* -**s**) large bag made of coarse material ▶ *v* (-**s**, -**ing**, -**ed**) (*Informal*) dismiss

sack[2] *n* (*pl* -**s**) plundering of a captured town
 ▶ *v* (-**s**, -**ing**, -**ed**) plunder (a captured town)
sackcloth *n* (*pl* -**s**) coarse fabric used for sacks, formerly worn as a penance
 sackcloths *n* ▷ **sackcloth**
 sacked *v* ▷ **sack**[1, 2]
 sacking *v* ▷ **sack**[1, 2]
 sacks *v*, *n* ▷ **sack**[1, 2]
 sacra *n* ▷ **sacrum**
sacrament *n* (*pl* -**s**) ceremony of the Christian Church, esp. Communion > **sacramental** *adj*
 sacramental *adj* ▷ **sacrament**
 sacraments *n* ▷ **sacrament**
sacred *adj* holy
sacrifice *n* (*pl* -**s**) giving something up ▶ *v* (-**es**, -**ing**, -**ced**) offer as a sacrifice > **sacrificial** *adj*
 sacrificed *v* ▷ **sacrifice**
 sacrifices *n*, *v* ▷ **sacrifice**
 sacrificial *adj* ▷ **sacrifice**
 sacrificing *v* ▷ **sacrifice**
sacrilege *n* (*pl* -**s**) misuse or desecration of something sacred > **sacrilegious** *adj*
 sacrileges *n* ▷ **sacrilege**
 sacrilegious *adj* ▷ **sacrilege**
sacristan *n* (*pl* -**s**) person in charge of the contents of a church
 sacristans *n* ▷ **sacristan**
 sacristies *n* ▷ **sacristy**
sacristy *n* (*pl* -**ties**) room in a church where sacred objects are kept
sacrosanct *adj* regarded as sacred, inviolable
sacrum [say-krum] *n* (*pl* -**cra**) wedge-shaped bone at the base of the spine
 sacs *n* ▷ **sac**
sad *adj* (-**dder**, -**ddest**) sorrowful, unhappy

> **sadly** adv > **sadness** n (pl -es)
sadden v (-s, -ing, -ed) make sad
  saddened v ▷ **sadden**
  saddening v ▷ **sadden**
  saddens v ▷ **sadden**
  sadder adj ▷ **sad**
  saddest adj ▷ **sad**
saddle n (pl -les) rider's seat on a horse or
  bicycle ▶ v (-les, -ling, -led) put a saddle on
  (a horse)
  saddled v ▷ **saddle**
saddler n (pl -s) maker or seller of saddles
  saddlers n ▷ **saddler**
  saddles n, v ▷ **saddle**
  saddling v ▷ **saddle**
saddo n (pl -s, -es) (BRIT) (Informal) socially
  inadequate or pathetic person
  saddoes n ▷ **saddo**
  saddos n ▷ **saddo**
sadism [say-dizz-um] n (pl -s) gaining of
  (sexual) pleasure from inflicting pain > **sadist**
  n (pl -s) > **sadistic** adj > **sadistically** adv
  sadisms n ▷ **sadism**
  sadist n ▷ **sadism**
  sadistic adj ▷ **sadism**
  sadistically adv ▷ **sadism**
  sadists n ▷ **sadism**
  sadly adv ▷ **sad**
  sadness n ▷ **sad**
  sadnesses n ▷ **sad**
sadomasochism n (pl -s) combination of
  sadism and masochism > **sadomasochist**
  n (pl -s)
  sadomasochisms n ▷ **sadomasochism**
  sadomasochist n ▷ **sadomasochism**
  sadomasochists n ▷ **sadomasochism**
safari n (pl -s) expedition to hunt or observe
  wild animals, esp. in Africa
  safaris n ▷ **safari**
safe adj (-r, -st) secure, protected ▶ n (pl -s)
  strong lockable container > **safely** adv
safeguard v (-s, -ing, -ed) protect ▶ n (pl -s)
  protection
  safeguarded v ▷ **safeguard**
  safeguarding v ▷ **safeguard**
  safeguards v, n ▷ **safeguard**
safekeeping n (pl -s) protection
  safekeepings n ▷ **safekeeping**
  safely adv ▷ **safe**
  safer adj ▷ **safe**
  safes n ▷ **safe**
  safest adj ▷ **safe**
  safeties n ▷ **safety**
safety n (pl -ties) state of being safe
saffron n (pl -s) orange-coloured flavouring

obtained from a crocus ▶ adj orange
  saffrons n ▷ **saffron**
sag v (sags, sagging, sagged) sink in the
  middle ▶ n (pl -s) droop
saga [sah-ga] n (pl -s) legend of Norse heroes
sagacious adj wise > **sagacity** n (pl -ties)
  sagacities n ▷ **sagacious**
  sagacity n ▷ **sagacious**
  sagas n ▷ **saga**
sage[1] n (pl -s) very wise man ▶ adj (-r, -st) (Lit)
  wise > **sagely** adv
sage[2] n (pl -s) aromatic herb with grey-green
  leaves
  sagely adv ▷ **sage**[1]
  sager adj ▷ **sage**[1]
  sages n ▷ **sage**[1, 2]
  sagest adj ▷ **sage**[1]
  sagged v ▷ **sag**
  sagging v ▷ **sag**
sago n (pl -s) starchy cereal from the powdered
  pith of the sago palm tree
  sagos n ▷ **sago**
  sags v, n ▷ **sag**
  said v ▷ **say**
sail n (pl -s) sheet of fabric stretched to catch
  the wind for propelling a sailing boat ▶ v (-s,
  -ing, -ed) travel by water
sailboard n (pl -s) board with a mast and single
  sail, used for windsurfing
  sailboards n ▷ **sailboard**
  sailed v ▷ **sail**
  sailing v ▷ **sail**
sailor n (pl -s) member of a ship's crew
  sailors n ▷ **sailor**
  sails n, v ▷ **sail**
saint n (pl -s) (CHRISTIANITY) person venerated
  after death as specially holy > **saintly** adj
  > **saintliness** n (pl -es)
  saintliness n ▷ **saint**
  saintlinesses n ▷ **saint**
  saintly adj ▷ **saint**
  saints n ▷ **saint**
sake[1] n (pl -s) benefit
sake[2], **saki** [sah-kee] n (pl -s) Japanese alcoholic
  drink made from fermented rice
  sakes n ▷ **sake**[1, 2]
  saki n ▷ **sake**[2]
  sakis n ▷ **sake**[2]
salaam [sal-ahm] n (pl -s) low bow of greeting
  among Muslims
  salaams n ▷ **salaam**
salacious adj excessively concerned with sex
salad n (pl -s) dish of raw vegetables, eaten as a
  meal or part of a meal
  salads n ▷ **salad**

salamander *n* (*pl* **-s**) amphibian which looks like a lizard
  salamanders *n* ▷ **salamander**
salami *n* (*pl* **-s**) highly spiced sausage
  salamis *n* ▷ **salami**
  salaried *adj* ▷ **salary**
  salaries *n* ▷ **salary**
salary *n* (*pl* **-ries**) fixed regular payment, usu. monthly, to an employee > **salaried** *adj*
sale *n* (*pl* **-s**) exchange of goods for money > **saleable** *adj* fit or likely to be sold
  saleable *adj* ▷ **sale**
  sales *n* ▷ **sale**
salesman, saleswoman (*pl* **-men, -women**) > **salesperson** (*pl* **-people**) *n* person who sells goods
salesmanship *n* (*pl* **-s**) skill in selling
  salesmanships *n* ▷ **salesmanship**
  salesmen *n* ▷ **salesman**
  salespeople *n* ▷ **salesman**
  salesperson *n* ▷ **salesman**
  saleswoman *n* ▷ **salesman**
  saleswomen *n* ▷ **salesman**
salient [say-lee-ent] *adj* prominent, noticeable ▶ *n* (*pl* **-s**) (MIL) projecting part of a front line
  salients *n* ▷ **salient**
saline [say-line] *adj* containing salt > **salinity** *n* (*pl* **-ties**)
  salinities *n* ▷ **saline**
  salinity *n* ▷ **saline**
saliva *n* (*pl* **-s**) liquid that forms in the mouth, spittle > **salivary** *adj*
  salivary *adj* ▷ **saliva**
  salivas *n* ▷ **saliva**
salivate *v* (**-tes, -ting, -ted**) produce saliva
  salivated *v* ▷ **salivate**
  salivates *v* ▷ **salivate**
  salivating *v* ▷ **salivate**
sallee *n* (*pl* **-s**) (AUST) SE Australian eucalyptus with a pale grey bark
  sallees *n* ▷ **sallee**
  sallied *v* ▷ **sally**
  sallies *n*, *v* ▷ **sally**
sallow *adj* (**-er, -est**) of an unhealthy pale or yellowish colour
  sallower *adj* ▷ **sallow**
  sallowest *adj* ▷ **sallow**
sally *n* (*pl* **-lies**) witty remark ▶ *v* (**-lies, -lying, -lied**) (*foll. by* **forth**) rush out
  sallying *v* ▷ **sally**
salmon *n* (*pl* **-s**) large fish with orange-pink flesh valued as food ▶ *adj* orange-pink
salmonella *n* (*pl* **-lae**) bacterium causing food poisoning
  salmonellae *n* ▷ **salmonella**

  salmons *n* ▷ **salmon**
salon *n* (*pl* **-s**) commercial premises of a hairdresser, beautician, etc.
  salons *n* ▷ **salon**
saloon *n* (*pl* **-s**) two-door or four-door car with body closed off from rear luggage area
  saloons *n* ▷ **saloon**
salt *n* (*pl* **-s**) white crystalline substance used to season food ▶ *v* (**-s, -ing, -ed**) season or preserve with salt > **salty** *adj* (**-tier, -tiest**)
saltbush *n* (*pl* **-es**) shrub that grows in alkaline desert regions
  saltbushes *n* ▷ **saltbush**
  salted *v* ▷ **salt**
  saltier *adj* ▷ **salt**
  saltiest *adj* ▷ **salt**
  salting *v* ▷ **salt**
saltire *n* (*pl* **-s**) (HERALDRY) diagonal cross on a shield
  saltires *n* ▷ **saltire**
saltpetre *n* (*pl* **-s**) compound used in gunpowder and as a preservative
  saltpetres *n* ▷ **saltpetre**
  salts *n*, *v* ▷ **salt**
  salty *adj* ▷ **salt**
salubrious *adj* favourable to health
saluki *n* (*pl* **-s**) tall hound with a silky coat
  salukis *n* ▷ **saluki**
salutary *adj* producing a beneficial result
salutation *n* (*pl* **-s**) greeting by words or actions
  salutations *n* ▷ **salutation**
salute *n* (*pl* **-s**) motion of the arm as a formal military sign of respect ▶ *v* (**-tes, -ting, -ted**) greet with a salute
  saluted *v* ▷ **salute**
  salutes *n*, *v* ▷ **salute**
  saluting *v* ▷ **salute**
salvage *n* (*pl* **-s**) saving of a ship or other property from destruction ▶ *v* (**-ges, -ging, -ged**) save from destruction or waste
  salvaged *v* ▷ **salvage**
  salvages *n*, *v* ▷ **salvage**
  salvaging *v* ▷ **salvage**
salvation *n* (*pl* **-s**) fact or state of being saved from harm or the consequences of sin
  salvations *n* ▷ **salvation**
salve *n* (*pl* **-s**) healing or soothing ointment ▶ *v* (**-ves, -ving, -ved**) soothe or appease
  salved *v* ▷ **salve**
salver *n* (*pl* **-s**) (silver) tray on which something is presented
  salvers *n* ▷ **salver**
  salves *n*, *v* ▷ **salve**
salvia *n* (*pl* **-s**) plant with blue or red flowers

salvias *n* ▷ salvia
salving *v* ▷ salve
salvo *n* (*pl* -s, -es) simultaneous discharge of guns etc.
  salvoes *n* ▷ salvo
  salvos *n* ▷ salvo
samaritan *n* (*pl* -s) person who helps people in distress
  samaritans *n* ▷ samaritan
samba *n* (*pl* -s) lively Brazilian dance
  sambas *n* ▷ samba
same *adj* identical, not different, unchanged > sameness *n* (*pl* -es)
  sameness *n* ▷ same
  samenesses *n* ▷ same
samovar *n* (*pl* -s) Russian tea urn
  samovars *n* ▷ samovar
sampan *n* (*pl* -s) small boat with oars used in China
  sampans *n* ▷ sampan
samphire *n* (*pl* -s) plant found on rocks by the seashore
  samphires *n* ▷ samphire
sample *n* (*pl* -s) part taken as representative of a whole ▶ *v* (-les, -ling, -led) take and test a sample of > sampling *n* (*pl* -s)
  sampled *v* ▷ sample
sampler *n* (*pl* -s) piece of embroidery showing the embroiderer's skill
  samplers *n* ▷ sampler
  samples *v, n* ▷ sample
  sampling *v, n* ▷ sample
  samplings *n* ▷ sample
samurai *n* (*pl* -rai) member of an ancient Japanese warrior caste
  sanatoria *n* ▷ sanatorium
sanatorium *n* (*pl* -riums, -ria) institution for invalids or convalescents
  sanatoriums *n* ▷ sanatorium
  sancta *n* ▷ sanctum
  sanctified *v* ▷ sanctify
  sanctifies *v* ▷ sanctify
sanctify *v* (-fies, -fying, -fied) make holy
  sanctifying *v* ▷ sanctify
sanctimonious *adj* pretending to be religious and virtuous
sanction *n* (*pl* -s) permission, authorization ▶ *v* (-s, -ing, -ed) allow, authorize
  sanctioned *v* ▷ sanction
  sanctioning *v* ▷ sanction
  sanctions *n, v* ▷ sanction
  sanctities *n* ▷ sanctity
sanctity *n* (*pl* -ties) sacredness, inviolability
  sanctuaries *n* ▷ sanctuary
sanctuary *n* (*pl* -ries) holy place

sanctum *n* (*pl* -tums, -ta) sacred place
  sanctums *n* ▷ sanctum
sand *n* (*pl* -s) substance consisting of small grains of rock, esp. on a beach or in a desert ▶ *v* (-s, -ing, -ed) smooth with sandpaper
sandal *n* (*pl* -s) light shoe consisting of a sole attached by straps
  sandals *n* ▷ sandal
sandalwood *n* (*pl* -s) sweet-scented wood
  sandalwoods *n* ▷ sandalwood
sandbag *n* (*pl* -s) bag filled with sand, used as protection against gunfire or flood water
  sandbags *n* ▷ sandbag
sandblast *v* (-s, -ing, -ed) ▶ *n* (*pl* -s) (clean with) a jet of sand blown from a nozzle under pressure
  sandblasted *v* ▷ sandblast
  sandblasting *v* ▷ sandblast
  sandblasts *v, n* ▷ sandblast
  sanded *v* ▷ sand
sander *n* (*pl* -s) power tool for smoothing surfaces
  sanders *n* ▷ sander
  sandier *adj* ▷ sandy
  sandiest *adj* ▷ sandy
  sanding *v* ▷ sand
sandpaper *n* (*pl* -s) paper coated with sand for smoothing a surface
  sandpapers *n* ▷ sandpaper
sandpiper *n* (*pl* -s) shore bird with a long bill and slender legs
  sandpipers *n* ▷ sandpiper
sands *n, v* ▷ sand ▶ *pl n* stretches of sand forming a beach or desert
sandstone *n* (*pl* -s) rock composed of sand
  sandstones *n* ▷ sandstone
sandstorm *n* (*pl* -s) desert wind that whips up clouds of sand
  sandstorms *n* ▷ sandstorm
sandwich *n* (*pl* -es) two slices of bread with a layer of food between ▶ *v* (-es, -ing, -ed) insert between two other things
  sandwiched *v* ▷ sandwich
  sandwiches *n, v* ▷ sandwich
  sandwiching *v* ▷ sandwich
sandy *adj* (-dier, -diest) covered with sand
sane *adj* (-r, -st) of sound mind > sanity *n* (*pl* -ties)
  saner *adj* ▷ sane
  sanest *adj* ▷ sane
  sang *v* ▷ sing
sangoma *n* (*pl* -s) (S AFR) witch doctor or herbalist
  sangomas *n* ▷ sangoma
sanguinary *adj* accompanied by bloodshed

sanguine *adj* cheerful, optimistic
sanitary *adj* promoting health by getting rid of dirt and germs
sanitation *n* (*pl* -s) sanitary measures, esp. drainage or sewerage
  sanitations *n* ▷ **sanitation**
  sanities *n* ▷ **sane**
  sanity *n* ▷ **sane**
  sank *v* ▷ **sink**
sap¹ *n* (*pl* -s) moisture that circulates in plants
sap² *v* (**saps, sapping, sapped**) undermine
sapient [say-pee-ent] *adj* (*Lit*) wise, shrewd
sapling *n* (*pl* -s) young tree
  saplings *n* ▷ **sapling**
  sapped *v* ▷ **sap²**
sapper *n* (*pl* -s) soldier in an engineering unit
  sappers *n* ▷ **sapper**
sapphire *n* (*pl* -s) blue precious stone ▶ *adj* deep blue
  sapphires *n* ▷ **sapphire**
  sapping *v* ▷ **sap²**
  saps *n* ▷ **sap¹** ▶ *v* ▷ **sap²**
  saraband *n* ▷ **sarabande**
sarabande, saraband *n* (*pl* -s) slow stately Spanish dance
  sarabandes *n* ▷ **sarabande**
  sarabands *n* ▷ **sarabande**
sarcasm *n* (*pl* -s) (use of) bitter or wounding ironic language > **sarcastic** *adj* > **sarcastically** *adv*
  sarcasms *n* ▷ **sarcasm**
  sarcastic *adj* ▷ **sarcasm**
  sarcastically *adv* ▷ **sarcasm**
  sarcophagi *n* ▷ **sarcophagus**
sarcophagus *n* (*pl* -gi, -guses) stone coffin
  sarcophaguses *n* ▷ **sarcophagus**
sardine *n* (*pl* -s) small fish of the herring family, usu. preserved tightly packed in tins
  sardines *n* ▷ **sardine**
sardonic *adj* mocking or scornful > **sardonically** *adv*
  sardonically *adv* ▷ **sardonic**
  saree *n* ▷ **sari**
  sarees *n* ▷ **sari**
  sargasso *n* ▷ **sargassum**
  sargassos *n* ▷ **sargassum**
sargassum, sargasso *n* (*pl* -s) type of floating seaweed
  sargassums *n* ▷ **sargassum**
sari, saree *n* (*pl* -s) long piece of cloth draped around the body and over one shoulder, worn by Hindu women
  saris *n* ▷ **sari**
sarmie *n* (*pl* -s) (S AFR) (*Slang*) sandwich
  sarmies *n* ▷ **sarmie**

sarong *n* (*pl* -s) long piece of cloth tucked around the waist or under the armpits, worn esp. in Malaysia
  sarongs *n* ▷ **sarong**
sarsaparilla *n* (*pl* -s) soft drink, orig. made from the root of a tropical American plant
  sarsaparillas *n* ▷ **sarsaparilla**
sartorial *adj* of men's clothes or tailoring
sash¹ *n* (*pl* -es) decorative strip of cloth worn round the waist or over one shoulder
sash² *n* (*pl* -es) wooden frame containing the panes of a window
  sashes *n* ▷ **sash¹, ²**
sassafras *n* (*pl* -rases) American tree with aromatic bark used medicinally
  sassafrases *n* ▷ **sassafras**
  sat *v* ▷ **sit**
satanic *adj* of Satan
satanism *n* (*pl* -s) worship of Satan
  satanisms *n* ▷ **satanism**
satay, saté [sat-ay] *n* (*pl* -s) Indonesian and Malaysian dish consisting of pieces of chicken, pork, etc., grilled on skewers and served with peanut sauce
  satays *n* ▷ **satay**
satchel *n* (*pl* -s) bag, usu. with a shoulder strap, for carrying books
  satchels *n* ▷ **satchel**
sate *v* (-tes, -ting, -ted) satisfy (a desire or appetite) fully
  sated *v* ▷ **sate**
satellite *n* (*pl* -s) man-made device orbiting in space ▶ *adj* of or used in the transmission of television signals from a satellite to the home
  satellites *n* ▷ **satellite**
  sates *v* ▷ **sate**
satiate [say-she-ate] *v* (-tes, -ting, -ted) provide with more than enough, so as to disgust
  satiated *v* ▷ **satiate**
  satiates *v* ▷ **satiate**
  satiating *v* ▷ **satiate**
  satieties *n* ▷ **satiety**
satiety [sat-tie-a-tee] *n* (*pl* -ties) feeling of having had too much
satin *n* (*pl* -s) silky fabric with a glossy surface on one side
  sating *v* ▷ **sate**
  satins *n* ▷ **satin**
satinwood *n* (*pl* -s) tropical tree yielding hard wood
  satinwoods *n* ▷ **satinwood**
satiny *adj* of or like satin
satire *n* (*pl* -s) use of ridicule to expose vice or folly > **satirical** *adj* > **satirist** *n* (*pl* -s)

satires *n* ▷ **satire**
satirical *adj* ▷ **satire**
satirist *n* ▷ **satire**
satirists *n* ▷ **satire**
satirize *v* (**-zes, -zing, -zed**) ridicule by means of satire
satirized *v* ▷ **satirize**
satirizes *v* ▷ **satirize**
satirizing *v* ▷ **satirize**
satisfaction *n* ▷ **satisfy**
satisfactions *n* ▷ **satisfy**
satisfactory *adj* ▷ **satisfy**
satisfied *v* ▷ **satisfy**
satisfies *v* ▷ **satisfy**
satisfy *v* (**-fies, -fying, -fied**) please, content > **satisfaction** *n* (*pl* **-s**) > **satisfactory** *adj*
satisfying *v* ▷ **satisfy**
satnav *n* (*pl* **-s**) (MOTORING) (*Informal*) satellite navigation
satnavs *n* ▷ **satnav**
satsuma *n* (*pl* **-s**) kind of small orange
satsumas *n* ▷ **satsuma**
saturate *v* (**-tes, -ting, -ted**) soak thoroughly > **saturation** *n* (*pl* **-s**)
saturated *v* ▷ **saturate**
saturates *v* ▷ **saturate**
saturating *v* ▷ **saturate**
saturation *n* ▷ **saturate**
saturations *n* ▷ **saturate**
saturnalia *n* (*pl* **-s**) wild party or orgy
saturnalias *n* ▷ **saturnalia**
saturnine *adj* gloomy in temperament or appearance
satyr *n* (*pl* **-s**) woodland god, part man, part goat
satyrs *n* ▷ **satyr**
sauce *n* (*pl* **-s**) liquid added to food to enhance flavour
saucepan *n* (*pl* **-s**) cooking pot with a long handle
saucepans *n* ▷ **saucepan**
saucer *n* (*pl* **-s**) small round dish put under a cup
saucers *n* ▷ **saucer**
sauces *n* ▷ **sauce**
saucier *adj* ▷ **saucy**
sauciest *adj* ▷ **saucy**
saucily *adv* ▷ **saucy**
saucy *adj* (**-cier, -ciest**) impudent > **saucily** *adv*
sauerkraut *n* (*pl* **-s**) shredded cabbage fermented in brine
sauerkrauts *n* ▷ **sauerkraut**
sauna *n* (*pl* **-s**) Finnish-style steam bath
saunas *n* ▷ **sauna**
saunter *v* (**-s, -ing, -ed**) walk in a leisurely manner, stroll ▶ *n* (*pl* **-s**) leisurely walk
sauntered *v* ▷ **saunter**
sauntering *v* ▷ **saunter**
saunters *v*, *n* ▷ **saunter**
sausage *n* (*pl* **-s**) minced meat in an edible tube-shaped skin
sausages *n* ▷ **sausage**
sauté [so-tay] *v* (**-tés, -téing** *or* **-téeing, -téed**) fry quickly in a little fat
sautéed *v* ▷ **sauté**
sautéeing *v* ▷ **sauté**
sautéing *v* ▷ **sauté**
sautés *v* ▷ **sauté**
savage *adj* (**-r, -st**) wild, untamed ▶ *n* (*pl* **-s**) uncivilized person ▶ *v* (**-ges, -ging, -ged**) attack ferociously > **savagely** *adv* > **savagery** *n* (*pl* **-ries**)
savaged *v* ▷ **savage**
savagely *adv* ▷ **savage**
savager *adj* ▷ **savage**
savageries *n* ▷ **savage**
savagery *n* ▷ **savage**
savages *n*, *v* ▷ **savage**
savagest *adj* ▷ **savage**
savaging *v* ▷ **savage**
savanna *n* ▷ **savannah**
savannah, savanna *n* (*pl* **-s**) extensive open grassy plain in Africa
savannahs *n* ▷ **savannah**
savannas *n* ▷ **savanna**
savant *n* (*pl* **-s**) learned person
savants *n* ▷ **savant**
save *v* (**-ves, -ving, -ved**) rescue or preserve from harm, protect ▶ *n* (*pl* **-s**) (SPORT) act of preventing a goal > **saver** *n* (*pl* **-s**)
saved *v* ▷ **save**
saveloy *n* (*pl* **-s**) (BRIT, AUST & NZ) spicy smoked sausage
saveloys *n* ▷ **saveloy**
saver *n* ▷ **save**
savers *n* ▷ **save**
saves *v*, *n* ▷ **save**
saving *v* ▷ **save** ▶ *n* (*pl* **-s**) economy
savings *n pl* money put by for future use
saviour *n* (*pl* **-s**) person who rescues another
saviours *n* ▷ **saviour**
savories *n* ▷ **savory**
savory *n* (*pl* **-ries**) aromatic herb used in cooking
savour *v* (**-s, -ing, -ed**) enjoy, relish (*foll. by* **of**) ▶ *n* (*pl* **-s**) characteristic taste or odour
savoured *v* ▷ **savour**
savourier *adj* ▷ **savoury**
savouries *n* ▷ **savoury**
savouriest *adj* ▷ **savoury**

savouring v ▷ **savour**
savours v, n ▷ **savour**
savoury adj (**-rier, -riest**) salty or spicy ▶ n (pl **-ries**) savoury dish served before or after a meal
savoy n (pl **-s**) variety of cabbage
savoys n ▷ **savoy**
savvied v ▷ **savvy**
savvies v, n ▷ **savvy**
savvy (Slang) v (**-vies, -vying, -vied**) understand ▶ n (pl **-vies**) understanding, intelligence
savvying v ▷ **savvy**
saw[1] n (pl **-s**) cutting tool with a toothed metal blade ▶ v (**-s, -ing, -ed, -ed** or **sawn**) cut with a saw
saw[2] ▷ **see**[1]
saw[3] n (pl **-s**) wise saying, proverb
sawdust n (pl **-s**) fine wood fragments made in sawing
sawdusts n ▷ **sawdust**
sawed v ▷ **saw**[1]
sawfish n (pl **-es**) fish with a long toothed snout
sawfishes n ▷ **sawfish**
sawing v ▷ **saw**[1]
sawmill n (pl **-s**) mill where timber is sawn into planks
sawmills n ▷ **sawmill**
sawn v ▷ **saw**[1]
saws n ▷ **saw**[1, 3] ▶ v ▷ **saw**[1]
sawyer n (pl **-s**) person who saws timber for a living
sawyers n ▷ **sawyer**
sax n (pl **-es**) (Informal) ▷ **saxophone**
saxes n ▷ **sax**
saxifrage n (pl **-s**) alpine rock plant with small flowers
saxifrages n ▷ **saxifrage**
saxophone n (pl **-s**) brass wind instrument with keys and a curved body > **saxophonist** n (pl **-s**)
saxophones n ▷ **saxophone**
saxophonist n ▷ **saxophone**
saxophonists n ▷ **saxophone**
say v (**-s, -ing, said**) speak or utter ▶ n (pl **-s**) right or chance to speak
saying n (pl **-s**) maxim, proverb ▶ v ▷ **say**
sayings n ▷ **saying**
says v, n ▷ **say**

> **saz** n (**sazes**). A saz is a Turkish musical instrument. This is a very useful word, and one to remember for when you get a Z in the later stages of the game, with little space left on the board. Saz scores 12 points.

scab n (pl **-s**) crust formed over a wound
scabbard n (pl **-s**) sheath for a sword or dagger
scabbards n ▷ **scabbard**
scabbier adj ▷ **scabby**
scabbiest adj ▷ **scabby**
scabby adj (**-bbier, -bbiest**) covered with scabs
scabies [skay-beez] n itchy skin disease
scabrous [skay-bruss] adj rough and scaly
scabs n ▷ **scab**
scaffold n (pl **-s**) temporary platform for workmen
scaffolding n (pl **-s**) (materials for building) scaffolds
scaffoldings n ▷ **scaffolding**
scaffolds n ▷ **scaffold**
scalar n (pl **-s**) ▶ adj (variable quantity) having magnitude but no direction
scalars n ▷ **scalar**
scald v (**-s, -ing, -ed**) burn with hot liquid or steam ▶ n (pl **-s**) injury by scalding
scalded v ▷ **scald**
scalding v ▷ **scald**
scalds v, n ▷ **scald**
scale[1] n (pl **-s**) one of the thin overlapping plates covering fishes and reptiles ▶ v (**-les, -ling, -led**) remove scales from > **scaly** adj (**-lier, -liest**)
scale[2] n (pl **-s**) (often pl) weighing instrument
scale[3] n (pl **-s**) graduated table or sequence of marks at regular intervals, used as a reference in making measurements ▶ v (**-les, -ling, -led**) climb
scaled v ▷ **scale**[1, 3]
scalene adj (of a triangle) with three unequal sides
scales n ▷ **scale**[1, 2, 3] ▶ v ▷ **scale**[1, 3]
scalier adj ▷ **scale**[1]
scaliest adj ▷ **scale**[1]
scaling v ▷ **scale**[1, 3]
scallop n (pl **-s**) edible shellfish with two fan-shaped shells
scalloped adj decorated with small curves along the edge
scallops n ▷ **scallop**
scallywag n (pl **-s**) (Informal) scamp, rascal
scallywags n ▷ **scallywag**
scalp n (pl **-s**) skin and hair on top of the head ▶ v (**-s, -ing, -ed**) cut off the scalp of
scalped v ▷ **scalp**
scalpel n (pl **-s**) small surgical knife
scalpels n ▷ **scalpel**
scalping v ▷ **scalp**
scalps n, v ▷ **scalp**
scaly adj ▷ **scale**[1]
scam n (pl **-s**) (Informal) dishonest scheme

scamp n (pl -s) mischievous child
scamper v (-s, -ing, -ed) run about hurriedly or in play ▶ n (pl -s) scampering
  scampered v ▷ **scamper**
  scampering v ▷ **scamper**
  scampers v, n ▷ **scamper**
scampi pl n large prawns
  scamps n ▷ **scamp**
  scams n ▷ **scam**
scan v (-s, -nning, -nned) scrutinize carefully ▶ n (pl -s) scanning
scandal n (pl -s) disgraceful action or event > **scandalous** adj
scandalize v (-zes, -zing, -zed) shock by scandal
  scandalized v ▷ **scandalize**
  scandalizes v ▷ **scandalize**
  scandalizing v ▷ **scandalize**
  scandalous adj ▷ **scandal**
  scandals n ▷ **scandal**
scandium n (pl -s) (CHEM) rare silvery-white metallic element
  scandiums n ▷ **scandium**
  scanned v ▷ **scan**
scanner n (pl -s) electronic device used for scanning
  scanners n ▷ **scanner**
  scanning v ▷ **scan**
  scans v, n ▷ **scan**
scansion n (pl -s) metrical scanning of verse
  scansions n ▷ **scansion**
scant adj (-er, -est) barely sufficient, meagre
  scanter adj ▷ **scant**
  scantest adj ▷ **scant**
  scantier adj ▷ **scanty**
  scantiest adj ▷ **scanty**
  scantily n ▷ **scanty**
scanty adj (-tier, -tiest) barely sufficient or not sufficient > **scantily** adv
scapegoat n (pl -s) person made to bear the blame for others
  scapegoats n ▷ **scapegoat**
scapula n (pl -lae, -las) shoulder blade > **scapular** adj
  scapulae n ▷ **scapula**
  scapular adj ▷ **scapula**
  scapulas n ▷ **scapula**
scar n (pl -s) mark left by a healed wound ▶ v (-s, -rring, -rred) mark or become marked with a scar
scarab n (pl -s) sacred beetle of ancient Egypt
  scarabs n ▷ **scarab**
scarce adj (-r, -st) insufficient to meet demand > **scarcity** n (pl -ties)
scarcely adv hardly at all

scarcer adj ▷ **scarce**
scarcest adj ▷ **scarce**
scarcities n ▷ **scarce**
scarcity n ▷ **scarce**
scare v (-res, -ring, -red) frighten or be frightened ▶ n (pl -s) fright, sudden panic
scarecrow n (pl -s) figure dressed in old clothes, set up to scare birds away from crops
  scarecrows n ▷ **scarecrow**
  scared v ▷ **scare**
scaremonger n (pl -s) person who spreads alarming rumours
  scaremongers n ▷ **scaremonger**
  scares v, n ▷ **scare**
scarf[1] n (pl scarves, -s) piece of material worn round the neck, head, or shoulders
scarf[2] n (pl -s) joint between two pieces of timber made by notching the ends and fastening them together ▶ v (-s, -ing, -ed) join in this way
  scarfed v ▷ **scarf**[2]
  scarfing v ▷ **scarf**[2]
  scarfs n ▷ **scarf**[1, 2] ▶ v ▷ **scarf**[2]
  scarier adj ▷ **scary**
  scariest adj ▷ **scary**
  scarification n ▷ **scarify**
  scarifications n ▷ **scarify**
  scarified v ▷ **scarify**
  scarifies v ▷ **scarify**
scarify v (-fies, -fying, -fied) scratch or cut slightly all over > **scarification** n (pl -s)
  scarifying v ▷ **scarify**
  scaring v ▷ **scare**
scarlatina n (pl -s) scarlet fever
  scarlatinas n ▷ **scarlatina**
scarlet adj, n (pl -s) brilliant red
  scarlets n ▷ **scarlet**
scarp n (pl -s) steep slope
scarper v (-s, -ing, -ed) (BRIT) (Slang) run away
  scarpered v ▷ **scarper**
  scarpering v ▷ **scarper**
  scarpers v ▷ **scarper**
  scarps n ▷ **scarp**
  scarred v ▷ **scar**
  scarring v ▷ **scar**
  scars n, v ▷ **scar**
  scarves n ▷ **scarf**[1]
scary adj (-rier, -riest) (Informal) frightening
scat[1] v (-s, -tting, -tted) (Informal) go away
scat[2] n (pl -s) jazz singing using improvised vocal sounds instead of words
scathing adj harshly critical
scatological adj preoccupied with obscenity, esp. with references to excrement
  > **scatology** n (pl -gies)

scatologies n ▷ scatology
scatology n ▷ scatological
scats n ▷ scat² ▶ v ▷ scat¹
scatted v ▷ scat¹
scatter v (-s, -ing, -ed) throw about in various
directions
scatterbrain n (pl -s) empty-headed person
scatterbrains n ▷ scatterbrain
scattered v ▷ scatter
scattering v ▷ scatter
scatters v ▷ scatter
scattier adj ▷ scatty
scattiest adj ▷ scatty
scatting v ▷ scat¹
scatty adj (-tier, -tiest) (Informal) empty-
headed
scavenge v (-ges, -ging, -ged) search for
(anything usable) among discarded material
scavenged v ▷ scavenge
scavenger n (pl -s) person who scavenges
scavengers n ▷ scavenger
scavenges v ▷ scavenge
scavenging v ▷ scavenge
scenario n (pl -rios) summary of the plot of a
play or film
scenarios n ▷ scenario
scene n (pl -s) place of action of a real or
imaginary event
sceneries n ▷ scenery
scenery n (pl -ries) natural features of a
landscape
scenes n ▷ scene
scenic adj picturesque
scent n (pl -s) pleasant smell ▶ v (-s, -ing, -ed)
detect by smell
scented v ▷ scent
scenting v ▷ scent
scents n, v ▷ scent
sceptic [skep-tik] n (pl -s) person who
habitually doubts generally accepted beliefs
> sceptical adj > sceptically adv > scepticism
n (pl -s)
sceptical adj ▷ sceptic
sceptically adv ▷ sceptic
scepticism n ▷ sceptic
scepticisms n ▷ sceptic
sceptics n ▷ sceptic
sceptre n (pl -s) ornamental rod symbolizing
royal power
sceptres n ▷ sceptre
schedule n (pl -s) plan of procedure for a
project ▶ v (-les, -ling, -led) plan to occur at a
certain time
scheduled v ▷ schedule
schedules n, v ▷ schedule

scheduling v ▷ schedule
schema n (pl -mata) overall plan or diagram
schematic adj presented as a plan or diagram
scheme n (pl -s) systematic plan ▶ v (-mes,
-ming, -med) plan in an underhand manner
> scheming adj, n (pl -s)
schemed v ▷ scheme
schemes n, v ▷ scheme
scheming v, adj n ▷ scheme
schemings n ▷ scheme
scherzi n ▷ scherzo
scherzo [skairt-so] n (pl -zos, -zi) brisk lively
piece of music
scherzos n ▷ scherzo
schism [skizz-um] n (pl -s) (group resulting
from) division in an organization
> schismatic adj, n (pl -s)
schismatic adj, n ▷ schism
schismatics n ▷ schism
schisms n ▷ schism
schist [shist] n (pl -s) crystalline rock which
splits into layers
schists n ▷ schist
schizoid adj abnormally introverted ▶ n (pl -s)
schizoid person
schizoids n ▷ schizoid
schizophrenia n (pl -s) mental disorder
involving deterioration of or confusion about
the personality > schizophrenic adj, n (pl -s)
schizophrenias n ▷ schizophrenia
schizophrenic adj, n ▷ schizophrenia
schizophrenics n ▷ schizophrenia
schmaltz n (pl -es) excessive sentimentality
> schmaltzy adj (-zier, -ziest)
schmaltzes n ▷ schmaltz
schmaltzier adj ▷ schmaltz
schmaltziest adj ▷ schmaltz
schmaltzy adj ▷ schmaltz
schnapps n (pl -es) strong alcoholic spirit
schnappses n ▷ schnapps
schnitzel n (pl -s) thin slice of meat, esp. veal
schnitzels n ▷ schnitzel
scholar n (pl -s) learned person
scholarly adj learned
scholars n ▷ scholar
scholarship n (pl -s) learning
scholarships n ▷ scholarship
scholastic adj of schools or scholars
school¹ n (pl -s) place where children are
taught or instruction is given in a subject ▶ v
(-s, -ing, -ed) educate or train
school² n (pl -s) shoal of fish, whales, etc.
schooled v ▷ school¹
schoolie n (pl -s) (AUST) schoolteacher or high-
school student

schoolies n ▷ schoolie
schooling v ▷ school[1]
schools n ▷ school[1, 2] ▶ v ▷ school[1]
schooner n (pl -s) sailing ship rigged fore-and-aft
schooners n ▷ schooner
sciatic adj of the hip
sciatica n (pl -s) severe pain in the large nerve in the back of the leg
sciaticas n ▷ sciatica
science n (pl -s) systematic study and knowledge of natural or physical phenomena
sciences n ▷ science
scientific adj of science > **scientifically** adv
scientifically adv ▷ scientific
scientist n (pl -s) person who studies or practises a science
scientists n ▷ scientist
scimitar n (pl -s) curved oriental sword
scimitars n ▷ scimitar
scintillate v (-tes, -ting, -ted) give off sparks
scintillated v ▷ scintillate
scintillates v ▷ scintillate
scintillating adj very lively and amusing ▶ v ▷ scintillate
scion [sy-on] n (pl -s) descendant or heir
scions n ▷ scion
scissors pl n cutting instrument with two crossed pivoted blades
scleroses n ▷ sclerosis
sclerosis n (pl -ses) abnormal hardening of body tissues
scoff[1] v (-s, -ing, -ed) express derision
scoff[2] v (-s, -ing, -ed) (Informal) eat rapidly
scoffed v ▷ scoff[1, 2]
scoffing v ▷ scoff[1, 2]
scoffs v ▷ scoff[1, 2]
scold v (-s, -ing, -ed) find fault with, reprimand ▶ n (pl -s) person who scolds > **scolding** n (pl -s)
scolded v ▷ scold
scolding v, n ▷ scold
scoldings n ▷ scold
scolds v, n ▷ scold
sconce n (pl -s) bracket on a wall for holding candles or lights
sconces n ▷ sconce
scone n (pl -s) small plain cake baked in an oven or on a griddle
scones n ▷ scone
scoop n (pl -s) shovel-like tool for ladling or hollowing out ▶ v (-s, -ing, -ed) take up or hollow out with or as if with a scoop
scooped v ▷ scoop
scooping v ▷ scoop
scoops n, v ▷ scoop

scoot v (-s, -ing, -ed) (Slang) leave or move quickly
scooted v ▷ scoot
scooter n (pl -s) child's vehicle propelled by pushing on the ground with one foot
scooters n ▷ scooter
scooting v ▷ scoot
scoots v ▷ scoot
scope n (pl -s) opportunity for using abilities
scopes n ▷ scope
scorch v (-es, -ing, -ed) burn on the surface ▶ n (pl -es) slight burn
scorched v ▷ scorch
scorcher n (pl -s) (Informal) very hot day
scorchers n ▷ scorcher
scorches v, n ▷ scorch
scorching v ▷ scorch
score n (pl -s) points gained in a game or competition ▶ v (-res, -ring, -red) gain (points) in a game
scored v ▷ score
scores n, v ▷ score ▶ pl n lots
scoring v ▷ score
scorn n (pl -s) open contempt ▶ v (-s, -ing, -ed) despise > **scornful** adj > **scornfully** adv
scorned v ▷ scorn
scornful adj ▷ scorn
scornfully adv ▷ scorn
scorning v ▷ scorn
scorns n, v ▷ scorn
scorpion n (pl -s) small lobster-shaped animal with a sting at the end of a jointed tail
scorpions n ▷ scorpion
scotch v (-es, -ing, -ed) put an end to
scotched v ▷ scotch
scotches v ▷ scotch
scotching v ▷ scotch
scoundrel n (pl -s) (Old-fashioned) cheat or deceiver
scoundrels n ▷ scoundrel
scour[1] v (-s, -ing, -ed) clean or polish by rubbing with something rough
scour[2] v (-s, -ing, -ed) search thoroughly and energetically
scoured v ▷ scour[1, 2]
scourer n (pl -s) small rough nylon pad used for cleaning pots and pans
scourers n ▷ scourer
scourge n (pl -s) person or thing causing severe suffering ▶ v (-ges, -ging, -ged) cause severe suffering to
scourged v ▷ scourge
scourges n, v ▷ scourge
scourging v ▷ scourge
scouring v ▷ scour[1, 2]

scours v ▷ scour[1, 2]

scout n (pl -s) person sent out to reconnoitre ▶ v (-s, -ing, -ed) act as a scout

scouted v ▷ scout

scouting v ▷ scout

scouts n, v ▷ scout

scowl v (-s, -ing, -ed) ▶ n (pl -s) (have) an angry or sullen expression

scowled v ▷ scowl

scowling v ▷ scowl

scowls v, n ▷ scowl

scrabble v (-les, -ling, -led) scrape at with the hands, feet, or claws

scrabbled v ▷ scrabble

scrabbles v ▷ scrabble

scrabbling v ▷ scrabble

scrag n (pl -s) thin end of a neck of mutton

scraggier adj ▷ scraggy

scraggiest adj ▷ scraggy

scraggy adj (-ggier, -ggiest) thin, bony

scrags n ▷ scrag

scram v (-s, -mming, -mmed) (Informal) go away quickly

scramble v (-les, -ling, -led) climb or crawl hastily or awkwardly ▶ n (pl -les) scrambling

scrambled v ▷ scramble

scrambler n (pl -s) electronic device that makes transmitted speech unintelligible

scramblers n ▷ scrambler

scrambles v, n ▷ scramble

scrambling v ▷ scramble

scrammed v ▷ scram

scramming v ▷ scram

scrams v ▷ scram

scrap[1] n (pl -s) small piece ▶ v (-s, -pping, -pped) discard as useless

scrap[2] n (pl -s) ▶ v (-s, -pping, -pped) (Informal) fight or quarrel

scrapbook n (pl -s) book with blank pages in which newspaper cuttings or pictures are stuck

scrapbooks n ▷ scrapbook

scrape v (-pes, -ping, -ped) rub with something rough or sharp ▶ n (pl -s) act or sound of scraping > **scraper** n (pl -s)

scraped v ▷ scrape

scraper n ▷ scrape

scrapers n ▷ scrape

scrapes v, n ▷ scrape

scraping v ▷ scrape

scrapped v ▷ scrap[1, 2]

scrappier adj ▷ scrappy

scrappiest adj ▷ scrappy

scrapping v ▷ scrap[1, 2]

scrappy adj (-ppier, -ppiest) fragmentary, disjointed

scraps v ▷ scrap[1, 2] ▶ n ▷ scrap[1, 2] ▶ pl n leftover food

scratch v (-es, -ing, -ed) mark or cut with claws, nails, or anything rough or sharp ▶ n (pl -es) wound, mark, or sound made by scratching ▶ adj put together at short notice > **scratchy** adj (-chier, -chiest)

scratchcard n (pl -s) ticket that reveals whether or not the holder has won a prize when the surface is removed by scratching

scratchcards n ▷ scratchcard

scratched v ▷ scratch

scratches v, n ▷ scratch

scratchier adj ▷ scratch

scratchiest adj ▷ scratch

scratching v ▷ scratch

scratchy adj ▷ scratch

scrawl v (-s, -ing, -ed) write carelessly or hastily ▶ n (pl -s) scribbled writing

scrawled v ▷ scrawl

scrawling v ▷ scrawl

scrawls v, n ▷ scrawl

scrawnier adj ▷ scrawny

scrawniest adj ▷ scrawny

scrawny adj (-nier, -niest) thin and bony

scream v (-s, -ing, -ed) utter a piercing cry, esp. of fear or pain ▶ n (pl -s) shrill piercing cry

screamed v ▷ scream

screaming v ▷ scream

screams v, n ▷ scream

scree n (pl -s) slope of loose shifting stones

screech v (-es, -ing, -ed) ▶ n (pl -es) (utter) a shrill cry

screeched v ▷ screech

screeches v, n ▷ screech

screeching v ▷ screech

screed n (pl -s) long tedious piece of writing

screeds n ▷ screed

screen n (pl -s) surface of a television set, VDU, etc., on which an image is formed ▶ v (-s, -ing, -ed) shelter or conceal with or as if with a screen

screened v ▷ screen

screening v ▷ screen

screens n, v ▷ screen

screes n ▷ scree

screw n (pl -s) metal pin with a spiral ridge along its length, twisted into materials to fasten them together ▶ v (-s, -ing, -ed) turn (a screw)

screwdriver n (pl -s) tool for turning screws

screwdrivers n ▷ screwdriver

screwed v ▷ screw

screwier adj ▷ screwy

screwiest adj ▷ screwy
screwing v ▷ screw
screws n, v ▷ screw
screwy adj (-wier, -wiest) (Informal) crazy or eccentric
scribble v (-les, -ling, -led) write hastily or illegibly ▶ n (pl -s) something scribbled
scribbled v ▷ scribble
scribbles v, n ▷ scribble
scribbling v ▷ scribble
scribe n (pl -s) person who copied manuscripts before the invention of printing
scribes n ▷ scribe
scrimmage n (pl -s) rough or disorderly struggle
scrimmages n ▷ scrimmage
scrimp v (-s, -ing, -ed) be very economical
scrimped v ▷ scrimp
scrimping v ▷ scrimp
scrimps v ▷ scrimp
scrip n (pl -s) certificate representing a claim to stocks or shares
scrips n ▷ scrip
script n (pl -s) text of a film, play, or TV programme
scripts n ▷ script
scriptural adj ▷ scripture
scripture n (pl -s) sacred writings of a religion > **scriptural** adj
scriptures n ▷ scripture
scrofula n (pl -s) tuberculosis of the lymphatic glands > **scrofulous** adj
scrofulas n ▷ scrofula
scrofulous adj ▷ scrofula
scroggin n (pl -s) (NZ) mixture of nuts and dried fruits
scroggins n ▷ scroggin
scroll n (pl -s) roll of parchment or paper ▶ v (-s, -ing, -ed) move (text) up or down on a VDU screen
scrolled v ▷ scroll
scrolling v ▷ scroll
scrolls n, v ▷ scroll
scrota n ▷ scrotum
scrotum n (pl -ta, -tums) pouch of skin containing the testicles
scrotums n ▷ scrotum
scrounge v (-ges, -ging, -ged) (Informal) get by cadging or begging > **scrounger** n (pl -s)
scrounged v ▷ scrounge
scrounger n ▷ scrounge
scroungers n ▷ scrounge
scrounges v ▷ scrounge
scrounging v ▷ scrounge
scrub¹ v (-s, -bbing, -bbed) clean by rubbing, often with a hard brush and water ▶ n (pl -s) scrubbing
scrub² n (pl -s) stunted trees
scrubbed v ▷ scrub¹
scrubbier adj ▷ scrubby
scrubbiest adj ▷ scrubby
scrubbing v ▷ scrub¹
scrubby adj (-bbier, -bbiest) covered with scrub
scrubs v ▷ scrub¹ ▶ n ▷ scrub¹, ²
scruff¹ n (pl -s) nape (of the neck)
scruff² n (pl -s) (Informal) untidy person
scruffier adj ▷ scruffy
scruffiest adj ▷ scruffy
scruffs n ▷ scruff¹, ²
scruffy adj (-ffier, -ffiest) unkempt or shabby
scrum, scrummage n (pl -s) (RUGBY) restarting of play in which opposing packs of forwards push against each other to gain possession of the ball
scrummage n ▷ scrum
scrummages n ▷ scrum
scrumptious adj (Informal) delicious
scrums n ▷ scrum
scrunch v (-es, -ing, -ed) crumple or crunch or be crumpled or crunched ▶ n (pl -es) act or sound of scrunching
scrunched v ▷ scrunch
scrunches v, n ▷ scrunch
scrunching v ▷ scrunch
scruple n (pl -s) doubt produced by one's conscience or morals ▶ v (-les, -ling, -led) have doubts on moral grounds
scrupled v ▷ scruple
scruples n, v ▷ scruple
scrupling v ▷ scruple
scrupulous adj very conscientious > **scrupulously** adv
scrupulously adv ▷ scrupulous
scrutinies n ▷ scrutiny
scrutinize v (-zes, -zing, -zed) examine closely
scrutinized v ▷ scrutinize
scrutinizes v ▷ scrutinize
scrutinizing v ▷ scrutinize
scrutiny n (pl -nies) close examination
scud v (-s, -dding, -dded) move along swiftly
scudded v ▷ scud
scudding v ▷ scud
scuds v ▷ scud
scuff v (-s, -ing, -ed) drag (the feet) while walking ▶ n (pl -s) mark caused by scuffing
scuffed v ▷ scuff
scuffing v ▷ scuff
scuffle v (-les, -ling, -led) fight in a disorderly manner ▶ n (pl -s) disorderly struggle

scuffled v ▷ **scuffle**
scuffles v, n ▷ **scuffle**
scuffling v ▷ **scuffle**
scuffs v, n ▷ **scuff**
scull n (pl -s) small oar ▶ v (-s, -ing, -ed) row (a boat) using sculls
sculled v ▷ **scull**
sculleries n ▷ **scullery**
scullery n (pl -ries) small room where washing-up and other kitchen work is done
sculling v ▷ **scull**
sculls n, v ▷ **scull**
sculptor n ▷ **sculpture**
sculptors n ▷ **sculpture**
sculptress n ▷ **sculpture**
sculptresses n ▷ **sculpture**
sculptural adj ▷ **sculpture**
sculpture n (pl -s) art of making figures or designs in wood, stone, etc. ▶ v (-res, -ring, -red) (also **sculpt**) represent in sculpture > **sculptor, sculptress** n (pl -s, -es) > **sculptural** adj
sculptured v ▷ **sculpture**
sculptures n, v ▷ **sculpture**
sculpturing v ▷ **sculpture**
scum n (pl -s) impure or waste matter on the surface of a liquid > **scummy** adj (-mmier, -mmiest)
scummier adj ▷ **scum**
scummiest adj ▷ **scum**
scummy adj ▷ **scum**
scums n ▷ **scum**
scungier adj ▷ **scungy**
scungiest adj ▷ **scungy**
scungy adj (-ier, -iest) (AUST & NZ) (Informal) sordid or dirty
scupper v (-s, -ing, -ed) (Informal) defeat or ruin
scuppered v ▷ **scupper**
scuppering v ▷ **scupper**
scuppers v ▷ **scupper**
scurf n (pl -s) flaky skin on the scalp
scurfs n ▷ **scurf**
scurried v ▷ **scurry**
scurries v, n ▷ **scurry**
scurrilous adj untrue and defamatory
scurry v (-ries, -rying, -ried) move hastily ▶ n (pl -ries) act or sound of scurrying
scurrying v ▷ **scurry**
scurvies n ▷ **scurvy**
scurvy n (pl -vies) disease caused by lack of vitamin C
scut n (pl -s) short tail of the hare, rabbit, or deer
scuts n ▷ **scut**
scuttle¹ n (pl -s) fireside container for coal

scuttle² v (-les, -ling, -led) run with short quick steps ▶ n (pl -s) hurried run
scuttle³ v (-les, -ling, -ed) make a hole in (a ship) to sink it
scuttled v ▷ **scuttle²,³**
scuttles n ▷ **scuttle¹,²** ▶ v ▷ **scuttle²,³**
scuttling v ▷ **scuttle²,³**
scythe n (pl -s) long-handled tool with a curved blade for cutting grass ▶ v (-thes, -thing, -thed) cut with a scythe
scythed v ▷ **scythe**
scythes n, v ▷ **scythe**
scything v ▷ **scythe**
sea n (pl -s) mass of salt water covering three quarters of the earth's surface
seaboard n (pl -s) coast
seaboards n ▷ **seaboard**
seafaring adj working or travelling by sea
seafood n (pl -s) edible saltwater fish or shellfish
seafoods n ▷ **seafood**
seagull n (pl -s) gull
seagulls n ▷ **seagull**
seal¹ n (pl -s) piece of wax, lead, etc. with a special design impressed upon it, attached to a letter or document as a mark of authentication ▶ v (-s, -ing, -ed) close with or as if with a seal
seal² n (pl -s) amphibious mammal with flippers as limbs > **sealskin** n (pl -s)
sealant n (pl -s) any substance used for sealing
sealants n ▷ **sealant**
sealed v ▷ **seal¹**
sealing v ▷ **seal¹**
seals n ▷ **seal¹,²** ▶ v ▷ **seal¹**
sealskin n ▷ **seal²**
sealskins n ▷ **seal²**
seam n (pl -s) line where two edges are joined, as by stitching ▶ v (-s, -ing, -ed) mark with furrows or wrinkles > **seamless** adj
seaman n (pl -men) sailor
seamed v ▷ **seam**
seamen n ▷ **seaman**
seamier adj ▷ **seamy**
seamiest adj ▷ **seamy**
seaming v ▷ **seam**
seamless adj ▷ **seam**
seams n, v ▷ **seam**
seamstress n (pl -es) woman who sews, esp. professionally
seamstresses n ▷ **seamstress**
seamy adj (-mier, -miest) sordid
seance [say-anss] n (pl -s) meeting at which spiritualists attempt to communicate with the dead

seances *n* ▷ **seance**
seaplane *n* (*pl* -s) aircraft designed to take off from and land on water
seaplanes *n* ▷ **seaplane**
sear *v* (-s, -ing, -ed) scorch, burn the surface of
search *v* (-es, -ing, -ed) examine closely in order to find something ▶ *n* (*pl* -es) searching
searched *v* ▷ **search**
searches *v*, *n* ▷ **search**
searching *adj* keen or thorough ▶ *v* ▷ **search**
searchlight *n* (*pl* -s) powerful light with a beam that can be shone in any direction
searchlights *n* ▷ **searchlight**
seared *v* ▷ **sear**
searing *adj* (of pain) very sharp ▶ *v* ▷ **sear**
sears *v* ▷ **sear**
seas *n* ▷ **sea**
seasick *adj* suffering from nausea caused by the motion of a ship > **seasickness** *n* (*pl* -es)
seasickness *n* ▷ **seasick**
seasicknesses *n* ▷ **seasick**
seaside *n* (*pl* -s) area, esp. a holiday resort, on the coast
seasides *n* ▷ **seaside**
season *n* (*pl* -s) one of four divisions of the year, each of which has characteristic weather conditions ▶ *v* (-s, -ing, -ed) flavour with salt, herbs, etc.
seasonable *adj* appropriate for the season
seasonal *adj* depending on or varying with the seasons
seasoned *adj* experienced ▶ *v* ▷ **season**
seasoning *v* ▷ **season** ▶ *n* (*pl* -s) salt, herbs, etc. added to food to enhance flavour
seasonings *n* ▷ **seasoning**
seasons *n*, *v* ▷ **season**
seat *n* (*pl* -s) thing designed or used for sitting on ▶ *v* (-s, -ing, -ed) cause to sit
seated *v* ▷ **seat**
seating *v* ▷ **seat**
seats *n*, *v* ▷ **seat**
seaweed *n* (*pl* -s) plant growing in the sea
seaweeds *n* ▷ **seaweed**
seaworthy *adj* (of a ship) in fit condition for a sea voyage
sebaceous *adj* of, like, or secreting fat or oil
secateurs *pl n* small pruning shears
secede *v* (-des, -ding, -ded) withdraw formally from a political alliance or federation > **secession** *n* (*pl* -s)
seceded *v* ▷ **secede**
secedes *v* ▷ **secede**
seceding *v* ▷ **secede**
secession *n* ▷ **secede**
secessions *n* ▷ **secede**

seclude *v* (-des, -ding, -ded) keep (a person) from contact with others
secluded *adj* private, sheltered ▶ *v* ▷ **seclude** > **seclusion** *n* (*pl* -s)
secludes *v* ▷ **seclude**
secluding *v* ▷ **seclude**
seclusion *n* ▷ **secluded**
seclusions *n* ▷ **secluded**
second[1] *adj* coming directly after the first ▶ *n* (*pl* -s) person or thing coming second ▶ *v* (-s, -ing, -ed) express formal support for (a motion proposed in a meeting) > **secondly** *adv*
second[2] *n* (*pl* -s) sixtieth part of a minute of an angle or time
second[3] [si-**kond**] *v* (-s, -ing, -ed) transfer (a person) temporarily to another job > **secondment** *n* (*pl* -s)
secondary *adj* of less importance
seconded *v* ▷ **second**[1, 3]
secondhand *adj* bought after use by another
seconding *v* ▷ **second**[1, 3]
secondly *adv* ▷ **second**[1]
secondment *n* ▷ **second**[3]
secondments *n* ▷ **second**[3]
seconds *v* ▷ **second**[1, 3] ▶ *n* ▷ **second**[1, 2] ▶ *pl n* inferior goods
secrecies *n* ▷ **secret**
secrecy *n* ▷ **secret**
secret *adj* kept from the knowledge of others ▶ *n* (*pl* -s) something kept secret > **secretly** *adv* > **secrecy** *n* (*pl* -cies)
secretarial *adj* ▷ **secretary**
secretariat *n* (*pl* -s) administrative office or staff of a legislative body
secretariats *n* ▷ **secretariat**
secretaries *n* ▷ **secretary**
secretary *n* (*pl* -ries) person who deals with correspondence and general clerical work > **secretarial** *adj*
secrete[1] *v* (-tes, -ting, -ted) (of an organ, gland, etc.) produce and release (a substance) > **secretion** *n* (*pl* -s) > **secretory** [sek-**reet**-or-ee] *adj*
secrete[2] *v* (-tes, -ting, -ted) hide or conceal
secreted *v* ▷ **secrete**[1, 2]
secretes *v* ▷ **secrete**[1, 2]
secreting *v* ▷ **secrete**[1, 2]
secretion *n* ▷ **secrete**[1]
secretions *n* ▷ **secrete**[1]
secretive *adj* inclined to keep things secret > **secretiveness** *n* (*pl* -es)
secretiveness *n* ▷ **secretive**
secretivenesses *n* ▷ **secretive**
secretly *adv* ▷ **secret**

secretory adj ▷ secrete[1]
secrets n ▷ secret
sect n (pl -s) subdivision of a religious or political group, esp. one with extreme beliefs
sectarian adj of a sect
section n (pl -s) part cut off ▶ v (-s, -ing, -ed) cut or divide into sections > sectional adj
  sectional adj ▷ section
  sectioned v ▷ section
  sectioning v ▷ section
  sections n, v ▷ section
sector n (pl -s) part or subdivision
  sectors n ▷ sector
  sects n ▷ sect
secular adj worldly, as opposed to sacred
secure adj (-r, -st) free from danger ▶ v (-res, -ring, -red) obtain > securely adv
  secured v ▷ secure
  securely adv ▷ secure
  securer adj ▷ secure
  secures v ▷ secure
  securest adj ▷ secure
  securing v ▷ secure
  securities n ▷ security
security n (pl -ties) precautions against theft, espionage, or other danger
sedan n (pl -s) (US, AUST & NZ) two-door or four-door car with the body closed off from the rear luggage area
  sedans n ▷ sedan
sedate[1] adj (-r, -st) calm and dignified > sedately adv
sedate[2] v (-tes, -ting, -ted) give a sedative drug to > sedation n (pl -s)
  sedated v ▷ sedate[2]
  sedately adv ▷ sedate[1]
  sedater adj ▷ sedate[1]
  sedates v ▷ sedate[2]
  sedatest adj ▷ sedate[1]
  sedating v ▷ sedate[2]
  sedation n ▷ sedate[2]
  sedations n ▷ sedate[2]
sedative adj having a soothing or calming effect ▶ n (pl -s) sedative drug
  sedatives n ▷ sedative
sedentary adj done sitting down, involving little exercise
sedge n (pl -s) coarse grasslike plant growing on wet ground
  sedges n ▷ sedge
sediment n (pl -s) matter which settles to the bottom of a liquid > sedimentary adj
  sedimentary adj ▷ sediment
  sediments n ▷ sediment
sedition n (pl -s) speech or action encouraging

rebellion against the government > seditious adj
seditions n ▷ sedition
seditious adj ▷ sedition
seduce v (-ces, -cing, -ced) persuade into sexual intercourse > seducer, seductress n (pl -s, -es) > seduction n (pl -s) > seductive adj
  seduced v ▷ seduce
  seducer n ▷ seduce
  seducers n ▷ seduce
  seduces v ▷ seduce
  seducing v ▷ seduce
  seduction n ▷ seduce
  seductions n ▷ seduce
  seductive adj ▷ seduce
  seductress n ▷ seduce
  seductresses n ▷ seduce
sedulous adj diligent or persevering > sedulously adv
  sedulously adv ▷ sedulous
see[1] v (-s, -ing, saw, seen) perceive with the eyes or mind
see[2] n (pl -s) diocese of a bishop
seed n (pl -s) mature fertilized grain of a plant ▶ v (-s, -ing, -ed) sow with seed
  seeded v ▷ seed
  seedier adj ▷ seedy
  seediest adj ▷ seedy
  seeding v ▷ seed
seedling n (pl -s) young plant raised from a seed
  seedlings n ▷ seedling
  seeds n, v ▷ seed
seedy adj (-dier, -diest) shabby
seeing conj in view of the fact that ▶ v ▷ see[1]
seek v (-s, -ing, sought) try to find or obtain
  seeking v ▷ seek
  seeks v ▷ seek
seem v (-s, -ing, -ed) appear to be
  seemed v ▷ seem
seeming adj apparent but not real > seemingly adv, v ▷ seem
  seemingly adv ▷ seeming
  seemlier adj ▷ seemly
  seemliest adj ▷ seemly
seemly adj (-lier, -liest) proper or fitting
  seems v ▷ seem
  seen v ▷ see[1]
seep v (-s, -ing, -ed) trickle through slowly, ooze > seepage n (pl -s)
  seepage n ▷ seep
  seepages n ▷ seep
  seeped v ▷ seep
  seeping v ▷ seep
  seeps v ▷ seep

seer n (pl -s) prophet
  seers n ▷ **seer**
seersucker n (pl -s) light cotton fabric with a
  slightly crinkled surface
  seersuckers n ▷ **seersucker**
  sees n ▷ **see²** ▶ v ▷ **see¹**
seesaw n (pl -s) plank balanced in the middle
  so that two people seated on either end ride
  up and down alternately ▶ v (-s, -ing, -ed)
  move up and down
  seesawed v ▷ **seesaw**
  seesawing v ▷ **seesaw**
  seesaws n, v ▷ **seesaw**
seethe v (-thes, -thing, -thed) be very agitated
  seethed v ▷ **seethe**
  seethes v ▷ **seethe**
  seething v ▷ **seethe**
segment n (pl -s) one of several sections into
  which something may be divided ▶ v (-s, -ing,
  -ed) divide into segments > **segmentation**
  n (pl -s)
  segmentation n ▷ **segment**
  segmentations n ▷ **segment**
  segmented v ▷ **segment**
  segmenting v ▷ **segment**
  segments n, v ▷ **segment**
segregate v (-tes, -ting, -ted) set apart
  > **segregation** n (pl -s)
  segregated v ▷ **segregate**
  segregates v ▷ **segregate**
  segregating v ▷ **segregate**
  segregation n ▷ **segregate**
  segregations n ▷ **segregate**
seine [sane] n (pl -s) large fishing net that
  hangs vertically from floats
  seines n ▷ **seine**
seismic adj relating to earthquakes
seismograph, seismometer n (pl -s)
  instrument that records the strength of
  earthquakes
  seismographs n ▷ **seismograph**
  seismological adj ▷ **seismology**
  seismologies n ▷ **seismology**
  seismologist n ▷ **seismology**
  seismologists n ▷ **seismology**
seismology n (pl -gies) study of earthquakes
  > **seismological** adj > **seismologist** n (pl -s)
  seismometer n ▷ **seismograph**
  seismometers n ▷ **seismograph**
seize v (-zes, -zing, -zed) take hold of forcibly or
  quickly (usu. foll. by **up**)
  seized v ▷ **seize**
  seizes v ▷ **seize**
  seizing v ▷ **seize**
seizure n (pl -s) sudden violent attack of an

illness
  seizures n ▷ **seizure**
seldom adv not often, rarely
select v (-s, -ing, -ed) pick out or choose ▶ adj
  chosen in preference to others > **selector**
  n (pl -s)
  selected v ▷ **select**
  selecting v ▷ **select**
selection n (pl -s) selecting
  selections n ▷ **selection**
selective adj chosen or choosing carefully
  > **selectively** adv > **selectivity** n (pl -ties)
  selectively adv ▷ **selective**
  selectivities n ▷ **selective**
  selectivity n ▷ **selective**
  selector n ▷ **select**
  selectors n ▷ **select**
  selects v ▷ **select**
selenium n (pl -s) (CHEM) nonmetallic element
  with photoelectric properties
  seleniums n ▷ **selenium**
self n (pl selves) distinct individuality or
  identity of a person or thing
selfish adj caring too much about oneself
  and not enough about others > **selfishly** adv
  > **selfishness** n (pl -es)
  selfishly adv ▷ **selfish**
  selfishness n ▷ **selfish**
  selfishnesses n ▷ **selfish**
selfless adj unselfish
selfsame adj the very same
sell v (-s, -ing, sold) exchange (something) for
  money (foll. by **for**) ▶ n (pl -s) manner of selling
  > **seller** n (pl -s)
  seller n ▷ **sell**
  sellers n ▷ **sell**
  selling v ▷ **sell**
sellotape n (pl -s)® type of adhesive tape ▶ v
  (-pes, -ping, -ped) stick with sellotape
  sellotaped v ▷ **sellotape**
  sellotapes n, v ▷ **sellotape**
  sellotaping v ▷ **sellotape**
sellout n (pl -s) performance of a show etc. for
  which all the tickets are sold
  sellouts n ▷ **sellout**
  sells v, n ▷ **sell**
selvage, selvedge n (pl -s) edge of cloth,
  woven so as to prevent unravelling
  selvages n ▷ **selvage**
  selvedge n ▷ **selvage**
  selvedges n ▷ **selvage**
  selves n ▷ **self**
semantic adj relating to the meaning of words
semantics n study of linguistic meaning
semaphore n (pl -s) system of signalling by

holding two flags in different positions to represent letters of the alphabet

semaphores n ▷ **semaphore**

semblance n (pl -s) outward or superficial appearance

semblances n ▷ **semblance**

semen n (pl -s) sperm-carrying fluid produced by male animals

semens n ▷ **semen**

semester n (pl -s) either of two divisions of the academic year

semesters n ▷ **semester**

semi n (pl -s) (BRIT & S AFR) (Informal) semidetached house

semibreve n (pl -s) musical note four beats long

semibreves n ▷ **semibreve**

semicolon n (pl -s) the punctuation mark (;)

semicolons n ▷ **semicolon**

semiconductor n (pl -s) substance with an electrical conductivity that increases with temperature

semiconductors n ▷ **semiconductor**

semidetached adj (of a house) joined to another on one side

semifinal n (pl -s) match or round before the final > **semifinalist** n (pl -s)

semifinalist n ▷ **semifinal**

semifinalists n ▷ **semifinal**

semifinals n ▷ **semifinal**

seminal adj original and influential

seminar n (pl -s) meeting of a group of students for discussion

seminaries n ▷ **seminary**

seminars n ▷ **seminar**

seminary n (pl -ries) college for priests

semiprecious adj (of gemstones) having less value than precious stones

semiquaver n (pl -s) musical note half the length of a quaver

semiquavers n ▷ **semiquaver**

semis n ▷ **semi**

semitone n (pl -s) smallest interval between two notes in Western music

semitones n ▷ **semitone**

semitrailer n (pl -s) (AUST) large truck in two separate sections joined by a pivoted bar

semitrailers n ▷ **semitrailer**

semolina n (pl -s) hard grains of wheat left after the milling of flour, used to make puddings and pasta

semolinas n ▷ **semolina**

senate n (pl -s) upper house of some parliaments; governing body of some universities

senates n ▷ **senate**

senator n (pl -s) member of a senate > **senatorial** adj

senatorial adj ▷ **senator**

senators n ▷ **senator**

send v (-s, -ing, sent) cause (a person or thing) to go to or be taken or transmitted to a place

sending v ▷ **send**

sendoff n (pl -s) demonstration of good wishes at a person's departure

sendoffs n ▷ **sendoff**

sends v ▷ **send**

sendup n (pl -s) (Informal) imitation

sendups n ▷ **sendup**

senile adj mentally or physically weak because of old age > **senility** n (pl -ties)

senilities n ▷ **senile**

senility n ▷ **senile**

senior adj superior in rank or standing ▶ n (pl -s) senior person > **seniority** n (pl -ties)

seniorities n ▷ **senior**

seniority n ▷ **senior**

seniors n ▷ **senior**

senna n (pl -s) tropical plant

sennas n ▷ **senna**

señor [sen-**nyor**] n (pl -ores) Spanish term of address equivalent to sir or Mr

señora [sen-**nyor**-a] n (pl -s) Spanish term of address equivalent to madam or Mrs

señoras n ▷ **señora**

señorita [sen-nyor-**ee**-ta] n (pl -s) Spanish term of address equivalent to madam or Miss

señoritas n ▷ **señorita**

señors n ▷ **señor**

sensation n (pl -s) ability to feel things physically

sensational adj causing intense shock, anger, or excitement

sensationalism n (pl -s) deliberate use of sensational language or subject matter > **sensationalist** adj, n (pl -s)

sensationalisms n ▷ **sensationalism**

sensationalist adj, n ▷ **sensationalism**

sensationalists n ▷ **sensationalism**

sensations n ▷ **sensation**

sense n (pl -s) any of the faculties of perception or feeling (sight, hearing, touch, taste, or smell ▶ v (-ses, -sing, -sed) perceive > **senseless** adj

sensed v ▷ **sense**

senseless adj ▷ **sense**

senses n, v ▷ **sense**

sensibilities n ▷ **sensibility**

sensibility n (pl -ties) ability to experience deep feelings

sensible *adj* (**-r, -st**) having or showing good sense > **sensibly** *adv*
sensibler *adj* ▷ sensible
sensiblest *adj* ▷ sensible
sensibly *adv* ▷ sensible
sensing *v* ▷ sense
sensitive *adj* easily hurt or offended > **sensitively** *adv* > **sensitivity** *n* (*pl* **-s**)
sensitively *adv* ▷ sensitive
sensitivities *n* ▷ sensitive
sensitivity *n* ▷ sensitive
sensitize *v* (**-zes, -zing, -zed**) make sensitive
sensitized *v* ▷ sensitize
sensitizes *v* ▷ sensitize
sensitizing *v* ▷ sensitize
sensor *n* (*pl* **-s**) device that detects or measures the presence of something, such as radiation
sensors *n* ▷ sensor
sensory *adj* of the senses or sensation
sensual *adj* giving pleasure to the body and senses rather than the mind > **sensually** *adv* > **sensuality** *n* (*pl* **-ties**) > **sensualist** *n* (*pl* **-s**)
sensualist *n* ▷ sensual
sensualists *n* ▷ sensual
sensualities *n* ▷ sensual
sensuality *n* ▷ sensual
sensually *adj* ▷ sensual
sensuous *adj* pleasing to the senses > **sensuously** *adv*
sensuously *adv* ▷ sensuous
sent *v* ▷ send
sentence *n* (*pl* **-s**) sequence of words capable of standing alone as a statement, question, or command ▶ *v* (**-ces, -cing, -ced**) pass sentence on (a convicted person)
sentenced *v* ▷ sentence
sentences *n, v* ▷ sentence
sentencing *n, v* ▷ sentence
sententious *adj* trying to sound wise
sentience *n* ▷ sentient
sentiences *n* ▷ sentient
sentient [sen-tee-ent] *adj* capable of feeling > **sentience** *n* (*pl* **-s**)
sentiment *n* (*pl* **-s**) thought, opinion, or attitude
sentimental *adj* excessively romantic or nostalgic > **sentimentalism** *n* (*pl* **-s**) > **sentimentality** *n* (*pl* **-ties**)
sentimentalism *n* ▷ sentimental
sentimentalisms *n* ▷ sentimental
sentimentalities *n* ▷ sentimentality
sentimentality *n* ▷ sentimental
sentimentalize *v* (**-zes, -zing, -zed**) make sentimental
sentimentalized *v* ▷ sentimentalize

sentimentalizes *v* ▷ sentimentalize
sentiments *n* ▷ sentiment
sentinel *n* (*pl* **-s**) sentry
sentinels *n* ▷ sentinel
sentries *n* ▷ sentry
sentry *n* (*pl* **-tries**) soldier on watch
sepal *n* (*pl* **-s**) leaflike division of the calyx of a flower
sepals *n* ▷ sepal
separable *adj* ▷ separate
separate *v* (**-tes, -ting, -ted**) act as a barrier between ▶ *adj* not the same, different > **separable** *adj* > **separately** *adv*
separated *v* ▷ separate
separately *adv* ▷ separate
separates *v* ▷ separate
separating *v* ▷ separate
separation *n* (*pl* **-s**) separating or being separated
separations *n* ▷ separation
separatism *n* ▷ separatist
separatisms *n* ▷ separatist
separatist *n* (*pl* **-s**) person who advocates the separation of a group from an organization or country > **separatism** *n* (*pl* **-s**)
separatists *n* ▷ separatist
sepia *adj, n* (*pl* **-s**) reddish-brown (pigment)
sepias *n* ▷ sepia
sepses *n* ▷ sepsis
sepsis *n* (*pl* **-ses**) poisoning caused by pus-forming bacteria
septet *n* (*pl* **-s**) group of seven performers
septets *n* ▷ septet
septic *adj* (of a wound) infected
septicaemia [sep-tis-**see**-mee-a] *n* (*pl* **-s**) infection of the blood
septicaemias *n* ▷ septicaemia
septuagenarian *n* (*pl* **-s**) person aged between seventy and seventy-nine
septuagenarians *n* ▷ septuagenarian
sepulchral [sip-**pulk**-ral] *adj* gloomy
sepulchre [**sep**-pull-ker] *n* (*pl* **-s**) tomb or burial vault
sepulchres *n* ▷ sepulchre
sequel *n* (*pl* **-s**) novel, play, or film that continues the story of an earlier one
sequels *n* ▷ sequel
sequence *n* (*pl* **-s**) arrangement of two or more things in successive order > **sequential** *adj*
sequences *n* ▷ sequence
sequential *adj* ▷ sequence
sequester *v* (**-s, -ing, -ed**) seclude
sequestered *v* ▷ sequester
sequestering *v* ▷ sequester
sequesters *v* ▷ sequester

sequestrate v (-tes, -ting, -ted) confiscate (property) until its owner's debts are paid or a court order is complied with > **sequestration** n (pl -s)

sequestrated v ▷ sequestrate

sequestrates v ▷ sequestrate

sequestrating v ▷ sequestrate

sequestration n ▷ sequestrate

sequestrations n ▷ sequestrate

sequin n (pl -s) small ornamental metal disc on a garment > **sequined** adj

sequined adj ▷ sequin

sequins n ▷ sequin

sequoia n (pl -s) giant Californian coniferous tree

sequoias n ▷ sequoia

seraglio [sir-ah-lee-oh] n (pl -s) harem of a Muslim palace

seraglios n ▷ seraglio

seraph n (pl -s, -aphim) member of the highest order of angels > **seraphic** adj

seraphic adj ▷ seraph

seraphim n ▷ seraph

seraphs n ▷ seraph

serenade n (pl -s) music played or sung to a woman by a lover ▶ v (-des, -ding, -ded) sing or play a serenade to (someone)

serenaded v ▷ serenade

serenades n, v ▷ serenade

serenading v ▷ serenade

serendipities n ▷ serendipity

serendipity n (pl -ties) gift of making fortunate discoveries by accident

serene adj (-r, -st) calm, peaceful > **serenely** adv > **serenity** n (pl -ties)

serenely adv ▷ serene

serener adj ▷ serene

serenest adj ▷ serene

serenities n ▷ serene

serenity n ▷ serene

serf n (pl -s) medieval farm labourer who could not leave the land he worked on > **serfdom** n (pl -s)

serfdom n ▷ serf

serfdoms n ▷ serf

serfs n ▷ serf

serge n (pl -s) strong woollen fabric

sergeant n (pl -s) noncommissioned officer in the army

sergeants n ▷ sergeant

serges n ▷ serge

serial n (pl -s) story or play produced in successive instalments ▶ adj of or forming a series

serialize v (-zes, -zing, -zed) publish or present as a serial

serialized v ▷ serialize

serializes v ▷ serialize

serializing v ▷ serialize

serials n ▷ serial

series n (pl series) group or succession of related things, usu. arranged in order

serious adj giving cause for concern > **seriously** adv > **seriousness** n (pl -es)

seriously adv ▷ serious

seriousness n ▷ serious

seriousnesses n ▷ serious

sermon n (pl -s) speech on a religious or moral subject by a clergyman in a church service

sermonize v (-zes, -zing, -zed) make a long moralizing speech

sermonized v ▷ sermonize

sermonizes v ▷ sermonize

sermonizing v ▷ sermonize

sermons n ▷ sermon

serpent n (pl -s) (Lit) snake

serpentine adj twisting like a snake

serpents n ▷ serpent

serrated adj having a notched or sawlike edge

serried adj in close formation

serum [seer-um] n (pl -s) watery fluid left after blood has clotted

serums n ▷ serum

servant n (pl -s) person employed to do household work for another

servants n ▷ servant

serve v (-s, -ing, -ed) work for (a person, community, or cause) ▶ n (pl -s) (TENNIS ETC.) act of serving the ball

served v ▷ serve

server n (pl -s) player who serves in racket games

servers n ▷ server

serves n, v ▷ serve

service n (pl -s) system that provides something needed by the public ▶ v (-ces, -cing, -ced) overhaul (a machine or vehicle)

serviceable adj useful or helpful

serviced v ▷ service

serviceman, servicewoman n (pl -men, -women) member of the armed forces

servicemen n ▷ serviceman

services n, v ▷ service ▶ pl n armed forces

servicewoman n ▷ serviceman

servicewomen n ▷ serviceman

servicing v ▷ service

serviette n (pl -s) table napkin

serviettes n ▷ serviette

servile adj too eager to obey people, fawning > **servility** n (pl -s)

servilities *n* ▷ servile
servility *n* ▷ servile
serving *v* ▷ serve
servitude *n* (*pl* -s) bondage or slavery
servitudes *n* ▷ servitude
sesame [sess-am-ee] *n* (*pl* -s) plant cultivated for its seeds and oil, which are used in cooking
sesames *n* ▷ sesame
session *n* (*pl* -s) period spent in an activity
sessions *n* ▷ session
set[1] *v* (-s, -tting, set) put in a specified position or state ▶ *n* (*pl* -s) scenery used in a play or film ▶ *adj* fixed or established beforehand
set[2] *n* (*pl* -s) number of things or people grouped or belonging together
setback *n* (*pl* -s) anything that delays progress
setbacks *n* ▷ setback
sets *v* ▷ set[1] ▶ *n* ▷ set[2]
sett, set *n* (*p* -s) badger's burrow
settee *n* (*pl* -s) couch
settees *n* ▷ settee
setter *n* (*pl* -s) long-haired gun dog
setters *n* ▷ setter
setting *n* (*pl* -s) background or surroundings ▶ *v* ▷ set
settings *n* ▷ setting
settle[1] *v* (-les, -ling, -led) arrange or put in order
settle[2] *n* (*pl* -s) long wooden bench with high back and arms
settled *v* ▷ settle[1]
settlement *n* (*pl* -s) act of settling
settlements *n* ▷ settlement
settler *n* (*pl* -s) colonist
settlers *n* ▷ settler
settles *v* ▷ settle[1] ▶ *n* ▷ settle[2]
settling *v* ▷ settle[1]
setts *n* ▷ sett
setup *n* (*pl* -s) way in which anything is organized or arranged
setups *n* ▷ setup
seven *adj*, *n* (*pl* -s) one more than six
sevens *n* ▷ seven
seventeen *adj*, *n* (*pl* -s) ten and seven > seventeenth *adj*, *n* (*pl* -s)
seventeens *n* ▷ seventeen
seventeenth *n* ▷ seventeen
seventeenths *n* ▷ seventeen
seventh *adj*, *n* (*pl* -s) (of) number seven in a series
sevenths *n* ▷ seventh
seventies *n* ▷ seventy
seventieth *n* ▷ seventy
seventieths *n* ▷ seventy

seventy *adj*, *n* (*pl* -ties) ten times seven > seventieth *adj*, *n* (*pl* -s)
sever *v* (-s, -ing, -ed) cut through or off > severance *n* (*pl* -s)
several *adj* some, a few
severally *adv* separately
severance *n* ▷ sever
severances *n* ▷ sever
severe *adj* (-r, -st) strict or harsh > severely *adv* > severity *n* (*pl* -ties)
severed *v* ▷ sever
severely *adv* ▷ severe
severer *adj* ▷ severe
severest *adj* ▷ severe
severing *v* ▷ sever
severities *n* ▷ severe
severity *n* ▷ severe
severs *v* ▷ sever
sew *v* (-s, -ing, -ed, sewn *or* -ed) join with thread repeatedly passed through with a needle
sewage *n* (*pl* -s) waste matter or excrement carried away in sewers
sewages *n* ▷ sewage
sewed *v* ▷ sew
sewer *n* (*pl* -s) drain to remove waste water and sewage > sewerage *n* (*pl* -s) system of sewers
sewerage *n* ▷ sewer
sewerages *n* ▷ sewer
sewers *n* ▷ sewer
sewing *v* ▷ sew
sewn *v* ▷ sew
sews *v* ▷ sew
sex *n* (*pl* -es) state of being male or female ▶ *v* (-es, -ing, -ed) find out the sex of > sexual *adj* > sexually *adv* > sexuality *n* (*pl* -ties)
sexagenarian *n* (*pl* -s) person aged between sixty and sixty-nine
sexagenarians *n* ▷ sexagenarian
sexed *v* ▷ sex
sexes *n*, *v* ▷ sex
sexier *adj* ▷ sexy
sexiest *adj* ▷ sexy
sexing *v* ▷ sex
sexism *n* (*pl* -s) discrimination on the basis of a person's sex > sexist *adj*, *n* (*pl* -s)
sexisms *n* ▷ sexism
sexist *n* ▷ sexism
sexists *n* ▷ sexism
sextant *n* (*pl* -s) navigator's instrument for measuring angles, as between the sun and horizon, to calculate one's position
sextants *n* ▷ sextant
sextet *n* (*pl* -s) group of six performers

sextets *n* ▷ **sextet**
sexton *n* (*pl* **-s**) official in charge of a church and churchyard
sextons *n* ▷ **sexton**
sexual *adj* ▷ **sex**
sexualities *n* ▷ **sex**
sexuality *n* ▷ **sex**
sexually *adv* ▷ **sex**
sexy *adj* (**-xier, -xiest**) sexually exciting or attractive

> **sez** *v*. Sez is an short informal form of **says**. This word can be very useful when there isn't much space on the board, as it gives a good score. Sez scores 12 points.
> **sh** *interj*. Sh is a sound people make to request silence or quiet. This is one of two two-letter words beginning with S that do not contain a vowel. It's useful when you want to connect a word beginning with H to one ending in S or vice versa. Sh scores 5 points.

shabbier *adj* ▷ **shabby**
shabbiest *adj* ▷ **shabby**
shabbily *adv* ▷ **shabby**
shabbiness *n* ▷ **shabby**
shabbinesses *n* ▷ **shabby**
shabby *adj* (**-bier, -biest**) worn or dilapidated in appearance > **shabbily** *adv* > **shabbiness** *n* (*pl* **-es**)
shack *n* (*pl* **-s**) rough hut
shackle *n* (*pl* **-s**) one of a pair of metal rings joined by a chain, for securing a person's wrists or ankles ▶ *v* (**-les, -ling, -led**) fasten with shackles
shackled *v* ▷ **shackle**
shackles *n*, *v* ▷ **shackle**
shackling *v* ▷ **shackle**
shacks *n* ▷ **shack**
shad *n* (*pl* **-s**) herring-like fish
shade *n* (*pl* **-s**) relative darkness ▶ *v* (**-des, -ding, -ded**) screen from light > **shady** *adj* (**-dier, -diest**) situated in or giving shade
shaded *v* ▷ **shade**
shades *n*, *v* ▷ **shade** ▶ *pl n* (*Slang*) sunglasses
shadier *adj* ▷ **shade**
shadiest *adj* ▷ **shade**
shading *v* ▷ **shade**
shadow *n* (*pl* **-s**) dark shape cast on a surface when something stands between a light and the surface ▶ *v* (**-s, -ing, -ed**) cast a shadow over > **shadowy** *adj* (**-wier, -wiest**)
shadowboxing *n* (*pl* **-s**) boxing against an imaginary opponent for practice
shadowboxings *n* ▷ **shadowboxing**

shadowed *v* ▷ **shadow**
shadowier *adj* ▷ **shadow**
shadowiest *adj* ▷ **shadow**
shadowing *v* ▷ **shadow**
shadows *n*, *v* ▷ **shadow**
shadowy *adj* ▷ **shadow**
shads *n* ▷ **shad**
shady *adj* ▷ **shade**
shaft *n* (*pl* **-s**) long narrow straight handle of a tool or weapon
shafts *n* ▷ **shaft**
shag¹ *n* (*pl* **-s**) coarse shredded tobacco ▶ *adj* (of a carpet) having a long pile
shag² *n* (*pl* **-s**) kind of cormorant
shaggier *adj* ▷ **shaggy**
shaggiest *adj* ▷ **shaggy**
shaggy *adj* (**-ggier, -ggiest**) covered with rough hair or wool
shagreen *n* (*pl* **-s**) sharkskin
shagreens *n* ▷ **shagreen**
shags *n* ▷ **shag¹, ²**
shah *n* (*pl* **-s**) formerly, ruler of Iran
shahs *n* ▷ **shah**
shake *v* (**-kes, -king, shook, -en**) move quickly up and down or back and forth ▶ *n* (*pl* **-s**) shaking (*Informal*)
shaken *v* ▷ **shake**
shakes *v*, *n* ▷ **shake**
shakier *adj* ▷ **shaky**
shakiest *adj* ▷ **shaky**
shakily *adv* ▷ **shaky**
shaking *v* ▷ **shake**
shaky *adj* (**-kier, -kiest**) unsteady > **shakily** *adv*
shale *n* (*pl* **-s**) flaky sedimentary rock
shales *n* ▷ **shale**
shall *v* (*past tense* **should**) used as an auxiliary to make the future tense or to indicate intention, obligation, or inevitability
shallot *n* (*pl* **-s**) kind of small onion
shallots *n* ▷ **shallot**
shallow *adj* (**-er, -est**) not deep > **shallowness** *n* (*pl* **-es**)
shallower *adj* ▷ **shallow**
shallowest *adj* ▷ **shallow**
shallowness *n* ▷ **shallow**
shallownesses *n* ▷ **shallow**
shallows *pl n* area of shallow water
sham *n* (*pl* **-s**) thing or person that is not genuine ▶ *adj* not genuine ▶ *v* (**-s, -mming, -mmed**) fake, feign
shamble *v* (**-les, -ling, -led**) walk in a shuffling awkward way
shambled *v* ▷ **shamble**
shambles *n* (*pl* disorderly event or place ▶ *v* ▷ **shamble**

shambling v ▷ shamble
shame n (pl -s) painful emotion caused by awareness of having done something dishonourable or foolish ▶ v (-mes, -ming, -med) cause to feel shame ▶ interj (S AFR) (Informal) exclamation of sympathy or endearment
shamed v ▷ shame
shamefaced adj looking ashamed
shameful adj causing or deserving shame > **shamefully** adv
shamefully adv ▷ shameful
shameless adj with no sense of shame
shames n, v ▷ shame
shaming v ▷ shame
shammed v ▷ sham
shammies n ▷ shammy
shamming v ▷ sham
shammy n (pl -mies) (Informal) piece of chamois leather
shampoo n (pl -s) liquid soap for washing hair, carpets, or upholstery ▶ v (-s, -ing, -ed) wash with shampoo
shampooed v ▷ shampoo
shampooing v ▷ shampoo
shampoos n, v ▷ shampoo
shamrock n (pl -s) clover leaf, esp. as the Irish emblem
shamrocks n ▷ shamrock
shams n, v ▷ sham
shandies n ▷ shandy
shandy n (pl -dies) drink made of beer and lemonade
shanghai v (-hais, -haiing, -haied) force or trick (someone) into doing something ▶ n (pl -s) (AUST & NZ) catapult
shanghaied v ▷ shanghai
shanghaiing v ▷ shanghai
shanghais v, n ▷ shanghai
shank n (pl -s) lower leg
shanks n ▷ shank
shanties n ▷ shanty[1,2]
shantung n (pl -s) soft Chinese silk with a knobbly surface
shantungs n ▷ shantung
shanty[1] n (pl -ties) shack or crude dwelling
shanty[2] n (pl -ties) sailor's traditional song
shantytown n (pl -s) slum consisting of shanties
shantytowns n ▷ shantytown
shape n (pl -s) outward form of an object ▶ v (-pes, -ping, -ped) form or mould > **shapeless** adj
shaped v ▷ shape
shapeless adj ▷ shape

shapelier adj ▷ shapely
shapeliest adj ▷ shapely
shapely adj (-lier, -liest) having an attractive shape
shapes n, v ▷ shape
shaping v ▷ shape
shard n (pl -s) broken piece of pottery or glass
shards n ▷ shard
share[1] n (pl -s) part of something that belongs to or is contributed by a person ▶ v (-res, -ring, -red) give or take a share of (something) > **shareholder** n (pl -s)
share[2] n (pl -s) blade of a plough
shared v ▷ share[1]
shareholder n ▷ share[1]
shareholders n ▷ share[1]
sharemilker n (pl -s) (NZ) person who works on a dairy farm belonging to someone else
sharemilkers n ▷ sharemilker
shares v ▷ share[1] ▶ n ▷ share[1,2]
sharing v ▷ share[1]
shark n (pl -s) large usu. predatory sea fish
sharks n ▷ shark
sharkskin n (pl -s) stiff glossy fabric
sharkskins n ▷ sharkskin
sharp adj having a keen cutting edge or fine point ▶ adv promptly ▶ n (pl -s) (MUSIC) symbol raising a note one semitone above natural pitch > **sharply** adv > **sharpness** n (pl -es)
sharpen v (-s, -ing, -ed) make or become sharp or sharper > **sharpener** n (pl -s)
sharpened v ▷ sharpen
sharpener n ▷ sharpen
sharpeners n ▷ sharpen
sharpening v ▷ sharpen
sharpens v ▷ sharpen
sharply adv ▷ sharp
sharpness n ▷ sharp
sharpnesses n ▷ sharp
sharps n ▷ sharp
sharpshooter n (pl -s) marksman
sharpshooters n ▷ sharpshooter
shatter v (-s, -ing, -ed) break into pieces
shattered adj (Informal) completely exhausted ▶ v ▷ shatter
shattering v ▷ shatter
shatters v ▷ shatter
shave v (-ves, -ving, -ved, -ved or shaven) remove (hair) from (the face, head, or body) with a razor or shaver ▶ n (pl -s) shaving
shaved v ▷ shave
shaven v ▷ shave
shaver n (pl -s) electric razor
shavers n ▷ shaver
shaves v, n ▷ shave

shaving v ▷ shave
shavings pl n parings
shawl n (pl -s) piece of cloth worn over a woman's head or shoulders or wrapped around a baby
shawls n ▷ shawl
she pron refers to: female person or animal previously mentioned
sheaf n (pl sheaves) bundle of papers
shear v (-s, -ing, -ed, -ed or shorn) clip hair or wool from > shearer n (pl -s)
sheared v ▷ shear
shearer n ▷ shear
shearers n ▷ shear
shearing v ▷ shear
shears pl n large scissors or a cutting tool shaped like these ▶ v ▷ shear
shearwater n (pl -s) medium-sized sea bird
shearwaters n ▷ shearwater
sheath n (pl -s) close-fitting cover, esp. for a knife or sword
sheathe v (-thes, -thing, -thed) put into a sheath
sheathed v ▷ sheathe
sheathes v ▷ sheathe
sheathing v ▷ sheathe
sheaths n ▷ sheath
sheaves n ▷ sheaf
shebeen n (pl -s) (SCOT, IRISH & S AFR) place where alcohol is sold illegally
shebeens n ▷ shebeen
shed[1] n (pl -s) building used for storage or shelter or as a workshop
shed[2] v (-s, -dding, shed) pour forth (tears)
shedding v ▷ shed[2]
sheds n ▷ shed[1] ▶ v ▷ shed[2]
sheen n (pl -s) glistening brightness on the surface of something
sheens n ▷ sheen
sheep n (pl sheep) ruminant animal bred for wool and meat
sheepdog n (pl -s) dog used for herding sheep
sheepdogs n ▷ sheepdog
sheepish adj embarrassed because of feeling foolish > sheepishly adv
sheepishly adv ▷ sheepish
sheepskin n (pl -s) skin of a sheep with the fleece still on, used for clothing or rugs
sheepskins n ▷ sheepskin
sheer[1] adj (-er, -est) absolute, complete
sheer[2] v (-s, -ing, -ed) change course suddenly
sheered v ▷ sheer[2]
sheerer adj ▷ sheer[1]
sheerest adj ▷ sheer[1]
sheering v ▷ sheer[2]

sheers v ▷ sheer[2]
sheet[1] n (pl -s) large piece of cloth used as an inner bed cover
sheet[2] n (pl -s) rope for controlling the position of a sail
sheets n ▷ sheet[1, 2]
sheikdom n ▷ sheikh
sheikdoms n ▷ sheikh
sheikh, sheik [shake] n (pl -s) Arab chief > sheikhdom, sheikdom n (pl -s)
sheikhdoms n ▷ sheikhdom
sheikhs n ▷ sheikh
sheiks n ▷ sheikh
sheila n (pl -s) (AUST & NZ) (Slang) girl or woman
sheilas n ▷ sheila
shekel n (pl -s) monetary unit of Israel
shekels n ▷ shekel ▶ pl n (Informal) money
shelf n (pl -ves) board fixed horizontally for holding things
shell n (pl -s) hard outer covering of an egg, nut, or certain animals ▶ v (-s, -lling, -lled) take the shell from
shellac n (pl -s) resin used in varnishes ▶ v (-cs, -cking, -cked) coat with shellac
shellacked v ▷ shellac
shellacking v ▷ shellac
shellacs n, v ▷ shellac
shelled v ▷ shell
shellfish n (pl -s) sea-living animal, esp. one that can be eaten, with a shell
shellfishes n ▷ shellfish
shelling v ▷ shell
shells n, v ▷ shell
shelter n (pl -s) structure providing protection from danger or the weather ▶ v (-s, -ing, -ed) give shelter to
sheltered v ▷ shelter
sheltering v ▷ shelter
shelters n, v ▷ shelter
shelve[1] v (-ves, -ving, -ved) put aside or postpone
shelve[2] v (-ves, -ving, -ved) slope
shelved v ▷ shelve[1, 2]
shelves v ▷ shelve[1, 2] ▶ n ▷ shelf
shelving n (pl -s) (material for) shelves ▶ v ▷ shelve[1, 2]
shenanigans pl n (Informal) mischief or nonsense
shepherd n (pl -s) person who tends sheep ▶ v (-s, -ing, -ed) guide or watch over (people) > shepherdess n fem (pl -s)
shepherded v ▷ shepherd
shepherdess n ▷ shepherd
shepherdesses n ▷ shepherd
shepherding v ▷ shepherd

shepherds *n*, *v* ▷ **shepherd**
sherbet *n* (*pl* -**s**) (BRIT, AUST & NZ) fruit-flavoured fizzy powder
 sherbets *n* ▷ **sherbet**
sheriff *n* (*pl* -**s**) (in the US) chief law enforcement officer of a county
 sheriffs *n* ▷ **sheriff**
 sherries *n* ▷ **sherry**
sherry *n* (*pl* -**ries**) pale or dark brown fortified wine

> **shh** *interj*. Shh is a sound people make to request silence or quiet. As it doesn't contain a vowel, shh can help you to clear an unpromising rack. Shh scores 9 points.

shibboleth *n* (*pl* -**s**) slogan or principle, usu. considered outworn, characteristic of a particular group
 shibboleths *n* ▷ **shibboleth**
 shied *v* ▷ **shy**[1, 2]
shield *n* (*pl* -**s**) piece of armour carried on the arm to protect the body from blows or missiles ▶ *v* (-**s**, -**ing**, -**ed**) protect
 shielded *v* ▷ **shield**
 shielding *v* ▷ **shield**
 shields *n*, *v* ▷ **shield**
 shies *v* ▷ **shy**[1, 2] ▶ *n* ▷ **shy**[2]
shift *v* (-**s**, -**ing**, -**ed**) move ▶ *n* (*pl* -**s**) shifting
 shifted *v* ▷ **shift**
 shiftier *adj* ▷ **shifty**
 shiftiest *adj* ▷ **shifty**
 shiftiness *n* ▷ **shifty**
 shiftinesses *n* ▷ **shifty**
 shifting *v* ▷ **shift**
shiftless *adj* lacking in ambition or initiative
 shifts *v*, *n* ▷ **shift**
shifty *adj* (-**tier**, -**tiest**) evasive or untrustworthy > **shiftiness** *n* (*pl* -**es**)
shillelagh [shil-**lay**-lee] *n* (*pl* -**s**) (in Ireland) a cudgel
 shillelaghs *n* ▷ **shillelagh**
shilling *n* (*pl* -**s**) former British coin, replaced by the 5p piece
 shillings *n* ▷ **shilling**
 shillyshallied *v* ▷ **shillyshally**
 shillyshallies *v* ▷ **shillyshally**
shillyshally *v* (-**lies**, -**lying**, -**lied**) (*Informal*) be indecisive
 shillyshallying *v* ▷ **shillyshally**
shimmer *v* (-**s**, -**ing**, -**ed**) ▶ *n* (*pl* -**s**) (shine with) a faint unsteady light
 shimmered *v* ▷ **shimmer**
 shimmering *v* ▷ **shimmer**
 shimmers *v*, *n* ▷ **shimmer**
shin *n* (*pl* -**s**) front of the lower leg ▶ *v* (-**s**,

-**nning**, -**nned**) climb by using the hands or arms and legs
shinbone *n* (*pl* -**s**) tibia
 shinbones *n* ▷ **shinbone**
shindig *n* (*pl* -**s**) (*Informal*) noisy party
 shindigs *n* ▷ **shindig**
shine *v* (-**s**, -**ing**, **shone**) give out or reflect light ▶ *n* (*pl* -**s**) brightness or lustre > **shiny** *adj* (-**nier**, -**niest**)
shiner *n* (*pl* -**s**) (*Informal*) black eye
 shiners *n* ▷ **shiner**
 shines *v*, *n* ▷ **shine**
shingle[1] *n* (*pl* -**s**) wooden roof tile ▶ *v* (-**les**, -**ling**, -**led**) cover (a roof) with shingles
shingle[2] *n* (*pl* -**s**) coarse gravel found on beaches
 shingled *v* ▷ **shingle**[1]
shingles *n* disease causing a rash of small blisters along a nerve ▷ **shingle**[1, 2] ▶ *v* ▷ **shingle**[1]
 shingling *v* ▷ **shingle**[1]
 shinier *adj* ▷ **shine**
 shiniest *adj* ▷ **shine**
 shining *v* ▷ **shine**
 shinned *v* ▷ **shin**
 shinning *v* ▷ **shin**
 shins *n*, *v* ▷ **shin**
 shinties *n* ▷ **shinty**
shinty *n* (*pl* -**ties**) game like hockey
 shiny *adj* ▷ **shine**
ship *n* (*pl* -**s**) large seagoing vessel ▶ *v* (-**s**, -**pping**, -**pped**) send or transport by carrier, esp. a ship
shipment *n* (*pl* -**s**) act of shipping cargo
 shipments *n* ▷ **shipment**
 shipped *v* ▷ **ship**
shipping *n* (*pl* -**s**) freight transport business ▶ *v* ▷ **ship**
 shippings *n* ▷ **shipping**
 ships *n*, *v* ▷ **ship**
shipshape *adj* orderly or neat
shipwreck *n* (*pl* -**s**) destruction of a ship through storm or collision ▶ *v* (-**s**, -**ing**, -**ed**) cause to undergo shipwreck
 shipwrecked *v* ▷ **shipwreck**
 shipwrecking *v* ▷ **shipwreck**
 shipwrecks *n*, *v* ▷ **shipwreck**
shipyard *n* (*pl* -**s**) place where ships are built
 shipyards *n* ▷ **shipyard**
shire *n* (*pl* -**s**) (BRIT) county
 shires *n* ▷ **shire**
shirk *v* (-**s**, -**ing**, -**ed**) avoid (duty or work) > **shirker** *n* (*pl* -**s**)
 shirked *v* ▷ **shirk**
 shirker *n* ▷ **shirk**

shirkers n ▷ **shirk**
shirking v ▷ **shirk**
shirks v ▷ **shirk**
shirt n (pl -s) garment for the upper part of the body
shirtier adj ▷ **shirty**
shirtiest adj ▷ **shirty**
shirts n ▷ **shirt**
shirty adj (-tier, -tiest) (CHIEFLY BRIT) (Slang) bad-tempered or annoyed
shiver[1] v (-s, -ing, -ed) tremble, as from cold or fear ▶ n (pl -s) shivering
shiver[2] v (-s, -ing, -ed) splinter into pieces
shivered v ▷ **shiver**[1, 2]
shivering v ▷ **shiver**[1, 2]
shivers v ▷ **shiver**[1, 2] ▶ n ▷ **shiver**[1]
shoal[1] n (pl -s) large number of fish swimming together
shoal[2] n (pl -s) stretch of shallow water
shoals n ▷ **shoal**[1, 2]
shock[1] v (-s, -ing, -ed) horrify, disgust, or astonish ▶ n (pl -s) sudden violent emotional disturbance > **shocker** n (pl -s)
shock[2] n (pl -s) bushy mass (of hair)
shocked v ▷ **shock**[1]
shocker n ▷ **shock**[1]
shockers n ▷ **shock**[1]
shocking adj causing horror, disgust, or astonishment ▶ v ▷ **shock**[1]
shocks v ▷ **shock**[1] ▶ n ▷ **shock**[1, 2]
shod v ▷ **shoe**
shoddier adj ▷ **shoddy**
shoddiest adj ▷ **shoddy**
shoddy adj (-dier, -diest) made or done badly
shoe n (pl -s) outer covering for the foot, ending below the ankle ▶ v (shoes, shoeing, shod) fit with a shoe or shoes
shoehorn n (pl -s) smooth curved implement inserted at the heel of a shoe to ease the foot into it
shoehorns n ▷ **shoehorn**
shoeing v ▷ **shoe**
shoes n, v ▷ **shoe**
shoestring n (pl -s) (foll. by **on a**) using a very small amount of money
shoestrings n ▷ **shoestring**
shone v ▷ **shine**
shonkier adj ▷ **shonky**
shonkiest adj ▷ **shonky**
shonky adj (-kier, -kiest) (AUST & NZ) (Informal) unreliable or unsound
shoo interj go away! ▶ v (-s, -ing, -ed) drive away as by saying 'shoo'
shooed v ▷ **shoo**
shooing v ▷ **shoo**

shook v ▷ **shake**
shoos v ▷ **shoo**
shoot v (-s, -ing, shot) hit, wound, or kill with a missile fired from a weapon ▶ n (pl -s) new branch or sprout of a plant
shooting v ▷ **shoot**
shoots v, n ▷ **shoot**
shop n (pl -s) place for sale of goods and services ▶ v (-s, -pping, -pped) visit a shop or shops to buy goods
shoplifter n (pl -s) person who steals from a shop
shoplifters n ▷ **shoplifter**
shopped v ▷ **shop**
shopping v ▷ **shop**
shops n, v ▷ **shop**
shopsoiled adj soiled or faded from being displayed in a shop
shore[1] n (pl -s) edge of a sea or lake
shore[2] v (-res, -ring, -red) (foll. by **up**) prop or support
shored v ▷ **shore**[2]
shores n ▷ **shore**[1] ▶ v ▷ **shore**[2]
shoring v ▷ **shore**[2]
shorn v ▷ **shear**
short adj (-er, -est) not long ▶ adv abruptly ▶ n (pl -s) drink of spirits
shortage n (pl -s) deficiency
shortages n ▷ **shortage**
shortbread, shortcake n (pl -s) crumbly biscuit made with butter
shortbreads n ▷ **shortbread**
shortcake n ▷ **shortbread**
shortcakes n ▷ **shortbread**
shortchange v (-ges, -ging, -ed) give (someone) less than the correct amount of change
shortchanged v ▷ **shortchange**
shortchanges v ▷ **shortchange**
shortchanging v ▷ **shortchange**
shortcoming n (pl -s) failing or defect
shortcomings n ▷ **shortcoming**
shorten v (-s, -ing, -ed) make or become shorter
shortened v ▷ **shorten**
shortening v ▷ **shorten**
shortens v ▷ **shorten**
shorter adj ▷ **short**
shortest adj ▷ **short**
shortfall n (pl -s) deficit
shortfalls n ▷ **shortfall**
shorthand n (pl -s) system of rapid writing using symbols to represent words
shorthanded adj not having enough workers
shorthands n ▷ **shorthand**

shortlist v (**-s, -ing, -ed**) put on a short list
  shortlisted v ▷ **shortlist**
  shortlisting v ▷ **shortlist**
  shortlists v ▷ **shortlist**
shortly adv soon
shorts n ▷ **short** ▶ pl n short trousers
shortsighted adj unable to see distant things
  clearly
shot n (pl -s) shooting ▶ v ▷ **shoot**
shotgun n (pl -s) gun for firing a charge of shot
  at short range
  shotguns n ▷ **shotgun**
  shots n ▷ **shot**
  should v ▷ **shall**
shoulder n (pl -s) part of the body to which an
  arm, foreleg, or wing is attached ▶ v (**-s, -ing,
  -ed**) bear (a burden or responsibility)
  shouldered v ▷ **shoulder**
  shouldering v ▷ **shoulder**
  shoulders n, v ▷ **shoulder**
shout n (pl -s) loud cry (Informal) ▶ v (**-s, -ing,
  -ed**) cry out loudly
  shouted v ▷ **shout**
  shouting v ▷ **shout**
  shouts n, v ▷ **shout**
shove v (**-ves, -ving, -ved**) push roughly ▶ n (pl
  -s) rough push
  shoved v ▷ **shove**
shovel n (pl -s) tool for lifting or moving loose
  material ▶ v (**-s, -lling, -lled**) lift or move as
  with a shovel
  shovelled v ▷ **shovel**
  shovelling v ▷ **shovel**
  shovels n, v ▷ **shovel**
  shoves n ▷ **shove**
  shoving v ▷ **shove**
show v (**-s, -ing, -ed, shown** or **showed**) make,
  be, or become noticeable or visible ▶ n (pl -s)
  public exhibition
showcase n (pl -s) situation in which
  something is displayed to best advantage
  showcases n ▷ **showcase**
showdown n (pl -s) confrontation that settles
  a dispute
  showdowns n ▷ **showdown**
  showed v ▷ **show**
shower n (pl -s) kind of bath in which a person
  stands while being sprayed with water ▶ v
  (**-s, -ing, -ed**) wash in a shower > **showery** adj
  (**-rier, -riest**)
  showered v ▷ **shower**
  showerier adj ▷ **shower**
  showeriest adj ▷ **shower**
  showering v ▷ **shower**
  showers n, v ▷ **shower**

showery adj ▷ **shower**
showier adj ▷ **showy**
showiest adj ▷ **showy**
showily adv ▷ **showy**
showing v ▷ **show**
showjumping n (pl -s) competitive sport of
  riding horses to demonstrate skill in jumping
  showjumpings n ▷ **showjumping**
showman n (pl -men) man skilled at
  presenting anything spectacularly
  > **showmanship** n (pl -s)
  showmanship n ▷ **showman**
  showmanships n ▷ **showman**
  showmen n ▷ **showman**
  shown v ▷ **show**
showoff n (pl -s) (Informal) person who shows
  off
  showoffs n ▷ **showoff**
showpiece n (pl -s) excellent specimen shown
  for display or as an example
  showpieces n ▷ **showpiece**
showroom n (pl -s) room in which goods for
  sale are on display
  showrooms n ▷ **showroom**
  shows v, n ▷ **show**
showy adj (**-wier, -wiest**) gaudy > **showily** adv
shrank v ▷ **shrink**
shrapnel n (pl -s) artillery shell filled with
  pellets which scatter on explosion
  shrapnels n ▷ **shrapnel**
shred n (pl -s) long narrow strip torn from
  something ▶ v (**-s, -dding, -dded** or **shred**) tear
  to shreds
  shredded v ▷ **shred**
  shredding v ▷ **shred**
  shreds n, v ▷ **shred**
shrew n (pl -s) small mouselike animal
  > **shrewish** adj
shrewd adj (**-er, -est**) clever and perceptive
  > **shrewdly** adv > **shrewdness** n (pl -es)
  shrewder adj ▷ **shrewd**
  shrewdest adj ▷ **shrewd**
  shrewdly adv ▷ **shrewd**
  shrewdness n ▷ **shrewd**
  shrewdnesses n ▷ **shrewd**
  shrewish adj ▷ **shrew**
  shrews n ▷ **shrew**
shriek n (pl -s) shrill cry ▶ v (**-s, -ing, -ed**) utter
  (with) a shriek
  shrieked v ▷ **shriek**
  shrieking v ▷ **shriek**
  shrieks n, v ▷ **shriek**
shrike n (pl -s) songbird with a heavy hooked
  bill
  shrikes n ▷ **shrike**

shrill adj (-er, -est) (of a sound) sharp and high-pitched > **shrillness** n (pl -es) > **shrilly** adv
  shriller adj ▷ **shrill**
  shrillest adj ▷ **shrill**
  shrillness n ▷ **shrill**
  shrillnesses n ▷ **shrill**
  shrilly adv ▷ **shrill**
shrimp n (pl -s) small edible shellfish (Informal)
shrimping n (pl -s) fishing for shrimps
  shrimpings n ▷ **shrimping**
  shrimps n ▷ **shrimp**
shrine n (pl -s) place of worship associated with a sacred person or object
  shrines n ▷ **shrine**
shrink v (-s, -ing, shrank or shrunk, shrunk or shrunken) become or make smaller ▶ n (pl -s) (Slang) psychiatrist
shrinkage n (pl -s) decrease in size, value, or weight
  shrinkages n ▷ **shrinkage**
  shrinking v ▷ **shrink**
  shrinks v, n ▷ **shrink**
shrivel v (-s, -lling, -lled) shrink and wither
  shrivelled v ▷ **shrivel**
  shrivelling v ▷ **shrivel**
  shrivels v ▷ **shrivel**
shroud n (pl -s) piece of cloth used to wrap a dead body ▶ v (-s, -ing, -ed) conceal
  shrouded v ▷ **shroud**
  shrouding v ▷ **shroud**
  shrouds n, v ▷ **shroud**
shrub n (pl -s) woody plant smaller than a tree
  shrubberies n ▷ **shrubbery**
shrubbery n (pl -ries) area planted with shrubs
  shrubs n ▷ **shrub**
shrug v (-s, -gging, -gged) raise and then drop (the shoulders) as a sign of indifference, ignorance, or doubt ▶ n (pl -s) shrugging
  shrugged v ▷ **shrug**
  shrugging v ▷ **shrug**
  shrugs v, n ▷ **shrug**
  shrunk v ▷ **shrink**
  shrunken v ▷ **shrink**
shudder v (-s, -ing, -ed) shake or tremble violently, esp. with horror ▶ n (pl -s) shaking or trembling
  shuddered v ▷ **shudder**
  shuddering v ▷ **shudder**
  shudders v, n ▷ **shudder**
shuffle v (-les, -ling, -led) walk without lifting the feet ▶ n (pl -s) shuffling
  shuffled v ▷ **shuffle**
  shuffles v, n ▷ **shuffle**
  shuffling v ▷ **shuffle**
shun v (-s, -nning, -nned) avoid

  shunned v ▷ **shun**
  shunning v ▷ **shun**
  shuns v ▷ **shun**
shunt v (-s, -ing, -ed) move (objects or people) to a different position
  shunted v ▷ **shunt**
  shunting v ▷ **shunt**
  shunts v ▷ **shunt**
shush interj be quiet!
shut v (-s, -tting, shut) bring together or fold, close
shutdown n (pl -s) closing
  shutdowns n ▷ **shutdown**
  shuts v ▷ **shut**
shutter n (pl -s) hinged doorlike cover for closing off a window
  shutters n ▷ **shutter**
  shutting v ▷ **shut**
shuttle n (pl -s) vehicle going to and fro over a short distance ▶ v (-les, -ling, -led) travel by or as if by shuttle
shuttlecock n (pl -s) small light cone with feathers stuck in one end, struck to and fro in badminton
  shuttlecocks n ▷ **shuttlecock**
  shuttled v ▷ **shuttle**
  shuttles n, v ▷ **shuttle**
  shuttling v ▷ **shuttle**
shy¹ adj (-er, -est) not at ease in company (foll. by **of**) ▶ v (shies, shying, shied) start back in fear (foll. by **away from**) > **shyly** adv > **shyness** n (pl -es)
shy² v (shies, shying, shied) throw ▶ n (pl shies) throw
  shyer adj ▷ **shy¹**
  shyest adj ▷ **shy¹**
  shying v ▷ **shy¹, ²**
  shyly adv ▷ **shy¹**
  shyness n ▷ **shy¹**
  shynesses n ▷ **shy¹**

> **si** n (sis). Si means the same as **te**, a musical note This is an unusual word which can be helpful when you want to form words in more than one direction Si scores 2 points

sibilant adj hissing ▶ n (pl -s) consonant pronounced with a hissing sound
  sibilants n ▷ **sibilant**
sibling n (pl -s) brother or sister
  siblings n ▷ **sibling**
sibyl n (pl -s) (in ancient Greece and Rome) prophetess
  sibyls n ▷ **sibyl**
sic (LATIN) thus: used to indicate that an odd spelling or reading is in fact accurate

sick adj (-er, -est) vomiting or likely to vomit
> **sickness** n (pl -es)
sicken v (-s, -zing, -ed) make nauseated or
disgusted
sickened v ▷ sicken
sickening v ▷ sicken
sickens v ▷ sicken
sicker adj ▷ sick
sickest adj ▷ sick
sickle n (pl -s) tool with a curved blade for
cutting grass or grain
sickles n ▷ sickle
sicklier adj ▷ sickly
sickliest adj ▷ sickly
sickly adj (-lier, -liest) unhealthy, weak
sickness n ▷ sick
sicknesses n ▷ sick
side n (pl -s) line or surface that borders
anything ▶ adj at or on the side
sideboard n (pl -s) piece of furniture for
holding plates, cutlery, etc. in a dining room
sideboards n ▷ sideboard ▶ pl n ▷ **sideburns**
sideburns, sideboards pl n man's side
whiskers
sidekick n (pl -s) (Informal) close friend or
associate
sidekicks n ▷ sidekick
sidelight n (pl -s) either of two small lights on
the front of a vehicle
sidelights n ▷ sidelight
sideline n (pl -s) subsidiary interest or source
of income
sidelines n ▷ sideline
sidelong adj sideways ▶ adv obliquely
sidereal [side-eer-ee-al] adj of or determined
with reference to the stars
sides n ▷ side
sidesaddle n (pl -s) saddle designed to allow
a woman rider to sit with both legs on the
same side of the horse
sidesaddles n ▷ sidesaddle
sidestep v (-s, -pping, -pped) dodge (an issue)
sidestepped v ▷ sidestep
sidestepping v ▷ sidestep
sidesteps v ▷ sidestep
sidetrack v (-s, -ing, -ed) divert from the main
topic
sidetracked v ▷ sidetrack
sidetracking v ▷ sidetrack
sidetracks v ▷ sidetrack
sidewalk n (pl -s) (US) paved path for
pedestrians, at the side of a road
sidewalks n ▷ sidewalk
sideways adv to or from the side
siding n (pl -s) short stretch of railway track

on which trains or wagons are shunted from
the main line
sidings n ▷ siding
sidle v (-les, -ling, -led) walk in a furtive
manner
sidled v ▷ sidle
sidles v ▷ sidle
sidling v ▷ sidle
siege n (pl -s) surrounding and blockading of
a place
sieges n ▷ siege
sienna n (pl -s) reddish- or yellowish-brown
pigment made from natural earth
siennas n ▷ sienna
sierra n (pl -s) range of mountains in Spain or
America with jagged peaks
sierras n ▷ sierra
siesta n (pl -s) afternoon nap, taken in hot
countries
siestas n ▷ siesta
sieve [siv] n (pl -s) utensil with mesh through
which a substance is sifted or strained ▶ v
(-ves, -ving, -ved) sift or strain through a sieve
sieved v ▷ sieve
sieves n, v ▷ sieve
sieving v ▷ sieve
sift v (-s, -ing, -ed) remove the coarser particles
from a substance with a sieve
sifted v ▷ sift
sifting v ▷ sift
sifts v ▷ sift
sigh n (pl -s) long audible breath expressing
sadness, tiredness, relief, or longing ▶ v (-s,
-ing, -ed) utter a sigh
sighed v ▷ sigh
sighing v ▷ sigh
sighs n, v ▷ sigh
sight n (pl -s) ability to see ▶ v (-s, -ing, -ed)
catch sight of
sighted v ▷ sight
sighting v ▷ sight
sightless adj blind
sights n, v ▷ sight
sightseeing n (pl -s) visiting places of interest
> **sightseer** n (pl -s)
sightseeings n ▷ sightseeing
sightseer n ▷ sightseeing
sightseers n ▷ sightseeing
sign n (pl -s) indication of something not
immediately or outwardly observable ▶ v (-s,
-ing, -ed) write (one's name) on (a document
or letter) to show its authenticity or one's
agreement
signal n (pl -s) sign or gesture to convey
information ▶ adj (Formal) very important

▶ v (-s, -lling, -lled) convey (information) by signal > **signally** adv
signalled v ▷ **signal**
signalling v ▷ **signal**
signally adv ▷ **signal**
signalman n (pl -**men**) railwayman in charge of signals and points
signalmen n ▷ **signalman**
signals n, v ▷ **signal**
signatories n ▷ **signatory**
signatory n (pl -**ries**) one of the parties who sign a document
signature n (pl -**s**) person's name written by himself or herself in signing something
signatures n ▷ **signature**
signed v ▷ **sign**
signet n (pl -**s**) small seal used to authenticate documents
signets n ▷ **signet**
significance n ▷ **significant**
significances n ▷ **significant**
significant adj important > **significantly** adv > **significance** n (pl -**s**)
significantly adv ▷ **significant**
signification n ▷ **signify**
significations n ▷ **signify**
signified v ▷ **signify**
signifies v ▷ **signify**
signify v (-**fies**, -**fying**, -**fied**) indicate or suggest > **signification** n (pl -**s**)
signifying v ▷ **signify**
signing n (pl -**s**) system of communication by gestures, as used by deaf people ▶ v ▷ **sign**
signings n ▷ **signing**
signor [see-**nyor**] n (pl -**s**) Italian term of address equivalent to sir or Mr
signora [see-**nyor**-a] n (pl -**s**) Italian term of address equivalent to madam or Mrs
signoras n ▷ **signora**
signorina [see-nyor-**ee**-na] n (pl -**s**) Italian term of address equivalent to madam or Miss
signorinas n ▷ **signorina**
signors n ▷ **signor**
signpost n (pl -**s**) post bearing a sign that shows the way
signposts n ▷ **signpost**
signs n, v ▷ **sign**
silage [**sile**-ij] n (pl -**s**) fodder crop harvested while green and partially fermented in a silo or plastic bags
silages n ▷ **silage**
silence n (pl -**s**) absence of noise or speech ▶ v (-**ces**, -**cing**, -**ced**) make silent > **silent** adj > **silently** adv
silenced v ▷ **silence**

silencer n (pl -**s**) device to reduce the noise of an engine exhaust or gun
silencers n ▷ **silencer**
silences n, v ▷ **silence**
silencing v ▷ **silence**
silent adj ▷ **silencet**
silently adv ▷ **silence**
silhouette n (pl -**s**) outline of a dark shape seen against a light background ▶ v (-**s**, -**ing**, -**ed**) show in silhouette
silhouetted v ▷ **silhouette**
silhouettes n, v ▷ **silhouette**
silhouetting v ▷ **silhouette**
silica n (pl -**s**) hard glossy mineral found as quartz and in sandstone
silicas n ▷ **silica**
silicon n (pl -**s**) (CHEM) brittle nonmetallic element widely used in chemistry and industry
silicone n (pl -**s**) tough synthetic substance made from silicon and used in lubricants, paints, and resins
silicones n ▷ **silicone**
silicons n ▷ **silicon**
silicoses n ▷ **silicosis**
silicosis n (pl -**ses**) lung disease caused by inhaling silica dust
silk n (pl -**s**) fibre made by the larva of a certain moth
silken adj ▷ **silky**
silkier adj ▷ **silky**
silkiest adj ▷ **silky**
silks n ▷ **silk**
silky (-**ier**, -**iest**), **silken** adj of or like silk
sill n (pl -**s**) ledge at the bottom of a window or door
sillier adj ▷ **silly**
silliest adj ▷ **silly**
silliness n ▷ **silly**
sillinesses n ▷ **silly**
sills n ▷ **sill**
silly adj (-**lier**, -**liest**) foolish > **silliness** n (pl -**es**)
silo n (pl -**los**) pit or airtight tower for storing silage or grains
silos n ▷ **silo**
silt n (pl -**s**) mud deposited by moving water ▶ v (-**s**, -**ing**, -**ed**) (foll. by **up**) fill or be choked with silt
silted v ▷ **silt**
silting v ▷ **silt**
silts n, v ▷ **silt**
silvan adj ▷ **sylvan**
silver n (pl -**s**) white precious metal ▶ adj made of or of the colour of silver
silverbeet n (pl -**s**) (AUST & NZ) leafy green

vegetable with white stalks
silverbeets *n* ▷ **silverbeet**
silverfish *n* (*pl* **-es**) small wingless silver-coloured insect
silverfishes *n* ▷ **silverfish**
silvers *n* ▷ **silver**
silverside *n* (*pl* **-s**) cut of beef from below the rump and above the leg
silversides *n* ▷ **silverside**
sim *n* (*pl* **-s**) computer game that simulates an activity such as flying or playing a sport
simian *adj, n* (*pl* **-s**) (of or like) a monkey or ape
simians *n* ▷ **simian**
similar *adj* alike but not identical > **similarity** *n* (*pl* **-s**) > **similarly** *adv*
similarities *n* ▷ **similar**
similarity *n* ▷ **similar**
similarly *adv* ▷ **similar**
simile [sim-ill-ee] *n* (*pl* **-s**) figure of speech comparing one thing to another, using 'as' or 'like'
similes *n* ▷ **simile**
similitude *n* (*pl* **-s**) similarity, likeness
similitudes *n* ▷ **similitude**
simmer *v* (**-s, -ing, -ed**) cook gently at just below boiling point
simmered *v* ▷ **simmer**
simmering *v* ▷ **simmer**
simmers *v* ▷ **simmer**
simper *v* (**-s, -ing, -ed**) smile in a silly or affected way ▶ *n* (*pl* **-s**) simpering smile
simpered *v* ▷ **simper**
simpering *v* ▷ **simper**
simpers *v, n* ▷ **simper**
simple *adj* (**-r, -st**) easy to understand or do > **simply** *adv* > **simplicity** *n* (*pl* **-ties**)
simpler *adj* ▷ **simple**
simplest *adj* ▷ **simple**
simpleton *n* (*pl* **-s**) foolish or half-witted person
simpletons *n* ▷ **simpleton**
simplicities *n* ▷ **simple**
simplicity *n* ▷ **simple**
simplification *n* ▷ **simplify**
simplifications *n* ▷ **simplify**
simplified *v* ▷ **simplify**
simplifies *v* ▷ **simplify**
simplify *v* (**-fies, -fying, -fied**) make less complicated > **simplification** *n* (*pl* **-s**)
simplifying *v* ▷ **simplify**
simplistic *adj* too simple or naive
simply *adv* ▷ **simpl**
sims *n* ▷ **sim**
simulate *v* (**-tes, -ting, -ted**) make a pretence of > **simulation** *n* (*pl* **-s**) > **simulator** *n* (*pl* **-s**)

simulated *v* ▷ **simulate**
simulates *v* ▷ **simulate**
simulating *v* ▷ **simulate**
simulation *n* ▷ **simulate**
simulations *n* ▷ **simulate**
simulator *n* ▷ **simulate**
simulators *n* ▷ **simulate**
simultaneous *adj* occurring at the same time > **simultaneously** *adv*
simultaneously *adv* ▷ **simultaneous**
sin[1] *n* (*pl* **-s**) breaking of a religious or moral law ▶ *v* (**-s, -nning, -nned**) commit a sin > **sinner** *n* (*pl* **-s**)
sin[2] (MATHS) sine
since *prep* during the period of time after ▶ *conj* from the time when ▶ *adv* from that time
sincere *adj* (**-r, -st**) without pretence or deceit > **sincerely** *adv* > **sincerity** *n* (*pl* **-ties**)
sincerely *adv* ▷ **sincere**
sincerer *adj* ▷ **sincere**
sincerest *adj* ▷ **sincere**
sincerities *n* ▷ **sincere**
sincerity *n* ▷ **sincere**
sine *n* (*pl* **-s**) (in trigonometry) ratio of the length of the opposite side to that of the hypotenuse in a right-angled triangle
sinecure [sin-ee-cure] *n* (*pl* **-s**) paid job with minimal duties
sinecures *n* ▷ **sinecure**
sines *n* ▷ **sine**
sinew *n* (*pl* **-s**) tough fibrous tissue joining muscle to bone > **sinewy** *adj* (**-wier, -wiest**)
sinewier *adj* ▷ **sinew**
sinewiest *adj* ▷ **sinew**
sinews *n* ▷ **sinew**
sinewy *adj* ▷ **sinew**
sinful *adj* guilty of sin > **sinfully** *adv*
sinfully *adv* ▷ **sinful**
sing *v* (**-s, -ing, sang, sung**) make musical sounds with the voice
singe *v* (**-ges, -geing, -ged**) burn the surface of ▶ *n* (*pl* **-s**) superficial burn
singed *v* ▷ **singe**
singeing *v* ▷ **singe**
singer *n* (*pl* **-s**) person who sings, esp. professionally
singers *n* ▷ **singer**
singes *v, n* ▷ **singe**
singing *v* ▷ **sing**
single *adj* one only ▶ *n* (*pl* **-s**) single thing ▶ *v* (**-les, -ling, -led**) (*foll. by* **out**) pick out from others > **singly** *adv*
singled *v* ▷ **single**
singles *n, v* ▷ **single** ▶ *pl n* game between two players

singlet n (pl -s) sleeveless vest
  singlets n ▷ singlet
  singling v ▷ single
  singly adv ▷ single
  sings v ▷ sing
singsong n (pl -s) informal singing session
  ▶ adj (of the voice) repeatedly rising and
  falling in pitch
  singsongs n ▷ singsong
singular adj (of a word or form) denoting one
  person or thing ▶ n (pl -s) singular form of a
  word > **singularity** n (pl -ties) > **singularly** adv
  singularities n ▷ singular
  singularity n ▷ singular
  singularly adv ▷ singular
  singulars n ▷ singular
sinister adj threatening or suggesting evil
  or harm
sink v (-s, -ing, sank, sunk or sunken) submerge
  (in liquid) ▶ n (pl -s) fixed basin with a water
  supply and drainage pipe
sinker n (pl -s) weight for a fishing line
  sinkers n ▷ sinker
  sinking v ▷ sink
  sinks v, n ▷ sink
  sinned v ▷ sin¹
  sinner n ▷ sin¹
  sinners n ▷ sin¹
  sinning v ▷ sin¹
  sins n, v ▷ sin¹
sinuous adj curving > **sinuously** adv
  sinuously adv ▷ sinuous
sinus [sine-uss] n (pl -nuses) hollow space in
  a bone, esp. an air passage opening into
  the nose
  sinuses n ▷ sinus
sip v (-s, -pping, -pped) drink in small
  mouthfuls ▶ n (pl -s) amount sipped
siphon n (pl -s) bent tube which uses air
  pressure to draw liquid from a container ▶ v
  (-s, -ing, -ed) draw off thus
  siphoned v ▷ siphon
  siphoning v ▷ siphon
  siphons n, v ▷ siphon
  sipped v ▷ sip
  sipping v ▷ sip
  sips v, n ▷ sip
sir n (pl -s) polite term of address for a man
sire n (pl -s) male parent of a horse or other
  domestic animal ▶ v (-res, -ring, -red) father
  sired v ▷ sire
siren n (pl -s) device making a loud wailing
  noise as a warning
  sirens n ▷ siren
  sires n, v ▷ sire

  siring v ▷ sire
sirloin n (pl -s) prime cut of loin of beef
  sirloins n ▷ sirloin
sirocco n (pl -s) hot wind blowing from N Africa
  into S Europe
  siroccos n ▷ sirocco
  sirs n ▷ sir
sis interj (S AFR) (Informal) exclamation of disgust
sisal [size-al] n (pl -s) (fibre of) plant used in
  making ropes
  sisals n ▷ sisal
siskin n (pl -s) yellow-and-black finch
  siskins n ▷ siskin
  sissier adj ▷ sissy
  sissies n ▷ sissy
  sissiest adj ▷ sissy
sissy adj (-ssier, -ssiest) ▶ n (pl -ssies) weak or
  cowardly (person)
sister n (pl -s) girl or woman with the same
  parents as another person ▶ adj closely
  related, similar > **sisterly** adj
sisterhood n (pl -s) state of being a sister
  sisterhoods n ▷ sisterhood
  sisterly adj ▷ sister
  sisters n ▷ sister
sit v (-s, -tting, sat) rest one's body upright on
  the buttocks
sitar n (pl -s) Indian stringed musical
  instrument
  sitars n ▷ sitar
sitcom n (pl -s) (Informal) situation comedy
  sitcoms n ▷ sitcom
site n (pl -s) place where something is, was, or
  is intended to be located ▷ **website** ▶ v (-tes,
  -ting, -ted) provide with a site
  sited v ▷ site
  sites n, v ▷ site
  siting v ▷ site
  sits v ▷ sit
  sitting v ▷ sit
situate v (-tes, -ting, -ted) place
  situated v ▷ situate
  situates v ▷ situate
  situating v ▷ situate
situation n (pl -s) state of affairs
  situations n ▷ situation
six adj, n (pl -es) one more than five
  sixes n ▷ six
sixteen adj, n (pl -s) six and ten > **sixteenth**
  adj, n (pl -s)
  sixteens n ▷ sixteen
  sixteenth n ▷ sixteen
  sixteenths n ▷ sixteen
sixth adj, n (pl -s) (of) number six in a series
  sixths n ▷ sixth

sixties n ▷ sixty
sixtieth n ▷ sixty
sixtieths n ▷ sixty
sixty adj, n (pl -s) six times ten > **sixtieth** adj,
n (pl -s)
sizable adj ▷ sizeable
size¹ n (pl -s) dimensions, bigness ▶ v (-zes,
-zing, -zed) arrange according to size
size² n (pl -s) gluey substance used as a
protective coating
sizeable, sizable adj quite large
sized v ▷ size¹
sizes n ▷ size¹, ² ▶ v ▷ size¹
sizing v ▷ size¹
sizzle v (-les, -ling, -led) make a hissing sound
like frying fat
sizzled v ▷ sizzle
sizzles v ▷ sizzle
sizzling v ▷ sizzle
skankier adj ▷ skanky
skankiest adj ▷ skanky
skanky adj (-kier, -kiest) (Slang) dirty or
unnattractive
skate¹ n (pl -s) boot with a steel blade or sets of
wheels attached to the sole for gliding over
ice or a hard surface ▶ v (-tes, -ting, -ted) glide
on or as if on skates
skate² n (pl -s) large marine flatfish
skateboard n (pl -s) board mounted on small
wheels for riding on while standing up
> **skateboarding** n (pl -s)
skateboarding n ▷ skateboard
skateboardings n ▷ skateboard
skateboards n ▷ skateboard
skated v ▷ skate¹
skates n ▷ skate¹, ² ▶ v ▷ skate¹
skating v ▷ skate¹
skedaddle v (-les, -ling, -led) (Informal) run off
skedaddled v ▷ skedaddle
skedaddles v ▷ skedaddle
skedaddling v ▷ skedaddle
skein n (pl -s) yarn wound in a loose coil
skeins n ▷ skein
skeletal adj ▷ skeleton
skeleton n (pl -s) framework of bones inside a
person's or animal's body ▶ adj reduced to a
minimum > **skeletal** adj
skeletons n ▷ skeleton
sketch n (pl -es) rough drawing ▶ v (-es, -ing,
-ed) make a sketch (of)
sketched v ▷ sketch
sketches n, v ▷ sketch
sketchier adj ▷ sketchy
sketchiest adj ▷ sketchy
sketching v ▷ sketch

sketchy adj (-chier, -chiest) incomplete or
inadequate
skew v (-s, -ing, -ed) make slanting or crooked
▶ adj slanting or crooked
skewed v ▷ skew
skewer n (pl -s) pin to hold meat together
during cooking ▶ v (-s, -ing, -ed) fasten with
a skewer
skewered v ▷ skewer
skewering v ▷ skewer
skewers n, v ▷ skewer
skewing v ▷ skew
skews v ▷ skew
skewwhiff adj (BRIT) (Informal) slanting or
crooked
ski n (pl -s) one of a pair of long runners
fastened to boots for gliding over snow or
water ▶ v (skis, skiing, skied) travel on skis
> **skier** n (pl -s)
skid v (-s, -dding, -dded) (of a moving vehicle)
slide sideways uncontrollably ▶ n (pl -s)
skidding
skidded v ▷ skid
skidding v ▷ skid
skids v, n ▷ skid
skied v ▷ ski
skier n ▷ ski
skiers n ▷ ski
skies n ▷ sky
skiff n (pl -s) small boat
skiffs n ▷ skiff
skiing v ▷ ski
skilful adj having or showing skill > **skilfully**
adv
skilfully adv ▷ skilful
skill n (pl -s) special ability or expertise
> **skilled** adj
skilled adj ▷ skill
skillet n (pl -s) small frying pan or shallow
cooking pot
skillets n ▷ skillet
skills n ▷ skill
skim v (-s, -mming, -mmed) remove floating
matter from the surface of (a liquid)
skimmed v ▷ skim
skimming v ▷ skim
skimp v (-s, -ing, -ed) not invest enough time,
money, material, etc.
skimped v ▷ skimp
skimpier adj ▷ skimpy
skimpiest adj ▷ skimpy
skimping v ▷ skimp
skimps v ▷ skimp
skimpy adj (-pier, -piest) scanty or insufficient
skims v ▷ skim

skin n (pl -s) outer covering of the body ▶ v (-s, -nning, -nned) remove the skin of > **skinless** adj

skinflint n (pl -s) miser
  skinflints n ▷ **skinflint**

skinhead n (pl -s) youth with very short hair
  skinheads n ▷ **skinhead**
  skinless adj ▷ **skin**
  skinned v ▷ **skin**
  skinnier adj ▷ **skinny**
  skinniest adj ▷ **skinny**
  skinning v ▷ **skin**

skinny adj (-nnier, -nniest) thin
  skins n, v ▷ **skin**

skint adj (BRIT) (Slang) having no money

skip[1] v (-s, -pping, -pped) leap lightly from one foot to the other ▶ n (pl -s) skipping

skip[2] n (pl -s) large open container for builders' rubbish
  skipped v ▷ **skip**[1]

skipper n (pl -s) ▶ v (-s, -ing, -ed) captain
  skippered v ▷ **skipper**
  skippering v ▷ **skipper**
  skippers n, v ▷ **skipper**
  skipping v ▷ **skip**[1]
  skips v ▷ **skip**[1] ▶ n ▷ **skip**[1, 2]

skirl n (pl -s) sound of bagpipes
  skirls n ▷ **skirl**

skirmish n (pl -es) brief or minor fight or argument ▶ v (-es, -ing, -ed) take part in a skirmish
  skirmished v ▷ **skirmish**
  skirmishes n, v ▷ **skirmish**
  skirmishing v ▷ **skirmish**

skirt n (pl -s) woman's garment hanging from the waist ▶ v (-s, -ing, -ed) border
  skirted v ▷ **skirt**
  skirting v ▷ **skirt**
  skirts n, v ▷ **skirt**
  skis n, v ▷ **ski**

skit n (pl -s) brief satirical sketch

skite v (-tes, -ting, -ted) ▶ n (pl -s) (AUST & NZ) boast
  skited v ▷ **skite**
  skites v, n ▷ **skite**
  skiting v ▷ **skite**
  skits n ▷ **skit**

skittish adj playful or lively

skittle n (pl -s) bottle-shaped object used as a target in some games

skittles n ▷ **skittle** ▶ pl n game in which players try to knock over skittles by rolling a ball at them

skive v (-ves, -ving, -ved) (BRIT) (Informal) evade work or responsibility

skived v ▷ **skive**
skives v ▷ **skive**
skiving v ▷ **skive**
skivvies n ▷ **skivvy**

skivvy n (pl -vies) (BRIT) female servant who does menial work

skua n (pl -s) large predatory gull
  skuas n ▷ **skua**
  skulduggeries n ▷ **skulduggery**

skulduggery n (pl -ries) (Informal) trickery

skulk v (-s, -ing, -ed) move stealthily
  skulked v ▷ **skulk**
  skulking v ▷ **skulk**
  skulks v ▷ **skulk**

skull n (pl -s) bony framework of the head

skullcap n (pl -s) close-fitting brimless cap
  skullcaps n ▷ **skullcap**
  skulls n ▷ **skull**

skunk n (pl -s) small black-and-white N American mammal which emits a foul-smelling fluid when attacked
  skunks n ▷ **skunk**

sky n (pl skies) upper atmosphere as seen from the earth

skydiving n (pl -s) sport of jumping from an aircraft and performing manoeuvres before opening one's parachute
  skydivings n ▷ **skydiving**

skylark n (pl -s) lark that sings while soaring at a great height
  skylarks n ▷ **skylark**

skylight n (pl -s) window in a roof or ceiling
  skylights n ▷ **skylight**

skyscraper n (pl -s) very tall building
  skyscrapers n ▷ **skyscraper**

slab n (pl -s) broad flat piece
  slabs n ▷ **slab**

slack adj (-er, -est) not tight ▶ n (pl -s) slack part ▶ v (-s, -ing, -ed) neglect one's work or duty > **slacker** n (pl -s) > **slackness** n (pl -es)
  slacked v ▷ **slack**

slacken v (-s, -ing, -ed) make or become slack
  slackened v ▷ **slacken**
  slackening v ▷ **slacken**
  slackens v ▷ **slacken**
  slacker n, adj ▷ **slack**
  slackers n ▷ **slack**
  slackest adj ▷ **slack**
  slacking v ▷ **slack**
  slackness n ▷ **slack**
  slacknesses n ▷ **slack**

slacks n, v ▷ **slack** ▶ pl n informal trousers

slag n (pl -s) waste left after metal is smelted ▶ v (-s, -gging, -gged) (foll. by **off**) (BRIT, AUST & NZ) (Slang) criticize

slagged v ▷ **slag**
slagging v ▷ **slag**
slags n, v ▷ **slag**
slain v ▷ **slay**
slake v (**-kes, -king, -ked**) satisfy (thirst or desire)
slaked v ▷ **slake**
slakes v ▷ **slake**
slaking v ▷ **slake**
slalom n (pl **-s**) skiing or canoeing race over a winding course
slaloms n ▷ **slalom**
slam v (**-s, -mming, -mmed**) shut, put down, or hit violently and noisily ▶ n (pl **-s**) act or sound of slamming
slammed v ▷ **slam**
slamming v ▷ **slam**
slams v, n ▷ **slam**
slander n (pl **-s**) false and malicious statement about a person ▶ v (**-s, -ing, -ed**) utter slander about > **slanderous** adj
slandered v ▷ **slander**
slandering v ▷ **slander**
slanderous adj ▷ **slander**
slanders n, v ▷ **slander**
slang n (pl **-s**) very informal language > **slangy** adj (**-gier, -giest**)
slangier adj ▷ **slang**
slangiest adj ▷ **slang**
slangs n ▷ **slang**
slangy adj ▷ **slang**
slant v (**-s, -ing, -ed**) lean at an angle, slope ▶ n (pl **-s**) slope > **slanting** adj
slanted v ▷ **slant**
slanting v, adj ▷ **slant**
slants v, n ▷ **slant**
slap n (pl **-s**) blow with the open hand or a flat object ▶ v (**-s, -pping, -pped**) strike with the open hand or a flat object
slapdash adj careless and hasty
slaphappy adj (Informal) cheerfully careless
slapped v ▷ **slap**
slapping v ▷ **slap**
slaps n, v ▷ **slap**
slapstick n (pl **-s**) boisterous knockabout comedy
slapsticks n ▷ **slapstick**
slash v (**-es, -ing, -ed**) cut with a sweeping stroke ▶ n (pl **-es**) sweeping stroke
slashed v ▷ **slash**
slashes v, n ▷ **slash**
slashing v ▷ **slash**
slat n (pl **-s**) narrow strip of wood or metal
slate¹ n (pl **-s**) rock which splits easily into thin layers

slate² v (**-tes, -ting, -ted**) (Informal) criticize harshly
slated v ▷ **slate²**
slates n ▷ **slate¹** ▶ v ▷ **slate²**
slating v ▷ **slate²**
slats n ▷ **slat**
slattern n (pl **-s**) (Old-fashioned) slovenly woman > **slatternly** adj
slatternly adv ▷ **slattern**
slatterns n ▷ **slattern**
slaughter v (**-s, -ing, -ed**) kill (animals) for food ▶ n (pl **-s**) slaughtering
slaughtered v ▷ **slaughter**
slaughterhouse n (pl **-s**) place where animals are killed for food
slaughterhouses n ▷ **slaughterhouse**
slaughtering v ▷ **slaughter**
slaughters v, n ▷ **slaughter**
slave n (pl **-s**) person owned by another for whom he or she has to work ▶ v (**-ves, -ing, -ved**) work like a slave
slaved v ▷ **slave**
slaver n (pl **-s**) person or ship engaged in the slave trade ▶ v [slav-ver] (**-s, -ing, -ed**) dribble saliva from the mouth
slavered v ▷ **slaver**
slaveries n ▷ **slavery**
slavering v ▷ **slaver**
slavers n, v ▷ **slaver**
slavery n (pl **-ries**) state or condition of being a slave
slaves v, n ▷ **slave**
slaving v ▷ **slave**
slavish adj of or like a slave
slay v (**-s, -ing, slew, slain**) kill
slaying v ▷ **slay**
slays v ▷ **slay**
sleazes n ▷ **sleaze**
sleazier adj ▷ **sleazy**
sleaziest adj ▷ **sleazy**
sleazy adj (**-zier, -ziest**) run-down or sordid > **sleaze** n (pl **-s**)
sled n (pl **-s**) ▶ v (**-s, -dding, -dded**) ▷
sledded v ▷ **sled**
sledding v ▷ **sled**
sledge¹ n (pl **-s**) carriage on runners for sliding on snow ▶ v (**-dges, -dging, -dged**) travel by sledge
sledge², **sledgehammer** n (pl **-s**) heavy hammer with a long handle
sledged v ▷ **sledge¹**
sledgehammer n ▷ **sledge**
sledgehammers n ▷ **sledge**
sledges n ▷ **sledge¹, ²** ▶ v ▷ **sledge¹**
sledging v ▷ **sledge¹**

sleds *n, v* ▷ **sled**
sleek *adj* (**-er, -est**) glossy, smooth, and shiny
  sleeker *adj* ▷ **sleek**
  sleekest *adj* ▷ **sleek**
sleep *n* (*pl* **-s**) state of rest characterized by
  unconsciousness ▶ *v* (**-s, -ing, slept**) be in
  or as if in a state of sleep > **sleepy** *adj* (**-pier,
  -piest**) > **sleepily** *adv* > **sleepiness** *n* (*pl* **-es**)
  > **sleepless** *adj*
sleeper *n* (*pl* **-s**) railway car fitted for sleeping
  in
  sleepers *n* ▷ **sleeper**
  sleepier *adj* ▷ **sleep**
  sleepiest *adj* ▷ **sleep**
  sleepily *adv* ▷ **sleep**
  sleepiness *n* ▷ **sleep**
  sleepinesses *n* ▷ **sleep**
  sleeping *v* ▷ **sleep**
  sleepless *adj* ▷ **sleep**
sleepout *n* (*pl* **-s**) (NZ) small building for
  sleeping in
  sleepouts *n* ▷ **sleepout**
sleepover *n* (*pl* **-s**) occasion when a person
  stays overnight at a friend's house
  sleepovers *n* ▷ **sleepover**
  sleeps *n, v* ▷ **sleep**
  sleepy *adj* ▷ **sleep**
sleet *n* (*pl* **-s**) rain and snow or hail falling
  together
  sleets *n* ▷ **sleet**
sleeve *n* (*pl* **-s**) part of a garment which covers
  the arm > **sleeveless** *adj*
  sleeveless *adj* ▷ **sleeve**
  sleeves *n* ▷ **sleeve**
sleigh *n* (*pl* **-s**) ▶ *v* (**-s, -ing, -ed**) sledge
  sleighed *v* ▷ **sleigh**
  sleighing *v* ▷ **sleigh**
  sleighs *n, v* ▷ **sleigh**
slender *adj* (**-er, -est**) slim
  slenderer *adj* ▷ **slender**
  slenderest *adj* ▷ **slender**
  slept *v* ▷ **sleep**
sleuth [slooth] *n* (*pl* **-s**) detective
  sleuths *n* ▷ **sleuth**
  slew[1] *v* ▷ **slay**
slew[2] *v* (**-s, -ing, -ed**) twist or swing round
  slewed *v* ▷ **slew**[2]
  slewing *v* ▷ **slew**[2]
  slews *v* ▷ **slew**[2]
slice *n* (*pl* **-s**) thin flat piece cut from something
  ▶ *v* (**-ces, -cing, -ced**) cut into slices
  sliced *v* ▷ **slice**
  slices *n, v* ▷ **slice**
  slicing *v* ▷ **slice**
slick *adj* (**-er, -est**) persuasive and glib ▶ *n* (*pl* **-s**)

patch of oil on water ▶ *v* (**-s, -ing, -ed**) make
  smooth or sleek
  slicked *v* ▷ **slick**
  slicker *adj* ▷ **slick**
  slickest *adj* ▷ **slick**
  slicking *v* ▷ **slick**
  slicks *n, v* ▷ **slick**
  slid *v* ▷ **slide**
slide *v* (**-des, -ding, slid**) slip smoothly along (a
  surface) ▶ *n* (*pl* **-s**) sliding
  slides *v, n* ▷ **slide**
  sliding *v* ▷ **slide**
  slier *adj* ▷ **sly**
  sliest *adj* ▷ **sly**
slight *adj* (**-er, -est**) small in quantity or extent
  ▶ *v* (**-s, -ing, -ed**) ▶ *n* (*pl* **-s**) snub > **slightly** *adv*
  slighted *v* ▷ **slight**
  slighter *adj* ▷ **slight**
  slightest *adj* ▷ **slight**
  slighting *v* ▷ **slight**
  slightly *adv* ▷ **slight**
  slights *v, n* ▷ **slight**
slim *adj* (**-mmer, -mmest**) not heavy or stout,
  thin ▶ *v* (**-s, -mming, -mmed**) make or become
  slim by diet and exercise > **slimmer** *n* (*pl* **-s**)
slime *n* (*pl* **-s**) unpleasant thick slippery
  substance
  slimes *n* ▷ **slime**
  slimier *adj* ▷ **slimy**
  slimiest *adj* ▷ **slimy**
  slimmed *v* ▷ **slim**
  slimmer *adj, n* ▷ **slim**
  slimmers *n* ▷ **slim**
  slimmest *adj* ▷ **slim**
  slimming *v* ▷ **slim**
  slims *v* ▷ **slim**
slimy *adj* (**-mier, -miest**) of, like, or covered
  with slime
sling[1] *n* (*pl* **-s**) bandage hung from the neck to
  support an injured hand or arm ▶ *v* (**-s, -ing,
  slung**) throw
sling[2] *n* (*pl* **-s**) sweetened drink with a spirit
  base
  slinging *v* ▷ **sling**[1]
  slings *n* ▷ **sling**[1, 2] ▶ *v* ▷ **sling**[1]
slink *v* (**-s, -ing, slunk**) move furtively or guiltily
  slinkier *adj* ▷ **slinky**
  slinkiest *adj* ▷ **slinky**
  slinking *v* ▷ **slink**
  slinks *v* ▷ **slink**
slinky *adj* (**-kier, -kiest**) (of clothes) figure-
  hugging
slip[1] *v* (**-s, -pping, -pped**) lose balance by sliding
  ▶ *n* (*pl* **-s**) slipping
slip[2] *n* (*pl* **-s**) small piece (of paper)

slip³ n (pl **-s**) clay mixed with water used for decorating pottery
slipknot n (pl **-s**) knot tied so that it will slip along the rope round which it is made
  slipknots n ▷ **slipknot**
  slipped v ▷ **slip¹**
slipper n (pl **-s**) light shoe for indoor wear
  slipperier adj ▷ **slippery**
  slipperiest adj ▷ **slippery**
  slippers n ▷ **slipper**
slippery adj (**-rier, -riest**) so smooth or wet as to cause slipping or be difficult to hold
  slippier adj ▷ **slippy**
  slippiest adj ▷ **slippy**
  slipping v ▷ **slip¹**
slippy adj (**-pier, -piest**) (Informal) slippery
  slips n ▷ **slip¹·²·³** ▶ v ▷ **slip¹**
slipshod adj (of an action) careless
slipstream n (pl **-s**) stream of air forced backwards by a fast-moving object
  slipstreams n ▷ **slipstream**
slipway n (pl **-s**) launching slope on which ships are built or repaired
  slipways n ▷ **slipway**
slit n (pl **-s**) long narrow cut or opening ▶ v (**-s, -tting, slit**) make a long straight cut in
slither v (**-s, -ing, -ed**) slide unsteadily
  slithered v ▷ **slither**
  slithering v ▷ **slither**
  slithers v ▷ **slither**
  slits n, v ▷ **slit**
  slitting v ▷ **slit**
sliver [sliv-ver] n (pl **-s**) small thin piece
  slivers n ▷ **sliver**
slob n (pl **-s**) (Informal) lazy and untidy person
  > **slobbish** adj
slobber v (**-s, -ing, -ed**) dribble or drool
  > **slobbery** adj
  slobbered v ▷ **slobber**
  slobbering v ▷ **slobber**
  slobbers v ▷ **slobber**
  slobbery adj ▷ **slobber**
  slobbish adj ▷ **slob**
  slobs n ▷ **slob**
sloe n (pl **-s**) sour blue-black fruit
  sloes n ▷ **sloe**
slog v (**-s, -gging, -gged**) work hard and steadily ▶ n (pl **-s**) long and exhausting work or walk
slogan n (pl **-s**) catchword or phrase used in politics or advertising
  slogans n ▷ **slogan**
  slogged v ▷ **slog**
  slogging v ▷ **slog**
  slogs v, n ▷ **slog**

sloop n (pl **-s**) small single-masted ship
  sloops n ▷ **sloop**
slop v (**-s, -pping, -pped**) splash or spill ▶ n (pl **-s**) spilt liquid
slope v (**-pes, -ping, -ped**) slant ▶ n (pl **-s**) sloping surface
  sloped v ▷ **slope**
  slopes v, n ▷ **slope** ▶ pl n hills
  sloping v ▷ **slope**
  slopped v ▷ **slop**
  sloppier adj ▷ **sloppy**
  sloppiest adj ▷ **sloppy**
  slopping v ▷ **slop**
sloppy adj (**-ppier, -ppiest**) careless or untidy
  slops v, n ▷ **slop** ▶ pl n liquid refuse and waste food used to feed animals
slosh v (**-es, -ing, -ed**) splash carelessly ▶ n (pl **-es**) splashing sound
  sloshed adj (Slang) drunk ▶ v ▷ **slosh**
  sloshes v, n ▷ **slosh**
  sloshing v ▷ **slosh**
slot n (pl **-s**) narrow opening for inserting something ▶ v (**-s, -tting, -tted**) make a slot or slots in
sloth [rhymes with **both**] n (pl **-s**) slow-moving animal of tropical America
slothful adj lazy or idle
  sloths n ▷ **sloth**
  slots n, v ▷ **slot**
  slotted v ▷ **slot**
  slotting v ▷ **slot**
slouch v (**-es, -ing, -ed**) sit, stand, or move with a drooping posture ▶ n (pl **-es**) drooping posture
  slouched v ▷ **slouch**
  slouches v, n ▷ **slouch**
  slouching v ▷ **slouch**
slough¹ [rhymes with **now**] n (pl **-s**) bog
slough² [sluff] v (**-s, -ing, -ed**) (of a snake) shed (its skin) or (of a skin) be shed
  sloughed v ▷ **slough²**
  sloughing v ▷ **slough²**
  sloughs n ▷ **slough¹** ▶ v ▷ **slough²**
sloven n (pl **-s**) habitually dirty or untidy person
  slovenlier adj ▷ **slovenly**
  slovenliest adj ▷ **slovenly**
slovenly adj (**-lier, -liest**) dirty or untidy
  slovens n ▷ **sloven**
slow adj (**-er, -est**) taking a longer time than is usual or expected ▶ v (**-s, -ing, -ed**) reduce the speed (of) > **slowly** adv > **slowness** n (pl **-es**)
slowcoach n (pl **-es**) (Informal) person who moves or works slowly
  slowcoaches n ▷ **slowcoach**

slowed v ▷ **slow**
slower adj ▷ **slow**
slowest adj ▷ **slow**
slowing v ▷ **slow**
slowly adv ▷ **slow**
slowness n ▷ **slow**
slownesses n ▷ **slow**
slows v ▷ **slow**
slowworm n (pl -s) small legless lizard
slowworms n ▷ **slowworm**
sludge n (pl -s) thick mud
sludges n ▷ **sludge**
slug¹ n (pl -s) land snail with no shell
slug² n (pl -s) bullet (Informal)
slug³ v (-s, -gging, -gged) hit hard ▶ n (pl -s) heavy blow
sluggard n (pl -s) lazy person
sluggards n ▷ **sluggard**
slugged v ▷ **slug³**
slugging v ▷ **slug³**
sluggish adj slow-moving, lacking energy > **sluggishly** adv > **sluggishness** n (pl -es)
sluggishly adv ▷ **sluggish**
sluggishness n ▷ **sluggish**
sluggishnesses n ▷ **sluggish**
slugs n ▷ **slug¹, ², ³** ▶ v ▷ **slug³**
sluice n (pl -s) channel carrying off water ▶ v (-ces, -cing, -ced) pour a stream of water over or through
sluiced v ▷ **sluice**
sluices n, v ▷ **sluice**
sluicing v ▷ **sluice**
slum n (pl -s) squalid overcrowded house or area ▶ v (-s, -mming, -mmed) temporarily and deliberately experience poorer places or conditions than usual
slumber v (-s, -ing, -ed) ▶ n (pl -s) (Lit) sleep
slumbered v ▷ **slumber**
slumbering v ▷ **slumber**
slumbers v, n ▷ **slumber**
slummed v ▷ **slum**
slumming v ▷ **slum**
slump v (-s, -ing, -ed) (of prices or demand) decline suddenly ▶ n (pl -s) sudden decline in prices or demand
slumped v ▷ **slump**
slumping v ▷ **slump**
slumps v, n ▷ **slump**
slums n, v ▷ **slum**
slung v ▷ **sling¹**
slunk v ▷ **slink**
slur v (-s, -rring, -rred) pronounce or utter (words) indistinctly ▶ n (pl -s) slurring of words
slurp (Informal) v (-s, -ing, -ed) eat or drink

noisily ▶ n (pl -s) slurping sound
slurped v ▷ **slurp**
slurping v ▷ **slurp**
slurps v, n ▷ **slurp**
slurred v ▷ **slur**
slurries n ▷ **slurry**
slurring v ▷ **slur**
slurry n (pl -ries) muddy liquid mixture
slurs v, n ▷ **slur**
slush n (pl -es) watery muddy substance > **slushy** adj (-shier, -shiest)
slushes n ▷ **slush**
slushier adj ▷ **slush**
slushiest adj ▷ **slush**
slushy adj ▷ **slush**
sly adj (**slyer, slyest** or **slier, sliest**) crafty > **slyly** adv > **slyness** n (pl -es)
slyer adj ▷ **sly**
slyest adj ▷ **sly**
slyly adv ▷ **sly**
slyness n ▷ **sly**
slynesses n ▷ **sly**
smack¹ v (-s, -ing, -ed) slap sharply ▶ n (pl -s) sharp slap ▶ adv (Informal) squarely or directly
smack² n (pl -s) slight flavour or trace ▶ v (-s, -ing, -ed) have a slight flavour or trace (of)
smack³ n (pl -s) small single-masted fishing boat
smacked v ▷ **smack¹, ²**
smacker n (pl -s) (Slang) loud kiss
smackers n ▷ **smacker**
smacking v ▷ **smack¹, ²**
smacks n ▷ **smack¹, ², ³** ▶ v ▷ **smack¹, ²**
small adj (-er, -est) not large in size, number, or amount ▶ n (pl -s) narrow part of the lower back > **smallness** n (pl -es)
smaller adj ▷ **small**
smallest adj ▷ **small**
smallholding n (pl -s) small area of farming land
smallholdings n ▷ **smallholding**
smallness n ▷ **small**
smallnesses n ▷ **small**
smallpox n (pl -es) contagious disease with blisters that leave scars
smallpoxes n ▷ **smallpox**
smalls n ▷ **small** ▶ pl n (Informal) underwear
smarmier adj ▷ **smarmy**
smarmiest adj ▷ **smarmy**
smarmy adj (-mier, -miest) (Informal) unpleasantly suave or flattering
smart adj (-er, -est) well-kept and neat ▶ v (-s, -ing, -ed) feel or cause stinging pain ▶ n (pl -s) stinging pain > **smartly** adv > **smartness** n (pl -es)

smarted v ▷ smart
smarten v (-s, -ing, -ed) make or become smart
smartened v ▷ smarten
smartening v ▷ smarten
smartens v ▷ smarten
smarter adj ▷ smart
smartest adj ▷ smart
smarting v ▷ smart
smartly adv ▷ smart
smartness n ▷ smart
smartnesses n ▷ smart
smarts v, n ▷ smart
smash v (-es, -ing, -ed) break violently and noisily ▶ n (pl -es) act or sound of smashing
smashed v ▷ smash
smasher n (pl -s) (Informal) attractive person or thing
smashers n ▷ smasher
smashes v, n ▷ smash
smashing adj (Informal) excellent ▶ v ▷ **smash**
smattering n (pl -s) slight knowledge
smatterings n ▷ smattering
smear v (-s, -ing, -ed) spread with a greasy or sticky substance ▶ n (pl -s) dirty mark or smudge
smeared v ▷ smear
smearing v ▷ smear
smears v, n ▷ smear
smell v (-s, -ing, smelt or -ed) perceive (a scent or odour) by means of the nose ▶ n (pl -s) ability to perceive odours by the nose
smelled v ▷ smell
smellier adj ▷ smelly
smelliest adj ▷ smelly
smelling v ▷ smell
smells v, n ▷ smell
smelly adj (-lier, -liest) having a nasty smell
smelt¹ v (-s, -ing, -ed) extract (a metal) from (an ore) by heating
smelt² n (pl smelt) small fish of the salmon family
smelt³ v ▷ smell
smelted v ▷ smelt¹
smelter n (pl -s) industrial plant where smelting is carried out
smelters n ▷ smelter
smelting v ▷ smelt¹
smelts v ▷ smelt¹
smile n (pl -s) turning up of the corners of the mouth to show pleasure, amusement, or friendliness ▶ v (-les, -ing, -led) give a smile
smiled v ▷ smile
smiles n, v ▷ smile
smiley n (pl -s) symbol depicting a smile or other facial expression, used in e-mail
smileys n ▷ smiley
smiling v ▷ smile
smirch v (-es, -ing, -ed) ▶ n (pl -es) stain
smirched v ▷ smirch
smirches v, n ▷ smirch
smirching v ▷ smirch
smirk n (pl -s) smug smile ▶ v (-s, -ing, -ed) give a smirk
smirked v ▷ smirk
smirking v ▷ smirk
smirks n, v ▷ smirk
smite v (-tes, -ting, smote, smitten) (Old-fashioned) strike hard
smites v ▷ smite
smith n (pl -s) worker in metal
smithereens pl n shattered fragments
smithies n ▷ smithy
smiths n ▷ smith
smithy n (pl -thies) blacksmith's workshop
smiting v ▷ smite
smitten v ▷ smite
smock n (pl -s) loose overall ▶ v (-s, -ing, -ed) gather (material) by sewing in a honeycomb pattern > **smocking** n (pl -s)
smocked v ▷ smock
smocking v, n ▷ smock
smockings n ▷ smock
smocks n, v ▷ smock
smog n (pl -s) mixture of smoke and fog
smogs n ▷ smog
smoke n (pl -s) cloudy mass that rises from something burning ▶ v (-kes, -king, -ked) give off smoke > **smokeless** adj > **smoker** n (pl -s) > **smoky** adj (-kier, -kiest)
smoked v ▷ smoke
smokeless adj ▷ smoke
smoker n ▷ smok
smokers n ▷ smok
smokes n, v ▷ smoke
smokier adj ▷ smoke
smokiest adj ▷ smoke
smoking v ▷ smoke
smoky adj ▷ smoke
smooch (Informal) v (-es, -ing, -ed) kiss and cuddle ▶ n (pl -es) smooching
smooched v ▷ smooch
smooches v, n ▷ smooch
smooching v ▷ smooch
smooth adj (-er, -est) even in surface, texture, or consistency ▶ v (-s, -ing, -ed) make smooth > **smoothly** adv
smoothed v ▷ smooth
smoother adj ▷ smooth
smoothest adj ▷ smooth

smoothie *n* (*pl* -**thies**) (*Informal*) charming but possibly insincere man
  smoothies *n* ▷ smoothie
  smoothing *v* ▷ smooth
  smoothly *adv* ▷ smooth
  smooths *v* ▷ smooth
smorgasbord *n* (*pl* -**s**) buffet meal of assorted dishes
  smorgasbords *n* ▷ smorgasbord
  smote *v* ▷ smite
smother *v* (-**s**, -**ing**, -**ed**) suffocate or stifle
  smothered *v* ▷ smother
  smothering *v* ▷ smother
  smothers *v* ▷ smother
smoulder *v* (-**s**, -**ing**, -**ed**) burn slowly with smoke but no flame
  smouldered *v* ▷ smoulder
  smouldering *v* ▷ smoulder
  smoulders *v* ▷ smoulder
smudge *v* (-**ges**, -**ging**, -**ged**) make or become smeared or soiled ▶ *n* (*pl* -**s**) dirty mark > **smudgy** *adj* (-**gier**, -**giest**)
  smudged *v* ▷ smudge
  smudges *v*, *n* ▷ smudge
  smudgier *adj* ▷ smudge
  smudgiest *adj* ▷ smudge
  smudging *v* ▷ smudge
  smudgy *adj* ▷ smudge
smug *adj* (-**gger**, -**ggest**) self-satisfied > **smugly** *adv* > **smugness** *n* (*pl* -**es**)
  smugger *adj* ▷ smug
  smuggest *adj* ▷ smug
smuggle *v* (-**les**, -**ling**, -**led**) import or export (goods) secretly and illegally > **smuggler** *n* (*pl* -**s**)
  smuggled *v* ▷ smuggle
  smuggler *n* ▷ smuggle
  smugglers *n* ▷ smuggle
  smuggles *v* ▷ smuggle
  smuggling *v* ▷ smuggle
  smugly *adv* ▷ smug
  smugness *n* ▷ smug
  smugnesses *n* ▷ smug
smut *n* (*pl* -**s**) obscene jokes, pictures, etc. > **smutty** *adj* (-**tier**, -**tiest**)
  smuts *n* ▷ smut
  smuttier *adj* ▷ smut
  smuttiest *adj* ▷ smut
  smutty *adj* ▷ smut
snack *n* (*pl* -**s**) light quick meal
  snacks *n* ▷ snack
snaffle *n* (*pl* -**s**) jointed bit for a horse ▶ *v* (-**les**, -**ling**, -**led**) (BRIT, AUST & NZ) (*Slang*) steal
  snaffled *v* ▷ snaffle
  snaffles *n*, *v* ▷ snaffle

  snaffling *v* ▷ snaffle
snag *n* (*pl* -**s**) difficulty or disadvantage ▶ *v* (-**s**, -**gging**, -**gged**) catch or tear on a point
  snagged *v* ▷ snag
  snagging *v* ▷ snag
  snags *n*, *v* ▷ snag
snail *n* (*pl* -**s**) slow-moving mollusc with a spiral shell
  snails *n* ▷ snail
snake *n* (*pl* -**s**) long thin scaly limbless reptile ▶ *v* (-**kes**, -**king**, -**ked**) move in a winding course like a snake
  snaked *v* ▷ snake
  snakes *n*, *v* ▷ snake
  snakier *adj* ▷ snaky
  snakiest *adj* ▷ snaky
  snaking *v* ▷ snake
snaky *adj* (-**kier**, -**kiest**) twisted or winding
snap *v* (-**s**, -**pping**, -**pped**) break suddenly ▶ *n* (*pl* -**s**) act or sound of snapping ▶ *adj* made on the spur of the moment
snapdragon *n* (*pl* -**s**) plant with flowers that can open and shut like a mouth
  snapdragons *n* ▷ snapdragon
  snapped *v* ▷ snap
snapper *n* (*pl* -**s**) food fish of Australia and New Zealand with a pinkish body covered with blue spots
  snappers *n* ▷ snapper
  snappier *adj* ▷ snappy
  snappiest *adj* ▷ snappy
  snapping *v* ▷ snap
  snappish *adj* ▷ snappy
snappy *adj* (-**ppier**, -**ppiest**) (*also* **snappish**) irritable
  snaps *v*, *n* ▷ snap
snapshot *n* (*pl* -**s**) informal photograph
  snapshots *n* ▷ snapshot
snare *n* (*pl* -**s**) trap with a noose ▶ *v* (-**res**, -**ring**, -**red**) catch in or as if in a snare
  snared *v* ▷ snare
  snares *n*, *v* ▷ snare
  snaring *v* ▷ snare
snarl[1] *v* (-**s**, -**ing**, -**ed**) (of an animal) growl with bared teeth ▶ *n* (*pl* -**s**) act or sound of snarling
snarl[2] *n* (*pl* -**s**) tangled mess ▶ *v* (-**s**, -**ing**, -**ed**) make tangled
  snarled *v* ▷ snarl[1, 2]
  snarling *v* ▷ snarl[1, 2]
  snarls *n*, *v* ▷ snarl[1, 2]
snatch *v* (-**es**, -**ing**, -**ed**) seize or try to seize suddenly ▶ *n* (*pl* -**es**) snatching
  snatched *v* ▷ snatch
  snatches *v*, *n* ▷ snatch
  snatching *v* ▷ snatch

snazzier *adj* ▷ **snazzy**
snazziest *adj* ▷ **snazzy**
snazzy *adj* (**-zzier, -zziest**) (*Informal*) stylish and flashy
sneak *v* (**-s, -ing, -ed**) move furtively ▶ *n* (*pl* **-s**) cowardly or underhand person > **sneaky** *adj* (**-kier, -kiest**)
sneaked *v* ▷ **sneak**
sneakers *pl n* canvas shoes with rubber soles
sneakier *adj* ▷ **sneak**
sneakiest *adj* ▷ **sneak**
sneaking *adj* slight but persistent ▶ *v* ▷ **sneak**
sneaks *v, n* ▷ **sneak**
sneaky *adj* ▷ **sneak**
sneer *n* (*pl* **-s**) contemptuous expression or remark ▶ *v* (**-s, -ing, -ed**) show contempt by a sneer
sneered *v* ▷ **sneer**
sneering *v* ▷ **sneer**
sneers *n, v* ▷ **sneer**
sneeze *v* (**-zes, -zing, -zed**) expel air from the nose suddenly, involuntarily, and noisily ▶ *n* (*pl* **-s**) act or sound of sneezing
sneezed *v* ▷ **sneeze**
sneezes *v, n* ▷ **sneeze**
sneezing *v* ▷ **sneeze**
snicker *n* (*pl* **-s**) ▶ *v* (**-s, -ing, -ed**) ▷ **snigger**
snickered *v* ▷ **snicker**
snickering *v* ▷ **snicker**
snickers *n, v* ▷ **snicker**
snide *adj* (**-r, -st**) critical in an unfair and nasty way
snider *adj* ▷ **snide**
snidest *adj* ▷ **snide**
sniff *v* (**-s, -ing, -ed**) inhale through the nose in short audible breaths ▶ *n* (*pl* **-s**) act or sound of sniffing
sniffed *v* ▷ **sniff**
sniffing *v* ▷ **sniff**
sniffle *v* (**-les, -ling, -led**) sniff repeatedly, as when suffering from a cold ▶ *n* (*pl* **-s**) slight cold
sniffled *v* ▷ **sniffle**
sniffles *v, n* ▷ **sniffle**
sniffling *v* ▷ **sniffle**
sniffs *v, n* ▷ **sniff**
snifter *n* (*pl* **-s**) (*Informal*) small quantity of alcoholic drink
snifters *n* ▷ **snifter**
snigger *n* (*pl* **-s**) sly disrespectful laugh, esp. one partly stifled ▶ *v* (**-s, -ing, -ed**) utter a snigger
sniggered *v* ▷ **snigger**
sniggering *v* ▷ **snigger**
sniggers *n, v* ▷ **snigger**

snip *v* (**-s, -pping, -pped**) cut in small quick strokes with scissors or shears ▶ *n* (*pl* **-s**) (*Informal*) bargain
snipe *n* (*pl* **-s**) wading bird with a long straight bill ▶ *v* (**-pes, -ping, -ped**) (*foll. by* **at**) shoot at (a person) from cover
sniped *v* ▷ **snipe**
sniper *n* (*pl* **-s**) person who shoots at someone from cover
snipers *n* ▷ **sniper**
snipes *n, v* ▷ **snipe**
sniping *v* ▷ **snipe**
snipped *v* ▷ **snip**
snippet *n* (*pl* **-s**) small piece
snippets *n* ▷ **snippet**
snipping *v* ▷ **snip**
snips *v, n* ▷ **snip**
snitch (*Informal*) *v* (**-es, -ing, -ed**) act as an informer ▶ *n* (*pl* **-es**) informer
snitched *v* ▷ **snitch**
snitches *v, n* ▷ **snitch**
snitching *v* ▷ **snitch**
snivel *v* (**-s, -lling, -lled**) cry in a whining way
snivelled *v* ▷ **snivel**
snivelling *v* ▷ **snivel**
snivels *v* ▷ **snivel**
snob *n* (*pl* **-s**) person who judges others by social rank > **snobbery** *n* (*pl* **-ries**) > **snobbish** *adj*
snobberies *n* ▷ **snob**
snobbery *n* ▷ **snob**
snobbish *adj* ▷ **snob**
snobs *n* ▷ **snob**
snoek *n* (*pl* **-s**) (S AFR) edible marine fish
snoeks *n* ▷ **snoek**
snood *n* (*pl* **-s**) pouch, often of net, loosely holding a woman's hair at the back
snoods *n* ▷ **snood**
snook *n* (*pl* **-s**) gesture of contempt
snooker *n* (*pl* **-s**) game played on a billiard table ▶ *v* (**-s, -ing, -ed**) leave (a snooker opponent) in a position such that another ball blocks the target ball
snookered *v* ▷ **snooker**
snookering *v* ▷ **snooker**
snookers *n, v* ▷ **snooker**
snooks *n* ▷ **snook**
snoop (*Informal*) *v* (**-s, -ing, -ed**) pry ▶ *n* (*pl* **-s**) snooping > **snooper** *n* (*pl* **-s**)
snooped *v* ▷ **snoop**
snooper *n* ▷ **snoop**
snoopers *n* ▷ **snoop**
snooping *v* ▷ **snoop**
snoops *v, n* ▷ **snoop**
snootier *adj* ▷ **snooty**

snootiest adj ▷ **snooty**
snooty adj (**-tier, -tiest**) (Informal) haughty
snooze (Informal) v (**-zes, -zing, -zed**) take a brief light sleep ▶ n (pl **-s**) brief light sleep
snoozed v ▷ **snooze**
snoozes v, n ▷ **snooze**
snoozing v ▷ **snooze**
snore v (**-res, -ring, -red**) make snorting sounds while sleeping ▶ n (pl **-s**) sound of snoring
snored v ▷ **snore**
snores v, n ▷ **snore**
snoring v ▷ **snore**
snorkel n (pl **-s**) tube allowing a swimmer to breathe while face down on the surface of the water ▶ v (**-s, -lling, -lled**) swim using a snorkel
snorkelled v ▷ **snorkel**
snorkelling v ▷ **snorkel**
snorkels n, v ▷ **snorkel**
snort v (**-s, -ing, -ed**) exhale noisily through the nostrils ▶ n (pl **-s**) act or sound of snorting
snorted v ▷ **snort**
snorting v ▷ **snort**
snorts v, n ▷ **snort**
snot n (pl **-s**) (Slang) mucus from the nose
snots n ▷ **snot**
snout n (pl **-s**) animal's projecting nose and jaws
snouts n ▷ **snout**
snow n (pl **-s**) frozen vapour falling from the sky in flakes ▶ v (**-s, -ing, -ed**) fall as or like snow > **snowy** adj (**-wier, -wiest**)
snowball n (pl **-s**) snow pressed into a ball for throwing ▶ v (**-s, -ing, -ed**) increase rapidly
snowballed v ▷ **snowball**
snowballing v ▷ **snowball**
snowballs n, v ▷ **snowball**
snowboard n (pl **-s**) board on which a person stands to slide across the snow > **snowboarding** n (pl **-s**)
snowboarding n ▷ **snowboard**
snowboardings n ▷ **snowboard**
snowboards n ▷ **snowboard**
snowdrift n (pl **-s**) bank of deep snow
snowdrifts n ▷ **snowdrift**
snowdrop n (pl **-s**) small white bell-shaped spring flower
snowdrops n ▷ **snowdrop**
snowed v ▷ **snow**
snowflake n (pl **-s**) single crystal of snow
snowflakes n ▷ **snowflake**
snowier adj ▷ **snow**
snowiest adj ▷ **snow**
snowing v ▷ **snow**

snowman n (pl **-men**) figure shaped out of snow
snowmen n ▷ **snowman**
snowplough n (pl **-s**) vehicle for clearing away snow
snowploughs n ▷ **snowplough**
snows n, v ▷ **snow**
snowshoes pl n racket-shaped shoes for travelling on snow
snowy adj ▷ **snow**
snub v (**-s, -bbing, -bbed**) insult deliberately ▶ n (pl **-s**) deliberate insult ▶ adj (of a nose) short and blunt
snubbed v ▷ **snub**
snubbing v ▷ **snub**
snubs v, n ▷ **snub**
snuff[1] n (pl **-s**) powdered tobacco for sniffing up the nostrils
snuff[2] v (**-s, -ing, -ed**) extinguish (a candle)
snuffed v ▷ **snuff**[2]
snuffing v ▷ **snuff**[2]
snuffle v (**-les, -ling, -led**) breathe noisily or with difficulty
snuffled v ▷ **snuffle**
snuffles v ▷ **snuffle**
snuffling v ▷ **snuffle**
snuffs n ▷ **snuff**[1] ▶ v ▷ **snuff**[2]
snug adj (**-gger, -ggest**) warm and comfortable ▶ n (pl **-s**) (in Britain and Ireland) small room in a pub > **snugly** adv
snugger adj ▷ **snug**
snuggest adj ▷ **snug**
snuggle v (**-les, -ling, -led**) nestle into a person or thing for warmth or from affection
snuggled v ▷ **snuggle**
snuggles v ▷ **snuggle**
snuggling v ▷ **snuggle**
snugly adv ▷ **snug**
snugs n ▷ **snug**

> **sny** n (**snys**). Sny is a Canadian word for a side channel of a river. This word doesn't contain a vowel, so it can help you to clear an awkward rack. Sny scores 6 points.

so adv to such an extent ▶ conj in order that ▶ interj exclamation of surprise, triumph, or realization
soak v (**-s, -ing, -ed**) make wet ▶ n (pl **-s**) soaking > **soaking** n (pl **-s**) adj
soaked v ▷ **soak**
soaking v, n, adj ▷ **soak**
soakings n ▷ **soak**
soaks v, n ▷ **soak**
soap n (pl **-s**) compound of alkali and fat, used with water as a cleaning agent ▶ v (**-s, -ing,**

-ed) apply soap to > **soapy** adj (**-pier, -piest**)
soaped v ▷ soap
soapier adj ▷ soap
soapiest adj ▷ soap
soaping v ▷ soap
soaps n, v ▷ soap
soapy adj ▷ soap
soar v (**-s, -ing, -ed**) rise or fly upwards
soared v ▷ soar
soaring v ▷ soar
soars v ▷ soar
sob v (**-s, -bbing, -bbed**) weep with convulsive
gasps ▶ n (pl **-s**) act or sound of sobbing
sobbed v ▷ sob
sobbing v ▷ sob
sober adj (**-er, -est**) not drunk ▶ v (**-s, -ing, -ed**)
make or become sober > **soberly** adv
sobered v ▷ sober
soberer adj ▷ sober
soberest adj ▷ sober
sobering v ▷ sober
soberly adv ▷ sober
sobers v ▷ sober
sobrieties n ▷ sobriety
sobriety n (pl **-ties**) state of being sober
sobriquet [so-brik-ay] n (pl **-s**) nickname
sobriquets n ▷ sobriquet
sobs v, n ▷ sob
soccer n (pl **-s**) football played by two teams of
eleven kicking a spherical ball
soccers n ▷ soccer
sociabilities n ▷ sociable
sociability n ▷ sociable
sociable adj friendly or companionable
> **sociability** n (pl **-ties**) > **sociably** adv
sociably adv ▷ sociable
social adj living in a community ▶ n (pl **-s**)
informal gathering > **socially** adv
socialism n (pl **-s**) political system which
advocates public ownership of industries,
resources, and transport
socialisms n ▷ socialism
socialist n (pl **-s**) ▶ adj
socialists n ▷ socialist
socialite n (pl **-s**) member of fashionable
society
socialites n ▷ socialite
socialize v (**-zes, -zing, -zed**) meet others
socially
socialized v ▷ socialize
socializes v ▷ socialize
socializing v ▷ socialize
socially adv ▷ social
socials n ▷ social
societies n ▷ society

society n (pl **-ties**) human beings considered
as a group
sociological adj ▷ sociology
sociologies n ▷ sociology
sociologist n ▷ sociology
sociologists n ▷ sociology
sociology n (pl **-gies**) study of human societies
> **sociological** adj > **sociologist** n (pl **-s**)
sock[1] n (pl **-s**) knitted covering for the foot
sock[2] (Slang) v (**-s, -ing, -ed**) hit hard ▶ n (pl **-s**)
hard blow
socked v ▷ sock[2]
socket n (pl **-s**) hole or recess into which
something fits
sockets n ▷ socket
socking v ▷ sock[2]
socks v ▷ sock[2] ▶ n ▷ sock[1, 2]
sod n (pl **-s**) (piece of) turf
soda n (pl **-s**) compound of sodium
sodas n ▷ soda
sodden adj soaked
sodium n (pl **-s**) (CHEM) silvery-white metallic
element
sodiums n ▷ sodium
sods n ▷ sod
sofa n (pl **-s**) couch
sofas n ▷ sofa
soft adj (**-er, -s**) easy to shape or cut > **softly** adv
soften v (**-s, -ing, -ed**) make or become soft
or softer
softened v ▷ soften
softening v ▷ soften
softens v ▷ soften
softer adj ▷ soft
softest adj ▷ soft
softly adv ▷ soft
software n (pl **-s**) computer programs
softwares n ▷ software
softwood n (pl **-s**) wood of a coniferous tree
softwoods n ▷ softwood
soggier adj ▷ soggy
soggiest adj ▷ soggy
sogginess n ▷ soggy
sogginesses n ▷ soggy
soggy adj (**-ggier, -ggiest**) soaked > **sogginess**
n (pl **-es**)
soigné, fem **soignée** [swah-nyay] adj well-
groomed, elegant
soil[1] n (pl **-s**) top layer of earth
soil[2] v (**-s, -ing, -ed**) make or become dirty
soiled v ▷ soil
soiling v ▷ soil
soils n ▷ soil[1] ▶ v ▷ soil[2]
soiree [swah-ray] n (pl **-s**) evening party or
gathering

soirees *n* ▷ **soiree**
sojourn [soj-urn] *n* (*pl* -s) temporary stay ▶ *v* (-s, -ing, -ed) stay temporarily
  sojourned *v* ▷ **sojourn**
  sojourning *v* ▷ **sojourn**
  sojourns *n*, *v* ▷ **sojourn**
solace [sol-iss] *n*, *v* (-ces, -cing, -ced) comfort in distress
  solaced *v* ▷ **solace**
  solaces *v* ▷ **solace**
  solacing *v* ▷ **solace**
solar *adj* of the sun
  solaria *n* ▷ **solarium**
solarium *n* (*pl* -riums, -ria) place with beds and ultraviolet lights used for acquiring an artificial suntan
  solariums *n* ▷ **solarium**
  sold *v* ▷ **sell**
solder *n* (*pl* -s) soft alloy used to join two metal surfaces ▶ *v* (-s, -ing, -ed) join with solder
  soldered *v* ▷ **solder**
  soldering *v* ▷ **solder**
  solders *n*, *v* ▷ **solder**
soldier *n* (*pl* -s) member of an army ▶ *v* (-s, -ing, -ed) serve in an army > **soldierly** *adj*
  soldiered *v* ▷ **soldier**
  soldiering *v* ▷ **soldier**
  soldierly *adj* ▷ **soldier**
  soldiers *n*, *v* ▷ **soldier**
sole¹ *adj* one and only
sole² *n* (*pl* -s) underside of the foot ▶ *v* (-les, -ling, -led) provide (a shoe) with a sole
sole³ *n* (*pl* -s) small edible flatfish
solecism [sol-iss-izz-um] *n* (*pl* -s) minor grammatical mistake
  solecisms *n* ▷ **solecism**
  soled *v* ▷ **sole²**
solely *adv* only, completely
solemn *adj* (-er, -est) serious, deeply sincere > **solemnly** *adv* > **solemnity** *n* (*pl* -ties)
  solemner *adj* ▷ **solemn**
  solemnest *adj* ▷ **solemn**
  solemnities *n* ▷ **solemn**
  solemnity *n* ▷ **solemn**
  solemnly *adv* ▷ **solemn**
solenoid [sole-in-oid] *n* (*pl* -s) coil of wire magnetized by passing a current through it
  solenoids *n* ▷ **solenoid**
  soles *n* ▷ **sole²,³** ▶ *v* ▷ **sole²**
solicit *v* (-s, -ing, -ed) request > **solicitation** *n* (*pl* -s)
  solicitation *n* ▷ **solicit**
  solicitations *n* ▷ **solicit**
  solicited *v* ▷ **solicit**
  soliciting *v* ▷ **solicit**

solicitor *n* (*pl* -s) (BRIT, AUST & NZ) lawyer who advises clients and prepares documents and cases
  solicitors *n* ▷ **solicitor**
solicitous *adj* anxious about someone's welfare > **solicitude** *n* (*pl* -s)
  solicits *v* ▷ **solicit**
  solicitude *n* ▷ **solicitous**
  solicitudes *n* ▷ **solicitous**
solid *adj* (-er, -est) (of a substance) keeping its shape ▶ *n* (*pl* -s) three-dimensional shape > **solidity** *n* (*pl* -ties) > **solidly** *adv*
  solidarities *n* ▷ **solidarity**
solidarity *n* (*pl* -ties) agreement in aims or interests, total unity
  solider *adj* ▷ **solid**
  solidest *adj* ▷ **solid**
  solidified *v* ▷ **solidify**
  solidifies *v* ▷ **solidify**
solidify *v* (-fies, -fying, -fied) make or become solid or firm
  solidifying *v* ▷ **solidify**
  solidities *n* ▷ **solid**
  solidity *n* ▷ **solid**
  solidly *adv* ▷ **solid**
  solids *n* ▷ **solid**
  soliloquies *n* ▷ **soliloquy**
soliloquy *n* (*pl* -quies) speech made by a person while alone, esp. in a play
  soling *v* ▷ **sole²**
solipsism *n* (*pl* -s) doctrine that the self is the only thing known to exist > **solipsist** *n* (*pl* -s)
  solipsisms *n* ▷ **solipsism**
  solipsist *n* ▷ **solipsism**
  solipsists *n* ▷ **solipsism**
solitaire *n* (*pl* -s) game for one person played with pegs set in a board
  solitaires *n* ▷ **solitaire**
solitary *adj* alone, single
solitude *n* (*pl* -s) state of being alone
  solitudes *n* ▷ **solitude**
solo *n* (*pl* -s) music for one performer ▶ *adj* done alone ▶ *adv* by oneself, alone > **soloist** *n* (*pl* -s)
  soloist *n* ▷ **solo**
  soloists *n* ▷ **solo**
  solos *n* ▷ **solo**
solstice *n* (*pl* -s) either the shortest (in winter) or longest (in summer) day of the year
  solstices *n* ▷ **solstice**
  solubilities *n* ▷ **soluble**
  solubility *n* ▷ **soluble**
soluble *adj* able to be dissolved > **solubility** *n* (*pl* -ties)
solution *n* (*pl* -s) answer to a problem
  solutions *n* ▷ **solution**

solvable *adj* ▷ solve
solve *v* (-ves, -ving, -ved) find the answer to (a problem) > **solvable** *adj*
  solved *v* ▷ solve
  solvencies *n* ▷ solvent
  solvency *n* ▷ solvent
solvent *adj* having enough money to pay one's debts ▸ *n* (*pl* -s) liquid capable of dissolving other substances > **solvency** *n* (*pl* -cies)
  solvents *n* ▷ solvent
  solves *v* ▷ solve
  solving *v* ▷ solve
sombre *adj* (-r, -st) dark, gloomy
  sombrer *adj* ▷ sombre
sombrero *n* (*pl* -s) wide-brimmed Mexican hat
  sombreros *n* ▷ sombrero
  sombrest *adj* ▷ sombre
some *adj* unknown or unspecified (*Informal*) ▸ *pron* certain unknown or unspecified people or things
  somebodies *n* ▷ somebody
somebody *pron* some person ▸ *n* (*pl* -dies) important person
somehow *adv* in some unspecified way
someone *pron* somebody
somersault *n* (*pl* -s) leap or roll in which the trunk and legs are turned over the head ▸ *v* (-s, -ing, -ed) perform a somersault
  somersaulted *v* ▷ somersault
  somersaulting *v* ▷ somersault
  somersaults *n, v* ▷ somersault
something *pron* unknown or unspecified thing or amount
sometime *adv* at some unspecified time ▸ *adj* former
sometimes *adv* from time to time, now and then
somewhat *adv* to some extent, rather
somewhere *adv* in, to, or at some unspecified or unknown place
  somnambulism *n* ▷ somnambulist
  somnambulisms *n* ▷ somnambulist
somnambulist *n* (*pl* -s) person who walks in his or her sleep > **somnambulism** *n* (*pl* -s)
  somnambulists *n* ▷ somnambulist
somnolent *adj* drowsy
son *n* (*pl* -s) male offspring
sonar *n* (*pl* -s) device for detecting underwater objects by the reflection of sound waves
  sonars *n* ▷ sonar
sonata *n* (*pl* -s) piece of music in several movements for one instrument with or without piano
  sonatas *n* ▷ sonata
song *n* (*pl* -s) music for the voice

songbird *n* (*pl* -s) any bird with a musical call
  songbirds *n* ▷ songbird
  songs *n* ▷ song
songster, songstress *n* (*pl* -s, -es) singer
  songsters *n* ▷ songster
  songstress *n* ▷ songster
  songstresses *n* ▷ songster
sonic *adj* of or producing sound
sonnet *n* (*pl* -s) fourteen-line poem with a fixed rhyme scheme
  sonnets *n* ▷ sonnet
  sonorities *n* ▷ sonorous
  sonority *n* ▷ sonorous
sonorous *adj* (of sound) deep or resonant > **sonorously** *adv* > **sonority** *n* (*pl* -ties)
  sonorously *adv* ▷ sonorous
  sons *n* ▷ son
soon *adv* in a short time
sooner *adv* rather
soot *n* (*pl* -s) black powder formed by the incomplete burning of an organic substance > **sooty** *adj* (-tier, -tiest)
soothe *v* (-thes, -thing, -thed) make calm
  soothed *v* ▷ soothe
  soothes *v* ▷ soothe
  soothing *v* ▷ soothe
soothsayer *n* (*pl* -s) seer or prophet
  soothsayers *n* ▷ soothsayer
  sootier *adj* ▷ soot
  sootiest *adj* ▷ soot
  soots *n* ▷ soot
  sooty *adj* ▷ soot
sop *n* (*pl* -s) concession to pacify someone ▸ *v* (-s, -pping, -pped) mop up or absorb (liquid)
  sophism *n* ▷ sophistry
  sophisms *n* ▷ sophistry
sophist *n* (*pl* -s) person who uses clever but invalid arguments
sophisticate *v* (-tes, -ting, -ted) make less natural or innocent ▸ *n* (*pl* -s) sophisticated person
sophisticated *adj* having or appealing to refined or cultured tastes and habits ▸ *v* ▷ sophisticate > **sophistication** *n* (*pl* -s)
  sophisticates *v, n* ▷ sophisticate
  sophisticating *v* ▷ sophisticate
  sophistication *n* ▷ sophisticated
  sophistications *n* ▷ sophisticated
  sophistries *n* ▷ sophistry
sophistry, sophism *n* (*pl* -ries, -s) clever but invalid argument
  sophists *n* ▷ sophist
sophomore *n* (*pl* -s) (us) student in second year at college
  sophomores *n* ▷ sophomore

soporific *adj* causing sleep ▸ *n* (*pl* -**s**) drug that causes sleep
  soporifics *n* ▷ **soporific**
  sopped *v* ▷ **sop**
  soppier *adj* ▷ **soppy**
  soppiest *adj* ▷ **soppy**
sopping *adj* completely soaked ▸ *v* ▷ **sop**
soppy *adj* (**soppier, soppiest**) (*Informal*) oversentimental
soprano *n* (*pl* -**s**) (singer with) the highest female or boy's voice
  sopranos *n* ▷ **soprano**
  sops *n, v* ▷ **sop**
sorbet *n* (*pl* -**s**) flavoured water ice
  sorbets *n* ▷ **sorbet**
sorcerer *n* (*pl* -**s**) magician > **sorceress** *n fem* (*pl* -**s**)
  sorcerers *n* ▷ **sorcerer**
  sorceress *n* ▷ **sorcerer**
  sorceresses *n* ▷ **sorcerer**
  sorceries *n* ▷ **sorcery**
sorcery *n* (*pl* -**ries**) witchcraft or magic
sordid *adj* (-**er, -est**) dirty, squalid > **sordidly** *adv* > **sordidness** *n* (*pl* -**es**)
  sordider *adj* ▷ **sordid**
  sordidest *adj* ▷ **sordid**
  sordidly *adv* ▷ **sordid**
  sordidness *n* ▷ **sordid**
  sordidnesses *n* ▷ **sordid**
sore *adj* (-**r, -st**) painful ▸ *n* (*pl* -**s**) painful area on the body ▸ *adv* (*Obs*) greatly > **soreness** *n* (*pl* -**es**)
sorely *adv* greatly
  soreness *n* ▷ **sore**
  sorenesses *n* ▷ **sore**
  sorer *adj* ▷ **sore**
  sores *n* ▷ **sore**
  sorest *adj* ▷ **sore**
sorghum *n* (*pl* -**s**) kind of grass cultivated for grain
  sorghums *n* ▷ **sorghum**
sorrel *n* (*pl* -**s**) bitter-tasting plant
  sorrels *n* ▷ **sorrel**
  sorrier *adj* ▷ **sorry**
  sorriest *adj* ▷ **sorry**
sorrow *n* (*pl* -**s**) grief or sadness ▸ *v* (-**s, -ing, -ed**) grieve > **sorrowful** *adj* > **sorrowfully** *adv*
  sorrowed *v* ▷ **sorrow**
  sorrowful *adj* ▷ **sorrow**
  sorrowfully *adv* ▷ **sorrow**
  sorrowing *v* ▷ **sorrow**
  sorrows *n, v* ▷ **sorrow**
sorry *adj* (-**rier, -riest**) feeling pity or regret
sort *n* (*pl* -**s**) group all sharing certain qualities or characteristics ▸ *v* (-**s, -ing, -ed**) arrange according to kind
  sorted *v* ▷ **sort**
sortie *n* (*pl* -**s**) relatively short return trip
  sorties *n* ▷ **sortie**
  sorting *v* ▷ **sort**
  sorts *n, v* ▷ **sort**
sot *n* (*pl* -**s**) habitual drunkard
  sots *n* ▷ **sot**
soubriquet [so-brik-ay] *n* (*pl* -**s**) ▷ **sobriquet**
  soubriquets *n* ▷ **soubriquet**
soufflé [soo-flay] *n* (*pl* -**s**) light fluffy dish made with beaten egg whites and other ingredients
  soufflés *n* ▷ **soufflé**
sough [rhymes with **now**] *v* (-**s, -ing, -ed**) (of the wind) make a sighing sound
  soughed *v* ▷ **sough**
  soughing *v* ▷ **sough**
  soughs *v* ▷ **sough**
  sought [sawt] *v* ▷ **seek**
souk [sook] *n* (*pl* -**s**) marketplace in Muslim countries, often open-air
  souks *n* ▷ **souk**
soul *n* (*pl* -**s**) spiritual and immortal part of a human being
soulful *adj* full of emotion
soulless *adj* lacking human qualities, mechanical
  souls *n* ▷ **soul**
sound[1] *n* (*pl* -**s**) something heard, noise ▸ *v* (-**s, -ing, -ed**) make or cause to make a sound
sound[2] *adj* (-**er, -est**) in good condition > **soundly** *adv*
sound[3] *v* (-**s, -ing, -ed**) find the depth of (water etc.)
sound[4] *n* (*pl* -**s**) channel or strait
  sounded *v* ▷ **sound**[1, 3]
  sounder *adj* ▷ **sound**[2]
  soundest *adj* ▷ **sound**[2]
  sounding *v* ▷ **sound**[1, 3]
soundings *pl n* measurements of depth taken by sounding
  soundly *adv* ▷ **sound**[2]
soundproof *adj* not penetrable by sound ▸ *v* (-**s, -ing, -ed**) make soundproof
  soundproofed *v* ▷ **soundproof**
  soundproofing *v* ▷ **soundproof**
  soundproofs *v* ▷ **soundproof**
  sounds *n* ▷ **sound**[1, 4] ▸ *v* ▷ **sound**[1, 3]
soundtrack *n* (*pl* -**s**) recorded sound accompaniment to a film
  soundtracks *n* ▷ **soundtrack**
soup *n* (*pl* -**s**) liquid food made from meat, vegetables, etc. > **soupy** *adj* (-**pier, -piest**)
soupçon [soop-sonn] *n* (*pl* -**s**) small amount

soupçons *n* ▷ soupçon
soupier *adj* ▷ soup
soupiest *adj* ▷ soup
soups *n* ▷ soup
soupy *adj* ▷ soup
sour *adj* (**-er, -est**) sharp-tasting ▶ *v* (**-s, -ing, -ed**) make or become sour > **sourly** *adv* > **sourness** *n* (*pl* **-s**)
source *n* (*pl* **-s**) origin or starting point
sources *n* ▷ source
soured *v* ▷ sour
sourer *adj* ▷ sour
sourest *adj* ▷ sour
souring *v* ▷ sour
sourly *adv* ▷ sour
sourness *n* ▷ sour
sournesses *n* ▷ sour
sours *v* ▷ sour
souse *v* (**-ses, -sing, -sed**) plunge (something) into liquid
soused *v* ▷ souse
souses *v* ▷ souse
sousing *v* ▷ souse
soutane [soo-**tan**] *n* (*pl* **-s**) Roman Catholic priest's cassock
soutanes *n* ▷ soutane
south *n* (*pl* **-s**) direction towards the South Pole, opposite north ▶ *adj* to or in the south ▶ *adv* in, to, or towards the south > **southerly** *adj* > **southern** *adj* > **southward** *adj, adv* > **southwards** *adv*
southerly *adj* ▷ south
southern *adj* ▷ south
southerner *n* (*pl* **-s**) person from the south of a country or area
southerners *n* ▷ southerner
southpaw *n* (*pl* **-s**) (*Informal*) left-handed person, esp. a boxer
southpaws *n* ▷ southpaw
souths *n* ▷ south
southward *adj, adv* ▷ south
southwards *adv* ▷ south
souvenir *n* (*pl* **-s**) keepsake, memento
souvenirs *n* ▷ souvenir
sou'wester *n* (*pl* **-s**) seaman's waterproof hat covering the head and back of the neck
sou'westers *n* ▷ sou'wester
sovereign *n* (*pl* **-s**) king or queen ▶ *adj* (of a state) independent > **sovereignty** *n* (*pl* **-ties**)
sovereigns *n* ▷ sovereign
sovereignties *n* ▷ sovereign
sovereignty *n* ▷ sovereign
soviet *n* (*pl* **-s**) formerly, elected council at various levels of government in the USSR ▶ *adj*

soviets *n* ▷ soviet
sow¹ [rhymes with **know**] *v* (**-s, -ing, -ed, sown** or **-ed**) scatter or plant (seed) in or on (the ground)
sow² [rhymes with **cow**] *n* (*pl* **-s**) female adult pig
sowed *v* ▷ sow¹
sowing *v* ▷ sow¹
sown *v* ▷ sow¹
sows *n* ▷ sow² ▶ *v* ▷ sow¹

> **sox** *pl n*. Sox is an informal word for **socks**. This is a good word to remember for when you find an X on your rack without the space or tiles to play a longer word. Sox scores 10 points.

soya *n* (*pl* **-s**) plant whose edible bean is used for food and as a source of oil
soyas *n* ▷ soya
sozzled *adj* (BRIT, AUST & NZ) (*Slang*) drunk
spa *n* (*pl* **-s**) resort with a mineral-water spring
space *n* (*pl* **-s**) unlimited expanse in which all objects exist and move ▶ *v* (**-ces, -cing, -ced**) place at intervals
spacecraft, spaceship *n* (*pl* **-s**) vehicle for travel beyond the earth's atmosphere
spacecrafts *n* ▷ spacecraft
spaced *v* ▷ space
spaces *n, v* ▷ space
spaceship *n* ▷ spacecraft
spaceships *n* ▷ spacecraft
spacesuit *n* (*pl* **-s**) sealed pressurized suit worn by an astronaut
spacesuits *n* ▷ spacesuit
spacing *v* ▷ space
spacious *adj* having a large capacity or area
spade¹ *n* (*pl* **-s**) tool for digging
spade² *n* (*pl* **-s**) playing card of the suit marked with black leaf-shaped symbols
spades *n* ▷ spade¹,²
spadework *n* (*pl* **-s**) hard preparatory work
spadeworks *n* ▷ spadework
spaghetti *n* (*pl* **-s**) pasta in the form of long strings
spaghettis *n* ▷ spaghetti
span *n* (*pl* **-s**) space between two points ▶ *v* (**-s, -nning, -nned**) stretch or extend across
spangle *n* (*pl* **-les**) small shiny metallic ornament ▶ *v* (**-les, -ling, -led**) decorate with spangles
spangled *v* ▷ spangle
spangles *n, v* ▷ spangle
spangling *v* ▷ spangle
spaniel *n* (*pl* **-s**) dog with long ears and silky hair
spaniels *n* ▷ spaniel

spank v (-s, -ing, -ed) slap with the open hand, on the buttocks or legs ▶ n (pl -s) such a slap
> **spanking** n (pl -s)
spanked v ▷ spank
spanking adj (Informal) outstandingly fine or smart ▶ v ▷ spank ▶ n ▷ spank
spankings n ▷ spank
spanks v, n ▷ spank
spanned v ▷ span
spanner n (pl -s) tool for gripping and turning a nut or bolt
spanners n ▷ spanner
spanning v ▷ span
spans n, v ▷ span
spar¹ n (pl -s) pole used as a ship's mast, boom, or yard
spar² v (-s, -rring, -rred) box or fight using light blows for practice
spare adj extra ▶ n (pl -s) duplicate kept in case of damage or loss ▶ v (-res, -ring, -red) refrain from punishing or harming
spared v ▷ spare
spares n, v ▷ spare
sparing adj economical ▶ v ▷ spare
spark n (pl -s) fiery particle thrown out from a fire or caused by friction ▶ v (-s, -ing, -ed) give off sparks
sparked v ▷ spark
sparkie n (pl -s) (NZ) (Informal) electrician
sparkies n ▷ sparkie
sparking v ▷ spark
sparkle v (-les, -ling, -led) glitter with many points of light ▶ n (pl -s) sparkling points of light
sparkled v ▷ sparkle
sparkler n (pl -s) hand-held firework that emits sparks
sparklers n ▷ sparkler
sparkles v, n ▷ sparkle
sparkling adj (of wine or mineral water) slightly fizzy ▶ v ▷ sparkle
sparks v, n ▷ spark
sparred v ▷ spar²
sparring v ▷ spar²
sparrow n (pl -s) small brownish bird
sparrowhawk n (pl -s) small hawk
sparrowhawks n ▷ sparrowhawk
sparrows n ▷ sparrow
spars n ▷ spar¹ ▶ v ▷ spar²
sparse adj (-r, -st) thinly scattered > **sparsely** adv > **sparseness** n (pl -es)
sparsely adv ▷ sparse
sparseness n ▷ sparse
sparsenesses n ▷ sparse
sparser adj ▷ sparse

sparsest adj ▷ sparse
spartan adj strict and austere
spas n ▷ spa
spasm n (pl -s) involuntary muscular contraction
spasmodic adj occurring in spasms
> **spasmodically** adv
spasmodically adv ▷ spasmodic
spasms n ▷ spasm
spastic n (pl -s) person with cerebral palsy ▶ adj suffering from cerebral palsy
spastics n ▷ spastic
spat¹ n (pl -s) slight quarrel
spat² v ▷ spit¹
spate n (pl -s) large number of things happening within a period of time
spates n ▷ spate
spatial adj of or in space
spats pl n coverings formerly worn over the ankle and instep ▶ n ▷ spat¹
spatter v (-s, -ing, -ed) scatter or be scattered in drops over (something) ▶ n (pl -s) spattering sound
spattered v ▷ spatter
spattering v ▷ spatter
spatters n, v ▷ spatter
spatula n (pl -s) utensil with a broad flat blade for spreading or stirring
spatulas n ▷ spatula
spawn n (pl -s) jelly-like mass of eggs of fish, frogs, or molluscs ▶ v (-s, -ing, -ed) (of fish, frogs, or molluscs) lay eggs
spawned v ▷ spawn
spawning v ▷ spawn
spawns n, v ▷ spawn
spay v (-s, -ing, -ed) remove the ovaries from (a female animal)
spayed v ▷ spay
spaying v ▷ spay
spays v ▷ spay
speak v (-s, -ing, spoke, spoken) say words, talk
speaker n (pl -s) person who speaks, esp. at a formal occasion
speakers n ▷ speaker
speaking v ▷ speak
speaks v ▷ speak
spear¹ n (pl -s) weapon consisting of a long shaft with a sharp point ▶ v (-s, -ing, -ed) pierce with or as if with a spear
spear² n (pl -s) slender shoot
speared v ▷ spear¹
spearhead v (-es, -ing, -ed) lead (an attack or campaign) ▶ n (pl -s) leading force in an attack or campaign
spearheaded v ▷ spearhead

spearheading v ▷ **spearhead**
spearheads v, n ▷ **spearhead**
spearing v ▷ **spear¹**
spearmint n (pl -s) type of mint
spearmints n ▷ **spearmint**
spears n ▷ **spear¹, ²** ▶ v ▷ **spear¹**
spec n (pl -s) (Informal) speculation
special adj distinguished from others of its
kind > **specially** adv
specialist n (pl -s) expert in a particular
activity or subject
specialists n ▷ **specialist**
specialities n ▷ **speciality**
speciality n (pl -ties) special interest or skill
specialization n ▷ **specialize**
specializations n ▷ **specialize**
specialize v (-zes, -zing, -zed) be a specialist
> **specialization** n (pl -s)
specialized v ▷ **specialize**
specializes v ▷ **specialize**
specializing v ▷ **specialize**
specially adv ▷ **special**
specie n coins as distinct from paper money
species n (pl **species**) group of plants or
animals that are related closely enough to
interbreed naturally
specific adj particular, definite ▶ n (pl -s)
drug used to treat a particular disease
> **specifically** adv
specifically adv ▷ **specific**
specification n (pl -s) detailed description of
something to be made or done
specifications n ▷ **specification**
specifics n ▷ **specific** ▶ pl n particular details
specified v ▷ **specify**
specifies v ▷ **specify**
specify v (-fies, -fying, -fied) refer to or state
specifically
specifying v ▷ **specify**
specimen n (pl -s) individual or part typifying
a whole
specimens n ▷ **specimen**
specious [spee-shuss] adj apparently true, but
actually false
speck n (pl -s) small spot or particle
speckle n (pl -s) small spot ▶ v (-les, -ling, -led)
mark with speckles
speckled v ▷ **speckle**
speckles n, v ▷ **speckle**
speckling v ▷ **speckle**
specks n ▷ **speck**
specs pl n (Informal) ▷ **spectacles** ▶ n ▷ **spec**
spectacle n (pl -s) strange, interesting, or
ridiculous sight
spectacles n ▷ **spectacle** ▶ pl n pair of glasses

for correcting faulty vision
spectacles n ▷ **spectacle**
spectacular adj impressive ▶ n (pl -s)
spectacular public show > **spectacularly** adv
spectacularly adv ▷ **spectacular**
spectaculars n ▷ **spectacular**
spectate v (-tes, -ting, -ted) watch
spectated v ▷ **spectate**
spectates v ▷ **spectate**
spectating v ▷ **spectate**
spectator n (pl -s) person viewing anything,
onlooker
spectators n ▷ **spectator**
spectra n ▷ **spectrum**
spectral adj ▷ **spectre**
spectre n (pl -s) ghost > **spectral** adj
spectres n ▷ **spectre**
spectroscope n (pl -s) instrument for
producing or examining spectra
spectroscopes n ▷ **spectroscope**
spectrum n (pl -tra) range of different
colours, radio waves, etc. in order of their
wavelengths
speculate v (-tes, -ting, -ted) guess, conjecture
> **speculation** n (pl -s) > **speculative** adj
> **speculator** n (pl -s)
speculated v ▷ **speculate**
speculates v ▷ **speculate**
speculating v ▷ **speculate**
speculation n ▷ **speculate**
speculations n ▷ **speculate**
speculative adj ▷ **speculate**
speculator n ▷ **speculate**
speculators n ▷ **speculate**
sped v ▷ **speed**
speech n (pl -es) act, power, or manner of
speaking
speeches n ▷ **speech**
speechless adj unable to speak because of
great emotion
speed n (pl -s) swiftness ▶ v (-s, -ing, **sped** or
-ed) go quickly
speedboat n (pl -s) light fast motorboat
speedboats n ▷ **speedboat**
speeded v ▷ **speed**
speedier adj ▷ **speedy**
speediest adj ▷ **speedy**
speedily adv ▷ **speedy**
speeding v ▷ **speed**
speedometer n (pl -s) instrument to show the
speed of a vehicle
speedometers n ▷ **speedometer**
speeds n, v ▷ **speed**
speedway n (pl -s) track for motorcycle racing
speedways n ▷ **speedway**

speedwell n (pl -s) plant with small blue flowers
  speedwells n ▷ **speedwell**
speedy adj (-dier, -diest) prompt > **speedily** adv
  speleologies n ▷ **speleology**
speleology n (pl -gies) study and exploration of caves
spell[1] v (-s, -ing, spelt or -ed) give in correct order the letters that form (a word)
spell[2] n (pl -s) formula of words supposed to have magic power
spell[3] n (pl -s) period of time of weather or activity
spellbound adj entranced
spellchecker n (pl -s) (COMPUTING) program that highlights wrongly spelled words in a word-processed document
  spellcheckers n ▷ **spellchecker**
  spelled v ▷ **spell**[1]
spelling n (pl -s) way a word is spelt ▶ v ▷ **spell**[1]
  spellings n ▷ **spelling**
  spells v ▷ **spell**[1] ▶ n ▷ **spell**[2, 3]
  spelt v ▷ **spell**[1]
spend v (-s, -ing, spent) pay out (money)
  spending v ▷ **spend**
  spends v ▷ **spend**
spendthrift n (pl -s) person who spends money wastefully
  spendthrifts n ▷ **spendthrift**
  spent v ▷ **spend**
sperm n (pl -s or sperm) male reproductive cell
spermaceti [sper-ma-**set**-ee] n (pl -s) waxy solid obtained from the sperm whale
  spermacetis n ▷ **spermaceti**
  spermatozoa n ▷ **spermatozoon**
spermatozoon [sper-ma-toe-**zoe**-on] n (pl -zoa) sperm
spermicide n (pl -s) substance that kills sperm
  spermicides n ▷ **spermicide**
  sperms n ▷ **sperm**
spew v (-s, -ing, -ed) vomit
  spewed v ▷ **spew**
  spewing v ▷ **spew**
  spews v ▷ **spew**
sphagnum n (pl -s) moss found in bogs
  sphagnums n ▷ **sphagnum**
sphere n (pl -s) perfectly round solid object > **spherical** adj
  spheres n ▷ **sphere**
  spherical adj ▷ **sphere**
sphincter n (pl -s) ring of muscle which controls the opening and closing of a hollow organ
  sphincters n ▷ **sphincter**
sphinx n (pl -es) enigmatic person

  sphinxes n ▷ **sphinx**
spice n (pl -s) aromatic substance used as flavouring ▶ v (-ces, -cing, -ced) flavour with spices
  spiced v ▷ **spice**
  spices n, v ▷ **spice**
  spicier adj ▷ **spicy**
  spiciest adj ▷ **spicy**
  spicing v ▷ **spice**
spicy adj (-cier, -ciest) flavoured with spices
spider n (pl -s) small eight-legged creature which spins a web to catch insects for food > **spidery** adj
  spiders n ▷ **spider**
  spidery adj ▷ **spider**
  spied v ▷ **spy**
spiel n (pl -s) speech made to persuade someone to do something
  spiels n ▷ **spiel**
  spies v, n ▷ **spy**
spigot n (pl -s) stopper for, or tap fitted to, a cask
  spigots n ▷ **spigot**
spike n (pl -s) sharp point ▶ v (-kes, -king, -ked) put spikes on > **spiky** adj (-kier, -kiest)
  spiked v ▷ **spike**
  spikes n, v ▷ **spike** ▶ pl n sports shoes with spikes for greater grip
  spikier adj ▷ **spike**
  spikiest adj ▷ **spike**
  spiking v ▷ **spike**
  spiky adj ▷ **spike**
spill[1] v (-s, -ing, spilt or spilled) pour from or as if from a container ▶ n (pl -s) fall > **spillage** n (pl -s)
spill[2] n (pl -s) thin strip of wood or paper for lighting pipes or fires
  spillage n ▷ **spill**[1]
  spillages n ▷ **spill**[1]
  spilled v ▷ **spill**[1]
  spilling v ▷ **spill**[1]
  spills n ▷ **spill**[1, 2] ▶ v ▷ **spill**[1]
  spilt v ▷ **spill**[1]
spin v (-s, -nning, spun) revolve or cause to revolve rapidly ▶ n (pl -s) revolving motion > **spinner** n (pl -s)
spinach n (pl -es) dark green leafy vegetable
  spinaches n ▷ **spinach**
spinal adj of the spine
spindle n (pl -s) rotating rod that acts as an axle
  spindles n ▷ **spindle**
  spindlier adj ▷ **spindly**
  spindliest adj ▷ **spindly**
spindly adj (-lier, -liest) long, slender, and frail

spine n (pl -s) backbone
spineless adj lacking courage
  spines n ▷ spine
spinet n (pl -s) small harpsichord
  spinets n ▷ spinet
  spinier adj ▷ spiny
  spiniest adj ▷ spiny
spinifex n (pl -es) coarse spiny Australian grass
  spinifexes n ▷ spinifex
spinnaker n (pl -s) large sail on a racing yacht
  spinnakers n ▷ spinnaker
  spinner n ▷ spin
  spinners n ▷ spin
spinney n (pl -s) (CHIEFLY BRIT) small wood
  spinneys n ▷ spinney
  spinning v ▷ spin
  spins v, n ▷ spin
spinster n (pl -s) unmarried woman
  spinsters n ▷ spinster
spiny adj (-nier, -niest) covered with spines
spiral n (pl -s) continuous curve formed by
  a point winding about a central axis at an
  ever-increasing distance from it ▶ v (-s, -lling,
  -lled) move in a spiral ▶ adj having the form
  of a spiral
  spiralled v ▷ spiral
  spiralling v ▷ spiral
  spirals n, v ▷ spiral
spire n (pl -s) pointed part of a steeple
  spires n ▷ spire
spirit¹ n (pl -s) nonphysical aspect of a person
  concerned with profound thoughts ▶ v (-s,
  -ing, -ed) carry away mysteriously
spirit² n (pl -s) liquid obtained by distillation
spirited adj lively ▶ v ▷ spirit¹
  spiriting v ▷ spirit¹
spirits n ▷ spirit¹, ² ▶ pl n emotional state ▶ v
  ▷ spirit¹
spiritual adj relating to the spirit ▶ n (pl -s)
  type of religious folk song originating among
  Black slaves in America > **spiritually** adv
  > **spirituality** n (pl -ties)
spiritualism n (pl -s) belief that the spirits of
  the dead can communicate with the living
  > **spiritualist** n (pl -s)
  spiritualisms n ▷ spiritualism
  spiritualist n ▷ spiritualism
  spiritualists n ▷ spiritualism
  spiritualities n ▷ spiritual
  spirituality n ▷ spiritual
  spiritually adv ▷ spiritual
  spirituals n ▷ spiritual
spit¹ v (-s, -tting, spat) eject (saliva or food)
  from the mouth ▶ n (pl -s) saliva
spit² n (pl -s) sharp rod on which meat is

skewered for roasting
spite n (pl -s) deliberate nastiness ▶ v (-tes,
  -ting, -ted) annoy or hurt from spite > **spiteful**
  adj > **spitefully** adv
  spited v ▷ spite
  spiteful adj ▷ spite
  spitefully adv ▷ spite
  spites n, v ▷ spite
spitfire n (pl -s) person with a fiery temper
  spitfires n ▷ spitfire
  spiting v ▷ spite
  spits n ▷ spit¹, ² ▶ v ▷ spit¹
  spitting v ▷ spit¹
spittle n (pl -s) fluid produced in the mouth,
  saliva
  spittles n ▷ spittle
spittoon n (pl -s) bowl to spit into
  spittoons n ▷ spittoon
spiv n (pl -s) (BRIT, AUST & NZ) (Slang) smartly
  dressed man who makes a living by shady
  dealings
  spivs n ▷ spiv
splash v (-es, -ing, -ed) scatter liquid on
  (something) ▶ n (pl -es) splashing sound
  splashed v ▷ splash
  splashes v, n ▷ splash
  splashing v, n ▷ splash
splatter v (-s, -ing, -ed) ▶ n (pl -s) splash
  splattered v ▷ splatter
  splattering v ▷ splatter
  splatters v, n ▷ splatter
splay v (-s, -ing, -ed) spread out, with ends
  spreading in different directions
  splayed v ▷ splay
  splaying v ▷ splay
  splays v ▷ splay
spleen n (pl -s) abdominal organ which filters
  bacteria from the blood
  spleens n ▷ spleen
splendid adj (-er, -est) excellent > **splendidly**
  adv > **splendour** n (pl -s)
  splendider adj ▷ splendid
  splendidest adj ▷ splendid
  splendidly adv ▷ splendid
  splendour n ▷ splendid
  splendours n ▷ splendid
splenetic adj spiteful or irritable
splice v (-ces, -cing, -ced) join by interweaving
  or overlapping ends
  spliced v ▷ splice
  splices v ▷ splice
  splicing v ▷ splice
splint n (pl -s) rigid support for a broken bone
splinter n (pl -s) thin sharp piece broken off,
  esp. from wood ▶ v (-s, -ing, -ed) break into

fragments
splintered v ▷ **splinter**
splintering v ▷ **splinter**
splinters n, v ▷ **splinter**
splints n ▷ **splint**
split v (**-s, -tting, split**) break into separate pieces ▶ n (pl -s) crack or division caused by splitting
splits v ▷ **split** ▶ n ▷ **split** ▶ pl n act of sitting with the legs outstretched in opposite directions
splitting v ▷ **split**
splodge n (pl -s) ▶ v (**-ges, -ging, -ged**) ▷ **splotch**
splodged v ▷ **splodge**
splodges n, v ▷ **splodge**
splodging v ▷ **splodge**
splotch n (pl -s) ▶ v (**-ches, -ching, -ched**) splash, daub
splotched v ▷ **splotch**
splotches n, v ▷ **splotch**
splotching v ▷ **splotch**
splurge v (**-ges, -ging, -ged**) spend money extravagantly ▶ n (pl -s) bout of extravagance
splurged v ▷ **splurge**
splurges v, n ▷ **splurge**
splurging v ▷ **splurge**
splutter v (**-s, -ing, -ed**) utter with spitting or choking sounds ▶ n (pl -s) spluttering
spluttered v ▷ **splutter**
spluttering v ▷ **splutter**
splutters v, n ▷ **splutter**
spoil v (**-s, -ing, -spoilt** or **-ed**) damage
spoiled v ▷ **spoil**
spoiling v ▷ **spoil**
spoils pl n booty ▶ v ▷ **spoil**
spoilsport n (pl -s) person who spoils the enjoyment of others
spoilsports n ▷ **spoilsport**
spoilt v ▷ **spoil**
spoke¹ v ▷ **speak**
spoke² n (pl -s) bar joining the hub of a wheel to the rim
spoken v ▷ **speak**
spokes n ▷ **spoke²**
spokesman, spokeswoman, spokesperson n (pl -men, -women, -persons, -people) person chosen to speak on behalf of a group
spokesmen n ▷ **spokesman**
spokespeople n ▷ **spokesman**
spokesperson n ▷ **spokesman**
spokespersons n ▷ **spokesman**
spokeswoman n ▷ **spokesman**
spokeswomen n ▷ **spokesman**
spoliation n (pl -s) plundering
spoliations n ▷ **spoliation**

sponge n (pl -s) sea animal with a porous absorbent skeleton ▶ v (**-ges, -ging, -ged**) wipe with a sponge > **spongy** adj (**-gier, -giest**)
sponged v ▷ **sponge**
sponger n (pl -s) (Slang) person who sponges on others
spongers n ▷ **sponger**
sponges n, v ▷ **sponge**
spongier adj ▷ **sponge**
spongiest adj ▷ **sponge**
sponging v ▷ **sponge**
spongy adj ▷ **sponge**
sponsor n (pl -s) person who promotes something ▶ v (**-s, -ing, -ed**) act as a sponsor for > **sponsorship** n (pl -s)
sponsored v ▷ **sponsor**
sponsoring v ▷ **sponsor**
sponsors n, v ▷ **sponsor**
sponsorship n ▷ **sponsor**
sponsorships n ▷ **sponsor**
spontaneities n ▷ **spontaneous**
spontaneity n ▷ **spontaneous**
spontaneous adj not planned or arranged > **spontaneously** adv > **spontaneity** n (pl -ties)
spontaneously adv ▷ **spontaneous**
spoof n (pl -s) mildly satirical parody
spoofs n ▷ **spoof**
spook n (pl -s) (Informal) ghost > **spooky** adj (**-kier, -kiest**)
spookier adj ▷ **spook**
spookiest adj ▷ **spook**
spooks n ▷ **spook**
spooky adj ▷ **spook**
spool n (pl -s) cylinder round which something can be wound
spools n ▷ **spool**
spoon n (pl -s) shallow bowl attached to a handle for eating, stirring, or serving food ▶ v (**-s, -ing, -ed**) lift with a spoon > **spoonful** n (pl -s)
spoonbill n (pl -s) wading bird of warm regions with a long flat bill
spoonbills n ▷ **spoonbill**
spooned v ▷ **spoon**
spoonerism n (pl -s) accidental changing over of the initial sounds of a pair of words, such as half-warmed fish for half-formed wish
spoonerisms n ▷ **spoonerism**
spoonful n ▷ **spoon**
spoonfuls n ▷ **spoon**
spooning v ▷ **spoon**
spoons n, v ▷ **spoon**
spoor n (pl -s) trail of an animal
spoors n ▷ **spoor**

sporadic *adj* intermittent, scattered
> **sporadically** *adv*
  sporadically *adv* ▷ **sporadic**
spore *n* (*pl* -s) minute reproductive body of some plants
  spores *n* ▷ **spore**
sporran *n* (*pl* -s) pouch worn in front of a kilt
  sporrans *n* ▷ **sporran**
sport *n* (*pl* -s) activity for pleasure, competition, or exercise *v* (-s, -ing, -ed) wear proudly > **sporty** *adj* (-tier, -tiest)
  sported *v* ▷ **sport**
  sportier *adj* ▷ **sport**
  sportiest *adj* ▷ **sport**
sporting *adj* of sport ▶ *v* ▷ **sport**
sportive *adj* playful
  sports *n*, *v* ▷ **sport**
sportsman, sportswoman *n* (*pl* -men, -women) person who plays sports
> **sportsmanlike** *adj* > **sportsmanship** *n* (*pl* -s)
  sportsmanlike *adj* ▷ **sportsman**
  sportsmanship *n* ▷ **sportsman**
  sportsmanships *n* ▷ **sportsman**
  sportsmen *n* ▷ **sportsman**
  sportswoman *n* ▷ **sportsman**
  sportswomen *n* ▷ **sportsman**
  sporty *adj* ▷ **sport**
spot *n* (*pl* -s) small mark on a surface (*Informal*) ▶ *v* (-s, -tting, -tted) notice
spotless *adj* absolutely clean > **spotlessly** *adv*
  spotlessly *adv* ▷ **spotless**
spotlight *n* (*pl* -s) powerful light illuminating a small area
  spotlights *n* ▷ **spotlight**
  spots *n*, *v* ▷ **spot**
  spotted *v* ▷ **spot**
  spottier *adj* ▷ **spotty**
  spottiest *adj* ▷ **spotty**
  spotting *v* ▷ **spot**
spotty *adj* (-ttier, -ttiest) with spots
spouse *n* (*pl* -s) husband or wife
  spouses *n* ▷ **spouse**
spout *v* (-s, -ing, -ed) pour out in a stream or jet (*Slang*) ▶ *n* (*pl* -s) projecting tube or lip for pouring liquids
  spouted *v* ▷ **spout**
  spouting *v* ▷ **spout**
  spouts *v*, *n* ▷ **spout**
sprain *v* (-s, -ing, -ed) injure (a joint) by a sudden twist ▶ *n* (*pl* -s) such an injury
  sprained *v* ▷ **sprain**
  spraining *v* ▷ **sprain**
  sprains *v*, *n* ▷ **sprain**
  sprang *v* ▷ **spring**
sprat *n* (*pl* -s) small sea fish

  sprats *n* ▷ **sprat**
sprawl *v* (-s, -ing, -ed) lie or sit with the limbs spread out ▶ *n* (*pl* -s) part of a city that has spread untidily over a large area
  sprawled *v* ▷ **sprawl**
  sprawling *v* ▷ **sprawl**
  sprawls *v*, *n* ▷ **sprawl**
spray[1] *n* (*pl* -s) (device for producing) fine drops of liquid ▶ *v* (-s, -ing, -ed) scatter in fine drops
spray[2] *n* (*pl* -s) branch with buds, leaves, flowers, or berries
  sprayed *v* ▷ **spray**[1]
  spraying *v* ▷ **spray**[1]
  sprays *v* ▷ **spray**[1] ▶ *n* ▷ **spray**[1, 2]
spread *v* (-s, -ing, spread) open out or be displayed to the fullest extent ▶ *n* (*pl* -s) spreading (*Informal*)
  spreading *v* ▷ **spread**
  spreads *v*, *n* ▷ **spread**
spreadsheet *n* (*pl* -s) computer program for manipulating figures
  spreadsheets *n* ▷ **spreadsheet**
spree *n* (*pl* -s) session of overindulgence, usu. in drinking or spending money
  sprees *n* ▷ **spree**
  sprier *adj* ▷ **spry**
  spriest *adj* ▷ **spry**
sprig *n* (*pl* -s) twig or shoot
  sprightlier *adj* ▷ **sprightly**
  sprightliest *adj* ▷ **sprightly**
  sprightliness *n* ▷ **sprightly**
  sprightlinesses *n* ▷ **sprightly**
sprightly *adj* (-lier, -liest) lively and brisk
> **sprightliness** *n* (*pl* -es)
  sprigs *n* ▷ **sprig**
spring *v* (-s, -ing, sprang *or* sprung) move suddenly upwards or forwards in a single motion, jump ▶ *n* (*pl* -s) season between winter and summer
springboard *n* (*pl* -s) flexible board used to gain height or momentum in diving or gymnastics
  springboards *n* ▷ **springboard**
springbok *n* (*pl* -s) S African antelope
  springboks *n* ▷ **springbok**
springer *n* (*pl* -s) small spaniel
  springers *n* ▷ **springer**
  springier *adj* ▷ **springy**
  springiest *adj* ▷ **springy**
  springing *v* ▷ **spring**
  springs *v*, *n* ▷ **springs**
springy *adj* (-gier, -giest) elastic
sprinkle *v* (-les, -ling, -led) scatter (liquid or powder) in tiny drops or particles over (something) > **sprinkler** *n* (*pl* -s)

sprinkled v ▷ **sprinkle**
sprinkler n ▷ **sprinkle**
sprinklers n ▷ **sprinkle**
sprinkles v ▷ **sprinkle**
sprinkling v ▷ **sprinkle** ▶ n (pl -s) small quantity or number
sprinklings n ▷ **sprinkling**
sprint n (pl -s) short race run at top speed ▶ v (-s, -ing, -ed) run a short distance at top speed > **sprinter** n (pl -s)
sprinted v ▷ **sprint**
sprinter n ▷ **sprint**
sprinters n ▷ **sprint**
sprinting v ▷ **sprint**
sprints n, v ▷ **sprint**
sprite n (pl -s) elf
sprites n ▷ **sprite**
sprocket n (pl -s) wheel with teeth on the rim, that drives or is driven by a chain
sprockets n ▷ **sprocket**
sprout v (-s, -ing, -ed) put forth shoots ▶ n (pl -s) shoot
sprouted v ▷ **sprout**
sprouting v ▷ **sprout**
sprouts v, n ▷ **sprout**
spruce[1] n (pl -s) kind of fir
spruce[2] adj (-r, -st) neat and smart
sprucer adj ▷ **spruce**[2]
spruces n ▷ **spruce**[1]
sprucest adj ▷ **spruce**[2]
sprung v ▷ **spring**
spry adj (-yer, -yest or **sprier**) (**spriest**) active or nimble
spryer adj ▷ **spry**
spryest adj ▷ **spry**
spud n (pl -s) (Informal) potato
spuds n ▷ **spud**
spume n (pl -s) ▶ v (-mes, -ming, -med) froth
spumed v ▷ **spume**
spumes v, n ▷ **spume**
spuming v ▷ **spume**
spun v ▷ **spin**
spunk n (pl -s) (Informal) courage, spirit > **spunky** adj (-kier, -kiest)
spunkier adj ▷ **spunk**
spunkiest adj ▷ **spunk**
spunks n ▷ **spunk**
spunky adj ▷ **spunk**
spur n (pl -s) stimulus or incentive ▶ v (-s, -rring, -rred) urge on, incite (someone)
spurge n (pl -s) plant with milky sap
spurges n ▷ **spurge**
spurious adj not genuine
spurn v (-s, -ing, -ed) reject with scorn
spurned v ▷ **spurn**

spurning v ▷ **spurn**
spurns v ▷ **spurn**
spurred v ▷ **spur**
spurring v ▷ **spur**
spurs n, v ▷ **spur**
spurt v (-s, -ing, -ed) gush or cause to gush out in a jet ▶ n (pl -s) short sudden burst of activity or speed
spurted v ▷ **spurt**
spurting v ▷ **spurt**
spurts v, n ▷ **spurt**
sputa n ▷ **sputum**
sputnik n (pl -s) early Soviet artificial satellite
sputniks n ▷ **sputnik**
sputter v (-es, -ing, -ed) ▶ n (pl -s) splutter
sputtered v ▷ **sputter**
sputtering v ▷ **sputter**
sputters v, n ▷ **sputter**
sputum n (pl -ta) spittle, usu. mixed with mucus
spy n (pl **spies**) person employed to obtain secret information ▶ v (**spies, spying, spied**) act as a spy
spying v ▷ **spy**
squabble v (-les, -ling, -led) ▶ n (pl -s) (engage in) a petty or noisy quarrel
squabbled v ▷ **squabble**
squabbles v, n ▷ **squabble**
squabbling v ▷ **squabble**
squad n (pl -s) small group of people working or training together
squadron n (pl -s) division of an air force, fleet, or cavalry regiment
squadrons n ▷ **squadron**
squads n ▷ **squad**
squalid adj (-er, -est) dirty and unpleasant
squalider adj ▷ **squalid**
squalidest adj ▷ **squalid**
squall[1] n (pl -s) sudden strong wind
squall[2] v (-s, -ing, -ed) cry noisily, yell ▶ n (pl -s) harsh cry
squalled v ▷ **squall**[2]
squalling v ▷ **squall**[2]
squalls v ▷ **squall**[2] ▶ n ▷ **squall**[1,2]
squalor n (pl -s) disgusting dirt and filth
squalors n ▷ **squalor**
squander v (-s, -ing, -ed) waste (money or resources)
squandered v ▷ **squander**
squandering v ▷ **squander**
squanders v ▷ **squander**
square n (pl -s) geometric figure with four equal sides and four right angles ▶ adj square in shape ▶ v (-res, -ring, -red) multiply (a number) by itself ▶ adv squarely, directly

squared v ▷ square
squarely adv in a direct way
squares n, v ▷ square
squaring v ▷ square
squash¹ v (-es, -ing, -ed) crush flat ▶ n (pl -es) sweet fruit drink diluted with water > **squashy** adj (-shier, -shiest)
squash² n (pl -es) marrow-like vegetable
squashed v ▷ squash¹
squashes n ▷ squash¹, ² ▶ v ▷ squash¹
squashier adj ▷ squash¹
squashiest adj ▷ squash¹
squashing v ▷ squash¹
squashy adj ▷ squash¹
squat v (-s, -tting, -tted) crouch with the knees bent and the weight on the feet ▶ n (pl -s) place where squatters live ▶ adj (-tter, -ttest) short and broad
squats v, n ▷ squat
squatted v ▷ squat
squatter n (pl -s) illegal occupier of unused premises ▶ adj ▷ squat
squatters n ▷ squatter
squattest n ▷ squat
squatting v ▷ squat
squaw n (pl -s) (Offens) Native American woman
squawk n (pl -s) loud harsh cry ▶ v (-s, -ing, -ed) utter a squawk
squawked v ▷ squawk
squawking v ▷ squawk
squawks v ▷ squawk
squaws n ▷ squaw
squeak n (pl -s) short shrill cry or sound ▶ v (-s, -ing, -ed) make or utter a squeak > **squeaky** adj (-kier, -kiest)
squeaked v ▷ squeak
squeakier adj ▷ squeak
squeakiest adj ▷ squeak
squeaking v ▷ squeak
squeaks n, v ▷ squeak
squeaky adj ▷ squeak
squeal n (pl -s) long shrill cry or sound ▶ v (-s, -ing, -ed) make or utter a squeal (Slang)
squealed v ▷ squeal
squealing v ▷ squeal
squeals n, v ▷ squeal
squeamish adj easily sickened or shocked
squeegee n (pl -s) tool with a rubber blade for clearing water from a surface
squeegees n ▷ squeegee
squeeze v (-zes, -zing, -zed) grip or press firmly ▶ n (pl -s) squeezing
squeezed v ▷ squeeze
squeezes v, n ▷ squeeze

squeezing v ▷ squeeze
squelch v (-es, -ing, -ed) make a wet sucking sound, as by walking through mud ▶ n (pl -es) squelching sound
squelched v ▷ squelch
squelches n ▷ squelch
squelching v ▷ squelch
squib n (pl -s) small firework that hisses before exploding
squibs n ▷ squib
squid n (pl -s) sea creature with a long soft body and ten tentacles
squids n ▷ squid
squiggle n (pl -s) wavy line > **squiggly** adj (-lier, -liest)
squiggles n ▷ squiggle
squigglier adj ▷ squiggle
squiggliest adj ▷ squiggle
squiggly adj ▷ squiggle
squint v (-s, -ing, -ed) have eyes which face in different directions ▶ n (pl -s) squinting condition of the eye ▶ adj crooked (-er, -est)
squinted v ▷ squint
squinter adj ▷ squint
squintest adj ▷ squint
squinting v ▷ squint
squints v, n ▷ squint
squire n (pl -s) country gentleman, usu. the main landowner in a community
squires n ▷ squire
squirm v (-s, -ing, -ed) wriggle, writhe ▶ n (pl -s) wriggling movement
squirmed v ▷ squirm
squirming v ▷ squirm
squirms v, n ▷ squirm
squirrel n (pl -s) small bushy-tailed tree-living animal
squirrels n ▷ squirrel
squirt v (-s, -ing, -ed) force (a liquid) or (of a liquid) be forced out of a narrow opening ▶ n (pl -s) jet of liquid
squirted v ▷ squirt
squirting v ▷ squirt
squirts n, v ▷ squirt
squish v (-es, -ing, -ed) ▶ n (pl -es) (make) a soft squelching sound > **squishy** adj (-shier, -shiest)
squished v ▷ squish
squishes n, v ▷ squish
squishier adj ▷ squish
squishiest adj ▷ squish
squishing v ▷ squish
squishy adj ▷ squish

squiz n (**squizzes**). Squiz is an informal word for a look or glance. This is a useful word to remember, both for when you have the most of the tiles to form it and when someone else plays **quiz** which you can then add an S to for a good score. Squiz scores 23 points.

st *interj*. St is a sound people make to request silence or quiet. This is one of two two-letter words beginning with S that do not contain a vowel. It's useful when you want to connect a word beginning with H to one ending in T or vice versa. St scores 2 points.

stab *v* (**-s, -bbing, -bbed**) pierce with something pointed ▶ *n* (*pl* **-s**) stabbing
  stabbed *v* ▷ **stab**
  stabbing *v* ▷ **stab**
  stabilities *n* ▷ **stable²**
  stability *n* ▷ **stable²**
  stabilization *n* ▷ **stabilize**
  stabilizations *n* ▷ **stabilize**
stabilize *v* (**-zes, -zing, -zed**) make or become stable > **stabilization** *n* (*pl* **-s**)
  stabilized *v* ▷ **stabilize**
stabilizer *n* (*pl* **-s**) device for stabilizing a child's bicycle, an aircraft, or a ship
  stabilizers *n* ▷ **stabilizer**
  stabilizes *v* ▷ **stabilize**
  stabilizing *v* ▷ **stabilize**
stable¹ *n* (*pl* **-s**) building in which horses are kept ▶ *v* (**-les, -ling, -led**) put or keep (a horse) in a stable
stable² *adj* (**-r, -st**) firmly fixed or established > **stability** *n* (*pl* **-ties**)
  stabled *v* ▷ **stable¹**
  stabler *adj* ▷ **stable²**
  stables *n, v* ▷ **stable¹**
  stablest *adj* ▷ **stable²**
  stabling *v* ▷ **stable¹**
  stabs *v, n* ▷ **stab**
staccato [stak-**ah**-toe] *adv* (MUSIC) with the notes sharply separated ▶ *adj* consisting of short abrupt sounds
stack *n* (*pl* **-s**) ordered pile ▶ *v* (**-s, -ing, -ed**) pile in a stack
  stacked *v* ▷ **stack**
  stacking *v* ▷ **stack**
  stacks *n, v* ▷ **stack**
  stadia *n* ▷ **stadium**
stadium *n* (*pl* **-diums, -dia**) sports arena with tiered seats for spectators
  stadiums *n* ▷ **stadium**
staff¹ *n* (*pl* **-s**) people employed in an organization ▶ *v* (**-s, -ing, -ed**) supply with personnel
staff² *n* (*pl* **staves**) set of five horizontal lines

on which music is written
  staffed *v* ▷ **staff¹**
  staffing *v* ▷ **staff¹**
  staffs *n, v* ▷ **staff¹**
stag *n* (*pl* **-s**) adult male deer
stage *n* (*pl* **-s**) step or period of development ▶ *v* (**-ges, -ging, -ged**) put (a play) on stage
stagecoach *n* (*pl* **-es**) large horse-drawn vehicle formerly used to carry passengers and mail
  stagecoaches *n* ▷ **stagecoach**
  staged *v* ▷ **stage**
  stages *n, v* ▷ **stage**
stagey *adj* (**-gier, -giest**) overtheatrical
stagger *v* (**-s, -ing, -ed**) walk unsteadily ▶ *n* (*pl* **-s**) staggering
  staggered *v* ▷ **stagger**
  staggering *v* ▷ **stagger**
  staggers *v, n* ▷ **stagger**
  stagier *adj* ▷ **stagey**
  stagiest *adj* ▷ **stagey**
  staging *v* ▷ **stage**
stagnant *adj* (of water or air) stale from not moving
stagnate *v* (**-tes, -ting, -ted**) be stagnant > **stagnation** *n* (*pl* **-s**)
  stagnated *v* ▷ **stagnate**
  stagnates *v* ▷ **stagnate**
  stagnating *v* ▷ **stagnate**
  stagnation *n* ▷ **stagnate**
  stagnations *n* ▷ **stagnate**
  stags *n* ▷ **stag**
staid *adj* (**-er, -est**) sedate, serious, and rather dull
  staider *adj* ▷ **staid**
  staidest *adj* ▷ **staid**
stain *v* (**-s, -ing, -ed**) discolour, mark ▶ *n* (*pl* **-s**) discoloration or mark > **stainless** *adj*
  stained *v* ▷ **stain**
  staining *v* ▷ **stain**
  stainless *adj* ▷ **stain**
  stains *v, n* ▷ **stain**
staircase, stairway *n* (*pl* **-s**) flight of stairs with a handrail or banisters
  staircases *n* ▷ **staircase**
stairs *pl n* flight of steps between floors, usu. indoors
  stairway *n* ▷ **staircase**
  stairways *n* ▷ **staircase**
stake¹ *n* (*pl* **-s**) pointed stick or post driven into the ground as a support or marker ▶ *v* (**-kes, -king, -ked**) support or mark out with stakes
stake² *n* (*pl* **-s**) money wagered ▶ *v* (**-kes, -king, -ked**) wager, risk
  staked *v* ▷ **stake¹, ²**

stakeholder n (pl -s) person who has a concern or interest in something, esp. a business
stakeholders n ▷ stakeholder
stakes v ▷ stake¹, ² ▶ n ▷ stake¹, ²
staking v ▷ stake¹, ²
stalactite n (pl -s) lime deposit hanging from the roof of a cave
stalactites n ▷ stalactite
stalagmite n (pl -s) lime deposit sticking up from the floor of a cave
stalagmites n ▷ stalagmite
stale adj (-r, -st) not fresh > **staleness** n (pl -es)
stalemate n (pl -s) (CHESS) position in which any of a player's moves would put his king in check, resulting in a draw
stalemates n ▷ stalemate
staleness n ▷ stale
stalenesses n ▷ stale
staler adj ▷ stale
stalest adj ▷ stale
stalk¹ n (pl -s) plant's stem
stalk² v (-s, -ing, -ed) follow or approach stealthily
stalked v ▷ stalk²
stalker n (pl -s) person who follows or stealthily approaches a person or an animal
stalkers n ▷ stalker
stalking v ▷ stalk²
stalking-horse n (pl -s) pretext
stalking-horses n ▷ stalking-horse
stalks n ▷ stalk¹ ▶ v ▷ stalk²
stall¹ n (pl -s) small stand for the display and sale of goods ▶ v (-s, -ing, -ed) stop (a motor vehicle or engine) or (of a motor vehicle or engine) stop accidentally
stall² v (-s, -ing, -ed) employ delaying tactics
stalled v ▷ stall¹, ²
stalling v ▷ stall¹, ²
stallion n (pl -s) uncastrated male horse
stallions n ▷ stallion
stalls n ▷ stall¹ ▶ v ▷ stall¹, ² ▶ pl n ground-floor seats in a theatre or cinema
stalwart [stawl-wart] adj strong and sturdy ▶ n (pl -s) stalwart person
stalwarts n ▷ stalwart
stamen n (pl -s) pollen-producing part of a flower
stamens n ▷ stamen
stamina n (pl -s) enduring energy and strength
staminas n ▷ stamina
stammer v (-s, -ing, ed) speak or say with involuntary pauses or repetition of syllables ▶ n (pl -s) tendency to stammer
stammered v ▷ stammer
stammering v ▷ stammer

stammers v, n ▷ stammer
stamp n (pl -s) piece of gummed paper stuck to an envelope or parcel to show that the postage has been paid ▶ v (-s, -ing, -ed) bring (one's foot) down forcefully
stamped v ▷ stamp
stampede n (pl -s) sudden rush of frightened animals or of a crowd ▶ v (-des, -ding, -ded) (cause to) take part in a stampede
stampeded v ▷ stampede
stampedes n, v ▷ stampede
stampeding v ▷ stampede
stamping v ▷ stamp
stamps n, v ▷ stamp
stance n (pl -s) attitude
stances n ▷ stance
stanch [stahnch] v (-es, -ing, -ed) ▷ staunch²
stanched v ▷ stanch
stanches v ▷ stanch
stanching v ▷ stanch
stanchion n (pl -s) upright bar used as a support
stanchions n ▷ stanchion
stand v (-s, -ing, stood) be in, rise to, or place in an upright position ▶ n (pl -s) stall for the sale of goods
standard n (pl -s) level of quality ▶ adj usual, regular, or average
standardization n ▷ standardize
standardize v (-zes, -zing, -zed) cause to conform to a standard > **standardization** n (pl -s)
standardized v ▷ standardize
standardizes v ▷ standardize
standardizing v ▷ standardize
standards n ▷ standard
standing adj permanent, lasting ▶ n (pl -s) reputation or status ▶ v ▷ stand
standings n ▷ standing
standoffish adj reserved or haughty
standpipe n (pl -s) tap attached to a water main to provide a public water supply
standpipes n ▷ standpipe
standpoint n (pl -s) point of view
standpoints n ▷ standpoint
stands v, n ▷ stand
standstill n (pl -s) complete halt
standstills n ▷ standstill
stank v ▷ stink
stanza n (pl -s) verse of a poem
stanzas n ▷ stanza
staple¹ n (pl -s) U-shaped piece of metal used to fasten papers or secure things ▶ v (-les, -ling, -led) fasten with staples
staple² adj of prime importance, principal ▶ n

(*pl* -**s**) main constituent of anything
stapled *v* ▷ **staple**[1]
stapler *n* (*pl* -**s**) small device for fastening papers together
staplers *n* ▷ **stapler**
staples *n* ▷ **staple**[1, 2] ▶ *v* ▷ **staple**[1]
stapling *v* ▷ **staple**[1]
star *n* (*pl* -**s**) hot gaseous mass in space, visible in the night sky as a point of light ▶ *v* (-**s**, -**rring**, -**rred**) feature or be featured in a main role ▶ *adj* leading, famous
starboard *n* (*pl* -**s**) right-hand side of a ship, when facing forward ▶ *adj* of or on this side
starboards *n* ▷ **starboard**
starch *n* (*pl* -**es**) carbohydrate forming the main food element in bread, potatoes, etc., and used mixed with water for stiffening fabric ▶ *v* (-**es**, -**ing**, -**ed**) stiffen (fabric) with starch
starched *v* ▷ **starch**
starches *n, v* ▷ **starch**
starchier *adj* ▷ **starchy**
starchiest *adj* ▷ **starchy**
starching *v* ▷ **starch**
starchy *adj* (-**chier**, -**chiest**) containing starch
stardom *n* (*pl* -**s**) status of a star in the entertainment or sports world
stardoms *n* ▷ **stardom**
stare *v* (-**res**, -**ring**, -**red**) look or gaze fixedly (at) ▶ *n* (*pl* -**s**) fixed gaze
stared *v* ▷ **stare**
stares *v, n* ▷ **stare**
starfish *n* (*pl* -**es**) star-shaped sea creature
starfishes *n* ▷ **starfish**
staring *v* ▷ **stare**
stark *adj* (-**er**, -**est**) harsh, unpleasant, and plain ▶ *adv* completely
starker *adj* ▷ **stark**
starkest *adj* ▷ **stark**
starling *n* (*pl* -**s**) songbird with glossy black speckled feathers
starlings *n* ▷ **starling**
starred *v* ▷ **star**
starrier *adj* ▷ **starry**
starriest *adj* ▷ **starry**
starring *v* ▷ **star**
starry *adj* (-**rrier**, -**rriest**) full of or like stars
stars *n, v* ▷ **star** ▶ *pl n* astrological forecast, horoscope
start *v* (-**s**, -**ing**, -**ed**) take the first step, begin ▶ *n* (*pl* -**s**) first part of something
started *v* ▷ **start**
starter *n* (*pl* -**s**) first course of a meal
starters *n* ▷ **starter**
starting *v* ▷ **start**

startle *v* (-**les**, -**ling**, -**led**) slightly surprise or frighten
startled *v* ▷ **startle**
startles *v* ▷ **startle**
startling *v* ▷ **startle**
starts *v, n* ▷ **start**
starvation *n* ▷ **starve**
starvations *n* ▷ **starve**
starve *v* (-**ves**, -**ving**, -**ved**) die or suffer or cause to die or suffer from hunger > **starvation** *n* (*pl* -**s**)
starved *v* ▷ **starve**
starves *v* ▷ **starve**
starving *v* ▷ **starve**
stash (*Informal*) *v* (-**es**, -**ing**, -**ed**) store in a secret place ▶ *n* (*pl* -**es**) secret store
stashed *v* ▷ **stash**
stashes *v, n* ▷ **stash**
stashing *v* ▷ **stash**
state *n* (*pl* -**s**) condition of a person or thing ▶ *adj* of or concerning the State ▶ *v* (-**tes**, -**ting**, -**ted**) express in words
stated *v* ▷ **state**
statehouse *n* (*pl* -**s**) (NZ) publicly-owned house rented to a low-income tenant
statehouses *n* ▷ **statehouse**
statelier *adj* ▷ **stately**
stateliest *adj* ▷ **stately**
stately *adj* (-**lier**, -**liest**) dignified or grand
statement *n* (*pl* -**s**) something stated
statements *n* ▷ **statement**
stateroom *n* (*pl* -**s**) private cabin on a ship
staterooms *n* ▷ **stateroom**
states *n, v* ▷ **state**
statesman, stateswoman *n* (*pl* -**men**, -**women**) experienced and respected political leader > **statesmanship** *n* (*pl* -**s**)
statesmanship *n* ▷ **statesman**
statesmanships *n* ▷ **statesman**
statesmen *n* ▷ **statesman**
stateswoman *n* ▷ **statesman**
stateswomen *n* ▷ **statesman**
static *adj* stationary or inactive ▶ *n* (*pl* -**s**) crackling sound or speckled picture caused by interference in radio or television reception
statics *n* ▷ **static**
stating *v* ▷ **state**
station *n* (*pl* -**s**) place where trains stop for passengers ▶ *v* (-**s**, -**ing**, -**ed**) assign (someone) to a particular place
stationary *adj* not moving
stationed *v* ▷ **station**
stationer *n* (*pl* -**s**) dealer in stationery
stationeries *n* ▷ **stationery**

stationers n ▷ **stationer**
stationery n (pl **-ries**) writing materials such as paper and pens
stationing v ▷ **station**
stations n, v ▷ **station**
statistic n (pl **-s**) numerical fact collected and classified systematically > **statistical** adj > **statistically** adv
statistical adj ▷ **statistic**
statistically adv ▷ **statistic**
statistician n (pl **-s**) person who compiles and studies statistics
statisticians n ▷ **statistician**
statistics n ▷ **statistic**
statuaries n ▷ **statuary**
statuary n (pl **-ries**) statues collectively
statue n (pl **-s**) large sculpture of a human or animal figure
statues n ▷ **statue**
statuesque adj (of a woman) tall and well-proportioned
statuette n (pl **-s**) small statue
statuettes n ▷ **statuette**
stature n (pl **-s**) person's height
statures n ▷ **stature**
status n (pl **-ses**) social position
statuses n ▷ **status**
statute n (pl **-s**) written law > **statutory** adj required or authorized by law
statutes n ▷ **statute**
statutory adj ▷ **statute**
staunch[1] adj (**-er**, **-est**) loyal, firm
staunch[2], **stanch** v (**-ches**, **-ching**, **-ched**) stop (a flow of blood)
staunched v ▷ **staunch**[2]
stauncher adj ▷ **staunch**[1]
staunches v ▷ **staunch**[2]
staunchest adj ▷ **staunch**[1]
staunching v ▷ **staunch**[2]
stave n (pl **-s**) one of the strips of wood forming a barrel
staves n ▷ **staff**[2]
stay[1] v (**-s**, **-ing**, **-ed**) remain in a place or condition ▶ n (pl **-s**) period of staying in a place
stay[2] n (pl **-s**) prop or buttress
stay[3] n (pl **-s**) rope or wire supporting a ship's mast
stayed v ▷ **stay**[1]
staying v ▷ **stay**[1]
stays n ▷ **stay**[1, 2, 3] ▶ v ▷ **stay**[1] ▶ pl n corset
stead n (pl **-s**) in someone's place
steadfast adj firm, determined > **steadfastly** adv
steadfastly adv ▷ **steadfast**

steadied v ▷ **steady**
steadier adj ▷ **steady**
steadiest adj ▷ **steady**
steadily adv ▷ **steady**
steadiness n ▷ **steady**
steadinesses n ▷ **steady**
steads n ▷ **stead**
steady adj (**-dier**, **-diest**) not shaky or wavering ▶ v (**-dies**, **-dying**, **-died**) make steady ▶ adv in a steady manner > **steadily** adv > **steadiness** n (pl **-es**)
steadying v ▷ **steady**
steak n (pl **-s**) thick slice of meat, esp. beef
steaks n ▷ **steak**
steal v (**-s**, **-ing**, **stole**, **stolen**) take unlawfully or without permission
stealing v ▷ **steal**
steals v ▷ **steal**
stealth n (pl **-s**) secret or underhand behaviour ▶ adj (of technology) able to render an aircraft almost invisible to radar > **stealthy** adj (**-thier**, **-thiest**) > **stealthily** adv
stealthier adj ▷ **stealth**
stealthiest adj ▷ **stealth**
stealthily adv ▷ **stealth**
stealths n ▷ **stealth**
stealthy adj ▷ **stealth**
steam n (pl **-s**) vapour into which water changes when boiled ▶ v (**-s**, **-ing**, **-ed**) give off steam
steamed v ▷ **steam**
steamer n (pl **-s**) steam-propelled ship
steamers n ▷ **steamer**
steaming v ▷ **steam**
steamroller n (pl **-s**) steam-powered vehicle with heavy rollers, used to level road surfaces ▶ v (**-s**, **-ing**, **-ed**) use overpowering force to make (someone) do what one wants
steamrollered v ▷ **steamroller**
steamrollering v ▷ **steamroller**
steamrollers n, v ▷ **steamroller**
steams n, v ▷ **steam**
steed n (pl **-s**) (Lit) horse
steeds n ▷ **steed**
steel n (pl **-s**) hard malleable alloy of iron and carbon ▶ v (**-s**, **-ing**, **-ed**) prepare (oneself) for something unpleasant > **steely** adj (**-lier**, **-liest**)
steeled v ▷ **steel**
steelier adj ▷ **steel**
steeliest adj ▷ **steel**
steeling v ▷ **steel**
steels n, v ▷ **steel**
steely adj ▷ **steel**
steep[1] adj (**-er**, **-est**) sloping sharply > **steeply**

adv > **steepness** *n* (*pl* -es)

steep² *v* (-s, -ing, -ed) soak or be soaked in liquid
  steeped *v* ▷ **steep²**
  steeper *adj* ▷ **steep¹**
  steepest *adj* ▷ **steep¹**
  steeping *v* ▷ **steep²**
steeple *n* (*pl* -s) church tower with a spire
steeplechase *n* (*pl* -s) horse race with obstacles to jump
  steeplechases *n* ▷ **steeplechase**
steeplejack *n* (*pl* -s) person who repairs steeples and chimneys
  steeplejacks *n* ▷ **steeplejack**
  steeples *n* ▷ **steeple**
  steeply *n* ▷ **steep¹**
  steepness *n* ▷ **steep¹**
  steepnesses *n* ▷ **steep¹**
  steeps *v* ▷ **steep²**
steer¹ *v* (-s, -ing, -ed) direct the course of (a vehicle or ship)
steer² *n* (*pl* -s) castrated male ox
steerage *n* (*pl* -s) cheapest accommodation on a passenger ship
  steerages *n* ▷ **steerage**
  steered *v* ▷ **steer¹**
  steering *v* ▷ **steer¹**
  steers *v* ▷ **steer¹** ▶ *n* ▷ **steer²**
stein [stine] *n* (*pl* -s) earthenware beer mug
  steins *n* ▷ **stein**
stellar *adj* of stars
stem¹ *n* (*pl* -s) long thin central part of a plant
  ▶ *v* (-s, -mming, -mmed) originate from
stem² *v* (-s, -mming, -mmed) stop (the flow of something)
  stemmed *v* ▷ **stem¹, ²**
  stemming *v* ▷ **stem¹, ²**
  stems *v* ▷ **stem¹, ²** ▶ *n* ▷ **stem¹**
stench *n* (*pl* -es) foul smell
  stenches *n* ▷ **stench**
stencil *n* (*pl* -s) thin sheet with cut-out pattern through which ink or paint passes to form the pattern on the surface below ▶ *v* (-s, -lling, -lled) make (a pattern) with a stencil
  stencilled *v* ▷ **stencil**
  stencilling *v* ▷ **stencil**
  stencils *n, v* ▷ **stencil**
stenographer *n* (*pl* -s) shorthand typist
  stenographers *n* ▷ **stenographer**
stent *n* (*pl* -s) surgical implant used to keep an artery open
stentorian *adj* (of a voice) very loud
  stents *n* ▷ **stent**
step *v* (-s, -pping, -pped) move and set down the foot, as when walking ▶ *n* (*pl* -s) stepping

stepladder *n* (*pl* -s) folding portable ladder with supporting frame
  stepladders *n* ▷ **stepladder**
  stepped *v* ▷ **step**
steppes *pl n* wide grassy treeless plains in Russia and Ukraine
  stepping *v* ▷ **step**
steps *pl n* stepladder ▶ *n, v* ▷ **step**
  stereo *adj* ▷ **stereophonic** ▶ *n* (*pl* -s) stereophonic record player
stereophonic *adj* using two separate loudspeakers to give the effect of naturally distributed sound
  stereos *n* ▷ **stereo**
stereotype *n* (*pl* -s) standardized idea of a type of person or thing ▶ *v* (-pes, -ping, -ped) form a stereotype of
  stereotyped *v* ▷ **stereotype**
  stereotypes *n, v* ▷ **stereotype**
  stereotyping *v* ▷ **stereotype**
sterile *adj* free from germs > **sterility** *n* (*pl* -ties)
  sterilities *n* ▷ **sterile**
  sterility *n* ▷ **sterile**
  sterilization *n* ▷ **sterilize**
  sterilizations *n* ▷ **sterilize**
sterilize *v* (-zes, -zing, -zed) make sterile
  > **sterilization** *n* (*pl* -s)
  sterilized *v* ▷ **sterilize**
  sterilizes *v* ▷ **sterilize**
  sterilizing *v* ▷ **sterilize**
sterling *n* (*pl* -s) British money system ▶ *adj* genuine and reliable
  sterlings *n* ▷ **sterling**
stern¹ *adj* (-er, -est) severe, strict > **sternly** *adv*
  > **sternness** *n* (*pl* -es)
stern² *n* (*pl* -s) rear part of a ship
  sterna *n* ▷ **sternum**
  sterner *adj* ▷ **stern¹**
  sternest *adj* ▷ **stern¹**
  sternly *adv* ▷ **stern¹**
  sternness *n* ▷ **stern¹**
  sternnesses *n* ▷ **stern¹**
  sterns *n* ▷ **stern²**
sternum *n* (*pl* -na, -nums) ▷ **breastbone**
  sternums *n* ▷ **sternum**
steroid *n* (*pl* -s) organic compound containing a carbon ring system, such as many hormones
  steroids *n* ▷ **steroid**
stethoscope *n* (*pl* -s) medical instrument for listening to sounds made inside the body
  stethoscopes *n* ▷ **stethoscope**
stevedore *n* (*pl* -s) person who loads and unloads ships
  stevedores *n* ▷ **stevedore**

stew n (pl -s) food cooked slowly in a closed pot
▶ v (-s, -ing, -ed) cook slowly in a closed pot
steward n (pl -s) person who looks after
passengers on a ship or aircraft > **stewardess**
n fem (pl -es)
stewardess n ▷ steward
stewardesses n ▷ steward
stewards n ▷ steward
stewed v ▷ stew
stewing v ▷ stew
stews n, v ▷ stew
stick¹ n (pl -s) long thin piece of wood
stick² v (-s, -ing, stuck) push (a pointed object)
into (something)
sticker n (pl -s) adhesive label or sign
stickers n ▷ sticker
stickier adj ▷ sticky
stickiest adj ▷ sticky
sticking v ▷ stick²
stickleback n (pl -s) small fish with sharp
spines on its back
sticklebacks n ▷ stickleback
stickler n (pl -s) person who insists on
something
sticklers n ▷ stickler
sticks n ▷ stick¹ ▶ v ▷ stick²
stickup n (pl -s) (Slang) robbery at gunpoint
stickups n ▷ stickup
sticky adj (-ckier, -ckiest) covered with an
adhesive substance
sties n ▷ sty
stiff adj (-er, -est) not easily bent or moved ▶ n
(pl -s) (Slang) corpse > **stiffly** adv > **stiffness**
n (pl -es)
stiffen v (-s, -ing, -ed) make or become stiff
stiffened v ▷ stiffen
stiffening v ▷ stiffen
stiffens v ▷ stiffen
stiffer adj ▷ stiff
stiffest adj ▷ stiff
stiffly adv ▷ stiff
stiffness n ▷ stiff
stiffnesses n ▷ stiff
stiffs n ▷ stiff
stifle v (-les, -ling, -led) suppress
stifled v ▷ stifle
stifles v ▷ stifle
stifling v ▷ stifle
stigma n (pl -mas, -mata) mark of social
disgrace
stigmas n ▷ stigma
stigmata pl n marks resembling the wounds
of the crucified Christ ▶ n ▷ stigma
stigmatize v (-zes, -zing, -zed) mark as being
shameful

stigmatized v ▷ stigmatize
stigmatizes v ▷ stigmatize
stigmatizing v ▷ stigmatize
stile n (pl -s) set of steps allowing people to
climb a fence
stiles n ▷ stile
stiletto n (pl -s) high narrow heel on a woman's
shoe
stilettos n ▷ stiletto
still¹ adv now or in the future as before ▶ adj
(-er, -est) motionless ▶ n (pl -s) photograph
from a film scene ▶ v (-s, -ing, -ed) make still
> **stillness** n (pl -es)
still² n (pl -s) apparatus for distilling alcoholic
drinks
stillborn adj born dead
stilled v ▷ still¹
stiller adj ▷ still¹
stillest adj ▷ still¹
stilling v ▷ still¹
stillness n ▷ still¹
stillnesses n ▷ still¹
stills n ▷ still¹, ² ▶ v ▷ still¹
stilted adj stiff and formal in manner
stilts pl n pair of poles with footrests for
walking raised from the ground
stimulant n (pl -s) something, such as a drug,
that acts as a stimulus
stimulants n ▷ stimulant
stimulate v (-tes, -ting, -ted) act as a stimulus
(on) > **stimulation** n (pl -s)
stimulated v ▷ stimulate
stimulates v ▷ stimulate
stimulating v ▷ stimulate
stimulation n ▷ stimulate
stimulations n ▷ stimulate
stimuli n ▷ stimulus
stimulus n (pl -li) something that rouses a
person or thing to activity
sting v (-s, -ing, stung) (of certain animals
or plants) wound by injecting with poison
▶ n (pl -s) wound or pain caused by or as if by
stinging
stingier adj ▷ stingy
stingiest adj ▷ stingy
stinginess n ▷ stingy
stinginesses n ▷ stingy
stinging v ▷ sting
stings v, n ▷ sting
stingy adj (-gier, -giest) mean or miserly
> **stinginess** n (pl -es)
stink n (pl -s) strong unpleasant smell ▶ v (-s,
-ing, stank or stunk) (stunk) give off a strong
unpleasant smell
stinking v ▷ stink

stinks n, v ▷ **stink**

stint v (-s, -ing, -ed) (foll. by **on**) be miserly with (something) ▸ n (pl -s) allotted amount of work

stinted v ▷ **stint**

stinting v ▷ **stint**

stints v, n ▷ **stint**

stipend [sty-pend] n (pl -s) regular allowance or salary, esp. that paid to a clergyman
> **stipendiary** adj receiving a stipend

stipendiary adj ▷ **stipend**

stipends n ▷ **stipend**

stipple v (-les, -ling, -led) paint, draw, or engrave using dots

stippled v ▷ **stipple**

stipples v ▷ **stipple**

stippling v ▷ **stipple**

stipulate v (-tes, -ting, -ted) specify as a condition of an agreement > **stipulation** n (pl -s)

stipulated v ▷ **stipulate**

stipulates v ▷ **stipulate**

stipulating v ▷ **stipulate**

stipulation n ▷ **stipulate**

stipulations n ▷ **stipulate**

stir v (-s, -rring, -rred) mix up (a liquid) by moving a spoon etc. around in it ▸ n (pl -s) a stirring

stirred v ▷ **stir**

stirring v ▷ **stir**

stirrup n (pl -s) metal loop attached to a saddle for supporting a rider's foot

stirrups n ▷ **stirrup**

stirs v, n ▷ **stir**

stitch n (pl -es) link made by drawing thread through material with a needle ▸ v (-es, -ing, -ed) sew

stitched v ▷ **stitch**

stitches n, v ▷ **stitch**

stitching v ▷ **stitch**

stoat n (pl -s) small mammal of the weasel family, with brown fur that turns white in winter

stoats n ▷ **stoat**

stock n (pl -s) total amount of goods available for sale in a shop ▸ adj kept in stock, standard ▸ v (-s, -ing, -ed) keep for sale or future use

stockade n (pl -s) enclosure or barrier made of stakes

stockades n ▷ **stockade**

stockbroker n (pl -s) person who buys and sells stocks and shares for customers

stockbrokers n ▷ **stockbroker**

stocked v ▷ **stock**

stockier adj ▷ **stocky**

stockiest adj ▷ **stocky**

stocking n (pl -s) close-fitting covering for the foot and leg ▸ v ▷ **stock**

stockings n ▷ **stocking**

stockist n (pl -s) dealer who stocks a particular product

stockists n ▷ **stockist**

stockpile v (-les, -ling, -led) store a large quantity of (something) for future use ▸ n (pl -s) accumulated store

stockpiled v ▷ **stockpile**

stockpiles v, n ▷ **stockpile**

stockpiling v ▷ **stockpile**

stocks n pl (HIST) instrument of punishment consisting of a wooden frame with holes into which the hands and feet of the victim were locked ▸ n, v ▷ **stock**

stocktaking n (pl -s) counting and valuing of the goods in a shop

stocktakings n ▷ **stocktaking**

stocky adj (-ckier, -ckiest) (of a person) broad and sturdy

stodge n (pl -s) (BRIT, AUST & NZ) heavy starchy food

stodges n ▷ **stodge**

stodgier adj ▷ **stodgy**

stodgiest adj ▷ **stodgy**

stodgy adj (-gier, -giest) (of food) heavy and starchy

stoep [stoop] n (pl -s) (S AFR) verandah

stoeps n ▷ **stoep**

stoic [stow-ik] n (pl -s) person who suffers hardship without showing his or her feelings ▸ adj (also **stoical**) suffering hardship without showing one's feelings > **stoically** adv
> **stoicism** [stow-iss-izz-um] n (pl -s)

stoical adj ▷ **stoic**

stoically adv ▷ **stoic**

stoicism n ▷ **stoic**

stoicisms n ▷ **stoic**

stoics n ▷ **stoic**

stoke v (-kes, -king, -ked) feed and tend (a fire or furnace) > **stoker** n (pl -s)

stoked v ▷ **stoke**

stoker n ▷ **stoke**

stokers n ▷ **stoke**

stokes v ▷ **stoke**

stoking v ▷ **stoke**

stole¹ v ▷ **steal**

stole² n (pl -s) long scarf or shawl

stolen v ▷ **steal**

stoles n ▷ **stole²**

stolid adj (-er, -est) showing little emotion or interest > **stolidly** adv

stolider adj ▷ **stolid**

stolidest *adj* ▷ **stolid**
stolidly *adv* ▷ **stolid**
stomach *n* (*pl* **-s**) organ in the body which digests food ▸ *v* (**-s, -ing, -ed**) put up with
stomached *v* ▷ **stomach**
stomaching *v* ▷ **stomach**
stomachs *n, v* ▷ **stomach**
stomp *v* (**-s, -ing, -ed**) (*Informal*) tread heavily
stomped *v* ▷ **stomp**
stomping *v* ▷ **stomp**
stomps *v* ▷ **stomp**
stone *n* (*pl* **-s**) material of which rocks are made ▸ *v* (**-nes, -ning, -ned**) throw stones at
stoned *adj* (*Slang*) under the influence of alcohol or drugs ▸ *v* ▷ **stone**
stones *n, v* ▷ **stone**
stonewall *v* (**-s, -ing, -ed**) obstruct or hinder discussion
stonewalled *v* ▷ **stonewall**
stonewalling *v* ▷ **stonewall**
stonewalls *v* ▷ **stonewall**
stoneware *n* (*pl* **-s**) hard kind of pottery fired at a very high temperature
stonewares *n* ▷ **stoneware**
stonier *adj* ▷ **stony**
stoniest *adj* ▷ **stony**
stonily *adv* ▷ **stony**
stoning *v* ▷ **stone**
stony *adj* (**-nier, -niest**) of or like stone
> **stonily** *adv*
stood *v* ▷ **stand**
stooge *n* (*pl* **-es**) actor who feeds lines to a comedian or acts as the butt of his jokes
stooges *n* ▷ **stooge**
stool *n* (*pl* **-s**) chair without arms or back
stools *n* ▷ **stool**
stoop *v* (**-s, -ing, -ed**) bend (the body) forward and downward ▸ *n* (*pl* **-s**) stooping posture
stooped *v* ▷ **stoop**
stooping *v* ▷ **stoop**
stoops *v, n* ▷ **stoop**
stop *v* (**-s, -pping, -pped**) cease or cause to cease from doing (something) ▸ *n* (*pl* **-s**) stopping or being stopped > **stoppage** *n* (*pl* **-s**)
stopcock *n* (*pl* **-s**) valve to control or stop the flow of fluid in a pipe
stopcocks *n* ▷ **stopcock**
stopgap *n* (*pl* **-s**) temporary substitute
stopgaps *n* ▷ **stopgap**
stopover *n* (*pl* **-s**) short break in a journey
stopovers *n* ▷ **stopover**
stoppage *n* ▷ **stop**
stoppages *n* ▷ **stop**
stopped *v* ▷ **stop**
stopper *n* (*pl* **-s**) plug for closing a bottle etc.

stoppers *n* ▷ **stopper**
stopping *v* ▷ **stop**
stops *v, n* ▷ **stop**
stopwatch *n* (*pl* **-es**) watch which can be stopped instantly for exact timing of a sporting event
stopwatches *n* ▷ **stopwatch**
storage *n* (*pl* **-s**) storing
storages *n* ▷ **storage**
store *v* (**-res, -ring, -red**) collect and keep (things) for future use ▸ *n* (*pl* **-s**) shop
stored *v* ▷ **store**
stores *v, n* ▷ **store** ▸ *n pl* stock of provisions
storey *n* (*pl* **-s**) floor or level of a building
storeys *n* ▷ **storey**
stories *n* ▷ **story**
storing *v* ▷ **store**
stork *n* (*pl* **-s**) large wading bird
storks *n* ▷ **stork**
storm *n* (*pl* **-s**) violent weather with wind, rain, or snow ▸ *v* (**-s, -ing, -ed**) attack or capture (a place) suddenly
stormed *v* ▷ **storm**
stormier *adj* ▷ **stormy**
stormiest *adj* ▷ **stormy**
storming *v* ▷ **storm**
storms *n, v* ▷ **storm**
stormy *adj* (**-mier, -miest**) characterized by storms
story *n* (*pl* **-ries**) description of a series of events told or written for entertainment
stoup [stoop] *n* (*pl* **-s**) small basin for holy water
stoups *n* ▷ **stoup**
stout *adj* (**-er, -est**) fat ▸ *n* (*pl* **-s**) strong dark beer > **stoutly** *adv*
stouter *adj* ▷ **stout**
stoutest *adj* ▷ **stout**
stoutly *adv* ▷ **stout**
stouts *n* ▷ **stout**
stove *n* (*pl* **-s**) apparatus for cooking or heating
stoves *n* ▷ **stove**
stow *v* (**-s, -ing, -ed**) pack or store
stowaway *n* (*pl* **-s**) person who hides on a ship or aircraft in order to travel free
stowaways *n* ▷ **stowaway**
stowed *v* ▷ **stow**
stowing *v* ▷ **stow**
stows *v* ▷ **stow**
straddle *v* (**-les, -ling, -led**) have one leg or part on each side of (something)
straddled *v* ▷ **straddle**
straddles *v* ▷ **straddle**
straddling *v* ▷ **straddle**
strafe *v* (**-fes, -fing, -fed**) attack (an enemy) with machine guns from the air

strafed v ▷ strafe
strafes v ▷ strafe
strafing v ▷ strafe
straggle v (**-les, -ling, -led**) go or spread in a rambling or irregular way > **straggler** n (pl **-s**) > **straggly** adj (**-lier, -liest**)
straggled v ▷ straggle
straggler n ▷ straggle
stragglers n ▷ straggle
straggles v ▷ straggle
stragglier adj ▷ straggle
straggliest adj ▷ straggle
straggling v ▷ straggle
straggly adj ▷ straggle
straight adj (**-er, -est**) not curved or crooked ▶ adv in a straight line ▶ n (pl **-s**) straight part, esp. of a racetrack > **straighten** v (**-s, -ing, -ed**)
straightaway adv immediately
straighten v ▷ straight
straightened v ▷ straight
straightening v ▷ straight
straightens v ▷ straighn
straighter adj ▷ straight
straightest adj ▷ straight
straightforward adj honest, frank
straightlaced adj ▷ straitlaced
straights n ▷ straight
strain[1] v (**-s, -ing, -ed**) cause (something) to be used or tested beyond its limits ▶ n (pl **-s**) tension or tiredness
strain[2] n (pl **-s**) breed or race
strained adj not natural, forced ▶ v ▷ strain[1]
strainer n (pl **-s**) sieve
strainers n ▷ strainer
straining v ▷ strain[1]
strains n ▷ strain[1, 2] ▶ v ▷ strain[1]
strait n (pl **-s**) position of acute difficulty
straitened adj not having much money
straitjacket n (pl **-s**) strong jacket with long sleeves used to bind the arms of a violent person
straitjackets n ▷ straitjacket
straitlaced, straightlaced adj prudish or puritanical
straits n ▷ strait ▶ n pl narrow channel connecting two areas of sea
strand[1] v (**-s, -ing, -ed**) run aground ▶ n (pl **-s**) (Poetic) shore
strand[2] n (pl **-s**) single thread of string, wire, etc.
stranded v ▷ strand[1]
stranding v ▷ strand[1]
strands n ▷ strand[1, 2] ▶ v ▷ strand[1]
strange adj (**-r, -st**) odd or unusual > **strangely** adv > **strangeness** n (pl **-es**)

strangely adv ▷ strange
strangeness n ▷ strange
strangenesses n ▷ strange
stranger n (pl **-s**) person who is not known or is new to a place or experience ▶ adj ▷ **strange**
strangers n ▷ stranger
strangest adj ▷ strange
strangle v (**-les, -ling, -led**) kill by squeezing the throat > **strangler** n (pl **-s**)
strangled v ▷ strangle
stranglehold n (pl **-s**) strangling grip in wrestling
strangleholds n ▷ stranglehold
strangler n ▷ strangle
stranglers n ▷ strangle
strangles v ▷ strangle
strangling v ▷ strangle
strangulation n (pl **-s**) strangling
strangulations n ▷ strangulation
strap n (pl **-s**) strip of flexible material for lifting, fastening, or holding in place ▶ v (**-s, -pping, -pped**) fasten with a strap or straps
strapped n ▷ strap
strapping adj tall and sturdy ▶ v ▷ strap
straps n, v ▷ strap
strata n ▷ stratum
stratagem n (pl **-s**) clever plan, trick
stratagems n ▷ stratagem
strategic [strat-**ee**-jik] adj advantageous > **strategically** adv
strategically adv ▷ strategic
strategies n ▷ strategy
strategist n ▷ strategy
strategists n ▷ strategy
strategy n (pl **-gies**) overall plan > **strategist** n (pl **-s**)
strathspey n (pl **-s**) Scottish dance with gliding steps
strathspeys n ▷ strathspey
stratification n ▷ stratified
stratifications n ▷ stratified
stratified adj divided into strata > **stratification** n (pl **-s**)
stratosphere n (pl **-s**) atmospheric layer between about 15 and 50 kilometres above the earth
stratospheres n ▷ stratosphere
stratum [**strah**-tum] n (pl **-ta**) layer, esp. of rock
straw n (pl **-s**) dried stalks of grain
strawberries n ▷ strawberry
strawberry n (pl **-ries**) sweet fleshy red fruit with small seeds on the outside
straws n ▷ straw
stray v (**-s, -ing, -ed**) wander ▶ adj having strayed ▶ n (pl **-s**) stray animal

strayed v ▷ stray
straying v ▷ stray
strays v, n ▷ stray
streak n (pl **-s**) long band of contrasting colour or substance ▶ v (**-s, -ing, -ed**) mark with streaks > **streaker** n (pl **-s**) > **streaky** adj (**-kier, -kiest**)
streaked v ▷ streak
streaker n ▷ streak
streakers n ▷ streak
streakier adj ▷ streak
streakiest adj ▷ streak
streaking v ▷ streak
streaks n, v ▷ streak
streaky adj ▷ streak
stream n (pl **-s**) small river ▶ v (**-s, -ing, -ed**) flow steadily
streamed v ▷ stream
streamer n (pl **-s**) strip of coloured paper that unrolls when tossed
streamers n ▷ streamer
streaming v ▷ stream
streamline v (**-nes, -ning, -ned**) make more efficient by simplifying
streamlined v ▷ streamline
streamlines v ▷ streamline
streamlining v ▷ streamline
streams n, v ▷ stream
street n (pl **-s**) public road, usu. lined with buildings
streetcar n (us) tram
streetcars n ▷ streetcar
streets n ▷ street
streetwise adj knowing how to survive in big cities
strength n (pl **-s**) quality of being strong > **strengthen** v (**-s, -ing, -ed**)
strengthen v ▷ strength
strengthened v ▷ strength
strengthening v ▷ strength
strengthens v ▷ strength
strengths n ▷ strength
strenuous adj requiring great energy or effort > **strenuously** adv
strenuously adv ▷ strenuous
streptococci n ▷ streptococcus
streptococcus [strep-toe-kok-uss] n (pl **-cocci**) bacterium occurring in chains, many species of which cause disease
stress n (pl **-es**) tension or strain ▶ v (**-es, -ing, -ed**) emphasize
stressed v ▷ stress
stresses n, v ▷ stress
stressing v ▷ stress
stretch v (**-es, -ing, -ed**) extend or be extended

▶ n (pl **-es**) stretching > **stretchy** adj (**-chier, -chiest**)
stretched v ▷ stretch
stretcher n (pl **-s**) frame covered with canvas, on which an injured person is carried
stretchers n ▷ stretcher
stretches v, n ▷ stretch
stretchier adj ▷ stretch
stretchiest adj ▷ stretch
stretching v ▷ stretch
stretchy adj ▷ stretch
strew v (**-s, -ing, -ed** or **strewn**) scatter (things) over a surface
strewed v ▷ strew
strewing v ▷ strew
strewn v ▷ strew
strews v ▷ strew
striated adj having a pattern of scratches or grooves
stricken adj seriously affected by disease, grief, pain, etc.
strict adj (**-er, -est**) stern or severe > **strictly** adv > **strictness** n (pl **-es**)
stricter adj ▷ strict
strictest adj ▷ strict
strictly adv ▷ strict
strictness n ▷ strict
strictnesses n ▷ strict
stricture n (pl **-s**) severe criticism
strictures n ▷ stricture
stridden v ▷ stride
stride v (**-des, -ding, strode, stridden**) walk with long steps ▶ n (pl **-s**) long step
stridencies n ▷ strident
stridency n ▷ strident
strident adj loud and harsh > **stridently** adv > **stridency** n (pl **-cies**)
stridently adv ▷ strident
strides v, n ▷ stride ▶ n pl progress
striding v ▷ stride
strife n (pl **-s**) conflict, quarrelling
strifes n ▷ strife
strike v (**-kes, -king, struck**) cease work as a protest ▶ n (pl **-s**) stoppage of work as a protest
striker n (pl **-s**) striking worker
strikers n ▷ striker
strikes v, n ▷ strike
striking adj impressive ▶ v ▷ strike
string n (pl **-s**) thin cord used for tying ▶ v (**-s, -ing, strung**) provide with a string or strings
stringed adj (of a musical instrument) having strings that are plucked or played with a bow
stringencies n ▷ stringent
stringency n ▷ stringent

stringent [strin-jent] *adj* strictly controlled or enforced > **stringently** *adv* > **stringency** *n (pl* **-cies**)

stringently *adv* ▷ **stringent**

stringier *adj* ▷ **stringy**

stringiest *adj* ▷ **stringy**

stringing *v* ▷ **string**

strings *n, v* ▷ **string** ▶ *n pl* restrictions or conditions

stringy *adj* (**-gier, -giest**) like string

stringybark *n (pl* **-s**) Australian eucalyptus with a fibrous bark

stringybarks *n* ▷ **stringybark**

strip¹ *v* (**-s, -pping, -pped**) take (the covering or clothes) off

strip² *n (pl* **-s**) long narrow piece

stripe *n (pl* **-s**) long narrow band of contrasting colour or substance > **striped, stripy, stripey** *adj* (**-pier, -piest**)

striped *adj* ▷ **stripe**

stripes *n* ▷ **stripe**

stripey *adj* ▷ **stripe**

stripier *adj* ▷ **stripe**

stripiest *adj* ▷ **stripe**

stripling *n (pl* **-s**) youth

striplings *n* ▷ **stripling**

stripped *v* ▷ **strip¹**

stripper *n (pl* **-s**) person who performs a striptease

strippers *n* ▷ **stripper**

stripping *v* ▷ **strip¹**

strips *v* ▷ **strip¹** ▶ *n* ▷ **strip²**

striptease *n (pl* **-s**) entertainment in which a performer undresses to music

stripteases *n* ▷ **striptease**

stripy *adj* ▷ **stripe**

strive *v* (**-ves, -ving, strove, striven**) make a great effort

striven *v* ▷ **strive**

strives *v* ▷ **strive**

striving *v* ▷ **strive**

strobe *n (pl* **-s**) ▷ **stroboscope**

strobes *n* ▷ **strobe**

stroboscope *n (pl* **-s**) instrument producing a very bright flashing light

stroboscopes *n* ▷ **stroboscope**

strode *v* ▷ **stride**

stroke *v* (**-kes, -king, -ked**) touch or caress lightly with the hand ▶ *n (pl* **-s**) light touch or caress with the hand

stroked *v* ▷ **stroke**

strokes *v, n* ▷ **stroke**

stroking *v* ▷ **stroke**

stroll *v* (**-s, -ing, -ed**) walk in a leisurely manner ▶ *n (pl* **-s**) leisurely walk

strolled *v* ▷ **stroll**

strolling *v* ▷ **stroll**

strolls *v, n* ▷ **stroll**

strong *adj* (**-er, -est**) having physical power > **strongly** *adv*

stronger *adj* ▷ **strong**

strongest *adj* ▷ **strong**

stronghold *n (pl* **-s**) area of predominance of a particular belief

strongholds *n* ▷ **stronghold**

strongly *adv* ▷ **strong**

strongroom *n (pl* **-s**) room designed for the safekeeping of valuables

strongrooms *n* ▷ **strongroom**

strontium *n (pl* **-s**) (CHEM) silvery-white metallic element

strontiums *n* ▷ **strontium**

strop *n (pl* **-s**) leather strap for sharpening razors

stroppier *adj* ▷ **stroppy**

stroppiest *adj* ▷ **stroppy**

stroppy *adj* (**-pier, -piest**) (*Slang*) angry or awkward

strops *n* ▷ **strop**

strove *v* ▷ **strive**

struck *v* ▷ **strike**

structural *adj* ▷ **structure**

structuralism *n (pl* **-s**) approach to literature, social sciences, etc., which sees changes in the subject as caused and organized by a hidden set of universal rules > **structuralist** *n (pl* **-s**) *adj*

structuralisms *n* ▷ **structuralism**

structuralist *n, adj* ▷ **structuralism**

structuralists *n* ▷ **structuralism**

structure *n (pl* **-s**) complex construction ▶ *v* (**-res, -ring, -red**) give a structure to > **structural** *adj*

structured *v* ▷ **structure**

structures *n, v* ▷ **structure**

structuring *v* ▷ **structure**

strudel *n (pl* **-s**) thin sheet of filled dough rolled up and baked, usu. with an apple filling

strudels *n* ▷ **strudel**

struggle *v* (**-les, -ling, -led**) work, strive, or make one's way with difficulty ▶ *n (pl* **-s**) striving

struggled *v* ▷ **struggle**

struggles *v, n* ▷ **struggle**

struggling *v* ▷ **struggle**

strum *v* (**-s, -mming, -mmed**) play (a guitar or banjo) by sweeping the thumb or a plectrum across the strings

strummed *v* ▷ **strum**

strumming *v* ▷ **strum**

strumpet n (pl -s) (Old-fashioned) prostitute
  strumpets n ▷ strumpet
  strums v ▷ strum
  strung v ▷ string
strut v (-s, -tting, -tted) walk pompously, swagger ▶ n (pl -s) bar supporting a structure
  struts v, n ▷ strut
  strutted v ▷ strut
  strutting v ▷ strut
strychnine [strik-neen] n (pl -s) very poisonous drug used in small quantities as a stimulant
  strychnines n ▷ strychnine
stub n (pl -s) short piece left after use ▶ v (-s, -bbing, -bbed) strike (the toe) painfully against an object
  stubbed v ▷ stub
  stubbier adj ▷ stubby
  stubbiest adj ▷ stubby
  stubbing v ▷ stub
stubble n (pl -s) short stalks of grain left in a field after reaping > **stubbly** adj (-lier, -liest)
  stubbles n ▷ stubble
  stubblier adj ▷ stubble
  stubbliest adj ▷ stubble
  stubbly adj ▷ stubble
stubborn adj (-er, -est) refusing to agree or give in > **stubbornly** adv > **stubbornness** n (pl -es)
  stubborner adj ▷ stubborn
  stubbornest adj ▷ stubborn
  stubbornly adv ▷ stubborn
  stubbornness n ▷ stubborn
  stubbornnesses n ▷ stubborn
stubby adj (-bbier, -bbiest) short and broad
  stubs n, v ▷ stub
stucco n (pl -oes) plaster used for coating or decorating walls
  stuccoes n ▷ stucco
  stuck v ▷ stick²
stud¹ n (pl -s) small piece of metal attached to a surface for decoration ▶ v (-s, -dding, -dded) set with studs
stud² n (pl -s) male animal, esp. a stallion, kept for breeding
  studded v ▷ stud¹
  studding v ▷ stud¹
student n (pl -s) person who studies a subject, esp. at university
  students n ▷ student
studied adj carefully practised or planned ▶ v ▷ study
  studies v, n ▷ study
studio n (pl -s) workroom of an artist or photographer
  studios n ▷ studio

studious adj fond of study > **studiously** adv
  studiously adv ▷ studious
  studs n ▷ stud¹, ² ▶ v ▷ stud¹
study v (-dies, -dying, -died) be engaged in learning (a subject) ▶ n (pl -dies) act or process of studying
  studying v ▷ study
stuff n (pl -s) substance or material ▶ v (-s, -ing, -ed) pack, cram, or fill completely
  stuffed v ▷ stuff
  stuffier adj ▷ stuffy
  stuffiest adj ▷ stuffy
stuffing n (pl -s) seasoned mixture with which food is stuffed ▶ v ▷ stuff
  stuffings n ▷ stuffing
  stuffs n, v ▷ stuff
stuffy adj (-ffier, -ffiest) lacking fresh air
stultifying adj very boring and repetitive
stumble v (-les, -ling, -led) trip and nearly fall ▶ n (pl -s) stumbling
  stumbled v ▷ stumble
  stumbles n ▷ stumble
  stumbling v ▷ stumble
stump n (pl -s) base of a tree left when the main trunk has been cut away ▶ v (-s, -ing, -ed) baffle
  stumped v ▷ stump
  stumpier adj ▷ stumpy
  stumpiest adj ▷ stumpy
  stumping v ▷ stump
  stumps n, v ▷ stump
stumpy adj (-pier, -piest) short and thick
stun v (-s, -nning, -nned) shock or overwhelm
  stung v ▷ sting
  stunk v ▷ stink
  stunned v ▷ stun
stunning adj very attractive or impressive ▶ v ▷ stun
  stuns v ▷ stun
stunt¹ v (-ts, -ing, -ed) prevent or impede the growth of > **stunted** adj
stunt² n (pl -s) acrobatic or dangerous action
  stunted v, adj ▷ stunt¹
  stunting v ▷ stunt¹
  stunts v ▷ stunt¹ ▶ n ▷ stunt²
  stupefaction n ▷ stupefy
  stupefactions n ▷ stupefy
  stupefied v ▷ stupefy
  stupefies v ▷ stupefy
stupefy v (-fies, -fying, -fied) make insensitive or lethargic > **stupefaction** n (pl -s)
  stupefying v ▷ stupefy
stupendous adj very large or impressive > **stupendously** adv
  stupendously adv ▷ stupendous

stupid *adj* (**-er, -est**) lacking intelligence
> **stupidity** *n* (*pl* **-ties**) > **stupidly** *adv*
  stupider *adj* ▷ **stupid**
  stupidest *adj* ▷ **stupid**
  stupidities *n* ▷ **stupid**
  stupidity *n* ▷ **stupid**
  stupidly *adv* ▷ **stupid**
stupor *n* (*pl* **-s**) dazed or unconscious state
  stupors *n* ▷ **stupor**
  sturdier *adj* ▷ **sturdy**
  sturdiest *adj* ▷ **sturdy**
  sturdily *adv* ▷ **sturdy**
sturdy *adj* (**-dier, -diest**) healthy and robust
> **sturdily** *adv*
sturgeon *n* (*pl* **-s**) fish from which caviar is
obtained
  sturgeons *n* ▷ **sturgeon**
stutter *v* (**-s, -ing, -ed**) speak with repetition
of initial consonants ▶ *n* (*pl* **-s**) tendency to
stutter
  stuttered *v* ▷ **stutter**
  stuttering *v* ▷ **stutter**
  stutters *v, n* ▷ **stutter**
sty *n* (*pl* **sties**) pen for pigs
stye *n* (*pl* **styes**) inflammation at the base of
an eyelash
  styes *n* ▷ **stye**
style *n* (*pl* **-s**) shape or design ▶ *v* (**-les, -ling,
-led**) shape or design
  styled *v* ▷ **style**
  styles *n, v* ▷ **style**
  styli *n* ▷ **stylus**
  styling *v* ▷ **style**
stylish *adj* smart, elegant, and fashionable
> **stylishly** *adv*
  stylishly *adv* ▷ **stylish**
stylist *n* (*pl* **-s**) hairdresser
stylistic *adj* of literary or artistic style
  stylists *n* ▷ **stylist**
stylize *v* (**-zes, -zing, -zed**) cause to conform to
an established stylistic form
  stylized *v* ▷ **stylize**
  stylizes *v* ▷ **stylize**
  stylizing *v* ▷ **stylize**
stylus *n* (*pl* **-li, -luses**) needle-like device on a
record player that rests in the groove of the
record and picks up the sound signals
  styluses *n* ▷ **stylus**
stymie *v* (**-mies, -mieing, -mied**) hinder or
thwart
  stymied *v* ▷ **stymie**
  stymieing *v* ▷ **stymie**
  stymies *v* ▷ **stymie**
styptic *n* (*pl* **-s**) ▶ *adj* (drug) used to stop
bleeding

  styptics *n* ▷ **styptic**
suave [swahv] *adj* smooth and sophisticated in
manner > **suavely** *adv*
  suavely *adv* ▷ **suave**
sub *n* (*pl* **-s**) subeditor ▶ *v* (**-s, -bbing, -bbed**) act
as a substitute
subaltern *n* (*pl* **-s**) British army officer below
the rank of captain
  subalterns *n* ▷ **subaltern**
subatomic *adj* of or being one of the particles
which make up an atom
  subbed *v* ▷ **sub**
  subbing *v* ▷ **sub**
subcommittee *n* (*pl* **-s**) small committee
formed from some members of a larger
committee
  subcommittees *n* ▷ **subcommittee**
subconscious *adj* happening or existing
without one's awareness ▶ *n* (*pl* **-es**)
(PSYCHOANALYSIS) that part of the mind of which
one is not aware but which can influence
one's behaviour > **subconsciously** *adv*
  subconsciouses *n* ▷ **subconscious**
  subconsciously *adv* ▷ **subconscious**
subcontinent *n* (*pl* **-s**) large land mass that is a
distinct part of a continent
  subcontinents *n* ▷ **subcontinent**
subcontract *n* (*pl* **-s**) secondary contract by
which the main contractor for a job puts
work out to others ▶ *v* (**-s, -ing, -ed**) put out
(work) on a subcontract > **subcontractor**
n (*pl* **-s**)
  subcontracted *v* ▷ **subcontract**
  subcontracting *v* ▷ **subcontract**
  subcontractor *n* ▷ **subcontract**
  subcontractors *n* ▷ **subcontract**
  subcontracts *n, v* ▷ **subcontract**
subcutaneous [sub-cute-**ayn**-ee-uss] *adj* under
the skin
subdivide *v* (**-des, -ding, -ded**) divide (a part of
something) into smaller parts > **subdivision**
n (*pl* **-s**)
  subdivided *v* ▷ **subdivide**
  subdivides *v* ▷ **subdivide**
  subdividing *v* ▷ **subdivide**
  subdivision *n* ▷ **subdivide**
  subdivisions *n* ▷ **subdivide**
subdue *v* (**-dues, -duing, -dued**) overcome
  subdued *v* ▷ **subdue**
  subdues *v* ▷ **subdue**
  subduing *v* ▷ **subdue**
subeditor *n* (*pl* **-s**) person who checks and
edits text for a newspaper or magazine
  subeditors *n* ▷ **subeditor**
subject *n* (*pl* **-s**) person or thing being dealt

with or studied ▶ *adj* being under the rule of a monarch or government ▶ *v* (**-s, -ing, -ed**) (*foll. by* **to**) cause to undergo > **subjection** *n* (*pl* **-s**)
subjected *v* ▷ **subject**
subjecting *v* ▷ **subject**
subjection *n* ▷ **subject**
subjections *n* ▷ **subject**
subjective *adj* based on personal feelings or prejudices > **subjectively** *adv*
subjectively *adv* ▷ **subjective**
subjects *n, v* ▷ **subject**
subjugate *v* (**-tes, -ting, -ted**) bring (a group of people) under one's control > **subjugation** *n* (*pl* **-s**)
subjugated *v* ▷ **subjugate**
subjugates *v* ▷ **subjugate**
subjugating *v* ▷ **subjugate**
subjugation *n* ▷ **subjugate**
subjugations *n* ▷ **subjugate**
subjunctive (GRAMMAR) *n* (*pl* **-s**) mood of verbs used when the content of the clause is doubted, supposed, or wished ▶ *adj* in or of that mood
subjunctives *n* ▷ **subjunctive**
sublet *v* (**-s, -letting, -let**) rent out (property rented from someone else)
sublets *v* ▷ **sublet**
subletting *v* ▷ **sublet**
sublimate *v* (**-tes, -ting, -ted**) (PSYCHOL) direct the energy of (a strong desire, esp. a sexual one) into socially acceptable activities > **sublimation** *n* (*pl* **-s**)
sublimated *v* ▷ **sublimate**
sublimates *v* ▷ **sublimate**
sublimating *v* ▷ **sublimate**
sublimation *n* ▷ **sublimate**
sublimations *n* ▷ **sublimate**
sublime *adj* (**-r, -st**) of high moral, intellectual, or spiritual value ▶ *v* (**-mes, -ming, -med**) (CHEM) change from a solid to a vapour without first melting > **sublimely** *adv*
sublimed *v* ▷ **sublime**
sublimely *adv* ▷ **sublime**
sublimer *adj* ▷ **sublime**
sublimes *v* ▷ **sublime**
sublimest *adj* ▷ **sublime**
subliminal *adj* relating to mental processes of which the individual is not aware
subliming *v* ▷ **sublime**
submarine *n* (*pl* **-s**) vessel which can operate below the surface of the sea ▶ *adj* below the surface of the sea
submarines *n* ▷ **submarine**
submerge *v* (**-ges, -ging, -ged**) put or go below the surface of water or other liquid

> **submersion** *n* (*pl* **-s**)
submerged *v* ▷ **submerge**
submerges *v* ▷ **submerge**
submerging *v* ▷ **submerge**
submersion *n* ▷ **submerge**
submersions *n* ▷ **submerge**
submission *n* (*pl* **-s**) submitting
submissions *n* ▷ **submission**
submissive *adj* meek and obedient
submit *v* (**-s, -tting, -tted**) surrender
submits *v* ▷ **submit**
submitted *v* ▷ **submit**
submitting *v* ▷ **submit**
subordinate *adj* of lesser rank or importance ▶ *n* (*pl* **-s**) subordinate person or thing ▶ *v* (**-tes, -ting, -ted**) make or treat as subordinate > **subordination** *n* (*pl* **-s**)
subordinated *v* ▷ **subordinate**
subordinates *n, v* ▷ **subordinate**
subordinating *v* ▷ **subordinate**
subordination *n* ▷ **subordinate**
subordinations *n* ▷ **subordinate**
suborn *v* (**-s, -ing, -ed**) (*Formal*) bribe or incite (a person) to commit a wrongful act
suborned *v* ▷ **suborn**
suborning *v* ▷ **suborn**
suborns *v* ▷ **suborn**
subpoena [sub-**pee**-na] *n* (*pl* **-s**) writ requiring a person to appear before a lawcourt ▶ *v* (**-nas, -naing, -naed**) summon (someone) with a subpoena
subpoenaed *v* ▷ **subpoena**
subpoenaing *v* ▷ **subpoena**
subpoenas *n, v* ▷ **subpoena**
subs *n, v* ▷ **sub**
subscribe *v* (**-bes, -bing, -bed**) pay (a subscription) > **subscriber** *n* (*pl* **-s**)
subscribed *v* ▷ **subscribe**
subscriber *n* ▷ **subscribe**
subscribers *n* ▷ **subscribe**
subscribes *v* ▷ **subscribe**
subscribing *v* ▷ **subscribe**
subscription *n* (*pl* **-s**) payment for issues of a publication over a period
subscriptions *n* ▷ **subscription**
subsection *n* (*pl* **-s**) division of a section
subsections *n* ▷ **subsection**
subsequent *adj* occurring after, succeeding > **subsequently** *adv*
subsequently *adv* ▷ **subsequent**
subservience *n* ▷ **subservient**
subserviences *n* ▷ **subservient**
subservient *adj* submissive, servile > **subservience** *n* (*pl* **-s**)
subside *v* (**-des, -ding, -ded**) become less

intense

subsided v ▷ subside

subsidence n (pl -s) act or process of subsiding

subsidences n ▷ subsidence

subsides v ▷ subside

subsidiaries n ▷ subsidiary

subsidiary adj of lesser importance ▶ n (pl -ries) subsidiary person or thing

subsidies n ▷ subsidy

subsiding v ▷ subside

subsidize v (-izes, -izing, -ized) help financially

subsidized v ▷ subsidize

subsidizes v ▷ subsidize

subsidizing v ▷ subsidize

subsidy n (pl -dies) financial aid

subsist v (-s, -ing, -ed) manage to live > **subsistence** n (pl -s)

subsisted v ▷ subsist

subsistence n ▷ subsist

subsistences n ▷ subsist

subsisting v ▷ subsist

subsists v ▷ subsist

subsonic adj moving at a speed less than that of sound

substance n (pl -s) physical composition of something

substances n ▷ substance

substantial adj of considerable size or value > **substantially** adv

substantially adv ▷ substantial

substantiate v (-tes, -ting, -ted) support (a story) with evidence > **substantiation** n (pl -s)

substantiated v ▷ substantiate

substantiates v ▷ substantiate

substantiating v ▷ substantiate

substantiation n ▷ substantiate

substantiations n ▷ substantiate

substantive n (pl -s) noun ▶ adj of or being the essential element of a thing

substantives n ▷ substantive

substitute v (-tes, -ting, -ted) take the place of or put in place of another ▶ n (pl -s) person or thing taking the place of (another) > **substitution** n (pl -s)

substituted v ▷ substitute

substitutes v, n ▷ substitute

substituting v ▷ substitute

substitution n ▷ substitute

substitutions n ▷ substitute

subsume v (-mes, -ming, -med) include (an idea, case, etc.) under a larger classification or group

subsumed v ▷ subsume

subsumes v ▷ subsume

subsuming v ▷ subsume

subterfuge n (pl -s) trick used to achieve an objective

subterfuges n ▷ subterfuge

subterranean adj underground

subtitle n (pl -s) secondary title of a book ▶ v (-les, -ling, -led) provide with a subtitle or subtitles

subtitled v ▷ subtitle

subtitles v, n ▷ subtitle ▶ pl n printed translation at the bottom of the picture in a film with foreign dialogue

subtitling v ▷ subtitle

subtle adj (-r, -st) not immediately obvious > **subtly** adv > **subtlety** n (pl -ties)

subtler adj ▷ subtle

subtlest adj ▷ subtle

subtleties n ▷ subtle

subtlety n ▷ subtle

subtly adv ▷ subtle

subtract v (-s, -ing, -ed) take (one number or quantity) from another > **subtraction** n (pl -s)

subtracted v ▷ subtract

subtracting v ▷ subtract

subtraction n ▷ subtract

subtractions n ▷ subtract

subtracts v ▷ subtract

subtropical adj of the regions bordering on the tropics

suburb n (pl -s) residential area on the outskirts of a city

suburban adj of or inhabiting a suburb

suburbia n (pl -s) suburbs and their inhabitants

suburbias n ▷ suburbia

suburbs n ▷ suburb

subvention n (pl -s) (Formal) subsidy

subventions n ▷ subvention

subversion n ▷ subvert

subversions n ▷ subvert

subversive adj, n ▷ subvert

subversives n ▷ subvert

subvert v (-s, -ing, -ed) overthrow the authority of > **subversion** n (pl -s) > **subversive** adj, n (pl -s)

subverted v ▷ subvert

subverting v ▷ subvert

subverts v ▷ subvert

subway n (pl -s) passage under a road or railway

subways n ▷ subway

succeed v (-s, -ing, -ed) accomplish an aim

succeeded v ▷ succeed

succeeding v ▷ succeed

succeeds v ▷ succeed

success n (pl -es) achievement of something

attempted
successes *n* ▷ **success**
successful *adj* having success > **successfully** *adv*
successfully *adv* ▷ **successful**
succession *n* (*pl* -**s**) series of people or things following one another in order
successions *n* ▷ **succession**
successive *adj* consecutive > **successively** *adv*
successively *adv* ▷ **successive**
successor *n* (*pl* -**s**) person who succeeds someone in a position
successors *n* ▷ **successor**
succinct *adj* (-**er**, -**est**) brief and clear > **succinctly** *adv*
succincter *adj* ▷ **succinct**
succinctest *adj* ▷ **succinct**
succinctly *adv* ▷ **succinct**
succour *v* (-**s**, -**ing**, -**ed**) ▶ *n* (*pl* -**s**) help in distress
succoured *v* ▷ **succour**
succouring *v* ▷ **succour**
succours *v*, *n* ▷ **succour**
succulence *n* ▷ **succulent**
succulences *n* ▷ **succulent**
succulent *adj* juicy and delicious ▶ *n* (*pl* -**s**) succulent plant > **succulence** *n* (*pl* -**s**)
succulent *n* ▷ **succulent**
succulents *n* ▷ **succulent**
succumb *v* (-**s**, -**ing**, -**ed**) (*foll. by* **to**) give way (to something overpowering)
succumbed *v* ▷ **succumb**
succumbing *v* ▷ **succumb**
succumbs *v* ▷ **succumb**
such *adj* of the kind specified ▶ *pron* such things
suchlike *pron* such or similar things
suck *v* (-**s**, -**ing**, -**ed**) draw (liquid or air) into the mouth ▶ *n* (*pl* -**s**) sucking
sucked *v* ▷ **suck**
sucker *n* (*pl* -**s**) (*Slang*) person who is easily deceived or swindled
suckers *n* ▷ **sucker**
sucking *v* ▷ **suck**
suckle *v* (-**les**, -**ling**, -**led**) feed at the breast
suckled *v* ▷ **suckle**
suckles *v* ▷ **suckle**
suckling *n* (*pl* -**s**) unweaned baby or young animal ▶ *v* ▷ **suckle**
sucklings *n* ▷ **suckling**
sucks *v*, *n* ▷ **suck**
sucrose [soo-kroze] *n* (*pl* -**s**) chemical name for sugar
sucroses *n* ▷ **sucrose**
suction *n* (*pl* -**s**) sucking

suctions *n* ▷ **suction**
sudden *adj* done or occurring quickly and unexpectedly > **suddenly** *adv* > **suddenness** *n* (*pl* -**es**)
suddenly *adv* ▷ **sudden**
suddenness *n* ▷ **suddenness**
suddennesses *n* ▷ **suddenness**
sudorific [syoo-dor-**if**-ik] *n* (*pl* -**s**) ▶ *adj* (drug) causing sweating
sudorifics *n* ▷ **sudorific**
suds *pl n* froth of soap and water, lather
sue *v* (-**ues**, -**uing**, -**ued**) start legal proceedings against
sued *v* ▷ **sue**
suede *n* (*pl* -**s**) leather with a velvety finish on one side
suedes *n* ▷ **suede**
sues *v* ▷ **sue**
suet *n* (*pl* -**s**) hard fat obtained from sheep and cattle, used in cooking
suets *n* ▷ **suet**
suffer *v* (-**s**, -**ing**, -**ed**) undergo or be subjected to > **sufferer** *n* (*pl* -**s**) > **suffering** *n* (*pl* -**s**) > **sufferance** *n* (*pl* -**s**)
sufferance *n* ▷ **suffer**
sufferances *n* ▷ **suffer**
suffered *v* ▷ **suffer**
sufferer *n* ▷ **suffer**
sufferers *n* ▷ **suffer**
suffering *n*, *v* ▷ **suffer**
sufferings *n* ▷ **suffer**
suffers *v* ▷ **suffer**
suffice [suf-**fice**] *v* (-**ces**, -**cing**, -**ced**) be enough for a purpose
sufficed *v* ▷ **suffice**
suffices *v* ▷ **suffice**
sufficiencies *n* ▷ **sufficiency**
sufficiency *n* (*pl* -**cies**) adequate amount
sufficient *adj* enough, adequate > **sufficiently** *adv*
sufficiently *adv* ▷ **sufficient**
sufficing *v* ▷ **suffice**
suffix *n* (*pl* -**es**) letter or letters added to the end of a word to form another word, such as -*s* and -*ness* in *dogs* and *softness*
suffixes *n* ▷ **suffix**
suffocate *v* (-**tes**, -**ting**, -**ted**) kill or be killed by deprivation of oxygen > **suffocation** *n* (*pl* -**s**)
suffocated *v* ▷ **suffocate**
suffocates *v* ▷ **suffocate**
suffocating *v* ▷ **suffocate**
suffocation *n* ▷ **suffocate**
suffocations *n* ▷ **suffocate**
suffragan *n* (*pl* -**s**) bishop appointed to assist an archbishop

suffragans n ▷ **suffragan**
suffrage n (pl -s) right to vote in public elections
suffrages n ▷ **suffrage**
suffragette n (pl -s) (in Britain in the early 20th century) a woman who campaigned militantly for the right to vote
suffragettes n ▷ **suffragette**
suffuse v (-ses, -sing, -sed) spread through or over (something) > **suffusion** n (pl -s)
suffused v ▷ **suffuse**
suffuses v ▷ **suffuse**
suffusing v ▷ **suffuse**
suffusion n ▷ **suffuse**
suffusions n ▷ **suffuse**
sugar n (pl -s) sweet crystalline carbohydrate found in many plants and used to sweeten food and drinks ▶ v (-s, -ing, -ed) sweeten or cover with sugar > **sugary** adj (-rier, -riest)
sugared v ▷ **sugar**
sugarier adj ▷ **sugar**
sugariest adj ▷ **sugar**
sugaring v ▷ **sugar**
sugars n, v ▷ **sugar**
sugary adj ▷ **sugar**
suggest v (-s, -ing, -ed) put forward (an idea) for consideration
suggested v ▷ **suggest**
suggestible adj easily influenced
suggesting v ▷ **suggest**
suggestion n (pl -s) thing suggested
suggestions n ▷ **suggestion**
suggestive adj suggesting something indecent > **suggestively** adv
suggestively adv ▷ **suggestive**
suggests v ▷ **suggest**
suicidal adj liable to commit suicide > **suicidally** adv
suicidally adv ▷ **suicide**
suicide n (pl -s) killing oneself intentionally
suicides n ▷ **suicide**
suing v ▷ **sue**
suit n (pl -s) set of clothes designed to be worn together ▶ v (-s, -ing, -ed) be appropriate for
suitabilities n ▷ **suitable**
suitability n ▷ **suitable**
suitable adj appropriate or proper > **suitably** adv > **suitability** n (pl -ties)
suitably adv ▷ **suitable**
suitcase n (pl -s) portable travelling case for clothing
suitcases n ▷ **suitcase**
suite n (pl -s) set of connected rooms in a hotel
suited v ▷ **suit**
suites n ▷ **suite**

suiting v ▷ **suit**
suitor n (pl -s) (Old-fashioned) man who is courting a woman
suitors n ▷ **suitor**
suits n, v ▷ **suit**
sulk v (-s, -ing, -ed) be silent and sullen because of resentment or bad temper ▶ n (pl -s) resentful or sullen mood > **sulky** adj (-kier, -kiest) > **sulkily** adv
sulked v ▷ **sulk**
sulkier adj ▷ **sulk**
sulkiest adj ▷ **sulk**
sulkily adv ▷ **sulk**
sulking v ▷ **sulk**
sulks v, n ▷ **sulk**
sulky adj ▷ **sulk**
sullen adj (-er, -est) unwilling to talk or be sociable > **sullenly** adv > **sullenness** n (pl -es)
sullener adj ▷ **sullen**
sullenest adj ▷ **sullen**
sullenly adv ▷ **sullen**
sullenness n ▷ **sullen**
sullennesses n ▷ **sullen**
sullied v ▷ **sully**
sullies v ▷ **sully**
sully v (-lies, -lying, -lied) ruin (someone's reputation)
sullying v ▷ **sully**
sulphate n (pl -s) salt or ester of sulphuric acid
sulphates n ▷ **sulphate**
sulphide n (pl -s) compound of sulphur with another element
sulphides n ▷ **sulphide**
sulphite n (pl -s) salt or ester of sulphurous acid
sulphites n ▷ **sulphite**
sulphonamide [sulf-on-a-mide] n (pl -s) any of a class of drugs that prevent the growth of bacteria
sulphonamides n ▷ **sulphonamide**
sulphur n (pl -s) (CHEM) pale yellow nonmetallic element
sulphuric, sulphurous adj of or containing sulphur
sulphurous adj ▷ **sulphuric**
sulphurs n ▷ **sulphur**
sultan n (pl -s) sovereign of a Muslim country
sultana n (pl -s) kind of raisin
sultanas n ▷ **sultana**
sultanate n (pl -s) territory of a sultan
sultanates n ▷ **sultanate**
sultans n ▷ **sultan**
sultrier n ▷ **sultry**
sultriest n ▷ **sultry**
sultry adj (-trier, -triest) (of weather or

sum n (pl **-s**) result of addition, total
  summaries n ▷ **summary**
  summarily adv ▷ **summary**
summarize v (**-izes, -izing, -ized**) make or be a
summary of (something)
  summarized v ▷ **summarize**
  summarizes v ▷ **summarize**
  summarizing v ▷ **summarize**
summary n (pl **-ries**) brief account giving the
main points of something ▶ adj done quickly,
without formalities > **summarily** adv
summation n (pl **-s**) summary
  summations n ▷ **summation**
summer n (pl **-s**) warmest season of the year,
between spring and autumn > **summery** adj
(**-rier, -riest**)
summerhouse n (pl **-s**) small building in a
garden
  summerhouses n ▷ **summerhouse**
  summerier adj ▷ **summer**
  summeriest adj ▷ **summer**
  summers n ▷ **summer**
summertime n (pl **-s**) period or season of
summer
  summertimes n ▷ **summertime**
  summery adj ▷ **summer**
summit n (pl **-s**) top of a mountain or hill
  summits n ▷ **summit**
summon v (**-s, -ing, -ed**) order (someone) to
come
  summoned v ▷ **summon**
  summoning v ▷ **summon**
summons n (pl **-es**) command summoning
someone ▶ v (**-es, -ing, -ed**) order (someone)
to appear in court ▶ v ▷ **summon**
  summonsed n ▷ **summons**
  summonses v, n ▷ **summons**
  summonsing v ▷ **summons**
sumo n (pl **-s**) Japanese style of wrestling
  sumos n ▷ **sumo**
sump n (pl **-s**) container in an internal-
combustion engine into which oil can drain
  sumps n ▷ **sump**
sumptuous adj lavish, magnificent
  > **sumptuously** adv
  sumptuously adv ▷ **sumptuous**
  sums n ▷ **sum**
sun n (pl **-s**) star around which the earth
and other planets revolve ▶ v (**-s, sunning,
sunned**) expose (oneself) to the sun's rays
  > **sunless** adj
sunbathe v (**-thes, -thing, -thed**) lie in the
sunshine in order to get a suntan
  sunbathed v ▷ **sunbathe**

  sunbathes v ▷ **sunbathe**
  sunbathing v ▷ **sunbathe**
sunbeam n (pl **-s**) ray of sun
  sunbeams n ▷ **sunbeam**
sunburn n (pl **-s**) painful reddening of the
skin caused by overexposure to the sun
  > **sunburnt, sunburned** adj
  sunburned adj ▷ **sunburn**
  sunburns n ▷ **sunburn**
  sunburnt adj ▷ **sunburn**
sundae n (pl **-s**) ice cream topped with fruit
etc.
  sundaes n ▷ **sundae**
sundial n (pl **-s**) device showing the time by
means of a pointer that casts a shadow on a
marked dial
  sundials n ▷ **sundial**
sundown n (pl **-s**) sunset
  sundowns n ▷ **sundown**
sundries pl n several things of various sorts
sundry adj several, various
sunflower n (pl **-s**) tall plant with large golden
flowers
  sunflowers n ▷ **sunflower**
  sung v ▷ **sing**
  sunk v ▷ **sink**
  sunken v ▷ **sink**
  sunless adj ▷ **sun**
  sunned v ▷ **sun**
  sunnier adj ▷ **sunny**
  sunniest adj ▷ **sunny**
  sunning v ▷ **sun**
sunny adj (**-nnier, -nniest**) full of or exposed
to sunlight
sunrise n (pl **-s**) daily appearance of the sun
above the horizon
  sunrises n ▷ **sunrise**
  suns n, v ▷ **sun**
sunset n (pl **-s**) daily disappearance of the sun
below the horizon
  sunsets n ▷ **sunset**
sunshine n (pl **-s**) light and warmth from
the sun
  sunshines n ▷ **sunshine**
sunspot n (pl **-s**) dark patch appearing
temporarily on the sun's surface
  sunspots n ▷ **sunspot**
sunstroke n (pl **-s**) illness caused by prolonged
exposure to intensely hot sunlight
  sunstrokes n ▷ **sunstroke**
suntan n (pl **-s**) browning of the skin caused by
exposure to the sun
  suntans n ▷ **suntan**
sup v (**-s, -pping, -pped**) take (liquid) by sips
  ▶ n (pl **-s**) sip

super adj (Informal) excellent
superannuated adj discharged with a pension, owing to old age or illness
superannuation n (pl -s) regular payment by an employee into a pension fund
superannuations n ▷ **superannuation**
superb adj excellent, impressive, or splendid > **superbly** adv
superbly adv ▷ **superb**
superbug n (pl -s) (Informal) bacterium resistant to antibiotics
superbugs n ▷ **superbug**
supercharged adj (of an engine) having a supercharger
supercharger n (pl -s) device that increases the power of an internal-combustion engine by forcing extra air into it
superchargers n ▷ **supercharger**
supercilious adj showing arrogant pride or scorn
superconductor n (pl -s) substance which has almost no electrical resistance at very low temperatures
superconductors n ▷ **superconductor**
superficial adj not careful or thorough > **superficially** adv > **superficiality** n (pl -ties)
superficialities n ▷ **superficial**
superficiality n ▷ **superficial**
superficially adv ▷ **superficial**
superfluities n ▷ **superfluous**
superfluity n ▷ **superfluous**
superfluous [soo-per-flew-uss] adj more than is needed > **superfluity** n (pl -ties)
superhuman adj beyond normal human ability or experience
superimpose v (-ses, -sing, -sed) place (something) on or over something else
superimposed v ▷ **superimpose**
superimposes v ▷ **superimpose**
superimposing v ▷ **superimpose**
superintend v (-s, -ing, -ed) supervise (a person or activity)
superintended v ▷ **superintend**
superintendent n (pl -s) senior police officer
superintendents n ▷ **superintendent**
superintending v ▷ **superintend**
superintends v ▷ **superintend**
superior adj greater in quality, quantity, or merit ▶ n (pl -s) person of greater rank or status > **superiority** n (pl -ties)
superiorities n ▷ **superior**
superiority n ▷ **superior**
superiors n ▷ **superior**
superlative [soo-per-lat-iv] adj of outstanding quality ▶ n (pl -s) (GRAMMAR) word expressing this

superlatives n ▷ **superlative**
superman n (pl -men) man with great physical or mental powers
supermarket n (pl -s) large self-service store selling food and household goods
supermarkets n ▷ **supermarket**
supermen n ▷ **superman**
supermodel n (pl -s) famous and highly-paid fashion model
supermodels n ▷ **supermodel**
supernatural adj of or relating to things beyond the laws of nature
supernova n (pl -vae, -vas) star that explodes and briefly becomes exceptionally bright
supernovae n ▷ **supernova**
supernovas n ▷ **supernova**
supernumeraries n ▷ **supernumerary**
supernumerary adj exceeding the required or regular number ▶ n (pl -ries) supernumerary person or thing
superpower n (pl -s) extremely powerful nation
superpowers n ▷ **superpower**
superscript n (pl -s) ▶ adj (character) printed above the line
superscripts n ▷ **superscript**
supersede v (-des, -ding, -ded) replace, supplant
superseded v ▷ **supersede**
supersedes v ▷ **supersede**
superseding v ▷ **supersede**
supersonic adj of or travelling at a speed greater than the speed of sound
superstition n (pl -s) belief in omens, ghosts, etc. > **superstitious** adj
superstitions n ▷ **superstition**
superstitious adj ▷ **superstition**
superstore n (pl -s) large supermarket
superstores n ▷ **superstore**
superstructure n (pl -s) structure erected on something else
superstructures n ▷ **superstructure**
supervene v (-nes, -ning, -ned) occur as an unexpected development
supervened v ▷ **supervene**
supervenes v ▷ **supervene**
supervening v ▷ **supervene**
supervise v (-ses, -sing, -sed) watch over to direct or check > **supervision** n (pl -s) > **supervisor** n (pl -s) > **supervisory** adj
supervised v ▷ **supervise**
supervises v ▷ **supervise**
supervising v ▷ **supervise**
supervision n ▷ **supervise**

supervisions *n* ▷ supervise
supervisor *n* ▷ supervise
supervisors *n* ▷ supervise
supervisory *adj* ▷ supervise
supine *adj* lying flat on one's back
supped *v* ▷ sup
supper *n* (*pl* -s) light evening meal
suppers *n* ▷ supper
supping *v* ▷ sup
supplant *v* (-s, -ing, -ed) take the place of, oust
supplanted *v* ▷ supplant
supplanting *v* ▷ supplant
supplants *v* ▷ supplant
supple *adj* (-r, -st) (of a person) moving and bending easily and gracefully > **suppleness** *n* (*pl* -es)
supplement *n* (*pl* -s) thing added to complete something or make up for a lack ▶ *v* (-s, -ing, -ed) provide or be a supplement to (something) > **supplementary** *adj*
supplementary *adj* ▷ supplement
supplemented *v* ▷ supplement
supplementing *v* ▷ supplement
supplements *n*, *v* ▷ supplement
suppleness *n* ▷ supple
supplenesses *n* ▷ supple
suppler *adj* ▷ supple
supplest *adj* ▷ supple
supplicant *n* (*pl* -s) person who makes a humble request
supplicants *n* ▷ supplicant
supplication *n* (*pl* -s) humble request
supplications *n* ▷ supplication
supplied *v* ▷ supply
supplier *n* ▷ supply
suppliers *n* ▷ supply
supplies *pl n* food or equipment ▶ *v* ▷ supply
supply *v* (-lies, -lying, -lied) provide with something required ▶ *n* (*pl* -lies) supplying > **supplier** *n* (*pl* -s)
supplying *v* ▷ supply
support *v* (-s, -ing, -ed) bear the weight of ▶ *n* (*pl* -s) supporting > **supportive** *adj*
supported *v* ▷ support
supporter *n* (*pl* -s) person who supports a team, principle, etc.
supporters *n* ▷ supporter
supporting *v* ▷ support
supportive *adj* ▷ support
supports *v*, *n* ▷ support
suppose *v* (-ses, -sing, -sed) presume to be true
supposed *adj* presumed to be true without proof, doubtful ▶ *v* ▷ suppose > **supposedly** *adv*
supposedly *adv* ▷ supposed

supposes *v* ▷ suppose
supposing *v* ▷ suppose
supposition *n* (*pl* -s) supposing
suppositions *n* ▷ supposition
suppositories *n* ▷ suppository
suppository *n* (*pl* -ries) solid medication inserted into the rectum or vagina and left to melt
suppress *v* (-es, -ing, -ed) put an end to > **suppression** *n* (*pl* -s)
suppressed *v* ▷ suppress
suppresses *v* ▷ suppress
suppressing *v* ▷ suppress
suppression *n* ▷ suppress
suppressions *n* ▷ suppress
suppurate *v* (-tes, -ting, -ted) (of a wound etc.) produce pus
suppurated *v* ▷ suppurate
suppurates *v* ▷ suppurate
suppurating *v* ▷ suppurate
supremacies *n* ▷ supremacy
supremacy *n* (*pl* -cies) supreme power
supreme *adj* highest in authority, rank, or degree
supremely *adv* extremely
supremo *n* (*pl* -s) (*Informal*) person in overall authority
supremos *n* ▷ supremo
sups *n*, *v* ▷ sup

suq *n* (**suqs**). A suq is an open-air marketplace in Arabic-speaking countries. This unusual word can be very useful. Usually, when you have a Q and a U, you will be looking to play words with QU in them. But look out for opportunities to play suq instead. Suq scores 12 points.

surcharge *n* (*pl* -s) additional charge
surcharges *n* ▷ surcharge
surd *n* (*pl* -s) (MATHS) number that cannot be expressed in whole numbers
surds *n* ▷ surd
sure *adj* (-r, -st) free from uncertainty or doubt ▶ *adv*, *interj* (*Informal*) certainly
surefooted *adj* unlikely to slip or stumble
surely *adv* it must be true that
surer *adj* ▷ sure
surest *adj* ▷ sure
sureties *n* ▷ surety
surety *n* (*pl* -ties) person who takes responsibility, or thing given as a guarantee, for the fulfilment of another's obligation
surf *n* (*pl* -s) foam caused by waves breaking on the shore ▶ *v* (-s, -ing, -ed) take part in surfing > **surfer** *n* (*pl* -s)

surface n (pl -s) outside or top of an object ▶ v (-ces, -cing, -ced) rise to the surface
surfaced v ▷ surface
surfaces n, v ▷ surface
surfacing v ▷ surface
surfboard n (pl -s) long smooth board used in surfing
surfboards n ▷ surfboard
surfed v ▷ surf
surfeit n (pl -s) excessive amount
surfeits n ▷ surfeit
surfer n ▷ surf
surfers n ▷ surf
surfing n (pl -s) sport of riding towards the shore on a surfboard on the crest of a wave ▶ v ▷ surf
surfings n ▷ surfing
surfs n, v ▷ surf
surge n (pl -s) sudden powerful increase ▶ v (-ges, -ging, -ged) increase suddenly
surged v ▷ surge
surgeon n (pl -s) doctor who specializes in surgery
surgeons n ▷ surgeon
surgeries n ▷ surgery
surgery n (pl -ries) treatment in which the patient's body is cut open in order to treat the affected part > **surgical** adj > **surgically** adv
surges n, v ▷ surge
surgical adj ▷ surgery
surgically adv ▷ surgery
surging v ▷ surge
surlier adj ▷ surly
surliest adj ▷ surly
surliness n ▷ surly
surlinesses n ▷ surly
surly adj (-lier, -liest) ill-tempered and rude > **surliness** n (pl -es)
surmise v (-ises, -ising, -ised) ▶ n (pl -s) guess, conjecture
surmised v ▷ surmise
surmises n, v ▷ surmise
surmising v ▷ surmise
surmount v (-s, -ing, -ed) overcome (a problem) > **surmountable** adj
surmountable adj ▷ surmount
surmounted v ▷ surmount
surmounting v ▷ surmount
surmounts v ▷ surmount
surname n (pl -s) family name
surnames n ▷ surname
surpass v (-es, -ing, -ed) be greater than or superior to
surpassed v ▷ surpass
surpasses v ▷ surpass

surpassing v ▷ surpass
surplice n (pl -s) loose white robe worn by clergymen and choristers
surplices n ▷ surplice
surplus n (pl -es) amount left over in excess of what is required
surpluses n ▷ surplus
surprise n (pl -ses) unexpected event ▶ v (-ses, -sing, -sed) cause to feel amazement or wonder
surprised v ▷ surprise
surprises n, v ▷ surprise
surprising v ▷ surprise
surreal adj bizarre > **surrealist** n (pl -s) adj > **surrealistic** adj
surrealism n (pl -s) movement in art and literature involving the combination of incongruous images, as in a dream
surrealisms n ▷ surrealism
surrealist n, adj ▷ surreal
surrealistic adj ▷ surreal
surrealists n ▷ surreal
surrender v (-s, -ing, -ed) give oneself up ▶ n (pl -s) surrendering
surrendered v ▷ surrender
surrendering v ▷ surrender
surrenders v, n ▷ surrender
surreptitious adj done secretly or stealthily > **surreptitiously** adv
surreptitiously adv ▷ surreptitious
surrogate n (pl -s) substitute
surrogates n ▷ surrogate
surround v (-s, -ing, -ed) be, come, or place all around (a person or thing) ▶ n (pl -s) border or edging
surrounded v ▷ surround
surrounding v ▷ surround
surroundings pl n area or environment around a person, place, or thing
surrounds v, n ▷ surround
surveillance n (pl -s) close observation
surveillances n ▷ surveillance
survey v (-s, -ing, -ed) view or consider in a general way ▶ n (pl -s) surveying > **surveyor** n (pl -s)
surveyed v ▷ survey
surveying v ▷ survey
surveyor n ▷ survey
surveyors n ▷ survey
surveys v, n ▷ survey
survival n (pl -s) condition of having survived
survivals n ▷ survival
survive v (-ves, -ing, -ved) continue to live or exist after (a difficult experience) > **survivor** n (pl -s)

survived v ▷ survive
survives v ▷ survive
surviving v ▷ survive
survivor n ▷ survive
survivors n ▷ survive
susceptibilities n ▷ susceptible
susceptibility n ▷ susceptible
susceptible adj liable to be influenced or affected by > **susceptibility** n (pl **-ties**)
sushi [soo-shee] n (pl **-s**) Japanese dish of small cakes of cold rice with a topping of raw fish
sushis n ▷ sushi
suspect v (**-s, -ing, -ed**) believe (someone) to be guilty without having any proof ▶ adj not to be trusted ▶ n (pl **-s**) person who is suspected
suspected v ▷ suspect
suspecting v ▷ suspect
suspects v, n ▷ suspect
suspend v (**-s, -ing, -ed**) hang from a high place
suspended v ▷ suspend
suspenders pl n straps for holding up stockings
suspending v ▷ suspend
suspends v ▷ suspend
suspense n (pl **-s**) state of uncertainty while awaiting news, an event, etc.
suspenses n ▷ suspense
suspension n (pl **-s**) suspending or being suspended
suspensions n ▷ suspension
suspicion n (pl **-s**) feeling of not trusting a person or thing
suspicions n ▷ suspicion
suspicious adj feeling or causing suspicion > **suspiciously** adv
suspiciously adv ▷ suspicious
sustain v (**-s, -ing, -ed**) maintain or prolong
sustained v ▷ sustain
sustaining v ▷ sustain
sustains v ▷ sustain
sustenance n (pl **-s**) food
sustenances n ▷ sustenance
suture [soo-cher] n (pl **-s**) stitch joining the edges of a wound
sutures n ▷ suture
suzerain n (pl **-s**) state or sovereign with limited authority over another self-governing state > **suzerainty** n (pl **-ties**)
suzerains n ▷ suzerain
suzerainties n ▷ suzerain
suzerainty n ▷ suzerain
svelte adj (**-r, -st**) attractively or gracefully slim
svelter adj ▷ svelte
sveltest adj ▷ svelte
swab n (pl **-s**) small piece of cotton wool used

to apply medication, clean a wound, etc.
▶ v (**-s, -bbing, -bbed**) clean (a wound) with a swab
swabbed v ▷ swab
swabbing v ▷ swab
swabs n, v ▷ swab
swaddle v (**-les, -ling, -led**) wrap (a baby) in swaddling clothes
swaddled v ▷ swaddle
swaddles v ▷ swaddle
swaddling v ▷ swaddle
swag n (pl **-s**) (Slang) stolen property
swagger v (**-s, -ing, -ed**) walk or behave arrogantly ▶ n (pl **-s**) arrogant walk or manner
swaggered v ▷ swagger
swaggering v ▷ swagger
swaggers v, n ▷ swagger
swagman n (pl **-men**) (AUST HIST) tramp who carries his belongings in a bundle on his back
swagmen n ▷ swagman
swags n ▷ swag
swain n (pl **-s**) (Poetic) suitor
swains n ▷ swain
swallow[1] v (**-s, -ing, -ed**) cause to pass down one's throat ▶ n (pl **-s**) swallowing
swallow[2] n (pl **-s**) small migratory bird with long pointed wings and a forked tail
swallowed v ▷ swallow[1]
swallowing v ▷ swallow[1]
swallows v ▷ swallow[1] ▶ n ▷ swallow[1, 2]
swam v ▷ swim
swamp n (pl **-s**) watery area of land, bog ▶ v (**-s, -ing, -ed**) cause (a boat) to fill with water and sink > **swampy** adj (**-pier, -piest**)
swamped v ▷ swamp
swampier adj ▷ swamp
swampiest adj ▷ swamp
swamping v ▷ swamp
swamps n, v ▷ swamp
swampy adj ▷ swamp
swan n (pl **-s**) large usu. white water bird with a long graceful neck ▶ v (**-s, -nning, -nned**) (Informal) wander about idly
swank (Slang) v (**-s, -ing, -ed**) show off or boast ▶ n (pl **-s**) showing off or boasting
swanked v ▷ swank
swankier adj ▷ swanky
swankiest adj ▷ swanky
swanking v ▷ swank
swanks v, n ▷ swank
swanky adj (**-kier, -kiest**) (Slang) expensive and showy, stylish
swanned n ▷ swan
swanning n ▷ swan
swans n, v ▷ swan

swap v (**-s, -pping, -pped**) exchange (something) for something else ▶ n (pl **-s**) exchange
  swapped v ▷ **swap**
  swapping v ▷ **swap**
  swaps v, n ▷ **swap**
sward n (pl **-s**) stretch of short grass
  swards n ▷ **sward**
swarm[1] n (pl **-s**) large group of bees or other insects ▶ v (**-s, -ing, -ed**) move in a swarm
swarm[2] v (**-s, -ing, -ed**) (foll. by **up**) climb (a ladder or rope) by gripping with the hands and feet
  swarmed v ▷ **swarm**[1, 2]
  swarming v ▷ **swarm**[1, 2]
  swarms v ▷ **swarm**[1, 2] ▶ n ▷ **swarm**[1]
  swarthier adj ▷ **swarthy**
  swarthiest adj ▷ **swarthy**
swarthy adj (**-thier, -thiest**) dark-complexioned
  swashbuckler n ▷ **swashbuckling**
  swashbucklers n ▷ **swashbuckling**
swashbuckling adj having the exciting behaviour of pirates, esp. those depicted in films > **swashbuckler** n (pl **-s**)
swastika n (pl **-s**) symbol in the shape of a cross with the arms bent at right angles, used as the emblem of Nazi Germany
  swastikas n ▷ **swastika**
swat v (**-s, -tting, -tted**) hit sharply ▶ n (pl **-s**) sharp blow
swatch n (pl **-es**) sample of cloth
  swatches n ▷ **swatch**
swath [swawth] n (pl **-s**) ▷ **swathe**
swathe v (**-thes, -thing, -thed**) wrap in bandages or layers of cloth ▶ n (pl **-s**) long strip of cloth wrapped around something (also **swath**)
  swathed v ▷ **swathe**
  swathes v, n ▷ **swathe**
  swathing v ▷ **swathe**
  swaths n ▷ **swath**
  swats v, n ▷ **swat**
  swatted v ▷ **swat**
  swatting v ▷ **swat**
sway v (**-s, -ing, -ed**) swing to and fro or from side to side ▶ n (pl **-s**) power or influence
  swayed v ▷ **sway**
  swaying v ▷ **sway**
  sways v, n ▷ **sway**
swear v (**-s, -ing, swore, sworn**) use obscene or blasphemous language
  swearing v ▷ **swear**
  swears v ▷ **swear**
swearword n (pl **-s**) word considered obscene or blasphemous
  swearwords n ▷ **swearword**
sweat n (pl **-s**) salty liquid given off through the pores of the skin ▶ v (**-s, -ing, -ed**) have sweat coming through the pores > **sweaty** adj (**-tier, -tiest**)
sweatband n (pl **-s**) strip of cloth tied around the forehead or wrist to absorb sweat
  sweatbands n ▷ **sweatband**
  sweated v ▷ **sweat**
sweater n (pl **-s**) (woollen) garment for the upper part of the body
  sweaters n ▷ **sweater**
  sweatier adj ▷ **sweat**
  sweatiest adj ▷ **sweat**
  sweating v ▷ **sweat**
  sweats n, v ▷ **sweat**
sweatshirt n (pl **-s**) long-sleeved cotton jersey
  sweatshirts n ▷ **sweatshirt**
sweatshop n (pl **-s**) place where employees work long hours in poor conditions for low pay
  sweatshops n ▷ **sweatshop**
  sweaty adj ▷ **sweat**
swede n (pl **-des**) kind of turnip
  swedes n ▷ **swede**
sweep v (**-s, -ing, swept**) remove dirt from (a floor) with a broom ▶ n (pl **-s**) sweeping
sweeping adj wide-ranging ▶ v ▷ **sweep**
  sweeps v, n ▷ **sweep**
sweepstake n (pl **-s**) lottery in which the stakes of the participants make up the prize
  sweepstakes n ▷ **sweepstake**
sweet adj (**-er, -est**) tasting of or like sugar ▶ n (pl **-s**) shaped piece of food consisting mainly of sugar > **sweetly** adv > **sweetness** n (pl **-es**) > **sweeten** v (**-s, -ing, -ed**)
sweetbread n (pl **-s**) animal's pancreas used as food
  sweetbreads n ▷ **sweetbread**
  sweetened v ▷ **sweet**
sweetener n (pl **-s**) sweetening agent that does not contain sugar
  sweeteners n ▷ **sweetener**
  sweetening v ▷ **sweet**
  sweetens v ▷ **sweet**
sweetheart n (pl **-s**) lover
  sweethearts n ▷ **sweetheart**
  sweetly adv ▷ **sweet**
sweetmeat n (pl **-s**) (Old-fashioned) sweet delicacy such as a small cake
  sweetmeats n ▷ **sweetmeat**
  sweetness n ▷ **sweet**
  sweetnesses n ▷ **sweet**
  sweets n ▷ **sweet**

swell v (-lls, -lling, -lled, swollen or swelled)
expand or increase ▶ n (pl -s) swelling or being
swollen ▶ adj (-er, -est) (US) (Slang) excellent
or fine
  swelled v ▷ swell
  sweller adj ▷ swell
  swellest adj ▷ swell
swelling n (pl -s) enlargement of part of the
body, caused by injury or infection ▶ v ▷ swell
  swells v, n ▷ swell
swelter v (-s, -ing, -ed) feel uncomfortably hot
  sweltered v ▷ swelter
sweltering adj uncomfortably hot ▶ v
  ▷ swelter
  swelters v ▷ swelter
  swept v ▷ sweep
swerve v (-ves, -ving, -ved) turn aside from a
course sharply or suddenly ▶ n (pl -s) swerving
  swerved v ▷ swerve
  swerves v, n ▷ swerve
  swerving v ▷ swerve
swift adj (-er, -est) moving or able to move
quickly ▶ n (pl -s) fast-flying bird with pointed
wings > **swiftly** adv > **swiftness** n (pl -es)
  swifter adj ▷ swift
  swiftest adj ▷ swift
  swiftly adv ▷ swift
  swiftness n ▷ swift
  swiftnesses n ▷ swift
  swifts n ▷ swift
swig n (pl -s) large mouthful of drink ▶ v (-s,
-gging, -gged) drink in large mouthfuls
  swigged v ▷ swig
  swigging v ▷ swig
  swigs n, v ▷ swig
swill v (-s, -ing, -ed) drink greedily ▶ n (pl -s)
sloppy mixture containing waste food, fed
to pigs
  swilled v ▷ swill
  swilling v ▷ swill
  swills v, n ▷ swill
swim v (-s, -mming, swam, swum) move along
in water by movements of the limbs ▶ n (pl -s)
act or period of swimming > **swimmer** n (pl -s)
  swimmer n ▷ swim
  swimmers n ▷ swim
  swimming v ▷ swim
swimmingly adv successfully and effortlessly
  swims v, n ▷ swim
swindle v (-les, -ling, -led) cheat (someone)
out of money ▶ n (pl -s) instance of swindling
> **swindler** n (pl -s)
  swindled v ▷ swindle
  swindler n ▷ swindle
  swindlers n ▷ swindle
  swindles v, n ▷ swindle
  swindling v ▷ swindle
swine n (pl -s) contemptible person
  swines n ▷ swine
swing v (-s, -ing, swung) move to and fro, sway
▶ n (pl -s) swinging
swingeing [swin-jing] adj punishing, severe
  swinging v ▷ swing
  swings v, n ▷ swing
swipe v (-ipes, -iping, -iped) strike (at) with a
sweeping blow ▶ n (pl -s) hard blow
  swiped v ▷ swipe
  swipes v, n ▷ swipe
  swiping v ▷ swipe
swirl v (-s, -ing, -ed) turn with a whirling
motion ▶ n (pl -s) whirling motion
  swirled v ▷ swirl
  swirling v ▷ swirl
  swirls v, n ▷ swirl
swish v (-es, -ing, -ed) move with a whistling
or hissing sound ▶ n (pl -es) whistling or
hissing sound ▶ adj (-er, -est) (Informal)
fashionable, smart
  swished v ▷ swish
  swisher adj ▷ swish
  swishes v, n ▷ swish
  swishest adj ▷ swish
  swishing v ▷ swish
switch n (pl -es) device for opening and closing
an electric circuit ▶ v (-ches, -ching, -ched)
change abruptly
switchback n (pl -s) road or railway with many
sharp hills or bends
  switchbacks n ▷ switchback
switchboard n (pl -s) installation in a
telephone exchange or office where
telephone calls are connected
  switchboards n ▷ switchboard
  switched v ▷ switch
  switches n, v ▷ switch
  switching v ▷ switch
swivel v (-s, -elling, -elled) turn on a central
point ▶ n (pl -s) coupling device that allows an
attached object to turn freely
  swivelled v ▷ swivel
  swivelling v ▷ swivel
  swivels v, n ▷ swivel
  swollen v ▷ swell
swoon v (-s, -ing, -ed) ▶ n (pl -s) faint
  swooned v ▷ swoon
  swooning v ▷ swoon
  swoons v, n ▷ swoon
swoop v (-s, -ing, -ed) sweep down or pounce
on suddenly ▶ n (pl -s) swooping
  swooped v ▷ swoop

swooping v ▷ swoop
swoops v, n ▷ swoop
swop v (-s, -pping, -pped) ▶ n (pl -s) ▷ swap
swopped v ▷ swop
swopping v ▷ swop
swops v, n ▷ swop
sword n (pl -s) weapon with a long sharp blade
swordfish n (pl -es) large fish with a very long upper jaw
swordfishes n ▷ swordfish
swords n ▷ sword
swordsman n (pl -men) person skilled in the use of a sword
swordsmen n ▷ swordsman
swore v ▷ swear
sworn v ▷ swear ▶ adj bound by or as if by an oath
swot (Informal) v (-s, -tting, -tted) study hard ▶ n (pl -s) person who studies hard
swots v, n ▷ swot
swotted v ▷ swot
swotting v ▷ swot
swum v ▷ swim
swung v ▷ swing

swy n (**swys**). Swy is an Australian gambling game. This is a very unusual word which doesn't contain a vowel, so it can be useful in helping you to clear a difficult rack. Swy scores 9 points.

sybarite [sib-bar-ite] n (pl -s) lover of luxury > **sybaritic** adj
sybarites n ▷ sybarite
sybaritic adj ▷ sybarite
sycamore n (pl -s) tree with five-pointed leaves and two-winged fruits
sycamores n ▷ sycamore
sycophancies n ▷ sycophant
sycophancy n ▷ sycophant
sycophant n (pl -s) person who uses flattery to win favour from people with power or influence > **sycophantic** adj > **sycophancy** n (pl -cies)
sycophantic adj ▷ sycophant
sycophants n ▷ sycophant
syllabi n ▷ syllabus
syllabic adj ▷ syllable
syllable n (pl -s) part of a word pronounced as a unit > **syllabic** adj
syllables n ▷ syllable
syllabub n (pl -s) dessert of beaten cream, sugar, and wine
syllabubs n ▷ syllabub
syllabus n (pl -buses, -bi) list of subjects for a course of study

syllabuses n ▷ syllabus
syllogism n (pl -s) form of logical reasoning consisting of two premises and a conclusion
syllogisms n ▷ syllogism
sylph n (pl -s) slender graceful girl or woman > **sylphlike** adj
sylphlike adj ▷ sylph
sylphs n ▷ sylph
sylvan adj (Lit) relating to woods and trees
symbioses n ▷ symbiosis
symbiosis n (pl -oses) close association of two species living together to their mutual benefit > **symbiotic** adj
symbiotic adj ▷ symbiosis
symbol n (pl -s) sign or thing that stands for something else > **symbolic** adj > **symbolically** adv
symbolic adj ▷ symbol
symbolically adv ▷ symbol
symbolism n (pl -s) representation of something by symbols > **symbolist** n (pl -s) adj
symbolisms n ▷ symbolism
symbolist n ▷ symbolism
symbolists n ▷ symbolism
symbolize v (-izes, -izing, -ized) be a symbol of
symbolized v ▷ symbolize
symbolizes v ▷ symbolize
symbolizing v ▷ symbolize
symbols n ▷ symbol
symmetrical adj ▷ symmetry
symmetrically adv ▷ symmetry
symmetries n ▷ symmetry
symmetry n (pl -tries) state of having two halves that are mirror images of each other > **symmetrical** adj > **symmetrically** adv
sympathetic adj feeling or showing sympathy > **sympathetically** adv
sympathetically adv ▷ sympathetic
sympathies n ▷ sympathy
sympathize v (-zes, -izing, -ized) feel or express sympathy > **sympathizer** n (pl -s)
sympathized v ▷ sympathize
sympathizer n ▷ sympathize
sympathizers n ▷ sympathize
sympathizes v ▷ sympathize
sympathizing v ▷ sympathize
sympathy n (pl -thies) compassion for someone's pain or distress
symphonic adj ▷ symphony
symphonies n ▷ symphony
symphony n (pl -nies) composition for orchestra, with several movements > **symphonic** adj
symposia n ▷ symposium
symposium n (pl -iums, -sia) conference for

discussion of a particular topic
symposiums n ▷ **symposium**
symptom n (pl -s) sign indicating the presence
of an illness > **symptomatic** adj
symptomatic adj ▷ **symptom**
symptoms n ▷ **symptom**

> **syn** adv. (**Syn**) is a Scots word for **since**.
> This is a good word to remember for
> when you have a shortage of vowels.
> Syn scores 6 points.

synagogue n (pl -s) Jewish place of worship
and religious instruction
synagogues n ▷ **synagogue**
sync, synch (Informal) n (pl -s) synchronization
▶ v (-s, -ing, -ed) synchronize
synced v ▷ **sync**
synched v ▷ **sync**
synching v ▷ **sync**
synchromesh adj (of a gearbox) having a
device that synchronizes the speeds of gears
before they engage
synchronization n ▷ **synchronize**
synchronizations n ▷ **synchronize**
synchronize v (-izes, -izing, -ized) (of two or
more people) perform (an action) at the same
time > **synchronization** n (pl -s)
synchronized v ▷ **synchronize**
synchronizes v ▷ **synchronize**
synchronizing v ▷ **synchronize**
synchronous adj happening or existing at the
same time
synchs n, v ▷ **sync**
syncing v ▷ **sync**
syncopate v (-tes, -ting, -ted) (MUSIC) stress
the weak beats in (a rhythm) instead of the
strong ones > **syncopation** n (pl -s)
syncopated v ▷ **syncopate**
syncopates v ▷ **syncopate**
syncopating v ▷ **syncopate**
syncopation n ▷ **syncopate**
syncopations n ▷ **syncopate**
syncope [sing-kop-ee] n (pl -s) (MED) a faint
syncopes n ▷ **syncope**
syncs n, v ▷ **sync**
syndicate n (pl -s) group of people or firms
undertaking a joint business project ▶ v
(-tes, -ting, -ted) publish (material) in several
newspapers > **syndication** n (pl -s)
syndicated v ▷ **syndicate**
syndicates n, v ▷ **syndicate**
syndicating v ▷ **syndicate**
syndication n ▷ **syndicate**
syndications n ▷ **syndicate**
syndrome n (pl -s) combination of symptoms
indicating a particular disease

syndromes n ▷ **syndrome**
synergies n ▷ **synergy**
synergy n (pl -gies) potential ability for people
or groups to be more successful working
together than on their own
synod n (pl -s) church council
synods n ▷ **synod**
synonym n (pl -s) word with the same
meaning as another > **synonymous** adj
synonymous adj ▷ **synonym**
synonyms n ▷ **synonym**
synopses n ▷ **synopsis**
synopsis n (pl -ses) summary or outline
syntactic adj ▷ **syntax**
syntax n (pl -es) (GRAMMAR) way in which words
are arranged to form phrases and sentences
> **syntactic** adj
syntaxes n ▷ **syntax**
syntheses n ▷ **synthesis**
synthesis n (pl -ses) combination of objects or
ideas into a whole
synthesize v (-izes, -izing, -ized) produce by
synthesis
synthesized v ▷ **synthesize**
synthesizer n (pl -s) electronic musical
instrument producing a range of sounds
synthesizers n ▷ **synthesizer**
synthesizes v ▷ **synthesize**
synthesizing v ▷ **synthesize**
synthetic adj (of a substance) made artificially
> **synthetically** adv
synthetically adv ▷ **synthetic**
syphilis n (pl -es) serious sexually transmitted
disease > **syphilitic** adj
syphilises n ▷ **syphilis**
syphilitic adj ▷ **syphilis**
syphon n (pl -s) ▶ v (-s, -ing, -ed) ▷ **siphon**
syphoned v ▷ **syphon**
syphoning v ▷ **syphon**
syphons n, v ▷ **syphon**
syringe n (pl -s) device for withdrawing or
injecting fluids, consisting of a hollow
cylinder, a piston, and a hollow needle ▶ v
(-ges, -ging, -ged) wash out or inject with
a syringe
syringed v ▷ **syringe**
syringes n, v ▷ **syringe**
syringing v ▷ **syringe**
syrup n (pl -s) solution of sugar in water
> **syrupy** adj (-pier, -piest)
syrupier adj ▷ **syrup**
syrupiest adj ▷ **syrup**
syrups n ▷ **syrup**
syrupy adj ▷ **syrup**
system n (pl -s) method or set of methods

> systematic *adj* > **systematically** *adv*
systematic *adj* ▷ **system**
systematically *adv* ▷ **system**
systematization *n* ▷ **systematize**
systematizations *n* ▷ **systematize**
systematize *v* (-izes, -izing, -ized) organize
using a system
systematization *n* (*pl* -s) systemizing
systematized *v* ▷ **systematize**

systematizes *v* ▷ **systematize**
systematizing *v* ▷ **systematize**
systemic *adj* affecting the entire animal or
body
systems *n* ▷ **system**
systole [siss-tol-ee] *n* (*pl* -s) regular contraction
of the heart as it pumps blood > **systolic** *adj*
systoles *n* ▷ **systole**
systolic *adj* ▷ **systole**

Tt

T is one of the most common consonants in Scrabble. There are only four two-letter words that begin with T, but they are easy to remember as there is one for every vowel except U. Like S, T begins a number of three-letter words that don't use vowels, which are well worth remembering. These are: **thy** (6 points), **try** (6), **tsk** (7), **twp** (8) and **tyg** (7). There are also some useful three-letter words using X: **tax**, **tix** and **tux** (10 each). If you have an X during a game, remember words like **text** (11), **texts** (12), **textile** (14), **textual** (14) and **texture** (14). The last three of these have seven letters, and so will earn you 50-point bonuses if you use all your tiles to form them.

ta interj (Informal) thank you

tab n (pl -s) small flap or projecting label

tabard n (pl -s) short sleeveless tunic decorated with a coat of arms, worn in medieval times

  tabards n ▷ tabard

  tabbies n ▷ tabby

tabby n (pl -bbies) ▶ adj (cat) with dark stripes on a lighter background

tabernacle n (pl -s) portable shrine of the Israelites

  tabernacles n ▷ tabernacle

tabla n (pl -bla, -blas) one of a pair of Indian drums played with the hands

  tablas n ▷ tabla

table n (pl -s) piece of furniture with a flat top supported by legs ▶ v (-les, -ling, -led) submit (a motion) for discussion by a meeting

  tabled v ▷ table

tableland n (pl -s) high plateau

  tablelands n ▷ tableland

tablespoon n (pl -s) large spoon for serving food

  tablespoons n ▷ tablespoon

tableau [tab-loh] n (pl -leaux) silent motionless group arranged to represent some scene

  tableaux n ▷ tableau

  tabled v ▷ table

  tables n, v ▷ table

tablet n (pl -s) pill of compressed medicinal substance

  tablets n ▷ tablet

  tabling v ▷ table

tabloid n (pl -s) small-sized newspaper with many photographs and a concise, usu. sensational style

  tabloids n ▷ tabloid

taboo n (pl -s) prohibition resulting from religious or social conventions ▶ adj forbidden by a taboo

  taboos n ▷ taboo

  tabs n ▷ tab

tabular adj arranged in a table

tabulate v (-tes, -ting, -ted) arrange (information) in a table > **tabulation** n (pl -s)

  tabulated v ▷ tabulate

  tabulates v ▷ tabulate

  tabulating v ▷ tabulate

  tabulation n ▷ tabulate

  tabulations n ▷ tabulate

tachograph n (pl -s) device for recording the speed and distance travelled by a motor vehicle

  tachographs n ▷ tachograph

tachometer n (pl -s) device for measuring speed, esp. that of a revolving shaft

  tachometers n ▷ tachometer

tacit [tass-it] adj implied but not spoken > **tacitly** adv

  tacitly adv ▷ tacit

taciturn [tass-it-turn] adj habitually uncommunicative > **taciturnity** n (pl -ties)

  taciturnities n ▷ taciturn

  taciturnity n ▷ taciturn

tack[1] n (pl -s) short nail with a large head ▶ v (-s, -ing, -ed) fasten with tacks

tack[2] n (pl -s) course of a ship sailing obliquely into the wind ▶ v (-s, -ing, -ed) sail into the wind on a zigzag course

tack[3] n (pl -s) riding harness for horses

  tacked v ▷ tack[1, 2]

  tackier adj ▷ tacky[1, 2]

tackies, takkies pl n (sing **tacky**) (S AFR)
(Informal) tennis shoes or plimsolls
  tackiest adj ▷ **tacky¹, ²**
  tacking v ▷ **tack¹, ²**
tackle v (-les, -ling, -led) deal with (a task)
(SPORT) ▶ n (pl -les) (SPORT) act of tackling an
opposing player
  tackled v ▷ **tackle**
  tackles v, n ▷ **tackle**
  tackling v ▷ **tackle**
  tacks n ▷ **tack¹, ², ³** ▶ v ▷ **tack¹, ²**
tacky¹ adj (-ckier, -ckiest) slightly sticky
tacky² adj (-ckier, -ckiest) (Informal) vulgar and
tasteless
  tacky³ n ▷ **tackies**
taco [tah-koh] n (pl -s) (MEXICAN COOKERY) tortilla
fried until crisp, served with a filling
  tacos n ▷ **taco**
tact n (pl -s) skill in avoiding giving offence
  > **tactful** adj > **tactfully** adv > **tactless** adj
  > **tactlessly** adv
  tactful adj ▷ **tact**
  tactfully adv ▷ **tact**
tactic n (pl -s) method or plan to achieve an
end > **tactical** adj > **tactician** n (pl -s)
  tactical adj ▷ **tactic**
  tactician n ▷ **tactic**
  tacticians n ▷ **tactic**
tactics pl n art of directing military forces in
battle ▶ n ▷ **tactic**
tactile adj of or having the sense of touch
  tactless adj ▷ **tact**
  tactlessly adv ▷ **tact**
  tacts n ▷ **tact**
tadpole n (pl -s) limbless tailed larva of a frog
or toad
  tadpoles n ▷ **tadpole**
taffeta n (pl -s) shiny silk or rayon fabric
  taffetas n ▷ **taffeta**
tag¹ n (pl -s) label bearing information ▶ v (-s,
-gging, -gged) attach a tag to
tag² n (pl -s) children's game where the person
being chased becomes the chaser upon being
touched ▶ v (-s, -gging, -gged) touch and
catch in this game
  tagged v ▷ **tag¹, ²**
  tagging v ▷ **tag¹, ²**
tagliatelle n pasta in long narrow strips
  tags n, v ▷ **tag¹, ²**
tail n (pl -s) rear part of an animal's body, usu.
forming a flexible appendage ▶ adj at the rear
  ▶ v (-s, -ing, -ed) (Informal) follow (someone)
secretly > **tailless** adj
tailback n (pl -s) (BRIT) queue of traffic
stretching back from an obstruction

  tailbacks n ▷ **tailback**
tailboard n (pl -s) removable or hinged rear
board on a truck etc.
  tailboards n ▷ **tailboard**
  tailed v ▷ **tail**
  tailing v ▷ **tail**
  tailless adj ▷ **tail**
tailor n (pl -s) person who makes men's clothes
  ▶ v (-s, -ing, -ed) adapt to suit a purpose
  tailored v ▷ **tailor**
  tailoring v ▷ **tailor**
  tailors n, v ▷ **tailor**
tailplane n (pl -s) small stabilizing wing at the
rear of an aircraft
  tailplanes n ▷ **tailplane**
tails adv with the side of a coin uppermost
that does not have a portrait of a head on it
  ▶ pl n (Informal) tail coat ▶ n, v ▷ **tail**
tailspin n (pl -s) uncontrolled spinning dive of
an aircraft
  tailspins n ▷ **tailspin**
tailwind n (pl -s) wind coming from the rear
  tailwinds n ▷ **tailwind**
taint v (-s, -ing, -ed) spoil with a small amount
of decay, contamination, or other bad quality
  ▶ n (pl -s) something that taints
  tainted v ▷ **taint**
  tainting v ▷ **taint**
  taints v, n ▷ **taint**
taipan n (pl -s) large poisonous Australian
snake
  taipans n ▷ **taipan**

> **taj** n (**tajes**). A taj is a tall conical
> cap worn by some Muslims. This
> unusual word can be helpful if you
> are struggling to use J because there
> aren't any good opportunities for
> longer words on the board. Taj scores
> 10 points.

take v (**takes, taking, took, taken**) remove
from a place ▶ n (pl -s) one of a series of
recordings from which the best will be used
takeaway n (pl -s) shop or restaurant selling
meals for eating elsewhere
  takeaways n ▷ **takeaway**
  taken v ▷ **take**
takeoff n (pl -s) (of an aircraft) act of leaving
the ground
  takeoffs n ▷ **takeoff**
takeover n (pl -s) act of taking control of a
company by buying a large number of its
shares
  takeovers n ▷ **takeover**
  takes v, n ▷ **take**
taking adj charming ▶ v ▷ **take**

takings *pl n* money received by a shop
 takkies *pl n* ▷ **tackies**
talc *n* (*pl* -**s**) talcum powder
 talcs *n* ▷ **talc**
tale *n* (*pl* -**s**) story
talent *n* (*pl* -**s**) natural ability > **talented** *adj*
 talented *adj* ▷ **talent**
 talents *n* ▷ **talent**
 tales *n* ▷ **tale**
talisman *n* (*pl* -**s**) object believed to have
 magic power > **talismanic** *adj*
 talismanic *adj* ▷ **talisman**
 talismans *n* ▷ **talisman**
talk *v* (-**s**, -**ing**, -**ed**) express ideas or feelings by
 means of speech ▶ *n* (*pl* -**s**) speech or lecture
talkative *adj* fond of talking
talkback *n* (*pl* -**s**) (NZ) broadcast in which
 telephone comments or questions from the
 public are transmitted live
 talkbacks *n* ▷ **talkback**
 talked *v* ▷ **talk**
talker *n* (*pl* -**s**) person who talks
 talkers *n* ▷ **talker**
 talking *v* ▷ **talk**
 talks *v*, *n* ▷ **talk**
tall (-**er**, -**est**) *adj* higher than average
tallboy *n* (*pl* -**s**) high chest of drawers
 tallboys *n* ▷ **tallboy**
 taller *adj* ▷ **tall**
 tallest *adj* ▷ **tall**
 tallied *v* ▷ **tally**
 tallies *v*, *n* ▷ **tally**
tallow *n* (*pl* -**s**) hard animal fat used to make
 candles
 tallows *n* ▷ **tallow**
tally *v* (-**lies**, -**lying**, -**lied**) (of two things)
 correspond ▶ *n* (*pl* -**lies**) record of a debt or
 score
 tallying *v* ▷ **tally**
talon *n* (*pl* -**s**) bird's hooked claw
 talons *n* ▷ **talon**
tamarind *n* (*pl* -**s**) tropical tree
 tamarinds *n* ▷ **tamarind**
tamarisk *n* (*pl* -**s**) evergreen shrub with slender
 branches and feathery flower clusters
 tamarisks *n* ▷ **tamarisk**
tambourine *n* (*pl* -**s**) percussion instrument
 like a small drum with jingling metal discs
 attached
 tambourines *n* ▷ **tambourine**
tame *adj* (-**r**, -**est**) (of animals) brought under
 human control ▶ *v* (-**mes**, -**ming**, -**med**) make
 tame > **tamely** *adv*
 tamed *v* ▷ **tame**
 tamely *adv* ▷ **tame**

tamer *n* (*pl* -**s**) person who tames wild animals
 ▶ *adj* ▷ **tame**
 tamers *n* ▷ **tamer**
 tames *v* ▷ **tame**
 tamest *adj* ▷ **tame**
 taming *v* ▷ **tame**
tamp *v* (-**s**, -**ing**, -**ed**) pack down by repeated
 taps
 tamped *v* ▷ **tamp**
tamper *v* (-**s**, -**ing**, -**ed**) (*foll. by* **with**) interfere
 tampered *v* ▷ **tamper**
 tampering *v* ▷ **tamper**
 tampers *v* ▷ **tamper**
 tamping *v* ▷ **tamp**
tampon *n* (*pl* -**s**) absorbent plug of cotton
 wool inserted into the vagina during
 menstruation
 tampons *n* ▷ **tampon**
 tamps *v* ▷ **tamp**
tan *n* (*pl* -**s**) brown coloration of the skin from
 exposure to sunlight ▶ *v* (-**s**, -**nning**, -**nned**)
 (of skin) go brown from exposure to sunlight
 ▶ *adj* (-**ner**, -**nest**) yellowish-brown
tandem *n* (*pl* -**s**) bicycle for two riders, one
 behind the other
 tandems *n* ▷ **tandem**
tandoori *adj* (of food) cooked in an Indian
 clay oven
tang *n* (*pl* -**s**) strong taste or smell > **tangy** *adj*
 (-**gier**, -**giest**)
tangent *n* (*pl* -**s**) line that touches a curve
 without intersecting it
tangential *adj* of superficial relevance only
 > **tangentially** *adv*
 tangentially *adv* ▷ **tangential**
 tangents *n* ▷ **tangent**
tangerine *n* (*pl* -**s**) small orange-like fruit of an
 Asian citrus tree
 tangerines *n* ▷ **tangerine**
tangible *adj* able to be touched > **tangibly** *adv*
 tangibly *adv* ▷ **tangible**
 tangier *adj* ▷ **tang**
 tangiest *adj* ▷ **tang**
tangle *n* (*pl* -**les**) confused mass or situation ▶ *v*
 (-**les**, -**ling**, -**led**) twist together in a tangle
 tangled *v* ▷ **tangle**
 tangles *n*, *v* ▷ **tangle**
 tangling *v* ▷ **tangle**
tango *n* (*pl* -**gos**) S American dance ▶ *v* (-**goes**,
 -**going**, -**goed**) dance a tango
 tangoed *v* ▷ **tango**
 tangoes *v* ▷ **tango**
 tangoing *v* ▷ **tango**
 tangos *v* ▷ **tango**
 tangs *n* ▷ **tang**

tangy *adj* ▷ **tang**
taniwha [tun-ee-fah] *n* (*pl* **-s**) (NZ) mythical Maori monster that lives in water
taniwhas *n* ▷ **taniwha**
tank *n* (*pl* **-s**) container for liquids or gases
tankard *n* (*pl* **-s**) large beer-mug, often with a hinged lid
tankards *n* ▷ **tankard**
tanker *n* (*pl* **-s**) ship or truck for carrying liquid in bulk
tankers *n* ▷ **tanker**
tanks *n* ▷ **tank**
tanned *v* ▷ **tan**
tanner *adj* ▷ **tan**
tanneries *n* ▷ **tannery**
tannery *n* (*pl* **-ries**) place where hides are tanned
tannest *adj* ▷ **tan**
tannin *n* (*pl* **-s**) vegetable substance used in tanning
tanning *v* ▷ **tan**
tannins *n* ▷ **tannin**
tans *n*, *v* ▷ **tan**
tansies *n* ▷ **tansy**
tansy *n* (*pl* **-sies**) yellow-flowered plant
tantalize *v* (**-zes, -zing, -zed**) torment by showing but withholding something desired > **tantalizing** *adj* > **tantalizingly** *adv*
tantalized *v* ▷ **tantalize**
tantalizes *v* ▷ **tantalize**
tantalizing *v*, *adj* ▷ **tantalize**
tantalizingly *adv* ▷ **tantalize**
tantalum *n* (*pl* **-s**) (CHEM) hard greyish-white metallic element
tantalums *n* ▷ **tantalum**
tantamount *adj* equivalent in effect to
tantrum *n* (*pl* **-s**) childish outburst of temper
tantrums *n* ▷ **tantrum**
tap[1] *v* (**taps, tapping, -pped**) knock lightly and usu. repeatedly ▸ *n* (*pl* **-s**) light knock
tap[2] *n* (*pl* **-s**) valve to control the flow of liquid from a pipe or cask ▸ *v* (**taps, tapping, tapped**) listen in on (a telephone call) secretly by making an illegal connection
tape *n* (*pl* **-s**) narrow long strip of material ▸ *v* (**tapes, taping, taped**) record on magnetic tape
taped *v* ▷ **tape**
taper *v* (**-s, -ing, -ed**) become narrower towards one end ▸ *n* (*pl* **-s**) long thin candle
tapered *v* ▷ **taper**
tapering *v* ▷ **taper**
tapers *v*, *n* ▷ **taper**
tapes *n*, *v* ▷ **tape**
tapestries *n* ▷ **tapestry**

tapestry *n* (*pl* **-tries**) fabric decorated with coloured woven designs
tapeworm *n* (*pl* **-s**) long flat parasitic worm living in the intestines of vertebrates
tapeworms *n* ▷ **tapeworm**
tapioca *n* (*pl* **-s**) beadlike starch made from cassava root, used in puddings
tapiocas *n* ▷ **tapioca**
taping *v* ▷ **tape**
tapir [tape-er] *n* (*pl* **-s**) piglike mammal of tropical America and SE Asia, with a long snout
tapirs *n* ▷ **tapir**
tapped *v* ▷ **tap**[1, 2]
tappet *n* (*pl* **-s**) short steel rod in an engine, transferring motion from one part to another
tappets *n* ▷ **tappet**
tapping *v* ▷ **tap**[1, 2]
taproot *n* (*pl* **-s**) main root of a plant, growing straight down
taproots *n* ▷ **taproot**
taps *n*, *v* ▷ **tap**[1, 2]
tar *n* (*pl* **-rs**) thick black liquid distilled from coal etc. ▸ *v* (**-s, -rring, -rred**) coat with tar
taramasalata *n* (*pl* **-s**) creamy pink pâté made from fish roe
taramasalatas *n* ▷ **taramasalata**
tarantella *n* (*pl* **-s**) lively Italian dance
tarantellas *n* ▷ **tarantella**
tarantula *n* (*pl* **-s**) large hairy spider with a poisonous bite
tarantulas *n* ▷ **tarantula**
tardier *adj* ▷ **tardy**
tardiest *adj* ▷ **tardy**
tardily *adv* ▷ **tardy**
tardiness *n* ▷ **tardy**
tardinesses *n* ▷ **tardy**
tardy *adj* (**-dier, -diest**) slow or late > **tardily** *adv* > **tardiness** *n* (*pl* **-es**)
tare *n* (*pl* **-s**) type of vetch plant
tares *n* ▷ **tare**
target *n* (*pl* **-s**) object or person a missile is aimed at ▸ *v* (**-gets, -geting, -geted**) aim or direct
targeted *v* ▷ **target**
targeting *v* ▷ **target**
targets *n*, *v* ▷ **target**
tariff *n* (*pl* **-s**) tax levied on imports
tariffs *n* ▷ **tariff**
tarn *n* (*pl* **-s**) small mountain lake
tarnish *v* (**-shes, -shing, -shed**) make or become stained or less bright ▸ *n* (*pl* **-es**) discoloration or blemish
tarnished *v* ▷ **tarnish**
tarnishes *v*, *n* ▷ **tarnish**

tarnishing v ▷ **tarnish**

tarns n ▷ **tarn**

tarot [tarr-oh] n (pl **-s**) special pack of cards used mainly in fortune-telling

tarots n ▷ **tarot**

tarpaulin n (pl **-s**) (sheet of) heavy waterproof fabric

tarpaulins n ▷ **tarpaulin**

tarragon n (pl **-s**) aromatic herb

tarragons n ▷ **tarragon**

tarred v ▷ **tar**

tarried v ▷ **tarry**

tarries v ▷ **tarry**

tarring v ▷ **tar**

tarry v (**tarries, tarrying, tarried**) (Old-fashioned) linger or delay

tarrying v ▷ **tarry**

tars n, v ▷ **tar**

tarsi n ▷ **tarsus**

tarsus n (pl **-si**) bones of the heel and ankle collectively

tart[1] n (pl **-s**) pie or flan with a sweet filling

tart[2] adj (**-er, -est**) sharp or bitter > **tartly** adv > **tartness** n (pl **-es**)

tart[3] n (pl **-s**) (Informal) sexually provocative or promiscuous woman

tartan n (pl **-s**) design of straight lines crossing at right angles, esp. one associated with a Scottish clan

tartans n ▷ **tartan**

tartar[1] n (pl **-s**) hard deposit on the teeth

tartar[2] n (pl **-s**) fearsome or formidable person

tartars n ▷ **tartar**[1,2]

tarter adj ▷ **tart**[2]

tartest adj ▷ **tart**[2]

tartly adv ▷ **tart**[2]

tartness n ▷ **tart**[2]

tartnesses n ▷ **tart**[2]

tartrazine [tar-traz-zeen] n (pl **-s**) artificial yellow dye used in food etc.

tartrazines n ▷ **tartrazine**

tarts n ▷ **tart**[1,3]

task n (pl **-s**) (difficult or unpleasant) piece of work to be done

taskmaster n (pl **-s**) person who enforces hard work

taskmasters n ▷ **taskmaster**

tasks n ▷ **task**

tassel n (pl **-s**) decorative fringed knot of threads

tassels n ▷ **tassel**

taste n (pl **-s**) sense by which the flavour of a substance is distinguished in the mouth ▶ v (**-tes, -ting, -ted**) distinguish the taste of (a substance)

tasted v ▷ **taste**

tasteful adj having or showing good taste > **tastefully** adv

tastefully adv ▷ **tasteful**

tasteless adj bland or insipid > **tastelessly** adv

tastelessly adv ▷ **tasteless**

tastes n, v ▷ **taste**

tastier adj ▷ **tasty**

tastiest adj ▷ **tasty**

tasting v ▷ **taste**

tasty adj (**-tier, -tiest**) pleasantly flavoured

tat n (pl **-s**) (BRIT) tatty or tasteless article(s)

tats n ▷ **tat**

tattered adj ragged or torn

tattier n ▷ **tatty**

tattiest n ▷ **tatty**

tattle v (**-les, -ling, -led**), n (pl **-les**) (BRIT, AUST & NZ) gossip or chatter

tattled v ▷ **tattle**

tattles n ▷ **tattle**

tattling v ▷ **tattle**

tattoo[1] n (pl **-s**) pattern made on the body by pricking the skin and staining it with indelible inks ▶ v (**-toos, -tooing, -tooed**) make such a pattern on the skin > **tattooist** n (pl **-s**)

tattoo[2] n (pl **-s**) military display or pageant

tattooed n ▷ **tattoo**[1]

tattooing n ▷ **tattoo**[1]

tattooist n ▷ **tattoo**[1]

tattooists n ▷ **tattoo**[1]

tattoos n ▷ **tattoo**[1,2] ▶ v ▷ **tattoo**[1]

tatty adj (**-tier, -tiest**) shabby or worn out

taught v ▷ **teach**

taunt v (**-s, -ing, -ed**) tease with jeers ▶ n (pl **-s**) jeering remark

taunted v ▷ **taunt**

taunting v ▷ **taunt**

taunts v, n ▷ **taunt**

taupe adj brownish-grey

taut adj (**-er, -est**) drawn tight

tauten v (**-s, -ing, -ed**) make or become taut

tautened v ▷ **tauten**

tautening v ▷ **tauten**

tautens v ▷ **tauten**

tauter adj ▷ **taut**

tautest adj ▷ **taut**

tautological adj ▷ **tautology**

tautologies n ▷ **tautology**

tautology n (pl **-gies**) use of words which merely repeat something already stated > **tautological** adj

tavern n (pl **-s**) (Old-fashioned) pub

taverns n ▷ **tavern**

tawdrier adj ▷ **tawdry**

tawdriest *adj* ▷ tawdry

tawdry *adj* (**-drier, -driest**) cheap, showy, and of poor quality

tawnier *adj* ▷ tawny

tawniest *adj* ▷ tawny

tawny *adj* (**-nier, -niest**) yellowish-brown

tax *n* (*pl* **-es**) compulsory payment levied by a government on income, property, etc. to raise revenue ▶ *v* (**-es, -ing, -ed**) levy a tax on > **taxable** *adj* > **taxpayer** *n* (*pl* **-s**)

taxable *adj* ▷ tax

taxation *n* (*pl* **-s**) levying of taxes

taxations *n* ▷ taxation

taxed *v* ▷ tax

taxes *n, v* ▷ tax

taxi *n* (*pl* **-s**) car with a driver that may be hired to take people to any specified destination ▶ *v* (**taxis, taxiing, taxied**) (of an aircraft) run along the ground before taking off or after landing

taxidermies *n* ▷ taxidermy

taxidermist *n* ▷ taxidermy

taxidermists *n* ▷ taxidermy

taxidermy *n* (*pl* **-mies**) art of stuffing and mounting animal skins to give them a lifelike appearance > **taxidermist** *n* (*pl* **-s**)

taxied *v* ▷ taxi

taxiing *v* ▷ taxi

taxing *v* ▷ tax

taxis *n, v* ▷ taxi

taxonomic *adj* ▷ taxonomy

taxonomies *n* ▷ taxonomy

taxonomist *n* ▷ taxonomy

taxonomists *n* ▷ taxonomy

taxonomy *n* (*pl* **-mies**) classification of plants and animals into groups > **taxonomic** *adj* > **taxonomist** *n* (*pl* **-s**)

taxpayer *n* ▷ tax

taxpayers *n* ▷ tax

te *n* (**tes**). Te is the seventh note of a musical scale. Although it won't earn you many points on its own, te is extremely useful as it allows you to connect a word beginning with T to one ending in E, or vice versa, which is very helpful as T and E are two of the most common tiles in the game. Te scores 2 points.

tea *n* (*pl* **-s**) drink made from infusing the dried leaves of an Asian bush in boiling water

teapot *n* (*pl* **-s**) container with a lid, spout, and handle for making and serving tea

teapots *n* ▷ teapot

teaspoon *n* (*pl* **-s**) small spoon for stirring tea

teaspoons *n* ▷ teaspoon

teach *v* (**-es, -ing, taught**) tell or show (someone) how to do something > **teaching** *n* (*pl* **-s**)

teacher *n* (*pl* **-s**) person who teaches, esp. in a school

teachers *n* ▷ teacher

teaches *v* ▷ teach

teaching *v, n* ▷ teach

teachings *n* ▷ teach

teak *n* (*pl* **-s**) very hard wood of an E Indian tree

teaks *n* ▷ teak

teal *n* (*pl* **-s**) kind of small duck

teals *n* ▷ teal

team *n* (*pl* **-s**) group of people forming one side in a game

teams *n* ▷ team

teamster *n* (*pl* **-s**) (*us*) commercial vehicle driver

teamsters *n* ▷ teamster

teamwork *n* (*pl* **-s**) cooperative work by a team

teamworks *n* ▷ teamwork

tear[1], **teardrop** *n* (*pl* **-s**) drop of fluid appearing in and falling from the eye

tear[2] *v* (**-s, -ing, tore, torn**) rip a hole in ▶ *n* (*pl* **-s**) hole or split

tearaway *n* (*pl* **-s**) wild or unruly person

tearaways *n* ▷ tearaway

teardrop *n* ▷ tear[1]

teardrops *n* ▷ tear[1]

tearful *adj* weeping or about to weep

tearing *v* ▷ tear[2]

tears *n* ▷ tear[1, 2] ▶ *v* ▷ tear[2]

teas *n* ▷ tea

tease *v* (**-ses, -sing, -sed**) make fun of (someone) in a provoking or playful way ▶ *n* (*pl* **-s**) person who teases > **teasing** *adj, n* (*pl* **-s**)

teased *v* ▷ tease

teasel, teazel, teazle *n* (*pl* **-s**) plant with prickly leaves and flowers

teasels *n* ▷ teasel

teases *v, n* ▷ tease

teasing *v, adj n* ▷ tease

teasings *n* ▷ tease

teat *n* (*pl* **-s**) nipple of a breast or udder

teats *n* ▷ teat

teazel *n* ▷ teasel

teazels *n* ▷ teasel

teazle *n* ▷ teasel

teazles *n* ▷ teasel

tech *n* (*pl* **-s**) (*Informal*) technical college

techie (*Informal*) *n* (*pl* **-s**) person who is skilled in the use of technology ▶ *adj* relating to or skilled in the use of technology

techies *n* ▷ techie

technetium [tek-**neesh**-ee-um] *n* (*pl* **-s**) (CHEM) artificially produced silvery-grey metallic element

technetiums n ▷ **technetium**

technical adj of or specializing in industrial, practical, or mechanical arts and applied sciences > **technically** adv

technicalities n ▷ **technicality**

technicality n (pl -s) petty point based on a strict application of rules

technically adv ▷ **technical**

technician n (pl -s) person skilled in a particular technical field

technicians n ▷ **technician**

technicolor adj garishly coloured

technique n (pl -s) method or skill used for a particular task

techniques n ▷ **technique**

techno n (pl -s) type of electronic dance music with a very fast beat

technocracies n ▷ **technocracy**

technocracy n (pl -cies) government by technical experts > **technocrat** n (pl -s)

technocrat n ▷ **technocracy**

technocrats n ▷ **technocracy**

technological adj ▷ **technology**

technologies n ▷ **technology**

technologist n ▷ **technology**

technologists n ▷ **technology**

technology n (pl -gies) application of practical or mechanical sciences to industry or commerce > **technological** adj > **technologist** n (pl -s)

technos n ▷ **techno**

techs n ▷ **tech**

tectonics n study of the earth's crust and the forces affecting it

teddies n ▷ **teddy**

teddy n (pl -dies) teddy bear

tedious adj causing fatigue or boredom > **tediously** adv

tediously adv ▷ **tedious**

tedium n (pl -s) monotony

tediums n ▷ **tedium**

tee n (pl -s) small peg from which a golf ball can be played at the start of each hole

teem[1] v (-s, -ing, -ed) be full of

teem[2] v (-s, -ing, -ed) rain heavily

teemed v ▷ **teem**[1, 2]

teeming v ▷ **teem**[1, 2]

teems v ▷ **teem**[1, 2]

teenage adj ▷ **teenager**

teenager n (pl -s) person aged between 13 and 19 > **teenage** adj

teenagers n ▷ **teenager**

teens pl n period of being a teenager

teepee n (pl -s) ▷ **tepee**

teepees n ▷ **teepee**

tees n ▷ **tee**

teeter v (-s, -ing, -ed) wobble or move unsteadily

teetered v ▷ **teeter**

teetering v ▷ **teeter**

teeters v ▷ **teeter**

teeth n ▷ **tooth**

teethe v (-thes, -thing, -thed) (of a baby) grow his or her first teeth

teethed v ▷ **teethe**

teethes v ▷ **teethe**

teething v ▷ **teethe**

teetotal adj drinking no alcohol > **teetotaller** n (pl -s)

teetotaller n ▷ **teetotal**

teetotallers n ▷ **teetotal**

telecommunications n communications using telephone, radio, television, etc.

telegram n (pl -s) formerly, a message sent by telegraph

telegrams n ▷ **telegram**

telegraph n (pl -s) formerly, a system for sending messages over a distance along a cable ▶ v (-s, -ing, -ed) communicate by telegraph > **telegraphic** adj > **telegraphist** n (pl -s)

telegraphed v ▷ **telegraph**

telegraphic adj ▷ **telegraph**

telegraphies n ▷ **telegraphy**

telegraphing v ▷ **telegraph**

telegraphist n ▷ **telegraph**

telegraphists n ▷ **telegraph**

telegraphs n, v ▷ **telegraph**

telegraphy n (pl -phies) science or use of a telegraph

telekinesis n (pl -eses) movement of objects by thought or willpower

telekineses n ▷ **telekinesis**

telemetries n ▷ **telemetry**

telemetry n (pl -tries) use of electronic devices to record or measure a distant event and transmit the data to a receiver

teleological adj ▷ **teleology**

teleologies n ▷ **teleology**

teleology n (pl -gies) belief that all things have a predetermined purpose > **teleological** adj

telepathic adj ▷ **telepathy**

telepathically adv ▷ **telepathy**

telepathies n ▷ **telepathy**

telepathy n (pl -thies) direct communication between minds > **telepathic** adj > **telepathically** adv

telephone n (pl -s) device for transmitting

sound over a distance ▶ v (-nes, -ning, -ned) call or talk to (a person) by telephone > **telephony** n (pl -nies) > **telephonic** adj
telephoned v ▷ **telephone**
telephones n, v ▷ **telephone**
telephonic adj ▷ **telephone**
telephonies n ▷ **telephone**
telephoning v ▷ **telephone**
telephonist n (pl -s) person operating a telephone switchboard
telephonists n ▷ **telephonist**
telephony n ▷ **telephone**
teleprinter n (pl -s) (BRIT) apparatus like a typewriter for sending and receiving typed messages by wire
teleprinters n ▷ **teleprinter**
telesales n selling of a product or service by telephone
telescope n (pl -s) optical instrument for magnifying distant objects ▶ v (-pes, -ping, -ped) shorten > **telescopic** adj
telescoped v ▷ **telescope**
telescopes n, v ▷ **telescope**
telescopic adj ▷ **telescope**
telescoping v ▷ **telescope**
televise v (-ses, -sing, -sed) broadcast on television
televised v ▷ **televise**
televises v ▷ **televise**
televising v ▷ **televise**
television n (pl -s) system of producing a moving image and accompanying sound on a distant screen > **televisual** adj
televisions n ▷ **television**
televisual adj ▷ **television**
telex n (pl -es) international communication service using teleprinters ▶ v (-es, -ing, -ed) transmit by telex
telexed v ▷ **telex**
telexes n, v ▷ **telex**
telexing v ▷ **telex**
tell v (-s, -lling, told) make known in words
teller n (pl -s) narrator
tellers n ▷ **teller**
tellies n ▷ **telly**
telling adj having a marked effect ▶ v ▷ **tell**
tells v ▷ **tell**
telltale n (pl -s) person who reveals secrets ▶ adj revealing
telltales n ▷ **telltale**
tellurium n (pl -s) (CHEM) brittle silvery-white nonmetallic element
telluriums n ▷ **tellurium**
telly n (pl -lies) (Informal) television
temerities n ▷ **temerity**

temerity [tim-**merr**-it-tee] n (pl -ties) boldness or audacity
temp (BRIT) (Informal) n (pl -s) temporary employee, esp. a secretary ▶ v (-s, -ing, -ed) work as a temp
temped v ▷ **temp**
temper n (pl -s) outburst of anger ▶ v (-s, -ing, -ed) make less extreme
tempera n (pl -s) painting medium for powdered pigments
temperas n ▷ **tempera**
temperament n (pl -s) person's character or disposition
temperamental adj having changeable moods > **temperamentally** adv
temperamentally adv ▷ **temperamental**
temperaments n ▷ **temperament**
temperance n (pl -s) moderation
temperances n ▷ **temperance**
temperate adj (of climate) not extreme
temperature n (pl -s) degree of heat or cold
temperatures n ▷ **temperature**
tempered v ▷ **temper**
tempering v ▷ **temper**
tempers n, v ▷ **temper**
tempest n (pl -s) violent storm
tempests n ▷ **tempest**
tempestuous adj violent or stormy
tempi n ▷ **tempo**
temping v ▷ **temp**
template n (pl -s) pattern used to cut out shapes accurately
templates n ▷ **template**
temple¹ n (pl -s) building for worship
temple² n (pl -s) region on either side of the forehead
temples n ▷ **temple¹, ²**
tempo n (pl -pi, -pos) rate or pace
temporal adj of time
temporarily adv ▷ **temporary**
temporary adj lasting only for a short time > **temporarily** adv
temporize v (-zes, -zing, -zed) gain time by negotiation or evasiveness
temporized v ▷ **temporize**
temporizes v ▷ **temporize**
temporizing v ▷ **temporize**
tempos n ▷ **tempo**
temps n, v ▷ **temp**
tempt v (-s, -ing, -ed) entice (a person) to do something wrong > **tempter, temptress** n (pl -s, -es)
temptation n (pl -s) tempting
temptations n ▷ **temptation**
tempted v ▷ **tempt**

tempter *n* ▷ tempt
tempters *n* ▷ tempt
tempting *adj* attractive or inviting ▶ *v* ▷ **tempt**
temptress *n* ▷ tempt
temptresses *n* ▷ tempt
tempts *v* ▷ tempt
ten *adj*, *n* (*pl* -s) one more than nine
tenable *adj* able to be upheld or maintained
tenacious *adj* holding fast > **tenaciously** *adv*
  > **tenacity** *n* (*pl* -ties)
  tenaciously *adv* ▷ **tenacious**
  tenacities *n* ▷ tenacious
  tenacity *n* ▷ tenacious
  tenancies *n* ▷ tenant
  tenancy *n* ▷ tenant
tenant *n* (*pl* -s) person who rents land or a
  building > **tenancy** *n* (*pl* -cies)
  tenants *n* ▷ tenant
tench *n* (*pl* -es) freshwater game fish of the
  carp family
  tenches *n* ▷ tench
tend¹ *v* (-s, -ing, -ed) be inclined
tend² *v* (-s, -ing, -ed) take care of
  tended *v* ▷ tend¹, ²
  tendencies *n* ▷ tendency
tendency *n* (*pl* -cies) inclination to act in a
  certain way > **tendentious** *adj* biased, not
  impartial
  tendentious *adj* ▷ tendency
tender¹ *adj* (-er, -est) not tough > **tenderly** *adv*
  > **tenderness** *n* (*pl* -es)
tender² *v* (-s, -ing, -ed) offer ▶ *n* (*pl* -s) such
  an offer
tender³ *n* (*pl* -s) small boat that brings supplies
  to a larger ship in a port
  tendered *v* ▷ tender²
  tenderer *adj* ▷ tender¹
  tenderest *adj* ▷ tender¹
  tendering *v* ▷ tender²
tenderize *v* (-zes, -zing, -zed) soften (meat)
  by pounding or treatment with a special
  substance
  tenderized *v* ▷ tenderize
  tenderizes *v* ▷ tenderize
  tenderizing *v* ▷ tenderize
  tenderly *adv* ▷ tender¹
  tenderness *n* ▷ tender¹
  tendernesses *n* ▷ tender¹
  tenders *n* ▷ tender², ³ ▶ *v* ▷ tender²
  tending *v* ▷ tend¹, ²
tendon *n* (*pl* -s) strong tissue attaching a
  muscle to a bone
  tendons *n* ▷ tendon
tendril *n* (*pl* -s) slender stem by which a
  climbing plant clings

tendrils *n* ▷ tendril
tends *v* ▷ tend¹, ²
tenement *n* (*pl* -s) (esp. in Scotland or the US)
  building divided into several flats
  tenements *n* ▷ tenement
tenet [ten-nit] *n* (*pl* -s) doctrine or belief
  tenets *n* ▷ tenet
tenner *n* (*pl* -s) (BRIT) (*Informal*) ten-pound note
  tenners *n* ▷ tenner
tennis *n* (*pl* -es) game in which players use
  rackets to hit a ball back and forth over a net
  tennises *n* ▷ tennis
tenon *n* (*pl* -s) projecting end on a piece of
  wood fitting into a slot in another
  tenons *n* ▷ tenon
tenor *n* (*pl* -s) (singer with) the second highest
  male voice ▶ *adj* (of a voice or instrument)
  between alto and baritone
  tenors *n* ▷ tenor
  tens *n* ▷ ten
tense¹ *adj* (-r, -st) emotionally strained ▶ *v*
  (-ses, -sing, -sed) make or become tense
tense² *n* (*pl* -s) (GRAMMAR) form of a verb
  showing the time of action
  tensed *v* ▷ tense¹
  tenser *adj* ▷ tense¹
  tenses *n* ▷ tense² ▶ *v* ▷ tense¹
  tensest *adj* ▷ tense¹
tensile *adj* of tension
  tensing *v* ▷ tense¹
tension *n* (*pl* -s) hostility or suspense
  tensions *n* ▷ tension
tent *n* (*pl* -s) portable canvas shelter
tentacle *n* (*pl* -s) flexible organ of many
  invertebrates, used for grasping, feeding, etc.
  tentacles *n* ▷ tentacle
tentative *adj* provisional or experimental
  > **tentatively** *adv*
  tentatively *adv* ▷ tentative
tenterhooks *pl n* tension
tenth *adj*, *n* (*pl* -s) (of) number ten in a series
  tenths *n* ▷ tenth
  tents *n* ▷ tent
tenuous *adj* slight or flimsy > **tenuously** *adv*
  tenuously *adv* ▷ tenuous
tenure *n* (*pl* -s) (period of) the holding of an
  office or position
  tenures *n* ▷ tenure
tepee, teepee [tee-pee] *n* (*pl* -s) cone-shaped
  tent, formerly used by Native Americans
  tepees *n* ▷ tepee
tepid *adj* (-er, -est) slightly warm
  tepider *adj* ▷ tepid
  tepidest *adj* ▷ tepid
tequila *n* (*pl* -s) Mexican alcoholic drink

tequilas *n* ▷ **tequila**
tercentenaries *n* ▷ **tercentenary**
tercentenary *adj, n (pl* -**ries**) (of) a three hundredth anniversary
term *n (pl* -**s**) word or expression ▶ *v* (-**s, -ing, -ed**) name or designate
termed *v* ▷ **term**
terminal *adj* (of an illness) ending in death ▶ *n (pl* -**s**) place where people or vehicles begin or end a journey > **terminally** *adv*
terminally *adv* ▷ **terminal**
terminals *n* ▷ **terminal**
terminate *v* (-**tes, -ting, -ted**) bring or come to an end > **termination** *n (pl* -**s**)
terminated *v* ▷ **terminate**
terminates *v* ▷ **terminate**
terminating *v* ▷ **terminate**
termination *n* ▷ **terminate**
terminations *n* ▷ **terminate**
terming *v* ▷ **term**
termini *n* ▷ **terminus**
terminologies *n* ▷ **terminology**
terminology *n (pl* -**gies**) technical terms relating to a subject
terminus *n (pl* -**ni, -nuses**) railway or bus station at the end of a line
terminuses *n* ▷ **terminus**
termite *n (pl* -**s**) white antlike insect that destroys timber
termites *n* ▷ **termite**
terms *n, v* ▷ **term** ▶ *pl n* conditions
tern *n (pl* -**s**) gull-like sea bird with a forked tail and pointed wings
ternary *adj* consisting of three parts
terns *n* ▷ **tern**
terrace *n (pl* -**s**) row of houses built as one block ▶ *v* (-**ces, -cing, -ced**) form into or provide with a terrace
terraced *v* ▷ **terrace**
terraces *n, v* ▷ **terrace** ▶ *pl n* (*also* **terracing**) tiered area in a stadium where spectators stand
terracing *v* ▷ **terrace**
terracotta *adj, n (pl* -**s**) (made of) brownish-red unglazed pottery ▶ *adj* brownish-red
terracottas *n* ▷ **terracotta**
terrain *n (pl* -**s**) area of ground, esp. with reference to its physical character
terrains *n* ▷ **terrain**
terrapin *n (pl* -**s**) small turtle-like reptile
terrapins *n* ▷ **terrapin**
terraria *n* ▷ **terrarium**
terrarium *n (pl* -**raria, -rariums**) enclosed container for small plants or animals
terrariums *n* ▷ **terrarium**

terrazzo *n (pl* -**s**) floor of marble chips set in mortar and polished
terrazzos *n* ▷ **terrazzo**
terrestrial *adj* of the earth
terrible *adj* very serious > **terribly** *adv*
terribly *adv* ▷ **terrible**
terrier *n (pl* -**s**) any of various breeds of small active dog
terriers *n* ▷ **terrier**
terries *n* ▷ **terry**
terrific *adj* great or intense
terrified *v, adj* ▷ **terrify**
terrifies *v* ▷ **terrify**
terrify *v* (-**fies, -fying, -fied**) fill with fear > **terrified** *adj* > **terrifying** *adj*
terrifying *v, adj* ▷ **terrify**
terrine [terr-reen] *n (pl* -**s**) earthenware dish with a lid
terrines *n* ▷ **terrine**
territorial *adj* ▷ **territory**
territories *n* ▷ **territory**
territory *n (pl* -**ries**) district > **territorial** *adj*
terror *n (pl* -**s**) great fear
terrorism *n (pl* -**s**) use of violence and intimidation to achieve political ends > **terrorist** *n (pl* -**s**) *adj*
terrorisms *n* ▷ **terrorism**
terrorist *n, adj* ▷ **terrorism**
terrorists *n* ▷ **terrorism**
terrorize *v* (-**zes, -zing, -zed**) force or oppress by fear or violence
terrorized *v* ▷ **terrorize**
terrorizes *v* ▷ **terrorize**
terrorizing *v* ▷ **terrorize**
terrors *n* ▷ **terror**
terry *n (pl* -**ries**) fabric with small loops covering both sides, used esp. for making towels
terse *adj* (-**r, -st**) neat and concise > **tersely** *adv*
tersely *adv* ▷ **terse**
terser *adj* ▷ **terse**
tersest *adj* ▷ **terse**
tertiary [**tur**-shar-ee] *adj* third in degree, order, etc.
tessellated *adj* paved or inlaid with a mosaic of small tiles
test *v* (-**s, -ing, -ed**) try out to ascertain the worth, capability, or endurance of ▶ *n (pl* -**s**) critical examination > **testing** *adj*
testament *n (pl* -**s**) proof or tribute
testaments *n* ▷ **testament**
testator [test-**tay**-tor], *fem* **testatrix** [test-**tay**-triks] *n (pl* -**s, -xes**) maker of a will
testators *n* ▷ **testator**
testatrix *n* ▷ **testator**

testatrixes *n* ▷ testator
tested *v* ▷ test
testes *n* ▷ testis
testicle *n* (*pl* -**s**) either of the two male
reproductive glands
testicles *n* ▷ testicle
testier *adj* ▷ testy
testiest *adj* ▷ testy
testified *v* ▷ testify
testifies *v* ▷ testify
testify *v* (-**fies, -fying, -fied**) give evidence
under oath
testifying *v* ▷ testify
testily *adv* ▷ testy
testimonial *n* (*pl* -**s**) recommendation of the
worth of a person or thing
testimonials *n* ▷ testimonial
testimonies *n* ▷ testimony
testimony *n* (*pl* -**nies**) declaration of truth
or fact
testiness *n* ▷ testy
testinesses *n* ▷ testy
testing *v, adj* ▷ test
testis *n* (*pl* -**tes**) testicle
testosterone *n* (*pl* -**s**) male sex hormone
secreted by the testes
testosterones *n* ▷ testosterone
tests *v, n* ▷ test
testy *adj* (-**tier, -tiest**) irritable or touchy
> testily *adv* > testiness *n* (*pl* -**es**)
tetanus *n* (*pl* -**es**) acute infectious disease
producing muscular spasms and convulsions
tetanuses *n* ▷ tetanus
tether *n* (*pl* -**s**) rope or chain for tying an
animal to a spot ▶ *v* (-**s, -ing, -ed**) tie up with
rope
tethered *v* ▷ tether
tethering *v* ▷ tether
tethers *n, v* ▷ tether
tetrahedra *n* ▷ tetrahedron
tetrahedron [tet-ra-**heed**-ron] *n* (*pl* -**drons, -dra**)
solid figure with four faces
tetrahedrons *n* ▷ tetrahedron
tetralogies *n* ▷ tetralogy
tetralogy *n* (*pl* -**gies**) series of four related
works
text *n* (*pl* -**s**) main body of a book as distinct
from illustrations etc. ▶ *v* (-**s, -ing, -ed**) send a
text message to (someone) > **textual** *adj*
textbook *n* (*pl* -**s**) standard book on a
particular subject ▶ *adj* perfect
textbooks *n* ▷ textbook
texted *v* ▷ text
textile *n* (*pl* -**s**) fabric or cloth, esp. woven
textiles *n* ▷ textile

texting *v* ▷ text
texts *n, v* ▷ text
textual *adj* ▷ text
textural *adj* ▷ texture
texture *n* (*pl* -**s**) structure, feel, or consistency
> textured *adj* > textural *adj*
textured *adj* ▷ texture
textures *n* ▷ texture
thalidomide [thal-**lid**-oh-mide] *n* (*pl* -**s**) drug
formerly used as a sedative, but found to
cause abnormalities in developing fetuses
thalidomides *n* ▷ thalidomide
thallium *n* (*pl* -**s**) (CHEM) highly toxic metallic
element
thalliums *n* ▷ thallium
than *conj, prep* used to introduce the second
element of a comparison
thane *n* (*pl* -**s**) (HIST) Anglo-Saxon or medieval
Scottish nobleman
thanes *n* ▷ thane
thank *v* (-**s, -ing, -ed**) express gratitude to
thanked *v* ▷ thank
thankful *adj* grateful
thanking *v* ▷ thank
thankless *adj* unrewarding or unappreciated
thanks *pl n* words of gratitude ▶ *interj* polite
expression of gratitude ▶ *v* ▷ thank
that *adj, pron* used to refer to something
already mentioned or familiar, or further
away ▶ *conj* used to introduce a clause ▶ *pron*
used to introduce a relative clause
thatch *n* (*pl* -**es**) roofing material of reeds or
straw ▶ *v* (-**ches, -ching, -ched**) roof (a house)
with reeds or straw
thatched *v* ▷ thatch
thatches *n, v* ▷ thatch
thatching *v* ▷ thatch
thaw *v* (-**s, -ing, -ed**) make or become unfrozen
▶ *n* (*pl* -**s**) thawing
thawed *v* ▷ thaw
thawing *v* ▷ thaw
thaws *n, v* ▷ thaw
the *adj* the definite article, used before a noun
theatre *n* (*pl* -**s**) place where plays etc. are
performed
theatres *n* ▷ theatre
theatrical *adj* of the theatre > **theatrically** *adv*
> theatricality *n* (*pl* -**ties**)
theatricalities *n* ▷ theatrical
theatricality *n* ▷ theatrical
theatrically *adv* ▷ theatrical
theatricals *pl n* (amateur) dramatic
performances
thee *pron* (Obs) you
theft *n* (*pl* -**s**) act or an instance of stealing

thefts n ▷ theft
their adj of or associated with them
theirs pron (thing or person) belonging to them
theism [thee-iz-zum] n (pl -s) belief in a God or gods > **theist** n (pl -s) adj > **theistic** adj
  theisms n ▷ theism
  theist n, adj ▷ theism
  theistic adj ▷ theism
  theists n ▷ theism
them pron refers to people or things other than the speaker or those addressed
  thematic adj ▷ theme
theme n (pl -s) main idea or subject being discussed > **thematic** adj
  themes n ▷ theme
  themselves pron ▷ they, them
then adv at that time
thence adv from that place or time
  theocracies n ▷ theocracy
theocracy n (pl -cies) government by a god or priests > **theocratic** adj
  theocratic adj ▷ theocracy
theodolite [thee-odd-oh-lite] n (pl -s) surveying instrument for measuring angles
  theodolites n ▷ theodolite
  theologian n ▷ theology
  theologians n ▷ theology
  theological adj ▷ theology
  theologically adv ▷ theology
  theologies n ▷ theology
theology n (pl -gies) study of religions and religious beliefs > **theologian** n (pl -s) > **theological** adj > **theologically** adv
theorem n (pl -s) proposition that can be proved by reasoning
  theorems n ▷ theorem
theoretical adj based on theory rather than practice or fact > **theoretically** adv
  theoretically adv ▷ theoretical
  theories n ▷ theory
  theorist n ▷ theory
  theorists n ▷ theory
theorize v (-zes, -zing, -zed) form theories, speculate
  theorized v ▷ theorize
  theorizes v ▷ theorize
  theorizing v ▷ theorize
theory n (pl -ries) set of ideas to explain something > **theorist** n (pl -s)
  theosophical adj ▷ theosophy
  theosophies n ▷ theosophy
theosophy n (pl -phies) religious or philosophical system claiming to be based on intuitive insight into the divine nature

> **theosophical** adj
therapeutic [ther-rap-pew-tik] adj curing
therapeutics n art of curing
  therapies n ▷ therapy
  therapist n ▷ therapy
  therapists n ▷ therapy
therapy n (pl -pies) curing treatment
  > **therapist** n (pl -s)
there adv in or to that place
thereby adv by that means
therefore adv consequently, that being so
thereupon adv immediately after that
therm n (pl -s) unit of measurement of heat
thermal adj of heat ▸ n (pl -s) rising current of warm air
  thermals n ▷ thermal
thermodynamics n scientific study of the relationship between heat and other forms of energy
thermometer n (pl -s) instrument for measuring temperature
  thermometers n ▷ thermometer
thermonuclear adj involving nuclear fusion
thermoplastic adj (of a plastic) softening when heated and resetting on cooling
thermosetting adj (of a plastic) remaining hard when heated
thermostat n (pl -s) device for automatically regulating temperature > **thermostatic** adj
  thermostatic adj ▷ thermostat
  thermostats n ▷ thermostat
  therms n ▷ therm
thesaurus [thiss-sore-uss] n (pl -ruses) book containing lists of synonyms and related words
  thesauruses n ▷ thesaurus
these adj, pron ▷ this
  theses n ▷ thesis
thesis n (pl theses) written work submitted for a degree
thespian n (pl -s) actor or actress ▸ adj of the theatre
  thespians n ▷ thespian
they pron refers to: people or things other than the speaker or people addressed
thiamine n (pl -s) vitamin found in the outer coat of rice and other grains
  thiamines n ▷ thiamine
thick adj (-er, -est) of great or specified extent from one side to the other > **thickly** adv
thicken v (-s, -ing, -ed) make or become thick or thicker
  thickened v ▷ thicken
  thickening v ▷ thicken
  thickens v ▷ thicken

thicker *adj* ▷ **thick**
thickest *adj* ▷ **thick**
thicket *n* (*pl* **-s**) dense growth of small trees
thickets *n* ▷ **thicket**
thickly *adv* ▷ **thick**
thickness *n* (*pl* **-es**) state of being thick
thicknesses *n* ▷ **thickness**
thickset *adj* stocky in build
thief *n* (*pl* **thieves**) person who steals
thieve *v* (**-ves, -ving, -ved**) steal > **thieving** *adj*
thieved *v* ▷ **thieve**
thieves *v* ▷ **thieve** ▶ *n* ▷ **thief**
thieving *v, adj* ▷ **thieve**
thigh *n* (*pl* **-s**) upper part of the human leg
thighs *n* ▷ **thigh**
thimble *n* (*pl* **-s**) cap protecting the end of the finger when sewing
thimbles *n* ▷ **thimble**
thin *adj* (**-nner, -nnest**) not thick ▶ *v* (**-s, -nning, -nned**) make or become thin > **thinly** *adv* > **thinness** *n* (*pl* **-es**)
thine *pron, adj* (*Obs*) (something) of or associated with you (thou)
thing *n* (*pl* **-s**) material object
things *n* ▷ **thing** ▶ *pl n* possessions, clothes, etc.
think *v* (**-s, -ing, thought**) consider, judge, or believe > **thinker** *n* (*pl* **-s**) > **thinking** *adj*, *n* (*pl* **-s**)
thinker *n* ▷ **think**
thinkers *n* ▷ **think**
thinking *v, adj, n* ▷ **think**
thinkings *n* ▷ **think**
thinks *v* ▷ **think**
thinly *adv* ▷ **thin**
thinned *v* ▷ **thin**
thinner *adj* ▷ **thin**
thinness *n* ▷ **thin**
thinnesses *n* ▷ **thin**
thinnest *adj* ▷ **thin**
thinning *v* ▷ **thin**
thins *v* ▷ **thin**
third *adj* of number three in a series ▶ *n* (*pl* **-s**) one of three equal parts
thirds *n* ▷ **third**
thirst *n* (*pl* **-s**) desire to drink ▶ *v* (**-s, -ing, -ed**) feel thirst > **thirsty** *adj* (**-tier, -tiest**) > **thirstily** *adv*
thirsted *v* ▷ **thirst**
thirstier *adj* ▷ **thirst**
thirstiest *adj* ▷ **thirst**
thirstily *adv* ▷ **thirst**
thirsting *v* ▷ **thirst**
thirsts *n, v* ▷ **thirst**
thirsty *adj* (**-tier, -tiest**) ▷ **thirst**

thirteen *adj, n* (*pl* **-s**) three plus ten
> **thirteenth** *adj, n* (*pl* **-s**)
thirteens *n* ▷ **thirteen**
thirteenth *n* ▷ **thirteen**
thirteenths *n* ▷ **thirteen**
thirties *n* ▷ **thirty**
thirtieth *n* ▷ **thirty**
thirtieths *n* ▷ **thirty**
thirty *adj, n* (*pl* **-ties**) three times ten
> **thirtieth** *adj, n* (*pl* **-s**)
this *adj, pron* used to refer to a thing or person nearby, just mentioned, or about to be mentioned ▶ *adj* used to refer to the present time
thistle *n* (*pl* **-s**) prickly plant with dense flower heads
thistles *n* ▷ **thistle**
thither *adv* (*Obs*) to or towards that place
thong *n* (*pl* **-s**) thin strip of leather etc.
thongs *n* ▷ **thong**
thoraces *n* ▷ **thorax**
thoracic *adj* ▷ **thorax**
thorax *n* (*pl* **-xes, -races**) part of the body between the neck and the abdomen > **thoracic** *adj*
thoraxes *n* ▷ **thorax**
thorn *n* (*pl* **-s**) prickle on a plant > **thorny** *adj* (**-ier, -iest**)
thornier *adj* ▷ **thorn**
thorniest *adj* ▷ **thorn**
thorns *n* ▷ **thorn**
thorny *adj* ▷ **thorn**
thorough *adj* complete > **thoroughly** *adv* > **thoroughness** *n* (*pl* **-es**)
thoroughbred *n* (*pl* **-s**) ▶ *adj* (animal) of pure breed
thoroughbreds *n* ▷ **thoroughbred**
thoroughfare *n* (*pl* **-s**) way through from one place to another
thoroughfares *n* ▷ **thoroughfare**
thoroughly *adv* ▷ **thorough**
thoroughness *n* ▷ **thorough**
thoroughnesses *n* ▷ **thorough**
those *adj, pron* ▷ **that**
thou *pron* (*Obs*) you
though *conj* despite the fact that ▶ *adv* nevertheless
thought *v* ▷ **think** ▶ *n* (*pl* **-s**) thinking > **thoughtful** *adj* considerate
thoughtful *adj* ▷ **thought**
thoughtless *adj* inconsiderate
thoughts *n* ▷ **thought**
thousand *adj, n* (*pl* **-s**) ten hundred
thousands *n* ▷ **thousand**
thousandth *adj, n* (*pl* **-s**) (of) number one

thousand in a series
thousandths *n* ▷ **thousandth**
thrall *n* (*pl* **-s**) state of being in the power of another person
  thralls *n* ▷ **thrall**
thrash *v* (**-es, -ing, -ed**) beat, esp. with a stick or whip
  thrashed *v* ▷ **thrash**
  thrashes *v* ▷ **thrash**
thrashing *n* (*pl* **-s**) severe beating ▶ *v* ▷ **thrash**
thread *n* (*pl* **-s**) fine strand or yarn ▶ *v* (**-s, -ing, -ed**) pass thread through
threadbare *adj* (of fabric) with the nap worn off
  threaded *v* ▷ **thread**
  threading *v* ▷ **thread**
  threads *n, v* ▷ **thread**
threat *n* (*pl* **-s**) declaration of intent to harm
threaten *v* (**-s, -ing, -ed**) make or be a threat to
  threatened *v* ▷ **threaten**
  threatening *v* ▷ **threaten**
  threatens *v* ▷ **threaten**
  threats *n* ▷ **threat**
three *adj, n* (*pl* **-s**) one more than two
  threes *n* ▷ **three**
threesome *n* (*pl* **-s**) group of three
  threesomes *n* ▷ **threesome**
  threnodies *n* ▷ **threnody**
threnody *n* (*pl* **-dies**) lament for the dead
thresh *v* (**-es, -ing, -ed**) beat (wheat etc.) to separate the grain from the husks and straw
  threshed *v* ▷ **thresh**
  threshes *v* ▷ **thresh**
  threshing *v* ▷ **thresh**
threshold *n* (*pl* **-s**) bar forming the bottom of a doorway
  thresholds *n* ▷ **threshold**
  threw *v* ▷ **throw**
thrice *adv* (*Lit*) three times
thrift *n* (*pl* **-s**) wisdom and caution with money > **thrifty** *adj*
  thrifts *n* ▷ **thrift**
  thrifty *adj* ▷ **thrif**
thrill *n* (*pl* **-s**) sudden feeling of excitement ▶ *v* (**-s, -ing, -ed**) (cause to) feel a thrill > **thrilling** *adj*
  thrilled *v* ▷ **thrill**
thriller *n* (*pl* **-s**) book, film, etc. with an atmosphere of mystery or suspense
  thrillers *n* ▷ **thriller**
  thrilling *v, adj* ▷ **thrill**
  thrills *n, v* ▷ **thrill**
thrive *v* (**-ves, -ving, -ved** *or* **throve, thrived** *or* **thriven**) flourish or prosper
  thrived *v* ▷ **thrive**

  thriven *v* ▷ **thrive**
  thrives *v* ▷ **thrive**
  thriving *v* ▷ **thrive**
throat *n* (*pl* **-s**) passage from the mouth and nose to the stomach and lungs
  throatier *adj* ▷ **throaty**
  throatiest *adj* ▷ **throaty**
  throats *n* ▷ **throat**
throaty *adj* (**-tier, -tiest**) (of the voice) hoarse
throb *v* (**-s, -bbing, -bbed**) pulsate repeatedly ▶ *n* (*pl* **-s**) throbbing
  throbbed *v* ▷ **throb**
  throbbing *v* ▷ **throb**
  throbs *v, n* ▷ **throb**
throes *pl n* violent pangs or pains
thrombosis *n* (*pl* **-oses**) forming of a clot in a blood vessel or the heart
  thromboses *n* ▷ **thrombosis**
throne *n* (*pl* **-s**) ceremonial seat of a monarch or bishop
  thrones *n* ▷ **throne**
throng *n* (*pl* **-s**) ▶ *v* (**-s, -ing, -ed**) crowd
  thronged *v* ▷ **throng**
  thronging *v* ▷ **throng**
  throngs *n, v* ▷ **throng**
throstle *n* (*pl* **-s**) song thrush
  throstles *n* ▷ **throstle**
throttle *n* (*pl* **-s**) device controlling the amount of fuel entering an engine ▶ *v* (**-les, -ling, -led**) strangle
  throttled *v* ▷ **throttle**
  throttles *n, v* ▷ **throttle**
  throttling *v* ▷ **throttle**
through *prep* from end to end or side to side of ▶ *adj* finished
throughout *prep, adv* in every part (of)
throughput *n* (*pl* **-s**) amount of material processed
  throughputs *n* ▷ **throughput**
  throve *v* ▷ **thrive**
throw *v* (**-s, -ing, threw, thrown**) hurl through the air ▶ *n* (*pl* **-s**) throwing
throwaway *adj* done or said casually
throwback *n* (*pl* **-s**) person or thing that reverts to an earlier type
  throwbacks *n* ▷ **throwback**
  throwing *v* ▷ **throw**
  thrown *v* ▷ **throw**
  throws *v, n* ▷ **throw**
thrush[1] *n* (*pl* **-es**) brown songbird
thrush[2] *n* (*pl* **-es**) fungal disease of the mouth or vagina
  thrushes *n* ▷ **thrush**[1, 2]
thrust *v* (**-s, -ing, thrust**) push forcefully ▶ *n* (*pl* **-s**) forceful stab

thrusting *v* ▷ **thrust**
thrusts *v, n* ▷ **thrust**
thud *n* (*pl* **-s**) dull heavy sound ▶ *v* (**-s, -dding, -dded**) make such a sound
thudded *v* ▷ **thud**
thudding *v* ▷ **thud**
thuds *n, v* ▷ **thud**
thug *n* (*pl* **-s**) violent man, esp. a criminal > **thuggery** *n* (*pl* **-ries**) > **thuggish** *adj*
thuggeries *n* ▷ **thug**
thuggery *n* ▷ **thug**
thuggish *adj* ▷ **thug**
thugs *n* ▷ **thug**
thumb *n* (*pl* **-s**) short thick finger set apart from the others ▶ *v* (**-s, -ing, -ed**) touch or handle with the thumb
thumbed *v* ▷ **thumb**
thumbing *v* ▷ **thumb**
thumbs *n, v* ▷ **thumb**
thump *n* (*pl* **-s**) (sound of) a dull heavy blow ▶ *v* (**-s, -ing, -ed**) strike heavily
thumped *v* ▷ **thump**
thumping *v* ▷ **thump**
thumps *n, v* ▷ **thump**
thunder *n* (*pl* **-s**) loud noise accompanying lightning ▶ *v* (**-s, -ing, -ed**) rumble with thunder > **thunderous** *adj* > **thundery** (**-rier, -riest**) *adj*
thunderbolt *n* (*pl* **-s**) lightning flash
thunderbolts *n* ▷ **thunderbolt**
thunderclap *n* (*pl* **-s**) peal of thunder
thunderclaps *n* ▷ **thunderclap**
thundered *v* ▷ **thunder**
thunderier *adj* ▷ **thunder**
thunderiest *adj* ▷ **thunder**
thundering *v* ▷ **thunder**
thunderous *adj* ▷ **thunder**
thunders *v, n* ▷ **thunder**
thunderstruck *adj* amazed
thundery *adj* ▷ **thunder**
thus *adv* therefore
thwack *v* (**-s, -ing, -ed**) ▶ *n* (*pl* **-s**) whack
thwacked *v* ▷ **thwack**
thwacking *v* ▷ **thwack**
thwacks *v, n* ▷ **thwack**
thwart *v* (**-s, -ing, -ed**) foil or frustrate ▶ *n* (*pl* **-s**) seat across a boat
thwarted *v* ▷ **thwart**
thwarting *v* ▷ **thwart**
thwarts *v, n* ▷ **thwart**
thy *adj* (*Obs*) of or associated with you (thou)
thylacine *n* (*pl* **-s**) extinct doglike Tasmanian marsupial
thylacines *n* ▷ **thylacine**
thyme [time] *n* (*pl* **-s**) aromatic herb

thymes *n* ▷ **thyme**
thymi *n* ▷ **thymus**
thymus *n* (*pl* **-muses, -mi**) small gland at the base of the neck
thymuses *n* ▷ **thymus**
thyroid *adj, n* (*pl* **-s**) (of) a gland in the neck controlling body growth
thyroids *n* ▷ **thyroid**
thyself *pron* (*Obs*) ▷ **thou**

ti *n* (**tis**). Ti means the same as **te.** This is a useful word when you want to form words in more than one direction. Ti scores 2 points.

tiara *n* (*pl* **-s**) semicircular jewelled headdress
tiaras *n* ▷ **tiara**
tibia *n* (*pl* **-biae, -bias**) inner bone of the lower leg > **tibial** *adj*
tibiae *n* ▷ **tibia**
tibial *adj* ▷ **tibia**
tibias *n* ▷ **tibia**
tic *n* (*pl* **-s**) spasmodic muscular twitch
tick[1] *n* (*pl* **-s**) mark (✓) used to check off or indicate the correctness of something ▶ *v* (**-s, -ing, -ed**) mark with a tick
tick[2] *n* (*pl* **-s**) tiny bloodsucking parasitic animal
tick[3] *n* (*pl* **-s**) (*Informal*) credit or account
ticked *v* ▷ **tick**[1]
ticket *n* (*pl* **-s**) card or paper entitling the holder to admission, travel, etc. (CHIEFLY US & NZ) ▶ *v* (**-s, -ing, -ed**) attach or issue a ticket to
ticketed *v* ▷ **ticket**
ticketing *v* ▷ **ticket**
tickets *n, v* ▷ **ticket**
ticking *n* (*pl* **-s**) strong material for mattress covers ▶ *v* ▷ **tick**[1]
tickings *n* ▷ **ticking**
tickle *v* (**-les, -ling, -led**) touch or stroke (a person) to produce laughter ▶ *n* (*pl* **-s**) tickling
tickled *v* ▷ **tickle**
tickles *v, n* ▷ **tickle**
tickling *v* ▷ **tickle**
ticklish *adj* sensitive to tickling
ticks *v* ▷ **tick**[1] ▶ *n* ▷ **tick**[1, 2, 3]
ticktack *n* (*pl* **-s**) (BRIT) bookmakers' sign language
ticktacks *n* ▷ **ticktack**
tics *n* ▷ **tic**
tidal *adj* ▷ **tide**
tiddler *n* (*pl* **-s**) (*Informal*) very small fish
tiddlers *n* ▷ **tiddler**
tiddlier *adj* ▷ **tiddly**[1, 2]
tiddliest *adj* ▷ **tiddly**[1, 2]
tiddly[1] *adj* (**-dlier, -dliest**) tiny
tiddly[2] *adj* (**-dlier, -dliest**) (*Informal*) slightly

drunk

tiddlywink *n* small plastic disc

tiddlywinks *n* game in which players try to flip small plastic discs into a cup

tide *n* (*pl* **-s**) rise and fall of the sea caused by the gravitational pull of the sun and moon > **tidal** *adj*

tides *n* ▷ **tide**

tidied *v* ▷ **tidy**

tidier *adj* ▷ **tidy**

tidies *v* ▷ **tidy**

tidiest *adj* ▷ **tidy**

tidily *adv* ▷ **tidy**

tidiness *n* ▷ **tidy**

tidinesses *n* ▷ **tidy**

tidings *pl n* news

tidy *adj* (**-dier, -diest**) neat and orderly ▶ *v* (**-dies, -dying, -died**) put in order > **tidily** *adv* > **tidiness** *n* (*pl* **-es**)

tidying *v* ▷ **tidy**

tie *v* (**ties, tying, tied**) fasten or be fastened with string, rope, etc. ▶ *n* (*pl* **-s**) long narrow piece of material worn knotted round the neck

tied *v* ▷ **tie** ▶ *adj* (BRIT) (of a cottage etc.) rented to the tenant only as long as he or she is employed by the owner

tier *n* (*pl* **-s**) one of a set of rows placed one above and behind the other

tiers *n* ▷ **tier**

ties *v*, *n* ▷ **tie**

tiff *n* (*pl* **-s**) petty quarrel

tiffs *n* ▷ **tiff**

tiger *n* (*pl* **-s**) large yellow-and-black striped Asian cat

tigers *n* ▷ **tiger**

tight *adj* (**-er, -est**) stretched or drawn taut > **tightly** *adv*

tighten *v* (**-s, -ing, -ed**) make or become tight or tighter

tightened *v* ▷ **tighten**

tightening *v* ▷ **tighten**

tightens *v* ▷ **tighten**

tighter *adj* ▷ **tight**

tightest *adj* ▷ **tight**

tightly *adv* ▷ **tight**

tightrope *n* (*pl* **-s**) rope stretched taut on which acrobats perform

tightropes *n* ▷ **tightrope**

tights *pl n* one-piece clinging garment covering the body from the waist to the feet

tigress *n* (*pl* **-s**) female tiger

tigresses *n* ▷ **tigress**

tiki *n* (*pl* **-s**) (NZ) small carving of a grotesque person worn as a pendant

tikis *n* ▷ **tiki**

tikka *adj* (INDIAN COOKERY) marinated in spices and dry-roasted

tilde *n* (*pl* **-s**) mark (~) used in Spanish to indicate that the letter 'n' is to be pronounced in a particular way

tildes *n* ▷ **tilde**

tile *n* (*pl* **-s**) flat piece of ceramic, plastic, etc. used to cover a roof, floor, or wall ▶ *v* (**-les, -ling, -led**) cover with tiles > **tiled** *adj*

tiled *v*, *adj* ▷ **tile**

tiles *n*, *v* ▷ **tile**

tiling *n* (*pl* **-s**) tiles collectively ▶ *v* ▷ **tile**

tilings *n* ▷ **tiling**

till¹ *conj*, *prep* until

till² *v* (**-s, -ing, -ed**) cultivate (land) > **tillage** *n* (*pl* **-s**)

till³ *n* (*pl* **-s**) drawer for money, usu. in a cash register

tillage *n* ▷ **till²**

tillages *n* ▷ **till²**

tilled *v* ▷ **till²**

tiller *n* (*pl* **-s**) lever to move a rudder of a boat

tillers *n* ▷ **tiller**

tilling *v* ▷ **till²**

tills *v* ▷ **till²** ▶ *n* ▷ **till³**

tilt *v* (**-s, -ing, -ed**) slant at an angle ▶ *n* (*pl* **-s**) slope

tilted *v* ▷ **tilt**

tilting *v* ▷ **tilt**

tilts *v*, *n* ▷ **tilt**

timber *n* (*pl* **-s**) wood as a building material > **timbered** *adj*

timbered *adj* ▷ **timber**

timbers *n* ▷ **timber**

timbre [tam-bra] *n* (*pl* **-s**) distinctive quality of sound of a voice or instrument

timbres *n* ▷ **timbre**

time *n* (*pl* **-s**) past, present, and future as a continuous whole ▶ *v* (**-mes, -ming, -med**) note the time taken by

timed *v* ▷ **time**

timeless *adj* unaffected by time

timelier *adj* ▷ **timely**

timeliest *adj* ▷ **timely**

timely *adj* (**-lier, -liest**) at the appropriate time

timepiece *n* (*pl* **-s**) watch or clock

timepieces *n* ▷ **timepiece**

times *n*, *v* ▷ **time**

timeserver *n* (*pl* **-s**) person who changes his or her views to gain support or favour

timeservers *n* ▷ **timeserver**

timetable *n* (*pl* **-s**) plan showing the times when something takes place, the departure and arrival times of trains or buses, etc.

timetables n ▷ timetable

timid adj (-er, -est) easily frightened > **timidly**
adv > **timidity** n (pl -**dies**)

timider adj ▷ timid

timidest adj ▷ timid

timidities n ▷ timid

timidity n ▷ timid

timidly adv ▷ timid

timing v ▷ time

timorous adj timid

timpani [tim-pan-ee] pl n set of kettledrums
> **timpanist** n (pl -**s**)

timpanist n ▷ timpani

timpanists n ▷ timpani

tin n (pl -**s**) soft metallic element

tincture n (pl -**s**) medicinal extract in a
solution of alcohol

tinctures n ▷ tincture

tinder n (pl -**s**) dry easily-burning material
used to start a fire > **tinderbox** n (pl -**es**)

tinderbox n ▷ tinder

tinderboxes n ▷ tinder

tinders n ▷ tinder

tine n (pl -**s**) prong of a fork or antler

tines n ▷ tine

ting n (pl -**s**) high metallic sound, as of a small
bell

tinge n (pl -**s**) slight tint ▶ v (-**ges, -geing, -ged**)
give a slight tint or trace to

tinged v ▷ tinge

tinges n, v ▷ tinge

tinging v ▷ tinge

tingle v (-**les, -ling, -led**) ▶ n (pl -**s**) (feel) a
prickling or stinging sensation

tingled v ▷ tingle

tingles v, n ▷ tingle

tingling v ▷ tingle

tings n ▷ ting

tinier adj ▷ tiny

tiniest adj ▷ tiny

tinker n (pl -**s**) travelling mender of pots and
pans ▶ v (-**s, -ing, -ed**) fiddle with (an engine
etc.) in an attempt to repair it

tinkered v ▷ tinker

tinkering v ▷ tinker

tinkers n, v ▷ tinker

tinkle v (-**les, -ling, -led**) ring with a high tinny
sound like a small bell ▶ n (pl -**s**) this sound
or action

tinkled v ▷ tinkle

tinkles v, n ▷ tinkle

tinkling v ▷ tinkle

tinned adj (of food) preserved by being sealed
in a tin

tinnier adj ▷ tinny

tinniest adj ▷ tinny

tinny adj (-**nnier, -nniest**) (of sound) thin and
metallic

tinpot adj (Informal) worthless or unimportant

tins n ▷ tin

tinsel n (pl -**s**) decorative metallic strips or
threads

tinsels n ▷ tinsel

tint n (pl -**s**) (pale) shade of a colour ▶ v (-**s, -ing,
-ed**) give a tint to

tinted v ▷ tint

tinting v ▷ tint

tints n, v ▷ tint

tiny adj (-**ier, -iest**) very small

tip[1] n (pl -**s**) narrow or pointed end of anything
▶ v (-**s, -pping, -pped**) put a tip on

tip[2] n (pl -**s**) money given in return for service
▶ v (-**s, -pping, -pped**) give a tip to

tip[3] v (-**s, -pping, -pped**) tilt or overturn ▶ n (pl
-**s**) rubbish dump

tipped v ▷ tip[1, 2, 3]

tipping v ▷ tip[1, 2, 3]

tipple v (-**les, -ling, -led**) drink alcohol
habitually, esp. in small quantities ▶ n (pl -**s**)
alcoholic drink > **tippler** n (pl -**s**)

tippled v ▷ tipple

tippler n ▷ tipple

tipplers n ▷ tipple

tipples v, n ▷ tipple

tippling v ▷ tipple

tips n, v ▷ tip[1, 2, 3]

tipsier adj ▷ tipsy

tipsiest adj ▷ tipsy

tipster n (pl -**s**) person who sells tips about
races

tipsters n ▷ tipster

tipsy adj (-**sier, -siest**) slightly drunk

tiptoe v (-**toes, -toeing, -toed**) walk quietly
with the heels off the ground

tiptoed v ▷ tiptoe

tiptoeing v ▷ tiptoe

tiptoes v ▷ tiptoe

tiptop adj of the highest quality or condition

tirade n (pl -**s**) long angry speech

tirades n ▷ tirade

tire v (-**res, -ring, -red**) reduce the energy of, as
by exertion > **tiring** adj

tired adj (-**er, -est**) exhausted ▶ v ▷ tire

tireder adj ▷ tired

tiredest adj ▷ tired

tireless adj energetic and determined

tires v ▷ tire

tiresome adj boring and irritating

tiring v, adj ▷ tire

tissue n (pl -**s**) substance of an animal body

or plant

tissues *n* ▷ **tissue**

tit¹ *n* (*pl* **-s**) any of various small songbirds

tit² *n* (*pl* **-s**) (*Slang*) female breast

titanic *adj* huge or very important

titanium *n* (*pl* **-s**) (CHEM) strong light metallic element used to make alloys

  titaniums *n* ▷ **titanium**

titbit *n* (*pl* **-s**) tasty piece of food

  titbits *n* ▷ **titbit**

tithe *n* (*pl* **-s**) esp. formerly, one tenth of one's income or produce paid to the church as a tax

  tithes *n* ▷ **tithe**

titian [tish-an] *adj* (of hair) reddish-gold

titillate *v* (**-tes, -ting, -ted**) excite or stimulate pleasurably > **titillating** *adj* > **titillation** *n* (*pl* **-s**)

  titillated *v* ▷ **titillate**

  titillates *v* ▷ **titillate**

  titillating *v*, *adj* ▷ **titillate**

  titillation *n* ▷ **titillate**

  titillations *n* ▷ **titillate**

titivate *v* (**-tes, -ting, -ted**) smarten up

  titivated *v* ▷ **titivate**

  titivates *v* ▷ **titivate**

  titivating *v* ▷ **titivate**

title *n* (*pl* **-s**) name of a book, film, etc.

titled *adj* aristocratic

  titles *n* ▷ **title**

  tits *n* ▷ **tit¹, ²**

titter *v* (**-s, -ing, -ed**) laugh in a suppressed way ▶ *n* (*pl* **-s**) suppressed laugh

  tittered *v* ▷ **titter**

  tittering *v* ▷ **titter**

  titters *v*, *n* ▷ **titter**

titular *adj* in name only

  tizzies *n* ▷ **tizzy**

tizzy *n* (*pl* **-zies**) (*Informal*) confused or agitated state

> **tix** *pl n*. Tix is an informal word for **tickets**. This is a good word if you are struggling to use an X towards the end of a game.

to *prep* indicating movement towards, equality or comparison, etc. ▶ *adv* to a closed position

toad *n* (*pl* **-s**) animal like a large frog

  toadied *v* ▷ **toady**

  toadies *n*, *v* ▷ **toady**

  toads *n* ▷ **toad**

toadstool *n* (*pl* **-s**) poisonous fungus like a mushroom

  toadstools *n* ▷ **toadstool**

toady *n* (*pl* **-dies**) ingratiating person ▶ *v* (**-dies, -dying, -died**) be ingratiating

  toadying *v* ▷ **toady**

toast¹ *n* (*pl* **-s**) sliced bread browned by heat ▶ *v* (**-s, -ing, -ed**) brown (bread) by heat

toast² *n* (*pl* **-s**) tribute or proposal of health or success marked by people raising glasses and drinking together ▶ *v* (**-s, -ing, -ed**) drink a toast to

toasted *v*, *n* ▷ **toast¹, ²**

toaster *n* (*pl* **-s**) electrical device for toasting bread

  toasters *n* ▷ **toaster**

  toasting *n*, *v* ▷ **toast¹, ²**

  toasts *n*, *v* ▷ **toast¹, ²**

tobacco *n* (*pl* **-os, -oes**) plant with large leaves dried for smoking

  tobaccoes *n* ▷ **tobacco**

tobacconist *n* (*pl* **-s**) person or shop selling tobacco, cigarettes, etc.

  tobacconists *n* ▷ **tobacconist**

  tobaccos *n* ▷ **tobacco**

toboggan *n* (*pl* **-s**) narrow sledge for sliding over snow ▶ *v* (**-s, -ing, -ed**) ride a toboggan

  tobogganed *v* ▷ **toboggan**

  tobogganing *v* ▷ **toboggan**

  toboggans *n*, *v* ▷ **toboggan**

toccata [tok-**kah**-ta] *n* (*pl* **-s**) rapid piece of music for a keyboard instrument

  toccatas *n* ▷ **toccata**

today *n* (*pl* **-s**) this day ▶ *adv* on this day

  todays *n* ▷ **today**

  toddies *n* ▷ **toddy**

toddle *v* (**-les, -ling, -led**) walk with short unsteady steps

  toddled *v* ▷ **toddle**

toddler *n* (*pl* **-s**) child beginning to walk

  toddlers *n* ▷ **toddler**

  toddles *v* ▷ **toddle**

  toddling *v* ▷ **toddle**

toddy *n* (*pl* **-dies**) sweetened drink of spirits and hot water

toe *n* (*pl* **-s**) digit of the foot ▶ *v* (**toes, toeing, toed**) touch or kick with the toe

  toed *v* ▷ **toe**

  toeing *v* ▷ **toe**

  toes *n*, *v* ▷ **toe**

toff *n* (*pl* **-s**) (BRIT) (*Slang*) well-dressed or upper-class person

toffee *n* (*pl* **-s**) chewy sweet made of boiled sugar

  toffees *n* ▷ **toffee**

  toffs *n* ▷ **toff**

tofu *n* (*pl* **-s**) soft food made from soya-bean curd

  tofus *n* ▷ **tofu**

tog *n* (*pl* **-s**) unit for measuring the insulating

power of duvets

toga [toe-ga] *n* (*pl* **-s**) garment worn by citizens of ancient Rome

  togas *n* ▷ **toga**

together *adv* in company ▶ *adj* (*Informal*) organized

toggle *n* (*pl* **-s**) small bar-shaped button inserted through a loop for fastening

  toggles *n* ▷ **toggle**

  togs *n* ▷ **tog**

toil *n* (*pl* **-s**) hard work ▶ *v* (**-s, -ing, -ed**) work hard

  toiled *v* ▷ **toil**

toilet *n* (*pl* **-s**) (room with) a bowl connected to a drain for receiving and disposing of urine and faeces

  toiletries *n* ▷ **toiletry**

toiletry *n* (*pl* **-ries**) object or cosmetic used to clean or groom oneself

  toilets *n* ▷ **toilet**

  toiling *v* ▷ **toil**

  toils *n*, *v* ▷ **toil**

token *n* (*pl* **-s**) sign or symbol ▶ *adj* nominal or slight

tokenism *n* (*pl* **-s**) policy of making only a token effort, esp. to comply with a law

  tokenisms *n* ▷ **tokenism**

  tokens *n* ▷ **token**

  told *v* ▷ **tell**

tolerable *adj* bearable > **tolerably** *adv*

  tolerably *adv* ▷ **tolerable**

tolerance *n* (*pl* **-s**) acceptance of other people's rights to their own opinions or actions > **tolerant** *adj* > **tolerantly** *adv* > **toleration** *n* (*pl* **-s**)

  tolerances *n* ▷ **tolerance**

  tolerant *adj* ▷ **tolerance**

  tolerantly *adv* ▷ **tolerance**

tolerate *v* (**-tes, -ting, -ted**) allow to exist or happen

  tolerated *v* ▷ **tolerate**

  tolerates *v* ▷ **tolerate**

  tolerating *v* ▷ **tolerate**

  toleration *n* ▷ **tolerance**

  tolerations *n* ▷ **tolerance**

toll[1] *v* (**-s, -ing, -ed**) ring (a bell) slowly and regularly, esp. to announce a death ▶ *n* (*pl* **-s**) tolling

toll[2] *n* (*pl* **-s**) charge for the use of a bridge or road

  tolled *v* ▷ **toll**[1]

  tolling *v* ▷ **toll**[1]

  tolls *n* ▷ **toll**[1, 2] ▶ *v* ▷ **toll**[1]

tom *n* (*pl* **-s**) male cat

tomahawk *n* (*pl* **-s**) fighting axe of the Native Americans

  tomahawks *n* ▷ **tomahawk**

tomato *n* (*pl* **-es**) red fruit used in salads and as a vegetable

  tomatoes *n* ▷ **tomato**

tomb *n* (*pl* **-s**) grave

tombola *n* (*pl* **-s**) lottery with tickets drawn from a revolving drum

  tombolas *n* ▷ **tombola**

tomboy *n* (*pl* **-s**) girl who acts or dresses like a boy

  tomboys *n* ▷ **tomboy**

  tombs *n* ▷ **tomb**

tombstone *n* (*pl* **-s**) gravestone

  tombstones *n* ▷ **tombstone**

tome *n* (*pl* **-s**) large heavy book

  tomes *n* ▷ **tome**

  tomfooleries *n* ▷ **tomfoolery**

tomfoolery *n* (*pl* **-ries**) foolish behaviour

tomorrow *adv*, *n* (*pl* **-s**) (on) the day after today

  tomorrows *n* ▷ **tomorrow**

  toms *n* ▷ **tom**

ton *n* (*pl* **-s**) unit of weight equal to 2240 pounds or 1016 kilograms or, in the US, 2000 pounds or 907 kilograms

tonal *adj* (MUSIC) written in a key > **tonality** *n* (*pl* **-ties**)

  tonalities *n* ▷ **tonal**

  tonality *n* ▷ **tonal**

tone *n* (*pl* **-s**) sound with reference to its pitch, volume, etc. ▶ *v* (**-nes, -ning, -ned**) harmonize (with) > **toneless** *adj*

  toned *v* ▷ **tone**

  toneless *adj* ▷ **tone**

  tones *n*, *v* ▷ **tone**

tongs *pl n* large pincers for grasping and lifting

tongue *n* (*pl* **-s**) muscular organ in the mouth, used in speaking and tasting

  tongues *n* ▷ **tongue**

tonic *n* (*pl* **-s**) medicine to improve body tone ▶ *adj* invigorating

  tonics *n* ▷ **tonic**

tonight *adv*, *n* (*pl* **-s**) (in or during) the night or evening of this day

  tonights *n* ▷ **tonight**

  toning *v* ▷ **tone**

tonnage *n* (*pl* **-s**) weight capacity of a ship

  tonnages *n* ▷ **tonnage**

tonne [tunn] *n* (*pl* **-s**) unit of weight equal to 1000 kilograms

  tonnes *n* ▷ **tonne**

  tons *n* ▷ **ton**

tonsil *n* (*pl* **-s**) small gland in the throat

  tonsillectomies *n* ▷ **tonsillectomy**

tonsillectomy *n* (*pl* **-mies**) surgical removal

of the tonsils

tonsillitis n (pl **-tises**) inflammation of the tonsils

tonsillitises n ▷ **tonsillitis**

tonsils n ▷ **tonsil**

tonsure n (pl **-s**) shaving of all or the top of the head as a religious or monastic practice ▷ **tonsured** adj

tonsured adj ▷ **tonsure**

tonsures n ▷ **tonsure**

too adv also, as well

took v ▷ **take**

tool n (pl **-s**) implement used by hand

tools n ▷ **tool**

toot n (pl **-s**) short hooting sound ▶ v (**-s, -ing, -ed**) (cause to) make such a sound

tooted v ▷ **toot**

tooth n (pl **teeth**) bonelike projection in the jaws of most vertebrates for biting and chewing ▷ **toothless** adj

toothless adj ▷ **tooth**

toothpaste n (pl **-s**) paste used to clean the teeth

toothpastes n ▷ **toothpaste**

toothpick n (pl **-s**) small stick for removing scraps of food from between the teeth

toothpicks n ▷ **toothpick**

tooting v ▷ **toot**

toots n, v ▷ **toot**

top[1] n (pl **-s**) highest point or part ▶ adj at or of the top ▶ v (**-s, -pping, -pped**) form a top on

top[2] n (pl **-s**) toy which spins on a pointed base

topaz [toe-pazz] n (pl **-es**) semiprecious stone in various colours

topazes n ▷ **topaz**

topee, topi [toe-pee] n (pl **-s**) lightweight hat worn in tropical countries

topees n ▷ **topee**

topi n ▷ **topee**

topiaries n ▷ **topiary**

topiary [tope-yar-ee] n (pl **-ries**) art of trimming trees and bushes into decorative shapes

topic n (pl **-s**) subject of a conversation, book, etc.

topical adj relating to current events ▷ **topicality** n (pl **-ties**)

topicalities n ▷ **topical**

topicality n ▷ **topical**

topics n ▷ **topic**

topis n ▷ **topee**

topless adj (of a costume or woman) with no covering for the breasts

topmost adj highest or best

topographer n ▷ **topography**

topographers n ▷ **topography**

topographical adj ▷ **topography**

topographies n ▷ **topography**

topography n (pl **-phies**) (science of describing) the surface features of a place ▷ **topographer** n (pl **-s**) ▷ **topographical** adj

topological adj ▷ **topology**

topologies n ▷ **topology**

topology n (pl **-gies**) geometry of the properties of a shape which are unaffected by continuous distortion ▷ **topological** adj

topped n ▷ **top**[1]

topping n (pl **-s**) sauce or garnish for food ▶ v ▷ **top**[1]

toppings n ▷ **topping**

topple v (**-les, -ling, -led**) (cause to) fall over

toppled v ▷ **topple**

topples v ▷ **topple**

toppling v ▷ **topple**

top-notch adj excellent, first-class

tops n ▷ **top**[1, 2] ▶ v ▷ **top**[1]

topsoil n (pl **-s**) surface layer of soil

topsoils n ▷ **topsoil**

toque [toke] n (pl **-s**) small round hat

toques n ▷ **toque**

tor n (pl **-s**) high rocky hill

torch n (pl **-es**) small portable battery-powered lamp ▶ v (**-es, -ing, -ed**) (Informal) deliberately set (a building) on fire

torched v ▷ **torch**

torches n, v ▷ **torch**

torching v ▷ **torch**

tore v ▷ **tear**[2]

toreador [torr-ee-a-dor] n (pl **-s**) bullfighter

toreadors n ▷ **toreador**

torment v (**-s, -ing, -ed**) cause (someone) great suffering ▶ n (pl **-s**) great suffering ▷ **tormentor** n (pl **-s**)

tormented v ▷ **torment**

tormenting v ▷ **torment**

tormentor n ▷ **torment**

tormentors n ▷ **torment**

torments v, n ▷ **torment**

torn v ▷ **tear**[2]

tornado n (pl **-s, -es**) violent whirlwind

tornadoes n ▷ **tornado**

tornados n ▷ **tornado**

torpedo n (pl **-es**) self-propelled underwater missile ▶ v (**-es, -ing, -ed**) attack or destroy with or as if with torpedoes

torpedoed v ▷ **torpedo**

torpedoes n, v ▷ **torpedo**

torpedoing v ▷ **torpedo**

torpid adj sluggish and inactive

torpor n (pl **-s**) torpid state

torpors n ▷ **torpor**

torque [tork] *n* (*pl* **-s**) force causing rotation
  torques *n* ▷ **torque**
torrent *n* (*pl* **-s**) rushing stream
torrential *adj* (of rain) very heavy
  torrents *n* ▷ **torrent**
torrid *adj* (**-er, -est**) very hot and dry
  torrider *adj* ▷ **torrid**
  torridest *adj* ▷ **torrid**
  tors *n* ▷ **tor**
torsion *n* (*pl* **-s**) twisting of a part by equal
  forces being applied at both ends but in
  opposite directions
  torsions *n* ▷ **torsion**
torso *n* (*pl* **-s**) trunk of the human body
  torsos *n* ▷ **torso**
tort *n* (*pl* **-s**) (LAW) civil wrong or injury for
  which damages may be claimed
tortilla *n* (*pl* **-s**) thin Mexican pancake
  tortillas *n* ▷ **tortilla**
tortoise *n* (*pl* **-s**) slow-moving land reptile with
  a dome-shaped shell
  tortoises *n* ▷ **tortoise**
tortoiseshell *n* (*pl* **-s**) mottled brown shell of
  a turtle, used for making ornaments ▶ *adj*
  having brown, orange, and black markings
  tortoiseshells *n* ▷ **tortoiseshell**
  torts *n* ▷ **tort**
tortuous *adj* winding or twisting
torture *v* (**-res, -ring, -red**) cause (someone)
  severe pain or mental anguish ▶ *n* (*pl* **-s**)
  severe physical or mental pain > **torturer**
  n (*pl* **-s**)
  tortured *v* ▷ **torture**
  torturer *n* ▷ **torture**
  torturers *n* ▷ **torture**
  tortures *v, n* ▷ **torture**
  torturing *v* ▷ **torture**
toss *v* (**-es, -ing, -ed**) throw lightly ▶ *n* (*pl* **-es**)
  tossing
  tossed *v* ▷ **toss**
  tosses *v, n* ▷ **toss**
  tossing *v* ▷ **toss**
tot¹ *n* (*pl* **-s**) small child
tot² *v* (**-s, -tting, -tted**) add (numbers) together
total *n* (*pl* **-s**) whole, esp. a sum of parts ▶ *adj*
  complete ▶ *v* (**-s, -lling, -lled**) amount to
  > **totally** *adv* > **totality** *n* (*pl* **-ties**)
totalitarian *adj* of a dictatorial one-party
  government > **totalitarianism** *n* (*pl* **-s**)
  totalitarianism *n* ▷ **totalitarian**
  totalitarianisms *n* ▷ **totalitarian**
  totalities *n* ▷ **total**
  totality *n* ▷ **total**
  totalled *v* ▷ **total**
  totalling *v* ▷ **total**

totally *adv* ▷ **total**
  totals *n, v* ▷ **total**
tote¹ *v* (**-tes, -ting, -ted**) carry (a gun etc.)
tote² *n* (*pl* **-s**) ▷ **totalizator**
  toted *v* ▷ **tote¹**
totem *n* (*pl* **-s**) tribal badge or emblem
  totems *n* ▷ **totem**
  totes *v* ▷ **tote¹** ▶ *n* ▷ **tote²**
  toting *v* ▷ **tote¹**
  tots *n* ▷ **tot¹** ▶ *v* ▷ **tot²**
  totted *v* ▷ **tot²**
totter *v* (**-s, -ing, -ed**) move unsteadily
  tottered *v* ▷ **totter**
  tottering *v* ▷ **totter**
  totters *v* ▷ **totter**
  totting *v* ▷ **tot²**
toucan *n* (*pl* **-s**) tropical American bird with
  a large bill
  toucans *n* ▷ **toucan**
touch *v* (**-es, -ing, -ed**) come into contact
  with ▶ *n* (*pl* **-es**) sense by which an object's
  qualities are perceived when they come into
  contact with part of the body ▶ *adj* of a non-
  contact version of particular sport
touché [too-shay] *interj* acknowledgment of
  the striking home of a remark or witty reply
touched *adj* emotionally moved ▶ *v* ▷ **touch**
  touches *v, n* ▷ **touch**
  touchier *adj* ▷ **touchy**
  touchiest *adj* ▷ **touchy**
touching *adj* emotionally moving ▶ *v* ▷ **touch**
touchline *n* (*pl* **-s**) side line of the pitch in some
  games
  touchlines *n* ▷ **touchline**
touchstone *n* (*pl* **-s**) standard by which a
  judgment is made
  touchstones *n* ▷ **touchstone**
touchy *adj* (**-chier, -chiest**) easily offended
tough *adj* (**-er, -est**) strong or resilient ▶ *n* (*pl* **-s**)
  (*Informal*) rough violent person > **toughness**
  n (*pl* **-es**)
toughen *v* (**-s, -ing, -ed**) make or become
  tough or tougher
  toughened *v* ▷ **toughen**
  toughening *v* ▷ **toughen**
  toughens *v* ▷ **toughen**
  tougher *adj* ▷ **tough**
  toughest *adj* ▷ **tough**
  toughness *n* ▷ **tough**
  toughnesses *n* ▷ **tough**
  toughs *n* ▷ **tough**
toupee [too-pay] *n* (*pl* **-s**) small wig
  toupees *n* ▷ **toupee**
tour *n* (*pl* **-s**) journey visiting places of interest
  along the way ▶ *v* (**-s, -ing, -ed**) make a tour

(of)

toured v ▷ **tour**

touring v ▷ **tour**

tourism n (pl -s) tourist travel as an industry

tourisms n ▷ **tourism**

tourist n (pl -s) person travelling for pleasure

tourists n ▷ **tourist**

touristy adj (Informal) (often derogatory) full of tourists or tourist attractions

tournament n (pl -s) sporting competition with several stages to decide the overall winner

tournaments n ▷ **tournament**

tourniquet [tour-nick-kay] n (pl -s) something twisted round a limb to stop bleeding

tourniquets n ▷ **tourniquet**

tours n, v ▷ **tour**

tousled adj ruffled and untidy

tout [rhymes with **shout**] v (-s, -ing, -ed) seek business in a persistent manner ▶ n (pl -s) person who sells tickets for a popular event at inflated prices

touted v ▷ **tout**

touting v ▷ **tout**

touts v, n ▷ **tout**

tow[1] v (-s, -ing, -ed) drag, esp. by means of a rope ▶ n (pl -s) towing

tow[2] n (pl -s) fibre of hemp or flax

toward n ▷ **towards**

towards, toward prep in the direction of

towbar n (pl -s) metal bar on a car for towing vehicles

towbars n ▷ **towbar**

towed v ▷ **tow**[1]

towel n (pl -s) cloth for drying things

towelling n (pl -s) material used for making towels

towellings n ▷ **towelling**

towels n ▷ **towel**

tower n (pl -s) tall structure, often forming part of a larger building

towers n ▷ **tower**

towing v ▷ **tow**[1]

town n (pl -s) group of buildings larger than a village

towns n ▷ **town**

township n (pl -s) small town

townships n ▷ **township**

towpath n (pl -s) path beside a canal or river, originally for horses towing boats

towpaths n ▷ **towpath**

tows n ▷ **tow**[1, 2] ▶ v ▷ **tow**[1]

toxaemia [tox-seem-ya] n (pl -s) blood poisoning

toxaemias n ▷ **toxaemia**

toxic adj poisonous > **toxicity** n (pl -ties)

toxicities n ▷ **toxic**

toxicity n ▷ **toxic**

toxicologies n ▷ **toxicology**

toxicology n (pl -gies) study of poisons

toxin n (pl -s) poison of bacterial origin

toxins n ▷ **toxin**

toy n (pl -s) something designed to be played with ▶ adj (of a dog) of a variety much smaller than is normal for that breed ▶ v (-s, -ing, -ed) play

toyed v ▷ **toy**

toying v ▷ **toy**

toys n, v ▷ **toy**

trace v (-ces, -cing, -ced) track down and find ▶ n (pl -s) track left by something > **traceable** adj

traceable adj ▷ **trace**

traced v ▷ **trace**

tracer n (pl -s) projectile which leaves a visible trail

traceries n ▷ **tracery**

tracers n ▷ **tracer**

tracery n (pl -ries) pattern of interlacing lines

traces v, n ▷ **trace** ▶ pl n strap by which a horse pulls a vehicle

trachea [track-kee-a] n (pl -cheae) windpipe

tracheae n ▷ **trachea**

tracheotomies n ▷ **tracheotomy**

tracheotomy [track-ee-ot-a-mee] n (pl -mies) surgical incision into the trachea

tracing n (pl -s) traced copy ▶ v ▷ **trace**

track n (pl -s) rough road or path ▶ v (-s, -ing, -ed) follow the trail or path of

tracked v ▷ **track**

tracking v ▷ **track**

tracks n, v ▷ **track**

tracksuit n (pl -s) warm loose-fitting suit worn by athletes etc., esp. during training

tracksuits n ▷ **tracksuit**

tract[1] n (pl -s) wide area

tract[2] n (pl -s) pamphlet, esp. a religious one

tractable adj easy to manage or control

traction n (pl -s) pulling, esp. by engine power

tractions n ▷ **traction**

tractor n (pl -s) motor vehicle with large rear wheels for pulling farm machinery

tractors n ▷ **tractor**

tracts n ▷ **tract**[1, 2]

trade n (pl -s) buying, selling, or exchange of goods ▶ v (-des, -ding, -ded) buy and sell > **trader** n (pl -s) > **trading** n (pl -s)

traded v ▷ **trade**

trademark n (pl -s) (legally registered) name or symbol used by a firm to distinguish its

goods
trademarks *n* ▷ **trademark**
trader *n* ▷ **trade**
traders *n* ▷ **trade**
trades *n*, *v* ▷ **trade**
tradesman *n* (*pl* -**men**) skilled worker
tradesmen *n* ▷ **tradesman**
trading *v*, *n* ▷ **trade**
tradings *n* ▷ **trad**
tradition *n* (*pl* -**s**) body of beliefs, customs, etc.
handed down from generation to generation
> **traditional** *adj* > **traditionally** *adv*
traditional *adj* ▷ **tradition**
traditionally *adv* ▷ **tradition**
traditions *n* ▷ **tradition**
traduce *v* (-**ces, -cing, -ced**) slander
traduced *v* ▷ **traduce**
traduces *v* ▷ **traduce**
traducing *v* ▷ **traduce**
traffic *n* (*pl* -**s**) vehicles coming and going on a
road ▶ *v* (-**s, -cking, -cked**) trade, usu. illicitly
> **trafficker** *n* (*pl* -**s**)
trafficked *v* ▷ **traffic**
trafficker *n* ▷ **traffic**
traffickers *n* ▷ **traffic**
trafficking *v* ▷ **traffic**
traffics *n*, *v* ▷ **traffic**
tragedian [traj-**jee**-dee-an], **tragedienne**
[traj-jee-dee-**enn**] *n* (*pl* -**s**) person who acts in
or writes tragedies
tragedians *n* ▷ **tragedian**
tragedies *n* ▷ **tragedy**
tragedy *n* (*pl* -**dies**) shocking or sad event
tragic *adj* of or like a tragedy > **tragically** *adv*
tragically *adv* ▷ **tragic**
tragicomedies *n* ▷ **tragicomedy**
tragicomedy *n* (*pl* -**s**) play with both tragic and
comic elements
trail *n* (*pl* -**s**) path, track, or road ▶ *v* (-**s, -ing,**
-**ed**) drag along the ground
trailed *v* ▷ **trail**
trailer *n* (*pl* -**s**) vehicle designed to be towed by
another vehicle
trailers *n* ▷ **trailer**
trailing *v* ▷ **trail**
trails *n*, *v* ▷ **trail**
train *v* (-**s, -ing, -ed**) instruct in a skill ▶ *n* (*pl* -**s**)
line of railway coaches or wagons drawn by
an engine
trained *v* ▷ **train**
trainee *n* (*pl* -**s**) person being trained
trainees *n* ▷ **trainee**
trainer *n* (*pl* -**s**) person who trains an athlete
or sportsman
trainers *n* ▷ **trainer**

training *v* ▷ **train**
trains *v*, *n* ▷ **train**
traipse *v* (-**pses, -psing, -psed**) (*Informal*) walk
wearily
traipsed *v* ▷ **traipse**
traipses *v* ▷ **traipse**
traipsing *v* ▷ **traipse**
trait *n* (*pl* -**s**) characteristic feature
traitor *n* (*pl* -**s**) person guilty of treason or
treachery > **traitorous** *adj*
traitorous *adj* ▷ **traitor**
traitors *n* ▷ **traitor**
traits *n* ▷ **trait**
trajectories *n* ▷ **trajectory**
trajectory *n* (*pl* -**ries**) line of flight, esp. of a
projectile
tram *n* (*pl* -**s**) public transport vehicle powered
by an overhead wire and running on rails laid
in the road
tramlines *pl n* track for trams
tramp *v* (-**s, -ing, -ed**) travel on foot, hike ▶ *n* (*pl*
-**s**) homeless person who travels on foot
tramped *v* ▷ **tramp**
tramping *v* ▷ **tramp**
trample *v* (-**les, -ling, -led**) tread on and crush
trampled *v* ▷ **trample**
tramples *v* ▷ **trample**
trampling *v* ▷ **trample**
trampoline *n* (*pl* -**s**) tough canvas sheet
attached to a frame by springs, used by
acrobats etc. ▶ *v* (-**nes, -ning, -ned**) bounce on
a trampoline
trampolined *v* ▷ **trampoline**
trampolines *n*, *v* ▷ **trampoline**
trampolining *v* ▷ **trampoline**
tramps *n* ▷ **tramp**
trams *n* ▷ **tram**
trance *n* (*pl* -**s**) unconscious or dazed state
trances *n* ▷ **trance**
tranche *n* (*pl* -**s**) portion of something large,
esp. a sum of money
tranches *n* ▷ **tranche**
tranquil *adj* (-**ler, -lest**) calm and quiet
> **tranquilly** *adv* > **tranquillity** *n* (*pl* -**ties**)
tranquiller *adj* ▷ **tough**
tranquillest *adj* ▷ **tough**
tranquillities *n* ▷ **tranquil**
tranquillity *n* ▷ **tranquil**
tranquillize *v* (-**zes, -zing, -zed**) make calm
tranquillized *v* ▷ **tranquillize**
tranquillizer *n* (*pl* -**s**) drug which reduces
anxiety or tension
tranquillizers *n* ▷ **tranquillizer**
tranquillizes *v* ▷ **tranquillize**
tranquillizing *v* ▷ **tranquillize**

tranquilly *adv* ▷ tranquil
transact *v* (**-s, -ing, -ed**) conduct or negotiate (a business deal)
  transacted *v* ▷ transact
  transacting *v* ▷ transact
transaction *n* (*pl* **-s**) business deal transacted
  transactions *n* ▷ transaction
  transacts *v* ▷ transact
transatlantic *adj* on, from, or to the other side of the Atlantic
transceiver *n* (*pl* **-s**) transmitter and receiver of radio or electronic signals
  transceivers *n* ▷ transceiver
transcend *v* (**-s, -ing, -ed**) rise above
  > **transcendence** *n* (*pl* **-s**) > **transcendent** *adj*
  transcended *v* ▷ transcend
  transcendence *n* ▷ transcend
  transcendences *n* ▷ transcend
  transcendent *adj* ▷ transcend
transcendental *adj* based on intuition rather than experience
  transcending *v* ▷ transcend
  transcends *v* ▷ transcend
transcribe *v* (**-bes, -bing, -bed**) write down (something said)
  transcribed *v* ▷ transcribe
  transcribes *v* ▷ transcribe
  transcribing *v* ▷ transcribe
transcript *n* (*pl* **-s**) copy
  transcripts *n* ▷ transcript
transducer *n* (*pl* **-s**) device that converts one form of energy to another
  transducers *n* ▷ transducer
transept *n* (*pl* **-s**) either of the two shorter wings of a cross-shaped church
  transepts *n* ▷ transept
  transsexual *n* ▷ transsexual
  transsexuals *n* ▷ transsexual
transfer *v* (**-fers, -ferring, -ferred**) move or send from one person or place to another ▶ *n* (*pl* **-s**) transferring > **transferable** *adj*
  transferable *adj* ▷ transfer
transference *n* (*pl* **-s**) transferring
  transferences *n* ▷ transference
  transferred *v* ▷ transfer
  transferring *v* ▷ transfer
  transfers *v, n* ▷ transfer
  transfiguration *n* ▷ transfigure
  transfigurations *n* ▷ transfigure
transfigure *v* (**-res, -ring, -red**) change in appearance > **transfiguration** *n* (*pl* **-s**)
  transfigured *v* ▷ transfigure
  transfigures *v* ▷ transfigure
  transfiguring *v* ▷ transfigure
transfix *v* (**-es, -ing, -ed**) astound or stun

transfixed *v* ▷ transfix
  transfixes *v* ▷ transfix
  transfixing *v* ▷ transfix
transform *v* (**-s, -ing, -ed**) change the shape or character of > **transformation** *n* (*pl* **-s**)
  transformation *n* ▷ transform
  transformations *n* ▷ transform
  transformed *v* ▷ transform
transformer *n* (*pl* **-s**) device for changing the voltage of an alternating current
  transformers *n* ▷ transformer
  transforming *v* ▷ transform
  transforms *v* ▷ transform
transfuse *v* (**-ses, -sing, -sed**) give a transfusion to
  transfused *v* ▷ transfuse
  transfuses *v* ▷ transfuse
  transfusing *v* ▷ transfuse
transfusion *n* (*pl* **-s**) injection of blood into the blood vessels of a patient
  transfusions *n* ▷ transfusion
transgress *v* (**-es, -ing, -ed**) break (a moral law) > **transgression** *n* (*pl* **-s**) > **transgressor** *n* (*pl* **-s**)
  transgressed *v* ▷ transgress
  transgresses *v* ▷ transgress
  transgressing *v* ▷ transgress
  transgression *n* ▷ transgress
  transgressions *n* ▷ transgress
  transgressor *n* ▷ transgress
  transgressors *n* ▷ transgress
  transience *n* ▷ transient
  transiences *n* ▷ transient
transient *adj* lasting only for a short time
  > **transience** *n* (*pl* **-s**)
transistor *n* (*pl* **-s**) semiconducting device used to amplify electric currents
  transistors *n* ▷ transistor
transit *n* (*pl* **-s**) movement from one place to another
transition *n* (*pl* **-s**) change from one state to another > **transitional** *adj*
  transitional *adj* ▷ transition
  transitions *n* ▷ transition
transitive *adj* (GRAMMAR) (of a verb) requiring a direct object
transitory *adj* not lasting long
  transits *n* ▷ transit
translate *v* (**-tes, -ting, -ted**) turn from one language into another > **translation** *n* (*pl* **-s**) > **translator** *n* (*pl* **-s**)
  translated *v* ▷ translate
  translates *v* ▷ translate
  translating *v* ▷ translate
  translation *n* ▷ translat

translations *n* ▷ translat
translator *n* ▷ translate
translators *n* ▷ translate
transliterate *v* (**-tes, -ting, -ted**) convert
to the letters of a different alphabet
> **transliteration** *n* (*pl* **-s**)
transliterated *v* ▷ transliterate
transliterates *v* ▷ transliterate
transliterating *v* ▷ transliterate
transliteration *n* ▷ transliterate
translucence *n* ▷ translucence
translucences *n* ▷ translucent
translucencies *n* ▷ translucent
translucency *n* ▷ translucent
translucent *adj* letting light pass through,
but not transparent > **translucency,**
translucence *n* (*pl* **-cies, -ces**)
transmigrate *v* (**-tes, -ting, -ted**) (of a soul)
pass into another body > **transmigration**
n (*pl* **-s**)
transmigrated *v* ▷ transmigrate
transmigrates *v* ▷ transmigrate
transmigrating *v* ▷ transmigrate
transmigration *n* ▷ transmigrate
transmigrations *n* ▷ transmigrate
transmission *n* (*pl* **-s**) transmitting
transmissions *n* ▷ transmission
transmit *v* (**-mits, -mitting, -mitted**) pass
(something) from one person or place to
another > **transmittable** *adj* > **transmitter**
n (*pl* **-s**)
transmits *v* ▷ transmit
transmittable *adj* ▷ transmit
transmitted *v* ▷ transmit
transmitter *n* ▷ transmit
transmitters *n* ▷ transmit
transmitting *v* ▷ transmit
transmogrified *v* ▷ transmogrify
transmogrifies *v* ▷ transmogrify
transmogrify *v* (**-fies, -fying, -fied**) (*Informal*)
change completely
transmogrifying *v* ▷ transmogrify
transmutation *n* ▷ transmute
transmutations *n* ▷ transmute
transmute *v* (**-tes, -ting, -ted**) change the form
or nature of > **transmutation** *n* (*pl* **-s**)
transmuted *v* ▷ transmute
transmutes *v* ▷ transmute
transmuting *v* ▷ transmute
transom *n* (*pl* **-s**) horizontal bar across a
window
transoms *n* ▷ transom
transparencies *n* ▷ transparency
transparency *n* (*pl* **-cies**) transparent quality
transparent *adj* able to be seen through, clear

> **transparently** *adv*
transparently *adv* ▷ transparent
transpiration *n* ▷ transpire
transpirations *n* ▷ transpire
transpire *v* (**-res, -ring, -red**) become known
> **transpiration** *n* (*pl* **-s**)
transpired *v* ▷ transpire
transpires *v* ▷ transpire
transpiring *v* ▷ transpire
transplant *v* (**-s, -ing, -ed**) transfer (an organ
or tissue) surgically from one part or body
to another ▶ *n* (*pl* **-s**) surgical transplanting
> **transplantation** *n* (*pl* **-s**)
transplantation *n* ▷ transplant
transplantations *n* ▷ transplant
transplanted *v* ▷ transplant
transplanting *v* ▷ transplant
transplants *v, n* ▷ transplant
transport *v* (**-s, -ing, -ed**) convey from one
place to another ▶ *n* (*pl* **-s**) business or system
of transporting > **transportation** *n* (*pl* **-s**)
transportation *n* ▷ transport
transportations *n* ▷ transport
transported *v* ▷ transport
transporter *n* (*pl* **-s**) large goods vehicle
transporters *n* ▷ transporter
transporting *v* ▷ transport
transports *v, n* ▷ transport
transpose *v* (**-ses, -sing, -sed**) interchange two
things > **transposition** *n* (*pl* **-s**)
transposed *v* ▷ transpose
transposes *v* ▷ transpose
transposing *v* ▷ transpose
transposition *n* ▷ transpose
transpositions *n* ▷ transpose
transsexual, transexual *n* (*pl* **-s**) person of
one sex who believes his or her true identity
is of the opposite sex
transsexuals *n* ▷ transsexual
transuranic [tranz-yoor-**ran**-ik] *adj* (of an
element) having an atomic number greater
than that of uranium
transverse *adj* crossing from side to side
transvestite *n* (*pl* **-s**) person who seeks sexual
pleasure by wearing the clothes of the
opposite sex > **transvestism** *n* (*pl* **-s**)
transvestism *n* ▷ transvestite
transvestisms *n* ▷ transvestite
transvestites *n* ▷ transvestite
trap *n* (*pl* **-s**) device for catching animals ▶ *v* (**-s,
-pping, -pped**) catch
trapdoor *n* (*pl* **-s**) door in floor or roof
trapdoors *n* ▷ trapdoor
trapeze *n* (*pl* **-s**) horizontal bar suspended from
two ropes, used by circus acrobats

trapezes *n* ▷ **trapeze**
trapezia *n* ▷ **trapezium**
trapezium *n* (*pl* -**ziums**, -**zia**) quadrilateral with two parallel sides of unequal length
trapeziums *n* ▷ **trapezium**
trapezoid [trap-piz-zoid] *n* (*pl* -**s**) quadrilateral with no sides parallel
trapezoids *n* ▷ **trapezoid**
trapped *n* ▷ **trap**
trapper *n* (*pl* -**s**) person who traps animals for their fur
trappers *n* ▷ **trapper**
trapping *n* ▷ **trap**
trappings *pl n* accessories that symbolize an office or position
traps *n*, *v* ▷ **trap**
trash *n* (*pl* -**es**) anything worthless > **trashy** *adj* (-**shier**, -**shiest**)
trashes *n* ▷ **trash**
trashier *adj* ▷ **trash**
trashiest *adj* ▷ **trash**
trashy *adj* ▷ **trash**
trauma [traw-ma] *n* (*pl* -**mata**, -**s**) emotional shock > **traumatic** *adj* > **traumatize** *v* (-**zes**, -**zing**, -**zed**)
traumas *n* ▷ **trauma**
traumata *n* ▷ **trauma**
traumatic *adj* ▷ **trauma**
traumatized *v* ▷ **trauma**
traumatizes *v* ▷ **trauma**
traumatizing *v* ▷ **trauma**
travail *n* (*pl* -**s**) (*Lit*) labour or toil
travails *n* ▷ **travail**
travel *v* (-**s**, -**lling**, -**lled**) go from one place to another, through an area, or for a specified distance ▶ *n* (*pl* -**s**) travelling, esp. as a tourist > **traveller** *n* (*pl* -**s**)
travelled *v* ▷ **travel**
traveller *n* ▷ **travel**
travellers *n* ▷ **travel**
travelling *v* ▷ **travel**
travelogue *n* (*pl* -**s**) film or talk about someone's travels
travelogues *n* ▷ **travelogue**
travels *v*, *n* ▷ **travel** ▶ *pl n* (account of) travelling
traverse *v* (-**ses**, -**sing**, -**sed**) move over or back and forth over
traversed *v* ▷ **traverse**
traverses *v* ▷ **traverse**
traversing *v* ▷ **traverse**
travesties *n* ▷ **travesty**
travesty *n* (*pl* -**ties**) grotesque imitation or mockery
trawl *n* (*pl* -**s**) net dragged at deep levels behind

a fishing boat ▶ *v* (-**s**, -**ing**, -**ed**) fish with such a net
trawled *v* ▷ **trawl**
trawler *n* (*pl* -**s**) trawling boat
trawlers *n* ▷ **trawler**
trawling *v* ▷ **trawl**
trawls *n*, *v* ▷ **trawl**
tray *n* (*pl* -**s**) flat board, usu. with a rim, for carrying things
trays *n* ▷ **tray**
treacheries *n* ▷ **treachery**
treacherous *adj* disloyal > **treacherously** *adv*
treacherously *adv* ▷ **treacherous**
treachery *n* (*pl* -**ries**) wilful betrayal
treacle *n* (*pl* -**s**) thick dark syrup produced when sugar is refined > **treacly** *adj* (-**lier**, -**liest**)
treacles *n* ▷ **treacle**
treaclier *adj* ▷ **treacle**
treacliest *adj* ▷ **treacle**
treacly *adj* ▷ **treacle**
tread *v* (-**s**, -**ing**, **trod**, **trodden** *or* **trod**) set one's foot on ▶ *n* (*pl* -**s**) way of walking or dancing
treading *v* ▷ **tread**
treadle [tred-dl] *n* (*pl* -**s**) lever worked by the foot to turn a wheel
treadles *n* ▷ **treadle**
treadmill *n* (*pl* -**s**) (HIST) cylinder turned by treading on steps projecting from it
treadmills *n* ▷ **treadmill**
treads *v*, *n* ▷ **tread**
treason *n* (*pl* -**s**) betrayal of one's sovereign or country > **treasonable** *adj*
treasonable *adj* ▷ **treason**
treasons *n* ▷ **treason**
treasure *n* (*pl* -**s**) collection of wealth, esp. gold or jewels ▶ *v* (-**res**, -**ring**, -**red**) prize or cherish
treasured *v* ▷ **treasure**
treasurer *n* (*pl* -**s**) official in charge of funds
treasurers *n* ▷ **treasurer**
treasures *n*, *v* ▷ **treasure**
treasuries *n* ▷ **treasury**
treasuring *v* ▷ **treasure**
treasury *n* (*pl* -**ries**) storage place for treasure
treat *v* (-**s**, -**ing**, -**ed**) deal with or regard in a certain manner ▶ *n* (*pl* -**s**) pleasure, entertainment, etc. given or paid for by someone else
treated *v* ▷ **treat**
treaties *n* ▷ **treaty**
treating *v* ▷ **treat**
treatise [treat-izz] *n* (*pl* -**s**) formal piece of writing on a particular subject
treatises *n* ▷ **treatise**
treatment *n* (*pl* -**s**) medical care

treatments *n* ▷ **treatment**

treats *v*, *n* ▷ **treat**

treaty *n* (*pl* **-ties**) signed contract between states

treble *adj* triple (MUSIC) ▶ *n* (*pl* **-s**) (singer with or part for) a soprano voice ▶ *v* (**-les, -ling, -led**) increase three times > **trebly** *adv*

trebled *v* ▷ **treble**

trebles *n*, *v* ▷ **treble**

trebling *v* ▷ **treble**

trebly *adv* ▷ **treble**

tree *n* (*pl* **-s**) large perennial plant with a woody trunk > **treeless** *adj*

treeless *adj* ▷ **tree**

trees *n* ▷ **tree**

trefoil [tref-foil] *n* (*pl* **-s**) plant, such as clover, with a three-lobed leaf

trefoils *n* ▷ **trefoil**

trek *n* (*pl* **-s**) long difficult journey, esp. on foot ▶ *v* (**-s, -kking, -kked**) make such a journey

trekked *v* ▷ **trek**

trekking *v* ▷ **trek**

treks *n*, *v* ▷ **trek**

trellis *n* (*pl* **-ises**) framework of horizontal and vertical strips of wood

trellises *n* ▷ **trellis**

tremble *v* (**-les, -ling, -led**) shake or quiver ▶ *n* (*pl* **-les**) trembling > **trembling** *adj*

trembled *v* ▷ **tremble**

trembles *v*, *n* ▷ **tremble**

trembling *v*, *adj* ▷ **tremble**

tremendous *adj* huge > **tremendously** *adv*

tremendously *adv* ▷ **tremendous**

tremolo *n* (*pl* **-s**) (MUSIC) quivering effect in singing or playing

tremolos *n* ▷ **tremolo**

tremor *n* (*pl* **-s**) involuntary shaking

tremors *n* ▷ **tremor**

tremulous *adj* trembling, as from fear or excitement

trench *n* (*pl* **-es**) long narrow ditch, esp. one used as a shelter in war

trenchant *adj* incisive

trencher *n* (*pl* **-s**) (HIST) wooden plate for serving food

trencherman *n* (*pl* **-men**) hearty eater

trenchermen *n* ▷ **trencherman**

trenchers *n* ▷ **trencher**

trenches *n* ▷ **trench**

trend *n* (*pl* **-s**) general tendency or direction

trendier *adj* ▷ **trendy**

trendies *n* ▷ **trendy**

trendiest *adj* ▷ **trendy**

trendiness *n* ▷ **trendy**

trendinesses *n* ▷ **trendy**

trends *n* ▷ **trend**

trendy *adj* (**-dier, -diest**) ▶ *n* (*pl* **-dies**) (*Informal*) consciously fashionable (person) > **trendiness** *n* (*pl* **-es**)

trepidation *n* (*pl* **-s**) fear or anxiety

trepidations *n* ▷ **trepidation**

trespass *v* (**-es, -ing, -ed**) go onto another's property without permission ▶ *n* (*pl* **-es**) trespassing > **trespasser** *n* (*pl* **-s**)

trespassed *v* ▷ **trespass**

trespasser *n* ▷ **trespass**

trespassers *n* ▷ **trespass**

trespasses *v*, *n* ▷ **trespass**

trespassing *v* ▷ **trespass**

tresses *pl n* long flowing hair

trestle *n* (*pl* **-s**) board fixed on pairs of spreading legs, used as a support

trestles *n* ▷ **trestle**

trevallies *n* ▷ **trevally**

trevally *n* (*pl* **-lies**) (AUST & NZ) any of various food and game fishes

trews *pl n* close-fitting tartan trousers

triad *n* (*pl* **-s**) group of three

triads *n* ▷ **triad**

trial *n* (*pl* **-s**) investigation of a case before a judge

trials *n* ▷ **trial** ▶ *pl n* sporting competition for individuals

triangle *n* (*pl* **-s**) geometric figure with three sides > **triangular** *adj*

triangles *n* ▷ **triangle**

triangular *adj* ▷ **triangle**

tribal *adj* ▷ **tribe**

tribalism *n* (*pl* **-s**) loyalty to a tribe

tribalisms *n* ▷ **tribalism**

tribe *n* (*pl* **-s**) group of clans or families believed to have a common ancestor > **tribal** *adj*

tribes *n* ▷ **tribe**

tribulation *n* (*pl* **-s**) great distress

tribulations *n* ▷ **tribulation**

tribunal *n* (*pl* **-s**) board appointed to inquire into a specific matter

tribunals *n* ▷ **tribunal**

tribune *n* (*pl* **-s**) people's representative, esp. in ancient Rome

tribunes *n* ▷ **tribune**

tributaries *n* ▷ **tributary**

tributary *n* (*pl* **-ries**) stream or river flowing into a larger one ▶ *adj* (of a stream or river) flowing into a larger one

tribute *n* (*pl* **-s**) sign of respect or admiration

tributes *n* ▷ **tribute**

trice *n* (*pl* **-s**) moment

triceps *n* (*pl* **-pses**) muscle at the back of the upper arm

tricepses *n* ▷ triceps
trices *n* ▷ trice
trichologies *n* ▷ trichology
trichologist *n* ▷ trichology
trichologists *n* ▷ trichology
trichology [trick-ol-a-jee] *n* (*pl* -gies) study
and treatment of hair and its diseases
> **trichologist** *n* (*pl* -s)
trick *n* (*pl* -s) deceitful or cunning action
or plan ▶ *v* (-s, -ing, -ed) cheat or deceive
> **trickery** *n* (*pl* -ries) > **trickster** *n* (*pl* -s)
tricked *v* ▷ trick
trickeries *n* ▷ trick
trickery *n* ▷ trick
trickier *adj* ▷ tricky
trickiest *adj* ▷ tricky
tricking *v* ▷ trick
trickle *v* (-les, -ling, -led) (cause to) flow in a
thin stream or drops ▶ *n* (*pl* -s) gradual flow
trickled *v* ▷ trickle
trickles *v*, *n* ▷ trickle
trickling *v* ▷ trickle
tricks *n*, *v* ▷ trick
trickster *n* ▷ trick
tricksters *n* ▷ trick
tricky *adj* (-kier, -kiest) difficult, needing
careful handling
tricolour [trick-kol-lor] *n* (*pl* -s) three-coloured
striped flag
tricolours *n* ▷ tricolour
tricycle *n* (*pl* -s) three-wheeled cycle
tricycles *n* ▷ tricycle
trident *n* (*pl* -s) three-pronged spear
tridents *n* ▷ trident
tried *v* ▷ try
triennial *adj* happening every three years
tries *v*, *n* ▷ try
trifle *n* (*pl* -s) insignificant thing or amount
trifles *n* ▷ trifle
trifling *adj* insignificant
trigger *n* (*pl* -s) small lever releasing a catch on
a gun or machine ▶ *v* (-s, -ing, -ed) (*usu. foll. by
off*) set (an action or process) in motion
triggered *v* ▷ trigger
triggering *v* ▷ trigger
triggers *n*, *v* ▷ trigger
trigonometries *n* ▷ trigonometry
trigonometry *n* (*pl* -ries) branch of
mathematics dealing with relations of the
sides and angles of triangles
trike *n* (*pl* -s) (*Informal*) tricycle
trikes *n* ▷ trike
trilateral *adj* having three sides
trilbies *n* ▷ trilby
trilby *n* (*pl* -bies) man's soft felt hat

trill *n* (*pl* -s) (MUSIC) rapid alternation between
two notes ▶ *v* (-s, -ing, -ed) play or sing a trill
trilled *v* ▷ trill
trilling *v* ▷ trill
trillion *n* (*pl* -s) one million million, 10^{12}
trillions *n* ▷ trillion
trills *n*, *v* ▷ trill
trilobite [trile-oh-bite] *n* (*pl* -s) small prehistoric
sea animal
trilobites *n* ▷ trilobite
trilogies *n* ▷ trilogy
trilogy *n* (*pl* -gies) series of three related books,
plays, etc.
trim *adj* (-mmer, -mmest) neat and smart ▶ *v*
(-s, -mming, -mmed) cut or prune into good
shape ▶ *n* (*pl* -s) decoration
trimaran [trime-a-ran] *n* (*pl* -s) three-hulled boat
trimarans *n* ▷ trimaran
trimmed *v* ▷ trim
trimmer *adj* ▷ trim
trimmest *adj* ▷ trim
trimming *n* (*pl* -s) decoration ▶ *v* ▷ trim
trimmings *n* ▷ trimming ▶ *pl n* usual
accompaniments
trims *v*, *n* ▷ trim
trinities *n* ▷ trinity
trinitrotoluene *n* (*pl* -s) TNT
trinitrotoluenes *n* ▷ trinitrotoluene
trinity *n* (*pl* -ties) group of three
trinket *n* (*pl* -s) small or worthless ornament or
piece of jewellery
trinkets *n* ▷ trinket
trio *n* (*pl* -s) group of three
trios *n* ▷ trio
trip *n* (*pl* -s) journey to a place and back, esp.
for pleasure ▶ *v* (-s, -pping, -pped) (cause to)
stumble
tripe *n* (*pl* -s) stomach of a cow used as food
tripes *n* ▷ tripe
triple *adj* having three parts ▶ *v* (-les, -ling,
-led) increase three times
tripled *v* ▷ triple
triples *v* ▷ triple
triplet *n* (*pl* -s) one of three babies born at
one birth
triplets *n* ▷ triplet
triplicate *adj* triple
tripling *v* ▷ triple
tripod [tripe-pod] *n* (*pl* -s) three-legged stand,
stool, etc.
tripods *n* ▷ tripod
tripos [tripe-poss] *n* (*pl* -poses) final
examinations for an honours degree at
Cambridge University
triposes *n* ▷ tripos

tripped v ▷ **trip**
tripper n (pl -**s**) tourist
  trippers n ▷ **tripper**
  tripping v ▷ **trip**
  trips n, v ▷ **trip**
triptych [trip-tick] n (pl -**s**) painting or carving on three hinged panels, often forming an altarpiece
  triptychs n ▷ **triptych**
trite adj (of a remark or idea) commonplace and unoriginal
tritium n (pl -**s**) radioactive isotope of hydrogen
  tritiums n ▷ **tritium**
triumph n (pl -**s**) (happiness caused by) victory or success ▶ v (-**s**, -**ing**, -**ed**) be victorious or successful
triumphal adj celebrating a triumph
triumphant adj feeling or showing triumph
  triumphed v ▷ **triumph**
  triumphing v ▷ **triumph**
  triumphs n, v ▷ **triumph**
triumvirate [try-**umm**-vir-rit] n (pl -**s**) group of three people in joint control
  triumvirates n ▷ **triumvirate**
trivet [triv-vit] n (pl -**s**) metal stand for a pot or kettle
  trivets n ▷ **trivet**
trivia pl n trivial things or details
trivial adj of little importance > **trivially** adv > **triviality** n (pl -**ties**)
  trivialities n ▷ **trivial**
  triviality n ▷ **trivial**
trivialize v (-**zes**, -**zing**, -**zed**) make (something) seem less important or complex than it is
  trivialized v ▷ **trivialize**
  trivializes v ▷ **trivialize**
  trivializing v ▷ **trivialize**
  trivially adv ▷ **trivial**
  trod v ▷ **tread**
  trodden v ▷ **tread**
troglodyte n (pl -**s**) cave dweller
  troglodytes n ▷ **troglodyte**
troika n (pl -**s**) Russian vehicle drawn by three horses abreast
  troikas n ▷ **troika**
troll n (pl -**s**) giant or dwarf in Scandinavian folklore
trolley n (pl -**s**) small wheeled table for food and drink
  trolleys n ▷ **trolley**
trollop n (pl -**s**) (Old-fashioned) promiscuous or slovenly woman
  trollops n ▷ **trollop**

trolls n ▷ **troll**
trombone n (pl -**s**) brass musical instrument with a sliding tube > **trombonist** n (pl -**s**)
  trombones n ▷ **trombone**
  trombonist n ▷ **trombone**
  trombonists n ▷ **trombone**
troop n (pl -**s**) large group ▶ v (-**s**, -**ing**, -**ed**) move in a crowd
  trooped v ▷ **troop**
trooper n (pl -**s**) cavalry soldier
  troopers n ▷ **trooper**
  trooping v ▷ **troop**
  troops n, v ▷ **troop** ▶ pl n soldiers
trope n (pl -**s**) figure of speech
  tropes n ▷ **trope**
  trophies n ▷ **trophy**
trophy n (pl -**phies**) cup, shield, etc. given as a prize
tropic n (pl -**s**) either of two lines of latitude at $23\frac{1}{2}°$N (**tropic of Cancer**) or $23\frac{1}{2}°$S (**tropic of Capricorn**) ▶ pl n part of the earth's surface between these lines
tropical adj of or in the tropics
  tropics n ▷ **tropic**
trot v (-**s**, -**tting**, -**tted**) (of a horse) move at a medium pace, lifting the feet in diagonal pairs ▶ n (pl -**s**) trotting
troth [rhymes with **growth**] n (pl -**s**) (Obs) pledge of devotion, esp. a betrothal
  troths n ▷ **troth**
  trots v, n ▷ **trot**
  trotted v ▷ **trot**
trotter n (pl -**s**) pig's foot
  trotters n ▷ **trotter**
  trotting v ▷ **trot**
troubadour [troo-bad-oor] n (pl -**s**) medieval travelling poet and singer
  troubadours n ▷ **troubadour**
trouble n (pl -**s**) (cause of) distress or anxiety ▶ v (-**les**, -**ling**, -**led**) (cause to) worry > **troubled** adj > **troublesome** adj
  troubled v, adj ▷ **trouble**
  troubles n, v ▷ **trouble**
troubleshooter n (pl -**s**) person employed to locate and deal with faults or problems
  troubleshooters n ▷ **troubleshooter**
  troublesome adj ▷ **trouble**
  troubling v ▷ **trouble**
trough [troff] n (pl -**s**) long open container, esp. for animals' food or water
  troughs n ▷ **trough**
trounce v (-**ces**, -**cing**, -**ced**) defeat utterly
  trounced v ▷ **trounce**
  trounces v ▷ **trounce**
  trouncing v ▷ **trounce**

troupe [troop] *n* (*pl* **-s**) company of performers
> **trouper** *n* (*pl* **-s**)
trouper *n* ▷ **troupe**
troupers *n* ▷ **troupe**
troupes *n* ▷ **troupe**
trouser *adj* of trousers
trousers *pl n* two-legged outer garment with legs reaching usu. to the ankles
trousseau [troo-so] *n* (*pl* **-seaux, -seaus**) bride's collection of clothing etc. for her marriage
trousseaus *n* ▷ **trousseau**
trousseaux *n* ▷ **trousseau**
trout *n* (*pl* **trout, trouts**) game fish related to the salmon
trouts *n* ▷ **trout**
trowel *n* (*pl* **-s**) hand tool with a wide blade for spreading mortar, lifting plants, etc.
trowels *n* ▷ **trowel**
truancies *n* ▷ **truant**
truancy *n* ▷ **truant**
truant *n* (*pl* **-s**) pupil who stays away from school without permission > **truancy** *n* (*pl* **-cies**)
truants *n* ▷ **truant**
truce *n* (*pl* **-s**) temporary agreement to stop fighting
truces *n* ▷ **truce**
truck[1] *n* (*pl* **-s**) railway goods wagon
truck[2] *n* (*pl* **-s**) commercial goods
trucker *n* (*pl* **-s**) truck driver
truckers *n* ▷ **trucker**
trucks *n* ▷ **truck**[1, 2]
truculence *n* ▷ **truculent**
truculences *n* ▷ **truculent**
truculent [truck-yew-lent] *adj* aggressively defiant > **truculence** *n* (*pl* **-s**)
trudge *v* (**-dges, -dging, -dged**) walk heavily or wearily ▶ *n* (*pl* **-s**) long tiring walk
trudged *v* ▷ **trudge**
trudges *v, n* ▷ **trudge**
trudging *v* ▷ **trudge**
true *adj* (**truer, truest**) in accordance with facts
> **truly** *adv*
truer *adj* ▷ **true**
truest *adj* ▷ **true**
truffle *n* (*pl* **-s**) edible underground fungus
truffles *n* ▷ **truffle**
trug *n* (*pl* **-s**) (BRIT) long shallow basket used by gardeners
trugs *n* ▷ **trug**
truism *n* (*pl* **-s**) self-evident truth
truisms *n* ▷ **truism**
truly *adv* ▷ **true**
trump[1] *n* (*pl* **-s**) ▶ *adj* (card) of the suit outranking the others ▶ *v* (**-s, -ing, -ed**) play a trump card on (another card)

trump[2] *n* (*pl* **-s**) (*Lit*) (sound of) a trumpet
trumped *v* ▷ **trump**[1]
trumpet *n* (*pl* **-s**) valved brass instrument with a flared tube ▶ *v* (**-s, -ing, -ed**) proclaim loudly
> **trumpeter** *n* (*pl* **-s**)
trumpeted *v* ▷ **trumpet**
trumpeter *n* ▷ **trumpet**
trumpeters *n* ▷ **trumpet**
trumpeting *v* ▷ **trumpet**
trumpets *n, v* ▷ **trumpet**
trumping *v* ▷ **trump**[1]
trumps *n* ▷ **trump**[1, 2] ▶ *pl n* suit outranking the others ▶ *v* ▷ **trump**[1]
truncate *v* (**-tes, -ting, -ted**) cut short
truncated *v* ▷ **truncate**
truncates *v* ▷ **truncate**
truncating *v* ▷ **truncate**
truncheon *n* (*pl* **-s**) club carried by a policeman
truncheons *n* ▷ **truncheon**
trundle *v* (**-les, -ling, -led**) move heavily on wheels
trundled *v* ▷ **trundle**
trundles *v* ▷ **trundle**
trundling *v* ▷ **trundle**
trunk *n* (*pl* **-s**) main stem of a tree
trunks *n* ▷ **trunk** ▶ *pl n* man's swimming shorts
truss *v* (**-es, -ing, -ed**) tie or bind up ▶ *n* (*pl* **-es**) device for holding a hernia in place
trussed *v* ▷ **truss**
trusses *v, n* ▷ **truss**
trussing *v* ▷ **truss**
trust *v* (**-s, -ing, -ed**) believe in and rely on ▶ *n* (*pl* **-s**) confidence in the truth, reliability, etc. of a person or thing
trusted *v* ▷ **trust**
trustee *n* (*pl* **-s**) person holding property on another's behalf
trustees *n* ▷ **trustee**
trustful, trusting *adj* inclined to trust others
trustier *adj* ▷ **trusty**
trustiest *adj* ▷ **trusty**
trusting *v* ▷ **trust** ▶ *adj* ▷ **trustful**
trusts *n, v* ▷ **trust**
trustworthy *adj* reliable or honest
trusty *adj* (**-tier, -tiest**) faithful or reliable
truth *n* (*pl* **-s**) state of being true
truthful *adj* honest > **truthfully** *adv*
truthfully *adv* ▷ **truthful**
truths *n* ▷ **truth**
try *v* (**tries, trying, tried**) make an effort or attempt ▶ *n* (*pl* **tries**) attempt or effort
trying *adj* (*Informal*) difficult or annoying ▶ *v*
▷ **try**
tryst *n* (*pl* **-s**) arrangement to meet
trysts *n* ▷ **tryst**

tsar, czar [zahr] *n* (*pl* **-s**) (HIST) Russian emperor
tsars *n* ▷ **tsar**

> **tsk** *interj.* Tsk is a sound people make
> to show disapproval. This is a useful
> word because it enables you to play K
> without using vowels, which is handy
> if your rack is low on vowel tiles. Tsk
> scores 7 points.

tsunami *n* (*pl* **-mis, -mi**) tidal wave, usu.
caused by an earthquake under the sea
tsunamis *n* ▷ **tsunami**
tuatara *n* (*pl* **-s**) large lizard-like New Zealand
reptile
tuataras *n* ▷ **tuatara**
tub *n* (*pl* **-s**) open, usu. round container
tuba [tube-a] *n* (*pl* **-s**) valved low-pitched brass
instrument
tubas *n* ▷ **tuba**
tubbier *adj* ▷ **tubby**
tubbiest *adj* ▷ **tubby**
tubby *adj* (**tubbier, tubbiest**) (of a person)
short and fat
tube *n* (*pl* **-s**) hollow cylinder
tuber [tube-er] *n* (*pl* **-s**) fleshy underground root
of a plant such as a potato > **tuberous** *adj*
tubercle [tube-er-kl] *n* (*pl* **-s**) small rounded
swelling
tubercles *n* ▷ **tubercle**
tubercular *adj* ▷ **tuberculosis**
tuberculin *n* (*pl* **-s**) extract from a bacillus used
to test for tuberculosis
tuberculins *n* ▷ **tuberculin**
tuberculosis [tube-berk-yew-**lohss**-iss] *n* (*pl*
-ses) infectious disease causing tubercles,
esp. in the lungs > **tubercular** *adj*
tuberculoses *n* ▷ **tuberculosis**
tuberous *adj* ▷ **tuber**
tubers *n* ▷ **tuber**
tubes *n* ▷ **tube**
tubing *n* (*pl* **-s**) length of tube
tubings *n* ▷ **tubing**
tubs *n* ▷ **tub**
tubular [tube-yew-lar] *adj* of or shaped like
a tube
tuck *v* (**-s, -ing, -ed**) push or fold into a small
space ▶ *n* (*pl* **-s**) stitched fold
tucked *v* ▷ **tuck**
tucker *n* (*pl* **-s**) (AUST & NZ) (*Informal*) food
tuckers *n* ▷ **tucker**
tucking *v* ▷ **tuck**
tucks *v, n* ▷ **tuck**
tufa [tew-fa] *n* (*pl* **-s**) porous rock formed as a
deposit from springs
tufas *n* ▷ **tufa**
tuffet *n* (*pl* **-s**) small mound or seat

tuffets *n* ▷ **tuffet**
tuft *n* (*pl* **-s**) bunch of feathers, grass, hair, etc.
held or growing together at the base
tufts *n* ▷ **tuft**
tug *v* (**-s, -gging, -gged**) pull hard ▶ *n* (*pl* **-s**)
hard pull
tugged *v* ▷ **tug**
tugging *v* ▷ **tug**
tugs *v, n* ▷ **tug**
tuition *n* (*pl* **-s**) instruction, esp. received
individually or in a small group
tuitions *n* ▷ **tuition**
tulip *n* (*pl* **-s**) plant with bright cup-shaped
flowers
tulips *n* ▷ **tulip**
tulle [tewl] *n* (*pl* **-s**) fine net fabric of silk etc.
tulles *n* ▷ **tulle**
tumble *v* (**-les, -ling, -led**) (cause to) fall, esp.
awkwardly or violently ▶ *n* (*pl* **-s**) fall
tumbled *v* ▷ **tumble**
tumbledown *adj* dilapidated
tumbler *n* (*pl* **-s**) stemless drinking glass
tumblers *n* ▷ **tumbler**
tumbles *v, n* ▷ **tumble**
tumbling *v* ▷ **tumble**
tumbrel *n* ▷ **tumbril**
tumbrels *n* ▷ **tumbril**
tumbril, tumbrel *n* (*pl* **-s**) farm cart used
during the French Revolution to take
prisoners to the guillotine
tumbrils *n* ▷ **tumbril**
tumescent [tew-**mess**-ent] *adj* swollen or
becoming swollen
tummies *n* ▷ **tummy**
tummy *n* (*pl* **-mies**) (*Informal*) stomach
tumour [tew-mer] *n* (*pl* **-s**) abnormal growth in
or on the body
tumours *n* ▷ **tumour**
tumuli *n* ▷ **tumulus**
tumult *n* (*pl* **-s**) uproar or commotion
> **tumultuous** [tew-**mull**-tew-uss] ▶ *adj*
tumults *n* ▷ **tumult**
tumultuous *adj* ▷ **tumult**
tumulus *n* (*pl* **-li**) burial mound
tun *n* (*pl* **-s**) large beer cask
tuna *n* (*pl* **-s**) large marine food fish
tunas *n* ▷ **tuna**
tundra *n* (*pl* **-s**) vast treeless Arctic region with
permanently frozen subsoil
tundras *n* ▷ **tundra**
tune *n* (*pl* **-s**) (pleasing) sequence of musical
notes ▶ *v* (**-nes, -ning, -ned**) adjust (a musical
instrument) so that it is in tune > **tuneful** *adj*
> **tunefully** *adv* > **tuneless** *adj* > **tuner** *n* (*pl* **-s**)
tuned *v* ▷ **tune**

tuneful *adj* ▷ **tune**
tunefully *adv* ▷ **tune**
tuneless *adj* ▷ **tune**
tuner *n* ▷ **tune**
tuners *n* ▷ **tune**
tunes *n*, *v* ▷ **tune**
tungsten *n* (*pl* -s) (CHEM) greyish-white metal
tungstens *n* ▷ **tungsten**
tunic *n* (*pl* -s) close-fitting jacket forming part of some uniforms
tunics *n* ▷ **tunic**
tuning *v* ▷ **tune**
tunnel *n* (*pl* -s) underground passage ▸ *v* (-s, -lling, -lled) make a tunnel (through)
tunnelled *v* ▷ **tunnel**
tunnelling *v* ▷ **tunnel**
tunnels *n*, *v* ▷ **tunnel**
tunnies *n* ▷ **tunny**
tunny *n* (*pl* -nies, -ny) tuna
tuns *n* ▷ **tun**
tup *n* (*pl* -s) male sheep
tups *n* ▷ **tup**
turban *n* (*pl* -s) Muslim, Hindu, or Sikh man's head covering, made by winding cloth round the head
turbans *n* ▷ **turban**
turbid *adj* muddy, not clear
turbine *n* (*pl* -s) machine or generator driven by gas, water, etc. turning blades
turbines *n* ▷ **turbine**
turbot *n* (*pl* -s) large European edible flatfish
turbots *n* ▷ **turbot**
turbulence *n* (*pl* -s) confusion, movement, or agitation > **turbulent** *adj*
turbulences *n* ▷ **turbulence**
turbulent *adj* ▷ **turbulence**
tureen *n* (*pl* -s) serving dish for soup
tureens *n* ▷ **tureen**
turf *n* (*pl* -s, **turves**) short thick even grass ▸ *v* (-s, -ing, -ed) cover with turf
turfed *v* ▷ **turf**
turfing *v* ▷ **turf**
turfs *n*, *v* ▷ **turf**
turgid [tur-jid] *adj* (-er, -est) (of language) pompous
turgider *adj* ▷ **turgid**
turgidest *adj* ▷ **turgid**
turkey *n* (*pl* -s) large bird bred for food
turkeys *n* ▷ **turkey**
turmeric *n* (*pl* -s) yellow spice obtained from the root of an Asian plant
turmerics *n* ▷ **turmeric**
turmoil *n* (*pl* -s) agitation or confusion
turmoils *n* ▷ **turmoil**
turn *v* (-s, -ing, -ed) change the position or direction (of) ▸ *n* (*pl* -s) turning > **turner** *n* (*pl* -s)
turncoat *n* (*pl* -s) person who deserts one party or cause to join another
turncoats *n* ▷ **turncoat**
turned *v* ▷ **turn**
turner *n* ▷ **turn**
turners *n* ▷ **turn**
turning *n* (*pl* -s) road or path leading off a main route ▸ *v* ▷ **turn**
turnings *n* ▷ **turning**
turnip *n* (*pl* -s) root vegetable with orange or white flesh
turnips *n* ▷ **turnip**
turnout *n* (*pl* -s) number of people appearing at a gathering
turnouts *n* ▷ **turnout**
turnover *n* (*pl* -s) total sales made by a business over a certain period
turnovers *n* ▷ **turnover**
turnpike *n* (*pl* -s) (BRIT) road where a toll is collected at barriers
turnpikes *n* ▷ **turnpike**
turns *v*, *n* ▷ **turn**
turnstile *n* (*pl* -s) revolving gate for admitting one person at a time
turnstiles *n* ▷ **turnstile**
turntable *n* (*pl* -s) revolving platform
turntables *n* ▷ **turntable**
turnup *n* (*pl* -s) turned-up fold at the bottom of a trouser leg
turnups *n* ▷ **turnup**
turpentine *n* (*pl* -s) (oil made from) the resin of certain trees
turpentines *n* ▷ **turpentine**
turpitude *n* (*pl* -s) wickedness
turpitudes *n* ▷ **turpitude**
turps *n* turpentine oil
turquoise *adj* blue-green ▸ *n* (*pl* -s) blue-green precious stone
turquoises *n* ▷ **turquoise**
turret *n* (*pl* -s) small tower
turrets *n* ▷ **turret**
turtle *n* (*pl* -s) sea tortoise
turtledove *n* (*pl* -s) small wild dove
turtledoves *n* ▷ **turtledove**
turtleneck *n* (*pl* -s) (sweater with) a round high close-fitting neck
turtlenecks *n* ▷ **turtleneck**
turtles *n* ▷ **turtle**
turves *n* ▷ **turf**
tusk *n* (*pl* -s) long pointed tooth of an elephant, walrus, etc.
tusks *n* ▷ **tusk**
tussle *n* (*pl* -s) ▸ *v* (-les, -ling, -led) fight or

scuffle
tussled v ▷ tussle
tussles n, v ▷ tussle
tussling v ▷ tussle
tussock n (pl -s) tuft of grass
tussocks n ▷ tussock
tutelage [tew-till-lij] n (pl -s) instruction or guidance, esp. by a tutor > **tutelary** [tew-till-lar-ee] ▶ adj
tutelages n ▷ tutelage
tutelary adj ▷ tutelage
tutor n (pl -s) person teaching individuals or small groups ▶ v (-s, -ing, -ed) act as a tutor to
tutored v ▷ tutor
tutorial n (pl -s) period of instruction with a tutor
tutorials n ▷ tutorial
tutoring v ▷ tutor
tutors n, v ▷ tutor
tutu n (pl -s) short stiff skirt worn by ballerinas
tutus n ▷ tutu

> **tux** n (**tuxes**). Tux is a short form of **tuxedo**. This is a very useful word, as U and T are common tiles, so look for opportunities to play it when you get an X. Tux scores 10 points.

tuxedo n (pl -s) (US & AUST) dinner jacket
tuxedos n ▷ tuxedo
twaddle n (pl -s) silly or pretentious talk or writing
twaddles n ▷ twaddle
twain n (pl -s) (Obs) two
twains n ▷ twain
twang n (pl -s) sharp ringing sound ▶ v (-s, -ing, -ed) (cause to) make a twang
twanged v ▷ twang
twanging v ▷ twang
twangs n, v ▷ twang
tweak v (-s, -ing, -ed) pinch or twist sharply ▶ n (pl -s) tweaking
tweaked v ▷ tweak
tweaking v ▷ tweak
tweaks v, n ▷ tweak
twee adj (Informal) (-r, -st) too sentimental, sweet, or pretty
tweed n (pl -s) thick woollen cloth > **tweedy** adj (-dier, -diest)
tweedier adj ▷ tweed
tweediest adj ▷ tweed
tweeds n ▷ tweed ▶ pl n suit of tweed
tweedy adj ▷ tweed
tweer adj ▷ twee
tweest adj ▷ twee
tweet n (pl -s) ▶ v (-s, -ing, -ed) chirp
tweeted v ▷ tweet

tweeter n (pl -s) loudspeaker reproducing high-frequency sounds
tweeters n ▷ tweeter
tweeting v ▷ tweet
tweets n, v ▷ tweet
tweezers pl n small pincer-like tool
twelfth adj, n (pl -s) (of) number twelve in a series
twelfths n ▷ twelfth
twelve adj, n (pl -s) two more than ten
twelves n ▷ twelve
twenties n ▷ twenty
twentieth adj, n ▷ twenty
twentieths n ▷ twenty
twenty adj, n (pl -ties) two times ten > **twentieth** adj, n (pl -s)
twerp n (pl -s) (Informal) silly person
twerps n ▷ twerp
twice adv two times
twiddle v (-les, -ling, -led) fiddle or twirl in an idle way
twiddled v ▷ twiddle
twiddles v ▷ twiddle
twiddling v ▷ twiddle
twig[1] n (pl -s) small branch or shoot
twig[2] v (-s, -gging, -gged) (Informal) realize or understand
twigged v ▷ twig[1]
twigging v ▷ twig[1]
twigs n ▷ twig[1] ▶ v ▷ twig[2]
twilight n (pl -s) soft dim light just after sunset
twilights n ▷ twilight
twill n (pl -s) fabric woven to produce parallel ridges
twills n ▷ twill
twin n (pl -s) one of a pair, esp. of two children born at one birth ▶ v (-s, -nning, -nned) pair or be paired
twine n (pl -es) string or cord ▶ v (-nes, -ning, -ned) twist or coil round
twined v ▷ twine
twines n, v ▷ twine
twining v ▷ twine
twinge n (pl -s) sudden sharp pain or emotional pang
twinges n ▷ twinge
twinkle v (-les, -ling, -led) shine brightly but intermittently ▶ n (pl -les) flickering brightness
twinkled v ▷ twinkle
twinkles v, n ▷ twinkle
twinkling v ▷ twinkle
twinned v ▷ twin
twinning v ▷ twin
twins n, v ▷ twin

twirl *v* (**-s, -ing, -ed**) turn or spin around quickly
  twirled *v* ▷ **twirl**
  twirling *v* ▷ **twirl**
  twirls *v* ▷ **twirl**
twist *v* (**-s, -ing, -ed**) turn out of the natural
  position ▶ *n* (*pl* **-s**) twisting
twisted *adj* (of a person) cruel or perverted
  ▶ *v* ▷ **twist**
twister *n* (*pl* **-s**) (BRIT) (*Informal*) swindler
  twisters *n* ▷ **twister**
  twisting *v* ▷ **twist**
  twists *v*, *n* ▷ **twist**
twit[1] *v* (**-s, -tting, -tted**) poke fun at (someone)
twit[2] *n* (*pl* **-s**) (*Informal*) foolish person
twitch *v* (**-es, -ing, -ed**) move spasmodically ▶ *n*
  (*pl* **-es**) nervous muscular spasm
  twitched *v* ▷ **twitch**
  twitches *v*, *n* ▷ **twitch**
  twitching *v* ▷ **twitch**
  twits *n* ▷ **twit**[2] ▶ *v* ▷ **twit**[1]
  twitted *v* ▷ **twit**[1]
twitter *v* (**-s, -ing, -ed**) (of birds) utter chirping
  sounds ▶ *n* (*pl* **-s**) act or sound of twittering
  twittered *v* ▷ **twitter**
  twittering *v* ▷ **twitter**
  twitters *v*, *n* ▷ **twitter**
  twitting *v* ▷ **twit**[1]
two *adj*, *n* (*pl* **-s**) one more than one
  twos *n* ▷ **two**

> **twp** *adj*. This is a Welsh word that
> means stupid or daft. This is a useful
> word because it contains no vowels,
> and can thus help when you have an
> awkward rack. Twp scores 8 points.

tycoon *n* (*pl* **-s**) powerful wealthy businessman
  tycoons *n* ▷ **tycoon**

> **tyg** *n* (**tygs**). A tyg is a cup with more
> than one handle. This word is useful
> because it uses no vowels, and can
> thus help when you are short of them.
> Tyg scores 7 points.

  tying *v* ▷ **tie**
tyke *n* (*pl* **-s**) (BRIT, AUST & NZ) (*Informal*) small
  cheeky child
  tykes *n* ▷ **tyke**
type *n* (*pl* **-s**) class or category ▶ *v* (**-pes, -ping,
  -ped**) print with a typewriter or word processor
typecast *v* (**-s, -ing, -ed**) continually cast (an
  actor or actress) in similar roles
  typecasted *v* ▷ **typecast**
  typecasting *v* ▷ **typecast**
  typecasts *v* ▷ **typecast**
  typed *v* ▷ **type**

types *n*, *v* ▷ **type**
typewriter *n* (*pl* **-s**) machine which prints a
  character when the appropriate key is pressed
  typewriters *n* ▷ **typewriter**
  typing *v* ▷ **type**
typist *n* (*pl* **-s**) person who types with a
  typewriter or word processor
  typists *n* ▷ **typist**
typhoon *n* (*pl* **-s**) violent tropical storm
  typhoons *n* ▷ **typhoon**
typhus *n* (*pl* **-uses**) infectious feverish disease
  typhuses *n* ▷ **typhus**
typical *adj* true to type, characteristic
  > **typically** *adv*
  typically *adv* ▷ **typical**
  typified *v* ▷ **typify**
  typifies *v* ▷ **typify**
typify *v* (**-fies, -fying, -fied**) be typical of
  typifying *v* ▷ **typify**
  typographer *n* ▷ **typography**
  typographers *n* ▷ **typography**
  typographical *adj* ▷ **typography**
  typographies *n* ▷ **typography**
typography *n* (*pl* **-phies**) art or style of printing
  > **typographical** *adj* > **typographer** *n* (*pl* **-s**)
tyrannical *adj* like a tyrant, oppressive
  tyrannies *n* ▷ **tyranny**
tyrannize *v* (**-zes, -zing, -zed**) exert power
  (over) oppressively or cruelly > **tyrannous** *adj*
  tyrannized *v* ▷ **tyrannize**
  tyrannizes *v* ▷ **tyrannize**
  tyrannizing *v* ▷ **tyrannize**
tyrannosaurus [tirr-ran-oh-**sore**-uss] *n* (*pl* **-es**)
  large two-footed flesh-eating dinosaur
  tyrannosauruses *n* ▷ **tyrannosaurus**
  tyrannous *n* ▷ **tyrannize**
tyranny *n* (*pl* **-nies**) tyrannical rule
tyrant *n* (*pl* **-s**) oppressive or cruel ruler
  tyrants *n* ▷ **tyrant**
tyre *n* (*pl* **-s**) rubber ring, usu. inflated, over the
  rim of a vehicle's wheel to grip the road
  tyres *n* ▷ **tyre**
tyro *n* (*pl* **-ros**) novice or beginner
  tyros *n* ▷ **tyro**

> **tzaddiq** *n* (**tzaddiqim, tzaddiqs**). A
> tzaddiq is a Hasidic Jewish leader.
> This is a fantastic word if you can get
> the necessary tiles. If someone has
> played add, you might be able to form
> it around that; if you can form the
> whole word using all your tiles you'll
> earn a 50-point bonus. Tzaddiq scores
> 27 points.

Uu

U can be a difficult tile to use effectively. Although there are quite a few two-letter words beginning with U, most of them are quite unusual, and so difficult to remember. Only **up** (4 points) and **us** (2) are immediately obvious, so it's well worth learning words like **ug** (3), **uh** (5), **um** (4), and **un**, **ur** and **ut** (2 each). Three-letter words beginning with U can also be difficult to remember. If you are trying to use a Q, X or Z, bear in mind that there aren't any valid three-letter words with these letters that start with U. Knowing this can save you valuable time. It's also helpful to remember that there aren't any particularly high-scoring two- or three-letter words starting with U.

ubiquities *n* ▷ **ubiquitous**

ubiquitous [yew-**bik**-wit-uss] *adj* being or seeming to be everywhere at once > **ubiquity** *n* (*pl* **-ties**)

ubiquity *n* ▷ **ubiquitous**

udder *n* (*pl* **-s**) large baglike milk-producing gland of cows, sheep, or goats

udders *n* ▷ **udder**

ug *v* (**ugs, ugging, ugged**). Ug is an old word meaning to loathe. The different verb forms of this word can be useful, and remember that if someone plays ug or its inflections, you can put B, L, M or T in front of it to form another valid word. Ug scores 3 points.

ugh *interj*. Ugh is a sound that people make when they dislike something or are disgusted by it. Together with uke, this is the highest-scoring three-letter word starting with U. Ugh scores 7 points.

uglier *adj* ▷ **ugly**

ugliest *adj* ▷ **ugly**

ugliness *n* ▷ **ugly**

uglinesses *n* ▷ **ugly**

ugly *adj* (**-lier, -liest**) of unpleasant appearance > **ugliness** *n* (*pl* **-es**)

uh *interj*. Uh is a sound that people make when they are unsure about something. This useful little word can help when you are trying to form words in more than one direction. Uh scores 5 points.

uke *n* (**ukes**). Uke is a short form of ukulele. Together with ugh, this is the highest-scoring three-letter word

starting with U. Uke scores 7 points.

ukelele *n* ▷ **ukulele**

ukeleles *n* ▷ **ukulele**

ukulele, ukelele [yew-kal-**lay**-lee] *n* (*pl* **-s**) small guitar with four strings

ukuleles *n* ▷ **ukulele**

ulcer *n* (*pl* **-s**) open sore on the surface of the skin or mucous membrane. > **ulceration** *n* (*pl* **-s**)

ulcerated *adj* made or becoming ulcerous

ulceration *n* ▷ **ulcer**

ulcerations *n* ▷ **ulcer**

ulcerous *adj* of, like, or characterized by ulcers

ulcers *n* ▷ **ulcer**

ulna *n* (*pl* **-nae, -nas**) inner and longer of the two bones of the human forearm

ulnae *n* ▷ **ulna**

ulnas *n* ▷ **ulna**

ulterior *adj* (of an aim, reason, etc.) concealed or hidden

ultimate *adj* final in a series or process > **ultimately** *adv*

ultimately *adv* ▷ **ultimate**

ultimatum [ult-im-**may**-tum] *n* (*pl* **-s**) final warning stating that action will be taken unless certain conditions are met

ultimatums *n* ▷ **ultimatum**

ultramarine *adj* vivid blue

ultrasonic *adj* of or producing sound waves with a higher frequency than the human ear can hear

ultraviolet *adj, n* (*pl* **-s**) (of) light beyond the limit of visibility at the violet end of the spectrum

ultraviolets *n* ▷ **ultraviolet**

ululate [**yewl**-yew-late] *v* (**-tes, -ting, -ted**) howl

or wail > **ululation** n (pl -**s**)
ululated v ▷ **ululate**
ululates v ▷ **ululate**
ululating v ▷ **ululate**
ululation n ▷ **ululate**
ululations n ▷ **ululate**

um interj. Um is a sound people make when hesitating in speech. If someone plays this word, remember that lots of words end in UM (dictum, podium and rostrum, for example) and look out for chances to play them. Um scores 4 points.

umber adj dark brown to reddish-brown
umbilical adj of the navel
umbrella n (pl -**s**) portable device used for protection against rain, consisting of a folding frame covered in material attached to a central rod
umbrellas n ▷ **umbrella**
umpire n (pl -**s**) official who rules on the playing of a game ▶ v (-**res, -ring, -red**) act as umpire in (a game)
umpired v ▷ **umpire**
umpires n, v ▷ **umpire**
umpiring v ▷ **umpire**
umpteen adj (Informal) very many > **umpteenth** n (pl -**s**) adj
umpteenth n, adj ▷ **umpteen**
umpteenths n ▷ **umpteen**

un pron. Un is a dialect word for one. If someone plays this, remember that you can form lots of words by placing letters after UN. Un scores 2 points.

unable adj lacking the necessary power, ability, or authority to (do something)
unaccountable adj unable to be explained > **unaccountably** adv
unaccountably adv ▷ **unaccountable**
unadulterated adj with nothing added, pure
unanimities n ▷ **unanimous**
unanimity n ▷ **unanimous**
unanimous [yew-**nan**-im-uss] adj in complete agreement > **unanimity** n (pl -**ties**)
unarmed adj without weapons
unassuming adj modest or unpretentious
unaware adj not aware or conscious
unawares adv by surprise
unbalanced adj biased or one-sided
unbearable adj not able to be endured > **unbearably** adv
unbearably adv ▷ **unbearable**
unbeknown adv without the knowledge of (a person)
unbend v (-**s, -ing, unbent**) (Informal) become

less strict or more informal in one's attitudes or behaviour > **unbending** adj
unbending v, adj ▷ **unbend**
unbends v ▷ **unbend**
unbent v ▷ **unbend**
unbidden adj not ordered or asked
unborn adj not yet born
unbosom v (-**s, -ing, -ed**) relieve (oneself) of (secrets or feelings) by telling someone
unbosomed v ▷ **unbosom**
unbosoming v ▷ **unbosom**
unbosoms v ▷ **unbosom**
unbridled adj (of feelings or behaviour) not controlled in any way
unburden v (-**s, -ing, -ed**) relieve (one's mind or oneself) of a worry by confiding in someone
unburdened v ▷ **unburden**
unburdening v ▷ **unburden**
unburdens v ▷ **unburden**
uncannier adj ▷ **uncanny**
uncanniest adj ▷ **uncanny**
uncannily adv ▷ **uncanny**
uncanny adj (-**nnier, -nniest**) weird or mysterious > **uncannily** adv
unceremonious adj relaxed and informal > **unceremoniously** adv
unceremoniously adv ▷ **unceremonious**
uncertain adj not able to be accurately known or predicted > **uncertainty** n (pl -**ties**)
uncertainties n ▷ **uncertain**
uncertainty n ▷ **uncertain**
uncle n (pl -**s**) brother of one's father or mother
unclean adj lacking moral, spiritual, or physical cleanliness
uncles n ▷ **uncle**
uncomfortable adj not physically relaxed
uncommon adj (-**er, -est**) not happening or encountered often > **uncommonly** adv
uncommoner adj ▷ **uncommon**
uncommonest adj ▷ **uncommon**
uncommonly adv ▷ **uncommon**
uncompromising adj not prepared to compromise
unconcerned adj lacking in concern or involvement > **unconcernedly** adv
unconcernedly adv ▷ **unconcerned**
unconditional adj without conditions or limitations
unconscionable adj having no principles, unscrupulous
unconscious adj lacking normal awareness through the senses ▶ n (pl -**es**) part of the mind containing instincts and ideas that exist without one's awareness > **unconsciously** adv > **unconsciousness** n

(pl -**es**)

unconsciouses n ▷ **unconscious**

unconsciously adv ▷ **unconscious**

unconsciousness n ▷ **unconscious**

unconsciousnesses n ▷ **unconscious**

uncooperative adj not willing to help other people with what they are doing

uncouth adj (-**er**, -**est**) lacking in good manners, refinement, or grace

uncouther adj ▷ **uncouth**

uncouthest adj ▷ **uncouth**

uncover v (-**s**, -**ing**, -**ed**) reveal or disclose

uncovered v ▷ **uncover**

uncovering v ▷ **uncover**

uncovers v ▷ **uncover**

unction n (pl -**s**) act of anointing with oil in sacramental ceremonies

unctions n ▷ **unction**

unctuous adj pretending to be kind and concerned

undecided adj not having made up one's mind

undeniable adj unquestionably true
> **undeniably** adv

undeniably adv ▷ **undeniable**

under prep, adv indicating movement to or position beneath the underside or base ▶ prep less than

underage adj below the required or standard age

underarm adj (SPORT) denoting a style of throwing, bowling, or serving in which the hand is swung below shoulder level ▶ adv (SPORT) in an underarm style

undercarriage n (pl -**s**) landing gear of an aircraft

undercarriages n ▷ **undercarriage**

underclass n (pl -**es**) class consisting of the most disadvantaged people, such as the long-term unemployed

underclasses n ▷ **underclass**

undercoat n (pl -**s**) coat of paint applied before the final coat

undercoats n ▷ **undercoat**

undercover adj done or acting in secret

undercurrent n (pl -**s**) current that is not apparent at the surface

undercurrents n ▷ **undercurrent**

undercut v (-**cuts**, -**cutting**, -**cut**) charge less than (a competitor) to obtain trade

undercuts v ▷ **undercut**

undercutting v ▷ **undercut**

underdog n (pl -**s**) person or team in a weak or underprivileged position

underdogs n ▷ **underdog**

underdone adj not cooked enough

underestimate v (-**tes**, -**ting**, -**ted**) make too low an estimate of

underestimated v ▷ **underestimate**

underestimates v ▷ **underestimate**

underestimating v ▷ **underestimate**

underfoot adv under the feet

undergarment n (pl -**s**) any piece of underwear

undergarments n ▷ **undergarment**

undergo v (-**goes**, -**going**, -**went**, -**gone**) experience, endure, or sustain

undergoes v ▷ **undergo**

undergoing v ▷ **undergo**

undergone v ▷ **undergo**

undergraduate n (pl -**s**) person studying in a university for a first degree

undergraduates n ▷ **undergraduate**

underground adj occurring, situated, used, or going below ground level ▶ n (pl -**s**) electric passenger railway operated in underground tunnels

undergrounds n ▷ **underground**

undergrowth n (pl -**s**) small trees and bushes growing beneath taller trees in a wood or forest

undergrowths n ▷ **undergrowth**

underhand adj sly, deceitful, and secretive

underlain v ▷ **underlie**

underlay v ▷ **underlie**

underlie v (-**lies**, -**lying**, -**lay**, **underlain**) lie or be placed under > **underlying** adj fundamental or basic

underlies v ▷ **underlie**

underline v (-**s**, -**ning**, -**d**) draw a line under

underlined v ▷ **underline**

underlines v ▷ **underline**

underling n (pl -**s**) subordinate

underlings n ▷ **underling**

underlining v ▷ **underline**

underlying v, adj ▷ **underlie**

undermine v (-**nes**, -**ning**, -**ned**) weaken gradually

undermined v ▷ **undermine**

undermines v ▷ **undermine**

undermining v ▷ **undermine**

underneath prep, adv under or beneath ▶ adj, n (pl -**s**) lower (part or surface)

underneaths n ▷ **underneath**

underpants pl n man's undergarment for the lower part of the body

underpass n (pl -**es**) section of a road that passes under another road or a railway line

underpasses n ▷ **underpass**

underpin v (-**pins**, -**pinning**, -**pinned**) give strength or support to

underpinned v ▷ **underpin**
underpinning v ▷ **underpin**
underpins v ▷ **underpin**
underprivileged *adj* lacking the rights and advantages of other members of society
underrate v (**-tes, -ting, -ted**) not realize the full potential of > **underrated** *adj*
underrated v, *adj* ▷ **underrate**
underrates v ▷ **underrate**
underrating v ▷ **underrate**
underseal n (*pl* **-s**) (CHIEFLY BRIT) coating of tar etc. applied to the underside of a motor vehicle to prevent corrosion
underseals n ▷ **underseal**
underside n (*pl* **-s**) bottom or lower surface
undersides n ▷ **underside**
understand v (**-s, -ing, -stood**) know and comprehend the nature or meaning of > **understandable** *adj* > **understandably** *adv*
understandable *adj* ▷ **understand**
understandably *adj* ▷ **understand**
understanding n (*pl* **-s**) ability to learn, judge, or make decisions ▶ *adj* kind and sympathetic ▶ v ▷ **understand**
understandings n ▷ **understanding**
understands v ▷ **understand**
understate v (**-tes, -ting, -ted**) describe or represent (something) in restrained terms > **understatement** n (*pl* **-s**)
understated v ▷ **understate**
understatement n ▷ **understate**
understatements n ▷ **understate**
understates v ▷ **understate**
understating v ▷ **understate**
understood v ▷ **understand**
understudied v ▷ **understudy**
understudies n, v ▷ **understudy**
understudy n (*pl* **-dies**) actor who studies a part in order to be able to replace the usual actor if necessary ▶ v (**-dies, -dying, -died**) act as an understudy for
understudying v ▷ **understudy**
undertake v (**-takes, -taking, -took, -taken**) agree or commit oneself to (something) or to do (something)
undertaken v ▷ **undertake**
undertaker n (*pl* **-s**) person whose job is to prepare corpses for burial or cremation and organize funerals
undertakers n ▷ **undertaker**
undertakes v ▷ **undertake**
undertaking n (*pl* **-s**) task or enterprise ▶ v ▷ **undertake**
undertakings n ▷ **undertaking**
undertone n (*pl* **-s**) quiet tone of voice

undertones n ▷ **undertone**
undertook v ▷ **undertake**
undertow n (*pl* **-s**) strong undercurrent flowing in a different direction from the surface current
undertows n ▷ **undertow**
underwear n (*pl* **-s**) clothing worn under the outer garments and next to the skin
underwears n ▷ **underwear**
underwent v ▷ **undergo**
underworld n (*pl* **-s**) criminals and their associates
underworlds n ▷ **underworld**
underwrite v (**-writes, -writing, -wrote, -written**) accept financial responsibility for (a commercial project)
underwriter n (*pl* **-s**) person who underwrites (esp. an insurance policy)
underwriters n ▷ **underwriter**
underwrites v ▷ **underwrite**
underwriting v ▷ **underwrite**
underwritten v ▷ **underwrite**
underwrote v ▷ **underwrite**
undesirable *adj* not desirable or pleasant, objectionable ▶ n (*pl* **-s**) objectionable person
undesirables n ▷ **undesirable**
undid v ▷ **undo**
undo v (**-does, -doing, -did, -done**) open, unwrap > **undone** *adj*
undoes v ▷ **undo**
undoing n (*pl* **-s**) cause of someone's downfall ▶ v ▷ **undo**
undoings n ▷ **undoing**
undone v, *adj* ▷ **undo**
undoubted *adj* certain or indisputable > **undoubtedly** *adv*
undoubtedly *adv* ▷ **undoubted**
undue *adj* greater than is reasonable, excessive > **unduly** *adv*
undulate v (**-tes, -ting, -ted**) move in waves > **undulation** n (*pl* **-s**)
undulated v ▷ **undulate**
undulates v ▷ **undulate**
undulating v ▷ **undulate**
undulation n ▷ **undulate**
undulations n ▷ **undulate**
unduly *adv* ▷ **undue**
undying *adj* never ending, eternal
unearth v (**-s, -ing, -ed**) reveal or discover by searching
unearthed v ▷ **unearth**
unearthing v ▷ **unearth**
unearthly *adj* ghostly or eerie
unearths v ▷ **unearth**
unease n (*pl* **-s**) feeling of anxiety

uneases n ▷ unease
uneasier adj ▷ uneasy
uneasiest adj ▷ uneasy
uneasily adv ▷ uneasy
uneasiness n ▷ uneasy
uneasinesses n ▷ uneasy
uneasy adj (-sier, -siest) (of a person) anxious
or apprehensive > **uneasily** adv > **uneasiness**
n (pl -es)
unemployed adj out of work
> **unemployment** n (pl -s)
unemployment n ▷ unemployed
unemployments n ▷ unemployed
unequivocal adj completely clear in meaning
> **unequivocally** adv
unequivocally adv ▷ unequivocal
unerring adj never mistaken, consistently
accurate
unexceptionable adj beyond criticism or
objection
unfailing adj continuous or reliable
> **unfailingly** adv
unfailingly adv ▷ unfailing
unfair adj (-er, -est) not right, fair, or just
> **unfairly** adv > **unfairness** n (pl -es)
unfairer adj ▷ unfair
unfairest adj ▷ unfair
unfairly adv ▷ unfair
unfairness n ▷ unfair
unfairnesses n ▷ unfair
unfaithful adj having sex with someone other
than one's regular partner > **unfaithfulness**
n (pl -es)
unfaithfulness n ▷ unfaithful
unfaithfulnesses n ▷ unfaithful
unfeeling adj without sympathy
unfit adj unqualified or unsuitable
unflappabilities n ▷ unflappable
unflappability n ▷ unflappable
unflappable adj (Informal) not easily upset
> **unflappability** n (pl -ties)
unfold v (-s, -ing, -ed) open or spread out from
a folded state
unfolded v ▷ unfold
unfolding v ▷ unfold
unfolds v ▷ unfold
unforgettable adj impossible to forget,
memorable
unfortunate adj unlucky, unsuccessful, or
unhappy > **unfortunately** adv
unfortunately adv ▷ unfortunate
unfrock v (-s, -ing, -ed) deprive (a priest in holy
orders) of his or her priesthood
unfrocked v ▷ unfrock
unfrocking v ▷ unfrock

unfrocks v ▷ unfrock
ungainlier adj ▷ ungainly
ungainliest adj ▷ ungainly
ungainly adj (-lier, -liest) lacking grace when
moving
ungodlier adj ▷ ungodly
ungodliest adj ▷ ungodly
ungodly adj (-lier, -liest) (Informal)
unreasonable or outrageous
ungrateful adj not grateful or thankful
unguarded adj not protected
unguent [ung-gwent] n (pl -s) (Lit) ointment
unguents n ▷ unguent
unhand v (-s, -ing, -ed) (Old-fashioned or lit)
release from one's grasp
unhanded v ▷ unhand
unhanding v ▷ unhand
unhands v ▷ unhand
unhappier adj ▷ unhappy
unhappiest adj ▷ unhappy
unhappily adv ▷ unhappy
unhappiness n ▷ unhappy
unhappinesses n ▷ unhappy
unhappy adj (-ppier, -ppiest) sad or depressed
> **unhappily** adv > **unhappiness** n (pl -es)
unhealthier adj ▷ unhealthy
unhealthiest adj ▷ unhealthy
unhealthy adj (-thier, -thiest) likely to cause
poor health
unhinge v (-ges, -ging, -ged) derange or
unbalance (a person or his or her mind)
unhinged v ▷ unhinge
unhinges v ▷ unhinge
unhinging v ▷ unhinge
unicorn n (pl -s) imaginary horselike creature
with one horn growing from its forehead
unicorns n ▷ unicorn
unification n ▷ unify
unifications n ▷ unify
unified v ▷ unify
unifies v ▷ unify
uniform n (pl -s) special identifying set of
clothes for the members of an organization,
such as soldiers ▶ adj regular and even
throughout, unvarying > **uniformly** adv
> **uniformity** n (pl -ties)
uniformities n ▷ uniform
uniformity n ▷ uniform
uniformly adv ▷ uniform
uniforms n ▷ uniform
unify v (-fies, -fying, -fied) make or become
one > **unification** n (pl -s)
unifying v ▷ unify
unilateral adj made or done by only one
person or group > **unilaterally** adv

unilaterally *adv* ▷ **unilateral**

unimpeachable *adj* completely honest and reliable

uninterested *adj* having or showing no interest in someone or something

union *n* (*pl* -s) uniting or being united

unionist *n* (*pl* -s) member or supporter of a trade union

  unionists *n* ▷ **unionist**

  unionization *n* ▷ **unionize**

  unionizations *n* ▷ **unionize**

unionize *v* (-zes, -zing, -zed) organize (workers) into a trade union > **unionization** *n* (*pl* -s)

  unionized *v* ▷ **unionize**

  unionizes *v* ▷ **unionize**

  unionizing *v* ▷ **unionize**

  unions *n* ▷ **union**

unique [yoo-neek] *adj* being the only one of a particular type > **uniquely** *adv*

  uniquely *adv* ▷ **unique**

unisex *adj* designed for use by both sexes

unison *n* (*pl* -s) complete agreement

  unisons *n* ▷ **unison**

unit *n* (*pl* -s) single undivided entity or whole

unitary *adj* consisting of a single undivided whole

unite *v* (-tes, -ting, -ted) make or become an integrated whole

  united *v* ▷ **unite**

  unites *v* ▷ **unite**

  unities *n* ▷ **unity**

  uniting *v* ▷ **unite**

  units *n* ▷ **unit**

unity *n* (*pl* -ties) state of being one

universal *adj* of or typical of the whole of mankind or of nature > **universally** *adv* > **universality** *n* (*pl* -ties)

  universalities *n* ▷ **universal**

  universality *n* ▷ **universal**

  universally *adv* ▷ **universal**

universe *n* (*pl* -s) whole of all existing matter, energy, and space

  universes *n* ▷ **universe**

  universities *n* ▷ **university**

university *n* (*pl* -ties) institution of higher education with the authority to award degrees

unkempt *adj* (of the hair) not combed

unknown *adj* not known ▶ *n* (*pl* -s) unknown person, quantity, or thing

  unknowns *n* ▷ **unknown**

unleaded *adj* (of petrol) containing less tetraethyl lead, in order to reduce environmental pollution

unless *conj* except under the circumstances that

unlike *adj* dissimilar or different ▶ *prep* not like or typical of

unlikely *adj* improbable

unload *v* (-s, -ing, -ed) remove (cargo) from (a ship, truck, or plane)

  unloaded *v* ▷ **unload**

  unloading *v* ▷ **unload**

  unloads *v* ▷ **unload**

unmask *v* (-s, -ing, -ed) remove the mask or disguise from

  unmasked *v* ▷ **unmask**

  unmasking *v* ▷ **unmask**

  unmasks *v* ▷ **unmask**

unmentionable *adj* unsuitable as a topic of conversation

unmistakable, unmistakeable *adj* not ambiguous, clear > **unmistakably, unmistakeably** *adv*

  unmistakably *adv* ▷ **unmistakable**

  unmistakeable *adj* ▷ **unmistakable**

  unmistakeably *adv* ▷ **unmistakable**

unmitigated *adj* not reduced or lessened in severity etc.

unmoved *adj* not affected by emotion, indifferent

unnatural *adj* strange and frightening because not usual

unnerve *v* (-ves, -ving, -ved) cause to lose courage, confidence, or self-control

  unnerved *v* ▷ **unnerve**

  unnerves *v* ▷ **unnerve**

  unnerving *v* ▷ **unnerve**

unnumbered *adj* countless

unorthodox *adj* (of ideas, methods, etc.) unconventional and not generally accepted

unpack *v* (-s, -ing, -ed) remove the contents of (a suitcase, trunk, etc.)

  unpacked *v* ▷ **unpack**

  unpacking *v* ▷ **unpack**

  unpacks *v* ▷ **unpack**

unparalleled *adj* not equalled, supreme

unpick *v* (-s, -ing, -ed) undo (the stitches) of (a piece of sewing)

  unpicked *v* ▷ **unpick**

  unpicking *v* ▷ **unpick**

  unpicks *v* ▷ **unpick**

unpleasant *adj* not pleasant or agreeable > **unpleasantly** *adv* > **unpleasantness** *n* (*pl* -s)

  unpleasantly *adv* ▷ **unpleasant**

  unpleasantness *n* ▷ **unpleasant**

  unpleasantnesses *n* ▷ **unpleasant**

unprintable *adj* unsuitable for printing for reasons of obscenity or libel

unprofessional *adj* contrary to the accepted code of a profession > **unprofessionally** *adv*
  unprofessionally *adv* ▷ **unprofessional**
unqualified *adj* lacking the necessary qualifications
unravel *v* (**-vels, -velling, -velled**) reduce (something knitted or woven) to separate strands
  unravelled *v* ▷ **unravel**
  unravelling *v* ▷ **unravel**
  unravels *v* ▷ **unravel**
unremitting *adj* never slackening or stopping
unrequited *adj* not returned
unrest *n* (*pl* **-s**) rebellious state of discontent
  unrests *n* ▷ **unrest**
unrivalled *adj* having no equal
unroll *v* (**-s, -ing, -ed**) open out or unwind (something rolled or coiled) or (of something rolled or coiled) become opened out or unwound
  unrolled *v* ▷ **unroll**
  unrolling *v* ▷ **unroll**
  unrolls *v* ▷ **unroll**
  unrulier *adj* ▷ **unruly**
  unruliest *adj* ▷ **unruly**
unruly *adj* (**-lier, -liest**) difficult to control or organize
unsavoury *adj* distasteful or objectionable
unscathed *adj* not harmed or injured
unscrupulous *adj* prepared to act dishonestly, unprincipled
unseat *v* (**-s, -ing, -ed**) throw or displace from a seat or saddle
  unseated *v* ▷ **unseat**
  unseating *v* ▷ **unseat**
  unseats *v* ▷ **unseat**
unsettled *adj* lacking order or stability
  unsightlier *adj* ▷ **unsightly**
  unsightliest *adj* ▷ **unsightly**
unsightly *adj* (**-lier, -liest**) unpleasant to look at
  unsociable *adj* ▷ **unsocial**
unsocial *adj* (*also* **unsociable**) avoiding the company of other people
unsound *adj* unhealthy or unstable
unstable *adj* (**-r, -st**) lacking stability or firmness
  unstabler *adj* ▷ **unstable**
  unstablest *adj* ▷ **unstable**
unsuitable *adj* not right or appropriate for a particular purpose > **unsuitably** *adv*
  unsuitably *adv* ▷ **unsuitable**
unsuited *adj* not appropriate for a particular task or situation
unswerving *adj* firm, constant, not changing

unthinkable *adj* out of the question, inconceivable
  untidier *adj* ▷ **untidy**
  untidiest *adj* ▷ **untidy**
  untidily *adv* ▷ **untidy**
  untidiness *n* ▷ **untidy**
  untidinesses *n* ▷ **untidy**
untidy *adj* (**-dier, -diest**) messy and disordered > **untidily** *adv* > **untidiness** *n* (*pl* **-es**)
untie *v* (**-ties, -tying, -tied**) open or free (something that is tied)
  untied *v* ▷ **untie**
  unties *v* ▷ **untie**
until *conj* up to the time that ▶ *prep* in or throughout the period before
  untimelier *adj* ▷ **untimely**
  untimeliest *adj* ▷ **untimely**
untimely *adj* (**-lier, -liest**) occurring before the expected or normal time
unto *prep* (*Old-fashioned*) to
untold *adj* incapable of description
untouchable *adj* above reproach or suspicion ▶ *n* (*pl* **-s**) member of the lowest Hindu caste in India
  untouchables *n* ▷ **untouchable**
untoward *adj* causing misfortune or annoyance
untrue *adj* (**-r, -st**) incorrect or false
  untruer *adj* ▷ **untrue**
  untruest *adj* ▷ **untrue**
untruth *n* (*pl* **-s**) statement that is not true, lie
  untruths *n* ▷ **untruth**
  untying *v* ▷ **untie**
unusual *adj* uncommon or extraordinary > **unusually** *adv*
  unusually *adv* ▷ **unusual**
unutterable *adj* incapable of being expressed in words > **unutterably** *adv*
  unutterably *adv* ▷ **unutterable**
unvarnished *adj* not elaborated upon
  unwieldier *adj* ▷ **unwieldy**
  unwieldiest *adj* ▷ **unwieldy**
unwieldy *adj* (**-dier, -diest**) too heavy, large, or awkward to be easily handled
unwind *v* (**-s, -ing, unwound**) relax after a busy or tense time
  unwinding *v* ▷ **unwind**
  unwinds *v* ▷ **unwind**
unwitting *adj* not intentional > **unwittingly** *adv*
  unwittingly *adv* ▷ **unwitting**
unwonted *adj* out of the ordinary
  unworthier *adj* ▷ **unworthy**
  unworthiest *adj* ▷ **unworthy**
unworthy *adj* (**-thier, -thiest**) not deserving

or worthy
unwound v ▷ **unwind**
unwrap v (**-s, -pping, -pped**) remove the wrapping from (something)
unwrapped v ▷ **unwrap**
unwrapping v ▷ **unwrap**
unwraps v ▷ **unwrap**
unwritten adj not printed or in writing
up prep, adv indicating movement to or position at a higher place ▶ adv indicating readiness, intensity or completeness, etc. ▶ adj of a high or higher position ▶ v (**-s, -pping, -pped**) increase or raise ▶ adv (also **upwards**) from a lower to a higher place, level, or condition
upbeat adj (Informal) cheerful and optimistic ▶ n (pl -s) (MUSIC) unaccented beat
upbeats n ▷ **upbeat**
upbraid v (**-s, -ing, -ded**) scold or reproach
upbraided v ▷ **upbraid**
upbraiding v ▷ **upbraid**
upbraids v ▷ **upbraid**
upbringing n (pl -s) education of a person during the formative years
upbringings n ▷ **upbringing**
update v (**-tes, -ting, -ted**) bring up to date
updated v ▷ **update**
updates v ▷ **update**
updating v ▷ **update**
upend v (**-s, -ing, -ed**) turn or set (something) on its end
upended v ▷ **upend**
upending v ▷ **upend**
upends v ▷ **upend**
upfront adj open and frank ▶ adv, adj (of money) paid out at the beginning of a business arrangement
upgrade v (**-des, -ding, -ded**) promote (a person or job) to a higher rank
upgraded v ▷ **upgrade**
upgrades v ▷ **upgrade**
upgrading v ▷ **upgrade**
upheaval n (pl -s) strong, sudden, or violent disturbance
upheavals n ▷ **upheaval**
upheld v ▷ **uphold**
uphill adj sloping or leading upwards ▶ adv up a slope ▶ n (pl -s) (S AFR) difficulty
uphills n ▷ **uphill**
uphold v (**-s, -ing, upheld**) maintain or defend against opposition > **upholder** n (pl -s)
upholder n ▷ **uphold**
upholders n ▷ **uphold**
upholding v ▷ **uphold**
upholds v ▷ **uphold**

upholster v (**-s, -ing, -ed**) fit (a chair or sofa) with padding, springs, and covering > **upholsterer** n (pl -s)
upholstered v ▷ **upholster**
upholsterer n ▷ **upholster**
upholsterers n ▷ **upholster**
upholsteries n ▷ **upholstery**
upholstering v ▷ **upholster**
upholsters v ▷ **upholster**
upholstery n (pl -ries) soft covering on a chair or sofa
upkeep n (pl -s) act, process, or cost of keeping something in good repair
upkeeps n ▷ **upkeep**
upland adj of or in an area of high or relatively high ground > **uplands** pl n area of high or relatively high ground
uplands pl n ▷ **upland**
uplift v (**-s, -ing, -ed**) raise or lift up ▶ n (pl -s) act or process of improving moral, social, or cultural conditions > **uplifting** adj
uplifted v ▷ **uplift**
uplifting v, adj ▷ **uplift**
uplifts v, n ▷ **uplift**
upload v (**-s, -ing, -ed**) transfer (data or a program) from one's own computer into the memory of another computer
uploaded v ▷ **upload**
uploading v ▷ **upload**
uploads v ▷ **upload**
upon prep on
upped v ▷ **up**
upper adj higher or highest in physical position, wealth, rank, or status ▶ n (pl -s) part of a shoe above the sole
uppermost adj highest in position, power, or importance ▶ adv in or into the highest place or position
uppers n ▷ **upper**
upping v ▷ **up**
uppish, uppity adj (BRIT) (Informal) snobbish, arrogant, or presumptuous
uppity adj ▷ **uppish**
upright adj vertical or erect ▶ adv vertically or in an erect position ▶ n (pl -s) vertical support, such as a post > **uprightness** n (pl -s)
uprightness n ▷ **upright**
uprightnesses n ▷ **upright**
uprights n ▷ **upright**
uprising n (pl -s) rebellion or revolt
uprisings n ▷ **uprising**
uproar n (pl -s) disturbance characterized by loud noise and confusion
uproarious adj very funny > **uproariously** adv
uproariously adv ▷ **uproarious**

uproars *n* ▷ uproar
uproot *v* (**-s, -ing, -ed**) pull up by or as if by the roots
　uprooted *v* ▷ uproot
　uprooting *v* ▷ uproot
　uproots *v* ▷ uproot
　ups *v* ▷ up
upset *adj* emotionally or physically disturbed or distressed ▶ *v* (**-s, -tting, upset**) tip over ▶ *n* (*pl* **-s**) unexpected defeat or reversal > **upsetting** *adj*
　upsets *v, n* ▷ upset
　upsetting *v, adj* ▷ upset
upshot *n* (*pl* **-s**) final result or conclusion
　upshots *n* ▷ upshot
upstage *adj* at the back half of the stage ▶ *v* (**-ges, -ging, -ged**) (*Informal*) draw attention to oneself from (someone else)
　upstaged *v* ▷ upstage
　upstages *v* ▷ upstage
　upstaging *v* ▷ upstage
upstairs *adv* to or on an upper floor of a building ▶ *n* upper floor
upstanding *adj* of good character
upstart *n* (*pl* **-s**) person who has risen suddenly to a position of power and behaves arrogantly
　upstarts *n* ▷ upstart
upstream *adv, adj* in or towards the higher part of a stream
upsurge *n* (*pl* **-s**) rapid rise or swell
　upsurges *n* ▷ upsurge
uptake *n* (*pl* **-s**) (*Informal*) quick *or* slow to understand or learn
　uptakes *n* ▷ uptake
uptight *adj* (*Informal*) nervously tense, irritable, or angry
upturn *n* (*pl* **-s**) upward trend or improvement > **upturned** *adj* facing upwards
　upturned *adj* ▷ upturn
　upturns *n* ▷ upturn
upward *adj* directed or moving towards a higher place or level
　upwards *adv* ▷ up

ur *interj*. Ur is a sound people make when hesitating in speech. If someone plays this, you may be able to use it to form words that begin with UR. Ur is also handy for connecting words beginning with U to those ending in R. Ur scores 2 points.

uranium *n* (*pl* **-s**) (CHEM) radioactive silvery-white metallic element, used chiefly as a source of nuclear energy
　uraniums *n* ▷ uranium

urban *adj* of or living in a city or town
urbane *adj* (**-r, -st**) characterized by courtesy, elegance, and sophistication > **urbanity** *n* (*pl* **-ties**)
　urbaner *adj* ▷ urbane
　urbanest *adj* ▷ urbane
　urbanities *n* ▷ urbane
　urbanity *n* ▷ urbane
　urbanization *n* ▷ urbanize
　urbanizations *n* ▷ urbanize
urbanize *v* (**-zes, -zing, -zed**) make (a rural area) more industrialized and urban > **urbanization** *n* (*pl* **-s**)
　urbanized *v* ▷ urbanize
　urbanizes *v* ▷ urbanize
　urbanizing *v* ▷ urbanize
urchin *n* (*pl* **-s**) mischievous child
　urchins *n* ▷ urchin
urethra [yew-reeth-ra] *n* (*pl* **-rae**) canal that carries urine from the bladder out of the body
　urethrae *n* ▷ urethra
urge *n* (*pl* **-s**) strong impulse, inner drive, or yearning ▶ *v* (**-urges, -urging, -urged**) plead with or press (a person to do something)
　urged *v* ▷ urge
　urgencies *n* ▷ urgent
　urgency *n* ▷ urgent
urgent *adj* requiring speedy action or attention > **urgency** *n* (*pl* **-cies**) > **urgently** *adv*
　urgently *adv* ▷ urgent
　urges *n, v* ▷ urge
　urging *v* ▷ urge
urinal *n* (*pl* **-s**) sanitary fitting used by men for urination
　urinals *n* ▷ urine
　urinary *adj* ▷ urine
urinate *v* (**-tes, -ting, -ted**) discharge urine > **urination** *n* (*pl* **-s**)
　urinated *v* ▷ urinate
　urinates *v* ▷ urinate
　urinating *v* ▷ urinate
　urination *n* ▷ urinate
　urinations *n* ▷ urinate
urine *n* (*pl* **-s**) pale yellow fluid excreted by the kidneys to the bladder and passed as waste from the body > **urinary** *adj*
　urines *n* ▷ urine
urn *n* (*pl* **-s**) vase used as a container for the ashes of the dead
　urns *n* ▷ urn
ursine *adj* of or like a bear
us *pron* ▷ we
usable *adj* able to be used
usage *n* (*pl* **-s**) regular or constant use
　usages *n* ▷ usage

use *v* (**-ses, -sing, -sed**) put into service or action ▸ *n* (*pl* **-s**) using or being used > **user** *n* (*pl* **-s**) > **useful** *adj* > **usefully** *adv* > **usefulness** *n* (*pl* **-es**) > **useless** *adj* > **uselessly** *adv* > **uselessness** *n* (*pl* **-es**)

used *adj* second-hand ▸ *v* ▷ **use**

  useful *adj* ▷ **use**

  usefully *adv* ▷ **use**

  usefulness *n* ▷ **use**

  usefulnesses *n* ▷ **use**

  useless *adj* ▷ **use**

  uselessly *adv* ▷ **use**

  uselessness *n* ▷ **use**

  uselessnesses *n* ▷ **use**

  user *n* ▷ **use**

username *n* (*pl* **-s**) (COMPUTERS) name entered into a computer for identification purposes

  usernames *n* ▷ **username**

  users *n* ▷ **use**

  uses *v, n* ▷ **use**

usher *n* (*pl* **-s**) official who shows people to their seats, as in a church ▸ *v* (**-s, -ing, -ed**) conduct or escort

  ushered *v* ▷ **usher**

usherette *n* (*pl* **-s**) female assistant in a cinema who shows people to their seats

  usherettes *n* ▷ **usherette**

  ushering *v* ▷ **usher**

  ushers *n, v* ▷ **usher**

  using *v* ▷ **use**

usual *adj* of the most normal, frequent, or regular type

usually *adv* most often, in most cases

  usurer *n* ▷ **usury**

  usurers *n* ▷ **usury**

  usuries *n* ▷ **usury**

usurp [yewz-**zurp**] *v* (**-s, -ing, -ed**) seize (a position or power) without authority > **usurpation** *n* (*pl* **-s**) > **usurper** *n* (*pl* **-s**)

  usurpation *n* ▷ **usurp**

  usurpations *n* ▷ **usurp**

  usurped *v* ▷ **usurp**

  usurper *n* ▷ **usurp**

  usurpers *n* ▷ **usurp**

  usurping *v* ▷ **usurp**

  usurps *v* ▷ **usurp**

usury *n* (*pl* **-ries**) practice of lending money at an extremely high rate of interest > **usurer** [yewz-yoor-er] ▸ *n* (*pl* **-s**)

  ut *n* (**uts**). Ut is a musical note. This unusual word is useful for connecting words beginning with U to those ending with T. Ut scores 2 points.

ute [yoot] *n* (*pl* **-s**) (AUST & NZ) (*Informal*) utility truck

utensil *n* (*pl* **-s**) tool or container for practical use

  utensils *n* ▷ **utensil**

  uteri *n* ▷ **uterus**

  uterine *adj* ▷ **uterus**

uterus [yew-ter-russ] *n* (*pl* **uteri**) womb > **uterine** *adj*

  utes *n* ▷ **ute**

utilitarian *adj* useful rather than beautiful

utilitarianism *n* (*pl* **-s**) (ETHICS) doctrine that the right action is the one that brings about the greatest good for the greatest number of people

  utilitarianisms *n* ▷ **utilitarianism**

  utilities *n* ▷ **utility**

utility *n* (*pl* **-ties**) usefulness ▸ *adj* designed for use rather than beauty

  utilization *n* ▷ **utilize**

  utilizations *n* ▷ **utilize**

utilize *v* (**-zes, -zing, -zed**) make practical use of > **utilization** *n* (*pl* **-s**)

  utilized *v* ▷ **utilize**

  utilizes *v* ▷ **utilize**

  utilizing *v* ▷ **utilize**

utmost, uttermost *adj, n* (*pl* **-s**) (of) the greatest possible degree or amount

  utmosts *n* ▷ **utmost**

utopia [yew-tope-ee-a] *n* (*pl* **-s**) any real or imaginary society, place, or state considered to be perfect or ideal > **utopian** *adj*

  utopian *adj* ▷ **utopia**

  utopias *n* ▷ **utopia**

utter¹ *v* (**-s, -ing, -ed**) express (something) in sounds or words

utter² *adj* total or absolute > **utterly** *adv*

utterance *n* (*pl* **-s**) something uttered

  utterances *n* ▷ **utterance**

  uttered *v* ▷ **utter¹**

  uttering *v* ▷ **utter¹**

  utterly *adv* ▷ **utter²**

  uttermost *adj, n* (*pl* **-s**) ▷ **utmost**

  uttermosts *n* ▷ **uttermost**

  utters *v* ▷ **utter¹**

uvula [yew-view-la] *n* (*pl* **-s**) small fleshy part of the soft palate that hangs in the back of the throat > **uvular** *adj*

  uvular *adj* ▷ **uvula**

  uvulas *n* ▷ **uvula**

uxorious [ux-or-ee-uss] *adj* excessively fond of or dependent on one's wife

Vv

If you have a V on your rack, the first thing to remember is that there are no valid two-letter words beginning with V. In fact, there are no two-letter words that end in V either, so you can't form any two-letter words using V. Remembering this will stop you wasting time trying to think of some. While V is useless for two-letter words, it does start some good three-letter words. **Vex** and **vox** (13 points each) are the best of these, while **vaw, vow** and **vly** (9 each) are also useful.

vac *n* (**vacs**). Vac is a short form of vacuum cleaner. This word can prove useful when you have a V but not much space to play it in. Remember that if you have the letters for vac, you might be able to form **cave** using an E that is already on the board. Vac scores 8 points.

vacancies *n* ▷ **vacancy**

vacancy *n* (*pl* -**cies**) unfilled job

vacant *adj* (of a toilet, room, etc.) unoccupied > **vacantly** *adv*

vacantly *adv* ▷ **vacant**

vacate *v* (-**tes, -ting, -ted**) cause (something) to be empty by leaving

vacated *v* ▷ **vacate**

vacates *v* ▷ **vacate**

vacating *v* ▷ **vacate**

vacation *n* time when universities and law courts are closed

vacations *n* ▷ **vacation**

vaccinate *v* (-**tes, -ting, -ted**) inject with a vaccine > **vaccination** *n* (*pl* -**s**)

vaccinated *v* ▷ **vaccinate**

vaccinates *v* ▷ **vaccinate**

vaccinating *v* ▷ **vaccinate**

vaccination *n* ▷ **vaccinate**

vaccinations *n* ▷ **vaccinate**

vaccine *n* (*pl* -**s**) substance designed to cause a mild form of a disease to make a person immune to the disease itself

vaccines *n* ▷ **vaccine**

vacillate [vass-ill-late] *v* (-**tes, -ting, -ted**) keep changing one's mind or opinions > **vacillation** *n* (*pl* -**s**)

vacillated *v* ▷ **vacillate**

vacillates *v* ▷ **vacillate**

vacillating *v* ▷ **vacillate**

vacillation *n* ▷ **vacillate**

vacillations *n* ▷ **vacillate**

vacua *n* ▷ **vacuum**

vacuous *adj* not expressing intelligent thought > **vacuity** *n* (*pl* -**ties**)

vacuum *n* (*pl* -**cuums, -cua**) empty space from which all or most air or gas has been removed ▶ *v* (-**s, -ing, -ed**) clean with a vacuum cleaner

vacuumed *v* ▷ **vacuum**

vacuuming *v* ▷ **vacuum**

vacuums *n* ▷ **vacuum**

vagabond *n* (*pl* -**s**) person with no fixed home, esp. a beggar

vagabonds *n* ▷ **vagabond**

vagaries *n* ▷ **vagary**

vagary [vaig-a-ree] *n* (*pl* -**ries**) unpredictable change

vagina [vaj-**jine**-a] *n* (*pl* -**s**) (in female mammals) passage from the womb to the external genitals > **vaginal** *adj*

vaginal *adj* ▷ **vagina**

vaginas *n* ▷ **vagina**

vagrancies *n* ▷ **vagrancy**

vagrancy *n* ▷ **vagrant**

vagrant [**vaig**-rant] *n* (*pl* -**s**) person with no settled home ▶ *adj* wandering > **vagrancy** *n* (*pl* -**cies**)

vagrants *n* ▷ **vagrant**

vague *adj* (-**guer, -guest**) not clearly explained > **vaguely** *adv*

vaguely *adv* ▷ **vague**

vaguer *adj* ▷ **vague**

vaguest *adj* ▷ **vague**

vain *adj* (-**er, -est**) excessively proud, esp. of one's appearance

vainer *adj* ▷ **vain**

vainest *adj* ▷ **vain**

vainglorious *adj* (*Lit*) boastful

valance [val-lenss] *n* (*pl* **-s**) piece of drapery round the edge of a bed
valances *n* ▷ **valance**
vale *n* (*pl* **-s**) (*Lit*) valley
valediction *n* (*pl* **-s**) farewell speech
valedictions *n* ▷ **valediction**
valedictory [val-lid-**dik**-tree] *adj* (of a speech, performance, etc.) intended as a farewell
valence [vale-ence] *n* (*pl* **-s**) molecular bonding between atoms
valences *n* ▷ **valence**
valencies *n* ▷ **valency**
valency *n* (*pl* **-cies**) power of an atom to make molecular bonds
valentine *n* (*pl* **-s**) (person to whom one sends) a romantic card on Saint Valentine's Day, 14th February
valentines *n* ▷ **valentine**
valerian *n* (*pl* **-s**) herb used as a sedative
valerians *n* ▷ **valerian**
vales *n* ▷ **vale**
valet *n* (*pl* **-s**) man's personal male servant
valets *n* ▷ **valet**
valetudinarian [val-lit-yew-din-**air**-ee-an] *n* (*pl* **-s**) person with a long-term illness
valetudinarians *n* ▷ **valetudinarian**
valiant *adj* brave or courageous
valid *adj* (**-er, -est**) soundly reasoned > **validity** *n* (*pl* **-ies**)
validate *v* (**-tes, -ting, -ted**) make valid > **validation** *n* (*pl* **-s**)
validated *v* ▷ **validate**
validates *v* ▷ **validate**
validating *v* ▷ **validate**
validation *n* ▷ **validate**
validations *n* ▷ **validate**
valider *adj* ▷ **valid**
validest *adj* ▷ **valid**
validities *n* ▷ **valid**
validity *n* ▷ **valid**
valise [val-**leez**] *n* (*pl* **-s**) (*Old-fashioned*) small suitcase
valises *n* ▷ **valise**
valley *n* (*pl* **-s**) low area between hills, often with a river running through it
valleys *n* ▷ **valley**
valour *n* (*pl* **-s**) (*Lit*) bravery
valours *n* ▷ **valour**
valuable *adj* having great worth
valuables *pl n* valuable personal property
valuation *n* (*pl* **-s**) assessment of worth
valuations *n* ▷ **valuation**
value *n* (*pl* **-s**) importance, usefulness ▶ *pl* moral principles ▶ *v* (**-ues, -uing, -ued**) assess the worth or desirability of > **valueless** *adj*

> **valuer** *n* (*pl* **-s**)
valued *v* ▷ **value**
valueless *adj* ▷ **value**
valuer *n* ▷ **value**
valuers *n* ▷ **value**
values *n, v* ▷ **value**
valuing *v* ▷ **value**
valve *n* (*pl* **-s**) device to control the movement of fluid through a pipe > **valvular** *adj*
valves *n* ▷ **valve**
valvular *adj* ▷ **valve**
vamp¹ *n* (*pl* **-s**) (*Informal*) sexually attractive woman who seduces men
vamp² *v* (**-s, -ing, -ed**) make (a story, piece of music, etc.) seem new by inventing additional parts
vamped *v* ▷ **vamp²**
vamping *v* ▷ **vamp²**
vampire *n* (*pl* **-s**) (in folklore) corpse that rises at night to drink the blood of the living
vampires *n* ▷ **vampire**
vamps *n, v* ▷ **vamp¹, ²**
van¹ *n* (*pl* **-s**) motor vehicle for transporting goods
van² *n* (*pl* **-s**) ▷ **vanguard**
vanadium *n* (*pl* **-s**) (CHEM) metallic element, used in steel
vanadiums *n* ▷ **vanadium**
vandal *n* (*pl* **-s**) person who deliberately damages property > **vandalism** *n* (*pl* **-s**) > **vandalize** *v* (**-zes, -zing, -zed**)
vandalism *n* ▷ **vandal**
vandalisms *n* ▷ **vandal**
vandalize *n* ▷ **vandal**
vandalized *n* ▷ **vandal**
vandalizes *n* ▷ **vandal**
vandalizing *v* ▷ **vandal**
vandals *n* ▷ **vandal**
vane *n* (*pl* **-s**) flat blade on a rotary device such as a weathercock or propeller
vanes *n* ▷ **vane**
vanguard *n* (*pl* **-s**) unit of soldiers leading an army
vanguards *n* ▷ **vanguard**
vanilla *n* (*pl* **-s**) seed pod of a tropical climbing orchid, used for flavouring
vanillas *n* ▷ **vanilla**
vanish *v* (**-es, -ing, -ed**) disappear suddenly or mysteriously
vanished *v* ▷ **vanish**
vanishes *v* ▷ **vanish**
vanishing *v* ▷ **vanish**
vanities *n* ▷ **vanity**
vanity *n* (*pl* **-ies**) (display of) excessive pride
vanquish *v* (**-es, -ing, -ed**) (*Lit*) defeat

(someone) utterly
vanquished v ▷ vanquish
vanquishes v ▷ vanquish
vanquishing v ▷ vanquish
vans n ▷ van¹, ²
vantage n (pl -s) position that gives one an overall view
vantages n ▷ vantage
vapid adj (-er, -est) lacking character, dull
vapider adj ▷ vapid
vapidest adj ▷ vapid
vaporize v ▷ vapour
vaporized v ▷ vapour
vaporizer n ▷ vapour
vaporizers n ▷ vapour
vaporizes v ▷ vapour
vaporizing v ▷ vapour
vaporous adj ▷ vapour
vapour n (pl -s) moisture suspended in air as steam or mist > **vaporize** v (-zes, -zing, -zed) > **vaporizer** n (pl -s) > **vaporous** adj
vapours n ▷ vapour
variabilities n ▷ variable
variability n ▷ variable
variable adj not always the same, changeable ▶ n (pl -s) (MATHS) expression with a range of values > **variability** n (pl -ties)
variables n ▷ variable
variant adj differing from a standard or type ▶ n (pl -s) something that differs from a standard or type
variants n ▷ variant
variation n (pl -s) something presented in a slightly different form
variations n ▷ variation
varied v, adj ▷ vary
variegated adj having patches or streaks of different colours > **variegation** n (pl -s)
variegation n ▷ variegate
variegations n ▷ variegate
varies adj ▷ vary
varieties n ▷ variety
variety n (pl -ies) state of being diverse or various
various adj of several kinds > **variously** adv
variously adv ▷ various
varnish n (pl -es) solution of oil and resin, put on a surface to make it hard and glossy ▶ v (-es, -ing, -ed) apply varnish to
varnished v ▷ varnish
varnishes n, v ▷ varnish
varnishing v ▷ varnish
vary v (-ries, -rying, -ried) change > **varied** adj
varying v ▷ vary
vascular adj (BIOL) relating to vessels

vase n (pl -s) ornamental jar, esp. for flowers
vasectomies n ▷ vasectomy
vasectomy n (pl -mies) surgical removal of part of the vas deferens, as a contraceptive method
vases n ▷ vase
vassal n (pl -s) (HIST) man given land by a lord in return for military service > **vassalage** n (pl -s)
vassalage n ▷ vassal
vassalages n ▷ vassal
vassals n ▷ vassal
vast adj (-er, -est) extremely large > **vastly** adv > **vastness** n (pl -es)
vaster adj ▷ vast
vastest adj ▷ vast
vastly adv ▷ vast
vastness n ▷ vast
vastnesses n ▷ vast
vat n (pl -s) large container for liquids
vats n ▷ vat
vaudeville n (pl -s) variety entertainment of songs and comic turns
vaudevilles n ▷ vaudeville
vault¹ n (pl -s) secure room for storing valuables
vault² v (-s, -ing, -ed) jump over (something) by resting one's hand(s) on it. ▶ n such a jump
vaulted adj having an arched roof ▶ v ▷ **vault²**
vaulting v ▷ vault²
vaults n, v ▷ vault¹, ²
vaunt v (-s, -ing, -ed) describe or display (success or possessions) boastfully > **vaunted** adj
vaunted adj, v ▷ vaunt
vaunting v ▷ vaunt
vaunts v ▷ vaunt

> **vaw** n (vaws). Vaw is a letter of the Hebrew alphabet. This is a very unusual word that can be useful when you are short of options. If you have the tiles for vaw, look out for opportunities to play **wave** or **wavy** using an E or Y that is already on the board. Vaw scores 9 points.

veal n (pl -s) calf meat
veals n ▷ veal
vector n (pl -s) (MATHS) quantity that has size and direction, such as force
vectors n ▷ vector
veer v (-s, -ing, -ed) change direction suddenly
veered v ▷ veer
veering v ▷ veer
veers v ▷ veer

> **veg** n (veges). Veg is a short form of **vegetable**. If someone plays this, look

out for opportunities to form **vegan** or **vegetate** from it. Veg scores 7 points.

vegan [vee-gan] n (pl -s) person who eats no meat, fish, eggs, or dairy products ▶ adj suitable for a vegan > **veganism** n (pl -s)
  veganism n ▷ **vegan**
  veganisms n ▷ **vegan**
  vegans n ▷ **vegan**
vegetable n (pl -s) edible plant ▶ adj of or like plants or vegetables
  vegetables n ▷ **vegetable**
vegetarian n (pl -s) person who eats no meat or fish ▶ adj suitable for a vegetarian > **vegetarianism** n (pl -s)
  vegetarianism n ▷ **vegetarian**
  vegetarianisms n ▷ **vegetarian**
  vegetarians n ▷ **vegetarian**
vegetate v (-tes, -ting, -ted) live a dull boring life with no mental stimulation
  vegetated v ▷ **vegetate**
  vegetates v ▷ **vegetate**
  vegetating v ▷ **vegetate**
vegetation n (pl -s) plant life of a given place
  vegetations n ▷ **vegetation**
  vehemence n ▷ **vehement**
  vehemences n ▷ **vehement**
vehement adj expressing strong feelings > **vehemence** n (pl -s) > **vehemently** adv
  vehemently adv ▷ **vehement**
vehicle n (pl -s) machine, esp. with an engine and wheels, for carrying people or objects > **vehicular** adj
  vehicles n ▷ **vehicle**
  vehicular adj ▷ **vehicle**
veil n (pl -s) piece of thin cloth covering the head or face ▶ v (-s, -ing, -ed) cover with or as if with a veil
veiled adj disguised ▶ v ▷ **veil**
  veiling v ▷ **veil**
  veils n, v ▷ **veil**
vein n (pl -s) tube that takes blood to the heart > **veined** adj
  veined adj ▷ **vein**
  veins n ▷ **vein**
veld, veldt n (pl -s) high grassland in southern Africa
  velds n ▷ **veld**
veldskoen, velskoen n (pl -s) (S AFR) leather ankle boot
  veldskoens n ▷ **veldskoen**
  veldts n ▷ **veld**
vellum n (pl -s) fine calfskin parchment
  vellums n ▷ **vellum**
  velocities n ▷ **velocity**
velocity n (pl -ties) speed of movement in a

given direction
velour, velours [vel-loor] n (pl -s) fabric similar to velvet
  velours n ▷ **velour**
  velskoen n ▷ **veldskoen**
  velskoens n ▷ **veldskoen**
velvet n (pl -s) fabric with a thick soft pile
velveteen n (pl -s) cotton velvet
  velveteens n ▷ **velveteen**
  velvetier adj ▷ **velvety**
  velvetiest adj ▷ **velvety**
  velvets n ▷ **velvet**
velvety adj (-tier, -tiest) soft and smooth
venal adj easily bribed
vend v (-s, -ing, -ed) sell > **vendor** n (pl -s)
  vended v ▷ **vend**
vendetta n (pl -s) prolonged quarrel between families, esp. one involving revenge killings
  vendettas n ▷ **vendetta**
  vending v ▷ **vend**
  vendor n ▷ **vend**
  vendors n ▷ **vend**
  vends v ▷ **vend**
veneer n (pl -s) thin layer of wood etc. covering a cheaper material
  veneers n ▷ **veneer**
venerable adj worthy of deep respect
venerate v (-tes, -ting, -ted) hold (a person) in deep respect > **veneration** n (pl -s)
  venerated v ▷ **venerate**
  venerates v ▷ **venerate**
  venerating v ▷ **venerate**
  veneration n ▷ **venerate**
  venerations n ▷ **venerate**
vengeance n (pl -s) revenge
  vengeances n ▷ **vengeance**
vengeful adj wanting revenge
venial [veen-ee-al] adj (of a sin or fault) easily forgiven
venison n (pl -s) deer meat
  venisons n ▷ **venison**
venom n (pl -s) malice or spite > **venomous** adj
  venomous adj ▷ **venom**
  venoms n ▷ **venom**
venous adj (ANAT) of veins
vent[1] n (pl -s) outlet releasing fumes or fluid ▶ v (-s, -ing, -ed) express (an emotion) freely
vent[2] n (pl -s) vertical slit in a jacket
  vented v ▷ **vent**[1]
ventilate v (-tes, -ting, -ted) let fresh air into > **ventilation** n (pl -s) > **ventilator** n (pl -s)
  ventilated v ▷ **ventilate**
  ventilates v ▷ **ventilate**
  ventilating v ▷ **ventilate**
  ventilation n ▷ **ventilate**

ventilations *n* ▷ ventilate
ventilator *n* ▷ ventilate
ventilators *n* ▷ ventilate
venting *v* ▷ vent¹
ventral *adj* relating to the front of the body
ventricle *n* (*pl* -**s**) (ANAT) one of the four cavities of the heart or brain
ventricles *n* ▷ ventricle
ventriloquism *n* ▷ ventriloquist
ventriloquisms *n* ▷ ventriloquist
ventriloquist *n* (*pl* -**s**) entertainer who can speak without moving his or her lips, so that a voice seems to come from elsewhere > **ventriloquism** *n* (*pl* -**s**)
ventriloquists *n* ▷ ventriloquist
vents *n*, *v* ▷ vent¹, ²
venture *n* (*pl* -**s**) risky undertaking, esp. in business ▶ *v* (-**res**, -**ring**, -**red**) do something risky
ventured *v* ▷ venture
ventures *n*, *v* ▷ venture
venturesome *adj* daring
venturing *v* ▷ venture
venue *n* (*pl* -**s**) place where an organized gathering is held
venues *n* ▷ venue
veracious *adj* ▷ veracity
veracities *n* ▷ veracity
veracity *n* (*pl* -**ties**) habitual truthfulness > **veracious** *adj*
veranda *n* ▷ verandah
verandah, veranda *n* (*pl* -**s**) open porch attached to a house
verandahs *n* ▷ verandah
verandas *n* ▷ verandah
verb *n* (*pl* -**s**) word that expresses the idea of action, happening, or being
verbal *adj* spoken > **verbally** *adv*
verbalize *v* (-**s**, -**ing**, -**ed**) express (something) in words
verbalized *v* ▷ verbalize
verbalizes *n* ▷ verbalize
verbalizing *v* ▷ verbalize
verbally *adv* ▷ verbal
verbatim [verb-**bait**-im] *adv*, *adj* word for word
verbena *n* (*pl* -**s**) plant with sweet-smelling flowers
verbenas *n* ▷ verbena
verbiage *n* (*pl* -**s**) excessive use of words
verbiages *n* ▷ verbiage
verbose [verb-**bohss**] *adj* (-**r**, -**st**) speaking at tedious length > **verbosity** *n* (*pl* -**ties**)
verboser *adj* ▷ verbose
verbosest *adj* ▷ verbose
verbosities *n* ▷ verbose

verbosity *n* ▷ verbose
verbs *n* ▷ verb
verdant *adj* (*Lit*) covered in green vegetation
verdict *n* (*pl* -**s**) decision of a jury
verdicts *n* ▷ verdict
verdigris [**ver**-dig-riss] *n* (*pl* -**es**) green film on copper, brass, or bronze
verdigrises *n* ▷ verdigris
verdure *n* (*pl* -**s**) (*Lit*) flourishing green vegetation
verdures *n* ▷ verdure
verge *n* (*pl* -**s**) grass border along a road
verger *n* (*pl* -**s**) (C OF E) church caretaker
vergers *n* ▷ verger
verges *n* ▷ verge
verifiable *adj* ▷ verify
verification *n* ▷ verify
verifications *n* ▷ verify
verified *v* ▷ verify
verifies *v* ▷ verify
verify *v* (-**fies**, -**fying**, -**fied**) check the truth or accuracy of > **verifiable** *adj* > **verification** *n* (*pl* -**s**)
verifying *v* ▷ verify
verily *adv* (*Obs*) in truth
verisimilitude *n* (*pl* -**s**) appearance of being real or true
verisimilitudes *n* ▷ verisimilitude
veritable *adj* rightly called, without exaggeration > **veritably** *adv*
veritably *adv* ▷ veritable
verities *n* ▷ verity
verity *n* (*pl* -**ies**) true statement or principle
vermicelli [ver-me-**chell**-ee] *n* (*pl* -**s**) fine strands of pasta
vermicellis *n* ▷ vermicelli
vermiform *adj* shaped like a worm
vermilion *adj* orange-red
vermin *pl n* (*pl* -**s**) animals, esp. insects and rodents, that spread disease or cause damage > **verminous** *adj*
verminous *adj* ▷ vermin
vermins *n* ▷ vermin
vermouth [**ver**-muth] *n* (*pl* -**s**) wine flavoured with herbs
vermouths *n* ▷ vermouth
vernacular [ver-**nak**-yew-lar] *n* (*pl* -**s**) most widely spoken language of a particular people or place
vernaculars *n* ▷ vernacular
vernal *adj* occurring in spring
vernier [**ver**-nee-er] *n* (*pl* -**s**) movable scale on a graduated measuring instrument for taking readings in fractions
verniers *n* ▷ vernier

veronica *n (pl -s)* plant with small blue, pink, or white flowers
veronicas *n* ▷ **veronica**
verruca [ver-**roo**-ka] *n (pl -s)* wart, usu. on the foot
verrucas *n* ▷ **verruca**
versatile *adj* having many skills or uses
> **versatility** *n (pl -ties)*
versatilities *n* ▷ **versatile**
versatility *n* ▷ **versatile**
verse *n (pl -s)* group of lines forming part of a song or poem
verses *n* ▷ **verse**
versification *n (pl -s)* writing in verse
versifications *n* ▷ **versification**
version *n (pl -s)* form of something, such as a piece of writing, with some differences from other forms
versions *n* ▷ **version**
verso *n (pl -s)* left-hand page of a book
versos *n* ▷ **verso**
versus *prep* in opposition to or in contrast with
vertebra *n (pl -rae)* one of the bones that form the spine > **vertebral** *adj*
vertebrae *n* ▷ **vertabra**
vertebral *adj* ▷ **vertebra**
vertebrate *n, adj (pl -s)* (animal) having a spine
vertebrates *n* ▷ **vertebrate**
vertex *n (pl -texes, -tices)* (MATHS) point on a geometric figure where the sides form an angle
vertexes *n* ▷ **vertex**
vertical *adj* straight up and down ▶ *n (pl -s)* vertical direction
verticals *n* ▷ **vertical**
vertices *n* ▷ **vertex**
vertiginous *adj* ▷ **vertigo**
vertigo *n (pl -s)* dizziness, usu. when looking down from a high place > **vertiginous** *adj*
vertigoes *n* ▷ **vertigo**
vervain *n (pl -s)* plant with spikes of blue, purple, or white flowers
vervains *n* ▷ **vervain**
verve *n (pl -s)* enthusiasm or liveliness
verves *n* ▷ **verve**
very *adv* more than usually, extremely ▶ *adj* absolute, exact
vesicle *n (pl -s)* (BIOL) sac or small cavity, esp. one containing fluid
vesicles *n* ▷ **vesicle**
vespers *pl n* (RC CHURCH) (service of) evening prayer
vessel *n (pl -s)* ship
vessels *n* ▷ **vessel**

vest *n (pl -s)* undergarment worn on the top half of the body ▶ *v (-s, -ing, -ed)* (foll. by **in** or **with**) give (authority) to (someone)
vested *v* ▷ **vest**
vestibule *n (pl -s)* small entrance hall
vestibules *n* ▷ **vestibule**
vestige [**vest**-ij] *n (pl -s)* small amount or trace
> **vestigial** *adj*
vestiges *n* ▷ **vestige**
vestigial *adj* ▷ **vestige**
vesting *v* ▷ **vest**
vestments *pl n* priest's robes
vestries *n* ▷ **vestry**
vestry *n (pl -ies)* room in a church used as an office by the priest or minister
vests *n, v* ▷ **vest**
vet[1] *n (pl -s)* ▷ **veterinary surgeon** ▶ *v (-s, -tting, -tted)* check the suitability of
vet[2] *n (pl -s)* (US, AUST & NZ) military veteran
vetch *n (pl -es)* climbing plant with a beanlike fruit used as fodder
vetches *n* ▷ **vetch**
veteran *n (pl -s)* person with long experience in a particular activity, esp. military service ▶ *adj* long-serving
veterans *n* ▷ **veteran**
veterinary *adj* concerning animal health
veto *n (pl -es)* official power to cancel a proposal ▶ *v (-es, -ing, -ed)* enforce a veto against
vetoed *v* ▷ **veto**
vetoes *n, v* ▷ **veto**
vetoing *v* ▷ **veto**
vets *n, v* ▷ **vet**[1, 2]
vetted *v* ▷ **vet**[1]
vetting *v* ▷ **vet**[1]
vex *v (-es, -ing, -ed)* frustrate, annoy
vexation *n (pl -s)* something annoying
> **vexatious** *adj*
vexations *n* ▷ **vexation**
vexatious *adj* ▷ **vexation**
vexed *v* ▷ **vex**
vexes *v* ▷ **vex**
vexing *v* ▷ **vex**
via *prep* by way of
viabilities *n* ▷ **viable**
viability *n* ▷ **viable**
viable *adj* able to be put into practice
> **viability** *n (pl -ties)*
viaduct *n (pl -s)* bridge over a valley
viaducts *n* ▷ **viaduct**
vial *n (pl -s)* ▷ **phial**
vials *n* ▷ **vial**
viands *pl n* (Obs) food
vibes *pl n* (Informal) emotional reactions

between people

vibrant [vibe-rant] *adj* vigorous in appearance, energetic

vibraphone *n* (*pl* -s) musical instrument with metal bars that resonate electronically when hit

vibraphones *n* ▷ vibraphone

vibrate *v* (-tes, -ting, -ted) move back and forth rapidly > **vibration** *n* (*pl* -s)

vibrated *v* ▷ vibrate

vibrates *v* ▷ vibrate

vibrating *v* ▷ vibrate

vibration *n* ▷ vibrate

vibrations *n* ▷ vibrate

vibrato *n* (*pl* -s) (MUSIC) rapid fluctuation in the pitch of a note

vibrator *n* (*pl* -s) device that produces vibratory motion, used for massage or as a sex aid > **vibratory** *adj*

vibrators *n* ▷ vibrate

vibratos *n* ▷ vibrato

vicar *n* (*pl* -s) (C OF E) member of the clergy in charge of a parish

vicarage *n* (*pl* -s) vicar's house

vicarages *n* ▷ vicarage

vicarious [vick-air-ee-uss] *adj* felt indirectly by imagining what another person experiences > **vicariously** *adv*

vicariously *adv* ▷ vicarious

vicars *n* ▷ vicar

vice[1] *n* (*pl* -s) immoral or evil habit or action

vice[2] *n* (*pl* -s) tool with a pair of jaws for holding an object while working on it

vice[3] *adj* serving in place of

viceregal *adj* ▷ viceroy

viceroy *n* (*pl* -s) governor of a colony who represents the monarch > **viceregal** *adj*

viceroys *n* ▷ viceroy

vices *n* ▷ vice[1, 2]

vicinities *n* ▷ vicinity

vicinity [viss-in-it-ee] *n* (*pl* -ties) surrounding area

vicious *adj* cruel and violent > **viciously** *adv*

viciously *adv* ▷ vicious

vicissitudes [viss-iss-it-yewds] *pl n* changes in fortune

victim *n* (*pl* -s) person or thing harmed or killed

victimization *n* ▷ victimize

victimizations *n* ▷ victimize

victimize *v* (-zes, -zing, -zed) punish unfairly > **victimization** *n* (*pl* -s)

victimized *v* ▷ victimize

victimizes *v* ▷ victimize

victimizing *v* ▷ victimize

victims *n* ▷ victim

victor *n* (*pl* -s) person who has defeated an opponent, esp. in war or in sport

victories *n* ▷ victory

victorious *adj* ▷ victory

victors *n* ▷ victor

victory *n* (*pl* -ries) winning of a battle or contest > **victorious** *adj*

victuals [vit-tals] *pl n* (*Old-fashioned*) food and drink

vicuña [vik-koo-nya] *n* (*pl* -s) S American animal like the llama

vicuñas *n* ▷ vicuña

video *n* (*pl* -s) ▷ video cassette (recorder) ▶ *v* (-s, -ing, -ed) record (a TV programme or event) on video ▶ *adj* relating to or used in producing television images

videoed *v* ▷ video

videoing *v* ▷ video

videos *n*, *v* ▷ video

videotext *n* (*pl* -s) means of representing on a TV screen information that is held in a computer

videotexts *n* ▷ videotext

vie *v* (vies, vying, vied) compete (with someone)

vied *v* ▷ vie

vies *v* ▷ vie

view *n* (*pl* -s) opinion or belief ▶ *v* (-s, -ing, -ed) think of (something) in a particular way

viewdata *n* (*pl* -as)® videotext service linking users to a computer by telephone

viewdatas *n* ▷ viewdatas

viewed *v* ▷ view

viewer *n* person who watches television

viewers *n* ▷ viewer

viewfinder *n* (*pl* -s) window on a camera showing what will appear in a photograph

viewfinders *n* ▷ viewfinder

viewing *v* ▷ view

views *n*, *v* ▷ view

vigil [vij-ill] *n* (*pl* -s) night-time period of staying awake to look after a sick person, pray, etc.

vigilance *n* ▷ vigilant

vigilances *n* ▷ vigilant

vigilant *adj* watchful in case of danger > **vigilance** *n* (*pl* -s)

vigilante [vij-ill-ant-ee] *n* (*pl* -s) person, esp. as one of a group, who takes it upon himself or herself to enforce the law

vigilantes *n* ▷ vigilante

vigils *n* ▷ vigil

vignette [vin-yet] *n* (*pl* -s) concise description of the typical features of something

vignettes *n* ▷ vignette

vigorous *adj* ▷ **vigour**
vigorously *adv* ▷ **vigour**
vigour *n* (*pl* -s) physical or mental energy
 > **vigorous** *adj* > **vigorously** *adv*
vigours *n* ▷ **vigour**
viking *n* (*pl* -s) (HIST) seafaring raider and
 settler from Scandinavia
vikings *n* ▷ **viking**
vile (-r, -st) *adj* very wicked > **vilely** *adv*
 > **vileness** *n* (*pl* -s)
vilely *adv* ▷ **vile**
vileness *n* ▷ **vile**
vilenesses *n* ▷ **vile**
viler *adj* ▷ **vile**
vilest *adj* ▷ **vile**
vilification *n* ▷ **vilify**
vilifications *n* ▷ **vilify**
vilified *v* ▷ **vilify**
vilifies *v* ▷ **vilify**
vilify *v* (-fies, -fying, -fied) attack the character
 of > **vilification** *n* (*pl* -s)
vilifying *v* ▷ **vilify**
villa *n* (*pl* -s) large house with gardens
village *n* (*pl* -s) small group of houses in a
 country area > **villager** *n* (*pl* -s)
villager *n* ▷ **village**
villagers *n* ▷ **village**
villages *n* ▷ **village**
villain *n* (*pl* -s) wicked person > **villainous** *adj*
 > **villainy** *n* (*pl* -nies)
villianies *n* ▷ **villian**
villainous *adj* ▷ **villain**
villains *n* ▷ **villain**
villas *n* ▷ **villa**
villein [vill-an] *n* (*pl* -s) (HIST) peasant bound in
 service to his lord
villeins *n* ▷ **villein**
villiany *n* ▷ **villian**

> **vim** *n* (**vims**). Vim means vigour or
> energy. This word can be helpful when
> you're stuck with unpromising letters,
> and gives a reasonable score for a
> three-letter word. Vim scores 8 points.

vinaigrette *n* (*pl* -s) salad dressing of oil and
 vinegar
vinaigrettes *n* ▷ **vinaigrette**
vindicate *v* (-tes, -ting, -ted) clear (someone)
 of guilt > **vindication** *n* (*pl* -s)
vindicated *v* ▷ **vindicate**
vindicates *v* ▷ **vindicate**
vindicating *v* ▷ **vindicate**
vindication *n* ▷ **vindicate**
vindications *n* ▷ **vindicate**
vindictive *adj* maliciously seeking revenge
 > **vindictiveness** *n* (*pl* -es) > **vindictively** *adv*

vindictively *adv* ▷ **vindictive**
vindictiveness *n* ▷ **vindictive**
vindictivenesses *n* ▷ **vindictive**
vine *n* (*pl* -s) climbing plant, esp. one
 producing grapes
vinegar *n* (*pl* -s) acid liquid made from wine,
 beer, or cider > **vinegary** *adj*
vinegars *n* ▷ **vinegar**
vinegary *adj* ▷ **vinegar**
vines *n* ▷ **vine**
vineyard [vinn-yard] *n* (*pl* -s) plantation of
 grape vines, esp. for making wine
vineyards *n* ▷ **vineyard**
vino [vee-noh] *n* (*pl* -s) (*Informal*) wine
vinos *n* ▷ **vino**
vintage *n* (*pl* -s) wine from a particular harvest
 of grapes ▶ *adj* best and most typical
vintages *n* ▷ **vintage**
vintner *n* (*pl* -s) dealer in wine
vintners *n* ▷ **vintner**
vinyl [vine-ill] *n* (*pl* -s) type of plastic, used in
 mock leather and records
vinyls *n* ▷ **vinyl**
viol [vie-oll] *n* (*pl* -s) early stringed instrument
 preceding the violin
viola[1] [vee-oh-la] *n* (*pl* -s) stringed instrument
 lower in pitch than a violin
viola[2] [vie-ol-la] *n* (*pl* -s) variety of pansy
violas *n* ▷ **viola**[1,2]
violate *v* (-tes, -ting, -ted) break (a law or
 agreement) > **violation** *n* > **violator** *n*
violated *v* ▷ **violate**
violates *v* ▷ **violate**
violating *v* ▷ **violate**
violation *n* ▷ **violate**
violations *n* ▷ **violate**
violator *n* ▷ **violate**
violators *n* ▷ **violate**
violence *n* (*pl* -s) use of physical force, usu.
 intended to cause injury or destruction
 > **violent** *adj* > **violently** *adv*
violences *n* ▷ **violence**
violent *adj* ▷ **violence**
violently *adv* ▷ **violent**
violet *n* (*pl* -s) plant with bluish-purple flowers
 ▶ *adj* bluish-purple
violets *n* ▷ **violet**
violin *n* (*pl* -s) small four-stringed musical
 instrument played with a bow. > **violinist**
 n (*pl* -s)
violinist *n* ▷ **violin**
violinists *n* ▷ **violin**
violins *n* ▷ **violin**
viols *n* ▷ **viol**
viper *n* (*pl* -s) poisonous snake

vipers *n* ▷ **viper**
virago [vir-**rah**-go] *n* (*pl* -**goes**, -**gos**) aggressive woman
viragoes *n* ▷ **virago**
viragos *n* ▷ **virago**
viral *adj* of or caused by a virus
virgin *n* (*pl* -**s**) person, esp. a woman, who has not had sexual intercourse ▶ *adj* not having had sexual intercourse > **virginity** *n* (*pl* -**ties**)
virginal *adj* like a virgin ▶ *n* early keyboard instrument like a small harpsichord
virginities *n* ▷ **virgin**
virginity *n* ▷ **virgin**
virgins *n* ▷ **virgin**
virile *adj* having the traditional male characteristics of physical strength and a high sex drive > **virility** *n* (*pl* -**ties**)
virilities *n* ▷ **virile**
virility *n* ▷ **virile**
virologies *n* ▷ **virology**
virologies *n* ▷ **virology**
virology *n* (*pl* -**gies**) study of viruses
virtual *adj* having the effect but not the form of > **virtually** *adv* practically, almost
virtually *adv* ▷ **virtual**
virtue *n* (*pl* -**s**) moral goodness
virtues *n* ▷ **virtue**
virtuosi *n* ▷ **virtuoso**
virtuosities *n* ▷ **virtuoso**
virtuosity *n* ▷ **virtuoso**
virtuoso *n* (*pl* -**sos**, -**si**) person with impressive esp. musical skill > **virtuosity** *n* (*pl* -**ies**)
virtuosos *n* ▷ **virtuoso**
virtuous *adj* morally good > **virtuously** *adv*
virtuously *adv* ▷ **virtuous**
virulent [vir-yew-lent] *adj* very infectious
virus *n* (*pl* -**es**) microorganism that causes disease in humans, animals, and plants
viruses *n* ▷ **virus**
visa *n* (*pl* -**s**) permission to enter a country, granted by its government and shown by a stamp on one's passport
visage [viz-zij] *n* (*pl* -**s**) (*Lit*) face
visages *n* ▷ **visage**
visas *n* ▷ **visa**
viscera [viss-er-a] *pl n* large abdominal organs
visceral [viss-er-al] *adj* instinctive
viscid [viss-id] *adj* sticky
viscose *n* (*pl* -**s**) synthetic fabric made from cellulose
viscoses *n* ▷ **viscose**
viscosities *n* ▷ **viscous**
viscosity *n* ▷ **viscous**
viscount [vie-count] *n* (*pl* -**s**) British nobleman ranking between an earl and a baron

viscountess [vie-count-iss] *n* (*pl* -**es**) woman holding the rank of viscount in her own right
viscountesses *n* ▷ **viscountess**
viscounts *n* ▷ **viscount**
viscous *adj* thick and sticky > **viscosity** *n* (*pl* -**ties**)
visibilities *n* ▷ **visibility**
visibility *n* (*pl* -**ties**) range or clarity of vision
visible *adj* able to be seen > **visibly** *adv*
visibly *adv* ▷ **visible**
vision *n* (*pl* -**s**) ability to see
visionaries *n* ▷ **visionary**
visionary *adj* showing foresight ▶ *n* (*pl* -**ries**) visionary person
visions *n* ▷ **vision**
visit *v* (-**s**, -**ing**, -**ed**) go or come to see ▶ *n* instance of visiting > **visitor** *n* (*pl* -**s**)
visitation *n* (*pl* -**s**) formal visit or inspection
visitations *n* ▷ **visitation**
visited *v* ▷ **visit**
visiting *v* ▷ **visit**
visitor *n* ▷ **visit**
visitors *n* ▷ **visit**
visits *v* ▷ **visit**
visor [vize-or] *n* (*pl* -**s**) transparent part of a helmet that pulls down over the face
visors *n* ▷ **visor**
vista *n* (*pl* -**s**) (beautiful) extensive view
vistas *n* ▷ **vista**
visual *adj* done by or used in seeing
visualization *n* ▷ **visualize**
visualizations *n* ▷ **visualize**
visualize *v* (-**zes**, -**zing**, -**zed**) form a mental image of > **visualization** *n* (*pl* -**s**)
visualized *v* ▷ **visualize**
visualizes *v* ▷ **visualize**
visualizing *v* ▷ **visualize**
vital *adj* essential or highly important > **vitally** *adv*
vitalities *n* ▷ **vitality**
vitality *n* (*pl* -**ties**) physical or mental energy
vitally *adv* ▷ **vital**
vitals *pl n* bodily organs necessary to maintain life
vitamin *n* (*pl* -**s**) one of a group of substances that are essential in the diet for specific body processes
vitamins *n* ▷ **vitamin**
vitiate [vish-ee-ate] *v* (-**tes**, -**ting**, -**ted**) spoil the effectiveness of
vitiated *v* ▷ **vitiate**
vitiates *v* ▷ **vitiate**
vitiating *v* ▷ **vitiate**
viticulture *n* (*pl* -**s**) cultivation of grapevines
viticultures *n* ▷ **viticulture**

vitreous *adj* like or made from glass
vitriol *n* (*pl* -s) language expressing bitterness
and hatred > **vitriolic** *adj*
  vitriolic *adj* ▷ vitriol
  vitriols *n* ▷ vitriol
  vituperation *n* ▷ vituperative
  vituperations *n* ▷ vituperative
vituperative [vite-**tyew**-pra-tiv] *adj* bitterly
abusive > **vituperation** *n* (*pl* -s)
viva¹ *interj* long live (a person or thing)
viva² *n* (*pl* -s) (BRIT) examination in the form of
an interview
vivace [viv-**vah**-chee] *adv* (MUSIC) in a lively
manner
vivacious *adj* full of energy and enthusiasm
> **vivacity** *n* (*pl* -ties)
  vivacities *n* ▷ vivacious
  vivacity *n* ▷ vivacious
  vivas *n* ▷ viva²
vivid *adj* (-er, -est) very bright > **vividly** *adv*
> **vividness** *n* (*pl* -es)
  vivider *adj* ▷ vivd
  vividest *adj* ▷ vivd
  vividly *adv* ▷ vivd
  vividness *n* ▷ vivid
  vividnesses *n* ▷ vivid
vivisection *n* (*pl* -s) performing surgical
experiments on living animals
> **vivisectionist** *n* (*pl* -s)
  vivisectionist *n* ▷ vivisection
  vivisectionists *n* ▷ vivisection
  vivisections *n* ▷ vivisection
vixen *n* (*pl* -s) female fox
  vixens *n* ▷ vixen
vizier [viz-**zeer**] *n* (*pl* -s) high official in certain
Muslim countries
  viziers *n* ▷ vizier
vizor *n* (*pl* -s) ▷ visor
  vizors *n* ▷ vizor

> **vly** *n* (**vlys**). Vly is a South African
> word meaning an area of low marshy
> ground. This is a good word to
> remember because it doesn't contain
> any vowels, making it useful when
> you are short of vowel tiles. Vly scores
> 9 points.

  vocabularies *n* ▷ vocabulary
vocabulary *n* (*pl* -ries) all the words that a
person knows
vocal *adj* relating to the voice
vocalist *n* (*pl* -s) singer
  vocalists *n* ▷ vocalist
  vocalization *n* ▷ vocalize
  vocalizations *n* ▷ vocalize
vocalize *v* (-zes, -zing, -zed) express with or

use the voice > **vocalization** *n* (*pl* -s)
  vocalizes *v* ▷ vocalize
  vocalizes *v* ▷ vocalize
  vocalizing *v* ▷ vocalize
  vocally *adv* ▷ vocal
vocals *pl n* singing part of a piece of pop music
> **vocally** *adv*
vocation *n* (*pl* -s) profession or trade
vocational *adj* directed towards a particular
profession or trade
  vocations *n* ▷ vocation
vociferous *adj* shouting, noisy
vodka *n* (*pl* -s) (Russian) spirit distilled from
potatoes or grain
  vodkas *n* ▷ vodka
vogue *n* (*pl* -s) popular style
  vogues *n* ▷ vogue
voice *n* (*pl* -s) (quality of) sound made when
speaking or singing ▶ *v* (-ces, -cing, -ced)
express verbally > **voiceless** *adj*
  voiced *v* ▷ voice
  voiceless *adj* ▷ voice
  voices *n, v* ▷ voice
  voicing *v* ▷ voice
void *adj* not legally binding ▶ *n* (*pl* -s) empty
space ▶ *v* (-s, -ing, -ed) make invalid
  voided *v* ▷ void
  voiding *v* ▷ void
  voids *n, v* ▷ void
voile [voyl] *n* (*pl* -s) light semitransparent
fabric
  voiles *n* ▷ voile
volatile *adj* liable to sudden change, esp. in
behaviour > **volatility** *n* (*pl* -ties)
  volatilities *n* ▷ volatile
  volatility *n* ▷ volatile
  volcanic *adj* ▷ volcano
volcano *n* (*pl* -noes, -nos) mountain with a
vent through which lava is ejected > **volcanic**
adj
  volcanoes *n* ▷ volcano
  volcanos *n* ▷ volcano
vole *n* (*pl* -s) small rodent
  voles *n* ▷ vole
volition *n* (*pl* -s) ability to decide things for
oneself
  volitions *n* ▷ volition
volley *n* (*pl* -s) simultaneous discharge of
ammunition ▶ *v* (-s, -ing, -ed) discharge
(ammunition) in a volley
volleyball *n* (*pl* -s) team game where a ball is
hit with the hands over a high net
  volleyballs *n* ▷ volleyball
  volleyed *v* ▷ volley
  volleying *v* ▷ volley

volleys n, v ▷ volley

volt n (pl -s) unit of electric potential

voltage n (pl -s) electric potential difference expressed in volts

voltages n ▷ voltage

voltmeter n instrument for measuring voltage

voltmeters n ▷ voltmeter

volts n ▷ volt

volubilities n ▷ voluble

volubility n ▷ voluble

voluble adj talking easily and at length > **volubility** n (pl -ties) > **volubly** adv

volubly adv ▷ voluble

volume n (pl -s) size of the space occupied by something

volumes n ▷ volume

volumetric adj relating to measurement by volume

voluminous adj (of clothes) large and roomy

voluntaries n ▷ voluntary

voluntarily adv ▷ voluntary

voluntary adj done by choice ▶ n (pl -ries) organ solo in a church service > **voluntarily** adv

volunteer n (pl -s) person who offers voluntarily to do something ▶ v (-s, -ing, -ed) offer one's services

volunteered v ▷ volunteer

volunteering v ▷ volunteer

volunteers n, v ▷ volunteer

voluptuaries n ▷ voluptuary

voluptuary n (pl -ries) person devoted to sensual pleasures

voluptuous adj (of a woman) sexually alluring through fullness of figure

volute n (pl -s) spiral or twisting turn, form, or object

volutes n ▷ volute

vomit v (-s, -ing, -ed) eject (the contents of the stomach) through the mouth ▶ n (pl -s) matter vomited

vomited v ▷ vomit

vomiting v ▷ vomit

vomits v, n ▷ vomit

voodoo n (pl -s) religion involving ancestor worship and witchcraft, practised by Black people in the West Indies, esp. in Haiti.

voodoos n ▷ voodoo

voracious adj craving great quantities of food > **voraciously** adv > **voracity** n (pl -ties)

voraciously adv ▷ voracious

voracities n ▷ voracious

voracity n ▷ voracious

vortex n (pl -texes, -tices) whirlpool

vortexes n ▷ vortex

vortices n ▷ vortex

vote n (pl -s) choice made by a participant in a shared decision, esp. in electing a candidate ▶ v (-tes, -ting, -ted) make a choice by a vote > **voter** n (pl -s)

voted v ▷ vote

voter n ▷ vote

voters n ▷ vote

votes n, v ▷ vote

voting v ▷ vote

votive adj done or given to fulfil a vow

vouch v (-es, -ing, -ed) give one's personal assurance about

vouched v ▷ vouch

voucher n (pl -s) ticket used instead of money to buy specified goods

vouchers n ▷ voucher

vouches v ▷ vouch

vouching v ▷ vouch

vouchsafe v (-fes, -fing, -fed) (Old-fashioned) give, entrust

vouchsafed v ▷ vouchsafe

vouchsafes v ▷ vouchsafe

vouchsafing v ▷ vouchsafe

vow n (pl -s) solemn and binding promise ▶ pl formal promises made when marrying or entering a religious order ▶ v (-s, -ing, -ed) promise solemnly

vowed v ▷ vow

vowel n (pl -s) speech sound made without obstructing the flow of breath

vowels n ▷ vowel

vowing v ▷ vow

vows n, v ▷ vow

> **vox** n (**voces**). Vox means a voice or sound. Along with **vex,** this is the highest-scoring three-letter word beginning with V. Vox scores 13 points.

voyage n (pl -s) long journey by sea or in space ▶ v (-ges, -ging, -ged) make a voyage > **voyager** n (pl -s)

voyaged v ▷ voyage

voyager n ▷ voyager

voyagers n ▷ voyager

voyages n, v ▷ voyage

voyaging v ▷ voyage

voyeur n (pl -s) person who obtains pleasure from watching people undressing or having sex > **voyeurism** n (pl -s)

voyeurism n ▷ voyeur

voyeurisms n ▷ voyeur

voyeurs n ▷ voyeur

> **vug** n (**vugs**). A vug is a small cavity in a rock. This is a very unusual word

that can be useful when you have an uninspiring combination of letters. Vug scores 7 points.

vulcanize v (-zes, -zing, -zed) strengthen (rubber) by treating it with sulphur
  vulcanized v ▷ **vulcanize**
  vulcanizes v ▷ **vulcanize**
  vulcanizing v ▷ **vulcanize**
vulgar adj (-er, -est) showing lack of good taste, decency, or refinement > **vulgarly** adv > **vulgarity** n (pl -ies)
  vulgarer adj ▷ **vulgar**
  vulgarest adj ▷ **vulgar**
vulgarian n (pl -s) vulgar (rich) person
  vulgarians n ▷ **vulgarian**
  vulgarities n ▷ **vulgar**
  vulgarities n ▷ **vulgar**
  vulgarly adv ▷ **vulgar**
  vulnerabilities n ▷ **vulnerable**
  vulnerability n ▷ **vulnerable**
vulnerable adj liable to be physically or emotionally hurt > **vulnerability** n (pl -s)
vulpine adj of or like a fox
vulture n (pl -s) large bird that feeds on the flesh of dead animals
  vultures n ▷ **vulture**
vulva n (pl -vae) woman's external genitals
  vulvae n ▷ **vulva**
  vying v ▷ **vie**

Ww

W is a useful tile to have on your rack as it earns 4 points on its own and produces a number of high-scoring short words. There are, however, only two two-letter words begin with W: **we** and **wo** (5 points each). If you know this, though, you won't waste time looking for others. There are lots of everyday three-letter words that earn good scores: **wax** (13) with its two old-fashioned variants **wex** and **wox** (also 13 each) and **way, who, why, wow** and **wry** (9 each). Don't forget **wok** (10) either, which can be as useful on the Scrabble board as in the kitchen!

wackier *adj* ▷ **wacky**
wackiest *adj* ▷ **wacky**
wackiness *n* ▷ **wacky**
wackinesses *n* ▷ **wacky**
wacky *adj* (**-ckier, -ckiest**) (*Informal*) eccentric or funny > **wackiness** *n* (*pl* **-es**)
wad *n* (*pl* **-s**) small mass of soft material
waddies *n* ▷ **waddy**
wadding *n* (*pl* **-s**) soft material used for padding or stuffing
waddings *n* ▷ **wadding**
waddle *v* (**-les, -ling, -led**) walk with short swaying steps ▶ *n* (*pl* **-s**) swaying walk
waddled *v, n* ▷ **waddle**
waddles *v* ▷ **waddle**
waddling *v* ▷ **waddle**
waddy *n* (*pl* **-ies**) heavy wooden club used by Australian Aborigines
wade *v* (**-des, -ding, -ded**) walk with difficulty through water or mud
waded *v* ▷ **wade**
wader *n* (*pl* **-s**) long-legged water bird ▶ *pl* angler's long waterproof boots
waders *n* ▷ **wader**
wades *v* ▷ **wade**
wadi [**wod**-dee] *n* (*pl* **-s**) (in N Africa and Arabia) river which is dry except in the wet season
wading *v* ▷ **wade**
wadis *n* ▷ **wadi**
wads *n* ▷ **wad**
wafer *n* (*pl* **-s**) thin crisp biscuit
wafers *n* ▷ **wafer**
waffle¹ (*Informal*) *v* (**-les, -ling, -led**) speak or write in a vague wordy way ▶ *n* (*pl* **-s**) vague wordy talk or writing
waffle² *n* (*pl* **-s**) square crisp pancake with a gridlike pattern

waffled *v* ▷ **waffle¹**
waffles *v, n* ▷ **waffle¹, ²**
waffling *v* ▷ **waffle¹**
waft *v* (**-s, -ing, -ed**) drift or carry gently through the air ▶ *n* (*pl* **-s**) something wafted
wafted *v* ▷ **waft**
wafting *v* ▷ **waft**
wafts *v, n* ▷ **waft**
wag *v* (**-s, -gging, -gged**) move rapidly from side to side ▶ *n* (*pl* **-s**) wagging movement
wage *n* (*pl* **-s**) (*often pl* payment for work done, esp. when paid weekly ▶ *v* (**-ges, -ging, -ged**) engage in (an activity)
waged *v* ▷ **wage**
wager *n, v* (**-s, -ing, -ed**) bet on the outcome of something
wagered *v* ▷ **wager**
wagering *v* ▷ **wager**
wagers *n, v* ▷ **wager**
wages *n, v* ▷ **wage**
wagged *v* ▷ **wag**
wagging *v* ▷ **wag**
waggle *v* (**-les, -ling, -led**) move with a rapid shaking or wobbling motion
waggled *v* ▷ **waggle**
waggles *v* ▷ **waggle**
waggling *v* ▷ **waggle**
waggon *n* ▷ **wagon**
waggons *n* ▷ **wagon**
waging *v* ▷ **wage**
wagon, waggon *n* (*pl* **-s**) four-wheeled vehicle for heavy loads
wagons *n* ▷ **wagon**
wags *v* ▷ **wag**
wagtail *n* (*pl* **-s**) small long-tailed bird
wagtail *n* ▷ **wagtails**
wahoo *n* (*pl* **-s**) food and game fish of tropical

seas

wahoos *n* ▷ **wahoo**

waif *n* (*pl* -**s**) young person who is, or seems, homeless or neglected

waifs *n* ▷ **waif**

wail *v* (-**s**, -**ing**, -**ed**) cry out in pain or misery ▶ *n* (*pl* -**s**) mournful cry

wailed *v* ▷ **wail**

wailing *v* ▷ **wail**

wails *v*, *n* ▷ **wail**

wain *n* (*pl* -**s**) (*Poetic*) farm wagon

wains *n* ▷ **wain**

wainscot, wainscoting *n* (*pl* -**s**) wooden lining of the lower part of the walls of a room

wainscoting *n* ▷ **wainscot**

wainscotings *n* ▷ **wainscot**

wainscots *n* ▷ **wainscot**

waist *n* (*pl* -**s**) part of the body between the ribs and hips

waistband *n* (*pl* -**s**) band of material sewn on to the waist of a garment to strengthen it

waistbands *n* ▷ **waistband**

waistcoat *n* (*pl* -**s**) sleeveless garment which buttons up the front, usu. worn over a shirt and under a jacket

waistcoats *n* ▷ **waistcoat**

waistline *n* (*pl* -**s**) (size of) the waist of a person or garment

waistlines *n* ▷ **waistline**

waists *n* ▷ **waist**

wait *v* (-**s**, -**ing**, -**ed**) remain inactive in expectation (of something) ▶ *n* (*pl* -**s**) act or period of waiting

waited *v* ▷ **wait**

waiter *n* (*pl* -**s**) man who serves in a restaurant etc. > **waitress** *n fem* (*pl* -**es**)

waiters *n* ▷ **waiter**

waiting *v* ▷ **wait**

waitress *n* ▷ **waiter**

waitresses *n* ▷ **waiter**

waits *v*, *n* ▷ **wait**

waive *v* (-**ves**, -**ving**, -**ved**) refrain from enforcing (a law, right, etc.)

waived *v* ▷ **waive**

waiver *n* (*pl* -**s**) act or instance of voluntarily giving up a claim, right, etc.

waivers *n* ▷ **waiver**

waives *v* ▷ **waive**

waiving *v* ▷ **waive**

waka *n* (*pl* -**s**) (NZ) Maori canoe

wakas *n* ▷ **waka**

wake¹ *v* (-**kes**, -**king**, **woke**, **woken**) rouse from sleep or inactivity ▶ *n* (*pl* -**s**) vigil beside a corpse the night before the funeral > **wakeful** *adj*

wake² *n* (*pl* -**s**) track left by a moving ship

wakeful *adj* ▷ **wake¹**

waken *v* (-**s**, -**ing**, -**ed**) wake

wakened *v* ▷ **waken**

wakening *v* ▷ **waken**

wakens *v* ▷ **waken**

wakes *n* ▷ **wake**¹, ²

waking *v* ▷ **wake¹**

walk *v* (-**s**, -**ing**, -**ed**) move on foot with at least one foot always on the ground ▶ *n* (*pl* -**s**) act or instance of walking > **walker** *n* (*pl* -**s**)

walkabout *n* (*pl* -**s**) informal walk among the public by royalty etc.

walkabouts *n* ▷ **walkabout**

walked *v* ▷ **walk**

walker *n* ▷ **walk**

walkers *n* ▷ **walk**

walking *v* ▷ **walk**

walkout *n* (*pl* -**s**) strike

walkouts *n* ▷ **walkout**

walkover *n* (*pl* -**s**) easy victory

walkovers *n* ▷ **walkover**

walks *v*, *n* ▷ **walk**

wall *n* (*pl* -**s**) structure of brick, stone, etc. used to enclose, divide, or support ▶ *v* (-**s**, -**ing**, -**ed**) enclose or seal with a wall or walls

wallabies *n* ▷ **wallaby**

wallaby *n* (*pl* -**bies**) marsupial like a small kangaroo

wallaroo *n* (*pl* -**s**) large stocky Australian kangaroo of rocky regions

wallaroos *n* ▷ **wallaroo**

walled *v* ▷ **wall**

wallet *n* (*pl* -**s**) small folding case for paper money, documents, etc.

wallets *n* ▷ **wallet**

walleye *n* (*pl* -**s**) fish with large staring eyes (*also* **dory**)

walleyes *n* ▷ **walleye**

wallflower *n* (*pl* -**s**) fragrant garden plant

wallflowers *n* ▷ **wallflower**

wallies *n* ▷ **wally**

walling *v* ▷ **wall**

wallop (*Informal*) *v* (-**s**, -**ing**, -**ed**) hit hard ▶ *n* (*pl* -**s**) hard blow

walloped *v* ▷ **wallop**

walloping (*Informal*) *n* thrashing ▶ *adj* large or great ▶ *v* ▷ **wallop**

wallops *v*, *n* ▷ **wallop**

wallow *v* (-**s**, -**ing**, -**ed**) revel in an emotion ▶ *n* (*pl* -**s**) act or instance of wallowing

wallowed *v* ▷ **wallow**

wallowing *v* ▷ **wallow**

wallows *v*, *n* ▷ **wallow**

wallpaper *n* (*pl* -**s**) decorative paper to cover

interior walls
wallpapers n ▷ **wallpaper**
walls n, v ▷ **wall**
wally n (pl -**ies**) (BRIT) (Slang) stupid person
walnut n (pl -**s**) edible nut with a wrinkled shell
walnuts n ▷ **walnut**
walrus n (pl -**ruses**, -**rus**) large sea mammal with long tusks
walruses n ▷ **walrus**
waltz n (pl -**es**) ballroom dance ▶ v (-**zes**, -**zing**, -**zed**) dance a waltz
waltzed v ▷ **waltz**
waltzes n, v ▷ **waltz**
waltzing v ▷ **waltz**
wampum [**wom**-pum] n (pl -**s**) shells woven together, formerly used by Native Americans for money and ornament
wampums n ▷ **wampum**
wan [rhymes with **swan**] adj (-**nner**, -**nnest**) pale and sickly looking
wand n (pl -**s**) thin rod, esp. one used in performing magic tricks
wander v (-**s**, -**ing**, -**ed**) move about without a definite destination or aim ▶ n (pl -**s**) act or instance of wandering > **wanderer** n (pl -**s**)
wandered v ▷ **wander**
wanderer n ▷ **wander**
wanderers n ▷ **wander**
wandering v ▷ **wander**
wanderlust n (pl -**s**) great desire to travel
wanderlusts n ▷ **wanderlust**
wanders v, n ▷ **wander**
wands n ▷ **wand**
wane v (-**nes**, -**ning**, -**ned**) decrease gradually in size or strength
waned v ▷ **wane**
wanes v ▷ **wane**
wangle v (-**les**, -**ling**, -**led**) (Informal) get by devious methods
wangled v ▷ **wangle**
wangles v ▷ **wangle**
wangling v ▷ **wangle**
waning v ▷ **wane**
wanner adj ▷ **wan**
wannest adj ▷ **wan**
want v (-**s**, -**ing**, -**ed**) need or long for ▶ n (pl -**s**) act or instance of wanting
wanted adj sought by the police ▶ v ▷ **want**
wanting adj lacking ▶ v ▷ **want**
wanton adj (-**er**, -**est**) without motive, provocation, or justification
wantoner adj ▷ **wanton**
wantonest adj ▷ **wanton**
wants v, n ▷ **want**
war n (pl -**s**) fighting between nations ▶ adj

of, like, or caused by war ▶ v (-**s**, -**rring**, -**rred**) conduct a war > **warring** adj
waratah n (pl -**s**) Australian shrub with crimson flowers
waratahs n ▷ **waratah**
warble v (-**les**, -**ling**, -**led**) sing in a trilling voice
warbled v ▷ **warble**
warbler n (pl -**s**) any of various small songbirds
warblers n ▷ **warbler**
warbles v ▷ **warble**
warbling v ▷ **warble**
ward n (pl -**s**) room in a hospital for patients needing a similar kind of care
warden n (pl -**s**) person in charge of a building and its occupants
wardens n ▷ **warden**
warder n (pl -**s**) prison officer > **wardress** n fem (pl -**es**)
warders n ▷ **warder**
wardress n ▷ **warder**
wardresses n ▷ **warder**
wardrobe n (pl -**s**) cupboard for hanging clothes in
wardrobes n ▷ **wardrobe**
wardroom n (pl -**s**) officers' quarters on a warship
wardrooms n ▷ **wardroom**
wards n ▷ **ward**
ware n (pl -**s**) articles of a specified type or material ▶ pl goods for sale
warehouse n (pl -**s**) building for storing goods prior to sale or distribution
warehouses n ▷ **warehouse**
wares n ▷ **ware**
warfare n (pl -**s**) fighting or hostilities
warfares n ▷ **warfare**
warhead n (pl -**s**) explosive front part of a missile
warheads n ▷ **warhead**
warier adj ▷ **wary**
wariest n ▷ **wary**
warily adv ▷ **wary**
wariness n ▷ **wary**
warinesses n ▷ **wary**
warlike adj of or relating to war
warlock n (pl -**s**) man who practises black magic
warlocks n ▷ **warlock**
warm adj (-**er**, -**est**) moderately hot ▶ v (-**s**, -**ing**, -**ed**) make or become warm > **warmly** adv
warmed v ▷ **warm**
warmer adj ▷ **warm**
warmest adj ▷ **warm**
warming v ▷ **warm**
warmly adv ▷ **warm**

warmonger *n* (*pl* -**s**) person who encourages war

warmongers *n* ▷ **warmonger**

warms *v* ▷ **warm**

warmth *n* (*pl* -**s**) mild heat

warmths *n* ▷ **warmth**

warn *v* (-**s**, -**ing**, -**ed**) make aware of possible danger or harm

warned *v* ▷ **warn**

warning *n* (*pl* -**s**) something that warns ▶ *v* ▷ **warn**

warnings *n* ▷ **warning**

warns *v* ▷ **warn**

warp *v* (-**s**, -**ing**, -**ed**) twist out of shape ▶ *n* (*pl* -**s**) state of being warped

warped *v* ▷ **warp**

warping *v* ▷ **warp**

warps *v*, *n* ▷ **warp**

warrant *n* (*pl* -**s**) (document giving) official authorization ▶ *v* (-**s**, -**ing**, -**ed**) make necessary

warranted *v* ▷ **warrant**

warranties *n* ▷ **warranty**

warranting *v* ▷ **warrant**

warrants *n*, *v* ▷ **warrant**

warranty *n* (*pl* -**ties**) (document giving) a guarantee

warred *v* ▷ **war**

warren *n* (*pl* -**s**) series of burrows in which rabbits live

warrens *n* ▷ **warren**

warrigal (AUST) *n* (*pl* -**s**) dingo ▶ *adj* wild

warrigals *n* ▷ **warrigal**

warring *v* ▷ **war**

warrior *n* (*pl* -**s**) person who fights in a war

warriors *n* ▷ **warrior**

wars *n*, *v* ▷ **war**

warship *n* (*pl* -**s**) ship designed and equipped for naval combat

warships *n* ▷ **warship**

wart *n* (*pl* -**s**) small hard growth on the skin

warts *n* ▷ **wart**

wary [ware-ree] *adj* (-**rier**, -**riest**) watchful or cautious > **warily** *adv* > **wariness** *n* (*pl* -**es**)

was *v* ▷ **be**

wash *v* (-**es**, -**ing**, -**ed**) clean (oneself, clothes, etc.) with water and usu. soap (*Informal*) ▶ *n* (*pl* -**es**) act or process of washing > **washable** *adj*

washable *adj* ▷ **wash**

washed *v* ▷ **wash**

washer *n* (*pl* -**s**) ring put under a nut or bolt or in a tap as a seal

washers *n* ▷ **washer**

washes *v*, *n* ▷ **wash**

washing *n* (*pl* -**s**) clothes to be washed ▶ *v* ▷ **wash**

washings *n* ▷ **washing**

washout *n* (*pl* -**s**) (*Informal*) complete failure

washouts *n* ▷ **washouts**

wasp *n* (*pl* -**s**) stinging insect with a slender black-and-yellow striped body

waspish *adj* bad-tempered

wasps *n* ▷ **wasp**

wastage *n* (*pl* -**s**) loss by wear or waste

wastages *n* ▷ **wastage**

waste *v* (-**tes**, -**ting**, -**ted**) use pointlessly or thoughtlessly ▶ *n* (*pl* -**s**) act of wasting or state of being wasted ▶ *pl* desert ▶ *adj* rejected as worthless or surplus to requirements

wasted *v* ▷ **waste**

wasteful *adj* extravagant > **wastefully** *adv*

wastefully *adv* ▷ **waste**

waster, wastrel *n* (*pl* -**s**) layabout

wasters *n* ▷ **waster**

wastes *v*, *n* ▷ **waste**

wasting *v* ▷ **waste**

wastrel *n* ▷ **waster**

wastrels *n* ▷ **waster**

watch *v* (-**es**, -**ing**, -**ed**) look at closely ▶ *n* (*pl* -**es**) portable timepiece for the wrist or pocket > **watchable** *adj* > **watcher** *n* (*pl* -**s**)

watchable *adj* ▷ **watch**

watchdog *n* (*pl* -**s**) dog kept to guard property

watchdogs *n* ▷ **watchdog**

watched *v* ▷ **watch**

watcher *n* ▷ **watch**

watchers *n* ▷ **watch**

watches *v*, *n* ▷ **watch**

watchful *adj* vigilant or alert > **watchfully** *adv*

watchfully *adv* ▷ **watchful**

watching *v* ▷ **watch**

watchman *n* (*pl* -**men**) man employed to guard a building or property

watchmen *n* ▷ **watchman**

watchword *n* (*pl* -**s**) word or phrase that sums up the attitude of a particular group

watchwords *n* ▷ **watchword**

water *n* (*pl* -**s**) clear colourless tasteless liquid that falls as rain and forms rivers etc. ▶ *v* (-**s**, -**ing**, -**ed**) put water on or into > **watery** *adj* (-**rier**, -**riest**)

watercolour *n* (*pl* -**s**) paint thinned with water

watercolours *n* ▷ **watercolour**

watercourse *n* (*pl* -**s**) bed of a stream or river

watercourses *n* ▷ **watercourse**

watercress *n* (*pl* -**es**) edible plant growing in clear ponds and streams

watercresses *n* ▷ **watercress**

watered *v* ▷ **water**

waterfall *n* (*pl* -**s**) place where the waters of a

river drop vertically
  waterfalls n ▷ **waterfall**
waterfront n (pl -s) part of a town alongside a body of water
  waterfronts n ▷ **waterfront**
  waterier adj ▷ **watery**
  wateriest adj ▷ **watery**
  watering v ▷ **water**
watermark n (pl -s) faint translucent design in a sheet of paper
  watermarks n ▷ **watermark**
watermelon n (pl -s) melon with green skin and red flesh
  watermelons n ▷ **watermelon**
waterproof adj not letting water through ▶ n (pl -s) waterproof garment ▶ v (-s, -ing, -ed) make waterproof
  waterproofed v ▷ **waterproof**
  waterproofing v ▷ **waterproof**
  waterproofs n, v ▷ **waterproof**
  waters n, v ▷ **water**
watershed n (pl -s) important period or factor serving as a dividing line
  watersheds n ▷ **watershed**
watersider n (pl -s) (NZ) person employed to load and unload ships
  watersiders n ▷ **watersider**
waterskiing n (pl -s) sport of riding over water on skis towed by a speedboat
  waterskiings n ▷ **waterskiing**
watertight adj not letting water through
  watery adj ▷ **water**
watt [wott] n (pl -s) unit of power
wattage n (pl -s) electrical power expressed in watts
  wattages n ▷ **wattage**
wattle [wott-tl] n (pl -s) branches woven over sticks to make a fence making fences
  wattles n ▷ **wattle**
  watts n ▷ **watt**
wave v (-ves, -ving, -ved) move the hand to and fro as a greeting or signal ▶ n (pl -s) moving ridge on water > **wavy** adj (-vier, -viest)
  waved v ▷ **wave**
wavelength n (pl -s) distance between the same points of two successive waves
  wavelengths n ▷ **wavelength**
waver v (-s, -ing, -ed) hesitate or be irresolute > **waverer** n (pl -s)
  wavered v ▷ **waver**
  waverer n ▷ **waver**
  waverers n ▷ **waver**
  wavering v ▷ **waver**
  wavers v ▷ **waver**
waves v, n ▷ **wave**

  wavier adj ▷ **wave**
  waviest adj ▷ **wave**
  waving v ▷ **wave**
  wavy adj ▷ **wave**
wax[1] n (pl -es) solid shiny fatty or oily substance used for sealing, making candles, etc. ▶ v (-es, -ing, -ed) coat or polish with wax > **waxy** adj (-xier, -xiest)
wax[2] v (-es, -ing, -ed) increase in size or strength
  waxed v ▷ **wax**[1, 2]
waxen adj made of or like wax
  waxes n, v ▷ **wax**[1, 2]
  waxier adj ▷ **wax**
  waxiest adj ▷ **wax**
  waxing v ▷ **wax**[1, 2]
waxwork n (pl -s) lifelike wax model of a (famous) person ▶ pl place exhibiting these
  waxworks n ▷ **waxwork**
  waxy adj ▷ **wax**[1]
way n (pl -s) manner or method
wayfarer n (Lit) traveller
  wayfarers n ▷ **wayfarer**
  waylaid v ▷ **waylay**
waylay v (-lays, -laying, -laid) lie in wait for and accost or attack
  waylaying v ▷ **waylay**
  waylays v ▷ **waylay**
  ways n ▷ **way**
wayside adj, n (pl -s) (situated by) the side of a road
  waysides n ▷ **wayside**
wayward adj erratic, selfish, or stubborn > **waywardness** n (pl -es)
  waywardness n ▷ **waywardness**
  waywardnesses n ▷ **wayward**
we pron (used as the subject of a verb) the speaker or writer and one or more others
weak adj (-er, -est) lacking strength
weaken v (-s, -ing, -ed) make or become weak
  weakened v ▷ **weaken**
  weakening v ▷ **weaken**
  weakens v ▷ **weaken**
  weaker adj ▷ **weak**
  weakest adj ▷ **weak**
weakling n feeble person or animal
  weaklings n ▷ **weakling**
weakly adv feebly
weakness n (-es) being weak
  weaknesses n ▷ **weakness**
weal n (pl -s) raised mark left on the skin by a blow
  weals n ▷ **weal**
wealth n (pl -s) state of being rich > **wealthy** adj (-thier, -thiest)

wealthier *adj* ▷ **wealth**
wealthiest *adj* ▷ **wealth**
wealthy *adj* ▷ **wealth**
wean *v* (**-s, -ing, -ed**) accustom (a baby or young mammal) to food other than mother's milk
weaned *v* ▷ **wean**
weaning *v* ▷ **wean**
weans *v* ▷ **wean**
weapon *n* (*pl* **-s**) object used in fighting
weaponries *n* ▷ **weapon**
weaponry *n* (*pl* **-ries**) weapons collectively
weapons *n* ▷ **weapon**
wear *v* (**-s, -ing, wore, worn**) have on the body as clothing or ornament ▶ *n* (*pl* **-s**) clothes suitable for a particular time or purpose > **wearer** *n* (*pl* **-s**)
wearer *n* ▷ **wear**
wearers *n* ▷ **wear**
wearied *v* ▷ **weary**
wearier *adj* ▷ **weary**
wearies *v* ▷ **weary**
weariest *adj* ▷ **weary**
wearily *adv* ▷ **weary**
weariness *n* ▷ **weary**
wearinesses *n* ▷ **weary**
wearing *v* ▷ **wear**
wearisome *adj* tedious
wears *n, v* ▷ **wear**
weary *adj* (**-rier, -riest**) tired or exhausted ▶ *v* (**-ries, -rying, -ried**) make or become weary > **wearily** *adv* > **weariness** *n* (*pl* **-es**)
wearying *v* ▷ **weary**
weasel *n* (*pl* **-s**) small carnivorous mammal with a long body and short legs
weasels *n* ▷ **weasel**
weather *n* (*pl* **-s**) day-to-day atmospheric conditions of a place ▶ *v* (**-s, -ing, -ed**) (cause to) be affected by the weather
weathercock, weathervane *n* device that revolves to show the direction of the wind
weathercocks *n* ▷ **weathercock**
weathered *v* ▷ **weather**
weathering *v* ▷ **weather**
weathers *v, n* ▷ **weather**
weathervanes *n* ▷ **weathervane**
weave *v* (**-s, -ving, wove** *or* **weaved, woven** *or* **weaved**) make (fabric) by interlacing (yarn) on a loom > **weaver** *n* (*pl* **-s**)
weaved *v* ▷ **weave**
weaver *n* ▷ **weave**
weavers *n* ▷ **weave**
weaves *v* ▷ **weave**
web *n* (*pl* **-s**) net spun by a spider > **webbed** *adj*
webbed *adj* ▷ **web**

webbing *n* (*pl* **-s**) strong fabric woven in strips
webbings *n* ▷ **web**
webcam *n* (*pl* **-s**) camera that transmits images over the Internet
webcams *n* ▷ **webcam**
webcast *n* (*pl* **-s**) broadcast of an event over the Internet
webcasts *n* ▷ **webcast**
weblog *n* (*pl* **-s**) person's online journal (*also* **blog**)
weblogs *n* ▷ **weblog**
webs *n* ▷ **web**
website *n* (*pl* **-s**) group of connected pages on the World Wide Web
websites *n* ▷ **website**
wed *v* (**-s, -dding, -dded** *or* **wed**) marry
wedded *v* ▷ **wed**
wedding *n* (*pl* **-s**) act or ceremony of marriage ▶ *v* ▷ **wed**
weddings *n* ▷ **wedding**
wedge *n* (*pl* **wedges**) piece of material thick at one end and thin at the other ▶ *v* (**-ges, -ging, -ged**) fasten or split with a wedge
wedged *v* ▷ **wedge**
wedges *n, v* ▷ **wedge**
wedging *v* ▷ **wedge**
wedlock *n* (*pl* **-s**) marriage
wedlocks *n* ▷ **wedlock**
wee *adj* (**-r, -st**) (BRIT, AUST & NZ) (*Informal*) small or short
weed *n* (*pl* **-s**) plant growing where undesired (*Informal*) ▶ *v* (**-s, -ing, -ed**) clear of weeds
weeded *v* ▷ **weed**
weedier *adj* ▷ **weedy**
weediest *adj* ▷ **weddy**
weeding *v* ▷ **weed**
weeds *n, v* ▷ **weed** ▶ *pl n* (*Obs*) widow's mourning clothes
weedy *adj* (**-dier, -diest**) (*Informal*) (of a person) thin and weak
week *n* (*pl* **-s**) period of seven days, esp. one beginning on a Sunday
weekday *n* (*pl* **-s**) any day of the week except Saturday or Sunday
weekdays *n* ▷ **weekday**
weekend *n* (*pl* **-s**) Saturday and Sunday
weekends *n* ▷ **weekend**
weeklies *n* ▷ **weekly**
weekly *adj, adv* happening, done, etc. once a week ▶ *n* (*pl* **-lies**) newspaper or magazine published once a week
weeks *n* ▷ **week**
weep *v* (**-s, -ing, wept**) shed tears
weepier *adj* ▷ **weepy**
weepiest *adj* ▷ **weepy**

weeping v ▷ weep
weeps v ▷ weep
weepy adj (-pier, -piest) liable to cry
weer adj ▷ wee
weest adj ▷ wee
weevil n (pl -s) small beetle which eats grain etc.
weevils n ▷ weevil
weft n (pl -s) cross threads in weaving
wefts n ▷ weft
weigh v (-s, -ing, -ed) have a specified weight
weighbridge n (pl -s) machine for weighing vehicles by means of a metal plate set into the road
weighbridges n ▷ weighbridge
weighed v ▷ weigh
weighing v ▷ weigh
weighs v ▷ weigh
weight n (pl -s) heaviness of an object ▶ v (-s, -ing, -ed) add weight to > **weightless** adj > **weightlessness** n
weighted v ▷ weight
weightier adj ▷ weighty
weightiest adj ▷ weighty
weightily adv ▷ weighty
weighting v ▷ weight ▶ n (pl -s) (BRIT) extra allowance paid in special circumstances
weightings n ▷ weighting
weightless adj ▷ weight
weightlessness n ▷ weight
weights n, v ▷ weight
weighty adj (-tier, -tiest) important or serious > **weightily** adv
weir n (pl -s) river dam
weird (-er, -est) adj strange or bizarre
weirder adj ▷ weird
weirdest adj ▷ weird
weirdo n (pl -s) (Informal) peculiar person
weirdos n ▷ weirdo
weirs n ▷ weir
welch v (-es, -ing, -ed) ▷ welsh
welched v ▷ welch
welches v ▷ welch
welching v ▷ welch
welcome v (-mes, -ming, -med) greet with pleasure ▶ n (pl -s) kindly greeting ▶ adj received gladly
welcomed v ▷ welcome
welcomes v, n ▷ welcome
welcoming v ▷ welcome
weld v (-s, -ing, -ed) join (pieces of metal or plastic) by softening with heat ▶ n (pl -s) welded joint > **welder** n (pl -s)
welded v ▷ weld
welder n ▷ weld

welders n ▷ weld
welding v ▷ weld
welds v, n ▷ weld
welfare n (pl -s) wellbeing
welfares n ▷ welfare
well[1] adv (better, best) satisfactorily ▶ adj in good health ▶ interj exclamation of surprise, interrogation, etc.
well[2] n (pl -s) hole sunk into the earth to reach water, oil, or gas ▶ v (-s, -ing, -ed) flow upwards or outwards
wellbeing n (pl -s) state of being well, happy, or prosperous
wellbeings n ▷ wellbeing
welled v ▷ well[2]
wellies pl n (BRIT & AUST) (Informal) wellingtons
welling v ▷ well[2]
wellingtons pl n (BRIT & AUST) high waterproof rubber boots
wells n, v ▷ well[2]
welsh v (-es, -ing, -ed) fail to pay a debt or fulfil an obligation
welshed v ▷ welsh
welshes v ▷ welsh
welshing v ▷ welsh
welt n (pl -s) raised mark on the skin produced by a blow
welter n (pl -s) jumbled mass
welters n ▷ welter
welterweight n (pl -s) boxer weighing up to 147lb (professional) or 67kg (amateur)
welterweights n ▷ welterweight
welts n ▷ welt
wen n (pl -s) cyst on the scalp
wench n (pl -es) (facetious) young woman
wenches n ▷ wench
wend v (-s, -ing, -ed) go or travel
wended v ▷ wend
wending v ▷ wend
wends v ▷ wend
wens n ▷ wen
went v ▷ go
wept v ▷ weep
were v form of the past tense of **be** used after we, you, they, or a plural noun ▷ be
werewolf n (pl -wolves) (in folklore) person who can turn into a wolf
werewolves n ▷ werewolf
west n (pl -s) (direction towards) the part of the horizon where the sun sets ▶ adj to or in the west ▶ adv in, to, or towards the west > **westerly** adj > **westward** adj, adv > **westwards** adv
westerly adj ▷ west
western adj of or in the west ▶ n (pl -s) film or

story about cowboys in the western US

westernize v (-zes, -zing, -zed) adapt to the customs and culture of the West

westernized v ▷ **westernize**

westernizes v ▷ **westernize**

westernizing v ▷ **westernize**

westerns n ▷ **western**

wests n ▷ **west**

westward adj ▷ **west**

westwards adv ▷ **west**

wet adj (-tter, -ttest) covered or soaked with water or another liquid (BRIT) (Informal) ▶ n moisture or rain (BRIT) (Informal) ▶ v (-s, -tting, **wet** or **wetted**) make wet

wetland n (pl -s) area of marshy land

wetlands n ▷ **wetland**

wetted v ▷ **wet**

wetter adj ▷ **wet**

wettest adj ▷ **wet**

wetting v ▷ **wet**

> **wex** n (**wexes**). Wex is an old word for **wax**. This gives a very good score for a three-letter word, and is a good one to look for when you have an X. Wex scores 13 points.

whack v (-s, -ing, -ed) strike with a resounding blow ▶ n (pl -s) such a blow

whacked adj exhausted ▶ v ▷ **whack**

whacking adj (Informal) huge ▶ v ▷ **whack**

whacks v, n ▷ **whack**

whale n (pl -s) large fish-shaped sea mammal

whaler n ship or person involved in whaling

whalers n ▷ **whaler**

whales n ▷ **whale**

whaling n (pl -s) hunting of whales for food and oil

whalings n ▷ **whaling**

wharf n (pl **wharves, wharfs**) platform at a harbour for loading and unloading ships

wharfie n (pl -s) (AUST) person employed to load and unload ships

wharfies n ▷ **wharfie**

wharfs n ▷ **wharf**

wharves n ▷ **wharf**

what pron which thing ▶ interj exclamation of anger, surprise, etc. ▶ adv in which way, how much

whatnot n (pl -s) (Informal) similar unspecified things

whatnots n ▷ **whatnot**

whatsoever adj at all

wheat n (pl -s) grain used in making flour, bread, and pasta > **wheaten** adj

wheatear n (pl -s) small songbird

wheatears n ▷ **wheatear**

wheaten adj ▷ **wheat**

wheats n ▷ **wheat**

wheedle v (-les, -ling, -led) coax or cajole

wheedled v ▷ **wheedle**

wheedles v ▷ **wheedle**

wheedling v ▷ **wheedle**

wheel n (pl -s) disc that revolves on an axle ▶ v (-s, -ing, -ed) push or pull (something with wheels)

wheelbarrow n (pl -s) shallow box for carrying loads, with a wheel at the front and two handles

wheelbarrows n ▷ **wheelbarrow**

wheelbase n (pl -s) distance between a vehicle's front and back axles

wheelbases n ▷ **wheelbase**

wheelchair n (pl -s) chair mounted on wheels for use by people who cannot walk

wheelchairs n ▷ **wheelchair**

wheeled v ▷ **wheel**

wheeling v ▷ **wheel**

wheels n, v ▷ **wheel**

wheeze v (-zes, -zing, -zed) breathe with a hoarse whistling noise ▶ n (pl -s) wheezing sound (Informal) > **wheezy** adj (-zier, -ziest)

wheezed v ▷ **wheeze**

wheezes v, n ▷ **wheeze**

wheezier adj ▷ **wheeze**

wheeziest adj ▷ **wheeze**

wheezing v ▷ **wheeze**

wheezy adj ▷ **wheeze**

whelk n (pl -s) edible snail-like shellfish

whelks n ▷ **whelk**

whelp n (pl -s) pup or cub ▶ v (-s, -ing, -ed) (of an animal) give birth

whelped v ▷ **whelp**

whelping v ▷ **whelp**

whelps n, v ▷ **whelp**

when adv at what time? ▶ conj at the time that ▶ pron at which time

whence adv, conj (Obs) from what place or source

whenever adv, conj at whatever time

where adv in, at, or to what place? ▶ pron in, at, or to which place ▶ conj in the place at which

whereabouts n present position ▶ adv at what place

whereas conj but on the other hand

whereby pron by which

wherefore (Obs) adv why ▶ conj consequently

whereupon conj at which point

wherever conj, adv at whatever place

wherewithal n (pl -s) necessary funds, resources, etc.

wherewithals n ▷ **wherewithals**

whet v (-s, -tting, -tted) sharpen (a tool)
whether conj used to introduce an indirect question or a clause expressing doubt or choice
  whets v ▷ whet
whetstone n (pl -s) stone for sharpening tools
  whetstones n ▷ whetstone
  whetted v ▷ whet
  whetting v ▷ whet
whey [way] n (pl -s) watery liquid that separates from the curd when milk is clotted
  wheys n ▷ whey
which adj, pron used to request or refer to a choice from different possibilities ▶ pron used to refer to a thing already mentioned
whichever adj, pron any out of several
whiff n (pl -s) puff of air or odour
  whiffs n ▷ whiff
whig n (pl -s) member of a British political party of the 18th–19th centuries that sought limited reform
  whigs n ▷ whig
while conj at the same time that ▶ n (pl -s) period of time
  whiles n ▷ while
whilst conj while
whim n (pl -s) sudden fancy
whimper v (-s, -ing, -ed) cry in a soft whining way ▶ n (pl -s) soft plaintive whine
  whimpered v ▷ whimper
  whimpering v ▷ whimper
  whimpers v, n ▷ whimper
  whims n ▷ whim
whimsical adj unusual, playful, and fanciful
  whimsies n ▷ whimsy
whimsy n (pl -ies) capricious idea
whin n (pl -s) (BRIT) gorse
whine n (pl -s) high-pitched plaintive cry
  ▶ v (-nes, -ning, -ned) make such a sound
  > **whining** n, adj (pl -s)
  whined v ▷ whine
  whines n, v ▷ whine
whinge (BRIT, AUST & NZ) (Informal) v (-ges, -geing, -ged) complain ▶ n (pl -s) complaint
  whinged v ▷ whinge
  whingeing v ▷ whinge
  whinges v, n ▷ whinge
  whining v, n adj ▷ whine
  whinings n ▷ whine
  whinnied v ▷ whinny
  whinnies v, n ▷ whinny
whinny v (-nnies, -nnying, -nnied) neigh softly
  ▶ n (pl -nnies) soft neigh
  whinnying v ▷ whinny
  whins n ▷ whin

whip n (pl -s) cord attached to a handle, used for beating animals or people ▶ v (-s, -pping, -pped) strike with a whip, strap, or cane
  whipped v ▷ whip
whippet n (pl -s) racing dog like a small greyhound
  whippets n ▷ whippet
  whipping v ▷ whip
  whips v, n ▷ whip
  whir v ▷ whirr
whirl v (-s, -ing, -ed) spin or revolve ▶ n (pl -s) whirling movement
  whirled v ▷ whirl
  whirling v ▷ whirl
whirlpool n (pl -s) strong circular current of water
  whirlpools n ▷ whirlpool
  whirls v, n ▷ whirl
whirlwind n (pl -s) column of air whirling violently upwards in a spiral ▶ adj much quicker than normal
  whirlwinds n ▷ whirlwind
whirr, whir n (pl -s) prolonged soft buzz ▶ v (-s, -rring, -rred) (cause to) make a whirr
  whirred v ▷ whirr
  whirring v ▷ whirr
  whirrs n, v ▷ whirr
  whirs n ▷ whirr
whisk v (-s, -ing, -ed) move or remove quickly ▶ n (pl -s) egg-beating utensil
  whisked v ▷ whisk
whisker n (pl -s) any of the long stiff hairs on the face of a cat or other mammal ▶ pl hair growing on a man's face
  whiskers n ▷ whisker
whiskey n (pl -s) Irish or American whisky
  whiskeys n ▷ whiskey
  whiskies n ▷ whisky
  whisking v, v ▷ whisk
  whisks n ▷ whisk
whisky n (pl -ies) spirit distilled from fermented cereals
whisper v (-s, -ing, -ed) speak softly, without vibration of the vocal cords ▶ n (pl -s) soft voice (Informal)
  whispered v ▷ whisper
  whispering v ▷ whisper
  whispers v, n ▷ whisper
whist n (pl -s) card game in which one pair of players tries to win more tricks than another pair
whistle v (-les, -ling, -led) produce a shrill sound, esp. by forcing the breath through pursed lips ▶ n (pl -s) whistling sound
  > **whistling** n, adj (pl -s)

whistled v ▷ **whistle**
whistles v, n ▷ **whistle**
whistling v, n ▷ **whistle**
whistlings n ▷ **whistle**
whists n ▷ **whist**
whit n (pl -s) not the slightest amount
white adj (-r, -st) of the colour of snow ▶ n
(pl -s) colour of snow > **whiteness** n (pl -es)
> **whitish** adj
whitebait n (pl -s) small edible fish
whitebaits n ▷ **whitebait**
whiten v (-s, -ing, -ed) make or become white
or whiter
whitened v ▷ **whiten**
whiteness n ▷ **white**
whitenesses n ▷ **white**
whitening v ▷ **whiten**
whitens v ▷ **whiten**
whiter adj ▷ **white**
whites n ▷ **white**
whitest adj ▷ **white**
whitewash n (pl -es) substance for whitening
walls ▶ v (-es, -ing, -ed) cover with whitewash
whitewashed v ▷ **whitewash**
whitewashes n, v ▷ **whitewash**
whitewashing v ▷ **whitewash**
whither adv (Obs) to what place
whiting n (pl -s) edible sea fish
whitings n ▷ **whiting**
whitish adj ▷ **white**
whittle v (-les, -ling, -led) cut or carve (wood)
with a knife
whittled v ▷ **whittle**
whittles v ▷ **whittle**
whittling v ▷ **whittle**
whiz v ▷ **whizz**
whizz, whiz v (-es, -ing, -ed) make a loud
buzzing sound (Informal) ▶ n (pl -es) loud
buzzing sound (Informal)
whizzed v ▷ **whizz**
whizzes v, n ▷ **whizz**
whizzing v ▷ **whizz**
who pron which person
whodunnit, whodunit [hoo-**dun**-nit] n (pl -s)
(Informal) detective story, play, or film
whodunnits n ▷ **whodunnit**
whoever pron any person who
whole adj containing all the elements or
parts ▶ n (pl -s) complete thing or system
> **wholly** adv
wholefood n (pl -s) food that has been
processed as little as possible
wholefoods n ▷ **wholefood**
wholehearted adj sincere or enthusiastic
wholemeal adj (of flour) made from the whole

wheat grain
wholes n ▷ **whole**
wholesale adj, adv dealing by selling goods
in large quantities to retailers > **wholesaler**
n (pl -s)
wholesaler n ▷ **wholesale**
wholesalers n ▷ **wholesale**
wholesome adj physically or morally
beneficial
wholly adv ▷ **whole**
whom pron ▷ **who**
whoop v, n (pl -s) shout or cry to express
excitement
whoopee interj (Informal) cry of joy
whoops n ▷ **whoop**
whopper n (pl -s) (Informal) anything unusually
large > **whopping** adj
whoppers n ▷ **whopper**
whopping adj ▷ **whopper**
whore [hore] n (pl -s) prostitute
whores n ▷ **whore**
whorl n (pl -s) ring of leaves or petals
whorls n ▷ **whorl**
whose pron of whom or of which
why adv for what reason ▶ pron because of
which
wick n (pl -s) cord through a lamp or candle
which carries fuel to the flame
wicked (-er, -est) adj morally bad > **wickedly**
adv > **wickedness** n (pl -s)
wickedly adv ▷ **wicked**
wickedness n ▷ **wicked**
wickednesses n ▷ **wicked**
wicker adj made of woven cane > **wickerwork**
n (pl -s)
wickerwork n ▷ **wicker**
wickerworks n ▷ **wicker**
wicket n (pl -s) set of three cricket stumps and
two bails
wickets n ▷ **wicket**
wicks n ▷ **wick**
wide adj (-r, -st) large from side to side ▶ adv to
the full extent > **widely** adv
widely adv ▷ **wide**
widen v (-s, -ing, -ed) make or become wider
widened v ▷ **widen**
widening v ▷ **widen**
widens v ▷ **widen**
wider adj ▷ **wide**
widespread adj affecting a wide area or a large
number of people
widest adj ▷ **wide**
widgeon n (pl -s) ▷ **wigeon**
widgeons n ▷ **widgeon**
widow n (pl -s) woman whose husband is dead

and who has not remarried > **widowed** adj
> **widowhood** n (pl **-s**)
  widowed adj ▷ **widow**
widower n (pl **-s**) man whose wife is dead and
who has not remarried
  widowers n ▷ **widower**
  widowhood n ▷ **widow**
  widowhoods n ▷ **widow**
  widows n ▷ **widow**
width n (pl **-s**) distance from side to side
  widths n ▷ **width**
wield v (**-s, -ing, -ed**) hold and use (a weapon)
  wielded v ▷ **wield**
  wielding v ▷ **wield**
  wields v ▷ **wield**
wife n (pl **wives**) woman to whom a man is
married
wig n (pl **-s**) artificial head of hair
wigeon n (pl **-s**) duck found in marshland
  wigeons n ▷ **wigeon**
wiggle v (**-les, -ling, -led**) move jerkily from
side to side ▶ n (pl **-les**) wiggling movement
  wiggled v ▷ **wiggle**
  wiggles v, n ▷ **wiggle**
  wiggling v ▷ **wiggle**
  wigs n ▷ **wig**
wigwam n (pl **-s**) Native American's tent
  wigwams n ▷ **wigwam**
wild adj (**-er, -est**) (of animals) not tamed or
domesticated > **wildly** adv > **wildness** n (pl
-es)
wildcat n (pl **-s**) European wild animal like a
large domestic cat
  wildcats n ▷ **wildcat**
wildebeest n (pl **-s**) gnu
  wildebeests n ▷ **wildebeest**
  wilder adj ▷ **wild**
wilderness n (pl **-es**) uninhabited uncultivated
region
  wildernesses n ▷ **wilderness**
  wildest adj ▷ **wild**
wildlife n (pl **-s**) wild animals and plants
collectively
  wildlifes n ▷ **wildlife**
  wildly adv ▷ **wild**
  wildness n ▷ **wild**
  wildnesses n ▷ **wild**
wilds pl n desolate or uninhabited place
wiles pl n tricks or ploys
wilful adj headstrong or obstinate > **wilfully**
adv
  wilfully adv ▷ **wilful**
  wilier adj ▷ **wily**
  wiliest adj ▷ **wily**
will¹ v (past **would**) used as an auxiliary to form

the future tense or to indicate intention,
ability, or expectation
will² n (pl **-s**) strong determination ▶ v (**-s,
-ing, -ed**) use one's will in an attempt to do
(something)
  willed v ▷ **will²**
willing adj ready or inclined (to do something)
▶ v ▷ **will²** > **willingly** adv > **willingness** n
(pl **-es**)
  willingly adv ▷ **willing**
  willingness n ▷ **willing**
  willingnesses n ▷ **willing**
willow n (pl **-s**) tree with thin flexible branches
  willowier adj ▷ **willowy**
  willowiest adj ▷ **willowy**
  willows n ▷ **willow**
willowy adj (**-wier, -wiest**) slender and graceful
willpower n (pl **-s**) ability to control oneself
and one's actions
  willpowers n ▷ **willpower**
  wills n, v ▷ **will²**
wilt v (**-s, -ing, -ed**) (cause to) become limp or
lose strength
  wilted v ▷ **wilt**
  wilting v ▷ **wilt**
  wilts v ▷ **wilt**
wily adj (**-lier, -liest**) crafty or sly
wimp n (pl **-s**) (Informal) feeble ineffectual
person
wimple n (pl **-s**) garment framing the face,
worn by medieval women and now by nuns
  wimples n ▷ **wimple**
  wimps n ▷ **wimp**
win v (**-s, -nning, won**) come first in (a
competition, fight, etc.) ▶ n (pl **-s**) victory, esp.
in a game > **winner** n (pl **-s**)
wince v (**-ces, -cing, -ced**) draw back, as if in
pain ▶ n (pl **-s**) wincing
  winced v ▷ **wince**
  winces v, n ▷ **wince**
winch n (pl **-es**) machine for lifting or hauling
using a cable or chain wound round a drum
▶ v (**-es, -ing, -ed**) lift or haul using a winch
  winched v ▷ **winch**
  winches n, v ▷ **winch**
  winching v ▷ **winch**
  wincing v ▷ **wince**
wind¹ n (pl **-s**) current of air ▶ v (**-s, -ing, -ed**)
render short of breath > **windy** adj (**-dier,
-diest**)
wind² v (**-s, -ing, wound**) coil or wrap around
  winded v ▷ **wind¹**
windfall n (pl **-s**) unexpected good luck
  windfalls n ▷ **windfall**
  windier adj ▷ **wind¹**

windiest *adj* ▷ **wind¹**
winding *v* ▷ **wind¹, ²**
windlass *n* (*pl* -es) winch worked by a crank
windlasses *n* ▷ **windlass**
windmill *n* (*pl* -s) machine for grinding or
pumping driven by sails turned by the wind
windmills *n* ▷ **windmill**
window *n* (*pl* -s) opening in a wall to let in
light or air
windows *n* ▷ **window**
windpipe *n* (*pl* -s) tube linking the throat and
the lungs
windpipes *n* ▷ **windpipe**
winds *n, v* ▷ **wind¹, ²**
windscreen *n* (*pl* -s) front window of a motor
vehicle
windscreens *n* ▷ **windscreen**
windsock *n* (*pl* -s) cloth cone on a mast at an
airfield to indicate wind direction
windsocks *n* ▷ **windsock**
windsurfing *n* (*pl* -s) sport of riding on water
using a surfboard propelled and steered by
a sail
windsurfings *n* ▷ **windsurfing**
windward *adj, n* (*pl* -s) (of or in) the direction
from which the wind is blowing
windwards *n* ▷ **windward**
windy *adj* ▷ **wind¹**
wine *n* (*pl* -s) alcoholic drink made from
fermented grapes
wines *n* ▷ **wine**
wing *n* (*pl* -s) one of the limbs or organs of a
bird, insect, or bat that are used for flying ▶ *pl*
sides of a stage ▶ *v* (-s, -ing, -ed) fly > **winged**
adj
winged *v, adj* ▷ **wing**
winger *n* (*pl* -s) (SPORT) player positioned on the
side of the pitch
wingers *n* ▷ **winger**
winging *v* ▷ **wing**
wings *n, v* ▷ **wing**
wink *v* (-s, -ing, -ed) close and open (an eye)
quickly as a signal ▶ *n* (*pl* -s) winking
winked *v* ▷ **wink**
winking *v* ▷ **wink**
winkle *n* (*pl* -s) shellfish with a spiral shell
winkles *n* ▷ **winkle**
winks *v, n* ▷ **wink**
winner *n* ▷ **win**
winners *n* ▷ **win**
winning *adj* gaining victory ▶ *v* ▷ **win**
winnings *pl n* sum won, esp. in gambling
winnow *v* (-s, -ing, -ed) (*pl* -s) separate (chaff)
from (grain)
winnowed *v* ▷ **winnow**

winnowing *v* ▷ **winnow**
winnows *v, n* ▷ **winnow**
winsome *adj* (-r, -st) charming or winning
winsomer *adj* ▷ **winsome**
winsomest *adj* ▷ **winsome**
winter *n* (*pl* -s) coldest season ▶ *v* (-s, -ing, -ed)
spend the winter
wintered *v* ▷ **winter**
wintering *v* ▷ **winter**
winters *n, v* ▷ **winter**
wintrier *adj* ▷ **wintry**
wintriest *adj* ▷ **wintry**
wintry *adj* (-rier, -riest) of or like winter
wipe *v* (-pes, -ping, -ped) clean or dry by
rubbing ▶ *n* (*pl* -s) wiping
wiped *v* ▷ **wipe**
wipes *v, n* ▷ **wipe**
wiping *v* ▷ **wipe**
wire *n* (*pl* -s) thin flexible strand of metal (*Obs*)
▶ *v* (-res, -ring, -red) equip with wires
wired *v* ▷ **wire**
wirehaired *adj* (of a dog) having a stiff wiry
coat
wireless *n* (*pl* -es) (*Old-fashioned*) ▷ **radio** ▶ *adj*
(of a computer network) connected by radio
rather than by cables or fibre optics
wirelesses *n* ▷ **wireless**
wires *n, v* ▷ **wire**
wirier *adj* ▷ **wiry**
wiriest *adj* ▷ **wiry**
wiring *n* (*pl* -s) system of wires ▶ *v* ▷ **wire**
wirings *n* ▷ **wiring**
wiry *adj* (-rier, -riest) lean and tough
wisdom *n* (*pl* -s) good sense and judgment
wisdoms *n* ▷ **wisdom**
wise¹ *adj* (-r, -st) having wisdom > **wisely** *adv*
wise² *n* (*pl* -s) (*Obs*) manner
wiseacre *n* (*pl* -s) person who wishes to seem
wise
wiseacres *n* ▷ **wiseacres**
wisecrack (*Informal*) *n* (*pl* -s) clever, sometimes
unkind, remark ▶ *v* (-s, -ing, -ed) make a
wisecrack
wisecracked *v* ▷ **wisecrack**
wisecracking *v* ▷ **wisecrack**
wisecracks *n, v* ▷ **wisecrack**
wisely *adv* ▷ **wise¹**
wiser *adj* ▷ **wise¹**
wises *n* ▷ **wise²**
wisest *adj* ▷ **wise¹**
wish *v* (-es, -ing, -ed) want or desire ▶ *n* (*pl* -es)
expression of a desire
wishbone *n* (*pl* -s) V-shaped bone above the
breastbone of a fowl
wishbones *n* ▷ **wishbone**

wished *v* ▷ **wish**
wishes *v*, *n* ▷ **wish**
wishful *adj* too optimistic
wishing *v* ▷ **wish**
wisp *n* (*pl* -s) light delicate streak > **wispy** *adj* (-pier, -piest)
wispier *adj* ▷ **wisp**
wispiest *adj* ▷ **wisp**
wisps *n* ▷ **wisp**
wispy *adj* ▷ **wisp**
wisteria *n* (*pl* -s) climbing shrub with blue or purple flowers
wisterias *n* ▷ **wisteria**
wistful *adj* sadly longing > **wistfully** *adv*
wistfully *adv* ▷ **wistful**
wit *n* (*pl* -s) ability to use words or ideas in a clever and amusing way
witch *n* (*pl* -es) person, usu. female, who practises (black) magic
witchcraft *n* (*pl* -s) use of magic
witchcrafts *n* ▷ **witchcraft**
witches *n* ▷ **witch**
with *prep* indicating presence alongside, possession, means of performance, characteristic manner, etc.
withdraw *v* (-drawing, -drew, -drawn) take or move out or away > **withdrawal** *n* (*pl* -s)
withdrawal *n* ▷ **withdraw**
withdrawals *n* ▷ **withdraw**
withdrawn *adj* unsociable ▶ *v* ▷ **withdraw**
withdraws *v* ▷ **withdraw**
withdrew *v* ▷ **withdraw**
wither *v* (-s, -ing, -ed) wilt or dry up
withered *v* ▷ **wither**
withering *adj* (of a look or remark) scornful ▶ *v* ▷ **wither**
withers *v* ▷ **wither** ▶ *pl n* ridge between a horse's shoulder blades
withheld *v* ▷ **withhold**
withhold *v* (-s, -ing, -held) refrain from giving
withholding *v* ▷ **withhold**
withholds *v* ▷ **withhold**
within *prep*, *adv* in or inside
without *prep* not accompanied by, using, or having
withstand *v* (-s, -ing, -stood) oppose or resist successfully
withstanding *v* ▷ **withstand**
withstands *v* ▷ **wwithstand**
withstood *v* ▷ **wwithstand**
witless *adj* foolish
witness *n* (*pl* -es) person who has seen something happen ▶ *v* (-es, -ing, -ed) see at first hand
witnessed *v* ▷ **witness**

witnesses *n*, *v* ▷ **witness**
witnessing *v* ▷ **witness**
wits *n* ▷ **wit**
witter *v* (-s, -ing, -ed) (CHIEFLY BRIT) chatter pointlessly or at unnecessary length
wittered *v* ▷ **witter**
wittering *v* ▷ **witter**
witters *v* ▷ **witter**
witticism *n* (*pl* -s) witty remark
witticisms *n* ▷ **witticism**
wittier *adj* ▷ **witty**
wittiest *adj* ▷ **witty**
wittily *adv* ▷ **witty**
wittingly *adv* intentionally
witty *adj* (-ttier, -ttiest) clever and amusing > **wittily** *adv*
wives *n* ▷ **wife**

> **wiz** *n* (**wizzes**). Wiz is a short form of **wizard.** This is the highest-scoring three-letter word beginning with W, and can be especially useful when there isn't much room to manoeuvre. Wiz scores 15 points.

wizard *n* (*pl* -s) magician > **wizardry** *n* (*pl* -ies)
wizardries *n* ▷ **wizard**
wizardry *n* ▷ **wizard**
wizards *n* ▷ **wizard**
wizened [wiz-zend] *adj* shrivelled or wrinkled

> **wo** *n* (**wos**). Wo is an old-fashioned spelling of **woe.** This unusual word is handy for joining words ending in W to those beginning in O. Wo scores 5 points.

woad *n* (*pl* -s) blue dye obtained from a plant, used by the ancient Britons as a body dye
woads *n* ▷ **woad**
wobbegong *n* (*pl* -s) Australian shark with brown-and-white skin
wobbegongs *n* ▷ **wobbegong**
wobble *v* (-les, -ling, -led) move unsteadily ▶ *n* (*pl* -s) wobbling movement or sound > **wobbly** *adj* (-lier, -liest)
wobbled *v* ▷ **wobble**
wobbles *v*, *n* ▷ **wobble**
wobblier *adj* ▷ **wobble**
wobbliest *adj* ▷ **wobble**
wobbling *v* ▷ **wobble**
wobbly *adj* ▷ **wobble**
wodge *n* (*pl* -s) (*Informal*) thick lump or chunk
wodges *n* ▷ **wodge**
woe *n* (*pl* -s) grief
woebegone *adj* looking miserable
woeful *adj* extremely sad > **woefully** *adv*
woefully *adv* ▷ **woeful**
woes *n* ▷ **woe**

wok n (pl -s) bowl-shaped Chinese cooking pan, used for stir-frying
woke v ▷ **wake**¹
woken v ▷ **wake**¹
woks n ▷ **wok**
wold n (pl -s) high open country
wolds n ▷ **wold**
wolf n (pl **wolves**) wild predatory canine mammal ▶ v eat ravenously
wolverine n (pl -s) carnivorous mammal of Arctic regions
wolverines n ▷ **wolverine**
wolves n ▷ **wolf**
woman n (pl **women**) adult human female > **womanhood** n (pl -s)
womanhood n ▷ **woman**
womanhoods n ▷ **woman**
womanish adj effeminate
womanizer n ▷ **womanizing**
womanizers n ▷ **womanizing**
womanizing n (pl -s) practice of indulging in casual affairs with women > **womanizer** n (pl -s)
womanizings n ▷ **womanizing**
womanly adj having qualities traditionally associated with a woman
womb n (pl -s) hollow organ in female mammals where babies are conceived and develop
wombat n (pl -s) small heavily-built burrowing Australian marsupial
wombats n ▷ **wombat**
wombs n ▷ **womb**
women n ▷ **woman**
won v ▷ **win**
wonder v (-s, -ing, -ed) be curious about ▶ n (pl -s) wonderful thing ▶ adj spectacularly successful > **wonderment** n (pl -s)
wondered v ▷ **wonder**
wonderful adj very fine > **wonderfully** adv
wonderfully adv ▷ **wonderful**
wondering v ▷ **wonder**
wonderment n ▷ **wonder**
wonderments n ▷ **wonder**
wonders v, n ▷ **wonder**
wondrous adj (Old-fashioned) wonderful
wonkier adj ▷ **wonky**
wonkiest adj ▷ **wonky**
wonky adj (-kier, -kiest) (BRIT, AUST & NZ) (Informal) shaky or unsteady
wont [rhymes with **don't**] adj accustomed ▶ n (pl -s) custom
wonts n ▷ **wont**
woo v (-s, -ing, -ed) try to persuade (Old-fashioned)

wood n (pl -s) substance trees are made of, used in carpentry and as fuel > **woody** adj (-dier, -diest)
woodbine n (pl -s) honeysuckle
woodbines n ▷ **woodbine**
woodcock n (pl -s) game bird
woodcocks n ▷ **woodcook**
woodcut n (pl -s) (print made from) an engraved block of wood
woodcuts n ▷ **woodcut**
wooded adj covered with trees
wooden adj made of wood
woodier adj ▷ **wood**
woodiest adj ▷ **wood**
woodland n (pl -s) forest
woodlands n ▷ **woodland**
woodlice n ▷ **woodlouse**
woodlouse n (pl -**lice**) small insect-like creature with many legs
woodpecker n (pl -s) bird which searches tree trunks for insects
woodpeckers n ▷ **woodpecker**
woods n ▷ **wood**
woodwind adj, n (pl -s) (of) a type of wind instrument made of wood
woodwinds n ▷ **woodwind**
woodworm n insect larva that bores into wood
woodworms n ▷ **woodworm**
woody adj ▷ **wood**
wooed v ▷ **woo**
woof¹ n (pl -s) cross threads in weaving
woof² n (pl -s) barking noise made by a dog
woofer n (pl -s) loudspeaker reproducing low-frequency sounds
woofers n ▷ **woofer**
woofs n ▷ **woof**¹, ²
wooing v ▷ **woo**
wool n (pl -s) soft hair of sheep, goats, etc. > **woollen** adj
woollen adj ▷ **wool**
woollier adj ▷ **woolly**
woolliest adj ▷ **woolly**
woolly adj (-llier, -lliest) of or like wool ▶ n knitted woollen garment
wools n ▷ **wool**
woomera n (pl -s) notched stick used by Australian Aborigines to aid the propulsion of a spear
woomeras n ▷ **woomera**
woos v ▷ **woo**
woozier adj ▷ **woozy**
wooziest adj ▷ **woozy**
woozy adj (-zier, -ziest) (Informal) weak, dizzy, and confused

word n (pl -**s**) smallest single meaningful unit of speech or writing ▶ v (-**s, -ing, -ed**) express in words

  worded v ▷ **word**

  wordier adj ▷ **wordy**

  wordiest adj ▷ **wordy**

wording n (pl -**s**) choice and arrangement of words ▶ v ▷ **word**

  wordings n ▷ **wording**

  words n, v ▷ **word**

wordy adj (-**dier, -diest**) using too many words

  wore v ▷ **wear**

work n (pl -**s**) physical or mental effort directed to making or doing something ▶ pl factory (Informal) ▶ adj of or for work ▶ v (-**s, -ing, -ed**) (cause to) do work > **workable** adj > **worker** n (pl -**s**)

  workable adj ▷ **work**

workaholic n (pl -**s**) person obsessed with work

  workaholics n ▷ **workaholic**

  worked v ▷ **work**

  worker n ▷ **work**

  workers n ▷ **work**

workhorse n (pl -**s**) person or thing that does a lot of dull or routine work

  workhorses n ▷ **workhorse**

workhouse n (pl -**s**) (in England, formerly) institution where the poor were given food and lodgings in return for work

  workhouses n ▷ **workhouse**

  working v ▷ **work**

workman n (pl -**men**) manual worker

workmanship n (pl -**s**) skill with which an object is made

  workmanships n ▷ **workmanship**

  workmen n ▷ **workman**

  works n, v ▷ **work**

workshop n (pl -**s**) room or building for a manufacturing process

  workshops n ▷ **w**

worktop n (pl -**s**) surface in a kitchen, used for food preparation

  worktops n ▷ **worktop**

world n (pl -**s**) the planet earth ▶ adj of the whole world

  worldlier adj ▷ **worldly**

  worldliest adj ▷ **worldly**

worldly adj (-**ier, -iest**) not spiritual

  worlds n ▷ **world**

worm n (pl -**s**) small limbless invertebrate animal ▶ pl illness caused by parasitic worms in the intestines ▶ v (-**s, -ing, -ed**) rid of worms > **wormy** adj (-**mier, -miest**)

  wormed v ▷ **worm**

  wormier adj ▷ **worm**

  wormiest adj ▷ **worm**

  worming v ▷ **worm**

  worms n, v ▷ **worm**

wormwood n (pl -**s**) bitter plant

  wormwoods n ▷ **wormwood**

  wormy adj ▷ **worm**

  worn v ▷ **wear**

  worried v, adj ▷ **worry**

  worries v, n ▷ **worry**

worry v (-**ies, -ying, -ied**) (cause to) be anxious or uneasy ▶ n (pl -**ies**) (cause of) anxiety or concern > **worried** adj > **worrying** adj, n

  worrying v, adj ▷ **worry**

  worse adj, adv ▷ **bad, badly**

worsen v (-**s, -ing, -ed**) make or grow worse

  worsened v ▷ **worsen**

  worsening v ▷ **worsen**

  worsens v ▷ **worsen**

worship v (-**s, -pping, -pped**) show religious devotion to ▶ n (pl -**s**) act or instance of worshipping > **worshipper** n (pl -**s**)

worshipful adj worshipping

  worshipped v ▷ **worship**

  worshipper n ▷ **worship**

  worshippers n ▷ **worship**

  worshipping v ▷ **worship**

  worships v, n ▷ **worship**

worst adj, adv ▷ **bad, badly** ▶ n worst thing

worsted [wooss-tid] n (pl -**s**) type of woollen yarn or fabric

  worsteds n ▷ **worsted**

worth prep having a value of ▶ n (pl -**s**) value or price > **worthless** adj

  worthier adj ▷ **worthy**

  worthiest adj ▷ **worthy**

  worthily adv ▷ **worthy**

  worthiness n ▷ **worthy**

  worthinesses n ▷ **worthy**

  worthless adj ▷ **worth**

  worths n ▷ **worth**

worthwhile adj worth the time or effort involved

worthy adj (-**thier, -thiest**) deserving admiration or respect ▶ n (Informal) notable person > **worthily** adv > **worthiness** n (pl -**es**)

  would v ▷ **will**[1]

wound[1] n (pl -**s**) injury caused by violence ▶ v (-**s, -ing, -ed**) inflict a wound on

wound[2] v ▷ **wind**[2]

  wounded v ▷ **wound**[1]

  wounding v ▷ **wound**[1]

  wounds n, v ▷ **wound**[1]

  wove v ▷ **weave**

  woven v ▷ **weave**

wow *interj* exclamation of astonishment ▶ *n* (*pl* -s) (*Informal*) astonishing person or thing

wows *n* ▷ **wow**

wowser *n* (*pl* -s) (AUST & NZ) (*Slang*) puritanical person

wowsers *n* ▷ **wowser**

> **wox** *n* (**woxes**). Wox is an old past tense of the verb **wax**. This gives a very good score for a three-letter word, and is a good one to look for when you have an X. Wox scores 13 points.

wrack *n* (*pl* -s) seaweed

wracks *n* ▷ **wrack**

wraith *n* (*pl* -s) ghost

wraiths *n* ▷ **wraith**

wrangle *v* (-les, -ling, -led) argue noisily ▶ *n* (*pl* -s) noisy argument

wrangled *v* ▷ **wrangle**

wrangles *v*, *n* ▷ **wrangle**

wrangling *v* ▷ **wrangle**

wrap *v* (-s, -pping, -pped) fold (something) round (a person or thing) so as to cover ▶ *n* (*pl* -s) garment wrapped round the shoulders

wrapped *v* ▷ **wrap**

wrapper *n* (*pl* -s) cover for a product

wrappers *n* ▷ **wrapper**

wrapping *n* (*pl* -s) material used to wrap ▶ *v* ▷ **wrap**

wrappings *n* ▷ **wrapping**

wraps *v*, *n* ▷ **wrap**

wrasse *n* (*pl* -s) colourful sea fish

wrasses *n* ▷ **wrasse**

wrath [roth] *n* (*pl* -s) intense anger > **wrathful** *adj*

wrathful *adj* ▷ **wrath**

wraths *n* ▷ **wrath**

wreak *v* (-s, -ing, -ed) cause (chaos)

wreaked *v* ▷ **wreak**

wreaking *v* ▷ **wreak**

wreaks *v* ▷ **wreak**

wreath *n* (*pl* -s) twisted ring or band of flowers or leaves used as a memorial or tribute

wreathed *adj* surrounded or encircled

wreaths *n* ▷ **wreath**

wreck *v* (-s, -ing, -ed) destroy ▶ *n* (*pl* -s) remains of something that has been destroyed or badly damaged, esp. a ship > **wrecker** *n* (*pl* -s)

wreckage *n* (*pl* -s) wrecked remains

wreckages *n* ▷ **wreckage**

wrecked *v* ▷ **wreck**

wrecker *n* ▷ **wreck**

wreckers *n* ▷ **wreck**

wrecking *v* ▷ **wreck**

wrecks *v*, *n* ▷ **wreck**

wren *n* (*pl* -s) small brown songbird

wrench *v* (-es, -ing, -ed) twist or pull violently ▶ *n* (*pl* -es) violent twist or pull

wrenched *v* ▷ **wrench**

wrenches *v*, *n* ▷ **wrench**

wrenching *v* ▷ **wrench**

wrens *n* ▷ **wren**

wrest *v* (-s, -ing, -ed) twist violently

wrested *v* ▷ **wrest**

wresting *v* ▷ **wrest**

wrestle *v* (-les, -ling, -led) fight, esp. as a sport, by grappling with and trying to throw down an opponent > **wrestler** *n* (*pl* -s) > **wrestling** *n* (*pl* -s)

wrestled *v* ▷ **wrestle**

wrestler *n* ▷ **wrestle**

wrestlers *n* ▷ **wrestle**

wrestles *v* ▷ **wrestle**

wrestling *v*, *n* ▷ **wrestle**

wrestlings *n* ▷ **wrestle**

wrests *v* ▷ **wrest**

wretch *n* (*pl* -es) despicable person

wretched [retch-id] *adj* (-er, -est) miserable or unhappy > **wretchedly** *adv* > **wretchedness** *n* (*pl* -es)

wretcheder *adj* ▷ **wretched**

wretchedest *adj* ▷ **wretched**

wretchedly *adv* ▷ **wretched**

wretchedness *n* ▷ **wretched**

wretchednesses *n* ▷ **wretched**

wretches *n* ▷ **wretch**

wrier *adj* ▷ **wry**

wriest *adj* ▷ **wry**

wriggle *v* (-les, -ling, -led) move with a twisting action ▶ *n* (*pl* -s) wriggling movement

wriggled *v* ▷ **wriggle**

wriggles *v*, *n* ▷ **wriggle**

wriggling *v* ▷ **wriggle**

wright *n* (*pl* -s) maker

wrights *n* ▷ **wright**

wring *v* (-s, -ing, wrung) twist, esp. to squeeze liquid out of

wringing *v* ▷ **wring**

wrings *v* ▷ **wring**

wrinkle *n* (*pl* -s) slight crease, esp. one in the skin due to age ▶ *v* (-les, -ling, -led) make or become slightly creased > **wrinkly** *adj* (-lier, -liest)

wrinkled *v* ▷ **wrinkle**

wrinkles *n*, *v* ▷ **wrinkle**

wrinklier *adj* ▷ **wrinkle**

wrinkliest *adj* ▷ **wrinkle**

wrinkling *v* ▷ **wrinkle**

wrinkly *adj* ▷ **wrinkle**

wrist *n* (*pl* -s) joint between the hand and

the arm
wrists *n* ▷ **wrist**
wristwatch *n* (*pl* **-es**) watch worn on the wrist
wristwatches *n* ▷ **wristwatch**
writ *n* (*pl* **-s**) written legal command
write *v* (**-tes, -ting, wrote, written**) mark paper
etc. with symbols or words > **writing** *n* (*pl* **-s**)
writer *n* (*pl* **-s**) author
writers *n* ▷ **writer**
writhe *v* (**-thes, -thing, -thed**) twist or squirm
in or as if in pain
writhed *v* ▷ **writhe**
writhes *v* ▷ **writhe**
writhing *v* ▷ **writhe**
writing *v, n* ▷ **write**
writings *n* ▷ **write**
writs *n* ▷ **writ**
written *v* ▷ **write**
wrong *adj* incorrect or mistaken ▶ *adv* in a
wrong manner ▶ *n* (*pl* **-s**) something immoral
or unjust ▶ *v* (**-s, -ing, -ed**) treat unjustly
> **wrongly** *adv* > **wrongful** *adj* > **wrongfully**
adv
wrongdoer *n* ▷ **wrongdoing**
wrongdoers *n* ▷ **wrongdoing**

wrongdoing *n* (*pl* **-s**) immoral or illegal
behaviour > **wrongdoer** *n* (*pl* **-s**)
wrongdoings *n* ▷ **wrongdoing**
wronged *v* ▷ **wrong**
wrongful *adj* ▷ **wrong**
wrongfully *adv* ▷ **wrong**
wronging *v* ▷ **wrong**
wrongly *adv* ▷ **wrong**
wrongs *n, v* ▷ **wrong**
wrote *v* ▷ **write**
wrought [rawt] *v* (*Lit*) ▷ **work** ▶ *adj* (of metals)
shaped by hammering or beating
wrung *v* ▷ **wring**
wry *adj* (**wrier, wriest** *or* **wryer**) (**wryest**) drily
humorous > **wryly** *adv*
wryer *adj* ▷ **wry**
wryest *adj* ▷ **wry**
wryly *adv* ▷ **wry**

wye *n* (**wyes**). Wye is the letter Y. If you
have W and Y on your rack, look for an
E on the board that will allow you to
play this especially if you can land on
a bonus square as a result. Wye scores
9 points.

Xx

Worth 8 points on its own, X is one of the best tiles in the game. It doesn't, however, start many two- and three-letter words. There are only two valid two-letter words, **xi** and **xu** (9 points each), beginning with X, and only one three-letter word, **xis.** Therefore, if you have an X on your rack and need to play short words, you're probably better off thinking of words that end in X or have X in them rather than those that start with X.

xebec *n* (**xebecs**). A xebec is an Algerian ship. This is a good high-scoring word. If you have an X, you'll probably only need one E as well as B and C to play it, as there is likely to be an available E on the board already. Xebec scores 16 points.

xenon *n* (*pl* **-s**) (CHEM) colourless odourless gas found in very small quantities in the air
xenons *n* ▷ **xenon**

xenophobia [zen-oh-**fobe**-ee-a] *n* (*pl* **-s**) fear or hatred of people from other countries
xenophobias *n* ▷ **xenophobia**

xi *n* (**xis**). Xi is the 14th letter of the Greek alphabet. The plural of this word is the only three-letter word that starts with X. Xi scores 9 points.

xoanon *n* (**xoanons**) A xoanon is a primitive carving of a god. If you have all the tiles for the plural, and are able to place them all on the board, you'll earn a 50-point bonus. Xoanon scores 13 points.

xu *n* (**xu**). The xu is a unit of currency in Vietnam. The plural form of this word is the same as its singular, so be sure to challenge anyone who adds an S to it! Xu scores 9 points.

xylem [**zy**-lem] *n* (*pl* **-s**) plant tissue that conducts water and minerals from the roots to all other parts
xylems *n* ▷ **xylem**

xylophone [**zile**-oh-fone] *n* (*pl* **-s**) musical instrument made of a row of wooden bars played with hammers
xylophones *n* ▷ **xylophone**

Yy

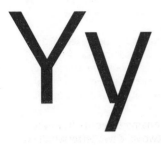

Y is a useful tile to have on your rack. It's worth 4 points on its own, and so often gives you good scores. There are only four two-letter words beginning with Y, but these are easy to remember as there's one for every vowel except I: **ya, ye, yo** and **yu** (5 points each). There are quite a few useful three-letter words: **yew** (9) and **yob** (8) and remember that yob was originally **boy** backwards: if you can't fit in yob, you may be able to use boy instead. And while his half-brother the **zo** (or **dzo** or **dso** or **zho**) gets all the attention, don't forget that the **yak** (10) earns quite a decent score!

ya *interj* (S AFR) yes
  yabbies *n* ▷ **yabby**
yabby *n* (*pl* -**bbies**) (AUST) small freshwater
  crayfish
yacht [yott] *n* (*pl* -**s**) large boat with sails or an
  engine, used for racing or pleasure cruising
  > **yachting** *n* (*pl* -**s**) > **yachtsman** *n* (*pl* -**men**)
  > **yachtswoman** *n* (*pl* -**women**)
  yachting *n* ▷ **yacht**
  yachtings *n* ▷ **yacht**
  yachts *n* ▷ **yacht**
  yachtsman *n* ▷ **yacht**
  yachtsmen *n* ▷ **yacht**
  yachtswoman *n* ▷ **yacht**
  yachtswomen *n* ▷ **yacht**
yak[1] *n* (*pl* -**s**) Tibetan ox with long shaggy hair
yak[2] *v* (**yaks, yakking, yakked**) (*Slang*) talk
  continuously about unimportant matters
yakka *n* (*pl* -**s**) (AUST & NZ) (*Informal*) work
  yakkas *n* ▷ **yakka**
  yakked *v* ▷ **yak**[2]
  yakking *v* ▷ **yak**[2]
  yaks *n* ▷ **yak**[1] ▶ *v* ▷ **yak**[2]
yam *n* (*pl* -**s**) tropical root vegetable
  yams *n* ▷ **yam**
yank *v* (-**s**, -**ing**, -**ed**) pull or jerk suddenly ▶ *n* (*pl*
  -**s**) sudden pull or jerk
  yanked *v* ▷ **yank**
  yanking *v* ▷ **yank**
  yanks *v*, *n* ▷ **yank**
yap *v* (-**s**, -**pping**, -**pped**) bark with a high-
  pitched sound (*Informal*) ▶ *n* (*pl* -**s**) high-
  pitched bark
  yapped *v* ▷ **yap**
  yapping *v* ▷ **yap**

yaps *v* ▷ **yap**
yard[1] *n* (*pl* -**s**) unit of length equal to 36 inches
  or about 91.4 centimetres > **yardstick** *n* (*pl*
  -**s**) standard against which to judge other
  people or things
yard[2] *n* (*pl* -**s**) enclosed area, usu. next to a
  building and often used for a particular
  purpose
  yards *n* ▷ **yard**[1, 2]
  yardstick *n* ▷ **yard**[1]
  yardsticks *n* ▷ **yard**[1]
yarmulke [yar-mull-ka] *n* (*pl* -**s**) skullcap worn
  by Jewish men
  yarmulkes *n* ▷ **yarmulke**
yarn *n* (*pl* -**s**) thread used for knitting or
  making cloth
  yarns *n* ▷ **yarn**
yashmak *n* (*pl* -**s**) veil worn by a Muslim
  woman to cover her face in public
  yashmaks *n* ▷ **yashmak**
yaw *v* (-**s**, -**ing**, -**ed**) (of an aircraft or ship) turn
  to one side or from side to side while moving
  yawed *v* ▷ **yaw**
  yawing *v* ▷ **yaw**
yawl *n* (*pl* -**s**) two-masted sailing boat
  yawls *n* ▷ **yawl**
yawn *v* (-**s**, -**ing**, -**ed**) open the mouth wide and
  take in air deeply, often when sleepy or bored
  ▶ *n* (*pl* -**s**) act of yawning > **yawning** *adj*
  yawned *v* ▷ **yawn**
  yawning ▷ **yawn**
  yawns *v*, *n* ▷ **yawn**
  yaws *v* ▷ **yaw**
ye [yee] *pron* (*Obs*) you
year *n* (*pl* -**s**) time taken for the earth to make

one revolution around the sun, about 365 days

yearling n (pl **-s**) animal between one and two years old

> **yearlings** n ▷ **yearling**

yearly adj, adv (happening) every year or once a year

yearn v (**-s, -ing, -ed**) want (something) very much > **yearning** n (pl **-s**) adj

> **yearned** v ▷ **yearn**

> **yearning** v, n ▷ **yearn**

> **yearnings** n ▷ **yearn**

> **yearns** v ▷ **yearn**

> **years** n ▷ **year**

yeast n (pl **-s**) fungus used to make bread rise and to ferment alcoholic drinks > **yeasty** adj

> **yeasts** n ▷ **yeast**

yebo interj (S AFR) (Informal) yes

yell v (**-s, -ing, -ed**) shout or scream in a loud or piercing way ▶ n (pl **-s**) loud cry of pain, anger, or fear

> **yelled** v ▷ **yell**

> **yelling** v ▷ **yell**

yellow n (pl **-s**) the colour of gold, a lemon, etc. ▶ adj (**-er, -est**) of this colour ▶ v (**-s, -ing, -ed**) make or become yellow

> **yellowed** v ▷ **yellow**

> **yellower** adj ▷ **yellow**

> **yellowest** adj ▷ **yellow**

yellowhammer n (pl **-s**) European songbird with a yellow head and body

> **yellowhammers** n ▷ **yellowhammer**

> **yellowing** v ▷ **yellow**

> **yellows** n, v ▷ **yellow**

> **yells** v, n ▷ **yell**

yelp v (**-s, -ing, -ed**) ▶ n (pl **-s**) (give) a short sudden cry

> **yelped** v ▷ **yelp**

> **yelping** v ▷ **yelp**

> **yelps** v, n ▷ **yelp**

yen¹ n (pl **yen**) monetary unit of Japan

yen² n (pl **yen**) (Informal) longing or desire

yeoman [yo-man] n (pl **-men**) (HIST) farmer owning and farming his own land

> **yeomen** n ▷ **yeoman**

yes interj expresses consent, agreement, or approval

yesterday adv, n (pl **-s**) (on) the day before today

> **yesterdays** n ▷ **yesterday**

yet conj nevertheless, still ▶ adv up until then or now

yeti n (pl **yetis**) large apelike creature said to live in the Himalayas

> **yetis** n ▷ **yeti**

yew n (pl **-s**) evergreen tree with needle-like leaves and red berries

> **yews** n ▷ **yew**

> **yex** v (**yexes, yexing, yexed**). Yex is a Scots word that means to hiccup or cough. This word gives you a good score, and the verb forms offer the chance to expand it if someone else plays it, or if you get the chance later on. Yex scores 13 points.

yield v (**-s, -ing, -ed**) produce or bear ▶ n (pl **-s**)

> **yielded** v ▷ **yield**

yielding adj submissive ▶ v ▷ **yield**

> **yields** v, n ▷ **yield**

> **yo** interj. Yo is an informal greeting. This is useful for connecting words ending in Y with ones beginning in O. Yo scores 5 points.

yob n (pl **-s**) (Slang) bad-mannered aggressive youth

yobbo n (pl **-bboes** or **-bbos**) yob

> **yobboes** n ▷ **yobbo**

> **yobbos** n ▷ **yobbo**

> **yobs** n ▷ **yob**

yodel v (**-s, -lling, -lled**) sing with abrupt changes between a normal and a falsetto voice

> **yodelled** v ▷ **yodel**

> **yodelling** v ▷ **yodel**

> **yodels** v ▷ **yodel**

yoga n (pl **-s**) Hindu method of exercise and discipline aiming at spiritual, mental, and physical wellbeing

> **yogas** n ▷ **yoga**

> **yoghurt** n ▷ **yogurt**

> **yoghurts** n ▷ **yogurt**

yogi n (pl **-s**) person who practises yoga

> **yogis** n ▷ **yogi**

yogurt, yoghurt n (pl **-s**) slightly sour custard-like food made from milk that has had bacteria added to it, often sweetened and flavoured with fruit

> **yogurts** n ▷ **yogurt**

> **yok** n (**yoks**). A yok is a noisy laugh. This unusual word is useful if there isn't much space on the board, as there's likely to be an O available to form it around. Yok scores 10 points.

yoke n (pl **-s**) wooden bar put across the necks of two animals to hold them together (Lit) ▶ v (**-kes, -king, -ked**) put a yoke on

> **yoked** v ▷ **yoke**

yokel n (pl **yokels**) (Offens) person who lives in the country and is usu. simple and old-fashioned

yokels *n* ▷ **yokel**
yokes *n*, *v* ▷ **yoke**
yoking *v* ▷ **yoke**
yolk *n* (*pl* -**s**) yellow part of an egg that provides food for the developing embryo
yolks *n* ▷ **yolk**
yonder *adj*, *adv* (situated) over there
yonks *pl n* (*Informal*) very long time
yore *n* (*pl* -**s**) (*Lit*) a long time ago
yores *n* ▷ **yore**
you *pron* refers to: the person or people addressed
young *adj* in an early stage of life or growth
▶ *pl n* young people in general
youngster *n* (*pl* -**s**) young person
youngsters *n* ▷ **youngster**
your *adj* of, belonging to, or associated with you > **yourself** *pron*
yours *pron* something belonging to you
yourself *pron* ▷ **your**
youth *n* (*pl* -**s**) time of being young > **youthful** *adj* > **youthfulness** *n* (*pl* -**es**)
youthful *adj* ▷ **youth**
youthfulness *adj* ▷ **youth**
youthfulnesses *adj* ▷ **youth**
youths *n* ▷ **youth**
yowl *v*, *n* (*pl* -**s**) (produce) a loud mournful cry

yowls *n* ▷ **yowl**
yttrium [it-ree-um] *n* (*pl* -**s**) (CHEM) silvery metallic element used in various alloys
yttriums *n* ▷ **yttrium**

> **yu** *n* (**yus**). Yu is a Chinese word that means precious jade. This word is good for connecting words ending in Y with ones beginning in U. Yu scores 5 points.

yucca *n* (*pl* -**s**) tropical plant with spikes of white leaves
yuccas *n* ▷ **yucca**
yuckier *adj* ▷ **yucky**
yuckiest *adj* ▷ **yucky**
yucky *adj* (-**ckier**, -**ckiest**) (*Slang*) disgusting, nasty

> **yuk** *interj*. Yuk is a noise people make to express disgust or dislike. This funny little word is worth remembering as it give a good score and uses an unpromising combination of letters. Yuk scores 10 points.

yuppie *n* (*pl* -**s**) young highly-paid professional person, esp. one who has a materialistic way of life ▶ *adj* typical of or reflecting the values of yuppies
yuppies *n* ▷ **yuppie**

Zz

Scoring the same as Q but easier to use, Z is the most valuable tile in Scrabble. There is only one two-letter word beginning with Z, **zo** (11 points), but remembering this will save you wasting time looking for others. There some very good three-letter words starting with Z, however. These include another variant of **zo**, **zho** (15), as well as **zax** and **zex** (19 each), **zap** (14), **zip** (14) and **zoo** (12).

zanier *adj* ▷ **zany**
zaniest ▷ **zany**

> **zanja** *n* (**zanjas**). A zanja is an irrigation canal. This unusual word is very useful because of its combination of J and Z. As there are many As in the game, if you are lucky enough to get J and Z together, you may well be able to play this somewhere. Zanja scores 21 points.
>
> **zanjero** *n* (**zanjeros**). A zanjero is a supervisor of irrigation canals. If you can use all your tiles to play zanjero, you'll earn a 50-point bonus. Zanjero scores 23 points.

zany [zane-ee] *adj* (**-nier, -niest**) comical in an endearing way
zap *v* (**-s, -pping, -pped**) (*Slang*) kill (by shooting)

> **zapped** *v* ▷ **zap**
> **zapping** *v* ▷ **zap**
> **zaps** *v* ▷ **zap**
>
> **zax** *n* (**zaxes**). A zax a small axe for cutting slates. This is great word combining X and Z. If you get a Z late in the game, check if X has already been played, and whether there is an opportunity to form zax or **zex**. Zax scores 19 points.

zeal *n* (*pl* **-s**) great enthusiasm or eagerness
zealot [zel-lot] *n* (*pl* **-s**) fanatic or extreme enthusiast

> **zealots** *n* ▷ **zealot**

zealous [zel-luss] *adj* extremely eager or enthusiastic > **zealously** *adv*

> **zealously** *adv* ▷ **zealous**
> **zeals** *n* ▷ **zeal**

zebra *n* (*pl* **-s**) black-and-white striped African animal of the horse family

zebras *n* ▷ **zebra**
zebu [zee-boo] *n* (*pl* **-s**) Asian ox with a humped back and long horns

> **zebus** *n* ▷ **zebu**
>
> **zed** *n* (**zeds**). Zed is the letter Z. This is a handy word when you have a Z but no space or letters for a longer word. Zed scores 13 points.
>
> **zee** *n* (**zees**). Zee is the American pronunciation of the letter Z. This word can be very useful because E is the most common tile in Scrabble, so keep it in mind if you draw a Z. Zee scores 12 points.

zenith *n* (*pl* **-s**) highest point of success or power

> **zeniths** *n* ▷ **zenith**

zephyr [zef-fer] *n* (*pl* **-s**) soft gentle breeze

> **zephyrs** *n* ▷ **zephyr**

zeppelin *n* (*pl* **-s**) (HIST) large cylindrical airship

> **zeppelins** *n* ▷ **zeppelin**

zero *n* (*pl* **-ros, -roes**) (symbol representing) the number 0 ▶ *adj* having no measurable quantity or size

> **zeroes** *n* ▷ **zero**
> **zeros** *n* ▷ **zero**

zest *n* (*pl* **-s**) enjoyment or excitement
zests *n* ▷ **zest**

> **zeuxite** *n* (**zeuxites**). Zeuxite is a mineral. This unusual word is great if you have the letters for it. If you can use all of your tiles to play zeuxite, you'll get a 50-point bonus. Zeuxite scores 23 points.
>
> **zex** *n* (**zexes**). Zex means the same as **zax**. If you get a Z late in the game, check if X has already been played, and whether there is an opportunity to form zax. Zex scores 19 points.

zho *n* (**zhos**) Zho is one of several spelling for a Tibetan animal bred from yaks and cattle. The other forms are **dso, dzo** and **zo**, and it's worth remembering all of them. Zho scores 15 points.

zigzag *n* (*pl* -**s**) line or course having sharp turns in alternating directions ▸ *v* (-**zags, -zagging, -zagged**) move in a zigzag ▸ *adj* formed in or proceeding in a zigzag
zigzagged *v* ▷ **zigzag**
zigzagging *v* ▷ **zigzag**
zigzags *n*, *v* ▷ **zigzag**
zinc *n* (*pl* -**s**) (CHEM) bluish-white metallic element used in alloys and to coat metal
zincs *n* ▷ **zinc**
zing *n* (*pl* -**s**) (*Informal*) quality in something that makes it lively or interesting
zings *n* ▷ **zing**
zip *n* (*pl* -**s**) fastener with two rows of teeth that are closed or opened by a small clip pulled between them ▸ *v* (-**s**, -**pping**, -**pped**) fasten with a zip
zipped *v* ▷ **zip**
zipping *v* ▷ **zip**
zips *n*, *v* ▷ **zip**
zircon *n* (*pl* -**s**) mineral used as a gemstone and in industry
zirconium *n* (*pl* -**s**) (CHEM) greyish-white metallic element that is resistant to corrosion
zirconiums *n* ▷ **zirconium**
zircons *n* ▷ **zircon**

zit *n* (**zits**). A zit is a pimple. This nasty little word can be very useful during a game, especially when there's not much space left on the board. Zit scores 12 points.

zither *n* (*pl* -**s**) musical instrument consisting of strings stretched over a flat box and plucked to produce musical notes
zithers *n* ▷ **zither**

zo *n* (**zos**). Zo is one of several spelling for a Tibetan animal bred from yaks and cattle. The other forms are **dso, dzo** and **zho,** and it's worth remembering all of them. If someone plays zo and you have a D, remember that you can form dzo from it. Zo is the only two-letter word beginning with Z, and scores 11 points.

zodiac *n* (*pl* -**s**) imaginary belt in the sky within which the sun, moon, and planets appear to move, divided into twelve equal areas, called signs of the zodiac, each named after a constellation
zodiacs *n* ▷ **zodiac**
zombi *n* ▷ **zombie**
zombie, zombi *n* (*pl* -**s**) person who appears to be lifeless, apathetic, or totally lacking in independent judgment
zombies *n* ▷ **zombie**
zombis *n* ▷ **zombie**
zonal *adj* ▷ **zone**
zone *n* (*pl* -**s**) area with particular features or properties ▸ *v* (-**nes**, -**ning**, -**ned**) divide into zones > **zonal** *adj*
zoned *v* ▷ **zone**
zones *n*, *v* ▷ **zone**
zoning *v* ▷ **zone**
zoo *n* (*pl* -**s**) place where live animals are kept for show
zoological *adj* ▷ **zoology**
zoologies *n* ▷ **zoology**
zoologist *n* ▷ **zoology**
zoologists *n* ▷ **zoology**
zoology *n* (*pl* -**gies**) study of animals > **zoologist** *n* (*pl* -**s**) > **zoological** *adj*
zoom *v* (-**s**, -**ing**, -**ed**) move or rise very rapidly
zoomed *v* ▷ **zoom**
zooming *v* ▷ **zoom**
zooms *v* ▷ **zoom**
zoos *n* ▷ **zoo**

zootaxy *n* (**zootaxies**). Zootaxy is the scientific classification of animals. If you're lucky enough to have the letters for this word, you can earn a 50-point bonus by using all of your tiles to form it. Zootaxy scores 26 points.

zucchini [zoo-**keen**-ee] *n* (*pl* -**ni**, -**nis**) (US & AUST) courgette
zucchinis *n* ▷ **zucchini**
zulu *n* (*pl* -**s**) member of a tall Black people of southern Africa
zulus *n* ▷ **zulu**
zygote *n* (*pl* -**s**) fertilized egg cell
zygotes *n* ▷ **zygote**